QUALITY SOFTWARE PROJECT MANAGEMENT

ISBN 0-13-091297-2

90000

9 780130 912978

Software Quality Institute Series

The Software Quality Institute Series is a partnership between the Software Quality Institute (SQI) at The University of Texas at Austin and Prentice Hall Professional Technical Reference (PHPTR). The books discuss real-life problems and offer strategies for improving software quality and software business practices.

Each publication is written by highly skilled, experienced practitioners who understand and can help solve the problems facing software professionals. SQI series topic areas include software development practices and technologies, management of software organizations, integration of high-quality software into other industries, business issues with reference to software quality, and related areas of interest

TITLES IN THE SOFTWARE QUALITY INSTITUTE SERIES

QUALITY SOFTWARE PROJECT MANAGEMENT

Robert T. Futrell
Donald F. Shafer
Linda I. Shafer

Prentice Hall PTR
Upper Saddle River, NJ 07458
www.phptr.com

Library of Congress Cataloging-in-Publication Data

Futrell, Robert.

   Quality software project management / Robert Futrell, Donald Shafer, Linda Shafer.
     p. cm. — (Software Quality Institute series)
   Includes bibliographical references and index.
   ISBN 0-13-091297-2 (pbk.)
    1. Computer software—Development—Management. I. Shafer, Donald. II. Shafer, Linda.
   III. Title. IV. Series.

   QA76.76.D47 F88 2001

   005.1'068—dc21

2001133050

Editorial/Production Supervision: *Argosy*
Acquisitions Editor: *Paul Petralia*
Editorial Assistant: *Richard Winkler*
Marketing Manager: *Debby van Dijk*
Manufacturing Manager: *Alexis R. Heydt-Long*

Development Editor: *Jennifer Blackwell*
Technical Editor: *Barry J. Busler*
Cover Design: *Nina Scuderi*
Cover Design Director: *Jerry Votta*
Series Design: *Gail Cocker-Bogusz*

© 2002 Prentice Hall PTR
A Division of Pearson Education, Inc.
Upper Saddle River, NJ 07458

The publisher offers discounts on this book when ordered in bulk quantities.
For more information, contact
Corporate Sales Department,
Prentice Hall PTR
One Lake Street
Upper Saddle River, NJ 07458
Phone: 800-382-3419; FAX: 201-236-7141
E-mail (Internet): corpsales@prenhall.com

Printed in the United States of America

10 9 8 7 6 5 4 3 2 1

ISBN 0-13-091297-2

Pearson Education LTD.
Pearson Education Australia PTY, Limited
Pearson Education Singapore, Pte. Ltd
Pearson Education North Asia Ltd
Pearson Education Canada, Ltd.
Pearson Educación de Mexico, S.A. de C.V.
Pearson Education—Japan
Pearson Education Malaysia, Pte. Ltd

To The University of Texas at Austin
Software Quality Institute

Contents

CHAPTER 8
Creating the Work Breakdown Structure

CHAPTER 9
Identifying the Tasks and Activities

CHAPTER 10
Software Size and Reuse Estimating   *305*

CHAPTER 11
Estimating Duration and Cost   *359*

CHAPTER 15
Scheduling the Work

CHAPTER 16
Eliciting Requirements

CHAPTER   17
Developing the Software Requirements Specification

CHAPTER 22
Analysis and Design Methods

CHAPTER 23
Validation and Verification

CHAPTER   24
Use of Tools

CHAPTER   25
Project Tracking and Control

CHAPTER 26
Continuous Process Improvement   1037

CHAPTER 27
Project Termination   1071

CHAPTER 28
Post-Performance Analysis   *1087*

CHAPTER 29
Reporting and Communicating   *1107*

CHAPTER 30
Software Quality Assurance

CHAPTER 31
Software Configuration Management

CHAPTER 32
Legal Issues in Software

CHAPTER 33
Summary

APPENDIX A
Supporting Organizations

Glossary   *1563*

Bibliography   *1575*

Index   *1611*

Foreword

A few years ago, a colleague at a management consulting firm invited me to give a presentation at a monthly meeting of the local chapter of a professional software organization. It turned out that there was an ulterior motive for the invitation: My colleague explained that his firm was involved in a huge project for a major client, and that several of the client's managers would be attending my presentation.

"Here's the problem," my colleague said to me. "We've got dozens of our programmers, analysts, network architects, database designers, and other technical people working on this project—and the client is perfectly happy to pay for them. But when we told them that we need to have a project manager and some support staff to help carry out the project management tasks, they balked. They don't understand why they should have to pay for project management—and the way they described it to us, it sounds like they don't believe that project management has any value." My task for the presentation, as it turned out, was to provide an eloquent explanation of why project management was important, with the indirect implication that it was worth paying for.

If such an event had taken place in the mid-1960s, perhaps it would not have been surprising. After all, as Futrell, Shafer, and Shafer point out in the first chapter of their book, it was not until 1968 that a famous NATO software engineering conference provided some public recognition of the importance of project management in what came to be known as the "software crisis." Even in 1975 or 1985, we could have forgiven a typical business person for not appreciating that successful IT projects require more than an army of clever technical people. But my experience took place in the 1990s, and I suspect that it is being repeated today, in various parts of the world. If nothing else, it demonstrates why there is such a desperate need for a thorough, detailed book like *Quality Software Project Management*.

The illusion that no project management resources are necessary to succeed with an IT project is only slightly more dangerous than the common misconception that project management is simple, intuitive, and easily learned by skimming through a "project management for dummies" book. A quick scan of the Amazon.com Web site indicates that there are roughly half a dozen books with some variation on that title; and while the books probably do serve a constructive purpose, I'm concerned about the common perception that a 22-year-old Java programmer, with a mere two years of experience in a technical discipline, can be promoted to the position of project manager with any reasonable hope of succeeding on a non-trivial project.

Becoming a *bona fide* project manager is not a quick or easy process—and if I can accomplish only one thing in this brief foreword, let me also emphasize that it's not equivalent to achieving competence with a software product like Microsoft Project. That particular program, as well as a dozen others like it, are enormously useful tools for carrying out some of the scheduling activities associated with a project. But as the authors describe in enormous detail in this book, there's more to project management than just drawing PERT charts and Gantt charts. Indeed, there are some 34 key competencies, as the authors point out; perhaps we can get away with mediocrity or minimal competence in one or two of those competencies, if the circumstances of the project allow it, but there are literally dozens of things we need to be good at if we're going to call ourselves "project managers" in the highly complex field of IT systems development.

The authors have been involved with a software project management certification program at the University of Texas at Austin's Software Quality Institute; in the best of worlds, IT organizations would send their fledgling project managers to such a program for a total immersion course—as well as sending their veteran project managers (most of whom have acquired only a haphazard understanding of the 34 key competencies through on-the-job training) for a refresher course. But for those of us who don't have the time, or whose employers don't have the budget or the foresight to send us to such a program, the next best thing is a book like *Quality Software Project Management*.

Chances are that you won't be able to read this book in a single sitting. It's not an "airplane book" that you can read on a quick flight from New York to Chicago; it's not even a "weekend book" that you can take to the beach for some summertime reading. You'll need to set aside an hour or two each evening over a period of several weeks or months to be able to absorb all of the guidelines, checklists, procedures, and advice from these eminently qualified practitioners of software project management. You should also take advantage of the Web site and additional resources provided by the authors and realize that mastery of project management is an ongoing process.

When I first started working in the computer field in the mid-1960s, my goal was to be the best assembly-language programmer on the planet. Of course, the computer I was working on at the time has long since disappeared, but there is still a great deal of honor and virtue to be associated with mastery of such technical skills as programming, testing, or database design. For many of us, though, a fascination with technical skills is eventually replaced by a dedication to project management skills because it doesn't take more than two or three projects to realize that success or failure is far more likely to be determined by management issues than technical issues. In my case, it took nearly a decade to make that shift in preferences and priorities. Simply wanting to become a project manager is not enough. I only wish that I had had a book like *Quality Software Project Management* to provide the foundation for skills and practices that I had to learn on my own, piece by piece. As for you, dear reader, rejoice: You do have such a book, and if you read it and study it carefully, it will not only speed up the learning process, but it may also help you avoid some unpleasant project disasters along the way!

Ed Yourdon

September, 2001

Preface

Quality Software Project Management was written by and for software practitioners who need a hands-on guide to the non-deterministic but leading-edge task of managing software development projects. The book takes its overall outline from the successful Software Project Management (SWPM) certification program at The University of Texas at Austin's Software Quality Institute, a division of the College of Engineering's Center for Lifelong Engineering Education (CLEE).

Software project managers and their development teams play a critical role in the success of modern businesses, be they high-tech or otherwise. These professionals and their knowledge of sound management practices and thorough software development, enhancement, and maintenance processes, can determine organizational success or failure.

The trend toward increased software quality is responsible for the promulgation of new standards to certify that development processes meet certain benchmarks. Certifications to standards are becoming more common as buyers demand tighter quality controls. Software project managers must be keenly aware of standards such as those published by the Institute of Electrical and Electronics Engineers (IEEE), as well as continually evolving practices, guided in part by the Software Engineering Institute's (SEI) Capability Maturity Model (CMM), and by a new emphasis on the management of small projects.

It is in recognition of these trends that UT's College of Engineering and its Software Quality Institute (SQI) created the SWPM certificate program in 1993. Since then, hundreds of software project managers have graduated from the program. Those managers are currently applying "best practices" to overcome the limitations of a tight labor force and to meet the rapidly changing needs of their customers and organizations in today's highly competitive marketplace. This book is a consolidation of teachings from that certification program as it has evolved over the years.

In addition to knowledge of the principles of software engineering, software project managers must incorporate skills for managing people, products, and process into their daily routine. For this reason, *Quality Software Project Management* is grounded in two interlaced bodies of knowledge developed by internationally recognized organizations: the Project Management Institute (PMI®) and the American Society for Quality (ASQ). SQI instructors, many of whom are certified software (CSQE) and project management professionals (PMP®), refine knowledge identified by those two organizations and contribute decades of their own industry experience with the most up-to-date practices. Quality, applicability, timeliness, portability, and profitability are all main areas of focus, both for the SWPM certificate program and for this book, on which it is based.

Software engineering principles and quality goals are necessary but not sufficient for the needs of today's marketplace. Shorter cycle times, completed with fewer resources, are also in demand. Products must be carefully targeted toward the specific functional requirements of increasingly sophisticated customers. Software developers and managers dealing with these challenging and often conflicting goals, must be highly skilled in planning, coordinating, and managing software projects. They must know how to tailor best practices to their current projects and to take advantage of their organization's past experience when constructing project plans. Establishing the proper metrics to monitor project performance is essential, as is having necessary multi-disciplinary team leadership skills. Furthermore, software project management must view the project "big picture" as it relates to their profession and to their career advancement.

Quality Software Project Management has evolved from the strong belief of the authors, and based on their experience, that with a defined process, quality software can be developed in a repeatable fashion. Figure 1 shows that methods, tools, and technology interrelate in complex and constant ways and require the process in order to achieve balance. These three entities are at the heart of quality, software, and project management, and will therefore be used throughout the text. A *method* is defined as a manner, means, or process for accomplishing something. A *tool* is defined as an implement or machine used to do work or perform a task. *Technology* is defined as the application of scientific knowledge in industry or business.

The experience of the authors is that the knowledge in this guide, applied by practitioners, along with the effective use of methods, tools, and techniques encapsulated in 34 competencies, will result in quality software. "Quality" incorporates the necessary functionality as well as other factors such as reliability, usability, etc. Figure 2 represents how ideas are turned into products through iterations of such use.

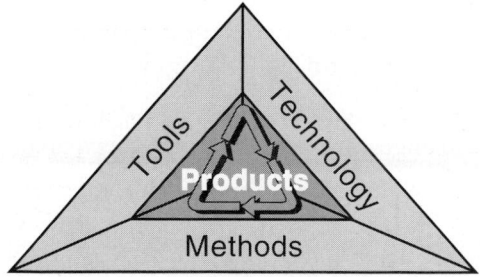

FIGURE 1
Methods, Tools, and Technology Relationships

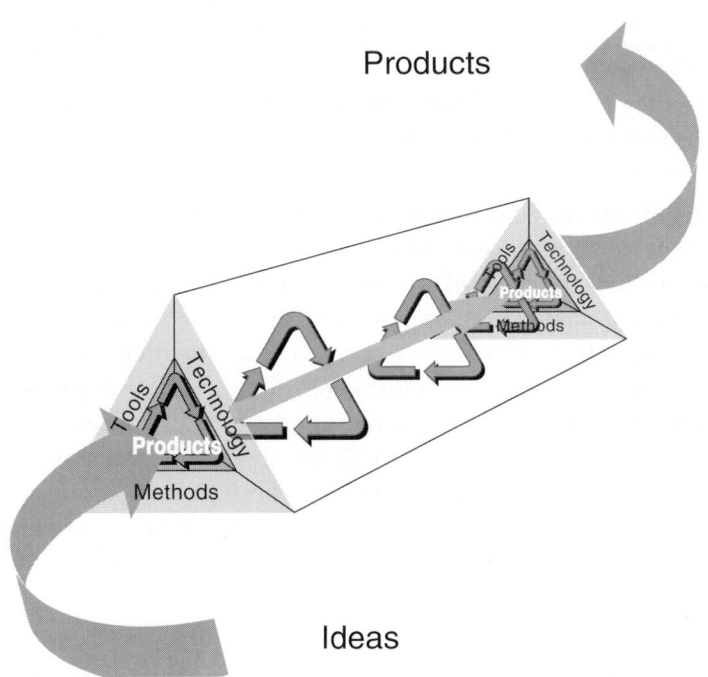

Products

Ideas

FIGURE 2
Transforming Ideas into Products

While based on the SWPM course materials, this book is not simply a recitation of them. The specific combined experience of these authors (almost 100 years worth) permeates the work and attempts to blend the thoughts of about 30 instructors into "one voice." A composite case study has been developed containing most of the common types of problems encountered in software projects. The project scenario reflects today's increasingly common need for rapid "Internet time" software development.

Using the Guide as a Course Text

If you are participating in either the online or the classroom presentation of The University of Texas at Austin Software Quality Institute's Software Project Management certification program, this will be your main text. If you are a professor or instructor of software engineering, this text will suffice for a semester-long course in software engineering plus project management. The bodies of knowledge for project management, software engineering, and software quality, recognized by several professional societies (IEEE, SEI, PMI, ASQ) are presented. If you are a student of project management and software engineering, please feel confident that real industry veterans have authored this text.

Acknowledgements

The authors of this text are "masters" not "philosophers," meaning that each has a Masters Degree, but none has a PhD at this time. In the original academic world of associates, bachelors, and masters, the masters of the trade knew how to apply their knowledge to "real" tasks. They were the practitioners. Philosophers were considered to be in a different category, focusing on theory and more ethereal concepts. Our current academic society assumes that philosophers are also masters of application. While there is no question that these philosophers deservedly receive the highest recognition, it also seems to be the case that, with the fields of software engineering and project management, the masters of application are often found in industry rather than in academia. Computer science is to software engineering as chemistry is to chemical engineering. The former is about the theory, and the latter is about practical application of the theory. A mathematician who wrestles with the theoretical question of whether an answer exists, has a different job than the engineer who needs to know the answer in order to use it. While paying homage to all of the theorists who have developed computer science, we hope to be some of the masters, who, in some small way, add to its application.

We wish to personally thank The University of Texas at Austin, Center for Lifelong Engineering Education, Software Quality Institute's staff for their unwavering, cheerful, consistent (and constant) help. They made the last eleven software project management certification program materials available to us, and professionally, efficiently, and effectively helped us get everything we needed. Candy Walser-Berry, Marilyn Robertson, Theresa Lestingi, Heather Wagner, Jayne Tune, Carolyn Stark—thanks! The Chinese railway case study became a real but fair student challenge due to the original work of Jack Odom and the acting skills of John McNeill. The employee owners of Athens Group provided material for Appendix B, "Real World Projects," and a wealth of metrics data. The instructors who shaped the SWPM lessons deserve special credit—many of them are cited in the reference sections of the individual chapters. We appreciate the SQI Board of Advisors who have volunteered their time, since 1993, to make a program of high quality. Thank you Paul Petralia and Jennifer Blackwell at Prentice Hall, and especially to Barry Busler of IBM. And, of course, we also appreciate and thank our children for cheering us on—a collection of four fabulous young women and one incredible young man.

Introduction

Fifty software engineers from 11 different countries, "all concerned professionally with software," attended a NATO Science Committee conference in Garmish, Germany in October 1968. While most discussions were focused on the technical aspects of design, production, implementation, distribution, and service of software, there were also reports on "the difficulties of meeting schedules and specifications on large software projects." This may have been the first public recognition of the importance of software project management—needless to say, those difficulties of "schedules and specifications" continue to trouble us today. Shortly afterward, 22 international leaders in software development from academia, industry, and research laboratories gathered at Hedsor Park, a corporate retreat near London, to commemorate the NATO conference and to analyze the future direction of software. These events became known as the first sober look at the impending "software crisis." Following this awakening to the serious impact software could have on human lives, improvements in the process of software development began to be introduced. Among them was the concept of a software life cycle (SLC) to represent the sequence of events that occur in software development. The definition of an SLC, as well as arguments for and against its *raison d'etre*, has been the subject of many conversations and publications in the software industry. By the late 1970s, the controversy resulted in the mantra, "Stop the life cycle, I want to get off!" Despite the differing views, the need for a documented software development process persisted. In 1970, W.W. Royce identified several phases in a typical SLC. Royce and Barry Boehm suggested that controlling the entry and the exit points from each phase in the process would improve quality and perhaps increase productivity. For example, the design of software module interfaces should be delayed until the requirements have been specified, thereby reducing the amount of rework. Their model was informally labeled the "waterfall model" SLC because it was graphically portrayed in a manner similar to Figure 1–1. Software development activities "flow" from block to block in the graphic.

In reality, most project activities do not proceed linearly. Often, developers are required to revert to a previous phase to follow up on issues that were not adequately addressed at that time. When, in the design phase, a missing or incorrect requirement is discovered, the developer

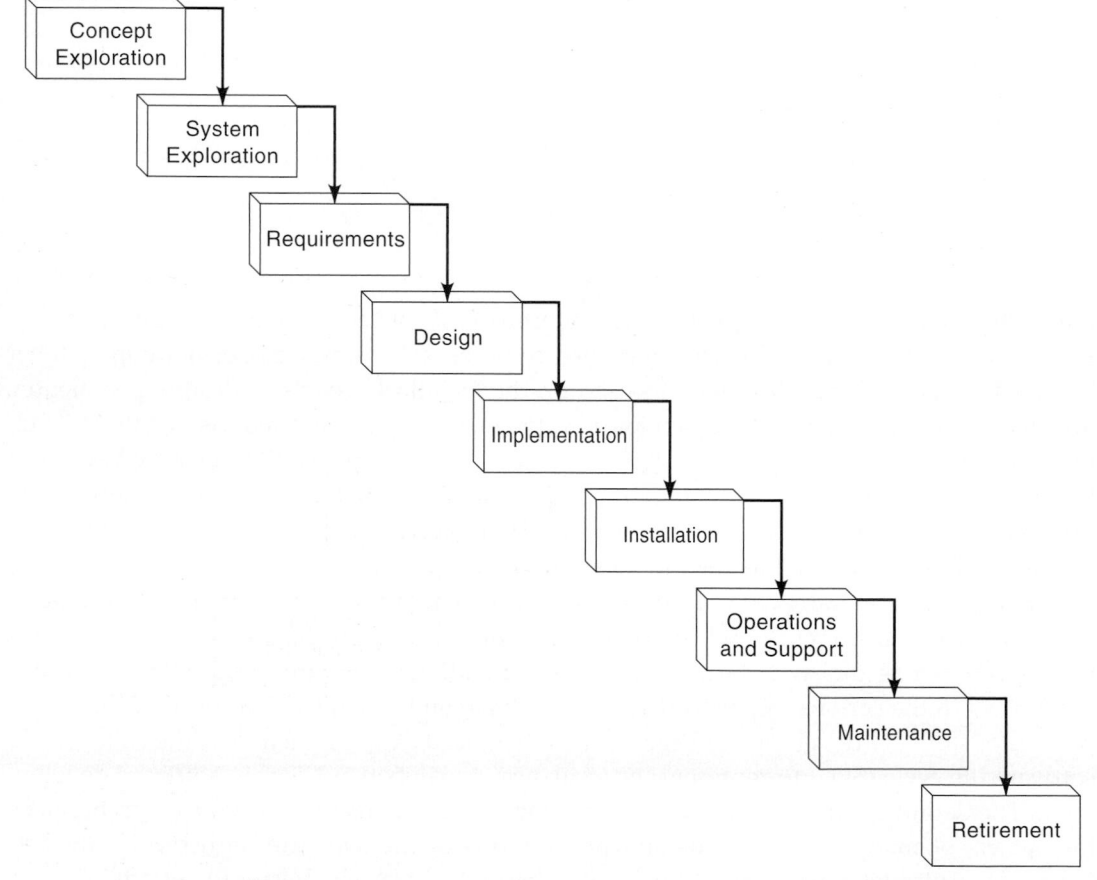

FIGURE 1–1
The "Waterfall" Software Life Cycle (SLC)

does not plow ahead, but revisits the requirements specifications phase. When the requirements specification is once again believed to be complete and correct, the design phase is reentered and begun again. To accommodate this iterative nature of software development, backward arrows were added to what was becoming the industry standard life cycle graphic, as illustrated in Figure 1–2.

Now, there are lots of people who feel that the waterfall model is old-fashioned or simplistic, having long ago outlived its usefulness—the very name seems wrong, since water cannot "fall" uphill to accommodate the backward arrows. All sorts of new models have been depicted to better show how the "real world" works, or how software can be developed faster, or how customers can become more engaged in the process to improve functionality. The spiral model, the evolutionary rapid prototyping model, the V-shaped model, and others

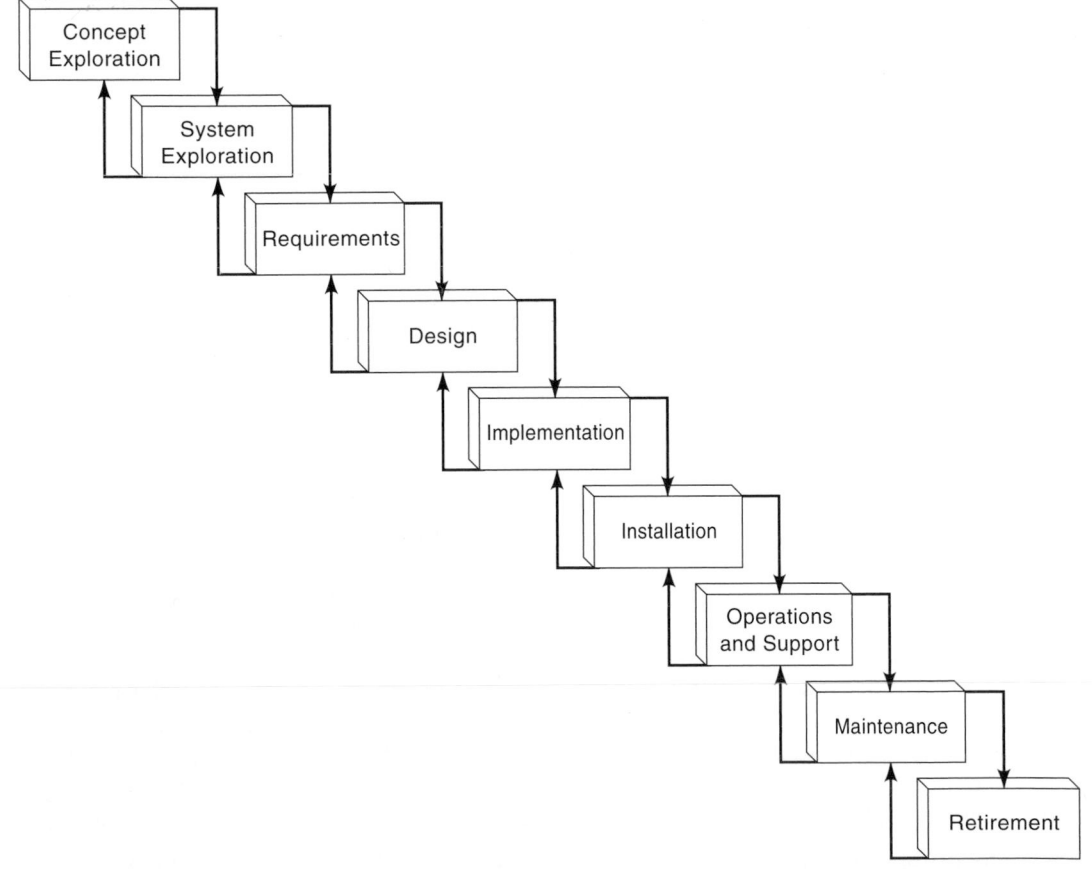

FIGURE 1–2
The Iterative "Waterfall" Model Software Life Cycle (SLC)

have emerged to solve one issue or another. Today, most practitioners might agree that there are so many different types of projects, a one size SLC cannot possibly fit all. The modern viewpoint is that unique projects require unique models, or combinations of models, to succeed. We will discuss the choice of appropriate SLC models, or modified versions of SLC models, in Chapter 4, "Selecting Software Development Life Cycles." We will describe several of the more modern SLCs, and how a project manager can decide which one to use. We will also explain the process groups from the Project Management Body of Knowledge® (PMBOK®) Guide—initiating processes, planning processes, executing processes, and closing processes—and how they map to software life cycle phases.

For simplicity's sake, each chapter in this book will describe project activities by pegging them to the common "waterfall with iterations" life cycle. Though many software practices have changed considerably since the 1970s, tens of thousands of developers learned to use the language of the first SLC as part of a common vocabulary. The terms *phase, iteration, entry criteria, exit criteria, concept exploration, maintenance,* and so forth, have been passed on to succeeding generations of analysts, designers, and programmers. No matter what kind of software project, or its size or scope, the phases of concept exploration through retirement will take place one way or another. The old faithful SLC provides a cradle-to-grave snapshot of project steps, be they large or small. It is for this reason that we have chosen to describe how each of the chapters in this book fits into the overall software process by looking at where we are in the product development life cycle.

Introduction to the 34 Competencies

In the early stages of software project management, the best programmers were promoted to the role of project manager because they demonstrated competence with the tools (programming languages, compilers, etc.) and often displayed knowledge of a domain, such as a scientific, business, or real-time application. They frequently did not succeed in this position because they were unprepared for situations outside of the technical realm. Now we know that every software manager needs skills far beyond knowing how to code. A working knowledge of software engineering is necessary to succeed, but a good software manager needs to excel in people and project management skills, too.

We have compiled a list of the essential competencies employed by the most successful software project managers and organized them into three categories: product, project, and people, as shown in Figure 1–3. This list came from the experiences of many practicing software project managers who contributed to the Software Project Management (SWPM) certificate program at The University of Texas at Austin from 1993 to 2001. It represents the Software Quality Institute's Body of Knowledge for Software Project Management (SQI BOK).

The remainder of this introductory chapter will discuss each of these categories in more detail, while chapters in the sections that follow will show how to use each skill in practical

Software   Project   Management

Product	Project	People
1. Assessing processes	12. Building a work breakdown structure	23. Appraising performance
2. Awareness of process standards		24. Handling intellectual property
3. Defining the product	13. Documenting plans	25. Holding effective meetings
4. Evaluating alternative processes	14. Estimating cost	26. Interaction and communication
5. Managing requirements	15. Estimating effort	27. Leadership
6. Managing subcontractors	16. Managing risks	28. Managing change
7. Performing the initial assessment	17. Monitoring development	29. Negotiating successfully
8. Selecting methods and tools	18. Scheduling	30. Planning careers
9. Tailoring processes	19. Selecting metrics	31. Presenting effectively
10. Tracking product quality	20. Selecting project management tools	32. Recruiting
11. Understanding development activities	21. Tracking process	33. Selecting a team
	22. Tracking project progress	34. Teambuilding

FIGURE 1–3
Thirty-Four Competencies that Every Software Project Manager Needs to Know

situations. Many of these techniques and skills will be further illustrated in sidebar stories and anecdotes.

Product Development Techniques

1. **Assessing processes**—Defining criteria for reviews
2. **Awareness of process standards**—Understanding process standards
3. **Defining the product**—Identifying customer environment and product requirements
4. **Evaluating alternative processes**—Evaluating various approaches
5. **Managing requirements**—Monitoring requirements changes
6. **Managing subcontractors**—Planning, managing, and monitoring performance
7. **Performing the initial assessment**—Assessing difficulty, risks, costs, and schedule
8. **Selecting methods and tools**—Defining selection processes
9. **Tailoring processes**—Modifying standard processes to suit a project
10. **Tracking product quality**—Monitoring the quality of an evolving product
11. **Understanding development activities**—Learning the software development cycle

Project Management Skills

12. **Building a work breakdown structure**—Building a WBS for a project
13. **Documenting plans**—Identifying key components
14. **Estimating cost**—Estimating cost to complete the project
15. **Estimating effort**—Estimating effort required to complete the project
16. **Managing risks**—Identifying and determining the impact and handling of risks
17. **Monitoring development**—Monitoring the production of software

18. **Scheduling**—Creating a schedule and key milestones
19. **Selecting metrics**—Choosing and using appropriate metrics
20. **Selecting project management tools**—Knowing how to select project management tools
21. **Tracking processes**—Monitoring compliance of project team
22. **Tracking project progress**—Monitoring progress using metrics

People Management Skills

23. **Appraising performance**—Evaluating teams to enhance performance
24. **Handling intellectual property**—Understanding the impact of critical issues
25. **Holding effective meetings**—Planning and running excellent meetings
26. **Interaction and communication**—Dealing with developers, upper management, and other teams
27. **Leadership**—Coaching project teams for optimal results
28. **Managing change**—Being an effective change agent
29. **Negotiating successfully**—Resolving conflicts and negotiating successfully
30. **Planning careers**—Structuring and giving career guidance
31. **Presenting effectively**—Using effective written and oral skills
32. **Recruiting**—Recruiting and interviewing team members successfully
33. **Selecting a team**—Choosing highly competent teams
34. **Teambuilding**—Forming, guiding, and maintaining an effective team

Views of the competencies throughout the book:

- Chapters are pegged to the sequence of activities in a software life cycle.
- Every chapter in this book will begin by describing when (in what phase or phases) the subject matter will be used during the SLC. For example, Chapter 16, "Eliciting Requirements," points out that this activity occurs primarily in the requirements phase, although it may begin as early as the concept exploration phase and continue through the design phase.
- Multiple competencies are addressed in each chapter. One or more of the 34 competencies will be most important to the subject of a chapter. In Chapter 16 the focus is on the skills of managing requirements, estimating cost, estimating effort, and presenting effectively, although others may be touched upon.

Surveying the Foundations

Before explaining the product, process, and people categories where the 34 project management (PM) competencies have been grouped, it will be helpful to define a few basic terms in order to create a shared vocabulary. We will offer practical descriptions of software, management, software engineering, project management, and process in addition to the important definitions listed in Box 1–1, to facilitate communication.

Box 1–1
Important Project Management Definitions

Task:	A generic term for work that is not included in the work breakdown structure, but potentially could be a further decomposition of work by the individuals responsible for that work. Also, the lowest level of effort on a project.
Activity:	An element of work performed during the course of a project. An activity normally has an expected duration, an expected cost, and expected resource requirements. Activities can be subdivided into tasks.
Phase:	A group of activities/tasks, producing a significant deliverable work product.
Project:	A unique, goal-oriented, time-bound, and constrained undertaking.
Program:	A large collection of related projects.
System:	An organized element acting as a whole.

Some of the terms can be confusing. For example, most of the 34 competencies that we address in this book apply equally well to projects and programs. Therefore, we may use the terms interchangeably when discussing them. Depending on the context, the abbreviation PM may mean: project manager, project management, program manager, or program management.

What Is "Software Project Management"?

This book is about the practice of *software*, *project*, and *management*. Which term is most important, and what do the words actually mean? And how do the 34 competencies fit into them? Many authors have proposed variations over the years, and the standards organizations themselves don't always agree. We need some practical definitions that fit our circumstances.

The following is a simple interpretation of these for our purposes:

Software is the program(s) that is (are) the product of a (software engineering) project. (See Box 1–2.) For *software*, we will rely on the Software Engineering Institute (SEI) and the Institute of Electrical and Electronics Engineers (IEEE), with supporting information on quality coming from the National Institute of Standards and Technology (NIST), the International Organization for Standards (ISO), the American National Standards Institute (ANSI), and the American Society for Quality (ASQ).

Box 1–2
Software Definition
Source: *www.bartleby.com*

---

soft·ware

The programs, routines, and symbolic languages that control the functioning of the hardware and direct its operation.

A *project* is a large or important undertaking that is planned. Calling it a "scheme" seems a little harsh. (See Box 1–3.) For *project*, we will rely on the Project Management Institute® (PMI®) and the IEEE.

Box 1–3
Project Definition
Source: *www.m-w.com/cgi-bin/dictionary*

---

proj·ect

1. a specific plan or design: SCHEME

2. a planned undertaking: as **(a)** a definitely formulated piece of research **(b)** a large usually government-supported undertaking **(c)** a task or problem engaged in usually by a group of students to supplement and apply classroom studies

---

Management is the practice of executing and controlling the project. (See Box 1–4.) For *management* we will turn to PMI® and the general practice of management as taught in Master of Business Administration (MBA) higher education.

Box 1–4
Management Definition
Source: *www.m-w.com/cgi-bin/dictionary*

---

man·age·ment

1. the act or art of managing: the conducting or supervising of something (as a business)

2. judicious use of means to accomplish an end

3. the collective body of those who manage or direct an enterprise

Simple as it sounds, the phrase *software project management* requires considerable study for the competencies associated with each word. As described in Figure 1–3, the 34 competencies are divided into product, project, and people skills, which correlate to the terms in the title of this book, "software," "project," and "management," respectively. Although the term "quality" appears in the title, there is not a separate competencies category for quality skills, as they permeate the entire set of competencies.

What Is Software Engineering?

According to Barry Boehm, *software engineering* is: A practical application of scientific knowledge in the design and construction of computer programs and the associated documentation required to develop, operate, and maintain them.[1] IEEE defines it as: a systematic approach to the development, operation, maintenance, and retirement of software.[2] And Stephen Schach describes software engineering as: a discipline whose aim is the production of quality software, software that is delivered on time, within budget, and that satisfies its requirements.[3]

We choose to use a blend of the preceding definitions to reflect the viewpoint of the software project manager: *Software engineering* is a disciplined, systematic approach to the development, operation, maintenance, and retirement of software through the practical application of scientific knowledge and processes.

What Is a Project?

Although we just examined the phrase *software project management* through dictionary definitions and professional standards organizations descriptions, the individual terms are important enough to bear further investigation.

Two noted authors of MBA textbooks and specialized courses in project management provide these definitions of "project":

Harold Kerzner defines a project to be any series of activities or tasks that have a specific objective to be completed within certain specifications, have defined start and end dates, have funding limits (if applicable), and consume resources (i.e., money, people, equipment).[4]

James Lewis views a project as a one-time job that has definite starting and ending points, clearly defined objectives, scope, and (usually) a budget; differentiated from repetitive activities such as production, order processing, and so on; a special activity with very tactical goals.[5]

Given these definitions, we can see how the well-known "PM Triangle" (Figure 1–4) was created. A project strives to deliver a product of a given scope, within a given cost and schedule, with a certain degree of quality. The PM's task is to balance performance (scope), time (schedule), and resources (cost). Yet, there are only so many degrees of freedom—it is rare that schedule, budget, and quality are abundant in unlimited quantities. We are forced to choose only one or two of the qualities as a primary pursuit. This is known in the vernacular as "the good-fast-cheap triangle—pick two."

We agree with quality guru Joseph Juran that a project is a problem scheduled for solution.

Not specific to software, the Project Management Institute includes a fairly well-received definition in its *PMBOK® Guide*. PMI® refers to a project as: a temporary endeavor undertaken to create a unique product or service with a definite beginning and end, different from ongoing, repetitive operations and requiring progressive elaboration of characteristics.[6]

These project definitions have a few things in common:

Objective. There must be a clearly defined goal or set of goals for the project. A project must accomplish something. If a project has multiple goals, they should be related to each other, and not conflict with one another.

Start and end points. A project is a temporary endeavor. It must have a clearly defined beginning and ending, usually expressed as dates. Software maintenance is usually an ongoing operation, not a project, but may have well-defined projects that occur within it, such as specific releases.

Uniqueness. A project is a one-time thing, not usually repeated exactly the same way. This does not imply that repeat performance is not a project. Building a house is usually classified as a project, even though contractors have built millions of houses. Although the pattern and process are basically the same (a template), there are enough differences in each house (such as lot and location, varying materials, and code and design changes) to distinguish it from others. Otherwise, it becomes an ongoing production line making

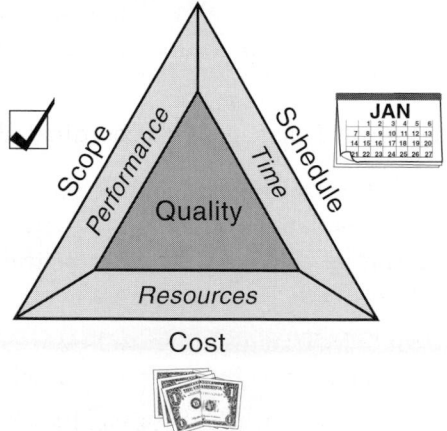

FIGURE 1-4
The Project Management Triangle

identical pieces in exactly the same way. The same is true for software professionals—we never build exactly the same software system, although we may copy it or port it.

Constraints. A project has cost, schedule, and quality performance constraints. These are the "big three" of the PM triangle that must be balanced and managed to achieve success.

So, our practical definition of this term in the software development realm is: A *project* is a unique, temporary endeavor with defined start and end dates to achieve one or more objectives within the constraints of cost, schedule, and quality performance.

What Is a Program?

Similar to a project, and often confused with it, is the *program*. Although many people refer to these interchangeably, the differences are mostly of scale. Let's look at some existing definitions as we did for *project*.

Kerzner defines a program as: the necessary first-level elements of a system (in the context of systems theory); a time-phased subsystem; and, borrowing from NASA, a relative series of undertakings that continue over a period of time (normally years), and that are designed to accomplish a broad technical or scientific goal in the long range plan.[7]

Don Shafer, in lectures to The University of Texas at Austin's Software Quality Institute, has described a program as usually a large endeavor, encompassing a broad goal, which can be composed of a number of projects; for example, the U.S. space program (manned—Gemini, moon lander, space shuttle, orbital lab, etc.).

The American Society for Quality™ (ASQ™) certifies software quality engineers by way of a Certified Software Quality Engineer (CSQE) exam. The Quality Council of Indiana publishes a primer for the exam (the *CSQE Primer*) that describes a program to be a group of related projects managed to obtain collective benefits, often with a strategic goal, which may involve a series of repetitive or cyclical undertakings.

PMI® succinctly states: A program is a group of related projects managed in a coordinated way. Programs usually include an element of ongoing activity.[8]

These definitions agree that a program is:

Large. Programs are usually larger than projects and are often composed of projects.

Lengthy. Programs usually span long time periods and extend beyond the time spans of projects.

General. Programs may have only "ballpark" ending dates and objectives defined for them. Often the objective for the program is very broad, such as you would find in a class of software product.

So, our definition becomes: A *program* is a large, lengthy endeavor with indistinct ending dates and objectives, composed of related projects, managed cooperatively.

What Is Project Management?

PMI® defines PM as: a set of proven principles, methods and techniques for the effective planning, scheduling, controlling and tracking of deliverable-oriented work (results) that help to establish a sound historical basis for future planning of projects.

Kerzner finds PM to be the planning, organizing, directing, and controlling of company resources (functional personnel) assigned to a specific project, for a relatively short-term objective that has been established to complete specific goals and objectives.

Common concepts in those statements are:

Management. Project management skills are a subset of general management skills.

Skills. Project management skills apply management skills to the achievement of project objectives. Those skills include planning, organizing, scheduling, directing, controlling, and tracking.

How does this relate to the Body of Knowledge? PMI describes the Project Management Body of Knowledge (e.g., critical path analysis and work breakdown structures) as intersecting the general management area of MBA knowledge (e.g., planning, organizing, staffing, executing, and controlling the operations of an ongoing enterprise), and both of those with the domain knowledge for the project (construction, biosciences, government contracting, consulting, etc.), as illustrated in Figure 1–5. For software projects, this domain area is usually some specialty of IT or Engineering (payroll, electrical engineering, automotive, real time).

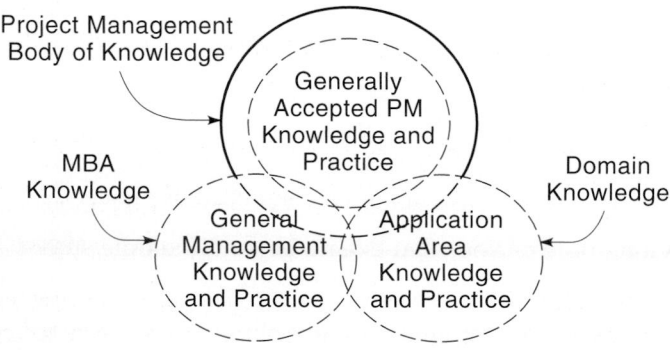

FIGURE 1–5
PMBOK Intersection with MBA Knowledge and Domain

So, we have this definition of PM as it applies to software: *Project management* is a specialization of general management studies that employs the standard management skills of planning, organizing, staffing, leading or directing, and controlling to achieve defined project objectives.

Generally, the same definition works for Program Management as well.

Some Other Useful Definitions

In addition to the terms *software, project, management, software project management, software engineering, program,* and *project management,* there are a few others that will be used repeatedly throughout the text. Next, we will briefly examine the terms *process, task, activity, phase,* and *system.*

What Is a Process?

PMI defines project management as being composed of proven principles, methods, and techniques. Most often, the methods and techniques are composed of work processes supported by tools.

Merriam-Webster's definition of *process* is in Box 1–5.

Box 1–5
Process Definition
Source: *www.m-w.com/cgi-bin/dictionary*

---

pro·cess

1. something going on

2a. a natural phenomenon marked by gradual changes that lead toward a particular result: a natural continuing activity or function

2b. a series of actions or operations conducing to an end; especially: a continuous operation or treatment especially in manufacture

---

In *Quality Process Management,* Gabriel Pall defines the term as: a bounded set of interrelated activities that takes one or more kinds of inputs and creates outputs that are of value to the customer by means of one or more transformations.[9] And IEEE simply states that a process is a sequence of steps performed for a given purpose.

Figure 1–6 depicts the input, transformation, and output relationships that define a process.

We will use this definition: A *process* is a series of actions that transform a set of inputs into a result.

For software project management, we define two types of processes—project and product—as shown in Table 1–1.

TABLE 1–1
Project and Product Processes

Project Processes	Product Processes
Describe and organize the work of the project	Specify and create the project product
Most are applicable, most of the time	Defined by the life cycle used
Defined by the PMI® *PMBOK® Guide*	Vary by application area
	Defined by the American Society of Quality (ASQ) Certified Software Quality Engineer (CSQE) Body of Knowledge (BOK)

What Is a Task? What Is an Activity?

Tasks and activities are often used interchangeably, causing some confusion. Unfortunately, there is no consensus within the software project management community for the relationship between activities and tasks. In some areas, activities are composed of tasks, and in others tasks are composed of activities. In our experience, activities have a higher order than tasks, and are primarily composed of tasks. Of course, what really matters is that the work is clearly described for the team members, not what it is named.

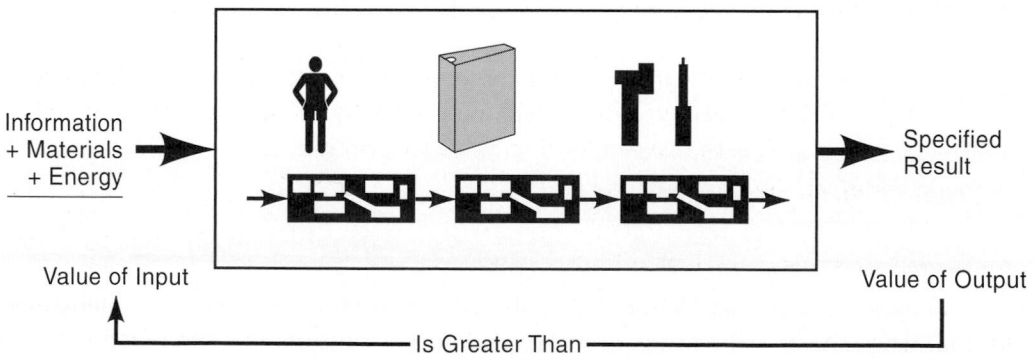

FIGURE 1–6
Process Input, Transformation, and Output

As a lower element in the hierarchy, tasks are relatively shorter in duration than activities, phases, projects, or programs. They are usually the lowest order of work element in a project, although some software project managers also define subtasks as a further division.

There are many defining characteristics of tasks and activities. Tasks usually are an assigned piece of work to be finished within a certain time period. Activities are often a grouping of tasks that can be carried out by one person or organizational unit, and/or that produce a single work product. Descriptions of *task* and *activity* provided by *Webster's* are:

Task: a usually assigned piece of work often to be finished within a certain time; implies work imposed by a person in authority or an employer or by circumstance.

Activity: an organizational unit for performing a specific function; also: its function or duties.[10]

Other authoritative definitions—from the PMBOK—are:

Activity: an element of work performed during the course of a project; an activity normally has an expected duration, expected cost, and expected resource requirements, and can be subdivided into tasks.

Task: a generic term for work that is not included in the work breakdown structure, but potentially could be a further decomposition of work by the individuals responsible for that work; also, the lowest level of effort on a project.[11]

The big thing is that tasks mean anything tracked that is not in the WBS. It really refers to what a professional learned in school. This is why everything is not broken down into the baby steps taught in a computer programming textbook. For years, the industry has argued over whether a task is part of an activity or an activity is part of a task. The 2000 edition of the PMBOK makes that distinction clear.

So, for software project management, we will use the following definitions:

Task is a generic term for work that is not included in the work breakdown structure, but potentially could be a further decomposition of work by the individuals responsible for that work. Also, it is the lowest level of effort on a project.

And an *activity* is an element of work performed during the course of a project. An activity normally has an expected duration, expected cost, and expected resource requirements. Activities can be subdivided into tasks.

What Is a Phase?

In any large, complex project, it is easy to become overwhelmed by the sheer number of tasks and activities that need to be completed. A convenient way to deal with this volume is to divide the project into groups of tasks that make it easier for us to understand and organize them. We will view activities as groups of tasks, and phases as groups of activities. Webster defines *phase* as a distinguishable part in a course, development, or cycle. SEI defines *phase* as a period of time. PMI refers to *project phase* as a collection of logically related project activities, usually culminating in the completion of a major deliverable. For the sake of our common vocabulary, our phases are represented in Figure 1–2 and in Figure 1–17.

Organizing tasks around a deliverable makes sense, and provides a logical checkpoint before moving into another set of tasks. It's not required, but a nice way to organize a large collection of tasks is around the production steps of deliverables and work products, with tasks grouped into activities, and activities grouped into phases.

So a definition we can use in software project management becomes: A *phase* is a collection of related activities or tasks that produce a deliverable or work product.

What Is a System?

Right behind "thing" as the most ambiguous word in the English language, "system" can mean just about anything for software. This ambiguity has historically been a root cause of problems in understanding software requirements. So, we will define it here for our purposes.

From business systems theory, a general definition is useful.

Kerzner says that a system is a group of elements organized and arranged so that the elements can act as a whole toward achieving a common goal; is a collection of interacting subsystems; and has boundaries that define it as an open system (which interacts with the surrounding environment) or a closed system (which is isolated from the surrounding environment).[12]

IEEE defines a system as a collection of components organized to accomplish a specific function or set of functions.

This means that any collection of organized elements oriented towards a goal can be a system. In software project management, we can have many systems: change management system, cost management system, configuration management system, project management information system, and performance measurement system.

We think of the software products of our projects as systems, often composed of hardware, software, and processes.

A key point about systems is that they have boundaries and may or may not interact with their surrounding environments. If they can stand alone and function independently they are *closed systems*. If they must interact with their environment to be effective they are *open systems*.

Regardless of whether the products produced by a software project are closed or open systems, programs and projects are almost always open systems, as much of the project manager's job involves interacting with other people and systems in a business environment.

Our definition of the term will be: A *system* is an organized group of elements with a boundary defining openness or closeness that acts as a whole toward achieving a common goal.

It is important for software project managers to understand the basic nature of systems as they run programs and projects made up of many interacting systems in organizations composed of many interacting systems. This is why their jobs are so complex.

Now we have a consistent language that includes a basic set of PM terms. Next, we will turn to brief descriptions of the SWPM essential software project management competencies, and how they will be addressed in this book. Each SLC phase requires the use of more than one competency, and each competency is used in more than one phase. The chapters are arranged to follow an SLC sequence, each chapter addressing applicable PM skills. As described earlier in this chapter, our focus is quality, software, project, and management. Quality underlies all; software (product), project, and management (people) each have a number of skills that should be possessed or acquired by a project manager. So, we will begin with a brief description of software, or product, competencies.

Product Development Techniques

At the end of the day, software project managers are responsible for delivering a product. Since that is our primary objective, we will examine product development techniques first, before project skills and people skills. Product development techniques, competencies 1 through 11, are shown in Table 1–2. A brief description of each competency will follow, while chapters appearing later in this handbook will describe each competency more fully.

TABLE 1–2
Product (Software) Competencies

Product (Software) Competency	Description	Chapter or Appendix
1. Assessing processes	Defining criteria for reviews	11. Estimating Duration and Cost 25. Project Tracking and Control 26. Continuous Process Improvement 30. Software Quality Assurance
2. Awareness of process standards	Understanding process standards	Appendix A. Supporting Organizations

(Continues)

TABLE 1–2 (Continued)
Product (Software) Competencies

Product (Software) Competency	Description	Chapter or Appendix
3. Defining the product	Identifying customer environment and product requirements	7. Defining the Goal and Scope of the Software Project
4. Evaluating alternative processes	Evaluating various approaches	4. Selecting Software Development Life Cycles 7. Defining the Goal and Scope of the Software Project 13. Choosing an Organizational Form
5. Managing requirements	Monitoring requirements changes	16. Eliciting Requirements 17. Developing the Software Requirements Specification
6. Managing subcontractors	Planning, managing, and monitoring performance	6. Selecting a Project Team 12. Assigning Resources 32. Legal Issues in Software
7. Performing the initial assessment	Assessing difficulty, risks, costs, and schedule	9. Identifying the Tasks and Activities 10. Software Size and Reuse Estimating 11. Estimating Duration and Cost 18. Determining Project Risks
8. Selecting methods and tools	Defining selection processes	24. Use of Tools 31. Software Configuration Management Appendix D. Understanding Systems Engineering

(Continues)

TABLE 1–2 (Continued)
Product (Software) Competencies

Product (Software) Competency	Description	Chapter or Appendix
9. Tailoring processes	Modifying standard processes to suit a project	4. Selecting Software Development Life Cycles 13. Choosing an Organizational Form 14. Considering Dependencies
10. Tracking product quality	Monitoring the quality of an evolving product	30. Software Quality Assurance
11. Understanding development activities	Learning the software development cycle	4. Selecting Software Development Life Cycles 5. Managing Domain Processes

Where Product Competencies Are Addressed

There are many approaches to the "sequence" of events that comprise the process of developing, controlling, managing, enhancing, and maintaining software. The word "sequence" appears in quotes because the process is not necessarily linear—iterations inside and between phases, or process steps, often occur. And, the process steps may occur in tandem—more than one task may be worked on during any given period of time, and a project member may be dividing time among multiple tasks.

Different types of projects require different types of process models: Software controlling an automobile air bag or medical CAT Scan machine will require extraordinary testing since human life is at stake. Software for an Internet catalog ordering system for used china and silver requires a great deal of attention to the user interface—a part of the system that should probably be prototyped. The safety needs of the latter system are minimal as compared to the others, so the same degree of testing is not necessary. The different degrees of testing are but one of many reasons different life cycles exist.

In Chapter 4 we will describe several of the more popular or widely used models, and how to know which one to use "as is," or to use as the basis for tailoring to your specific project. Since we need a common framework for discussion, we will talk in terms of a "plain vanilla" waterfall with iterations (Figure 1–2), instead of one of the newer, more specialized SLCs.

A Brief Description of Product Management Skills

Product competencies 1 through 11 are briefly described in the following sections.

Product Competency 1:
Assessing Processes—Defining Criteria for Reviews   *Review* describes the activity of evaluating or assessing work products. Reviews should take place frequently and at certain milestones in the life of a project, certainly at the end of a phase. Once we determine the appropriate life cycle, we will know its phases and can then determine where end-of-phase product reviews should occur. Reviews can and should take place in process as well. In Chapter 30, "Software Quality Assurance," we will describe the review event: what should be reviewed, when the reviews should occur, who should attend, and how the review should be conducted. Also included are the quality control aspects that reviews must address, such as the cost of quality and defect counts. The triangles in our IEEE 1074-inspired waterfall model (Figure 1–7) show that it is necessary for a development team to pass a review of the just-completed phase before proceeding to the next. In addition to end-of-phase product reviews, internal and external deliverables from within each phase are also candidates for review. Reviews of early estimates of effort and cost will improve the overall, committed project cost/schedule estimates as described in Chapter 11, "Estimating Duration and Cost."

As detailed in Chapter 25, "Project Tracking and Control," items to be reviewed also include actual versus estimated cost, actual versus estimated schedule, percent of project completion, risk control, and many other project metric "barometers."

Finally, the assessment process forms the foundation for continually assessing how effective and appropriate our processes function in our development environment, as described in Chapter 26, "Continuous Process Improvement." Here, reviews will focus on the assessment and improvement of productivity, the improvement of cycle time, and other process-related artifacts.

Product Competency 2:
Awareness of Process Standards—Understanding Process Standards   Raising awareness of the standards that impact a project manager's success is the goal of Appendix A, "Supporting Organizations." Professional organizations provide the PM with guidance on organizations, projects, analysis, design, coding, testing, and more.

Organizations that support the software development process are responsible for many of these standards. Table 1–3 lists some of these organizations.

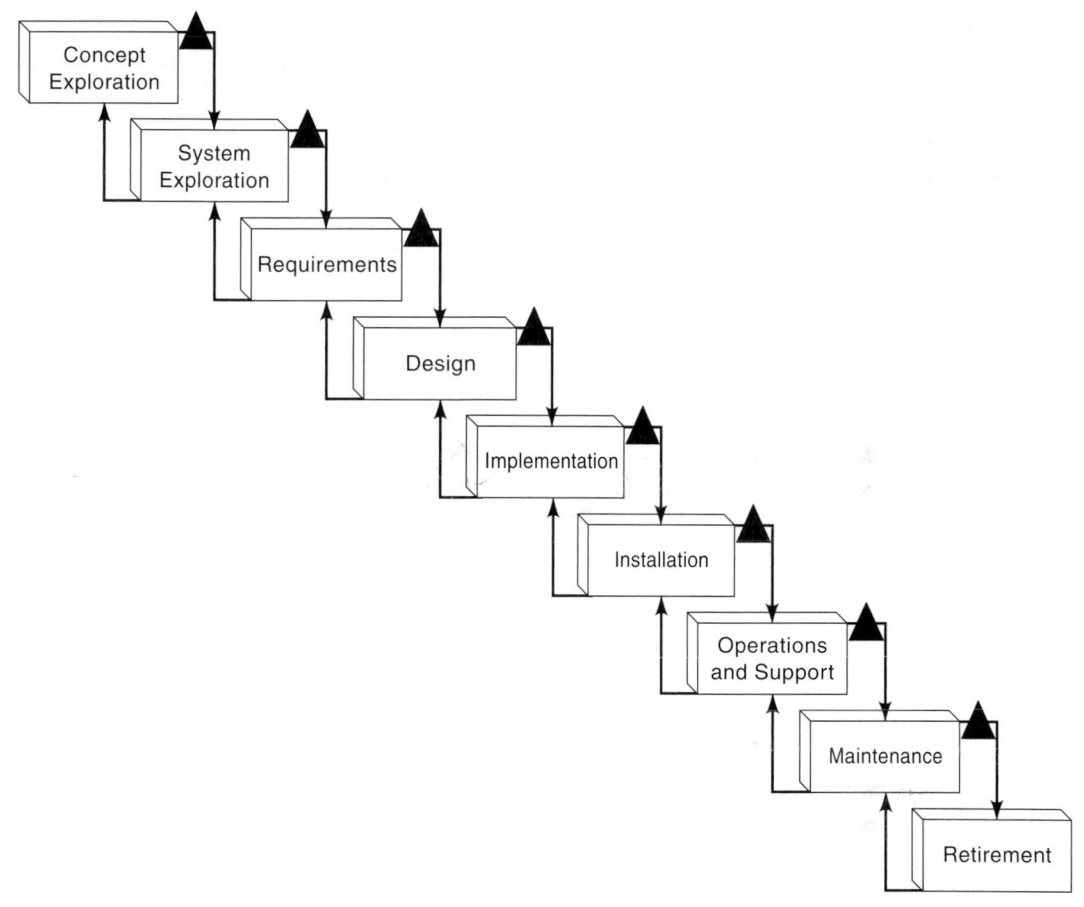

FIGURE 1–7
Phase Reviews in the Iterative Waterfall Software Life Cycle

TABLE 1–3
Organizations that Support the Software Development Process with Industry Standards

Label	Organization	Primary Focus	Of Interest for SWPM	URL
PMI®	Project Management Institute®	General project management	Project Management Body of Knowledge® (PMBOK®) Guide	www.pmi.org
ASQ™	American Society of Quality™	Quality improvement	Software Quality Engineering Body of Knowledge (Certified Software Quality Engineer [CSQE] BOK)	www.asq.org
IEEE	Institute of Electrical and Electronics Engineers	Engineering standards	Software Engineering Standards Collection	www.ieee.org
ISO	International Organization for Standardization	International standards	ISO 9000 Quality Standards; ISO/IEC 12207 IT-software life cycle process standard	www.iso.ch
ANSI	American National Standards Institute	National standards for the U.S.	Guide for application of ISO/IEC 12207 to software engineering project management	www.ansi.org
NIST	National Institute of Standards and Technology	Technology, measurements, and standards for U.S. industry	Malcolm Baldrige National Quality Award for Performance Excellence (MBNQA)	www.nist.gov
SEI	Software Engineering Institute	Software engineering	Capability Maturity Model for Software v.1.1 (CMM™)	www.sei.cmu.edu

Product Competency 3:
Defining the Product—Identifying Customer Environment and Product

Requirements   Chapter 7, "Defining the Goal and Scope of the Software Project," covers the process governing those activities. The project manager must be competent in relating the customer environment and overall product requirements to the product definition as built by the development team.

This product definition is accomplished through the use of project deliverables shown in Appendix F, "Project Artifact Templates." In that appendix, each of the standard project individual work products will be recalled, as well as the relationships that bind them: software project management plan (SPMP), risk management plan, communication plan, software configuration management plan (SCM plan), software quality assurance plan (SQA plan), and test plan.

Upon completion of these plans, the project manager, project team, and customer will have a common understanding of the product definition. The plans are constructed according to templates provided by the standards organizations listed in Table 1–3.

Product Competency 4:
Evaluating Alternative Processes—Evaluating Various Approaches   There

are as many ways to organize project personnel as there are variations on the standard waterfall life cycle. The ability to pick and choose from a plethora of toolkits means the "evaluation of various approaches." By definition, projects are unique, a characteristic that distinguishes them from ongoing operations. Because of this uniqueness, each project may have different goals, objectives, development standards, life cycles, and team structures. A crucial competency for software project managers is to be able to evaluate the various options and select the most appropriate for each project.

Some of the ways that a project manager may evaluate alternative processes are by selecting a life cycle (Chapter 4, "Selecting Software Development Life Cycles"), defining standards for development based on an approved charter, goals, and scope (Chapter 7, "Defining the Goal and Scope of the Software Project"), and choosing an organizational form.

Product Competency 5:
Managing Requirements—Monitoring Changes in Requirements   The im-

portant and difficult part of getting the requirements correct is eliciting them from the stakeholders. Communication issues, varying expectations, differing needs, and many more barriers make the job complex. Chapter 16, "Eliciting Requirements," describes several methods for extracting and formulating true requirements for the software requirements specification, and determining the value of each. Requirements elicitation techniques that will be covered include: interviewing, using use cases and scenario analysis, role playing, storyboarding, forming focus groups, using story boards, building prototypes/modeling, using Joint Application Design® (JAD) and similar techniques, using groupware, brainstorming and idea reduction, and selecting appropriate requirements elicitation techniques.

Defining correct requirements is perhaps the most important part of a software development project. Chapter 17, "Developing the Software Requirements Specification," describes the construction of the software requirements specification (SRS) document itself, beginning with the exploratory activity of helping the customer determine his true wants and needs. Related to this competency, we will study the mastery of requirements engineering, requirements gathering using object models, and an introduction to the SRS template and the evolution of the SRS.

Chapter 23, "Validation and Verification," covers techniques for validating the actual contents of the SRS once the requirements have been gathered and documented into the specifications template. This is another example of where the review activity should be used. More on these will be covered in discussions on executing the software project processes (Chapters 19–24). We will describe how and when techniques like these may be helpfully applied. We'll consider inspections (inspection procedures, inspection forms, and more), prototypes, quality function deployment (QFD), and tools—the set of support systems for the methods and processes.

Product Competency 6:
Managing Subcontractors—Planning, Managing, and Monitoring

Performance   Subcontractor management begins when the project manager determines that some or all of the project work will be outsourced. Clearly, this competency is critical to project success in times of increasingly scarce personnel resources. Chapter 6, "Selecting a Project Team," is the starting place to develop the competence, through the study of project staffing. It presents some basic personality models for understanding people in the context of a high performance team and describes techniques for recruiting and building such teams. These include identifying and understanding personalities, knowing the characteristics of an effective software project team, selecting team members according to a process, and contracting for personnel resources.

Chapter 12, "Assigning Resources," moves to the next step after selecting the project team. Resources include people, software, hardware, facilities, and anything else needed to execute the project plans. We'll discuss issues such as: using named resources versus generic labels; balancing cost ability and availability; determining resource leveling methods; making build versus buy decisions (building products in-house versus buying a commercial-off-the-shelf [COTS] product), and subcontracting versus in-house development.

Every software project manager must build some competency in the basic legal issues surrounding software development. Chapter 32, "Legal Issues in Software," discusses the fundamentals of business law relating to contracts, licenses, and intellectual property. This includes contracting issues such as the procurement cycle and identifying, managing, and protecting intellectual property—patents, trademarks, trade secrets, copyrights, and trade dress.

Product Competency 7:
Performing the Initial Assessment—Assessing Difficulty, Risks, Costs, and
Schedule   Chapter 9, "Identifying the Tasks and Activities," describes the preparation of software development task descriptions within each life cycle process. Also included are references to the usual and customary integral processes necessary to run the project. When assessing the difficulties of initiating the software development project, these areas must be mastered: project management, software quality assurance, unit and system testing, configuration management, contract management, and communicating and reporting.

The key to successful software project planning is good estimating. In the software domain, task duration is usually dependent on software size. Chapter 10, "Software Size and Reuse Estimating," describes useful estimating techniques for sizing software, including: counting measures, reusing software, and understanding software estimation methods.

With a size estimate and some historical data, duration and costs can be estimated. Chapter 11, "Estimating Duration and Cost," details what the elements of a cost estimate are and how to prepare one. This includes effort measures, components cost estimation, estimation accuracy, productivity measures, and parametric models.

Chapter 18, "Determining Project Risks," describes how to analyze the constructed plan for risks and produce a major project deliverable: the risk management plan. We describe the nature of risk management, models, risk identification, where to look for risks, risk analysis, quantification tools, risk response development, rating and ranking risks, preparing the risk management plan, and periodic risk changes reporting.

Product Competency 8:
Selecting Methods and Tools—Defining Selection Processes   Project managers' application of sound software development methods, techniques and tools, coupled with project management practices, determines organizational success or failure.

We use these three concepts throughout the handbook. For consistency, these are the definitions used for each leg of the triangle in Figure 1–8: A *method* is a manner, means, or process for accomplishing something. A *tool* is an implement or machine used to do work or perform a task. *Technology* is the application of scientific knowledge in industry or business.

In Chapter 24, "Use of Tools," we discuss the use of certain common tools available for planning and controlling software development projects. This will focus on the important characteristics of the tools a SWPM uses, not specific software products, and is intended as a guide for selection. Specific applications are discussed in other chapters. We will look at: computer aided software engineering (CASE) tools in both object-oriented (OO) environments and structured environments; software size and estimating tools such as COCOMO and SLIM; and project planning, tracking, and control tools for planning, scheduling, effort reporting, and resource leveling. Many of these tools are Internet- and Web-enabled.

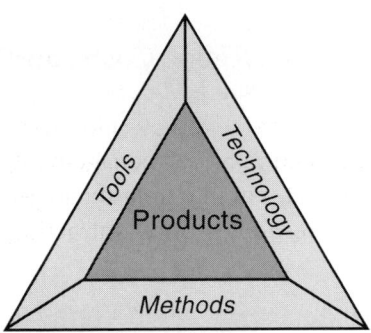

FIGURE 1–8
Methods, Tools, and Technology Relationships

Required from the beginning of a project, a configuration management (CM) system must be available for the duration. Every single project deliverable, beginning with Concept Exploration and Requirements Elicitation documentation, must be kept under configuration control. Chapter 31, "Software Configuration Management," covers the issues and basics for a sound software project CM system: principles, basic requirements, planning and organizing, tools, and internal and external artifacts. Project management competencies also span the problem domain (type of application) and branch out to the entire system (including hardware) to be developed. Appendix D, "Understanding Systems Engineering," provides insight into the systems engineering required for any product. The key areas covered are the system engineering process, life cycles, and methods. These are often somewhat different than those for pure software systems.

Product Competency 9:
Tailoring Processes—Modifying Standard Processes to Suit a Project As discussed with competency 1, "Assessing Processes," it is often advantageous to customize or tailor processes, procedures, and life cycles to meet the specific needs of a project. The tailoring activity typically begins with the project manager's selection of the most appropriate life cycle for a project. Chapter 4, "Selecting Software Development Life Cycles," covers the characteristics of various software project life cycles and provides guidelines for selecting an appropriate one for a given software project.

Typical organizational structures are not applicable to all software projects. It is important for the project manager to recognize the type of organizational structure best suited for the project at hand, considering the environment in which it will operate. The forms of organization defined in Chapter 13, "Choosing an Organizational Form," include: functional, project expediter, project coordinator, and matrix. Each of these will be defined and discussed in terms of advantages and disadvantages.

Tailoring the project processes and environment must be done with consideration to all dependencies. Most tasks are not performed in isolation on a project. Identifying proper dependencies is a key part of getting the schedule right. Chapter 14, "Considering Dependencies," discusses some of those "tailorable" dependencies common in software development projects, including: company-wide support, configuration management, project management, and SQA; potential problem identification—high fan-in or fan-out, circular relationships, identifying the critical path, and the critical chain through unique resources; and contracting relationships.

There are no prescriptions here, but only suggestions as to how the modification of tried and true methods can benefit the project. Flexibility and "out of the box" thinking are often required for appropriateness, effectiveness, and efficiency.

Product Competency 10:
Tracking Product Quality—Monitoring the Quality of an Evolving

Product   Quality of product is the responsibility of the entire development team and of all the stakeholders. The project manager is responsible for putting the processes in place to monitor the product's quality as it evolves through its life cycle. The task, "Identify Quality Improvement Needs," may be seen in Figure 1–17 under "Software Quality Management." Because it occurs during multiple development phases, it is one of several "integral tasks."

Chapter 30, "Software Quality Assurance," provides the foundations of quality improvement as they relate to project execution. The following topics will be covered: defining quality, its characteristics, and measures; understanding a brief history of the quality movement—Shewhart, Deming, Juran, and Crosby; understanding important quality concepts—continuous improvement and the Deming control circle plan-do-check-act (PDCA); managing change—being a change agent; implementing software quality; and becoming familiar with software industry issues.

Software Quality Assurance (SQA) will be covered, focusing on: defining software quality, tracking process quality, tracking product quality, understanding assessment processes, and assuring the quality (preparing quality assurance assessment instruments and becoming familiar with the IEEE SQA plan).

Product Competency 11:
Understanding Development Activities—Learning the Software

Development Cycle   As with competencies 1, "Assessing Processes," and 9, "Tailoring Processes," the waterfall model (Figure 1–2) is the typical starting point in learning the software development cycle. Each of the described processes—beginning with concept exploration and ending with system retirement—requires specific competencies. The waterfall model is most certainly not the best life cycle model for all software projects. We refer to it here because it is well established and understood. It provides a form for the major phases occurring in every software project.

Along with simply learning the life cycle models, the software project manager must understand the basic domain processes of the respective domain for which the software is being developed. Merely understanding computer science or software engineering is akin to understanding only how to operate a bulldozer when trying to be a civil engineer. Software engineers and computer scientists may concentrate only on understanding the tools. To be a successful project manager, it is crucial to know the domain to which the tool will be applied. Chapter 5, "Managing Domain Processes," describes how to identify as well as manage those domain-specific processes. Acting as the communication bridge between the developers and the consumer, the project manager must be able to understand the customer and product environments as they relate to software products and define the product in software engineering terminology. Now that we've explored the software product to be developed, it's time to explore how it will be built. Understanding what the product should be required defining it (requirements) and redefining it (requirements management), and putting into place the organizational infrastructure necessary to support turning the requirements into software. That infrastructure included setting up the processes and standards, and methods and tools that will be used. Knowing how to evaluate alternative processes and tailor the ones chosen led us to the appropriate infrastructure. Having a method for managing contractors and determining the initial project risks, costs, and schedule set the stage for actually developing the product. As soon as all of this is in place, the project team is up to speed on development techniques, and quality tracking procedures have been identified, the time for execution has arrived. The project competencies are all about using the product skills. Execution of development, as well as monitoring, tracking, and measuring it, results in implementation.

Project Management Skills _____

Just as with *product* skills, each of the *project* management skills from the 34 competencies will be covered in this book. They are shown in Table 1–2 as competencies 12 through 22. A brief description of each will appear in this section, while chapters appearing later in the book will describe each competency more fully.

Where Project Competencies Are Addressed

Now we will outline the essential project management skills required to achieve software project management competency. The brief explanation of the project management skills, competencies 12 through 22, will be introduced here to serve as a roadmap and as a review guide. The chapters in this handbook that more fully describe each competency are forward referenced in Table 1–4.

TABLE 1–4
Project Competencies

Project Competency	Description	Chapter
12. Building a work breakdown structure	Building a work breakdown structure for a project	4. Selecting Software Development Life Cycles 8. Creating the Work Breakdown Structure 9. Identifying the Tasks and Activities
13. Documenting plans	Identifying key components	4. Selecting Software Development Life Cycles 7. Defining the Goal and Scope of the Software Project 17. Developing the Software Requirements Specification 28. Post Performance Analysis 30. Software Quality Assurance 31. Software Configuration Management Appendix A. Supporting Organizations
14. Estimating cost	Estimating cost to complete a project	10. Software Size and Reuse Estimating 11. Estimating Duration and Cost 12. Assigning Resources 16. Eliciting Requirements
15. Estimating effort	Estimating effort required to complete a project	10. Software Size and Reuse Estimating 11. Estimating Duration and Cost 12. Assigning Resources

(Continues)

TABLE 1–4 (Continued)
Project Competencies

Project Competency	Description	Chapter
		16. Eliciting Requirements 17. Developing the Software Requirements Specification
16. Managing risks	Determining impact and handling of risks	18. Determining Project Risks 21. Software Metrics
17. Monitoring development	Monitoring the production of software	24. Use of Tools 25. Project Tracking and Control 26. Continuous Process Improvement 30. Software Quality Assurance
18. Scheduling	Creating a schedule and key milestones	7. Defining the Goal and Scope of the Software Project 14. Considering Dependencies 15. Scheduling the Work
19. Selecting metrics	Choosing appropriate metrics	21. Software Metrics 24. Use of Tools Appendix A. Supporting Organizations
20. Selecting project management tools	Knowing how to select PM tools	24. Use of Tools
21. Tracking process	Monitoring compliance of project team	5. Managing Domain Processes 21. Software Metrics 25. Project Tracking and Control 26. Continuous Process Improvement 30. Software Quality Assurance
22. Tracking project progress	Monitoring progress using metrics	21. Software Metrics 30. Software Quality Assurance

The project competencies listed in Table 1–4 are what most people think of as project management skills. But they are only part of the picture, as product and people competencies are important as well. In addition, they do not stand alone, but fit into a more global view. Figure 1–9 demonstrates how the project life cycle fits within the phases of the product life cycle, which, in turn, is a segment of the phases found in a typical overall business life cycle.

A Brief Description of Project Management Skills

Project competencies 12 through 22 are briefly described in the following sections.

Project Competency 12:
Building a Work Breakdown Structure—Building a WBS for a Project

The backbone of any project is the work breakdown structure (WBS). It describes the steps necessary to carry out the project and their relationship to each other. Not as straightforward as it first appears, there is an art to creating a good WBS that is useful and usable. Chapter 8, "Creating the Work Breakdown Structure," and Chapter 9, "Identifying the Tasks and Activities," describe the project management skill of creating a WBS. The material in Chapter 4, "Selecting Software Development Life Cycles," influences these.

Chapters 19–24 describe how to use the WBS as a tool to run the project, and Chapter 25, "Project Tracking and Control," illustrates the use of other helpful measurement tools.

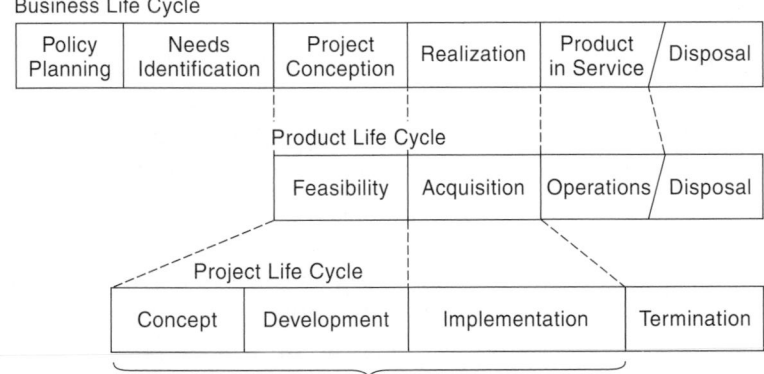

FIGURE 1–9
The Business, Product, and Project Life Cycles
Source: Project Management Institute (1996). *A Guide to the Project Management Body of Knowledge.* Sylva, NC: PMI Publication Division.

Product and project competencies are necessary, but not sufficient, for project success. The best process analysts, requirements crafters, toolsmiths, designers, coders, and project managers on the planet cannot salvage a project devoid of people competencies. Developers and customers are not abstract problems, but human beings with classical needs. They like to be led, coached, negotiated with, recruited, and selected, with dignity, by project managers who are competent and honest. Ask anyone in our industry if they have ever been in an ineffective meeting, on an unproductive team, the recipient of an insensitive performance review, or had their career aspirations ignored, and you will likely turn up a "yes" for every offense. Project management is not just about developing the product, it is about the journey—products cannot be developed without people. The framers of the 34 competencies believed that all people-related activities are integral tasks, used throughout the software life cycle.

Project Competency 13:
Documenting Plans—Identifying Key Components   Documenting plans and other project artifacts, an important aspect of project management, is often forgotten or ignored. Documentation ranges from program code analysis and reverse engineering of legacy systems, to functional specifications, user manuals, and project plans.

Programmers, good at developing software and maintaining custom applications, usually have neither the skills nor the desire to write user manuals. When forced, programmers who write manuals do so at a level too complex for the average user to understand. Unfortunately, user documentation is often misunderstood, cannot be found in the manual or online, or is missing altogether.

Thoroughness, logical organization, and step-by-step instructions lead to usable documentation. It should never be, but often is, left until the end of the project.

For any project, large or small, short or long, a few basic documents are essential for success. They are the authority that transcends the tribal memory of the team. The core document is the project management plan—the team's map for the project journey. Other documents will also be needed depending on size, scope, and other requirements—they include a project charter, business justification, risk management plan, configuration management plan, SQA plan, communications plan, requirements and design specifications, a test plan, acceptance instrument, and post process analysis. The project management skill of how to prepare each of these documents is discussed throughout the book as they apply at each phase of the product development life cycle.

We will address documentation in at least ten chapters. Our case study illustrates the differences between a project drifting on fading memories, and one centered on a documented foundation.

Project Competency 14:
Estimating Cost—Estimating Cost Required to Complete a Project   Along
with schedule and scope, forecasting and managing costs represent basic and necessary skills. These competencies are not easy—it has been said that the only thing harder than forecasting the future is changing the past.

Knowledge of software size is paramount, as it is the foundation for effort and cost estimation. Chapter 10, "Software Size and Reuse Estimating," explores well-respected size estimation methods. The accuracy of the software product size estimate feeds the accuracy of the effort estimate (Chapter 11, "Estimating Duration and Cost"). An effort estimate leads directly to labor costs, and can be added to other costs such as materials and overhead to produce a reasonable overall cost figure for the software project. Figure 1–10 shows the estimated trend for using senior designers on a software development project.

Software size largely depends on the requirements, which we will cover in Chapter 16, "Eliciting Requirements."

In Chapter 12, "Assigning Resources," we will see how resource assignments can dramatically affect project costs through such factors as overtime, perks, and experience level.

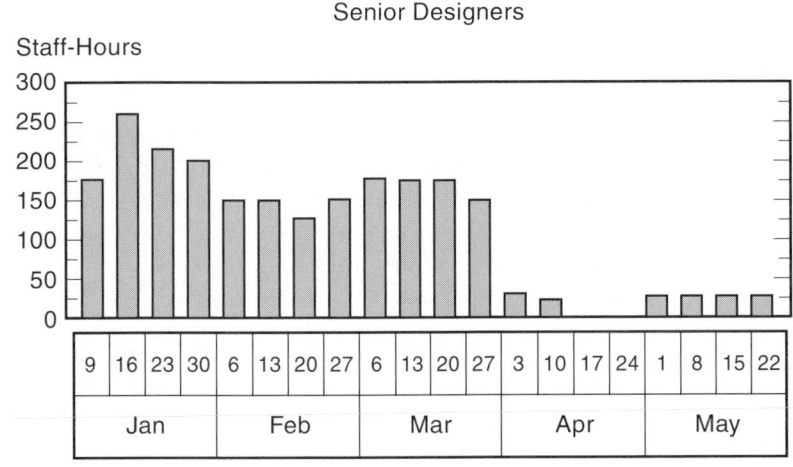

FIGURE 1–10
Estimating Effort

Project Competency 15:
Estimating Effort—Estimating Effort Required to Complete a Project   Fundamental to cost estimating is approximating the effort necessary to build the software product. Of course, effort estimation depends on size estimation, which in turn depends on a thorough understanding of the product requirements. Figure 1–10 is an example of one of the many graphical tools than can aid a PM in forecasting and tracking effort.

In Chapter 16, "Eliciting Requirements," and in Chapter 17, "Developing the Software Requirements Specification," we will cover how to get the requirements right. From there, we can use Chapter 10, "Software Size and Reuse Estimating," and Chapter 11, "Estimating Duration and Cost," to complete the estimation picture.

Project Competency 16:
Managing Risks—Determining Impact and Handling of Risks   It has been said that the best project managers are good risk managers. Handling risks is a key skill for any manager, but it is crucial for software project managers because so much can (and often does) go wrong—software projects are thought of as more complex because the product is intangible, and therefore difficult to test or assess.

In Chapter 18, "Determining Project Risks," we look at some models for risk management, identification, and control, offering guidance on which one fits best in certain situations. In Chapter 21, "Software Metrics," we see how software project metrics can be used to monitor project risks.

Project Competency 17:
Monitoring Development—Monitoring the Production of Software   Once the team begins the production of software, the project manager must monitor the production process in several ways. These include software production and quality metrics, effort and cost data, value achievement, and process improvement.

The project management skill here is in knowing what to monitor when, where to measure, and how much effort to expend. It is important to keep up with both code dependencies and personnel dependencies. Few activities are more unproductive than having to wait for needed resources. Chapter 21, "Software Metrics," and Chapter 22, "Analysis and Design Methods," discuss many of these items in detail. Chapter 25, "Project Tracking and Control," relates them to the goals of the project.

Project Competency 18:
Scheduling—Creating a Schedule and Key Milestones   The schedule is derived from the WBS and includes step duration, significant milestones, any work products to be produced, and who is responsible for them. Usually represented as a Gantt chart, but equally useful as a table, the schedule adds flesh to the WBS backbone, bringing the project to life.

Good scheduling requires technique and is an art form similar to the creation of a WBS. It starts with knowing the scope of the project, covered in Chapter 7, "Defining the Goal and Scope of the Software Project," and is refined in Chapter 14, "Considering Dependencies." In Chapter 15, "Scheduling the Work," we teach the ability to schedule a software project in the "real world."

Project Competency 19:
Selecting Metrics—Choosing Appropriate Metrics   Metrics are the yardstick for a software development project. They serve as an early warning system, a way to keep your finger on the pulse. If a project is veering off course, a metrics "detection system" will allow it to be brought back in line before it becomes unmanageable. When we suspect that we need process improvements, metrics can be used to turn an opinion into justification for effort, supported by data. Figure 1–11 is an example of defect tracking—one of many metrics tools.

In Chapter 21, "Software Metrics," we discuss the concepts behind the most commonly used software metrics and how to select an appropriate one for a given project. Support and resources for metrics are discussed in Appendix A, "Supporting Organizations." In Chapter 24, "Use of Tools," we show how to use certain tools to monitor the selected metrics. These skills are then illustrated in the case study.

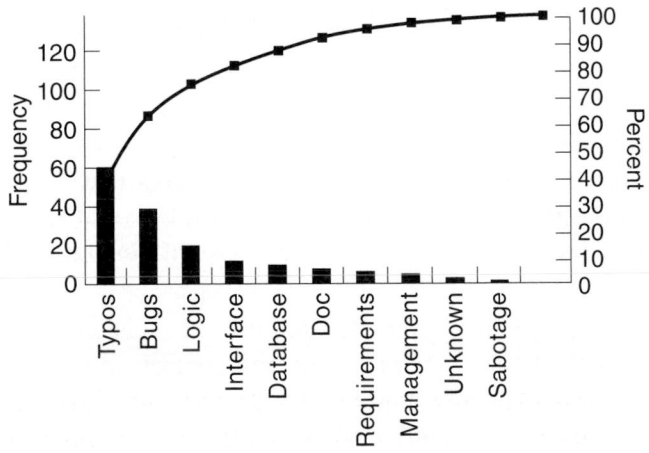

FIGURE 1–11
Software Metrics

Project Competency 20:
Selecting Project Management Tools—Knowing How to Select PM Tools

Every project manager should understand the criteria for selecting and using appropriate software project management tools. The use of tools will not guarantee quality software, on-time software, or within-budget software, but they do serve as aides. There is no silver bullet that will replace the activities of taking time to decide upon the appropriate tools, plan for them, and train their users.

Basic tools range from simple personal information managers (PIMs) to centralized enterprise-wide resource management, tracking, and scheduling tools. Others include configuration management tools from simple source version control systems, to full product data management systems (PDMs) and integrated CASE tools. Selection criteria and a categorization for the tools are presented in Chapter 24, "Use of Tools."

Project Competency 21:
Tracking Process—Monitoring Compliance of the Project Team   Part of the
software quality assurance function, this skill involves tracking project execution against defined processes, recognizing deviations, and knowing what to do about them.

In Chapter 2, "A Case in Point," little or no process tracking is performed, since there is little or no defined process, and the project spins out of control. Chapter 5, "Managing Domain Processes," and Chapter 21, "Software Metrics," discuss how to define and manage project domain processes using metrics, while Chapter 25, "Project Tracking and Control," Chapter 30, "Software Quality Assurance," and Chapter 26, "Continuous Process Improvements," show the skills needed to monitor compliance of the project team to defined processes.

Project Competency 22:
Tracking Project Progress—Monitoring Progress Using Metrics   Many pro-
jects burn energy but don't get anywhere. A key project management skill is being able to track real progress, not just effort. This skill relates to metric selection and development monitoring, and includes earned value analysis and project buffer management.

Figures 1–12 and 1–13 show but two of the many software tracking tools that graph progress metrics. As shown in Figure 1–17, tracking progress is an integral task that spans the life cycle (note "Implement Problem Reporting Methods," under "Project Management and Control").

The chapters on controlling a software project, Chapters 25–26, introduce methods and tools for tracking progress. Chapter 25 is all about project tracking and control, and shows how to use these tools to assess the real progress being made by the project team. The case study uses few progress tracking techniques so they think they are 90 percent complete all the time.

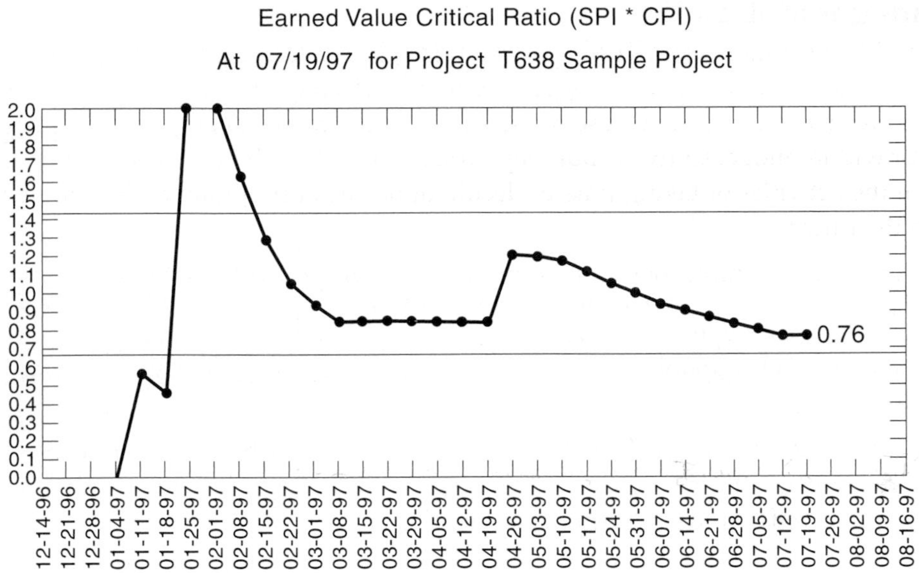

Earned Value Critical Ratio (SPI * CPI)
At 07/19/97 for Project T638 Sample Project
2.0
1.9
1.8
1.7
1.6
1.5
1.4
1.3
1.2
1.1
1.0
0.9
0.8
0.7
0.6
0.5
0.4
0.3
0.2
0.1
0.0
0.76
12-14-96
12-21-96
12-28-96
01-04-97
01-11-97
01-18-97
01-25-97
02-01-97
02-08-97
02-15-97
02-22-97
03-01-97
03-08-97
03-15-97
03-22-97
03-29-97
04-05-97
04-12-97
04-19-97
04-26-97
05-03-97
05-10-97
05-17-97
05-24-97
05-31-97
06-07-97
06-14-97
06-21-97
06-28-97
07-05-97
07-12-97
07-19-97
07-26-97
08-02-97
08-09-97
08-16-97

CR key	
0.9 < CR < 1.1	OK
0.8 < CR < 1.2	Check
0.6 < CR < 1.4	Problem

FIGURE 1–12
Tracking Software Progress

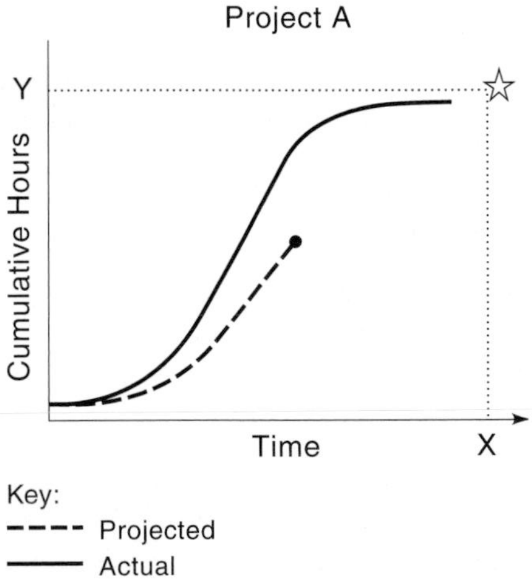

Project A
Y
Cumulative Hours
Time
X
Key:
Projected
Actual

FIGURE 1–13
Tracking Progress

People Management Skills

Just as with *product* skills and *project* skills, each of the *people* management skills from the 34 competencies will be covered in this book. They are shown in Table 1–2 as competencies 23 through 34. A brief description of each will appear in this section, while chapters appearing later in the book will describe each competency more fully.

Where People Management Skills Are Addressed

We now turn to a brief explanation of the people management skills, competencies 23 through 34. Each competency will be introduced here to serve as a roadmap and as a review guide. The chapters in this handbook that more fully describe each competency are forward referenced in Table 1–5.

We want to emphasize the competencies necessary to select and build a project team, infuse the team members with enthusiasm, encourage them through difficult issues, and help each member plan a career to ensure life after the project.

As integral tasks, people skills are essential for the successful completion of every phase in the SLC. For those of us who were not born with the ability to lead, capably negotiate win-win situations, or give presentations, it is comforting to know that each of these skills can be learned.

This introduction will provide a brief description of each of the 12 people skills and discuss how they support the other 22 competencies. The *what*—what project and product competencies are supported by each of the people skills—and the *when*—in which phase of the software development life cycle the people skills are applied—are outlined. The *why* and the *how* of each of the people skills will be presented in depth in later chapters, as referenced in Figure 1–14.

Often thought of as the softer side of software project management, people management may actually be the most important piece of the software-project-support composition: people,

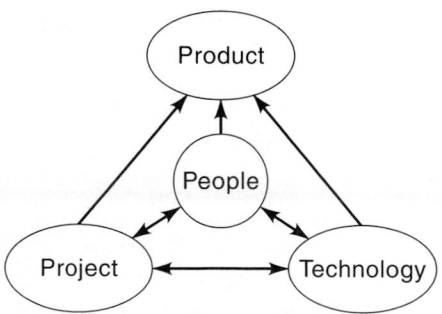

FIGURE 1–14
People Skills in Perspective

TABLE 1–5
People Competencies

People Competency	Description	Chapter
23. Appraising performance	Evaluating teams to enhance performance	29. Reporting and Communicating
24. Handling intellectual property	Understanding the impact of critical issues	32. Legal Issues in Software
25. Holding effective meetings	Planning and running excellent meetings	3. Process Overview 4. Selecting Software Development Life Cycles 5. Managing Domain Processes 6. Selecting a Project Team 7. Defining the Goal and Scope of the Software Project 8. Creating the Work Breakdown Structure 9. Identifying the Tasks and Activities 10. Software Size and Reuse Estimating 11. Estimating Duration and Cost 12. Assigning Resources 13. Choosing an Organizational Form 14. Considering Dependencies 15. Scheduling the Work 16. Eliciting Requirements 17. Developing the Software Requirements Specification 18. Determining Project Risks 19. Introduction to Software Engineering 20. Reliability 21. Software Metrics

(Continues)

TABLE 1–5 (Continued)
People Competencies

People Competency	Description	Chapter
25. Holding effective meetings *(continued)*	Planning and running excellent meetings *(continued)*	22. Analysis and Design Methods 23. Validation and Verification 24. Use of Tools 25. Project Tracking and Control 26. Continuous Process Improvement 27. Project Termination 28. Post Performance Analysis 29. Reporting and Communicating 30. Software Quality Assurance 31. Software Configuration Management 32. Legal Issues in Software
26. Interaction and communication	Dealing with developers, upper management, and other teams	3. Process Overview 4. Selecting Software Development Life Cycles 5. Managing Domain Processes 6. Selecting a Project Team 7. Defining the Goal and Scope of the Software Project 8. Creating the Work Breakdown Structure 9. Identifying the Tasks and Activities 10. Software Size and Reuse Estimating 11. Estimating Duration and Cost 12. Assigning Resources 13. Choosing an Organizational Form 14. Considering Dependencies

TABLE 1–5 (Continued)
People Competencies

People Competency	Description	Chapter
26. Interaction and communication *(continued)*	Dealing with developers, upper management, and other teams *(continued)*	15. Scheduling the Work 16. Eliciting Requirements 17. Developing the Software Requirements Specification 18. Determining Project Risks 19. Introduction to Software Engineering 20. Reliability 21. Software Metrics 22. Analysis and Design Methods 23. Validation and Verification 24. Use of Tools 25. Project Tracking and Control 26. Continuous Process Improvement 27. Project Termination 28. Post Performance Analysis 29. Reporting and Communicating 30. Software Quality Assurance 31. Software Configuration Management 32. Legal Issues in Software
27. Leadership	Coaching project teams for optimal results	6. Selecting a Project Team 25. Project Tracking and Control 26. Continuous Process Improvement 29. Reporting and Communicating
28. Managing change	Being an effective change agent	29. Reporting and Communicating

(Continues)

TABLE 1–5 (Continued)
People Competencies

People Competency	Description	Chapter
29. Negotiating successfully	Resolving conflicts and negotiating successfully	6. Selecting a Project Team 7. Defining the Goal and Scope of the Software Project 12. Assigning Resources 13. Choosing an Organizational Form 16. Eliciting Requirements 24. Use of Tools 29. Reporting and Communicating 32. Legal Issues in Software
30. Planning careers	Structuring and giving career guidance	6. Selecting a Project Team 12. Assigning Resources 28. Post Performance Analysis 29. Reporting and Communicating
31. Presenting effectively	Using effective written and oral skills	7. Defining the Goal and Scope of the Software Project 17. Developing the Software Requirements Specification 18. Determining Project Risks 25. Project Tracking and Control 27. Project Termination 29. Reporting and Communicating 32. Legal Issues in Software
32. Recruiting	Recruiting and interviewing team members successfully	6. Selecting a Project Team 12. Assigning Resources 29. Reporting and Communicating
33. Selecting a team	Choosing highly competent teams	6. Selecting a Project Team 29. Reporting and Communicating

(Continues)

TABLE 1–5 (Continued)
People Competencies

People Competency	Description	Chapter
34. Teambuilding	Forming, guiding, and maintaining an effective team	12. Assigning Resources 13. Choosing an Organizational Form 25. Project Tracking and Control 26. Continuous Process Improvement 29. Reporting and Communicating

process, product (see Figure 1–14). True, the organization will soon be out of business if a software product isn't created, but it's equally true that the software won't meet requirements, won't be of high quality, or maybe won't even exist if the project team doesn't pull together toward a common vision and have an effective leader. An organization may have an SEI Level 5 world-class process, but without the proper recruiting, team selection, team building, and care of team members (appraisal, career planning), there won't be a functioning team to follow it. Researchers may have a superior invention, but without interaction, effective presentations, effective meetings, negotiation skills, and change management the product will never get out the door.

Because they are used in every project phase and software development life cycle phase and in the continuous support of quality, it is difficult to cleanly peg each people skill to a specific PMI project process phase, SLC phase, or SQI competency. So we'll describe where multiple skills can be applied and which skills may be especially important to getting a process or product phase task completed.

For example, negotiation and managing change may be two people skills required continuously, whereas team selection obviously takes place only near the beginning of a project—usually in the PMI project planning project phase (which corresponds to the concept exploration and/or system exploration software development life cycle phase) as in Figure 1–15.

Multiple competencies are frequently required during any given life cycle phase, and one SQI competency may support others. Managing people on a software project requires applying people skills, software engineering and development knowledge, and project management smarts at the same time. As long as each skill is mastered, it becomes natural to use several in unison. There will be a section in this book on mastering each of the people management skills, and it will be assumed that project managers need to employ one or more of them every step of the way.

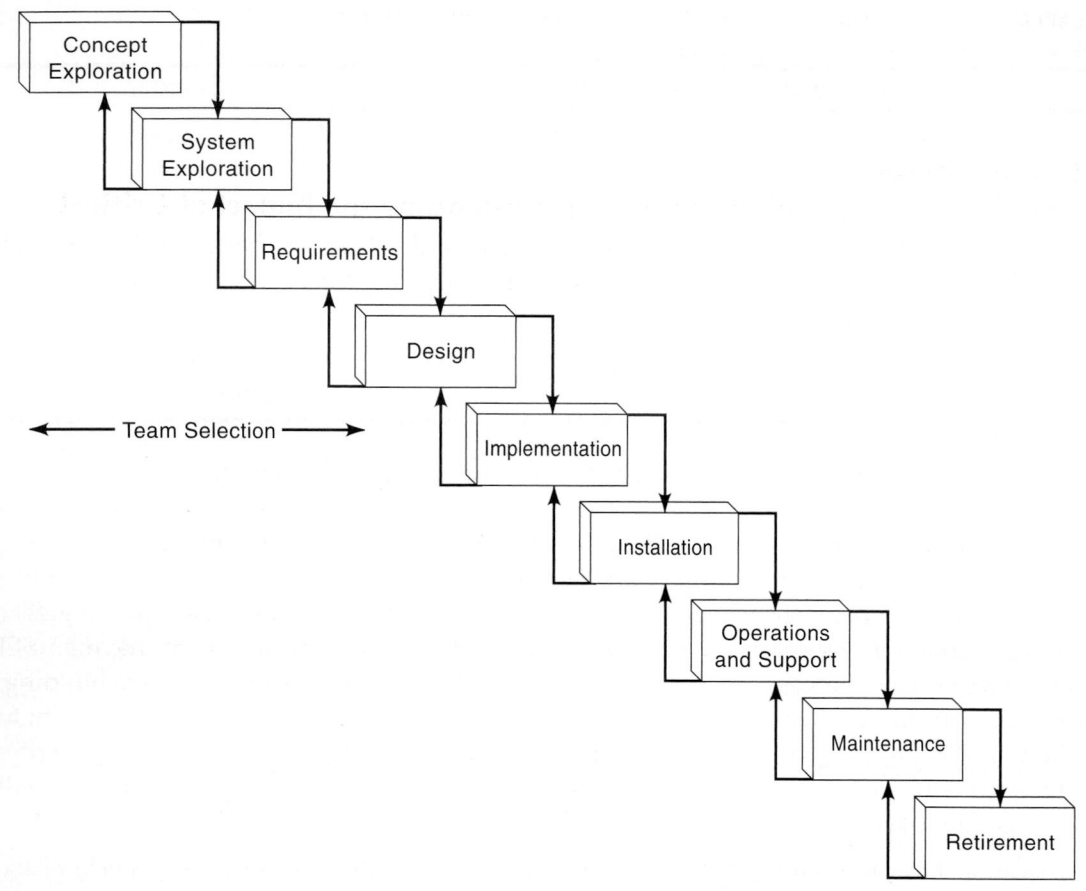

FIGURE 1–15
Selecting a Project Team

A Brief Description of People Management Skills

People competencies 23 through 34 are briefly described in the following sections.

People Competency 23:
Appraising Performance—Evaluating Teams to Enhance Performance

How do you know if your team is performing well—as a team and not just as a group of individuals? In addition to constant project tracking to ensure the team is meeting milestones and delivering project artifacts, it is important to ask them how they think they are doing. When a team is in the "performing" stage, players should have settled into their appropriate roles. At that point, each team member can evaluate the other members. As the manager and collector of information, you will immediately be able to see the high and low performers and spot the supportive, team-spirited, goal-oriented staff.

Appraisal will be discussed in Chapters 29–32.

People Competency 24:
Handling Intellectual Property—Understanding the Impact of Critical

Issues   Every software project manager should understand the basic legal issues surrounding software development. This section discusses the fundamentals of business law relating to contracts, licenses, and intellectual property.

Intellectual property will be discussed in Chapter 32, "Legal Issues in Software."

People Competency 25:
Effective Meetings—Planning and Running Excellent Meetings   Poor meeting management wastes more time than all other negative forces that occur on a project. It also contributes to ineffective project communications. For informal internal brainstorming sessions, formal project reviews, inspection logging meetings, or even one-on-one problem solving discussions, a few basic skills and items are needed. This integral skill is incredibly useful throughout the life of a project. If the kick-off meeting for a project is ineffective, an unfortunate tone is set for the remainder. Our case study demonstrates a well-run meeting, as well as a kick-off fiasco.

Effective meetings will be discussed in Chapter 29, "Reporting and Communicating."

People Competency 26:
Interaction and Communication—Dealing with Developers, Upper

Management, and Other Teams   Part of communications management, the people management skill of interaction includes personal exchanges with individuals through any medium. It applies at any level, but is especially important in formal reporting and communications with sponsors, customers, and upper management. A clear understanding of at least one good personality model (e.g., Myers-Briggs Type Indicator®) is required to effectively manage the interplay among all project players. If personalities are not recognized, understood, and handled effectively, serious personnel situations can arise, adding an unneeded risk to project success. Suboptimal interaction between team members due to personality interactions may have a detrimental effect on the outcome of the project. Fortunately, this is an area that has received a great deal of attention since the 1940s and many techniques exist for turning negative situations into positive ones for the project.

Just as a teaser, consider what happens to communications and interactions when a team is expanded from four to six people. The communication/interaction pathways expand from five to 16. What's the big deal? You, as the project manager, must make sure the pathways stay open (Figure 1–16).

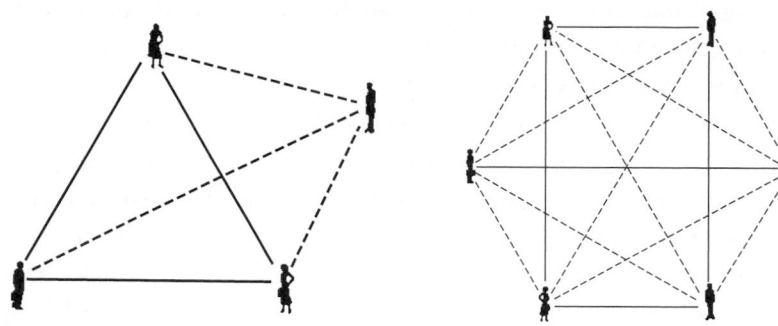

FIGURE 1–16
The Complexity of Communication Networks

People Competency 27:
Leadership—Coaching Project Teams for Optimal Results   Leaders redirect

life's emotional energies, for themselves and for others, stage revolutions, and develop other leaders. They coach and teach constantly; they are able to organize their ideas and thoughts into teachable points. Their values, such as honesty, integrity, and the sanctity of an agreement, are clearly articulated via their own behavior. Leaders walk the walk; they don't just talk the talk.

There is a world of difference between a manager and a leader. A leader has a vision that he or she can communicate to the team and can, in turn, feel assured that the team subscribes to it, believes in it, and is willing to work for it. A vision is a long-term strategic goal, which can be reached by a series of shorter-term tactical activities. A true leader is able to chart the map used by the team to navigate from "here" to the vision and can keep the team on the road with the rewards of tactical milestones. Some say the answer to "How do you recognize a leader?" is "Look around to see if he or she has followers." Having followers requires relationships, which are built on trust.

Leadership is discussed in Chapters 29–32.

People Competency 28:
Managing Change—Being an Effective Change Agent   As we know, change is

inevitable. "The only thing that is constant is change." In the software industry, we couldn't ignore it if we wanted to—technology is moving at a fast clip. At the same time, change is unpleasant for many people, high tech software developers included, because it takes us out of our comfort zone. From relatively small changes, like converting to a newer version of an operating system or moving offices, to a huge change like opening up a new product line, the project manager must be knowledgeable about how to navigate uncharted waters. Long projects are bound to see turnover in team members, which requires learning how to accept the loss of a member and learning how to get along with a new one.

As with all of the people management skills, a project manager can learn how to be an effective change agent. You may acquire the "tools" necessary to recognize when change is on the horizon, which team members will be the most affected and how, and how to energize and prepare the team for the future. Luckily for us, psychiatrists and psychologists have studied the effects of change for decades and we have a wealth of research from which to borrow. In the last few years, quite a few notables have addressed the role of change agent in the software industry.

People Competency 29:
Negotiating Successfully—Resolving Conflicts and Negotiating
Successfully   Negotiation is often the key to making the rest of the skills and techniques effective. It is universally applicable and absolutely necessary to most interactions, formal or informal. Conflict is inevitable when managing scarce resources against escalating requirements and increasing time pressure; the project manager must become the peacemaker. We will visit some correct and some not-so-good negotiation examples in the case studies.

Negotiation skills will be discussed in Chapter 29, "Reporting and Communicating."

People Competency 30:
Planning Careers—Structuring Teams and Giving Career Guidance
"Choose a job you love, and you will never have to work a day in your life." Is it possible to teach your staff how to learn to love work? Maybe. When team members have a stake in planning their place in the organization, they can look forward to a "life after the project." Uncertainty about the next assignment, especially near the closing phases of a project, is one of the most challenging aspects of people management. Project managers must be highly attuned to the fine art of individual staff member performance evaluation in order to determine what makes each person tick. Within reason and within organizational policy boundaries, every effort must be made to match individual skills and proclivities to project roles. Some organizational behaviorists believe that there is no such thing as a "personality problem" on a project team, but there are frequent instances of the wrong person in the wrong position. Whatever the origin, frustration with a career often presents itself in the form of anger or even project sabotage.

People Competency 31:
Presenting Effectively—Using Effective Written and Oral Skills   Project managers are required to make presentations on the "state of the project" on multiple levels. Making presentations is an integral task, closely aligned with communications management. It is the

critically important people management skill of presenting information concisely and effectively, to be received and understood correctly. The basic principles of graphic design, public speaking, business writing, and presenting numbers and statistics unambiguously are discussed. Both good and bad examples appear in the case example and in the case problem. For example, misused statistics can show a false picture of project progress, but may be hidden behind a confusing project presentation to management. When presentations go well, especially the all-important project status review meeting, then concise, communicative, and accurate graphics and text are almost always in play.

Presentation skills will be discussed in Chapter 29, "Reporting and Communicating."

People Competency 32:
Recruiting—Recruiting and Interviewing Successful Team Members
Interviewing potential recruits, a workable process for selecting team members, includes defining the skill set necessary for the task and may mean resumé searching and phone screening. During the interview, the savvy PM will know how to effectively use open-ended questions and recognize trait versus experience data.

It has been said that the best way to find team members is through the "network." Sometimes, this works—specializations in the software industry form subcommunities such as database, state government business analysts, language experts, Internet-savvy programmers, and many other "cultures" from which talent may be drawn. Word gets around, especially within a geographic area, and those with good reputations are invited again and again to participate on projects within and outside of their current places of business. But much of the time, project managers must rely on advertising or search firms to find talent. Sometimes, the applicant files are high on quantity and low on quality. When interviewing those who appear to be good candidates, there is much more than technical skills to consider. An interviewer can use techniques such as active listening and behavioral interviewing to determine if the interviewee will fit in with other team members and uphold the group vision.

Recruiting and interviewing will be discussed in Chapter 6, "Selecting a Project Team."

People Competency 33:
Selecting a Team—Choosing Highly Competent Teams   Staffing a project requires the ability to understand people in the context of a high performance team. Basic personality models are helpful, as is knowledge of recruiting and building such teams. As identifying and understanding personalities is an important aspect of selecting a team, models from psychology, especially Myers-Briggs Personality Type models, will be described. Others include the Kiersey Temperament Sorter (© 1997–2001 Dr. David W. Kiersey) and the Enneagram.

No matter how effective a team is, it must be right for the job at hand. A team of Java programmers may be able to develop the next killer app, but they might not comprise the right team to automate a day-care center (currently big business) if the team doesn't include a knowledgeable business analyst. Assuming the correct mix of talents can be determined, the manager must also be able to ascertain the competency of each team member and of the total team (the whole is not the sum of the parts). Dr. Bill Curtis tells us that productivity varies wildly between the "best" and "worst" programmers, depending on their experience, domain knowledge, and innate smarts.[13]

Recruiting and interviewing will be discussed in Chapter 6, "Selecting a Project Team."

People Competency 34:
Teambuilding—Forming, Guiding, and Maintaining an Effective Team

Building the right team requires mixing personalities for better team performance. We will discuss the team development model in terms of the classic five stages: forming, storming, norming, performing, and adjourning. There are successful techniques for turning individuals into a team that may be employed.

If all members of a team are highly compatible, they will look back on the project as enjoyable, but they may remember a "failure" in terms of project accomplishments. Just as the sand must be present in the oyster to create a pearl, a bit of dispute among team members often gives birth to original ideas. It is best if the team consists of introverts and extroverts, sensing and intuitive types, and thinkers and feelers. Constant and total agreement on issues is boring, unproductive, and inbred. Teams are effective when lively technical discussions can take place without harm to personal feelings.

There are several well-known software team organizations. We will discuss them and their strengths and weaknesses in Chapter 6, "Selecting a Project Team."

Summary _____

Now that we have described the content of *Quality Software Project Management* in terms of where each competency is used in the IEEE software life cycle phases, we are ready to move on to initiating, planning, executing, controlling, and closing a software project. Figure 1–17, the IEEE 1074 Software Product Development Life Cycle Model, identifies the referenced phases and lists the software development specific activities for each. This is the main product development life cycle model used throughout this practitioner's guide.

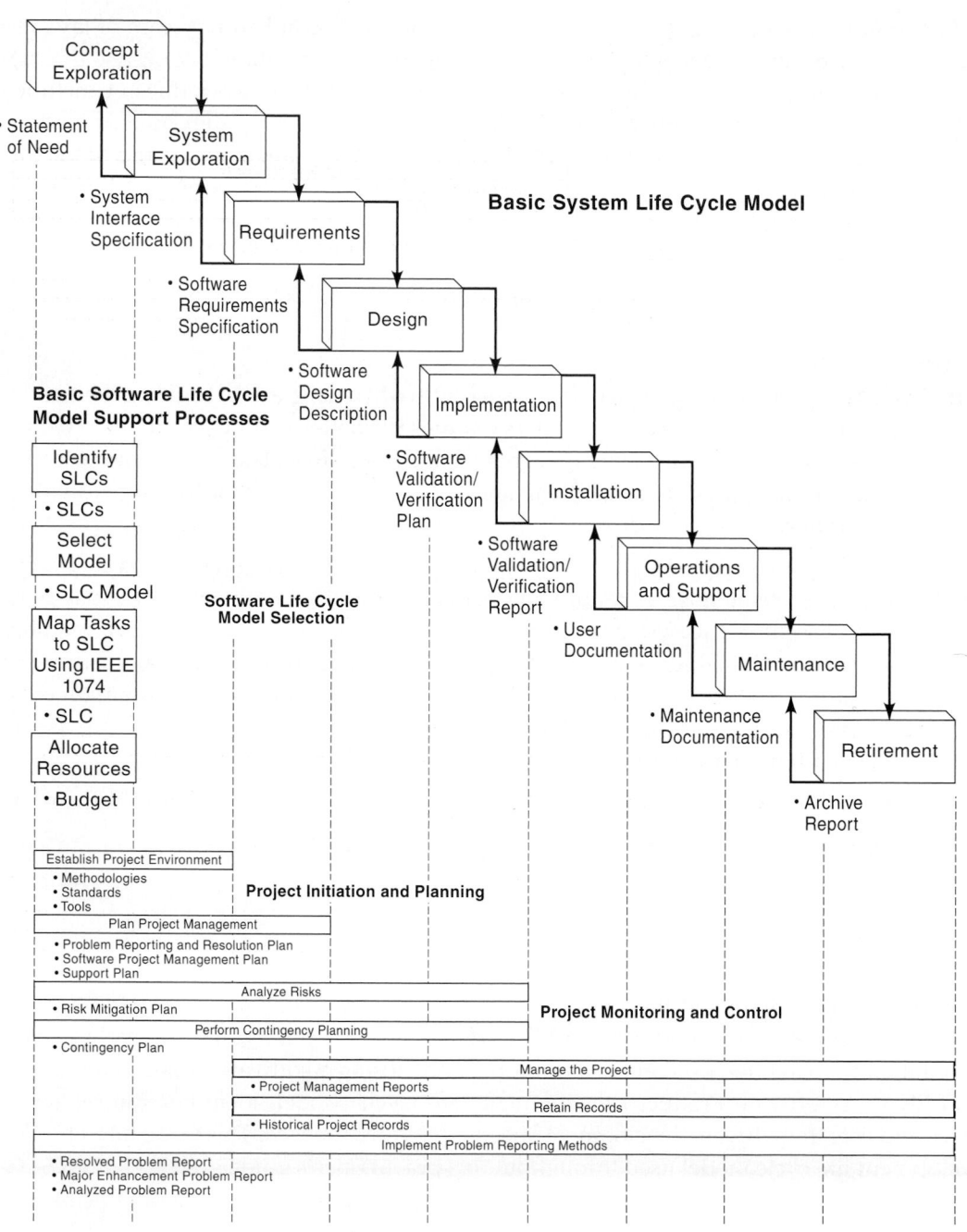

FIGURE 1–17

IEEE 1074 Software Product Development Life Cycle Model

(Continues)

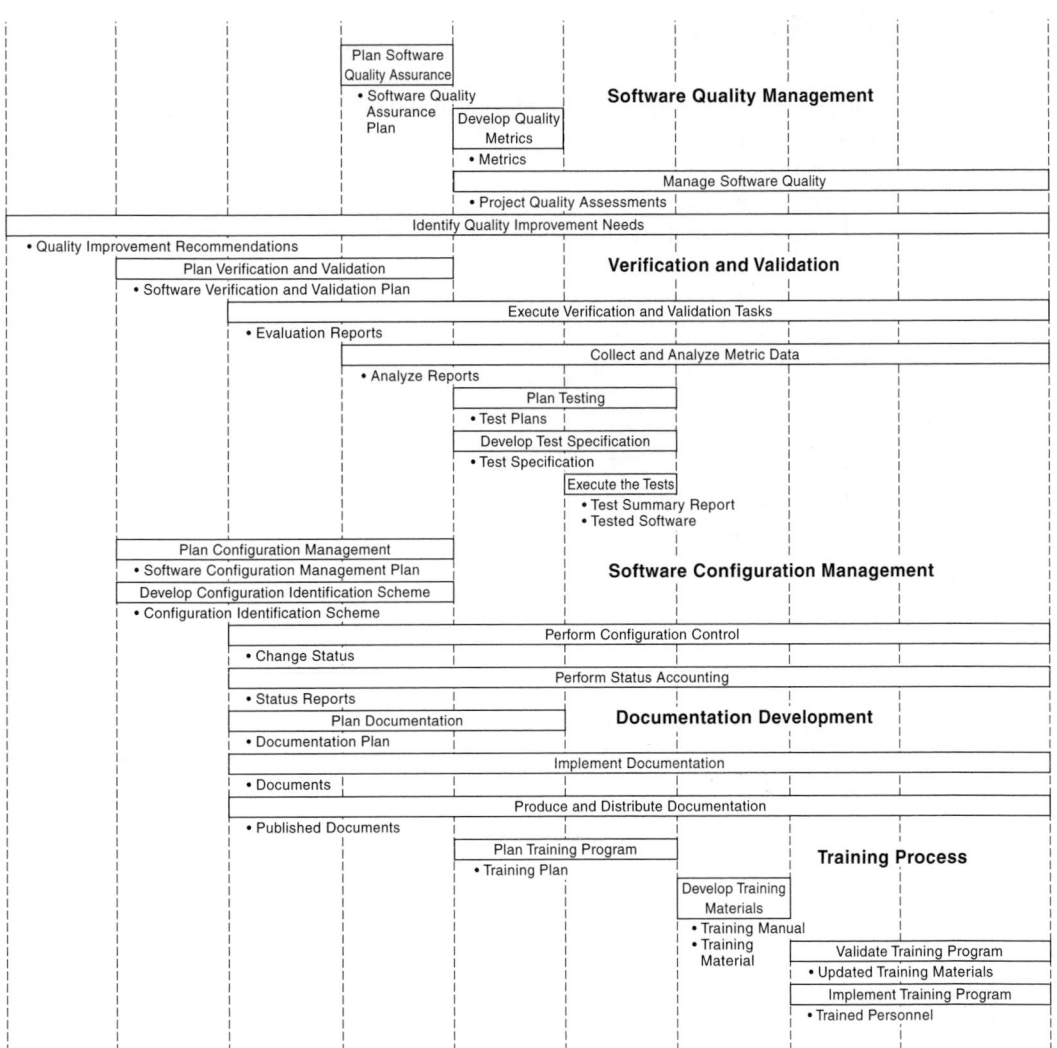

FIGURE 1–17 (Continued)
IEEE 1074 Software Product Development Life Cycle Model

Problems for Review_____

1. Arrange the following definitions into a hierarchy from top level to bottom:

   Activity

   Phase

   Program

   Project

   System

   Task

2. After reading the descriptions in this chapter, define the following terms in your own words:

   34 competencies

   Activity

   Management

   People skills

   Phase

   PM triangle

   Process

   Product skills

   Program

   Project

   Project management

   Project skills

   Software

   Software engineering

   Software life cycle

   Software project management (SWPM)

   System

   Task

3. Visit the Web sites of three of the listed standards organizations. How does the presentation of materials promoted by their organization aid you in adopting their standards? How does the Web presentation detract from your adoption? Based on the information presented, compare and contrast the standards promoted by each of the three organizations.

4. If you were going to begin the process of tailoring a process for your organization, how would the techniques of alternative processes and development activities affect your decisions?

5. Give examples of methods, tools, and technologies that you use in your day-to-day business activities.

6. Go to the Web site *www.pmi.org* and peruse the PMI PMBOK. Download Chapter 3, "Project Management Processes," to see how this book fits the software development life cycle into the PM phases of initiating, planning, executing, controlling, and closing.

7. Look on the Web for descriptions of some of the instruments used to indicate basic personality types. A typical search on MBTI (Myers-Briggs Type Indicator) will return links like these:

www.personalitytype.com/quiz.html

www.teamtechnology.co.uk/tt/h-articl/mb-simpl.htm

keirsey.com/

Citations

[1]Boehm, Barry (1976). *Software Engineering Economics.* Englewood Cliffs, NJ: Prentice Hall. p. 16.

[2]Institute of Electrical and Electronics Engineers (1983). "IEEE Std 610.12-1990 Standard Glossary of Software Engineering Terminology." *Software Engineering Standards Collection.* New York, NY: Institute of Electrical and Electronics Engineers. p. 76.

[3]Schach, Stephen R. (1999). *Classical and Object-Oriented Software Engineering,* 4th ed. Boston, MA: McGraw-Hill. p. 4.

[4]Kerzner, Harold (1998). *Project Management: A Systems Approach to Planning, Scheduling, and Controlling,* 6th ed. New York, NY: John Wiley & Sons. p. 2.

[5]Lewis, James P. (1995). *Project Planning, Scheduling, and Control: A Hands-On Guide to Bringing Projects in on Time and on Budget,* rev ed. Chicago, IL: Irwin. pp. 2–3.

[6]Project Management Institute (1996). *A Guide to the Project Management Body of Knowledge.* Sylva, NC: PMI Publication Division. p. 167.

[7]See note 4. p. 70.

[8]See note 6.

[9]Adopted from Pall, Gabriel A. (1987). *Quality Process Management.* Englewood Cliffs, NJ: Prentice-Hall.

[10]*www.m-w.com/cgi-bin/dictionary.* Merriam-Webster's Collegiate® Dictionary Online.

[11]Project Management Institute (2000). *A Guide to the Project Management Body of Knowledge.* Sylva, NC: PMI Publication Division. pp. 43, 55.

[12]Kerzner, Harold (1998*). Project Management: A Systems Approach to Planning, Scheduling, and Controlling,* 6th ed. New York, NY: John Wiley & Sons. pp. 69–72.

[13]Curtis, Bill, Herb Krasner, and Neil Iscoe (1988). "A Field Study of the Software Design Process for Large Systems." *Communications of the ACM,* 31(11):1268–1287.

A Case in Point

The case study method has been used throughout project management training to frame the student within the real world. This practitioner's handbook makes extensive use of the Chinese Railway Passenger Reservation System Prototype Case Study. The case study is designed to parallel a real-life client situation. For that reason, in may areas there may be more data provided than actually used for the prototype. There will be ambiguous situations where information may conflict. Many pieces of data will be presented without adequate discussion—very much like the real world. This case study is useful for instructors as a graded project with class project teams providing their solutions. The entire case is solved with all instructor materials in the Instructor's Workbook for the handbook. The Chinese Railway Passenger Reservation System will be visited in each chapter with further information and new tasks from the client.

A second extensive case study, the elevator control problem, will be used as the example in Appendix F, "Project Artifact Templates," for a complete set of project management artifacts. Where technical software engineering concepts are being compared and contrasted, as in classical versus object-oriented modeling notation, the elevator problem will be used as reference.

The Chinese Railway Passenger Reservation System Prototype takes place outside of your corporation's home country and thus some of the constraints will be different from what you are typically accustomed. The opportunity to develop this prototype will allow you to gain the expertise needed to compete for the final project. To have a chance in being named one of the competitors to build the actual information system, you must have a successful prototype. The first step in this process is the competition with other organizations to build a system feasibility prototype.

You have been sent as a team to establish a project plan to build this limited prototype of the Chinese Railway Passenger Reservation System. The following is a list of the known conditions of your work:

- None of your team speaks the language of this country and you must rely on interpreters to speak with those who do not speak English.
- This country will not allow you to bring programmers or analysts into the country to work on this project. You will be limited to bringing only your team to manage the project and must work with the personnel and equipment resources supplied by the Chinese Railroad Ministry (CRM).
- The local programmers have a fairly solid computer science background but lack most typical software engineering skills. Also, they are weak in object-oriented development skills (they have read and studied OO development) and telecommunications skills. Only recently has China been able to buy telecommunications software from the U.S. and other western countries.
- The CRM prides itself on having state-of-the-art hardware and software. While this is not necessarily true, there is sufficient hardware and software available for a workstation-based client/server approach. Even though there are object-oriented software packages readily available, none of the personnel at the CRM have experience developing object-oriented systems.
- The CRM attempted to develop a full-blown reservation system before and failed miserably. This was prior to good telecommunications technology being available, so the conditions were fairly rustic.
- You will be allowed to interview whatever customers, employees, and managers you need to enable you to accurately develop the project plan.

Background Information on the Chinese Railway System_____

There are more than 52,000 km of rail in China and it is estimated that 3.7 million Chinese and visitors use the country's railway system daily. This vast rail network covers every province but Tibet. In China, train tickets can usually be purchased at the China International Travel Service (CITS) desk in major tourist hotels. Larger cities also have advance-booking offices or a foreign desk at the train station. Depending on the distance traveled, tickets are

FIGURE 2–1
Map of China
Source: Map produced by the Central Intelligence Agency and found online in the University of Texas at Austin Perry-Castañeda Library Map Collection (*www.lib.utexas.edu/maps/cia99/china_sm99.jpg*).

valid from one to seven days: 250 km/2 days, 500 km/3 days, 1000 km/3 days, 2000 km/6 days. Purchasing a train ticket in China can be a fun but frustrating endeavor. Foreign travelers should be advised to plan ahead or use the services of one of the CITS offices in major country capitals worldwide. Please reference Figure 2–1 for a map of China and Box 2–1 for contact information for CITS.

BOX 2–1
CITS Contact Information

Address:	6 East Chang'an Street
	Beijing
	CHINA
Phone:	86-1-5128931 Beijing Railway Station

Tickets are sold for four different classes: hard-seat, hard-sleeper, soft-seat, and soft-sleeper; although not all of these are available for every train. The conditions in these classes will vary from train to train. All trains, cars, and berths are numbered and the ticket should show all of these numbers. Hard-seat is generally a padded upright seat in a coach-type car. This class of travel is the loudest and most crowded. Hard-seat is not recommended for foreigners; however, it may be acceptable for short day trips. Hard-sleeper is a sleeper carriage with doorless compartments. Bunks are arranged in tiers and the lower bunks are used as seats during the day. Soft-seat is generally found on shorter routes. This ticket offers a more traditional coach setting with reclining seats. Soft-sleeper offers four bunks in a modest closed compartment. This is the luxury class of the People's Railroad, offering clean washrooms, carpets, and many times, air conditioning. Soft-class cars are usually located in the center of the train near the chief assistant's (conductor's) office.

Dining cars are usually available on train journeys of longer length (12 hours or more). An attendant announces breakfast, lunch, and dinner. Train attendants will sometimes serve hot tea in the soft-class. The dining car is usually in the center of the train. At station stops you can sometimes buy food from vendors from your window. For longer trips it is worth bringing a few of your own supplies. The larger train stations will have soft-class and hard-class waiting rooms and smaller stations will have a designated waiting area. Signs are posted with the train number and destination telling passengers where to queue. Almost all of the stations will have left-luggage rooms.

Prices are based on the class of service and length of the journey. There are surcharges for express service. Tickets purchased through the CITS, for foreigners, are higher in price than those available to the People's Republic Chinese. However, purchasing these cheaper and technically illegal People's tickets in China can be quite an adventure and is recommended for the budget traveler with time to spend. A tourist-priced ticket for a hard-sleeper express from Beijing to Shanghai (1,462 km) is approximately 46 Yuan (£5.75 or nearly $10.00).

Train numbers usually reveal something about the different train types:

- Numbers one to 90 are express and have all classes of service. There is a surcharge for the service and speed.
- Numbers 100 to 350 make more stops and have fewer sleeping berths. There is not much of a price difference between these and the special express.
- Numbers 400 to 500 are slower, older trains making several stops. There are limited classes and services available on these trains.
- Number 700 is the suburban route train.

Railroad Building in China[1]

A major challenge facing China is how to maintain an eight-percent growth rate this year amid the severe financial crisis gripping much of East Asia. Domestic demand stimulation, especially injection of massive infrastructure investments, is part of the answer. This includes large-scale railroad building; indeed railroad construction has evolved into one of the major engines for China's national economy.

On March 29, the State Council made a decision concerning the ninth Five-Year Plan. It decided to invest $30 billion in railroad building during the next five years, or $11 billion more than the figure for the eighth Five-Year Plan. It plans to build 5,340 km of new railroads and 2,580 km of double-tracks for present lines, electrify 4,400 km of railways, and add another 1,000 km to the local railroad system—thus increasing the nation's total operating mileage to 68,000 km in the third year of the plan and over 70,000 km by the fifth and last year of the plan.

Railroads play a decisive role in the transportation system of China, a country with a vast territory and a huge population. The country now has 65,000 km of railroads in operation, including over 11,000 km of which are electrified. More than 15,000 locomotives, 34,000 passenger trains, and 540,000 freight trains are currently in service across the country. Annual total passenger-transport volume stands at 920 million people, with cargo volume amounting to 1.62 billion tons.

Nevertheless, the system still fails to satisfy the needs of the country's modernization drive and growing international trade. In fact, transportation density for the major railroads has exceeded the saturation point, and utilization has come close to the limit of loading capacity. In the central and western parts of the country, low density of railroads coupled with a flawed layout of the original railroad network, has long been hampering the exploitation of huge natural resources. Thus, the backward national railroad system has become a major bottleneck for China's booming economy.

Under these circumstances, the accelerated expansion of the railroad system will play a significant role in boosting nationwide economic growth by bringing about more even development in different regions, absorbing excess labor, and promoting a unified national market.

As is well known, railroad construction requires a huge investment and involves a long chain of related industries. Larger investments in this field will, like a locomotive engine, drive the expansion of a large number of secondary industries such as iron and steel, machinery, energy, building materials, and electronic equipment.

The relevant infrastructure projects for the coming five years will be arranged as follows:

- Accelerated construction of passenger lines with an emphasis on the building or technical revamping of those that link major economic zones, thus extending routes across the country; special attention will be focused on southwest China, where the transportation deficiency is acute;

- Accelerated building of new, all-purpose railroads, with an emphasis toward the central and western parts of the country;

- Renovation of existing railroads through modernizing equipment further by taking advantage of the latest high-tech processes;

- Prioritizing these projects to maximize their social and economic impact.

The ninth Five-Year Plan envisages a T-shaped railroad network. An East-West "big artery" will be built along the Yangtze (Changjiang) River starting from Sichuan Province in Southwest

China. It will be connected to another North-South "big artery" along the East coast, starting from Harbin in northeast China.

This plan turns out to conform with the vision of Dr. Sun Yat Sen, put forth in his national construction program decades ago. Construction of this grandiose T-shaped railroad network would add wings to the economic development of China's vast hinterland in the southwest.

Meanwhile, on the agenda will also be construction of the first high-speed railroad linking Beijing and Shanghai. The new 1,300 km railroad, with a capacity for speeds of up to 250 km per hour, is planned for completion in ten years. Its construction would greatly improve the current situation, which lags far behind the transportation needs of the vast region between the two major cities.

Expansion of China's national railroad system on such an unprecedented scale in the coming five years should lay down a solid foundation for pushing the entire Chinese economy to new heights. By happy coincidence, it would serve the same purpose as did the construction of six transcontinental railroads in the United States in the last century. This locomotive will certainly pull the train of China toward an earlier realization of the long-cherished national dream of modernization.

Chinese Business Environment[2] _____

Westinghouse Power Contract

During Commerce Department Under-Secretary David Aaron's visit to Beijing, Westinghouse Power Generation announced on April 16 the signing of a $170 million power plant contract in China. Under the terms of the contract, Westinghouse and its consortium partners, Black & Veatch of Kansas City, Kansas, and CMEC of China, will design and supply the turbine and boiler islands for the 700 megawatt, two-unit, coal-fired Yuzhou Power Plant in He Nan Province. The Westinghouse scope includes supply of the turbine-generator equipment and consortium management. The Asian Development Bank is financing the project. Westinghouse currently has eight joint ventures in China and, with its licensees and joint-venture partners, is supplying over 50,000 megawatts of electricity throughout the region. Project construction is expected to begin later this year and the plant will enter commercial operation in three years.

Non-State Group in IFC Loan

The International Finance Corp. (IFC), the World Bank's private-sector financing arm, signed an unprecedented cooperation project on March 27 involving a Chinese non-state financing house. The deal covers a $30 million IFC loan for Orient Finance Co.—a member of Orient Group and the first non-state finance company in China. Javed Hamid, director of IFC's East and Southeast Asian operations, said the project reflected IFC's keen interest in supporting the development of China's capital market and its private sectors. Hamid said the company would be increasingly active in supporting private business while playing a role in the reform of state firms. IFC, which has already provided $1.15 billion in loans and investment for China, plans to supply another $400 million in the first year of the ninth Five-Year Plan. Hamid said IFC is also seeking to take part in the development of China's financial market by cooperating with local rating firms, banks, insurance companies, and securities brokerages.

Globalstar Gearing Up

On April 21, Globalstar announced that China Telecom (Hong Kong) Group Ltd. had agreed to invest $37.5 million to become a full partner in Globalstar L.P. China Telecom, along with CHINASAT (China Telecommunications Broadcast Satellite Corporation), will retain the sole rights to provide Globalstar services in China. Both companies are expected to be wholly owned and supervised by China's newly-formed Ministry of Information Industry (MII). "The addition of China Telecom as a full partner solidifies Globalstar's commitment to bringing the promise of mobile satellite communications to China's 1.2 billion people," said Bernard L. Schwartz, chairman and CEO of Globalstar L.P., and of Loral Space and Communications, Globalstar's largest equity owner. China Telecom and CHINASAT will manage all Globalstar operations in China. The Globalstar system, comprising 48 low-earth-orbiting (LEO) satellites and a global network of ground stations, will allow people in areas with inadequate or non-existing telecommunications infrastructure to make or receive calls or transmit data. The first four Globalstar satellites were successfully launched on February 14th.

Mineral Resource Priorities

Attracting foreign investment into China's mineral sector and raising the standard of the country's natural-resource management remain priorities for the new Minister of Land and Natural Resources. According to Zhou Yongkang, "The goal of sustained economic development requires us to seek markets and supply sources both at home and abroad. The creation of the Ministry of Land and Natural Resources will promote utilization of natural resources and help foreign investors to conduct their business activities in China more effectively." In the past few years, foreign investment has been restricted to major sectors such as oil exploration and coal mining.

Project Description _____

The Chinese Railroad Ministry (CRM) is requesting proposals to build a prototype of an automated railway reservation system (ARRS). The cornerstone of this proposal will be the project plan. The project plan will be evaluated on its merits as a feasible development plan and process description. There is serious competition between prospective providers. If the organization is successful in convincing the CRM of the prototype's feasibility and portraying a successful ARRS, the organization will be given preferential consideration to manage the overall development of the final ARRS.

You do not yet have the benefit of a completed requirements analysis or design. The information provided here is intended to give you enough data to scope the effort and build the initial project plan.

Submitted plans are evaluated on their management approach and appropriateness to the project at hand. The CRM fully expects the winning vendor to update its plan as the project progresses.

Some overall statistics on train travel in China are as follows:

- There are over 10,000 train stations in China.

- Some of the peak travel lines experience extremely heavy traffic. Between Beijing and Shanghai the number of passengers traveling averages in the millions each month.

- Some of the remote regions have as few as one train per week.

- It is believed everyone in China uses a train *at least once a year* (there are 1.2 billion people in China).

Your Project Management Situation

You are the matrixed project manager of a team to build a limited prototype of the Chinese Railway Passenger Reservation System. Following is a list of the known conditions of your work:

- None of your team speaks the language of this country and you must rely on interpreters to speak with those who do not speak English.

- China will not allow you to bring programmers or analysts into the country to work on this project. You will be limited to bringing only a four-person management team to manage the project and must work with the personnel and equipment resources supplied by the Chinese Railroad Ministry (CRM). The limit to the number of the in-country team includes you as the project manager.

- The local programmers have a fairly solid computer science background but lack most typical software engineering skills. Also, they are weak in object-oriented development skills (they have read and studied OO development) and telecommunications skills. Only recently has China been able to buy telecommunications software from the U.S. and other western countries.

- The CRM prides itself on having state-of-the-art hardware and software. While this is not necessarily true, there is sufficient hardware and software available for a workstation-based client/server approach. Even though there are object-oriented software packages readily available, none of the personnel at the CRM have experience developing object-oriented systems.

- The CRM attempted to develop a full-blown reservation system before and failed miserably. This was prior to good telecommunications technology being available, so the conditions were fairly rustic.

- You will be allowed to interview whatever customers, employees, and managers you need to enable you to accurately develop the project plan.

Resources   The CRM wishes to use its own programmers for this project. This means the winning vendor organization will be expected to act as a management team and will be allowed to bring only that team into the country. Since the CRM also has excellent equipment resources, the vendor organization may not bring additional production equipment into the country.

You will have access to 26 software development professionals:

- One development manager who speaks and writes English well;

- Three analysts who have had extensive experience in developing applications, none of whom speak English, although all read English and have a fair ability to write in English;

- One programmer/analyst who has extensive telecommunications skills and communicates fairly well in English;

- 11 programmers with five or more years of experience in developing extensive applications—three have excellent English communication skills;

- 10 programmers with less than five years of experience; the ministry is extremely interested in these people receiving on-the-job training so they must be used; only two can communicate in English.

The CRM will also provide a facilitator to help make arrangements with government authorities, make travel arrangements, and serve as a host in China.

Your Corporation and You

Your corporation generates a billion dollars a year in revenue from the sale of telecommunications equipment and software. With sales offices throughout the Asia Pacific (AsiaPac) market area, a cellular phone assembly plant in Guangzhou, and part-ownership in a semiconductor fabrication plant in Taiwan, your company feels it has the experience and deep cultural knowledge to succeed in any high-technology Chinese project. Although mainly thought of as a hardware company, your corporate software initiative team sponsored the development of a Software Engineering Institute (SEI) Level 5 Capability Maturity Model (CMM) group in Bangalore, India, and a software design company in Australia. They have also just completed a very high-profile acquisition of a computer aided software engineering (CASE) tool company. Your company was focused on this acquisition because the corporate planning group convinced the executive management team that this company's tools will be able to lift all the corporation's software developers to at least Level 4. The corporation has stood behind this commitment by requiring all new projects to use the CASE tool and its object-oriented development methodology with unified modeling language (UML) representation and instant Java code generation. All software organizations now have a training budget identified with continental U.S. development organizations to be trained first. The training plan will have all software development organizations trained worldwide within the next 15 months. AsiaPac organizations will be the last to be trained.

This is the first hardware company for which you have been employed. After graduating from engineering school with a bachelor's degree in electrical engineering, you went to work for a company that built factory automation tools. After five years with that company, your current employer recruited you. You have been employed as a software developer and software tools project development manager for seven years with your current employer. Six months ago, you completed the Project Management Institute's Project Management Professional certification course, took the examination, and earned the PMP designation. After earning your PMP, you were transferred to a matrixed software project management organization whose mission is to work closely with international marketing groups and use all the varied hardware and software capabilities within the corporation to win new international business.

The CRM project is a perfect fit for your current organization (see Figure 2–2) and will receive a high level of executive support and scrutiny. Your organization is purely matrixed in that you have no engineers on your staff. You are one of 10 professional project managers, but only two of you focus exclusively on software projects. The remainder of the 28 professionals in your organization are marketers. There are 12 support people who focus on marketing communications, documentation preparation, and marketing reference library management. Your organization's leader is a corporate vice president and is funded out of the total corporate marketing allocations. Although not a profit-and-loss organization, *per se*, the vice president is measured annually on the amount of projects that move into productization. All the marketing staff's annual bonuses are tied to productization of their projects.

Your Project Deliverables

The CRM project requires a complete project plan in order to do the evaluation to determine whether or not your company will be one of the competitors for the final project. The CRM executive management team, reporting directly to the Minister of Chinese Railroads, will do this evaluation. There is no prescribed format provided for the project plan.

Along with the project plan, a prototype showing the functional requirements for the system must be delivered for demonstration by the project team in China. The CRM would like to have an operational prototype within one month of the vendor organization's arrival in the country. The following is a description of the system to date: the prototype is to provide a reservation system that includes three cities; the trains originate in either Guangzhou or

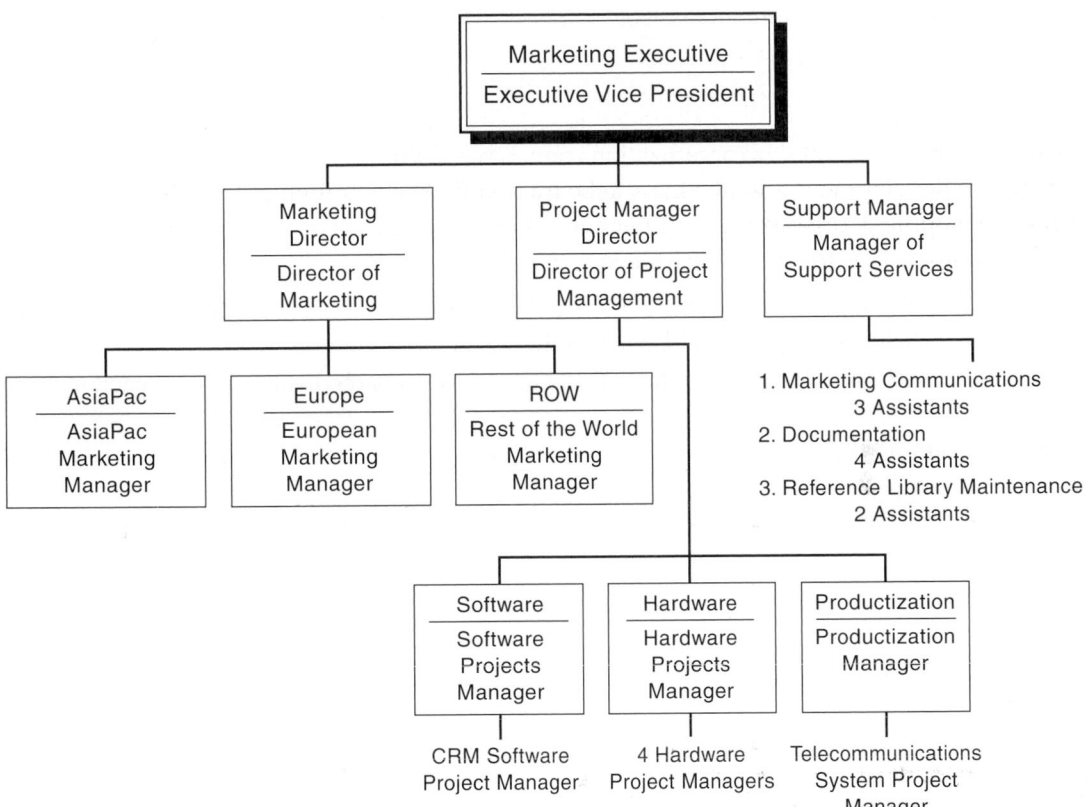

FIGURE 2–2
Company Organization Chart

Shanghai and pass through and pick up passengers in Nanjing. Please reference Figure 2–3 for a detailed map of the routes.

The CRM would like to test the prototype in a live (actual-use) test during a low-usage period under the following circumstances:

- Five trains travel *from* city Guangzhou or Shanghai each day and five travel *to* city Guangzhou or Shanghai each day. Two of the trains traveling *from* Granzhou or Shanghai stop at Nanjing each day and one of the trains traveling *to* Guanzhou or Shanghai stops at Nanjing each day. No trains originate in Nanjing.

- Trains have always been oversold during peak periods, which is a known problem.

- There are five classes of tickets:

1. Sleeping (soft)—compartment-style coaches with 4 passengers per compartment
2. Sleeping (hard)—compartment-style coaches with 6 passengers per compartment

3. Sitting (soft)—typical first-class coach
4. Sitting (hard)—tourist-class coach
5. Standing (hard and soft sitting coaches only)

- Seat assignments are made at the time of the reservation.
- Reservations are to be allowed up to one month prior to a particular trip. This period will be expanded in the future.
- Reservations that are made over the phone must be purchased in person within 24 hours after making the reservation. No reservations are allowed less than 48 hours before a trip.
- During the last 48 hours, available seats will be sold on a first-come, first-served basis.
- Passenger lists are provided for the conductors of each coach of each train at each stop on the route.
- Occasionally CRM trains may become non-operational. A new train will be dispatched, but a delay of up to a few days could occur.
- Trains will be assumed to be of a constant size: two soft-sleeping coaches (12 compartments each), two hard-sleeping coaches (12 compartments each), two soft-sitting coaches (60 seats), and nine hard-sitting coaches (80 seats each).

Although scalping of tickets is popular, CRM wishes to discourage such practices and therefore wants to track ticket sales by buyer.

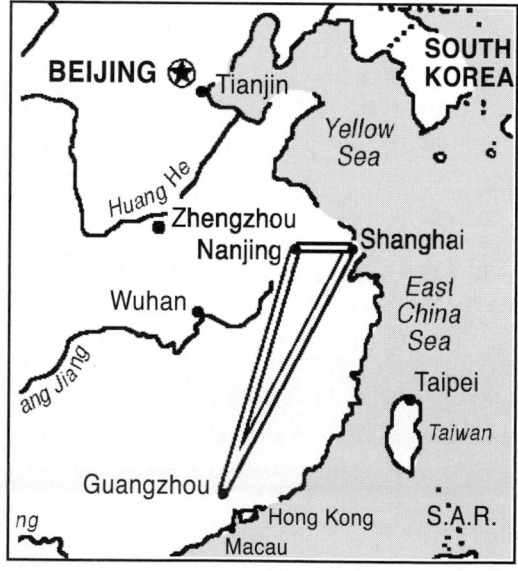

FIGURE 2–3

Detail Map Area of Train System

Source: See Figure 2–1. Portion of map enlarged, with detailed area of the train system added by the authors.

The CRM has need of several management reports. They include:

1. Number of reservations made for each departure date/train
2. Number of customers turned away because of full trains for each departure/train
3. Number of no-shows for each departure
4. Number and names of people who show up without reservations for each departure
5. Lists of "high buyers" (possible scalpers) of train tickets, along with number of tickets and departures on associated sales

The number of reservations during the test period may be around 25,000 per day. The volume varies significantly by hour, day, and season.

Your Schedule

You were notified 30 days ago at the weekly staff meeting that the AsiaPac marketing manager had made contact with one of the Ministry of Railroads' automation managers. There was discussion of a potential automation contract being released. At today's meeting, the marketing executive and AsiaPac marketing manager informed the team that this was going to be a real project and that you were going to be the project manager. This was also to have the highest priority for the organization and was going to be pitched as a "must win" project to the executive management. According to the marketing manager, the project plan and prototype had to be ready within 90 days. Management feels this is easily doable because you will be using the CASE tool technology so recently acquired.

Your Competition

The marketing department is working on a complete competitive analysis to be finished in 45 days. At this time they don't see any other company as qualified as we are to complete this job.

Your Project Team

The AsiaPac marketing manager is your "customer" for this project. You can look to her to get the required research and Chinese contacts made. You have use of three analysts in the Bangalore software development center, the Australian design center manager, two documentation specialists from your organization, and three field applications managers from the Taiwan office. If you need any other resources, all you have to do is make the request and your organization's executive will provide what you need.

A Final Note: Potential Market for Software _____

You marketing manager has just completed her MBA with an international concentration. She feels that other Southeast Asian countries will also need this kind of reservation system. In order to cover marketing's investment in the prototype, you must ensure that it will also be applicable to the Thai, Vietnamese, Kampuchean, and Burmese Railroads. She has set a date for 90 days from now when you will demo the software to one of these country's railway ministries. You also need to get a picture of the bridge on the River Kwai as the opening background for the PowerPoint presentation.

Citations

[1]*www.capitolwebservices.com/china2thou/9805p3.htm*. Chunlei, Zhao (1998). "Railroad Building as a Locomotive for Growth." *China 2000: The Monthly Newsletter*. May.

[2]*www.china2thou.com*. Business Briefs. *China 2000: The Monthly Newsletter*. May 1988.

Web Pages for Further Information

home.tronet.de/joachim.fabry/html/body_asien.html. In Asia, Asien Mittlerer Osten 1912 Hunslet 4-6-4 tank engine "Sir Ralph Home" Sabah Museum, East Malaysia—China Academy of Railway Sciences—China Rail—devoted to China Railways and Beijing transit including photos and maps; by Allen Zagel.

info-s.com/travel1.html. The Info Service—Topographical Pictures Tour in China—Tourism Info.

vlad.tribnet.com/2000/page/china.html. Vladivostok News: China page, "Good fences make good neighbors," Robert Frost once wrote. For Russia and China, who share a 4,300-kilometer border, building a good fence is not easy. In northeast Asia, the border between the two has opened up since the break up of the Soviet Union.

www.china2thou.com/9805p3.htm. China 2000—Railroad building, May 1998 Cover Article Agriculture in China with the population to hit 1.6 billion by 2030, grain production is a top priority. Railroad building: Major investments in this sector meet key transportation needs and drive growth.

www.china2thou.com/9805p4.htm. China 2000—Tourism: Progress has already been made in China's tourism since 1978, when China remained virtually closed to the world.

www.chinavista.com/business/ciec/en/ciec19990518.html. Economic Brief—Shanxi eyes tourism to spur economy.

www.chinesebusinessworld.com/tourism. Budget Travel—China—China Cities—China at a Glance—China National Tourism Administration.

www.frommers.com/features/articles/9803_1b.html. Arthur Frommer's Budget Travel Magazine: March 1998 Articles—Traveling Within China.

www.lib.utexas.edu/Libs/PCL/Map_collection/map_sites/cities_sites.html. City Map Sites. The Perry-Castañeda Library Map Collection, The University of Texas at Austin, Updated 2/14/00.

www.links2go.com/more/severn.dmu.ac.uk/~mlp/crsg.html. Links2Go: China Railways Home Page, The, Links and topics related to China Railways Home Page.

www.lonelyplanet.com/letters/nea/chi_pc.htm. Lonely Planet—Travelers' reports on China.

www.netlizard.com/travel/1travel.html. Nonstop Travel Guide: Worldwide Online Travel Information, comprehensive travel information online, from destinations to subways.

www.netscout.net/oneworld/countries_a-c.htm. Nations Online: countries of the world A–C—Republic of China, China National Tourism Administration—The China Tourism Website—China Internet Information Center.

www.newpaltz.edu/geography/links.html. SUNY New Paltz Department of Geography WWW Links Page—Environment Issues—China—National Tourism Administration—World Geography | Latin America | China and More.

www.odci.gov/cia/publications/factbook/geos/ch.html. 2000, The World Fact Book, CIA. Background: For most of its 3,500 years of history, China led the world in agriculture, crafts, and science, then fell behind in the 19th century when the Industrial Revolution gave the West clear superiority in military and economic affairs. In the first half of the 20th century, China continued to suffer from major famine, civil unrest, military defeat, and foreign occupation. After World War II, the Communists under Mao Zedong established a dictatorship that, while ensuring China's autonomy, imposed strict controls over all aspects of life and cost the lives of tens of millions of people. After 1978, Mao's successor Deng Xiaoping decentralized economic decision-making; output quadrupled in the next 20 years. Political controls remain tight at the same time that economic controls have been weakening. Present issues are: incorporating Hong Kong into the Chinese system, closing down inefficient state-owned enterprises, modernizing the military, fighting corruption, and providing support to tens of millions of displaced workers.

www.tradeport.org/ts/countries/china/isa/isar0014.html. China: Retail Sector—Number of Internet users in China—Understand your export financing options with Sanwa.

www.wanghuhotel.com/8e.htm. Vacation Train Travel in China. Hangzhou Wanghu Travel Agency is a specialized one attached to Hangzhou Wanghu Hotel. Its main task is to organize and receive domestic and foreign tourists for sightseeing in Hangzhou and other parts of the country. It also provides services for conferences and touring after conferences. With the great economic strength and fine reputation of Wanghu Hotel, and its close relations with big domestic hotels, travel agencies, airports, and railroad stations, Wanghu Travel Agency can extend various excellent services to guests in time. The advanced facilities of the hotel and vigorous and dedicated professional contingent of the agency show its unique advantage in guest reception. Based on the aim of guests and reputation above everything, Wanghu Travel Agency does hope to have extensive cooperation with friends of the same trade and people from all walks of life.

www.zhuhai.com.cn/projects/english/1/railway.htm. Zhuhai zhuhai-guangzhou railway, Guangzhou-Zhuhai Railroad Project Undertaker: Zhuhai Guangzhou-Zhuhai Railroad Co. Brief Introduction to the Project.

Process Overview

Process management is one of the activities that project managers must consider before they can begin any project in earnest. This activity lays out the framework for how progress on a project may be measured. The authors of this book used a process to divide up the chapters, produce the information, review it, and get it to the publishers for integration into a completed book. Process management ensures the correct execution of the organization's procedures, policies, and life-cycle model. For example, this addresses the question, "Were all the files tested and checked for quality before being released to the customer?" Process management controls the software development activities. For example, it might check to ensure that a change request existed and was approved for fixing and that the associated design, documentation, and review activities were completed before allowing the code to be "checked in" again.

"Process" is defined in Box 3–1.

BOX 3–1
Process Definition

> **process**
>
> a bounded set of interrelated activities that takes one or more kinds of inputs and creates outputs that are of value to the customer by means of one or more transformations

A process represents activities, tools, methods, and practices that transform inputs, or raw materials, into outputs, or finished products, as shown in Figure 3–1. With software engineering, the transformation (production and evolution) is from user's requirements into software. IEEE 610 defines *process* as "a sequence of steps performed for a given purpose—for example, the software development process." In *Managing the Software Process*, Watts Humphrey says:

> Software development can be exceedingly complex and there are often many alternative ways to perform the various tasks. A defined process can help guide the software professionals through these choices in an orderly way. With an established process definition they can better understand what they should do, what they can expect from their co-workers, and what they are expected to provide in return. This allows them to focus on doing their job... Software engineering, however, is not a routine activity that can be structured and regimented like a repetitive manufacturing or clerical procedure. We are dealing with an intellectual process that must dynamically adjust to the creative needs of the professionals and their tasks. A trade-off is thus required between the individual need for flexibility and the organizational need for standards and consistency. Some of the factors to be considered are:

1. Since software projects have differences, their software engineering processes must have differences as well.
2. In the absence of a universal software engineering process, organizations and projects must define processes that meet their own unique needs.
3. The process used for a given project must consider the experience level of the members, current product status and the available tools and facilities.[1]

This chapter provides an understanding of the basics of process management and how it fits into the front end of the project life cycle. Key foundation documents in process management are IEEE 1074 and 1074.1. The specific understanding and application of 1074 and 1074.1 to evolve a project's life cycle will be stressed in this chapter. The life cycles that are used in the practitioner's guide are direct derivations from 1074.

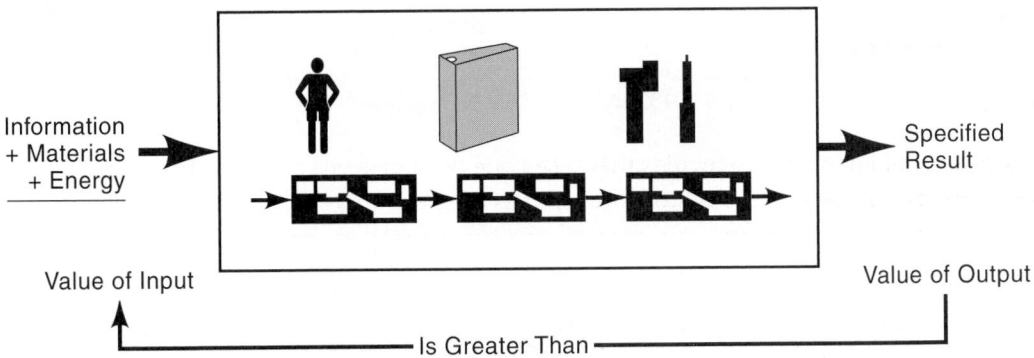

FIGURE 3–1
Process Flow

Key Chapter 3 Points_____

Process defines our level of quality. Without having a defined process, there is nothing to manage against. Process and quality are not free. There is a cost in establishing a managed, repeatable process. As project managers, we must continue to ask ourselves, "Why is quality important?" and "What is our optimum level of quality?" What is "good enough"? As shown in Box 3–2, 99.9% sounds like a really high quality rating, but when human life or health is at stake, it may not be good enough.

The Software Project Managers Network (*www.spmn.com*) has developed a list of 16 best practices. These are the management and technical practices with the highest return on investment (ROI) in developing and sustaining large-scale software-intensive systems, as ranked by the U.S. Department of Defense:

1. Formal risk management
2. Empirical cost and schedule estimation
3. Metrics-based project management
4. Earned value tracking
5. Defect tracking against quality targets
6. People-aware program management
7. Configuration management
8. End-to-end requirements tracing
9. System-architecture–based software design

BOX 3–2
What Is "Good Enough"?

If 99.9% Were "Good Enough"

- 27,800 pieces of mail would be lost each hour.[a]

- We would experience 1 hour of unsafe drinking water each month.

- 3,000,000 incorrect drug prescriptions would be filled each year.[b]

- 9,703 checks would be deducted from the wrong bank accounts each hour.[c]

- Doctors would drop 370 newborn babies at birth every day.[d]

- 8,605 commercial aircraft takeoffs would annually result in crashes.[e]

Notes:

[a]*www.usps.com/history/anrpt00/index1.htm*. "Every day, we handle 668 million pieces of mail."
[b]*www.nacds.org/user-documents/2001_projections.PDF*. 3 billion projected for all of 2001.
[c]*www.calacreek.com/consumer/banking/chkfraud.html*. "ACA estimates that in the year 2000, 85 billion checks will be processed…"
[d]*www.prb.org/Content/NavigationMenu/Other_reports/2000-2002/sheet1.html*.
[e]*www.bts.gov/publications/airactstats/AAS_1999.pdf*.

---

10. Data and database interoperability
11. Formal definition and control of interfaces
12. Visible and inspectable design
13. Cost-justified and quality-justified reuse
14. Formal inspections
15. Managing tests as assets
16. Frequent compile and smoke testing

These 16 best practices are addressed in chapters of this practitioner's guide. This chapter looks at how all of them are integrated into the management of a process.

Where We Are in the Product Development Life Cycle

We are at the very beginning of the life cycle. In fact, we are before the beginning. Process management starts with deciding on the life cycle to use for the project, as shown in Figure 3–2.

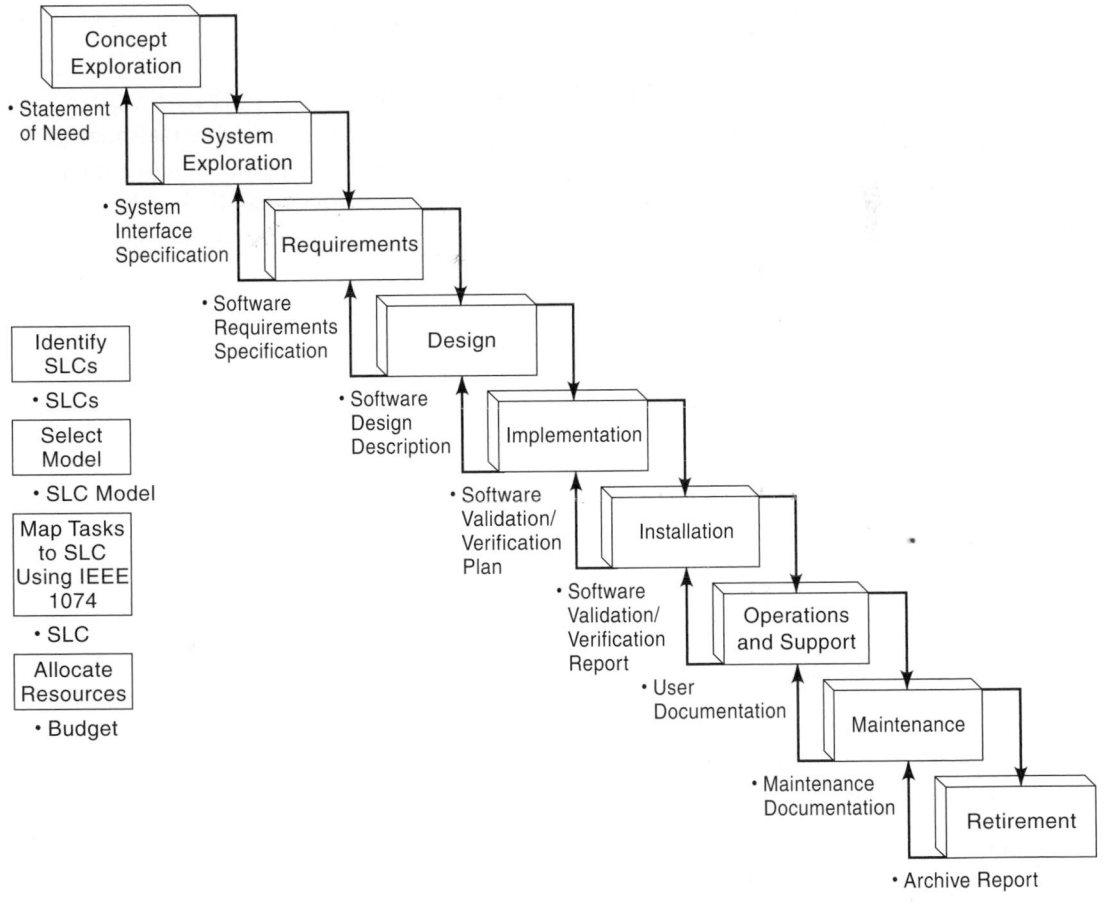

FIGURE 3–2
Where Process Tailoring Occurs in the Product Development Life Cycle

Chapter 3 Relation to the 34 Competencies

This chapter relates to both product and people competencies. Managing the process of product development is a critical skill for project managers. The first two competencies to be mastered by a project manager are assessing processes and awareness of process standards. The other product competencies that must be mastered in understanding process are number 8, selecting methods and tools, and number 9, tailoring processes. Each project is different. A project manager must be able to assess the current state of organizational processes and modify that to fit the project needs by changing product development methods or adding tools.

The project competency that must be mastered is number 21, tracking process. For an organization to become more mature in the processes used to build products, the organization must be measuring what and how it executes product development. This tracking process to gather process metrics must be built into the overall development process from the beginning. Defining an organization's product development processes is a critical competency for project managers.

Process management fits within the following six competencies:

Product Development Techniques

1. **Assessing processes**—Defining criteria for reviews
2. **Awareness of process standards**—Understanding process standards
8. **Selecting methods and tools**—Defining selection processes
9. **Tailoring processes**—Modifying standard processes to suit a project

Project Management Skills

21. **Tracking process**—Monitoring compliance of the project team

People Management Skills

28. **Managing change**—Being an effective change agent

Learning Objectives for Chapter 3

Upon completion of this chapter, the reader should be able to:

- Define a process;
- Explain why having a process is important in the production of software;
- Describe reasons for tailoring software processes;
- Explain why process improvement leads to product improvement.

SEI contends that processes can be developed and maintained in a way similar to the way products are developed and maintained. There must be:

- Requirements that define what process is to be described.
- An architecture and design that provide information on how the process will be defined.

- Implementation of the process design in a project or organizational situation.
- Validation of the process description via measurement.
- Deployment of the process into widespread operation within the organization or project for which the process is intended.

Software process assets, entities maintained by the organization for use by projects in developing, tailoring, maintaining, and implementing their software processes typically include:

- The organization's standard software process (including the software process architecture and software process elements, as defined in the glossary).
- The descriptions of software life cycles approved for use (this will be discussed in Chapter 4, "Selecting Software Development Life Cycles").
- The guidelines and criteria for tailoring the organization's standard software process.
- The organization's software process database.
- The library of software process-related documentation.

A mature software process, with respect to the Capability Maturity Model (CMM) is effective in building organizational capability and is defined, documented, trained, practiced, supported, maintained, controlled, verified, validated, measured, and able to improve.

SEI CMM Level 3 Is the Defined Level _____

The software process for both management and engineering activities is documented, standardized, and integrated into an organization-wide software process. All projects use a documented and approved version of the organization's process for developing and maintaining software.

Two key process areas (KPAs) for Level 3 deal specifically with process.

Organizational Process Focus

The purpose of organizational process focus is to establish the organizational responsibility for software process activities that improve the organization's overall software process capability. It involves developing and maintaining an understanding of the organizations' and projects' software processes and coordinating the activities to assess, develop, maintain, and improve these processes.

Goals:

1. Software process development and improvement activities are coordinated across the organization.
2. The strengths and weaknesses of the software processes used are identified relative to a process standard.
3. Organization-level process development and improvement activities are planned.

Activities:

1. The software process is assessed periodically, and action plans are developed to address the assessment findings.

2. The organization develops and maintains a plan for its software process development and improvement activities.

3. The organization and projects' activities for developing and improving software processes are coordinated at the organization level.

4. The use of the organization's software process database is coordinated at the organizational level.

5. New processes, methods, and tools in limited use in the organization are monitored, evaluated, and, where appropriate, transferred to other parts of the organization.

6. Training for the organization and projects' software processes is coordinated across the organization.

7. The groups involved in implementing the software processes are informed of the organization and projects' activities for software process development and improvement.

Organizational Process Definition

The purpose of organizational process definition is to develop and maintain a usable set of software process assets that improve process performance across the projects and provide a basis for cumulative, long-term benefits to the organization. It involves developing and maintaining the organization's standard software process, along with related process assets, such as descriptions of software life cycles, process tailoring guidelines and criteria, the organization's software process database, and a library of software process-related documentation.

Goals:

1. A standard software process for the organization is developed and maintained.

2. Information related to the use of the organization's standard software process by the software projects is collected, reviewed, and made available.

Activities:

1. The organization's standard software process is developed and maintained according to a documented procedure.

2. The organization's standard software process is documented according to established organizational standards.

3. Descriptions of software life cycles that are approved for use by the projects are documented and maintained.

4. Guidelines and criteria for the projects' tailoring of the organization's standard software process are developed and maintained.
5. The organization's software process database is established and maintained.
6. A library of software process-related documentation is established and maintained.

Figure 3–3 shows the triangle formed by the people, technology, and process determinants of our software project and product success. These are the three major elements that determine the cost of the software produced, the project's performance to schedule, and the ultimate delivered quality of the product. Along with the applicable members of the 34 competencies, this chapter will provide instruction in these two tools:

1. The evolution of the Plan-Do-Check-Act Cycle into a model that is used to evaluate all of the project management and software engineering knowledge areas and processes to clarify what is in place versus what is needed before determining how to proceed.
2. IEEE 1074-1997, "IEEE Standard for Developing Software Life Cycle Processes," is the most comprehensive tool for determining a software development life cycle and the attendant support processes.

Process Management Begins at the Front End

Process management starts with defining a project or organizational approach to developing products. The process front end shown in Figure 3–4 captures all the information that can be used to define a process. As an ongoing organization, this is a representation of knowledge base of previous project and product metrics and artifacts. For a new organization or an organization "new" to process, this represents the areas to "visit" to gather the information and data needed to establish a product development process. As we define the analysis cycles for process development, this figure will be again used to show the customization of basic processes for the organization.

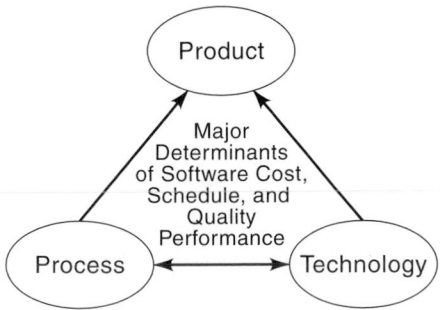

FIGURE 3–3
Project Success Determinants

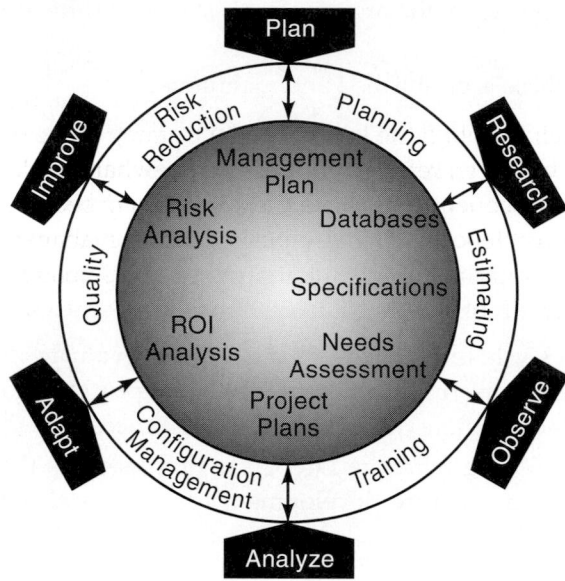

FIGURE 3–4
Process Front End

Process Management Defined

Process management is the discipline of defining, implementing, and maintaining the work processes within an organization. The goal of process management is to create an environment for improving quality and productivity. The foundation of a successful process management system is a defined framework that fits the organization's objective and culture. Building a process management system is a progressive, iterative task that requires a strategic commitment of the organization.

The fundamental process management premise is this: "The quality of a product (e.g., a software system) is governed by the quality of the process used to produce it." This fundamental premise, combined with the definition of *process*, gives us a definition for *process management*. So, then, *process* is defined as a management paradigm for increasing quality through:

1. Formal process definition
2. Process measurement
3. Feedback and control
4. Improvement
5. Optimization

The Process of Process Management

W. Edwards Deming brought the first easily understandable framework for process management from his work in Japan after World War II. Deming encouraged the Japanese to adopt a systematic approach to problem solving, which later became known as the Deming Cycle or Plan-Do-Check-Act (PDCA) Cycle. Deming, however, referred to it as the Shewhart Cycle, named after his teacher, W.A. Shewhart. He subsequently replaced *check* with *study* because that word reflects the actual meaning more accurately. Deming also pushed senior managers to become actively involved in their company's quality improvement programs. His greatest contribution to the Japanese is the message regarding a typical business system. It explained that the consumers are the most important part of a production line. Meeting and exceeding the customers' requirements is the task that everyone within an organization needs to accomplish. Furthermore, the management system has to enable everyone to be responsible for the quality of his output to his internal customers.

Deming's four steps had these tasks:

1. **Plan** the short-term objective:
   - Determine the time frame.
   - Decide what data will be needed.
   - Decide what each member will do as part of the project team effort.

2. **Do** what the plan said:
   - Collect the data.
   - Design studies or devices.
   - Train people on data collection and analysis.

3. **Check** to see that the plan was carried out:
   - Compare project studies to plan.
   - If the plan was not carried out, then do it.
   - Look for lessons for future use.
   - Discuss adjustments in approaches.
   - Determine courses of action and changes.

4. **Act** on the recommendations of the team:
   - Implement fixes, adjustments, and so on.
   - Inform others of needed changes.
   - Improve communications from processes to processes.

As can be seen in Figure 3–5, Kaoru Ishikawa expanded Deming's four steps into six:

Plan:

1. Determine goals and targets.
2. Determine methods of reaching goals.

Do:

3. Engage in education and training.
4. Implement work.

Check:

5. Check the effects of implementation.

Act:

6. Take appropriate action.

Using these six steps, we start to customize our own software product development process definition. Managing software projects is different from managing other projects with tangible deliverables. We must recognize that difference up front as we are deciding on a life cycle set of processes. We can quantify the core knowledge areas of software engineering that must be

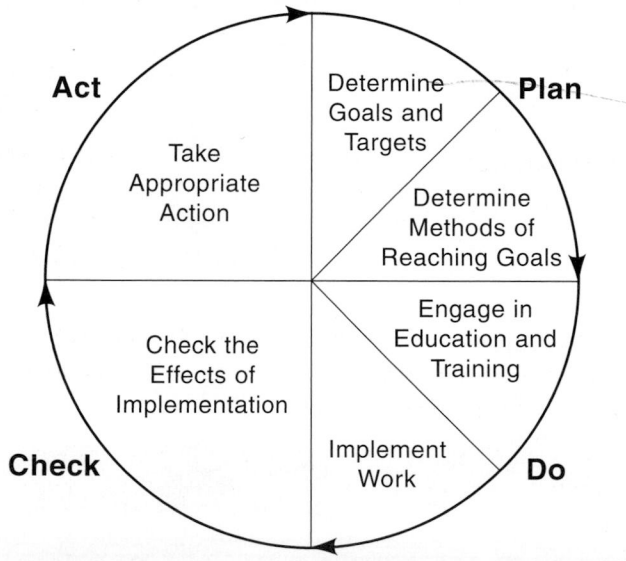

FIGURE 3–5
Deming/Shewhart/Ishikawa Cycle
Source: Ishikawa, K., D.J. Lu. trans. (1988). *What is Total Quality Control? The Japanese Way.* Englewood Cliffs, NJ: Prentice Hall.

investigated: software project management planning, metrics databases, libraries of specifications and project plans, completed project ROI analyses, and risk analysis plans for completed projects. We view all these core knowledge areas through specific software engineering processes: planning, estimating, training, performing configuration management, maintaining quality, and performing risk reduction. We then change our basis Deming/Shewhart/Ishikawa Cycle into our process front-end cycle, where the major steps of the process are external to the software engineering processes and the core knowledge areas. Referring back to Figure 3–4, these six new steps map to the original PDCA Cycle in this fashion:

Plan maps to Plan.

Do maps to Research, Observe, and Analyze.

Check maps to Adapt.

Act maps to Improve.

Remember that a process is a management paradigm for increasing quality through (1) formal process definition, (2) process measurement, (3) feedback and control, (4) improvement, and (5) optimization. Our process front end provides the structure for these quality steps:

1. **Formal process definition** is done through using the Process Front End model to analyze the current process for developing software products within the project manager's organization. The Process Front End model works as a focusing mechanism to acquire best practices from the body of knowledge existing outside the organization for new software development products and projects.

2. **Process measurement** can begin as soon as the process has been defined. The front-end process and any resulting software development life cycle act as a process map for taking measurements. A metrics program must be defined that uses the processes, activities, deliverables, and transitions as points at which to measure the overall process for achievement of quality goals.

3. **Feedback and control** occur after a series of cycles has been executed and metrics have been collected and analyzed. The formal process definition has its own built-in feedback loops where control can be exercised based on the process measurements.

4. **Improvement** is the inherent goal of any software engineering process. The ability to repeat processes that succeed and modify processes that fall short of expectation is one of the quality benefits of a formal process.

5. **Optimization** occurs as improvements are made to repeatable processes. A formal process moves toward optimization because the measurement data that is acquired allows project and process managers to modify the process itself to produce the highest quality results.

IEEE 1074—Process Map for Software Life Cycle Process

IEEE 1074 provides a process for creating a software life cycle process (SLCP). The SLCP is defined as the project-specific description of the process that is based on a project's software life cycle (SLC) and the integral and project management processes used by the organization. These integral processes include configuration management, metrics, quality assurance, risk reduction, and the acts of estimating, planning, and training. It is primarily the responsibility of the project manager and the process architect for a given software project to create the SLCP.

This methodology begins with the selection of an appropriate software life cycle model (SLCM) for use on the specific project. It continues through the creation of the SLC, using the selected SLCM and the activities described in Table 3–1. The methodology concludes with the augmentation of the SLC with an organization's support processes to create the SLCP. The activities described in the 1074 mapping table cover the entire life cycle of a software project, from concept exploration through the eventual retirement of the software system. 1074 does not address nonsoftware activities, such as contracting, purchasing, or hardware development. It also does not mandate the use of a specific SLCM. 1074 presumes that the project manager and process architect are already familiar with a variety of SLCMs, with the criteria for choosing among them, and with the criteria for determining the attributes and constraints of the desired end system and the development environment that affects this selection. An example of life cycle derivation is shown in Figure 3–6.

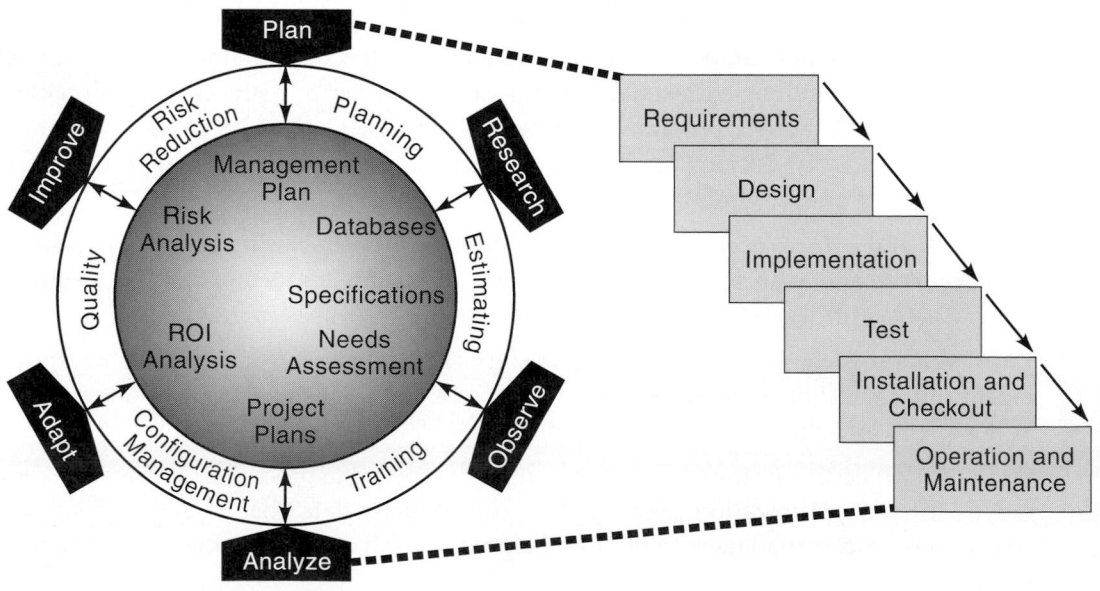

FIGURE 3–6
Deriving the Software Life Cycle

TABLE 3–1

IEEE 1074 Process Mapping

Category	Process	Activity
I. Software Life Cycle Model Process	A. Software Life Cycle Model	1. Identify Candidate SLC Models 2. Select Project Model
II. Project Management Processes	A. Project Initiation	1. Map Activities to SLC Model 2. Allocate Project Information 3. Establish Project Environment 4. Plan Project Management
	B. Project Monitoring and Control	1. Analyze Risks 2. Perform Contingency Planning 3. Manage the Project 4. Retain Records 5. Implement Problem Reporting Method
	C. Software Quality Management	1. Plan Software Quality Management 2. Define Metrics 3. Manage Software Quality 4. Identify Quality Improvement Needs
III. Predevelopment Processes	A. Concept Exploration	1. Identify Ideas or Needs 2. Formulate Potential Approaches 3. Conduct Feasibility Studies 4. Plan System Transition 5. Refine and Finalize the Idea or Need
	B. System Allocation	1. Analyze Functions 2. Develop System Architecture 3. Decompose System Requirements

(Continues)

TABLE 3–1 (Continued)
IEEE 1074 Process Mapping

Category	Process	Activity
IV. Development Processes	A. Requirements	1. Define and Develop Software Requirements 2. Define Interface Requirements 3. Prioritize and Integrate Software Requirements
	B. Design	1. Perform Architecture Design 2. Design Database 3. Design Interfaces 4. Select or Develop Algorithms 5. Perform Detailed Design
	C. Implementation	1. Create Test Data 2. Create Source 3. Generate Object Code 4. Create Operating Documentation 5. Plan Integration 6. Perform Integration
V. Post-Development Processes	A. Installation	1. Plan Installation 2. Distribute Software 3. Install Software 4. Accept Software in Operational Environment
	B. Operation and Support	1. Operate the System 2. Provide Technical Assistance and Consulting 3. Maintain Support Request Log
	C. Maintenance	1. Reapply Software Life Cycle
	D. Retirement	1. Notify User 2. Conduct Parallel Operations 3. Retire System

(Continues)

TABLE 3–1 (Continued)
IEEE 1074 Process Mapping

Category	Process	Activity
VI. Integral Processes	A. Verification and Validation	1. Plan V&V 2. Execute V&V Tasks 3. Collect and Analyze Metric Data 4. Plan Testing 5. Develop Test Requirements 6. Execute the Tests
	B. Software Configuration Management	1. Plan Configuration Management 2. Develop Configuration Identification 3. Perform Configuration Control 4. Perform Status Accounting
	C. Documentation Development	1. Plan Documentation 2. Implement Documentation 3. Produce and Distribute Documentation
	D. Training	1. Plan the Training Program 2. Develop Training Materials 3. Validate the Training Program 4. Implement the Training Program

1074 is useful to any organization that is responsible for managing and performing software projects. It can be used where software is the total system or where software is part of a larger system. It works for pure software product organizations, internal information technology (IT) shops, software consultants, and pure project management organizations that procure and implement commercial-off-the-shelf (COTS) software products. The 1074 product is the SLCP that is required for a specific software project.

Although 1074 describes the creation of a single, overall SLCP that is to be used for a project, the user of this standard should recognize that an SLCP can itself include lower-level SLCPs. This is the same concept as in configuration management, in which a particular configuration item can include subordinate configuration items. This standard applies equally to the development of SLCPs at any level.

1074 consists of six major process categories:

1. Software life cycle model process
2. Project management processes
3. Predevelopment processes
4. Development processes
5. Post-development processes
6. Integral processes

Within the processes, there are 17 subprocesses and a total of 65 activities in the subprocesses. The 1074 mapping table summarizes these.

1074 is not a prescriptive, specific SLCM. It cannot exist without an organization's SLC. 1074 does not presume to use any specific software development methodology, nor does it recommend one. It is not self-limiting—more stringent requirements may be added, if desired. Table 3–1 shows the IEEE 1074 map of category to process to activity.

How to Use 1074

1074 is a step-by-step guide to implementing the nine steps described to produce an SLCP. In keeping with the customization nature of this IEEE standard, practitioners have found that the steps specified in the standard can be further simplified to the following six steps.

Step 1. Select the SLCM. This starting point allows the project manager to select the life cycle model with which he has the most experience, one proposed by the organization, a model requested by the customer, or a new model that research has shown may have promising quality improvement results. For this description, we will select the simplest model to implement, the basic waterfall model shown in Figure 3–7.

Initially, the project manager or process architect shall identify the SLCM to which the activities will be mapped. This step encompasses locating, evaluating, selecting, and acquiring an SLCM. It is possible for an organization to have multiple SLCMs; however, only one model is to be selected for a project. Mixing models within projects adds to confusion and nondeterministic collection of project metrics. It is suggested that the process architect or project manager follow the following five steps to evaluate and select an SLCM:

1. Identify all the SLCMs that are available to the development project.
2. Identify the attributes that apply to the desired end system and the development environment.

3. Identify any constraints that might be imposed on the selection.

4. Evaluate the various SLCMs based on past experience and organizational capabilities.

5. Select the SLCM that will best satisfy the project attributes and constraints.

Step 2. Compare activities to SLCM requirements. Having selected an SLCM, the project manager performs a detailed mapping of the activities against the SLCM. This involves matching the activities against the major phases of the SLCM. This step provides a checklist to ensure that all activities are mapped and that all SLCM requirements are covered by one or more activities. The easiest way to accomplish this is to take the 1074 map and add columns for each of the major SLCM phases. Using our basic waterfall model, we would add columns titled Requirements, Design, Implementation, Test, Installation and Checkout, and Operation and Maintenance. Figure 3–8 shows this. At each cell in which a 1074 activity is used in a life cycle phase, a check is placed. When all the activities are analyzed to see where (and if) they fit a phase, the table is sorted so that the activities with no phase cell checks are at the bottom. Do not delete them from the table; in this iterative process they may be needed in a later step.

Wrapped into this step are Steps 3 and 4 from 1074. Step 3 is to develop and justify the list of activities not used. Although that is a noble effort, it is usually quite easy in a review session to decide what is in and what is out. Practitioners have found that keeping detailed reasons for not selecting an activity for a specific project does not aid in making this decision for the next project. 1074 Step 4 is to list activities and invocations. The list of activities already exists in the 1074 modified map. Invocations are nothing more than the triggers into the support processes, such as configuration management, that are used in the phase.

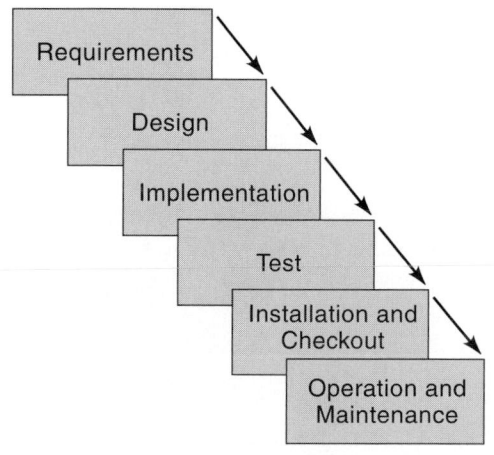

FIGURE 3–7
Step 1—Consider the Basic Waterfall Process Model

Step 3. Place the activities in time sequence. Table 3–2 represents the activities map with dates placed in the phase cell. The order in which activities will be performed will be determined by three major factors:

1. The selected SLCM will dictate an initial ordering of activities. As mapping progresses, the actual order in which activities will be performed will be established. This will usually differ from the original order of the 1074 activities map.
2. Schedule constraints may require the overlapping of activities in the SLCM and may thus impact the ordering. In this case, activities may be mapped for parallel execution rather than for serial execution. This provides the project manager with a first order look at the feasibility of the schedule.
3. The ordering of activities may be impacted by the entry and exit criteria of associated activities. This will be further analyzed in Step 4.

When this is completed, the table is sorted again so that the activities are in date order.

Step 4. Check information flow. The input and output information tables in 1074 specify the information that is to be used and generated by each activity. This step verifies that the information flow into and out of the activities will support the relative order into which they have been mapped. Although it is unlikely that this will cause a major rearrangement or modification of the mapping, it is a necessary check to be sure that all information will be available when and where needed. Figure 3–9 shows this for the Establish Project Environment activity.

Step 5. Assign activity output to deliverables. Each SLCM process requires and defines the format and content of its own set of outputs. These products are the specific artifacts that the SLCM delivers. Note that the term *artifact* does not imply any particular medium. This step

1074 Activities			Life Cycle Phase				
Category	Process	Activity	Requirements	Design	Code	Test	Implement
I. Software Life Cycle Model Process	A. Software Life Cycle Model	1. Identify Candidate SLC Models					
		2. Select Project Model					
II. Project Management Processes	A. Project Initiation	1. Map Activities to SLC Model					
		2. Allocate Project Information					
		3. Establish Project Environment					
		4. Plan Project Management					
	B. Project Monitoring and Control	1. Analyze Risks					
		2. Perform Contingency Planning					
		3. Manage the Project					
		4. Retain Records					
		5. Implement Problem Reporting Method					
	C. Software Quality Management	1. Plan Software Quality Management					
		2. Define Metrics					
		3. Manage Software Quality					
		4. Identify Quality Improvement Needs					

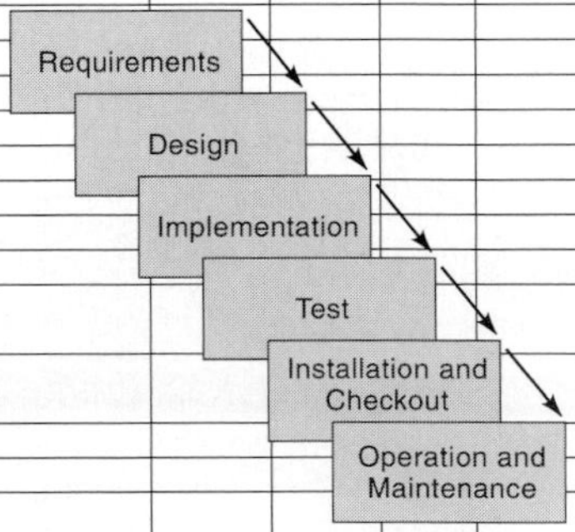

FIGURE 3–8
Step 2—Compare Activities to SLCM Requirements

compares the output information that is generated by each activity with the SLCM-required artifacts into which it must go. Once again, the order of the mapping, this time from Step 4, might have to be modified. If a particular artifact, as specified by the selected SLCM, is to be created at a particular point in the development schedule, all the activities that contribute information to be recorded in that document must have had an opportunity to generate it.

Step 6. Add life cycle support processes. This step in 1074 is discussed as adding an organizational process asset (OPA): 1074 defines OPAs as "artifacts that defines some portion of an organization's software project environment." Practitioners define the life cycle support processes as the project-specific processes based on a project's SLC and the integral and project management processes used by the organization. These integral processes include configuration management, metrics, quality assurance, risk reduction, and the activities of estimating, planning, and training. These are already included in the 1074 map and have been addressed once. The purpose of this step is to ensure that all phases of the SLC have adequately accounted for the effort required by the project management and integral process activities. This step is a further sanity check on the project estimates and schedule.

After Step 6 is completed, the project and organization will have in place an SLC process. Figure 3–10 shows how the information used in the SLC process definition just described fits within an organization. The processes on the left side of the figure are all the activities listed on the 1074 map. As a project manager, you have used this map, referenced process improvement models such as the Software Engineering Institutes' Capability Maturity Model and the selected life cycle model, to derive your SLCM. From this model, you derived the specific subset of the model for your project's SLC. After that, you begin to turn activity artifacts into deliverables such as your project's software development plan.

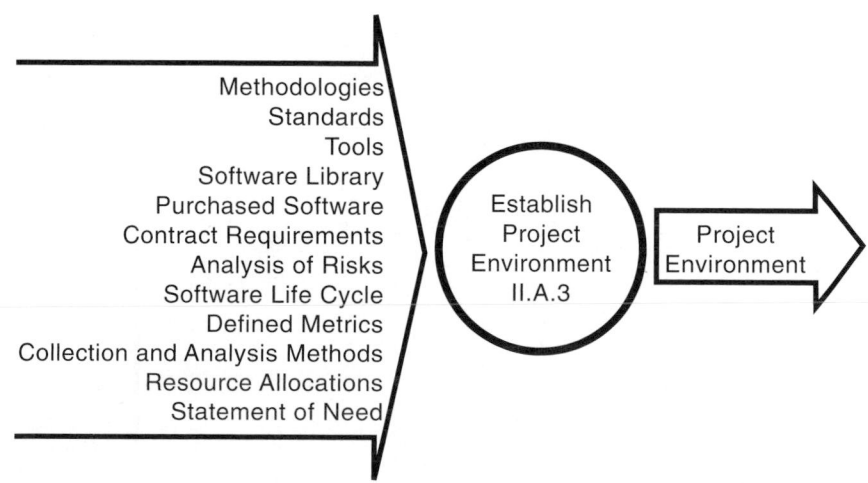

FIGURE 3–9
Step 4—Check Information Flow

TABLE 3–2

Step 3—Place the Activities in Time Sequence

Category	Process	Activity	Requirements	Design	Code	Test	Implement
				Life Cycle Phases			
I. Software Life Cycle Model Process	A. Software Life Cycle Model	1. Identify Candidate SLC Models	1-Jan				
II. Project Management Processes	B. Project Monitoring and Control	1. Analyze Risks	15-Jan				
II. Project Management Processes	B. Project Monitoring and Control	2. Perform Contingency Planning	21-Jan				
I. Software Life Cycle Model Process	A. Software Life Cycle Model	2. Select Project Model	1-Feb				
II. Project Management Processes	C. Software Quality Management	1. Plan Software Quality Management	1-Mar				
II. Project Management Processes	C. Software Quality Management	2. Define Metrics	15-Mar				
II. Project Management Processes	A. Project Initiation	4. Plan Project Management	15-Apr				

(Continues)

TABLE 3-2 (Continued)

Step 3—Place the Activities in Time Sequence

			Life Cycle Phases
II. Project Management Processes	A. Project Initiation	3. Establish Project Environment	30-Apr
II. Project Management Processes	B. Project Monitoring and Control	5. Implement Problem Reporting Method	30-Apr
II. Project Management Processes	A. Project Initiation	1. Map Activities to SLC Model	1-May
II. Project Management Processes	A. Project Initiation	2. Allocate Project Information	1-Jun
II. Project Management Processes	C. Software Quality Management	4. Identify Quality Improvement Needs	15-Jul
II. Project Management Processes	B. Project Monitoring and Control	3. Manage the Project	
II. Project Management Processes	B. Project Monitoring and Control	4. Retain Records	
II. Project Management Processes	C. Software Quality Management	3. Manage Software Quality	

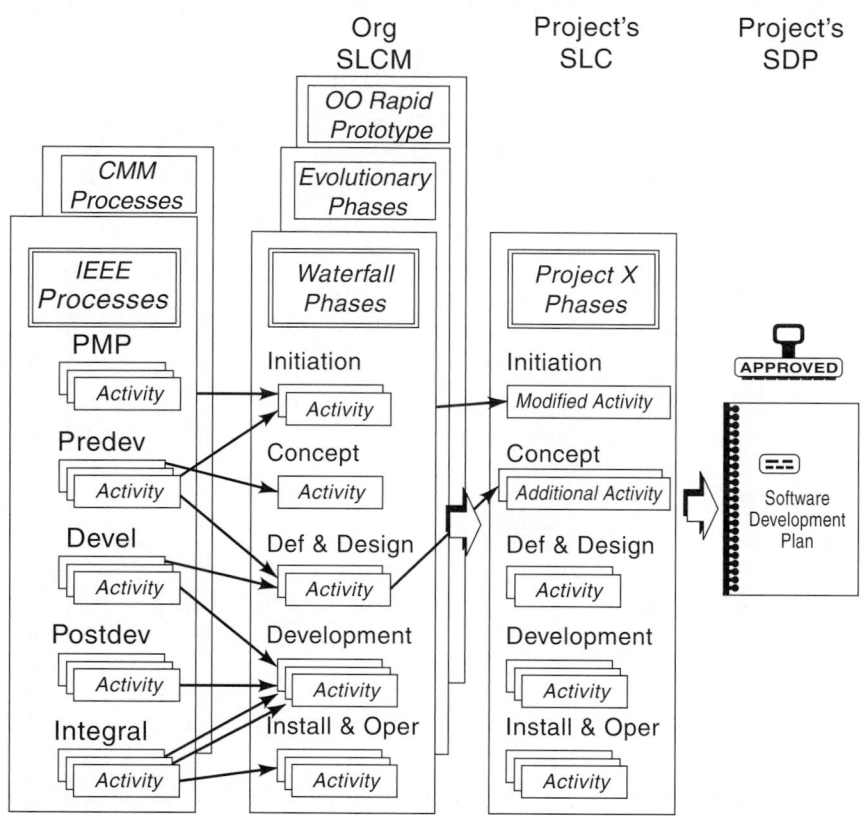

FIGURE 3–10
Organizational Relationship of SLCM

1074 Applied

Using the process defined in IEEE 1074 for defining a software development life cycle is one of the most valuable tools available. The idea of a roll-your-own life cycle is critical to cycle time reduction and continuous process improvement. A couple examples of how it is used will introduce its flexibility.

Customized Software Development Process _____

Figure 3–11 represents a 1074-derived SLCM for a custom software development organization. The organization develops custom software products that are then turned over to the client organization to operate and maintain. Early visibility into proof of concept, feasibility, and design were

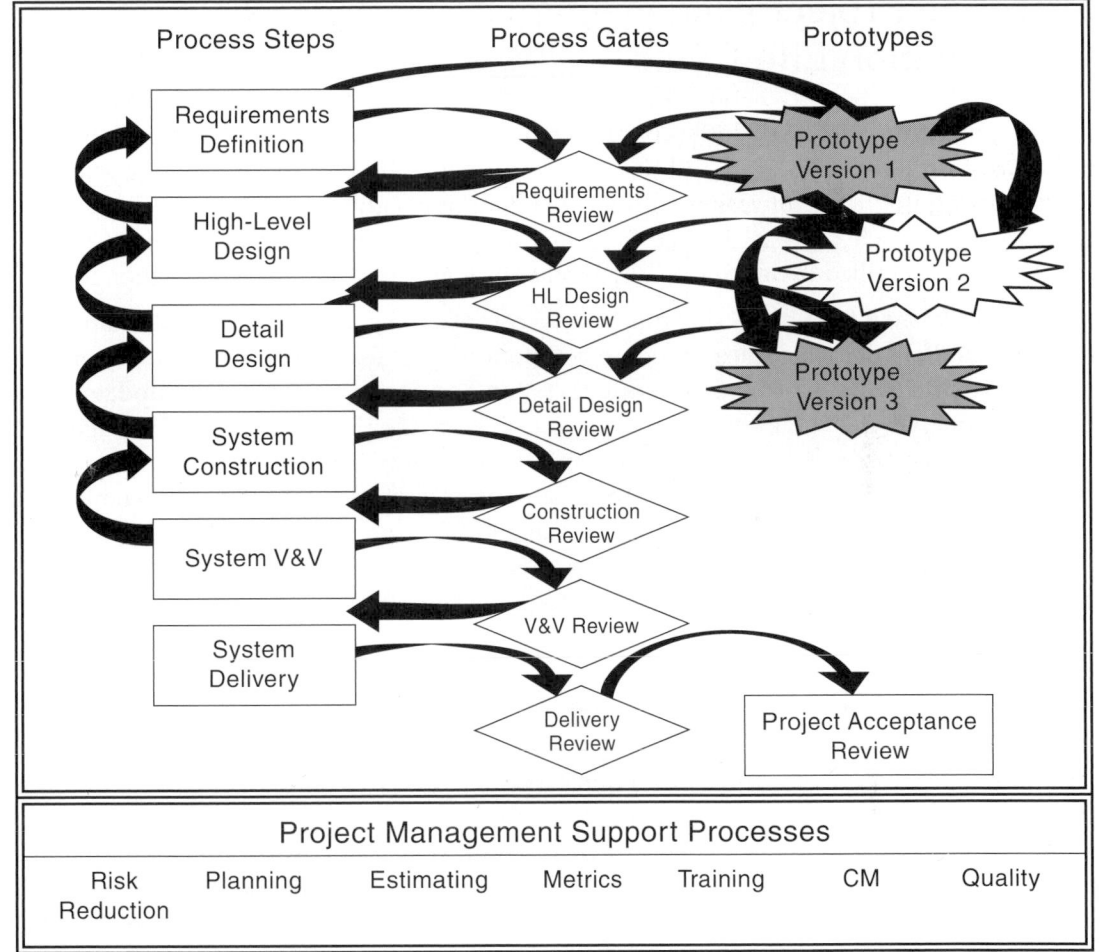

FIGURE 3–11
Customized Software Development Process

very important, so prototypes were incorporated early in the life cycle. A pure, evolutionary prototyping life cycle was not used because the clients desired formal review steps and a time-boxed process step to measure performance. Thus, this organization began with a straightforward waterfall model and extended it with prototypes, reviews, and the integral processes directly from 1074.

Software Project Management Organization Life Cycle

A project management office consists of project managers, technical writers, and a minimal set of information technology specialists needed to formalize its process of software selection. Working for a public organization with its attendant oversight required a well-thought-out and formal life cycle process. Taking the waterfall model as a starting point, the 1074 map and steps were applied to develop a COTS software acquisition and implementation model.

Figure 3–12 shows the detail that this office accomplished in applying the 1074 map to the basic waterfall model. The office ended up with four major life cycle processes: requirements analysis, architecture definition, system integration and test, and technology update. Each phase has defined deliverables. Great detail was given to the place that project management and integral processes play within the organization. Prototyping was accounted for in the first two phases to be able to search for the best-of-breed software solutions while remaining within the framework of the public agencies' request for information and request for proposal guidelines. Special care was taken in the areas of configuration management and documentation to be able to turn over a complete software system to clients.

Summary

Project managers who undertake process management before beginning a project will reap the benefits. The framework for manager and team behavior and methods for measuring progress toward project goals will be well defined and easy to follow for the duration of the project. To make the best use of the software management tools available, the organization's procedures and policies and the project's life cycle model will be determined. Also, the team will be familiar with them well before the project begins in earnest. Then, no one has to rethink what processes they should be following, and everyone can concentrate on the building the system requirements.

Process management starts with defining a project or organizational approach to developing products. Figure 3–13 shows information that can be used to define a process. As an ongoing organization, this is a representation of the knowledge base of previous project and product metrics and artifacts. For a new organization or an organization new to process, this represents the areas that would be considered for adoption. As we define the analysis cycles for process development, this figure will be used again to show the customization of basic processes for an organization.

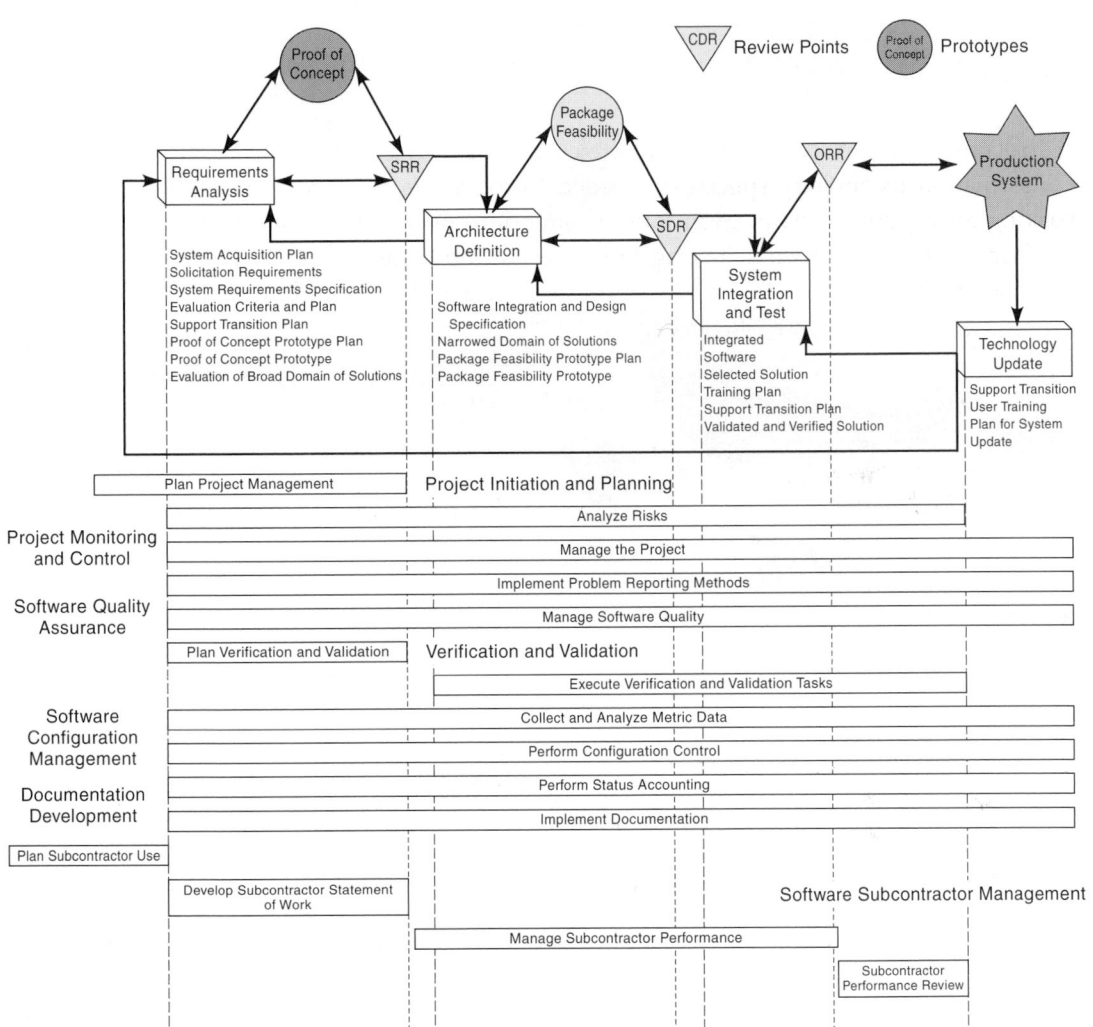

FIGURE 3–12
Commercial-off-the-Shelf (COTS) Development Process Model

The conclusive result of applying process management is the elimination of the fuzzy front end of any project and a rapid move to the project concept definition, candidate architectures, and initial market and system requirements.

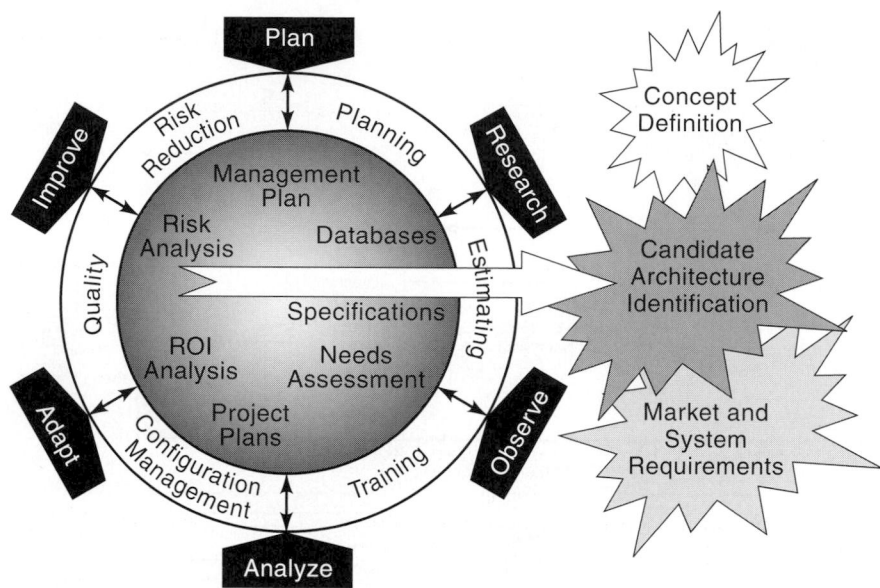

FIGURE 3–13
Process Front-End Results

Problems for Review

1. Name the process assets in your organization. Why are they considered assets?
2. Who should be responsible for an organization's software process activities?

Visit the Case Study

You have presented your initial project estimate to your internal customer, the marketing manager for AsiaPac. She has reviewed the amount of time you have estimated to derive the basic process map for the CRM prototype from IEEE 1074. Although she has never used 1074, she has used the eXtreme programming model and feels that that is the one to use. She will be out of the country in five days and will not approve the planning portion of your project plan because you can merely use the eXtreme model. Prepare a position paper convincing her that the planning stage of your project plan is important and that project processes are more than a programming model.

Citations

[1]Humphrey, Watts (1989). *Managing the Software Process*, 1st ed.; reprinted with corrections August 1990. Reading, MA: Addison-Wesley.

References

Deming, W. Edwards (2000). *Out of the Crisis*, 1st ed. Cambridge, MA: MIT Press.

Deming, W. Edwards (2000). *The New Economics: For Industry, Government, Education*, 2nd ed. Cambridge, MA: MIT Press.

Humphrey, Watts (1989). *Managing the Software Process*, 1st ed.; reprinted with corrections, August 1990. Reading, MA: Addison-Wesley.

IEEE 1074-1997 (1998). "IEEE Standard for Developing Software Life Cycle Processes." New York, NY: The Institute of Electrical and Electronics Engineers.

Ishikawa, K., Lu, D.J. trans (1988). *What is Total Quality Control? The Japanese Way.* Englewood Cliffs, NJ: Prentice Hall.

Paulk, Mark C., Charles V. Weber, Bill Curtis, and Mary Beth Chrissis (1994). *The Capability Maturity Model: Guidelines for Improving the Software Process*, 1st ed. Reading, MA: Addison-Wesley.

Shewhart, Walter A., and W. Edwards Deming (1986). *Statistical Method from the Viewpoint of Quality Control*, 1st ed. New York, NY: Dover Pubs.

Web Pages for Further Information

standards.ieee.org/. The IEEE Standards Association (IEEE-SA) is an international membership organization serving today's industries with a complete portfolio of standards programs.

www.incose.org/. The International Council on Systems Engineering is a not-for-profit membership organization founded in 1990. INCOSE is an international authoritative body promoting the application of an interdisciplinary approach and means to enable the realization of successful systems.

www.psmsc.com/. "Practical Software and Systems Measurement: A Foundation for Objective Project Management," was developed to meet today's software and system technical and management challenges. It describes an issue-driven measurement process that will address the unique technical and business goals of an organization. The guidance in PSM represents the best practices used by measurement professionals within the software and system acquisition and engineering communities.

www.spmn.com/. The Mission of the Software Program Managers Network is to enable managers of large-scale, software-intensive development or maintenance projects to more effectively manage and succeed by identifying and conveying to them management best practices, lessons learned, and direct support.

Selecting Software Development Life Cycles

By definition, a *project* is a unique undertaking, resulting in a unique *product*. It follows, then, that a project is likely to employ a unique *process* for product development. How does a project manager go about the formulation of an appropriate process, or life cycle, to follow to achieve the project goals? Rather than starting from scratch with each project, the software manager is well served to begin with a generic, proven approach and customize it. There are multiple "starter" life cycles from which to choose. Some of the most widely used ones will be presented here, along with guidelines for selecting an appropriate one and guidelines for tailoring it to the needs of a specific project.

Chapter 1, "Introduction," explained how and why the organization of this book follows a software product development life cycle. It's simply a way to discuss the 34 product, project, and people competencies in a logical order. Based on our process framework (Figure 4–1), defining the product (product competency 3) occurs before estimating its cost (project competency 14), so the former is presented before the latter. By following the process framework, we are also following the five major project phases published in the Project Management Institute's Body of Knowledge (PMBOK): initiation, planning, executing, controlling, and closing. Selecting and customizing a software development life cycle for a specific project occurs during the PMI planning phase.

Where We Are in the Product Development Life Cycle_____

Where are we in the product development life cycle model that serves as our map? As shown in Figure 4–1, we are very close to the beginning. When the project manager is developing the software project management plan (SPMP), he will be considering the activities, grouped into phases, that constitute a development approach.

The waterfall used here provides a convenient platform to present the 34 competencies. We hope that you will not assume that we are advocating the waterfall model as a software

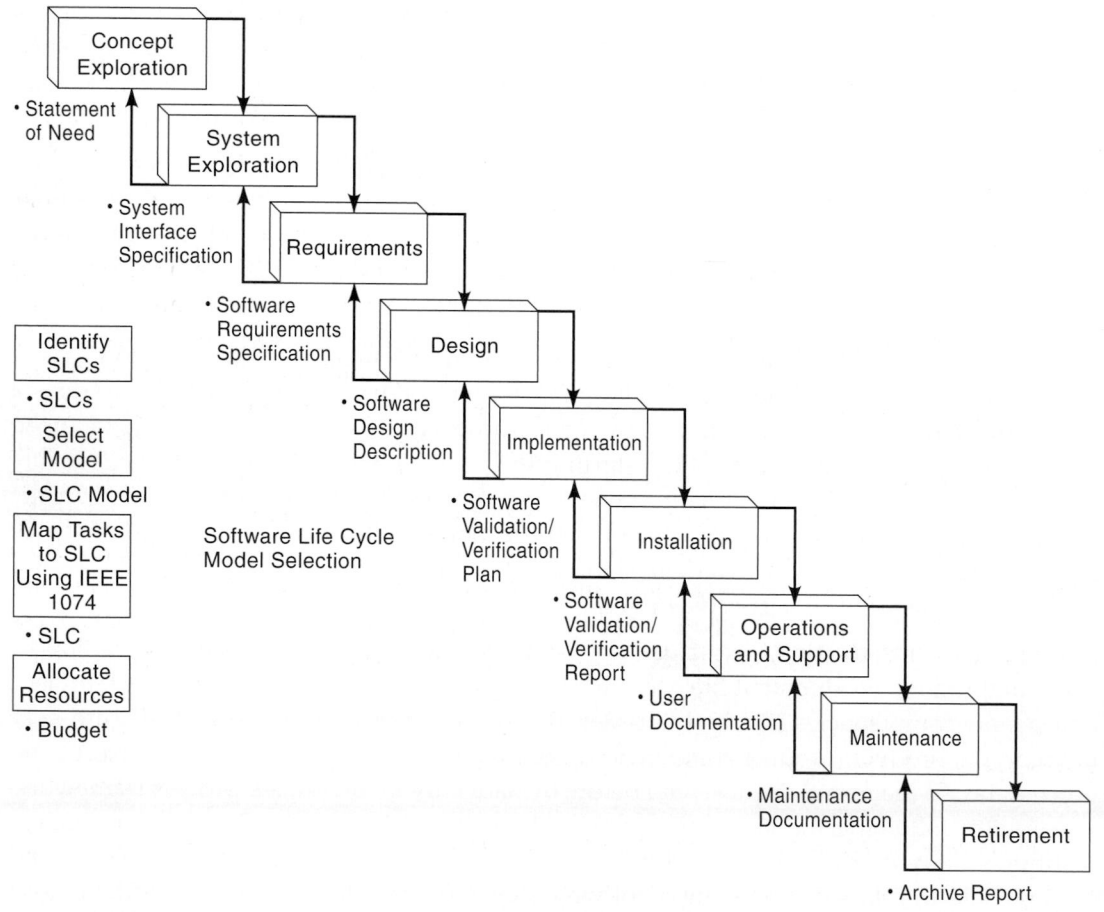

FIGURE 4–1
Selection of a Project-Specific Life Cycle Occurs at the Beginning of the Project

development life cycle for *all* new projects. It does work sometimes, under some circumstances, but it is often not the most appropriate life cycle model to apply to a software development project.

One size certainly does not fit all. A project manager will always want to research and settle on an approach that is most appropriate for the product under development—and do it early in the game. The best choice may turn out to be the waterfall, but it will very likely be a more modern model.

Chapter 4 Relation to the 34 Competencies

Selecting and tailoring a development life cycle impacts all three areas of product development techniques, project management skills, and people management skills. Under product development techniques, a project manager must first be aware of process standards (competency 2), be able to assess them for applicability to a given project (competency 1), evaluate alternative processes (competency 4), and, if necessary, tailor the life cycle process (competency 9). The selection of methods and tools (competency 8) may also be affected by the selection of a life cycle.

Under project management skills, competency 19, selecting metrics, is affected. For example, if a project manager wants to show that holding reviews early in the life cycle reduces overall cost of development, he must keep track of review results. Managing risks, competency 16, is in play especially with some of the newer life cycle models that have been created especially for the identification and control of risk. As we will see with the spiral model, risk is assessed at the end of each development phase. The life cycle provides the outline for tracking project progress. For example, if an organization knows that the first three phases of a project have been completed and that, typically, those phases comprise 67% of the overall effort, some idea of where the project tracks with the schedule can be had. Life cycle phases often provide the highest-level work breakdown structure (WBS) activities (competency 12), which are later broken down into tasks. Under people management skills, a life cycle can aid a project manager in appraising the performance of a team member (competency 23). For example, if a developer has been assigned to gather system specifications in the requirements phase but skips to the coding phase instead, he may be in need of a software engineering education.

Learning Objectives for Chapter 4

Upon completion of this chapter, the reader should be able to:

- Describe several different life cycle approaches;
- Demonstrate the ability to select a life cycle model based on project characteristics;
- Demonstrate the ability to customize a life cycle for a specific project.

What Is a Software Development Life Cycle? _____

Chapter 3, "Process Overview," defines a process, as shown in Figure 4–2, and describes the importance of following a process on a software development project.

A software process framework, or skeleton, describes what is to be performed in each phase of a development project via the activities of that phase. By *phase* we mean a distinguishable stage in the development process. Life cycle phases represent distinct and successive periods with entry and exit criteria. For example moving from the requirements phase to the design phase entails sign-offs from all stakeholders that the requirements are as complete as they can be at this point in time. This means that (at least some of) the exit criteria from the requirements phase is met and that (at least some of) the entrance criteria to the design phase are met.[1,2]

Chapter 3 discussed inputs, outputs, transformations, checkpoints, and milestones typically associated with a phase. The framework, however, does not represent the order or sequence in which these phases and activities will be conducted. A software development life cycle model is but one type of process that represents order.

A software life cycle model (SLCM) graphically describes how development activities will be performed by depicting the "sequence" of the activities. The sequence may or may not be linearly sequential because the phases may follow one another, repeat themselves, or run concurrently. Figure 4–3 is a simple, generic process framework showing that the overall process consists of major phases, which consist of activities that produce deliverables.

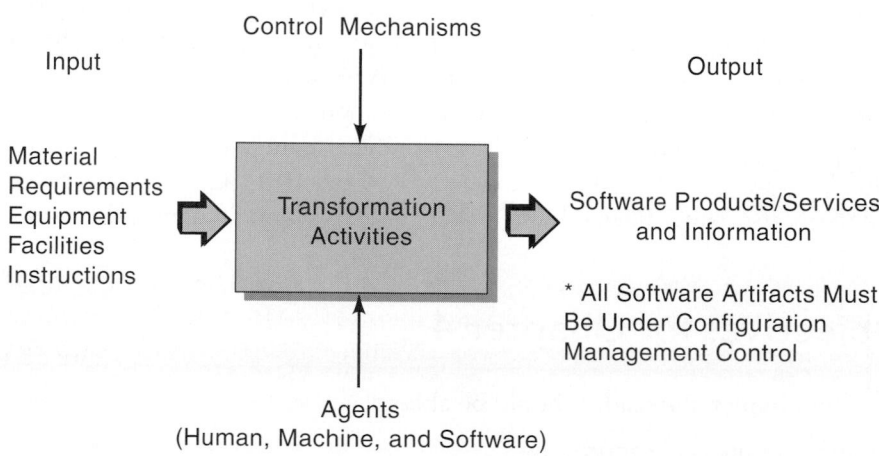

Control Mechanisms

Input

Output

Material
Requirements
Equipment
Facilities
Instructions

Transformation
Activities

Software Products/Services
and Information

* All Software Artifacts Must
Be Under Configuration
Management Control

Agents
(Human, Machine, and Software)

FIGURE 4–2
A Generic Process Phase

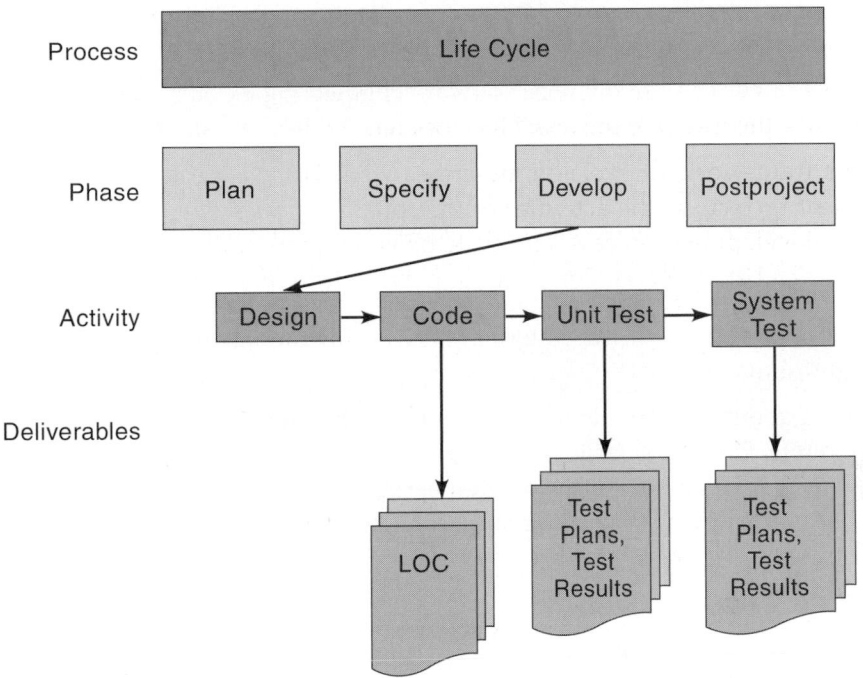

FIGURE 4–3
A Generic Process Framework

An SLCM is the framework, or scaffold, for defining the repeatable process that the software engineer applies to the development of software. It defines the explicit practices that the software engineer can use to consistently produce high-quality software systems. The concept of the software life cycle applies to all software projects, whether large or small.

Why Are Software Development Life Cycles Important? _____

To be successful, software project managers and their peers, customers, staff, and managers must have communications tools, such as common terminology and an agreed-upon development life cycle. The life cycle is the map that guides all project stakeholders forward and helps them understand whether they "are there yet."

Concerning maps in general, others have said it well:

- "If you don't know where you are going, you will probably end up somewhere else."
  —Laurence J. Peter

- "You've got to be very careful if you don't know where you're going, because you might not get there."—Yogi Berra

Dr. Barry Boehm, the father of so many wise software engineering axioms, has provided us with several "maps" of the software process. His work has not become stale—the formats of his maps have evolved and improved with the times. For the critics of the waterfall life cycle model, it is only fair to point out that Boehm said, as least as early as 1981, that using the term *sequential* to describe software development phases is a "convenient oversimplification," and described prototyping and incremental development as alternatives to the waterfall sequence. As will be described later in this chapter, he was the first to propose the popular spiral model. Beginning with the waterfall, each of his models has become more progressive and insightful than the last.

Boehm began writing about software development maps when he published his seminal work, *Software Engineering Economics*. In it, he referred to a "Software Engineering Goal Structure," pointing out that successful software engineering depends not only on having a successful software *product*, but also on having successful software development *processes*. This structure is illustrated in Figure 4–4.

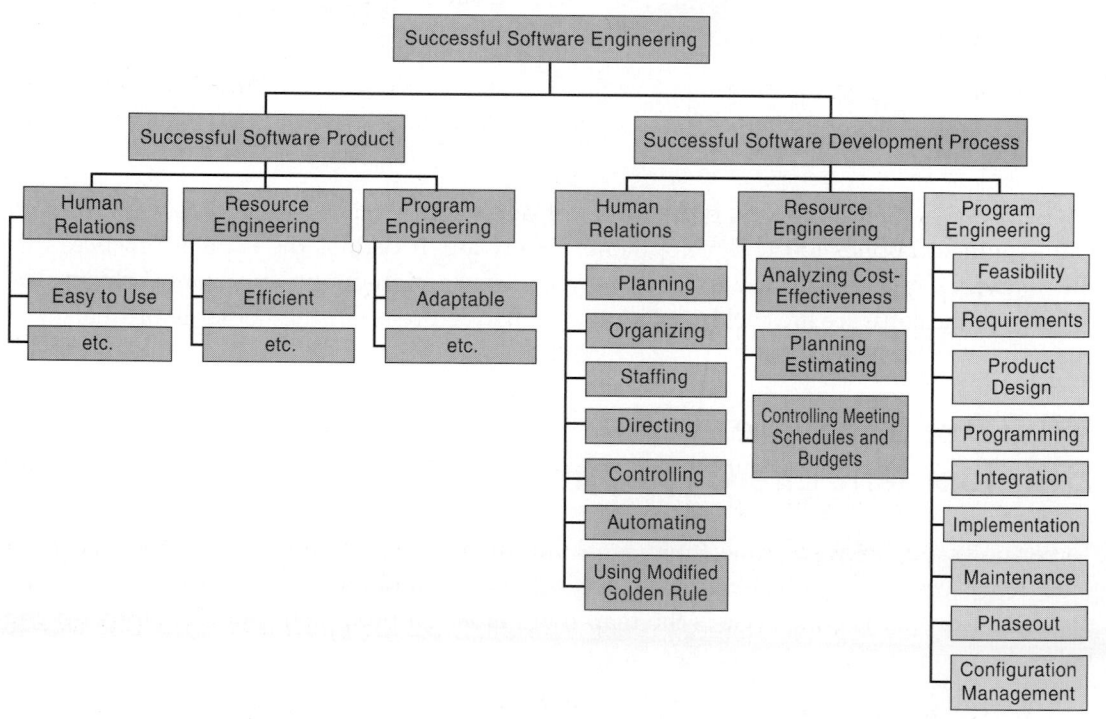

FIGURE 4–4
Boehm's Software Engineering Goal Structure
Source: Boehm, Barry (1981). *Software Engineering Economics.*

Human relations, resource engineering, and program engineering are critical success factor categories in both process and product. The *product* has several characteristics in each category, such as ease of use (human relations), efficiency (resource engineering), and adaptability (program engineering). One of the processes, the software development process, also requires supporting success factors. Human relations requires planning, organizing, staffing, directing, controlling, automating, and using the "Modified Golden Rule": Managers should not do unto programmers as they would have the programmers do unto them because managers and programmers are motivated by different factors. Process resource engineering requires analyzing cost-effectiveness, planning and estimating, and controlling meeting schedules and budgets. Under *process program engineering*, the success factors are feasibility validation, requirements validation, product design verification and validation, programming verification and validation, integration verification and validation, implementation verification and validation, maintenance verification and validation, phaseout, and configuration management (CM). These program engineering factors become the corresponding life cycle phases (except for CM, which is an integral task), as illustrated in Figure 4–5.

What interests us at this point is the fact that some sort of map to project activities and their chronology is required to manage a software project. Boehm's early theories on achievement of subgoals (Figure 4–4) as a necessity for a successful software product continue to remain viable today.

A standard for IT-systems of the Federal Republic of Germany included reasons for the necessity of a standardized process. This standard helps to achieve the following objectives:

- Improvement and guarantee of the quality:
  - The completeness of the results to be delivered can best be guaranteed by a standardized procedure.
  - Defined interim results make early assessment procedures possible.
  - Uniform product contents alleviate the readability of the products and the assessment procedures.
- The costs for the whole life cycle can be checked:
  - The generation of relevant project-specific development standards and its assessment will be simplified.
  - The standardized procedure makes the cost calculation more transparent. Any risks in connection with the costs can be recognized better.
  - Uniform standards reduce friction losses between customer and contractor, as well as between main contractor and subcontractor.
  - Standardized procedures allow for the reduction in the use of resources.
  - In case of a standardized procedure, universal approaches to the solutions become transparent and can thus be reused.

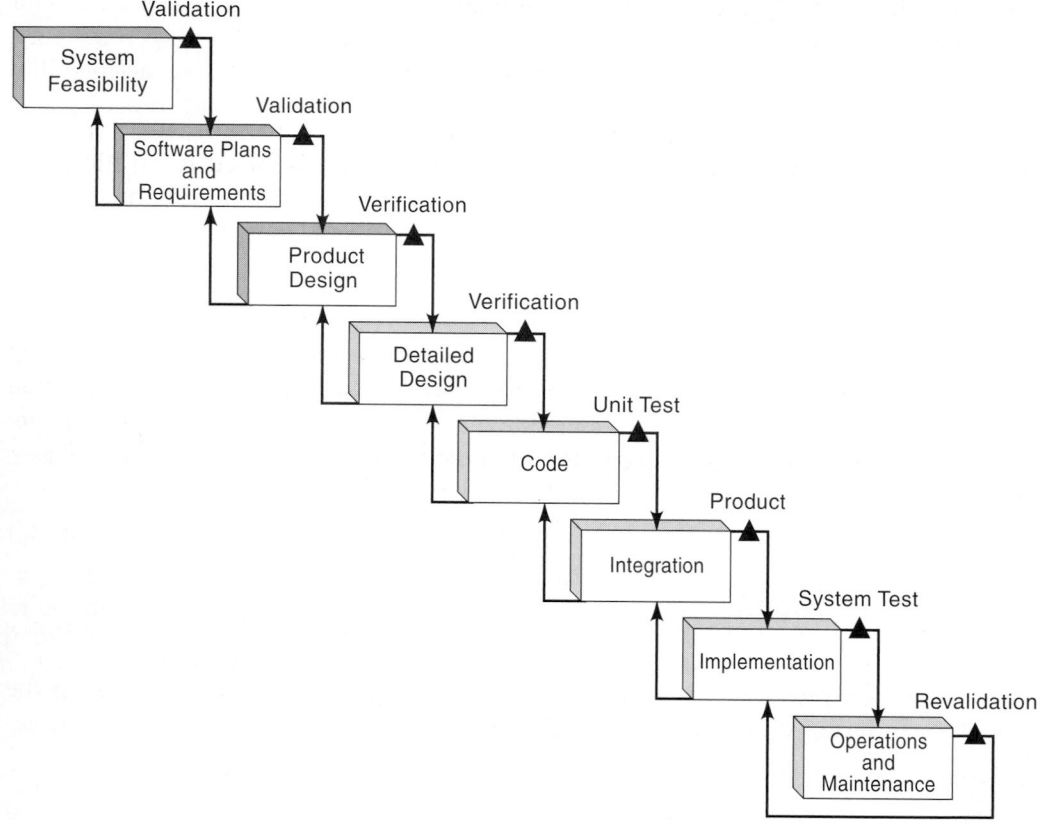

FIGURE 4–5
Major Features of the Iterative Waterfall Model with Verification and Validation

- Undesirable developments are recognized at an earlier stage.

- The training costs are reduced.

• Communication between the different parties is improved, and there is a reduction in the dependence of the customer on the contractor:

- Using defined terms reduces misunderstandings between all parties involved.

- The user, the purchaser, and the developer will be supported when formulating their requirements and when describing their parts or results.

- The interim results/final results are standardized to such an extent that other parties involved or staff of other companies are able to settle in without very much effort, if necessary.[3]

Selection and Tailoring of Software Development Life Cycles Is a Quality Objective_____

A defined software process provides organizations with a consistent process framework while permitting adjustment to unique needs. The conflicting needs for customization and standardization can be met by establishing a process architecture with standard unit or "kernel" process steps and rules for describing and relating them. Customization is then achieved through their interconnection into process models.[4]

The SEI CMM and the Life Cycle _____

Quality software project management is based upon the interlaced bodies of knowledge from three sources: software engineering (ACM, IEEE), project management (PMI), and quality (ASQ). The Software Engineering Institute (SEI) at Carnegie Mellon University incorporates all three. The Capability Maturity Model (CMM), a publicly available product, serves as a software process framework that is based on actual practices, that reflects the best of the state of the practice, and that reflects the needs of individuals performing software process improvement and software process appraisals. The way in which quality software project management conforms to the SEI CMM will be referred to many times in future chapters. Because the CMM is well known in software engineering circles, there is little need to redefine it here. We will provide only a brief description to show support for a life cycle. A short summary of the CMM maturity levels follows.

> The CMM provides a framework for organizing...evolutionary steps into five maturity levels that lay successive foundations for continuous process improvement....A maturity level is a well-defined evolutionary plateau toward achieving a mature software process. Each maturity level comprises a set of process goals that, when satisfied, stabilize an important component of the software process....Organizing the CMM into the five levels shown in (Figure 4–6) prioritizes improvement actions for increasing software process maturity....The five levels can be briefly described as:

> **Initial.** The software process is characterized as *ad hoc*, and occasionally even chaotic. Few processes are defined, and success depends on individual effort and heroics.

> **Repeatable.** Basic project management processes are established to track cost, schedule, and functionality. The necessary process discipline is in place to repeat earlier successes on projects with similar applications.

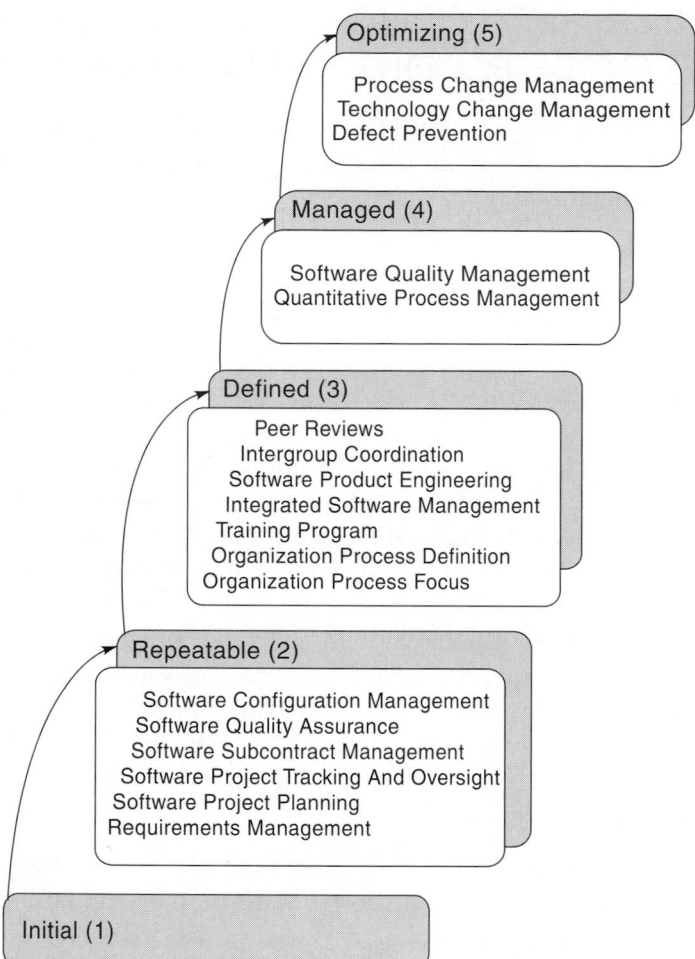

Figure 4–6
SEI CMM Key Process Areas by Maturity Level

Defined. The software process for both management and engineering activities is documented, standardized, and integrated into a standard software process for the organization. All projects use an approved, tailored version of the organization's standard software process for developing and maintaining software.

Managed. Detailed measures of the software process and product quality are collected. Both the software process and products are quantitatively understood and controlled.

Optimizing. Continuous process improvement is enabled by quantitative feedback from the process and from piloting innovative ideas and technologies.[5]

Each maturity level is decomposed into several key process areas that indicate where an organization should focus to improve its software process. Each key process area (KPA) identifies a cluster of related activities that, when performed collectively, achieve a set of goals considered important for enhancing process capability. The goals of each key process area summarize its key practices and can be used in determining whether an organization or project has effectively implemented the key process area. The goals signify the scope, boundaries, and intent of each KPA.

The KPAs at Level 2 focus on the software project's concerns related to establishing basic project management controls. We will return to this level when we discuss project competencies.

For now, we need to know that a repeatable process (Level 2) enables an organization to be more structured and manageable. Life cycles, the topic of this chapter, provide a definition of what is meant by the process to be performed and the product to be built by the process. Having such a definition available provides a common language and eases transitions as developers come on board, particularly if they lack experience.

Having a repeatable process (Level 2) does not, however, automatically mean having a good process. Generally, processes improve when an organization achieves SEI Level 3 (L3), the defined level. L3 addresses both project and organizational issues, as the organization establishes an infrastructure that institutionalizes effective software engineering and management processes across all projects. Two KPAs, organizational process definition and integrated software management, reference the subject of life cycles. In the discussion of these two KPAs, the mention of the software life cycle will be **bolded**. KPA descriptions are from *The Capability Maturity Model.*[6]

Organization Process Definition

> The purpose of the Level 3 KPA organization process definition is to develop and maintain a usable set of software process assets that improve process performance across the projects....Process definition involves developing and maintaining the organization's standard software process, along with related process assets, such as descriptions of **software life cycles**, process tailoring guidelines and criteria, ...[7]

A goal of organization process definition is to develop and maintain a standard software process for the organization.

Activities include documenting and maintaining descriptions of **software life cycles** that are approved for use by the projects. Examples of **software life cycles** include waterfall, overlapping waterfall, spiral, serial build, and single prototype/overlapping waterfall.

Guidelines and criteria for the projects' tailoring of the organization's standard software process are developed and maintained. The tailoring guidelines and criteria cover selecting and tailoring the **software life cycle** for the project, and tailoring the organization's standard software process to accommodate the **software life cycle** and the project's characteristics.

Examples of tailoring include adapting the process for a new product line or host environment, customizing the process for a specific project or class of projects, and elaborating and adding detail to the process so that the resulting project's defined software process can be enacted.

Integrated Software Management

The purpose of the Level 3 KPA integrated software management is to integrate the software engineering and management activities into a coherent, defined software process that is tailored from the organization's standard software process and related process assets, described in "Organization Process Definition."

Goals are for the project's defined software process to be a tailored version of the organization's standard software process, and for the project to be planned and managed according to the project's defined software processes. Activities include tailoring the organization's standard software process according to a documented procedure to develop the project's defined software process. This procedure typically specifies that a **software life cycle** is selected from those approved by the organization, to satisfy the project's contractual and operational constraints; modified, if necessary, in ways permitted by the organization's tailoring guidelines and criteria; and documented according to the organization's standards.

International Organization for Standardization (ISO)/IEC 12207 _____

The SEI is not the only quality or standards organization concerned with software processes and life cycles. As early as 1989, it was recognized that the standard imposed upon defense and other government contractors, Department of Defense Standard (DOD STD) 2167A, was not well suited to use with projects employing object-oriented design (OOD) or Rapid Application Development (RAD) methods. A new Military Standard (MIL STD) 498 was intended to correct issues with these methods, and it does indeed solve some of the problems. A third approach, International Organization for Standardization (ISO)/IEC 12207, which developed independently from MIL STD 498, is another step forward. It describes the major component processes of a complete software life cycle, their interfaces with one another, and the high-level relations that govern their interactions.

As shown in Figure 4–7, ISO/IEC 12207 lists 12 engineering activities, following process implementation, that are similar to the phases in a typical SLCM:

1. System requirement analysis;
2. System architectural design;
3. Software requirements analysis;

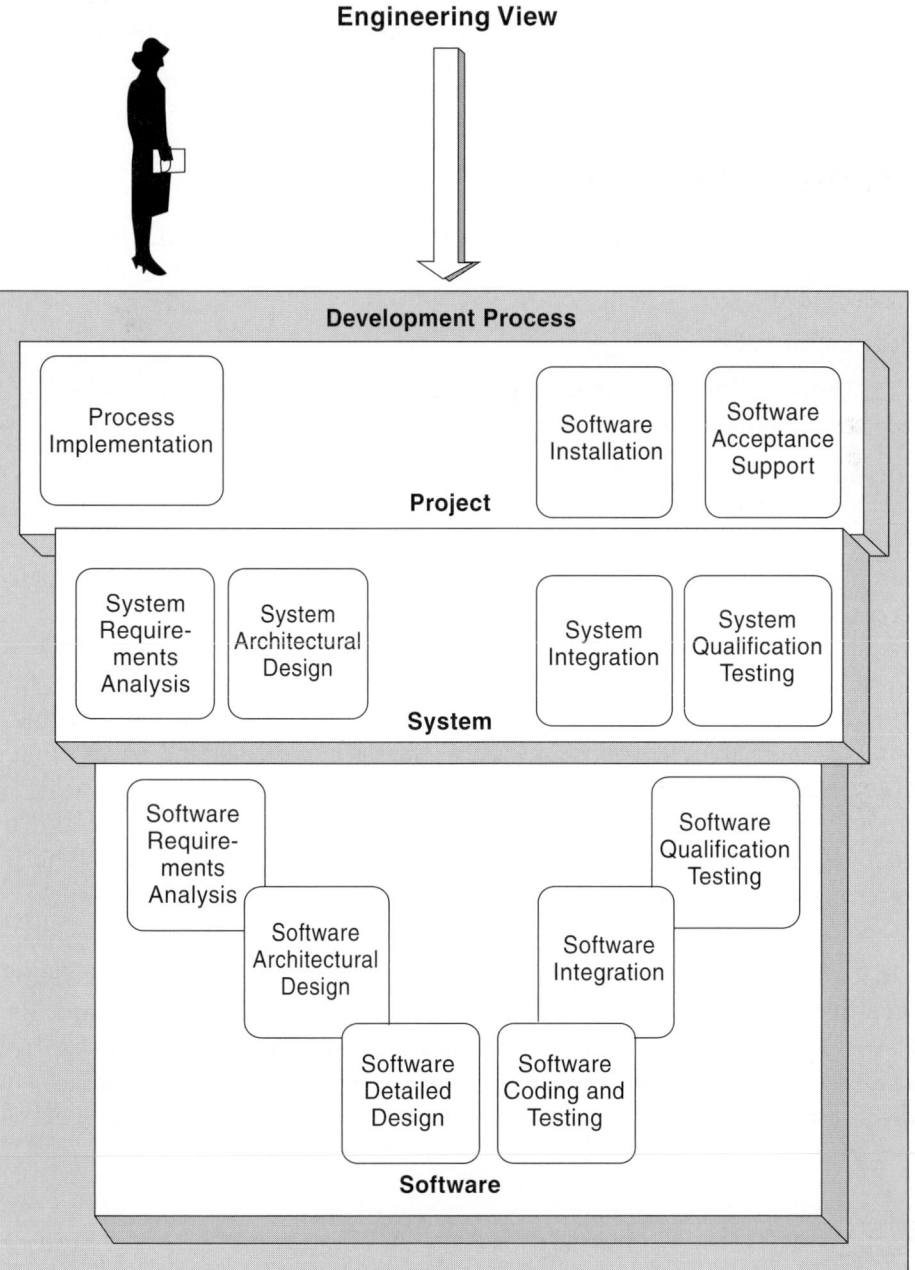

FIGURE 4–7
Engineering View of ISO/IEC 12207

4. Software architectural design;

5. Software detailed design;

6. Software coding and testing;

7. Software integration;

8. Software qualification testing;

9. System integration;

10. System qualification testing;

11. Software installation;

12. Software acceptance test.

The ISO/IEC 12207 approach has been described as an implementation of a *Plan-Do-Check-Act* (PDCA) cycle, discussed in Chapter 3, "Process Overview."

The intent is that the engineer should check the output of an engineering task before it becomes input to the next task. "The activities of the ISO/IEC 12207 development process have independence from one another ... they are not ordered in a waterfall sequence and, ... there are no requirements in the international standard that dictate which of them must be executed first and which next." In fact, ISO/IEC 12207 says explicitly, in paragraph 5.3.1.1, that "these activities and tasks may overlap or interact and may be performed iteratively or recursively." Paragraph 1.5 states that "this international standard does not prescribe a specific life cycle model or software development method." Paragraph 5.3.1.1 states that, unless the contract stipulates one, "the developer shall define or select a software life cycle model appropriate to the scope, magnitude, and complexity of the project. The activities and tasks of the development process shall be selected and mapped onto the life cycle model." The intent and effect of the language in the international standard are to provide flexibility in ordering activities, and to choose development models to avoid the waterfall bias of other standards.[8]

Individuals and organizations respected in the software, project management, and quality arenas are in agreement on the necessity of process and life cycle process, in particular. PMI, Boehm, IT-Systems of the Federal Republic of Germany, the SEI, and the ISO have all recommended having a software development life cycle, one that is carefully selected and tailored for project suitability.

Software Development Life Cycle Models _____

The most well-known and widely used software development life cycles include: the waterfall, V-shaped, evolutionary rapid prototyping, rapid application development, incremental, and spiral models. In the following sections, each model will be described; strengths and weaknesses of each will be discussed, and examples of modified models and guidance on tailoring will be provided. Tables 4–1 through 4–4 will offer criteria to assist the project manager in selecting an appropriate life cycle model for a given project.

The Waterfall Software Development Life Cycle Model

The "classic" waterfall model, despite recent bad press, has served the software engineering community well for many years. Understanding its strengths and flaws improves the ability to assess other, often more effective life cycle models that are based on the original.

In the earliest days of software development, code was written and then debugged. It was common to forego planning altogether and, starting with a general idea of the product, informally design, code, debug, and test until the software was ready for release. The process looked something like the one in Figure 4–8. There are several things "wrong" with such a process (or lack thereof). Primarily, because there was no formal design or analysis, it is impossible to know when you are done. There is no way to assess whether the requirements or the quality criteria have been satisfied.

The waterfall model was first identified in 1970 as a formal alternative to the *code-and-fix* software development method prevalent at the time. It was the first to formalize a framework for software development phases, placing emphasis on up-front requirements and design activities and on producing documentation during early phases.

Execution of the waterfall model begins at the upper left of Figure 4–9 and progresses through the orderly sequence of steps. It assumes that each subsequent phase will begin when activities in the current phase have been completed. Each phase has defined entry and exit criteria: inputs and outputs. Internal or external project deliverables are output from each phase, including documentation and software. Requirements analysis documents are passed to system engineers, who hand off high-level design documents to software architects, who hand off detailed specifications to coders, who hand off code to testers.

FIGURE 4–8
"Do Until Done" Process Model

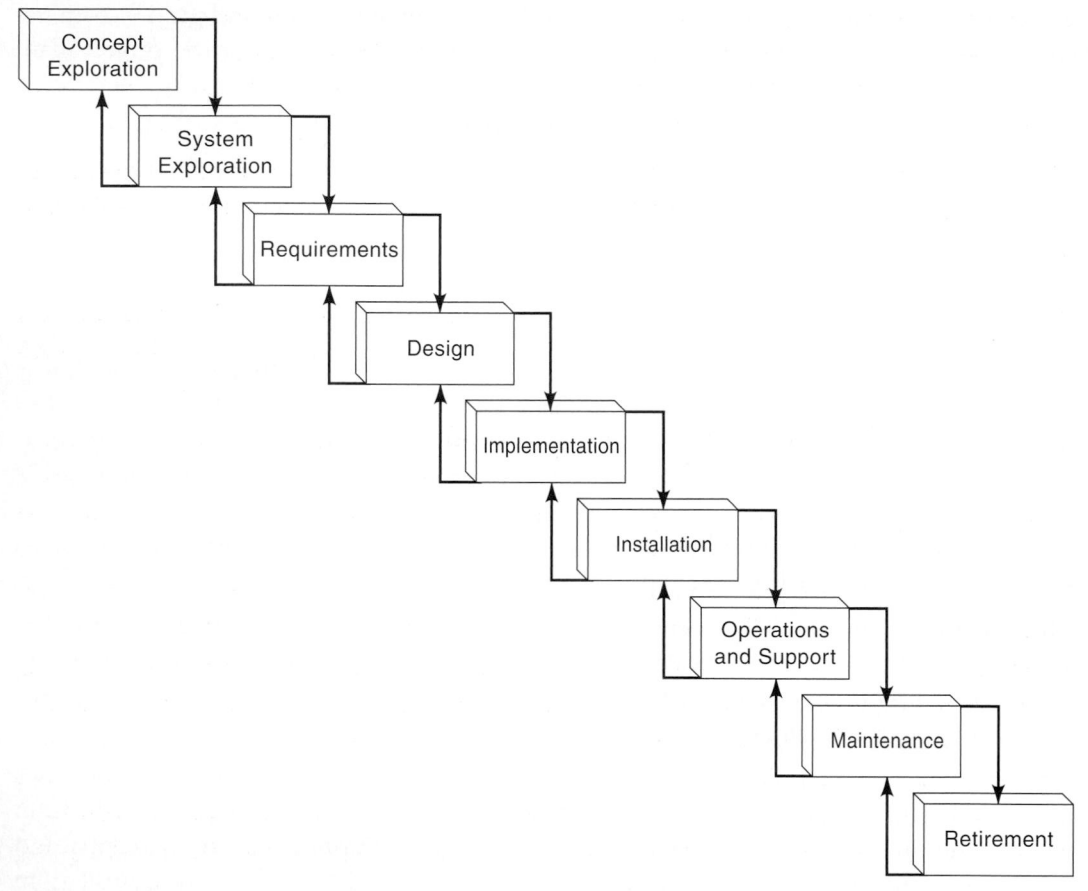

FIGURE 4–9
Classic Waterfall Model with Feedback

Transition from one phase to the next is accomplished by passing a formal review, a way to provide customers insight into the development process and to check on product quality. Typically, passing the review indicates an agreement among the project team members and the customer that the phase has ended and the next one can begin. The end of a phase is a convenient place for a project milestone.

In conjunction with certain phase completions, a baseline is established that "freezes" the products of the development at that point. If a need is identified to change these products, a formal change process is followed to make the change.

At critical points on the waterfall model, baselines are established, the last of which is the product baseline. This final baseline is accompanied by an acceptance review.

Other software development life cycles have evolved from attempts to optimize the waterfall model. Software prototyping helps provide the complete understanding of the requirements; the incremental and spiral models allow the phases identified in the classic waterfall to be revisited repeatedly before declaring a product to be final.

The salient attributes of the waterfall model are that it is a formal method, a type of top-down development, composed of independent phases executed sequentially and subject to frequent review.

A Brief Description of the Phases in the Waterfall Model   The following is a brief description of each phase of the waterfall model, from concept exploration through retirement, including the integration phases:

- **Concept exploration**—Examines requirements at the system level, to determine feasibility.

- **System allocation process**—May be skipped for software-only systems. For systems that require the development of both hardware and software, the required functions are mapped to software or hardware based on the overall system architecture.

- **Requirements process**—Defines software requirements for the system's information domain, function, behavior, performance, and interfaces. (Where appropriate, this includes the functional allocation of system requirements to hardware and software.)

- **Design process**—Develops and represents a coherent, technical specification of the software system, including data structures, software architecture, interface representations, and procedural (algorithmic) detail.

- **Implementation process**—Results in the transformation of the software design description to a software product. Produces the source code, database, and documentation constituting the physical transformation of the design. If the software product is a purchased application package, the major activities of implementation are the installation and testing of the software package. If the software product is custom developed, the major activities are programming and testing code.

- **Installation process**—Involves software being installed, checked out, and formally accepted by the customer, for the operational environment.

- **Operation and support process**—Involves user operation of the system and ongoing support, including providing technical assistance, consulting with the user, recording user requests for enhancements and changes, and handling corrections or errors.

- **Maintenance process**—Concerned with the resolution of software errors, faults, failures, enhancements, and changes generated by the support process. Consists of iterations of development, and supports feedback of anomaly information.

- **Retirement process**—Removing an existing system from its active use, by either ceasing its operation or replacing it with a new system or an upgraded version of the existing system.

- **Integral tasks**—Involves project initiation, project monitoring and control, quality management, verification and validation, configuration management, document development, and training throughout the entire life cycle.

Strengths of the Waterfall Model

We can see that the waterfall model has many strengths when applied to a project for which it is well suited. Some of these strengths are:

- The model is well known by nonsoftware customers and end-users (it is often used by other organizations to track nonsoftware projects).
- It tackles complexity in an orderly way, working well for projects that are well understood but still complex.
- It is easy to understand, with a simple goal—to complete required activities.
- It is easy to use as development proceeds one phase after another.
- It provides structure to a technically weak or inexperienced staff.
- It provides requirements stability.
- It provides a template into which methods for analysis, design, code, test, and support can be placed.
- It works well when quality requirements dominate cost and schedule requirements.
- It allows for tight control by project management.
- When correctly applied, defects may be found early, when they are relatively inexpensive to fix.
- It is easy for the project manager to plan and staff.
- It allows staff who have completed their phase activities to be freed up for other projects.
- It defines quality control procedures. Each deliverable is reviewed as it is completed. The team uses procedure to determine the quality of the system.
- Its milestones are well understood.
- It is easy to track the progress of the project using a timeline or Gantt chart—the completion of each phase is used as a milestone.

Weaknesses of the Waterfall Model

We can also note weakness of the model when it is applied to a project for which it is not well suited:

- It has an inherently linear sequential nature—any attempt to go back two or more phases to correct a problem or deficiency results in major increases in cost and schedule.
- It does not handle the reality of iterations among phases that are so common in software development because it is modeled after a conventional hardware engineering cycle.
- It doesn't reflect the problem-solving nature of software development. Phases are tied rigidly to activities, not how people or teams really work.

- It can present a false impression of status and progress—"35 percent done" is a meaningless metric for the project manager.

- Integration happens in one big bang at the end. With a single pass through the process, integration problems usually surface too late. Previously undetected errors or design deficiencies will emerge, adding risk with little time to recover.

- There is insufficient opportunity for a customer to preview the system until very late in the life cycle. There are no tangible interim deliverables for the customer; user responses cannot be fed back to developers. Because a completed product is not available until the end of the process, the user is involved only in the beginning, while gathering requirements, and at the end, during acceptance testing.

- Users can't see quality until the end. They can't appreciate quality if the finished product can't be seen.

- It isn't possible for the user to get used to the system gradually. All training must occur at the end of the life cycle, when the software is running.

- It is possible for a project to go through the disciplined waterfall process, meet written requirements, but still not be operational.

- Each phase is a prerequisite for succeeding activities, making this method a risky choice for unprecedented systems because it inhibits flexibility.

- Deliverables are created for each phase and are considered frozen—that is, they should not be changed later in the life cycle of the product. If the deliverable of a phase changes, which often happens, the project will suffer schedule problems because the model did not accommodate, nor was the plan based on managing a change later in the cycle.

- All requirements must be known at the beginning of the life cycle, yet customers can rarely state all explicit requirements at that time. The model is not equipped to handle dynamic changes in requirements over the life cycle, as deliverables are "frozen." The model can be very costly to use if requirements are not well known or are dynamically changing during the course of the life cycle.

- Tight management and control is needed because there is no provision for revising the requirements.

- It is document-driven, and the amount of documentation can be excessive.

- The entire software product is being worked on at one time. There is no way to partition the system for delivery of pieces of the system. Budget problems can occur because of commitments to develop an entire system at one time. Large sums of money are allocated, with little flexibility to reallocate the funds without destroying the project in the process.

- There is no way to account for behind-the-scenes rework and iterations.

When to Use the Waterfall Model   Because of its weaknesses, application of the waterfall model should be limited to situations in which the requirements and the implementation of those requirements are very well understood.

The waterfall model performs well for product cycles with a stable product definition and well-understood technical methodologies.

If a company has experience in building a certain genre of system—accounting, payroll, controllers, compilers, manufacturing—then a project to build another of the same type of product, perhaps even based on existing designs, could make efficient use of the waterfall model. Another example of appropriate use is the creation and release of a new version of an existing product, if the changes are well defined and controlled. Porting an existing product to a new platform is often cited as an ideal project for use of the waterfall.

In all fairness, critics of this model must admit that the modified version of the waterfall is far less rigid than the original, including iterations of phases, concurrent phases, and change management. Reverse arrows allow for iterations of activities within phases. To reflect concurrence among phases, the rectangles are often stacked or the activities within the phases are listed beneath the rectangles showing the concurrence. Although the modified waterfall is much more flexible than the classic, it is still not the best choice for rapid development projects.

Waterfall models have historically been used on large projects with multiple teams and team members.

The V-Shaped Software Development Life Cycle Model

The V-shaped model was developed to assist the project team in planning and designing for the testability of a system. The model places a strong emphasis on the verification and validation activities of the product. It illustrates that the testing of the product is discussed, designed, and planned in the early phases of the development life cycle. The customer acceptance test plan is developed during the planning phase, the system integration test plan is developed during the analysis and design phases, and so on. This test plan development activity is represented by the dotted lines between the rectangles of the V.

The V-shaped model, shown in Figure 4–10, was designed as a variation of the waterfall model; therefore, it has inherited the same sequence structure. Each subsequent phase is begun at the completion of the deliverables of the current phase. It is representative of a comprehensive approach to defining the phases of the software development process. It emphasizes the relationship between the analytical and design phases that precede coding with the testing phases that follow coding. The dotted lines indicate that these phases should be considered in parallel.

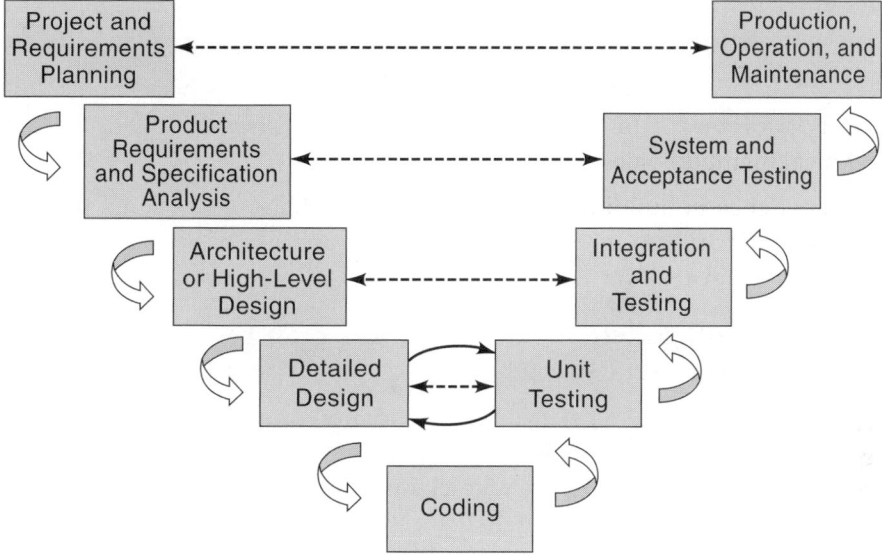

FIGURE 4–10
The V-Shaped Software Development Life Cycle Model

Phases in the V-Shaped Model   The following list contains a brief description of each phase of the V-shaped model, from project and requirements planning through acceptance testing:

- **Project and requirements planning**—Determines the system requirements and how the resources of the organization will be allocated to meet them. (Where appropriate, this phase allocates functions to hardware and software.)

- **Product requirements and specification analysis**—Includes analysis of the software problem at hand and concludes with a complete specification of the expected external behavior of the software system to be built.

- **Architecture or high-level design**—Defines how the software functions are to implement the design.

- **Detailed design**—Defines and documents algorithms for each component that was defined during the architecture phase. These algorithms will be translated into code.

- **Coding**—Transforms the algorithms defined during the detailed design phase into software.

- **Unit testing**—Checks each coded module for errors.

- **Integration and testing**—Interconnects the sets of previously unit-tested modules to ensure that the sets behave as well as the independently tested modules did during the unit-testing phase.

- **System and acceptance testing**—Checks whether the entire software system (fully integrated) embedded in its actual hardware environment behaves according to the software requirements specification.
- **Production, operation, and maintenance**—Puts software into production and provides for enhancements and corrections.
- **Acceptance testing** (not shown)—Allows the user to test the functionality of the system against the original requirements. After final testing, the software and its surrounding hardware become operational. Maintenance of the system follows.

Strengths of the V-Shaped Model   When applied to a project for which it is well suited, the V-shaped model offers several strengths:

- The model emphasizes planning for verification and validation of the product in the early stages of product development. Emphasis is placed on testing by matching the test phase or process with the development process. The unit testing phase validates detailed design. The integration and testing phases validate architectural or high-level design. The system testing phase validates the product requirements and specification phase.
- The model encourages verification and validation of all internal and external deliverables, not just the software product.
- The V-shaped model encourages definition of the requirements before designing the system, and it encourages designing the software before building the components.
- It defines the products that the development process should generate; each deliverable must be testable.
- It enables project management to track progress accurately; the progress of the project follows a timeline, and the completion of each phase is a milestone.
- It is easy to use (when applied to a project for which it is suited).

Weaknesses of the V-Shaped Model   When applied to a project for which it is *not* well suited, the weaknesses of the V-shaped model are evident:

- It does not easily handle concurrent events.
- It does not handle iterations of phases.
- The model is not equipped to handle dynamic changes in requirements throughout the life cycle.
- The requirements are tested too late in the cycle to make changes without affecting the schedule for the project.
- The model does not contain risk analysis activities.

It is often graphically shown (as in Figure 4–10) without the integral tasks. This is an easily remedied issue, mentioned here only to remind the reader that integral tasks are present with the use of all life cycle models.

The V-shaped model may be modified to overcome these weaknesses by including itera-tion loops to handle the changing of requirements beyond the analysis phase.

When to Use the V-Shaped Model   Like its predecessor, the waterfall model, the V-shaped model works best when all knowledge of requirements is available up-front. A common modification to the V-shaped model, to overcome weaknesses, includes the addition of iteration loops to handle the changing of requirements beyond the analysis phase.

It works well when knowledge of how to implement the solution is available, technology is available, and staff have proficiency and experience with the technology.

The V-shaped model is an excellent choice for systems that require high reliability, such as hospital patient control applications and embedded software for air-bag chip controllers in automobiles.

The Prototype Software Development Life Cycle Model

Fred Brooks's classic, *The Mythical Man-Month*, is as fresh today as it was in 1975. Technology has changed the world in drastic ways, but many foibles of software project management remain the same. Decades ago, Brooks said:

> In most projects, the first system built is barely usable. It may be too slow, too big, awkward to use, or all three. There is no alternative but to start again, smarting but smarter, and build a redesigned version in which these problems are solved....

> When a new system concept or new technology is used, one has to build a system to throw away, for even the best planning is not so omniscient as to get it right the first time.

> The management question, therefore, is not whether to build a pilot system and throw it away. You will do that. The only question is whether to plan in advance to build a throwaway, or to promise to deliver the throwaway to customers....[9]

It is this concept of building a pilot, or prototype system that led to the "structured," "evolu-tionary" rapid prototyping model, the RAD model, and the spiral model. In his later, equally wise work, "No Silver Bullet, the Essence and Accidents of Programming," Brooks believes that most software development errors still have to do with getting the system concept wrong, not the syntax or the logic. Software development will always be difficult, and there will never be a magic panacea or silver bullet. He offers a positive note in the application of rapid prototyping techniques:

> The hardest single part of building a software system is deciding precisely what to build. No other part of the conceptual work is as difficult as establishing the detailed technical requirements, including all the interfaces to people, to machines,

and to other software systems. No other part of the work so cripples the resulting system if done wrong. No other part is more difficult to rectify later.

Therefore, the most important function that the software builder performs for the client is the iterative extraction and refinement of the product requirements. For the truth is, the client does not know what he wants.

One of the most promising of the current technological efforts, and one which attacks the essence, not the accidents, of the software problem, is the development of approaches and tools for rapid prototyping of systems as part of the iterative specification of requirements.[10]

Watts Humphrey, best known as the inspiration for the SEI CMM, supports Brooks in the importance of requirements and evolution:

There is a basic principle of most systems that involve more than minor evolutionary change: The system will change the operational environment. Since the users can only think in terms of the environment they know, the requirements for such systems are always stated in the current environment's terms. These requirements are thus necessarily incomplete, inaccurate, and misleading. The challenge for the system developer is to devise a development process that will discover, define, and develop to real requirements. This can only be done with intimate user involvement, and often with periodic prototype or early version field tests. Such processes always appear to take longer but invariably end up with a better system much sooner than with any other strategy.[11]

Definitions of Prototyping   According to Connell and Shafer, an evolutionary rapid prototype is:

An easily modifiable and extensible working model of a proposed system, not necessarily representative of a complete system, which provides users of the application with a physical representation of key parts of the system before implementation. An easily built, readily modifiable, ultimately extensible, partially specified, working model of the primary aspects of a proposed system.[12]

And Bernard Boar defined a prototype as "a strategy for performing requirements determination wherein user needs are extracted, presented, and developed by building a working model of the ultimate system—quickly and in context."[13]

Description of the Structured Evolutionary Prototyping Model   Prototyping is the process of building a working replica of a system. The prototype is the equivalent of a mock-up, or "breadboard," in the hardware world.

Evolutionary programs are conducted within the context of a plan for progression toward an ultimate capability. This strategy also requires the development of increments of software demonstrable to the user, who is involved throughout the entire development process.

A "quick" partial implementation of the system is created before or during the requirements definition phase. The end users of the system use the rapid prototype and then supply feedback to the project team for further refinement of the requirements of the system. This refinement process continues until the user is satisfied. When the requirements definition process has been completed, through the development of rapid prototypes, the detailed design is derived and the rapid prototype is fine-tuned using code or external utilities to create a final working product. Ideally, the prototyping model is evolvable—nothing wasted—and of high quality— no skimping on documentation, analysis, design, testing, and so on. Hence, the name is "structured rapid prototyping model," as shown in Figure 4–11.

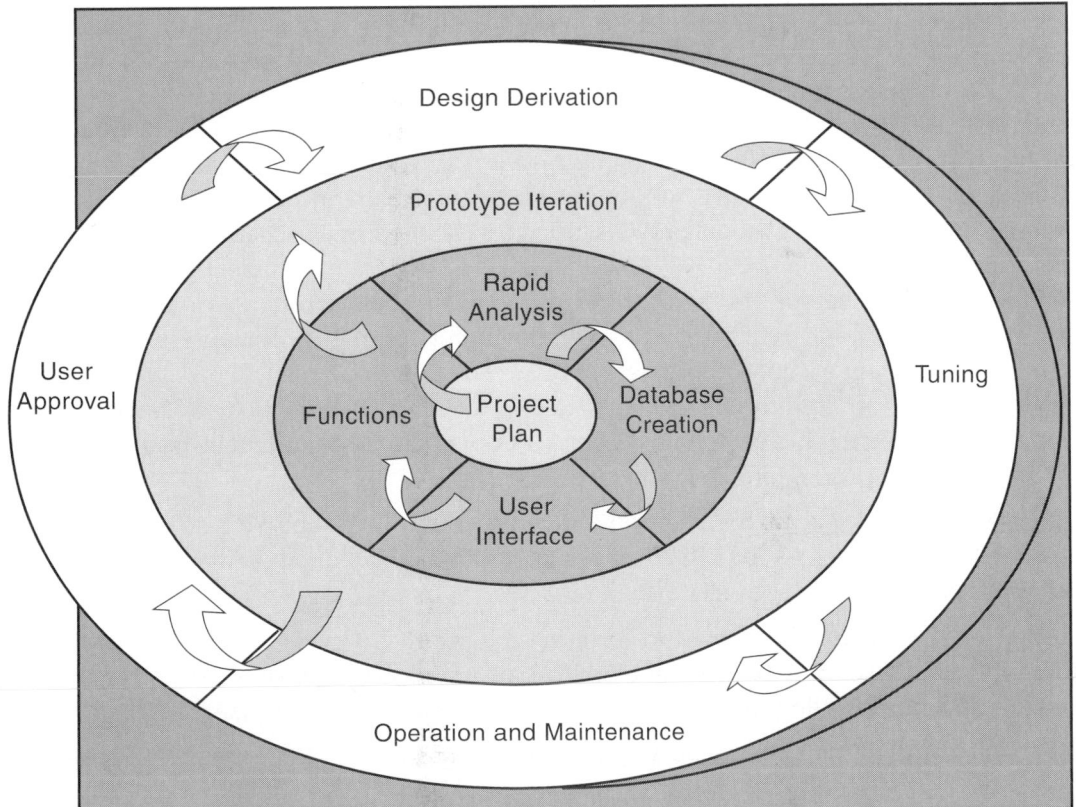

FIGURE 4–11
The Structured Evolutionary Rapid Prototyping Model

The life cycle begins in the center of the ellipse. User and designer develop a preliminary project plan from preliminary requirements. Using rapid analysis techniques, user and designer work together to define the requirements and specifications for the critical parts of the envisioned system. Project planning is the first activity of the rapid analysis phase, producing a document outlining rough schedules and deliverables.

The project plan is created, and then a rapid analysis is performed, followed by database, user interface, and function creation. The second activity is rapid analysis, during which preliminary user interviews are used to develop an intentionally incomplete high-level paper model of the system. A document containing the partial requirements specification is output from this task and used to build the initial prototype that is created in the next three phases. The designer constructs a model (using tools), a partial representation of the system that includes only those basic attributes necessary for meeting the customer's requirements. Next the rapid prototype iteration loop begins. The designer demonstrates the prototype; the user evaluates its performance. Problems are identified then, and the user and designer work together to eliminate them. The process continues until the user is satisfied that the system represents the requirements. The project team will remain in this loop until the user has agreed that the rapid prototype accurately reflects the system requirements. Creation of the database is the first of these phases. After the initial database is set up, menu development may begin, followed by function development—a working model. The model is then demonstrated to the user for suggestions for improvements, which are incorporated into successive iterations until the working model proves satisfactory. Then formal user approval of the prototype's functionality is obtained. Next, a preliminary system design document is produced. The prototype iteration phase is the heart—through scenarios provided by the working model, the user may role-play and request successive refinements to the model until all functional requirements are met. When the user approval has been obtained, the detail design is derived from the rapid prototype and the system is tuned for production use. It is within this tuning phase that the rapid prototype becomes a fully operational system instead of a partial system during the prototyping iteration loop.

A detailed design may be derived from the prototypes. The prototype then is tuned using code or external utilities, as required. The designer uses validated requirements as a basis for designing the production software.

Additional work may be needed to construct the production version: more functionality, different system resources to meet full workload, or timing constraints. Stress testing, benchmarking, and tuning follow, and then comes operation maintenance as usual.

The final phase is operation and maintenance, which reflects the activities to move the system into a production state.

There is no "right" way to use the prototype approach. The result may be thrown away, used as a foundation for enhancement, or repackaged as a product, depending on the original objectives, the process used, and the desired quality. Clearly, cost and schedules benefit from *evolutionary* prototyping because no components are "thrown away."

Strengths of the Structured Evolutionary Rapid Prototyping Model   When applied to a suitable project, the strengths of the structured evolutionary rapid prototyping model can be seen in the following ways:

- The end user can "see" the system requirements as they are being gathered by the project team—customers get early interaction with system.
- Developers learn from customers' reactions to demonstrations of one or more facets of system behavior, thereby reducing requirements uncertainties.
- There is less room for confusion, miscommunication, or misunderstanding in the definition of the system requirements, leading to a more accurate end product—customer and developer have a baseline to work against.
- New or unexpected user requirements can be accommodated, which is necessary because reality can be different from conceptualization.
- It provides a formal specification embodied in an operating replica.
- The model allows for flexible design and development, including multiple iterations through life cycle phases.
- Steady, visible signs of progress are produced, making customers secure.
- Communications issues between customers and developers are minimized.
- Quality is built in with early user involvement.
- The opportunity to view a function in operation stimulates a perceived need for additional functionality.
- Development costs are saved through less rework.
- Costs are limited by understanding the problem before committing more resources.
- Risk control is provided.
- Documentation focuses on the end product, not the evolution of the product.
- Users tend to be more satisfied when involved throughout the life cycle.

Weaknesses of the Structured Evolutionary Rapid Prototyping Model
When applied to a project for which it is *not* suited, the weaknesses of this model can be seen in the following ways:

- The model may not be accepted due to a reputation among conservatives as a "quick-and-dirty" method.
- Quick-and-dirty prototypes, in contrast to evolutionary rapid prototypes, suffer from inadequate or missing documentation.

- If the prototype objectives are not agreed upon in advance, the process can turn into an exercise in hacking code.
- In the rush to create a working prototype, overall software quality or long-term maintainability may be overlooked.
- Sometimes a system with poor performance is produced, especially if the tuning stage is skipped.
- There may be a tendency for difficult problems to be pushed to the future, causing the initial promise of the prototype to not be met by subsequent products.
- If the users cannot be involved during the rapid prototype iteration phase of the life cycle, the final product may suffer adverse effects, including quality issues.
- The rapid prototype is a partial system during the prototype iteration phase. If the project is cancelled, the end user will be left with only a partial system.
- The customer may expect the exact "look and feel" of the prototype. In fact, it may have to be ported to a different platform, with different tools to accommodate size or performance issues, resulting in a different user interface.
- The customer may want to have the prototype delivered rather than waiting for full, well-engineered version.
- If the prototyping language or environment is not consistent with the production language or environment, there can be delays in full implementation of the production system.
- Prototyping is habit-forming and may go on too long. Undisciplined developers may fall into a code-and-fix cycle, leading to expensive, unplanned prototype iterations.
- Developers and users don't always understand that when a prototype is evolved into a final product, traditional documentation is still necessary. If it is not present, a later retrofit can be more expensive than throwing away the prototype.
- When customers, satisfied with a prototype, demand immediate delivery, it is tempting for the software development project manager to relent.
- Customers may have a difficult time knowing the difference between a prototype and a fully developed system that is ready for implementation.
- Customers may become frustrated without the knowledge of the exact number of iterations that will be necessary.
- A system may become overevolved; the iterative process of prototype demonstration and revision can continue forever without proper management. As users see success in requirements being met, they may have a tendency to add to the list of items to be prototyped until the scope of the project far exceeds the feasibility study.
- Developers may make less-than-ideal choices in prototyping tools (operating systems, languages, and inefficient algorithms) just to demonstrate capability.

- Structured techniques are abandoned in the name of analysis paralysis avoidance. The same "real" requirements analysis, design, and attention to quality for maintainable code is necessary with prototyping, as with any other life cycle model (although they may be produced in smaller increments).

When to Use the Structured Evolutionary Rapid Prototyping Model

A project manager may feel confident that the structured evolutionary rapid prototyping model is appropriate when several of the following conditions are met:

- When requirements are not known up-front;
- When requirements are unstable or may be misunderstood or poorly communicated;
- For requirements clarification;
- When developing user interfaces;
- For proof-of-concept;
- For short-lived demonstrations;
- When structured, evolutionary rapid prototyping may be used successfully on large systems where some modules are prototyped and some are developed in a more traditional fashion;
- On new, original development (as opposed to maintenance on an existing system);
- When there is a need to reduce requirements uncertainty—reduces risk of producing a system that has no value to the customer;
- When requirements are changing rapidly, when the customer is reluctant to commit to a set of requirements, or when application not well understood;
- When developers are unsure of the optimal architecture or algorithms to use;
- When algorithms or system interfaces are complex;
- To demonstrate technical feasibility when the technical risk is high;
- On high-technology software-intensive systems where requirements beyond the core capability can be generally but not specifically identified;
- During software acquisition, especially on medium- to high-risk programs;
- In combination with the waterfall model—the front end of the project uses prototyping, and the back end uses waterfall phases for system operational efficiency and quality;
- Prototyping should always be used with the analysis and design portions of object-oriented development.

Rapid prototyping is well suited for user-interface intensive systems, such as display panels for control devices, interactive online systems, first-of-a-kind products, and decision support systems such as command and control or medical diagnosis, among others.

The Rapid Application Development (RAD) Software Development Life Cycle Model

In the 1980s, IBM responded to the constricting nature of formal methods, such as the waterfall model, with the use of a rapid application development (RAD) approach. James Martin's book *Rapid Application Development* introduced this approach to the software community. With RAD, the user is involved in *all* phases of the life cycle—not only requirements definition, but design, development, test, and final delivery as well. User involvement is increased from the norm by the use of a development tool or environment that allows product evaluation in all stages of its development. The availability of graphical user interface development tools and code generators made it possible. Tools such as Oracle Designer/2000, Java Jbuilder 3, Linux, Visual C++, Visual Basic 6, SAS, and other applications have entire books dedicated to using them as rapid application tools.

RAD is characterized by the quick turnaround time from requirements definition to completed system. It follows a sequence of evolutionary system integrations or prototypes that are reviewed with the customer, discovering requirements along the way. The development of each integrated delivery is restricted to a well-defined period of time, usually about 60 days, called a time-box.

Factors that allow a system to be created in the 60 days of the time-box, without sacrificing quality, include the use of high-powered development tools, a high reuse factor, and knowledgeable and dedicated resources.

The critical end-user roles shift work from programming and testing to planning and design. More work is created for users at the front of the life cycle, but they are rewarded with a system that is built more quickly.

A Brief Description of the Phases in the RAD Model   The RAD model, shown in Figure 4–12, represents the phases of its life cycle development process and the user involvement throughout the phases (the curved line).

- **Requirements planning phase**—Requirements are gathered using a workshop technique called joint requirements planning (JRP), a structured discussion of the business problems at hand.

- **User description**—Joint application design (JAD) is used to harness user involvement; the project team often uses automated tools to capture information from the users during this nontechnical design of the system.

- **Construction phase ("do until done")**—This phase combines detailed design, the build (coding and testing), and the release to the customer inside a time-box. It is heavily dependent on the use of code generators, screen generators, and other types of productivity tools.

- **Cutover**—This phase includes acceptance testing by the users, installation of the system, and user training.

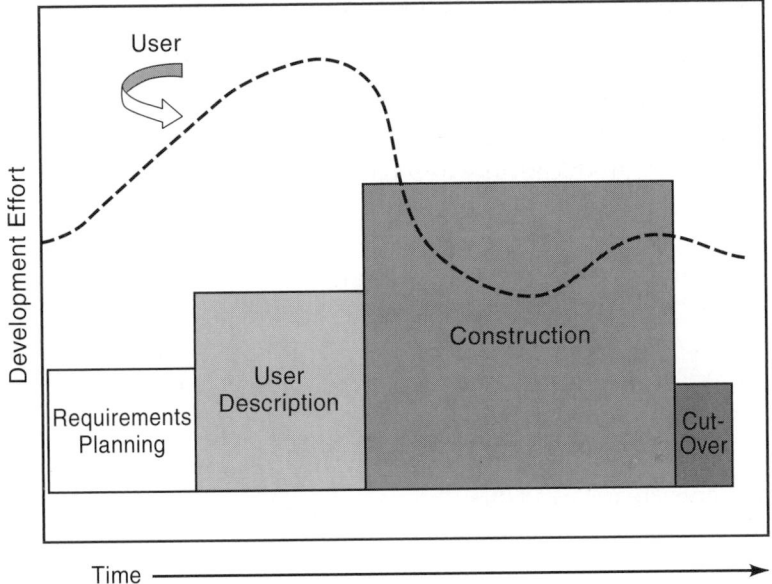

FIGURE 4–12
The Rapid Application Development Model

Strengths of the RAD Model   When applied to a project for which it is well suited, strengths of the RAD model include the following:

- Cycle time for the full product can be reduced due to the use of powerful development tools.
- Fewer developers are required because the system is developed by a project team familiar with the problem domain.
- Quick initial views of the product are possible.
- Reduced cycle time and improved productivity with fewer people spell lower costs.
- The time-box approach mitigates cost and schedule risk.
- It makes effective use of off-the-shelf tools and frameworks.
- Ongoing customer involvement minimizes the risk of not achieving customer satisfaction and ensures that the system meets the business needs and that the operational utility of the product is sound.
- Each time-box includes analysis, design, and implementation (phases are separated from activities).
- Constant integrations isolate problems and encourage customer feedback.
- The focus moves from documentation to code—what you see is what you get (WYSIWYG).

- It uses modeling approaches and tools—business modeling (how information flows, where it is generated, by whom, where it goes, how it is processed); data modeling (data objects and attributes and relationships identified); process modeling (data objects transformed); application generation (fourth-generation techniques).
- It reuses existing program components.

Weaknesses of the RAD Model Weaknesses of this model when applied to a project for which it is *not* well suited include the following:

- If the users cannot be involved consistently throughout the life cycle, the final product will be adversely affected.
- This model requires highly skilled and well-trained developers in the use of the chosen development tools to achieve the rapid turnaround time.
- It requires a system that can be properly modularized.
- It can fail if reusable components are not available.
- It may be hard to use with legacy systems and many interfaces.
- It requires developers and customers who are committed to rapid-fire activities in an abbreviated time frame.
- Blindly applied, no bounds are placed on the cost or completion date of the project.
- Teams developing commercial projects with RAD can overevolve the product and never ship it.
- There is a risk of never achieving closure—the project manager must work closely with both the development team and the customer to avoid an infinite loop.
- An efficient, accelerated development process must be in place for quick response to user feedback.

When to Use the RAD Model A project manager may feel confident that the RAD model is appropriate when several of the following conditions are met:

- On systems that may be modularized (component-based construction) and that are scalable;
- On systems with reasonably well-known requirements;
- When the end user can be involved throughout the life cycle;
- When users are willing to become heavily involved in the use of automated tools;
- On projects requiring short development times, usually about 60 days;
- On systems that can be time-boxed to deliver functionality in increments;
- When reusable parts are available through automated software repositories;
- On systems that are proof-of-concept, noncritical, or small;
- When cost and schedule are not a critical concern (such as internal tool development);
- On systems that do not require high performance, especially through tuning interfaces;

- When technical risks are low;

- On information systems;

- When the project team is familiar with the problem domain, skilled in the use of the development tools, and highly motivated.

The Incremental Software Development Life Cycle Model

Incremental development is the process of constructing a partial implementation of a total system and slowly adding increased functionality or performance. This approach reduces the cost incurred before an initial capability is achieved. It also produces an operational system more quickly by emphasizing a building-block approach that helps control the impact of changing requirements.

The incremental model performs the waterfall in overlapping sections, producing usable functionality earlier. This may involve a complete up-front set of requirements that are implemented in a series of small projects, or a project may start with general objectives that are refined and implemented in groups.

Boehm describes the incremental approach as combining elements of the linear sequential model and prototyping, and advocates developing the software in increments of functional capability. He reports that his experience is that this refinement of the waterfall model works equally well on extremely large as well as on small projects. In a short example of a product delivered in three increments, increment 1 would provide basic algorithms and basic output of results, increment 2 would add some valuable production-mode capabilities such as the ability to file and retrieve previous runs, and increment 3 would add various nice-to-have features for the user interface and added computational features.

The incremental model describes the process of prioritizing requirements of the system and then implementing them in groups. Generally, increments become smaller, implementing fewer requirements each time. Each subsequent release of the system adds function to the previous release, until all designed functionality has been implemented. This approach reduces costs, controls the impact of changing requirements, and produces an operational system more quickly by developing the system in a building-block fashion.

The early phases of the life cycle (planning, analysis, and design) consider the entire system to be developed. During these phases, the increments and the functions within them are defined for development. *Each increment* then proceeds through the remaining phases of the life cycle: code, test, and delivery.

A set of functions that are the core, or highest priority requirements critical to the success of the project, or that will reduce risk is constructed, tested, and implemented first. Subsequent iterations expand on the core, gradually adding increased functionality or performance.

Functions are added in significant increments to meet user needs in a cohesive fashion. Each additional function is validated against the entire set of requirements.

The linear sequences may be staggered over calendar time, with each one producing a deliverable increment of software, as shown in Figure 4–13.

This type of development can be combined with other models. It is often integrated with the spiral model, the V-shaped model, and the waterfall model to reduce costs and risks in the development of a system.

Strengths of the Incremental Model   When applied to a project for which it is well suited, strengths of the incremental model include the following:

- Funds for a total product development need not be expended up-front because a major function or high-risk function is developed and delivered first.
- An operational product is delivered with each increment.
- Lessons learned at the end of each incremental delivery can result in positive revisions for the next; the customer has an opportunity to respond to each build.
- The use of the successive increments provides a way to incorporate user experience into a refined product in a much less expensive way than total redevelopment.

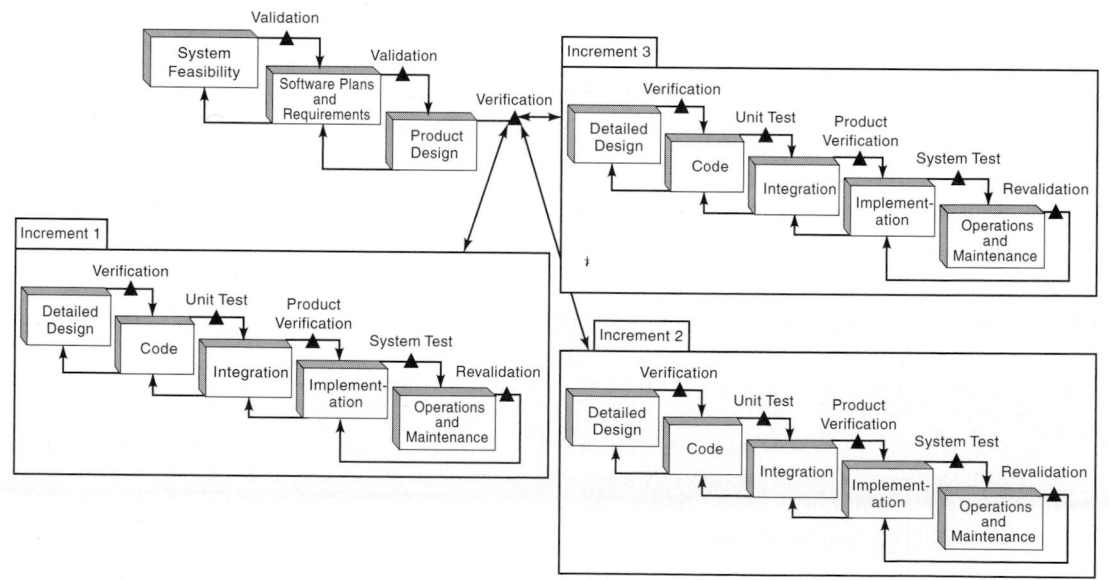

FIGURE 4–13
The Incremental Model

- The "divide and conquer" rule allows the problem to be broken down into manageable pieces, preventing the development team from becoming overwhelmed with lengthy requirements.
- Limited staff can be used, with the same team working sequentially to deliver each increment, keeping all teams working (labor distribution curve may be leveled out through the time-phasing of project effort).
- Starting the next build during the transition phase of the last smoothes staffing exchanges.
- Project momentum can be maintained.
- Costs and schedule risks may be revisited at the end of each incremental delivery.
- Initial delivery cost is lowered.
- Initial delivery schedule is faster, perhaps allowing response to a market window.
- Risk of failure and changing requirements is reduced.
- User needs are more controllable because the development time for each increment is so small.
- Because the leap from present to future does not occur in one move, the customer can adjust to new technology in incremental steps.
- Customers can see the most important, most useful functionality early.
- Tangible signs of progress keeps schedule pressure to a manageable level.
- Risk is spread across several smaller increments instead of concentrating in one large development.
- Requirements are stabilized (through user buy-in) during the production of a given increment by deferring nonessential changes until later increments.
- Understanding of the requirements for later increments becomes clearer based on the user's ability to gain a working knowledge of earlier increments.
- The increments of functional capability are much more helpful and easy to test than the intermediate level products in level-by-level top-down development.

Weaknesses of the Incremental Model   When applied to a project for which it is *not* well suited, weaknesses of this model include the following:

- The model does not allow for iterations within each increment.
- The definition of a complete, fully functional system must be done early in the life cycle to allow for the definition of the increments.
- Because some modules will be completed long before others, well-defined interfaces are required.
- Formal reviews and audits are more difficult to implement on increments than on a complete system.

- There can be a tendency to push difficult problems to the future to demonstrate early success to management.
- The customer must realize that the total cost will not be lower.
- Use of general objectives, rather than complete requirements, in the analysis phase can be uncomfortable for management.
- It requires good planning and design: Management must take care to distribute the work; the technical staff must watch dependencies.

When to Use the Incremental Model   A project manager may feel confident that the incremental model is appropriate when several of the following conditions are met:

- When most of the requirements are understood up-front but are expected to evolve over time;
- When there is a short market window and a need to get basic functionality to the market quickly;
- On projects that have lengthy development schedules, usually over one year;
- With an even distribution of different priority features;
- On low- to medium-risk programs;
- On a project with new technology, allowing the user to adjust to the system in smaller incremental steps rather than leaping to a major new product;
- When considerations of risk, funding, schedule, size of program, complexity of program, or need for early realization of benefits indicate that a phased approach is the most prudent;
- When it is too risky to develop the whole system at once;
- When deliveries occur at regular intervals.

The Spiral Software Development Life Cycle Model

The spiral model, introduced by Dr. Barry Boehm and published in *IEEE Computer*, 1988, addresses these concerns about the waterfall model: It does not adequately address changes, it assumes a relatively uniform and orderly sequence of development steps, and it does not provide for such methods as rapid prototyping or advanced languages.

The spiral model encompasses the strengths of the waterfall model while including risk analysis, risk management, and support and management processes. It also allows for the development of the product to be performed using a prototyping technique or rapid application development through the use of fourth-generation (and beyond) languages and development tools.

It reflects the underlying concept that each cycle involves a progression that addresses the same sequence of steps as the waterfall process model, for each portion of the product and for each of its levels of complexity, from an overall statement of need to the coding of each individual program.

As shown in Figure 4–14, each quadrant of the model has a purpose and supporting activities. The quadrants are listed here:

- **Determine objectives, alternatives, and constraints**—Objectives such as performance, functionality, ability to accommodate change, hardware/software interface, and critical success factors are identified. Alternative means of implementing this portion of the product (build, reuse, buy, subcontract, etc.) are determined; constraints imposed on the application of the alternatives (cost, schedule, interface, environmental limitations, etc.) are determined. Risks associated with lack of experience, new technology, tight schedules, poor processes, and so on are documented.

- **Evaluate alternatives, and identify and resolve risks**—Alternatives relative to the objectives and constraints are evaluated; the identification and resolution of risks (risk management,

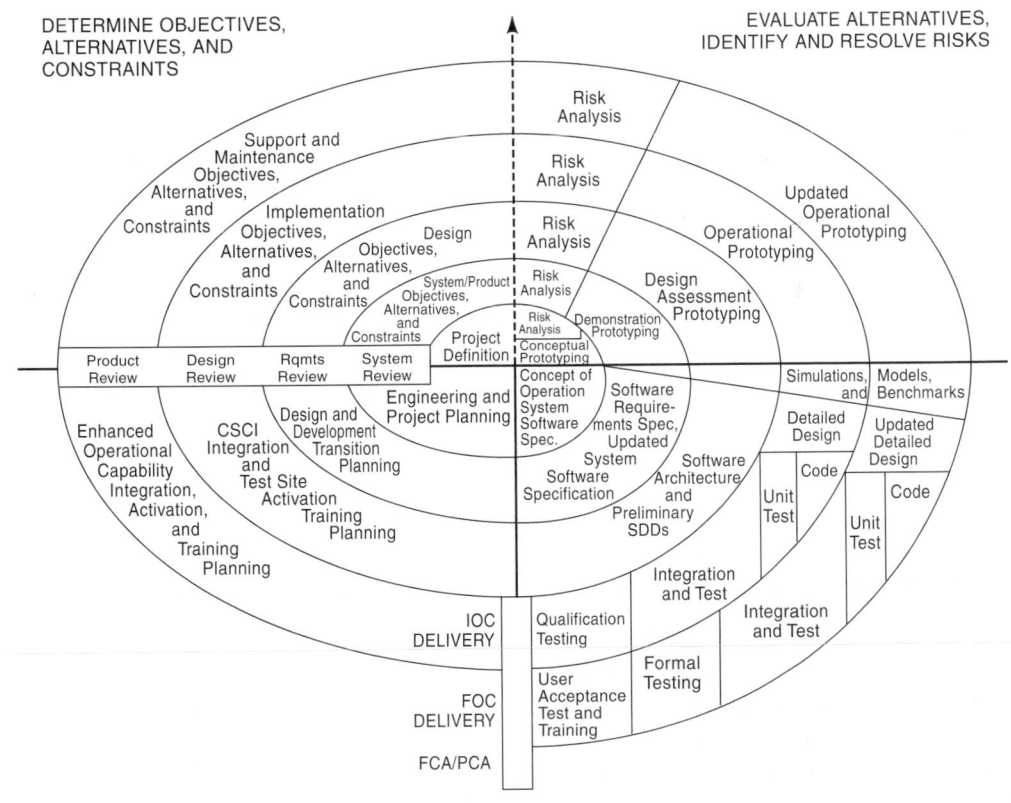

FIGURE 4–14
The Spiral Model

cost-effective strategy for resolving sources, evaluation of remaining risks where money could be lost by continuing system development [go/no-go decisions], etc.) occurs.

- **Develop next-level product**—Typical activities in this quadrant could be creation of a design, review of a design, development of code, inspection of code, testing, and packaging of the product. The first build is the customer's first look at the system. After this, a planning phase begins—the program is reset to respond to customer's reaction. With each subsequent build, a better idea of customer requirements is developed. The degree of change from one build to the next diminishes with each build, eventually resulting in an operational system.

- **Plan next phase**—Typical activities in this quadrant could be development of the project plan, development of the configuration management plan, development of the test plan, and development of the installation plan.

To read the spiral model shown in Figure 4–14, start in the center in Quadrant 1 (determine objectives, alternatives, and constraints), explore risks, make a plan to handle risks, commit to the approach for the next iteration, and move to the right.

For each iteration, determine objectives, alternatives, and constraints; identify and resolve risks; evaluate alternatives; develop the deliverables for that iteration and verify that they are correct; plan the next iteration; and commit to an approach for the next iteration, if you decide to have one.

There is no set number of loops through the four quadrants—as many should be taken as are appropriate, and iterations may be tailored for a specific project.

A salient factor is that coding is de-emphasized for a much longer period than with other models. The idea is to minimize risk through successive refinements of user requirements. Each "mini-project" (travel around the spiral) addresses one or more major risks, beginning with the highest. Typical risks include poorly understood requirements, poorly understood architecture, potential performance problems, problems in the underlying technology, and so on. Chapter 18, "Determining Project Risks," will describe the most common software project risks and techniques for their mitigation. The first build, the initial operational capability (IOC), is the customer's first chance to "test-drive" the system, after which another set of planning activities takes place to kick off the next iteration. It is also important to note that the model does not dispense with traditional structured methods—they appear at the end (outside loop) of the spiral. Design through user acceptance testing appears before final operational capability (FOC), just as they do in the waterfall model.

When using a prototyping approach, there may be a tendency for developers to dismiss good system development practices and misuse the model as an excuse for "quick-and-dirty" development. Proper use of the spiral model or one of its simpler variants will help prevent "hacking" and instill discipline. As seen in Figure 4–14, after much analysis and risk assessment, the "tail" of the spiral shows a set of waterfall-like disciplined process phases.

Addressed more thoroughly than with other strategies, the spiral method emphasizes the evaluation of alternatives and risk assessment. A review at the end of each phase ensures commitment to the next phase, or, if necessary, identifies the need to rework a phase. The advantages of the spiral model are its emphasis on procedures, such as risk analysis, and its adaptability to different life cycle approaches. If the spiral method is employed with demonstrations, baselining, and configuration management, you can get continuous user buy-in and a disciplined process.[14]

Strengths of the Spiral Model   When applied to a project for which it is well suited, strengths of the spiral model include the following:

- The spiral model allows users to see the system early, through the use of rapid prototyping in the development life cycle.
- It provides early indications of insurmountable risks, without much cost.
- It allows users to be closely tied to all planning, risk analysis, development, and evaluation activities.
- It splits a potentially large development effort into small chunks in which critical, high-risk functions are implemented first, allowing the continuation of the project to be optional. In this way, expenses are lessened if the project must be abandoned.
- The model allows for flexible design by embracing the strengths of the waterfall model while allowing for iteration throughout the phases of that model.
- It takes advantage of the strengths of the incremental model, with incremental releases, schedule reduction through phased overlap of releases, and resources held constant as the system gradually grows.
- It does not rely on the impossible task of getting the design perfect.
- It provides early and frequent feedback from users to developers, ensuring a correct product with high quality.
- Management control of quality, correctness, cost, schedule, and staffing is improved though reviews at the conclusion of each iteration.
- It provides productivity improvement through reuse capabilities.
- It enhances predictability through clarification of objectives.
- All the money needed for the project need not be allocated up-front when the spiral model is adopted.
- Cumulative costs may be assessed frequently, and a decrease in risk is associated with the cost.

Weaknesses of the Spiral Model   When applied to a project for which it is *not* well suited, weaknesses of the spiral model include the following:

- If the project is low-risk or small, this model can be an expensive one. The time spent evaluating the risk after each spiral is costly.

- The model is complex, and developers, managers, and customers may find it too complicated to use.
- Considerable risk assessment expertise is required.
- The spiral may continue indefinitely, generated by each of the customer's responses to the build initiating a new cycle; closure (convergence on a solution) may be difficult to achieve.
- The large number of intermediate stages can create additional internal and external documentation to process.
- Use of the model may be expensive and even unaffordable—time spent planning, resetting objectives, doing risk analysis, and prototyping may be excessive.
- Developers must be reassigned during nondevelopment-phase activities.
- It can be hard to define objective, verifiable milestones that indicate readiness to proceed through the next iteration.
- The lack of a good prototyping tool or technique can make this model clumsy to use.
- The industry has not had as much experience with the spiral model as it has with others.

Some users of this technique have found the original spiral model to be complex and have created a simplified version, shown in Figure 4–15.

Another version, a modified view of the spiral model from the Software Productivity Consortium, may be seen in Figure 4–16.

When to Use the Spiral Model   A project manager may feel confident that the spiral model is appropriate when several of the following conditions are met:

- When the creation of a prototype is the appropriate type of product development;
- When it is important to communicate how costs will be increasing and to evaluate the project for costs during the risk quadrant activities;
- When organizations have the skills to tailor the model;
- For projects that represent a medium to high risk;
- When it is unwise to commit to a long-term project due to potential changes in economic priorities, and when these uncertainties may limit the available time frame;
- When the technology is new and tests of basic concepts are required;
- When users are unsure of their needs;
- When requirements are complex;
- For a new function or product line;
- When significant changes are expected, as with research or exploration;
- When it is important to focus on stable or known parts while gathering knowledge about changing parts;

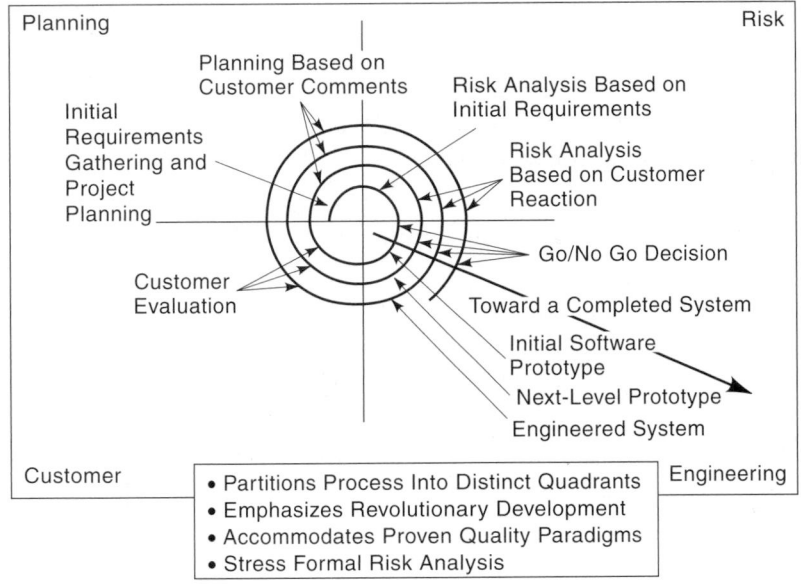

Planning

Risk

Planning Based on
Customer Comments

Initial
Requirements
Gathering and
Project
Planning

Risk Analysis Based on
Initial Requirements

Risk Analysis
Based on Customer
Reaction

Go/No Go Decision

Customer
Evaluation

Toward a Completed System

Initial Software
Prototype

Next-Level Prototype

Engineered System

Customer

- Partitions Process Into Distinct Quadrants
- Emphasizes Revolutionary Development
- Accommodates Proven Quality Paradigms
- Stress Formal Risk Analysis

Engineering

FIGURE 4–15
A Simplified View of the Spiral Model

- For large projects;
- For organizations that cannot afford to allocate all the necessary project money up-front, without getting some back along the way;
- On long projects that may make managers or customers nervous;
- When benefits are uncertain and success is not guaranteed;
- To demonstrate quality and attainment of objectives in short period of time;
- When new technologies are being employed, such as first-time object-oriented approaches;
- With computation-intensive systems, such as decision support systems;
- With business projects as well as aerospace, defense, and engineering projects, where the spiral model already enjoys popular use.

Tailored Software Development Life Cycle Models

Sometimes a project manager can pluck a life cycle model from a book and run with it. Other times, there seems to be nothing that quite fits the project needs, although one of the widely used and pretested models comes close. Need a life cycle that considers risk, but the spiral seems like overkill? Then start with the spiral and pare it down. Required to deliver

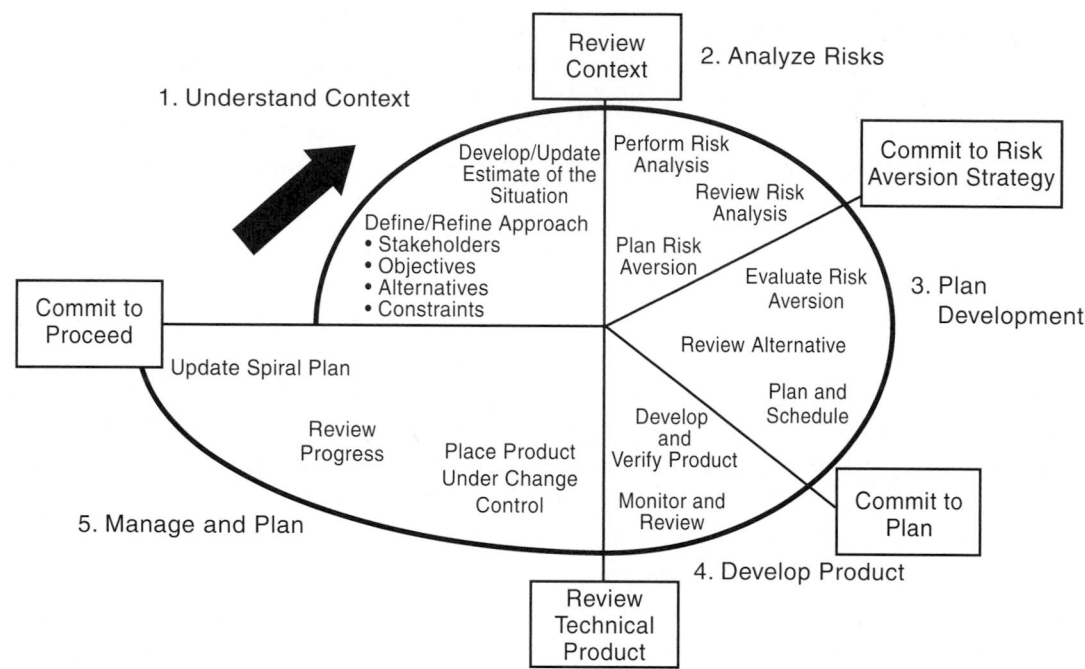

FIGURE 4–16
A Modified View of the Spiral Model
Source: Software Productivity Consortium.

functionality in increments but must consider serious reliability issues? Then combine the incremental model with the V-shaped model. Several examples of tailored models follow.

Fast Track   A fast-track life cycle methodology speeds up, or bypasses, one or more of the life cycle phases or development processes. Many or most of the normal development steps are executed as usual, while the formality or scope of others may be reduced.

Tailoring of the life cycle is required for a fast-track approach best used on nonmajor software development and acquisition projects. Fast tracking may be needed to serve a time criticality such as being the first to market for a commercial product, or a national threat for a government agency. In addition to a shortened life cycle, one tailored for fast tracking is usually less formal. The overall life of the delivered product may be short, indicating a short maintenance phase.

Fast-track projects should be attempted only in organizations accustomed to discipline. An institutionalized, defined development environment minimizes risk when employing this type of extreme measure. With a clearly defined, stable set of requirements and a method in place to accommodate changes, fast-track projects have an increased chance of success.

Concurrent Engineering   Concurrent engineering (CE) is concerned with making better products in less time. A basic tenet of the approach is that all aspects of the product's life cycle should be considered as early as possible in the design-to-manufacturing process. Early consideration of later phases of the life cycle brings to light problems that will occur downstream and, therefore, supports intelligent and informed decision-making throughout the process.[15]

Although borrowed from other engineering disciplines, concurrent engineering works for software as well. Especially on large projects, status tracking by major phases in a life cycle may be an oversimplified model. A snapshot in time would show that there are usually several activities (requirements gathering, design, coding, testing, etc.) going on simultaneously. In addition, any internal or external project deliverable may be in one of several states (being developed, being reviewed, being revised, waiting for the next step, etc.). Concurrent engineering considers all aspects of the life cycle as early as possible. Concurrent process models allow an accurate view of what state the project is in—what activities are being conducted and how the deliverables are progressing.

When using this approach, it is wise to assess technical risks involved to determine whether the technology being attempted is compatible with an accelerated strategy, leave some room in the schedule, assess the technological process periodically to see if it is still compatible with the plan, and, as with more traditional life cycles, ensure that there is a provision for testing and evaluation because there is extreme risk in skipping these activities.

The spiral model, being risk-driven, is a good model to use in guiding multistakeholder concurrent engineering of software-intensive systems. It offers a cyclic approach for incrementally growing a system's definition and implementation, as well as providing anchor-point milestones for ensuring continued stakeholder commitment.

Win-Win Spiral Model   Boehm also offers a modified spiral model called the "win-win spiral model," shown in Figure 4–17. It contains more customer-focused phases by adding Theory W activities to the front of each cycle. *Theory W* is a management approach elevating the importance of the system's key stakeholders (user, customer, developer, maintainer, interfacer, etc.), who must all be "winners" if the project is declared a success. In this negotiation-based approach, the cycles contain these phases or steps: Identify next-level stakeholders; identify stakeholders' win conditions; reconcile win conditions; establish next-level objectives, constraints, and alternatives; evaluate process and product alternatives and resolve risks; define the next level of the product and process, including partitions; validate the product and process definitions; and review and comment.

Not shown in Figure 4–17, but an important step, is to then plan the next cycle and update the life-cycle plan, including partitioning the system into subsystems to be addressed in parallel cycles. This can include a plan to terminate the project if it is too risky or infeasible. Secure the management's commitment to proceed as planned.

Benefits of the win-win spiral model have been noted as: faster software via facilitated collaborative involvement of relevant stakeholders, cheaper software via rework and maintenance reduction, greater stakeholder satisfaction up-front, better software via use of architecture-level quality-attribute trade-off models, and early exploration of many architecture options.[16]

Evolutionary/Incremental   Due to their nature, the evolutionary/incremental acquisitions often encounter complications. Questions arise because each incremental build provides but a small part of the capability of the system to be acquired. In addition to normal development decision criteria, additional questions must be answered:

- Is the decision to develop this functionality for this amount of money a good idea?
- Is this the time to address the functionality question (user priorities, dictates of the evolution itself)?
- Is this a reasonable price for the functionality being added (or are we "gold-plating" one functional area before developing all required capabilities)?
- Will we run out of money before we complete the required system?

Incremental V   Figure 4–18 shows a combination model fashioned by Krasner. In *Constructing Superior Software*, he is approaching the software development life cycle model from teamwork considerations.

> Fashioning a good project life cycle model is a worthwhile up-front investment that puts all project staff on the same page ... such as the traditional V model blended with the incremental, iterative development model. This model attempts to

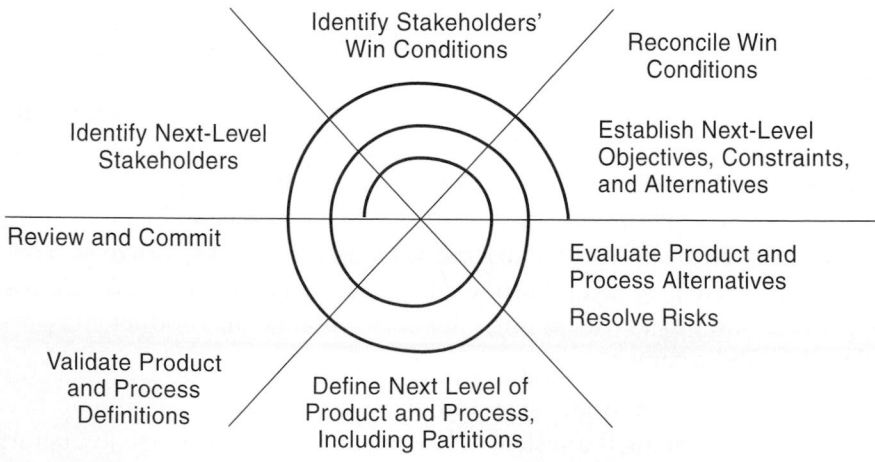

FIGURE 4–17
The Win-Win Spiral Model

balance the need for management controls with the need for technical innovation and situation dynamics. The keys to success of the Incremental V model are what happen at the control ... points. These are the formal mechanisms when management and development must jointly make explicit decisions to proceed to the next phase. Along with periodic management reviews and previews, these control points force the discussion of issues, risks, and alternatives. The meaning of each control point should be explicitly defined within the overall process. Behind such a high-level model are concrete plans based on rigorous estimates and well-defined milestones that lead down the path to success.[17]

Object-Oriented Rapid Prototyping   It is common to wonder why the subtle differences between the structured rapid prototyping, RAD, and spiral models matter—all three are user-involved, evolutionary approaches. The waterfall, V-shaped, and incremental models also have characteristics in common, such as the entry and exit phase criteria. The spiral can be thought of as an overlay of incremental, with the addition of risk management. All the models have some sort of scoping, requirements gathering, designing, developing, testing, and implementation activities.

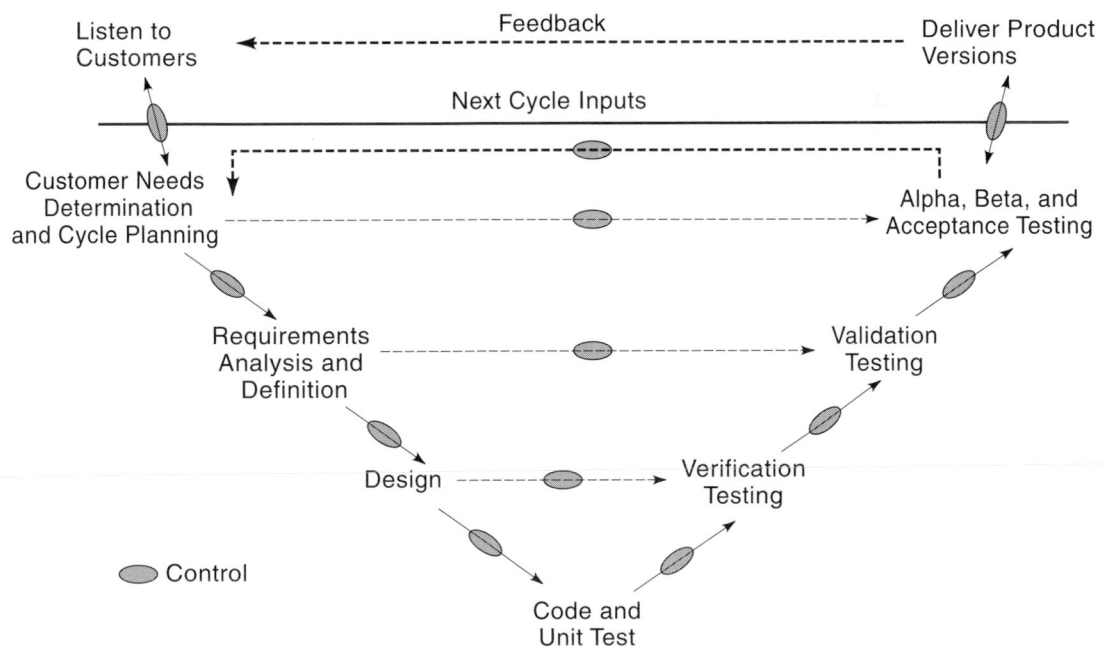

FIGURE 4–18
Incremental V Project Process Model

In fact, most life cycles are adaptations and combinations, and all software evolves. Commercial products are always evolving, and government and IT shops call the later evolutionary loops "maintenance."

The project manager should feel free to select and customize a software development life cycle to suit the project needs, but he must also remember the importance of naming the phases and clearly demarking the transition from "developing" to "implementing." The importance of the implementation or deployment line is all about control and management. There is a need for every software product to be considered "in production" at some point in time, or customers don't know when to pay the bill, users have no assurance of when functionality is stable, and the project team will not be able to baseline the product for configuration management purposes.

Selecting an Appropriate
Software Development Life Cycle Model _____

The selection of an appropriate life cycle model for a project can be accomplished by using the following process:

1. Examine the following project characteristic categories, as demonstrated in Tables 4–1 through 4–4:

   Requirements: Table 4–1

   Project team: Table 4–2

   User community: Table 4–3

   Project type and risk: Table 4–4

2. Answer the questions presented for each category by circling a yes or no in the matrices provided.
3. Rank the importance of the category, or question within the category, in terms of the project for which you a selecting a life cycle model.
4. Total the number of circled responses for each column in the matrices to arrive at an appropriate model.
5. Use the category ranking to resolve conflicts between models if the totals are close or the same.

Project Characteristic Categories

A brief description of the characteristics of requirements, project team, user community, and project type and risk follow. Tables 4–1 through 4–4 provide a set of matrices for use in steps 1–5 of the life cycle model selection process described in the preceding section.

Requirements   The requirements category (Table 4–1) consists of questions related to things that have been requested by the user for the project. They are sometimes termed as functions or features of the system that will be provided by the project.

TABLE 4–1

Selecting a Life Cycle Model Based on Characteristics of Requirements

Requirements	Waterfall	V-Shaped	Prototype	Spiral	RAD	Incremental
Are the requirements easily defined and/or well known?	Yes	Yes	No	No	Yes	No
Can the requirements be defined early in the cycle?	Yes	Yes	No	No	Yes	Yes
Will the requirements change often in the cycle?	No	No	Yes	Yes	No	No
Is there a need to demonstrate the requirements to achieve definition?	No	No	Yes	Yes	Yes	No
Is a proof of concept required to demonstrate capability?	No	No	Yes	Yes	Yes	No
Do the requirements indicate a complex system?	No	No	Yes	Yes	No	Yes
Is early functionality a requirement?	No	No	Yes	Yes	Yes	Yes

Project Team   Whenever possible, it is best to select the people for the project team before selecting the life cycle model. The characteristics of this team (Table 4–2) are important in the selection process because they are responsible for the successful completion of the cycle, and they can assist in the selection process.

TABLE 4–2
Selecting a Life Cycle Model Based on Characteristics of the Project Team

Project Team	Waterfall	V-Shaped	Prototype	Spiral	RAD	Incremental
Are the majority of team members new to the problem domain for the project?	No	No	Yes	Yes	No	No
Are the majority of team members new to the technology domain for the project?	Yes	Yes	No	Yes	No	Yes
Are the majority of team members new to the tools to be used on the project?	Yes	Yes	No	Yes	No	No
Are the team members subject to reassignment during the life cycle?	No	No	Yes	Yes	No	Yes
Is there training available for the project team, if required?	No	Yes	No	No	Yes	Yes
Is the team more comfortable with structure than flexibility?	Yes	Yes	No	No	No	Yes

(Continues)

TABLE 4–2 (Continued)
Selecting a Life Cycle Model Based on Characteristics of the Project Team

Project Team	Waterfall	V-Shaped	Prototype	Spiral	RAD	Incremental
Will the project manager closely track the team's progress?	Yes	Yes	No	Yes	No	Yes
Is ease of resource allocation important?	Yes	Yes	No	No	Yes	Yes
Does the team accept peer reviews and inspections, management/ customer reviews, and milestones?	Yes	Yes	Yes	Yes	No	Yes

User Community   The early project phases can provide a good understanding of the user community (Table 4–3) and the expected relationship with the project team for the duration of the project. This understanding will assist you in selecting the appropriate model because some models are dependent on high user involvement and understanding of the project.

Project Type and Risk   Finally, examine the type of project and the risk (Table 4–4) that has been identified to this point in the planning phase. Some models are designed to accommodate high-risk management, while others are not. The selection of a model that accommodates risk management does not mean that you do not have to create an action plan to minimize the risk identified. The model simply provides a framework within which this action plan can be discussed and executed.

TABLE 4–3
Selecting a Life Cycle Model Based on Characteristics of the User Community

User Community	Waterfall	V-Shaped	Prototype	Spiral	RAD	Incremental
Will the availability of the user representatives be restricted or limited during the life cycle?	Yes	Yes	No	Yes	No	Yes
Are the user representatives new to the system definition?	No	No	Yes	Yes	No	Yes
Are the user representatives experts in the problem domain?	No	No	Yes	No	Yes	Yes
Do the users want to be involved in all phases of the life cycle?	No	No	Yes	No	Yes	No
Does the customer want to track project progress?	No	No	Yes	Yes	No	No

TABLE 4–4

Selecting a Life Cycle Model Based on Characteristics of Project Type and Risk

Project Type and Risk	Waterfall	V-Shaped	Prototype	Spiral	RAD	Incremental
Does the project identify a new product direction for the organization?	No	No	Yes	Yes	No	Yes
Is the project a system integration project?	No	Yes	Yes	Yes	Yes	Yes
Is the project an enhancement to an existing system?	No	Yes	No	No	Yes	Yes
Is the funding for the project expected to be stable throughout the life cycle?	Yes	Yes	Yes	No	Yes	No
Is the product expected to have a long life in the organization?	Yes	Yes	No	Yes	No	Yes
Is high reliability a must?	No	Yes	No	Yes	No	Yes
Is the system expected to be modified, perhaps in ways not anticipated, post-deployment?	No	No	Yes	Yes	No	Yes

(Continues)

TABLE 4–4 (Continued)
Selecting a Life Cycle Model Based on Characteristics of Project Type and Risk

Project Type and Risk	Waterfall	V-Shaped	Prototype	Spiral	RAD	Incremental
Is the schedule constrained?	No	No	Yes	Yes	Yes	Yes
Are the module interfaces clean?	Yes	Yes	No	No	No	Yes
Are reusable components available?	No	No	Yes	Yes	Yes	No
Are resources (time, money, tools, people) scarce?	No	No	Yes	Yes	No	No

Customizing the Life Cycle Model

The selection of the appropriate model is but the first step in utilizing a life cycle model on a project. The next step is customizing it to the needs of a specific project—the actual phases and activities chosen should assist the project manager in tracking the project to the model.

As we are reminded by the SEI CMM, there are no prescriptions: "Guidelines and criteria for the projects' tailoring of the organization's standard software process are developed and maintained" and "The project's defined software process is a tailored version of the organization's standard software process."

The life cycles, their phases, and their activities suggested here can be used as a starting point in defining those you need. When the customization of the model is completed, the model becomes more meaningful to the project team and the user community. It can be used as a reference point during status reporting sessions, demonstrations, risk assessment sessions, and delivery of the final product.

What if during the course of the project something changes that causes the team to think that a different model may be more appropriate? Can the model be changed during the execution of the project? The answer is, yes, it can be changed, but it should be done with careful consideration to the impacts of the project. Ultimately, it is better to change the model than to attempt to use one that is not well suited to meet the needs of the project.

The steps in life cycle selection and customization are these:

1. Become familiar with the various models.
2. Review and analyze the types of work performed: development, enhancement, maintenance, and so on.
3. Select the most appropriate life cycle, using the criteria matrices: high risk, user interface, high reliability, time to market/release, user priorities, clarity of requirements, expected life of system, technology, size and complexity, potential parallelism, and interfaces to existing and new systems.
4. Review the life cycle approach to standards required of your organization, your customer, or the type of project—ISO, IEEE, and so on.
5. Identify a set of phases and phase activities.
6. Establish internal and external deliverables.
7. Define templates and content guides for deliverables.
8. Determine review, inspection, verification, validation checkpoints, and milestones.
9. Evaluate the effectiveness of the life cycle framework, and implement improvements where needed.

A frequent method of customizing life cycles is to combine models. Two examples are shown in Figures 4–19 and 4–20.

Summary

There are many "models" or representations of the software life cycle, all showing a logical flow of activity, an orderly progression from the identification of a need to production software. Each model is a process framework consisting of phases designed to guarantee the integrity of their subcomponent activities. Each phase reduces project risk by employing entry and exit criteria to determine how to proceed; each phase results in an internal or external deliverable.

Software development life cycles are sometimes called software life cycle management methodologies, to encompass all the standards and procedures that affect planning, requirements gathering and analysis, design, development, and implementation of a software system. For any life cycle to be effective, it must be carefully selected and often customized (adapted and evolved) to specific project goals and objectives.

Rather than starting from scratch, some popular, generic models provide good beginnings. Each model has its peculiar strengths and weaknesses, and each is well suited for certain types of projects.

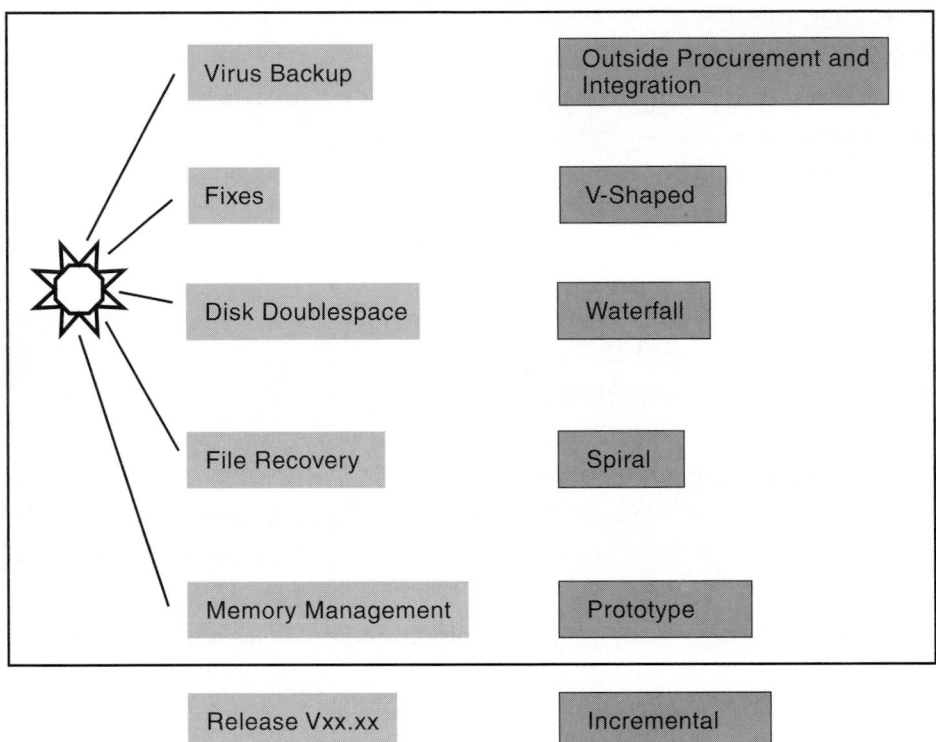

FIGURE 4–19
A Software Company's Product Release Using Combined Models

The model selected for a project or the models used by an organization should meet the needs of the organization, the type of work to be done, and the skills and tools of the software practitioners using the model(s).

By recognizing the power of life cycle models within the process framework, you can assist your organization in becoming flexible. Each project in the organization can use a different life cycle model that is customized, while continuing to operate within the same process framework to assist management with providing baseline information across projects. The integration of life cycle models with the process framework is yet another step in achieving a higher level of maturity in software development. The organization will have recognized the need for a process to develop software that is consistent, while providing for flexibility in the implementation of that process through the use of the customized life cycle models.

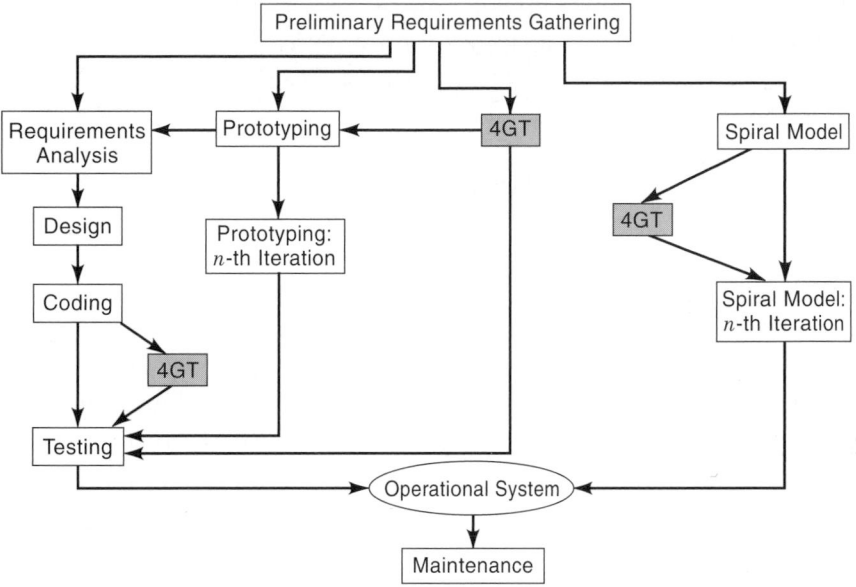

FIGURE 4–20
A Software Development Life Cycle Using Combined Models

Problems for Review _____

For each of the four problem scenarios, select an appropriate software development life cycle model and describe the advantage.

1. A corporation is rewriting its Accounts Payable system to move it from an old batch-type mainframe to a Web-enabled system. No new functionality will be added. The statement of work calls for a conversion "as is." Only the input and output subsystems will be altered for the new environment. Because it is a financial application, testing and verification will be emphasized within the development activities. The schedule allows five months for the project, with two people working on it. What do you think is the most appropriate life cycle approach? What is the advantage of this approach for this project?

2. An electronics corporation has recently decided to venture into a business area developing personal digital assistants (PDAs, like Palm Pilots). The PDA would incorporate a cellular modem. The company has considerable previous experience on product lines similar to this and believes that a cheaper price could present a value-added challenge to the PDA market. It would like to have a working model to present at a national electronics

fair coming up 90 days from now. What do you think is the most appropriate life cycle approach? What is the advantage of this approach for this project?

3. A corporation has recently completed a three-year process to develop a global configuration management system. It is now ready to move into the next phase, where new releases will be issued approximately every three months. An average of 12 new features and an appropriate number of bug fixes will be included in each release spread across teams composed of one to three engineers, located in India, Russia, and the United States. Development times for the new features can range from one to five months. Some features can require multiple releases for full implementation. What do you think is the most appropriate life cycle approach? What is the advantage of this approach for this project?

4. A company has created a new small-business division to develop a specialized wireless protocol operating system. Approximately 12 persons will be transferred from key areas of the company to form the base for the venture. Some 23 additional people will be hired from the outside, the bulk of whom are engineers. It has already been decided that object-oriented tools and approaches will be used with Java as the language. None of the participants has any prior knowledge of these techniques, but all will go through ten days of training when they come on board. In addition, a consortium-partner of the company has just released a new development platform (its first). This will be the development platform of choice. Training is also being scheduled for the new platform. The primary wireless supplier has been having major financial difficulties due to cutbacks and has laid off about 35% of its work force. What do you think is the most appropriate life cycle approach? What is the advantage of this approach for this project?

Visit the Case Study

The marketing executive vice president of your business unit has just approved for release this feature set of the CASE tool developed and sold by your new subsidiary. Here are the highlights of the feature set:

xTRemeObjectMaker delivers simultaneous round-trip engineering so that models built by modelers are actually used by developers and remain always up-to-date throughout the project. It even reverse-engineers source code from any compilers compliant with the Java and Swing class. It also delivers simultaneous round-trip engineering of EJBs from any source.

xTRemeObjectMaker encourages more efficient and effective development, with automatic generation of modeling patterns, design patterns, refactorings, and EJBs. xTRemeObjectMaker lets development teams establish exactly how they want code constructed, with mandatory and optional controls at the project and the developer levels.

xTRemeObjectMaker supports true team development by keeping models, code, and documentation in sync. It includes a leading multiuser multiplatform Web-enabled version-control system, and it can also autointegrate with most leading version-control systems on the Windows platform.

xTRemeObjectMaker automatically generates an XML-enabled portfolio of always up-to-date documentation—including Javadoc2 multiframe HTML doc, multiplatform Rich Text Format (RTF) reports, and both government-standard and corporate-standard documentation using xml_Java as the scripting language.

xTRemeObjectMaker supports customizable requirements traceability, allowing a team to track requirements data for any model elements, using any requirements-gathering methods across any domain of clients.

xTRemeObjectMaker delivers detailed visual support for UML diagrams, with significantly more comprehensive support than any other modeling product.

xTRemeObjectMaker scales to even the largest of projects; it is as scalable as any file-based version-control system. xTRemeObjectMaker includes project and subproject support for projects with hundreds or thousands of classes.

xTRemeObjectMaker includes very extensive view management, including a regular-expression language for defining custom view-management options to help define custom view "filters" via an embedded XML server.

xTRemeObjectMaker features a multilevel open object-oriented API. In fact, the majority of xTRemeObjectMaker's features are actually implemented using configuration files and the underlying API that is made available to all users at the graphical level. This allows the development of advanced scripts to generate metrics, perform a QA audit, generate sequence diagrams from source code, and autosync with third-party tool interfaces.

xTRemeObjectMaker integrates with leading development tools. Invoke any editor directly from within xTRemeObjectMaker. Add and invoke any other development tool, including a debugger. Invoke a compiler, and the following happens: xTRemeObjectMaker catches and displays error messages; double-click, and xTRemeObjectMaker takes a developer to that point in the model and source so that he can fix the error. xTRemeObjectMaker includes all the Sun JDK tools.

xTRemeObjectMaker provides complete supports for XML, DTD, and DDL. A pure Java application, xTRemeObjectMaker naturally runs on NT, 98/95, and Linux.

With these features, why are you wasting time on defining a life cycle? The marketing executive is holding your boss responsible for answering why you are not already generating code with this tool for the prototype. You, the project manager, must answer this question before tomorrow's staff meeting.

Citations

[1]*dictionary.cambridge.org/.* © Cambridge University Press 2000.

[2]*www.m-w.com/netdict.htm.* Merriam-Webster's WWWebster Dictionary.

[3]*www.informatik.uni-bremen.de/uniform/gdpa/vmodel/vm1.htm.* V-Model Development Standard for IT-Systems of the Federal Republic of Germany, pp. 6–7.

[4]Humphrey, Watts (1989). *Managing the Software Process,* 1st ed. Reading, MA: Addison-Wesley. Reprinted with corrections, August 1990, p. 167.

[5]Paulk, Mark C., Charles V. Weber, Bill Curtis, and Mary Beth Chrissis (1994). *The Capability Maturity Model: Guidelines for Improving the Software Process,* 1st ed. Reading, MA: Addison-Wesley, pp. 15–17.

[6]See note 5.

[7]See note 5.

[8]*www.stsc.hill.af.mil/crosstalk/1996/aug/isoiec.asp.* Gray, Lewis (1996). "ISO/IEC 12207 Software Lifecycle Processes." *Crosstalk,* August.

[9]Brooks, Fred (1975). *The Mythical Man-Month: Essays on Software Engineering,* 1st ed. Reading, MA: Addison-Wesley, p. 116.

[10]Brooks, Fred (1986). "No Silver Bullet—Essence and Accidents of Software Engineering." *Information Processing,* North-Holland: Elsevier Science Publishers.

[11]See note 4.

[12]Connell, John, and Linda Shafer (1989). *Structured Rapid Prototyping: An Evolutionary Approach to Software Development,* 1st ed. Englewood Cliffs, NJ: Prentice Hall, p. 23.

[13]Boar, Bernard (1984). *Application Prototyping: A Requirements Definition Strategy for the 80's,* 1st ed. New York, NY: John Wiley & Sons, p. 7.

[14]Boehm, Barry (1981). *Software Engineering Economics,* 1st ed. Englewood Cliffs, NJ: Prentice Hall, p. 42.

[15]*http://itc.fgg.uni-lj.si/ICARIS/LIST/msg00007.html.* "The Application of Multi-agent Systems to Concurrent Engineering." Description of "Concurrent Engineering" on the homepage for *Concurrent Engineering: Research and Applications (CERA).* West Bloomfield, MI: CERA Institute.

[16]Boehm, Barry, et al. (1998). "Using WINWIN Spiral Model: A Case Study." *IEEE Computer,* 31(7):33–44.

[17]Krasner, Herb (1999). "Teamwork Considerations for Superior Software Development." *Constructing Superior Software,* 1st ed. Indianapolis, IN: Macmillan Technical Publishing, p. 180.

References

Boehm, Barry (1988). "A Spiral Model of Software Development and Enhancement." *IEEE Computer,* 21(5):61–72.

Cantor, Murray R. (1998). *Object-Oriented Project Management with UML*, 1st ed. New York, NY: John Wiley & Sons, Inc.

Department of the Air Force, Software Technology Support Center (1996). "Guidelines for Successful Acquisition and Management of Software Intensive Systems." Version 2.0, June.

Deutsch, Michael S., and Ronald R. Willis (1988). *Software Quality Engineering: A Total Technical and Management Approach*, 1st ed. Englewood Cliffs, NJ: Prentice Hall PTR/Sun Microsystems Press.

Graham, Ian (1995). *Migrating to Object Technology*, 1st ed. Reading, MA: Addison-Wesley.

IEEE 1074-1997 (1998). "IEEE Standard for Developing Software Life Cycle Processes." New York, NY: The Institute of Electrical and Electronics Engineers.

Martin, James (1991). *Rapid Application Development*, 1st ed. New York, NY: Macmillan.

McConnell, Steve (1996). *Rapid Development: Taming Wild Software Schedules*, 1st ed. Redmond, WA: Microsoft Press.

Pressman, Roger S. (1993). "Understanding Software Engineering Practices: Required at SEI Level 2 Process Maturity." *Software Engineering Training Series*, Software Engineering Process Group, July 30.

Pressman, Roger S. (2001). *Software Engineering: A Practitioner's Approach*, 5th ed. Boston, MA: McGraw-Hill.

Royce, W.W. (1970). "Managing the Development of Large Software Systems: Concepts and Techniques." *Proceedings WESCON*, August. Los Alamitos, CA.

www.software.org/pub/darpa/erd/erdpv010004.html. DeSantis, Richard, John Blyskal, Assad Moini, and Mark Tappan (1997). SPC-97057 CMC Version 01.00.04, Herndon, VA: Software Productivity Consortium.

Web Pages for Further Information _____

stsc.hill.af.mil/crosstalk/1995/jan/comparis.asp. Abstract: "A Comparison of Software Development Methodologies. Reed Sorensen, Software Technology Support Center." Purpose and Scope: This article introduces and compares software development methodologies. This information will help you recognize which methodologies may be best suited for use in various situations. Software Technology Support Center (STSC) of the United States Air Force (USAF), "Guidelines for Successful Acquisition and Management of Software-Intensive Systems." *CrossTalk, The Journal of Defense Software Engineering*

stsc.hill.af.mil/crosstalk/1996/aug/isoiec.asp. Abstract: "ISO/IEC 12207 Software Lifecycle Processes." Lewis Gray. Ada PROS, Inc. This article describes ISO/IEC 12207. It shows how the standard solves some of the problems with DOD-STD-2167A that motivated the development of MIL-STD-498. Software Technology Support Center (STSC) of United States Air Force (USAF), "Guidelines for Successful Acquisition and Management of Software-Intensive Systems," *CrossTalk, The Journal of Defense Software Engineering*.

www.software.org/pub.darpa/erd/erdpv010004.html.

www.stsc.hill.af.mil/. Software Technology Support Center (STSC) of United States Air Force (USAF), "Guidelines for Successful Acquisition and Management of Software-Intensive Systems," *CrossTalk, The Journal of Defense Software Engineering*, Version 2.0, 1996.

Managing Domain Processes 5

Domain processes are the interrelated activities specific to the functioning of the organization for which a software project is developed. The measure of quality for a software project is based on how well the software solves specific domain-related problems. For the software customer, the view is from his business domain, not that of a computer scientist or software engineer. To deliver quality software, the project manager must understand the domain for which the software solves specific needs.

There are basic questions to answer to understand the domain in which the project manager is working. These questions result in a matrix set where product class domains are mapped to product types and the software components delivered.

After the domain has been categorized, the difference between the project and product life cycles must be understood. These differences are very apparent for both commercial and public projects. Understanding that development is just the first step in a product's life cycle is important in communicating the necessity for quality project management practices to customers.

Domain processes that are common to all organizations are criteria definitions for project selection models, project portfolio analysis, and the communication of basic financial ratios for project analysis. Each of these common domain process management activities will be discussed in this chapter.

Chapter 3, "Process Overview," provided an understanding of the basics of process management and how that fits into the front end of the project life cycle. Chapter 4, "Selecting Software Development Life Cycles," provided the descriptions of commonly used software development life cycles and the selection criteria for each. The final chapter in this section on initiating a software project covers the selection of teams. This chapter frames the project with respect to the domain in which it will ultimately function. This is the project manager's opportunity to frame the software delivered in the voice of the customer.

Managing domain processes requires a framing of the software development project within the organization. Figure 5–1 shows how the corporate, product, and project life cycles relate. The corporate business life cycle produces many products. These products are in different life cycle phases at any one point in time. A product life cycle begins after a need has been identified and when project conception is begun. A healthy corporation has many products and a managed number of projects under development. Each product may have one or more than one project in execution at any one time to complete the product family. Projects have a defined start and end point. In the product life cycle, a project begins after feasibility and is executed within the product acquisition phase. The project begins at initiation based on acquisition needs and ends at delivery, when the project deliverables are placed into operation.

The goal of any computer-based system is to provide assistance in meeting an organizational goal or objective, to support a business goal, and/or to develop a product that is sold to generate business revenue. Computer-based systems are more than software. Building quality software requires that hardware, people, data, documentation, and procedures be accounted for somewhere within the development life cycle.

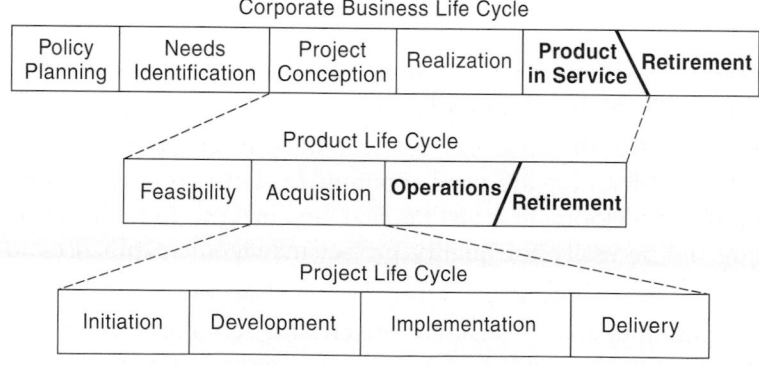

FIGURE 5–1
Life Cycle Relationships

A project manager must be able to define criteria for project selection. There will always be more projects than resources to adequately execute those projects. One of the key topics in this chapter is the definition of those criteria and taking them into a model structure for decision.

The ability to analyze a portfolio of projects and select the "best" one based on all known information is a skill that all project managers need to possess. Portfolio management looks at projects from the point of view of a return on investment based on what an organization feels is an effective internal rate of return. This financial view of selecting projects is appropriate for any size of organization, in any stage of maturity. It levels projects to a common comparative measure: money.

Understanding basic financial ratios for project analysis is part of evaluating projects for selection and existing projects within an ongoing portfolio. In this chapter, we will review the major ratios with respect to the DuPont financial analysis model. Detailed information is in Appendix C, "Creating the Business Plan."

Where We Are in the Product Development Life Cycle

Managing domain processes is initiated during the concept exploration phase, as shown in Figure 5–2. As the project concept is defined, the domain processes frame the concept in the target operating environment. Eventual delivery of a quality product requires the project manager to understand the customer's domain in which the software will operate.

Chapter 5 Relation to the 34 Competencies

Managing domain processes involves several project management skills, including:

Product Development Techniques

   4. **Evaluating alternative processes**—Evaluating various approaches
  11. **Understanding development activities**—Learning the software development cycle

Project Management Skills

  21. **Tracking process**—Monitoring compliance of the project team

People Management Skills

  25. **Holding effective meetings**—Planning and running excellent meetings

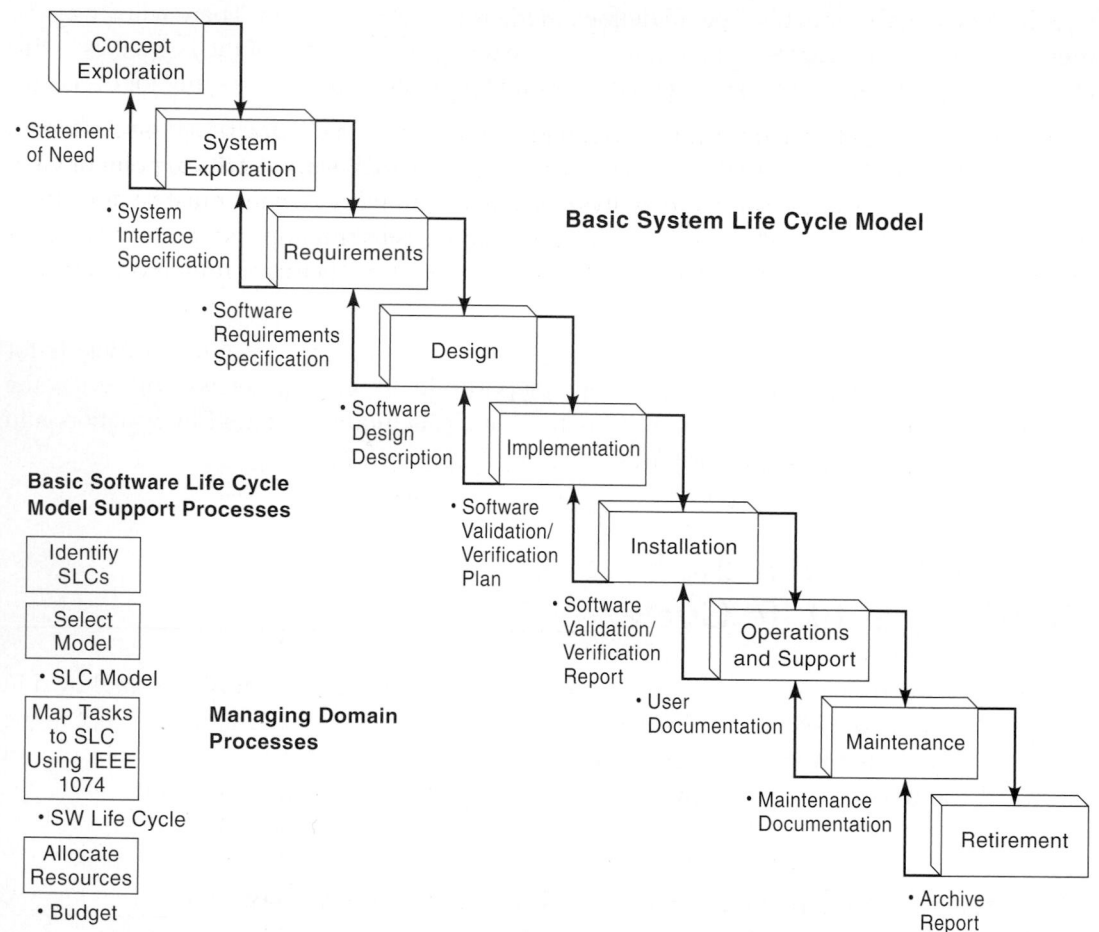

FIGURE 5–2
Managing Domain Processes Occurs During the Concept Exploration Phase

Learning Objectives for Chapter 5 _____

Upon completion of this chapter, the reader should be able to:

- Explain the domain processes that must be incorporated into the concept exploration phase of every project;
- Explain how domain processes differ for the six classes of product domains;
- Map product domain types to critical product components;
- Define the organization's project portfolio and classify the projects with respect to their economic impact.

Defining the Process Domain_____

Domain processes are the interrelated activities that are specific to the functioning of the organization for which a software project is developed. The first step is to determine the domain in which the product will eventually be used. For all domain analysis, the critical point of view is that of the ultimate end-user. Valid analyses and evaluations of options must be done from this view. If there is no "real" customer available, then we must rely on a secondary "voice of the customer." This is usually someone from the marketing organization. Even when a matrix is viewed from the "developer's" perspective, the customer is ever present.

The measure of quality for a software project is based on how well the software solves specific domain-related problems. For the software customer, the view is from his business domain, not that of a computer scientist or software engineer. For this reason, to deliver quality software, the project manager must understand the domain for which the software solves specific needs. For software product development, there are six classes of product domains:

1. Consumer
2. Business
3. Industrial
4. Real-time
5. Really timely
6. Scientific

Individuals buy *consumer* products for personal use. This use could be at home, while traveling, or at work. The key here is that the consumer market is a mass market and is usually addressing a price-sensitive purchaser. Examples of consumer products utilizing software are cellular phones, automobiles, televisions, personal computers, and personal digital assistants.

The majority of software products are targeted at the *business* product domain. Here the key is providing a cost-effective product to the business customer that will improve overall business profits. These products are usually expensive compared to consumer products and have maintenance, service, and installation services available as a necessary part of the product. Examples of these types of products are database tools such as Oracle™, enterprise resource planning products such as PeopleSoft™, development tool suites such as WebSphere™ and VisualAge™, and operating systems such as Solaris™.

Industrial products are a specific subclass of business products. These are software tools that are purchased for the specific purposes of machine automation, factory automation and integration, and embedded control software. These are special-purpose and usually focused on a specific industry such as automotive, food processing, and semiconductor fabrication. This domain has the highest percentage of product customization and integration with legacy systems. Examples of these products are factory automation software from FactoryWorks™, embedded development systems from Wind River, and process modeling tools such as Hewlett-Packard's Vee™.

Real-time products are used to control processes that have a defined and finite time budget. Real-time systems are used for data collection of events that last less than a microsecond. Real-time products control embedded medical devices such as pacemakers, where information must literally be processed between heartbeats. These products also work in the interface between the collection of analog data such as voice or music and its conversion to digital data that can be stored on a magnetic disk or CD-ROM. All real-time software is written specifically for the target hardware on which it executes.

Really timely, as opposed to real-time, software products must execute within a time budget that does not irritate the end user. Examples of this are the software that runs ATM machines and does credit card verification while ordering over the Internet. Most really timely software products are a part of either business or industrial software products. They are broken out as a subclass because of the potential for causing customer irritability if they do not function effectively.

Scientific products simulate real-world activities using mathematics. Real-world objects are turned into mathematical models. Executing formulas simulates the actions of the real-world objects. For example, some of an airplane's flight characteristics can be simulated in the computer. Rivers, lakes, and mountains can be simulated. Virtually any object with known characteristics can be modeled and simulated. Simulations use enormous calculations and often require supercomputer speed. As personal computers become more powerful, more laboratory experiments will be converted into computer models that can be interactively examined by students without the risk and cost of the actual experiments. Members of this product domain are Matlib™ for large mathematical formula development, Analytica™ for developing large-scale business models, and Expert Choice for developing large-scale decision support systems. Scientific software products are usually special-purpose tool kits for problem solving.

The question now arises, "What about the government market?" For the six classes of software product domains as defined, all of them could be "government" customers. Where the separation of government from private customers comes into play is in the areas of business plans, legal concerns, contracting, and risk analysis.

Four classes of product systems look at ways that the software product will be built and delivered from the developer's perspective. These four have different product development plans and life cycles. Although all product development is an iterative process, in the real business world there is usually an existing product portfolio. During the conceptual stage, the project manager will have worked on the product concept and selected a preliminary life cycle. That earlier work influences the selection of one or more of these product system classes:

1. New software product
2. Re-engineering of existing product

3. Component integration

4. Heroic maintenance

A *new software product* starts with a set of requirements and moves through its development life cycle to delivery. It will use some sort of development tools and possibly object libraries, where appropriate. This is building a truly new software product for taking advantage of a new technology such as the Internet or using a new set of programming tools such as Java. It may also be a new market opportunity because of changes in government regulations such as telecommunications or banking deregulation.

Re-engineering existing product is simply that. This product already exists in a form that may use outmoded software technology or be hosted on obsolete hardware. An example would be a DOS-based data collection system that would be re-engineered to run on Linux.

Taking available commercial-off-the-shelf (COTS) products and integrating them into a product is *component integration*. An example of this type of product is taking an available embedded database tool along with a script-generation tool and a graphical user interface (GUI) generator to produce a new product that is used for integrating factory equipment into the overall manufacturing execution system.

Heroic maintenance occurs when a company wants to wring the last bit of revenue out of an existing software product that has been passed over for re-engineering. Software product companies take great care in the management and timing of the releases of new capabilities within their product portfolios. When completely new products or massively re-engineered products are released, there is always a potential to cannibalize existing customer sales instead of having new customers buy the new product. Timing decisions may result in the delay of the newest product and the release of the old product with heroic work done to dress it up in new clothes. An example of this is once again our DOS system: Instead of re-engineering the entire system, the command-line interface was replaced with a pseudo-GUI. This is known in the software industry as "same dog, new collar!"

The first matrix to be developed by the project manager involves identifying the product domain type, illustrated in Figure 5–3. This product domain type resides at the intersection of the six product domain classes and the product type classes. A software product can be defined to exist in multiple cells on this matrix. For example, suppose that there is a new, Web-based software product for registering personal DVD movies in a trading club in which points are earned to borrow (or a small fee is paid, if points are insufficient). This product would "live" in the consumer and really timely product domain classes as both a new software product and component integration. Although the concept of the product is new and new software would be developed, there are many libraries of components available for use. This example is represented in the matrix with an X in the relevant cell.

Another example product is an enhancement to an existing factory-integration product to take information from past process steps and determine the optimum process for the product through the factory based on past production yield information and customer orders. We can

1. Identify the Product Domain Type	Consumer	Business	Industrial	Real-Time	Really Timely	Scientific
New Hardware/Software Product	X	O	O	O	X	O
Re-engineering Existing Product		O	O	O		O
Component Integration	X				X	
Heroic Maintenance						

FIGURE 5–3
Step 1—Identify the Product Domain Type

tell immediately that this will be re-engineering an existing product, but some new software also will be developed. This product may touch four of the product domain classes: business, industrial, real-time, and scientific. Business could be touched because of accessing historic information on production yields. Industrial and real-time apply because it will be operating on factory automation equipment. The scientific piece comes in with the optimization algorithms necessary for determining the best individual product flow through the factory. This example is represented in the matrix with an O in the relevant cell.

The third part of defining the process domain is the product component classes. This set of classes is also viewed from the perspective of the end-user. There are six members of the class, and the key question to ask is, "What does the customer expect to have delivered?" The software development project manager must discover whether the end-user has a product expectation. Six product component classes exist:

1. Software
2. Hardware
3. People
4. Database
5. Documentation
6. Procedures

If a project is to develop a "pure" software product, the end-user has an expectation that he will get an installation set of media or an access key to a remote site to download the product. This is the way most consumer software is purchased—the only items received are the media or a digital file.

Many products are turnkey: The developed software is hosted on hardware. Buying a cellular phone usually dictates the software running within the hardware. Although the software is a critical system component, the customer purchases the hardware.

People are a critical part of many software products. Enterprise-wide software systems used for financial management, factory control, and product development may require consulting services to be "purchased" along with the software to aid in product installation, integration, and adoption into a specific environment.

Database products, although most definitely software, are separated as a distinct class because of the expectations that accompany the purchase of this class of complex software. A database product is usually purchased as a separate, general-purpose tool kit to be used as an adjunct to all of a company's other information systems. More "software" products are delivered with an embedded database package within the product. It is important for the customer to realize that he is purchasing not only the "new" software, but also a database product.

Documentation is almost always a part of the product. In some cases, it may be books and manuals purchased as a "shrink-wrapped," off-the-shelf software product. Many complex enterprise software products have third-party authors writing usage and tips books sold through commercial bookstores. If downloaded, the digital files may include a "readme" file and possibly complete soft copy documentation. Acquiring software from some sources such as SourceForge (*www.SourceForge.com*) may provide no documentation other that the software's source code.

Procedures or business rules are a final component class. In situations in which the customer is buying systems and software used for decision support, equipment control, and component integration, it is important for the customer to understand the procedure deliverables. Usually the custom development of the business rules for an organization are done by either the organization itself or consultants hired from the software company. This can be a very gray area, and it is important that the project manager understand all of the project deliverables early in the development life cycle, especially those that can cause customer dissatisfaction and demonstrate a lack of quality.

Now that the third set of domain classes has been defined, the project manager can fill out the last two matrices. The next one to complete is the identification of the critical product components, shown in Figure 5–4. This matrix is a table of the product component classes matched with the classes of product systems. This matrix provides us with the deliverables for the defined product based on whether it is new software, re-engineered software, a component integration product, or the heroic maintenance of a legacy product within the company's portfolio. Remember, the Web example is the X and the factory integration is the O.

For example, our Web-based software product for registering personal DVD movies was determined to be both a new software product and component integration. The critical product components for this product are software and documentation. It is Web-based and runs from a browser running on the customer's personal hardware. The customer will see no database, people, or procedures. The only documentation may be the instructions on the Web page itself.

Our other example product, an enhancement to an existing factory integration product, involves re-engineering an existing product and some new software development. Based on how the product is to be marketed, the customer will see all the component classes except hardware. He will expect software to be delivered along with a field applications engineer to do the installation and acceptance testing within the customer's factory. The customer will also expect a database to keep the real-time product status and yield information along with the procedures for running the optimization algorithms. Documentation will be critical to both a company's engineers doing the installation and the customers after the product is accepted.

The third matrix that the project manager produces to define the domain is to link the product domains to the delivered components. This matrix shown in Figure 5–5 is a table of

2. Identify Critical Product Components	Software	Hardware	People	Database	Documentation	Procedures
New Hardware/Software Product	X O		O	O	X O	O
Re-engineering Existing Product	O		O	O	O	O
Component Integration	X				X	
Heroic Maintenance						

FIGURE 5–4
Step 2—Identify Critical Product Components

the product component classes matched with the product domain classes. This matrix provides us with the deliverables for the defined product based on whether it is going to be installed into a consumer, business, industrial, real-time, really timely, or scientific domain.

Using our two examples, the Web-based software product for registering personal DVD movies in a trading club would "live" in the consumer and really timely product domain classes. The deliverables would be software and documentation. The second example, an enhancement to an existing factory integration product, touches four of the product domain classes: business, industrial, real-time, and scientific. The deliverable components are software, people, database, documentation, and procedures.

Chapter 4, "Selecting Software Development Life Cycles," provided the descriptions of commonly used software development life cycles and the selection criteria for each. When compared to the overall company versus product life cycles, the software development life cycle is assumed within the acquisition phase of the product life cycle. Figure 5–1 shows this.

A project manager must understand the relationship within his organization of software development within product life cycles. A typical product development life cycle begins with a development or acquisition phase during which the product is built or acquired. Figure 5–6 represents the product development phase. The project manager works hand in hand with the product manager to plan for the manufacturing of the product. This phase is the production

3. Link Product Domains with Components	Software	Hardware	People	Database	Documentation	Procedures
Consumer	X				X	
Business	O		O	O	O	O
Industrial	O		O	O	O	O
Real-Time	O		O	O	O	O
Really Timely	X				X	
Scientific	O		O	O	O	O

FIGURE 5–5
Step 3—Link Product Domains with Components

ramp. Investment is made on the infrastructure for product manufacturing, and first products are built. After the production ramp, the software portion of the product is out of the hands of the software project manager, except for problem fixes.

Figure 5–7 shows the entire product life cycle plotted in months versus thousands of dollars invested. The dollars of investment on the left side of the graph and below the zero line is the estimated investment in the product. The dollars above the zero line are the estimated revenue dollars that the product will earn. This type of information is usually developed by marketing and is a critical part of the return on investment that the product will make.

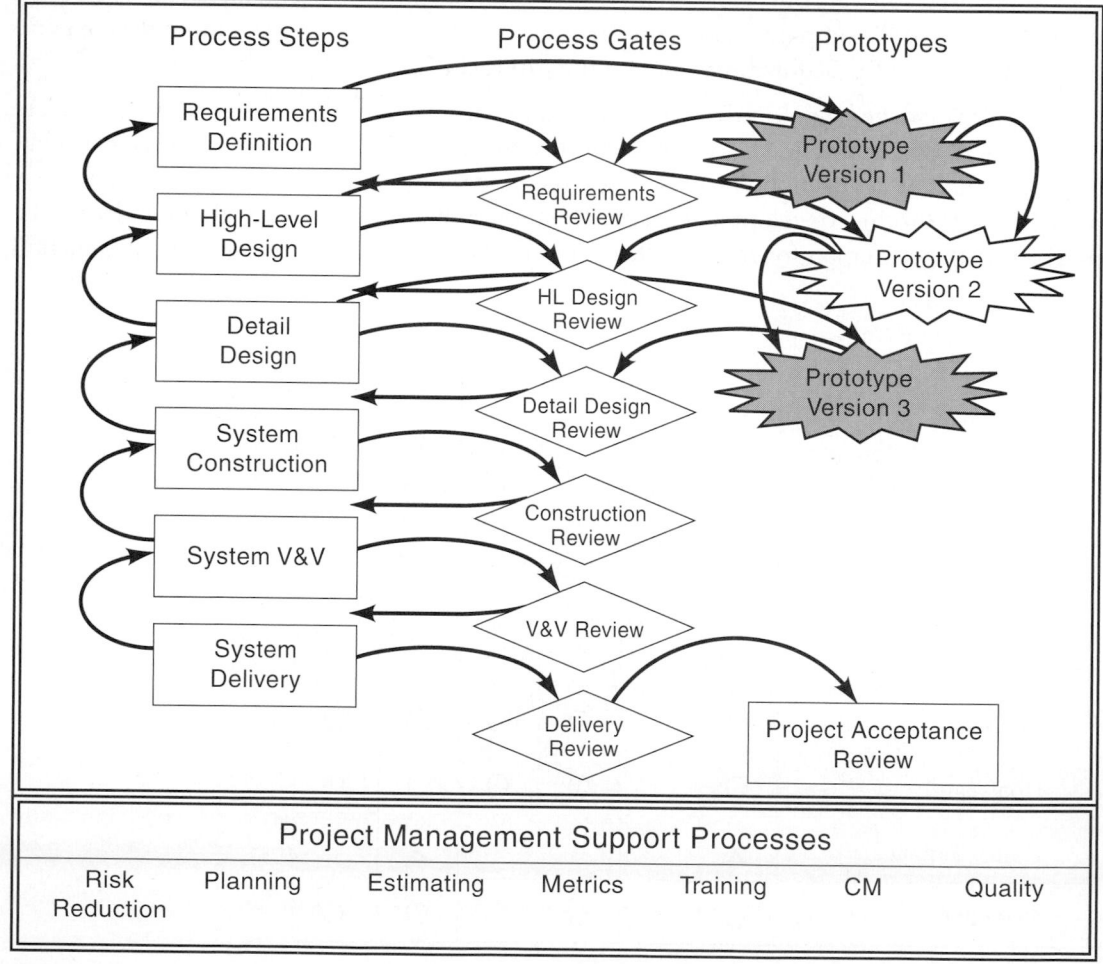

Figure 5–6
Software Development Life Cycle

Finally, the relationship between the development and product life cycles is graphically represented in Figure 5–8. This relationship is critical to keep in mind as the project manager works through the product development process. In the product world, the product life cycle drives decisions and investment. Only the investment part of the software development life cycle is important to product managers planning product portfolios.

Project Selection Models _____

Selection of projects is a key business process and is essential to the ongoing economic health of the organization. This process involves the project managers, product line managers and business unit executives, *and* all the stakeholders in and out of the business organization. Getting the correct set of stakeholders involved in project selection and definition is critical to the ultimate project development success. Figure 5–9 shows the relationship among all the main entities.

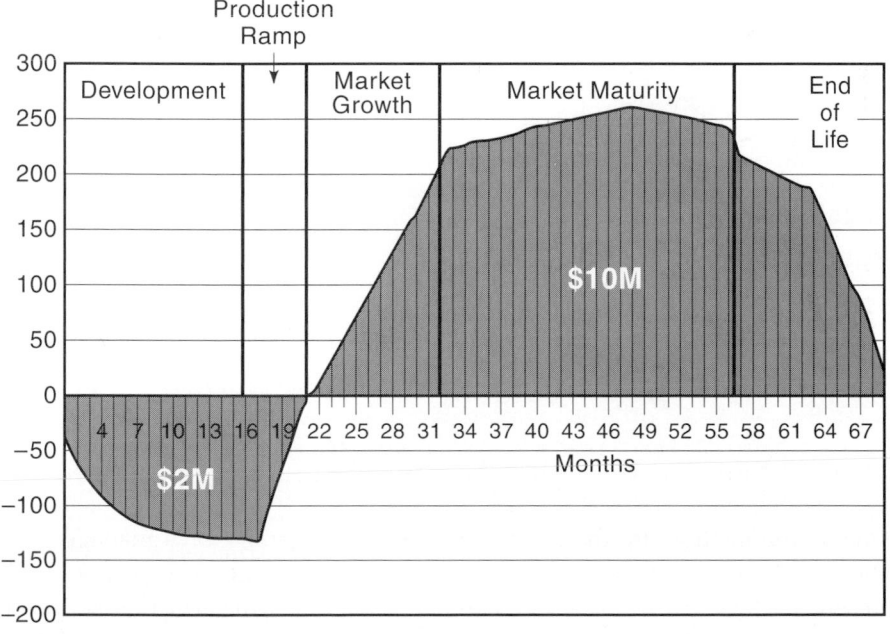

FIGURE 5–7
Software Product Life Cycle

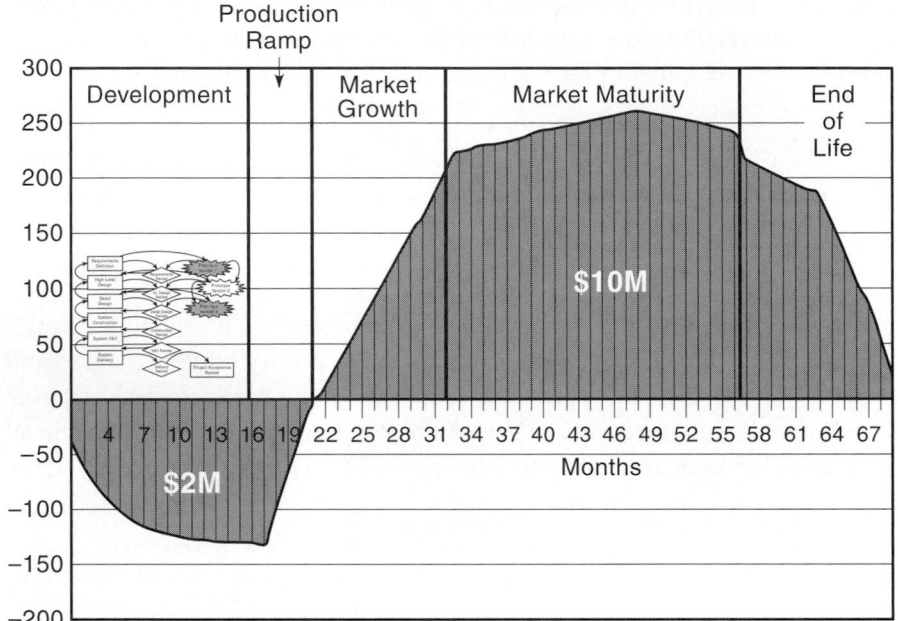

FIGURE 5–8
Software Product and Development Life Cycles

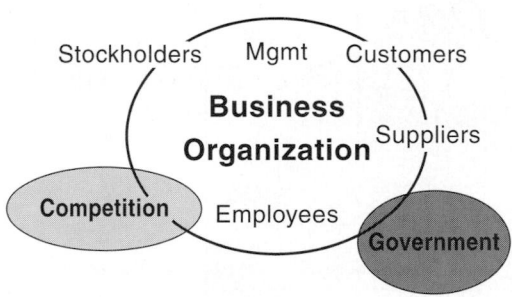

FIGURE 5–9
Private Enterprise Stakeholders' Map

Within the business organization are the employees and the organization's management. The majority of the stakeholder entities reside outside the organization. The corporation's stockholders, represented through the Board of Directors, have a fiduciary interest in the financial success of the company. In that respect, they are concerned that projects are selected that will provide an adequate return on investment. Customers are concerned about the release of state-of-the-art products that meet their needs at an economic cost. Customers do not readily change from competent suppliers because the internal "switching" cost of changing major software systems is excessively high.

The organization's suppliers are stakeholders in that they want to continue providing development teams with the best in software and hardware development products. Companies such as Microsoft, Sun, and Oracle have extensive programs for their development partners and work hand in hand with them to produce industry-specific products that use their development and internal tools.

The government is a stakeholder in consumer product decisions—at times, a very proactive partner. Government regulations touch not only product strategies but also employees in areas from workplace safety to immigration laws to hazardous materials regulation. Many software products must be subjected to lengthy government agency approvals because they are installed in medical devices, provide for aircraft safety, or monitor hazardous materials.

Finally, competition is a stakeholder in product selection criteria. Although they may not have an active voice, decisions made in the same marketplaces influence decisions to develop new products. A competitor's missteps may signal an opening for a new product. A very strong product with loyal clients may be a model for an organization to follow in releasing a complementary product in another market. Competition also touches employees in their efforts to recruit the best developers.

Those project managers in the public sector have a similar stakeholders' map with which to work. Figure 5–10 shows that relationship.

Internally the organization could operate in a similar fashion to the business organization. The external stakeholders are very different. The owners and the customers are one and the same—citizens. Therefore, the government organization, by its nature, is subject to enormous amounts of political pressure. The suppliers have a similar stakeholder position, but with

FIGURE 5–10
Government Stakeholders' Map

more regulation and barriers to entry. Many suppliers will not work with government development groups because of the onerous amounts of paperwork required and the high risks associated with completion of joint government and private-sector projects.

Competition plays an important role in this stakeholder map. Governmental agencies are tasked with creating their own competition by either "privatizing" agencies such as the U.S. Postal Service or passing laws that encourage competition in previously regulated industries, such as banking and telecommunications. A project manager in a governmental organization needs to pay special attention to pending regulation changes and efforts to build private competition to public organizations. Just as in private industry, the competition is looking to hire the best employees. Many companies look at the public sector as the "farm league" for their technical hires.

After the organization-wide and project-specific stakeholders have been mapped, the next process is to define the selection criteria for a project. The selection process evaluates individual projects or groups of projects and then chooses to implement some set of them to achieve the objectives of the organization. This practitioner's guide will not discuss how an organization sets its goals and objectives. For the domain process of project selection, it is assumed that the project manager and the project selection team understand and have available the organization's current objectives as a business or governmental organization. If these objectives do not exist, the selection process must be halted until those are defined. If a project selection team does not know the organization's goals and objectives, selecting a project is the least of the organization's worries.

Project selection must be based on sound strategy and usually involves more than one stakeholder department. An interdisciplinary team executes the selection process because enough information common to all projects and product areas is required so that sound selection decisions can be made. Risk is a major driver in the selection process because of both the development risk and the market risk. Can the product be built? And can the product be sold?

In preparing for the project selection decision, these questions must be answered:

1. What stakeholders are included in this project selection decision?
2. What is the team's familiarity with the technology of the product?
3. What is the team's familiarity with the market for this product?
4. How technically complex is the product to build?
5. How complex is the product to explain to an end-user?
6. What is the organization's experience in developing this type of product?
7. What is the estimated product development effort in dollars?
8. How is the project life cycle defined?
9. How is the product life cycle defined?
10. What is the risk in developing this product?

11. What is the risk in *not* developing this product?
12. Is this project a "sacred cow," suggested by executives or owners?
13. Is this project an operating necessity that must support existing organization systems?
14. Is this project a competitive necessity to keep abreast of competition?
15. Is this a product line extension to our current portfolio?

The answers to these questions become the foundation of an organization's project selection model. A typical method for this involves the project selection team reviewing the statement of need document produced in the concept exploration phase and then answering these questions. When consensus is reached that the project should move forward, a project manager and organization owner should be assigned. A preliminary software project management plan should be developed and the project development environment should be established.

Project Portfolio Management

Projects have a defined start point and an end point based on the deliverables produced. While projects are executing, they are part of the organization's project portfolio. A project portfolio is a group of projects carried out under the sponsorship and/or management of an organization. They are grouped together for these reasons:

- They are part of the same product family.
- They compete for scarce resources.
- Project deliverables and interim development artifacts are interdependent.
- There are multiple and conflicting organization objectives in making selection.
- Selection criteria are qualitative or quantitative, based on specific organization objectives.
- Political objectives play a role.

Different models can be used for portfolio selection. The models must be linked to corporate strategy, as opposed to simple profit maximization or furthering of a single product. By grouping projects into portfolios, the development process is aided in its conversion from chaotic to manageable by strategic concentration of product focus. There ends up being fewer projects in focused areas that can capitalize on research and development investments, strategic alliances and partnerships, and potential technology breakthroughs.

Portfolio models define a strategic domain process within an organization. This differs from company to company, absolutely must involve executive management, and determines direction, focus, and budget allocations for the projects that will build the organization's products. The criteria development for a portfolio model must be reviewed at regular intervals to ensure that the adopted strategy is updated to suit the current business and economic environment.

Portfolio models consider relative value of projects and resource interactions. They can be *ad hoc* in response to market conditions—market-driven portfolios. They can be rule based and prescriptive—drop any project with an internal rate of return below 15%. Portfolio models can take a broad definition of projects and include large numbers of optional projects for comparison. This type of portfolio model may involve pair-wise comparison of project attributes using a method such as analytic hierarchy process.[1]

There are three classes of portfolio models to understand. The first is a pure economic return model that uses financial measures of internal rate of return, net present value, marginal cost of capital, return on investment and assets and invested capital, and weighted average cost of capital (WACC). Figure 5–11 shows how this model is applied in its simplest fashion. Over time, the line that tracks the cost of asset deployment rises and falls with respect to the WACC. Projects that have a return above this moving line are earning a return above the WACC. Those that are below the line need to be evaluated for termination. This model can be used to both track historic trends and predict the future cost of asset deployment. Appendix C has a complete discussion on all the financial measures to be used in an economic project selection model.

In the economic model, a project is in or out of the portfolio based on how it performs relative to a financial "hurdle rate." This rate could be any of the internal rates of return used in the evaluating organization. For the figure, WACC is used. Over time, the WACC per project is calculated and plotted. Because WACC is a percentage, another line over time may be plotted, and that could be cost of assets deployed. There can be a return on investment (ROI) line plotted based on WACC. At any point in time, a project that falls below the ROI could be canceled. In the case of Figure 5–11, projects 2, 3, and 5 would be canceled for being below the ROI. Project 3 might be evaluated because it is still above the cost of assets deployed.

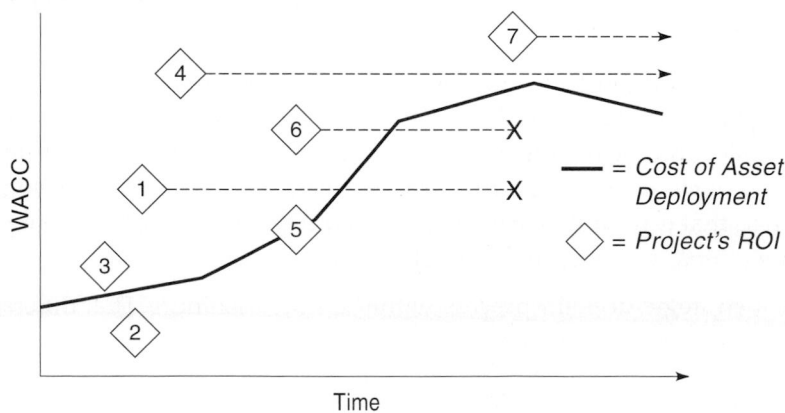

FIGURE 5–11
Economic Return Model Project Selection

Cost-benefit models are the second class of portfolio evaluation models. Employing benefit/cost analysis techniques, these models compare project alternatives when some benefits are not tangible (e.g. internal projects or public projects). Relative benefits are determined for each project and are factored by cost or relative cost. Projects are then ranked according to the benefit-to-cost ratio, where a higher ratio is better.

Market research models are the third class and are used almost exclusively for new products. Inadequate market analysis has been determined to be the number-one cause of product failure. Some techniques for the market research approach are focus groups, market surveys, consumer panels, and test marketing.

When the class of portfolio model to implement has been decided upon, the method for scoring the results of the model must be determined. A weighted scoring technique measures the amount of model conformance defined based on the class of the portfolio model chosen. Importance weights are developed for each measure, and the portfolio team scores each project on all measures. The average of the sum of weighted scores for each project is calculated, and projects are ranked according to result. Portfolio matrices display project portfolio decision data in two or three dimensions of risk, length of project, cost, and other factors critical to the selection model.

The Delphi scoring model is an excellent method to be used along with weighted scoring to take advantage of experts' decisions for validation of the organization's unique portfolio model. An effective strategy for aggregating information from the expertise of decision makers, this technique employs interaction among group members who are isolated from each other to preclude forceful group members from dominating the discussion and stifling contributions of other group members. The experts are separated and given questionnaires soliciting their opinions and reasons for them. These questionnaires are then circulated anonymously to each other group member. After each round of questionnaires, information is consolidated and again circulated anonymously among group members. This is a strategy to maximize decision-making benefits of a group while limiting some of its weaknesses.

For mature and experienced development and marketing organizations, optimization models are employed to combine the selection, scoring, validation, and presentation techniques. Optimization handles resource constraints and interdependence due to mutual exclusivity or precedence. Maximizing return on specific objectives and preparing an optimum product and project schedule are outputs of optimization. This fits into a portfolio selection framework in which the process is:

- Simple (logical series of steps)
- Flexible (users can select their favorite models)
- Repeatable (different analysts can get "close" to the same result)
- Documented (how did we make that decision?)
- Extendable (environment constraints will change)

Understanding Financial Processes _____

The final domain process for the project manager to understand is the financial aspect of the project. Many of the techniques are included in the economic selection models previously discussed and in Appendix C. The understanding that the project manager needs is one of the interrelationships among the various ways that a financial evaluation is done on a project or business unit. The most widely used technique is shown in Figure 5–12.

Fundamentally, any project selection or portfolio analysis criteria decision that influences product prices, per-unit costs, volume, or efficiency will impact profit margin or turnover ratio. And any decision that affects the amount and type of debt and equity used will impact the financial structure as well as cost. The domain of financial analysts and the office of the chief financial officer for many organizations use this analysis technique to decide on the funding of projects.

These financial concepts are important to understand because every business in the world is competing for capital. Money flows where the perceived risk adjusted return is greatest. If we as project managers and marketers of products and services to businesses understand these financial concepts, we can better understand where we might be able to maximize help to our customers. Helping our customers as stakeholders in our projects leads to the success of our projects and products.

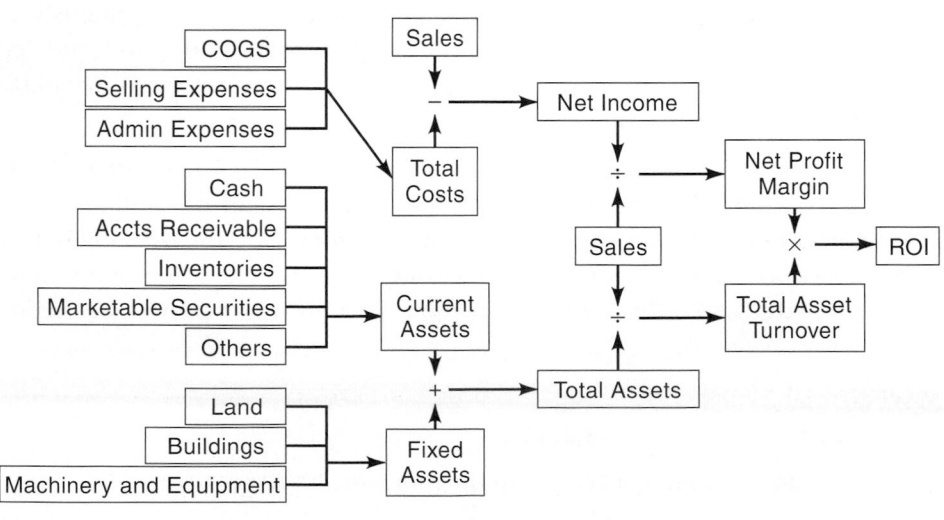

FIGURE 5–12
DuPont Financial Model

Summary

Domain processes are the interrelated activities specific to the functioning of the organization for which a software project is developed. The measure of quality for a software project is based on how well the software solves specific domain-related problems. For the software customer, the view is from his business domain, not that of a computer scientist or software engineer. To deliver quality software, the project manager must understand the domain for which the software solves specific needs.

Domain processes that are common to all organizations are defined criteria for project selection models, project portfolio analysis, and the communication of basic financial ratios for project analysis. Each of these common domain process management activities was discussed in this chapter.

Managing domain processes requires a framing of the software development project within the organization. Figure 5–1 showed how the corporate, product, and project life cycles relate. The corporate business life cycle produces many products. These products are in different life cycle phases at any one point in time. A product life cycle begins after a need has been identified and when project conception has begun. A healthy corporation has many products and a managed number of projects under development. Each product may have one or more than one project in execution at any one time to complete the product family. Projects have a defined start and end point. In the product life cycle, a project begins after feasibility and is executed within the product acquisition phase. The project begins at initiation based on acquisition needs and ends at delivery, when the project deliverables are placed into operation.

A project manager must be able to define criteria for project selection. There will always be more projects than resources to adequately execute those projects. One of the key topics in this chapter is defining those criteria and putting them into a model structure for decision. The ability to analyze a portfolio of projects and select the "best" one based on all known information is a skill that all project managers need to possess. Portfolio management looks at projects from the point of view of a return on investment based on what an organization feels is an effective internal rate of return. This financial view of selecting projects is appropriate for any size of organization in any stage of maturity. It levels projects to a common comparative measure: money.

Problems for Review

1. You are the only project manager in a new software application tool company. This is your first product. How does project selection management work for you?
2. Using the domain categorization matrices, develop a set for each one of these products:
   a. An enhancement to your company's payroll system;

b. A new avionics system for the latest single-engine Cessna private aircraft;

c. A GPS addition to the Palm OS for the new wireless Palm Pilot;

d. New code to handle the latest transmission in the next model year's Ford Explorer.

3. How would you apply the DuPont model in a government organization?

4. How would you plan to use portfolio management processes if you were an information resource manager for your state's Office of the Attorney General?

Visit the Case Study _____

Over the objections of the marketing manager, your boss has accepted the 1074 plan for the life cycle. The only issue is that the CASE tool is still a line item on your business unit executive's bonus plan. You can use whatever life cycle you want, but you must use the corporate CASE tool for all the support processes. How will you modify your project plan to use xTRemeObjectMaker? Is there an impact on the final deliverable to the CRM? What is the cost when you go to install the prototype and bid on the total project? A cost sheet has not yet been prepared for xTRemeObjectMaker, but it will cost in the neighborhood of a single-site Oracle development system license.

Citations _____

[1]Saaty, Thomas L. (1990). "Multicriteria Decision Making." *The Analytic Hierarchy Process: Planning Priority Setting, Resource Allocation,* Volume I, AHP Series, extended edition. New York, NY: McGraw-Hill.

Web Pages for Further Information_____

quote.yahoo.com/. Yahoo! financial data Web site for all types of corporate financial information.

www.investorguide.com/EDGAR.htm. Search engine that takes the EDGAR information and develops a real-time index for easy retrieval.

www.sb.gov.bc.ca/smallbus/workshop/sample.html. URL to sample business plan.

www.sec.gov/edgarhp.htm. Security and Exchange Commission's Electronic Data Gathering, Analysis and Retrieval System.

Selecting a
Project Team

The selection of a project team occurs early in the life cycle of a software development project. The selection of team members, the stages of team building that occur, and the way in which the team morphs all support and affect the remainder of the activities in the life cycle. The information presented in this chapter forms the background needed to fully understand how individual personalities affect the ability of a team to create positive synergy.

Many project teams exhibit behavioral characteristics of a single personality. Some are productive, some are seemingly dysfunctional, and others exhibit wide mood swings. The manifestation of a team's character is based on the dynamics of the team members—the emergent personality critically affects the accomplishment of project goals. Team members may be added or deleted as the project leader discovers conflicts, but such changes come with a price: Any change in membership will require the group to go through team formation stages all over again before the team can perform.

A team personality is complete with spoken and unspoken rules and constantly shifting relationships. As new members join the team and existing ones depart, the character of the team changes. It may also change as the project moves through the phases of its life cycle. A dominant personality (or two) usually emerges soon after formation, and the dynamics of the workgroup change over time. As the project progresses through initial stages of confusion and later stages of ideal cooperation, the leader must recognize the signs of dysfunctionality and act accordingly to halt the unwelcome transformation. This is no simple task because the human personality is far more complex than any science or technology rooted in physics. Yet, if left unattended, the negative aspects of clashing personalities can wreak havoc on the project and sometimes destroy individual team members.

Chapter 29, "Reporting and Communicating," will describe communication aspects of a project team; Chapter 25, "Project Tracking and Control," will discuss how to track team progress. Selecting the right team members and correctly building the team at the beginning of the project life cycle will facilitate these skills. To understand how to apply leadership to project teams, we'll first explore individual uniqueness, then project team dynamics, and, finally, specific leadership techniques.

Where We Are in the Product Development Life Cycle

Information in this chapter begins in the early stages of a project, during initiation. However, project teams constantly morph, especially with large or lengthy projects. The selection and formation of a project team supports the entire life cycle and is therefore integral to every phase, but the first team formation occurs early in the project, as shown in Figure 6–1. This is the background necessary to fully understand personalities of individuals and how personalities of teams, which are greater than the sum of the parts, are formed.

Chapter 6 Relation to the 34 Competencies

Selecting a project team fits within the following ten competencies:

Product Development Techniques

   6. **Managing subcontractors**—Planning, managing, and monitoring performance
  11. **Understanding development activities**—Learning the software development cycle

Project Management Skills

  14. **Estimating cost**—Estimating cost to complete the project
  15. **Estimating effort**—Estimating effort required to complete the project
  16. **Managing risks**—Identifying and determining the impact and handling of risks

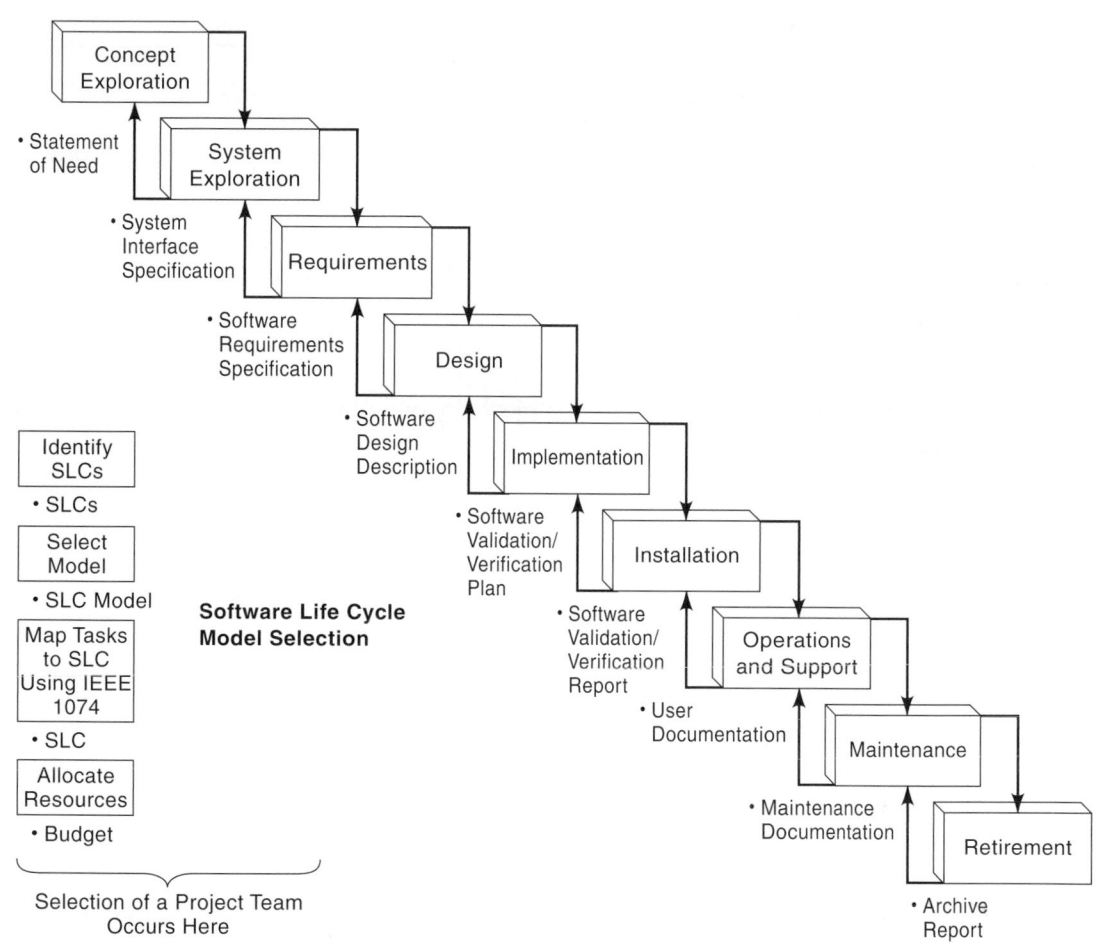

FIGURE 6–1
Selection of Project Team Occurs at the Beginning of the Life Cycle

People Management Skills

26. **Interaction and communication**—Dealing with developers, upper management, and other teams
27. **Leadership**—Coaching project teams for optimal results
32. **Recruiting**—Recruiting and interviewing team members successfully
33. **Selecting a team**—Choosing highly competent teams
34. **Teambuilding**—Forming, guiding, and maintaining an effective team

Learning Objectives for Chapter 6 _____

Upon completion of this chapter, the reader should be able to:

- Explain the importance of selecting team members with a mix of personality types, to comprise a software development project team;
- Describe various personality typing models;
- Discuss individual work styles and the impact that they can have on a project;
- Describe the phases of team development;
- Describe communication paths;
- Discuss decentralized versus centralized project documentation and the effects on the project team communication;
- Discuss leadership styles and how they affect the team.

Selecting a Project Team _____

The IEEE-CS/ACM joint task force on Software Engineering Ethics and Professional Practices (SEEPP) has developed a code of ethics for software engineers. It contains eight sets of guiding principles:

1. **Public**—Software engineers shall act consistently with the public interest.
2. **Client and employer**—Software engineers shall act in a manner that is in the best interests of their client and employer, and that is consistent with the public interest.
3. **Product**—Software engineers shall ensure that their products and related modifications meet the highest professional standards possible.
4. **Judgment**—Software engineers shall maintain integrity and independence in their professional judgment.
5. **Management**—Software engineering managers and leaders shall subscribe to and promote an ethical approach to the management of software development and maintenance.
6. **Profession**—Software engineers shall advance the integrity and reputation of the profession consistent with the public interest.
7. **Colleagues**—Software engineers shall be fair to and supportive of their colleagues.
8. **Self**—Software engineers shall participate in lifelong learning regarding the practice of their profession, and promote an ethical approach to the practice of the profession.

Principles 7 and 8 contain language that is pertinent to the formation and maintenance of teams. As we delve into the "personalities of project teams," it is relevant that we, as project managers and leaders, keep in mind that we are the guardians of our staff. In addition to maintaining awareness of our own actions toward the team, we can encourage the team to behave ethically toward each other as well as themselves.

Principle 7: Colleagues

Software engineers shall be fair to and supportive of their colleagues. In particular, software engineers shall, as appropriate:

7.01. Encourage colleagues to adhere to this code.

7.02. Assist colleagues in professional development.

7.03. Credit fully the work of others and refrain from taking undue credit.

7.04. Review the work of others in an objective, candid, and properly documented way.

7.05. Give a fair hearing to the opinions, concerns, or complaints of a colleague.

7.06. Assist colleagues in being fully aware of current standard work practices, including policies and procedures for protecting passwords, files and other confidential information, and security measures in general.

7.07. Not unfairly intervene in the career of any colleague; however, concern for the employer, the client, or public interest may compel software engineers, in good faith, to question the competence of a colleague.

7.08. In situations outside their own areas of competence, call upon the opinions of other professionals who have competence in that area.

Principle 8: Self

Software engineers shall participate in lifelong learning regarding the practice of their profession and shall promote an ethical approach to the practice of the profession. In particular, software engineers shall continually endeavor to:

8.01. Further their knowledge of developments in the analysis, specification, design, development, maintenance, and testing of software and related documents, together with the management of the development process.

8.02. Improve their ability to create safe, reliable, and useful quality software at reasonable cost and within a reasonable time.

8.03. Improve their ability to produce accurate, informative, and well-written documentation.

8.04. Improve their understanding of the software and related documents on which they work and of the environment in which they will be used.

8.05. Improve their knowledge of relevant standards and the law governing the software and related documents on which they work.

8.06. Improve their knowledge of this code, its interpretation, and its application to their work.

8.07. Not give unfair treatment to anyone because of any irrelevant prejudices.

8.08. Not influence others to undertake any action that involves a breach of this code.

8.09. Recognize that personal violations of this code are inconsistent with being a professional software engineer.

A leader must understand at least one model of determining individual and team personalities thoroughly to be able to assess the health of relationships on project teams. Understanding several models gives the leader even more insight. In addition to being versed in current project management technology, managers today must be equipped to select, form, motivate, and lead increasingly complex teams. Most software projects are so complex that no single individual can accomplish the goal; project teams are required to meet the technological challenges. As IBM's Fred Brooks pointed out in his landmark paper "No Silver Bullet" in 1987, no single tool will solve all the problems of the day, technical or otherwise.

To ensure project, program, and business success, the contemporary company must recognize that project teams and their managers require a careful blend of structure and flexibility, dictating and delegating, speaking and listening, and managing and leading. This is, of course, in addition to the required technical savvy.

The Software Engineering Institute offers a People Capability Maturity Model® (P-CMM®), which adapts the maturity framework of the Capability Maturity Model® for Software (CMM®) for managing and developing an organization's work force. The motivation for the P-CMM is to radically improve the ability of software organizations to attract, develop, motivate, organize, and retain the talent needed to continuously improve software development capability. The P-CMM is designed to allow software organizations to integrate workforce improvement with software process improvement programs guided by the SW-CMM. The P-CMM can also be used by any kind of organization as a guide for improving its people-related and work-force practices. Bill Curtis, along with William E. Hefley and Sally Miller, is a primary author of the P-CMM.

Experts such as Bill Curtis tell us that the largest variable in the success of a project is the skill of the people on the project team. The project manager's job is not to throw away whole teams and hire new ones for specific projects, but to get the most performance out of employees, new or existing, through management and leadership. When people on a team don't perform in concert, the result is cacophony, at best, and possibly an unfinished symphony.

This chapter explores methods and approaches to aid a project or program manager in understanding the developing personality of a project team. It will also provide guidance on the selection, structure, motivation, and maintenance of a project team.

The Whole Is the Sum of the Parts _____

The personality of a project is comprised of individuals who, in turn, have complex personalities. Taibi Kahler suggests, Observing people is like observing holograms. A hologram consists of hundreds of thousands of independent images, each of which portrays a complete object from a slightly different angle. Combined, these images create a three-dimensional display. When we view the entire display, we "get the whole picture." When we perceive a person, we "get the whole picture" of an entire personality, consisting of separate units of behavior linked in sequences or patterns. Some patterns are natural, healthy and constructive. Others are learned, negative behaviors that we exhibit when distressed.[1]

As an organization deploys the project management methodologies, care must be taken not to become so involved in the technical aspects, such as project registers and scheduling tools, that we lose sight of the real strength of the business—its people and the rich diversity of experience that they hold. The project leader must gain skill in handling people, seeing their holographic facets, and recognizing their healthy and unhealthy behavior patterns, not merely employing the processes and tools of the methodology.

Many project managers achieve their rank by having been technical experts in a given domain. A key skill, often unnatural among technical leaders, is the ability to recognize the mix of personalities that a project team possesses and maximize that mix for productivity. A team is made up of independent images, just as is each person. Several models are available from the behavioral sciences to help us with the composite. Each of us harbors a little bit of darkness within our individual personality. Management theory contains several personality models that explain how the team's collective unconstructive traits may be controlled.

Individual Personality Type

Starting with the individual, several personality models have been derived from Carl Jung's theory of "psychological types." The Myers-Briggs Type Indicator (MBTI), the Fundamental Interpersonal Relations Orientation—Behavior (FIRO-B) model, the Keirsey Temperament Sorter, the Kahler Process Communication Model (PCM), and the WorkStyle Patterns™ Inventory from the McFletcher Corporation, represent a few. There are more than 150 models published, but we will discuss seven that are readily implementable.

Myers-Briggs Type Indicator   The Myers-Briggs Personality Type Indicator may be the most popular and widespread, having been in use for more than 40 years. With millions of people assessed all over the world, its validity is continually updated and debated. It is usually administered and interpreted by professionals formally trained in its use. MBTI identifies four bipolar dimensions of behavior, measuring self-reported preferences on each one, which allows for 16 different personality descriptions, identified by 4-letter codes. The type dimensions are illustrated in Table 6–1.

Much can be found on the Web about MBTI, including an abbreviated version of the test instrument and a discussion that relates the model to leadership. For the technical disciplines, many personality types (about 60%) fall into the ISTJ type. Regional or national culture can provide a modifying context for expressing type, as discussed in a later section.

TABLE 6–1
Myers-Briggs Type Indicator (MBTI)

MBTI Type Dimension	Characteristics
Introvert (**I, E**) Extrovert	*Source and Direction of Energy:* **I**: From internal concentration (is drained of energy by being around others) **E**: From external contact ("plugs into" the energy of others)
Sensing (**S, N**) i**N**tuitive	*Preferred Method of Information Reception:* **S**: Prefers empirical, sensory data **N**: Prefers meaningful patterns and abstractions
Thinking (**T, F**) Feeling	*Way of Information Processing:* **T**: Makes decisions according to their impersonal logic **F**: Makes a decision according to their personal values
Judging (**J, P**) Perceiving	*Way of Living Out Processed Information:* **J**: Organizes all life events and acts strictly according to their plans **P**: Inclined to improvisation and seeking different alternatives

FIRO-B Instrument   Another tool that requires certification to administer is the Fundamental Interpersonal Relations Orientation-Measuring Behavior (FIRO-B), a multiple-choice questionnaire developed by William C. Schutz, Ph.D. It is an efficient measure of interpersonal relationships, and it has been normalized by data from tens of thousands of individuals across 15 occupations.[2] It measures three fundamental dimensions of interpersonal relationships in a very short period of time. Most behavioral test instruments tend to ask a lot of questions, so the brevity of the FIRO-B is a welcome relief from "test fatigue."

According to Schutz, all humans possess three basic needs, to a greater or lesser degree. They are the needs for *inclusion*, *control*, and *affection*.[3] Inclusion is the inner drive "to establish and maintain a satisfactory relation with people with respect to interaction and association." It has to do with being "in" or "out." A person may need inclusion from others or might need to reach out to others, expressing inclusion. Control is "the need to establish and maintain a satisfactory relation with people with respect to control and power." It has to do with being on top or on the bottom. As with inclusion, it works in two directions, but a high need for both getting and giving power are not usually found in the same person. The third need of the triad is "the need to establish and maintain a satisfactory relationship with others with respect to love and affection." It has to do with being close or far. As shown in Table 6–2, in the FIRO-B Model, the six inner needs are the desires of a well-balanced individual.

TABLE 6–2
The FIRO-B Model

Direction	Inclusion	Control	Affection
Wants from others	Acceptance	Guidance	Closeness
Expresses to others	Interest	Leadership	Liking

Schutz claims that the needs profile of a person is shaped by that person's parents or care-givers in childhood, and these needs are not likely to change in a lifetime.

Applying the FIRO-B postulate of compatibility to teams helps determine which individuals will work well together and which ones will clash. In some cases, it is desirable to have team members who possess similar traits (two people are compatible if both express and desire little affection); in other cases, it is best to mix complementary traits (it might not work if two people on the same team have a high need for control but they have different goals). Schutz's principle of group interaction is that each of the three needs comes to prominence at different points of the group's life cycle:

> The typical sequence is: inclusion→control→affection. During initial meetings, members try to determine where they fit and how much they're willing to invest in the group. This is the inclusion phase. As these primary identity issues are resolved, the emphasis switches to questions of control. What are the ground rules? Who will be the leader? How much responsibility will be shared? When this struggle is resolved, the group slides into the affection phase, which centers on positive attraction, pairing, jealousy, and hostility… this sequence recurs in groups that continue to meet.[4]

Later, we'll see that this sequence closely follows a popular model of team formation behavior.

Keirsey Temperament Sorter   Closely related to MBTI is the Keirsey Temperament Sorter, derived from the work of David Keirsey in his book *Please Understand Me*.[5] It is accessible via the Internet, does not require professional administration, and offers the personality test instrument in four languages (Spanish, Portuguese, German, and Norwegian).[6] Keirsey's model identifies four temperament types, with variants as described in Table 6–3.

Kahler Process Communication Model   The Kahler Process Communication Model (PCM) is a six-part description based on transactional analysis, which analyzes personalities by observing how one conducts transactions with others (their "miniscripts"). It is administered and interpreted by formally trained professionals enabling you to understand, motivate, and communicate more effectively with others on a project team. PCM has profiled more than a half-million people in 20 different countries, and is used by NASA to evaluate astronaut candidates.[7] The six personality types identified in PCM are described in Table 6–4.

TABLE 6–3

Keirsey Temperament Sorter

Keirsey's Type (with MBTI Labels)	Characteristics
Guardians, SJs Supervisors (ESTJ) Inspectors (ISTJ) Providers (ESFJ) Protectors (ISFJ)	**Concrete** in communicating **Cooperative** in implementing goals; can become highly skilled in logistics
Artisans, SPs Promoters (ESTP) Crafters (ISTP) Performers (ESFP) Composers (ISFP)	**Concrete** in communicating **Utilitarian** in implementing goals; can become highly skilled in **tactical variation**
Idealists, NFs Teachers (ENFJ) Counselors (INFJ) Champions (ENFP) Healers (INFP)	**Abstract** in communicating **Cooperative** in implementing goals; can become highly skilled in **diplomatic integration**
Rationals, NTs Field Marshals (ENTJ) Masterminds (INTJ) Inventors (ENTP) Architects (INTP)	**Abstract** in communicating **Utilitarian** in implementing goals; can become highly skilled in **strategic analysis**

TABLE 6–4

Kahler Process Communication Model (PCM)

PCM Type	Characteristics
Dreamer	Imaginative, reflective, calm, introspective, directable Motivated into action by things and people
Workaholic	Logical, responsible, organized, time-oriented Perceptions through logic, things
Reactor	Warm, sensitive, compassionate, kind, empathetic, nurturing Perceptions through feelings and emotions
Rebel	Spontaneous, creative, playful, expressive, energetic Reactions through likes and dislikes
Persister	Dedicated, observant, conscientious, tenacious Evaluates through opinions
Promoter	Adaptable, persuasive, charming, resourceful Action-oriented

A key feature of this model is that it accounts for a person's changes in apparent personality over the course of his lifetime. These phase shifts are important for a team leader to identify because they may be misinterpreted as a Dr. Jekyll–Mr. Hyde transformation. The PCM model requires a full-day class from a trained professional to understand and apply it effectively.[8]

Non-Jungian sources for personality models are the Enneagram,[9, 10] and Richard Bandler's Neuro-Linguistic Programming (NLP).[11]

Enneagram   The Enneagram, a centuries-old nine-part model with roots in the Middle East, measures nine basic defensive styles and gives breakthrough feedback and strategies for managing individual stress. The nine parts to the Enneagram model are related as illustrated in Figure 6–2.

The Enneagram has been related to the MBTI types as illustrated in Table 6–5.[12]

Model Usage   When used properly, surprising results are often obtained from using any one of these models, revealing the reasons why certain people do or don't work well together.

It is important for a project manager to gain some skill in recognizing personality patterns and predicting their interaction. Mostly, the models mentioned divide personalities into patterns of behavior describing a map of an individual's personality.[13–18] It is important to remember that these are only maps to a territory, not the territory itself. The models, when applied with experience and caution, *are* a big help. As a leader, you should thoroughly understand at least one of these models to help you read and deal with individual and team personalities.

Cultural Influences

Cultural patterns are another dimension to individual and team personalities. The cultural diversity of many modern companies is well known, and global project teams are becoming more common. Cultural patterns vary by country and region, and affect team members' expectations. Cultures can influence individual personality expression by providing a framework of

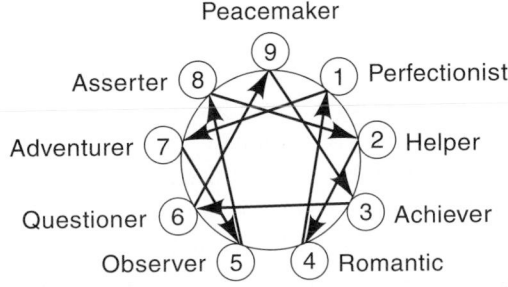

FIGURE 6–2
The Enneagram

TABLE 6–5
MBTI and Enneagram Types

Enneagram Types	MBTI Types
Perfectionist	Judging
Helper	Extrovert, Feeling
Achiever	Extrovert, Sensing, Judging
Romantic	iNtuitive, Feeling, Perceiving
Observer	Introvert, Thinking
Questioner	Introvert
Adventurer	Extrovert, iNtuitive
Asserter	Extrovert, iNtuitive, Thinking, Perceiving
Peacemaker	iNtuitive, Perceiving

norms within which personality types operate. For example, the United States is an apparent MBTI extroverted culture, as compared to the apparent introverted cultures in the United Kingdom and Japan. Also, German participants are typically prepared for meetings and stick closely to the agenda (MBTI SJ behavior), while Latin American participants are ready to improvise and feel free to start on unexpected topics (NP behavior). Latinos also easily speak their mind (E), while Scandinavians need to express themselves only if they disagree with a decision (I).[19] In Asia, the members' relationships are considered most important (NF), whereas, in Western countries (United States and European), money and tasks are usually weighted more heavily (ST). Some older American women, having grown up in the South or the Southwest, may fear ageism (the United States is not a culture of "respect for elders," as in Japan) and may have trouble discussing money matters. American businesspeople frequently jump right into "making the deal," whereas Latin Americans, Asians, and Europeans carefully build a trusting relationship first.

To understand cultural patterns better, project managers can take short classes available to increase sensitivity to cultural issues. If you have a multinational project team, the members may be divided by the common business language of a company's English (well, American, actually). A good way to gain some quick vocabulary with which to build trust (it helps to show that you are trying even if you aren't proficient) is to take a short immersion course in one or more of your project team members' languages (e.g., Berlitz). It will help you with the basics but also allow you to absorb some of the local cultural patterns. This will help you to read individuals' motives and actions better because language is inextricably related to culture.

Personal Motivation

Kahler suggests that understanding a person's "home-base" psychological needs (birth), in addition to the phase of life in which he is currently operating (environment), will give rise to an understanding of what motivates the person individually and in teams. Table 6–6 shows motivators for the previous personality structure.

TABLE 6–6
PCM Motivators

PCM Type	PCM Motivators
Dreamer	Solitude and direction Time alone to reflect and to be creative
Workaholic	Work recognition: awards, bonuses, pat on the back Structured time and a plan
Reactor	A pleasant environment (both places and people) Comfort and relaxation
Rebel	Frequent interaction with others Personal contact and fun
Persister	Recognition of achievements due to strong commitment to a mission or goal
Promoter	Risk taking High finance

Channels of communication are as important as perceptions for each type—a PCM workaholic would probably rather have "just the facts" than be nurtured.

With a handle on personal motivation, the team manager/leader also discovers what to avoid and what behavior is causing distress and therefore lack of productivity, as illustrated in Table 6–7.

In understanding personal motivation for each team member's performance, individual drivers can be discovered. Does an individual value peer recognition, career path enhancement, financial reward, self-sabotage, or something else?

Several theories relating to motivation in management literature help provide maps to this territory as well. Some of the more useful ones are shown in Table 6–8.[20]

A modern project manager must understand the basics of these models for managing motivation in people and organizations. Much information on these models of organizational behavior can be found in general management literature because they are usually part of any MBA program. See the references for recommended reading.[13, 21]

TABLE 6–7
Leadership Behaviors

PCM Type	Managers Should Avoid These Behaviors	Or They May See These Reactions
Dreamer	*Laissez-faire* style Overstimulating environment	Withdrawal Not finishing tasks
Workaholic	Being too personal Canceling projects with no logical reason	Criticism of others Frustration about fairness, money, order, and so on
Reactor	Autocratic style Pointing out mistakes	Overadaptation to others Self-doubt Criticism
Rebel	Restricting to time frames Preaching	Negativity Complaints Blame
Persister	Autocratic style Power plays Redefinition	Crusades Verbal attacks Righteousness
Promoter	Wishy-washy style Confrontation	Arguments Negative drama Rule breaking

TABLE 6–8
Models of Individual Motivation

Motivation Model	Brief Description	Creator
Expectancy Theory	An effort-performance relationship exists. People perform if they expect to be rewarded.	Victor Vroom
Path-Goal Model	Clarify the path to a performer's perceived goal, and they will work to achieve it.	Robert House
Goal-Setting Theory	Commitment increases if performers set their own goals.	Edwin Locke

(Continues)

TABLE 6–8 (Continued)
Models of Individual Motivation

Motivation Model	Brief Description	Creator
Hawthorne Effect	Just the act of measuring will influence the outcome of a social experiment. When watched, people perform as the watchers expect them to.	Elton Mayo
Force Field Analysis	Status quo is maintained by driving and restraining forces in opposition. Change agents must identify these and change them to implement any lasting organizational change.	Kurt Lewin
Theory X and Theory Y	Predispositioned attitudes toward people: X: People are inherently lazy and must be forced to work. Y: People will be self-directed and creative if favorably motivated.	Douglas McGregor
Theory Z	Actually, Organization Type Z: Combines the best of American and Japanese management in a humanistic manner.	William Ouchi
Motivator/Hygiene Theory	Motivator: An element of work that satisfies a performer's needs Hygiene: Factors that must be present for any motivation	Frederick Herzberg
Hierarchy of Needs	People have a needs hierarchy: Physiological (food) Safety (security, shelter) Love (social belonging) Self-esteem (ego) Self-actualization (fulfillment)	Abraham Maslow

Parts Need to Work Together

Seemingly obvious but often overlooked is the importance of choosing a good team (when possible) and preparing the members for the project. A large number of projects fail because the team never "jells." Many times, project leaders are given team members based on personnel availability rather than being able to choose them. Nevertheless, preparation by the project manager to understand individual personalities and team dynamics is the key to creating a successful working group.

Hire for Trait and Train for Skill

It is much easier to start with a positive, jelled team that might deteriorate later than to start with a dysfunctional team in the first place. Whenever possible, select team members for their compatible and complementary personality traits rather than their demonstrated skill in a particular area. This seems contrary to popular belief at first, but it makes sense when you understand that it is easier to train people in a new technical (and often rapidly changing) skill than to change their personality. Most people enjoy learning new things anyway. The training need not be formal. The general ability to rapidly learn and adjust to constantly changing information is often more valuable than deep experience in one or two skill areas, assuming that basic competency in the core technologies. Of course, if the person's personality does not fit the task, stress results and less desirable characteristics begin to appear.

McFletcher WorkStyle Patterns Inventory   A useful instrument for explaining behavior is the WorkStyle Patterns™ Inventory (WSPI) from the McFletcher Corporation. The purpose of the assessment is to identify how a person *prefers to approach work* versus *the approach that the position or current assignment requires*, and it may be administered by a facilitator certified by McFletcher. Analysis of discrepancies between a person's preferred workstyle and their actual workstyle can produce various degrees of stress, which may be manifested in a variety of ways.

McFletcher defines two kinds of stress: personal and organizational. Typical personal responses to stress include apathy or low productivity, irritability and frequent complaints, and health disorders or illnesses. Personal stress usually occurs because you want to perform more activities of a specific kind than the position requires.

Organizational stress can be observed through misunderstandings of work expectations, product quality and customer service problems, missed deadlines, and high turnover. Organizational stress may result when the position requires more activities of a specific kind than you are inclined to perform.

According to the inventory, a person may fall into one of the categories indicated in Table 6–9.

TABLE 6–9
McFletcher WorkStyle Inventory Model

Category	Focus	Types
Worker	Task	Specialist
		Perfecter
		Technician
		Worker
		Superworker
		Independent Worker
Supervisor	Project	Guardian
		Supervisor
Manager	Organization	Adaptor
		Synthesist
		Innovator
		Challenger
		Manager
		Promoter
		Appraiser
		Project Manager

Each of these profiles is explained in depth, and the contribution to the organization of each is described in the inventory booklet. The inventory (questionnaire) scores are graphed as a discrepancy of *preference* versus *actual position*, as shown in the example in Figure 6–3.

The sample graph in Figure 6–3 shows profile scores for a team leader with a preferred workstyle of independent worker and an actual position workstyle of supervisor. He prefers to work independently through managing his own work. The position requires coordinating the work of others. Perhaps the team leader wants to perform more direct computer work, whereas his position requires more coordinating, coaching, and scheduling activities than he is inclined to do.[22] This is typical for many technologists promoted to a position of leadership. This team leader may want to consider obtaining some coaching or even making a job change.

The work styles of each team member may be plotted on a summary chart, validating a complementary mix of work styles or exposing a conflict or imbalance. For example, if everyone wants to redesign the health-care system, there may be no one left to administer care to the patient.

The Skill Gap   Again, a leader's ability to quickly assess a person's personality characteristics will go well beyond the one-sided balance sheet of accomplishments called a resumé. In fact, resumés can be terribly misleading.

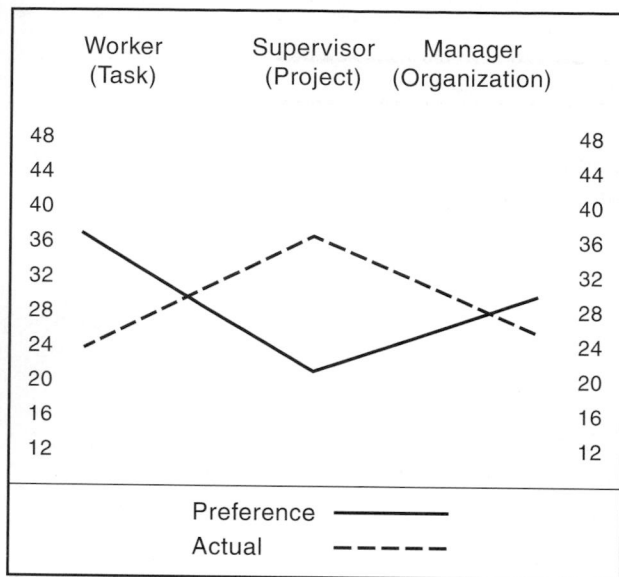

FIGURE 6–3
Sample McFletcher WorkStyle Inventory

When Bill Curtis, a behavioral scientist and coauthor of the Capability Model for Software, was at ITT in the early 1980s, he conducted a study of how the skill of programmers could impact a technical project schedule. He seeded a Fortran program with bugs and then timed a sampling of ITT's programmers on how long it took them to find all the seeded errors.[23] All of the participants were Fortran programmers by trade. The results were astonishing. The differences in technical skill performance varied by 20 to 1. That is, it took the worst programmer 20 times longer to find the bugs than the best programmer. This kind of variation has more impact to a project than any method or process followed. Imagine trying to build and hold to a plan with this kind of variation underlying the schedule!

Curtis also discovered that there was little correlation of skill, as measured by the test, to the individuals' education, experience, and qualifications as represented in their resumés. This revelation means that it is critical for the project manager to understand the subtleties of personality differences. Managers/leaders who are trained in motivational theory are better at observing different types and responding to their needs. When appropriate, such managers are also capable of employing professional personality-typing instruments to deepen understanding of the team's needs. Examples of such instruments are those offered by Alignment Products and Processes from the previously mentioned McFletcher Corporation.

Understand Group Dynamics

A leader must recognize how teams form to be able to lead them properly. A well-known model of team formation is the five-stage model shown in Table 6–10.

TABLE 6–10
Team Formation Model

Stage	Description
Forming	Members find out: what they will be doing, the styles of acceptable leadership, and possible kinds of interpersonal and task relationships. Characterized by: courtesy, confusion, caution, and commonality.
Storming	Members begin resisting the influence of the group. There is conflict over competing approaches to reaching the group's goals. Characterized by: tension, criticism, and confrontation.
Norming	Resistance is overcome as the group: establishes its rules and standards, develops intragroup cohesiveness, and delineates task standards and expectations. Characterized by: cooperation, collaboration, cohesion, and commitment.
Performing	The group is ready to focus attention on task accomplishment. Issues of interpersonal relations, member status, and division of tasks are settled. Characterized by: challenge, creativity, group consciousness, and consideration of members.
Adjourning	The group has fulfilled its purpose or died. Characterized by: compromise, communication, consensus, and closure.

This model depicts the process of how a group decides on its operating profile. The profile is different for every group and is time- and place-dependent. This is why there is one set of accepted behavior for team members in a project meeting and a different set at the local pub, even though membership may be the same.[24, 25]

Every team experiences this cycle and often repeats it many times during the course of a project. Each time a new member joins the team or an old member departs, the team norms must be recalibrated for the new team situation. The stages needn't occur in order, either, as some teams cycle back and forth between them. Teams may iterate between storming and norming several times before moving on to performing. Sometimes, this is misinterpreted as a Dr. Jekyll–to–Mr. Hyde transformation taking place. It is the leader's responsibility to recognize the state of the team at any moment and take actions that will move the team toward the performing stage in the least amount of time, using the correct techniques for each personality type.

Recognize Teamicide

Teamicide is the result of group dynamics in the organizational environment that become stuck in the storming stage, causing the members to retreat into the roots of their personalities, often destructively. DeMarco and Lister devoted an entire chapter in their book, *Peopleware*, to "Teamicide," referring to it as the inhibition of team formation and the disruption of project sociology. They list teamicide techniques as environmental things that a leader should watch for to avoid killing teamwork.[26] These include defensive management, bureaucracy, physical separation, fragmentation of people's time, quality reduction of the product, phony deadlines, and clique control.

A technical project leader should look for signs that any of these are occurring and take action to correct them immediately. DeMarco and Lister give us some hints:

- **Defensive management**—Allow the staff to make their own decisions, even if they sometimes make a mistake. Giving them the freedom to make errors is a sign of trust.
- **Bureaucracy**—Avoid turning developers into bureaucrats. Allow the team to believe in its own goals, and express your belief in it (and them) as well.
- **Physical separation**—Place workers together so that casual interaction may occur. When people are on the same team, they tend to go into "quiet mode" at the same time and suffer less interruption of their thought flow.
- **Fragmentation of time**—Limit the number of projects, and, therefore, teams, that a person is assigned to. There is high overhead in "switching gears" when moving from one team culture to another.
- **Quality reduction of the product**—A developer's self-esteem suffers when he is required to build a product of lower quality than what he is capable of. Don't allow "cost-reduced" products to become "quality-reduced" products. Promote a sense of pride.

- **Phony deadlines**—Tight deadlines are sometimes a necessity and can even present an enjoyable challenge to the team. However, phony deadlines are not tight deadlines, and teams know the difference.
- **Clique control**—Managers don't usually work in jelled teams. Instead, they achieve peer acceptance via roles. Even so, the importance of allowing a team to remain together should not be forgotten as one moves up the management ladder. On jelled teams, team activities are pleasurable, and energy is produced by team interaction.

Working Together Requires a Framework_____

A team can sing at the same time but not talk at the same time. The difference is a common sheet of music. This is the framework provided by project management competencies.

The project leader must read the team's collective personality, select an appropriate infrastructure suitable for it, and maintain its rhythm throughout the project. It should become part of the group's norm. Following the methodology becomes a group rule that spans cultures and personalities, and serves as a foundation for regrouping if (or when) the team falls back to the storming stage and some of the jell melts.

Communication and Team Size

Many of the causes of teamicide are under the control of a project leader. Team size in relation to the project size (see Table 6–11), if inappropriate for the task, may contribute to teamicide. This is a consequence of the mythical man-month phenomenon described in Fred Brooks' 1975 classic *The Mythical Man-Month*.[27] Note that a staff month is usually described as 40 hours of effort, which may be spread over a period of time that is less than or, more frequently, more than a calendar month.

TABLE 6–11
Project/Team Sizes

Project Size	Staff Months	Calendar Months	Typical Staff Size
Small	Less than 6	Less than 3	Less than 3
Medium	6–48	3–9	3–15
Large	More than 48	More than 9	More than 15

What works for a small project with a small team may not scale to a medium or large project. Certain economies and characteristics of team personality are primarily dependent on team size. Two of the most important are communication and dispersion.

Team Communication

Communication among the team members is fundamental to the accomplishment of the project's tasks. To prevent teamicide, everyone, managers and team members alike, must attempt to use the preferred channel of communication to transmit information so that the receiver can truly hear the message. Preferred communications channels for Kahler's PCM are shown in Table 6–12. You probably don't want to say to a reactor, "I don't care how you feel about it, you must take the lead to improve the bottom line!"

TABLE 6–12
Preferred Channel for Communication

PCM Type	Preferred Channel for Communication	Examples
Dreamer	Direct	Allow private time: "Work on this at home"
Workaholic	Informative	Clarify issues: Provide facts and data
Reactor	Nurturative	Verbal "strokes": "I'm pleased you are here to work on this"
Rebel	Emotive	Playful interaction: "Wow, what a wonderful idea!"
Persister	Informative	Acknowledge beliefs: "What is your opinion?"
Promoter	Direct	Focus on excitement and activity: "Go for it!"

Other communication issues within a project leader's control are bureaucracy and clique repression. Bureaucracy involves too much overhead for the communications channel. Cliques are "clubby" groups of people who establish exclusive subgroups within a team. Cliques cause *information isolation*.

As the team size grows, the number of two-way communications paths increases rapidly according to the formula,

$$\frac{n(n-1)}{2}$$

where n is the number of participating team members, producing the rapidly rising curve in Figure 6–4.

This creates overhead in the form of bureaucracy and increases the potential for error and misunderstanding (especially when the team members' native languages are not the same).

For example, the number of communication paths in various-size projects that we looked at earlier gets complicated very quickly (see Table 6–13). For illustration, very large projects of 50 people or more (typically a program) are also shown.

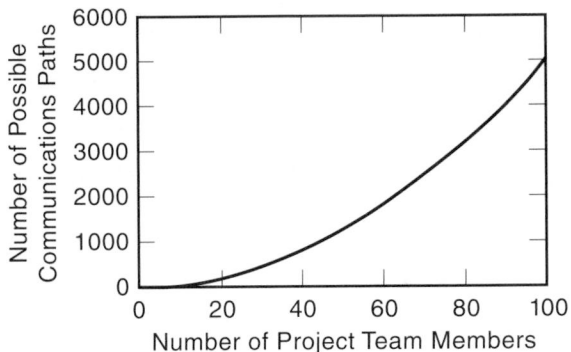

FIGURE 6–4
Communications Paths Growth

TABLE 6–13
Example Communications Paths

Project Size	Calendar Months	Typical Staff Size (n)	Maximum Number of Two-Way Communications Paths
Small	Less than 3	Less than 3	1
Medium	3–9	3–15	3–105
Large	More than 9	More than 15	Hundreds
Very Large (Program)	More than 1 year	More than 50	Thousands

As team size grows, the tendency for cliques to form goes up, often around geographic centers. This phenomenon is why the leader must provide a strong framework for the team to operate within. Even simple things such as providing a common team glossary help tremendously. The project leader must decide how much communication is enough and when it is too much.

Those personalities in the project team that require structure, ritual, and direction (e.g., PCM: dreamers, promoters; MBTI: SPs; Keirsey: guardian SJs) will want them more than the independents and rebels of the group. The People Capability Maturity Model (P-CMM), from the Software Engineering Institute is a framework to start with, but the project leader must judiciously adopt only the procedures that fit the team and project size, to minimize communication errors.

A useful tool from the P-CMM set is the Functional Responsibility Matrix, shown in Figure 6–5.

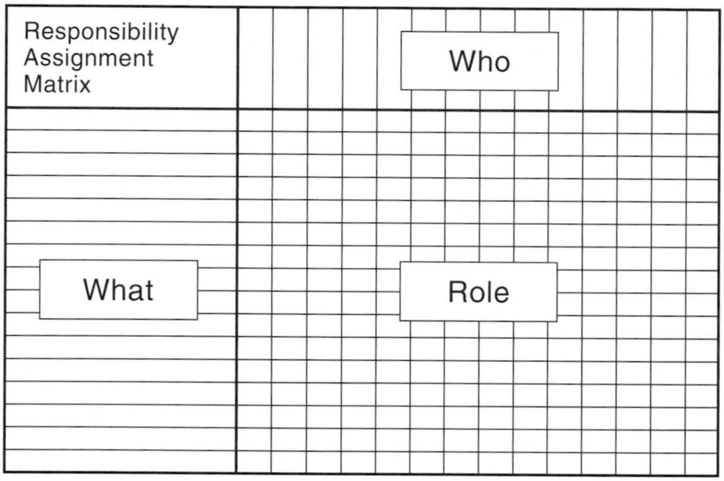

FIGURE 6–5
Functional Responsibility Matrix

The Functional Responsibility Matrix defines the boundaries between members' responsibilities for different project tasks. Almost all personality models comprehend boundary infractions because humans are, by nature, territorial. Territorial issues are a basic cause for team disharmony as they touch deep-rooted personality traits in many of the models.

The leader must also collect and present information in a way that is compatible with the members' and the team's personality. This is where understanding group dynamics and personality type is extremely important. If there is too much bureaucracy and too many cliques, then even the most patient of teams will rebel.

Team Dispersion

The management of a project team is much more difficult when it is geographically dispersed. Both distance apart and time zones around the globe affect the dynamics of team interactions.

Geography Issues   Communication and dispersion are the limiting realities for any work team spread over a wide physical area, where the team members will not likely interact face-to-face. This is because most of the team interaction models assume that team members are physically close and can use all their senses to detect the useful individual personality clues of other team members. Telecommunications technologies such as conference calls, videoconferencing, and email help but are not good substitutes for face-to-face interaction and full-body communication. The project manager must create a team environment with whatever is available.

If at all possible, at least one face-to-face team meeting should occur at the beginning, and another one should occur at the end of a project. The initial meeting sets the style and form for future interpersonal interactions that will span the middle part of the project's life cycle. This is critical in the early stages of a project, when understanding of the project's requirements is growing. The last meeting will provide the closure necessary to minimize personal emotional baggage moving to the next project (as well as significantly enhance the post-project metrics collection activities).

Time Considerations   Time shifts are an important issue as well. All teams require both asynchronous (done alone without coordination with other team members) and synchronous (done together in time and place) tasks.

When team members are geographically dispersed, a mutually agreeable time and place for synchronous tasks must be chosen. Most often, this is the project leader's home location and time zone, but there is great advantage to rotating this parameter of a project's infrastructure. If moved to other team members' locations or times, cross-cultural sharing is enhanced, burdens of travel or inconvenience are shared, and everyone reaches a deeper level of team personality understanding.

Structure and Ritual

This is the engine of a project. It is the framework to which the team personalities will react and anchor. Without it, misinterpretations and confusion begin to spread like wildfire.

Provide a Strong Framework   One of the most important things a leader can do is to set up a project office as a hub of information about the project. This is where the P-CMM project documents can reside, along with the working documents of the team. A project office is a concept, not necessarily a physical place. A decentralized project office is most common, but not best. It means that documents and tools are geographically dispersed into different team members' control. It is usually characterized by much emailing of documents and files, with not all team members sharing common platforms and software. This leads to territoriality and configuration management issues. A decentralized project office is represented in Figure 6–6.

A centralized project office is a concept of commonality and colocation. It may involve only one geographic location under one team member's control; be a physical space such as a project lab, conference room, or office; or be a virtual space on a remote system. Figure 6–7 depicts the centralized project office concept.

At a minimum, the project office should contain the charter and statement of work for the team. A schedule for work tasks is usually required, but the level of detail varies with the size

Project Documents
Maintained Locally

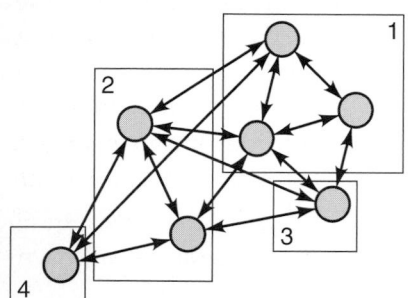

Members at Four Different Locations

FIGURE 6–6
Decentralized Project Office

and scope of the project. The functional responsibility matrix is also a good tool to keep central-ized when the project and team size is medium to large, or if the small team has serious person-ality issues (territoriality).

Practice Rituals   Our lives are ruled by small rituals that we've learned since birth, such as our eating and sleeping habits, our home and work processes, and our social interactions. These provide a "comfort zone" for us in which to deal with the uncertainties that we encounter every day. Abraham Maslow said that without the basics under control, we find it harder to realize our full potential and work on team problems.[28]

Project Documents
Maintained Centrally

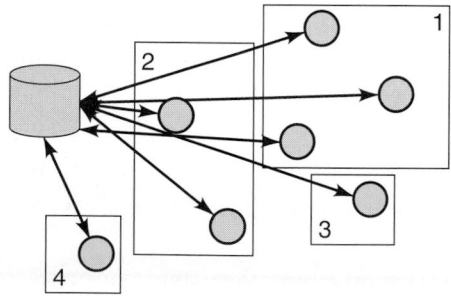

Members at Four Different Locations

FIGURE 6–7
Centralized Project Office

For project teams, this means that a regular schedule of exchanges (the synchronous part of projects) and "free" time (the unstructured part set aside for individual task accomplishment) is required. The leader must define this pattern and communicate it to the team as early in the project as possible. Daily expectations must be set for each individual to follow, or they will begin to drift apart as a team.

Peoplework, Not Paperwork   The amount of framework to provide for a given project is a matter of judgment for the team leader. Too much becomes stifling, but not enough encourages out-of-control behavior. The best guidance for this is to leverage the experience of practicing project professionals.

Providing the Total Solution_____

The total solution requires more than just technology and process today. Referring again to Fred Brooks' "No Silver Bullet,"[29] no single tool or approach will solve all problems. Even the P-CMM implementation must be viewed as a framework around which to manage the constant transformations of a team's personality. It must be used in conjunction with human and team personality assessment, applied with judgment, to increase a project's chance for success.

Managing Creativity

One of the criticisms of most frameworks is that they create bureaucracy and stifle creativity. In excess, this is true. But the absence of a good framework makes leading project teams immensely difficult and actually harms creativity. This is where the leader must decide how much is required for the situation at hand.

Creativity thrives in an environment that is safe and bounded. Children at play on a gym in a field with no boundaries show a reluctance to explore the area, clinging to the gym in the center because they fear violation of an unidentified boundary. If the boundaries are clearly marked with a fence or marker, the children feel free to explore every inch of the bounded area and do not cling to the center. This same phenomenon occurs with professionals in a project setting. Given clear and well-defined boundaries, creativity is set free. The trick for the leader is to read the personalities correctly and set the boundaries in the right place—not too tight, but not too loose.

When to Lead and When to Manage

This chapter is about leadership of project teams, but much of it concerns management. What's the difference between leadership and management?

Management is about following policies and procedures, and doing things right as an agent of the project and organization. It is about execution and compliance. It is getting the project team to perform at its best to pursue the project's goal. Management is about following processes. Following the P-CMM is a management activity.

Leadership is about conjuring up and following a vision, and communicating that vision to the project team. Leadership is about figuring out the right things to do and building a fire in the followers to do them. It is about passion and pursuing the leader's goal. Leadership is about setting direction. Creating the team charter and communicating it to the team are leadership activities. These concepts are summarized in Figure 6–8. It is best if the leader's goals and the project's goals are the same.

Knowing when to lead and when to manage requires an understanding of the project's personality. Should "good" be encouraged or "evil" quashed? What does the situation call for?

A useful model for both leadership and management is Hersey and Blanchard's Situational Leadership Model.[30] In the model, the kind of leadership to apply at a given time moves on a spectrum among four leadership styles, based on performer's maturity, as described in Table 6–14. The model is shown in Figure 6–9.

Each of the styles is a combination of task behavior (concern for the doing the job, shown on the y-axis) and relationship behavior (concern for the support of the followers who must do the job—the performers, shown on the x-axis). The curved shape suggests a typical "journey" of styles through an individual's situations, from S1 to S4 (right to left movement). This is similar to the journey that a team makes in the forming-storming-norming model described earlier.

Figure 6–10 suggests the leaders' role in each of the four styles. In telling, the leader tells the performers not only what to do, but how to do it. The leader's role becomes less aggressive in selling and participating, until the leader is just an observer in delegating.

In every case, the actions of the leader are determined by the readiness of the performers at the moment. Performer readiness is described in terms of their maturity, which is a combination of their willingness to do the task and their ability to do it (knowledge of how to do the task), as shown in Figure 6–11.

Leaders	Managers
Set Direction	Follow Process
Do the Right Thing	Do Things Right

FIGURE 6–8
Leadership vs. Management

TABLE 6–14
Situational Leadership Behavior

Leader's Style	Leader's Behavior	Performer's Maturity
Telling	Give strong direction for what to do, and how to do it, with little regard for the feelings of the performers	Unwilling Unable
Selling	Give softer direction, with a high degree of sensitivity to the feelings of the performers	Unwilling Able
Participating	Show a high degree of concern for the feelings of the performers, and join in to help them do the task	Willing Unable
Delegating	Just give them the task, and observe from a distance	Willing Able

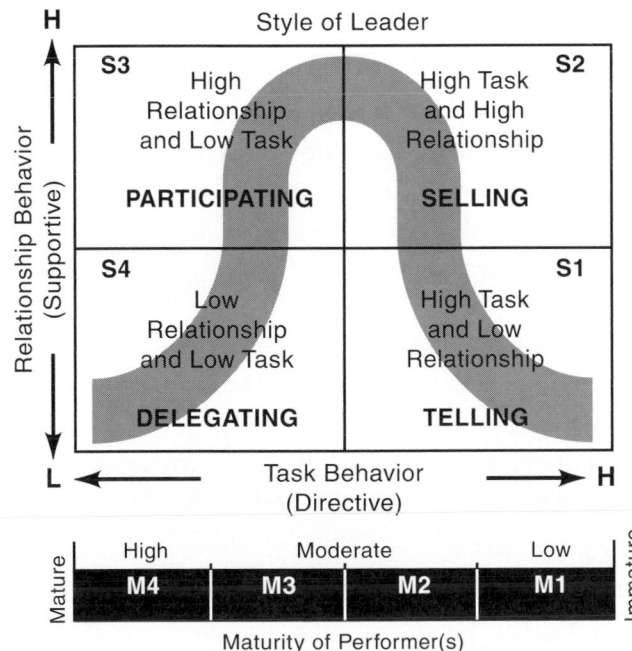

FIGURE 6–9
Situational Leadership Model

Style of Leader

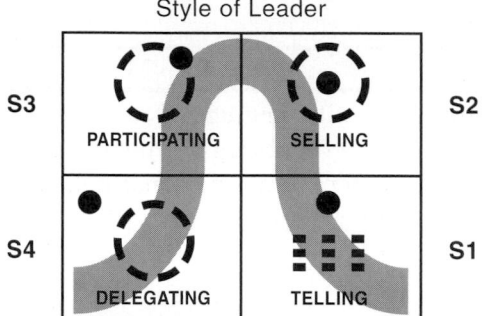

FIGURE 6–10
Leader's Role in Situational Leadership

Performer's Readiness

Willing	Willing	Unwilling	Unwilling
M4	**M3**	**M2**	**M1**
Able	Unable	Able	Unable

FIGURE 6–11
Performer's Readiness in Situational Leadership

If the performers are both unwilling and unable to do the task, their maturity is M1 and the leader should adopt a telling management style (S1). This is the drill sergeant approach.

If the leader assesses the performers as willing to do the task but not very able (perhaps lacking some skill or knowledge), their maturity is M3, so the leader should adopt the S3 style of leadership (participating). This is a "Let me show you how" style in which the leader participates *with the performers* to accomplish the task.

If the performers are both willing and able to do the task (M4), the leader should adopt the delegating style (S4). This is the research lab manager's approach. The leader must only throw the task to them, and they will perform it with little supervision.

S4 is the easiest style for the leader, but it does not permit as much rest as you might think. If the team runs into difficulty with the task, the leader must step in, assess the situation, and act accordingly.

Situational leadership is why leaders must be able to read individual and team personalities well. It is one of the primary remedies for helping a team toward maximum performance.

Summary _____

This chapter explored the problem of why a project team seemingly turns from a well-mannered Dr. Jekyll to a malevolent Mr. Hyde. We have briefly discussed different models available for reading individual and team personalities, including the Myers-Briggs Type Indicator (MBTI), the Keirsey Temperament Sorter, the Kahler Fundamental Interpersonal Relations Orientation—Measuring Behavior (FIRO-B), the Process Communication Model (PCM), the Enneagram, and the McFletcher WorkStyle Patterns Inventory (WSPI).

A leader must understand at least one of these thoroughly to be able to assess individual personalities as they relate to others in a project team. Understanding several models gives the leader even more insight. We encourage you to investigate at least one of these models further, perhaps with professional assistance.

We have looked at some basic elements of project team leadership, such as personality, culture, and motivation, and explored them as they apply to the group dynamics of project management. Several models of personal and team motivation were identified. A team's formation and its subsequent transition to a performing workgroup were described, and suggestions were made for actions that the leader can take to minimize the potential for a team transformation into dysfunctionality during this process. The impact of team and project size, and time and distance issues were also explored.

The importance of performed rituals and a sound project structure for project team performance was discussed, with the caveat that the leader's judgment is the best guide for how much framework to provide. The leader should promote peoplework, not paperwork.

The leader must provide a proper communication environment to create the total project solution. A centralized project office is the most effective way to achieve smooth communication across geographically dispersed teams.

After individual personalities have been read and the team's personality has been established, the leader must know when and how to lead and manage the team to the project's conclusion. Employing the situational leadership model was discussed as a vehicle for success.

Application of these models, tools, and techniques can help keep a project team mild-mannered and orderly.

Problems for Review_____

1. The dimensions of psychological type measure which one of the following?

   Intelligence

   Achievement

   Preference

   Psychopathology

2. Using the personality types "communication styles" in Table 6–15 as a guide, suppose that you are preparing a presentation about your current project for a general audience. Considering your four-letter type preference, describe two ways to communicate effectively in your speech with each of the opposite types of your preference. For example, if you are an I type on extroversion/introversion, describe how you would appeal to an E.

   Extroversion/Introversion (E/I)

   My type is: _____

   My approach to my opposite is:

   1.

   2.

   Sensing/Intuition (S/N)

   My type is: _____

   My approach to my opposite is:

   1.

   2.

   Thinking/Feeling (T/F)

   My type is: _____

   My approach to my opposite is:

   1.

   2.

   Judgment/Perception (J/P)

   My type is: _____

   My approach to my opposite is:

   1.

   2.

3. Give at least two reasons why teams are necessary in today's work environment. What are the four stages in a team's life cycle?

How to Recognize Communication Styles:	
E	Engages you to learn about project, wants to discuss it first
I	Reflects about project before discussing it, wants to read about it first
S	Keeps conversation on facts, figures, real experience
N	Describes what the project means, how it relates to things or improves them
T	Accuracy, logic, and research count more than personal relationship
F	Personal, cares about human reactions; personal relationship counts more than project
J	Feels important sticking to goals, priorities, schedules
P	Feels happy increasing options, realistically adapting

How to Communicate with Different Personality Types About Projects:

E (Extroversion)	I (Introversion)	S (Sensing)	N (Intuition)
• Need a good verbal presentation. • Want to engage you to learn about project; allow for questions, interruptions, or dialogue. • May decide quickly and verbally; watch for this and do not "oversell." • Cover the major points at a fast pace; do not go into too much detail. • Do not presume that an E will remember you next week; use reminders such as phone calls, mailings, updates. This feeds the E need for variety, contact, and action. • Want to do something now about an external need or crisis; be ready to deliver.	• Need a good written proposal to review. • Need time to reflect about detail or the implications of a project. • Do not usually decide quickly unless they have thought it through beforehand. • Should not be bothered too much with telephone calls, literature, or updates; tell him in advance about the next planned contact. • Even in crisis or urgent needs, an I will take time to do the right thing after deliberating; do not rush.	• Begin with facts, build to "big picture." • Use simple, practical examples. • Emphasize implementation, the next step. • See systems as a number of facts/projects. • Stay in here-and-now.	• Begin with the "big picture," fill in facts. • Make connections between facts and ideas. • Comment on unseen implications and future projections. • Discuss project as part of system. • Show interest in creative ideas or enthusiasms.

(Continues)

TABLE 6–15 (Continued)
How to Communicate with Different Personality Types About Projects

How to Communicate with Different Personality Types About Projects:			
E (Extroversion)	**I (Introversion)**	**S (Sensing)**	**N (Intuition)**
• What you say counts more than how you say it. • Be logical, researched. • Be low-key, conservative, businesslike. • Emphasize soundness, reliability, statistics. • Avoid generalizations, repetition, incoherence.	• How you say it counts more than what you say. • Emphasize human benefits. • Use eye contact, smile, be warm and personal. • Support service or project with first-hand testimonials and personal feedback. • Show genuine interest in the client as a person.	• Justify project through precedent. • No surprises! • Find out the schedules, priorities, criteria, and goals of the client, and stick to them. • Stay organized. • Give feedback so that the J "stays on track" toward goals.	• Allow for last-minute adjustments. • Concentrate on increasing present adaptability, options. • Diplomatically remind P that a decision must be made within certain time constraints. • Allow time for enjoyment.

Source: Dr. Richard Grant, instructor for The University of Texas at Austin, Software Quality Institute, Software Project Management Certification Program.

Visit the Case Study _____

Your company has reorganized all the marketing groups to flatten the reporting structures. Your boss, the project management director, was moved to a line organization in Florida. At the same time, Ms. Patel, the marketing director for AsiaPac, became the marketing manager for the Bangalore Software Development (BSD). With her new responsibilities in BSD and the need to show revenue, she is going to move all the CRM work to Bangalore. The only slot that will remain in the line marketing organization is you, the CRM project manager. Get to BSD and staff the in-process CRM project. What is the impact on your project plan?

Citations _____

[1]Kahler, Taibi, and Hedges Capers (1974). "The Miniscript." *Transactional Analysis Journal*, 4(1):27–42.

[2]*www.selbymillsmith.com*. Selby MillSmith, Chartered Occupational Psychologists, *FIRO-B Instrument*.

[3]Schutz, William (1996). *The Interpersonal Underworld*. Palo Alto, CA: Science and Behavior Books. First published in 1958 as *FIRO: A Three Dimensional Theory of Interpersonal Behavior*, New York, NY: Holt, Rinehart, and Winston.

[4]See note 3.

[5]Keirsey, David, and Marilyn Bates (1984). *Please Understand Me, An Essay on Temperament Styles.* Amherst, NY: Prometheus Books.

[6]*www.keirsey.com.* Keirsey Temperament Sorter.

[7]See note 1.

[8]Personal experience of the authors, Robert T. Futrell and Linda I. Shafer, who taught a course in "Progam Management Methodology," in 1998 at Motorola.

[9]Baron, Renee, and Elizabeth Wagele (1994). *The Enneagram Made Easy: Discover the 9 Types of People.* San Francisco, CA: Harper Collins Press.

[10]Palmer, Helen (1991). *The Enneagram: Understanding Yourself and the Others in Your Life.* San Francisco, CA: Harper.

[11]*www.purenlp.com/whatsnlp.htm.* Richard Bandler (1996). *What Is NLP?* The First Institute of Neuro-Linguistic Programming™ and Design Human Engineering™.

[12]See note 10.

[13]Bowditch, James L., and Anthony F. Buono (2001). *A Primer on Organizational Behavior*, 5th ed. New York, NY: John Wiley & Sons.

[14]Hergenhahn, B.R. (1990). *An Introduction to Theories of Personality.* Englewood Cliffs, NJ: Prentice Hall.

[15]Hirsh, Sandra, and Jean Kummerow (1989). *LIFETypes.* New York, NY: Warner Books, Inc.

[16]Maples, M.F., and C. Sieber (1998). "Gestalt Theory." *Counseling and Psychotherapy: Theories and Interventions*, D. Capuzzi and D. Gross, eds. Boston, MA: Merrill-Macmillan.

[17]Rothwell, J.D (2001). *In Mixed Company: Small Group Communication*, 4th ed. Fort Worth, TX: Harcourt College Publishers.

[18]Tuckman, Bruce W. (1965). "Developmental Sequence in Small Groups." *Psychological Bulletin*, 63:384–399.

[19]Chevrier, Sylvia, as reported by Larraine Segil in "Global Work Teams: A Cultural Perspective." *PM Network*, March 1999.

[20]Bowditch, James L., and Anthony F. Buono (2001). *A Primer on Organizational Behavior.* 5th ed. New York, NY: John Wiley & Sons.

[21]Hersey, Paul, Kenneth Blanchard, and Dewey Johnson (1996). *Management of Organizational Behavior: Utilizing Human Resources,* 7th ed. Upper Saddle River, NJ: Prentice Hall.

[22]McFletcher Corporation (1993). *WorkStyle Patterns™ Inventory.* Scottsdale, AZ.

[23]Curtis, Bill, personal communciation, 1993.

[24]See note 16.

[25]See note 18.

[26]DeMarco, Tom, and Timothy Lister (1987). *Peopleware: Productive Projects and Teams.* New York, NY: Dorset House.

[27]Brooks, Fredrick P. (1995). *The Mythical Man-Month: Essays on Software Engineering,* anniversary edition (originally published 1975). Reading, MA: Addison-Wesley.

[28]See note 20.

[29]Brooks, Fredrick P. (1987). "No Silver Bullet: Essence and Accidents of Software Engineering." *IEEE Computer,* 20(4):10–19.

[30]See note 21.

Suggested Readings

Kummerow, Jean M., Nancy J. Barger, and Linda K. Kirby (1997). *Worktypes.* New York, NY: Warner Books.

Kroeger, Otto, and Janet Theusen (1992). *Talk Type at Work.* New York, NY: Delacorte Press.

Tieger, Paul D., and Barbara Barron-Tieger (1995). *Do What You Are: Discover the Perfect Career for You Through the Secrets of Personality Type,* 2nd ed. Boston, MA: Little, Brown.

Tieger, Paul D., and Barbara Barron-Tieger (1997). *Nurture by Nature: Understand Your Child's Personality Type—and Become a Better Parent,* 1st ed. Boston, MA: Little, Brown.

Web Pages for Further Information

www.computer.org/tab/swecc/. The IEEE-CS/ACM joint task force on Software Engineering Ethics and Professional Practices (SEEPP) has developed a Code of Ethics for Software Engineers. It contains eight sets of guiding principles.

www.humanmetrics.com/JungType.htm. An abbreviated version of the MBTI test instrument.

www.keirsey.com. The Keirsey Temperament Sorter, derived from the work of David Keirsey in his book *Please Understand Me.*

www.tajnet.org/articles/kahler-miniscript-addendum.html. Article by Taibi Kahler, Ph.D.

www.typeworks.com/leadersh.htm. A discussion that relates the model to leadership.

Defining the Goal and Scope of the Software Project

Up to this point, we have described processes and life cycles as a framework for performing software project management. This chapter describes the beginning of formal project creation. In this chapter, we describe how the project and product processes fit together to define a unique project instance. The five steps of any project are *why, what, how, do it,* and *did it.* These steps are where the five PMI® project processes of initiating, planning, executing, controlling, and closing are executed, regardless of the nature of the project. We saw how the five steps mapped into business, product, and project life cycles.

We'll see what is required to define the goal and scope of a unique software development project. The techniques to be described are the S.M.A.R.T. method for goal and objective completeness, and the Is/Is Not technique for goal and objective clarification. The goal and scope become the key content for the important documents that define the project. These include the charter, scope of work statement, and software project management plan (SPMP).

Where We Are in the Product Development Life Cycle

Where are we in the basic software life cycle model that serves as our map? The first three steps of Figure 7–1 are where the goal and scope of the project get defined. In concept exploration, the goal of the system is identified at a high level in the statement of need. In the system exploration and requirements steps, the scope is refined until it is understood and manageable.

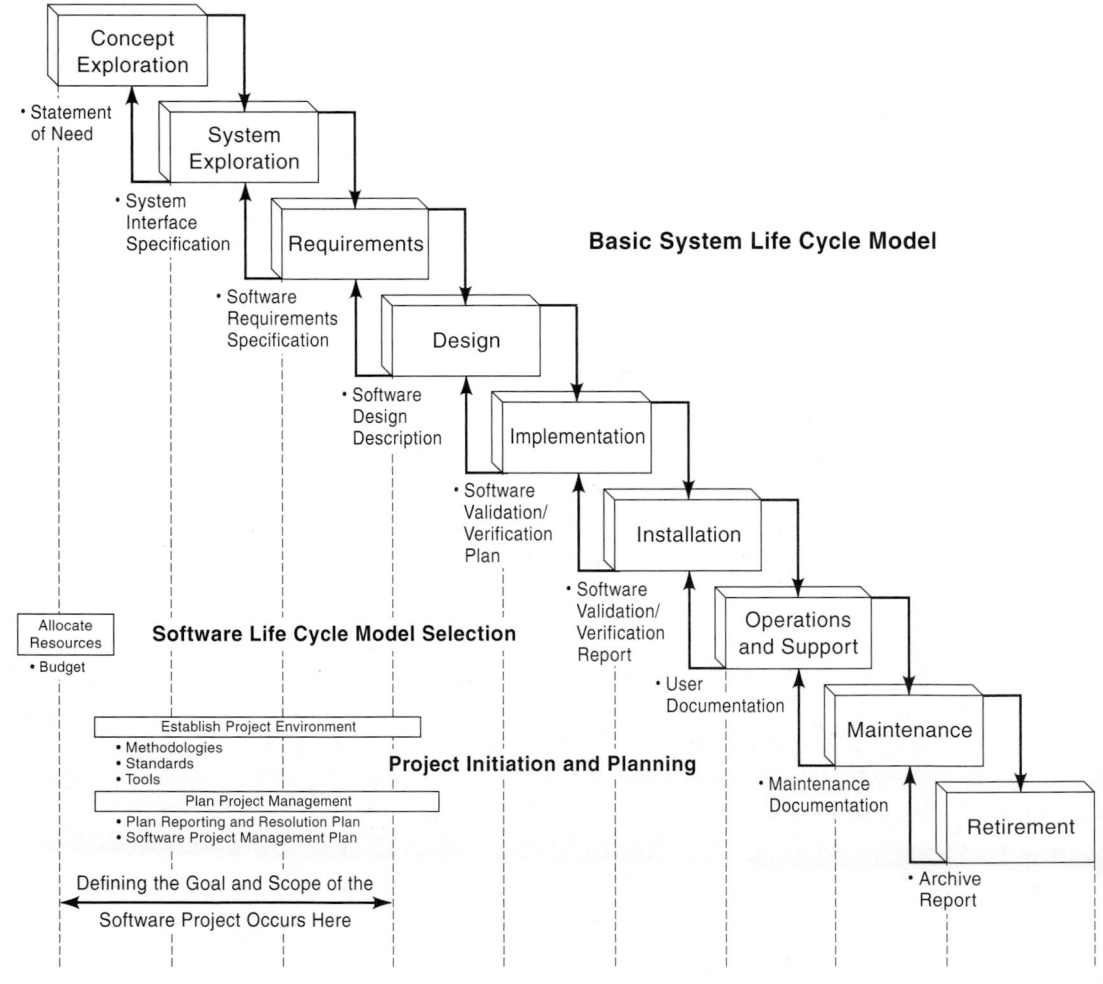

FIGURE 7–1
Where Defining the Goal and Scope of the Software Project Occurs in the Life Cycle

Chapter 7 Relation to the 34 Competencies _____

This chapter concerns the competencies shown in Figure 7–2. Defining the project goal and scope directly relate to the initial assessment and product definition techniques of product development, and the project management skills related to estimating and documenting, using the people management competencies of leadership, negotiation, and communication and interaction.

Product Development Techniques

3. **Defining the product**—Identifying customer environment and product requirements
7. **Performing the initial assessment**—Assessing difficulty, risks, costs, and schedule

Project Management Skills

12. **Building a work breakdown structure**—Building a work breakdown structure for a project
13. **Documenting plans**—Identifying key components
14. **Estimating cost**—Estimating cost to complete the project
15. **Estimating effort**—Estimating effort required to complete the project

People Management Skills

26. **Interaction and communication**—Dealing with developers, upper management, and other teams

Software   Project   Management

Product	Project	People
1. Assessing processes	**12. Building a work breakdown**	23. Appraising performance
2. Awareness of process standards	**structure**	24. Handling intellectual property
3. Defining the product	**13. Documenting plans**	25. Holding effective meetings
4. Evaluating alternative processes	**14. Estimating cost**	**26. Interaction and communication**
5. Managing requirements	**15. Estimating effort**	**27. Leadership**
6. Managing subcontractors	16. Managing risks	28. Managing change
7. Performing the initial assessment	17. Monitoring development	**29. Negotiating successfully**
8. Selecting methods and tools	18. Scheduling	30. Planning careers
9. Tailoring processes	19. Selecting metrics	**31. Presenting effectively**
10. Tracking product quality	20. Selecting project	32. Recruiting
11. Understanding development	management tools	33. Selecting a team
activities	21. Tracking process	34. Teambuilding
	22. Tracking project progress	

FIGURE 7–2
How Defining the Goal and Scope of a Software Project Relates to the 34 Competencies

27. **Leadership**—Coaching project teams for optimal results
29. **Negotiating successfully**—Resolving conflicts and negotiating successfully
31. **Presenting effectively**—Using effective written and oral skills

Learning Objectives for Chapter 7 _____

The main point of this chapter is to define the goal and scope of the project so clearly that measuring progress is easy and there is no ambiguity that the project goals have been achieved.

There are several techniques and tools available to the project manager to define the goal and scope clearly. Among them are the Is/Is Not technique and the S.M.A.R.T. goal checklist.

Upon completion of this chapter, the reader should be able to:

- Explain why project planning is valuable;
- Describe the value and contents of a project charter, scope of work statement, and software project management plan;
- Create usable goal and objective statements;
- Explain how to make crisp, clean boundaries around the project's scope;
- Describe the five project process steps for any project, and explain how they relate to the product processes of business and software development;
- Show how the project charter, statement of work (SOW), software project management plan (SPMP), and software requirements specification (SRS) relate to each other.

Project Planning _____

Why plan? Won't the plans just change anyway? Why waste a lot of time and effort writing down what we think we're going to do, just to have blind luck change it all before we're done? Why not "just do it" and handle whatever happens whenever it happens? These are good questions in a world changing at Internet speed. Whatever life cycle roadmap you choose, uncertainties abound, and your team may end up achieving something different than what it originally envisioned.

Referring to the mountains of planning documents prepared for the historic D-Day invasion of Europe on June 6, 1944, Gen. Dwight Eisenhower said, "Plans are nothing. But planning is everything." He recognized that extremely well-thought-out and detailed plans are also extremely fragile in the face of fate and uncertainty. But he also knew that the depth of understanding of the problem space that came from the work to prepare the plans would enable his team to react intelligently to new situations. They would be better prepared to seize new opportunities and avoid serious mistakes. Good luck is where preparation meets opportunity.

Project planning is the process that lays the framework for how the project will be run. It includes the definition of the project's objectives, selection of an appropriate life cycle, and establishment of the policies, procedures, and processes necessary to achieve the objectives. How much framework you need to write down depends, in part, on how mature your organizational environment is. If your team is a freshly hired group of people from many different backgrounds who haven't worked together, with you or your organization, more structure is required to guide them. If most of your team has been working together for a while, only a skeleton framework and simple checklist is required. The team probably already has enough cultural heritage to flesh out the plans well enough using established reporting structures, definitions, and work products.

The old jokes about planning are "Ready, fire, aim," and "You go ahead and get started coding while I go upstairs and find out what they want." Also, many projects have followed the tongue-in-cheek life cycle shown in Box 7–1. Let's hope your projects don't follow this life cycle!

Box 7–1
A Commonly Encountered Life Cycle in Low-Maturity Organizations

Phase 1—Project Initiation
Phase 2—Wild Enthusiasm
Phase 3—Disillusionment
Phase 4—Chaos
Phase 5—Search for the Guilty
Phase 6—Punishment of the Innocent
Phase 7—Promotion of the Nonparticipants
Phase 8—Definition of the Requirements

Regardless of the life cycle chosen for the project, there will be two distinct sets of processes followed:

- Project processes: Describe how the project team will define and execute the product development processes (see Figures 7–3 and 7–4)
- Product processes: Describe how the software product will be built (see Figure 7–1)

The product processes are introduced in Chapters 3–5, and are discussed in detail in Chapters 19–24. The project processes were introduced in Chapter 3, "Process Overview," and will be discussed in detail here as we look into how to execute a specific instance of a project plan.

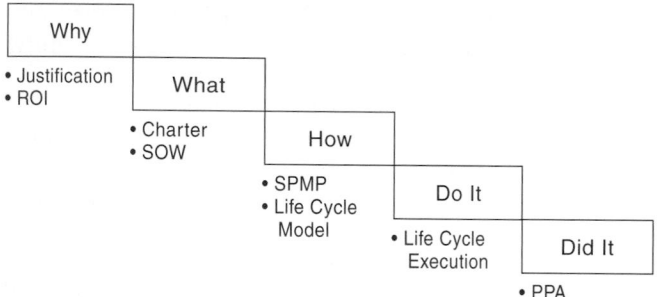

FIGURE 7–3
Project Process Framework

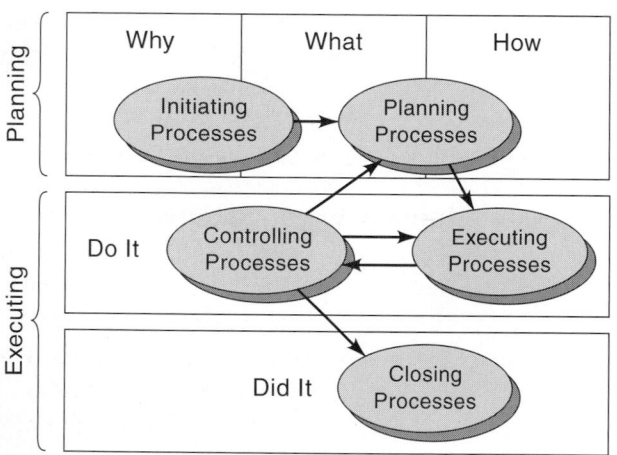

FIGURE 7–4
Project Process Integration Map

Why

Every project needs a good reason to exist, and this step ensures that there is at least one. Using business analysis suitable for the organization, the project manager should perform an opportunity analysis and prepare a return on investment (ROI) statement for the project. This *raison d'etre* may be just a statement indicating that the project has high strategic value and must be accomplished for other projects to exist, or it may be a complete ROI prepared by financial experts showing net present value (NPV), internal rate of return (IRR), payback period (PBP), or other acceptable calculations. Whatever the justification is, it should be recorded and usually becomes part of the project charter.

What

When a good reason is identified for proceeding with the software project, the goal and scope of the project can be defined to distinguish it from ongoing operations. Called a project charter, this is usually a simple outline statement of what the project will accomplish, including major deliverables, a rough high-level schedule, an initial estimate of resources needed, and the expected return to the organization for the effort invested. The charter has two purposes:

1. To formally document the existence of a software development project and to separate the work of the project from ongoing operations such as maintenance and support; and

2. To obtain management approval for the work to be done and to get commitment for the resources to do it.

The charter may take the form of a legal contract and statement of work (SOW) for external work to be executed by a third party outside the project manager's direct control. In this case, the details of the "how" may be left up to the contractor.

How

With the authority granted by charter approval, the software project manager can employ the many other software engineering and people skills needed to define the product and manage a team to develop and deliver it. This is the heart of software project planning. The major work product of this step is the software project management plan (SPMP). The SPMP explains (in an appropriate level of detail for the maturity of the performing organization) how the life cycle steps will be performed. These may vary for every project even though the basic life cycle used is the same. This is the roadmap that the project team will follow to prepare the software deliverables and meet customer expectations. Usually for large or long-duration projects, iterative planning is used, with detail planning done only for the next immediate step of the life cycle as the project progresses.

Do It

When the SPMP is completed and approved (by the customer or by management), the team can execute the plan, following the life cycle steps chosen for this particular project instance. Even if a spiral model using rolling wave planning is chosen, the SPMP should be the roadmap to guide the team toward project completion. This step uses most of the information presented in this book for the 34 competencies.

Did It

Commensurate with good process management, an evaluation step should be performed before closing out the software development project. This is the post-performance analysis (PPA) step, and it results in a PPA report documenting lessons learned and recommendations for project or product process improvements for the next similar project that the organization attempts.

These five steps are required for every project, large or small, short duration or long, regardless of the project's intended output. The variables of size, scope, cost, schedule, complexity, and risk determine how much rigor and documentation is required in each step, and which development life cycle should be used. Even a small project such as assembling a child's bicycle for a birthday present is a project that requires thinking through these five steps. But it isn't likely that you would make an effort to document it for posterity.

The Project Management Institute (PMI®) cites five processes necessary for any project, or phases within a project: *initiating, planning, executing, controlling,* and *closing*.[1]

Figure 7–4 shows that the *initiating* processes are where the *why* step is handled. It includes enough of the *what* step to describe the project at a high level. The rest of the *what* step and the entire *how* step are handled in the *planning* processes. The *do it* step is composed of the *executing* and *controlling* processes, and the *did it* step is covered by the *closing* processes.

For the product processes shown in Figure 7–1, the project planning process starts in *concept exploration* by ensuring that you are pursuing a solution to the right problem for your customer, or much effort is wasted. This is where the *why* of a project is explored.

In Chapter 16, "Eliciting Requirements," and Chapter 17, "Developing the Software Requirements Specification," we will look into the development of detailed requirements.

Planning is an iterative process, usually done repeatedly during the course of a project as conditions change and new knowledge is gained. But the objectives set early should remain fairly static; otherwise, the project will wander aimlessly and should be cancelled and then redefined. Objectives are usually interrelated. If some objectives conflict, management must prioritize them or the project will not be successful.

The general approach fits into the framework described in Figure 7–5.

What Is "The Goal"?

Every project needs at least one goal. Most have multiple goals. Sometimes these are called the project objectives or are collectively referred to as the mission of the project. Actually, we believe that the mission of the project is to accomplish the goals and objectives. Whatever label is used, defining them clearly and crisply can be one of the simplest and most beneficial things done during the whole software development project. A fuzzy goal will most likely lead to fuzzy results. Managing software projects well is mostly about managing expectations and foreseeing risks.

The software project manager always has at least one goal: to *finish* the project. This comes from the definition of what a software project is: a *unique, temporary* endeavor with defined

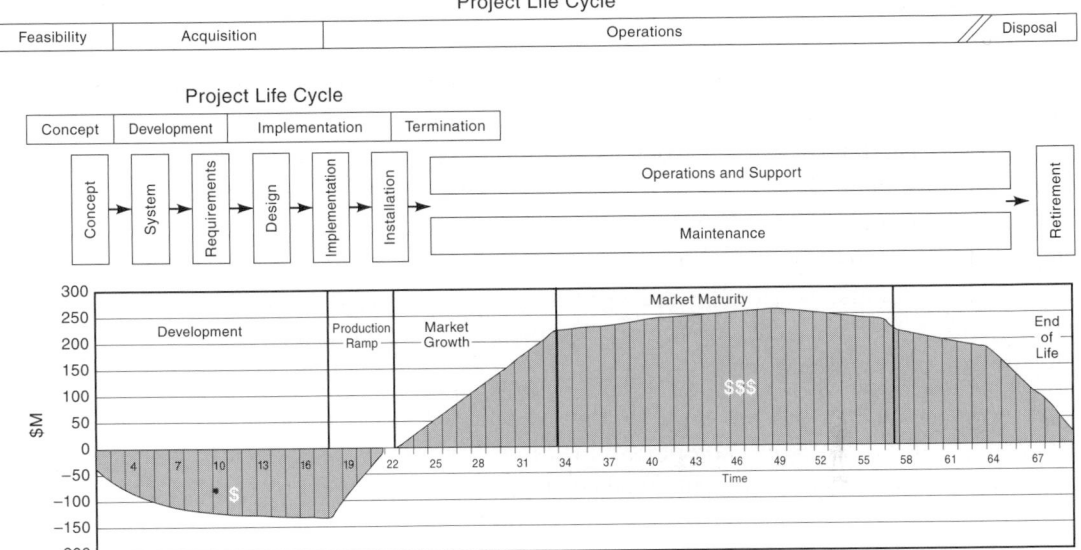

FIGURE 7–5

Relationship of Project and Product Life Cycles for a Software Project

start and end dates to achieve one or more *objectives* within the *constraints* of *cost, schedule,* and *quality* performance.

Often, what seems like an obvious software project goal may not be seen the same way by everyone. This is why it is important to write it down and interpret it for the project team. For example, a software development project to build a Web-based timesheet data entry system may be viewed as:

- An internal tool development effort by the engineering manager;
- A training exercise by the recently hired programmers;
- A requirement before starting a new software development project for an external customer by the general manager;
- A marketing tool to demonstrate the capabilities of the development team by the sales staff.

Each of these views implies a different level of robustness, ease of use, and maintainability for the final end-product software deliverable. Unfortunately, many project managers would simply state that the project goal is to "build a timesheet data entry system," and leave it at that, inviting misinterpretation later. To clarify the goal for all stakeholders, this project could have the goal and objectives defined as in Box 7–2.

This statement is what some call "the elevator speech." It is a clear but concise description of the project that could be conveyed to the CEO informally on the spur of the moment in a short elevator ride, without prior notice. In the example, it states that the project is for internal

Box 7–2
Example Goal Statement

> **Goal:** Build and successfully deploy a Web-based timesheet data application entry system for the engineering department's internal use before the beginning of the next major external software product development project.

use (implying internal benefit but no revenue directly associated with it), it includes successful deployment (not just development), it specifies who the customer is (the engineering department), and it cites a time frame (before the beginning of the next major external software product development project).

It is very valuable for the overall goal of the project to be stated in terms that are easily understood and repeated. At any project meeting, anyone on the project team should be able to recite the project goal statement, if asked. This keeps the project focused and may be used as the opening to the "elevator speech" about the project by anyone asked to explain what they are doing to an uninformed observer.

Setting Clear Objectives

In the previous example, the objectives in the goal statement have certain characteristics that make it clear. Most objectives tell *what*. The best ones also imply *why*. Good project objectives are:

- Focused on *deliverables*, not just processes: The customer ultimately cares about the final end product (timesheet system), not the processes needed to get to the end product (SPMP, SRS, etc.).

- Measurable and testable ($, %, Mkt. Share, Dates): There is something quantifiable to measure and test, usually quality-related ("successful" implies that acceptance criteria are defined).

- Action-oriented: The goal implies actions to achieve (the verbs *build* and *deploy* complement the noun *system*).

- Conversational: The goal could be recited and explained in a few seconds (the elevator ride).

- Doable (within your authority): The goal is reasonable and does not imply trying to solve world hunger (many accounting applications like this have been done before).

- Communicated: The team knows it, and it is published in the project charter (it's also the elevator speech).

Setting clear objectives goes a long way toward starting a successful software project.[2]

When objectives have been set, measurable subobjectives for some or all may be defined so that cost and performance may be tracked. Rather than the "big bang" approach of having one or just a few objectives, it is good project practice to set up a number of smaller measurement posts along the way. Many small milestones are better than one big one at the end of the project. The team should have a part in establishing their own objectives and subobjectives. A useful technique for defining clear objectives is the S.M.A.R.T. method. S.M.A.R.T. is comprised of the initials for: specific, measurable, achievable, realistic, and time-bound.

For any objective, determine the specific results and performance targets necessary to meet expectations. Are the objectives specific? Do you and your sponsor/customer both agree on the results needed for each of your project's objectives? Are the objectives measurable? How will you know that you are achieving results? What does "meet expectations" mean to you and your customer for each of the objectives? Are the objectives achievable and attainable? Why or why not? What support would you need to attain them? Are the objectives realistic and relevant? Do they address the customer's requirements and real needs? Do they align with the key success factors for the organization, the business goals, and the strategies? Are your objectives time-bound? Are there specific dates by which the objectives should be achieved? Is there a clearly understood reason for each of the dates? What is the driver behind the dates (e.g., your customer's customer needs the product then)?

The following is an example of a (relatively) short-duration objective that is part of a larger quality systems improvement project in a large multinational corporation. Note that it is specific and measurable, achievable for the average corporate quality department, both realistic and relevant to the department and corporation long-term goals, and time-bound (in this case, a specific due date, not a specific duration, as in "within six months from project start").

Benchmark two other companies' automated line-manufacturing processes according to ISO 9000 standards. Complete the project by the end of the third quarter at a maximum budget of $30,000.

What Is the Scope of Work?

Often part of the SPMP, but sometimes a separate document (or several), is the scope of work, statement of work (SOW), or, sometimes, statement of requirements (SOR), although this may get confused with the software requirements specification (SRS), which contains the detailed requirements. The SOW contains just enough specific details and specifications of components packaged so that they can be given to a subcontractor for execution. The SOW may be incorporated within, may be referenced as an appendix in the SPMP, or may reside in a completely separate document if it needs to be separated from the main document for security or other reasons.

Setting Boundary Conditions

It is usually easier for a project team to identify what the software project should include than what it should *not* include. The goal and objectives statements describe what is to be part of the final project scope. What is often harder to describe is what it will not include, but this is absolutely necessary to help define the edges of the project scope. Later, preparation of the SRS will detail the contents of what is included more finely.

Use the Is/Is Not technique to help draw crisp boundaries around the project scope and its objectives individually. This technique is simple. For each goal or objective, your team uses brainstorming techniques to define what it is and make a list for the team (see Figure 7–6). Next, brainstorm a list of what it is not, and make that into a list. Both lists can then be used to make a list of assumptions about the project.

This exercise pulls out hidden assumptions that team members had about the project scope or its work products. It is better to find that out early rather than get deep into the project and discover misunderstandings about the project objectives and scope. For instance, using the example goal statement in Box 7–2, we might say that the project:

Is:

- internal;
- a timesheet data-entry system;
- Web-based;
- for the engineering department;
- to be deployed before we begin the next major external project;

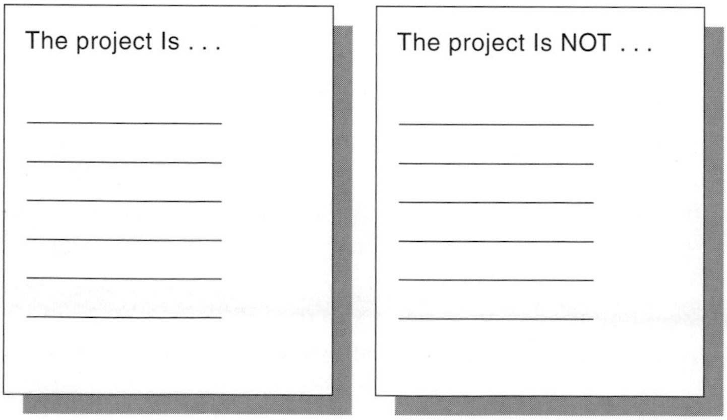

FIGURE 7–6
Is/Is Not Technique

- to be successful per existing application deployment criteria;
- to serve as a training project to familiarize the team with the new project management process.

Is not:

- intended for use by other departments or external customers;
- a full-blown labor accounting system;
- intended to be accessed by PDAs or wireless Web cell phones;
- required to interface to existing earned value management programs such as MS Project;
- to be in beta test mode when the next external project begins;
- to use outside contractors for development.

These characterizations become a way to crisply define the edges of the project's scope. They translate easily into assumptions to be recorded for the project charter and SPMP. The assumptions then become the first risks of the project because if any of them is violated, the project scope is breached.

Sometimes the scope of work is large enough to warrant its own document, instead of appearing as statements in a charter. However, at this early stage in the life cycle, the scope of work is just a rough planning item. Sometimes, this document is referred to as the statement of work (SOW), statement of requirements (SOR), or software requirements specification (SRS). Often, the SOW/SOR/SRS is subdivided into pieces that fully describe what a subcontractor is expected to do, in relation to the overall requirements. In these cases, the SOW/SOR/SRS may contain nonspec items from the project management plan, such as status reporting protocol, payment schedules, and legal statements. Details and templates for SOW construction vary with industry and domain, but they generally carry the specifications of the product to be built in a format that can be separated from the other processes of the project.

Project Charter

A charter includes the business need, the product description, and major assumptions. See Box 7–3.

Box 7–3
Charter Definition
Source: *www.dictionary.com*

char·ter

A document that formally recognizes the existence of a project

Now that the individual objectives have been identified and the overall project scope is understood and has been agreed upon, it is time to prepare the project charter. Basically, the project manager will capture the high-level objectives and the scope, and then add other pertinent high-level information so that a sponsor or customer can approve it. Often, the charter is the basic document needed for project selection in the organization's project portfolio management process, in which this project would be compared to others in a cost/benefit sense and funded, if selected. Project selection models and techniques are outside the scope of this book. See the references listed at the end of this chapter for more information.

Project Charter Contents

The charter may sometimes be called by other names, such as the project initiation document (PID), scope baseline, or just contract (usually for external work). It may be produced in many forms, such as a narrative document (most common), a fill-in-the-blank form (paper or software application), or spreadsheets for extensive financial justification.

The charter contains the why and what of the project processes discussed at the beginning of this chapter. It should contain brief statements (very *brief*—don't qualify every phrase!) about the following:

- **Objectives**: What the desired outcomes are
- **Functions**: Major features and/or processes
- **Performance**: Generalized specifications
- **Constraints**: Limitations of the environment
- **Scope**: Boundaries of the project
- **Costs/benefits**: Rough order of magnitude estimates

Be sure to answer the usual questions about a project that uninformed observers tend to ask: What is the reason for the project? Is it to seize an opportunity, solve a problem, increase revenues, decrease costs, or a combination of these? Be sure to have an answer for the typical newspaper reporter's questions: Who? What? Where? Why? When?

Typically, the charter is a short one- to three-page letter, memo, or email document—just enough to secure management or customer approval for the project. Sometimes the charter is labeled as the SPMP and uses its framework but includes only the sections pertinent to the selection process at this early point. Sometimes it is better to make it a separate document and merge it later because executives don't like to see large documents come their way (such as SPMPs with lots of extra sections, revision blocks and change control, specifications, appendices, etc.). Remember that the purpose of the charter is to concisely represent the project at a high level, to get management approval and support (and a signature). From there, you can flesh out the rest of the project planning because you will have the authority of approved sponsorship (and funding).[3]

The Software Project Management Plan _____

This is the most important document of a project. It defines how the project is supposed to be executed and what it is going to produce. Next in importance would be the SRS. The SPMP should contain definitive project information that includes:

- **Charter**: Elements from the project charter that define the project, including deliverables
- **Organization**: How the project will be organized and executed to produce the deliverables
- **Process**: Details of the managerial and technical processes that will be used during the project
- **Work breakdown**: Work breakdown and work package details
- **Schedule**: Schedule, dependencies, and resources
- **Budget**: Budgetary and definitive estimates

All of these items are related, and the SPMP actually evolves over a period of time as the various items come together. The process usually starts, though, with incorporating the elements of the approved charter into the SPMP. Because the project is approved beyond the concept stage, it can proceed to the definition (what) and planning (how) stages, where the detailed planning takes place.

Major Elements of SPMP

Usually completed from a template such as that described by IEEE 1058, "Standard for Software Project Management Plans," the SPMP describes the how of the project processes discussed earlier in this chapter.[4] It describes how the project team will implement the life cycle software development processes of the chosen life cycle.

The project charter information is integrated into appropriate sections of the SPMP. The rest of the document contains sections that include these:

- Project overview and deliverables
- Project organization
- Managerial processes
- Technical processes
- Work packages, schedule, and budget

Other chapters in this book provide details about how to identify and represent the information necessary to complete an SPMP. The depth and breadth of the coverage for each section is a matter of judgment according the type and scope of the project. When completed and approved, the SPMP becomes the benchmark for controlling the project during execution (the *do it* step).

How These Project Planning Documents Relate

As shown in Figure 7–7, the flow of information starts with defining the goal, objectives, and high-level scope of the proposed software project. These items are usually presented in a project charter document. For a large project, or one to be sublet through a contracting process, the charter may be supported by a scope of work document containing more details outlining the work to be performed.

When the charter containing the why and what for the project has gained management approval, then the information in it is integrated into the SPMP where the details of how the project will be executed are described at a level suitable for the size and scope of the project, as well as the maturity of the project team and organization.

Summary

In this chapter, we have described how the project and product processes fit together to define a unique project instance. The five steps of any project are *why*, *what*, *how*, *do it*, and *did it*. These steps are where the five PMI® project processes of *initiating*, *planning*, *executing*, *controlling*, and *closing* are executed, regardless of the nature of the project. We saw how the five steps mapped into business, product, and project life cycles.

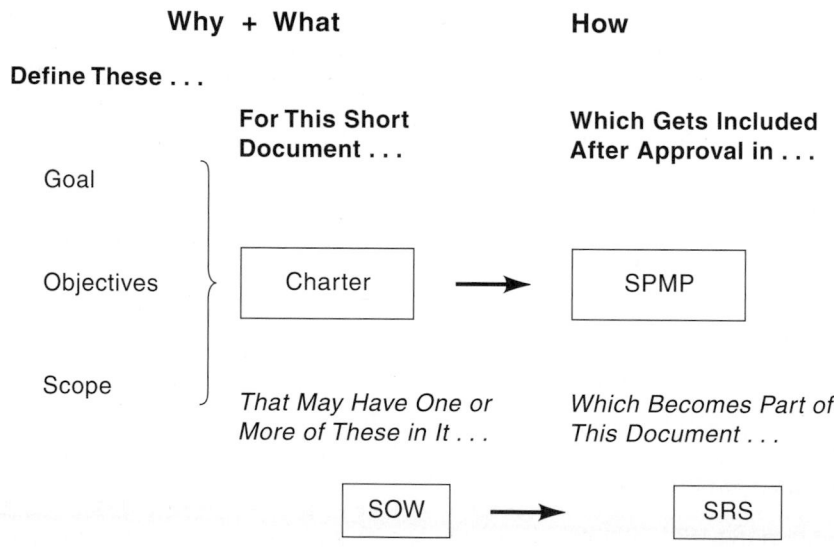

FIGURE 7–7
Relationship of Planning Documents

We've seen what is required to define the goal and scope of a unique software development project. The techniques described were the S.M.A.R.T. method for goal and objective completeness, and the Is/Is Not technique for goal and objective clarification. The goal and scope become the key content for the important documents that define the project. These include the charter, scope of work statement, and SPMP.

Problems for Review

1. What is (are) the goal(s) for the case project?
2. Define the S.M.A.R.T. features of the goal for the case project.
3. What is the case project's scope?
4. Explain the difference between project scope and the project's goal.

Visit the Case Study

You have had the PMP approved by the management chain in your department. Mr. Lu, the CRM direct interface for your corporation, wants a teleconference with you and the project leads. His management has approved the scope of the original prototype but wants a co-proposal for a second prototype to follow within 60 days of the first prototype. This would be an extension to the ARRS that would include Beijing, Zhengzhou, Shanghai, and Tianjin. This is excellent news for your corporate management because you have a major manufacturing facility in Tianjin.

Citations

[1]Project Management Institute (1996). *A Guide to the Project Management Body of Knowledge*. Sylva, NC: PMI Publication Division.

[2]Kerzner, Harold (1998). *Project Management: A Systems Approach to Planning, Scheduling, and Controlling*, 6th ed. New York, NY: John Wiley & Sons.

[3]Lewis, James P. (1995). *Project Planning, Scheduling, and Control: A Hands-On Guide to Bringing Projects in on Time and on Budget*, rev. ed. Chicago, IL: Irwin.

[4]IEEE (1993). "IEEE 1058 Standard for Software Project Management Plans." *IEEE Software Engineering Standards Collection*. New York, NY: Institute of Electrical and Electronics Engineers.

Suggested Readings

Adams, John R. (1997). *The Principles of Project Management.* Sylva, NC: PMI Publication Division.

Lewis, James P. (2000). *The Project Manager's Desk Reference: A Comprehensive Guide to Project Planning, Scheduling, Evaluation, and Systems,* 2nd ed. New York, NY: McGraw-Hill.

Web Pages for Further Information

dictionary.com/. Dictionary.com, online English Dictionary.

www.pmi.org/. Project Management Institute (PMI®). This is the premier organization in the United States representing PM interests. It is the certifying body for Project Management Professionals (PMP). Since its founding in 1969, PMI® has grown to be the organization of choice for project management professionalism. With more than 60,000 members worldwide, PMI is the leading nonprofit professional association in the area of project management. PMI establishes project management standards and provides seminars and educational programs and professional certification that more organizations desire for their project leaders.

www.sei.cmu.edu/activities/str/indexes/glossary/. SEI Glossary.

Creating the Work Breakdown Structure

If you've got a project charter and an excited customer, why go to the trouble to build a work breakdown structure? After all, aren't you a software engineering professional? The work breakdown structure (WBS) is the heart of a project plan, as most of the other parts of a project are built from it. The WBS is the tool used to document all the work that must be done to develop and deliver the software in a satisfactory manner. Although it may seem that the information that it contains is redundant with some of the other various documents that a software development project generates (scope of work, software requirements specification, design document, etc.), it serves to consolidate information from many sources into one place and into an organized format, convenient for planning, estimating, and tracking.

A WBS serves as a framework around which to build the project schedule. It helps you move from the top-level activity of the project (the *do it* activity) down through a set of simpler, smaller activities designed to build the software product deliverable, until the activities become small enough to manage well. It helps everyone understand the relationships of tasks and activities to each other in an illustrated way. It helps ensure that all the work is represented and that no work steps have been omitted. It also helps the project team divide the work to be done into small, well-defined tasks and activities. Of course, the WBS also facilitates planning, estimating, and scheduling, and it is a basis for monitoring the project and for historical data collection. (See Figure 10–3 for an illustration of how building the WBS is part of the big picture for software estimating.) It allows us to dismiss, "We're 90% done," and replace it with, "We've completed 97 of 234 planned activities." Weighted tasks and activities become meaningful and can be associated with a cost estimate.

Where We Are in the Product Development Life Cycle

Where are we in the product development life cycle model that serves as our map? As shown in Figure 8–1, we are still near the beginning, actually preconcept exploration. As discussed in Chapter 7, "Defining the Goal and Scope of the Software Project," we are in the *why, what*, and *how* planning steps of the project process framework for a given project instance (shown in Figure 8–2). In the *why* step, we need to know which software development life cycle model will likely be used, and we need to have it broken down into enough detail to make a rough order of magnitude estimate of the work. This is required to develop a reasonable return on investment (ROI) for the project work. In the *what* step, we use it to predict the expected work product outputs from the software development life cycle selected. In the *how* step, we need the WBS to make budgetary and detailed estimates of the work to be done, and to develop a realistic schedule. There will be more on how to use what is known at this point in the project's life to do software product sizing and estimating (Chapter 10, "Software Size and Reuse Estimating," and Chapter 11, "Estimating Duration and Cost"), and then to prepare a realistic schedule for the work to be done (Chapter 14, "Considering Dependencies," and Chapter 15, "Scheduling the Work").

Chapter 8 Relation to the 34 Competencies

This chapter concerns the competencies shown next. Creating the work breakdown structure (WBS) is one of the most important parts of any project because it creates the centerpiece of any project plan around which all activities derive. After the project goal and scope are defined at a high level and appropriate approvals are obtained, then fleshing out and customizing the work according to the defined life cycle model chosen begins. This process directly relates to the competencies of product definition and process tailoring, and to building the WBS. It indirectly relates to documenting plans and estimates, and it uses the people skills of interaction and communication, leadership, negotiation, and often presentation.

Product Development Techniques

3. **Defining the product**—Identifying customer environment and product requirements
9. **Tailoring processes**—Modifying standard processes to suit a project

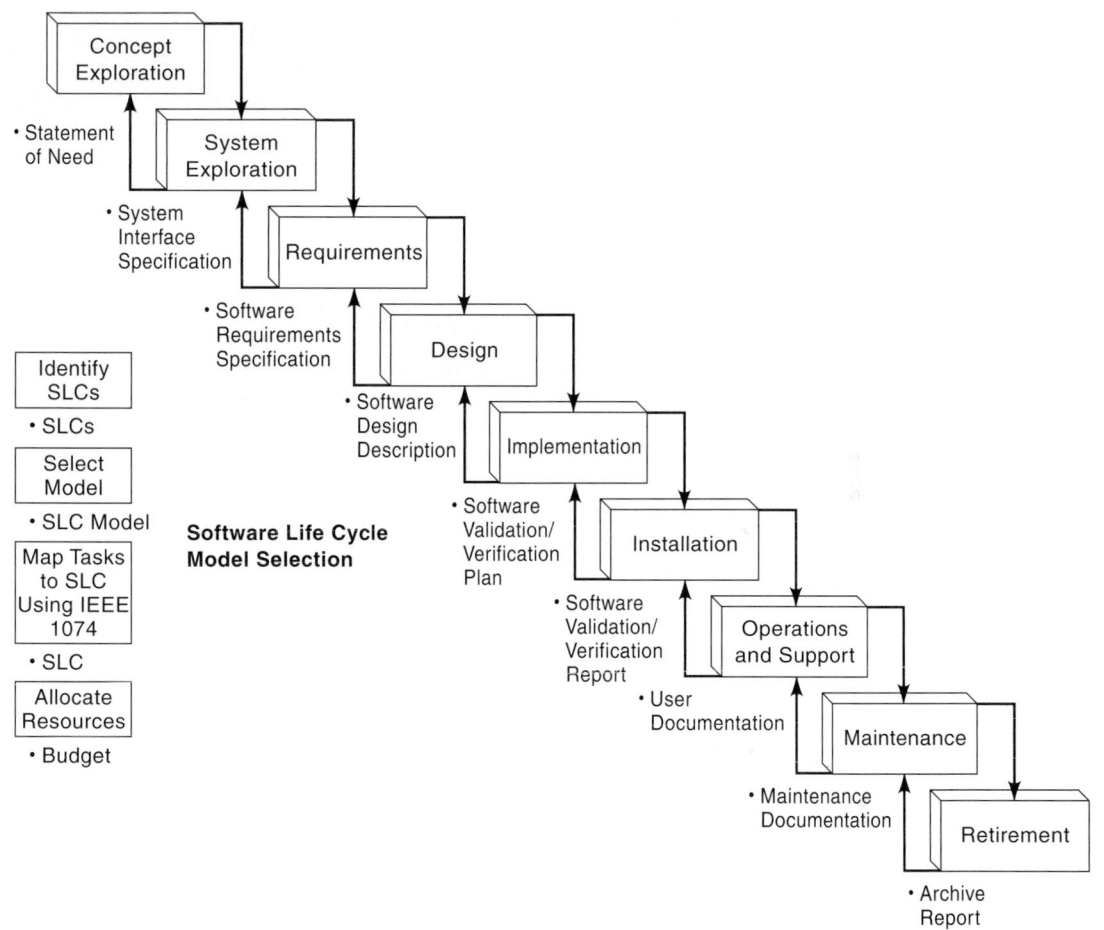

FIGURE 8–1
Product Development Life Cycle

Project Management Skills

12. **Building a work breakdown structure**—Building a WBS for a project
13. **Documenting plans**—Identifying key components
14. **Estimating cost**—Estimating cost to complete a project
15. **Estimating effort**—Estimating effort required to complete a project

People Management Skills

26. **Interaction and communication**—Dealing with developers, upper management, and other teams
27. **Leadership**—Coaching project teams for optimal results

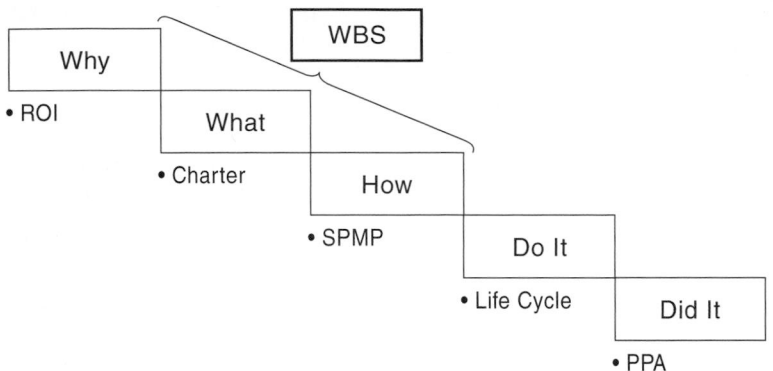

FIGURE 8–2
Project Process Framework

29. **Negotiating successfully**—Resolving conflicts and negotiating successfully
31. **Presenting effectively**—Using effective written and oral skills

Learning Objectives for Chapter 8 _____

Upon completion of this chapter, the reader should be able to:

• Describe several different WBS architectures;
• Describe the major approaches to constructing a WBS;
• Explain why a software WBS is needed;
• Explain how a software WBS is used in a software development project;
• Define what a WBS is and what milestones are;
• List and describe the steps to build a software WBS.

What Is a Work Breakdown Structure? _____

Simply stated, a WBS is a hierarchical list of the work activities required to complete a project. It will include managerial, administrative, integral, or developmental activities for:

• Doing the software development;
• Managing the project;
• Providing support for all of the project's activities;

- Any other activities required to meet the objectives of the project and the customer requirements, such as the creation of documents, training programs, tools for development, acquisitions, travel, and so on.

The WBS is a description of the work to be performed, broken down into its key components, to the lowest level. By partitioning the project into manageable pieces this way, each component can be sized (see Chapter 10) and its effort can be estimated (see Chapter 11). For software projects, most of the development effort is directly related to the size and complexity of the desired software product. Figure 10–3 is a depiction of the *what* and *how* implementation steps for a software development project. In this framework, the product-oriented WBS identifies activities at a level useful in locating available staff with the proper skills (see Chapter 6, "Selecting a Project Team"). When the number of staff members and the skills of each are determined, the effort estimates (see Chapter 10) can then be applied to a calendar to determine the duration of the project and when project milestones are due (see Chapter 15, "Scheduling the Work"). The resulting project schedule is typically shown as a Gantt chart (see Chapter 15). This completes the *how* planning step, and the project can be executed. In execution, each WBS activity can be tracked throughout the project.

A product-oriented WBS contains process steps to build the product, organized around the product components. It drives the planning for the *what* and *how* steps, and provides the foundation for tracking of work activities, cost, and schedule in the *do it* step by giving the engineer or manager a global view. It is the "table of contents" for the work of the project. As such, it is an indispensable tool for the project manager.

Remember that the triple constraint for projects is composed of scope, schedule, and cost. They relate directly to the software size, calendar due date, and resource effort that make software project managers lose sleep at night. The starting point, how to identify the goal and scope, was described in Chapter 7. Now let's look at cost and schedule. As stated earlier, we need a product-oriented WBS to make budgetary and detailed estimates of the work to be done and to develop a realistic schedule. Specifically, we need the WBS for the following three project activities:

Cost estimating

- To make sure that all activities get estimated;
- To make sure that each element of the estimate corresponds to a necessary activity;
- To "roll up" costs of individual elements into total costs for subelements and for the system as a whole.

Cost accounting

- To assign work and "charge it" to appropriate cost centers based on specific WBS elements;
- To determine the actual cost of each element.

Schedule performance

- To monitor which activities are complete;
- To measure project progress.

As shown in Figure 8–3, the WBS can be related to cost accounts created for a project to control costs, and to the organizational breakdown structure created (or perhaps inherited from a parent organization) to manage the work. The WBS can map these together with a specific scheduled work item after the schedule has been built (see Chapter 15). On a large software project, this provides a cost basis for how much each piece of the final software system will cost to build, which is an important factor to pass on to future estimators of similar software products (see Chapter 11).

Work breakdowns can be described in a number of different ways. An example of a common WBS viewed as a tree is shown in Figure 8–4. The tree view is most useful for high-level breakdowns of the work in the why and what steps of the project process framework.

Another representation for a WBS usually seen when the project planning gets detailed in the how step is as an indented list, illustrated in Figure 8–5. The indentations indicate the hierarchy as the levels do in a tree view. This is an excellent way to view the hierarchical structure of the work, when the work involves a lot of activities. Most people can readily relate to an outline format. Large indented lists are easily managed with a simple spreadsheet, permitting sorting in a variety of ways (by WBS code, responsibility, start date, etc.). Most project management scheduling tools can show the WBS as an indented list, but few show it as a tree. This

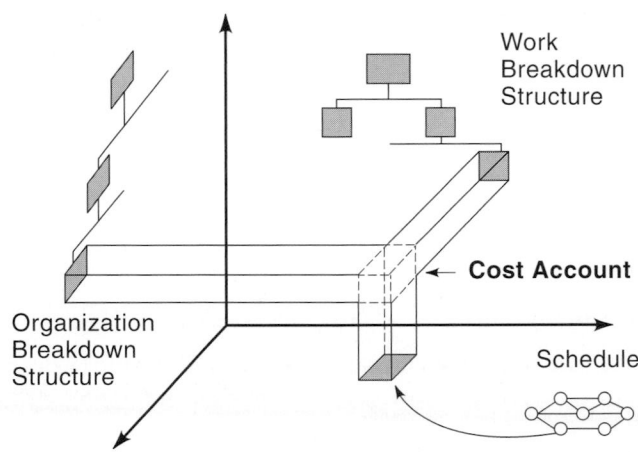

FIGURE 8–3

WBS Relationship to Cost Control

Source: Struckenbruck, Linn C., ed. (1981). *The Implementation of Project Management: the Professional's Handbook.* Reading, MA: Addison-Wesley.

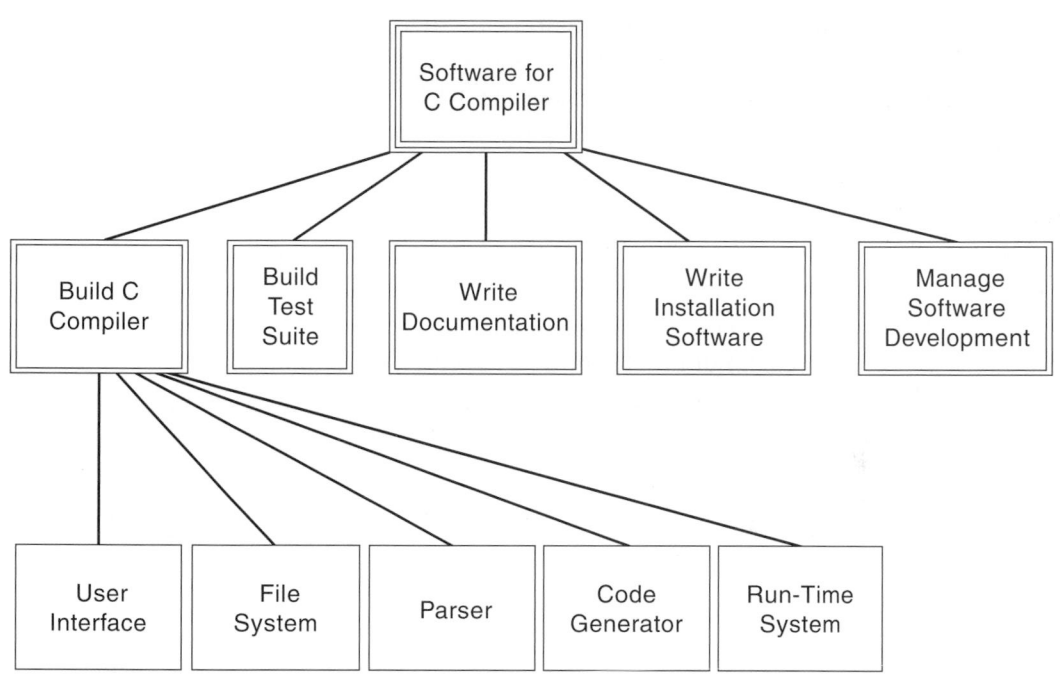

FIGURE 8–4
A Sample Work Breakdown Structure Shown as a Tree
Courtesy of Dennis J. Frailey, Principal Fellow, Raytheon Company, Plano, TX.

is perhaps because the graphical tree can get extremely large and messy-looking on a project with many activities. However, plugs-ins can sometimes add this functionality to scheduling software tools (see the Web references for this chapter).

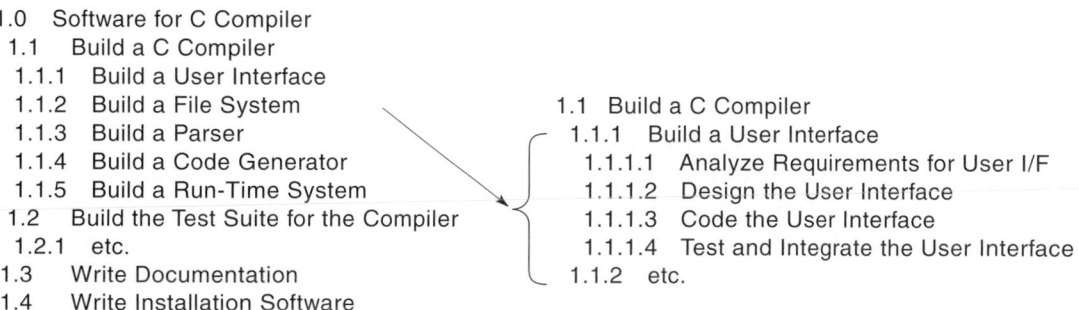

FIGURE 8–5
A Sample Work Breakdown Structure Shown as an Indented List
Courtesy of Dennis J. Frailey, Principal Fellow, Raytheon Company, Plano, TX.

Note in Figure 8–5 the use of a numbering scheme to label the items in the WBS. This is extremely helpful in distinguishing such generic activities as design, code, test, and document among several software components. In the example, 1.1.1.3 is the activity for coding the user interface, whereas 1.4 contains the activity for coding the installer script. It helps to be specific when labeling activities in a project. The numbering scheme removes ambiguity from the labeling. Most project scheduling software can automatically provide indenting and WBS or outline numbering. Notice also that similar work can be done at different levels of the WBS.

A WBS may be created for the two most common views of the project:

- A *product* view depicting hierarchical relationships among product elements (routines, modules, subsystems, etc.). But don't confuse this with a bill of materials.
- A *project* view depicting hierarchical relationships among work activities (process elements). This is often divided along organizational lines.

Both sets of elements and activities need to be considered in sizing and estimating the software to be built (see Chapters 10 and 11).

Typically, there is a unique work breakdown for each different life cycle that might be used by the organization. Even though most software development life cycles share many common activities such as decomposing system requirements, performing architectural design, creating test data, and managing the project, the ordering of these activities in each life cycle may be different. Some activities may be omitted under certain circumstances, such as prototype development, or for very small projects. Many organizations create WBSs to match these predefined life cycles of processes and activities (from a template such as IEEE 1074) that fit the typical kinds of projects that they do, such as completely new Web-based system applications, major enhancements to an existing system, or ad hoc special database projects. Many times, these are defined according to the size of the project: large, medium, or small. This concept was illustrated in Figure 3–10. Some sample activity lists for seven predefined life cycles are presented in Chapter 9, "Identifying the Tasks and Activities."

Approaches to Building a WBS

A WBS can be organized in many ways, but it is usually best to arrange the activities around major work products and customer deliverables that will satisfy the customer's requirements. We make a distinction here between work products (anything tangible produced by the project, such as the charter, SOW, SPMP, SRS, SDD, code, test suites, etc.) and deliverables (work products that the customer cares about, executable code modules, documentation, etc.). Notice in Figure 8–3 that the hierarchical "tree" of information is:

- the compiler.
- the basic parts of the compiler.
- the steps of the development process to build the basic parts of the compiler.

The first of these is the deliverable, the second are the major work product components of the deliverable, and the third are activities that would create the major components. This progression shows how the actions in the WBS branches directly correlate to the deliverable to be produced. Organizing a WBS around deliverables and the actions to produce those deliverables helps keep unnecessary work from being done on the project. Work that does not drive toward a deliverable is called "gold plating" and is not desirable.

Although organizing a WBS around the project's deliverables and work products is a good way to avoid planning extra work into the project, other arrangements are also possible. Sometimes it is more convenient to segment the work by organization at the top level rather than by deliverables or work products. This can provide a measure of control for the project by having the natural organizations that already exist be responsible for portions of the final work product. This enhances command and control of the software project. Several possible arrangements for a work breakdown structure are illustrated in Figure 8–6 as the basic elements of the project. Other elements could also be used, such as deliverables, skills, responsibilities, or chronology. In Figure 8–6, all the approaches assume that system-level decomposition has taken place and that only the software items are considered. Under System, the breakdown might have included hardware, software, and business processes.

The WBS can be created from the top down or from the bottom up, as illustrated in Figure 8–7. The top-down approach involves successive decomposition. The bottom-up approach uses brainstorming and affinity diagramming. Usually, at the beginning of a project when

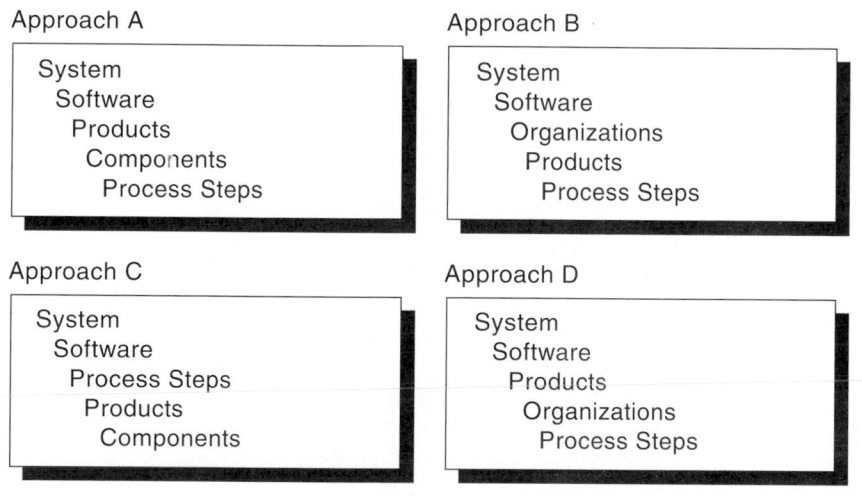

Approach A
```
System
  Software
    Products
      Components
        Process Steps
```

Approach B
```
System
  Software
    Organizations
      Products
        Process Steps
```

Approach C
```
System
  Software
    Process Steps
      Products
        Components
```

Approach D
```
System
  Software
    Products
      Organizations
        Process Steps
```

Many Others Are Possible

FIGURE 8–6
Several Possible Arrangements for a Work Breakdown Structure, Shown as an Indented List
Courtesy of Dennis J. Frailey, Principal Fellow, Raytheon Company, Plano, TX.

still in the *what* and *how* steps, the top-down approach is used. Often the tree view is used to depict the WBS because it doesn't have too many levels yet. This is a convenient representation for the project charter documents, and it helps the project manager identify the big components of work that will need to be done and to make rough order of magnitude (ROM) estimates for the work. These estimates will usually be based on a broad rule of thumb, such as extrapolation from previous similar software development projects or the gross size (large, medium, small) of the project and the type of software development life cycle anticipated. See Chapters 10 and 11 for more information on the detailed estimation of software.

The top-down approach is often used when the work has been done before and the project team understands the steps well. The top-down approach involves starting with the topmost item (usually a software deliverable, such as "Completed Software for C Compiler") and breaking it down from there, getting progressively more granular at each level. This continues until chunks of work that can reasonably be done by "one unit of resource" in a "relatively short period of time" have been reached. "One unit of resource" may be one person, one section, one department, or other organizational breakdown that makes sense for the work to be done. "Relatively short period of time" may mean one day, week, fortnight, month, or other unit that is of reasonable granularity for the scale of the project scope to provide good measurement during the execution of the project. Generally, for software development projects, a rule of thumb is to break down the work until the work can be done by one person or group over a

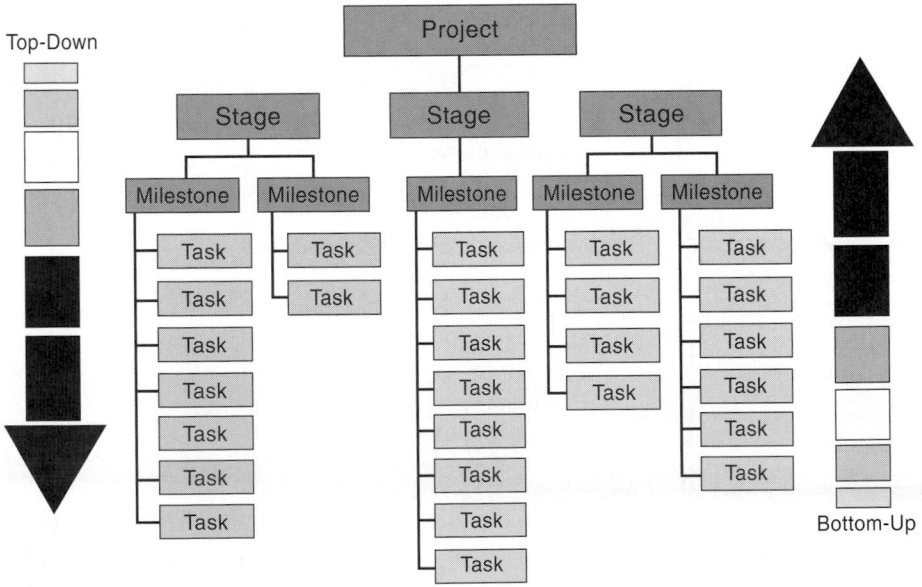

FIGURE 8–7
Build a WBS Top-Down or Bottom-Up

one- to two-week period, producing one work product. This provides a good yardstick for preventing the "big bang" approach to managing deliverables.

The bottom-up approach is a good fit for a new type of project, when the project team is not very familiar with the steps that would be performed. This approach is usually done by brainstorming everything that could be done during the project and then grouping the activities into similar levels of granularity (rough size of the work to be done) and arranging all the activities into ever-higher groupings until the top-level item is reached. This is affinity diagramming.

For either approach, avoid too much detail and granularity because it can make for very fragile plans. Don't plan in any more detail than you can manage. For example, if it is thought to take about two weeks to design a certain code module, then breaking that down into the detail steps of data element identification, data flow diagram creation, and customer review is too much detail. At some point, the project manager relies on the engineering education of the team. One common fault is to produce too much detail at the initial planning stages. You should stop when you have a sufficient description of the activity to provide clear instruction for the people who will actually do the work and to have a reasonable estimate for the total effort involved. You need the former to allocate (or delegate) the activity; you need the latter to finish the planning.

Use teams and subgroups for chunks of work rather than individuals, trying to divide the work into natural groupings corresponding to organizational units. Arrange the work so that whole organizational units have responsibility to execute activities at the lowest levels of the WBS. Also, because it is difficult to organize and manage work more than three to four levels deep in a WBS, try to limit the depth of the tree or indented list to something manageable. A very large tree is cumbersome to understand and navigate. Think of it as if it were a phone tree menu for a voicemail box. Too many sublevels frustrate the user and lead to confusion. Keep it as simple as possible, yet still express the structure and hierarchy of the project work. In Chapters 10 and 11, you will see how to use what is known about the desired software product to add more levels of breakdown to the product-oriented WBS as more information becomes known. Known as "progressive elaboration of characteristics," this is a cornerstone of most software development projects.

Defining Project Milestones

Milestones deserve special mention. A milestone is a significant event in a project, usually associated with a major work product or deliverable. They mark passage points in the journey toward completion, and every project should have enough of them, spread evenly throughout the schedule so that it is easy to measure achievement toward the final goal. With too few, you get the "big bang" project, where no one really knows until the very end if the project is on schedule. But too many can bog down the project's pace. An even spacing on a schedule calendar is desirable. Milestones have zero duration. They only mark a point in time when something important has been completed. They can be defined for the end of one or more activities, or for a work product or deliverable, or for a designated group of these. It is best to use language that indicates completion, such as "Done" or "Complete." In the C compiler example of Figure 8–5, the milestone for item 1.0 would be "Software for C Compiler Completed."

Stages or phases are not milestones but are collections of related product activities. However, milestones can be used to mark a stage or phase completion, as illustrated in Figure 8–7.

Creating Work Packages

The lowest level of the WBS is where the work gets done. These are the "leaves" on the tree representation, or the farthest indented activities in the indented list. These are called work packages and usually result in a work product being delivered. Work packages define the work product in such a way that each is clearly distinguished from all other work packages in the project. They are usually described with all the information necessary for a qualified person to carry out the work. For software development projects, these usually correspond to the lowest identifiable objects or modules to be created in a deliverable system. The contents of a work package may include:

- Description of the work product expected—software element to be produced;
- The staffing requirements—who or how many people will do this activity;
- Names of responsible individual(s)—who is responsible for seeing that it is completed;
- The scheduled start and end dates—when the activity is expected to start and to end;
- The budget assigned (dollars, hours, or other unit)—the effort estimate for the activity;
- The acceptance criteria for the work—defect level or other quality measure.

If the project staff already know these things, which is common in organizations where the same group of software engineers work together every day, then writing up a formal work package is unnecessary because they already know the tasks needed to complete the activity. However, when more control is needed to organize a group that has never worked together before and has no common software culture to provide a framework, then writing down the work package information is very helpful because it minimizes ambiguity about their assignments. It may also occur that a work package for a project becomes the scope of work for a whole subproject, which is further divided into more activities, managed as a project under the larger effort. The way to distinguish a subproject from a standalone project is to ask whether the subproject could stand alone on its own, without the larger project for context. A subproject's work product deliverable may be a standalone piece of software useful in contexts outside the scope of the current project. Creating custom software utilities is a good example of a software subproject. Most project management scheduling tools, such as Microsoft Project, have a place for notes about each activity and a way to print them as assignment handouts. This is great for getting a newly hired diverse group of software engineers to use the same processes.

Building a WBS for Software

The WBS is the key work product needed to do software project estimating. In many projects, what hurts you the most are not the things that you estimate poorly, but the things that you forget to include at all. In preparation for sizing the work to be done (see Chapters 10 and 11), follow the process in this section as a framework for estimating. As stated earlier, there is a top-down and a bottom-up approach to building any WBS. In planning any project, follow the simple rule: If an item is too complicated to manage, it becomes a list of simpler items. Here are five steps to constructing a WBS for a software project:

1. Identify the work concerning the software product (separate from hardware and work processes).
2. Find any higher system WBS (separate the software from other systems and components).
3. Determine the software WBS architecture (how to organize this software product and project).
4. Populate the software WBS architecture (identify all the parts and activities to produce them).
5. Determine cost categories for software (prepare for estimation activities).

Identify the Work Concerning Software

Go through the available documentation (that is, whatever is available to you at this point in the project) and make a complete list of all items that might impact the cost of building the software. Many possible source documents might be available:

- SOW (usually the best item to start with);
- Specifications, concept of operation;
- Requirements documents of many kinds;
- Design documents;
- Standards (internal and external);
- Customer conversations;
- Test criteria or expectations.

The list should include the what and where of each item, for trace reasons, as illustrated in Figure 8–8. This helps ensure that nothing is overlooked.

Document	Paragraph	Description
SOW	1.3.4	Design Software for Compiler
SOW	2.3.3	Travel for Design Reviews
...	...	...
Contract	7.13.2.a	Follow ISO Standard 5432f
Rqmts. Doc.	3.4	Use Data Compression
...	...	...
Customer	6/5/99 Mtg.	Code All Software in C++

FIGURE 8–8
Example List of Items Affecting Software Work
Courtesy of Dennis J. Frailey, Principal Fellow, Raytheon Company, Plano, TX.

Find Any Higher System WBS

Determine whether there is a WBS for any higher system (higher project or program) and how the software fits in. Many organizations have a standard WBS architecture that defines where the software will appear. Many project managers for systems development projects will establish a WBS that has requirements applicable to software broken out separately. Figure 8–9 shows two such possible breakouts. It is important to find out where the software fits relative to higher-level activities because this may affect how the software project portions are structured and run. For example, the systems project manager may have a specific approach to the ordering of WBS items, the number of levels to show, where to show certain kinds of costs, and so on.

The approach on the left in Figure 8–9 shows software as an embedded item under hardware in a systems project. The right side shows software as a separate but equal item with the hardware. Separate but equal may tend to isolate software planning from the rest of the system, resulting in inconsistent interpretations of requirements.

Determine the Software WBS Architecture

Determine a logical structure (architecture) for the software portion(s) of the WBS. As described earlier and illustrated in Figure 8–6, there are many possible architectures for a software WBS. Some organizations have a standard software WBS architecture to ensure consistency and make it easier to track costs. Different software products and different software development life cycles followed may need different WBS structures. Figure 8–10 shows possible software architectures using approaches A and C from Figure 8–6.

Populate the Software WBS

Populate the chosen WBS structure with activities that address the work identified in the available documentation (SOW, etc., from Step 1). Derived from the information in Figures 8–8 and 8–10, the cross-reference matrix in Figure 8–11 shows standard WBS items for the software on the right. On the left are the corresponding source documents, paragraph numbers, and descriptions that caused creation of the WBS items on the right. This enables you to be sure that all work is accounted for, and it reduces the chances that something will be omitted from the WBS. If a single SOW paragraph is reflected in several WBS elements (or vice versa), you can make several separate entries in the cross-reference matrix. This is where the WBS can become a requirements trace tool, or can be supplemented by one. Sometimes the standard

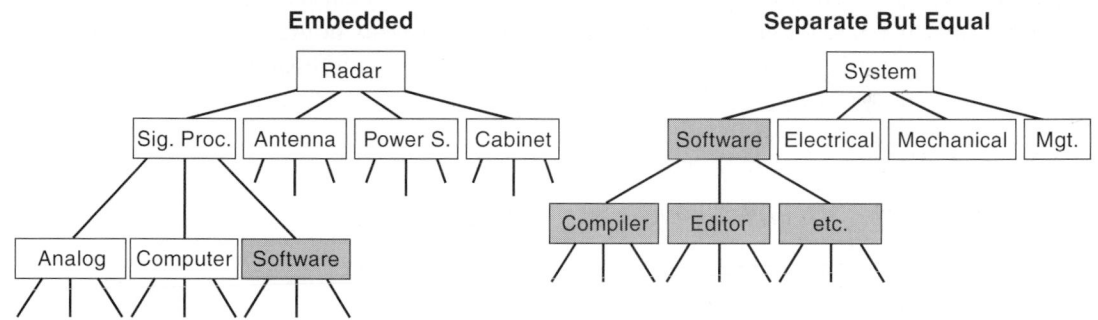

FIGURE 8–9
Example Higher Level WBS Showing Where Software Might Be Placed
Courtesy of Dennis J. Frailey, Principal Fellow, Raytheon Company, Plano, TX.

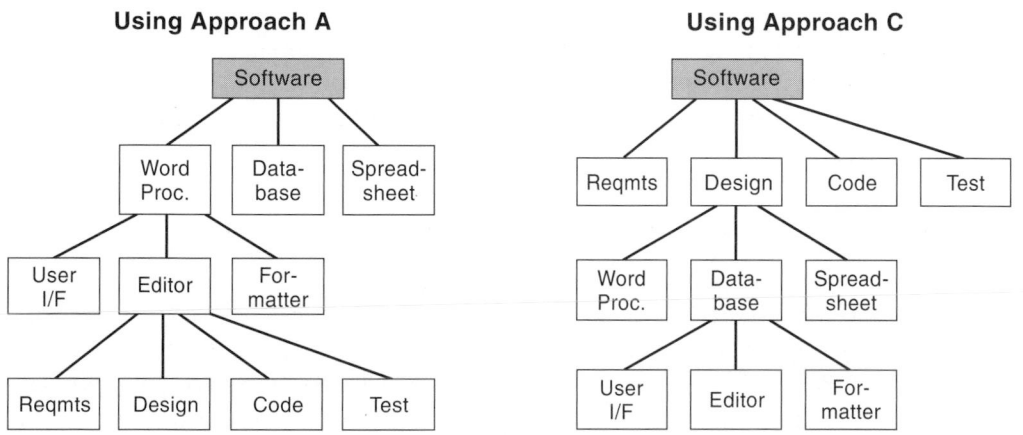

FIGURE 8–10
Example WBS Architectures for Software from Figure 8–6
Courtesy of Dennis J. Frailey, Principal Fellow, Raytheon Company, Plano, TX.

WBS is more detailed than what the source documents state. In such cases, always trace to the highest level that makes sense, to avoid excessive detail.

Determine Cost Categories for Software

Determine the cost-estimating category for each element in the WBS. This final step is not always necessary for every project, but it will be important for those that track unit-level costs in a WBS (see Figure 8–3). If this step is not done here, it needs to be done later, during the cost estimating process. Some projects use only one category of costs for simplicity. Typically, only hours are estimated. More complex projects may require more categories because different units are needed. The cost-estimating category determines how the cost for each item will be estimated as shown in Figure 8–12. Things such as capital equipment are usually estimated in currency, whereas effort is usually estimated in hours, weeks, or months of labor, which can readily be translated into units of currency. Overhead items such as project management, change control, and configuration management are estimated by using a proportional add-on to the basic software effort (a percentage).

Applying the Five WBS-Building Steps

Some items from Step 1 will be scattered throughout many WBS elements. An example is the need to use a particular standard or a particular programming language for the project. Some items from Step 1 will not seem to fit anywhere because some items in the organization's standard WBS may not be explicitly stated in source documents for this project. Examples of such items are training, project management, facilities needs, and development tools.

Info Source	Requirement	Software WBS Item
SOW 1.1.1	Develop C Compiler	1.0 Software for C Compiler
SPEC 2.0	Develop Compiler	1.1 Build a C Compiler
SPEC 2.1	User I/F for PC	1.1.1 Build a User I/F
PROC STD 3.4	Requirements Analysis	1.1.1.1 RA for User I/F
PROC STD 3.5	Design	1.1.1.2 Design for User I/F
....	....	....
SPEC 2.2	File System	1.1.2 Build a File System
....	....	....
SPEC 3.0	Test Company Stds	1.2 Build the Test Suite
....	....	....
SOW 2.3.4	Provide User Guide	1.3 Write Documentation
....	....	....

FIGURE 8–11
Example Cross-Reference Matrix for Software from Figure 8–6
Courtesy of Dennis J. Frailey, Principal Fellow, Raytheon Company, Plano, TX.

Doc	Para	WBS #	Description	Category
SOW	1.3.4	1.1.2.2	Design Software for Compiler	Software
....	....	....		
SOW	2.3.3	1.7.1	Travel for Design Reviews	Actual $ Cost
....				

FIGURE 8–12
Example Cost Categories
Courtesy of Dennis J. Frailey, Principal Fellow, Raytheon Company, Plano, TX.

These project-supporting functions are usually shown as a separate branch on the WBS tree. After the WBS is created and validated, with its accompanying and supporting items such as the cross-reference matrix, it can serve as a framework for all the activities that will be done on the software development project. It is the software project's table of contents.

Summary

In this chapter, we defined the work breakdown structure (WBS) and showed how important it is to the project. You've seen how to construct a framework for any software development project around a product-oriented WBS. We also discussed the top-down and bottom-up approaches to building a WBS.

Studying the WBS has prepared you for Chapter 9 where you will see how to populate a WBS with appropriate tasks, and for Chapters 10 and 11 where you will see how the size of the defined work products and the effort to produce them are determined.

Problems for Review

1. Where should milestones be represented in a WBS? Why?
2. What is the value of a product-oriented WBS to a software development project manager?

Visit the Case Study

Mr. Lu has wonderful news for you, the CRM ARRS project manager. His new assistant, Dr. Zhou, the first PMI-certified PMP in mainland China, will be going to the Bangalore Development Center for a 90-day exchange assignment arranged by your corporation's manufacturing manager in Tianjin. She wants to develop a detailed software project management template for the CRM and use your project as the lighthouse system. What do you need to do to reconcile your existing project plan to this new requirement? How will you adjust your prototype life cycle WBS to accommodate that of a full-blown software development project?

Suggested Readings

Archibald, Russell D. (1992). *Managing High-Technology Programs and Projects*, 2nd ed. New York, NY: John Wiley & Sons.

Brown, Karen A., and Nancy Lea Hyer (2001). "Mind Mapping as a WBS Development Tool." PMI 2001 Seminar and Symposium, Nashville, TN.

Cleland, David I. (1994). *Project Management: Strategic Design and Implementation*, 2nd ed. New York, NY: McGraw-Hill.

Goldratt, Eliyahu M., and Jeff Cox (1993). *The Goal: A Process of Ongoing Improvement*, 2nd ed. Aldershot, Hampshire, England: Gower.

Kerzner, Harold (1998). *Project Management: A Systems Approach to Planning, Scheduling, and Controlling*, 6th ed. New York, NY: John Wiley & Sons.

King, David (1992). *Project Management Made Simple: A Guide to Successful Management of Computer Systems Projects*. Englewood Cliffs, NJ: Yourdon Press.

Lavold, Gary D. (1998). "Developing Using the Work Breakdown Structure." *Project Management Handbook*, 2nd ed., David I. Cleland and William R. King, eds. New York, NY: Van Nostrand Reinhold.

Lewis, James P. (1995). *Project Planning, Scheduling, and Control: A Hands-On Guide to Bringing Projects in on Time and on Budget*, rev ed. Chicago, IL: Irwin.

Lewis, James P. (1998). *Mastering Project Management: Applying Advanced Concepts of Systems Thinking, Control and Evaluation, Resource Allocation*. New York, NY: McGraw-Hill.

Lewis, James P. (1998). *Team-Based Project Management*. New York, NY: American Management Association.

Lewis, James P. (2000). *The Project Manager's Desk Reference: A Comprehensive Guide to Project Planning, Scheduling, Evaluation, and Systems*. New York, NY: McGraw-Hill.

Paulk, Mark C., et al. (1994). *The Capability Maturity Model: Guidelines for Improving the Software Process*. Reading, MA: Addison-Wesley. Section 7.2, "Software Project Planning" and Section 7.3, "Software Project Tracking and Oversight."

Pressman, Roger S. (2001). *Software Engineering: A Practitioner's Approach*, 5th ed. Boston, MA: McGraw-Hill.

Warner, Paul (1998). "How to Use the Work Breakdown Structure." *Field Guide to Project Management*, David I. Cleland, ed. New York, NY: John Wiley & Sons.

Web Pages for Further Information _____

varatek.com/howtowbs0.html. Work Breakdown Structure Development. "How To Create A Project Work Breakdown Structure (WBS)." Varatek Software, Inc.

www.4pm.com/articles/wbs.html. "Work Breakdown Structure: Important Project Design Issue or Clerical Task?"

www.acq.osd.mil/pm/newpolicy/wbs/wbs.html. MIL-HDBK-881, "Work Breakdown Structures (WBS) for Defense Material Items."

www.dir.state.tx.us/eod/qa/contents.htm. State of Texas, Department of Information Resources, Internal Quality Assurance Guidelines.

www.jsc.nasa.gov/bu2/PCEHHTML/pceh.htm. Parametric Cost Estimating Handbook.

www.pmi.org/publictn/pmboktoc.htm. PMI's *A Guide to the Project Management Body of Knowledge (PMBOK® Guide).*

Identifying the Tasks and Activities

As described in Chapter 8, "Creating the Work Breakdown Structure," building a product-oriented work breakdown structure (WBS) involves decomposing a large activity (the whole project) into successively smaller activities (top-down approach) until the work is described in detail to manage properly. Alternatively, it involves brainstorming everything that needs to be done as detailed activities and arranging them until enough are present to carry out and manage the work (bottom-up approach). In either case, identifying the right activities for the work is paramount.

The triple constraint for any project (scope, schedule, cost) is largely dependent on getting the scope right because it usually drives the schedule and cost of a software development project. In Chapter 10, "Software Size and Reuse Estimating," we'll see how the product-oriented WBS is the primary determinant of the scope and cost portions for software projects, as product size is the primary determinant of effort for software, an intellectual product. In this chapter, we explore the identification of tasks and activities that software engineers use to produce the elements of a product-oriented WBS, and we consider how to arrange them for best effect in the life cycle models described in Chapter 4, "Selecting Software Development Life Cycles."

The tie to the software development life cycle models will be done through a series of checklists. Once the project manager has decided on a life cycle model, these checklists can be used to identify tasks and activities.

Where We Are in the Product Development Life Cycle

Where are we in the basic software life cycle model that serves as our map? As shown in Figure 4–1 and in Figure 9–1, we are still at the beginning of the software life cycle and are deeply involved in the *what* step of project planning, as shown in Figure 9–2.

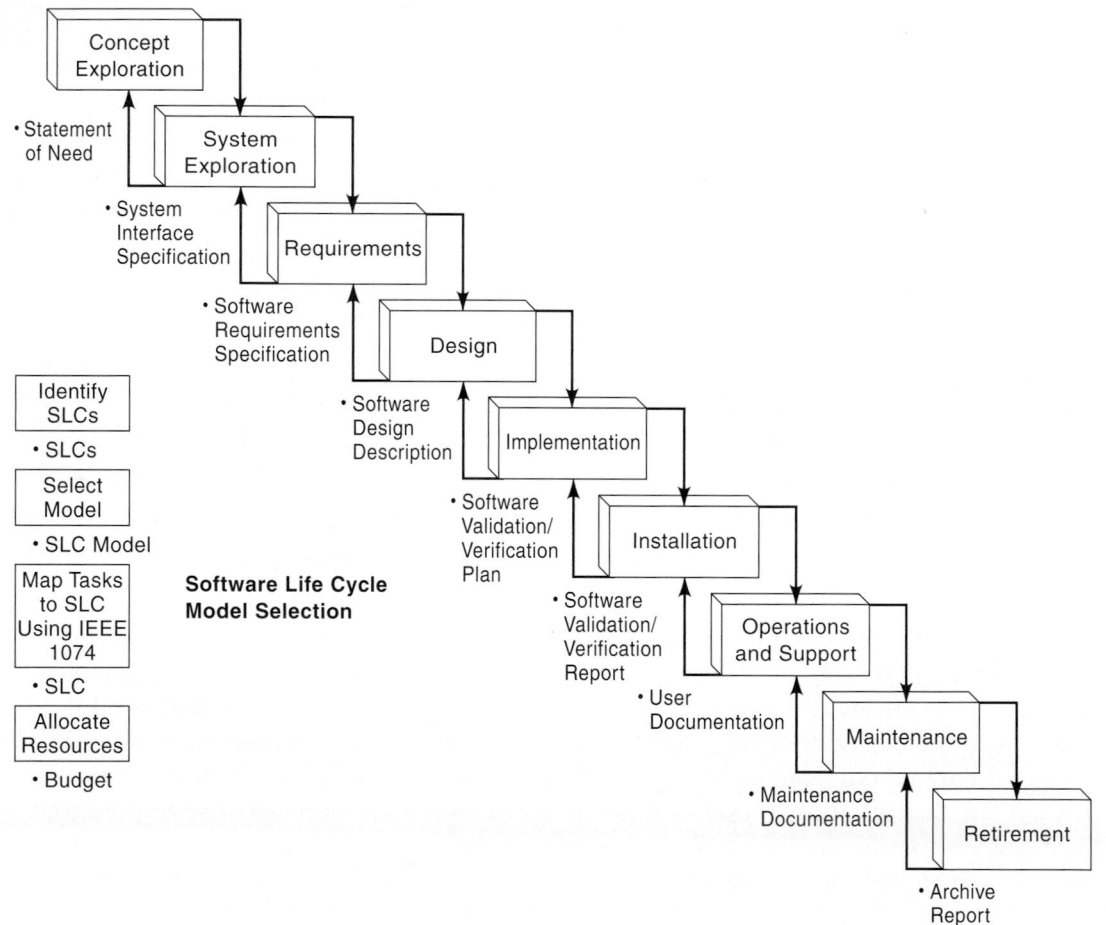

FIGURE 9–1
Product Development Life Cycle

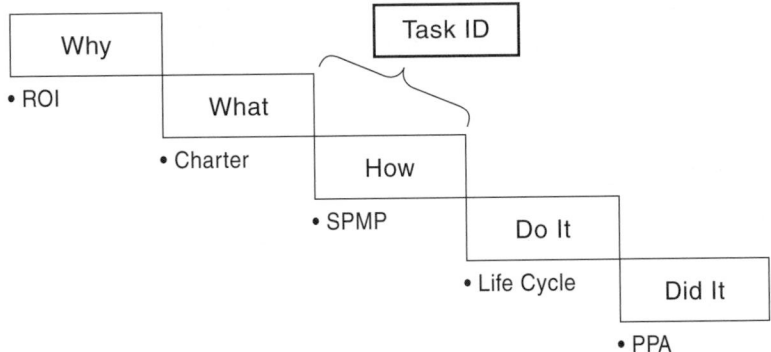

FIGURE 9–2
Project Process Framework

Chapter 9 Relation to the 34 Competencies _____

This chapter concerns the competencies shown next. For identifying tasks and activities, the key product development technique needed is an awareness of the processes of software development using different life cycles. Life cycles must be evaluated and tailored to the individual needs of each project. A general understanding of software development activities (software engineering) and how to define the software product are competencies needed for task and activity identification.

The project management skills needed here are a continuation of those needed for building the WBS, such as documenting plans in an arranged structure and finding tasks and activities that can be used to create a schedule. Activity ID requires the people skills of leadership, interface, and communication, and the ability to present ideas effectively throughout the identification process.

Product Development Techniques

1. **Assessing processes**—Defining criteria for reviews
3. **Defining the product**—Identifying customer environment and product requirements
4. **Evaluating alternative processes**—Evaluating various approaches
9. **Tailoring processes**—Modifying standard processes to suit a project
11. **Understanding development activities**—Learning the software development cycle

Project Management Skills

12. **Building a work breakdown structure**—Building a WBS for a project
13. **Documenting plans**—Identifying key components
18. **Scheduling**—Creating a schedule and key milestones

People Management Skills

26. **Interaction and communication**—Dealing with developers, upper management, and other teams

27. **Leadership**—Coaching project teams for optimal results

31. **Presenting effectively**—Using effective written and oral skills

Learning Objectives for Chapter 9 _____

Upon completion of this chapter, the reader should be able to:

- Define a task and an activity, describe the difference between, and tell which is used where;
- Prepare a meaningful activity label;
- List several sources for software engineering activities;
- Demonstrate the ability to map activities to each of the life cycles discussed in Chapter 4;
- Identify the characteristics of a useful and meaningful activity for a WBS;
- List at least three common types of activities found in every software project;
- Explain how to construct a customized WBS;
- Find at least five uses of the same activity among the life cycles presented in Chapter 4;
- Use the checklists provided to identify tasks and activities in different software development life cycle models.

Characteristics of Tasks and Activities _____

How hard can it be to identify the work that needs to done for a software project? It's mostly common sense, isn't it? What seems like a straightforward assignment can be riddled with opportunities for poor results. The first thing to address is what tasks and activities are. These were first visited in Chapter 1, "Introduction," where we introduced some of the important definitions for understanding software project management. The PMBOK® offers these definitions:

> **Activity**—An element of work performed during the course of a project. An activity normally has an expected duration, an expected cost, and expected resource requirements. Activities can be subdivided into tasks.

> **Task**—A generic term for work that is not included in the WBS but that potentially could be a further decomposition of work by the individuals responsible for that work. Also, the lowest level of effort on a project.

This means that, technically, a WBS is composed only of activities, and those activities are composed of task effort. The task effort is what a professional is educated for and is expected to know how to do. For software engineers, task effort would encompass designing, coding, compiling, debugging, and documenting. Skills in various programming languages and with an assortment of software development tools fall into the task realm for a software project. Those are things that you would expect a skilled software practitioner to already know how to do. In this chapter, we focus on the activities that take place in a software development project.

Whether considered tasks or activities, the characteristics of activity identification that we will discuss are the label, size, and source.

Meaningful Label

Many developers seem to believe that the SPMP is just one large task called *do it*. But that is not a very descriptive label, and we know that software development is more than that (a lot more). So, we want to describe the work with more accuracy and meaning. The most obvious requirement for an activity ID is that it should clearly describe the work to be done. However, too many developers and managers don't use enough verbs in their activity labels that are supposed to describe processes. Instead of an activity label such as "build a C compiler," it might appear as just "C compiler." This leaves ambiguity as to exactly what is meant by the label. Is it to build the whole thing, or just some parts? Does it include the test suite and documentation? Or does it really mean "completed C compiler" as a major deliverable? Try to avoid a whole WBS with nothing but a hierarchy of nouns. There have to be some verbs somewhere because the verbs supply the action to get the work done. Of course, putting too many words in an activity label is also not a good practice because it makes the WBS unwieldy. It is best to keep the labels as short, simple sentences with a verb and a noun. Many people call this "bullet language," referring to the abbreviated wording for presentation slides. This is acceptable because further explanation and qualification can occur in notes about the activity or in the work package information for it.

Optimal Activity Size

Just how big is a unit of work? "Optimal" for software development projects means whatever fits the scale and scope of the current project. There is no one number for this. As mentioned in Chapter 8, activities should be chunks of work that can reasonably be done by "one unit of resource" in a "relatively short period of time." "One unit of resource" could mean any reasonable organizational segment, down to the individual, and "relatively short period of time" could mean any time period that provides adequate measurement for goal achievement and that the project team is willing to measure.

Initially, your best guess, or "gut feel," provides a guide for determining how big a chunk of work should be. Later, when the requirements for the software product are refined (Chapter 16,

"Eliciting Requirements") and the software size can be estimated (Chapter 10, "Software Size and Reuse Estimating") to help determine the effort needed (Chapter 11, "Estimating Duration and Cost"), a more accurate sizing of activities can occur.

Remember that one of the characteristics of a project is "progressive elaboration of characteristics." This means that you cannot be expected to have all the detail needed for the project plans at the start of the project. You learn as you go, increasing the amount of detail in near-term plans. So, a large activity may be further broken down into smaller activities as the detail becomes known. For example, at the beginning of the project, the activity may be "design interfaces." As more information is known about the requirements and design, it may be broken into the subactivities "design main functions menu" and "design utility menu." Again, break down work only as far as is practical for the work to be understood and manageable for the organizational maturity of the project's environment.

Source

From where do you get a list of activities and tasks to run a software development project and build a software product? The source depends on whether there is any project precedent. If neither you nor your organization has done a project like this before or has any other history to draw from, then the detailed work steps to create it must be invented. An approach to invention of product development activities using brainstorming with the project team and stakeholders is described later. If there is a project precedent, reviewing the activities used on it can provide some guidance for activity identification. Even if no precedent exists, professional organizations such as the SEI, ISO, or IEEE provide sources for software development activities. The SEI models have been discussed elsewhere. ISO/IEC 12207 lists 12 engineering activities following process implementation that are similar to the phases in a typical software life cycle model:

1. System requirement analysis
2. System architectural design
3. Software requirements analysis
4. Software architectural design
5. Software detailed design
6. Software coding and testing
7. Software integration
8. Software qualification testing
9. System integration
10. System qualification testing
11. Software installation
12. Software acceptance testing

The IEEE publishes a standard for life cycle model definitions that contains 17 processes of 65 activities that cover the essential activities of software development. These will be studied in the next section.

The Activity ID Process

There are really only two ways that tasks and activities are identified for a project: They are part of a pre-existing WBS for a software development life cycle, or they are invented anew for a unique development project situation. Either way, customization occurs. We'll look at both approaches and explore how to select and organize tasks for a software development project. First, in this chapter, let's look at how we use these sources as a guide to activity identification for a given software project. Then, in Chapter 14, "Considering Dependencies," we'll look at ways to invent them when no guide exists already.

Adapting Life Cycle Activities for Common Situations

IEEE 1074 provides a set of 17 processes and 65 activities that software projects may need to carry out the work of software engineering organized by where they fit in the basic product development life cycle that serves as our map (Figure 4–1). These are shown in Table 9–1, which is a tabular form of Figure 4–1, with activities added. The 34 competencies that every software project manager should know directly relate to the 65 software development project activities shown, and they are explained in more detail elsewhere in this book.

Development (product) activities may include analysis, high-level design, low-level design, coding, testing, and other tasks that occur in the life cycle phases. Managerial activities may include project planning, tracking, control, risk analysis, and so on. Support activities may include documentation of deliverables such as a user's manual, operations guides, network communications, and so on. All of these kinds of activities are part of a product-oriented project WBS. We call managerial, administrative, and support tasks *integral tasks*, traversing one or more (sometimes all) of the development tasks. Other integral tasks include configuration management procedures, software quality assurance practices, risk analysis and management, software development tools and techniques, methods of conducting reviews of in-process deliverables, metrics to be collected and analyzed, definition and documentation of standards (rules for in-process deliverables), and any other activities required to meet customer requirements, such as creation of documents, training programs, tool development, or acquisition.

The challenge for every software development project manager is to map the activities in Table 9–1 into a life cycle model that fits the current project situation, and then describe them in enough detail for the organization's personnel to understand and execute. Each of the activities in the table may need further breakdown to be useful to your project team. For example, "plan configuration management" may be all that is needed for a project in an

Development Phase	Life Cycle Processes	Activities
Software Life Cycle Model Planning	1. Map the SLCM to project needs	1. Identify candidate SLCMs 2. Select project model
Project Management	2. Project initiation	3. Map activities to the SLCM 4. Allocate project resources 5. Establish project environment 6. Plan project management
	3. Project monitoring and control	7. Analyze risks 8. Perform contingency planning 9. Manage the project 10. Retain records 11. Implement problem reporting method
	4. Software quality management	12. Plan software quality management 13. Define metrics 14. Manage software quality 15. Identify quality improvement needs
Predevelopment	5. Concept exploration	16. Identify ideas or needs 17. Formulate potential approaches 18. Conduct feasibility studies 19. Plan system transition (if applicable) 20. Refine and finalize the idea or need
	6. System allocation	21. Analyze functions 22. Develop system architecture 23. Decompose system requirements
Development	7. Requirements	24. Define and develop software requirements 25. Define interface requirements 26. Prioritize and integrate software requirements
	8. Design	27. Perform architectural design 28. Design database (if applicable) 29. Design interfaces 30. Select or develop algorithms (if applicable) 31. Perform detailed design
	9. Implementation	32. Create test data 33. Create source code 34. Generate object code

(Continues)

Development Phase	Life Cycle Processes	Activities
		35. Create operating documentation
		36. Plan integration
		37. Perform integration
Post-Development	10. Installation	38. Plan installation
		39. Distribute software
		40. Install software
		41. Accept software in operational environment
	11. Operation and support	42. Operate the system
		43. Provide technical assistance and consulting
		44. Maintain support request log
	12. Maintenance	45. Reapply software life cycle
	13. Retirement	46. Notify user(s)
		47. Conduct parallel operations (if applicable)
		48. Retire system
Integral	14. Verification and validation	49. Plan verification and validation
		50. Execute verification and validation tasks
		51. Collect and analyze metric data
		52. Plan testing
		53. Develop test requirements
		54. Execute the tests
	15. Software configuration management	55. Plan configuration management
		56. Develop configuration identification
		57. Perform configuration control
		58. Perform status accounting
	16. Documentation development	59. Plan documentation
		60. Implement documentation
		61. Produce and distribute documentation
	17. Training	62. Plan the training program
		63. Develop training materials
		64. Validate the training program
		65. Implement the training program

organization in which a sophisticated configuration management (CM) system and process are in place and in which the staff is trained for its proper use. The activity may need only a minimal work package description, such as "arrange for CM support from department coordinator." No separate software configuration management plan (SCMP) document is needed. It may instead just be a section in the project's software project management plan (SPMP). However, for a new organization, this activity may involve considerably more work, including the design of a CM system and the selection, purchasing, installation, and training for a supporting software configuration management toolset. This would imply that a separate (and probably very detailed) SCMP should be developed. The scope of these two activity extremes is very different, as is the effort to carry them out.

One other thing to note about the activities in Table 9–1 is that all the activities follow the guidelines mentioned earlier for a proper activity label. The action levels have verbs and nouns, making their meaning more precise.

Software Development Life Cycle Activities

The actual construction of customized software development life cycles is covered in Chapter 4. Here, we will look at the common types of life cycle models derived from different arrangements of the activities in Table 9–1. We will look at the activities and corresponding descriptions for the following software development life cycles described in more detail in Chapter 4:

- Waterfall model
- V-shaped model
- Structured evolutionary rapid prototyping model
- Rapid application development (RAD) model
- Incremental model
- Spiral model

Each of these life cycle models has a different set of activities and tasks for the main development portions. The integral process activities (e.g., configuration management, verification, documentation) are all the same for each model. Table 9–2 shows the checklist for those common tasks and activities. It should be used as a companion to all of the other life cycle checklists.

TABLE 9–2
Integral Activities for All Life Cycle Models

Integral activities—Support activities occurring throughout the life cycle	
• Project monitoring and control	• Analyze risks
	• Perform contingency planning
	• Manage the project
	• Retain records
	• Implement problem reporting method
• Software quality management	• Plan software quality management
	• Define metrics
	• Manage software quality
	• Identify quality improvement needs
• Verification and validation	• Plan verification and validation
	• Execute verification and validation tasks
	• Collect and analyze metric data
• Software configuration management	• Plan configuration management
	• Develop configuration identification
	• Perform configuration control
	• Perform status accounting
• Documentation development	• Plan documentation
	• Implement documentation
	• Produce and distribute documentation
• Training	• Plan the training program
	• Develop training materials
	• Validate the training program
	• Implement the training program

You will note that many of these life cycles derived from sources such as IEEE 1074 include both product development and ongoing maintenance operations in their design. Recall Figure 7–5. Do not lose sight of the fact that the actual development project ends when the software products are developed and ongoing operations and maintenance activities begin. Operations and maintenance activities (sometimes called "sustaining") typically occupy a much larger portion of the lifetime of the average software product and should not be included when referring to the development project. This conforms to the relative sizes of the cost curve areas in Figure 9–3.

In most organizations, software maintenance activities are often more than meets the eye. There are at least three types of maintenance activities:

- **Corrective (about 20%)**—Removing defects in the product deliverables (software, manuals, training, etc.)
- **Adaptive (about 20%)**—Accommodating changing environments (platform changes, rules and regulation changes such as tax rates, and laws governing official data reporting)
- **Perfective (about 60%)**—Adding capabilities or changing features as requested by users

The sum of these types of maintenance activities constitutes about two-thirds of the total costs for an average software product during its lifetime. Because perfection at initial release is unlikely for most software products, some corrective maintenance can be expected to

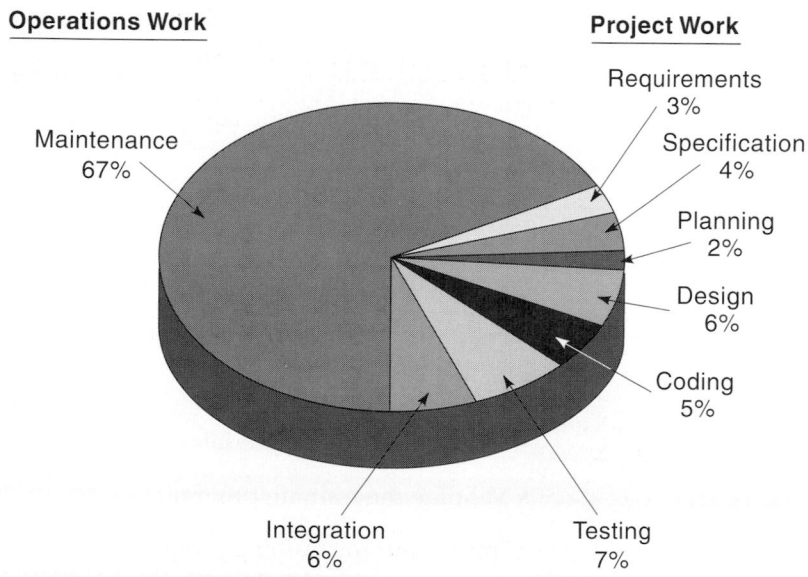

Operations Work

Project Work

Maintenance 67%

Requirements 3%

Specification 4%

Planning 2%

Design 6%

Coding 5%

Integration 6%

Testing 7%

FIGURE 9–3
Typical Software Maintenance Life Cycle Cost Distribution
Source: Stephen Schach (1992). *Practical Software Engineering*. Irwin and Aksen Associates. p. 5.

occur in any operations phase of a product's full life cycle. This should be factored into the operations budget for the sustaining organization. The adaptive and perfective types, however, could probably be treated as a separate development project to prepare a major release of the software product. These are the types of maintenance that result from changing environments and increased problem knowledge during the course of the original software product development project. Some of the life cycle models discussed next include these operations and maintenance activities in their descriptions, and some do not.

Another thing to note about the activity arrangements for a WBS in the models is that, even though some models are depicted as circular, they must be "straightened" for representation in a project WBS. Their circular, looping, iterative nature comes from doing certain activities repeatedly. For instance, the spiral model can be thought of as a straight line if it is "uncoiled" and flattened. The project planner must use judgment and experience to decide how many loops through the spiral to plan for.

Waterfall Model Activities

As described in Chapter 4 and depicted in Figure 4–9, the waterfall model is a linear arrangement of most of the activities in Table 9–1. These are arranged into phases using the processes and activities shown in Table 9–3.

TABLE 9–3
Waterfall Model Checklist of Potential Activities and Tasks

Life Cycle Phase	
Potential Activities	**Potential Tasks**
Concept exploration—Examining requirements at the system level to determine feasibility	
• Identify ideas or needs	
• Formulate potential approaches	
• Conduct feasibility studies	
• Plan system transition (if applicable)	
• Refine and finalize the idea or need	
System allocation process—Mapping functions to software or hardware based on the overall system architecture	
• Analyze functions	
• Develop system architecture	

(Continues)

TABLE 9–3 (Continued)
Waterfall Model Checklist of Potential Activities and Tasks

Life Cycle Phase	
Potential Activities	**Potential Tasks**

• Decompose system requirements

Requirements process—Defining software requirements for the system's information domain and function, behavior, performance, and interfaces

• Define and develop software requirements

• Define interface requirements

• Prioritize and integrate software requirements

Design process—Developing and representing a coherent, technical specification of the software system, including data structures, software architecture, interface representations, and procedural (algorithmic) detail

• Perform architectural design

• Design the database (if applicable)

• Design interfaces

• Select or develop algorithms (if applicable)

• Perform detailed design

Implementation process—Transforming the software design description into a software product, producing source code, databases, and documentation, whether developed, purchased, or a blend

• Create test data

• Create source code

• Generate object code

• Create operating documentation

• Plan integration

• Perform integration

(Continues)

TABLE 9–3 (Continued)
Waterfall Model Checklist of Potential Activities and Tasks

Life Cycle Phase	
Potential Activities	**Potential Tasks**

Installation process—Installing and checking out the software in the operational environment and getting formal customer acceptance of the software

- Plan installation

- Distribute software

- Install software

- Accept software in operational environment

Operation and support process—Involving user operation of the system and ongoing support, including providing technical assistance, consulting with the user, and recording user requests for enhancements and changes, and handling corrections or errors

- Operate the system

- Provide technical assistance and consulting

- Maintain support request log

Maintenance process—Resolving requests to address software errors, faults, failures, enhancements, and changes generated by the support process

- Reapply a software life cycle (initiate a development project)

Retirement process—Removing an existing system from its active use, either by ceasing its operation, replacing it with a completely new system, or replacing it with an upgraded version of the existing system

- Notify user(s)

- Conduct parallel operations (if applicable)

- Retire system

Integral activities—See Table 9–2.

V-Shaped Model Activities

The V-shaped model, described in Chapter 4 and shown in Figure 4–10, is a linear arrangement of most of the activities in Table 9–1, similar to the waterfall model. The checklist for the V-shaped model's tasks and activities is shown in Table 9–4.

TABLE 9–4
V-Shaped Model Checklist of Potential Activities and Tasks

Life Cycle Phase	
Potential Activities	**Potential Tasks**
Project and requirements planning—Determining the system requirements and how the resources of the organization will be allocated to meet them	
• Initiate the project	• Map activities to the SLCM
	• Allocate project resources
	• Establish project environment
	• Plan project management
• Explore the concept	• Identify ideas or needs
	• Formulate potential approaches
	• Conduct feasibility studies
	• Plan system transition (if applicable)
	• Refine and finalize the idea or need
• Manage software quality	• Plan software quality management
	• Define metrics
Product requirements and specification analysis—Analysis and specification of the expected external behavior of the software system to be built	
• Analyze system allocation	• Analyze functions
	• Develop system architecture
	• Decompose system requirements
• Identify software requirements	• Define and develop software requirements
	• Define interface requirements

TABLE 9–4 (Continued)
V-Shaped Model Checklist of Potential Activities and Tasks

Life Cycle Phase	
Potential Activities	**Potential Tasks**
	• Prioritize and integrate software requirements

Architecture or high-level design—Defining how the software functions are to implement the design

• Perform high-level design

• Perform architectural design

• Design the database (if applicable)

• Design interfaces

Detailed design—Defining and documenting algorithms for each component that was defined during the architecture phase

• Select or develop algorithms (if applicable)

• Perform detailed design

Coding—Transforming the algorithms defined during the detailed design phase into software

• Create source code

• Generate object code

• Create operating documentation

Unit testing—Checking each coded module for errors

• Plan testing

• Develop test requirements

• Create test data

• Execute the tests

Integration and testing—Interconnecting the sets of previously unit-tested modules to ensure that the sets behave as well as the independently tested modules did during the unit testing phase

(Continues)

TABLE 9–4 (Continued)
V-Shaped Model Checklist of Potential Activities and Tasks

Life Cycle Phase	
Potential Activities	**Potential Tasks**

- Plan integration

- Perform integration

- Plan testing

- Develop test requirements

- Create test data

- Execute the tests

System testing—Checking whether the entire software system (fully integrated) embedded in its actual hardware environment behaves according to the software requirements specification

- Plan testing

- Develop test requirements

- Create test data

- Execute the tests

Acceptance testing—Allowing the users to test the functionality of the system against the original requirements. After final testing, the software and its surrounding hardware become operational. Maintenance of the system follows.

- Plan installation

- Distribute software

- Install software

- Plan testing

- Develop test requirements

- Create test data

- Execute the tests

- Accept software in operational
  environment

(Continues)

TABLE 9–4 (Continued)
V-Shaped Model Checklist of Potential Activities and Tasks

Life Cycle Phase	
Potential Activities	**Potential Tasks**

Production, operation, and maintenance—Putting software into production and providing for enhancement and corrections

- Operate the system
- Provide technical assistance and consulting
- Maintain support request log

Integral activities—See Table 9–2.

Structured Evolutionary Rapid Prototyping Model Activities

The structured evolutionary rapid prototyping model, described in Chapter 4 and illustrated in Figure 4–11, is a circular arrangement of most of the activities in Table 9–1, but it is done linearly several times, with more robust deliverables each time. One version of the structured evolutionary rapid prototyping model's tasks and activities is shown in Table 9–5.

TABLE 9–5
Rapid Prototyping Model Checklist of Potential Activities and Tasks

Life Cycle Phase	
Potential Activities	**Potential Tasks**

Joint project planning—User and designer jointly developing a preliminary project plan outlining rough schedules and deliverables

• Initiate the project	• Map activities to the SLCM
	• Allocate project resources
	• Establish project environment
	• Plan project management
• Explore the concept	• Identify ideas or needs
	• Formulate potential approaches
	• Conduct feasibility studies

(Continues)

TABLE 9–5 (Continued)
Rapid Prototyping Model Checklist of Potential Activities and Tasks

Life Cycle Phase	
Potential Activities	**Potential Tasks**
	• Plan system transition
	• Refine and finalize the idea or need

Develop paper prototype—User and designer work together to define the requirements and specifications for the critical parts of the envisioned system to produce an intentionally incomplete high-level paper model

Rapid analysis—User and designer jointly designing from preliminary requirements

• Analyze system allocation	• Analyze functions
	• Develop preliminary system architecture
	• Decompose preliminary system requirements
• Identify preliminary software requirements	• Conduct preliminary user interviews
	• Define and develop preliminary software requirements
	• Define preliminary interface requirements
	• Prioritize and integrate software requirements

Database creation—Jointly identify the preliminary database elements

• Perform preliminary architectural design

• Design the preliminary database

Design the user interface—Jointly define how the software should interact with the user

• Design preliminary interfaces

Design the algorithmic functions

• Select or develop algorithms (on paper only)

(Continues)

TABLE 9–5 (Continued)
Rapid Prototyping Model Checklist of Potential Activities and Tasks

Life Cycle Phase	
Potential Activities	**Potential Tasks**

Create partial requirements specification—Used to build the initial prototype

Produce software prototype of system—Using the rapid analysis requirements specification

Implement system—Building software from specifications and evaluation results

- Create test data

- Create source code

- Generate object code

- Plan installation

- Install software

Evaluate system—Jointly review software prototype

Repeat production of software prototype—Incorporating changes learned during evaluation (if necessary). This step may be repeated several times. Use judgment to plan for cycles of learning.

Update requirements specification—Used to build the revised prototype

Repeat rapid analysis—User and designer jointly redesigning from revised requirements

• Analyze system allocation	
• Identify revised software requirements	• Conduct preliminary user interviews
	• Refine and further develop software requirements
	• Define revised interface requirements
	• Prioritize and integrate software requirements

Revise database—Jointly identify the revised database elements

- Perform revised architectural design

(Continues)

TABLE 9–5 (Continued)
Rapid Prototyping Model Checklist of Potential Activities and Tasks

Life Cycle Phase	
Potential Activities	**Potential Tasks**

• Revise the database design

Revise the user interface—Jointly redefine how the software should interact with the user

• Design preliminary interfaces

Revise the algorithmic functions

• Select or develop algorithms

Accept prototype software functionality—User formally approves the prototype's functionality

Derive production software detailed design—Detailed design is derived from the accepted rapid prototype

• Refine algorithms

• Perform detailed design

• Produce production system design document

Implement production system—Transform the production software design description into a software product, producing source code, databases, and documentation, whether developed, purchased, or a blend

Coding—Transforming the detailed design into a production system

• Create source code

• Generate object code

• Create operating documentation

Integration—Combining software components

• Plan integration

• Perform integration

Testing—Validating the production design implementation

• Plan testing

(Continues)

TABLE 9–5 (Continued)
Rapid Prototyping Model Checklist of Potential Activities and Tasks

Life Cycle Phase	
Potential Activities	**Potential Tasks**

• Develop test requirements

• Create test data

• Execute the tests

Install production system—Install and check out the software in the operational environment, tuning as necessary to get formal customer acceptance of the production software

• Plan installation

• Distribute software

• Install software

• Accept software in production operational environment

Operation and support process—Involving user operation of the system and ongoing support, including providing technical assistance, consulting with the user, recording user requests for enhancements and changes, and handling corrections or errors.

• Operate the system

• Provide technical assistance and consulting

• Maintain support request log

Maintenance process—Resolving requests to address software errors, faults, failures, enhancements, and changes generated by the support process

• Reapply a software life cycle (initiate a new development project)

Retirement process—Removing an existing system from its active use, either by ceasing its operation, replacing it with a completely new system, or replacing it with an upgraded version of the existing system

• Notify user(s)

• Conduct parallel operations

(Continues)

TABLE 9–5 (Continued)
Rapid Prototyping Model Checklist of Potential Activities and Tasks

Life Cycle Phase	
Potential Activities	**Potential Tasks**
• Retire system	

Operation and maintenance—Moving the software into a production state

• Distribute software

• Install software

• Accept software in operational environment

• Operate the system

• Provide technical assistance and consulting

• Maintain support request log

Integral activities—See Table 9–2.

Rapid Application Development (RAD) Model Activities

The RAD model, described in Chapter 4 and shown in Figure 4–12, is a special case of a linear model. In the RAD model, the emphasis is on an extremely short development cycle using component-based construction. It is used mainly for information systems applications, especially for client/server architectures.

The activities in Table 9–1 are still used to populate the RAD WBS. A typical RAD model's tasks and activities are shown in Table 9–6.

Incremental Model Activities

The incremental model, described in Chapter 4 and shown in Figure 4–13, is another linear model using the activities in Table 9–1. Actually, it can be a more or less standard life cycle using one of the other models (waterfall, V-shaped, RAD, spiral, etc.). However, in incremental models, the complete system is designed early in the project, and the system is delivered and implemented in discrete component releases, typically with ever-increasing functionality. Often, the development activities for each discrete component overlap. The number of components to build is decided early in the project. The tasks and activities for an example incremental model delivering three components for a complete system are shown in Table 9–7.

TABLE 9–6
RAD Model Checklist of Potential Activities and Tasks

Life Cycle Phase	
Potential Activities	**Potential Tasks**
Plan and activate the project	
• Initiate the project	• Map activities to the SLCM
	• Allocate project resources
	• Establish project environment
	• Plan project management

Requirements planning phase

Concept exploration—Examining requirements at the system level to determine feasibility, using the joint requirements planning (JRP) approach

• Identify ideas or needs

• Formulate potential approaches

• Conduct feasibility studies

• Plan system transition

• Refine and finalize the idea or need

System allocation process—Mapping functions to software or hardware based on the overall system architecture, using the joint requirements planning (JRP) approach

• Analyze functions

• Develop system architecture

• Decompose system requirements

Requirements process—Defining software requirements for the system's information domain and function, behavior, performance, and interfaces, using the joint requirements planning (JRP) approach

• Define and develop software requirements

(Continues)

TABLE 9–6 (Continued)
RAD Model Checklist of Potential Activities and Tasks

Life Cycle Phase	
Potential Activities	**Potential Tasks**

• Define interface requirements

• Prioritize and integrate software requirements

User description phase

Design process—Developing and representing a coherent, technical specification of the software system, including data structures, software architecture, interface representations, and procedural (algorithmic) detail, using the Joint Application Design (JAD) approach

• Perform architectural design

• Design the database

• Design interfaces

• Select or develop algorithms

• Construction phase

Design process—Developing and representing a coherent, technical specification of the software system, including data structures, software architecture, interface representations, and procedural (algorithmic) detail, done within a strict time frame

• Perform architectural design

• Design the database

• Design interfaces

• Select or develop algorithms

• Perform detailed design

Implementation process—Transforming the software design description into a software product, producing source code, databases, and documentation, whether developed, purchased, or a blend

• Create test data

• Create source code

(Continues)

TABLE 9–6 (Continued)
RAD Model Checklist of Potential Activities and Tasks

Life Cycle Phase	
Potential Activities	**Potential Tasks**

- Generate object code

- Create operating documentation

- Plan integration

- Perform integration

- Plan testing

- Develop test requirements

- Execute the tests

Cut-over phase

Installation process—Installing and checking out the software in the operational environment, and getting formal customer acceptance of the software

- Plan installation

- Distribute software

- Install software

- Accept software in operational environment

Integral activities—See Table 9–2.

TABLE 9–7
Incremental Model Checklist of Potential Activities and Tasks

Life Cycle Phase	
Potential Activities	**Potential Tasks**
Plan and activate the project	
• Initiate the project	• Map activities to the SLCM
	• Allocate project resources
	• Establish project environment

TABLE 9–7 (Continued)
Incremental Model Checklist of Potential Activities and Tasks

Life Cycle Phase	
Potential Activities	**Potential Tasks**
	• Plan project management

System feasibility

Concept exploration—Examining requirements at the system level to determine feasibility

• Identify ideas or needs

• Formulate potential approaches

• Conduct feasibility studies

• Plan system transition

• Refine and finalize the idea or need

System allocation process—Mapping functions to software or hardware based on the overall system architecture

• Analyze functions

• Develop system architecture

• Decompose system requirements

Software plans and requirements

Requirements process—Defining software requirements for the system's information domain, function, behavior, performance, and interfaces

• Define and develop software requirements

• Define interface requirements

• Prioritize and integrate software requirements

Design process—Developing and representing a coherent, technical specification of the software system, including data structures, software architecture, interface representations, and some procedural (algorithmic) detail

• Perform architectural design

(Continues)

TABLE 9–7 (Continued)
Incremental Model Checklist of Potential Activities and Tasks

Life Cycle Phase	
Potential Activities	**Potential Tasks**

- Design the database

- Design interfaces

- Select or develop algorithms

Product Design: Increment 1

Design process—Developing and representing a coherent, technical specification of the software system, including data structures, software architecture, interface representations, and procedural (algorithmic) detail

- Select or develop algorithms

- Perform detailed design

Code process—Transforming the software design description into a software product, producing source code and databases

- Create test data

- Create source code

- Generate object code

Integration process—Combining elements into a working component system

- Plan integration

- Perform integration

Implementation process—Transforming the software components into an initial installed software product release, with documentation. Installing and checking out the software in the operational environment, and getting formal customer acceptance of the software for Increment 1.

- Create operating documentation

- Plan installation

- Distribute software

- Install software

TABLE 9–7 (Continued)
Incremental Model Checklist of Potential Activities and Tasks

Life Cycle Phase	
Potential Activities	**Potential Tasks**

• Accept software in operational environment

Operation and maintenance process—Involving user operation of the system and ongoing support, including providing technical assistance, consulting with the user, recording user requests for enhancements and changes, and handling corrections or errors

Operations process—Using the system in production

• Operate the system

• Provide technical assistance and consulting

• Maintain support request log

Maintenance process—Resolving requests to address software errors, faults, failures, enhancements, and changes generated by the support process

• Reapply a software life cycle (initiate a development project)

Product Design: Increment 2

Design process—Developing and representing a coherent, technical specification of the software system, including data structures, software architecture, interface representations, and procedural (algorithmic) detail

• Select or develop algorithms

• Perform detailed design

Code process—Transforming the software design description into a software product, producing source code and databases

• Create test data

• Create source code

• Generate object code

Integration process—Combine elements into a working component system

• Plan integration

(Continues)

TABLE 9–7 (Continued)
Incremental Model Checklist of Potential Activities and Tasks

Life Cycle Phase

Potential Activities	Potential Tasks

- Perform integration

Implementation process—Transforming the software components into an initial installed software product release, with documentation. Installing and checking out the software in the operational environment, and getting formal customer acceptance of the software for Increment 2.

- Create operating documentation

- Plan installation

- Distribute software

- Install software

- Accept software in operational environment

Operation and maintenance process—Involving user operation of the system and ongoing support, including providing technical assistance, consulting with the user, recording user requests for enhancements and changes, and handling corrections or errors

Operations process—Using the system in production

- Operate the system

- Provide technical assistance and consulting

- Maintain support request log

Maintenance process—Resolving requests to address software errors, faults, failures, enhancements, and changes generated by the support process

- Reapply a software life cycle (initiate a development project)

Product Design: Increment 3

Design process—Developing and representing a coherent, technical specification of the software system, including data structures, software architecture, interface representations, and procedural (algorithmic) detail

(Continues)

TABLE 9–7 (Continued)
Incremental Model Checklist of Potential Activities and Tasks

Life Cycle Phase	
Potential Activities	**Potential Tasks**

• Select or develop algorithms

• Perform detailed design

Code process—Transforming the software design description into a software product, producing source code and databases

• Create test data

• Create source code

• Generate object code

Integration process—Combining elements into a working component system

• Plan integration

• Perform integration

Implementation process—Transforming the software components into an initial installed software product release, with documentation. Installing and checking out the software in the operational environment, and getting formal customer acceptance of the software for Increment 3.

• Create operating documentation

• Plan installation

• Distribute software

• Install software

• Accept software in operational environment

Operation and maintenance process—Involving user operation of the system and ongoing support, including providing technical assistance, consulting with the user, recording user requests for enhancements and changes, and handling corrections or errors

Operations process—Using the system in production

• Operate the system

(Continues)

TABLE 9–7 (Continued)
Incremental Model Checklist of Potential Activities and Tasks

Life Cycle Phase	
Potential Activities	**Potential Tasks**

- Provide technical assistance and consulting

- Maintain support request log

Maintenance process—Resolving requests to address software errors, faults, failures, enhancements, and changes generated by the support process

- Reapply a software life cycle (initiate a development project)

Retirement process—Removing the existing system from its active use, either by ceasing its operation, replacing it with a completely new system, or replacing it with an upgraded version of the existing system

- Notify user(s)

- Conduct parallel operations

- Retire system

Integral activities—See Table 9–2.

Spiral Model Activities

As discussed in Chapter 4, there are several variations of the spiral model. All are similar to the rapid prototyping model described earlier in this chapter. The spiral model described and illustrated in Figure 4–14 is used here as an example. All the spiral models are a circular arrangement of most of the activities in Table 9–1, but done linearly several times, with more robust deliverables each time. One version of the spiral model's tasks and activities is shown in Table 9–8.

The activity lists shown here are only representative as a life cycle framework for the six common life cycles discussed. Each can (and should) be modified to fit the circumstances of an individual project. Other rearrangements or rewording of the activities is not only possible, but also probable.

For situations in which no framework already exists (which may be only for portions of one of the life cycles discussed), a brainstorming approach is needed to invent the activities. Techniques for this are covered in Chapter 14.

TABLE 9–8
Spiral Model Checklist of Potential Activities and Tasks

Life Cycle Phase	
Potential Activities	**Potential Tasks**

First Pass: Project Definition Cycle

Determine objectives, alternatives, and constraints—Defining the requirements and specifications for the critical parts of the envisioned system regarding performance, functionality, ability to accommodate change, hardware/software interface, critical success factors, and so on

Project definition—Developing a preliminary objective and project plan outlining rough schedules and deliverables

• Initiate the project	• Map activities to the SLCM
	• Allocate project resources
	• Establish project environment
	• Plan project management
• Explore the concept	• Identify ideas or needs
	• Formulate potential approaches
	• Conduct feasibility studies
	• Plan system transition
	• Refine and finalize the idea or need

Evaluate alternatives, and identify and resolve risks—Evaluating alternatives relative to the objectives and constraints; identifying and resolving risks

Develop conceptual prototype of selected system portion—Defining the requirements and specifications for the riskiest parts of the envisioned system to enable evaluation and a risk assessment; separate into portions by risk

Design analysis—Designing from preliminary requirements

• Analyze system allocation	• Analyze functions
	• Develop preliminary system architecture
	• Decompose preliminary system requirements

(Continues)

TABLE 9–8 (Continued)
Spiral Model Checklist of Potential Activities and Tasks

Life Cycle Phase	
Potential Activities	**Potential Tasks**
• Identify preliminary software requirements	• Conduct preliminary user interviews
	• Define and develop preliminary software requirements
	• Define preliminary interface requirements
	• Prioritize and integrate software requirements

Develop next level product—Building a prototype using the information gained in the previous phase

• Create partial requirements specification at system level; includes concept of operation that will be used to build the demonstration prototype design

Plan next phase—Using information from the develop next level product phase to plan for the next project phase step

• Replan project management

• Reformulate potential approaches

• Replan system transition

• Refine the idea or need

• Conduct system-level concept review; accept the demonstration prototype system concept

Second Pass: Requirements Review Cycle

Determine objectives, alternatives, and constraints—Defining the requirements and specifications for the critical parts of the envisioned system regarding performance, functionality, ability to accommodate change, hardware/software interface, critical success factors, and so on

TABLE 9–8 (Continued)
Spiral Model Checklist of Potential Activities and Tasks

Life Cycle Phase	
Potential Activities	**Potential Tasks**

Potential Activities	Potential Tasks
• Analyze functions for system/product level	
• Develop system architecture	
• Decompose system requirements	
• Define and develop software requirements	
• Define interface requirements	
• Prioritize and integrate software requirements for system/product level	

Evaluate alternatives, and identify and resolve risks—evaluating alternatives relative to the objectives and constraints; identifying and resolving risks

Develop demonstration prototype of selected system portion—Refining the requirements and specifications for the riskiest parts of the envisioned system to enable evaluation and a risk assessment; separate into portions by risk

Potential Activities	Potential Tasks
• **Conduct feasibility studies**—Perform simulations and benchmarks	
• **Design analysis**—Design from preliminary requirements	
• Analyze risks	
• Perform contingency planning	
• Analyze system allocation further	• Analyze functions further
	• Develop preliminary system architecture further
	• Decompose preliminary system requirements further
• Identify product software requirements further	• Conduct user interviews further

(Continues)

TABLE 9–8 (Continued)
Spiral Model Checklist of Potential Activities and Tasks

Life Cycle Phase	
Potential Activities	**Potential Tasks**
	• Define and develop software requirements further
	• Define interface requirements further
	• Prioritize and integrate software requirements further
• **Database creation**—Identify the preliminary database elements	• Perform preliminary architectural design
	• Design the preliminary database
• **Design the user interface**—Define how the software should interact with the user	• Design preliminary interfaces
• **Design the algorithmic functions**	• Select or develop algorithms (on paper only)

Develop next level product—Building a prototype using the information gained in the previous phase

• Create complete requirements specification; includes detail that will be used to build the design assessment prototype design

Plan next phase—Using information from the next level product phase step to perform transition planning for the next project phase step

• Replan project management

• Reformulate potential approaches

• Replan system transition

• Refine the idea or need

• Conduct requirements review; accept the design assessment prototype design

(Continues)

TABLE 9–8 (Continued)
Spiral Model Checklist of Potential Activities and Tasks

Life Cycle Phase	
Potential Activities	**Potential Tasks**

Third Pass: Design Review Cycle

Determine objectives, alternatives, and constraints—Defining the requirements and specifications for the critical parts of the envisioned system regarding performance, functionality, ability to accommodate change, hardware/software interface, critical success factors, and so on

- Analyze functions for design level

- Develop system architecture further

- Decompose system requirements further

- Define and develop software requirements further

- Define interface requirements further

- Prioritize and integrate requirements for the design level

Evaluate alternatives, and identify and resolve risks—Evaluating alternatives relative to the objectives and constraints; identifying and resolving risks

Develop demonstration prototype of selected system portion—Refining the requirements and specifications for the riskiest parts of the envisioned system to enable evaluation and a risk assessment; separate into portions by risk

- **Conduct feasibility studies**—Perform simulations and benchmarks

- **Design analysis**—Design from accepted requirements

- Analyze risks

- Perform contingency planning

• Analyze system allocation further	• Analyze functions further
	• Develop preliminary system architecture further

(Continues)

TABLE 9–8 (Continued)
Spiral Model Checklist of Potential Activities and Tasks

Life Cycle Phase	
Potential Activities	**Potential Tasks**
	• Decompose preliminary system requirements further
• Identify product software requirements further	• Conduct user interviews further
	• Define and develop software requirements further
	• Define interface requirements further
	• Prioritize and integrate software requirements further
• **Database creation**—Identifying the database elements	• Refine architectural design
	• Refine the database design
• **Design the user interface**—Defining how the software should interact with the user	• Refine interface design
• **Design the algorithmic functions**	• Refine algorithms (on paper only)

Develop next level product—Building a prototype using the information gained in the previous phase

• **Derive software detailed design**—Detailed design is derived from the accepted requirements	• Refine algorithms
	• Perform detailed design
	• Produce system design document (SDD)

Plan next phase—Using information from the next level product phase step to perform transition planning for the next project phase step

• Replan project management

• Reformulate potential approaches

(Continues)

TABLE 9–8 (Continued)
Spiral Model Checklist of Potential Activities and Tasks

Life Cycle Phase	
Potential Activities	**Potential Tasks**

- Replan system transition

- Refine the idea or need

- Conduct design review; accept the operational prototype design

Fourth Pass: Initial Operational Capability (IOC) Product Review Cycle

Determine objectives, alternatives, and constraints—Defining the requirements and specifications for the critical parts of the envisioned system regarding performance, functionality, ability to accommodate change, hardware/software interface, critical success factors, and so on

- Analyze functions for product level

- Develop system architecture further

- Decompose system requirements further

- Define and develop software requirements further

- Define interface requirements further

- Prioritize and integrate requirements for the operational level

Evaluate alternatives, and identify and resolve risks—Evaluating alternatives relative to the objectives and constraints; identifying and resolving risks

Develop demonstration prototype of selected system portion—Refine the requirements and specifications for the riskiest parts of the envisioned system to enable evaluation and a risk assessment; separate into portions by risk

- **Design analysis**—Designing from accepted product design	- Analyze risks
	- Perform contingency planning
	- Analyze system allocation further

(Continues)

TABLE 9–8 (Continued)
Spiral Model Checklist of Potential Activities and Tasks

Life Cycle Phase	
Potential Activities	**Potential Tasks**
	• Analyze functions further
	• Develop product system architecture further
• **Database creation**—Identifying the database elements	• Refine architectural design
	• Refine the database design
• **Design the user interface**—Defining how the software should interact with the user	• Refine interface design
• **Design the algorithmic functions**	• Refine algorithms (on paper only)

Develop next level product—Building a prototype using the information gained in the previous phase

Create an operational prototype—Transforming the software design document description into the initial operational capability (IOC) software product, producing source code, databases and documentation, whether developed, purchased, or a blend

• **Conduct feasibility studies**—Performing simulations and benchmarks	
• **Coding**—Transforming the detailed design into an operational system	• Create source code
	• Generate object code
	• Create operating documentation
• **Integration**—Combining software components	• Plan integration
	• Perform integration
• **Testing**—Validating the production design implementation	• Plan testing
	• Develop test requirements

TABLE 9–8 (Continued)
Spiral Model Checklist of Potential Activities and Tasks

Life Cycle Phase	
Potential Activities	**Potential Tasks**
	• Create test data
	• Execute the tests
• **Install production system**—Installing and checking out the software in the operational environment, tuning as necessary to get formal customer acceptance of the production software	• Plan installation
	• Distribute software
	• Install software

Plan next phase—Using information from the next level product phase step to perform transition planning for the next project phase step

• **Evaluate system**—Review operational prototype

• Replan project management

• Reformulate potential approaches

• Replan system transition

• Refine the idea or need

• Conduct product review; accept the operational prototype

Fifth Pass: Final Operational Capability (FOC) Product Review Cycle

Determine objectives, alternatives, and constraints—Defining the requirements and specifications for the critical parts of the envisioned system regarding performance, functionality, ability to accommodate change, hardware/software interface, critical success factors, and so on

• Analyze functions for FOC level

• Develop system architecture further

TABLE 9–8 (Continued)
Spiral Model Checklist of Potential Activities and Tasks

Life Cycle Phase	
Potential Activities	**Potential Tasks**

• Decompose system requirements further

• Define and develop software requirements further

• Define interface requirements further

• Prioritize and integrate requirements for the final operational level

Evaluate alternatives, and identify and resolve risks—Evaluating alternatives relative to the objectives and constraints; identifying and resolving risks

Develop final operational capability (FOC) system design—Refining the operational prototype for the specified system

• **Design analysis**—Designing from accepted product design	• Analyze risks
	• Perform contingency planning
	• Analyze system allocation further
	• Analyze functions further
	• Develop product system architecture further
• **Database creation**—Identifying the database elements	• Refine architectural design
	• Refine the database design
• **Design the user interface**—Defining how the software should interact with the user	• Refine interface design
• **Design the algorithmic functions**	• Refine algorithms

Develop next level product—Building a prototype using the information gained in the previous phase

(Continues)

TABLE 9–8 (Continued)
Spiral Model Checklist of Potential Activities and Tasks

Life Cycle Phase	
Potential Activities	**Potential Tasks**

Create the final operational capability (FOC) system—Transforming the updated software design document description into the final operational capability (FOC) software product, producing source code, databases, documentation and training whether developed, purchased, or a blend

Potential Activities	Potential Tasks
• **Conduct feasibility studies**—Performing simulations and benchmarks	
• **Coding**—Transforming the detailed design into an operational system	• Create source code
	• Generate object code
	• Create operating documentation
• **Integration**—Combining software components	• Plan integration
	• Perform integration
• **Testing**—Validating the final operational capability (FOC) design implementation	• Plan testing
	• Develop test requirements
	• Create test data
	• Execute the tests
• **Install production system**—Installing and checking out the software in the operational environment, tuning as necessary to get formal customer acceptance of the production software	• Plan installation
	• Distribute software
	• Install software
	• Perform training

(Continues)

TABLE 9–8 (Continued)
Spiral Model Checklist of Potential Activities and Tasks

Life Cycle Phase	
Potential Activities	**Potential Tasks**

Plan next phase—Using information from the next level product phase step to perform transition planning for the next project phase step

• **Evaluate system**—Reviewing operational prototype	• Replan project management
	• Reformulate potential approaches
	• Replan system transition
	• Refine the idea or need
	• Conduct FOC product review; accept the operational system

Operation and maintenance—Moving the software into a production state

• Distribute software

• Install software

• Accept software in operational environment

• Operate the system

• Provide technical assistance and consulting

• Maintain support request log

Retirement process—Removing an existing system from its active use, either by ceasing its operation, replacing it with a completely new system, or replacing it with an upgraded version of the existing system

• Notify user(s)

• Conduct parallel operations

• Retire system

Integral activities—See Table 9–2.

Summary

In this chapter, we described the characteristics of tasks and activities that comprise a WBS for a project. We explored the differences between a task and an activity, and how they relate to the WBS. We showed how the 65 activities from the 17 processes of IEEE 1074 could appear as life cycle templates of activities, ready for tailoring. And we explored the role of maintenance in the software development life cycle.

Problems for Review

1. Explain the difference between a task and an activity for a software development project. Give an example of each.
2. Identify which activities are not present in each of the life cycle work breakdowns discussed.
3. Give an example of an "optimally sized" activity from your own work experiences.

Visit the Case Study

Dr. Zhou has reviewed your project plan with great thoroughness. She has discovered that your WBS is inconsistent. As a project manager, she assumes that you are aware that the PMBOK™ definition of a task is "a generic term for work that is not included in the work breakdown structure." You attached a copy of your project management plan's network, Gantt chart, and resource loading charts from Microsoft™ Project. All these charts refer to tasks that you are executing. Dr. Zhou, Mr. Lu, and now Ms. Patel want to know why you are working on these things not included in your WBS when you say that the risk of schedule slippage is so high. Please explain this in a PowerPoint presentation to be given at tomorrow's 7:00 a.m. NetMeeting conference.

References

Kerzner, H. (1995). *Project Management: A Systems Approach to Planning, Scheduling, and Controlling,* 5th ed. Van Nostrand Reinhold.

Lewis, James P. (1995). *Project Planning, Scheduling, and Control: A Hands-On Guide to Bringing Projects in on Time and on Budget.* McGraw-Hill.

Paulk, Mark C., et al. (1994). *The Capability Maturity Model: Guidelines for Improving the Software Process,* Addison-Wesley SEI Series in Software Engineering. Section 7.2, Software Project Planning and Section 7.3, Software Project Tracking and Oversight.

Pressman, Roger S. (2001). *Software Engineering: A Practitioner's Approach*, 5th ed. McGraw-Hill. Chapter 5, "Software Project Planning," and Chapter 7, "Project Scheduling and Tracking."

Web Pages for Further Information

stsc.hill.af.mil/crosstalk/1996/apr/project.asp. Lynn Satterthwaite. "Project Management: Some Lessons Learned—April 1996." Software Technology Support Center.

www.pmi.org/publictn/pmboktoc.htm. PMI's *A Guide to the Project Management Body of Knowledge (PMBOK® Guide)*, Chapter 6.

www.pmi.org/standards/wbspractice.htm. Cindy Berg and Kim Colenso (2000). "Work Breakdown Structure Practice Standard Project—WBS vs. Activities." *PM Network*, April.

www.worldbank.org/worldlinks/english/training/world/webproj/define/develop/develop2.htm. Building a Collaborative Web Project, World Links for Development Program (WorLD) Training Materials.

Software Size and Reuse Estimating

Predicting the "size" of a software system becomes progressively easier as the project advances. The first time an attempt is made, at the front end of the life cycle, little is known except for high-level customer requirements. This is equivalent to requesting a custom-built home, beginning with only an idea of the layout—the square footage may be estimated by architect and client, but it may well change as requirements are clarified and blueprints evolve. Near the end of a software development project, there are fewer tasks remaining and stable specifications, allowing for far more accurate estimation. Of course, we can't wait until near the end to provide estimates—we are required to estimate cost, calendar time, and effort seemingly way too early. At no other time are the estimates so important than at the beginning of a project, yet we are so unsure of them. Go/no-go decisions are made, contracts are won and lost, and jobs appear and fade away based on these estimates. As unconfident and uncomfortable as we may be, we must provide these estimates.

There are two major steps in determining how long a project will take and how much it will cost. The first is to estimate its size; the second is to use size along with other environmental factors to estimate effort and its associated cost. Sizing is the prediction of coding needed to fulfill requirements. Estimation is the prediction of resources needed to complete a project of predicted size, taking into account factors of calendar time, staff, and budget constraints.

We will discuss the second step in Chapter 11, "Estimating Duration and Cost." Here, in Chapter 10, we are concerned with the first step, which is estimating the size of the software project. Size may be measured in various units, according to what is appropriate for the project and for your organization.

Software size has been defined in terms of lines of code (LOC), function points, feature points, number of bubbles on a data flow diagram (DFD), a count of process/control specifications (PSPECS/CSPECS), number of module boxes on a structure chart, number of major entities and/or relationships on an entity relationship diagram (ERD), "shalls" versus "wills" in a government requirements document, number of pages of user documentation, objects and/or classes on an object model, and many other ways. Do not be concerned if some of these terms are foreign because we'll discuss some of the more popular definitions. Whether we are estimating the end product, as with LOC, or some abstraction or model of it, as with object classes, we are guessing about something that doesn't yet exist. This is what makes size estimation so difficult.

Where We Are in the Product Development Life Cycle

Estimating the size and reuse potential of software occurs during the early stages of project planning. In terms of our generic life cycle model, planning takes place during the concept exploration, system exploration, and requirements phases (see Figure 10–1). Estimating size and effort will occur many times during the life cycle, increasing confidence with each occurrence—after initial customer requirements, after analysis, after design, and so on. Our process model describing the phases of the life cycle (see Chapter 4, "Selecting Software Development Life Cycles") serves us well in indicating where estimates and re-estimates should occur. A good practice for project managers is to require size estimates and re-estimates as exit criteria from each phase.

Chapter 10 Relation to the 34 Competencies

The estimate of the size of the software product, which is then used to estimate the effort and cost of the project, falls under the project competencies umbrella. Software size estimates, adjusted for reuse, are recorded in the project plan; therefore, a third project competency, documenting plans, also has a relationship to this chapter. An estimate of software size is a metric that should be maintained as the project progresses. Lastly, knowledge of software size also feeds the scheduling of the project.

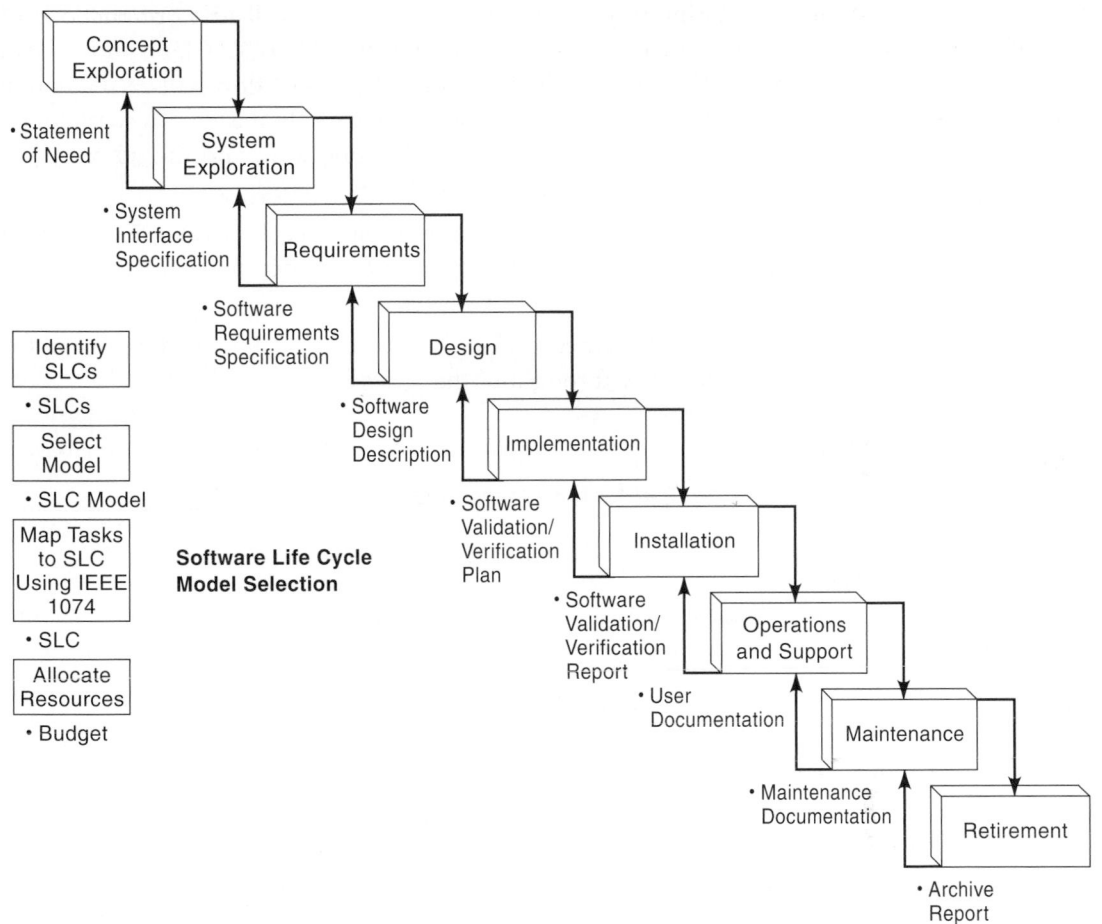

FIGURE 10–1
Software Size and Reuse Estimation Occurs at the Beginning of the Life Cycle

Project Management Skills

12. **Building a work breakdown structure**—Product and project tasks are decomposed into small enough increments to be estimated in size.

13. **Documenting plans**—Decomposed product and project tasks lead to size, effort, and cost estimation, and then ultimately to the project schedule. All are represented in the software project management plan (SPMP); estimation risks are documented in a separate risk plan or as a segment in the SPMP.

14. **Estimating cost** and 15. **Estimating effort**—Predictions of size lead to predictions of effort. For example, if we estimate that we have to produce 500 LOC (size), and we can produce an average of 5 LOC/hour (productivity rate), then the effort will be 100 hours. If we have a small team of two people who can split the load, then each can work for 50 hours. Effort leads to cost—if one developer makes $65 per hour, and the other makes $55 per hour, then the software will cost $6,000 ($3,250 + $2,750).

18. **Scheduling**—Effort also leads to schedule. In our example, if each developer can put in 25 productive hours each week and can work in parallel (no dependencies), then the 500 LOC product is estimated to be delivered in two weeks.

19. **Selecting metrics**—Units of size are a metric. Once chosen (LOC, in the previous example), they will be referred to consistently throughout the project.

Learning Objectives for Chapter 10 _____

By the end of this chapter, the reader should be able to:

• Explain why the sizing of software is an important estimating technique, when it should occur in the life cycle, and how it reduces risk and enhances the maturity of an organization;

• Describe how the work breakdown structure (WBS) influences the ability to estimate software size;

• List several models frequently used in the software industry to estimate size;

• Explain LOC, function points, feature points, model blitz, and Delphi software size estimating methods;

• Summarize the advantages and disadvantages of each of the models;

• Describe, for each model, its applicability, degree of accuracy, and cost effectiveness;

• Explain the impact of reused software components upon the size estimate.

The SEI CMM and Estimating _____

The Software Engineering Institute (SEI) Capability Maturity Model (CMM) introduced in Chapter 4 supports activities described in this chapter. Software project planning is a key process area for maturity Level 2, the repeatable level. Sizing software products and projects is an element of project planning.

> The purpose of Software Project Planning is to establish reasonable plans for performing the software engineering and for managing the software project…. Software Project Planning involves developing estimates for the work to be performed

establishing the necessary commitments, and defining the plan to perform the work.... The software planning begins with a statement of the work to be performed and other constraints and goals that define and bound the software project (those established by the practices of the Requirements Management key process area). The software planning process includes steps to *estimate the size of the software work products* and the resources needed, produce a schedule, identify and assess software risks, and negotiate commitments. Iterating through these steps may be necessary to establish the plan for the software project (i.e., the software development plan).... This plan provides the basis for performing and managing the software project's activities and addresses the commitments to the software project's customer according to the resources, constraints, and capabilities of the software project.

> Paulk, Weber, Curtis, and Chrissis, *The Capability Maturity Model: Guidelines for Improving the Software Process*[1]

Goals of SEI CMM Level 2, Key Process Area (KPA): Software Project Planning (PP)

Goal 1—Software estimates are documented for use in planning and tracking the software project.

Ability to Perform, associated with KPA PP, Goal 1

Ability 4—The software managers, software engineers, and other individuals involved in the software project planning are trained in the software estimating and planning procedures applicable to their areas of responsibility.

Activities Performed

Activity 5—A software life cycle with predefined stages of manageable size is identified or defined.

Activity 8—Software work products that are needed to establish and maintain control of the software project are identified.

Activity 9—Estimates for the size of the software work products (or changes to the size of software work products) are derived according to a documented procedure.

1. Size estimates are made for all major software products and activities.
2. Software work products are decomposed to the granularity needed to meet the estimating objectives.
3. Historical data is used where available.
4. Size estimating assumptions are documented.
5. Size estimates are documented, reviewed, and agreed to.

Problems and Risks with Estimating Software Size

The following sections describe why software project managers and developers have such an inordinate problem with estimating their tasks, and why the estimates they do provide are so fraught with risk.

The Problem with Estimating

Software Engineers are notoriously poor estimators. We know this because 15 percent of all software projects fail to meet their goals and overruns of 100–200 percent are common in software projects. As an industry, we are not poor performers, although it may seem that way, because the prediction of performance is poor. There are many reasons why we set unreasonable expectations, and few will deny that estimating is a complex task.

When performance doesn't meet the estimate, there are two possible causes: poor performance or poor estimates. In the software world, we have ample evidence that our estimates stink, but virtually no evidence that people in general don't work hard enough or intelligently enough.

—Tom DeMarco, *Why Does Software Cost So Much?*[2]

DeMarco is right. Developers are frequently blamed for being obstreperous, unresponsive and uncaring toward the customer, unable to do the job, or just plain lazy. Most of the time, none of these accusations is true. The truth is that developers have been asked to do the impossible. Correcting this impression relies on what DeMarco calls the management of expectations. And it all begins with the estimation of software size.

It's not an easy task, though. Among the numerous reasons estimating is so difficult:

- The problem may not be well understood by developers and/or customers; either or both may be missing facts or might have them distorted by unsubstantiated opinions and biases.
- There is little or no historical data upon which to base future estimates.
- Estimators may become frustrated when trying to describe how big a system will be before it is built—maybe even before it is designed.
- The developing organization has no standard estimating process (or, where standards exist, they are not followed), resulting in a lack of consistency in the estimation process.
- Management and/or customer demand quick estimates and possibly misunderstand that code can be written right away, skipping analysis and design steps.
- Stakeholders believe that requirements can be fixed at the beginning of a project, or customers believe that they cannot afford time for requirements specification.

- Management uses estimates as performance or motivational goals.
- Developers are optimistic and desire to please their management, peers, and customers.
- Mistakes are hidden rather than being reported and evaluated, resulting in false impressions of past performance.
- Assessment abilities are impaired by egos involved in performance.
- Early estimates and schedules are viewed as performance goals; estimates are made prematurely, before the concept exploration is complete; and confusion arises between desired versus realistic schedules.
- Reluctance to re-estimate arises.
- Insufficient visibility into other parts of the system (legacy system interfaces, hardware, etc.) may require additional software and therefore may affect size; incomplete understanding of system-level constraints or special system limitations exists.
- Inequality in estimating and development abilities and/or experience exists among managers, analysts, designers, developers, testers, and implementers.

It is little wonder that the very complexity and difficulty of predicting software size culminates in project risks.

The Risks of Estimating

The general principles of software project management risk will be discussed in Chapter 18, "Determining Project Risks." Many of the typical software risks originate with estimates of size, effort, cost, and schedule, which are based on the "problem with estimating." Here is a brief review of some risks resulting from the problem, along with a brief set of suggestions for mitigating those risks.

Some Software Project Management
Risks Associated with Estimating Size   Whenincompleteorincorrectestimatesare given, there is an obvious risk of disappointing the customer, possibly losing future business. Equally serious is the misestimate of a fixed-price contract—a too-optimistic estimate will result in the contractor losing money (perhaps a great deal) as well as losing face.

Inaccurate estimates will require adjustments to the schedule, to squeeze the optimal one into a shorter time frame, which almost always results in the introduction of defects.

Some Suggestions to Mitigate Size-Related Risks   There are ways to diminish the effects of size estimation risks, all of which are good project management practices in any case:

- Produce a WBS, decomposed to the lowest level possible, to use in a "divide and conquer" approach; small components are easier to estimate.

- Review assumptions with all stakeholders, including operations, maintenance, and support departments.
- Wherever possible, do the research into past organizational experiences instead of just guessing. This can often be done in the absence of historical data. Anecdotal evidence can be illuminating.
- Stay in close communication, using a common language, with developers working on other components of the system (perhaps in parallel).
- Update estimates at frequent intervals, as shown in Figure 10–2. Estimation accuracy does improve over the course of the life cycle.
- Use multiple size estimating methods to increase confidence.
- Educate software development staff in estimation methods.

Both Boehm[3] and Capers Jones have published graphs that are surprising in the possible degree of estimating inaccuracy in the early stages of the life cycle—particularly because these are the figures upon which we usually base initial project go/no-go decisions. When customers ask for ballpark estimates, they deserve to know that the "ballpark" is not terribly accurate—it is usually in the range of +/− 35% above or below the final actual size/effort/ schedule/cost (estimates are too low more frequently than they are too high). Again, this phenomenon is illustrated in Figure 10–2.

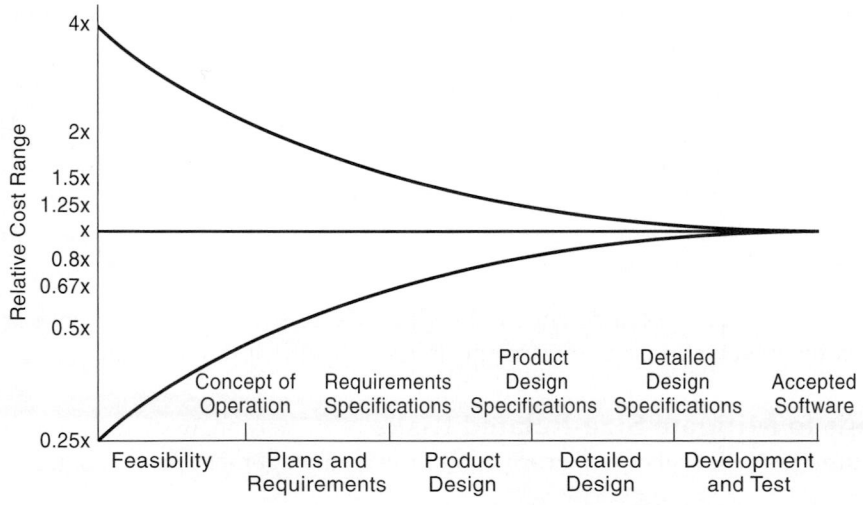

FIGURE 10–2
Estimating Accuracy

Getting Started with Software Sizing: Estimating Begins with Planning _____

Sizing is the prediction of product deliverables (internal and external) needed to fulfill the project requirements. Estimation is the prediction of effort (resources) needed to produce the deliverables.

Sizing and estimating activities fall in the middle of the sequence of planning tasks for a software project. As shown in Figure 10–3, defining the goal and scope of the software project, creating the WBS, and identifying the tasks and activities (Chapters 7–9) precede the sizing task. Following the prediction of software size are the tasks of estimating duration and cost (Chapter 11), which are used to assign resources (Chapter 12), consider dependencies (Chapter 14), and schedule the work (Chapter 15).

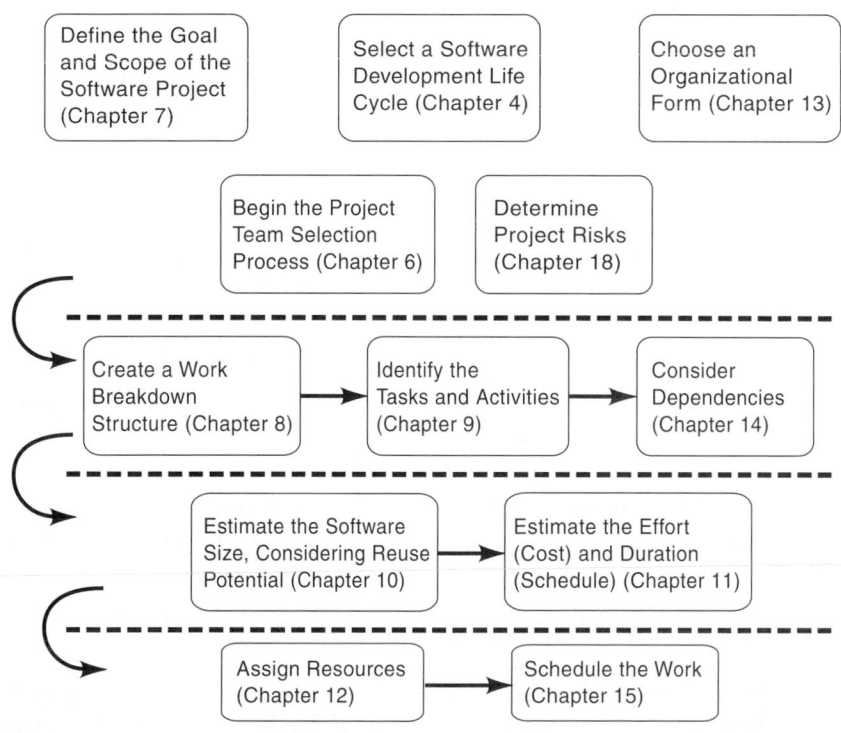

FIGURE 10–3
The Big Picture of Software Estimation

The WBS—"Decomposing" a Project into Tasks

Recall from Chapter 8, "Creating the Work Breakdown Structure," that a WBS is a description of the work to be performed, broken down into key elements or tasks. A task may be managerial, administrative, integral, or developmental. By partitioning the project into these manageable pieces, each element, or task, may be sized and its effort (expressed in person hours, weeks, months, etc.) may be estimated. The WBS identifies tasks at a level useful in locating available staff with the proper skills. After the number of staff members and the skills of each are determined, the effort estimates may then be applied to a calendar to determine the duration of the project and project milestones—the resulting project schedule is typically portrayed as a Gantt chart. Lastly, each task is defined, estimated, and tracked throughout the project.

There are multiple views of the WBS—a *product* view depicts hierarchical relationships among product elements (routines, modules, subsystems, etc.), while a *project* view depicts hierarchical relationships among work activities (process elements). In sizing and estimating for schedule predictions, both sets of elements and activities need to be considered. Development (product) tasks may include analysis, high-level design, low-level design, coding, testing, and so on, which occurs in the life cycle phases. Managerial tasks may include project planning, tracking, control, risk analysis, and so on.

Support tasks may include documentation of deliverables such as users' manual, operations' guides, and network communications. We call managerial, administrative, and support tasks *integral tasks*, traversing one or more (sometimes all) of the development tasks. Other integral tasks include: configuration management procedures, software quality assurance practices, risk analysis and management, software development tools and techniques, methods of conducting reviews of in-process deliverables, metrics to be collected and analyzed, definition and documentation of standards (rules for in-process deliverables), and any other activities required to meet customer requirements, such as creation of documents, training programs, tool development, or acquisition.

The WBS drives planning, providing the foundation for tracking of work activities, cost, and schedule by giving the engineer or manager a global view. It allows us to organize and illustrate the work to be done, ensure that all necessary work has been identified; divide the work into small, well-defined tasks; facilitate planning, estimating and scheduling of the project, to provide a basis for data monitoring and historical data collection; and identify contractual tasks and deliverables. It allows us to dismiss, "We're 90% done," and replace it with "We've completed 97 of 234 tasks." Weighted tasks become meaningful and can be associated with a cost estimate.

The WBS becomes our table of contents, a hierarchical list of the work activities required to complete a project. As such, it becomes an indispensable tool in sizing and estimating process activities.

Recall from Chapter 3, "Process Overview," that every process has inputs, transformations, and outputs. The following additional inputs are useful to the sizing and estimating process (where outputs are estimated size, effort, duration [schedule], and cost):

- Project proposal or statement of work (SOW);
- Project initiation documentation;
- Statement of requirements:
    - Performance to be achieved;
    - Specific features to be included;
    - How the results will be evaluated;
- Constraints;
- Processes and standards to be used:
    - How the software will be developed;
    - Rules that will be followed and quality criteria that will be used;
- Contract for services, if applicable;
- Prior experience on similar tasks;
- Historical estimating and actual data for your organization;
- Programming languages to be used;
- Reusable software information;
- System design information;
- Initial concepts of software architecture—major components;
- Goal and scope of the project, including tasks to be performed and products to be delivered.

Of course, it is unlikely that all of these inputs will be available to the process of size estimation, but the more, the better. Following the identification of *what* to size, as rendered in the WBS, the business of sizing software can begin in earnest.

Estimating the Size of Software Under Development (Sizing)

Conversions for values of length, volume, capacity, mass, and area to and from the metric system remind us that what we choose for units and unit names is not as important as that we communicate about them in a common language. The same is true of software sizing—as long as we choose a measure and stick with it, comparisons of actual data to planned estimates may be tracked over time to provide feedback for improvement. Some of the more popular units of measure for software include the following examples. If you are not familiar with all the terms, no matter—the point is that any "observable" physical incarnation of software, even before it becomes software, that is countable will suffice for a unit of size.

Examples of Size Measures

In our exploration of different units of measurement for software, we'll take a look at some of the most commonly used ones, including:

- Lines of code (LOC);
- Function points;
- Feature points;
- Number of bubbles on a data flow diagram (DFD);
- Number of entities on an entity relationship diagram (ERD);
- Count of process/control (PSPEC/CSPEC) boxes on a structure chart;
- Number of "shalls" versus "wills" in a government specification;
- Amount of documentation;
- Number of objects, attributes, and services on an object diagram.

There are lots of academic arguments over which is best, and there is merit to measuring whichever fits your application best. It doesn't matter which one you choose as long as you use it consistently and remember that historical data is your best ally.

Lines of Code as a Unit of Size   How do you know how many LOC will be produced before they are written or even designed? Why does anyone think that LOC has any bearing on how much effort will be required when product complexity, programmer ability/style, or the power of the programming language are not taken into consideration? How can a vast difference in the number of LOC needed to do equivalent work be explained? Questions like these have caused the LOC measure to become infamous, yet it is still the most widely used metric. The relationship between LOC and effort is not linear. Despite the introduction of new languages, the average programmer productivity rate remains, over the last two decades, at about 3,000 delivered LOC/programmer year. This tells us that no matter how languages improve, how hard managers push, or how fast or how much overtime programmers work, cycle time improvements cannot come directly from squeezing more out of programming productivity. The real concerns involve software functionality and quality, not the number of LOC produced.

Estimating LOC Using Expert Opinions and Bottom-Up Summations
We will assume that our WBS contains many levels of decomposition in the product/project hierarchy. Requirements on the WBS product hierarchy have been decomposed into actual software system components, beginning at a generic subsystem level (such as Accounts Receivable or Accounts Payable, in a financial system) and refined into a very precise level or primitive level of abstraction (such as Editor or GET/PUT I/O routines or Screen Formatter). This lowest level can rarely be known at the time of the initial sizing; it is usually completed much later in the project. However, typically several levels of abstraction can be determined

even at very early stages of project planning. The most complete WBS that can be derived will be the most helpful in accurate sizing that leads to accurate estimating.

When the WBS has been decomposed to the lowest level possible at this time, a "statistical" size may be created through a sizing and summing process. The size of each component may be obtained by asking experts who have developed similar systems, or by asking potential developers of this system to estimate the size of each box on the lower levels of the WBS. When the sizes are summed, the total is called a "bottom-up" size estimate. A much better size estimate is usually obtained if each estimator is asked to provide an optimistic, pessimistic, and realistic size estimate. Then a beta distribution may be formed by multiplying the realistic size estimate by 4, adding the optimistic and pessimistic, and dividing the total by 6. This weighted average is a comfort to the inherent uncertainty of estimating. For example, if a given window object appears on the WBS for a system, the supporting code required to process the editing for that window might be estimated at between 200 and 400 lines of code, with a belief that it will be closer to 200. Requesting the estimator to think about optimistic and pessimistic scenarios might produce this final estimate:

$$\frac{200 + (250 \times 4) + 400}{6} = 266 \text{ LOC}$$

The number of thousands of source lines of code (KSLOC) delivered is a common metric, carried through to estimations of productivity, which are usually expressed as KSLOC/SM or KLOC/SM (where SM = staff-month). Barry Boehm, one of the most highly regarded researchers in this area, has been looking for many years for a better product metric to correlate with effort and schedule, but he has not found one. LOC is a universal metric because all software products are essentially made of them.

Guidelines for Counting LOC

Counting lines of existing code manually is far too tedious and time-consuming, so most organizations purchase or build an automated LOC counter. This can raise some tricky questions about what exactly is a line of code. Again, it doesn't matter so much how you define LOC, as long as the definition is used consistently. The following counting guidelines have been in use for many years, both for the recording of existing program size and for the estimation of size for programs to be developed:

- Ensure that each "source code line" counted contains only one source statement (if two executable statements appear on one line, separated by a semicolon, then the count is two; if one executable statement is spread across two "physical" lines, then the count is one. Programming languages allow for all manner of coding options, but it is usually pretty easy to determine a single executable statement because the compiler or interpreter has to do it.

- Count *all* delivered, executable statements—the end user may not directly use every statement, but the product may need it for support (i.e., utilities).

- Count data definitions once.
- Do not count lines that contain only comments.
- Do not count debug code or other temporary code such as test software, test cases, development tools, prototyping tools, and so on.
- Count each invocation, call, or inclusion (sometimes called compiler directive) of a macro as part of the source in which it appears (don't count reused source statements).
- Translate the number of lines of code to assembly language equivalent lines so that comparisons may be made across projects.

The first and second columns of Table 10–1 represent a widely used method of translating SLOC in various languages to the average number of basic assembler SLOC. (Note that SLOC and LOC are used interchangeably.) Many project managers want a translation of all languages into basic assembler so that an apples-to-apples comparison may be made across projects. Another use of this data is to project from a known language into a conversion language. For example, suppose a 50,000 LOC system written in C will be converted to C++. Using numbers from Table 10–1, the basic Assembler SLOC for C is 2.5, so the 50,000 SLOC system written in C would be equivalent to 125,000 if written in Assembler (50,000 × 2.5). A 125,000 Assembler language system, if written in C++, would be equivalent to 125,000/6, or 20,833 SLOC.

Estimating LOC by Analogy

One way to estimate the size of an undeveloped software system is to compare its functionality with existing ones. Imagine that you have an existing software component, Module A, which will have to be rebuilt for a new system. A is 2,345 LOC, and you believe that the new Module A' will be more efficient (you've learned through maintaining the original A how to make the code tighter), yet you also know that there are some additional features that can be added. Then, A' may be estimated at 3,000 LOC.

This is certainly not a very accurate method because A' may be written in a different programming language, in a different application domain, using different algorithms, with a different level of complexity, with untried functionality, in a different level of reality (simulation, emulation, actual application).

Consider another example: software converted from COBOL, using no design technique, to software written in C++, using an object-oriented design. The size decreased because it was designed better the second time, and the functionality and quality went up. However, the cost per line of code was 10% higher. Is this a productivity loss as it might appear? Of course it is not. It was an improvement in productivity as well as functionality and maintainability.

TABLE 10–1
Conversion from Programming Language to Basic Assembler SLOC to SLOC per Function Point

Language	Basic Assembler SLOC (Level)	Average SLOC per Function Point
Basic Assembler	1	320
Autocoder	1	320
Macro Assembler	1.5	213
C	2.5	128–150
DOS Batch Files	2.5	128
Basic	3	107
LOTUS Macros	3	107
ALGOL	3	105–106
COBOL	3	105–107
FORTRAN	3	105–106
JOVIAL	3	105–107
Mixed Languages (default)	3	105
Pascal	3.5	91
COBOL (ANSI 85)	3.5	91
RPG	4	80
MODULA-2	4.5	80
PL/I	4.5	80
Concurrent PASCAL	4	80
FORTRAN 95	4.5	71
BASIC (ANSI)	5	64
FORTH	5	64
LISP	5	64
PROLOG	5	64

(Continues)

TABLE 10–1 (Continued)
Conversion from Programming Language to Basic Assembler SLOC to SLOC per Function Point

Language	Basic Assembler SLOC (Level)	Average SLOC per Function Point
LOGO	5.5	58
Extended Common LISP	5.75	56
RPG III	5.75	56
C++	6	53
JAVA	6	53
YACC	6	53
Ada 95	6.5	49
CICS	7	46
SIMULA	7	46
Database Languages	8	40
CLIPPER DB and dBase III	8	40
INFORMIX	8	40
ORACLE and SYBASE	8	40
Access	8.5	38
DBase IV	9	36
FileMaker Pro	9	36
Decision Support Languages	9	35
FOXPRO 2.5	9.5	34
APL	10	32
Statistical languages (SAS)	10	32
DELPHI	11	29
Object-Oriented Default	11	29
OBJECTIVE-C	12	27

(Continues)

TABLE 10–1 (Continued)
Conversion from Programming Language to Basic Assembler SLOC to SLOC per Function Point

Language	Basic Assembler SLOC (Level)	Average SLOC per Function Point
Oracle Developer/2000	14	23
SMALLTALK	15	21
awk	15	21
EIFFEL	15	21
UNIX Shell Scripts (PERL)	15	21
4th Generation Default	16	20
Application Builder	16	20
COBRA	16	20
Crystal Reports	16	20
Datatrieve	16	20
CLIPPER	17	19
Database Query Languages (SQL)	25	13–16
HTML 3.0	22	15
Information Engineering Facility (IEF)/Information Engineering Workbench (IEW)	23	14
EASYTRIEVE+	25	13
SQL (ANSI)	25	13
Spreadsheet Languages (EXCEL)	50	6
QUATTRO PRO	51	6
Graphic Icon Languages	75	4

Advantages of Using LOC as a Unit of Measure
Advantages of using lines of code as a unit of software measurement include:

- It is widely used and universally accepted.
- It permits comparison of size and productivity metrics between diverse development groups.
- It directly relates to the end product.
- LOC are easily measured upon project completion.
- It measures software from the developer's point of view—what he actually does (write lines of code).
- Continuous improvement activities exist for estimation techniques—the estimated size can be easily compared with the actual size during post-project analysis. (How accurate was the estimate? Why was it off by a certain percent? What can be learned for the next project's size estimation?)

Disadvantages of Using LOC
Disadvantages of using lines of code as a unit of software measurement include the following:

- LOC is difficult to estimate for new software early in the life cycle.
- Source instructions vary with the type of coding languages, with design methods, and with programmer style and ability.
- There are no industry standards (such as ISO) for counting lines of code.
- Software involves many costs that may not be considered when just sizing code—"fixed costs" such as requirements specifications and user documents are not included with coding.
- Programmers may be rewarded for large LOC counts if management mistakes them for productivity; this penalizes concise design. Source code is not the essence of the desired product—functionality and performance are.
- LOC count should distinguish between generated code and hand-crafted code—this is more difficult than a "straight count" that could be obtained from a compiler listing or code-counting utility.
- LOC cannot be used for normalizing if platforms or languages are different.
- The only way to predict a LOC count for new software to be developed is by analogy to functionally similar existing software products and by expert opinion, both imprecise methods.
- Code generators often produce excess code that inflates or otherwise skews the LOC count.

Unfortunately, productivity is often measured by LOC produced. If a programmer's average output increases from 200 LOC per month to 250 LOC per month, a manager may be tempted to conclude that productivity has improved. This is a dangerous perception that often results in encouraging developers to produce more LOC per design. Not only is the developer rewarded with a seemingly higher productivity rating, but he is also perceived to produce cleaner code. Many organizations use this metric to measure quality:

$$\frac{\text{\# of defects}}{\text{\# of lines of code}}$$

If the denominator is inflated, then the quality may appear artificially high. The coding phase of most projects typically consumes only an insignificant 7% of total effort to a maximum of only about 20% of total effort. It is, of course, the quality of code that is important, not the volume.

These issues led the thinkers of the software revolution to cast about for another way to measure. Enter function points.

Function Points as a Unit of Size   The function point (FP) method is based on the idea that software size is better measured in terms of the number and complexity of the functions that it performs than on the number of lines of code that represent it. The first work to be published about function points was written in the late 1970s by A.J. Albrecht of IBM, for transaction-oriented systems. Capers Jones, of Software Productivity Research, Inc, expanded Albrecht's ideas into a large and widely recognized body of knowledge. In 1986, a nonprofit group, the International Function Point User Group (IFPUG), was formed to disseminate information about the metric. In 1987, the British government adopted a modified function point for the standard software productivity metric. 1994 saw the publication of Release 4.0 of the IFPUG Standard *Function Point Counting Practices Manual* and Release 1.0 of the IFPUG Standard *Guidelines to Software Measurement*.

Function points measure categories of end-user business functions. They are determined in a more methodological way than are LOC counts. A really straightforward analogy is that of a physical house to software: The number of square feet is to the house as LOC is to software; the number of bedrooms and bathrooms is to the house as function points are to software. The former looks only at size; the latter looks at size and function.

Function points are intended to do the following:

- Measure categories of end-user business functions;
- Address the problem of attempting to estimate LOC too early in the life cycle;
- Determine the number and complexity of outputs, inputs, database inquiries, files or data structures, and external interfaces associated with the software system.

A quick overview of the function point process is:

1. Count the functions in each category (categories are: outputs, inputs, inquiries, data structures, and interfaces).
2. Establish the complexity of each—simple, medium, complex.

3. Establish weights for each complexity.
4. Multiply each function by its weight and then sum up to get total function points.
5. Convert function points to LOC using the formula:

$$LOC = Points \times ADJ \times Conversion\ factor$$

where ADJ is an adjustment for the general characteristics of the application.

The conversion factor, based on historical experience for the application and programming language, represents the average number of lines of code to implement a simple function. Why do this last step? Because most automated tools that estimate effort, cost, and schedule require LOC as input. Now we'll describe the FP process in more detail.

Guidelines for Counting Function Points

Figure 10–4 shows the basic steps in counting function points; each will be described later. Each step has an output that is used in the next step. Table 10–2 shows the input, transformation, and output of each step in FP counting. This worksheet is left blank, as a template for your future use.

Step 1. Count Number of Functions in Each Category

General Guidelines for Counting

- Count only software requirements functions.
- Count logical representations. When any input, output, and so on requires different processing logic, each one of those logical representations is a unique function point.

The first rough cut at estimating the size of the system to be developed entails examination of the major system components. How much output is produced? How much input is necessary to produce the output? How much data is stored?

Count the number of items: outputs, inputs, inquiries, and files. The preliminary architecture provides the basis for this counting activity. Some people can begin with architecture in the form of textual requirements, but having an architecture in graphical form is very helpful. The weighting factors applied to all of these visibly external aspects of software are a set of empirical constants derived from trial and error.

Counting Outputs

The following list includes "hints" to keep in mind when counting outputs:

- External outputs are things produced by the software that go to the outside of the system.
- Outputs are units of business information produced by the software for the end user (application-oriented).
- Examples include screen data, report data, error messages, and so on.

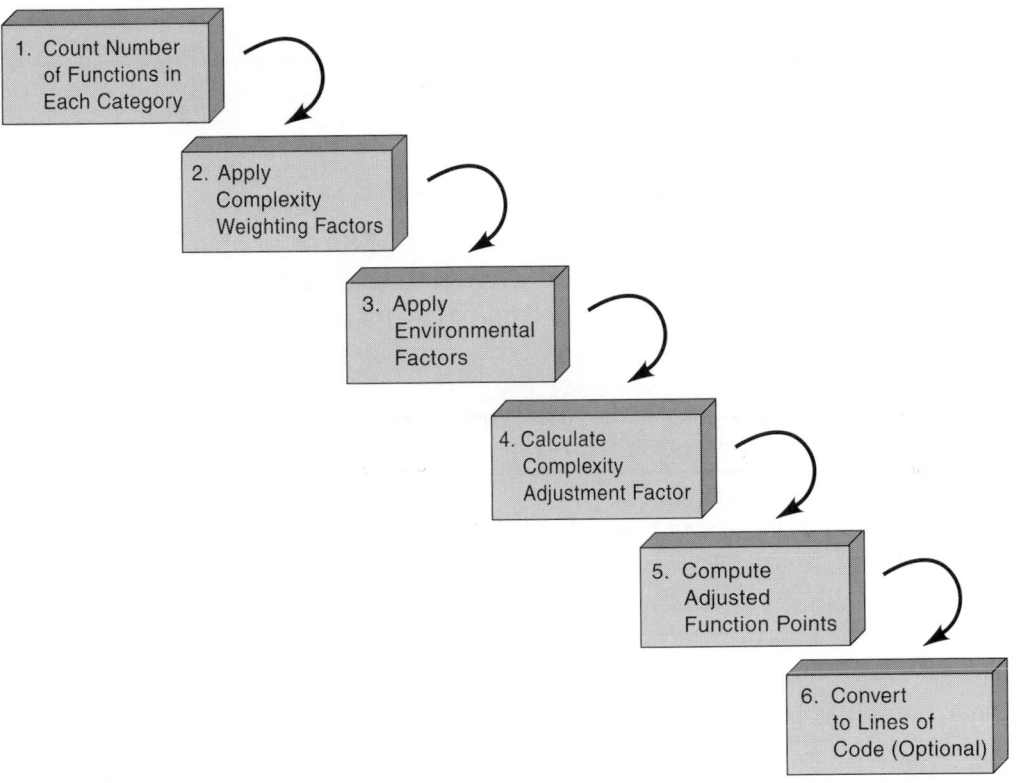

FIGURE 10–4
Basic Steps in Function Point Analysis

TABLE 10–2
Function Point Analysis Worksheet

Step 1. Count Number of Functions in Each Category
Step 2. Apply Complexity Weighting Factors

	Simple	Average	Complex	Function Points
Number of Outputs	____ × 4	____ × 5	____ × 7	
Number of Inputs	____ × 3	____ × 4	____ × 6	
Number of Inquiry Outputs	____ × 4	____ × 5	____ × 7	

(Continues)

TABLE 10–2 (Continued)
Function Point Analysis Worksheet

Number of Inquiry Inputs	____ × 3	____ × 4	____ × 6
Number of Files	____ × 7	____ × 10	____ × 15
Number of Interfaces	____ × 5	____ × 7	____ × 10

Total (FP):

Step 3. Apply Environmental Factors

Environmental Factor	Rating (0, 1, 2, 3, 4, 5)
Data Communications	
Distributed Computing	
Performance Requirements	
Constrained Configuration	
Transaction Rate	
Online Inquiry and/or Entry	
End-User Efficiency	
Online Update	
Complex Processing	
Reusability	
Ease of Conversion/Install	
Ease of Operation	
Used at Multiple Sites	
Potential for Function Change	

Total (N):

(Continues)

TABLE 10–2 (Continued)
Function Point Analysis Worksheet

Step 4. Calculate Complexity Adjustment Factor (CAF)

$$CAF = 0.65 + (0.01 \times N) =$$

Step 5. Compute Adjusted Function Points (AFP)

$$AFP = FP \, (Raw) \times CAF =$$

Step 6. Convert to LOC (Optional)

$$LOC = AFP \times LOC/AFP =$$

- Count each unique unit of output that leaves the application boundary. An output unit is unique if it has a different format and/or requires different processing logic.
- For those using structured methods (Chapter 22, "Analysis and Design Methods"), an output is a data flow of information produced by the software for the end-user. The number of outputs leaving the application boundary may easily be counted on a context or source/sink diagram.

Each output is added to one of three totals, depending on its complexity: a total for simple outputs, a total for average outputs, and a total for complex outputs. The separation allows each type to be multiplied by a weighting factor—a complex output will require more effort to create than will an average or a simple output. Guidelines for determining complexity are found in Table 10–3.

TABLE 10–3
Function Point Analysis Outputs Weighting Factors

	1–5 Data Items Referenced	6–19 Data Items Referenced	20 or More Data Items Referenced
0 or 1 File Referenced	Simple (4)	Simple (4)	Average (5)
2 or 3 Files Referenced	Simple (4)	Average (5)	Complex (7)
4 or More Files Referenced	Average (5)	Complex (7)	Complex (7)

Counting Inputs

Remember the following when counting inputs:

- External inputs are things received by the software from outside of the system.
- Inputs are units of business information input by the user to the software for processing or storage.
- Count each unique unit of input.

As with outputs, inputs are separated into simple, average, and complex for weighting. Guidelines for determining complexity are found in Table 10–4.

TABLE 10–4

Function Point Analysis Inputs Weighting Factors

	1–5 Data Items Referenced	6–19 Data Items Referenced	20 or More Data Items Referenced
0 or 1 File Referenced	Simple (3)	Simple (3)	Average (4)
2 or 3 Files Referenced	Simple (3)	Average (4)	Complex (6)
4 or More Files Referenced	Average (4)	Complex (6)	Complex (6)

Counting Inquiries (Output/Input)

When counting inquiries, keep the following in mind:

- External inquiries are specific commands or requests that the software performs, generated from the outside. It is online input that causes a software response.
- Inquiries are direct accesses to a database that retrieve specific data, use simple keys, are real-time (requires an immediate response), and perform no update functions.
- Count each unique unit of inquiry. An inquiry is considered unique in either of two cases:
    - It has a format different from others in either its input or output portions.
    - It has the same format, both input and output, as another inquiry but requires different processing logic in either.
- Inquiries with different input and output portions will have different complexity weighting factors, as explained later.
- Queries are not inquiries. Queries are usually classified as either inputs or outputs because they often use many keys and include operations or calculations on data.

Inquiries are separated into simple, average, and complex. Guidelines for determining complexity are found in Table 10–5.

TABLE 10–5
Function Point Analysis Inquiries Weighting Factors

Output Part (Note: Select the Greatest Value—Output or Input)	1–5 Data Items Referenced	6–19 Data Items Referenced	20 or More Data Items Referenced
0 or 1 File Referenced	Simple (4)	Simple (4)	Average (5)
2 or 3 Files Referenced	Simple (4)	Average (5)	Complex (7)
4 or More Files Referenced	Average (5)	Complex (7)	Complex (7)
Input Part (Note: Select the Greatest Value—Output or Input)	**1–5 Data Items Referenced**	**6–19 Data Items Referenced**	**20 or More Data Items Referenced**
0 or 1 File Referenced	Simple (3)	Simple (3)	Average (4)
2 or 3 Files Referenced	Simple (3)	Average (4)	Complex (6)
4 or More Files Referenced	Average (4)	Complex (6)	Complex (6)

Counting Data Structures (Files)

Things to keep in mind when counting data structures (files) include:

- Internal files are logical files within the program.
- Data structures (previously known as "files") are each primary logical group of user data permanently stored entirely within the software system boundary.
- Data structures are available to users via inputs, outputs, inquiries, or interfaces.

Data structures are separated into simple, average, and complex. Guidelines for determining complexity are found in Table 10–6.

Counting Interfaces

When counting interfaces, keep these thoughts in mind:

- External files are machine-generated files used by the program.
- Interfaces are data (and control) stored outside the boundary of the software system being evaluated.
- Data structures shared between systems are counted as both interfaces and data structures.
- Count each data and control flow in each direction as a unique interface.

TABLE 10–6
Function Point Analysis Files Weighting Factors

Note: Count of Logical Relationships, Not Physical Record Types	1–9 Data Items Referenced	20–50 Data Items Referenced	51 or More Data Items Referenced
1 Logical Record Format/Relationship	Simple (7)	Simple (7)	Average (10)
2–5 Logical Record Format/Relationships	Simple (7)	Average (10)	Complex (15)
6 or More Logical Record Format/Relationships	Average (10)	Complex (15)	Complex (15)

Interfaces are separated into simple, average, and complex. Guidelines for determining complexity are found in Table 10–7.

TABLE 10–7
Function Point Analysis Interfaces Weighting Factors

Note: Number of Logical Relationships, Not Physical Record Types	1–9 Data Items Referenced	20–50 Data Items Referenced	51 or More Data Items Referenced
1 Logical Record Format/Relationship	Simple (5)	Simple (5)	Average (7)
2–5 Logical Record Format/Relationships	Simple (5)	Average (7)	Complex (10)
6 or More Logical Record Format/Relationships	Average (7)	Complex (10)	Complex (10)

Step 2. Apply Complexity Weighting Factors

• Multiply each the number of each type (simple, average, complex) within each category (output, input, inquiries [output/input], data structure [files], interfaces) by the appropriate weighting factor. The weighting factors given in Tables 10–3 through 10–7 and shown in Table 10–2 are time-tested values, but they may certainly be changed if deemed necessary.

- Add the totals for each category. When filled out, Steps 1 and 2 will look like the top section of Table 10–10.
- Notice that the total results in a "raw function point" count.

Step 3. Apply Environmental Factors

Adjust the raw function point total to account for environmental factors that affect the entire software development process. Many aspects of your surroundings might affect the software development process. Some of these aspects affect the project positively, and others tip the scales in the negative direction; all are considered as they uniquely apply to a specific project.

Table 10–8 contains a detailed definition of each of the 14 environmental factors, or influential adjustment factors, as well as guidelines for choosing the weight of the environmental factor.

Here's how the environmental weighting works. Using Table 10–8, rate each factor on a scale of 0 to 5 (where 0 means not applicable). To help get a feel for one end of the rating spectrum, Table 10–9 contains examples of software systems that would rate high—a rating number 4 or 5 on the scale.

Sum the factor ratings (Fn) to calculate a total environmental influence factor (N).

$$N = sum (Fn)$$

Use the Function Point Worksheet in Table 10–2 to record the values.

Refer to Table 10–10 to see how Step 3 looks when filled in.

TABLE 10–8
Function Points Analysis Environmental Factors Descriptions

Environmental Factor	Rating (0, 1, 2, 3, 4, 5)
Data Communications	Data or control information is sent or received over data communication facilities. Online systems always have some data communications influence.
Distributed Computing	Application uses data stored, accessed or processed on a storage or processing system other than the one(s) used for the main system.
Performance Requirements	User-approved demands have been made for exceptionally high throughput or fast response times.

(Continues)

TABLE 10–8 (Continued)
Function Points Analysis Environmental Factors Descriptions

Environmental Factor	Rating (0, 1, 2, 3, 4, 5)
Constrained Configuration	Application will be run in a heavily used, tight, or crowded configuration.
Transaction Rate	Network traffic is high, screens are heavy with information and graphics, frequency of screen transmission is high.
Online Inquiry and/or Entry	Heavily interactive.
End-User Efficiency	Additional human factor considerations are required.
Online Update	Dynamic database updates, distributed databases.
Complex Processing	High security, heavy transaction processing, complex algorithms, interrupt control logic.
Reusability	Code designed for reusability must be of high quality.
Ease of Conversion/Install	Conversions and installations require planning documents that have been tested.
Ease of Operation	Effective but easy startup, backup, error recovery, and shutdown procedures. Minimal manual activities.
Used at Multiple Sites	Account for differences in business functions.
Potential for Function Change	Modular, table-driven, user-maintained, flexible query capability, and so on.

Step 4. Calculate Complexity Adjustment Factor (CAF)

As stated earlier in this chapter, Barry Boehm postulated that the level of uncertainty in estimates is a function of the life cycle phase. Capers Jones supports the theory with empirical data, stating that environmental factors would have a maximum impact of +/– 35% on the raw function point total. It is considered maximum impact because if the FP analysis is conducted at the beginning of the life cycle, there is the largest swing in potential inaccuracy, as illustrated in Figure 10–2. To account for this uncertainty when the level of knowledge is low, a complexity adjustment factor (CAF) is applied to the environmental factors total.

TABLE 10–9
Function Points Analysis Environmental Factors, Examples of Systems with High Scores

Environmental Factors	Examples of High-Scoring Systems
1. Complex Data Communications	A program for a multinational bank that must handle electronic monetary transfers from financial institutions around the world.
2. Distributed Processing	A Web search engine in which the processing is performed by more than a dozen server computers working in tandem.
3. Stringent Performance Objectives	An air-traffic-control system that must continuously provide accurate, timely positions of aircraft from radar data.
4. Heavily Used Configuration	A university system in which hundreds of students register for classes simultaneously.
5. Fast Transaction Rates	A banking program that must perform millions of transactions overnight to balance all books before the next business day.
6. Online Data Entry	Mortgage approval program for which clerical workers enter data interactively into a computer system from paper applications filled out by prospective home owners.
7. User-Friendly Design	Software for computer kiosks with touch screens in which consumers at a subway station can purchase tickets using their credit cards.
8. Online Updating of Data	Airline system in which travel agents can book flights and obtain seat assignments. The software must be able to lock and then modify certain records in the database to ensure that the same seat is not sold twice.
9. Complex Processing	Medical software that takes a patient's various symptoms and performs extensive logical decisions to arrive at a preliminary diagnosis.
10. Reusability	A work processor that must be designed so that its menu toolbars can be incorporated into other applications, such as a spreadsheet or report generator.
11. Installation Ease	An equipment-control application that nonspecialists will install on an offshore oil rig.

(Continues)

TABLE 10–9 (Continued)
Function Points Analysis Environmental Factors, Examples of Systems with High Scores

Environmental Factors	Examples of High-Scoring Systems
12. Operational Ease	A program for analyzing huge numbers of historical financial records that must process the information in a way that would minimize the number of times that computer operators have to unload and reload different tapes containing the data.
13. Multiple Sites	Payroll software for a multinational corporation that must take into account the distinct characteristics of various countries, including different currencies and income tax rules.
14. Flexibility	A financial forecasting program that can issue monthly, quarterly, or yearly projections tailored to a particular business manager, who might require that the information be broken down by specific geographic regions and product lines.

Source: www.ifpug.org.

$$CAF = 0.65 + (0.01 \times N)$$

where N is the sum of the weighted environmental factors.

Because there are 14 suggested environmental factors, each weighted on a scale of 0–5, the smallest value for N would be 0 (none of the 14 factors is applicable); the largest value for N would be 70 (each of the 14 factors is high—a rating of 5). Plugging in these boundary conditions, minimum CAF = 0.65 + (0.01 × 0) = 0.65. Maximum CAF = 0.65 + (0.01 × 70) = 1.35. (1.35 – 0.65 = 0.70) The earliest estimates of size and effort may be off by a factor +/– 35%.

Step 4 is illustrated in Table 10–10.

Table 10–8 shows Jones's suggestions for environmental factors, but you may create your own values if you feel that straight function point analysis is too generic for use in your case. Our advice, however, is to keep your metrics simple so that metrics-gathering does not become a significant life cycle phase all on its own. Metrics, like other good software engineering techniques, should speed you up, not slow you down.

Step 5. Compute Adjusted Function Points

$$\text{adjusted function points (AFP)} = \text{raw function points} \times CAF$$

Step 5 may be observed in Table 10–10.

Step 6. Convert to LOC (Optional)

Function points give us a way of predicting the size of potential software programs or systems through analysis of its intended functionality from the user's point of view. Programming languages have varying but characteristic levels, where the level is the average number of executable statements required to implement one function point. We may choose to convert function points to LOC for several reasons, including:

- To measure and compare the productivity or size of programs or systems that are written in multiple languages;
- To use the standard unit of measure for input into estimating tools (discussed in Chapter 11);
- To convert the size of a program or application in any language to the equivalent size if the application were written in a different language.

Upon completion of Steps 1–5, sufficient data is available to permit a reasonably accurate conversion from function points to LOC.

A partial function-point-to-language conversion is shown in Table 10–1 to illustrate the translation of function points to LOC (the first and third columns). Not all of the IFPUG-approved language conversions are listed in the table (it is quite lengthy), and it is continually evolving as new languages are developed.

$$\text{LOC} = \text{adjusted function points} \times \text{LOC per adjusted function point}$$
$$\text{AFP} \times \# \text{ of LOC per AFP} = \text{LOC}$$

The example of the completed Function Points Analysis Worksheet can again be noted in Table 10–10.

Advantages of Function Point Analysis

Some of the advantages to the use of function points as a unit of software measurement include:

- It can be applied early in the software development life cycle—project sizing can occur in the requirements or design phase.
- It is independent of programming language, technology, and techniques, except for the adjustments at the end.

TABLE 10–10
Function Points Analysis Worksheet Example

Step 1. Count Number of Functions in Each Category
Step 2. Apply Complexity Weighting Factors

	Simple	Average	Complex	Function Points
Number of Outputs	$12 \times 4 = 48$	$11 \times 5 = 55$	$5 \times 7 = 35$	$48 + 55 + 35 = 138$
Number of Inputs	$8 \times 3 = 24$	$9 \times 4 = 36$	$6 \times 6 = 36$	$24 + 36 + 36 = 96$
Number of Inquiry Outputs	$5 \times 4 = 20$	$7 \times 5 = 35$	$3 \times 7 = 21$	$20 + 35 + 21$
Number of Inquiry Inputs	$5 \times 3 = 15$	$8 \times 4 = 32$	$4 \times 6 = 24$	$15 + 32 + 24 = 71$
Number of Files	$12 \times 7 = 84$	$3 \times 10 = 30$	$2 \times 15 = 30$	$84 + 30 + 30 = 144$
Number of Interfaces	$9 \times 5 = 45$	$6 \times 7 = 42$	$4 \times 10 = 40$	$45 + 42 + 40 = 127$
			Total (FP):	**652 "Raw" Function Points**

Step 3. Apply Environmental Factors

Environmental Factor	Rating (0, 1, 2, 3, 4, 5)
Data Communications	5
Distributed Computing	5
Performance Requirements	3
Constrained Configuration	0
Transaction Rate	5
Online Inquiry and/or Entry	4
End-User Efficiency	5
Online Update	4
Complex Processing	2
Reusability	2

(Continues)

TABLE 10–10 (Continued)
Function Points Analysis Worksheet Example

Environmental Factor	Rating (0, 1, 2, 3, 4, 5)
Ease of Conversion/Install	3
Ease of Operation	4
Used at Multiple Sites	5
Potential for Function Change	4
Total (N):	**51**

Step 4. Calculate Complexity Adjustment Factor (CAF)

$CAF = 0.65 + (0.01 \times N) = 0.65 + (0.01 \times 51) = 1.16$

Step 5. Compute Adjusted Function Points (AFP)

$AFP = FP \text{ (Raw)} \times CAF = 652 \times 1.16 = 756.32$

Step 6. Convert to LOC (Optional)

$LOC \text{ for the C Language} = AFP \times LOC/AFP = 756.32 \times 128 = 96,808.96 \text{ LOC}$

- Function points provide a reliable relationship to effort (if you can determine the right functions to measure).
- Creation of more function points per hour (week or month) is an easily understood, desirable productivity goal (as opposed to the creation of more LOC per hour [week or month], which is less meaningful, perhaps paradoxically).
- Users can relate more easily to this measure of size. They can more readily understand the impact of a change in functional requirements.
- The productivity of projects written in multiple languages may be measured.
- Function points provide a mechanism to track and monitor scope creep. Function points may be counted early and often—function point counts at the end of requirements, analysis, design, and implementation can be compared. If the number of function points is increasing with each count, then the project has become better defined or the project has grown in size (dangerous unless the schedule and/or cost is renegotiated).

- Function points can be used for graphical user interface (GUI) systems, for client/server systems, and with object-oriented development.
- Function points may be counted by senior-level users (clients or customers) as well as technicians.
- Environmental factors are considered.

As with all sizing and estimating models, adaptations and calibrations are encouraged. What is counted, how weights are applied, and what environmental factors are considered are all modifiable. For example, in the silicon chip industry, where physical units are tested via software, device components could be counted instead of inputs and outputs.

Disadvantages of Function Point Analysis

Disadvantages to the use of function point analysis include the following:

- It requires subjective evaluations, with much judgment involved.
- Results depend on technology used to implement it.
- Many effort and cost models depend on LOC, so function points must be converted.
- There is more research data on LOC than on function points.
- It is best performed after the creation of a design specification.
- It is not well-suited to non-MIS applications (use feature points instead).

Table 10–1 has another use in that an existing program may be examined for its function point count. For example, if you had an application consisting of 500 SLOC system in C++, the table would indicate that you have $6 \times 500 = 3,000$ function points. This technique, called "backfiring," can be used to build a rough size measure for a portfolio of applications. The portfolio can become the extremely useful historical database, which can be used for estimating future projects as well as calibrating sizing and estimating models.

How many function points are in a system that is considered to be very large? Some large military applications approach 400,000, the full SAP/R3 is 300,000, Windows 98 is about 100,000, and IBM's MVS is also about 100,000. Software Productivity Research, Inc., generated this data from its database of 8,500 projects from more than 600 organizations.

Feature Points as a Unit of Size   Feature points are an extension of the function point method designed to deal with different kinds of applications, such as embedded and/or real-time systems. In 1986, Software Productivity Research developed feature point analysis for system software. Pure function point counts applied to non-MIS software can result in a misleading metric because the applications are usually heavy in algorithmic complexity but light on external inputs and outputs. A feature point is a new category of function that represents complex algorithms and control (stimulus/response). The complexity of the algorithm is defined in terms of the number of "rules" required to express that algorithm. Feature points are generally used for:

- Real-time software such as missile defense systems;
- Systems software (e.g., operating systems, compilers);
- Embedded software such as radar navigation packages or chips in automobile air bags;
- Engineering applications such as Computer-Aided Design (CAD), Computer-Integrated Manufacturing (CIM), and mathematical software;
- Artificial intelligence (AI) software;
- Communications software (e.g., telephone switching systems);
- Process control software such as refinery drivers.

Feature points are basically function points that are sensitive to high algorithmic complexity, where an algorithm is a bounded set of rules (executable statements) required to solve a computational problem.

Guidelines for Counting Feature Points

Figure 10–5 shows the basic steps in counting feature points; each will be described later. The Feature Point Worksheet appears in Table 10–11.

Step 1. Count Feature Points

This is the same as counting function points—count inputs, outputs, files (data structures), inquiries, and interfaces.

The filled-out Feature Point Worksheet in Table 10–13 serves as an example for each of the seven steps.

Step 2. Continue the Feature Point Count by Counting the Number of Algorithms

An algorithm is a bounded computational problem that is included within a specific computer program.

Significant and countable algorithms deal with a definite, solvable, bounded problem with a single entry and a single exit point.

Developers who use data flow diagrams or structure charts in design often equate an algorithm to a basic process specification or module specification.

Step 3. Weigh Complexity

Use "average" weights instead of simple, average, or complex (note that the average for feature points is different from the average for function points) for inputs, outputs, files (data structures), inquiries, and interfaces. Weigh algorithms with a simple, average, and complex multiplier.

The average complexity factor for "files" is reduced from 10 to 7 to reflect the reduced significance of logical files in computation-intensive software.

The default weighting factor for algorithms is 3. The value can vary over a range of 1 to 10. Algorithms that require basic arithmetic operations and few decision rules are assigned a

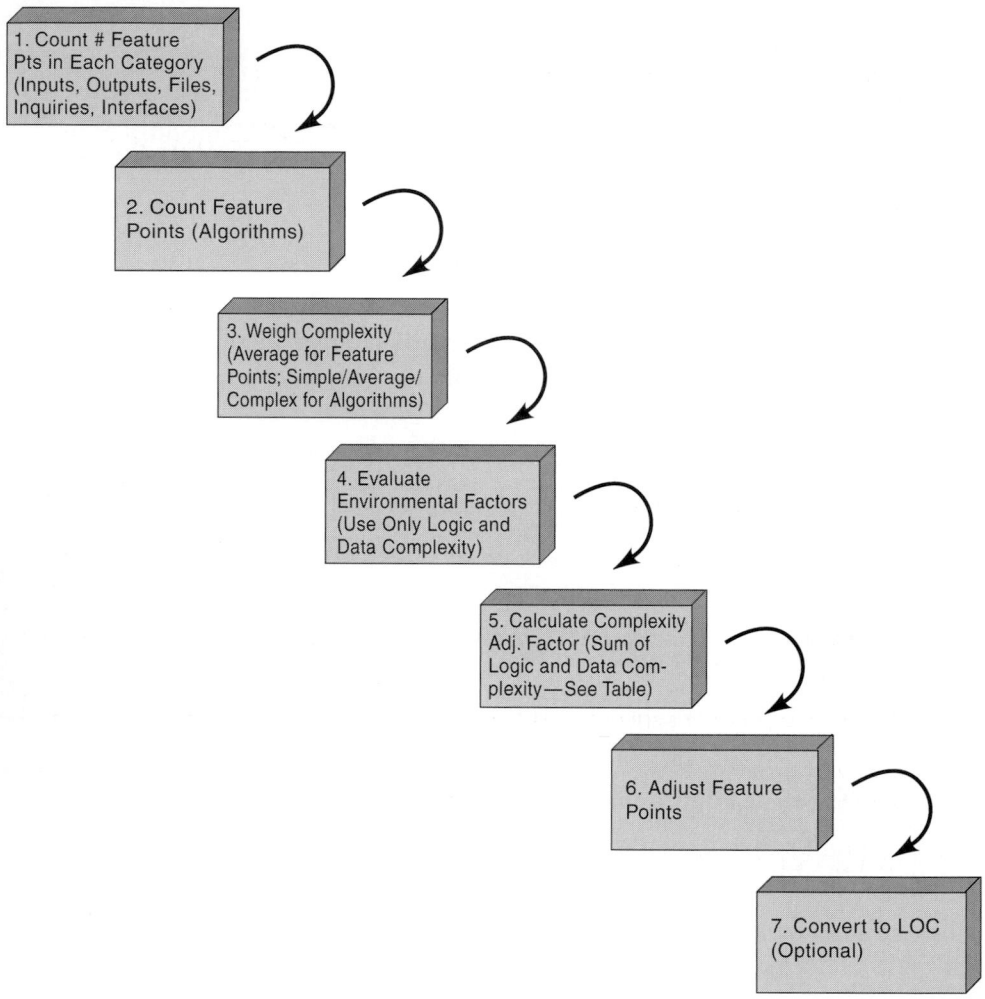

FIGURE 10–5
Basic Steps in Feature Point Analysis

value of 1. Algorithms requiring complex equations, matrix operation, and difficult logical processing are assigned a value of 10. Algorithms that are significant and therefore should be counted have these characteristics:

- Deals with a solvable, bounded, definite problem;
- Must be finite and have an end;
- Is precise and unambiguous;

TABLE 10–11
Feature Point Analysis Worksheet

Step 1. Count Feature Points

	Average	Feature Points
Number of Inputs	___ × 4	
Number of Outputs	___ × 5	
Number of Files (Data Structures)	___ × 7	
Number of Inquiries	___ × 4	
Number of Interfaces	___ × 7	

Step 2. Count the Number of Algorithms

	Average	Feature Points
Number of Algorithms	___ × 3	
	Total (FP):	

Step 3. Weigh Complexity
Step 4. Evaluate Environmental Factors
Step 5. Calculate the Complexity Adjustment Factor (CAF)

Logic Values (Select One)
Simple Algorithms and Calculations—1
Majority of Simple Algorithms—2
Average Complexity of Algorithms—3
Some Difficult Algorithms—4
Many Difficult Algorithms—5

Data Values (Select One)
Simple Data—1
Numerous Variables, but Simple Relationships—2
Multiple Fields, Files, and Interactions—3
Complex File Structures—4
Very Complex Files and Data Relationships—5

Total (CAF):

(Continues)

TABLE 10–11 (Continued)
Feature Point Analysis Worksheet

Step 6. Multiply the Raw Feature Point Count by the CAF

Raw FP × CAF =

Step 7. Convert to Lines of Code (Optional)

LOC = AFP × LOC/AFP =

- Has an input or starting value;
- Has output or produces a result;
- Is implementable—each step is capable of executing on a computer;
- Is capable of representation via one of the standard programming constructs: sequence, if-then-else, do-case, do-while, and do-until.

Step 4. Evaluate Environmental Factors

Instead of the 14 environmental factors used in function point analysis, feature point uses only two: logic complexity and data complexity. The range is from 1 to 5.

Logic Values

1—Simple algorithms and calculations

2—Majority of simple algorithms

3—Average complexity of algorithms

4—Some difficult algorithms

5—Many difficult algorithms

Data Values

1—Simple data

2—Numerous variables, but simple relationships

3—Multiple fields, files, and interactions

4—Complex file structures

5—Very complex files and data relationships

Sum the logic and data complexity factor values, yielding a number between 2 and 10.

Step 5. Calculate the Complexity Adjustment Factor

Use Table 10–12 to calculate the complexity adjustment factor.

TABLE 10–12

Feature Point Complexity Adjustment Factor

Sum of Logic and Data Complexity	Complexity Adjustment Factor
2	0.6
3	0.7
4	0.8
5	0.9
6	1.0
7	1.1
8	1.2
9	1.3
10	1.4

Step 6. Multiply the Raw Feature Point Count by the Complexity Adjustment Factor

Step 7. Convert to Lines of Code Using the Function Point Translation Table (Optional)

TABLE 10–13

Feature Point Analysis Worksheet Example

Step 1. Count Feature Points

	Average	Feature Points
Number of Inputs	12×4	48
Number of Outputs	15×5	75
Number of Files (Data Structures)	22×7	154
Number of Inquiries	17×4	68
Number of Interfaces	8×7	56

(Continues)

TABLE 10–13 (Continued)
Feature Point Analysis Worksheet Example

Step 2. Count the Number of Algorithms

	Average	Feature Points
Number of Algorithms	43×3	129
Total (FP):	530 "Raw" Feature Points	

Step 3. Weigh Complexity
Step 4. Evaluate Environmental Factors
Step 5. Calculate the Complexity Adjustment Factor (CAF)

Logic Values (Select One)
Simple Algorithms and Calculations—1
Majority of Simple Algorithms—2
Average Complexity of Algorithms—3
→**Some Difficult Algorithms—4**
Many Difficult Algorithms—5

Data Values (Select One)
Simple Data—1
Numerous Variables, but Simple Relationships—2
→**Multiple Fields, Files, and Interactions—3**
Complex File Structures—4
Very Complex Files and Data Relationships—5

Total (CAF): 4 + 3 = 7 Complexity Adjustment Factor

Step 6. Multiply the Raw Feature Point Count by the CAF

Raw FP × CAF = 530 × 7 = 3,710 Adjusted Feature Points

Step 7. Convert to Lines of Code (Optional)

LOC for the Java Language = AFP × LOC/AFP = 3,710 × 53 = 196,630 LOC

Advantages of Feature Point Analysis

Advantages of feature point analysis are essentially the same as those for function point analysis, with the additional advantage of being an excellent approach to use in the size estimation of algorithmically intensive systems.

Disadvantages of Feature Point Analysis

The primary disadvantage of feature point analysis is the subjective classification of algorithmic complexity.

Object Points   Counting "object points" to determine software size is an approach developed for object-oriented technology. Conducted at a more macro level than function points, it assigns one object point to each unique class or object, such as a screen, output report, and so on. The rest of the process is similar to that of function and feature points, but the conversion factors are different.

Model Blitz   Estimating gets better with each passing phase because more knowledge about project needs is gained in each phase. A great deal of knowledge is revealed in the analysis and design phase, in which models are produced (Chapter 22) that allow for increasingly accurate size estimates. Until that phase of the project is reached, there will probably be some useful but very high-level analysis models produced in the planning phase. They may be used as another method, simple but quick, for estimating size.

The concept of blitz modeling is based on Tom DeMarco's bang metric. Counting component pieces of the system (design elements) and multiplying the count by a productivity factor (on the average, how many lines of procedural code this takes to implement, based on historical precedent), results in rough estimates. For example, if high-level data flow diagrams or object models are produced as part of concept exploration or planning, their components may be observed for size. Imagine that there are 20 object classes and it is known by observation of existing systems that classes are implemented on average as five procedural programs per class. Also imagine that it is known by observation of existing systems that the average size procedural program (C language) is 75 LOC. Then the size can quickly be calculated as:

Number of processes (object classes) × Number of programs per class × Average Program Size
= Estimated Size

20 object classes × 5 programs per class × 75 LOC per program = 7,500 LOC estimated

This is known as a "blitz" of early feasibility documents. Components of any model (process bubbles, data flows, data repositories, entities, relationships, objects, attributes, services, etc.) may be multiplied by a factor that has been developed as a result of previous projects. Other examples are as follows: If it is known that each process bubble on a Level 0 DFD roughly corresponds to four actual SQL language programs, and it is also known that the average size for programs in the SQL library is 350 LOC, then a simple multiplication will suffice for the initial size count. Say that there are seven major process bubbles:

$$\text{Number of processes (DFD bubbles)} \times \text{Number of programs per bubble}$$
$$\times \text{Average Program Size} = \text{Estimated Size}$$

$$7 \text{ bubbles} \times 4 \text{ programs per bubble} \times 350 \text{ LOC per program} = 9{,}800 \text{ LOC estimated}$$

If a high-level global object model is produced during the feasibility scoping phase, and it is *known from historical evidence* that each service corresponds to two C++ programs and that company standards encourage confining each service packet to 100 LOC or less, then multiplying as follows will provide a good start in the estimation of the size of the system in LOC:

$$\text{Number of services} \times 2 \times 100$$

The key phrase here is "known from historical evidence." A historical database is essential to improving estimating accuracy. The database should contain a record of the actual delivered size for each software component. The amount of effort expended to create the component of that size must also be tracked. As the numbers of data points grow, so does the accuracy of the average number of LOC per program and the average amount of effort required building a component. When actual component sizes and their corresponding amounts of development effort are known, then average "productivity" is also known (size ÷ effort).

DeMarco suggests, with the bang metric, that function-strong systems (e.g., real time) be computed separately from data-strong systems. Functions-strong systems rely on a count of indivisible functional primitives as defined by a data flow diagram. Data-strong systems rely on a count of objects in the system-global data model. Each will have a weighting factor (WF) applied.

An example with function-strong systems is this: WF (average number of modules needed to complete this function) is three, the number of processes plus control specifications (functions) is eight, and the average size per function is 78 LOC. Then:

$$\text{WF} \times \text{(Number of process and control specifications)}$$
$$\times \text{average LOC for this type of module} = \text{LOC}$$

$$3 \text{ modules needed for function} \times 8 \text{ functions} \times 78 \text{ LOC} = 1{,}872 \text{ LOC}$$

How does this differ from the feature point analysis presented during the feasibility scoping phase? Not by much. A project manager may choose to perform feature point analysis during the feasibility scoping phase, when only high-level models such as context-level DFDs exist, and then refine that estimation during the planning phase, when there is more project knowledge and more documentation, such as a Level 0 DFD, along with a Level 1 DFD for a few of the major subsystems. Any of these models may be used during any phase. If they are applied consistently, the expectation is that sizing and estimating accuracy will increase.

Advantages of Model Blitz

Some of the advantages of using the Model Blitz method include:

- It is easy to use with structured methods (data flow diagrams, entity relationship diagrams, etc.) and with object-oriented classes, services, and so on.
- Accuracy increases with use of historical data.
- Continuous improvement activities are used for estimation techniques—the estimated size can be easily compared with the actual size during post-project analysis. (How accurate was the estimate? Why was it off by a certain percent? What can be learned for the next project's size estimation?)

Disadvantages of Model Blitz

Disadvantages of using Model Blitz include:

- It requires use of design methodology.
- Estimation cannot begin until design is complete.
- It requires historical data.
- It does not evaluate environmental factors.

Wideband Delphi   Another popular and simple technique for estimating size and for estimating effort is the Wideband Delphi group consensus approach. The Delphi technique originated at the Rand Corporation decades ago; the name was derived from the Oracle of Delphi in Greek mythology. It was used successfully at Rand to predict the future of major world technologies.

This is a disciplined method of using the experience of several people to reach an estimate that incorporates all of their knowledge.

In software engineering circles, the original Delphi approach has been modified. The "pure" approach is to collect expert opinion in isolation, feed back anonymous summary results, and iterate until consensus is reached (without group discussion).

Guidelines for Conducting Wideband Delphi Group Consensus

Because the Delphi approach can take a very long time, the concept of Wideband Delphi was introduced to speed up the process. This improved approach uses group discussion.

Steps in Conducting Wideband Delphi

There are six major steps in conducting Wideband Delphi:

1. Present experts with a problem and a response form.
2. Conduct a group discussion.
3. Collect expert opinion anonymously.
4. Feed back a summary of results to each expert.
5. Conduct another group discussion.
6. Iterate as necessary until consensus is reached.

Group discussions are the primary difference between pure Delphi and Wideband Delphi. The summary of results in Step 4 is presented in Figure 10–6.

Here's another way to look at the Wideband Delphi process:

- Get a few experts (typically three to five). Include experience in all of the "risk" areas—application domain, programming language, algorithms, target hardware, operating systems, and so on.
- Meet with them to discuss issues and describe the software to them. Bring specifications, other source documents, WBS, and so on. Let them add their own information and questions. Have everyone take notes.

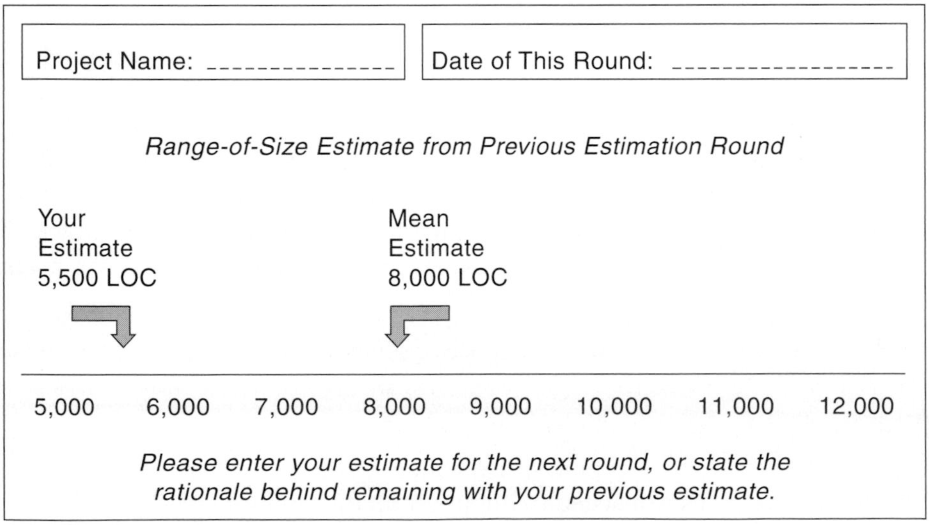

Project Name: _____ Date of This Round: _____

Range-of-Size Estimate from Previous Estimation Round

Your
Estimate
5,500 LOC

Mean
Estimate
8,000 LOC

| 5,000 | 6,000 | 7,000 | 8,000 | 9,000 | 10,000 | 11,000 | 12,000 |

Please enter your estimate for the next round, or state the rationale behind remaining with your previous estimate.

FIGURE 10–6
Delphi Software Size Estimation Results Summary Form

- Ask each expert to develop an estimate, including a minimum, expected, and maximum rating. Allow the experts to remain independent and anonymous.
- Record anonymous estimates on a graph.
- Meet and have each expert discuss his estimate, assumptions, and rationale.
- Seek consensus on assumptions. This may result in action items to gather factual data.
- If possible, reach a consensus estimate.
- If no consensus can be reached, break until you can gather additional data; then repeat.
- Stop repeating when you reach consensus or two consecutive cycles do not change much and there is no significant additional data available (agree to disagree). At the end, there is a consensus estimate on an expected value. There should also be a minimum and a maximum so that the degree of confidence in the estimate can be understood.

Advantages of Wideband Delphi

The advantages of Wideband Delphi include the following:

- Implemention is easy and inexpensive.
- It takes advantage of the expertise of several people.
- All participants become better educated about the software.
- It does not require historical data, although it is useful if available.
- It is used for high-level and detailed estimation.
- Results are more accurate and less "dangerous" than LOC estimating.
- It aids in providing a global view of project to team members.

Disadvantages of Wideband Delphi

The disadvantages of Wideband Delphi include the following:

- It is difficult to repeat with a different group of experts.
- You can reach consensus on an incorrect estimate. Because you all "buy in," you may not be skeptical enough when actual data shows it is wrong.
- You can develop a false sense of confidence.
- You may fail to reach a consensus.
- Experts may be all biased in the same subjective direction.

The Effects of Reuse on Software Size _____

Many software programs are derived from previous programs. This may result in savings of cost and/or time, and it may result in increased quality. But reuse can also cost more, take longer, and yield lower quality.

Just about anything can be reused—code, test code, test cases, test procedures, documentation, design specifications, designs, requirements specifications, and so on.

Reuse terminology includes:

- New code—code developed for a new application without including large portions of previously written code
- Modified code—code developed for a previous application that is suitable for a new application after a *modest amount of modification*
- Reused code—code developed for a previous application that is suitable for a new application *without change of any kind*
- Legacy code—code developed for a previous application that is believed to be of use for a new application

Why is it "modified" if you change it only a little bit? Totally reused code has identical documentation, identical test procedures and code, and only one copy to maintain in the configuration management library. Even if a single comment line is changed, two copies of the code, test code, documentation, and so on must be maintained in the configuration management library. If only one line of executable code is changed, tests and documentation must change as well.

When using legacy code, beware that it may have poor documentation, it may lack test code or procedures, it may not be designed well, and it may have lax quality standards.

The first step in estimating systems that may reuse code is to separate new code from modified and reused code. This is because modified and reused code can almost never just be added in—there are changes required for the integration, and size and effort increases to accommodate those changes. An example appears in Table 10–14.

TABLE 10–14
Separate New, Modified, and Reused Lines of Code

Item	New LOC	Modified LOC	Reused LOC	Total LOC
Component 1	1,233	0	0	1,233
Component 2	0	988	0	988
Component 3	0	0	781	781
Component 4	560	245	0	805
Component 5	345	549	420	1,314
Total	2,138	1,782	1,201	5,121

How do you count how much of a component is modified or reused? Consider Component 4 and Component 5 in Table 10–15. A rule of thumb is to examine the smallest level known for a unit or module (typically about 100 LOC). If the unit is not changed at all, it is "reused." If the unit has changed, by even one comment or executable statement, it is "modified." If more than 50% of the unit is changed, consider it to be "new." In addition, once the modified code has been identified, you may want to separate it into categories representing the type of modification. A widely used approach is to separate modifications for the sake of correcting defects from the modifications for adding enhancements. Table 10–14 might look something like Table 10–15 once this separation is made.

TABLE 10–15
Different Kinds of Modified Code

Item	New LOC	Modified to Fix Bugs	Modified to Add Enhancements	Reused LOC	Total LOC
Component 1	1,233	0	0	0	1,233
Component 2	0	988	0	0	988
Component 3	0	0	0	781	781
Component 4	560	0	245	0	805
Component 5	345	302	247	420	1,314
Total Delivered LOC	2,138	1,782	1,782	1,201	5,121

After estimating the total delivered size, reused code will be converted to "equivalent" new code. The conversion process is based on how much less effort will be expended for reused or modified software than for new software. Usually a conversion factor is established to reflect the amount of effort saved by reuse. Assuming that there is historical justification of the conversion factors, a simple calculation can then be done. Returning to the example in Table 10–16, we can apply reuse factors indicating that reused software takes only about 30% as much effort as new software, and modified software takes about 60% as much effort as new software. This indicates that the total effort to develop these 5,121 LOC will be comparable to that of producing 3,567 lines of new code.

Reuse factors come from experience. The 30% and 60% factors were observed on hundreds of projects. However, these are averages, and the range is wide. The best indicator of size and effort in your organization is actual data from the organization—keeping track of estimates and actuals in a historical database.

Typical reuse factors are shown in Table 10–17.

TABLE 10–16
Applying Reuse Factors

Item	New LOC	Modified LOC	Reused LOC	Total LOC
Total	2,138	1,782	1,201	5,121
Factor	100%	60%	30%	—
Net	2,138	1,069	360	3,567

TABLE 10–17
Typical Reuse Factors

Ease of Use	Reused	Modified
Easy	10%	25%
Average	30%	60%
Hard	40%	75%

Becoming More Accurate with Reuse

We can get more accurate if we are willing to look more closely at the process and the reuse characteristics. Returning to our example, the first step is to examine the process and then determine the percent of the total effort expended in each step in the development of new code.

Suppose that we know that our organization spends 18% of its time in requirements, 25% in design, 25% in code and test, and 32% in integration (there are only four life cycle phases in this example).

As shown in Figure 10–18, new code will require that every bit of that effort must be expended. However, modified and reused code will require less effort.

Instead of 100%, let's say that modified code requires only 20% of requirements effort, and reused code requires only 10%.

Instead of 100% of design effort, we'll say that only 40% will be required for modified software and no design (0%) is required for reused software. The 40% is because we may have to plan how to test the modified software, and maybe we must design the rest of the software in a special way. The value of pure reuse begins to become apparent.

Instead of 100% of the coding and unit testing effort required for new software, modified software requires only 70%, and, again, reused software is essentially "free." For only "pure" reused code will this be zero. If just one single line of code is changed, then it has been modified.

Integration effort doesn't get a break, even with modified or reused code. Even for pure reused code, integration often requires 50%–100%.

For each phase of the process, the effect of reuse can be determined after the percent of effort for each reuse category is determined. Table 10–18 shows that inclusion of reused and modified code wherever possible is indeed a size, effort, schedule, and cost savings.

TABLE 10–18
Applying an Accurate Estimating Method to Reused and Modified Code

	Process Step	Requirements	Design	Code	Integration	
	Percent	18%	25%	25%	32%	
Delivered						**Equivalent**
2,138	New	100%	100%	100%	100%	**2,138**
1,782	Modified	20%	40%	70%	100%	**1,124**
1,201	Reused	10%	0%	0%	100%	406
5,121						**3,668**

Estimation of Effort

After the size of a software product has been estimated, we can proceed to estimate the effort required to produce it. Such is the topic of Chapter 11, "Estimating Duration and Cost."

Summary _____

Sizing, estimating, and scheduling are inextricably intertwined during the project planning process. It's really impossible to create a realistic schedule (who's going to do what and when, dependencies, overlapping activities, culminating in the product delivery date) without knowing the amount of effort required for each task (e.g., person-months). It's equally difficult to estimate the amount of effort that a task will require without knowing how "big" it is. Therefore, sizing precedes estimating, which precedes scheduling. Each of these critical project activities may be performed using a variety of techniques. The ability to estimate is critical to a maturing software organization.

Poor estimates are problematic, increasing risk, which can be mitigated by standard estimating methods. All the methods begin with the best possible understanding of the project breakdown, as shown in the WBS.

There are five useful and well-known techniques for sizing, all building upon the WBS:

- Counting lines of code (LOC) as a measure of size;
- Counting function points as a measure of size;
- Counting feature points as a measure of size;
- Performing a model blitz (also known as the DeMarco bang metric and as bottom-up estimating);
- Applying Wideband Delphi.

Reuse of existing components is not all "gravy." There is a price to pay for integration; existing components may not have been designed for quality and reuse. There exists a set of empirically derived weighting factors to apply during reuse estimation.

The software industry often reverts to LOC metrics, the unit of measure that software practitioners find familiar, comfortable, and easy to use. Whatever technique is used, estimating the size of a product is important because it contributes to the single most important task of a project: setting realistic expectations. Unrealistic expectations based on inaccurate estimates are the single largest cause of software failure. Often, it is not project team performance that is poor, but only the prediction of performance. Accurate estimates providing for improved project control are vital to the management of the project; inaccurate estimates typically lead to last-minute panic, resulting in the introduction of defects.

To produce accurate estimates, you first need to know how much software is to be produced. This is the software size that must be expressed early in the development life cycle in units that are readily observable and easy to communicate.

A summary for an estimating checklist might include:

- Has a firm foundation been established for the estimate of software size?
- Have customers, managers, and developers been trained in the basics of sizing and estimating?
- Has historical data, if used, been applied correctly?
- Have models been used correctly?
- Has the estimation method been mapped/calibrated to the development process?
- Have reasonable assumptions been made about product and process factors that affect productivity?
- Do aggressive goals have realistic strategies for accomplishment?
- Have any alternative estimating methods been used for comparison?
- Have multiple methods been used? (No one method is reliable enough, in most cases. When two methods disagree, you may be missing some facts.)

- Have all functions been included? (Many are easy to overlook or underestimate, such as control, powerup, power failure, diagnostics, operating systems, and so on.)
- Have you been cautious not to underscope what you don't understand?

   Most importantly when estimating software size, remember:

- History is your ally.
- Use multiple methods, both to learn and to reduce risk.
- Account for reuse.

The authors especially thank Richard Fairley, who has designed and taught many excellent courses in sizing and estimating, for his mentorship.

Problems for Review

1. Explain why or why not LOC is an appropriate software size metric in your organization.
2. Select a current, future, or past project in your organization and describe whether function points or feature points would be the most appropriate method of relating the size of the system.
3. List the phases of the life cycle in use in your organization, and attach the percent of effort that you believe is spent, on average, in each phase. If you don't have a standard life cycle in use, list the phases of a life cycle that you believe would make a good standard; then apply the percent of effort that you think would be effective to spend on each phase.

Visit the Case Study

Ms. Patel, your AsiaPac marketing manager, presented the ARRS Market Requirements Document (MRD) to the corporation's productization steering committee. The corporation put in place an across-the-board goal of turning "software investment into paying products," and each marketing manager was required to build a preliminary MRD for any software being built in their areas of responsibility. The BSD was established as an SEI Level 5 organization and adopted the measurement-driven software management (MDSM) process of the Software Reuse Business Model (SRBM).

   BSD MDSM has these attributes:

- Measurement and management. Reuse impact analysis must be regarded as an aspect of an overall metrics program, thus dependent on that program. A program of systematic measurement is a planned, systematic effort that regularly measures the process and the products that it creates throughout the life cycle.

- Reuse and domain management. A program manager has a multiproject perspective and a general responsibility for managing the delivery of a family of similar projects within a domain. Part of this function is managing reuse across the members of the family. The program manager makes investment decisions based on the estimated value of a reuse capability applied over multiple programs, either current or expected, in a domain.
- Reuse and program management. A program manager has a single-program perspective. The program manager does this, in part, by helping to refine the estimated impact of the reuse program for a domain on the program's particular system. Furthermore, the program manager should be alert to potential opportunities for cost-effective reuse within the scope of the program.
- Typical reuse cost questions. Regarding reuse cost analysis in particular, some typical questions addressed are:
    1. What would be the likely decrease in the cost of delivering a new system for a given percentage of reuse in deliverable artifacts?
    2. What is the cost avoidance for an average percentage of reuse across a family of such systems?
    3. How many systems in a particular domain must realize expected reuse benefits for a given investment in reuse to pay off?
    4. What is the expected cost of developing each system of a family, given a particular reuse investment strategy?
    5. What is the return on investment that should be expected for a given reuse investment strategy?

The main action item that came out of her presentation was to answer these standard questions for the ARRS. Unfortunately, Ms. Patel is traveling to meetings in Australia the remainder of this week. Because she knows that you, as the project manager, studied the SEI CMM and has worked before with BSD, she is letting you answer these in an email to the corporate market productization board. The members meet again next Tuesday in Chicago at 3:30 p.m.

Citations

[1]Paulk, Mark C., Charles V. Weber, Bill Curtis, and Mary Beth Chrissis (1994). *The Capability Maturity Model: Guidelines for Improving the Software Process*, 1st ed. Reading, MA: Addison-Wesley.

[2]DeMarco, Tom (1995). *Why Does Software Cost So Much? and Other Puzzles of the Information Age*. New York, NY: Dorset House.

[3]Boehm, Barry (1981). *Software Engineering Economics*. Englewood Cliffs, NJ: Prentice Hall.

Suggested Readings _____

Albrecht, Allan J. (1979). "Measuring Application Development Productivity." *Proceedings of the IBM Application Development Symposium*, October 1979. Monterey, CA. pp. 83–92.

Albrecht, Allan J., and John E. Gaffney, Jr. (1993). "Software Function, Source Lines of Code, and Development Effort Prediction: A Software Science Validation." *IEEE Transactions on Software Engineering*, SE-9(6):639–648. New York, NY: The Institute of Electrical and Electronics Engineers.

DeMarco, Tom, and Barry W. Boehm (1998). *Controlling Software Projects: Management, Measurement, and Estimates*. Englewood Cliffs, NJ: Prentice Hall PTR/Sun Microsystems Press.

Florac, William A., and Anita D. Carleton (1999). *Measuring the Software Process*. Reading, MA: Addison-Wesley.

Garmus, David, and David Herron (2001). *Function Point Analysis: Measurement Practices for Successful Software Projects*. Boston, MA: Addison-Wesley.

Jones, Capers (1986). *Programming Productivity*. New York, NY: McGraw-Hill.

Jones, Capers (1997). *Applied Software Measurement: Assuring Productivity and Quality*, 2nd ed. New York, NY: McGraw-Hill.

Kemerer, Chris F. (1987). "An Empirical Validation of Software Cost Estimation Models." *Communications of the ACM*, 30(5):416–429. New York: NY: Association for Computing Machinery.

Stutzke, Richard D. (2001). *Software Estimation: Projects, Products, Processes*. Reading, MA: Addison-Wesley.

Von Mayrhauser, Anneliese (1990). *Software Engineering: Methods and Management*. Boston, MA: Academic Press.

www.ifpug.org. International Function Point Users Group (1990). Function Points as Asset Reporting to Management.

www.ifpug.org. International Function Point Users Group (1994). Function Point Counting Practices Manual, Release 4.0. IFPUG Standards.

www.ifpug.org. International Function Point Users Group (1994). Guidelines to Software measurement, Release 1.0. IFPUG Standards.

Web Pages for Further Information _____

kapis.www.wkap.nl/kapis/CGI-BIN/WORLD/journalhome.htm?1382-3256. Victor R. Basili, Editor-in-Chief; Warren Harrison, Associate Editor, Empirical Software Engineering.

ifpug.org. International Function Point User's Group (IFPUG) Web site.

ourworld.compuserve.com/homepages/softcomp/fpfaq.htm. "Frequently Asked Questions (and Answers) Regarding Function Point Analysis." Copyright 1996–1997 by Software Composition Technologies, Inc.

www.dacs.dtic.mil/databases/url/key.hts?keycode=4:7&islowerlevel=1. Cost Estimation: Function Points Analysis. The Data & Analysis Center for Software (DACS) is a Department of Defense (DoD) Information Analysis Center (IAC).

www.qpmg.com/fp-intro.htm. Roger Heller, "An Introduction to Function Points," Q/P Management Group, Inc.

www.sciam.com/1998/1298issue/1298jones.html#further. Jones, Capers, "Sizing Up Software: Unlike oil, steel or paper, software is an intangible commodity."

www.softwaremetrics.com/Articles/default.htm. Longstreet Consulting, Inc.

www.spr.com/index.htm. Software Productivity Research.

www.spr.com/library/0funcmet.htm. Capers Jones, Chairman, Software Productivity Research, Inc. "What Are Function Points?"

www.stsc.hill.af.mil/crosstalk/. Software Estimation: Challenges and Research.

www.stsc.hill.af.mil/CrossTalk/1995/nov/Living.asp. Lawrence Bernstein and Alex Lubashevsky, AT&T, "Living with Function Points."

Estimating Duration and Cost

Chapter 10, "Software Size and Reuse Estimating," described methods for estimating the size of a software project, typically in thousands of software lines of code (KSLOC or KLOC). After the size has been established, the answers to other questions that are important to all stakeholders may also be estimated. Most customers and sponsors are less interested in how big the product will be than in how long it will take to produce it and how much it will cost. When a project manager has an idea of the total number of staff-months that will be required, he can begin to plan for recruiting, training, rotating, and other staffing management concerns. This chapter describes how to build upon the estimate of size, whether it is in KLOC, object points, function points, feature points, or another unit of measure.

Where We Are in the Product Development Life Cycle

Estimating the effort, duration, and cost of software occurs during the early stages of project planning, just after estimating the size. In terms of our generic life cycle model, planning takes place during the concept exploration, system exploration, and requirements phases (see Figure 11–1). Estimating size and effort will occur many times during the life cycle, increasing confidence with each occurrence—after initial customer requirements, after analysis, after design, and so on. Our process model describing the phases of the life cycle serves us well in indicating where estimates and re-estimates should occur. A good practice for project managers is to require size estimates and re-estimates as exit criteria from each phase.

Please note that the life cycle shown here is not the entire picture. It shows only some of the phases and activities that are associated with the sizing and estimation process.

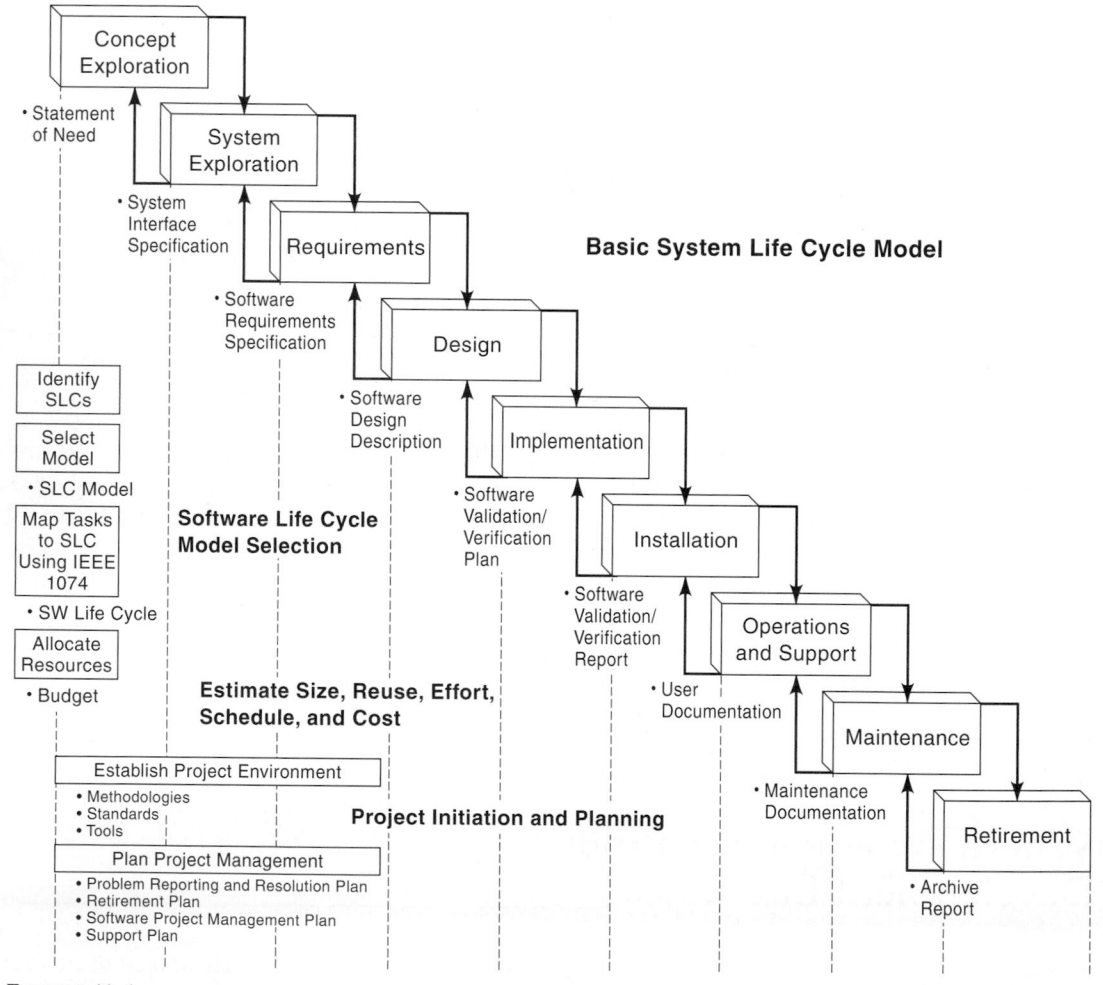

FIGURE 11–1
Initial Software Effort and Schedule (Duration) Estimation Occurs Early in the Project Life Cycle

Chapter 11 Relation to the 34 Competencies_____

The process of estimating effort, schedule, and cost falls under the project competencies umbrella (see Figure 11–2). These estimates are recorded in the project plan; therefore, a third project competency, documenting plans, is a skill that comes into play. The estimates are also metrics that should be maintained as the project progresses.

Product Development Techniques

4. **Evaluating alternative processes**—Estimate using at least two techniques.

8. **Selecting methods and tools**—Estimating is a method with a series of process steps; there are many tools available to support the process, both manual and automated.

9. **Tailoring processes**—All estimating models may be calibrated to reflect an organization's environment.

Project Management Skills

13. **Documenting plans**—Decomposed product and project tasks lead to size, effort, and cost estimation, and then ultimately to the project schedule. All are represented in the software project management plan (SPMP). Estimation risks are documented in a separate risk plan or as a segment in the SPMP.

14. **Estimating cost** and 15. **Estimating effort**—Predictions of size lead to predictions of effort.

18. **Scheduling**—Knowledge of effort also leads to schedule estimation.

19. **Selecting metrics**—Units of size are a metric. Once chosen (size, estimated effort months [hours, days, weeks], estimated schedule duration, estimated cost), they will be referred to consistently throughout the project. They will be used in comparing estimates to actual results.

People Management Skills

It is difficult to list separate people competencies because almost all of them are required in almost every activity of software development. With estimating effort, schedule and cost, the following people skills are particularly helpful:

24. Handling intellectual property

25. Holding effective meetings

26. Interaction and communication

27. Leadership

28. Managing change

29. Negotiating successfully

31. Presenting effectively

Software
Product

1. Assessing processes
2. Awareness of process standards
3. Defining the product
4. **Evaluating alternative processes**
5. Managing requirements
6. Managing subcontractors
7. Performing the initial assessment
8. **Selecting methods and tools**
9. **Tailoring processes**
10. Tracking product quality
11. Understanding development activities

Project
Project

12. Building a work breakdown structure
13. **Documenting plans**
14. **Estimating cost**
15. **Estimating effort**
16. Managing risks
17. Monitoring development
18. **Scheduling**
19. **Selecting metrics**
20. Selecting project management tools
21. Tracking process
22. Tracking project progress

Management
People

23. Appraising performance
24. **Handling intellectual property**
25. **Holding effective meetings**
26. **Interaction and communication**
27. **Leadership**
28. **Managing change**
29. **Negotiating successfully**
30. Planning careers
31. **Presenting effectively**
32. Recruiting
33. Selecting a team
34. Teambuilding

FIGURE 11–2
Estimating and the 34 Competencies

Learning Objectives for Chapter 11 _____

By the end of this chapter, the reader should be able to:

- List the major steps in software size, effort, duration and cost estimating;

- Name two models frequently used in the software industry to estimate effort and schedule;

- Distinguish among regression, mathematical, and empirical estimating models;

- Explain the basic concepts of the COCOMO estimating model;

- Explain the basic concepts of the SLIM estimating model;

- Summarize the advantages and disadvantages of each of the models;

- Apply the use of an estimating model to an actual software development project.

The SEI CMM and Estimating _____

The Software Engineering Institute (SEI) Capability Maturity Model (CMM) supports activities described here. Software project planning is a key process area for maturity Level 2, the repeatable level. The KPAs in Level 2 are a necessary foundation for the mature processes that follow in subsequent levels—planning the project is essential in the support of the software engineering, measurement, and continuous improvement activities occurring in levels 3 (defined), 4 (managed), and 5 (optimized).

The importance of software estimation is emphasized by a specific goal (Goal 1) in the project planning KPA. Because the plan provides the basis for performing the product development activities and managing those activities, its significance is paramount. A subset of the goals, abilities, and activities associated with project planning is listed next.[1]

A Goal of SEI CMM Level 2, Key Process Area (KPA): Software Project Planning (PP)

Goal 1.   Software *estimates* are documented for use in planning and tracking the software project.

Ability to Perform, associated with KPA PP, Goal 1

Ability 4. The software managers, software engineers, and other individuals involved in the software project planning are *trained in the software estimating* and planning procedures applicable to their areas of responsibility.

Activities Performed

Activity 10. *Estimates for the software project's effort and costs* are derived according to a documented procedure.

This procedure typically specifies that:

1. Estimates for the *software project's effort and costs* are related to the size estimates of the software work products (or the size of the changes).

2. Productivity data (historical and/or current) are used for the estimates when available; sources and rationale for these data are documented.

   - The *productivity and cost data* are from the organization's projects when possible.

   - The *productivity and cost data* take into account the effort and significant costs that go into making the software work products.

Examples of significant costs that go into making the software work products include: direct labor expenses, overhead expenses, travel expenses, and computer use cost.

3. *Effort, staffing, and cost estimates* are based on past experience.

   - Similar projects should be used when possible.

   - Time phasing of activities is derived.

   - Distributions of the *effort, staffing, and cost estimates* over the software life cycle are prepared.

4. Estimates and the assumptions made in deriving the estimates are documented, reviewed, and agreed to.

Activity 11. *Estimates for the project's critical computer resources* are derived according to a documented procedure.

Critical computer resources may be in the host environment, in the integration and testing environment, in the target environment, or in any combination of these.

This procedure typically specifies that:

1. Critical computer resources for the project are identified.
   Examples of critical computer resources include: computer memory capacity, computer processor use, and communications channel capacity.

2. Estimates for the critical computer resources are related to the estimates of the *size* of the software work products, the operational processing load, and the communications traffic.

3. Estimates of the critical computer resources are documented, reviewed, and agreed to.

Activity 12. The *project's software schedule* is derived according to a documented procedure. This procedure typically specifies that:

1. The *software schedule* is related to the *size estimate* of the software work products (or the size of changes), and the *software effort and costs.*

2. The *software schedule* is based on past experience. Similar projects are used when possible.

3. The *software schedule* accommodates the imposed milestone dates, critical dependency dates, and other constraints.

4. The *software schedule* activities are of appropriate duration and the milestones are of appropriate time separation to support accuracy in progress measurement.

5. Assumptions made in deriving the *schedule* are documented.

6. The software *schedule* is documented, reviewed, and agreed to.

A software engineering process group (SEPG) can help immeasurably in improving software cost estimation. Frequently, the starting point is a short course in software estimation given to project managers as well as estimators, if they are different people. The SEPG can also define the standards for collecting all project metrics, including effort, schedule, and cost estimation figures. They can be the party responsible for calibrating estimation models as the number of data points grows. The SEPG works well in tight coordination with SQA/SQE activities of defining and documenting policies, processes, and procedures, including those for cost estimation. These working groups can plan and help managers execute training and purchase and license estimation tools.

Recall that we have some idea, however vague, about the product to be built by the time we begin to estimate size. Estimating is an iterative process (Figure 11–3), so we will get some requirements; estimate size, effort, schedule, and cost; create or update the work breakdown structure (WBS); forecast resource needs; check the software project management plan (SPMP) to see if anything needs to be updated; model as much of the requirements as we have; create or update the software requirements specification (SRS) document; go back to the requirements gathering; and repeat the cycle until the SRS is sufficient for design.

In Figure 11–1, the estimating process is shown occurring with the integral task of planning for project management. The planning activities occur in parallel with the development life cycle phases of concept exploration, system exploration, and requirements. Figures 11–3 and 11–6 show more precise steps in estimating. The process inside Steps 1–5 shown here in Figure 11–3 (eliciting requirements, estimating size, estimating effort, estimating schedule and cost) are further defined in Figure 11–6.

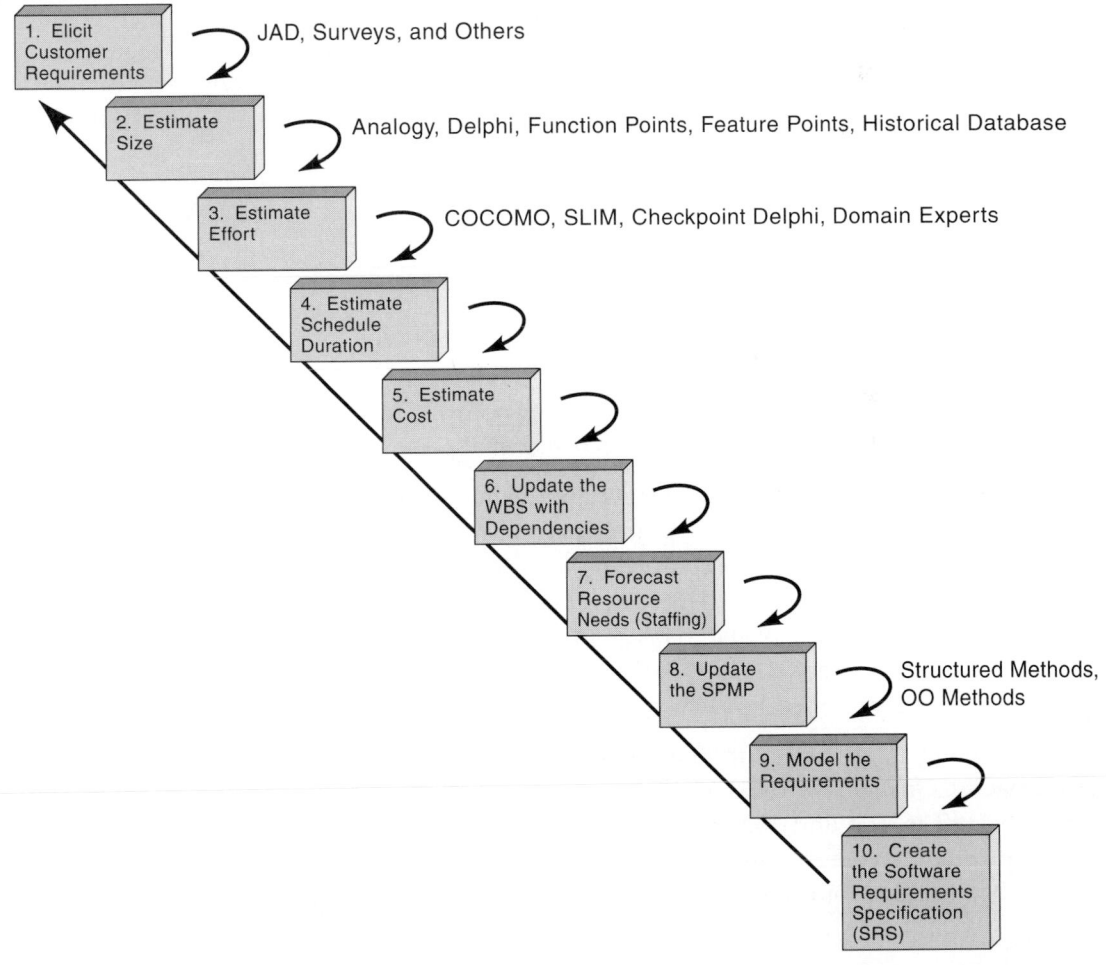

FIGURE 11–3
Steps in Sizing and Estimating

One of the widely published and frequently quoted experts in the field of estimation, Capers Jones, claims that our first estimations are typically off by a factor of four. As the project progresses and more knowledge is gained, the updated estimates begin to converge on the actual. It's a chicken-and-egg situation—it's hard to estimate if requirements are not solid, yet, if we don't estimate something, we'll never get a contract (permission or funding) to move forward. These figures, shown in Figure 10–2, were first proposed by Dr. Barry Boehm and later were corroborated by Jones.

Sizing is an important first step because all the following steps build upon it. Even if size is estimated in function points or object points, they are translated into thousands of lines of code (KLOC) before being placed into formulas or fed into estimating tools. Whether we like them or not (many do not), no other unit of measure has surfaced in the last 30 years that provides the same sort of universal acceptance. Size is typically estimated by analogy (comparisons to completed projects that are similar in scope and complexity), by a wideband Delphi process, or by counting function points, feature points, or object points. Whatever method is used by a project manager to arrive at his first size estimate for a project, size will be the basis for our discussion of effort, schedule, and cost estimating.

Effort Measures

By "effort" in the software estimation process, we mean the amount of person-effort, or labor, that will be required to perform a task. It can be measured in any units, as long as the unit is kept consistent. However, the *de facto* standard is staff-hours (person-hours), staff-days (person-days), or, most commonly, staff-months (person-months).

On a given project, the project manager and team can determine the unit of measure and stick with it, resulting in good communication and meaningful comparisons. Just beware that if productivity measures are compared between and among organizations, the definition of *staff-month* must be the same. (Does everyone agree that a staff-month is 320 hours, based on four weeks comprised of five days made up of eight hours? Sometimes the answer is "no.") Also be aware that a staff-month means one person working for one month (or two people working for two weeks each or some other combination).

One of our main topics in this chapter is the effort-schedule-cost estimating tool, COCOMO (COnstructive COst MOdel), which assumes that there are 19 productive staff-days per staff-month and 152 staff-hours per staff-month. These figures are arrived at by allowing for the average number of vacation days and holidays in the U.S.—they would need to be modified for other countries.

In the words of Dr. Dennis Frailey, "If you measure effort consistently, you can understand what it costs, compare different projects, and predict future performance." Like lines of code, there are many ways to measure effort and many arguments why each is good or bad. You cannot make meaningful evaluations if each project measures effort differently. As listed by Dr. Frailey, typical inputs to effort estimate include:

- Tasks to be performed (WBS)
    - Software development tasks (design, code, test)
    - Additional development tasks (requirements, system)
    - Support tasks (CM, QA, management)
    - Tasks requiring additional labor (documents, etc.)
- Additional dollar costs (travel, equipment, etc.)
- Size estimate for software
- Historical data on effort and productivity
- High-level schedule
- Process and methods
- Programming language
- Operating system for target system
- Tools to be used
- Staff experience level

Simple effort calculation is based on historical data: **Size × Historical Productivity = Effort**

Regardless of what unit is measured, reliance on good historical data is the best way to achieve accuracy.

Suppose that historical data showed the following productivity:

For complex software: 4 SLOC per staff-day
For simple software: 8 SLOC per staff-day

Therefore, if new software is estimated to be 8,000 SLOC, then

If it is complex, it should take 2,000 staff-days.
If it is simple, it should take 1,000 staff-days.

Typical values for productivity rates are:
- 50–300 SLOC/month (2–15 SLOC/day) for high-order language
- 60–500 SLOC/month for assembly language

Lower numbers are for government projects with very severe constraints, such as embedded real-time systems with life-critical safety characteristics. Higher numbers are for commercial applications with few constraints. Even higher numbers can be achieved if you use 4GLs, high levels of reuse, and so on.

Here's an example:

The effort for complex software varies from 2 to 8 SLOC per staff-day, with a mean of 5 SLOC per staff-day. In this case, the expected effort for a 5,000 SLOC program might be 1,000 staff-days. But it could be as high as 2,500 staff-days or as low as 625 staff-days.

Use of alternative methods and re-estimations are the best hedge against project risk associated with inaccurate (usually optimistic) estimates. The goal, as shown in Figure 11–4, is to match what is achievable with what is desirable.

The biggest challenge in software development, shown in Figures 11–4 and 11–5, is to deliver a fully functional, high-quality product on time within budget using forecasted assets.

The Steps in Estimating

In general, the steps in the software effort and cost estimation process are shown in Figure 11–6. We'll cover these next.

Step 1. Establish Cost-Estimation Objectives

- Understand how the estimates will be used. Will they be used to bid on a fixed-price contract? For external funding requests?

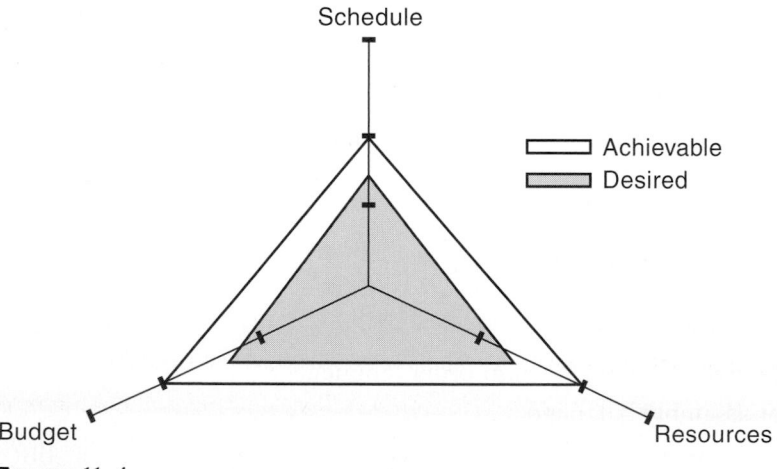

FIGURE 11–4
The Estimating Paradigm

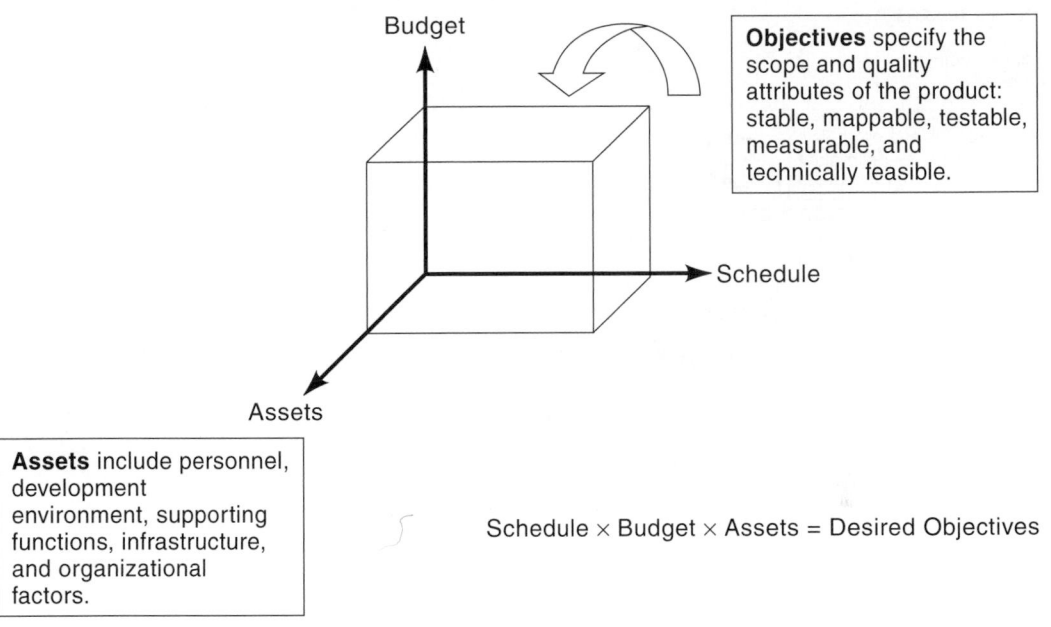

Budget

Objectives specify the scope and quality attributes of the product: stable, mappable, testable, measurable, and technically feasible.

Schedule

Assets

Assets include personnel, development environment, supporting functions, infrastructure, and organizational factors.

Schedule × Budget × Assets = Desired Objectives

FIGURE 11–5
The Estimating Paradigm as a Box
Source: Fairley, Dick. *Software Cost Estimation.*

- Tailor estimating objectives to decision-making information:
    - Absolute estimates are necessary for labor or resource planning.
    - Relative estimates may be used for either/or decisions.
    - Liberal versus conservative estimates heightens decision confidence.
- Re-examine estimation objectives as the process proceeds, and modify them where appropriate. Estimates will change as more project knowledge is gained.

Step 2. Develop a Plan for Estimation Activities; Plan for Resources

- A plan sets accurate expectations for the cost and value of the estimation process.
- View the estimation activities as a "miniproject." Estimation, like all other software activities, serves better when more effort is put into it (you get what you pay for). An estimate produced in 30 minutes will not be as accurate as one built upon individual developer's estimates of component parts of the system based on a carefully constructed WBS. The

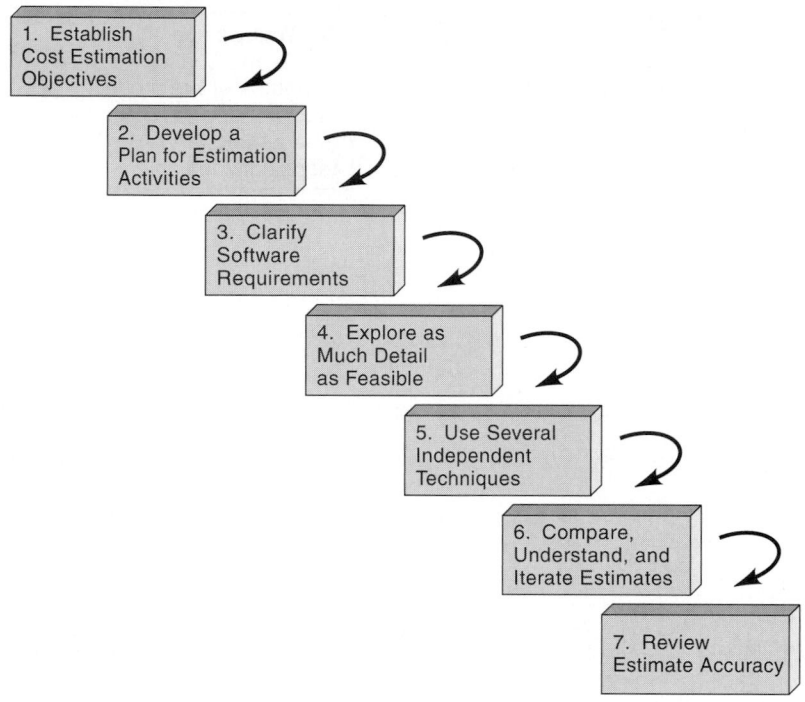

FIGURE 11–6
Steps in Estimating

miniplan includes an early set of notes on the why, what, when, who, where, how, and how much of your estimating activity.

Step 3. Clarify Software Requirements

• Pin down the requirements to the extent necessary to meet your estimating objectives.

• Make the software specifications as specific and unambiguous as possible, preferably quantifiable. Each specification must be testable so that a clear pass/fail test is defined for determining whether the developed software will satisfy the specification.

• When you can't clarify, document any assumptions.

Step 4. Explore as Much Detail as Feasible

• Remain consistent with estimating objectives.

• The more detail is explored, the better technical understanding there will be and the more accurate the estimates will be.

- The more pieces of software we estimate, the more the law of large numbers reduces estimate variance.
- The more we think through all the software functions, the less likely we will miss the costs of the less obvious functions.

Step 5. Use Several Independent Techniques

- No one method is better than others in all aspects.
- Strengths and weaknesses of various methods are complementary.
- A combination of techniques helps avoid the weaknesses of any single method.

Step 6. Compare, Understand, and Iterate Estimates

- Each person has a unique experience, role, and set of incentives (optimist/pessimist phenomenon).
- The use of multiple independent estimation techniques allows investigation into why estimates may differ, frequently an enlightening activity. Iterations converge into realistic estimates.
- Pareto's Law phenomenon applies: Eighty percent of the cost is contained in 20 percent of the components. Examine and iterate these components in greater detail.

Step 7. Review Estimate Accuracy

- Calibrate estimation techniques and models.
- As with size estimation, several models are available for estimating effort. Most of them are based on philosophies that are fundamentally mathematical, experiential, or based on regression.

Given that software estimates are imperfect, comparison of estimates with actuals provides an improved basis for management of the remainder of a given project or for future ones. Software projects are unpredictable and frequently are rescoped. The project manager re-estimates to reflect major changes. In software, unlike many other industries, the same product is never built twice. In addition to estimates taking into account the differences between a new project's specifications and previous ones, the differences in the development and delivery environment must also be considered—and with the fast-paced changes in technology, there may be no historical data upon which to base the new environment.

Some of the most widely used models for determining effort (and, therefore, cost) are the Delphi method, which is nonautomated and used for estimating effort in exactly the same way that it is used for estimating size (refer to Chapter 10), a regression-based model (we will look at COCOMO), a mathematical model (we will look at SLIM), and empirical models. This chapter will focus on the regression model and the mathematical model, and the formulas and tools that support them. No discussion of software sizing and estimating would be complete without mention of an empirical model from Software Productivity Research (SPR), a wholly owned subsidiary of Artemis Management Systems and a leader in software estimation and planning. Led by software development luminary Capers Jones, SPR provides a tool, SPR KnowledgePLAN®, for software estimation and planning. It contains a project wizard that simplifies the process of developing estimates, a sizing wizard that walks users through the sizing process, a goals wizard that helps users identify and achieve key project goals, and templates that help the user quick-start a project. The name most commonly associated with COCOMO is Dr. Barry Boehm. Lawrence Putnam, Sr., is associated with Quantitative Software Measurement (QSM, product is SLIM), and Capers Jones is associated with SPR (KnowledgePLAN®). Each of these experts is considered to be among the top problem solvers in the software estimation and measurement field, has published multiple full-length texts and articles, and has collected data from thousands of software projects.

COCOMO: A Regression Model

The COnstructive COst MOdel (COCOMO) is arguably the most widely used estimating technique. It is a regression-based model developed by Dr. Barry W. Boehm when he was at TRW in the early 1970s. He began by analyzing 63 software projects of various types. The projects were observed for actual size (LOC), actual effort expended, and actual schedule duration. Regression analysis was then used to develop exponential equations that best describe the relationship between the scattered data points.

Regression Models in General

A regression model is derived from a statistical interpretation of historical data to describe a mean or "typical" relationship between variables.

Definitions:
Regression analysis is:

- The use of regression to make quantitative predictions of one variable from the values of another.
- A statistical technique used to find relationships between variables for the purpose of predicting future values.
- Procedures for finding the mathematical function that best describes the relationship between a dependent variable and one or more independent variables. In linear regression, the relationship is constrained to be a straight line, and least-squares analysis is used to determine the best fit.

Linear models are: Statistical models in which the value of a parameter for a given value of a factor is assumed to be equal to $a + bx$, where a and b are constants. The models predict a linear regression.

In multiple regression, the dependent variable is considered to depend on more than a single independent variable.

Figure 11–7 shows a scattergram on the left and an attempt at fitting a line through the data points on the right. In this example, cavities are expected to increase with grams of sugar consumed.

COCOMO Modes

Boehm plotted his observed 63 projects, but because of the amount of scatter in the data, he developed multiple equations in an attempt to fit a line for use in future predictions, as shown in Figure 11–8. The technique that he used, and his advice to those who want to repeat the experiment, is to keep the equation simple and then apply additional explanatory factors later. Complicated statistics at this point will not gain much because the data is typically noisy anyway.

COCOMO refers to three modes, which categorize the complexity of the system and the development environment (see Table 11–1).

Organic   The organic mode is typified by systems such as payroll, inventory, and scientific calculation. Other characterizations are that the project team is small, little innovation is required, constraints and deadlines are few, and the development environment is stable.

Semidetached   The semidetached mode is typified by utility systems such as compilers, database systems, and editors. Other characterizations are that the project team is medium-size,

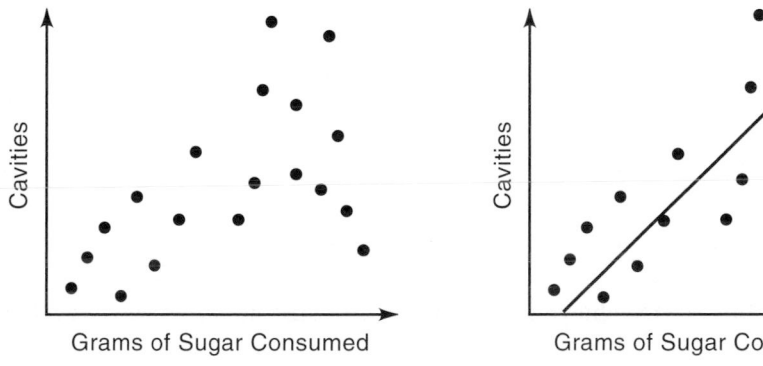

FIGURE 11–7
Scatter Plot, Fitted Line

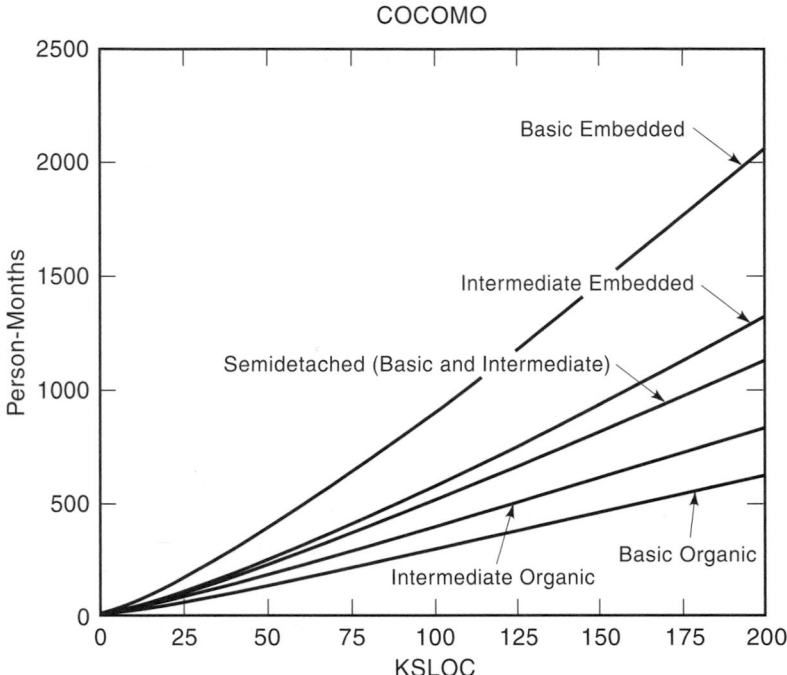

FIGURE 11–8
Boehm's Original 63 Projects
Source: Adapted from Boehm, Barry (1976). *Software Engineering Economics.* Englewood Cliffs, NY: Prentice Hall. p. 76.

some innovation is required, constraints and deadlines are moderate, and the development environment is somewhat fluid.

Embedded   The embedded mode is typified by real-time systems such as those for air traffic control, ATMs, or weapon systems. Other characterizations are that the project team is large, a great deal of innovation is required, constraints and deadlines are tight, and the development environment consists of many complex interfaces, including those with hardware and with customers.

COCOMO Levels

Three levels of detail allow the user to achieve greater accuracy with each successive level.

Basic   This level uses only size and mode to determine the effort and schedule. It is useful for fast, rough estimates of small to medium-size projects.

TABLE 11–1
COCOMO Mode Characteristics

Mode	Product Size	Project/Team Size	Innovation	Deadline and Constraints	Development Environment
Organic	Typically 2–50 KLOC	Small project, small team—development team is familiar with the application language and tools	Little	Not Tight	Stable, In-House
Semi–detached	Typically 50–300 KLOC	Medium project, medium team—team is average in terms of abilities	Medium	Medium	Medium
Embedded	Typically over 300 KLOC	Large project requiring a large team	Greater	Severe Constraints	Complex HW/ Customer Interfaces

Intermediate   This level uses size, mode, and 15 additional variables to determine effort. The additional variables are called "cost drivers" and relate to product, personnel, computer, and project attributes that will result in more effort or less effort required for the software project. The product of the cost drivers is known as the environmental adjustment factor (EAF).

Detailed   This level builds upon intermediate COCOMO by introducing the additional capabilities of phase-sensitive effort multipliers and a three-level product hierarchy. The intermediate level may be tailored to phase and product level to achieve the detailed level. An example of phase-sensitive effort multipliers would be consideration of memory constraints when attempting to estimate the coding or testing phases of a project. At the same time, though, memory size may not affect the effort or cost of the analysis phase. This will become more obvious after the effort multipliers (or cost drivers) are described. Phase-sensitive multipliers are generally reserved for use in mature organizations and require the use of an automated tool.

A three-level product hierarchy consists of system, subsystem, and module, much like the arrangement of a WBS. Large projects may be decomposed into at least three levels so that each of the cost drivers introduced in intermediate COCOMO is assigned to that level likely to be most influenced by variations in the cost driver. For example, an engineer's language experience may apply only at the module level, an analyst's capability may apply at a subsystem level and a module level, and required reliability may apply at the system, subsystem, and module level. As with the phase-sensitive multipliers, this will make more sense after the cost drivers are described. As with the phase-sensitive multipliers, mature organizations with automated tools are the heaviest users.

Basic COCOMO

Effort Estimation   KLOC is the only input variable. An exponential formula is used to calculate effort, as shown in Box 11–1.

Box 11–1
COCOMO Basic Effort Formula

Effort (E) = a × (Size)^b

where

a and b = constants derived from regression analysis (depends on the project)

Size = thousands of lines of code (KLOC)

E = effort expressed in staff-months

As pointed out by Dr. Frailey, effort is measured in staff-months (19 days per month or 152 working hours per month), the constants a and b can be determined by a curve fit procedure (regression analysis), matching project data to the equation. Most organizations do not have enough data to perform such an analysis and begin by using Boehm's three levels of difficulty that seem to characterize many software projects. Box 11–2 shows the basic formulas; Table 11–2 lists the effort and development time formulas for each mode.

The same-size project yields different amounts of effort when it is considered to be of different modes:

Suppose that a project was estimated to be 200 KLOC. Putting that data into the formula

Effort = a × (Size)^b

Box 11–2
Basic COCOMO Effort Formulas for Three Modes

> **Effort for Organic Mode: E = 2.4 × (Size)$^{1.05}$**
>
> **Effort for Semidetached Mode: E = 3.0 × (Size)$^{1.12}$**
>
> **Effort for Embedded Mode: E = 3.6 × (Size)$^{1.20}$**

TABLE 11–2
Basic COCOMO Effort and Development Time Formulas

Mode	a	b	Effort Formula Effort = a × (Size)^b	Development Time Formula
Organic	2.4	1.05	E = 2.4 × (S)$^{1.05}$	TDEV = 2.5 × (E)$^{0.38}$ Months
Semidetached	3.0	1.12	E = 3.0 × (S)$^{1.12}$	TDEV = 2.5 × (E)$^{0.35}$ Months
Embedded	3.6	1.20	E = 3.6 × (S)$^{1.20}$	TDEV = 2.5 × (E)$^{0.32}$ Months

Effort for the organic mode would be estimated at $2.4 \times (200)^{1.05} = 2.4(260.66) = 626$ staff-months.

Effort for the semidetached mode would be estimated at $3.0 \times (200)^{1.12} = 3.0(377.71) = 1,133$ staff-months. Effort for the embedded mode would be estimated at $3.6 \times (200)^{1.20} = 3.6(577) = 2,077$ staff-months.

After effort is estimated, an exponential formula is also used to calculate a project duration, or completion time (time to develop, TDEV). Project duration is expressed in months.

Basic COCOMO Project Duration Estimation   Boehm devised three formulas (see Box 11–3) to be used for development time in the same fashion as he did with effort.

Box 11–3
Basic COCOMO Project Duration Estimate

> **Project Duration for Organic Mode: TDEV = 2.5 × (E)$^{0.38}$**
>
> **Project Duration for Semidetached Mode: TDEV = 2.5 × (E)$^{0.35}$**
>
> **Project Duration for Embedded Mode: TDEV = 2.5 × (E)$^{0.32}$**

When effort (E) and development time (TDEV) are known, the average staff size (SS) to complete the project may be calculated, as shown in Box 11–4.

Box 11–4
Basic COCOMO Average Staff Estimate

Average Staff: SS = Effort ÷ TDEV

Basic COCOMO Average Staff and Productivity Estimation   When average staff size (SS) is known, the productivity level may be calculated, as shown in Box 11–5.

Box 11–5
Basic COCOMO Productivity Estimate

Productivity: P = Size ÷ Effort

Basic COCOMO Examples   Two examples of basic COCOMO follow. One is simple, and the other is of medium complexity.

Basic COCOMO Example 1
A development project is sized at 7.5 KLOC and is evaluated as being simple—in the organic mode.

The basic COCOMO equation for effort (E) in staff-months (SM) is:

$$\text{Effort (SM)} = 2.4(\text{KLOC})^{1.05} = 2.4(7.5)^{1.05} = 2.4(8.49296) = 20 \text{ staff-months}$$

Development time (TDEV) can also be found by using the basic COCOMO formulas:

$$\text{TDEV} = 2.5(\text{SM})^{0.38} = 2.5(20)^{0.38} = 2.5(3.1217) = 8 \text{ months}$$

The average number of staff members (S):

$$\text{Staff} = \text{Effort} \div \text{TDEV} = 20 \text{ staff-months} \div 8 \text{ months} = 2.5 \text{ staff members on average}$$

The productivity rate (P):

$$\text{Productivity} = \text{Size} \div \text{Effort} = 7{,}500 \text{ LOC} \div 20 \text{ staff-months} = 375 \text{ LOC/staff-month}$$

Basic COCOMO Example 2
A development project is estimated to be about 55 KLOC when complete and is believed to be of medium complexity. It will be a Web-enabled system with a robust back-end database. It is assumed to be in the semidetached mode.

For a rough estimate of the effort that will be required to complete the project, use the formula:

$$E \text{ (effort in staff-months)} = 3.0(KLOC)^{1.12}$$

$$E \text{ (effort in staff-months)} = 3.0(55)^{1.12}$$

$$E = 3.0(88.96)$$

$$E = 267 \text{ staff-months}$$

To determine how long it will take to complete the project, use the formula:

$$TDEV = 2.5 \times (E)^{0.35}$$

$$TDEV = 2.5 \times (267)^{0.35}$$

$$TDEV = 2.5(7.07)$$

$$TDEV = 17.67 \text{ months}$$

To obtain a rough estimate of how many developers will be needed, use the formula:

$$S \text{ (average staff)} = \text{effort} \div TDEV$$

$$S \text{ (average staff)} = 267 \div 17.67$$

$$S \text{ (average staff)} = 15.11$$

To determine a rough estimate of the productivity rate, use the formula:

$$P \text{ (productivity)} = \text{size} \div \text{effort}$$

$$P \text{ (productivity)} = 55,000 \div 267$$

$$P \text{ (productivity)} = 206 \text{ LOC/staff-month}$$

Basic COCOMO offers a way to calculate a set of quick estimates for effort, development time, staffing, and productivity rates, given knowledge only of size and mode. It can be arrived at with no more than a calculator. However, you get what you pay for. It doesn't take much to derive effort using the basic level, and the results won't be worth much more than a very, very rough estimate. To refine the estimation process, Boehm gives guidance in "tuning" via what he calls a complexity adjustment factor described in intermediate COCOMO.

Basic COCOMO Phase Distribution of Effort and Schedule   In addition to estimating development effort and schedule, it is often necessary to estimate how the effort is distributed among the primary life cycle activities. COCOMO takes a pretty simplistic view of the life cycle phases, considering only plans and requirements, product design, coding, and integration and test as the four development phases, and maintenance as the final life cycle phase. Any of these activities may be going on during any of the phases: requirements analysis, product design, coding, test planning, verification and validation, project office functions, configuration management and quality assurance, documentation, and so on.

Let's look at an example of phase distribution of effort and schedule (see Table 11–3).

Suppose that an embedded mode project is sized at 80 KLOC.

$$E \text{ (effort in staff-months)} = 3.6(\text{KLOC})^{1.20} = 3.6(80)^{1.20} = 3.6(192.18) = 692 \text{ staff-months}$$
$$TDEV \text{ (development time)} = 2.5(E)^{0.32} = 2.5(692)^{0.32} = 2.5(8.106) = 20 \text{ months}$$

TABLE 11–3
Basic COCOMO Phase Distribution of Effort and Schedule Example, Where Estimated SM = 692 and
Estimated TDEV = 20

	Plans and Requirements	Product Design	Coding	Integration and Test	Total
Effort (%) (% of effort spent in each major phase, based on historical data)	10%	12%	50.5%	27.5%	100% effort spread over four major phases
Effort (SM) = typical % of effort spent in this phase × estimated SM	.1 × 692 SM = 6.92 months	.12 × 692 SM = 83.04 months	.505 × 692 SM = 349.46 months	.275 × 692 SM = 190.3 months	692 months total staff-months
Schedule (%) (% of schedule spent on each major phase, based on historical data)	4%	33%	38%	25%	100% schedule spread over four major phases
Schedule (Months) = typical % of schedule spent on this phase × estimated TDEV	.04 × 20 = .8 months	.33 × 20 = 6.6 months	.38 × 20 = 7.6 months	.25 × 20 = 5 months	20 months duration (schedule)
Average # Personnel per major phase (Effort [SM]/ Schedule [Months])	6.92 ÷ .8 = 8.65 average persons	83.04 ÷ 6.6 = 12.5818 average persons	349.46 ÷ 7.6 = 45.98 average persons	190.3 ÷ 5 = 38.06 average persons	692 ÷ 20 = 34.6 average persons

Intermediate COCOMO

Intermediate COCOMO uses size and modes just like the basic model, plus 15 additional variables called cost drivers, which will be explained, and modified effort equations (Table 11–4). The idea is that there are characteristics of a given project that drive the cost (effort) up or down.

Intermediate COCOMO Effort Estimation   Inputs to intermediate COCOMO are KLOC (just as with basic COCOMO) and cost driver ratings, which further refine and improve the estimate. The equation appears in Box 11–6.

Box 11–6
Intermediate COCOMO Formula

> **Effort (E) = a × (Size)^b × C**

Note that constants for exponents and coefficients are different for *each mode* (see Box 11–7 and Table 11–4).

Box 11–7
Intermediate COCOMO Formula: Coefficients and Exponents Change from Basic

> **Effort for Organic Mode: E = 3.2 × (Size)$^{1.05}$ × C**
>
> **Effort for Semidetached Mode: E = 3.0 × (Size)$^{1.12}$ × C**
>
> **Effort for Embedded Mode: E = 2.8 × (Size)$^{1.20}$ × C**

TABLE 11–4
Intermediate COCOMO Effort Formulas

Mode	a	b	Effort Formula Effort = a × (Size)^b × C
Organic	3.2	1.05	E = 3.2 × (S)$^{1.05}$ × C
Semidetached	3.0	1.12	E = 3.0 × (S)$^{1.12}$ × C
Embedded	2.8	1.20	E = 2.8 × (S)$^{1.20}$ × C

Cost Drivers   The concept of the effort adjustment factor (EAF) is that it has the effect of increasing or decreasing the effort, and therefore cost, depending on a set of environmental factors. These environmental factors are also known as cost adjustment factors [C_is], or cost drivers. There are two steps in determining this multiplying factor:

Step 1 is to assign numerical values to the cost drivers.

Step 2 is to multiply the cost drivers together to generate the effort adjustment factor, C.

EAF is the product of the cost adjustment factors, as shown in Box 11–8.

When multiplied together, the cost adjustment factors can affect project cost and schedule estimates by 10 times or more!

Box 11–8
Product of Cost Drivers Is the Effort Adjustment Factor

$$\textbf{EAF} = \textbf{C1} \times \textbf{C2} \times \ldots \times \textbf{Cn}$$

$$[\textbf{C}_i = \textbf{i}^{\textbf{th}} \textbf{ cost adjustment factor}]$$

$C_i = 1$ implies the cost driver does not apply

$C_i > 1$ implies increased cost due to this factor

$C_i < 1$ implies decreased cost due to this factor

Cost drivers are grouped into four categories, as shown in Table 11–5.

Product Attributes   Some of the attributes that will drive the cost of a project up or down have to do with the product itself or with the nature of the job to be done. They include:

- Required reliability—applies mainly to real-time applications;
- Database size—applies mainly to data-processing applications;
- Product complexity—execution time constraints.

Computer Attributes   Other attributes have to do with the computer platform as a support tool, as well as with the job to be done:

- Execution time constraint—applies when processor speed is barely sufficient;
- Main storage constraints—applies when memory size is barely sufficient;
- Virtual machine volatility—includes hardware and operating system of target machine;

TABLE 11–5
Intermediate COCOMO Cost Driver Categories

Product	Computer	Personnel	Project
Required Software Reliability (RELY)	Execution Time Constraint (TIME)	Analyst Capability (ACAP)	Use of Modern Programming Practices (MODP)
Database Size (DATA)	Main Storage Constraint (STOR)	Application Experience (AEXP)	Use of Software Tools (TOOL)
Product Complexity (CPLX)	Virtual Machine Volatility (VIRT)	Programmer Capability (PCAP)	Required Development Schedule (SCED)
	Computer Turnaround Time (TURN)	Virtual Machine Experience (VEXP)	
		Programming Language Experience (LEXP)	

- Computer turnaround time—used for development (not too much of a problem now).

Project Attributes   Still others relate to practices and tools:

- Modern programming practices—structured techniques or OO;
- Modern programming tools—CASE, good debuggers, test-generation tools;
- Schedule compression (or expansion)—deviation from ideal can never help, but shorter is worse than longer.

Personnel Attributes   Some attributes describe the people who do the job. These cost drivers tend to have high potential for cost increase or decrease:

- Analyst capability;
- Application experience;
- Programmer capability;
- Virtual machine experience—includes operating system and hardware;
- Programming language experience—includes tools and practices.

Other Cost Drivers   Although product, computer, personnel, and project attributes are the four categories that are commonly associated with applications of the intermediate

COCOMO model, additional attributes are often added by a project manager aware of other organizational (or project) strengths and/or weaknesses. Some common ones include:

- Requirements volatility—some is expected, but too much can be a big problem;
- Development machine volatility—unstable OS, compilers, CASE tools, and so on;
- Security requirements—used for classified programs;
- Access to data—sometimes very difficult;
- Impact of standards and imposed methods;
- Impact of physical surroundings.

Cost drivers are selected for their general significance to all software development projects and are independent of project size.

Each cost driver determines a multiplying factor that estimates the effect of the attribute on the amount of effort.

Numerical values of the cost drivers, multiplied together, generate the adjustment factor, C, as shown in Box 11–9.

Box 11-9
Product of Cost Drivers

$$C = \mathbf{RELY} \times \mathbf{DATA} \times \mathbf{CPLX} \times \mathbf{TIME} \times \mathbf{STOR} \times \mathbf{VIRT} \times \mathbf{TURN} \times \mathbf{ACAP}$$

$$\times \mathbf{AEXP} \times \mathbf{PCAP} \times \mathbf{VEXP} \times \mathbf{LEXP} \times \mathbf{MODP} \times \mathbf{TOOL} \times \mathbf{SCED}$$

Because cost drivers are multiplicative, when a cost driver has no effect on effort, its value is 1, leaving the final value of C unchanged. Such cost drivers are considered normal or "nominal." For example, if the programming language experience (LEXP) of the team in a given organization is better than that of any other organization in town, the LEXP value would still remain 1 because superior language ability is the norm in that environment. The estimator is searching for circumstances that will cause the effort to expand (the product of all cost drivers is greater than 1) or contract (the product of all cost drivers is less than 1) from the customary in an environment. Usually, when more effort is required, it is because the technology is new, the team is newly formed or consists of novices in the domain area, the complexity of the technological problem is great, or some other circumstance differs from the standard. When less effort is required, it is usually because the class of problem has been successfully tackled before.

Figure 11–9 shows the effect of the cost drivers moving from extra high to very low values. Product complexity (CPLX) for example, takes a value of 0.70 if very low and 1.60 if very high. It becomes apparent how the product of the cost drivers (C) affects the effort estimation. If CPLX were the only cost driver that was not nominal and raw effort was 24 staff-months, the degree of complexity could cause the effort to range from 16.8 staff-months to 38.4 staff-months.

Note the "bathtub" curve as SCED moves from very low to very high. To what can this phenomenon be attributed?

The suggested values of the original 15 cost drivers are listed in Table 11–6. The rationale behind the assigned values is described in Table 11–7.

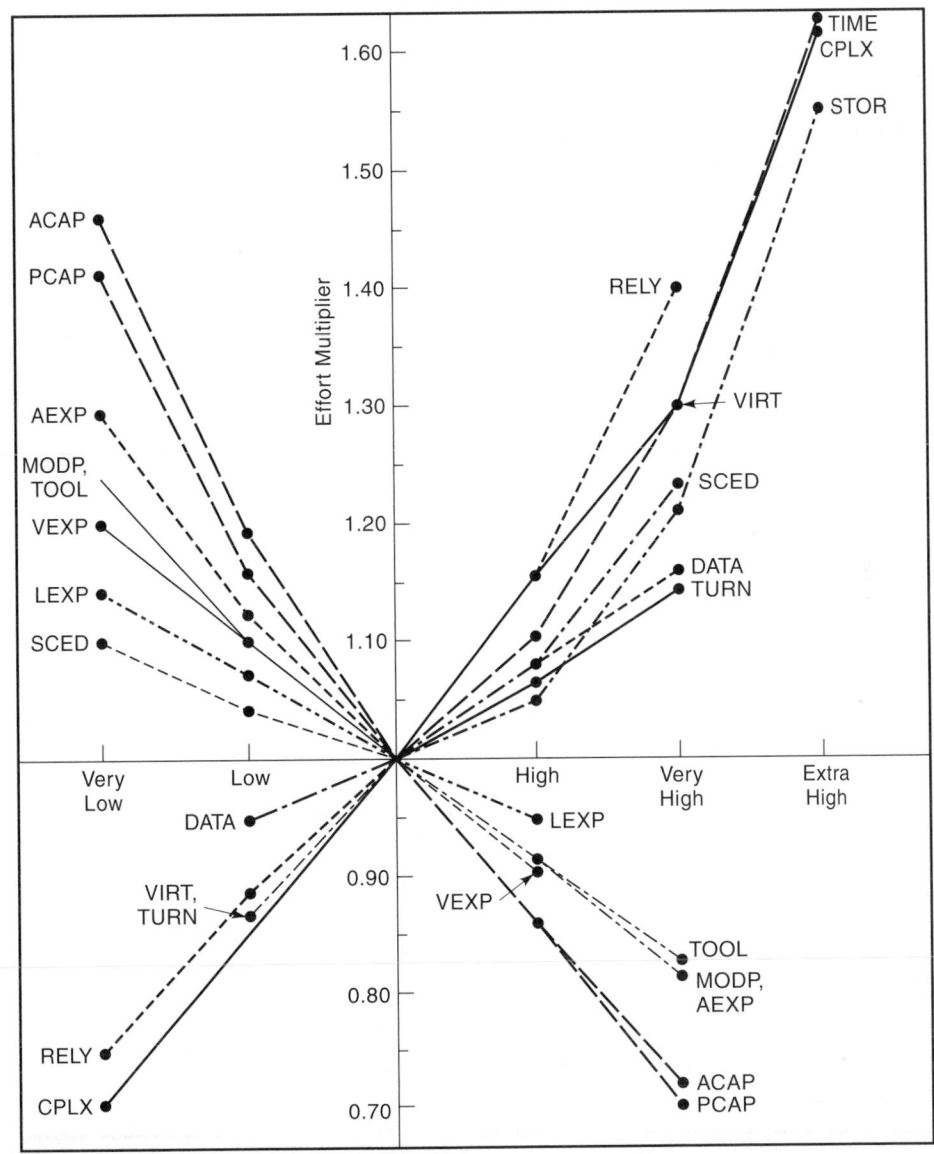

FIGURE 11–9
The Effect of Cost Drivers

TABLE 11–6
Intermediate COCOMO Software Development Cost Driver Values

Cost Drivers	Ratings					
	Very Low	Low	Nominal	High	Very High	Extra High
Product Attributes						
Required Software Reliability (RELY)	.75	.88	1.00	1.15	1.40	
Database Size (DATA)		.94	1.00	1.08	1.16	
Product Complexity (CPLX)	.70	.85	1.00	1.15	1.30	1.65
Computer Attributes						
Execution Time Constraint (TIME)			1.00	1.11	1.30	1.66
Main Storage Constraint (STOR)			1.00	1.06	1.21	1.56
Virtual Machine Volatility (VIRT)		.87	1.00	1.15	1.30	
Computer Turnaround Time (TURN)		.87	1.00	1.07	1.15	
Personnel Attributes						
Analyst Capability (ACAP)	1.46	1.19	1.00	.86	.71	
Application Experience (AEXP)	1.29	1.13	1.00	.91	.82	
Programmer Capability (PCAP)	1.42	1.17	1.00	.86	.70	
Virtual Machine Experience (VEXP)	1.21	1.10	1.00	.90		
Programming Language Experience (LEXP)	1.14	1.07	1.00	.95		

(Continues)

TABLE 11–6 (Continued)
Intermediate COCOMO Software Development Cost Driver Values

Cost Drivers	Ratings					
	Very Low	Low	Nominal	High	Very High	Extra High
Project Attributes						
Use of Modern Programming Practices (MODP)	1.24	1.10	1.00	.91	.82	
Use of Software Tools (TOOL)	1.24	1.10	1.00	.91	.82	
Required Development Schedule (SCED)	1.23	1.08	1.00	1.04	1.10	

TABLE 11–7
Intermediate COCOMO Software Cost Driver Ratings

Cost Driver Ratings						
	Very Low	Low	Nominal	High	Very High	Extra High
Product Attributes						
RELY	Effect: slight inconvenience	Low, easily recoverable losses	Moderate recoverable losses	High financial loss	Risk to human life	
DATA		DB bytes/ Prog. DSI < 10	10 < DB bytes/Prog. ELOC < 100	100 < DB bytes, Prog. ELOC — 1000	DB bytes/ Prog. ELOC => 1000	
CPLX	See separate CPLX tables	See separate CPLX tables	See separate CPLX tables	See separate CPLX tables	See separate CPLX tables	See separate CPLX tables

(Continues)

TABLE 11–7 (Continued)
Intermediate COCOMO Software Cost Driver Ratings

			Cost Driver Ratings			
	Very Low	**Low**	**Nominal**	**High**	**Very High**	**Extra High**
Computer Attributes						
TIME			<= 50% use of available exec. time	70% use of available exec. time	85% use of available exec. time	95% use of available exec. time
STOR			<= 50% use of available storage	70% use of available storage	85% use of available storage	95% use of available storage
VIRT		Changes: Major 12 mos; Minor 1 mo	Change: Major 6 mos: Minor 2 wks	Change: Major 2 mos; Minor 1 wk	Change: Major 2 wks; Minor 2 days	
TURN		Interactive	Average turnaround (<4 hrs)	4–12 hours	>12 hrs	
Personnel Attributes						
ACAP	15th percentile	35th percentile	55th percentile	75th percentile	90th percentile	
AEXP	<= 4 months experience	1 year	3 years	6 years	12 years	
PCAP	15th percentile	35th percentile	55th percentile	75th percentile	90th percentile	
VEXP	<= 1 month experience	4 mos	1 year	3 years		
LEXP	<= 1 month experience	4 mos	1 year	3 years		
Project Attributes						
MODP	No use	Beginning use	Some uses	General use	Routine use	

TABLE 11–7 (Continued)
Intermediate COCOMO Software Cost Driver Ratings

			Cost Driver Ratings			
	Very Low	**Low**	**Nominal**	**High**	**Very High**	**Extra High**
TOOL	Basic microprocessor tools	Basic mini tools	Basic midi/maxi tools	Strong maxi prog./test tools	Add req. des, mgnt, doc tools	
SCED	75% of nominal	85% of nominal	100% of nominal	130% of nominal	160% of nominal	

The model, having a strong sensitivity to CPLX, presents definitions of rating values for that cost driver in a separate table. Tables 11–8 through 11–11 show how CPLX is defined for five different applications: control operations, computational operations, device-dependent operations, data management operations, and requirements and product design.

TABLE 11–8
CPLX Effort Adjustment Table for Control Operations

Description	Rating
Straight-line code with few nonnested SP operators: DOs, CASEs, IFTHENELSEs; simple predicates	Very Low
Straightforward nesting of SP operators; mostly simple predicates	Low
Mostly simple nesting; some intermodule control; decision tables	Nominal
Highly nested SP operators with many compound predicates; queue and stack control; considerable intermodule control	High
Re-entrant and recursive coding; fixed-priority interrupt handling	Very High
Multiple resource scheduling with dynamically changing priorities; microcode-level coding	Extra High

TABLE 11–9
CPLX Effort Adjustment Table for Computational Operations

Description	Rating
Evaluation of simple expressions, such as A = B + C * (D – E)	Very Low
Evaluation of moderate-level expressions, such as, D = SQRT (B ** 2 – 4.0 * A * C)	Low
Use of standard math and statistical routines; basic matrix/ vector operations	Nominal
Basic numerical analysis: multivariate interpolation, ordinary differential equations, basic truncation/round-off concerns	High
Difficult but structured numerical analysis: near-singular matrix equations, partial differential equations	Very High
Difficult and unstructured numerical analysis: highly accurate analysis of noisy stochastic data	Extra High

TABLE 11–10
CPLX Effort Adjustment Table for Device-Dependent Operations

Description	Rating
Simple read, write statements with simple formats	Very Low
No cognizance needed of particular processor or I/O device characteristics. I/O done at GET/PUT level; no cognizance or overlap	Low
I/O processing includes device selection, status checking, and error processing	Nominal
Operations at physical I/O level (physical storage address translations; seeks, reads, etc.); optimized I/O overlap	High
Routines for interrupt diagnosis, servicing, masking; communication line handling	Very High
Device timing-dependent coding, microprogrammed operations	Extra High

TABLE 11-11
CPLX Effort Adjustment Table for Data Management Operations

Description	Rating
Simple arrays in main memory	Very Low
Single file subsetting with no data structure changes, no edits, no intermediate files	Low
Multifile input and single file output; simple structural changes, simple edits	Nominal
Special purpose subroutines activated by data stream contents; complex data restructuring at record level	High
A generalized, parameter-driven file structuring routine; file building, command processing, search optimization	Very High
Highly coupled, dynamic relational structures; natural language data management	Extra High

Intermediate COCOMO Examples   Two examples of intermediate COCOMO follow. One uses normal values for the cost drivers; the other changes ACAP and PCAP ratings to high.

Intermediate COCOMO Example 1
A 10 KLOC embedded-mode software product is to perform communications processing functions on a commercial microprocessor.

- The embedded mode formula gives nominal effort:

$$E_n = 2.8(10)^{1.20} = 2.8(15.85) = 44 \text{ staff-months}$$

- An evaluation of the project environment yields choices for cost driver multiplier values. These values are shown in Table 11–12.
- The adjustment factor is applied to the nominal effort:

$$E = 2.8(10)^{1.20} \times C = 44 \times 1.17 = 51 \text{ staff-months}$$

Intermediate COCOMO Example 2
A project is estimated at 44 staff-months (SM). Using more capable personnel on the project decreases both the ACAP and PCAP ratings from nominal (1.00) to high (0.86), but the staff cost increases from $5,000 to $6,000 per SM. Assume that all other cost drivers are rated nominal (1.00).

TABLE 11–12
Cost Driver Values for the Intermediate COCOMO Example 1

Cost Driver	Situation	Rating	Effort Multiplier
RELY	Local use of system. No serious recovery problems.	Nominal	1.00
DATA	30,000 bytes.	Low	0.94
CPLX	Communications processing.	Very high	1.30
TIME	Will use 70% of available time.	High	1.11
STOR	45K of 64K store (70%).	High	1.06
VIRT	Based on commercial microprocessor hardware.	Nominal	1.00
TURN	2-hour average turnaround time.	Nominal	1.00
ACAP	Good senior analysts.	High	0.86
AEXP	3 years.	Nominal	1.00
PCAP	Good senior programmers.	High	0.86
VEXP	6 months.	Low	1.10
LEXP	12 months.	Nominal	1.00
MODP	Most techniques in use over 1 year.	High	0.91
TOOL	At basic minicomputer tool level.	Low	1.10
SCED	10 months.	Nominal	1.00
EAF	$C = 1.00 \times 0.94 \times 1.30 \times 1.11 \times 1.06 \times 1.00 \times 1.00 \times 0.86 \times 1.00 \times 0.86 \times 1.10 \times 1.00 \times 0.91 \times 1.10 \times 1.00$	$C = 1.17$	

Effort Adjustment Factor (EAF) = C
= RELY × DATA × CPLX × TIME × STOR × VIRT × TURN × ACAP × AEXP × PCAP × VEXP ×
LEXP × MODP × TOOL × SCED = $1.00 \times 1.00 \times 1.00 \times 1.00 \times 1.00 \times 1.00 \times 1.00 \times 0.86 \times 1.00 \times 0.86 \times 1.00 \times 1.00 \times 1.00 \times 1.00 \times 1.00 = 0.74$

staff-month adjustment: 44 SM × 0.74 = 32.6

cost differential: 44 SM @ \$5,000/SM = \$220,000
32.6 SM @ \$6,000/SM = \$195,600
\$ 24,400

Conclusion: In this example, upgrading of the personnel more than pays for itself in the form of overall project savings.

Cost drivers behave like dial settings in that they help "tune" raw size until the level of effort becomes reasonable to support the development of the software, adhering to functional requirements. As illustrated in Figure 11–10, using size as a base, the output-staffing plan (effort spread over time) will change with cost driver settings.

Although these 15 cost drivers are a good jump-start for environments that have little or no historical data upon which to draw, they are not expected to serve every organization in the same way or even one organization over a long span of time. What worked for TRW under Boehm's leadership in the late 1970s and early 1980s will not work for anyone else—and probably wouldn't even work for TRW in the 1990s. The idea is to use the model (not the actual data) and tailor it for a given environment. Boehm strongly suggests adding, changing, and deleting cost drivers as well as changing the values assigned to the ratings (extra high to very low). The data from the original 63 projects may be used until actual data is gathered, but after the actual data is available, it should replace the original and the model should be calibrated until it is tuned for a given type of application, a given organizational environment, or both. Many vendors supply automated tools to produce estimates, given size and complexity; many of the same tools provide automated support for adding actual data and calibrating the model by changing the exponent, the coefficient, the cost driver values, or all three. Having five data points (projects where size, time duration, and effort are observable) is enough to create a calibrated model.

Detailed COCOMO

This is the most complex version of the COCOMO model. It involves the following additional steps:

- The program is decomposed into specific products and components of products. Boehm calls this the three-level product hierarchy: system, subsystem, and module. The top level, the system level, is used to apply major overall project relations such as nominal effort and schedule equations, and to apply the nominal project effort and schedule breakdowns by phase. The lowest level, the module level, is described by the number of KLOC in the module and by the cost drivers that tend to vary at the lowest level. The second level, the subsystem level, is described by the remainder of the cost drivers that tend to vary from subsystem to subsystem but that tend to be the same for all the modules within a subsystem.

- Cost drivers are analyzed separately for each component.
  Subsystems and modules inherit the system cost drivers. They are RELY, VIRT, TURN, MODP, TOOL, and SCED.
  Modules inherit the subsystem cost drivers. They are DATA, TIME, STOR, ACAP, AEXP (these tend to be the same for all modules within a subsystem).
  The module cost drivers are KLOC, AAF, CPLX, PCAP, VEXP, and LEXP.

AAF is new—it considers the adaptation of existing modules.

More information is available earlier when modifying existing software—this data leads to more accurate estimations. Given that much software under construction is not totally new development and the reuse of existing modules is encouraged by newer methods (i.e., object-oriented), use of detailed COCOMO is often worth the extra effort.

It should be noted that the cost of reuse is never zero. There is always effort expended to understand the existing code and to interface to it. The cost to rewrite a system may be less than to continue to maintain it (if it has suffered entropy of structure), but it will be more expensive than to build a "new" system of comparable size and complexity from scratch. Some believe that the economic breakeven point occurs when only 20% of the code is modified; reuse is not cost-effective above the breakeven point.

- The project development activities are partitioned into phases. Boehm used four major phases: requirements (RQ), product design (PD), detailed design (DD), and coding and unit test (CUT) for development. Integration and testing (IT) and maintenance (MN) describe the entire life cycle. Phases may be used to partition systems, subsystems, and/or modules. Different effort multipliers are used for each phase. Different values of the cost driver multipliers are set for each of the three levels in the product hierarchy (system, subsystem, module) and each phase (RPD, DD, CUT, IT) within the hierarchies.

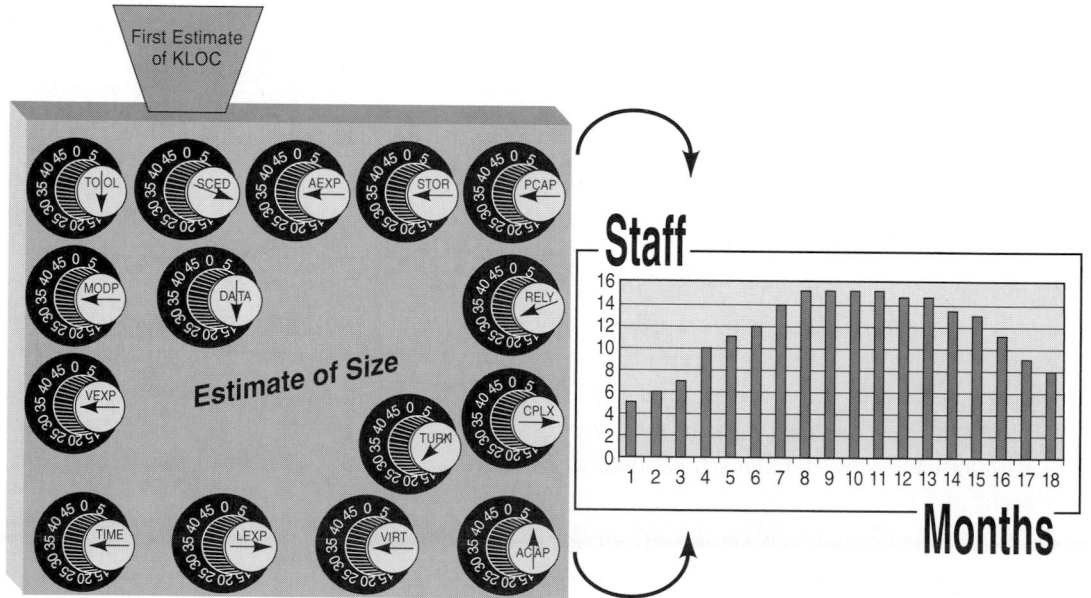

FIGURE 11–10
Cost Drivers Tune Staffing

Scheduling Using COCOMO

After the size, and, from the size, the overall effort, have been estimated, then the activity of scheduling can begin. Scheduling includes refining the WBS, if necessary, and assigning staff members' responsibility for specific tasks. Scheduling also includes determining a start and end date for each task, as well as noting dependencies between and among tasks and promoting parallelism where possible. With dependencies, one task needs input from one or more others and therefore must wait for the other(s) to complete before it can begin; with parallelism, two or more tasks may be worked on at the same time. The two most widely used methods of graphically representing tasks, dependencies, parallelism, and time, are the Gantt chart and the Pert chart. Each is easily produced using an automated tool.

Tailoring of COCOMO

An organization may want to develop a specially calibrated version that will more accurately reflect its particular practices and capabilities. There are three different ways to recalibrate and tailor the intermediate COCOMO equations to local conditions, based on a local historical database for n projects: recalibrate the effort equation coefficient, tailor the mode (recalibrate the exponent and coefficient), and revise the cost drivers. We won't go into the formulas and details of recalibrating the models here, but the instructions may be found in Boehm's *Software Engineering Economics*.

One thing to note is that a database of at least five projects is required to accurately recalibrate the coefficient. A database of at least 10 projects is required to accurately recalibrate the exponent.

Advantages of COCOMO

The advantages of COCOMO include:

- Actual data "backfitted" from many real programs can supply a set of COCOMO constants and adjustment factors that fit an organization well.
- It is a repeatable process.
- The method allows the addition of unique adjustment factors associated with an organization.
- It is versatile enough to support different "modes" and "levels."
- It works well on projects that are not dramatically different in size, complexity, or process.
- It is highly calibrated, based on previous experience.
- It is thoroughly documented.
- It is easy to use.

Disadvantages of COCOMO

The disadvantages of COCOMO include:

- It ignores requirements volatility (but an organization may add this as an extra adjustment factor in computing EAF).
- It ignores documentation and other requirements.
- It ignores customer attributes—skill, cooperation, knowledge, and responsiveness.
- It oversimplifies the impact of security issues.
- It ignores software safety issues.
- It ignores the software development environment.
- It ignores personnel turnover levels.
- It ignores many hardware issues.
- All the levels are dependent on the size estimate—the accuracy of the size drives the accuracy of effort, development time, staffing, and productivity estimates.
- Experience-based estimation may be flawed because of obsolescence of the historical data used or because the estimators' memory of past projects is flawed.
- It is dependent on the knowledge of cost drivers and/or the amount of time spent in each phase.

Other potential issues noted by Dr. Frailey include these:

- The COCOMO model primarily represents development effort (from the planning phase through the implementation phase). Maintenance, rework, porting, and reuse are issues that don't fit cleanly into the same model. These activities may also be estimated using a variation of the basic model.
- COCOMO assumes a very basic level of effort for configuration management and quality assurance, allowing about 5% of the total budget for both (based on typical commercial practice at the time COCOMO was established). It can take two to four times this much with modern software engineering practices and typical complexity of modern software products.
- Your data may not match the data used to develop COCOMO—if not, your company must collect the data needed to correlate the model.
- COCOMO assumes a basic waterfall process model: 30% design, 30% coding, and 40% integration and testing.
- COCOMO excludes:
  - Requirements development and specification, which is often not used in some commercial applications. Even though this portion of the estimate is commonly viewed as the responsibility of a systems engineering or systems analysis function, it is often underscoped unless software engineers are invited to participate in the cost estimate.

As shown in Figure 11–11, an increase of 20% is generally needed for the requirements phase—even more when object-oriented methods are in use.

- Management (it does include line management but not overall management);

- Overhead costs;

- Travel and other incidental costs;

- System integration and test support;

- Field test support;

- Computers;

- Supplies;

- Office space.

Boehm originally divided effort as 30% design, 30% code and unit testing, and 40% integration and testing.

If you add 20% to the total for requirements analysis, it becomes 17% requirements analysis, 25% design, 25% code and unit testing, and 33% integration and testing.

Time is more heavily tilted toward requirements analysis and design, but specifics depend on the process being used. Typical numbers for time are 30% requirements, 30% design, 15% code, and 25% integration and testing.

Some Typical Barriers to Faster Schedule or Lower Cost

Common barriers to "faster, cheaper" goals include:

- Lack of adequate equipment, software, tools, people, and so on;
- Slow approval cycles;
- Poor coordination with other disciplines, other companies, and so on;
- Poorly educated customers and managers;
- Irascible and irrational customers and managers;
- Intentional barriers such as competitors.

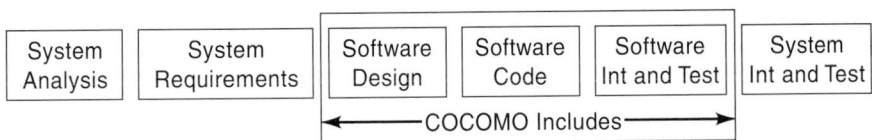

FIGURE 11–11
Phases Included by COCOMO

Here's the bottom line: Keep data, especially estimates versus actuals (Figure 11–12). The more facts you have, the better off you will be during negotiations. Prepare to re-estimate early and often. Use a model and a modeling tool, where possible; consider environmental factors, and calibrate the model/tool to your organization.

COCOMO II

COCOMO II is a revised and extended version of the model, built upon the original COCOMO. It more easily allows the estimation of object-oriented software, software created via spiral or evolutionary models, and applications developed from commercial-off-the-shelf software. It was created, in part, to develop software cost database and tool support capabilities for continuous model improvement and to provide a quantitative analytic framework and a set of tools and techniques for evaluating the effects of software technology improvements on software life cycle costs and schedules.

During the earliest conceptual stages of a project, the model uses object point estimates to compute effort. During the early design stages, when little is known about project size or project staff, unadjusted function points are used as an input to the model. After an architecture has been selected, design and development begin with SLOC input to the model.

COCOMO II provides likely ranges of estimates that represent one standard deviation around the most likely estimate. Accommodating factors that received little attention in the first version, COCOMO now adjusts for software reuse and re-engineering where automated

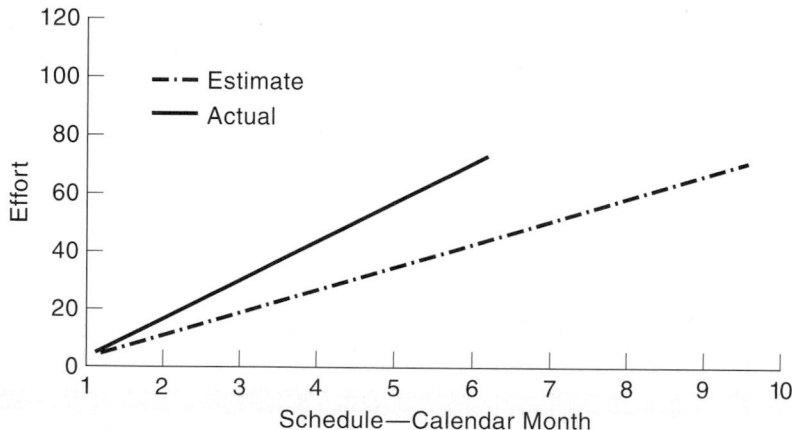

FIGURE 11–12
Track Estimates Versus Actuals

tools are used for translation of existing software. COCOMO II also accounts for requirements volatility in its estimates.

Whereas the exponent on size in the effort equations in the original COCOMO varies with the development mode, COCOMO II uses scaling factors to generalize and replace the effects of the development mode.

The COCOMO II application composition model uses object points to perform estimates. The model assumes the use of integrated CASE tools for rapid prototyping. Objects include screens, reports, and modules in third-generation programming languages. The number of raw objects is estimated, the complexity of each object is estimated, and the weighted total (object-point count) is computed. The percentage of reuse and anticipated productivity is also estimated. With this information, an effort estimate can be computed.

COCOMO II explicitly handles the availability of additional information in later stages of a project, the nonlinear costs of reusing software components, and the effects of several factors on the diseconomies of scale. (Some of these are the turnover rate of the staff, the geographic dispersion of the team, and the "maturity" of the development process as defined by the SEI.) The model also revises some coefficient values and eliminates discontinuities present in the old model (related to "development modes" and maintenance vs. adaptation).

COCOMO II is really three different models:

- **The application composition model**—Suitable for projects built with modern GUI-builder tools. Based on new object points.
- **The early design model**—Used to get rough estimates of a project's cost and duration before the entire architecture has been determined. It uses a small set of new cost drivers and new estimating equations, and it is based on unadjusted function points or KSLOC.
- **The post-architecture model**—The most detailed COCOMO II model, to be used after the development of the project's overall architecture. It has new cost drivers, new line counting rules, and new equations.

In collaboration with Rational, Inc., COCOMO II integrates phases and milestones with those of the Rational Unified Process and has provided phase and activity distribution estimators for COCOMO II.

SLIM: A Mathematical Model

With regression modeling, the emphasis is on constructing a formula that best represents scattered data points. In mathematical modeling, the emphasis is on matching the data to the form of an existing mathematical function. In the early 1960s, Peter V. Norden of IBM concluded that research and development projects exhibit well-defined and predictable staff loading patterns that fit the mathematical formula for a Rayleigh distribution (Box 11–10), as shown in Figure 11–13.

Box 11–10
The Norden-Rayleigh Function

$m(t) = 2K$ at $\exp(-at^2)$

where $m(t)$ = staffing requirement (number of persons) at any time "t" (in years) during the life of the project

K = total project effort in staff-years (SY)

a = acceleration factor

The acceleration factor is given by: $a = 1 \div 2t_d^2$

Where t_d = time of delivery = development time

Later, in the 1970s, Lawrence H. Putnam (Quality Software Management, QSM) applied Norden's observations to the software life cycle, validating the existence of an optimum staffing

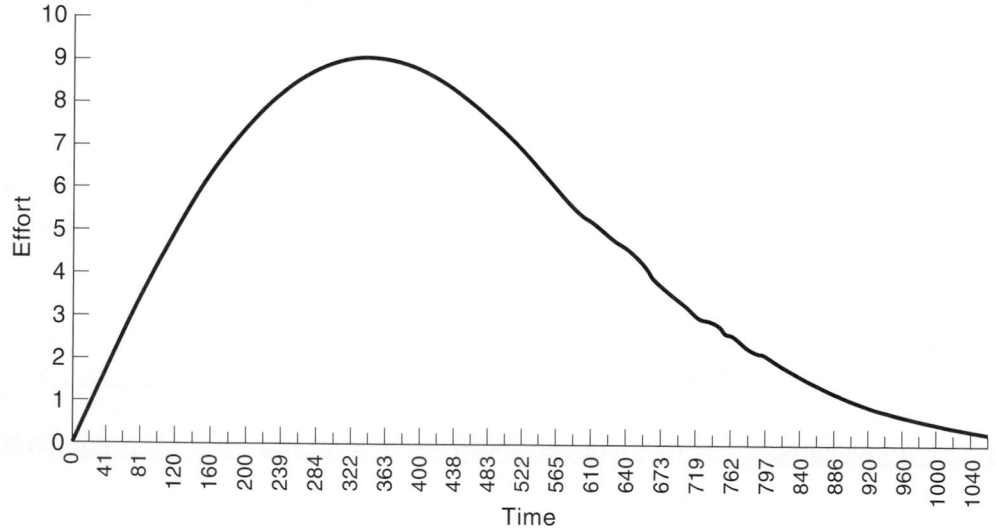

FIGURE 11–13
The Rayleigh Staffing Curve

shape for a given project. He began with 50 U.S. Army projects and now has empirical evidence for several thousand. Based on statistical analysis of these projects (QSM has been collecting data on completed projects since 1975), Putnam found that the relationship among the three principal elements of software estimating—size, schedule, and effort—matched the Norden/ Rayleigh function. As size goes up, so do effort, time, and defects, but in different types of relationships (exponential, logarithmic). He concluded that reducing size is one way to reduce schedule, effort, and number of defects. Size can be reduced a number of ways, including "requirements scrubbing" (eliminating "gold plating" or nonessential features), phased or incremental delivery, reuse, and commercial-off-the-shelf products.

Like Boehm, Putnam used scatter diagrams and curve-fitting techniques to find relationships in his observed data. After plotting the major trend line that represents all observed data points (size versus months), the mean was calculated (50% of the projects fell above the line and 50% of the projects fell below the line), along with values for +1σ (only 16% of the data points fell above this line; 84% of the data points fell below this line) and for –1σ (only 16% of the data points fell below this line; 84% of the data points fell above this line), as shown in Figure 11–14. If a project is estimated to fall above the +1σ line, the indication is that it is not practical to build the product now—this has become known as the Impractical Zone. If a project is estimated to fall below –1σ, the indication is that it is not possible to build the product this fast (this has become known as the Impossible Zone, although many project managers have been known to forge ahead anyway).

QSM's Software Lifecycle Management (SLIM) process consists of methodologies tied together with the decision-support tools, SLIM-Estimate©, SLIM-Control©, and SLIM-Metrics©. SLIM-Estimate© supports estimating and planning, SLIM-Control© supports tracking and forecasting, and SLIM-Metrics© supports data capture and analysis.

The software production relationship is described in Box 11–11.

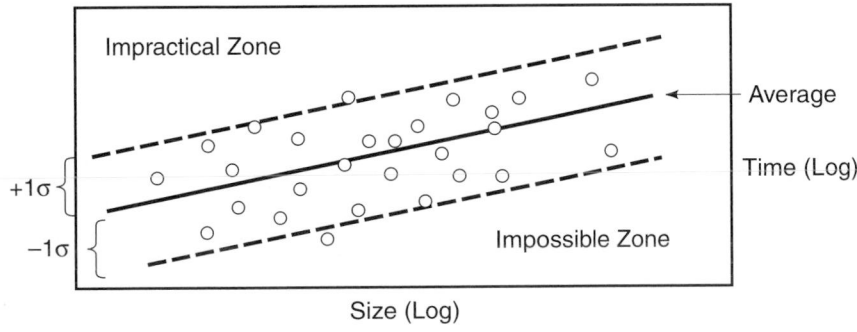

FIGURE 11–14
Impractical/Impossible Zones

Box 11-11
The QSM SPR Relationship

Deliverable Software (Size) = Effort ÷ Time at a Productivity Level

As with almost all sizing and estimating models, the estimating paradigm illustrated by triangle (Figure 11–4) or box (Figure 11–5) applies. There are only so many degrees of freedom. If productivity goes up, the schedule is extended, or resources are added, the size is able to increase as well (the inverse relationship also holds true).

All sizing and estimating methods and processes encourage the collection of actual data. The benefit of using an automated tool is that most of them provide "starter sets" of data based on observed projects. SLIM is particularly helpful in this regard because data from more than 5,500 projects has been captured. Putnam's software equation links the size of the software to development time and overall effort. The equation was derived by linking two mathematical definitions of productivity: size/staff power and Putnam's formula relating productivity and difficulty (see Box 11–12).

Box 11-12
The Putnam Equation
Source: Putnam, Larry H. and William Myers (1992). *Measures for Excellence: Reliable Software on Time, Within Budget*. Englewood Cliffs, NJ: Yourdon Press.

Product = Productivity × Effort × Time

$$S = C \times K^{1/3} \times t_d^{4/3}$$

where
S = software size in LOC
C = environmental factor, dependent on the state of technology
K = total effort for the overall project
t_d = delivery time constraint (schedule) in years

The environmental factor may be calculated, then, by:

$$C = S/K^{1/3} t_d^{4/3}$$

K and t_d are determined from historical data for previous projects of size S. The tailored value of C can then be used to calculate future estimates.

The technology constant, C, combines the effect of using tools, languages, methodology, quality assurance procedures, standards, and so on. It is determined on the basis of historical data (past projects). The values of the technology constant can vary from as little as 610 up to 57,314. C is determined from project size, area under effort curve, and project duration.

Rating: C = 2,000—poor, C = 8,000—good, C = 11,000—excellent

For example, assume that the technology constant, C, is estimated to be 4,000 (not great, but not poor) and size is estimated as 200,000 LOC. Then, plugging these numbers into the formula,

Total lifetime effort B = $(1/T^4)\,(S/C)^3$

Total lifetime effort B = $(1/T^4)\,(200,000/4,000)^3 = (1/T^4)\,(50)^3$

Development effort E = 0.3945 B

If target development period is two years, then

Total lifetime effort B = $(1/16)\,(50)^3 = 7,812.5$ staff-years

Development effort E = 0.3945 B = 3,082 staff-years

Putnam's recommended figures for C for different types of projects are:

- Real-time embedded—1,500;
- Batch development—4,894;
- Supported and organized—10,040;

Effort and productivity change when development time varies between two and three years:

T	E	B
2	3,082	7,814
2.5	1,262	3,200
3	609	1,543

Focusing on the productivity level is one major difference between the Boehm and Putnam models. It can be calculated based on the size, time, and effort values from previously completed projects. Putnam combines attributes of both the process and the product in his definition of productivity, and he separates the wide range of productivity values into an index ranging from 0 to 40. He calls this the process productivity index (PI), based on product attributes such as algorithm complexity and process attributes such as standards and team capabilities. Putnam is careful to explain that the PI is not a fair quantification of personal productivity because some of the attributes may not be within the control of the development team.

The PI makes a huge difference in the effort, schedule, and cost of a project. Organizations can improve their PI, just as they can improve their SEI CMM maturity level. Application types exhibit different PIs. For example, business systems average 17.3, scientific systems average 14.8, telecommunications average 11.4, real-time systems average 8.3, and microcode systems average 6.3.

Size and productivity are constants, while time and effort can be adjusted to some degree. According to Fred Brooks (Brooks' Law), adding people to a late project usually only makes it later. There is a minimum time solution and a minimum effort/cost solution.

Basic steps in estimating with the mathematical model are made palatable with the use of automated tools:

Step 1:   Estimate software size.

Application of a beta distribution is one way to do this (or expert opinion, analogy, Wideband Delphi).

$$S_n = (S_{min} + 4\,S_i + S_{max}) \div 6$$

where:

S_n = the predicted nominal size of the software product

S_{min} = the minimum possible size

S_i = the most likely size (50% probable)

S_{max} = the maximum possible size

Step 2:   Determine productivity and environmental factors (PI, C).

Step 3:   Identify the development constraints (maximum cost, etc.).

Step 4:   Construct a planning zone (feasible region versus the impractical or impossible zones) similar to Figure 11–15.

Step 5:   Find an acceptable planning point.

The QSM model default is based on four phases (users may customize this): requirements, design, code, and integration. The third phase is determined by estimated size and PI; phases 1 and 2 are determined as percentages of phase 3 values by analysis of historical data; and phase 4 is an extrapolation of the phase 3 staffing curve. (See Figure 11–16.)

Advantages of the SLIM Model

Advantages of the SLIM model include:

- Provides a comprehensive set of software development management tools that support the entire software program life cycle.

- Helps to enforce good habits within engineering and management team (software project planning, and software project tracking and oversight key process areas within the SEI CMM Level 2).

- Offers value-added effective planning, especially on large projects.

- Uses linear programming, statistical simulation, program evaluation, and review techniques to derive a software cost estimate. (Linear programming allows the user to impose a maximum cost, a maximum schedule, and high and low bounds on staffing, and to have an appropriate range of time and effort solutions returned.)
- Allows "design to cost" if the user elects to enter size and desired number of staff-months.
- Enables a software cost estimator to perform the following functions:
    - Calibration—Fine-tune the model to represent the local software development environment by interpreting a historical database of past projects.
    - Build—Create an information model of the software system, collecting software characteristics, personal attributes, computer attributes, and so on.
    - Software sizing—Use an automated version of the LOC costing technique.
- Allows an organization to tailor life cycle phases and milestones fit a given environment.
- Simplifies strategic decision making.
- Provides an optimal staffing policy in the context of the development environment.
- Supports "what-if" analysis.
- Generates reports and graphs for:
    - monthly staffing profiles
    - monthly budget profiles

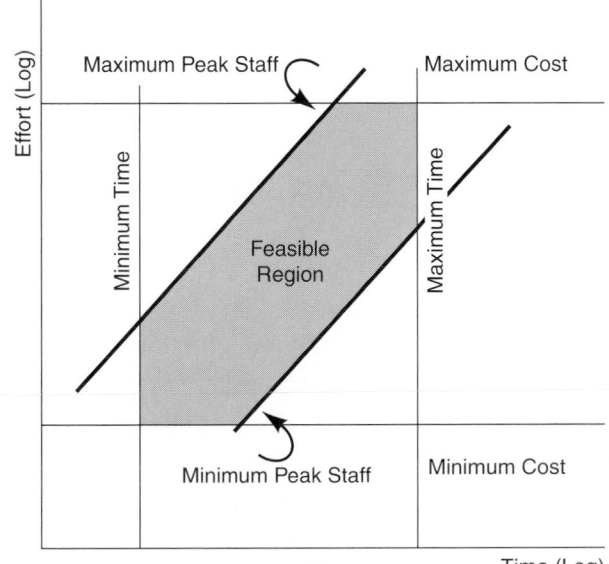

FIGURE 11–15
Planning Zone

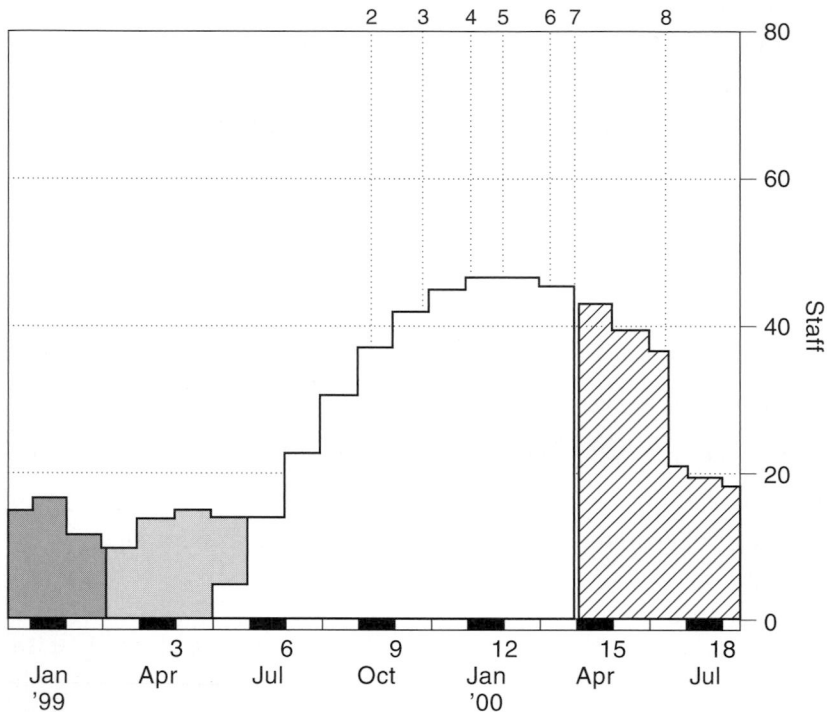

FIGURE 11–16
Staffing Profile

- risk profiles for cost, schedule, and effort
- forecasts of software reliability
- forecasts of beginning and ending milestones
- Provides defect rate information.
- SLIM will output minimal time and associated cost and effort, including a sensitivity analysis showing how the values change as the size estimate varies from one to three standard deviations.

Disadvantages of the SLIM Model

Disadvantages of the SLIM model include:

- It works best on large projects (some say anything where software size is greater than 5,000 lines, effort is greater than 1.5 person-years, and development time is more than 6 months).
- To use the model, the software size must be identified in advance.

- Estimates are extremely sensitive to the technology factor.
- The model is extremely sensitive to compression of the delivery time (t_d).
- The model is extremely sensitive to the size estimate.
- With the environmental factor, many important factors must be modeled, many of which may be difficult to determine.
- It assumes a waterfall life cycle, which does not map to incremental iterative (spiral) development process or the Rational Unified Process.
- Users must remember to add phases and integral tasks such as program management.
- The tool is complex—it is not usually a 2- to 5-minute job to update a model.
- The model often shows that total effort of small projects may be less than the effort of their sum if they were one large project. The user must be careful not to chop large projects into too many smaller ones, considering interface issues.

Summary

Estimating product size, staff effort, project schedule, and cost are inextricably intertwined during the project planning process, which occurs for the first time near the beginning of the project life cycle and many times thereafter, usually at the end of each major phase. Estimating accuracy is often very poor at the beginning of a project, but it improves with project knowledge gained with every phase, culminating in an exact estimate matching the actual size, effort, schedule, and cost (Figure 11–17).

Effort (person-hours) and duration (calendar days) for the project must be estimated to enable managers to assess product costs, return on investment, time to market, and quality. The estimation process is a difficult one because projects must often satisfy conflicting goals as well as provide specified functionality within specified performance criteria, within a specified cost and schedule, and with some desired level of quality. These multiple constraints complicate the estimation process. In addition, estimates are required before the specifications are well known. An architectural or high-level design barely scratches the surface in terms of providing quantifiable, testable requirements, yet the first estimate typically precedes this activity.

The estimating process falls primarily in the realm of project management skills of documenting plans, estimating cost, estimating effort, scheduling, and selecting metrics. Yet, as with all software project management activities, most of the people management skills come into play as well.

An organization that documents, follows, and continually improves its estimating process will satisfy a goal of the SEI CMM Level 2 key process area, software project planning. Goal 1 specifically states, "Software estimates are documented for use in planning and tracking the software project."

The biggest challenge in software development is to deliver a fully functional, high-quality product on time within budget, using forecasted assets. These constraints are referred to as the software estimation paradigm.

The first step in software estimation is to determine the size of the product. Size is usually expressed in KLOC, but it may also be expressed in function points, feature points, object points, or other units of measurement. A unit other than KLOC is usually translated into KLOC before moving on to the next step of estimating effort, schedule, and cost. Translation tables exist for translating almost any modern widely used language into a LOC count. Methods for estimating the size include Wideband Delphi, analogy, expert judgment, function point analysis, feature point analysis, object point analysis, and so on.

Empirical models, regression models, and mathematical models are used to estimate effort, the amount of labor required to create a software product of a given size. Here, we discussed regression models only. All the effort-estimating models depend on size.

When the effort, usually expressed in staff-months, is known, then the schedule and cost may be derived. Schedule is based on productivity factors, number of staff available, and phase distribution of effort.

COCOMO, a regression model, is the most widely used and best known of all the estimating models. COCOMO supplies three modes—organic, semidetached, and embedded—and three levels of complexity—basic, intermediate, and detailed. A "mode" simply describes the type of project—big, small, simple, complex, and so on. A "level" describes the amount of

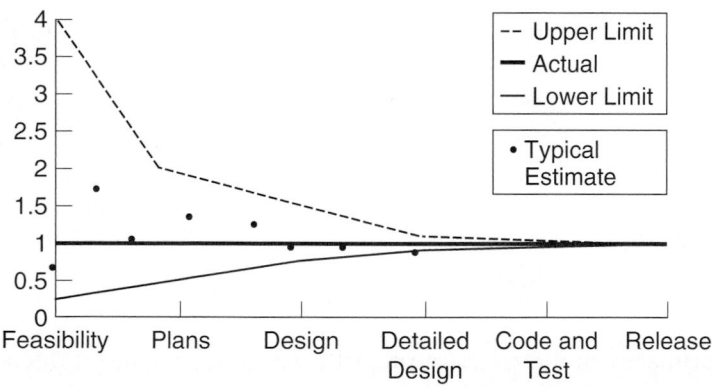

Grady and Caswell report that typical estimates are 20–25% optimistic, even for experienced estimators.

FIGURE 11–17

Grady and Caswell Corroborate Jones

Source: Grady, Robert B., and Deborah L. Caswell, *Software Metrics: Establishing a Company-Wide Program*, 1st ed. Englewood Cliffs, NJ: Prentice Hall.

input—more input results in a more accurate estimate. The original author of COCOMO is Dr. Barry Boehm; his work was researched at TRW and is continued at the University of Southern California.

Basic COCOMO relies on a formula arrived at by curve fitting to a set of observed data points and applying simple regression analysis. Intermediate COCOMO improves the basic model by adding cost drivers, or environmental factors that increase or decrease the effort involved in developing the product. Detailed COCOMO provides additional analysis tools by estimating according to WBS levels (three-level hierarchy: system, subsystem, module) and by adjusting formulas for each life cycle phase. Most people use the intermediate model, which can easily be performed with a spreadsheet. Several automated tools exist to calculate the estimations.

COCOMO, like all estimating models and tools, has advantages and disadvantages. It is easy to use and provides a common language for communication in the software project planning/management community. On the other hand, it must be calibrated to an organization's historical data to be really useful. Probably its greatest weakness is that it is founded upon an estimate of product size in LOC. However, neither Dr. Boehm nor the creator of other models and tools has described a better way to begin—even when starting with functionality instead of size, a translation of functions into size must occur before effort, schedule, and cost estimations can be continued.

COCOMO may be tailored for a specific organization. The means of calibration depends on historical data, and the formulas are in the public domain. Boehm's classic (though dense) book, *Software Engineering Economics*, contains all.

The original work that Boehm and his colleagues did at TRW in 1975–1980 must be translated into today's terms. Dr. Boehm, a professor at the University of Southern California, continues to update his findings and publishes regularly on the Web. A new work titled *Software Cost Estimation with Cocomo II* was published in 2000. A new user of the COCOMO model (I or II) should: 1. Collect data, 2. Run the COCOMO model, and 3. If a mismatch is suspected, then recalibrate the model for the environment (and restructure equations). This chapter simply describes how Boehm did his now-famous research, to explain the metamodel and offer directions for constructing organization-specific models. COCOMO II is more modern: It supports evolutionary, risk-driven, and collaborative software processes; fourth-generation languages and application generators; commercial-off-the-shelf and reuse-driven software approaches; fast-track software development approaches; and software process maturity initiatives.

Another model, the mathematical model, is best known as the Software Lifecycle Management (SLIM) tool from QSM. With SLIM, the estimator can invoke a linear programming analysis that considers development constraints on both cost and effort and that provides a month-by-month distribution of effort and a consistency check with data collected for software systems of similar size.

The SLIM model is based on Putnam's own analysis of the software life cycle in terms of the Rayleigh distribution of project personnel level versus time. The algorithm used is:

$$\text{size} = C \times K^{1/3} \times t_d^{4/3}$$

Size is the lines of code, K is the total life-cycle effort (in working years), and t is development time (in years). Estimating the size, effort, schedule, and cost of a new software project is an inexact science, so experts strongly recommend that more than one method be used for sizing as well as for estimating.

A summary for an estimating checklist might include:

- Has a firm foundation been established for the estimate of software size?
- Have customers, managers, and developers been trained in the basics of sizing and estimating?
- Has historical data, if used, been applied correctly?
- Have models been used correctly?
- Has the estimation method been mapped/calibrated to the development process?
- Have reasonable assumptions been made about product and process factors that affect productivity?
- Do aggressive goals have realistic strategies for accomplishment?
- Have any alternative estimating methods been used for comparison?
- Have multiple methods been used? No one method is reliable enough, in most cases. When two methods disagree, you may be missing some facts.
- Has the model clearly defined the costs it is estimating and the costs it is excluding?
- In tracking estimates, are the estimates close to the actual costs expended on the projects?
- Is the model objective? Does it allocate most of the software cost variance to poorly calibrated subjective factors (such as complexity)? The planner doesn't need a result that the tool can be manipulated to produce.
- Does the model accommodate the estimation of subsystems and units? Does it give (accurate) phase and activity breakdown?
- Is the tool stable? Do small differences in inputs produce small differences in output cost estimates?
- Does the model cover the class of software projects whose costs you need to estimate?
- Does the model avoid the use of information that will not be well known until the project is complete?
- Does the model avoid the use of highly redundant factors or factors that make no appreciable contribution to the results?

In addition to taking care with tool selection, Boehm and other experts have given us good advice to heed:

- Measure the difference between the actuals and the plan to determine the amount of variance.
- Establish a baseline (phases, milestones, size, effort/staffing/cost, defects).
- Use templates for efficiency and consistency.
- Back up positions with data.
- Try to negotiate solutions with a better than 50% probability of success.
- Collect data from completed projects in a nonintrusive and automated way.
- Maintain a master database that contains the data from every completed project.
- As the number of collected projects grows, use statistical analysis techniques to stratify the data into various meaningful subsets.
- Budget and plan for re-estimation. Execute re-estimates based upon new and/or revised information (predictors, assumptions). The uncertainty present at the beginning of a project warrants regular reviews, coupled with risk re-assessment.
- Don't let the forecast get stale.

There are similarities in the models. Even though we call one "mathematical," they all rely on mathematical formulas (see Table 11–13). Although we call one "empirical," they all rely on the observation of actual projects. Each estimating model has its own particular strengths and weaknesses, which is one of the reasons to use more than one for the sizing activity as well as for the effort-, schedule-, and cost-estimating activity. Estimating is a process, even a mini-project, to be documented, taught, and consistently followed.

TABLE 11–13
COCOMO, SLIM Equation, and Parameter Comparison

Model Name	Schedule Equation	Parameters
Basic and Intermediate COCOMO	Schedule $= 2.5$ Effort^c	Organic: $c = 0.38$ Semidetached: $c = 0.35$ Embedded: $c = 0.32$
COCOMO 2.0	Schedule $= c \left[\text{Effort}^{0.33 + 0.2\,(b-1.01)} \right] \frac{\text{SCED}\%}{100}$ $b = 1.01 + \frac{1}{100} \sum \text{SF}_j$	$c = 3.0$ $\text{SF}_j = $ scale factor $\text{SCED}\% = $ schedule compression/ expansion parameter
Putnam's SLIM	Simplified Model: $\text{Effort} = 8.14 \left(\frac{\text{SLOC}}{P} \right)^{3/7}$	$P = $ productivity parameter

Problems for Review_____

1. Are all estimating models mathematical? Empirical? Regression? Please explain.
2. Based on the following brief descriptions of a project:

   a. Determine the type of project.

   b. Using basic COCOMO:

      i. Calculate the amount of effort it will take to develop this project.

      ii. Calculate the development time based on the effort estimate.

   c. Using intermediate COCOMO:

      i. Calculate the amount of effort it will take to develop this project.

      ii. Calculate the development time based on the effort estimate.

   d. Compare the results from b and c.

   e. Recalculate the estimate, using intermediate COCOMO with all cost drivers set at their lowest levels.

   f. Recalculate the estimate, using intermediate COCOMO with all cost drivers set at their highest levels.

   g. Calculate the amount of effort to develop this project and the development time if the project were broken into four projects running in parallel. The size of each would be 500 KLOC. How does the estimated total of the four projects compare with the estimate for one big project?

Brief project description:

- The estimated size of the software project is 2 million LOC.
- Analysts and developers have experience in developing similar systems.
- Analysts have an average of seven years of experience.
- Although the system is similar to some previously developed, it will entail some innovative design, increasing the risk and requiring the use of a spiral model of development.
- The company will spare no expense to acquire the latest software development tools.
- The system architecture is complete; hardware development will proceed in parallel with software development.
- The company has received a government grant for extensive server farms—plenty of storage will be available for the largest of databases.
- The system has a real-time component that will require modeling of the system behavior.
- Programmers are experienced, but not in the language chosen for implementation.
- Development processes are in place; the organization is an SEI Level 2: Repeatable.
- Developer's experience with the operating system is adequate.

Visit the Case Study

Your corporation's marketing productization board has taken a special interest in the ARRS project based on your extremely positive answers to the reuse questions. Mr. Adams has been assigned from the board to monitor your project for immediate productization. He has asked you to evaluate the impact on being able to productize the ARRS as an open-source tool kit for building rail-based transportation system's software.

Citations

[1]Paulk, Mark C., Charles V. Weber, Bill Curtis, and Mary Beth Chrissis (1994). *The Capability Maturity Model: Guidelines for Improving the Software Process*, 1st ed. Reading, MA: Addison-Wesley, SEI Series in Software Engineering.

References

Boehm, Barry (1976). *Software Engineering Economics*. Englewood Cliffs, NJ: Prentice Hall.

DeMarco, Tom (1995). *Why Does Software Cost So Much? and Other Puzzles of the Information Age*. New York, NY: Dorset House.

Grady, Robert B., and Deborah L. Caswell (1987). *Software Metrics: Establishing a Company-Wide Program*, 1st ed. Englewood Cliffs, NJ: Prentice Hall.

Suggested Readings

Abdel-Hamid, Tarek, and Stuart E. Madnick (1991). *Software Project Dynamics: An Integrated Approach*. Upper Saddle River, NJ: Prentice Hall.

Basili, Victor (1980). *Tutorial on Models and Metrics for Software Management and Engineering*. New York, NY: Institute of Electrical and Electronics Engineers.

Boehm, Barry W., et al. (2000). *Software Cost Estimation with Cocomo II*. Englewood Cliffs, NJ: Prentice Hall.

Brooks, Fredrick P. (1995). *The Mythical Man-Month: Essays on Software Engineering*, anniversary ed. (originally published 1975). Reading, MA: Addison-Wesley.

Connell, John, and Linda Shafer (1987). *The Professional User's Guide to Acquiring Software*. New York, NY: Van Nostrand Reinhold.

DeMarco, Tom (1982). *Controlling Software Projects*. Upper Saddle River, NJ: Prentice Hall.

Fairley, R.E. "Recent Advances in Software Estimation Techniques." *IEEE 14th International Conference on Software Engineering*, New York, NY: IEEE Computer Society Press. pp. 382–391.

Halstead, Maurice (1977). *Elements of Software Science*. New York, NY: Elsevier North-Holland.

Humphrey, Watts (1989). *Managing the Software Process*. Reading, MA: Addison-Wesley.

Jones, Capers (1997). *Applied Software Measurement*, 2nd ed. New York, NY: McGraw-Hill.

Jones, Capers (1986). *Programming Productivity*, 1st ed. New York, NY: McGraw-Hill.

Norden, Peter V. (1958). "Curve Fitting for a Model of Applied Research and Development Scheduling." *IBM Journal of Research and Development*, Endicott, NY. 2(3).

Putnam, Lawrence H. (1978). "A General Empirical Solution to the Macro Software Sizing and Estimating Problem." *IEEE Transactions on Software Engineering*, SE4(7):345–361.

Sommerville, Ian (2000). *Software Engineering*, 6th ed. Workingham, England: Addison-Wesley.

Stutzke, Richard D. (2001). *Software Estimation: Projects, Products, Processes*. Addison-Wesley.

Von Mayrhauser, Anneliese (1990). *Software Engineering: Methods and Management*. Boston, MA: Academic Press.

Walston, C.E., and C.P. Felix (1977). "A Method of Programming Measurement and Estimation." *IBM Systems Journal*, 16(1):54–73.

Yourdon, Edward (1997). *Death March*. Upper Saddle River, NJ: Yourdon Press/Prentice Hall.

Web Pages for Further Information

ca.com/products/superproject.htm. Computer Associates.

mijuno.larc.nasa.gov/dfc/societies/Ispa.html. The International Society of Parametric Analysts.

www.bjmath.com/bjmath/least/curve.htm. Richard Reid, "Curve Fitting" (reference "Schaums Outline Series: Theory and problems of Probability and Statistics" by Murray R. Spiegal, Ph.D.).

www.costengineer.com.au/prod01.shtml. Expert Estimation.

www.cpsc.ucalgary.ca/~hongd/SENG/621/report2.html#2.6.5. Danfeng Hong, "Software Cost Estimation," Department of Computer Science, University of Canada, Alberta, Canada.

www.dacs.dtic.mil/databases/url/key.hts?keycode=4:7&islowerlevel=1. The Data & Analysis Center for Software (DACS) is a Department of Defense (DoD) Information Analysis Center (IAC). Cost Estimation: Function Points Analysis.

www.iconixsw.com/spec_sheets/CoCoPro.html. CoCoPro estimating tool.

www.jsc.nasa.gov/bu2/. NASA Johnson Space Center (JSC) Cost Estimating Group.

www.pricesystems.com/prices.htm. PRICE-S estimating tool from PRICE Systems.

www.qsm.com/products.html. SLIM estimating tool from Quantitative Software Management, Lawrence Putnam, President.

www.rcinc.com/. Resource Calculations, Inc., provides sizing and cost modeling tools including ASSET-R, SSM, and SOFTCOST-R.

www.rcinc.com/softcostr.html. Softcost-R estimating tool.

www.resourcedesigninc.com/RDImain.html. Ecomodeler provides automated front-end project building software for World Construction Set from Viewscape3D Ltd.

www.sciam.com/1998/1298issue/1298jones.html#further. Capers Jones, "Sizing Up Software: Unlike oil, steel or paper, software is an intangible commodity."

www.sepo.nosc.mil/revic.html. REVIC estimating tool.

www.SoftstarSystems.com/. Softstar Systems offer Costar, an automated implementation of COCOMO.

www.softwaremetrics.com/Articles/default.htm. Longstreet Consulting Inc.

www.spr.com/index.htm. Software Productivity Research provides software measurement, assessment, and estimation products and services. Capers Jones is chairman and founder.

www.spr.com/library/0funcmet.htm. Jones, Capers, Chairman, Software Productivity Research, Inc., "What are Function Points?"

www.stsc.hill.af.mil/crosstalk/. Software Estimation: Challenges and Research.

www.stsc.hill.af.mil/CrossTalk/1995/nov/Living.asp. Lawrence Bernstein and Alex Lubashevsky, AT&T, "Living with Function Points."

www.sunset.usc.edu/cocomo2.0/cocomo.html. COCOMO estimating tool.

www.wwk.com/coolsoft.html. COOLSoft™ Quantitative Tool for Software Development Cost Estimation.

Assigning Resources

When you have a WBS list of customized activities that match the life cycle you have chosen for a project, you are ready to assign resources to them. This should be easy, right? The database people get the database assignments, and the testers get the testing assignments. Not so fast. There are several dimensions to the resource assignment problem that a software development project manager should know about and consider when parceling out the work. All programmers are not created equal. Jealousy and bickering can erupt over choice assignments, creating more work for the project manager to manage conflict within the team. Career paths intersect and fork. And workloads get unbalanced, leading to project schedule and morale problems.

To address these issues, we will look at the project manager's role in staffing a project and making resource choices. These are part of human resource management. We'll learn about a concept and tool that can help people match themselves to assignments. We'll see how a simple spreadsheet tool can make project roles clear and also provide tracking for deliverables. These are essential skills and competencies for the software project manager today. It's not *all* about transactions. It's about relationship management, too.

Where We Are in the Product Development Life Cycle

Where are we in the basic software life cycle model that serves as our map? As shown in Figure 4–1 and Figure 12–1, we are still at the beginning of the software life cycle. But because we have created a product-oriented WBS, which answers the *what* question for us, we can move on to the *how* step, where we will determine *how* to do the *what*, as shown in Figure 12–2.

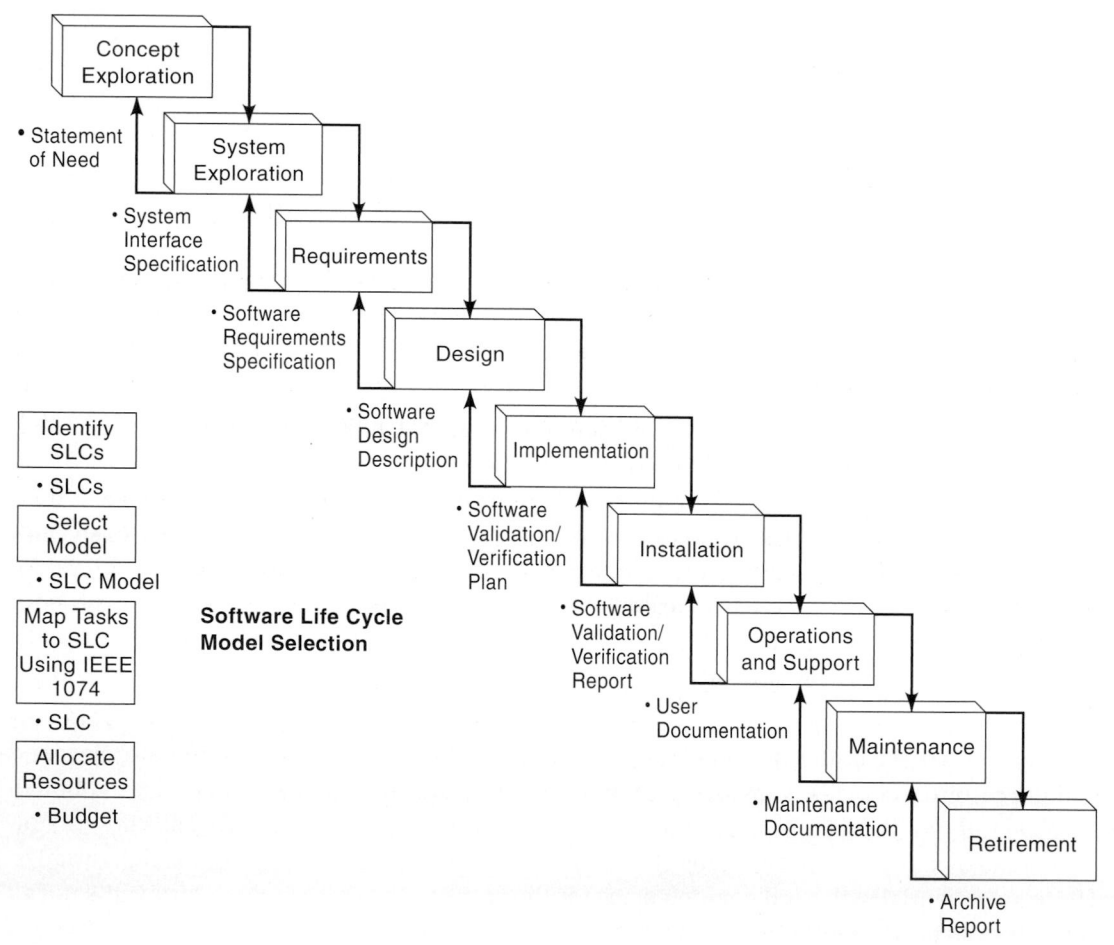

FIGURE 12–1
Product Development Life Cycle

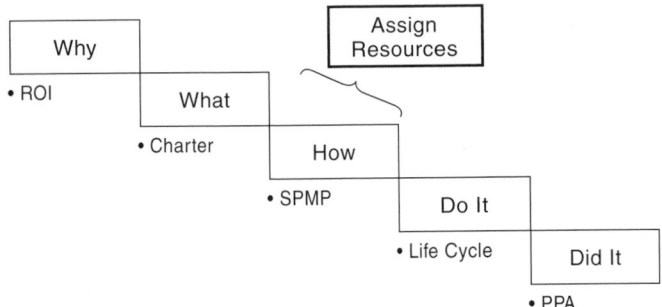

FIGURE 12–2
Project Process Framework

Chapter 12 Relation to the 34 Competencies _____

This chapter relies on the competencies shown here. For resource assignments, the key product development technique needed is an awareness of the processes of software development using different life cycles. Life cycles must be evaluated and tailored to the individual needs of each project. A general understanding of software development activities (software engineering) and how to define the software product are competencies needed for task and activity identification.

The project management skills needed here are a continuation of those needed for building the WBS, such as documenting plans in an arranged structure and finding tasks and activities that can be used to create a schedule. Activity ID requires the people skills of leadership, interface, and communication, as well as the ability to present ideas effectively throughout the identification process.

People management skills are needed the most here. Interaction and communications skills are vital to selecting the right people for the right activities. You may have to recruit people to your project, through interviews and a personnel-hiring process. Performance appraisal skills also are necessary to track progress and support career planning. Selecting and building a team come into play as you assemble resources for the activities. These are the skills and competencies to be touched on in this chapter.

Product Development Techniques

6. **Managing subcontractors**—Planning, managing, and monitoring performance
11. **Understanding development activities**—Learning the software development cycle

Project Management Skills

18. **Scheduling**—Creating a schedule and key milestones
21. **Tracking process**—Monitoring compliance of the project team

People Management Skills

23. **Appraising performance**—Evaluating teams to enhance performance
26. **Interaction and communication**—Dealing with developers, upper management, and other teams
29. **Negotiating successfully**—Resolving conflicts and negotiating successfully
30. **Planning careers**—Structuring and giving career guidance
32. **Recruiting**—Recruiting and interviewing team members successfully
33. **Selecting a team**—Choosing highly competent teams
34. **Teambuilding**—Forming, guiding, and maintaining an effective team

Learning Objectives for Chapter 12 _____

Upon completion of this chapter, the reader should be able to:

• Describe several different roles necessary for a software project;

• Describe the contents and purpose of a staffing management plan;

• Explain how to use a responsibility assignment matrix on a software project;

• Justify fitting a person to a role based on characteristics other than a specific skill;

• List and describe the characteristics of any role.

Organizational Planning _____

When you have a WBS list of customized activities that match the life cycle you have chosen for a project, you are ready to assign resources to them. But there are several important dimensions to the resource assignment process. For every activity in the project, you have to understand what the responsibilities and authority are and determine how the person performing the activity will be held accountable for results. You have to arrange and describe reporting relationships and roles on certain tasks. You have to balance career goals with project needs, optimize human interaction, and minimize barriers to achievement. These are not easy tasks for any project manager.

The project manager is responsible for the planning necessary to staff the project, which includes the functions of:

- Identifying and documenting the project roles and skills needed;
- Assigning responsibilities to individuals;
- Establishing reporting relationships.

Identifying and Documenting the Project Roles and Skills Needed

The project manager has to decide *who does what* and *who decides what* on the project. Deciding who does what is an exercise in career planning, balancing learning opportunities against accomplishing work on time and managing egos. The specific skills needed for each activity must be considered. It is sometimes valuable to list them if this is a new activity category for you or your team. This documentation is a necessity if the skill sets needed are very large and diverse. Then weigh the skills needed against what you know about each candidate's career objectives and ego needs.

Types of Roles

It may seem to be irrelevant to getting the job done (after all, this is *work*), but for the duration of a project team, matching the right people to assignments has a big payoff in team harmony and productivity. Sure, we're all software engineers, but within that profession are many specialties:

- Database designers;
- Configuration management experts;
- Human interface designers;
- Webmasters;
- Quality assurance (QA) specialists;
- Network specialists;
- System architects;
- Programming language experts (C, C++, Java, etc.);
- Buildmasters;
- Test engineers.

Recognize that the list may include some skills that aren't the usual software engineering set that we normally think of, but these may be crucial to getting the project done right. For example, there is often a person on a team who doesn't neatly fit into one of the formal classifications cited, but, because of his personality and social skills, is a necessary catalyst for getting things done. Sometimes these people get a "gopher" classification because they are not the lead on anything, but they get involved as helpers in everything. Their contributions are hard to measure on paper, but when they are not involved in tasks and activities, things seem to go slower, if any progress at all is made. They promote harmony among the team, act as intermediaries between cantankerous and egocentric team members with other specialties, and often provide a kind of "social glue" that is hard to define but absolutely necessary for team productivity. These "catalysts" or "glue" are often a necessary ingredient to make a workable project team. Recognize this, and plan for them accordingly.

For the more formal categories of skills, recognize that the skill sets needed may change over time, as the project moves through its various life cycle phases. Architects and designers are typically needed more at the front end of the life cycle. Programmers, webmasters, and network specialists are most needed in the middle phases. Buildmasters and testers become key toward the end of the development life cycle. Software QA specialists and configuration management experts tend to be needed throughout the life cycle. Exact needs and timing are determined by the development life cycle chosen for the project.

Characteristics of Roles

For every activity defined in the project, a set of roles requiring specific skill sets (or combinations) may be defined. For every role, the project manager must define three job aspects:

- Responsibility—The obligation to perform an assigned activity with or without detailed guidance or specific authority.
- Authority—The right to perform, command, or make decisions.
- Accountability—Assuming a liability for an activity or something of value in a project.

We know what happens when we assign responsibility to people who have no recognized authority within the organization to get it done. Estimates for completion become unreliable because the assigned person has an *obligation* to perform, but no *right* to perform, in the eyes of others in the organization; getting cooperation and assistance becomes difficult, if not impossible. Be sure that everyone recognizes the authority and responsibility boundaries for every role in the project.

Often overlooked when defining roles is the accountability aspect. The project manager should define a method for measuring the accomplishments for every role. This minimizes the problems of performance appraisals for project work later.

For instance, consider a test engineer. *Responsibilities* might include:

- Collaborating with architects and designers;
- Designing the test case;
- Generating test data;
- Running unit and regression test suites;
- Reporting results.

Authority might be granted within the project organization to include:

- Participating in design and inspection meetings;
- Exercising final authority for all test-related activities;
- Authorizing component builds;
- Reporting official test results and product quality metrics.

Accountability for the test engineers may be defined as quantifiable and easily measured parameters such as:

- Number of design and inspection meetings attended;
- Quantity and quality of tests prepared and executed;
- Percentage of successful component builds using components passing a quality gate;
- Accuracy and timeliness of reported test results and product quality metrics.

Definitions for each role may not be documented if the project team is small and well integrated, if the organization is so small that role boundaries are almost nonexistent and everyone does everything whenever it needs doing (common in many startup software development companies), or if the maturity level of the project organization is low. However, in large internal organizations running multiple projects, a standard set of role definitions can and should be developed. The organization's human resource professionals can often help in creating these standard definitions.

Another dimension to every role assignment is *reliability,* which is extremely important to the project manager. This, however, is assumed for most individuals taking project role assignments and is not usually documented as part of the role. It may be reflected in past performance appraisals or information from other project managers and leaders. Reliability refers to moral qualities as well as judgment, knowledge, skill, and habit. It implies that one is willing to put one's best effort into accomplishing the assigned activity. Implied or not, the project manager wants to be sure that everyone taking on project responsibilities can be relied upon to carry them out.

Assigning Responsibilities to Individuals

As project manager, your role in staff acquisition and assignment is to determine the specific time, cost, and resource commitments required to complete the project. This must be done for every activity. Some of these cannot be completed until after more planning has occurred, such as detailed activity estimates (Chapter 11, "Estimating Duration and Cost") derived from software size estimates (Chapter 10, "Software Size and Reuse Estimating"). It is also part of the project manager's role to negotiate with resource controllers for the services of the people with the needed skills, if necessary.

Comprehending Roll-On and Roll-Off

The project manager must also develop a roll-on and roll-off plan for each of the resources needed. This recognizes that showing five weeks of a Java developer starting on March 1 in your project plan to build a needed component assumes that the Java developer "hits the ground running" and doesn't waste time figuring out who's doing what, where everything is, what the overall architecture is, or how the Java development will fit into the product architecture and project plan. Instead, the resource should be reserved or acquired early enough for orientation before the skills are directly needed on the project. For resources from neighboring departments in a larger organization, this may need to be only a short period because the common company culture (acronyms, procedures, expectations, etc.) will carry over. But for new recruits, college hires, or geographically remote transfers (especially from culturally different areas or countries), this may take a considerable amount of time. This need seems obvious to most of us, but it is often overlooked in preparing software development project plans.

After completion of the activity, the person may need to execute roll-off activities before actually being removed from active participation in the project. Roll-off activities may include knowledge transfer to remaining team members, cleanup of local files and work spaces, documentation and hand-off of passwords, identification of the locations of project work products, or other actions needed when a team member leaves.

Typically, this roll-on and roll-off time is not included in effort estimates calculated from component sizes. It is usually not a good idea to just expand the activity estimates to include this time. If the estimates were made by a team or were made assuming that an average-skilled engineer would perform them, then the source of the resource was probably not included in the calculation. Of course, if the person to do the work is already identified, then roll-on and roll-off time can be included in the effort and time estimate when that person is asked to supply it.

Resource Assignment Strategy

Let's explore some strategies for assigning resources to activities. Resource assignment is not simply a case of handing out the various activities on your final lists to the people you have available; it is far more subtle (and powerful) than that. As a project manager, you have to look far beyond the single project; indeed any individual project can be seen as merely a single step in your team's development. The allocation of people to activities should thus be seen as a means of increasing the skills and experience of your team. When the project is complete, the team should have gained.

In simple terms, consider what each member of your team is capable of and allocate sufficient complexity of activities and tasks to match that (and to stretch them slightly). If at all possible, *activities should be molded to fit the people,* which is far more effective than the other way around. For example, if Joe is to learn something new on this project, the task or activity assigned to him may be simplified, with Mary assigned responsibility to guide him and check the work. If Andie is to develop her career, sufficient activities are combined so that her responsibility increases beyond what she has held before. If Perry lacks confidence, the activities assigned to him should be broken into smaller units, which can be completed (and celebrated) frequently.

Sometimes activities can be grouped together and assigned to one person or group for best effect. For instance, some activities that seem to be independent may benefit from being done together because they use common ideas, information, and talents. Assigning only one person to do them removes the startup time for one of them. Sometimes assigning two people where one would be the minimum necessary allows them to help each other, providing career growth.

Fitting a Person to a Role

Through his research at ITT in the 1980s, Bill Curtis discovered that it is better to hire people because of their traits than because of a specific skill as described on their resumes. Whenever possible, select team members for their compatible and complementary personality traits rather than their demonstrated skill in a particular area. This seems contrary to popular belief at first, but it makes sense when you understand that it is easier to train people in a new technical (and often rapidly changing) skill that is needed than to change their personality traits. Most people enjoy learning new things anyway. The training need not be formal. The general ability to rapidly learn and adjust to constantly changing information is often more valuable than deep experience in one or two skill areas, assuming basic competency in the core technologies. Of course, if the person's personality does not fit the activity very well, then stress results and disharmony begins to appear.

A useful instrument for identifying the potential of poor task and activity performance is the WorkStyle Patterns™ Inventory (WSPI) from the McFletcher Corporation. The purpose of the assessment is to identify how a person prefers to approach work versus the approach that his position or activity assignment requires; it may be administered by a facilitator certified by McFletcher. Analysis of discrepancies between a person's preferred workstyle and his actual workstyle can produce various degrees of stress, which may be manifested in a variety of ways.

McFletcher defines two kinds of stress: personal and organizational. Typical personal responses to stress include apathy and/or low productivity, irritability and frequent complaints, and health disorders or illnesses. Personal stress usually occurs because the person wants to perform more activities of a specific kind than the position requires. Organizational stress can be observed through misunderstandings of work expectations, product quality and customer service problems, missed deadlines, and high turnover. Organizational stress may result when the position requires more activities of a specific kind than the person is inclined to perform.

According to the inventory, a person may fall into one of the categories indicated in Table 12–1. Each of these profiles is explained in depth, and the contribution to the organization of each is described in the inventory booklet. The inventory (questionnaire) scores are graphed as a discrepancy of preference versus actual position, as shown in the example in Figure 12–3.

TABLE 12–1
McFletcher WorkStyle Inventory Model

Category	Focus	Types
Worker	Task	• Specialist • Perfecter • Technician • Worker • Superworker • Independent Worker
Supervisor	Project	• Guardian • Supervisor
Manager	Organization	• Adaptor • Synthesist • Innovator • Challenger • Manager • Promoter • Appraiser • Project Manager

The sample graph in Figure 12–3 shows profile scores for a team leader with a preferred workstyle of an independent worker and an actual position workstyle of supervisor. This person prefers to work independently through managing his or her own work. The position requires coordinating the work of others. Perhaps the team leader wants to perform more direct computer work, whereas the position requires more coordinating, coaching, and scheduling activities than he is inclined to do. This is typical for many technologists promoted to a position of leadership. This team leader may want to consider obtaining some coaching or even making a job change.

With this tool, the workstyles of each team member may be plotted on a summary chart, validating a complementary mix of workstyles, or exposing a conflict or imbalance.

Developing the Project Staffing Management Plan

As resource assignments that consider job and team fit, career plans, and project needs are made to activities in the WBS, a project-staffing plan takes shape. Typically, this information

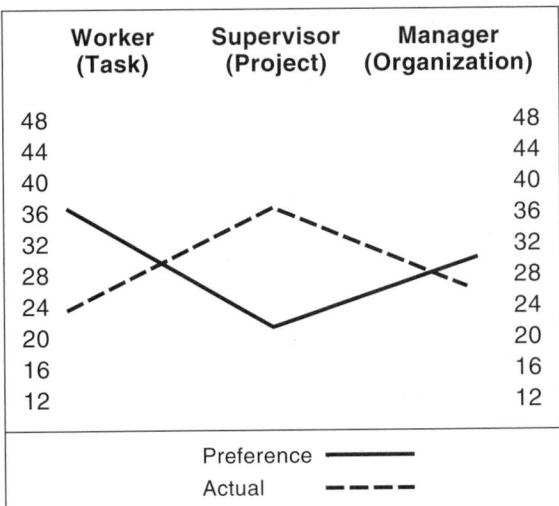

FIGURE 12–3
Sample McFletcher WorkStyle Inventory

is entered into a project management scheduling tool, such as Microsoft Project or an equivalent, and a staffing plan can start to be generated. Ultimately, this information becomes part of the software project management plan (SPMP), discussed elsewhere. The staffing plan will show how many of each role the project will need and when they will be needed. Some of this information will need to come from the dependency and scheduling activities described in Chapter 14, "Considering Dependencies," and Chapter 15, "Scheduling the Work." The staffing management plan is especially helpful for large development projects where many skilled people must be hired to fulfill project requirements months or years into the future. Typically, these are represented as histograms, with units expressed as hours or full-time equivalents (FTEs). An example staffing plan histogram is shown in Figure 12–4.

The staffing management plan contains information about skill, amount needed, schedule timing, and how the staffing will be done for each type of role. It may be formal or informal, highly detailed or broadly framed, based on the needs of the project and the organizational maturity of the organization. If the resources must be searched for and hired into the team, search professionals will want to have a staffing pool description available, which contains such information as:

- Skills and competencies needed;
- Experience level desired;
- Cost (salary) targets;
- Personal characteristics and interests for team fit;
- Availability requirements.

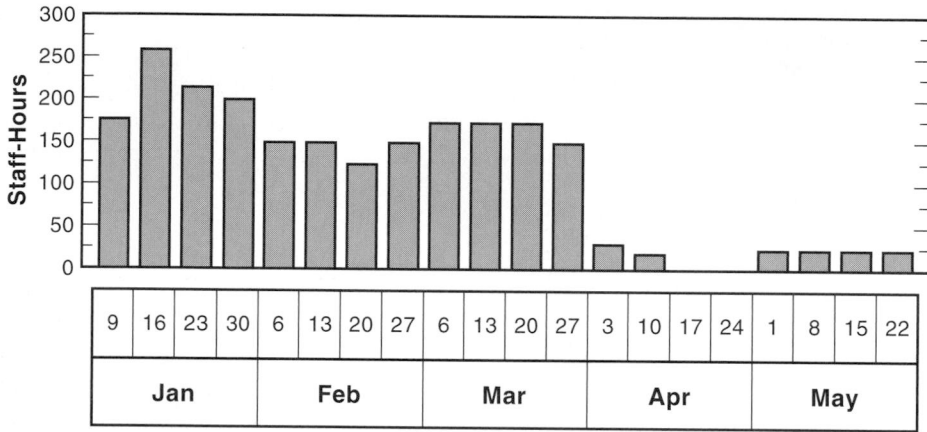

FIGURE 12–4
Staffing Plan Histogram

The search professional may need many other characteristics beyond those shown here. The staffing plan may also contain information about the reporting relationships needed to execute the project.

Establishing Reporting Relationships

When the staffing management plan has been started and assignment of people to roles has been done, the project manager can then define the reporting relationships expected to carry out the project's activities. Organizations get depicted for a software development project in many ways. The first and most obvious representation of reporting relationships is the classic organization chart. In large project organizations, these can get messy-looking if taken to the lowest levels of the organization. Sometimes they bruise egos, too. Another kind of chart depicting relationships is the organization breakdown structure (OBS) for the project, which relates parts of the organization to the work breakdown structure (WBS) elements and shows which organizational units are responsible for which work packages. Basically, the organization chart shows who gets direction from whom, and it identifies the paths of control for execution of the project activities in the WBS. The OBS shows which pieces of the total product are assigned to a given work group. These are useful representations for large projects, but they become cumbersome for small projects, where the WBS is relatively small and individuals execute the work packages.

Another useful tool is the project directory. This is simply a list of people working on the project, with appropriate contact information and group identity. It may even list stakeholders who are not part of the direct project team. This is useful to help maintain project stake-holder relationships. Even if all the team members come from the same company, grouping the project members in a separate directory is handy and useful. It also helps provide a sense of group identity. When the team members are widely dispersed and come from different companies or organizations (such as subcontractors), the directory becomes even more valuable.

Responsibility Assignment Matrix

One of the most useful tools for dealing with resource assignments is the responsibility assignment matrix (RAM). This sometimes appears under other names, such as responsibility matrix, staffing matrix, linear responsibility chart (LRC), or some variation of these names. The RAM clearly identifies an individual's responsibilities and roles for work products and activities. It defines *who* does *what* for the project activities, and it can easily be expanded into a work product progress tracking sheet. The basic components of a responsibility assignment matrix (RAM) are illustrated in Figure 12–5.

Where more than one person is assigned to a particular task, the RAM can identify who has the lead responsibility, who has backup, and who approves or validates. It helps the project manager sort out the *responsibility, authority,* and *accountability* for a task. Personality and job fit are major determinants of a person's *reliability* in a role. Typical role assignments may be:

- **A**pproval—Approves the item as complete (**L** approves, if not indicated);
- **L**ead—Has final responsibility for producing the item;

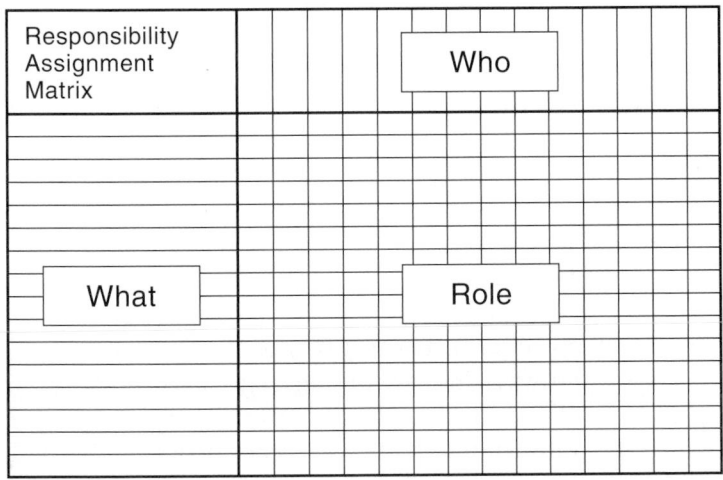

FIGURE 12–5
Responsibility Assignment Matrix

- **S**econdary—Is the lead person's backup for the item, else is a **C** and **R**;
- **C**ontributor—Materially contributes to the item (includes **R**);
- **R**eviewer—Has reviewer duties only for the item;
- (None)—Is not expected to participate in producing or approving the item.

An example resource assignment matrix using the A, L, S, C, and R codes for a software development project is shown in Figure 12–6. It also shows how the RAM can be used to balance the workloads and to ensure that leadership roles are equitably distributed. Additional columns can be added to the right to track work product status.

Resource Leveling

Often the needs for skills on the project are not convenient for the resource suppliers. That is, the timing of their involvement is spotty, or "lumpy," as viewed on the resource histogram in Figure 12–4. Ideally, you would like the roll-on and roll-off activities to occur *only once* for each resource on the project. For a software development project, we would like to concentrate the activities of the test engineers in the last few months of the development cycle rather than get them involved too much too early. This means that we should, if possible, try to schedule their activities on the various product components together, to maximize efficiency of their use. Sometimes this is essential (such as with contracted labor) because the same resource may not be available later in the project. Another example might be as illustrated in Figure 12–7, where, according to the scheduled work, we need too much of a resource in one or a few time periods, exceeding availability. In this case, we want to spread out the activities (flatten the histogram) so that usage never exceeds availability and we more efficiently use them while they are available (fill in the valleys between the peaks). This almost always lengthens the time needed to complete the work, as illustrated by the arrow in Figure 12–7, but it makes the usage of the resource more efficient. We will discuss more of the effects of resource leveling when we discuss dependencies in Chapter 14, and scheduling in Chapter 15.

Project Management Resource Activities During Execution

Assigning resources to activities in a development project is only part of the project manager's job. Another big part is developing those resources into a working, high-performance team capable of tackling difficult assignments and adjusting to changing project circumstances as required. The leader must manage all the different interfaces with other people and groups related to the product and the project. This is interface management, and it involves identifying, documenting, scheduling, communicating, and monitoring these interfaces throughout the course of the project.

Project X

Deliverable or Work Product (v2.2 12/1/98)

Item #	WBS #	Deliverable or Work Product	Completed	Advisory Cmte	Steering Cmte	Senior Advisor	Senior Advisor	PDM Advisor	Cust-Domain Expt	Program Mgr	Program Mgr	Systems Eng	Systems Eng	Systems Eng	Data Mgr	Tech Dev Lead	Tech Develop.	Tech Develop.	Tech Develop.	Tech Develop.	Technical Advisor	Approver (A)	Lead Developer (L)	Second Lead (S)	Contributor (C)	Reviewer (R)
	1.0	Initiate Project			A					L		S	C										1	1	1	1
1	1.2.2	Initial SW Project Mgmt Plan (SPMP)	X			R				L	R	R	L									0	1	1	0	1
2	1.2.3	Initial Web Site	X							R	R	R	L									0	1	0	0	2
3	1.2.4	Initial Calendar—Now Up-to-Date	X			A						L										1	1	0	0	0
4	1.2.5	Initial Config. Mgmt Plan (SCMP)—ADR	X							R		L	R									0	1	0	0	0
5	1.2.6	Initial Communications Plan (CP)	X	C					R	R		L	R									0	1	0	2	2
6	1.2.7	Initial Risk Management Plan (RMP)	X						R	C		L	R									0	1	1	2	2
7	1.2.8	Initial WBS	X						R	S		S	C									0	1	1	2	1
8	1.4	Q4 '97 Advisory Committee Workshop Summary	X	C						L												0	1	1	0	1
9	1.5	Initial SW Quality Assur Plan (SQAP)	X									L										0	1	0	0	0
	2.0	Preliminary Registry								R		R	L	S								0	0	1	0	2
10	2.4	Preliminary Registry SRS	X							R		R	L	S								0	1	1	0	2
11	2.6	Preliminary Registry Loading Document	X							R		R	L	S								0	1	1	0	2
	3.0	Research and Evaluate Automated Tools			A																					
12	3.1.6	Tool Evaluation Matrix	X		A	R			R	C		L	C									1	1	0	2	2
13	3.2.2	Tool Evaluation Report	X		A	R			R	C		L	C									1	1	0	2	2
	4.0	Containment—Document Rel Proc																								
14	4.2.8	QS 9000 Rel Procs for TX	X			A			R	S		L	C									1	1	1	1	1
15	4.3.1	Worksheet for Registry Data Entry	X			A			R	S		L	C									1	1	1	1	1
16	4.3.2	Test Prog Rel Proc Matrix (Stop Light)	X			A			R	S		L	C									1	1	1	1	1
17	4.4	Test Sites/Testers Report from Registry	X			A			R	S		L	C									1	1	1	1	1
18	4.5.5	QS 9000 Rel Procs (Updated)	X			A			R	S		L	C									1	1	1	1	1
		Close System Phase 1 Project																								
102	12.0	Post-Project Analysis Report			A	A			A	C	C	L	C									2	1	0	2	0
		Total		1	9	0	0	10	10	15		14	17	2								2	1	0	2	0

KEY:

A	Approval	Approves the item as complete (L approves if not indicated)
L	Lead	Has final responsibility for producing the item
S	Secondary	Is the lead person's backup for the item, also is a C and R
C	Contributor	Materially contributes to the item (includes R)
R	Reviewer	Has reviewer duties only for the item
None		Is not expected to participate in producing or approving the item

FIGURE 12–6
Example Responsibility Assignment Matrix

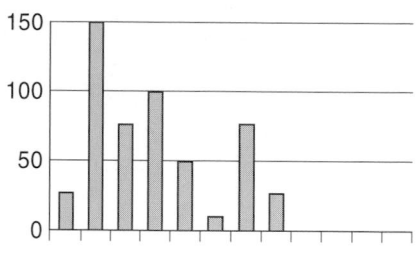 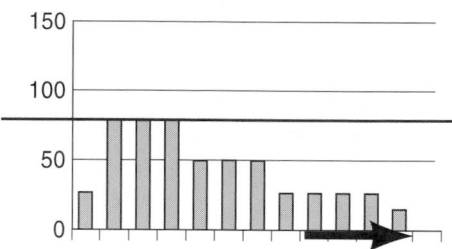

FIGURE 12–7
Resource Leveling

Three kinds of interfaces need attention: personal, organizational, and system. The *personal* interface deals with all conflicts involving people in or related to the project. Because projects invariably have many opportunities for conflict, the project manager is faced with being referee and peacemaker between individuals. The *organizational* interface deals with conflicts due to varying organizational goals and the different management styles of the project and resource supplying organizations. The project manager must bridge the differences and smooth communication both inside and outside the immediate organization or project. The *system* interface deals with the product, facility, or other nonpeople interfaces developed by the project. This typically includes all the technical problems of the project.

So, the project manager must manage these interfaces to balance and optimize human interaction and minimize barriers to completing the work.

Summary

In this chapter, we looked at how to assign resources when there is a WBS list of customized activities that match the chosen life cycle. The several dimensions to the resource assignment problem that a software development project manager should know about were discussed and analyzed while establishing the resource assignments. All programmers are not created equal. Jealousy and bickering can erupt over choice assignments, creating more work for the project manager to manage conflict within the team. Career paths intersect and fork. And workloads get unbalanced, leading to project schedule and morale problems.

In addressing all of these issues, the project manager's role in staffing a project and making resource choices was analyzed. These are part of human resource management. This chapter explored the roles found in software development projects, and you learned some strategies for fitting people to the roles. You saw the need for a staffing management plan and resource leveling in resource assignment for a project. The use of responsibility matrices was presented as one of the tools to use in assigning project resources as well.

Problems for Review _____

1. Describe a role you have had in your career that had only one of the three job aspects of responsibility, authority, and accountability. Were you successful in the role?

2. Under what specific circumstances would a responsibility assignment matrix not be needed? Why?

3. What additional information would you add to a responsibility assignment matrix, and why?

Visit the Case Study _____

Mr. Adams has reviewed the estimate done for the ARRS tool kit product and is not satisfied. Through discussions with Ms. Patel, he has three options for you to investigate in regard to project staffing:

1. Use the CRM personnel as originally planned, but improve their abilities through a boot-camp training program in software engineering.

2. Let the CRM folks continue on their own, and have the product built 100% by the BSD.

3. Outsource the development to the SourceForge (*www.sourceforge.net*) alliance and manage the development in parallel with the CRM.

Suggested Readings _____

Kerzner, Harold (1998). *Project Management: A Systems Approach to Planning, Scheduling, and Controlling,* 6th ed. New York, NY: John Wiley & Sons, Inc.

Lewis, James P. (1995). *Project Planning, Scheduling, and Control: A Hands-On Guide to Bringing Projects in on Time and on Budget,* revised edition. New York, NY: McGraw-Hill.

Paulk, Mark C., et al. (1994). *The Capability Maturity Model: Guidelines for Improving the Software Process.* New York, NY: Addison-Wesley.

Pressman, Roger S. (2001). *Software Engineering: A Practitioner's Approach,* 5th ed. New York, NY: McGraw-Hill.

Web Pages for Further Information _____

computer.org/software/. IEEE Software Magazine.

www.pmi.org/publictn/pmboktoc.htm. PMI's *A Guide to the Project Management Body of Knowledge (PMBOK® Guide),* Chapter 7.

www.sei.cmu.edu/. The Software Quality Institute.

www.swebok.org/. Guide to the Software Engineering Body of Knowledge. A project of the IEEE Computer Society, Software Engineering Coordinating Committee.

www2.umassd.edu/SWPI/sei/tr25f/tr25_12b.html. Software Project Planning, a key process area for level 2: Repeatable.

www2.umassd.edu/SWPI/sei/tr25f/tr25_12c.html. Software Project Tracking and Oversight, a key process area for level 2: Repeatable.

Choosing an Organizational Form

Just as there are many product development life cycles to choose from when planning a software development project, there are many organizational forms to choose from. How many kinds are there? Where did they come from? Where are they going? Which one is best under what circumstances? Exactly what is an organization, anyway? These are some of the questions that a software project manager might worry about when planning for a software development project.

This chapter describes what an organization is and discusses the typical organizational forms pertinent to a software project. Then we can discuss pros and cons of each form. It is important for the project manager to recognize which type of organization the project will operate within, and which type is best suited for the project at hand.

Where We Are in the Product Development Life Cycle

Where are we in the basic software life cycle model that serves as our map? As shown in Figure 13–1, we are still at the beginning of the product development life cycle, planning the project. In particular, we are planning *how* to do the project that we already defined in Chapters 7–9. The location of the organizational form selection activities is depicted in Figure 13–2.

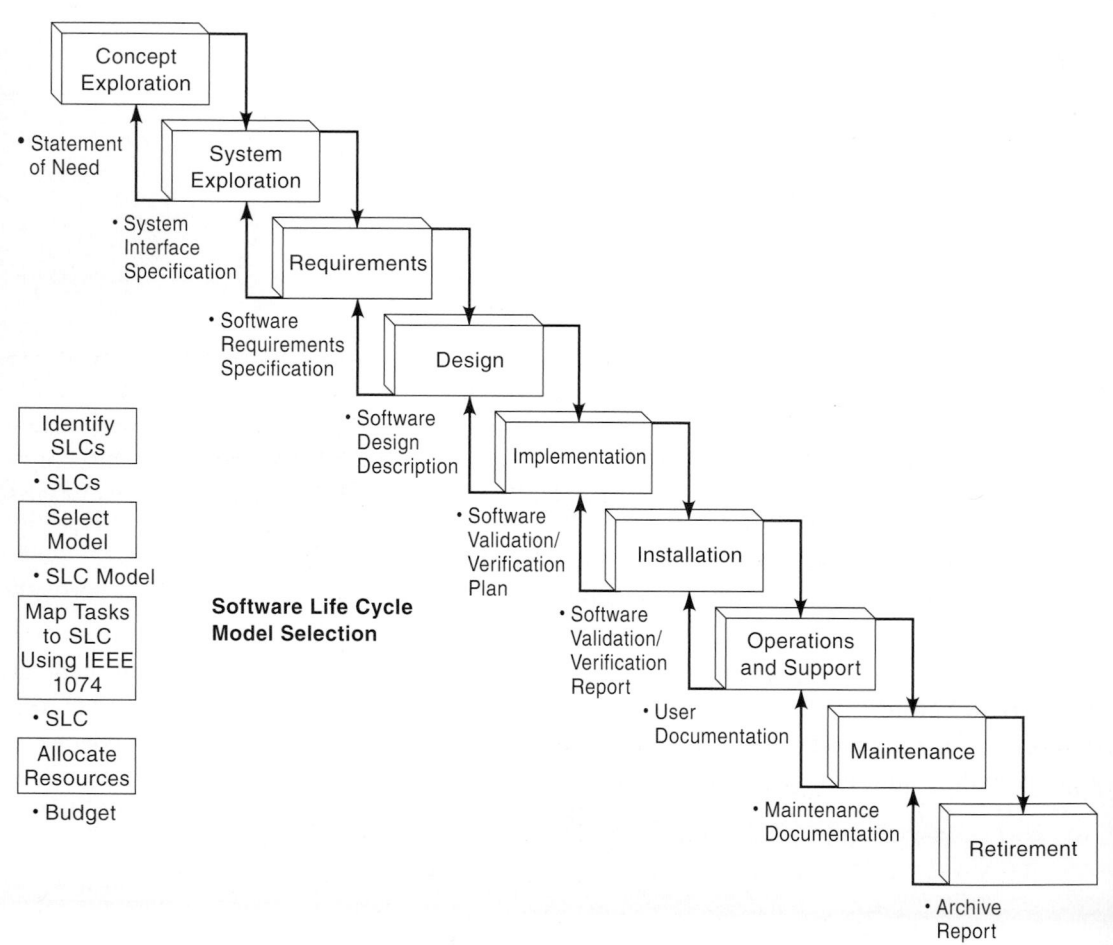

FIGURE 13–1
Product Development Life Cycle

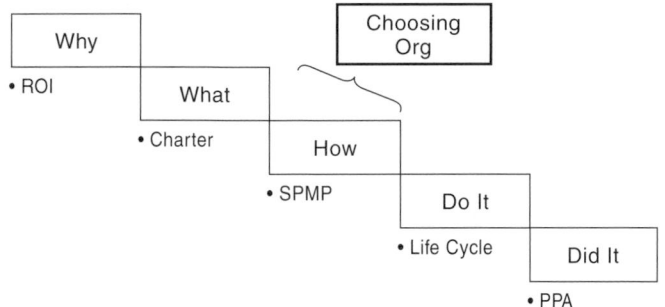

FIGURE 13–2
Project Process Framework

Chapter 13 Relation to the 34 Competencies _____

To properly understand and select an appropriate organizational form for a software development project, you must have an understanding of the competencies indicated.

Of course, in product development techniques, you must understand development activities and also know how to evaluate various approaches and how to select methods and tools. Tailoring existing structures to fit the current project is important to organizational design and has bearing on how to effectively manage and control any subcontracting relationships that may be needed. The project management skills required involve selecting project management tools and processes, as well as documenting the organizational choices made and the reasons for them. The people management skills needed are the leadership, interaction, and communication skills to appropriately select the organizational form and manage the changes necessary to implement a new organizational structure. All the preceding affect recruiting a staff and building them into an effective team, while furthering their careers from the work of the project. Your skill with these competencies helps determine the success chances for your software development project.

Product Development Techniques

4. **Evaluating alternative processes**—Evaluating various approaches
6. **Managing subcontractors**—Planning, managing, and monitoring performance
8. **Selecting methods and tools**—Defining selection processes
9. **Tailoring processes**—Modifying standard processes to suit a project
11. **Understanding development activities**—Learning the software development cycle

Project Management Skills

13. **Documenting plans**—Identifying key components
20. **Selecting project management tools**—Knowing how to select PM tools

People Management Skills

26. **Interaction and communication**—Dealing with developers, upper management, and other teams
27. **Leadership**—Coaching project teams for optimal results
28. **Managing change**—Being an effective change agent
30. **Planning careers**—Structuring and giving career guidance
32. **Recruiting**—Recruiting and interviewing team members successfully
33. **Selecting a team**—Choosing highly competent teams
34. **Teambuilding**—Forming, guiding, and maintaining an effective team

Learning Objectives for Chapter 13

Upon completion of this chapter, the reader should be able to:

- Describe how organizations evolved into the forms we have today;
- List and describe the organizational structures that a project may operate within;
- Describe a generic model of an organization;
- Evaluate which organizational form is best under what conditions;
- Define what an organization is, using at least four characteristics;
- List the forms of power that a person might have in an organization;
- List the steps and describe ways to make an organizational change effective.

What Is an Organization?

At this point in a project management life cycle, we are performing the *how* planning activities to build the *what* that the customer wants. When we have the work breakdown structure (WBS) developed enough to represent the work to do, we can consider possible organizational breakdowns to get it done. But what is an organization, and why is this a big deal? It's a big deal because the wrong organizational structure can make managing the development project much harder than it has to be. It's like boating: Choose the wrong vessel for the situation, and you may work much harder to make progress—or, worse yet, sink! If you have a large crew and stormy weather ahead, then you probably want a large, sturdy vessel capable of carrying a lot people, comfortably sheltered, with command and control all on the same ship, firmly planted on the bridge with the captain, in whose hands everyone's destiny lies. If there is good weather expected, a looser approach could be taken, using perhaps several smaller vessels in a loose flotilla, each with a captain, following general directions from existing navigation maps.

To get grounded in some basic organizational theory to help you understand the various organizational forms better, let's look at some classic organizational ideas and characteristics.

How Did Organizations Evolve?

Why do we have organizations in the first place? Aren't they all the same? No. Organizations go back thousands of years. Obviously, some form of organization was needed to build the pyramids in Egypt and Central America. Family and military needs drove other types. Families usually had a household leader, who coordinated the agricultural work necessary to survive. Military rank-and-file organizations were developed to attack and defend. These were the seeds of the organizational forms that we see around us today.

In the Agricultural Age, the concept of a "project" was not well formed. Most production took place on farms or in small villages. Trading, and often any necessary integration, was done in marketplaces. With the invention of the steam engine, the Industrial Age dawned, and large machines began to dominate the production scene. This meant that workers no longer could stay on the farms, but had to collect at large places called factories to produce products. A managerial structure was needed to control the activities of these largely uneducated workers. The most readily available structure was the military's, with its hierarchical chain of command. Indeed, much of our current organizational thinking is hierarchical, derived from military structures (CEOs are like generals, VPs are like colonels, division heads are like majors, department heads are like captains, etc.). This may be why people at the lowest parts of an organization are often called the "troops."

Much of our current corporate structure comes from the heritage of Henri Fayol (1841–1925), a French mining engineer at the Comambault Co. in the late 1800s, and a German named Max Weber (pronounced *vay*-bur), among others. Weber (1864–1920) is considered "The Father of Bureaucracy." In fact, *bureaucracy* is derived from the German word for "management by the office" (as opposed to "by the person," which is patrimonial management), and it did not originally have the bad connotation we give it today. Fayol is credited with invention of many of the organizing ideas that we call the "principles of management." Fayol and Weber's "principles of management" are characterized as:

- Division of work;
- Centralization;
- Authority;
- Discipline;

- Hierarchical structure;
- Functionally oriented;
- Silos of specialty;
- Decision and promotion path that is vertical within a silo, with project activities divided by specialties and disciplines.

Organizing around these principles is why we typically have all the marketing people in the marketing department, the engineering people in the engineering department, and so on. At the turn of the century, most workers were illiterate, so all decisions in a specialty had to be made by management at ever-higher echelons and then passed down to the "troops" at the bottom, who were merely considered "cogs" in the machinery. This was okay because the world didn't change at Internet speed yet, and the troops really didn't have enough education to make very big decisions.

Around the turn of the 19th Century, a mechanical engineer named Fredrick Taylor began what came to be known as the scientific management approach. This was all about efficiency experts and time and motion studies. He spawned a number of disciples, such as Frank and Lillian Gilbreth of *Cheaper by the Dozen* fame, and Henry L. Gantt, who gave us the now famous Gantt chart. Later, their ideas of workers as "cogs" gave way to the concepts of productivity achieved through employee satisfaction and empowerment that we know of today. As the education level of the average worker grew, the need for hierarchical management faded, and, in the face of cost and poor-quality pressures in the 1980s, gave way to flatter organizations with fewer managers and less direct command and control. Instead, empowered teams emerged to make decisions at a lower level in the organization, across functional department boundaries. The matrix approach to management that emerged in the 1960s (explained later in this chapter) using cross-functional teams from the 1980s has become the most prevalent form of organization seen in project work today.

Are Organizational Styles Changing?

As we enter the knowledge economy of the Information Age at the turn of the 20th Century and things seem to move much faster (at Internet speed) than ever before, organizational styles continue to shift at an ever-faster rate. Figure 13–3 illustrates how the hierarchical forms of organization are shifting toward flatter, more loosely structured, team-based styles. You could say that there is a parallel here to the differences between classical structured programming on mainframes and object-oriented programming in client/server environments.

This illustration recognizes that there are both formal and informal organizations in existence in any situation. The formal one is expressed in the organization chart. The informal one is a web of relationships that typically crosses formal boundaries (the World Wide Web was aptly named and is a good metaphor for a peer-to-peer network that crosses formal organizational boundaries). The team-based organizational model is one in which members may belong to several teams with different goals. Hopefully, all the team goals achieve some

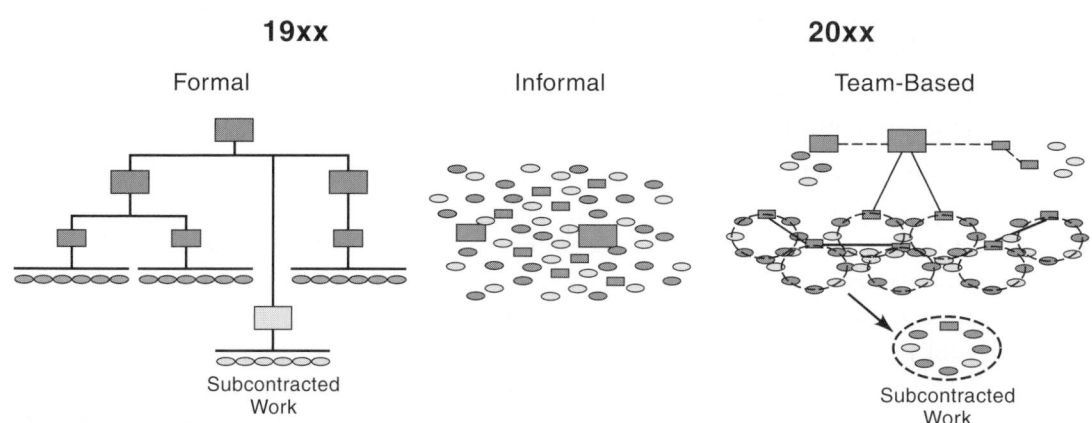

FIGURE 13–3
Shifting Organizational Styles

strategic purpose set by the strategic apex of the larger organization. Some of these teams may be focused on improvement of ongoing operations or may be project teams focused on one-time project objectives. As depicted in Figure 13–3, you can see how information flow could wind through the organization very rapidly, as people carry information from one team meeting to another. This is the "grapevine" that seems to carry news faster than official company communiqués.

Characteristics of an Organization

Several dimensions must be considered in the assessment of the organizational climate for managing a software development project in an organization:

- Model;
- Maturity;
- Thickness;
- Size;
- Dispersion;
- Structure.

But first, let's define what an organization is. Management literature contains several definitions:

- "An organization is a system that exchanges materials, personnel, manpower, and energy with the environment."—James L. Bowditch and Anthony F. Buono[1]

- "An organization is group of people with stated and formal goals."—Paul Hersey and Kenneth H. Blanchard[2]

- "Organizations can be defined as groups of people who must coordinate their activities in order to meet organizational objectives."—Harold Kerzner[3]

Some of these emphasize different characteristics. The definition that we'll use separates a collection from a group, and a group from an organization. A *collection* is just a bunch of people who are not interacting, with or without a common purpose. People in an elevator are a usually just a random collection of people sharing a public space. They become a group if they begin to interact with one another, and they become an organization if a goal is defined and some rules for group behavior are put in place (implicitly or explicitly). So, an *organization* is an interacting group of people with a unifying goal. A bunch of random people (a collection) who get trapped in an elevator soon become a group, and then an organization, with the unifying goal of trying to get out. Significant interaction begins. Goals, roles, and rules are verbally established. Leaders and specialists emerge, and, hopefully, so do they eventually.

But this is just a word model. Some kind of visual organizational model should be depicted. Management and organizational behavior literature is full of them, so they are not hard to find. But mapping an organization to some kind of model is important because it gives us a framework for understanding and change.

Generic Model of an Organization

It seems that there are almost as many organizational models as there are organizations in the world. Let's look at a generic model for an organization to understand the basic elements. Henry Mintzberg described a generic organization as having five main parts:

- Strategic apex—leadership that sets strategic direction;
- Middle line management—translation of strategic direction into tactical plans;
- Operating core—execution of the plans to produce the product/service;
- Technostructure—technical infrastructure supporting the operating core;
- Support staff—people infrastructure supporting all the organization's parts.

These are illustrated in Figure 13–4. Some call this the "mushroom cloud" depiction of an organization (a joke). But the center represents the main function of the business (to produce services such as software engineering and products such as software executable products). The technostructure usually consists of the engineering functions that define the main business (semiconductor manufacturing, Web design services, etc.), and the support staff includes administrative services, computer and network support, human resources, and so on).

You can think of any project organization as needing the same elements to be effective. If the project operates within a larger organization, then it may rely on the technostructure and support staff for many of its basic operating needs. The strategic management for a project

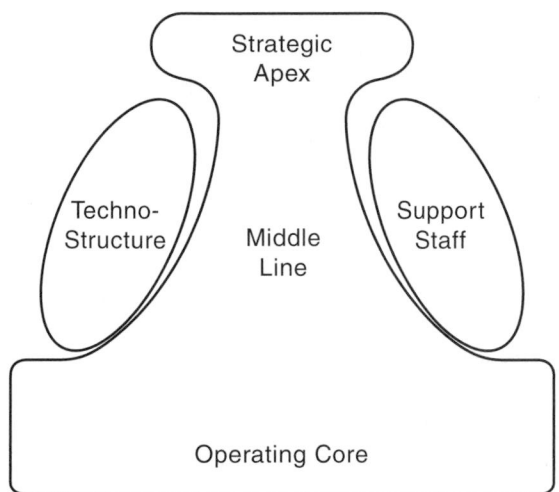

FIGURE 13–4

A Generic Organizational Structure

Source: Mintzberg, Henry (1993). *Structures in Fives: Designing Effective Organizations*. New York, NY: Prentice Hall. p. 11.

comes from the project manager, through interpretations of the goals of the customer, expressed in requirements. The support staff and technostructure for software engineering projects include configuration management, network support, and administrative services such as copying and supply management. The operating core for a software project are the software engineers who construct and implement the design using computer technology, often in small teams led by middle line managers or subproject managers.

Does Organization Size Matter?

Obviously, size is an important characteristic for an organization performing projects and programs. The size of the desired system product determines the size of the organization needed to produce it. The number of human interactions available and necessary in a project organization is one determinant of the project management climate in an organization. More people are not necessarily better, though.

If the size of the effort is important, what size is important in most businesses? Projects and programs operate within a larger business systems context, and, indeed, many businesses are completely organized around projects. Startup companies tend to have a lot of projects going on at once to put some revenue-generating products into service as quickly as possible. These businesses are totally organized around products and services, which must be market-sensitive. It is useful to consider a range of possible projects within two dimensions: staff size and project length. Figure 13–5 shows that not enough staff working on a project that stretches out too long results in an insensitivity to the marketplace, whereas too many people working on a "crash" project is impossible to manage. New products and major assets tend to follow a band moving from the lower left to the upper right. The scales for the x- and y-axes in this figure, and the width of the "sweet spot" band, will vary for most companies, but the general principle and relationships hold true.

Dispersed or Collocated

Another factor related to size is dispersion. The more widely dispersed a project team organization is, the more complicated it is for the people within it to interact. Today's telecommunications technologies have blurred many boundaries, but there is still nothing like face-to-face human interaction for getting things done. Figure 13–6 illustrates dispersed and collocated team member's interactions. The collocated team members share the same room, floor, building, or office campus (1), whereas the dispersed team members are in separate facilities (1, 2, 3, and 4), perhaps halfway around the world from each other. This situation produces special problems for the software development project manager. Cultural differences emerge, and it becomes physically harder to communicate due to time shifts, language issues, and the difficulty of maintaining a common technical and project infrastructure. See Appendix E, "Distance Project Management," for more information about running a project using distance project management.

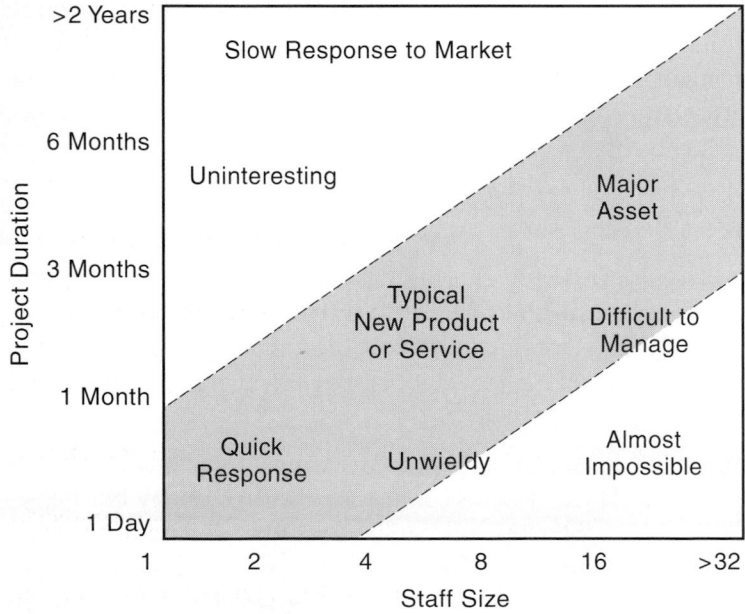

FIGURE 13–5
Market Sensitivities to Project Size and Duration

Collocated Team Members   Dispersed Team Members

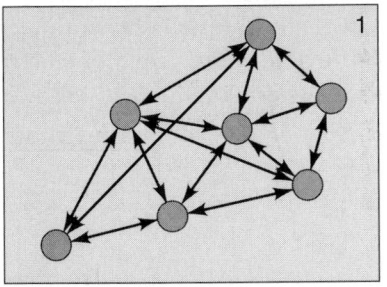 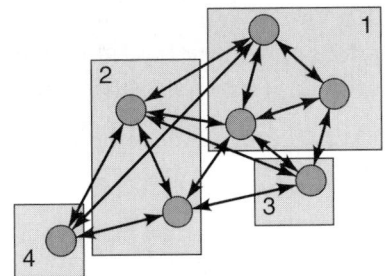

FIGURE 13-6
Dispersed and Collocated Project Team Organizations

The Relative Power of the Project Manager

Another important dimension for a project organization is how much authority and power the project manager has. We can think of an ideal software development project manager as the CEO of the project, with everyone involved reporting to him (and no one else). Unfortunately, this is rarely the case. But a project manager with no power is unlikely to get anything done. Power over others can come from several sources. According to Hersey and Blanchard, the types of power that a project manager might have are:

1. **Legitimate**—the perception that it is appropriate for the leader to make decisions due to title or position in the organization;
2. **Reward**—the perceived ability to provide things that people would like to have;
3. **Connection**—the perceived association with influential persons or organizations;
4. **Coercive**—the perceived ability to provide sanctions or consequences for nonperformance;
5. **Expert**—the perception that the leader has relevant education, experience, and expertise;
6. **Information**—the perceived access to or possession of useful information;
7. **Referent**—the perceived attractiveness of interacting with another person.

Numbers 1, 2, 3, and 4 in the list are based on a person's position in the organization and are called the *positional power* types. Numbers 5, 6, and 7 are called the *personal power* types. Technically oriented software engineers who rise to project leadership often have a great deal of expert and informational power. If they are well liked, then they also have referent power. Their leadership position gives them varying amounts of positional power, depending on the organization structure of the surrounding environment.

Organizational Maturity

Consider the maturity of the organization. Startups seem to behave differently from long-established corporations. They are typically characterized as flexible, fluid, energetic, and usually small. Maturity has to do with the formality of the processes they define and follow.

Characteristics of immature organizations include:

- *Ad hoc* processes, improvised by their practitioners and management;
- Processes and rules that are not rigorously followed or enforced;
- High dependence on current practitioners;
- Likeliness of having cost and schedule problems;
- Product or service functionality and quality compromised to meet schedule;
- Quality that is difficult to predict.

To an outsider looking in, an immature organization's processes may look like Figure 13–7.

In contrast, some characteristics of mature organizations are:

- Processes that are defined, documented, and continuously improving;
- Documented processes that are consistent with the way work actually gets done;
- Visible support by management and engineering;
- Well-controlled, audited, and enforced policies;
- Product and process measurements that are gathered and used;
- Disciplined use of technology.

A mature organization's processes may look more like Figure 13–8 to an outsider.

FIGURE 13–7
Immature Processes as Observed from Outside the Organization

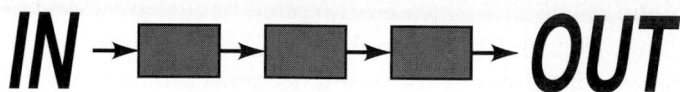

FIGURE 13–8
Mature Processes as Observed from Outside the Organization

Related closely to maturity is thickness or thinness of the organization's culture. Well-understood and followed norms, rules, and processes characterize a thick culture. The IBM of the 1980s was routinely described as a thick corporate culture, with long-established and set ways to behave, embodied in many formal processes for doing almost anything. Many analysts thought that it got too thick to be responsive to the rapidly changing computer marketplace. Thin cultures tend to be far looser and more individualistic. Your average dotcom startup company fits that model.

Organizational Structures

Now that we have a basic understanding of organizations in general, we can look at the common forms that a software development project manager may encounter. In the 1960s and 1970s, several forms of organization were being discussed in the literature. These are shown in Table 13–1.

TABLE 13–1
Types of Organizations

Types of Organizations		Organization of the Skills	Skill Specialists Report To
Functional		Grouped into functional specialties	Functional group leader only
Matrix	*Weak, balanced,* or *strong,* depending on the relative power of the functional and project leaders	Grouped into functional specialties, but assigned to projects as needed	Functional group leader, **and** to project leader(s)
Projectized		All skills needed are assigned to the project full-time	Project leader only
A Combination of the Above		Varies	Varies

In a 1977 article in the *Project Management Quarterly* ("Organizational Alternatives for Project Management"), Robert Youker proposed that the various organizational forms in the literature at the time fell on a spectrum. This made it easier to grasp which forms might be appropriate for a given type of project. The spectrum has the classical highly structured functional organization on one side (where functional specialists report only to the functional area leader) and organizations that are totally "owned" by project managers on the other (where everyone, regardless of specialty, reports to a project manager who is not one of the functional managers). In between are several forms of the matrix organization. Let's examine some of them.

Functional Organizations

The functional organization is what most of us think of as a "standard" old-fashioned organization (the 19xx side of Figure 13–3). It is the style in which people are divided into their functional specialties (remember Fayol's Principles of Management, discussed earlier?), and report to a functional area manager. For instance, all the software engineers in a company would be in the engineering department and would report to the engineering department manager. The same would be true for the operations people and the marketing people, and so on. A typical functional organization chart would look something like Figure 13–9.

The advantages of a purely functional organizational form are that it:

- Clearly defines authority—each specialist reports to only one manager;
- Eliminates duplication of functions—all engineers are in one group, marketing personnel is in another, and so on;
- Encourages technical competence and specialization—engineers sit near other engineers;
- Provides career paths for specialized skills—people see a career path within the department;
- Focuses attention on key functions—concentration on core competencies is encouraged.

There are some important disadvantages as well. The functional form:

- Lacks customer orientation and has "walls" to throw work over to the next function in a process;
- Implies a long decision cycle because it requires going up functional silos to get cross-group decisions;
- Has no single function accountable for the overall project, so project leaders have little power;

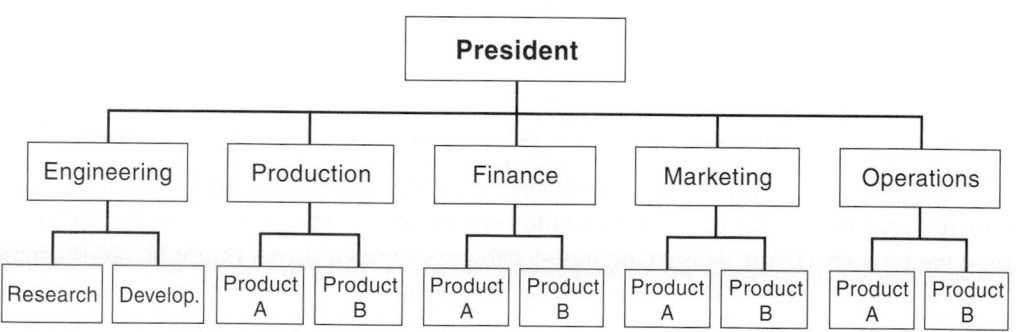

FIGURE 13–9
Typical Functional Organization
Source: Cable, Dwayne, and John R. Adams. *Organizing for Project Management.* pp. 11–20.

- Makes it difficult to coordinate activities across specialized functions due to the long decision cycle;
- Allows for conflicts between functional areas and bickering because of lack of customer focus.

A purely functional organization has no cross-functional projects. Anyone trying to lead a project requiring resources in other departments would have to get permission to borrow time from each of the functional managers' specialists when they were needed on the project. The project organization chart would need to cut across the functional silos of the larger organization. Two derivatives of this form are the project expediter organization and the project coordinator organization.

Project Expediter Organization   The expediter in a functional organization has very little authority to do anything. Most of the power of the position is derived from the manager that the expediter reports to, which is usually very low in the hierarchy. This kind of project organization fits highly functional organizations and small projects. The project workers remain in their functional organizations. The expediter must be a *very* persuasive person to be effective, motivating workers with no real authority. This requires a lot of personal power for the project manager. The expediter role is characterized as:

- Holding a staff assistant role;
- Making few decisions;
- Being responsible for the arrival of material and completion of tasks;
- Being primarily responsible for communications about the project;
- Needing special people skills and unique technical abilities;
- Forwarding decisions by superiors to people on the project.

An expediter organization is illustrated in Figure 13–10.

Project Coordinator   This subset of the functional form is very similar to the expediter form, but the coordinator usually reports to a manager higher in the functional hierarchy. The project coordinator has authority to assign work, but he shares this authority with the workers' functional managers. The coordinator organization form is illustrated in Figure 13–11.

Some of the disadvantages of this form are:

- Upper management is usually reluctant to relinquish power and authority to project managers.
- Upper management is usually not ready to cope with the problems of shared authority.
- Line-staff project managers who report to division heads have no authority or control over the portions of the project in other divisions.

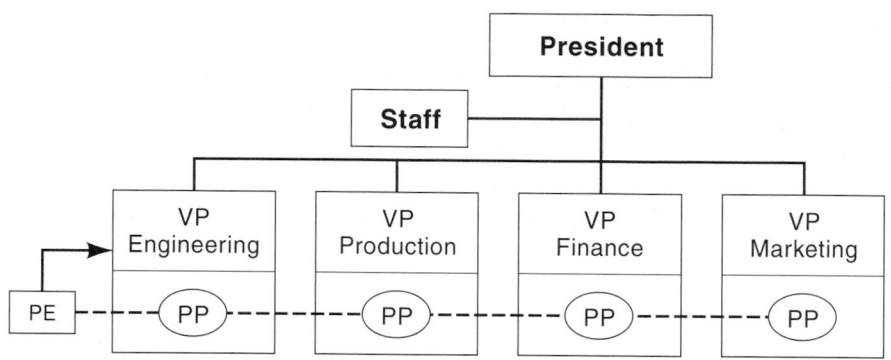

PE—Project Expeditor/Manager
PP—People Working on Various Aspects of the Project

FIGURE 13–10
Project Expediter Organization
Source: Cable, Dwayne, and John R. Adams. *Organizing for Project Management.* pp. 11–20.

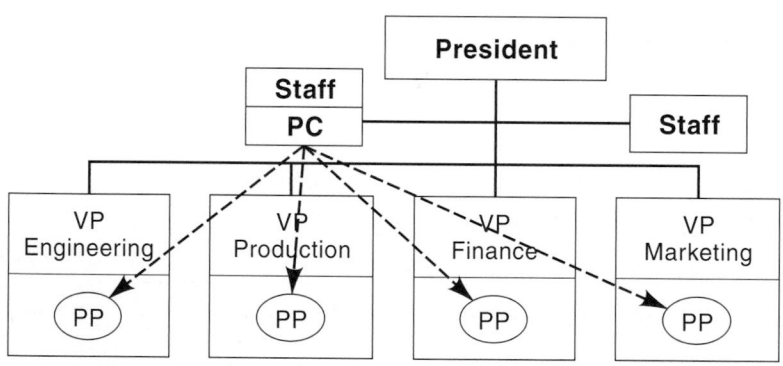

PC—Project Coordinator/Manager
PP—People Working on Various Aspects of the Project

FIGURE 13–11
Project Coordinator Organization
Source: Cable, Dwayne, and John R. Adams. *Organizing for Project Management.* pp. 11–20.

In either form, the project manager has little positional power to get things done. The coordinator form gives the project manager a little more power because he reports higher in the larger organization. In either organization, it is very difficult for a project manager to get anything done on time because the various specialists needed will take their direction from the (very powerful) functional managers.

Matrix Organizations

Matrix management is a relatively new invention, coming into view in the 1960s and put into practice in the 1970s. In matrix organizations, there is a balance of power established between the functional and project managers. The project worker in a matrix organization has a multiple command system of accountability and responsibility. Although it varies from organization to organization, we can usually find several chains of command inside a matrix organization. They can be linked by function, geographic location, or project, product, or client. A typical matrix structure is illustrated in Figure 13–12.

Usually three types of matrix organizations are described: weak, balanced, and strong. The differences are in the relative balance of power between the functional manager and the project manager. The matrix organization is the most commonly encountered form today.

The characteristic advantages of a matrix are manifold:

- Enables project objectives to be clearly communicated;
- Permits project integration to be done across functional lines;
- Makes efficient use of resources;
- Enhances information flow within an organization;
- Retains functional disciplinary teams;

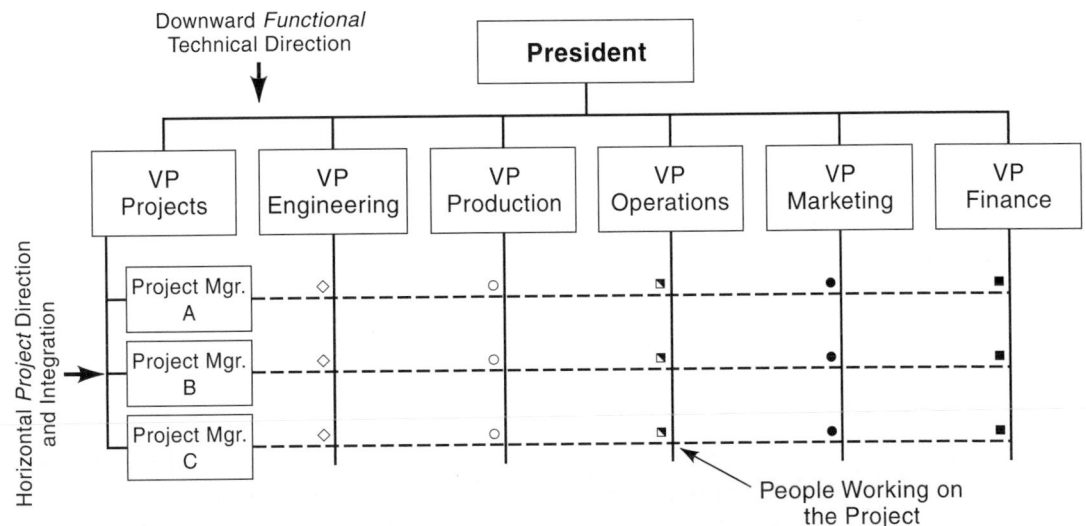

FIGURE 13–12

Matrix Organization

Source: Cable, Dwayne, and John R. Adams. *Organizing for Project Management.* pp. 11–20.

- Encourages higher morale;
- Develops project managers;
- Makes project termination less traumatic;
- Makes conflicts minimal and more easily resolved.

But the matrix is not without drawbacks:

- Project personnel must report to (at least) *two* bosses.
- It is complex to monitor and control.
- Resource allocation and project priorities can conflict.
- Functional and project management may have differing priorities.
- It requires extensive efforts to establish policies and procedures that work.
- More administrative personnel are required to manage the organization.
- It creates duplication of effort across projects.

Projectized Organizations

Projectized organizations are newer still, associated with thinking in the 1980s and 1990s, even though the first actual "project" credited with following the principles of project management was the Manhattan Project to build the first atomic bomb in the 1940s. In projectized organizations, the project manager (sometimes called a program manager) has total authority and acts like a mini-CEO. All personnel assigned to the project report to project manager, usually in a vertical organization, so the company becomes like a layered matrix. The projectized organization is illustrated in Figure 13–13. Examples of projectized organizations are the large defense contracts for avionics in aircraft projects and any pure construction project. Also, the motion picture industry utilizes this form for each movie produced.

The clear advantages for a project in this form of organization are that it establishes a unity of command and promotes more effective communication.

The disadvantages are that it fosters duplication of facilities and inefficient use of resources, and project team members work themselves out of a job (at project completion).

This latter one is especially important as, toward the end of the current project, the workers' attention begins to shift to pursuing their next project. This should be considered when planning the final activities in a projectized organization.

So how do you apply these structures to a software development project situation? There is no one answer for any given project, but rather a spectrum of possibilities. The terms (*projectized, functional, matrix*, etc.) have many variations. Robert Youker's Table 13–2 suggests a guide to selecting the right kind of organizational structure.

To use the chart, consider the characteristics of your development project and circle the descriptions in each row that seem to best apply. When the characterization is complete, look

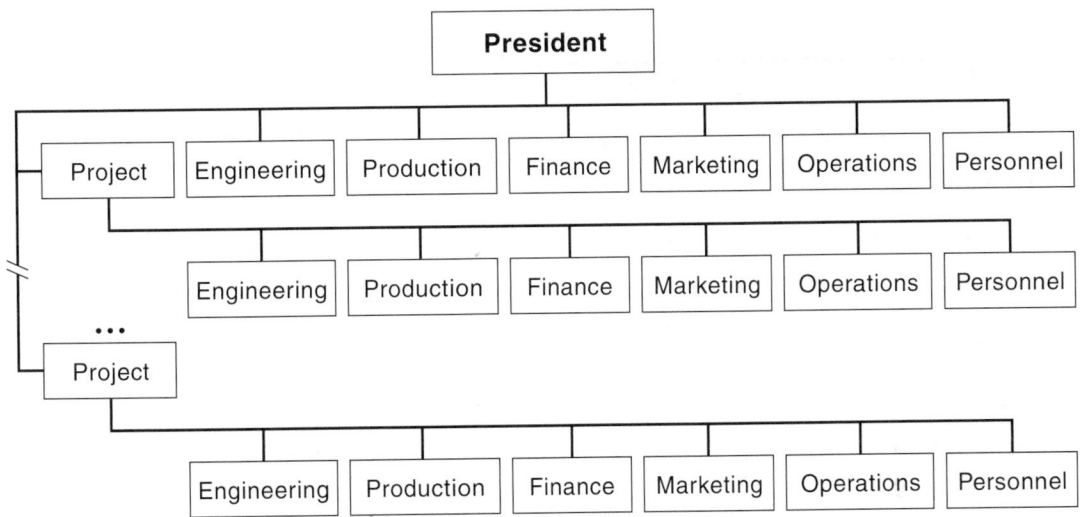

FIGURE 13-13
Projectized Organization
Source: Cable, Dwayne, and John R. Adams. *Organizing for Project Management*. pp. 11–20.

at the column(s) where most of the circled descriptions are, for a sense of which organizational structure would fit your project best.

Most modern organizations today employ some kind of blend of these forms, depending on specific needs. Many of us who have worked in industry or government for a while are familiar with the pros and cons mentioned for these different types of organizations. The majority of organizations have a constant power struggle between the functional and project managers. Figure 13–14 illustrates this concept.

Implementing an Organizational Structure _____

When you have chosen an organizational structure suitable to the conditions of your project environment, you may find some resistance to implementing it, especially if you have a low power base. This section will give you some background to help implement a change in the cultural fabric for the project team.

Suppose that the characteristics of your project as indicated by analysis using Table 13–1 show that a strong matrix organization would give the project the best chance of success. But long-entrenched functional managers in your organization have most of the power and outweigh project managers by a considerable margin. How do you "sell" sponsors on the idea for changing the organization to one in which the software development project manager

TABLE 13–2

Characteristics of Projects by Organizational Structure

Project Characteristics	Functional	Matrix		Projectized
		Weak	**Strong**	
Uncertainty	Low	Moderate	High	High
Technology	Standard	Standard	Complex	New
Complexity	Low	Low	Medium	High
Duration	Short	Medium	Medium	Long
Size	Small	Small	Medium	Large
Importance	Low	Moderate	Moderate	High
Customer	Diverse	Diverse	3 or 4	One
Interdependency (Within)	Low	Medium	Medium	High
Interdependency (Between)	High	Medium	Medium	Low
Time Criticality	Low	Moderate	Moderate	High
Resource Criticality	Depends	Depends	Depends	Depends
Differentiation	Low	Low	High	Medium

Source: Youker, Robert (1977). "Organizational Alternatives for Project Management." *Project Management Quarterly,* 8(1):21.

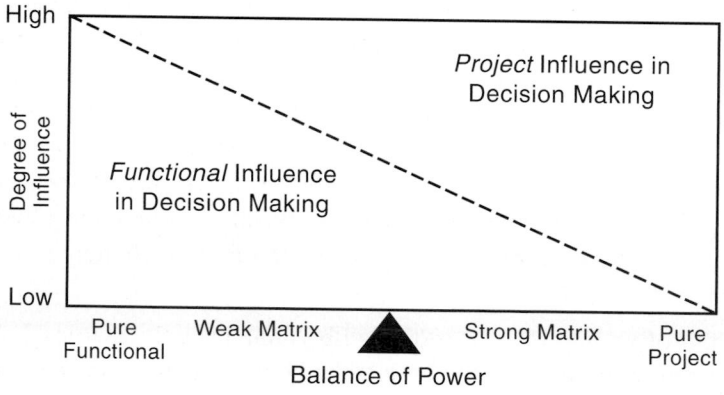

FIGURE 13–14

Relative Balance of Power Between Functional and Project Managers

Source: Cable, Dwayne, and John R. Adams. *Organizing for Project Management.* pp. 11–20.

has more power than the functional department heads? This can be a political minefield, but a few important ideas can help you navigate it.

First, recognize—and then convince your associates—that special project circumstances require a special organization. Emphasize that a project is a *temporary endeavor* to achieve certain goals and that this doesn't represent a permanent power shift. Sometimes the entrenched functional managers don't believe in project management concepts at all (whether they will admit it or not) because they did not rise to their position of power in the organization by using them.

Understand that any organization's culture is in equilibrium and that any change to it seems threatening. What you want is a change in overall group behavior, to recognize and accept the new organizational approach. People go through four stages when implementing a major change to their world:

1. **Awareness**—People get *familiar with the terms* that represent an initiative or a new process and have a perception of the accompanying issues.

2. **Questioning/understanding**—People get an *understanding* of what the change or initiative is and *appreciate* its implications and importance to their organization.

3. **Acceptance**—People have the *knowledge* needed to be intellectually prepared and understand how the initiative affects their job and/or functional organization, and how they can contribute to the success/failure.

4. **Ownership**—People become *personally committed* to making the initiative successful in their department and at their job.

These stages must be passed through to achieve the change. When Stage 4 is reached, people will embrace the changes and try to make them work. Stages 1, 2, and 3 require individual attitude adjustments through knowledge. Figure 13–15 shows that personal power is a good approach to changing knowledge and individual attitudes toward a change. This is persuasion through expert and information power, mixed with charisma. Positional power can mandate group behavior (like having a powerful sponsor announce a change), but it doesn't have too much effect on changing individual attitudes. The impact of approaching the change from the personal power side in the lower left diminishes the farther to the upper right you go. Likewise, the impact of positional power from the upper right diminishes as you move toward the lower left of the figure. So, the cultural change problem must be approached from both directions.

Recognize that fear of change provides much of the resistance in most organizations. Change is scary because it involves the unknown and leaves the comfort of the status quo. Kurt Lewin proposed a model implementing cultural changes in an organization called Force Field Analysis (see Figure 13–16). The model basically says that there are a set of restraining forces and a set of driving forces that are in equilibrium in any cultural situation. To implement a change, you must insightfully inspect the culture to identify these forces and

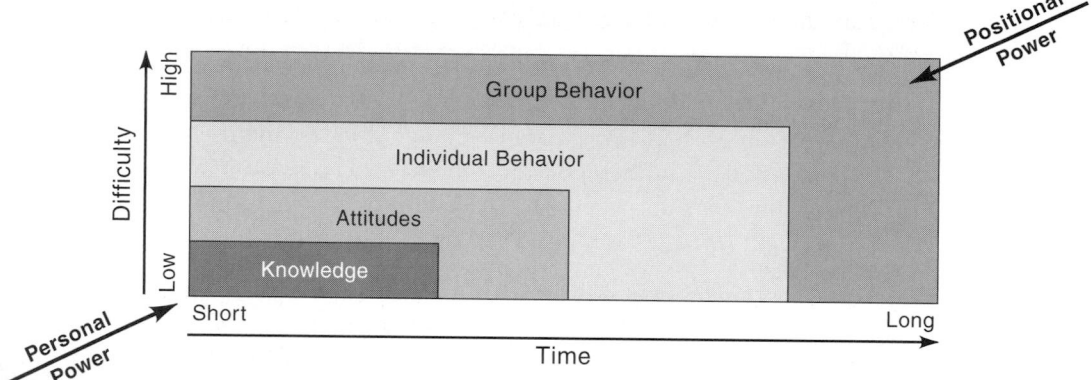

FIGURE 13–15
The Path to Modified Group Behavior
Source: Hersey, Paul, and Kenneth H. Blanchard (1993). *Management of Organizational Behavior,* 6th ed. Englewood Cliffs, NJ: Prentice Hall.

then take specific actions that reduce the restraining forces and strengthen the driving forces. Often this just means rewarding the behavior that you really want and not rewarding what you don't want. Rewards could be material or social, but they must directly reinforce the desired behavior. Mandating organizational changes without changing the reward structure guarantees failure. People instinctively know where their bread is buttered.

Lastly, recognize that change is, by nature, disruptive. We believe that organizational changes will lead to a better situation than before the change. Critics often point to poorer performance amid the confusion of a change implementation and say that things are worse.

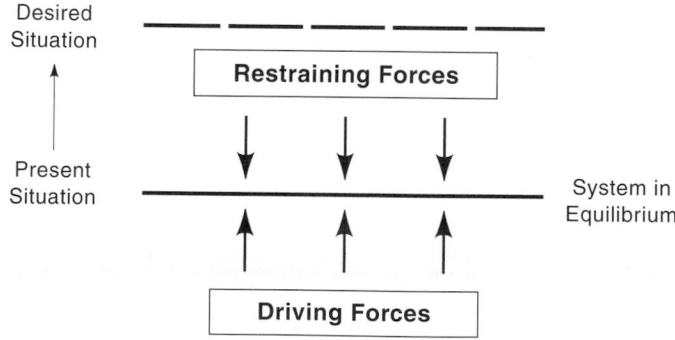

FIGURE 13–16
Force Field Analysis Model

They are usually right, but with some patience things usually do get better. As illustrated in Figure 13–17, change implementation is usually not a linear path to better performance. All change is disruptive, but it usually leads to better performance over time.

Summary

In this chapter, we have shown you how to choose an organizational form that would be suited to your project, or vice versa. We looked into the characteristics of an organization and explored its history and future possibilities, and we discussed some of the characteristics that make an organization effective.

We also looked at the pros and cons for each of the types of organizations, to understand why projects happen the way they do. This information will be useful in navigating the political and social landscapes of your future projects.

Problems for Review

1. Research indicates that the matrix structure is often confusing because it has multiple roles for people, with resulting confusion about these roles. Unfortunately, not all program managers, project managers, and project engineers possess the necessary skills to operate in this environment. Stuckenbruck has stated: "The path to success is strewn with the bodies of project managers who were originally functional line managers and then went into project management." What do you feel is the major cause of this downfall? Explain your response.

2. Under what circumstances would a purely functional organization be better for a software development project? Cite an example.

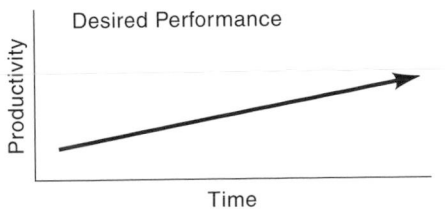 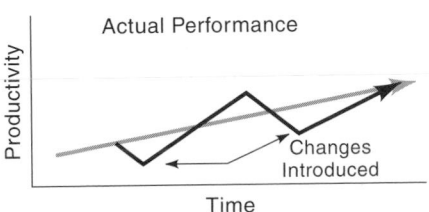

FIGURE 13–17
Change Implementation Effects are Nonlinear

Visit the Case Study

During a business meeting in Guangzhou between Mr. Lu and Ms. Patel's corporate boss, Mr. Lu intimated that it looked like your company is now the only remaining competitor. The competition announced a worldwide reorganization and a move of its old corporate headquarters from Seattle to Dallas. Because of the move, all the Asia work would be managed out of the Japanese subsidiary. This subsidiary stopped taking on pure software project 18 months ago after purchasing a suite of semiconductor foundries from a failing telecommunications company.

The way to cinch the deal was to have a strong development presence in Asia. Of course, the CRM could not relax the previous in-country staffing limitations, but, being a creative company, Mr. Lu was sure that you could solve that minor issue. This project is a must-win for your corporation. How will you organize your project to take advantage of this information? What will be the impact on your current project plan?

Citations

[1]Bowditch, James L., and Anthony F. Buono (1996). *A Primer on Organizational Behavior*, 4th ed. New York, NY: Jossey-Bass.

[2]Hersey, Paul, and Kenneth H. Blanchard (1993). *Management of Organizational Behavior*, 6th ed. Englewood Cliffs, NJ: Prentice Hall.

[3]Kerzner, Harold (1998). *Project Management: A Systems Approach to Planning, Scheduling, and Controlling*, 6th ed. New York, NY: John Wiley & Sons, Inc.

References

Bowditch, James L., and Anthony F. Buono (1996). *A Primer on Organizational Behavior*, 4th ed. New York, NY: Jossey-Bass.

Hersey, Paul, and Kenneth H. Blanchard (1993). *Management of Organizational Behavior*, 6th ed. Englewood Cliffs, NJ: Prentice Hall.

Mintzberg, Henry (1983). *Structures in Fives: Designing Effective Organizations*. New York, NY: Prentice Hall.

Suggested Readings

Frame, J. Davidson (1987). *Managing Projects in Organizations*. New York, NY: Jossey-Bass.

Frame, J. Davidson (1994). *The New Project Management*. New York, NY: Jossey-Bass.

Kerzner, Harold (1998). *Project Management: A Systems Approach to Planning, Scheduling, and Controlling*, 6th ed. New York, NY: John Wiley & Sons, Inc.

Lewis, James P. (1995). *Project Planning, Scheduling, and Control: A Hands-On Guide to Bringing Projects in on Time and on Budget*, revised edition. New York, NY: McGraw-Hill.

Martin, Charles C. (1976). *Project Management: How to Make It Work*. Amacom.

Paulk, Mark C., et al. (1994). *The Capability Maturity Model: Guidelines for Improving the Software Process*. New York, NY: Addison-Wesley.

Pressman, Roger S. (2001). *Software Engineering: A Practitioner's Approach*, 5th ed. New York, NY: McGraw-Hill.

Web Pages for Further Information

www.pmi.org/pmi2001/papers/quality.htm. "Quality in Project Management: Organizing for Continuous Improvement in Project Management."

www.pmi.org/publictn/pmboktoc.htm. PMI's *A Guide to the Project Management Body of Knowledge (PMBOK® Guide)*.

Considering Dependencies

Most activities are not performed in isolation on a project. Identifying proper dependencies is a key part of getting the schedule right. This chapter discusses some considerations for dependencies common in software development projects, with references to the life cycle models of Chapter 4, the work breakdown structures of Chapter 8, the activity identification of Chapter 9, and the resource assignments of Chapter 12.

We will discuss what dependencies are, and some of the types found in scheduling activities. We'll explore some typical dependencies in a software development project. And we'll look at a brainstorming technique for identifying activities and dependencies when life cycle model activities are not already available to modify into a workable project plan. All of these explorations will help us build a realistic and believable schedule in Chapter 15, "Scheduling the Work." In this chapter, we'll be introduced to some of the concepts of activity representation in a network diagram and we'll complete the coverage in Chapter 15 on scheduling, when we bring all the pieces together to build an actual schedule.

Remember that what we are trying to do is build a realistic schedule that is acceptable to sponsorship, management, and the customer, and which the development team can believe in and follow. This means that the planning activities we are describing (defining the goal and scope, creating the work breakdown structure, identifying the tasks and activities, estimating

461

the size and duration, assigning resources, considering dependencies, and scheduling the work) should be done with as much involvement of the identified development team members as is practical. Their involvement ensures that the project plan and schedules are *theirs*, not yours, which greatly increases the chances for successful completion of the project.

Where We Are in the Product Development Life Cycle

Where are we in the basic software life cycle model that serves as our map? As shown in Figure 14–1, we are still at the beginning of the product development life cycle, planning the project. In particular, we are still planning *how* to do the project that we already defined in Chapters 7, 8, and 9. The location of dependency consideration activities is depicted in Figure 14–2.

Chapter 14 Relation to the 34 Competencies

Understanding dependencies in a software development project requires the *product* development techniques of understanding development activities and tailoring the processes to meet the needs of the current project. The *project* management skills needed are a little bit of estimating costs and effort (especially for inventing new activities), building a WBS, scheduling, and, of course, documenting the plans as you go. To do these things effectively, you need the *people* management skills of interaction and good communications, of holding effective meetings, and of building a working team through leadership. These competencies are shown below.

Product Development Techniques

9. **Tailoring processes**—Modifying standard processes to suit a project
11. **Understanding development activities**—Learning the software development cycle

Project Management Skills

12. **Building a WBS**—Building a work breakdown structure for a project
13. **Documenting plans**—Identifying key components
14. **Estimating costs**—Estimating cost to complete the project
15. **Estimating effort**—Estimating effort required to complete the project
18. **Scheduling**—Creating a schedule and key milestones

People Management Skills

25. **Holding effective meetings**—Planning and running excellent meetings
26. **Interaction and communication**—Dealing with developers, upper management, and other teams

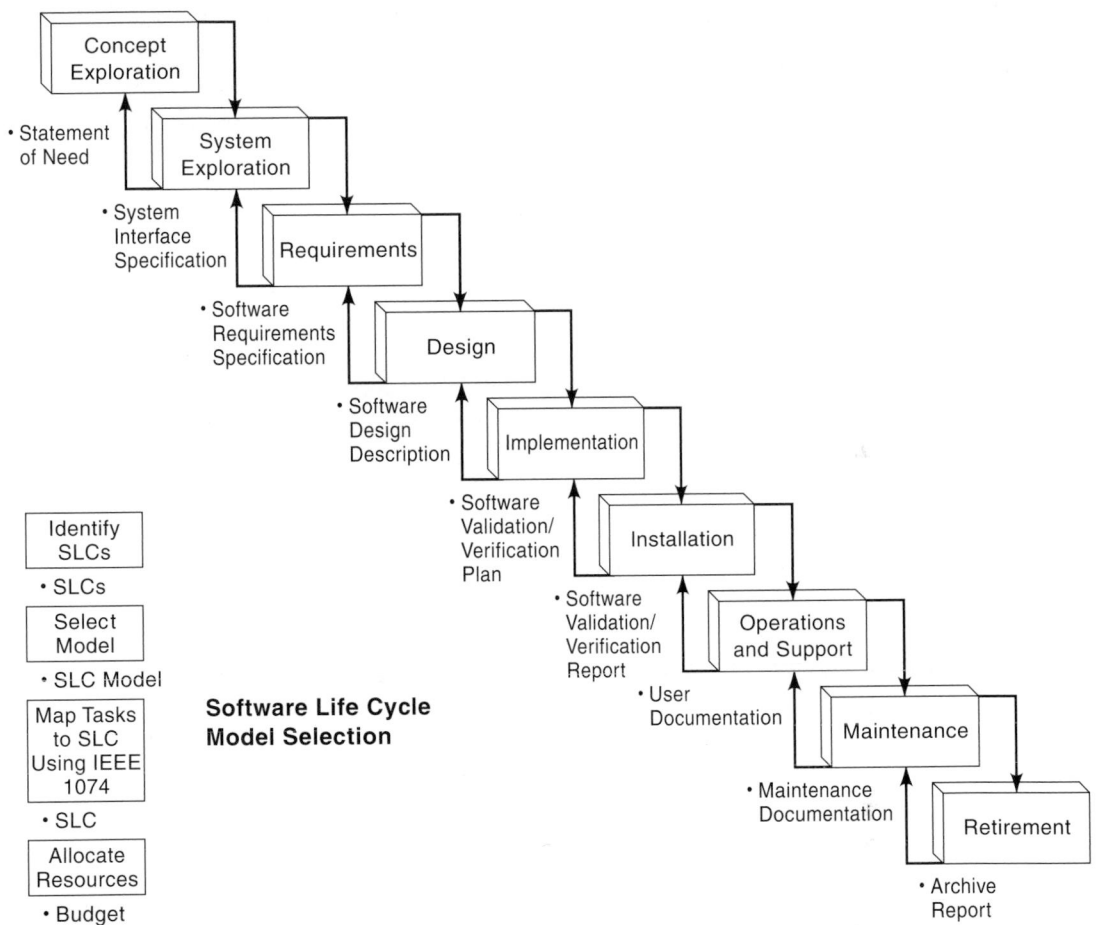

FIGURE 14-1
Product Process Framework

27. **Leadership**—Coaching project teams for optimal results
34. **Teambuilding**—Forming, guiding, and maintaining an effective team

Learning Objectives for Chapter 14 _____

Upon completion of this chapter, the reader should be able to:

- Describe several different ways that one activity can depend on another in a network;
- Identify new activities and dependencies using the nominal group technique;

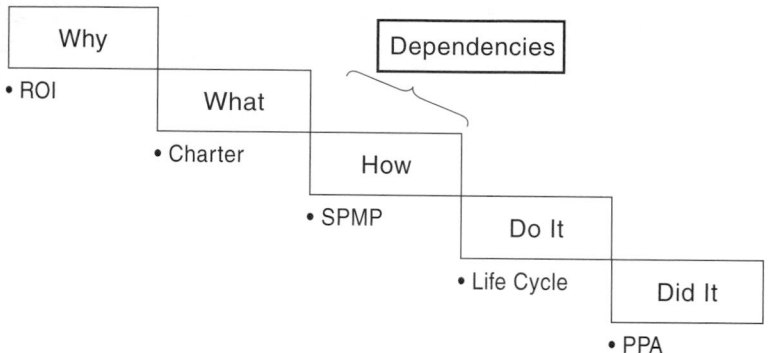

FIGURE 14–2
Project Process Framework

- Explain what lag and lead dependencies are used for;
- Describe at least three different types of dependencies;
- Define dependencies in the context of projects;
- Describe the uncertainty principle;
- Explain the difference between a hard and a soft dependency.

What Are Dependencies?

Dependencies are one form of constraint for any project. Remember the triple constraint illustrated in Figure 1–4? It says that scope, schedule, and cost are the triple constraints of any project, with quality measurement permeating all three parts. Hard deadlines and specific minimum functionality levels are to be considered constraints to your planning.

Dependencies are any relationship connections between activities in a project that may impact their scheduling. And there are usually many, many dependencies in a software development project. If the work were completely linear, every activity would depend on one other activity (except for "get started"), and the project would take forever to complete (the sum of all the activity durations estimated in Chapters 10 and 11). If there were no dependencies, everything could be started at the same time and the project would take as long as the longest single activity. Neither of these happens, of course. But they illustrate the extremes within which you want to build a *realistic* schedule.

After the product-oriented work breakdown structure has been defined, we often assume that certain dependencies between branches are implied. However, the WBS is not a structure well suited to showing dependencies. It does show relationships hierarchically, but it does not show cross-branch dependencies. A better representation for dependencies is the network diagram. How to build a network diagram will be discussed in Chapter 15, but for now, just consider that there is a dependency relationship between two activities represented as a straight line with an arrowhead pointing in the direction of the dependent activity. It means the second (dependent) activity depends on the first activity. A simple two-activity dependency is shown in Figure 14–3, as Gantt chart activity bars.

You and your project team must find as many of these dependencies amongst the activities in your project WBS as you can. Any you fail to find will likely cause their activities to form a default relationship. Most project management scheduling tools assume no relationship between activities when first entered into the tool. However, as soon as they are linked, a completely linear relationship is assumed (just like those in Figure 14–3). Reality is usually somewhere in between.

Types of Software Development Dependencies _____

As stated earlier, dependencies can be categorized a number of ways. One way is to consider internal versus external dependencies. Another way is to see them as activity-limited or resource-limited. Yet another way is to look at the strength of the dependency. All of these dependencies may not be as clean as you would hope for, and may have some special consequences in the schedule. Nonetheless, all must be identified and understood to build a realistic project schedule.

External versus Internal Dependencies

External dependencies for the development project would include any connections to the work products of other projects. These may be higher-level projects (see Step 2, "Find Any Higher System WBS," in the "Building a WBS for Software" section of Chapter 8) with dependencies on your project's work products or deliverables. Your project may be dependent on other development activities parallel to the software development. An example of this is when there is a higher-level WBS describing a total turnkey system solution under development that includes hardware (customized, or just assembled), software (what you are

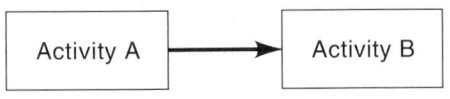

Activity B depends on Activity A

FIGURE 14–3
Simple Dependency Relationship

responsible for), and installation and training (you may or may not be responsible for all or part of this).

Another source for external dependencies is stakeholders. Stakeholders are anyone who has an interest in the project and who might influence it in a positive or negative way. An early project planning activity is to identify stakeholders and plan to manage relationships with them during the course of the project. This minimizes the chances that someone will "come out of nowhere" and destroy the project, since managing expectations and monitoring requirements changes is a big part of managing a software development project.

Stakeholders include, at a minimum: the project team, the sponsor, the functional manager(s), the customer(s), and the user(s). Sometimes the customers' customer or the user's users are included as well. Stakeholder management happens early and throughout the project, and includes communication and soliciting of stakeholder input for planning and scheduling, not just in requirements analysis, but throughout the planning process. Often, it is recommended to assign responsibility to the members of the project team to manage stakeholders on a one-to-one basis. This need not be a time-consuming activity, but the chances for surprise diminish if people on the project take explicit actions (such as occasional emails and short update visits or phone calls) to keep the stakeholders connected to the project and its goal. This is relationship management and is just as important to the success of the project as the technical parts, because projects in business are not just about transactions, but are about relationships, too. The objective of stakeholder management is to obtain and retain stakeholder buy-in to the project's objectives and plans. Individual stakeholder contacts can be selected using a variety of criteria, such as:

- Existing social relationship with a stakeholder—was there already an acquaintance in another context;

- Shared domain—both are database gurus or GUI experts who have attended similar conferences;

- Expect to work together later—maybe as a tester, installer, or beta user of the developed product;

- Common location or language—share the same workplace, campus, city, country, or time zone.

Examples of stakeholder dependencies that are important to many software development projects are major business events important to the customer, or to their customers. If you are developing a software system for a client to resell in the client's specialized marketplace, the customer's marketing team may have events such as trade shows at which they would want to show early versions of the software (often beta versions). This is an important dependency to know about for your project schedule, as it implies some kind of working version to be ready by some (immovable) date. This can really put a lot of pressure on a project team trying to develop a working product for a real deliverable later. It should be treated as a hard project constraint (on the *schedule* side of the triple constraint triangle). Experience suggests that this kind of event can be overlooked in the planning steps of the project life cycle because they may be on the periphery of knowledge of the direct customer from whom you get most of your requirements information.

Another major source of external dependencies are suppliers. They are also stakeholders, but are usually much closer to the project than most external stakeholders. Often, there are specific contractual relationships that can dictate firm constraints for the project. An example of a supplier dependency might be an interface to a third-party system that your software must communicate with. You may be dependent on another project's schedule in another department, company, or location over which you have little or no control. These become constraints for your project and cause a high need for contingency planning.

Internal dependencies abound in a software development project because the modules, components, and processes are so interrelated. Many of them are a direct result of relationships between components in the product-oriented WBS. For instance, the complete system build is dependent on all of the code for the components being compiled and ready. There are also many integral process dependencies in a software development project. These would include configuration management, project management, and software quality assurance. These tend to be very project specific, but some examples of common dependencies are:

- Project plan sign-offs and approvals;
- Requirements sign-offs and approvals;
- Internal or external management review cycles;
- Configuration item identification;
- Software quality audits.

It is recommended that these dependencies are represented as milestones in the software development project plan. Often, there is more than one activity that must be finished to recognize them anyway. Showing external dependencies as explicit milestones shows that your project is dependent on inputs out of your control. These must be kept visible and monitored frequently, as slips in them can cascade throughout the rest of your project plans. Describing project milestones was described in Chapter 8.

Resource versus Activity Dependencies

Another way to view dependency types is based on whether they are resource-driven or activity-driven. Most schedules are derived using the critical path method (CPM, described in Chapter 15) and are presented as Gantt charts. Gantt charts show only the dependencies between the activities in the project and so are activity-driven. They don't show the resource constraints underlying them. This is why executing a resource-leveling algorithm against them in a project management scheduling tool such as Microsoft Project seems to scramble all the activity dates and make the project end-date extend further.

Once you map the availability of resources into the schedule, you get a resource-constrained schedule. A resource-constrained schedule says that some activities cannot start when the predecessor activities have been completed because the resources to do them are not available yet. For example, even though integration and regression testing are scheduled to begin immediately after unit coding and testing have been completed, the testers are not available then, so those activities must slip out until the tester resources become free. This kind of dependency on resource availability becomes very constraining with some types of equipment resources, such as special test harnesses or new devices under development. Resource constraint dependencies can also occur because of calendar windows of availability, such as scheduled test time on a production network, or even the vacation schedules of key members of your project team. Another resource-driven dependency cause can be cost oriented, such as the need to wait until a more favorable time frame for access costs to diminish. An example of this kind of cost-oriented resource constraint could be using teleconferencing facilities at non-peak hours. In Chapter 15, we'll see how to adjust an activity-driven schedule to comprehend resource availability.

Now let's look at a few technical relationships between activities to help us understand how the different software development activities we saw in Chapter 9, "Identifying the Tasks and Activities," might relate.

Possible Dependency Relationships

Dependencies can be classified a number ways. One of the most common ways is by the type of their start-finish relationships. Others include classification by their category, and by their source. First, let's look at their start-finish relationships.

Finish-to-Start (FS)   In the finish-to-start (FS) relationship, one activity starts only when the preceding activity finishes. This is the most common type of activity dependency and is the default relationship for linked activities in most project management scheduling tools. The finish-to-start relationship is shown in Figure 14–4.

An example of a finish-to-start dependency could be that the activity "find cause" must finish before the activity "fix problem" begins, because you can't fix it until you know what

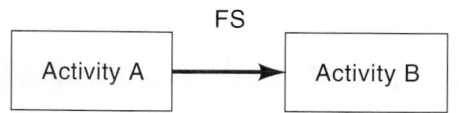

Activity B cannot start until Activity A is finished

FIGURE 14–4

Finish-to-Start Dependency Relationship

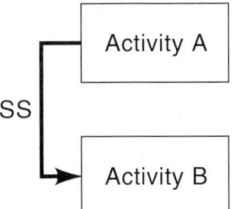

Activity B starts when Activity A starts

FIGURE 14–5
Start-to-Start Dependency Relationship

to fix. Other illustrations are that "build tests" must finish before "execute tests" starts, and "install software" must finish before "execute software" starts.

Start-to-Start (SS)   The start-to-start (SS) dependency means that one activity can start if and only if the other activity starts. Also a common type of relationship in software development projects, it is extremely useful for kicking-off a set of simultaneous activities based on a trigger event. An example would be starting the activities "perform project planning," "perform risk assessment," and "perform configuration management" at the same time that "start project" begins. The start-to-start activity relationship is illustrated in Figure 14–5.

Finish-to-Finish (FF)   The finish-to-finish (FF) relationship is similar to the start-to-start relationship, in that one activity must tie in with another, but it must finish at the same time. That is, one activity cannot end until the other one does. An example of this relationship could be that the "manage the project" activity cannot end until the "obtain project completion approval" activity is done. This dependency is illustrated in Figure 14–6.

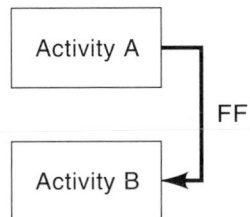

Activity B cannot be finished until Activity A is finished

FIGURE 14–6
Finish-to-Finish Dependency Relationship

Start-to-Finish (SF)   Rarest of all these relationships is the start-to-finish (SF). It means that the first activity cannot finish until the next activity starts. This is similar to the common finish-to-start relationship, except that the dependencies are reversed. It is useful to tie a working activity to a milestone (an event activity with zero duration often linked to several different activity accomplishments), such that the activity cannot end until the milestone is achieved (all the other activities have finished). An example of this might be that the "support customer" activity cannot finish until the "contract ends" milestone occurs. The start-to-finish relationship is shown in Figure 14–7.

Special Types of Relationships

Lag and lead relationships, hard versus soft dependencies, and the uncertainty principle all can be present to impact the straightforward start and finish relationships.

Lag and Lead Relationships   Useful dependency modifiers are the lag and lead types that can occur with any of the other dependencies discussed so far. Basically, the start or finish of one of the other dependency types is slipped-out (lagged) or pulled-up (led) by a certain time period. A lag is usually indicated with a positive number and a lead uses a negative number added to the start of finish times of their connected activities. This is a useful relationship for activities with a fixed duration connection to some other activity. For instance, you may want to always lag "apply second coat of paint" by two days after "apply first coat of paint" finishes to allow for drying time. The example in Figure 14–8 shows activity C lagging the finish of activity A by 10 days, even though activity B can start right away.

Hard vs. Soft Dependencies   Yet another way to look at dependencies is to rate their strength of connection. Some connections are physical, that is, it is physically impossible for activity B to start until activity A finishes. For example, it is impossible for the "allow paint to dry" activity to occur before the "apply paint" activity begins. And gravity prevents us from doing the "install roof" activity until the "erect walls" activity finishes. Similarly, we cannot

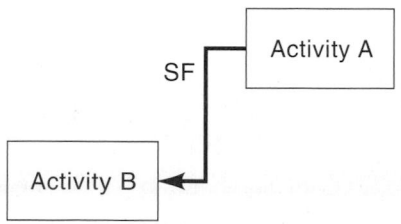

Activity B cannot be finished until Activity A is started

FIGURE 14–7
Start-to-Finish Dependency Relationship

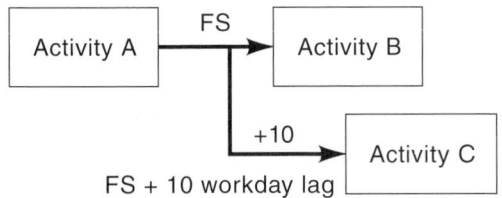

Activity B is finish-to-start with Activity A, but
Activity C cannot be started until 10 days *after*
Activity A is finished (a lag of 10 days)

FIGURE 14–8
Lag Relationship

achieve the "code compiled" milestone until the "write code" activity finishes, and we cannot start the "review design specification" activity until the "draft design specification" at least begins. These connections are said to be "hard logic" or "mandatory dependencies." They cannot be broken, and so the activities involved must be sequential, lengthening the total project duration.

However, some dependencies are discretionary, and may allow activities to overlap. An example would be that "paint living room" and "paint bedroom" could occur simultaneously. Often, it is not obvious that the dependency is discretionary. For instance, to non-builders it first appears that "build slab foundation," "build walls," and "build chimney" are sequential hard-logic activities. However, most construction managers have learned that framing the walls can begin at the same time as foundation construction by building them laying down on the ground next to the slab. Then when the slab's concrete cures enough to walk on, they can erect the pre-built walls onto the slab and nail the corners together. Software projects are full of these discretionary dependencies. For example, "draft design specification" need not wait to start until *after* "complete requirements document" has finished. It may start at the same time, or lag slightly behind, thus allowing the schedule to be compressed a bit. These so-called "soft-logic" dependencies are the project manager's key to constructing an aggressive, but realistic, schedule.

Hard and soft dependencies are summarized in Box 14–1.

The Uncertainty Principle   So far we have talked about dependencies as if we knew all the relationships. Unfortunately, there is always guesswork in planning because no one can predict the future very well. A project schedule is just an educated guess about how things might go if all the relationships and assumptions hold up. It is no better than the people making the guess, but usually, there are no others with more knowledge about the particular problem or product that the project was chartered to solve or build. Sometimes you plan a

BOX 14–1
Dependencies by Strength of Connection

Type	Also Known As	Description
Hard-logic	• Mandatory dependencies • Logical dependencies	A strong connection where an activity cannot start until a preceding one is completed
Soft-logic	• Discretionary dependencies • Preferred logic • Preferential logic	A weak connection between activities that is defined by the project team according to best practices or judgment

schedule with assumptions about dependencies and then find out later that your assumptions were wrong. All you can do is make the best guesses possible with the facts available, and plan to re-plan later.

You can also explicitly allow for the unknowns of the future through the use of contingency buffers, or management reserve. This is usually shown in a Gantt chart schedule as a separate activity bar, prior to a milestone. But it doesn't appear in a WBS since it is not an activity that you can assign people to. It is just there to absorb the uncertainty of the future. Of course, if you do *no* planning whatsoever, then your whole project is just one long activity bar—a big guess.

In Chapter 15 on scheduling techniques, and in Chapter 18 on determining project risks, we will look more into how to handle the inherent uncertainty in any software development project.

Brainstorming Dependencies and Activities _____

In Chapter 9 we looked at identification of the activities and tasks that might be needed in a software development project. Specifically, we saw how the 65 activities from 17 software engineering processes described in IEEE 1074 could be arranged according to a specific life cycle model to form a usable work breakdown structure. We could use those IEEE 1074 activities because the project we wanted to do fit an existing life cycle model closely enough to reuse most of the activities. But what if there is no precedent for the kind of project you are going to do? What if there is no existing life cycle model already defined?

In this case, you must invent the activities through brainstorming with your project team, group them and arrange them into a WBS, and then find all the dependencies using the information presented earlier in this chapter. To help with the invention of new activities, use the nominal group technique described in the next section. It is simple to use and extremely valuable for collecting balanced input and ideas from those on the project team. Then you can lead the team in finding dependencies amongst the activities as described in the "Process for Identifying New Dependencies" section.

Nominal Group Technique

Andre Delbecq and Andrew Van de Ven, based on research funded by the University of Wisconsin and the U.S. Department of Health, Education, and Welfare (HEW), developed the "nominal group technique" in 1968. The technique is an excellent way to get balanced participation in most data gathering efforts. It is good for:

- Problem solving—looking for root causes of problems, or solution approaches;
- Creative decision making—for estimates, and tough choices;
- Idea generating situations—completely new input is required.

The reason it works is that it allows for *every* team member to rank items without being pressured by others. This is especially valuable in teams where a few dominant personalities do all the talking, and the majority just follows along quietly. The process is illustrated in Box 14–2.

Box 14–2
Nominal Group Technique Process

1. Each participant privately generates a list of inputs (project activities to achieve the goal, using the proper activity methods discussed in Chapter 9, such as verb and noun, bullet language, etc.).

2. Round robin, each participant provides one new item for the common list (everyone gets a turn). No talking during this part. List items with letters not numbers.

3. Group discusses items as needed after list is complete to eliminate duplicates, sound-alikes, etc.

4. Each person privately ranks the *n* most important items.

5. Using these anonymous votes, the leader calculates a team ranking for each item.

6. Group discusses the resulting ranking, anomalies, etc.

7. Repeat steps 4, 5, and 6 until a consensus top set is reached. Usually, this is no more than two or three rounds.

   The goal of this exercise is to generate a list of activities that the team believes will satisfy the goals of the project, as stated in the project's charter. This is a substitute for not having a WBS template matched to a life cycle already. It is usually good to write each activity on adhesive notepaper (like 3M's Post-its, which we will generically call "stickies" here), and use a large white board or wall space to capture them where everyone can see them all. Typically, only a few rounds are needed to get a list of activities that can be used to populate a WBS. Next, we'll see a process for using the activities on stickies to build the WBS.

Process for Identifying New Dependencies

One problem you will notice with the resulting list of activities on stickies from the nominal group technique session is that many of the activities have different granularity. That is, if durations were estimated for them, some would take only an hour or two to do (like "perform software build") but others would take weeks or months (like "design production system"). The solution to this problem is to group the items in a hierarchical fashion (*a la* WBS) using affinity diagramming. This just means putting all the stickies with activities that have common elements together on one part of the whiteboard, and separate them from the rest. You may have to try several different ideas for commonality. Sometimes rewriting a few activities can help them fit together better. A general rule of thumb is to have detail one level below the level that day-to-day management will occur.

The next step is to arrange the stickies into a product-oriented work breakdown structure using the guidelines discussed in Chapter 8. Arrange them into logical groupings from highest-level activities to lowest. When you get this settled down into a good representation that the team agrees on, capture it on paper (but leave the stickies up there). You will have a useful WBS from which to derive dependencies.

Next you can find the dependencies between all the activities by carefully considering each activity and rearranging the stickies on the whiteboard using the information supplied in this chapter. It is best to start with the deliverable in mind, at the end of the project. Ask the question, "What is the last thing that the project does?" Put that on the whiteboard as the final item that closes the project. Then successively work backward from the last item asking the question, "What will have to be done in order to accomplish ...?" This should keep you from adding activities that don't directly relate to producing the deliverable, keeping "gold plating" to a minimum.

Using erasable markers (because you are likely to change them several times), draw lines connecting the stickies according to the dependency types discussed earlier. Work through the whole project like this, establishing dependencies appropriate for the task. Be sure that you don't end up with any "dangles" as shown in Figure 14–9, which would indicate a string of activities that don't produce anything. The resulting dependency map is almost a complete network diagram, as shown in the bottom part of Figure 15–10. We'll look more closely at network diagramming in Chapter 15 on scheduling.

To summarize the process, follow the steps below:

1. **Brainstorm an activity list**—Use the nominal group technique to build a list of possible activities for the project on stickies.

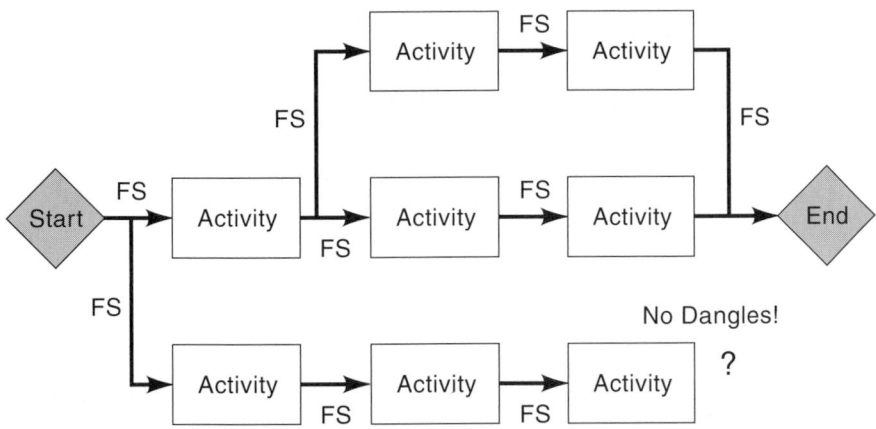

FIGURE 14–9
Watch Out for Dangles!

2. **Find affinity collections**—Logically "group" activities by identifying the work that must or will be performed together. The level of detail and number of high-level items will be governed by the nature of the project. Disregard duration and resources at this point.

3. **Find highest WBS levels**—Summarize the groupings by work product output to derive the higher levels of the WBS.

4. **Capture WBS representation**—Copy all the WBS information to paper. It becomes part of the project plan.

5. **Find dependencies**—Working from the end to the beginning, logically arrange stickies on the whiteboard. Using markers, draw the dependency relationships between activities, being careful to look for all interdependencies.

Summary _____

In this chapter, we have described dependencies from several angles. We've looked at them as being internal or external, activity-limited or resource-limited, and weak or strongly related. We have examined the ways in which one activity might be linked to another, such as the FS, SS, FF, and SF links.

These dependencies become very important in the construction of a network from the product-oriented WBS discussed in Chapter 8. The techniques of scheduling, discussed in Chapter 15, rely heavily on the dependency relationships created when building a project plan.

Problems for Review

1. What is the hardest challenge facing software development project managers regarding dependency relationships, and why does it have such a strong effect on project schedules?
2. Describe a situation in which you would need to use a lag time in a software development life cycle.

Visit the Case Study

You have been selected to attend your company's one-week "charm school" for new managers. Although you have been a project manager for years you have never been to this company's management training. In your opinion, the ARRS project cannot function with you being gone for 5 days at a retreat house in Arizona. Not only will you be gone all of next week, but there is pre-work that has to be completed and presented at the Sunday evening kick-off session. Your assignment is to analyze all of the outside influences that impact your most critical project. In your case, this is the ARRS. Your plan is to build a dependency diagram of all the project influencers. Get this finished before you leave on your Sunday airplane flight.

Suggested Readings

Berg, Cindy, and Kim Colenso (2000). "Work Breakdown Structure Practice Standard Project—WBS vs. Activities." *PM Network.* April 2000.

Kerzner, Harold (1998). *Project Management: A Systems Approach to Planning, Scheduling, and Controlling,* 6th ed. New York, NY: John Wiley & Sons, Inc.

Lewis, James P. (1995). *Project Planning, Scheduling, and Control: A Hands-On Guide to Bringing Projects in on Time and on Budget,* revised edition. New York, NY: McGraw-Hill.

Paulk, Mark C., et al. (1994). *The Capability Maturity Model: Guidelines for Improving the Software Process.* New York, NY: Addison-Wesley.

Pressman, Roger S. (2001). *Software Engineering: A Practitioner's Approach,* 5th ed. New York, NY: McGraw-Hill.

Web Pages for Further Information

www.ee.ed.ac.uk/~gerard/Management/art8.html. Gerard M. Blair, "Planning a Project."

www.pmi.org/publictn/pmboktoc.htm. PMI's *A Guide to the Project Management Body of Knowledge (PMBOK® Guide),* Chapter 6.

Scheduling the Work 15

The schedule is derived from the WBS and includes activity duration, significant milestones and work products to be produced, and who is responsible for them. Usually represented as a Gantt chart, but equally useful as a table, the schedule adds flesh to the WBS backbone, bringing the project to life. Here is where the activity estimates come together with the WBS to form a workable schedule.

Good scheduling requires technique, and is almost an art form similar to the creation of a WBS. It starts with knowing the scope of the project, covered in Chapter 7, "Defining the Goal and Scope of the Software Project," and is refined in Chapter 14, "Considering Dependencies." In this chapter, we show some of the art of scheduling a software project in the real world as a necessary project management skill. The case study project follows no firm schedule so it drifts toward disaster. In this chapter, we look at some ways to prevent this kind of aimlessness.

Where We Are in the Product Development Life Cycle

Where are we in the basic software life cycle model that serves as our map? As shown in Figure 15–1, we are still at the beginning of the product development life cycle, planning the project. In particular, we are still planning *how* to do the project that we already defined in Chapters 7, 8, 9, 10, 11, 12, and 13. We are near the end of the *how* step, as the last significant work product is the project schedule as an addendum to the software project management plan (SPMP). The location of scheduling activities is depicted in Figure 15–2.

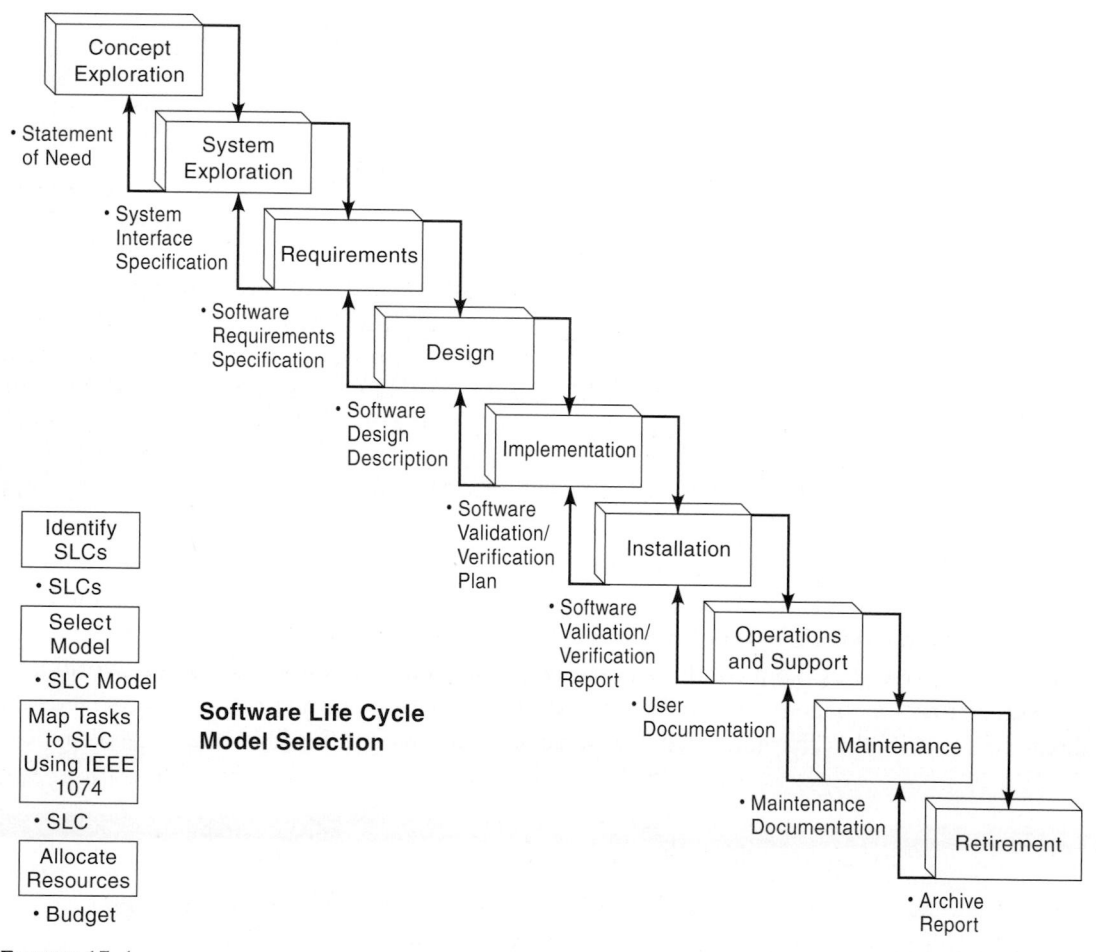

FIGURE 15–1
Product Process Framework

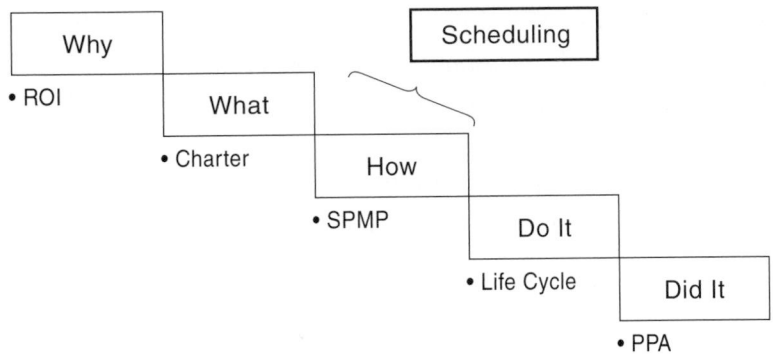

FIGURE 15–2
Project Process Framework

Chapter 15 Relation to the 34 Competencies _____

The art of scheduling exercises the *product* development skills of evaluating alternative processes in light of their scheduling implications, especially for subcontracted parts of the work. The *project* management skills used are WBS building (mostly for refinement) and scheduling. A big part of risk management is done in creating the schedule, since the risk plan is always made against a given schedule plan. Of course, understanding scheduling for selecting and using project management scheduling tools is also a needed skill. As in many of the other project planning activities, the *people* management skills needed include negotiating, leading a team to effective performance, and the interaction and communication needed to run good meetings.

Product Development Techniques

4. **Evaluating alternative processes**—Evaluating various approaches
6. **Managing subcontractors**—Planning, managing, and monitoring performance

Project Management Skills

12. **Building a work breakdown structure**—Building a work breakdown structure for a project
13. **Documenting plans**—Identifying key components
16. **Managing risks**—Identifying and determining the impact and handling of risks
18. **Scheduling**—Creating a schedule and key milestones
20. **Selecting project management tools**—Knowing how to select PM tools

People Management Skills

25. **Holding effective meetings**—Planning and running excellent meetings
26. **Interaction and communication**—Dealing with developers, upper management, and other teams
27. **Leadership**—Coaching project teams for optimal results
29. **Negotiating successfully**—Resolving conflicts and negotiating successfully
31. **Presenting effectively**—Using effective written and oral skills
34. **Teambuilding**—Forming, guiding, and maintaining an effective team

Learning Objectives for Chapter 15

Upon completion of this chapter, the reader should be able to:

- Build a real project schedule using the critical path method;
- Explain what the critical chain is and how it differs from the critical path;
- Describe several different schedule representations;
- Explain how uncertainty affects the scheduling of projects;
- Draw a scheduling network diagram using two different methods;
- Explain the reasons behind resource leveling;
- Explain the difference between an activity-constrained and a resource-constrained schedule.

Why Schedule?

What a question! Why even mess with all the details of trying to figure out what real dates a project scheduling algorithm tells us the project can be finished by, when the date will be declared unacceptable and pulled up anyway? This is a real problem facing many software development project managers today. They think, "Why not just slap the date they want up there and 'just do it' anyway you can, starting now?"

This attitude results from a lack of understanding of what a real project schedule is, on the part of the customer, sponsor, and the project manager. The big picture of the project is contained in the software development project plan. It describes *how* the project objectives (the *what*) can be met. One element of that is the schedule. It reflects all the relationships of all the activities, as best understood by the project team, mapped to a real-world calendar that comprehends true productive working hours, and allows for the inevitable uncertainty of the future. Normally, the schedule (usually expressed as a Gantt chart) is made an appendix to the SPMP. This is because it is a relatively volatile part of the plan, getting updated frequently during the tracking of the project. For any document, things that get updated a lot should be part of an appendix, because they are easier to maintain that way.

The Game

The lack of understanding of the true nature of a project schedule, and how it is built, causes management to see it as some kind of black magic, where they see a bunch of requirements go in, some hocus pocus with formulas and function points happens, and a date pops out, along with resource needs (cost = money). These are the three parts of the triple constraint (scope, schedule, and cost). Since software development is mostly a people-intensive process, managers and customers often play a game where whatever date and cost pops out, they will ask for it cheaper and sooner, thus getting the best possible price and schedule from the project team. Knowing this, many project managers pad their estimates and plans, expecting a demand for cuts. And so the game is played on both sides, padding and cutting, until an agreement is reached, or exhaustion occurs.

The right approach is to use the project team's deeper understanding of the tools and problem space to craft a realistic schedule based on solid estimating (Chapters 10 and 11) and scheduling (Chapters 8, 9, 12, 13, 14, and 15) methods. These can be defended because they are based on the best facts and methods available (and can be demonstrated). The schedule should be aggressive, reflecting a healthy work ethic, but realistic. It should understand that no one works 100 percent of their time on anything, over a long period. Due to vacations, illness, personal time off, interruptions, legacy system support, mentoring, job changes, and a host of similar reasons, the average productive time of an individual developer available to any given project is about 60 to 70 percent of their expected work hours over a year. For someone whose workday is 8 a.m. to 5 p.m. for a 40–hour workweek for 52 weeks a year, this is ($40 \times 52 =$) 2,080 hours, and 60 to 70 percent of that is 1,248 to 1,456 hours per year, or 24 to 28 hours per week. If you can get more than that, that's great. It will give you some lift and perhaps allow an early finish or additional features in the final product. But if you get less than that, others on your project team will be pressed to make up the slack to meet due dates (that you and the team committed to), and you will experience pressure, overtime, team disharmony, and perhaps product quality problems.

The Uncertainty of Scheduling the Future

Recognize the uncertainty principle at work (see Chapter 14). The planned schedule is just the team's best guess of the future. It does have some allowance for uncertainty management with time reserves built into it, just as management builds cost reserves into their business plans. But you and the team are not psychic and cannot predict the future with accuracy (if management or your customer can, then you and your project team can remove the uncertainty buffers and contingencies from your schedule, and management and the customer can absorb any overruns!). If they are better than most at predicting future events, then they should probably retire and just trade in the stock and commodity markets.

Remember that the output of the project is a deliverable (what the customer cares about) by a certain date, *with a certain percentage probability of meeting the date*. When you and the project team jointly construct the WBS, estimate the activity durations, and build the schedule, you will add enough contingency buffers to comprehend reasonable uncertainty, and give you about a 95 percent confidence level in the predicted end date. This 95 percent probability distribution is shown graphically in Figure 15–3.

Letting you and your team get squeezed down to a 5 percent confidence level doesn't really gain much for you, management, or the customer. Business is full of risks and rewards, so it is good practice when announcing expected completion dates to also mention the *probability of achievement*. For example, say "Our analysis of the work required indicates the project can be completed as described (the *scope*) with 19,500 hours of effort by 15 full-time-equivalents (the *cost*) by November 15th (the *schedule*) *with an 85 percent probability.*" Software development project management is mostly about managing expectations using industry-accepted approaches and technology. So, try not to get into the game of padding and cutting. Don't invalidate your estimation methods by reducing your estimates. They are not negotiable; they are estimates. Instead, rely on your team's best technical judgment for the activities, and insert contingency buffers into the schedule in enough places to absorb the uncertainty of estimation (usually at the end of major phases). If management or the customer says the finish date is too

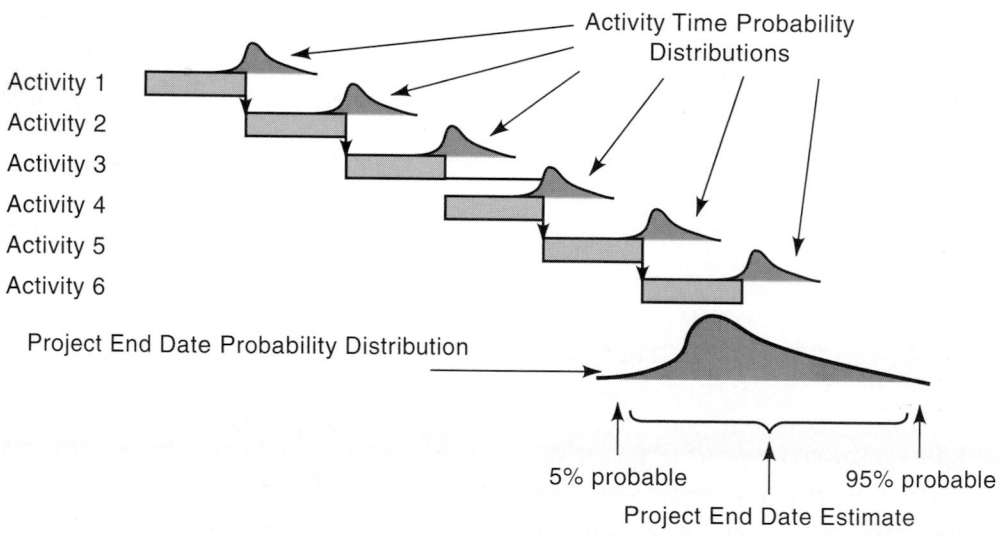

FIGURE 15–3
Uncertainty of the Project End Date Estimate

late for them, then ask what date is acceptable and treat that as a project constraint. Now your planning should manipulate the resources needed, and perhaps look for additional soft dependencies to overlap more activities and try to achieve a high-confidence-level schedule for the customer's desired finish date. If you cut features (reduce scope) then you can remove their portion from the estimates in the calculations. All of this means that you really should be targeting to finish all the planned work well *before* the due date.

The Psychology of Estimating

Chapters 10 and 11 describe an excellent set of software estimation methods and tools for helping us to create activity effort estimates. But in the end, judgment is applied and a "final number" must be put into the plan. Let's look for a moment at how the average software engineer thinks through this judgment. When presented with an activity estimation problem, the estimator's thought process before announcing their estimate goes something like this:

> "Based on my COCOMO analysis, the effort estimate is about *three weeks* for this component."

> "But there are a lot of uncertainties yet to be uncovered, so I'll *double the effort estimate* to cover them."

> "And I won't be able to focus on just this activity because I'm contributing to two other projects."

> "So I'll report my effort estimate for this activity on this project as *10 weeks*."

This process is illustrated in Figure 15–4. What's happening here is that the estimator is padding the estimate to account for the uncertainty in the situation. They don't want to be held accountable for the three-week estimate (with only a 50 percent chance of achieving that). Instead, they want about a 99 percent chance of meeting expectations, so they end up following an old rule-of-thumb estimating trick called "double it and add some." Essentially, about two thirds of the total time allotted for the activity is just contingency buffer. The effect is that the estimator gets to manage the use of the buffer to their benefit (to keep them from looking bad by being late with their part).

Once scheduled this way, people tend to exhibit what Eliyahu Goldratt called the "student syndrome," where they procrastinate on their planned activities in order to finish up the ones they were already committed to, on this or another project, because they had nearer-term deadlines to worry about.[1] They use up the uncertainty they planned into each activity at the beginning, leaving the bulk of the real work to be started at about the two-thirds point in the available activity time. This is OK if their initial COCOMO (or SLIM) estimate was right. But if not, they go into crash mode to finish the activity by the date they committed to. Goldratt named this phenomenon after the way students tend to put off doing their term paper until the night before it is due.

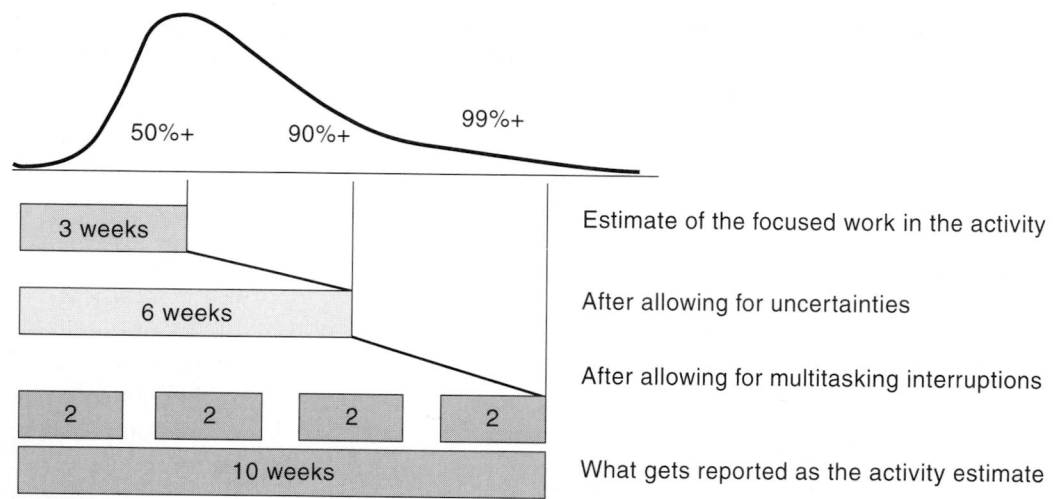

FIGURE 15–4
Another View of the Uncertainty Distribution

Unfortunately, if done for every activity in the WBS and translated to the project schedule, this causes all the uncertainty of the project schedule to be managed by the individuals on the team, rather than by the project team as a whole. And, if they all have student syndrome, then there is nothing but *outward pressure* on the project's finish date. This helps explain why most software development projects run late and few finish early.

A better way to manage the uncertainty is to try to extract the initial raw estimates and put those durations into the project plan, recognizing that each one will only have a 50 percent probability of completion. These are aggressive estimates. Move the uncertainty portions of the activities into explicit phase, or project, buffers so the project team can manage the uncertainty of *all the activities* as the project is executed and tracked (see Chapter 25, "Project Tracking and Control"). Figure 15–5 illustrates how the durations for individual activities are reduced, and the uncertainty time is moved to a project-level contingency buffer where it can be more effectively managed.

Since the calculated estimates have only a 50 percent chance of meeting their effort estimate, some will finish late and their estimated finish dates will slip out. Any slippage should be *subtracted* from the phase or project's contingency buffer. However, some others will finish early because of the 50 percent estimate. The time gained from those should be *added* to the phase or project's buffer. This means that on average, buffer consumption should be close to averaging out. In any case, the whole project team can watch the buffer consumption as it expands and contracts during project execution, and take appropriate action to keep the real 95 percent confidence-level project due date protected from the vagaries of uncertainty. We'll look into this more in Chapter 25 when we discuss project tracking and control.

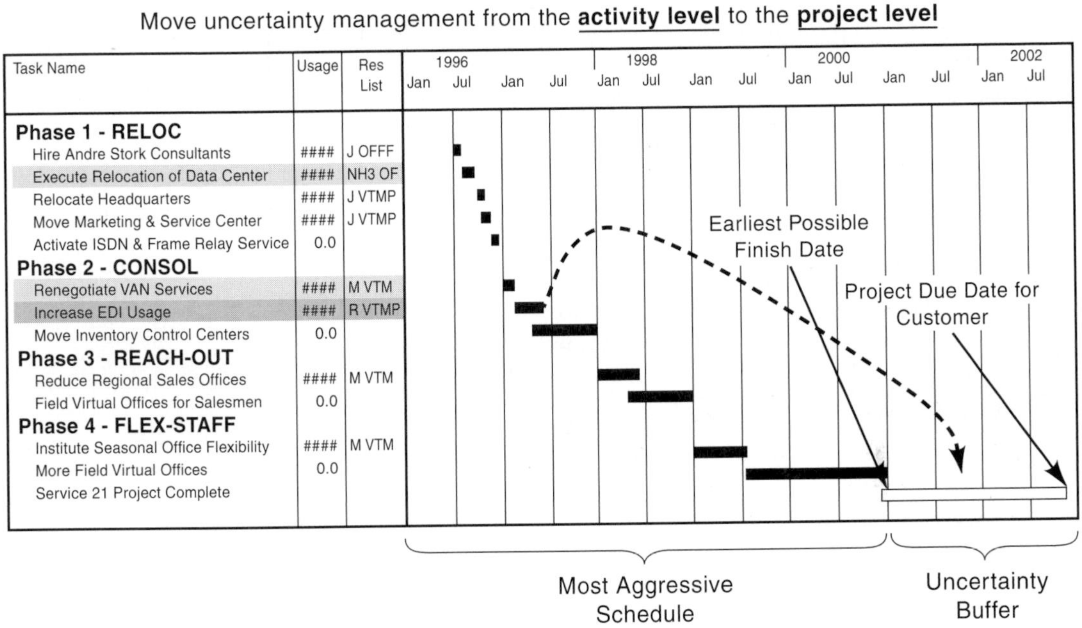

Move uncertainty management from the **activity level** to the **project level**

Task Name	Usage	Res List	1996 Jan Jul	Jan Jul	1998 Jan Jul	Jan Jul	2000 Jan Jul	Jan Jul	2002 Jan Jul
Phase 1 - RELOC									
Hire Andre Stork Consultants	####	J OFFF							
Execute Relocation of Data Center	####	NH3 OF							
Relocate Headquarters	####	J VTMP							
Move Marketing & Service Center	####	J VTMP							
Activate ISDN & Frame Relay Service	0.0								
Phase 2 - CONSOL									
Renegotiate VAN Services	####	M VTM							
Increase EDI Usage	####	R VTMP							
Move Inventory Control Centers	0.0								
Phase 3 - REACH-OUT									
Reduce Regional Sales Offices	####	M VTM							
Field Virtual Offices for Salesmen	0.0								
Phase 4 - FLEX-STAFF									
Institute Seasonal Office Flexibility	####	M VTM							
More Field Virtual Offices	0.0								
Service 21 Project Complete									

Earliest Possible Finish Date

Project Due Date for Customer

Most Aggressive Schedule

Uncertainty Buffer

FIGURE 15–5
Move Activity Uncertainty to Project-Level Contingency Buffers

Scheduling Fundamentals

There are a number of ways to represent a schedule. Let's look at some of them and learn what they show best. We'll look at the three most common forms of presenting a project schedule: table, Gantt chart, and network diagram.

Table

This is the simplest form for representing a project schedule. It is non-graphical and is just a list of the activities with a start and finish date. Other information can be provided, if desired. This is a great way to show a very long list of project activities, since the graphical methods tend to get messy with very large projects. A sample schedule table is shown in Figure 15–6.

Gantt Chart

The most commonly used schedule representation is the Gantt chart, sometimes called a bar chart. Invented by Henry L. Gantt during World War I, it was used to schedule the logistics of getting men and materials to the many ships on the U.S. coast for transport to Europe. In

Task Name	WBS	Duration	Start	Finish
Serve Meal	0	300.3 mins	9/18	9/19
Prepare Setting Activity	1	30 mins	9/18	9/19
Wash Tableware	1.1	20 mins	9/18	9/19
Set Table	1.2	10 mins	9/19	9/19
Setting Ready	1.3	0 mins	9/19	9/19
Make Food Activity	2	296.3 mins	9/18	9/19
Make Menu Activity	2.1	20 mins	9/18	9/19
Review Last Meal	2.1.1	5 mins	9/18	9/19
Construct New Menu	2.1.2	15 mins	9/19	9/19
Shop for Food Activity	2.2	130 mins	9/19	9/19
Make Shopping List	2.2.1	10 mins	9/19	9/19
Buy All Ingredients	2.2.2	2 hrs	9/19	9/19
Prepare Food Activity	2.3	146.3 mins	9/19	9/19
Prepare Appetizers	2.3.1	30 mins	9/19	9/19
Prepare Ingredients	2.3.2	45.3 mins	9/19	9/19
Cook Food	2.3.3	70 mins	9/19	9/19
Food Ready	2.4	0 days	9/19	9/19
Serve Meal Activity	3	5 mins	9/19	9/19
Move Food to Table	3.1	4 mins	9/19	9/19
Announce Meal Ready	3.2	1 min	9/19	9/19
Meal Served	3.3	0 days	9/19	9/19

FIGURE 15–6
A Sample Schedule Shown as a Table

fact, you may already be familiar with it even if you've not been involved with any projects at all.

The Gantt chart, seen in Figure 15–7, is a simple illustration of activities listed down the left side, with an activity bar shown to the right under a scale representing time. True Gantt charts do not show dependencies, but many project-scheduling tools have options to draw dependency lines between activity bars. There is a variation of the Gantt chart called a milestone chart, which is just a Gantt chart with the activities omitted so it only shows the milestones.

Visually, the Gantt chart can represent the sequence of activities to be done on a project. The activity list can be sorted by start date (giving the familiar cascade look, down and to the right, as shown in Figure 15–7), by finish date (showing the order for presenting work products and deliverables), or by some other feature such as WBS code or level. For very large projects

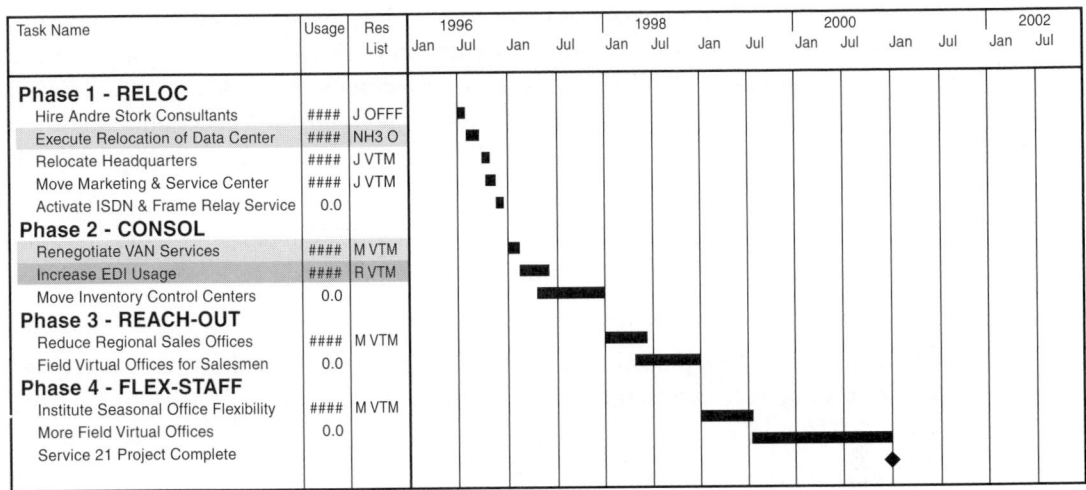

Task Name	Usage	Res List	1996 Jan	Jul	Jan	Jul	1998 Jan	Jul	Jan	Jul	2000 Jan	Jul	Jan	Jul	2002 Jan	Jul
Phase 1 - RELOC																
Hire Andre Stork Consultants	####	J OFFF														
Execute Relocation of Data Center	####	NH3 O														
Relocate Headquarters	####	J VTM														
Move Marketing & Service Center	####	J VTM														
Activate ISDN & Frame Relay Service	0.0															
Phase 2 - CONSOL																
Renegotiate VAN Services	####	M VTM														
Increase EDI Usage	####	R VTM														
Move Inventory Control Centers	0.0															
Phase 3 - REACH-OUT																
Reduce Regional Sales Offices	####	M VTM														
Field Virtual Offices for Salesmen	0.0															
Phase 4 - FLEX-STAFF																
Institute Seasonal Office Flexibility	####	M VTM														
More Field Virtual Offices	0.0															
Service 21 Project Complete																

FIGURE 15–7
Example of a Gantt Chart

with many activities and lots of detail to show, Gantt charts can get cumbersome. For large projects, sometimes project managers print the schedules out on large format stock and "wallpaper" the office with them. This is great for seeing the "big picture," but is difficult to maintain.

Network Diagram

The network diagram, also called a logic chart, a PERT chart, or some combination of these, is a graphical representation showing an ordered list of symbols (usually boxes or circles) that indicate activity name and precedence, and often include other information, as well (such as duration estimate, start and finish dates, and responsibility). There are a number of different names for methods that use network diagrams, including:

- GERT—graphical evaluation and review technique;
- PERT—program evaluation and review technique;
- CPM—critical path method;
- PDM—precedence diagramming method;
- ADM—arrow diagramming method.

The first three methods are regarded as analysis techniques. The last two are simply diagramming methods. Because PERT and CPM were invented at about the same time in the 1950s, they are sometimes lumped together and called PERT/CPM referring to a generic analysis process using a network diagram. GERT is also an analysis process, but it allows for conditional and probabilistic treatment of both precedence and duration estimates, making it very complex to use. PERT allows for probabilistic treatment of the activity duration estimates by using a three-point estimate instead of a single-point estimate, but assumes the network logic is fixed. CPM assumes that both the activity estimates and the precedence logic are fixed, making it the simplest to use. PERT and CPM use the same network diagramming approaches.

There are two basic ways to represent activities in a network. The basic network diagram is a collection of nodes and arrows. The basic information represented is:

- Activity name or Node ID—often using the WBS code;
- Earliest start—the earliest time period that the activity can start, based on prior activities' completions, or other project constraints (like fixed dates);
- Earliest finish—the earliest time period that the activity can finish;
- Duration—the number of time periods of work remaining for the activity;
- Latest start—the latest time period that the activity can start without impacting the next milestone;
- Latest finish—the latest time period that the activity can finish without impacting the next milestone.

One representation puts the activity information on nodes and is called an activity-on-node representation (AON). It is illustrated in Figure 15–8. The other puts the activity information on the arrows between the nodes and is called activity-on-arrow (AOA). It is illustrated in Figure 15–9. AOA representations may need to show dummy arrows ("activities" with no resources or time, usually shown as dashed lines) between nodes to indicate precedence when more than one activity follows. These dummy activities make reading AOA diagrams more complex. PDM is an AON method, and ADM is an AOA method of diagramming.

An AOA network is illustrated in Figure 15–10, and two AON networks are represented in Figure 15–11. AOA representations are seldom used today. Whichever network representation is used, the principles remain the same. For our purposes of network analysis, we will use the AON representation. In an AON network, there is a *start* node, usually placed on the left, and an *end* node, placed to the right. All the nodes in-between represent activities in the

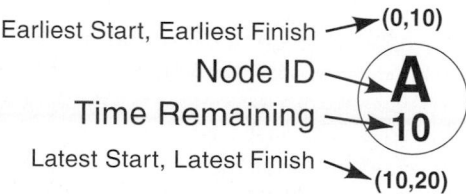

FIGURE 15–8
AON Activity Information Representation

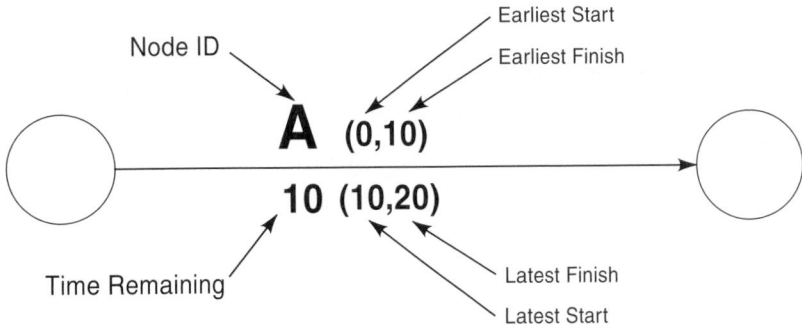

FIGURE 15-9
AOA Activity Information Representation

project WBS. There is a one-to-one correspondence of activities to network nodes. Although they could be represented as boxes, circles, or whatever shape is preferred for a node, we will represent nodes as shown in Figure 15–8.

You'll notice that all of these network diagrams show precedence very well. This is their major strength. It is easy to follow a path of activities from left to right, and to see how various activity sequences relate to each other. These diagrams are widely used to construct project plans from scratch when no WBS template exists, that is, when you are inventing the project activities from a brainstorming session (as discussed in Chapter 14). The weakness of these diagrams is the same as for the Gantt and other graphical representations. For large projects with lots of activities, they get very messy and hard to follow. But they are a great way to get started with planning and to get a WBS under control.

PERT and CPM Scheduling

These two methods of schedule analysis have been around since the 1950s, and form the foundation of what the profession knows about scheduling today. CPM (critical path method) was developed by DuPont in 1958–59, and uses fixed-time estimates for each activity. PERT (program evaluation and review technique) was developed for the U.S. Navy Special Projects Office Polaris missile submarine project by the consultants Booz, Allen, and Hamilton during the same years.

Both PERT and CPM use network-diagramming techniques to illustrate activity precedence. But most scheduling today is done using CPM. First we'll look at the major difference between the two methods (point estimate or weighted average), and then see how to use network diagramming for CPM analysis.

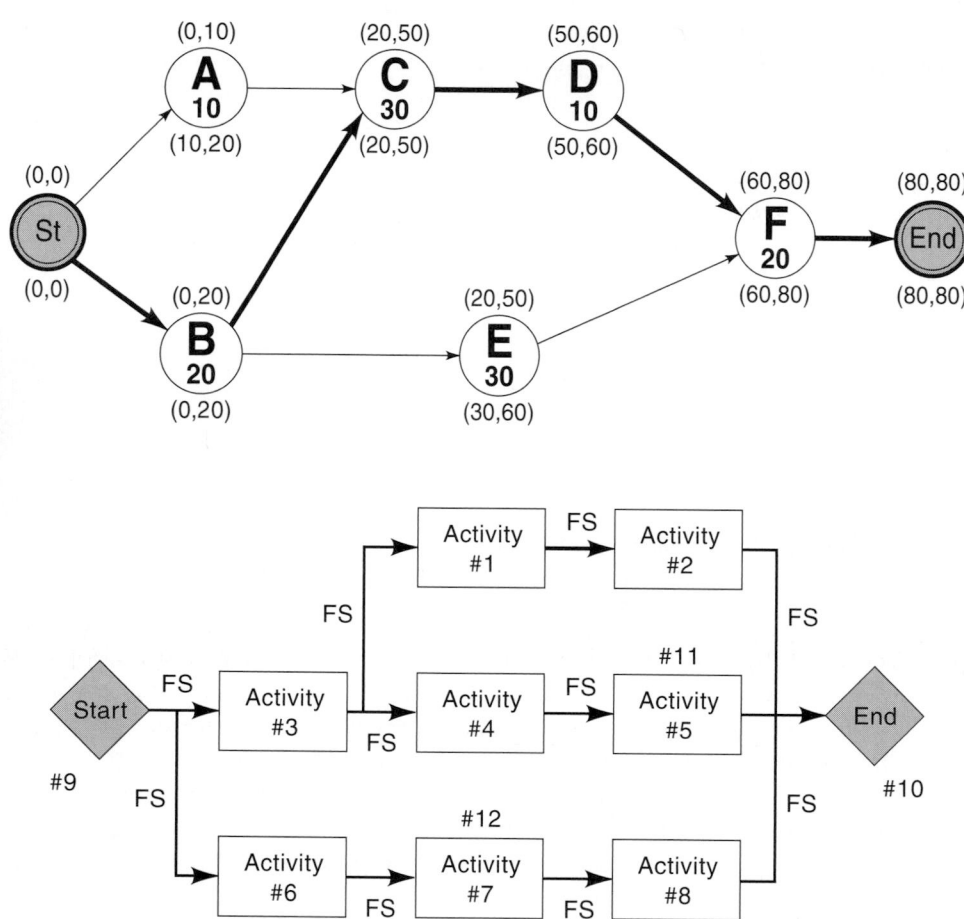

FIGURE 15–10
Sample AON Network Diagrams

PERT

PERT's time estimates involve the *beta* probability distribution to capture three estimates (optimistic, most likely, and pessimistic) of the duration of an activity. The PERT beta distribution is shown in Figure 15–12.

The beta distribution was chosen for PERT instead of the normal distribution because it more closely resembles people's behavior when estimating. We are naturally optimistic, which skews the results to the left. Some call the beta distribution the "Murphy's Law distribution." Note that the tails of the distribution intersect the X-axis and do not trail off toward the sides (they are not asymptotic). This means that there is no chance at all of an actual

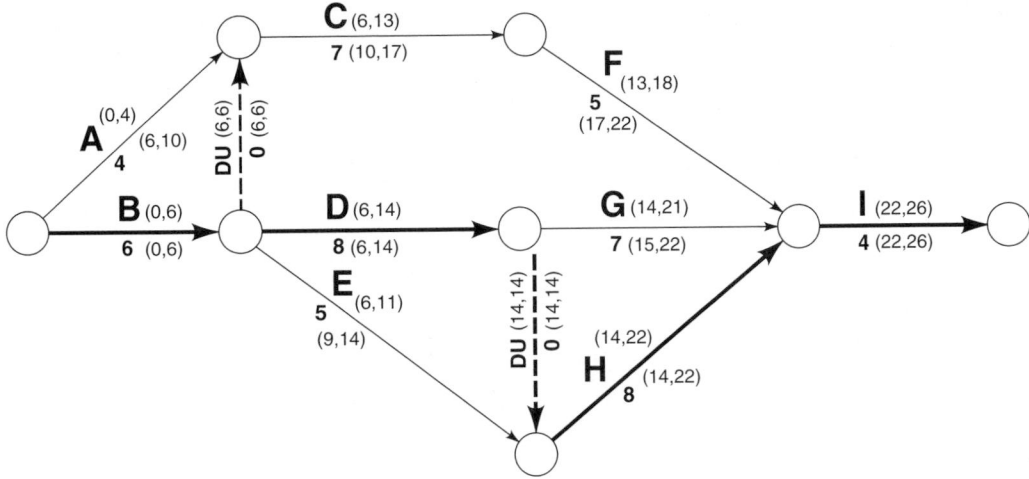

FIGURE 15–11
Sample AOA Network Diagram

duration being zero or infinity. If the actual duration is shorter than the most likely, it will not be *much* shorter (to the left), but if it is longer, then it could be *a lot* longer (to the right). The message is "when things go badly, they go *very* badly." Actually, since we only use three estimates in PERT, you would get a triangular distribution if plotted. The PERT and triangular distributions are shown together in Figure 15–13.

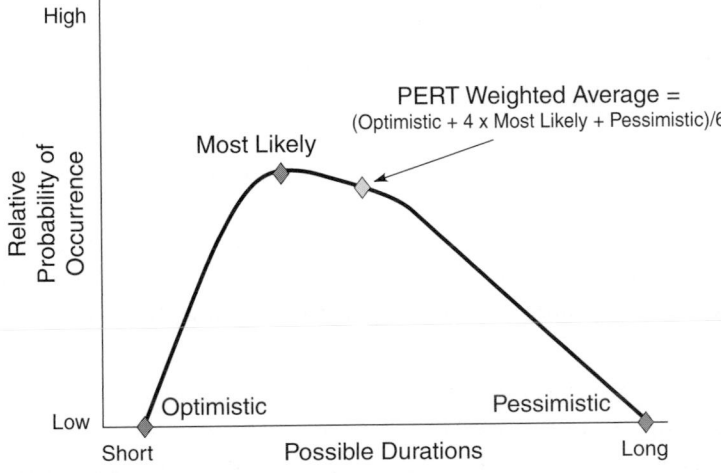

FIGURE 15–12
PERT Beta Distribution

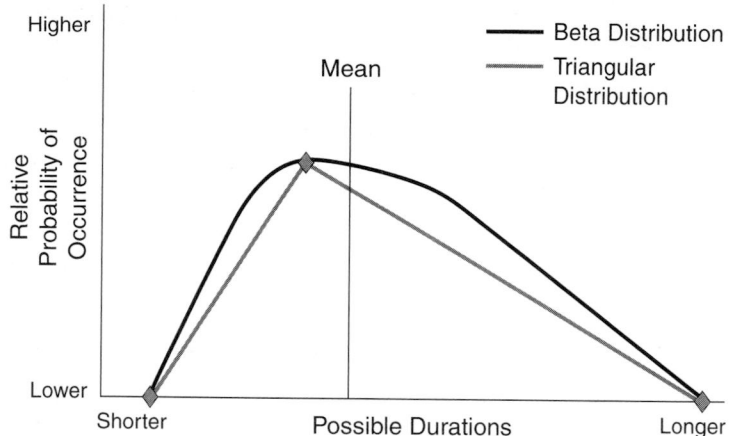

FIGURE 15–13
Triangular and Beta Distributions Compared

The formula for the weighted average of PERT is actually the mean of the triangular distribution used as an approximation of the beta, by experimentation. This is because in the 1950s, computing power to crunch the actual mean of the beta distribution was not available. The formula for computing the weighted average is:

$$\text{PERT Weighted Average} = \frac{\text{Optimistic} + 4(\text{Most Likely}) + \text{Pessimistic}}{6}$$

Since scheduling a lot of activities with three estimates is computationally messy, and many people argue that three "estimates" are not that much more accurate than one "estimate," most project management scheduling software uses the CPM method for scheduling. This results in the fixed-length activity bars we are used to seeing in most Gantt charts. You can compute the three values for each activity in your project plan, and plug them into your Gantt, but if any duration or estimate changes, you must recompute. This is not practical for most project schedules. However, you can use an aftermarket plug-in tool such as @Risk from Palisade Corporation, to plug in the three values and get the resulting PERT mean for your activity durations.[2]

CPM

The critical path method analyzes the precedence of activities to predict the total project duration. Its focus is on the *float*, also known as slack, free float, and path float, available between activities. The method calculates which sequence of activities (path through the network) has the least amount of schedule flexibility. The path with zero flexibility is called the *critical path,* because it will have zero float between all of its activities.

CPM analysis starts with a WBS that has single point estimates for each activity and uses PDM to relate precedence in a network. With the network drawn, you can then perform a two-pass analysis through the network of activities and calculate the node quantities for each activity. Once this is done, you will see the critical path. The critical path for the top network (using circle nodes) in Figure 15–10 is path B–C–D–F, and in Figure 15–11, it is path B–D–H–I. The critical path for the bottom network in Figure 15–10 cannot be determined yet because there is no duration information for the nodes.

To perform the two-path analysis, you first make a *forward pass* through the network, beginning at the start node, which begins with zeros for both earliest start and earliest finish. In Figure 15–10, they are noted at the top of the node as a numbered pair. At node A, the earliest start time will be zero, and the earliest finish time will be zero *plus* however long it takes to do A. In this case it will be 0 + 10 = 10. Continue following the arrow to C where the earliest start cannot yet be computed because we first need to know the data from node B. Go back to the start node and do the same calculation for B as was done for A. In this case, B will have an earliest start of zero, and an earliest finish of 20 (0 + 20 = 20). With this information, you can now compute C's earliest start time as the longest of A or B (A was 10 and B was 20, so in this case that's 20). *Add* the duration for C of 30 to get C's earliest finish time of (20 + 30 =) 50. Continue this process through D and F calculating the earliest start and finish times for each node. Be sure that you traverse each path in the network that feeds into a node to be calculated, or else you will not have all the information necessary to calculate the next earliest start time. The end node's earliest finish time is the total length of the longest path through the network, and is the length of the project (80 in the example of Figure 15–10).

With the forward pass complete, you are ready to do the *backward pass.* Starting at the end node, calculate the latest start and latest finish for each node in the network all the way back to the start node. This time, put the calculated numbers in the pair at the bottom of each node. This will be (80,80) for the end node in Figure 15–10. For node F, the latest start time will be the (known) finish time of 80 *minus* the duration for F (20), so it will be 80 − 20 = 60, and the latest start/finish pair will be shown as (60,80). For node D, a similar calculation occurs where the latest finish time is the same as the latest start time for node F (just calculated as 60), so 60 minus D's duration of 10 will be 50, and the pair will be (50,60). For node E, the calculation begins with the latest start of F (60) and subtracts E's duration from it (30) giving a latest start time of 30, so the number pair is (30,60). This process continues until you reach the start node and all number pairs have been calculated. The start node should calculate to (0,0).

Notice that for the forward pass, we:

- start at the *start* node.
- compute the *top* pair of numbers.
- always *add* the duration to the connecting node's earliest *finish* time.

And note that for the backward pass, we:

- start at the *end* node.
- compute the *bottom* pair of numbers.
- always *subtract* the duration from the connecting node's earliest *start* time.

When completed, each node shows its float as the difference between (either) the earliest start and latest start, or the earliest finish and the latest finish. It doesn't matter which number you use from each pair (start or finish) at a node, as long as both are the first or both are the last. Since the duration used to calculate them is the same number, you will get the same results. This float time means that the activity could start anytime between the earliest start and the latest start, yet still not lengthen the total length of the network (which is the total time for the project).

The *critical path* will show up as the path indicated by nodes with zero float. The critical paths are indicated in the networks in Figures 15–10 and 15–11 as heavy lines. For Figure 15–10, the critical path is B–C–D–F, and for Figure 15–11, it is B–D–H–I. Being on the critical path means that if duration grows for any of these nodes, the finish time for the whole project will grow. Conversely, if any of their durations shrink, then the finish time will also shrink. But (and this is a big "but"), any change in the duration of any node *may change the critical path*, so you would need to recalculate after each node change. Now you see why this is best left to computers! But at least you will now understand what the computer is doing to your schedule.

Notice that in all the calculations we've done to calculate float and find the critical path, we've not considered the availability of *any* of the resources necessary to actually do the activities. In most organizations, this is a major oversight as the resource availability is what usually constrains the schedule. This is the big weakness of CPM. It is an activity-oriented method that provides activity-constrained schedules. To put more realism into the schedule, we need to map the resources' actual availability to create a resource-constrained schedule.

Leveling Resource Assignments _____

When all the resources (Chapter 12) have been assigned to the scheduled and precedence-linked (Chapter 14) activities from the WBS (Chapter 8), and the activity-constrained schedule is prepared, the resource overloads can be identified. Usually, at this first pass of the schedule, you find an uneven distribution of resource needs, as shown in Figure 15–14, because they were not part of the CPM scheduling algorithm.

It is usually desirable to smooth out the demand for resources over the course of a project to minimize resource idle time between the peaks of demand. *Load leveling* is the process of rescheduling tasks that have available slack to achieve a more balanced distribution of resource usage.

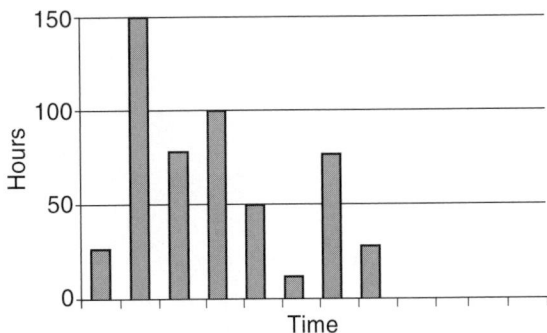

FIGURE 15–14
Uneven Resource Loading

There are two basic types of algorithms for leveling: those based on linear programming techniques, and those based on enumerative math techniques.

Most project scheduling tools will do resource leveling for you, but they do not provide an optimal solution, so you must use judgment when applying them. You must consider:

- Activity shifting—sliding start/end dates forward or backward to avoid a resource over allocation;
- Activity splitting—breaking an activity into two or more pieces to accommodate resource availability;
- Activity stretching—using less of a given resource continuously, making the activity duration longer;
- Resource substitution—changing resources for higher performance, more efficiency, etc.;
- Allocating overtime—accepting the overload, and paying for it;
- Resource depletion—assigning a resource using something other than a flat effort distribution.

The project manager must consider the effects of fixed or imposed dates on leveling issues ("must start/finish on" dates). These are treated as project constraints and cause rigidity in the schedule, making everything difficult to work with. Of course, some dates simply must remain fixed, like the due date for all Year2000 (Y2K) projects. Generally, when leveling is applied to an unleveled schedule, the project end date and all deliverable dates move farther out as shown in Figure 15–15.

Most of the project management scheduling tools today (like Microsoft Project) handle the complexities of schedule representations for you, and it is unlikely that you will ever have to do network calculations by hand for even a small-sized project, but it is still important to understand what's going on inside these scheduling tools for schedule calculations.

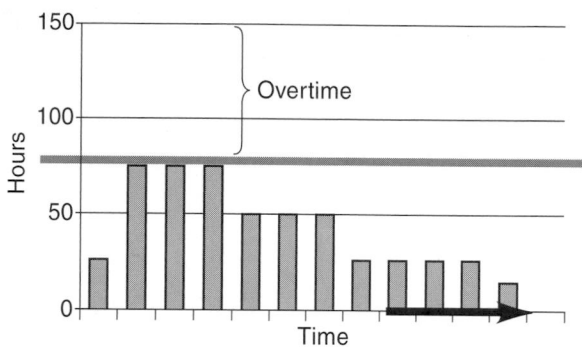

FIGURE 15–15
Leveled Resource Loading

Map the Schedule to a Real Calendar

One of the things that seems to baffle most new project managers is how to construct a workable schedule. Often, since they know they want a Gantt chart when they are done (because they saw one in a management review once), they start with that view of their WBS in a scheduling software tool like Microsoft Project. Sometimes they don't even have a work breakdown structure yet and just start from scratch with a blank Gantt view and a table to the left side. Then they add dated activity entries on the WBS, or directly with the Gantt bars, and manipulate them until the dates look like they "feel right." Then they add some precedence relationships and adjust it all a little bit. Lastly, they add resources to the picture and get very disturbed when the leveling algorithms rearrange their carefully laid out Gantt chart, changing the start and end dates for many activities, and splitting others. So they "undo" it and just show a summary of the major components' start and finish dates. This is a "feel" schedule, not a "real" one.

There are at least two things wrong when a schedule is created this way:

1. The project team was not involved in the preparation of the plan, which means that it will be the project manager's plan, not the project team's plan.

2. They don't understand how to map the information they *do* have together to create a "real" schedule (as opposed to a "feel" schedule).

The Gantt view, or any other view for that matter, only reflects the underlying information from the WBS, activity precedence, resource assignments, and the (fixed sized, usually average time) work estimates for each activity. When mapped together properly and overlaid on a "real" calendar of available work time, a "real" schedule results. To adjust this realistic schedule, the underlying elements must be changed (with good reasons), not the start and end dates.

To understand how to map everything together and get a "real" schedule, we will explore the relationship of the four major components of a scheduled activity:

- Work—staff time of estimated effort;
- Units—the number of resources available to complete the activity;
- Duration—work time needed to complete the activity;
- Dates—calendar time needed to complete the activity.

The triple constraint's elements of scope, schedule, and cost have a relationship to these components. The *work* is the total staff time of effort estimated from the estimation processes described in Chapters 10 and 11. Its output would be something like:

> Work: *"Design the GUI: 48 staff-days"*

The *units* would be the number of resources available to do the work. Perhaps for this example, it would be something like:

> Units: *"Able, Baker, Charlie, and Dawn will do it"*

The *duration* would be the actual number of workdays needed for the resources to do the work, which may be calculated from the work to do and units available:

> Duration: *"48 Staff-days / 4 People = 12 Workdays on task"*

The calendar dates for this would come from applying an actual calendar to the 12 days needed, assuming that everyone was working full time in a normal Monday through Friday 40-hour workweek:

> Dates: *"We need 2 weeks and 2 workdays to design the GUI"*

The first three parts would remain fairly constant no matter when the work was to be done, assuming that the same people were involved. This last part is very calendar dependent, obviously, and is sensitive to the exact days that the work falls on. If any of the resource units were unavailable during the work period, the expected end date of the work would move accordingly. It is a fixed-sized pie.

This relationship is a lot like the distance-time-speed relationship in Box 15–1.

Box 15–1
Distance-Time-Speed Relationship

$$\frac{Distance}{Speed} = Time$$

If I want to go from New York to Los Angeles in my car, and average 60 miles per hour when driving, then it will take 50 hours of driving to reach L.A. But, I won't be able to drive 24 hours a day, so if I choose to drive for only 8 hours each day, then it will take me 6.25 days to make the trip. The only way to do it quicker is to either drive faster or longer per day. The same is true for the triple constraint parameters. If I want to "Build the GUI," and it takes 48 staff-hours and I have four people to do it, then it will take 12 days to build it. If I want it faster, then I have to reduce the scope (limited-function GUI perhaps), change my four people's work hours (add overtime), or add more people. Be careful with adding people to an activity, though, as the more people that get involved, the less efficient the communications, exchanges, and division of work (this is the famous "Mythical Man Month" that Fred Brooks warned us about).

Critical Chain Scheduling

So far, we have talked only about the classical project management scheduling techniques (PERT, CPM, PDM, etc). Now that you have grounding in what "classical PM" is all about, let's look at some recent thinking in the scheduling field. Since the 1950s when PERT and CPM were introduced, there really weren't any major new developments in scheduling technology until 1997, when Dr. Eliyahu Goldratt applied his theory of constraints (TOC) to the practice of project management producing a book called *Critical Chain*.

TOC is a way of thinking and problem solving similar to TQM, and is applicable to just about any discipline. It is derived from systems theory, and from the knowledge that all systems have constraints within them. The trick is to identify the constraints and arrange the system to concentrate on and exploit the constraints in any way possible, thereby reducing the constraints and improving the whole system. There are five steps to Goldratt's TOC focusing method:

1. Identify the system's constraints.
2. Decide how to exploit the system's constraints.
3. Subordinate everything else to the above decision.
4. Elevate the system's constraints.
5. If a constraint has been broken, go back to Step 1.

The idea is to focus on increasing the *throughput* of the total system by reducing *work-in-process (WIP)* and *operating expense* (the cost of running the system). Goldratt makes much of the fact that most of us concentrate on optimizing the pieces of a system, and not the system itself. He faults our accounting conventions for treating inventories (WIP) as assets, when in fact they are big liabilities because they decrease throughput. The manufacturing improvement concepts of "just-in-time" production introduced in the 1980s are a reflection of that fact. He also faults many production optimization techniques like manufacturing requirements planning (MRP) and line-balancing for focusing on local optimizations at the expense of the *total system's* throughput.

Goldratt's theory of constraints was introduced in 1984 in a book called *The Goal*, where he applied it to a factory production situation. The book was very well received as it was written like a novel instead of a textbook or theory paper. In 1990, he wrote the *Theory of Constraints* to detail the principles of the theory.

In 1997, Goldratt wrote *Critical Chain* in which he applied TOC to project management and scheduling. It also is presented as a novel and is easy to read. Others have begun to expand on his writings, such as Robert Newbold's *Project Management in the Fast Lane: Applying the Theory of Constraints* of 1998.

In *Critical Chain*, Goldratt says that a project schedule is a lot like a factory, except that a progress line of work is moving through a number of activities, instead of a product being made in a sequence of machines. He describes some common problems with the way project scheduling has been handled in recent years, such as yielding to the student syndrome, and doing too much multitasking to get optimum organizational throughput.

He focuses on handling the uncertainties in any project plan, which is just good risk management, and advocates putting contingency buffers in strategic places in a project schedule.

One main focus is on handling scarce resources. Goldratt observed that an organization is a system, and like every system, it has constraints. Indeed, every software development organization seems to have a few bottlenecks, whether they are key technical individuals who seem to have a large role in most of the active projects, or a sub-group such as testing, that paces the total engineering throughout potential of the whole organization. These key constraints tend to be on the critical path in every project they are involved in. If these bottlenecks could be alleviated, then the throughput of the whole organization could be improved.

Identifying key constraining resources (which Goldratt calls "Herbies" after the slowest scout in a Boy Scout troop hiking anecdote mentioned in *The Goal*), and wrapping the activities around their availability, with appropriate buffers for activities feeding their work, will yield better results than simply trying to schedule all activities to occur as soon as possible (the default scheduling condition in most scheduling tools today).

Goldratt's approach is to build a project schedule from the final end deliverable backwards toward the beginning of the project, focusing on utilizing the "Herbies" as efficiently as possible, even if it means others in the organization might be idle for a time. He argues that it is better for them to be idle, and be ready to perform when the "Herbie" is ready and available, than to get involved in something else, possibly causing a slip in a critical path activity. Goldratt calls the chain of activities where "Herbies" are involved, the "Critical Chain," noting that it is OK for certain machines in a factory line to be idle, as long as the pace of the constraining machine remains optimized.

Figure 15–16 illustrates how a critical chain schedule might look. In this project, the critical chain is indicated as a heavy line through several activities and stops at the Early Finish Date (it does not go through the project buffer). Some of these activities have been identified as critical through a CPM analysis, and some are critical because the resource needed for them demands it. For instance, the resource needed for 1B, 2B, and 3B is the same, so those activities cannot be done simultaneously. CPM analysis would not have them on the critical path. Instead, these resource-constrained activities are shown serially, with a special buffer in front of them. These "feeding buffers" are designed to protect the critical chain activities from slippage of the preceding activities (1C, 2A, and 3A) due to student syndrome or the uncertainty of the future. If they do slip, there should be some time to absorb the slippage before their output is needed for the critical chain activity, else a non-critical activity might cause the whole project schedule to slip.

It is important to realize that the critical path and the critical chain are not the same thing. The critical path is the longest path through the network when only activities are considered. A critical chain is the longest path through the network considering both activities and resources.

Buffer sizing and management are important issues in critical chain scheduling. How big should a buffer be? The general guideline is to make them 50 percent of the total time for all

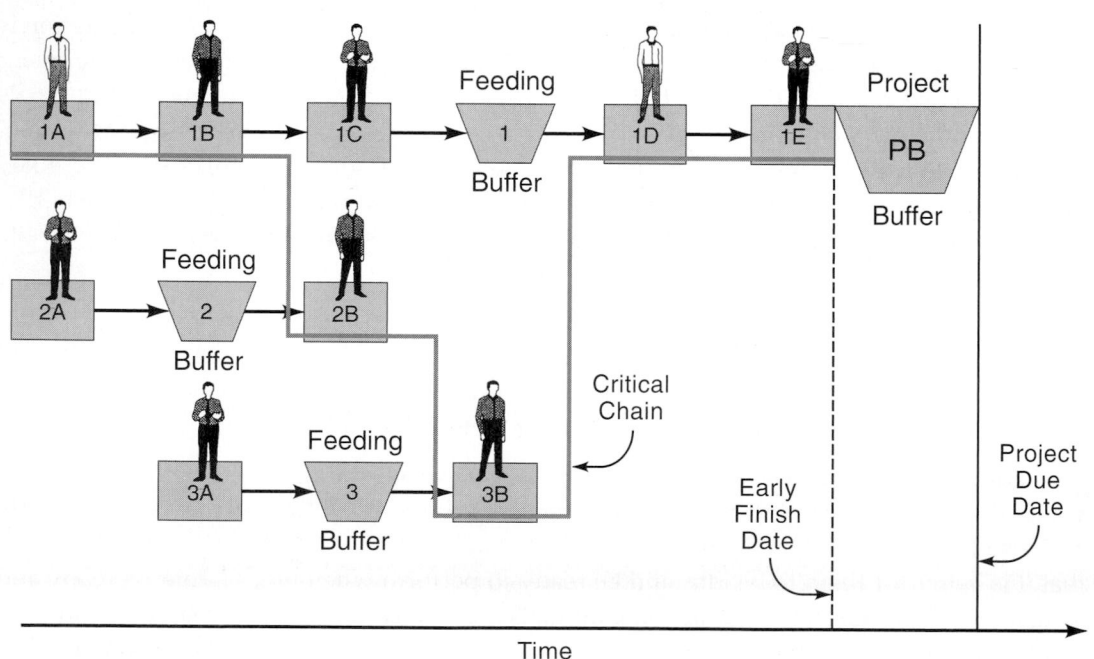

FIGURE 15–16
Critical Chain Schedule Construction

the preceding activities that they buffer, if those activities were estimated with a only a 50 percent probability of achievement. If the probability for each activity was conservatively estimated at closer to 95 percent, then the buffers should be much smaller, around 5 percent. Remember, the purpose of the buffers is to absorb the inevitable uncertainty of planning future events. The more of it that you can manage at the feeding and project levels, the better the project can control deliverable dates. We'll look at how to use these buffers for monitoring and controlling the project in Chapter 25.

Goldratt's techniques are not new, but his fresh approach to the common problems we see today has breathed new life into how we view activity scheduling with constrained resources. He focuses us on the resource-constrained schedule instead of the activity-constrained schedule, and on uncertainty management (buffer placement)—the right places to focus for optimum project throughput.

Unfortunately, most PM tools today don't comprehend uncertainty very well. PERT incorporates a probability distribution around any task due date, but the computations get very messy in a large schedule, so PM tools usually use CPM instead (fixed task estimates). Neither incorporates the concept of resource constraints very much, or the use of buffer management to handle uncertainties. Only a few tools are emerging to focus on the CPM ideas of the critical chain and buffer management. See the Web resources in Chapter 14 for links to some of these.

However, you can explicitly handle uncertainty in your project schedule by inserting buffers as activities at strategic points. Figure 15–17 shows one possibility for inserting buffers at the ends of major work stages.

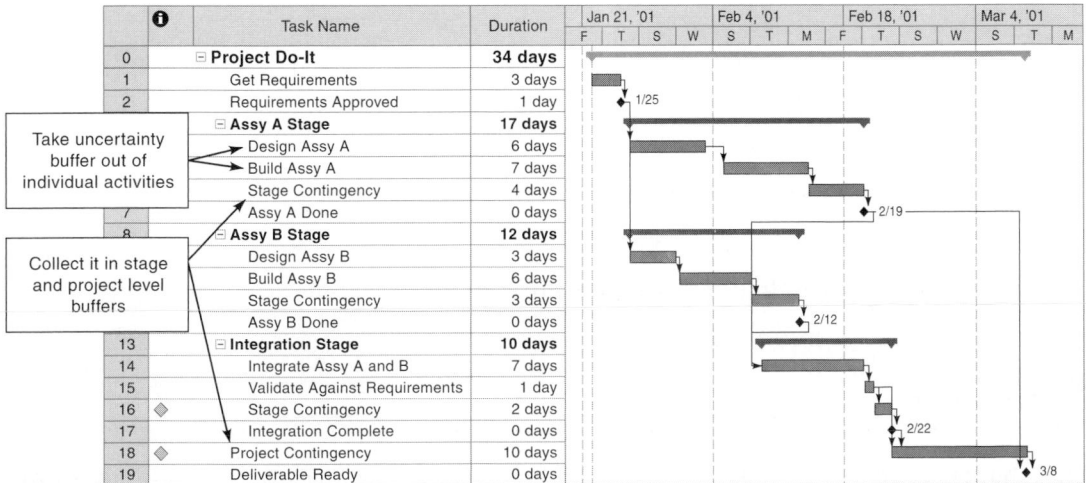

FIGURE 15–17
Critical Chain Schedule Construction

Complete Process for Building a Real Schedule _____

To summarize the whole CPM schedule building and analysis process, here are the steps from concept through critical path identification to schedule tuning and documentation:

1. Develop the work breakdown structure (WBS)

   a. What activities must be done?

   b. Who will do each one?

   c. What materials/supplies are required?

   d. How much will each activity cost?

2. Identify activity dependencies

   a. What can be done first?

   b. What can be done next?

   c. What can be done in parallel?

3. Develop a network diagram (PDM) from the WBS and dependency information

4. Do the CPM analysis computations

   a. Forward pass to find early times

   b. Backward pass for late times

   c. Is total duration acceptable?

5. Find and analyze critical path activities

   a. Can any be shortened?

   b. If so, will the critical path change?

6. Perform resource allocation

   a. Level resources

   b. Is total duration still acceptable?

7. Convert the network to Gantt chart

8. Develop the cost baseline and spending curves

Summary _____

This chapter covers the details of constructing a project schedule from a work breakdown structure with dependencies. Several approaches were presented describing the processes of the critical path method and the critical chain method for schedule construction.

We also presented the different ways a schedule network could be represented, along with several approaches to network diagramming. We discussed the effects of psychology and probability on project planning.

Problems for Review

1. What are the major difficulties with PERT, and how can they be overcome?

2. Why do you think that CPM methods are still used today in most scheduling software, even though computing power today is many times that of the 1950s? Do you think software tools should use PERT, or is CPM adequate, since it is all just "guestimating" anyway?

3. Do you think the critical chain methodology is different from that described in the PMBOK? Explain.

4. Which do you think would be a better measure of project performance: EVA or CPM's buffer management? Why?

Visit the Case Study

Ms. Patel has gotten your PMP approved and all the issues of tasks versus work packages have been resolved with Dr. Zhou. You feel that the correct organization form has been chosen, in spite of the BSD reorganization. Now it is time to put together the final work schedule. What are the remaining pieces of information that you need? Ms. Patel is in the final budget planning cycle for the next fiscal year and needs a firm number from you on the ARRS project. Produce your ARRS schedule.

Citations

[1] *www.goldratt.com/.* Critical Chain.

[2] *www.palisade.com/html/risk_for_project.html.* @Risk.

Suggested Readings

Kerzner, Harold (1998). *Project Management: A Systems Approach to Planning, Scheduling, and Controlling,* 6th ed. New York, NY: John Wiley & Sons, Inc.

Lewis, James P. (1995). *Project Planning, Scheduling, and Control: A Hands-On Guide to Bringing Projects in on Time and on Budget*, revised edition. New York, NY: McGraw-Hill.

Moder, Joseph J., et al. (1983). *Project Management with CPM, PERT, and Precedence Diagramming*, 3rd ed. New York, NY: Van Nostrand.

O'Brien, James J. (1969). *Scheduling Handbook.* New York, NY: McGraw-Hill.

Paulk, Mark C., et al. (1994). *The Capability Maturity Model: Guidelines for Improving the Software Process.* New York, NY: Addison-Wesley.

Pressman, Roger S. (2001). *Software Engineering: A Practitioner's Approach*, 5th ed. New York, NY: McGraw-Hill.

Web Pages for Further Information_____

stsc.hill.af.mil/crosstalk/1995/mar/metrics.asp. Metrics Tools: Effort and Schedule by David R. Erickson and A. Todd Steadman, STSC.

www.pmi.org/publictn/pmboktoc.htm. PMI's *A Guide to the Project Management Body of Knowledge (PMBOK® Guide)*, Chapter 6.

Eliciting Requirements

16

Almost everyone involved in software engineering or software project management during the last 20 years is well aware of the importance of requirements. We rarely hear of a success story declaring victory over the ever-elusive set of specs, but we often hear poor requirements cited as public enemy number one. As developers and managers, we're cautioned about the exorbitant cost to the project of a missed or incorrect requirement—the most expensive error to correct and the most damaging to customer relations. We're advised of the meaninglessness of a fuzzy requirement, and we're counseled about tester angst over an imprecise one. If we are far enough off the mark with requirements, we may be building a completely different system than the one actually desired; we may slip the bounds of the contractual agreement. Even when starting out on the right foot, requirements volatility can wreak havoc on the best-laid plans. Our goal is to understand the problem we have pledged to solve, even though we have multiple customers, often with conflicting needs. Each stakeholder has his own view of what is needed and wanted, each has a "filter" of the world, and each has individual learning and communication styles. If we fail to listen and communicate effectively, the "right" requirements will be discovered too late, if ever. Methods exist to aid requirements elicitation, albeit none is an exact science. Given that requirements form the foundation for the software product, it's well worth our time to adopt as many approaches as possible to triumph over this most challenging, yet crucial, step in the development process.

Where We Are in the Product Development Life Cycle

As shown in Figure 16–1, requirements begin to be gathered at the very beginning of the product development life cycle and continue in a gathering-refinement cycle through concept exploration, system exploration, and requirements analysis. In fact, they never stop being gathered, as most modern projects recognize an iterative development life cycle (e.g., spiral, prototyping, incremental delivery), but there comes a time when they, or a subset of them, are solid enough for the development team to move on. The activity of gathering or eliciting software requirements may begin in earnest as soon as the system requirements are firm. Once gathered, the requirements are then packaged into an official document, the Software Requirements Specification (SRS). The requirements are modeled, communicated back to the customer, and used as the basis for the software design.

Chapter 16 Relation to the 34 Competencies

Requirements elicitation, so critical to the project and product, relies upon many of the 34 competencies, as reflected in Figure 16–2.

Product Development Techniques

3. **Defining the product**—The software requirements are the very definition of the software product.

5. **Managing requirements**—As described in the first key process area mentioned, in the first meaningful level of SEI CMM maturity (Level 2: Repeatable), the requirements must be controlled (not changed without approvals), and baselined for driving project plans, products, and activities.

6. **Managing subcontractors**—If subcontractors are involved, proper communication of precise requirements is essential.

7. **Performing the initial assessment**—Only when it is known what the software product will be, can risks be assessed and estimates of size, cost, effort, and schedule made.

8. **Selecting methods and tools**—Methods such as those described in this chapter (e.g., interviewing, brainstorming) may be selected to support the elicitation of requirements. Automated tools support many of these methods.

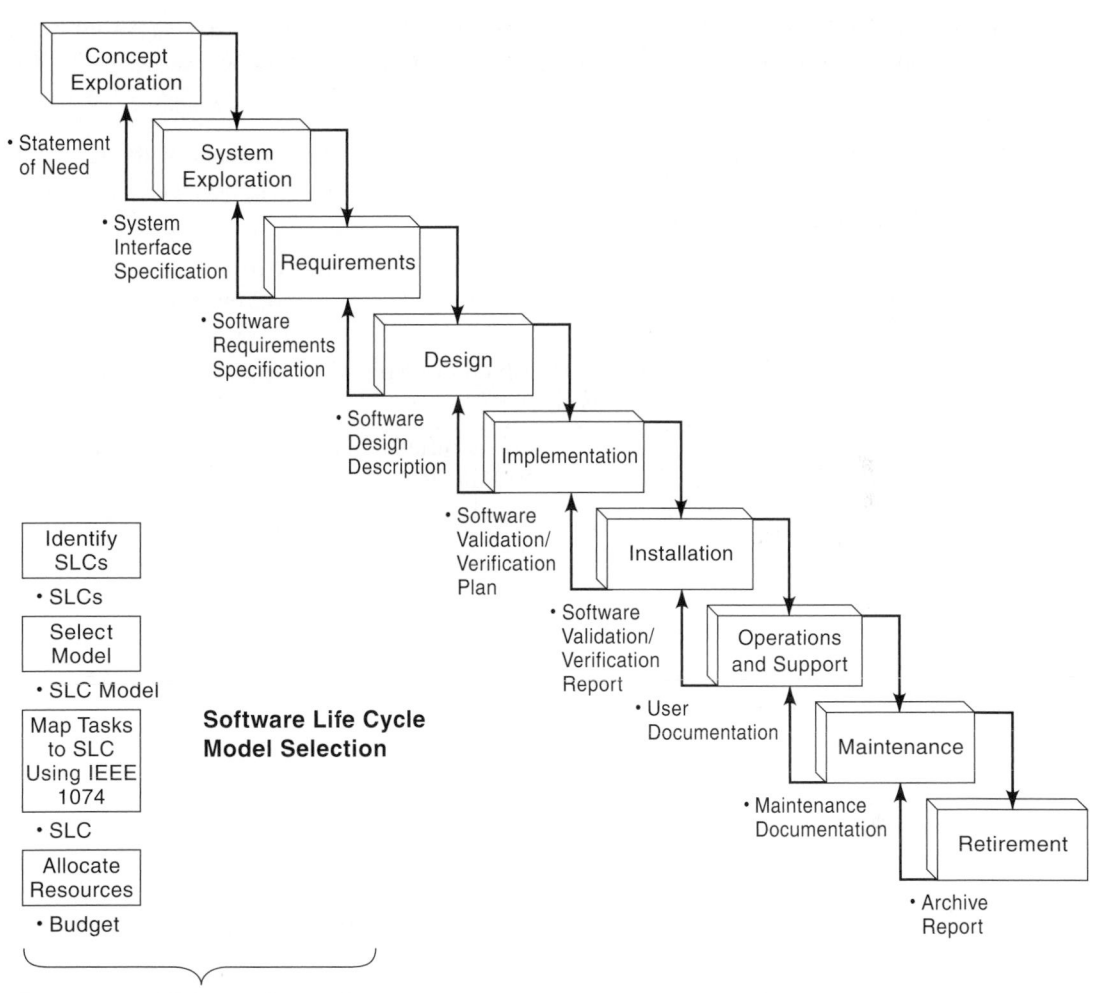

Requirements Elicitation Occurs Here

FIGURE 16–1
Requirements Elicitation Occurs at the Beginning of the Life Cycle

Project Management Skills

12. **Building a work breakdown structure**—Many project managers prefer to build a product WBS. To do so, the requirements defining the product must be known.

16. **Managing risks**—There are many risks to be managed in the requirements elicitation stage—the risk of goldplating, of poor negotiation for incremental release specifications, of gathering untestable requirements, and so on.

19. **Selecting metrics**—Requirements volatility is a useful metric that must begin with the observation of the number, type, and complexity of each requirement.

People Management Skills

25. **Holding effective meetings**—As will be described in this chapter, most of the methods for eliciting requirements occur in the setting of a planned meeting between customers, users, and analysts.

26. **Interaction and communication**—At no other time in a software project is communication so important as during requirements gathering. The development team is trying to "get inside the heads" of the stakeholders. The old saw about the requirement, "Build me a sports car," when the customer envisions a Porsche and the developer envisions a Sports Utility Vehicle (SUV), remains true.

29. **Negotiating successfully**—It is rare that the customer will be able to receive all desired requirements in the first version of the software. Prioritizing requirements and determining release schedules requires mature and fair negotiation.

31. **Presenting effectively**—Requirements elicitation is an iterative affair—we listen a little, feed back a little, and do it again. The manner in which the requirements, as understood by the project team, is presented to the stakeholders marks the beginning of a project-long relationship.

Software   Project   Management

Product	Project	People
1. Assessing processes	**12. Building a work breakdown structure**	23. Appraising performance
2. Awareness of process standards		24. Handling intellectual property
3. Defining the product	13. Documenting plans	**25. Holding effective meetings**
4. Evaluating alternative processes	14. Estimating cost	**26. Interaction and communication**
5. Managing requirements	15. Estimating effort	27. Leadership
6. Managing subcontractors	**16. Managing risks**	28. Managing change
7. Performing the initial assessment	17. Monitoring development	**29. Negotiating successfully**
8. Selecting methods and tools	18. Scheduling	30. Planning careers
9. Tailoring processes	**19. Selecting metrics**	**31. Presenting effectively**
10. Tracking product quality	20. Selecting project management tools	32. Recruiting
11. Understanding development activities	21. Tracking process	33. Selecting a team
	22. Tracking project progress	34. Teambuilding

FIGURE 16–2
Eliciting Requirements' Relationship to the 34 Competencies

Learning Objectives for Chapter 16 _____

Upon completion of this chapter, the reader should be able to:

- Describe where requirements elicitation occurs in the product development life cycle;
- List the product, project, and people competencies from the SQI BOK that are necessary for successful requirements gathering;
- Describe requirements management, both in general and in connection to the SEI CMM;
- Describe critical success factors and how they apply to software requirements;
- Describe the criticality of accurate requirements elicitation for the success of software development;
- Identify the characteristics of a well-written requirement (e.g., primitive, testable);
- List the types of software requirements;
- List several methods used in the elicitation of software requirements;
- Describe interviewing, brainstorming, mind mapping, FAST, JAD, and use case techniques for eliciting requirements;
- Discuss the challenges of gathering software requirements.

Background for Requirements Management _____

Several excellent guides to requirements elicitation have been published; therefore, our intent is not to rearticulate them, but to make the reader aware of them and the power of their use. Gerald Weinberg,[1] Roger Pressman,[2] and Barry Boehm[3] have suggested steps to gather and understand the necessary software requirements and prepare them for specifications in the SRS, as discussed in Chapter 17. We do not pretend to know of superior approaches, but we do desire to present a practical description and guide to consolidating the wisdom of these authorities.

In this chapter we'll discuss "Gather" and "Analyze" from Weinberg's steps shown in Figure 16–3. We will also reference a set of very high-level models that could help with gathering and analyzing requirements. The majority of modeling activities will take place in the analysis and design phases, as described in Chapter 22.

From Pressman's requirements engineering steps, shown in Figure 16–4, we'll cover requirements elicitation (understanding what the customer wants) and requirements analysis and negotiation (analyzing need, negotiating a reasonable solution). Pressman's requirements

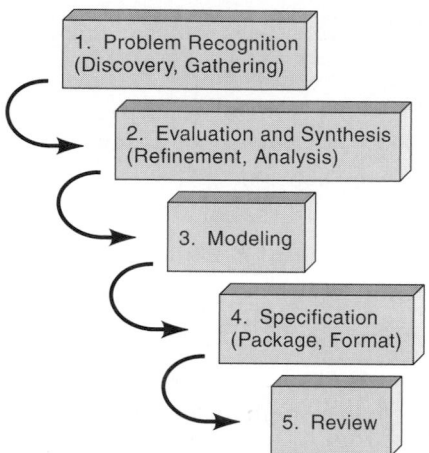

FIGURE 16–3
Weinberg's Steps in Analyzing Requirements
Source: Adapted from Donald C. Gause and Gerald M. Weinberg (1989). *Exploring Requirements: Quality Before Design*. New York, NY: Dorset House.

specification step is covered in Chapter 17; Pressman's system modeling step is covered in Chapter 22.

Requirements engineering steps include:

- Requirements elicitation—understanding what the customer wants;
- Requirements analysis and negotiation—analyzing need, negotiating a reasonable solution;
- Requirements specification—specifying the solution unambiguously;
- System modeling;
- Requirements validation—validating the specification;
- Requirements management.

From Boehm's model, shown in Figure 16–5, win conditions, negotiation, mutual gain, trade-offs, and win-win agreements apply when prioritizing requirements and preparing them for the specification activities.

Software requirements engineering is the process of determining what is to be produced in a software system. It has the widely recognized goal of determining the needs for, and the intended external behavior of, a system design. The process of requirements engineering is regarded as one of the most important aspects of building a software system. Within a project, it is a general term used to encompass all the activities related to requirements. The four specific steps in software requirements engineering are: requirements elicitation, requirements analysis, requirements specification, and requirements validation.

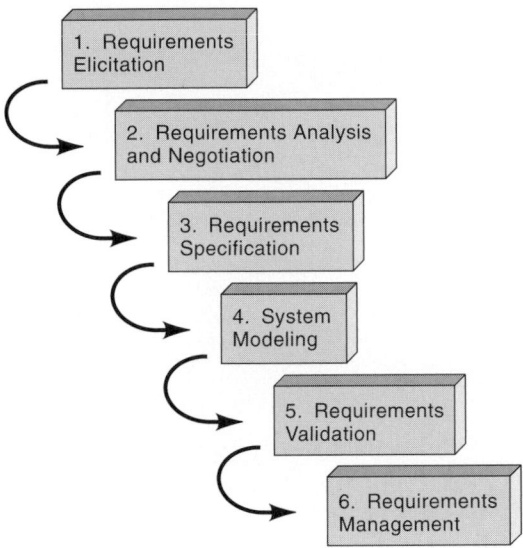

FIGURE 16–4
Pressman's Requirements Engineering Steps

Requirements Management and the SEI CMM _____

Requirements management is a key process area (KPA) for SEI CMM Level 2, the repeatable level. The purpose is to "establish a common understanding between the customer and the software project of the customer's requirements that will be addressed by the software project."[4] The customer may be a stakeholder other than the external user, such as the system engineering group, the marketing group, or another internal organization. The CMM views this KPA as managing system requirements that have already been gathered and subdivided into hardware and software requirements. Nonetheless, these requirements allocated to software are often just bare bones and must be fleshed out via further requirements-gathering activities with the customer.

The goals for the requirements management KPA, along with related activities, are listed below.

Goals

Goal 1: System requirements allocated to software are controlled to establish a baseline for software engineering and management use.

Goal 2: Software plans, products, and activities are kept consistent with the system requirements allocated to software.

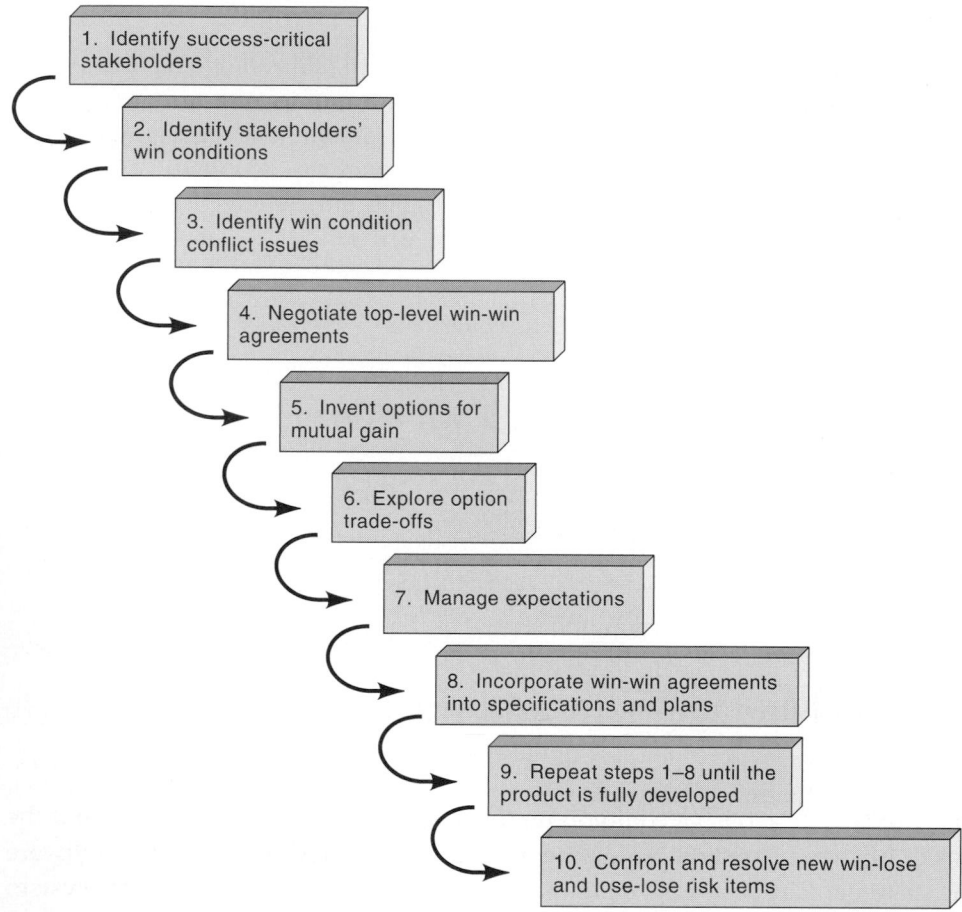

FIGURE 16–5

Boehm's Requirements Engineering Steps
Source: Adapted from Barry W. Boehm, et al. (1994). "Software Requirements as Negotiated Win Conditions."
Proceedings of ICRE, April, pp. 74–83.

Activities Performed

Activity 1: The software engineering group reviews the allocated requirements before they are incorporated into the software project.

1. Incomplete and missing allocated requirements are identified.

2. The allocated requirements are reviewed to determine whether they are:

   • feasible and appropriate to implement in software;

   • clearly and properly stated;

- consistent with each other;
- testable.

3. Any allocated requirements identified as having potential problems are reviewed with the group responsible for analyzing and allocating system requirements and necessary changes are made.

4. Commitments resulting from the allocated requirements are negotiated with the affected groups.

Activity 2: The software engineering group uses the allocated requirements as the basis for software plans, work products, and activities.

Activity 3: Changes to the allocated requirements are reviewed and incorporated into the software project.

Critical Success Factors as Applied to Software Requirements

Requirements are often viewed as a set of critical success factors (CSFs) for a software product. Descriptions of CSFs make the link seen reasonable:

- Those limited number of areas where "things must go right";
- Those managerial or enterprise areas that must be given special and continual attention to bring about high performance;
- Those factors predicting success on projects;
- Events or circumstances that require the special attention of managers;
- Those factors in which success is necessary in order that each of the major project participants in a project has the maximum chance of achieving the goals;
- Achieving quality targets.

There is a temptation to create CSFs with simplistic characteristics, such as "find a solution to the defined problem," but we shouldn't give in because there is too much ambiguity in this sort of definition of success. In order to proceed with requirements specification and design, requirements that will make the project results successful to the user community and other stakeholders need specificity.

CSFs, when clearly identified as critical requirements, can be tested and measured and can assist the analyst with controlling scope-creep. This does not give the analyst license to ignore the additional or remaining requirements, but does keep the project focused on those that were defined as the most significant during this crucial requirements gathering phase. The use of CSFs has been demonstrated to be especially effective in the rapid prototyping, RAD, and spiral models due to the rapidly changing environment of these life cycles.

CSFs are directly related to strategic and business plan objectives and goals. For each critical success factor there is an associated key indicator that provides the measure, and a standard of performance or allowable variance from planned performance. CSFs for software projects are usually thought of as completing certain milestones or other key indicators that provide a reading of performance. For our purposes here, we will limit our discussion to CSFs for the product and keep in mind that some requirements are simply more essential than others. We will use the definitions of CSFs to help identify them. This will come in handy when functions must inevitably be scrubbed or delayed in the prioritization process.

What Is a Software Requirement?

A software requirement is a capability that somebody needs or wants. It can be a component of an entire new application, a new feature for an existing application (an enhancement), or a request to correct a current shortcoming.

IEEE defines a *requirement* as: (a) a condition or capability needed by a user to solve a problem or achieve an objective; (b) a condition or capability that must be met or possessed by a system or system component to satisfy a contract, standard, specification, or other formally imposed document; (c) a documented representation of a condition or capability as in definition (a) or (b).[5]

Types of Software Requirements

A requirement may be conscious (known, spoken)—something a stakeholder believes to be necessary. There are also "unconscious requirements," forgotten (unspoken) by the stakeholder because they aren't needed right now, or they are unknown because they are needed only by another stakeholder, or they are satisfied by some existing process, manual or automated. Weinberg and others suggest there are also "undreamed-of requirements" (unknown, unspoken)—those that the stakeholder doesn't know can be had.

A conscious, forgotten, or unknown requirement may be functional or nonfunctional. Functional requirements specify what the software has to do. They are traceable to a specific source, often to use cases or business rules. They are often called "product features."

Nonfunctional requirements are mostly quality requirements that stipulate how well the software does what it has to do. Nonfunctional quality requirements that are especially important to users include specifications of desired performance, availability, reliability, usability, and flexibility. Nonfunctional quality requirements that are especially important to developers and maintainers include specifications of desired configurability and integratability of the software system, as well as maintainability, portability, and testability. Nonfunctional requirements may also be implicit requirements for changeability, reusability, and interoperability.

Some functional/nonfunctional requirements cannot be satisfied by one, or even a small set of, system components and are therefore dependent on other parts of the system. These require systemwide properties and a superset of quality requirements.

Some requirements are architectural, such as component-naming compatibility, interface-ability, upgradability, and "system buildability."

Other requirements are constraints, such as system design constraints, standards conformance, legal issues, and organizational issues. Constraints can come from users or organizations and may be functional or nonfunctional.

What Makes a "Good" Software Requirement? _____

In Chapter 17, "Developing the Software Requirements Specification," the translation of software requirements into software specifications is described. Here, during requirements elicitation, we are not so interested in formatting as we are in creating; the emphasis is on group activities designed to ensure that *all* requirements are considered, from *every* stakeholder's point of view. While we're gathering requirements, we can employ some simultaneous thoughts on what will make them viable software specifications—it never hurts to look ahead and make the next step a little easier.

There are attributes of quality that should permeate requirements. As we will see in Chapter 30, "Software Quality Assurance," these "-ilities" that originated with McCall in the 1970s continue to be a significant guide for distinguishing "good" software requirements from those that are less than first-rate. Weigers points out that there are characteristics that individual requirement statements should exhibit, and desirable characteristics of the SRS document as a whole.[6] We want to achieve both. According to Boehm, one of the most powerful tests for the "goodness" of a requirement is its testability. These experts suggest that if test cases can be written against a requirement, then it is unambiguous and measurable and, most importantly, we will be able to tell when it has been satisfied.

We can keep the following quality attributes in mind as we gather software requirements. Each requirement should be:

- Correct—a quality that can only be ensured by the customer or user representative;
- Possible (feasible)—a quality that requires knowledge of the environment on the part of the developer; available tools, techniques, people, and budgets must be able to satisfy the final requirements;
- Necessary—a quality that can be determined between the developers and stakeholders in an interview or elicitation session; there are many features that are nice to have, but in the ranking of requirements for development and implementation of the first software version, "gold plating" is discouraged; one test for necessity is to trace the source of the requirement back to a use case scenario;

- Prioritized—a quality that developers and stakeholders can determine; as we will explore in greater depth toward the end of this chapter, von Mayerhauser suggests three levels of priority: very important; absolutely necessary (to be implemented in the next release, essential); important, but not necessary for the next release (conditional); and purely optional (nice to have, but implementation will depend on resources and schedule);[7]
- Unambiguous—a quality that IEEE tells us means that there is only one interpretation; easy to read and understand;
- Concise—with only the information necessary to proceed to the next development step; associated history, costs, schedule, and so on, are housed elsewhere;
- Verifiable (testable, measureable)—a quality that means a person or machine can check that the software meets the requirement.

In addition to the quality of the individual requirement, we can pay attention to the future needs of the quality of the complete SRS:

- Complete—a quality that can be ensured by stakeholder review and means that all significant requirements are included (functional, performance, external, etc.);
- Consistent—a quality that the developers usually ensure and equals consistency among internal documents;
- Changeable—requirements changes are a fact of life;
- Traceable—a quality shared by stakeholder and developer that means the requirement can explicitly reference its source in an earlier document, such as that produced from a Joint Application Design (JAD) session; requirements should also be traceable forward to the SRS, then to design and code.

Gause and Weinberg remind us of the importance of clarity. They have an outstanding example of how a seemingly straightforward statement is prey to multiple interpretations. Taking a short familiar children's verse:

> Mary had a little lamb
>
> Its fleece was white as snow
>
> And everywhere that Mary went,
>
> The lamb was sure to go.

Here's how a different emphasis can result in a different meaning.

> *Mary* had a little lamb, might lead us to believe that the point to the first line is that it is Mary's lamb in question, not Tom's, Dick's, or Harry's.

> Mary *had* a little lamb, might lead us to believe that the point to the first line is that she no longer has the lamb.

> Mary had *a* little lamb seems to indicate that Mary had only one lamb, not several.

Mary had a little *lamb* makes us wonder what other pets, that she didn't have, might have been an option—a dog, cat, cow, goat, parakeet?

Mary had a little lamb appears to emphasize that someone else (John?) still has his little lamb.

Mary had a little lamb could be meant to be contrasted with Pallas, who still has four large turtles.

Suppose we take the definition of "had" to be "trick, fool"; the definition of "lamb" as "a person easily cheated or deceived esp. in trading securities"; "fleece" as "to strip of money or property by fraud or extortion";[8] and "snow" as "slang: to deceive, persuade, or charm glibly."[9] Gause and Weinberg go on to say that the poem could be construed as being about

...a charmingly glib but fraudulent person named Mary who tricked a small, help-less, gullible stock trader and stripped him of all worldly goods through deceit and extortion. Is it any wonder that

Everywhere that Mary went,

The lamb was sure to go.

What else could the poor lamb do after she fleeced him?

In short, the poem is making an editorial comment on today's business climate ...[10]

The commonly held view that the poem is about an innocent young lady with a loyal pet is naïve in the extreme—not as naïve, though, as sophisticated adults who pick some line out of a requirements document and, without giving it a second thought, proceed to develop a product based on a single, wrong interpretation.

Requirements Elicitation Methods

We will look at interviewing, brainstorming, mind mapping, facilitated application specification technique (FAST), Joint Application Design (JAD), and use case scenarios as viable methods for eliciting software requirements. These are some suggested activities and thoughts that are common to all:

- Actual users need to be involved in the requirements-gathering process rather than surrogates.
- All stakeholders should be identified; a representative from each type of stakeholder should be involved in requirements gathering.
- Ambiguous requirements should be identified as candidates for prototyping.

- Customers and sponsors are not always the users of the delivered application, but they are the entities that pay for the requirements-gathering work, as well as for the final system.
- Domain constraints that could limit the functionality or performance of the system or software under development should be identified.
- Each stakeholder will have a natural bias, including one toward his or her organization.
- Focus groups are not part of the methodology, as they are not composed of decision-making individuals.
- If only software is under development, the technical environment (e.g., computing architecture, operating system, telecommunications needs) into which the product will be placed must be defined.
- If the entire system (hardware and software) is under development, system requirements must exist before software requirements elicitation should take place.
- Inputs to the requirements elicitation methods process include a vision statement, high-level business objectives for the project, statement of need, feasibility statement, statement of scope, and the project plan.
- Outputs from the requirements elicitation methods process include a list of prioritized requirements organized by function, domain constraints, a set of use case scenarios, and prototypes, if applicable.
- The rationale for each requirement should be recorded.
- Use case scenarios and mind mapping may be used alone, or as subtechniques under the interviewing, brainstorming, FAST, or JAD methods.
- With the appropriate people present, elicitation methods result in decisions.

With these common elements of requirements elicitation in mind, we'll move on to a discussion of some of the methods.

Interviews

In the chronicle of requirements gathering, interviewing is almost always used at some point. Even when the recommended brainstorming, mind mapping, FAST, and/or JAD techniques are used, it is usually necessary to understand the level of detail that follows concept exploration by interviewing at least some of the stakeholders.

In the past, analysts have simply made an appointment with representatives of the stakeholders, asked them what they want, and expected to gather all requirements in this fashion. Unfortunately, uncovering requirements using this method alone can be pretty tough. Among other issues, it is very difficult to meet face-to-face with enough stakeholders to represent all of the varied experiences and needs; in our global economy, they are likely to be located all over the world. Interviewing is, however, very useful as a first step in getting a handle on software requirements. It is widely believed that 50 percent of key intelligence information comes from human sources.

We recommend reading a few other works that concentrate solely on interviewing in general, such as *Basic Interviewing Techniques*, by Bruno Vanasse, or publications that specifically address software requirements elicitation, such as Gause and Weinberg's *Exploring Requirements: Quality Before Design*. There are some steps in interviewing that are so important and so basic that they can be presented here without contradicting other sources.

Steps in Interviewing   The steps in interviewing are: create the questions, select the interviewees, plan contacts, conduct the interview, close the meeting, and determine where to go from here.

Create the questions. Interviewing begins with the question, or set of questions, that will lead to the most knowledge about true requirements (what is really needed, not what is wanted or only thought to be needed). There should be some indicators from the original request for service, the concept exploration documents, and the software project management plan (SPMP) that can be used to create a template of interview questions.

Select the interviewees. Selected stakeholders will provide the human source for interviews, providing the most relevant and precise information than any other source. Most likely, it will be impossible to interview every stakeholder and representatives must be chosen. They should have know-how, accessibility, and the potential to credibly and reliably answer your questions.

There are several groups to consider in the hierarchy of interviewees:

Entry-level personnel—Because they have not had the opportunity to gain much experience, they will not be able to contribute a great deal. However, they are worthy of an interview because of their fresh perspective and the possibility of an unexpected "pearl of information."

Mid-level stakeholders—Based on experience, these stakeholders know the intricacies of the operational and/or technical side of the domain and can provide detailed insights. The project lead should always be interviewed.

Managers or other special customers—CEOs and VPs who are knowledgeable of the domain and the impact of project success are definitely a stakeholder group to be interviewed. The executive sponsor should always be interviewed, if at all possible.

Academics—If there are such stakeholders, they can open your eyes to a different perspective.

Typical "users" of the system—This group is perhaps the most important because they will spend more time interacting with the system that anyone else. They may be revolutionary thinkers, which is good, but they may also be biased toward existing systems.

"Rising stars"—If they exist in the organization for which the software is under development, these soon-to-be-leaders in their field may provide cutting-edge thinking and information.

A multiplicity of human sources helps to verify the reliability of collected information.

Plan contacts. If time permits, do some research on the source you wish to contact and the perspective the individual has on the project—what is his "stake" as a stakeholder? Everyone is busy, so plan to limit the interview to what he wants to get out of the software; consideration of perspectives of other stakeholders will occur during brainstorming, FAST, or JAD sessions.

The first contact is often by telephone or email. Some guidelines are:

- Most people will be able to participate in a more relaxed interview on a Tuesday, Wednesday, or Thursday. They are likely to be less distracted by other work and in a better mood to talk.
- When calling, remember to use a pleasant tone of voice.
- Identify yourself clearly.
- State the purpose of your call or email.
- State how this stakeholder was chosen to be on the interview list.
- Confirm that he is the right person to answer questions and that the questions may be considered official.
- Give an estimated length of time for the interview.
- If available and needed, offer some compensation for travel and time given.
- Establish a time and place for the meeting, or a time for subsequent communication.
- Describe the exchange of information and the feedback mechanism.
- Ask for permission to study artifacts that portray the way the stakeholder currently does business.
- Describe the importance of a face-to-face encounter.
- If you encounter problems, leave your contact number in case the source changes their mind.

Conduct the interview. Interviews can be conducted over the phone, in person, or over the Internet (video conference, chat, email). However, the best way to perform interviews remains in the direct face-to-face human encounter. The most important factor for getting information in the interview is to get the right climate, one of comfort and confidence, between you and the interviewee.

1. **Establish the climate.** Once an atmosphere of trust and rapport has been established, it is possible to ask some very general and searching questions. The following actions will help in establishing that climate:
   - Ask for permission to take notes during the interview.
   - Exhibit a genuine human interest in the person's stake in the software.
   - Listen. The best motivator for an interviewee is your complete attention.

- Start with smaller stuff and go to more sensitive issues.
- Be direct and honest.
- Be modest—nobody wants to talk to a "know-it-all."
- Keep to the subject matter, unless you can tap on a shared experience that will contribute to understanding requirements needs.
- Ask to see the environment in which the product will be used.
- Offer future help or part of project report—make clear the exchange of information is a two-way street.

2. **Ask questions.**

Keep them simple. Questions should be short and contain only one part. Two or three questions rolled into one can lead to compound requirements statements that are difficult to interpret and test.

Bracket data. For example, "Does ABC Corp. sell between 15 and 30 million, or between 30 and 60 million dollars worth of widgets?"

Keep an open mind. While it is important to prepare a set of questions, do not read from the questionnaire, nor only stick to it. There may be "golden nuggets" that can be discovered only by following the flow of the conversation, listening to the source, and branching into space that may be more pertinent than the prepared questions. Some of the interviewees may be experts in their field, so when they provide information it may be useful to ask them for an analysis—the "so what?" and "what if?" questions that provide additional insight.

Ask context-free business, process, and product questions, such as these suggested by Gause and Weinberg:

- Are there any problems this system could create?
- Are there reasons for wanting to solve this problem that might not be obvious?
- At what level of granularity would you like to see it?
- Describe the environment in which the system will operate.
- In what way will the system change the way you are doing things now?
- In what ways will the system help you to be more efficient?
- Is either data or functionality shared by other departments or business areas in the organization?
- Is there anyplace else the solution could be obtained?
- What current problems should this system solve?
- What data, needed by you, exists in other systems?

- What information will the new system deliver that you currently don't get?
- What is the most important business goal of the proposed system?
- What kind of performance issues do you have (if any)?
- What problems do you want this system to solve?
- What software application packages are you currently using?
- What will the new system accomplish (functionality) that is not currently achieved by an existing manual or automated system?
- Who is the client for the product?

3. **If the interview stalls ...**
   Perhaps the interviewee does not have, nor can have access to, the information you need. Once this is established, thank the person for his or her time and leave a good impression of your visit by leaving a contact number in case that person finds something for you.

   On the other hand, the interviewee may not feel like giving you the information. In this case, perhaps emphasizing his or her expertise and its positive impact on the system may get the interview past this hurdle.

   At times, the interview may need to be redirected by asking precise questions and giving examples of the type of answers needed or analysis required.

Close the meeting. Remember to re-motivate the person, because you never know when you could need her help again or when she may volunteer further information. Here are some suggestions:

- Ask if there are questions the interviewee has for you.
- Ask if there are other questions that should have been brought up.
- Leave a future objective, in the form of a future question or point of interest for you.
- Offer to share the requirements documents and Software Requirements Specifications (SRS).
- Leave a way to be contacted if more information is forthcoming.
- Ask if you can contact the interviewee if you think of another question.
- Ask if there is someone else that should be interviewed.
- Ask if there is hard-copy or electronic material to be taken and studied.
- Ask meta-questions about the effectiveness of the process—did the questions seem relevant?

Determine where to go from here. Do the following:

- Contact the source to thank him or her for participating.
- Document the interview findings.
- Prepare input for the next step of the process—brainstorming, FAST, JAD, or perhaps, go directly to the requirements specification.

Brainstorming Sessions

> No idea is so outlandish that it should not be considered with a searching but at the same time steady eye.
>
> —Winston Churchill

Brainstorming is a conference technique by which a group attempts to find a solution for a specific problem by amassing all the ideas spontaneously by its members.

> It is easier to tone down a wild idea than to think up a new one.
>
> —Alex Osborn

The concept of brainstorming is explained in a body of knowledge, published in a myriad of books and articles (see the References section for a few). Here, we will simply summarize the suggested roles and rules of brainstorming as they apply to software project requirements elicitation. "Professional" requirements gatherers will want to study the works in the original, practice them under a master brainstorming facilitator, and contact a vendor for specialized training and automated tools. Others may find enough information in this chapter to proceed. An important point for the requirements elicitation process is that brainstorming is a great way to lead into JAD sessions and use case development sessions, as described later in this chapter.

Basically, brainstorming uses group effect to generate ideas and solve problems. It focuses on quickly generating ideas without evaluation or clarification. Anything goes—ideas may be wild, crazy, or impractical. Following idea generation, they are evaluated, and the ones to pursue are evaluated.

Definition of Brainstorming   Brainstorming is a group technique that may be used during the requirements-gathering process to promote creative thinking. It facilitates defining the "problem" to be solved by the life cycle activities to follow—including writing the software requirements specification, analyzing and modeling the requirements, and designing the software.

Brainstorming is used in many business applications as a way of generating a lot of new ideas, quickly. In this particular business situation, we are trying to brainstorm the needs of stakeholders in order to avoid unpleasant surprises later in the project. The more requirements that can be generated up front, the better. Even if they can't all be delivered at once, or in the first version, or ever, there is an advantage to having them documented. If a new generation of users requests a feature that has been thought out and postponed or deleted, time and effort will be saved since the interviewing, brainstorming, FAST, or JAD records document when the idea was first proposed and why it was not implemented.

A group technique, brainstorming is intended to generate lots of ideas, with the full understanding that they may not all be useful. The theory is that having a long list of requirements from which to choose is far superior to starting with a blank slate. Items in the long list can be categorized, prioritized, and pruned.

Alex Osborn is given credit for the central concept of brainstorming.[11] In 1941, as an advertising executive, he was looking for ways to stimulate new ideas, instead of inhibiting them, in formal meetings. He said groups could "think up" ideas by using a group process where all ideas are welcomed—none are criticized, ideas are allowed to build upon each other, wild and exaggerated ideas are encouraged, and large quantities of ideas are produced. His theory was that a greater quantity of original ideas gave rise to a greater quantity of useful ideas. Individuals alone will seldom, if ever, produce the volume or creativity of ideas made by a small group of individuals engaged in brainstorming techniques.

Osborn found that when natural inhibitions are reduced, people are far more willing to put forth useful ideas that they might otherwise feel were of no value. In fact, sometimes the more "far out" or zany the idea is, the more it changes the way others think—a way to get started with what we now call "thinking out of the box."

The development of this original technique was revolutionary—brainstorming is now used by nearly all of the world's largest companies and has become synonymous with "creative thinking" in most vocabularies.

A brainstorming session entails a group of people who free themselves from social inhibitions to generate as many ideas as possible so that original thoughts are free to surface. All participants are encouraged to say whatever ideas come to mind, whether they seem relevant or not. No one will be criticized for any idea, no matter how goofy it seems, as the responsibility of the participant is to generate views, not to vet them.

Dictionary definitions of "brainstorm" include: a sudden inspiration; a bright idea; a severe outburst of excitement, often as a result of a transitory disturbance of cerebral activity; a sudden mental aberration. Various modern authors have characterized the brainstorming process as:

- a part of problem solving that involves the creation of new ideas *by suspending judgment;*
- a technique that maximizes the ability to generate new ideas;
- a time dedicated to generating a large number of ideas regardless of their initial worth;
- designed to obtain the maximum number of ideas relating to a specific area of interest;
- the creation of an optimal state of mind for generating new ideas;
- the free association of different ideas to form new ideas and concepts;
- where a group of people can put social inhibitions and rules aside with the aim of generating new ideas and solutions.

As we will see, the definitions give way to "rules" to be followed in a brainstorming session.

Roles for a Brainstorming Session
There are three roles for participants in a brainstorming session: leader, scribe, and team member.

Leader
The leader is also called the facilitator, or moderator. Trained to be a good listener, the leader is responsible for making the brainstorming process an easy one, and the session itself run smoothly. He or she will encourage the participants, ensure proper individual and group behavior, and assist the scribe in capturing ideas. The leader will follow a published agenda and restart the creative process if it falters. The leader will ask for ideas to be shouted out, but will also accept written ones.

Scribe
The scribe will record every idea in such a way that everyone in the room can see it. Flip charts and markers, white boards, or overhead transparencies work for this, as does the projection of a computer screen. If using flip charts, remove each filled piece of paper and tape it to the wall so that everyone can see it. In a small group, the leader could also be the scribe, but it is difficult to keep the meeting moving *and* capture each idea correctly. In a large group, two or three scribes may be necessary.

Participants
In software development there are usually several stakeholders representing varying points of view. Brainstorming sessions are a wonderful venue for them to learn to empathize with each others' points of view. The good news is that differing personalities and vantage points will result in more creativity and a broader outlook. The risk is if the participants can't stop protecting their own needs for the sake of the process. Group sizes can number between four and 30 people, but seasoned leaders have recommended groups of five to 10 (the ideal group is six or seven). More people allows for the opportunity for diversity, but can lead to nervousness or frustration if there is not time to express all ideas. The primary responsibility of participants is to produce ideas and thoughts (requirements in this case), and to stimulate thoughts in others.

Rules for a Brainstorming Session
The rules for a brainstorming session have been published in many ways, with each often overlapping the other. We'll optimize our time here by consolidating rules from multiple publications into one comprehensive list.

Rules for Leaders
- Allow ideas to be expressed verbally (preferred) or in a written note.
- Allow silence when appropriate.

- Collect as many ideas as possible from all participants, with no criticisms or judgments made while ideas are being generated.
- Communicate the ground rules of the session.
- Don't allow criticism, discussion, or debate.
- Don't allow serious or derisive commentary.
- Encourage wild or exaggerated ideas.
- Establish the purpose or topic.
- For the most part, keep a fast pace to reduce inhibitions and evaluation.
- Help the participants mutate and combine ideas.
- Help the participants with the generation of ideas.
- Set a time limit.
- Use all the time allotted.

Rules for Scribes
- Don't describe an idea in detail—just capture its essence.
- If necessary, ask for a brief clarification.
- Use the speaker's own words.
- Write down each idea as stated, in short words or phrases.
- Write ideas so that all participants can see them.

Rules for Participants
- "Hitchhike," "piggyback," or build, on the ideas of others.
- Allow yourself to "be in the moment"—become absorbed by the process and think freely.
- Assume different personalities.
- Be creative in contributions.
- Be open to new, original ideas.
- Be patient with silence.
- Be willing to take risks.
- Build and expand on the ideas of others.
- Contribute only one idea at a time.
- Create improvements and variations of recorded ideas.
- Don't bother with providing explanations.
- Don't evaluate the ideas of others; don't criticize or judge.
- Don't give nonverbal clues that could be construed as criticism or judgment of others' ideas.
- Don't interrupt others.

- Don't place too much importance on any one idea.
- Generate as many ideas as possible.
- Generate as many ideas as possible in a short period of time—quantity now, quality later.
- Keep each idea short.
- Let your imagination soar.
- Reflect later.
- Take turns making contributions.
- Think fast.
- Write down your idea and pass it to the scribe.

Brainstorming Rules in General

- All ideas are welcome—there is no such thing as a "wrong" idea, or a silly one, or a dumb one, or one that is too far out.
- Each idea presented belongs to the group, not to the person who said it.
- Every point of view is valuable.
- Have the right number of people in the session.
- Have the right people in the session.
- Talking about the ideas will take place after brainstorming is complete.

An Expansion of Some of the Most Important Brainstorming Rules

Postpone and withhold judgment of ideas. Ideas can be discussed following the brainstorming session, but no judgment may be passed during the meeting. No one should suggest that an idea might not work or could have negative side effects. All ideas are potentially good (even if they don't seem so, they may be modified to produce great benefit); any discussion is likely to evolve into criticism or compliments. The evaluation of ideas takes up valuable time and effort that should be devoted to the creation of ideas instead.

Encourage wild and exaggerated ideas. It's easier to tame a wild idea than it is to think up a new and workable one. Wacky and seemingly unworkable ideas may inspire valid ones by stimulating new thought patterns. No idea is too bizarre or nonsensical—producing them will reduce inhibitions in others as well.

Quantity over quality, for now. It is easier to pare down a long list of ideas, or to create one good idea from combining lots of little ideas, than to try to supplement a puny one. The chances of finding a good idea improve with a long list. The leader should consistently help extract as many ideas from the participants as is possible during the course of the session.

"Hitchhike" on ideas. Most creative people are also good listeners. Leaders should encourage taking recorded ideas and expanding upon them, adding extra thoughts, adapting and improving them, using them as inspiration for original ideas, or for combinations of ideas. Each idea has a principle or concept that is useful.

All participants and all ideas have equal worth. Viewpoints can and should be different, but they are all valid. Unique perspectives on situations bring a richness of solutions.

Suggestions for a Brainstorming Session   In addition to roles and rules for a brainstorming session, experience has shown that a number of subtle techniques will add to the chances for success:

- Allow the group to determine the actual length of short breaks, as the freedom to start and stop when they are ready is a relaxing ingredient. Refreshments are helpful.

- At the opening of the brainstorming session, have a brief warm-up on an unrelated but fun topic. This will help set the mood and increase the comfort level of those who have not attended such sessions before. When the main session begins, the creative juices will be flowing and an unrestrictive mood will prevail.

- Be sensitive to the fact that many employees fear making mistakes in their jobs—fear of their managers, of losing their job, of demotion, of loss of status—and they are being asked to submit wild ideas that may not work. Creating a safe environment for them is a crucial part of allowing their creativity to surface. If properly set up, the brainstorming session is ideal because all participants have agreed not to judge. "Crazy" ideas are actually encouraged.

- Consider the concept of mind mapping to augment brainstorming, as discussed in the next section of this chapter.

- Don't trust first impressions that may make ideas seem unappealing; consider "seeds" of ideas.

- If the flow of ideas seems to be drying up, ask small groups to congregate around different flip charts and discuss the ideas on them. Another technique is to ask each person to write some ideas on a piece of paper and exchange it with someone else to discuss and build upon. List alternatives; "stuck" thinking doesn't mean "stopped" thinking.

- It works well to have the participants' seats arranged in a circle with no "head" of the table. U-shaped tables are also effective.

- Look for underlying concepts behind common things; use the process of "association."

- Make refreshments available during the entire session, limiting the time lost to breaks. A "stretch" period should still occur every few minutes.

- Place flip charts and markers within easy reach of each participant. Supplying the participants with notepads and pens facilitates the notation of personal ideas during the active moments, ensuring that no idea gets lost.

- Provide a set of things for the participants to manipulate with their hands to stimulate the thought process. Crayons with paper, and colored children's modeling clay are two good examples.

- Provide the participants with comfortable chairs.

- Provide visual variety in the room, giving participants something to look at while someone is suggesting an idea—it can be uncomfortable for either or both if everyone is looking the contributor in the face.
- Realize that if anyone needs a microphone to be heard, the group is too large for brainstorming.
- Reserve a room that is large enough to provide space for the participants to move around with comfort, but not so large that it seems cavernous and makes the group feel small in comparison.
- Restrict brainstorming sessions to two hours or less; break the period into 15-minute-or-less segments.
- Return to the posted ideas for reflection and perhaps combination or expansion, as the brainstorming session traverses peaks and valleys of rapid idea generation.
- Seat very small groups at a table covered in butcher paper for free-form writing. Participants should not be seated at too great a distance from each other.
- The leader may become part of the group and play an equal role in idea generation.
- Upon restarting the session following a break, ask people to sit in a different place and meet their new neighbors before starting again.
- When addressing the group, use "we" instead of calling participants by their names. This will enhance group bonding and reinforce the concepts of group effort and group responsibility.

Brainstorming Session Agenda   The following is a proposed agenda for a brainstorming session, consolidated from a number of sources (see the References section):

1. Introduce the session. Review the topic of the brainstorming session, discuss the rules, and introduce the participants.

2. Conduct a warm-up. Provide a warm-up activity (five to 10 minutes) that helps the group get used to the feelings of a safe environment, as well as the excitement that can be mounted through idea generation. The subject of the warm-up is neutral, something understood by all (for example, ideas for new kitchen gadgets or automobile accessories), and not related to the topic at hand in any way. In addition to fostering creativity with the warm-up subject, the leader could discuss the rules and ask the group to suggest additions or changes to make the session a particularly effective one.

3. Brainstorm. Ask for reasonable ideas, radical ideas, ideas that might work in a strange way, and ideas that just spring to mind. Work for 10 to 15 minutes and call time. Stop before all of the excitement wanes. If the group is in the "white heat of inspiration," allow them five more minutes. Take a break and then resume, always following the rules. Neither force a break nor force a return from a break. If ideas appear to be drying up, process the ideas and review them for clarity; ensure that every participant understands

them. Combine and categorize similar ideas and delete duplicates. Determine the criteria for evaluation.

4. Establish a consensus. Ask the group to vote on a small of number ideas to consider first (10 to 15, or about one-third of the refined idea list). Give each participant the same number of points to allocate to the idea list. Allow time for thinking about the "voting," then ask each participant to anonymously submit their allocations.

5. End the session. Thank the participants for taking part, allow them to finish if they are in the middle of writing, ask them to fill out an evaluation form, and tell them when the collated ideas will be fed back to them. Invite latent ideas.

Preparation for Brainstorming   As with projects, brainstorming sessions that are planned and prepped will have a much greater chance for success. The following are "must do's":

- Identify and invite the participants, the scribe, and the session leader; distribute information about the location, time, place, expected length of session, and RSVP-by-date.

- Identify the specific software system or subsystem to be developed and publish appropriate documentation (e.g., concept exploration summaries, interview summaries, project planning objectives) to all group members.

- Define brainstorming and brainstorming session rules and roles for your organization and distribute them to the participants.

- Ensure the room is properly equipped with comfortable chairs, appropriately shaped or arranged tables, flip charts, white boards, Post-its, projected computer monitors, refreshments, and manipulable "toys" (clay, crayons, kaleidoscope, etc.).

Follow-up to a Brainstorming Session   Typically, it is the leader who edits the ideas after a session. We recommend that he or she involve another person or two who is familiar with the application under development.

First, discard ideas that are unusable or incomplete (don't throw them away—document them for the record, but remove them from the list of ideas under consideration). Use valid criteria for removal of ideas and take care not to remove any too early. Remove duplicates if any still remain. If the session team had time to provide their short list of unanimously recommended ideas, this step is already completed. All of the ideas should be in one sectioned list, in some computerized format (e.g., an Excel worksheet).

Arrange the remaining ideas into three categories:

Valid. Appears to be a needed, testable requirement.

Possible. May be a requirement.

Not Likely. Probably is not a valid requirement.

Document the findings for input to the software requirements specification. They will not only help in turning requirements into specifications, they will help in determining which specifications will be delivered in the first implementation of the product. The prioritization process will be discussed later in this chapter.

Mind Mapping   Mind mapping is a concept that may be used in conjunction with brainstorming, or alone. The idea is that the use of keywords, along with pictures, symbols, and color can capture the way our brain perceives subject matter. For many people, particularly those whose learning style is visual, recall of details is easier in this nonlinear language style, making it particularly useful for quick summarization. Mind map advocates contend that 90 percent of written words are not useful in the task of recalling content, but that this "right-brained" activity provides highly effective visual tips. The development of this basic technique is attributed to Tony Buzan and Joseph Novak.[12]

The following is a brief history and some combined definitions:

- A mind map is a drawing, or sketch, of central and associated ideas that are represented by pictures (icons, graphics), and keywords that are written on lines (arcs, vectors) attached to the pictures.
- Every mind map is unique in its form and content. This is especially relevant for the task of recalling information.
- Keywords and connections between the keywords are easily seen due to the lines connecting them.
- Mind mapping makes possible the transformation of complex net-like fields of knowledge into a manageable structure.
- The central idea is presented clearly by its central location on the map (drawing); the relative importance of each idea becomes obvious by its placement—ideas of greater importance are closer to the center, those of less importance are closer to the boundaries.
- The idea of mind maps is to integrate a range of information concerning the central topic into a wholistic structure.
- The transparent and essentially wide-open mind mapping scheme facilitates the generation of new ideas in the creative aspects of note-taking.
- These constructs allow the informational content to be memorized and recalled with greater ease and increased efficiency.
- This type of structure makes it possible to integrate new information easily and without compromising the readability of the structure through deletions and cramped insertions.

In the construction of mind maps, the requirements elicitor will:

1. Select memorable keywords.
2. Connect keywords by writing them on lines and connecting the lines.

3. Structure the content of the mind map differently from the linear structure of the written page. Instead of beginning at the top of the page and proceeding vertically, sentence by sentence, a mind map begins in the center of the drawing and radiates outward from the main topic.

Group-based mind mapping, such as the activities that accompany brainstorming, involve the drawing of a group-created set of central ideas that are mounted on the wall in an "art gallery" of ideas. Individuals then visit each drawing and add inspired, connected words and sketches. Eventually, the subject will be documented in a way that allows quick and easy recall of the issues/solutions/requirements.

Facilitated Application Specification Techniques (FAST)

FAST is similar enough to brainstorming and to JAD that we will provide only cursory coverage here. This is not to belittle the process in any way—FAST is an important part of the software PM's vocabulary because it was developed to be a method specifically for gathering software requirements. But rather than attempt to rewrite existing texts, we will only summarize FAST and refer you to other works, such as Pressman's *Software Engineering*.[13]

The general rules for FAST will seem familiar, as they are similar to those for brainstorming:

- Conduct the meeting at a neutral site, attended by developers and customers.
- Establish rules for preparation and participation.
- Publish an informal agenda.
- Invite a facilitator to control the meeting.
- Prepare a definition mechanism—worksheets, flip charts, wall stickies, and so on.
- Participants should agree not to critique or debate.
- Share a goal:
    1. Identify the problem.
    2. Propose elements of the solution.
    3. Negotiate different approaches.
    4. Specify a preliminary set of solution requirements.

Preparation for a FAST session might include:

- making a list of objects that are:
    1. part of the environment that surrounds the system;
    2. produced by the system;
    3. used by the system.
- making a list of services (processes or functions) that manipulate or interact with the objects.
- making a list of constraints and performance criteria.

Activities during a FAST session typically include:

- presentation of prepared lists of objects, services, constraints, and performance for discussion (as separate entries so they can be moved, combined, etc.).
- creation of a combined list, where redundant entries are eliminated, and new ideas are added.
- consensus on the list, gained from the participants by the facilitator.
- work, by teams, on "mini-specifications," or discrete portions of the known software requirements:
    1. discuss mini-specifications;
    2. identify externally observable data objects;
    3. evaluate the flow and content of information;
    4. define and elaborate software functionality;
    5. understand the software "behavior";
    6. establish interface characteristics;
    7. uncover design constraints.
- maintenance of a "parking lot list of issues" to be resolved later.
- creation of validation criteria.
- assignments for the next step of drafting the SRS (see Chapter 17).

Joint Application Design

In addition to one-on-one interviews, interviews in small groups, brainstorming, and FAST sessions (with or without mind mapping), another type of extremely effective facilitated meeting is the Joint Application Design (JAD). As with the other requirements elicitation methods, it has been described in numerous other works. Wood and Silver wrote the definitive book in 1989, which remains popular today.[14] Here, we will present an overview of the JAD process; Appendix G, "Joint Application Design in Use," offers a glimpse into a recently completed real-life JAD exercise held between two major, just-merged, U.S. companies.

Definition of JAD   Joint Application Design (JAD) is a registered trademark of IBM Corporation. It is a team approach to requirements elicitation, focusing on improving the group process and getting the right people involved from the beginning of a project. Toby Crawford and Chuck Morris at IBM developed the initial concept of JAD in 1977. Through a marriage of the IBM methodology, business systems planning, and their own innovative methods, they got IT professionals and end-users to agree on requirement and design specifications. Since 1977, JAD has emerged as the most widely used tool for requirements definition. It isn't just for requirements, though—it is employed in the creation of other plans, designs, and policies throughout the software life cycle. Development organizations now realize that a methodology with a high degree of user interaction (including prototyping and RAD) leads to higher-quality software.

JAD sessions are similar to brainstorming sessions, but they aren't quite the same animal. Brainstorming sessions last about two hours; JAD sessions tend to last about three days. Brainstorming sessions are about rapid-fire production of ideas; JAD sessions can produce high-level, but specific, software models of function, data, and behavior.

JAD is a structured and disciplined session led by a facilitator. It is based upon communication through documentation, fixed requirements, and rules of work. As the JAD methodology evolved, it began to use CASE and other software tools during the sessions to capture work products such as data flow diagrams (DFDs), entity relationship diagrams (ERDs), state transition diagrams, and all commonly used object-oriented diagrams.

A 1989 study by Capers Jones of 60 development projects found that 35 percent of the functionality was missed without JAD, while less than 10 percent of the functionality was missed when JAD was incorporated into the requirements elicitation process. Projects combining JAD and prototyping did even better at managing requirements refinement.[15]

Roles in JAD

Developers
The role of the developer is to assist stakeholders to formulate their needs, which are usually solutions to existing problems. The stakeholders share ownership of the software requirements.

Participants
Like the participant roles in brainstorming, these invited stakeholders are the most important part of this process. The knowledge and skill level of the invitees are crucial to the session's success. Having the right people allows decisions to be made rapidly and models to be developed that are correct, even if incomplete.

The Facilitator/Process Consultant
As with brainstorming, the facilitator keeps the session focused and flowing, and prevents or minimizes the acting out of unproductive human emotions such as attacks or defensiveness. The facilitator owns neither the process nor the product, but is present to help the stakeholders with their product creation process.

Scribe
As with brainstorming sessions, the JAD scribe(s) documents ideas and helps with timekeeping.

JAD Sessions   According to Wood, JAD provides a concentrated workshop for making decisions with everyone present who has the authority to make those decisions. She recommends phases of project definition and research to deal with fact-finding and information gathering, preparation for the JAD session, and the JAD session itself, to validate the gathered information. As with brainstorming, the JAD session will be supported with a properly out-fitted room, including access to white boards, flip charts, markers, appropriately shaped and spaced worktables, projectors, wall charts, refreshment tables, and so on.

Ground rules/guidelines for JAD sessions mirror those for brainstorming sessions:

- There are no "dumb" questions.
- All participants are equal.
- Silence means agreement, even (especially) if you're absent.
- Any team member can request to go around the room and get explicit agreement from each person on a given issue.
- No "speeches" are given.
- No side conversations are allowed.
- All team members are involved for the full period of time (three days are recommended).
- One user scenario will be addressed at a time.
- Brainstorming is for quantity, not quality.
- Define terms and capture three-letter acronyms (TLAs).
- All team members participate with an open mind.
- All team members support each other, learn, grow, and relax and have a little fun.

Output from a JAD Session
It makes sense that the two groups, developers and stakeholders, will jointly own all deliver-ables from the JAD session where the joint authorship occurred. Frequently, these software-specific artifacts will include:

- a data context diagram (see Figure 16–6);
- a Level 0 data flow diagram;
- a Level 1 data flow diagram;
- a global data model—entity relationship diagram (see Figure 16–7);
- a list of primary objects;
- a high-level object model (see Figure 16–8);
- candidate responsibilities and collaborators for each object;
- a list of primary processes/use cases;
- other data flow diagrams, state diagrams, decision trees, or decision tables where needed;
- data requirements for each process;
- a list of assumptions;
- documentation for the resolution or assignment of open issues.

Output from a JAD session used to elicit requirements paves the way for the next step—the creation of the SRS.

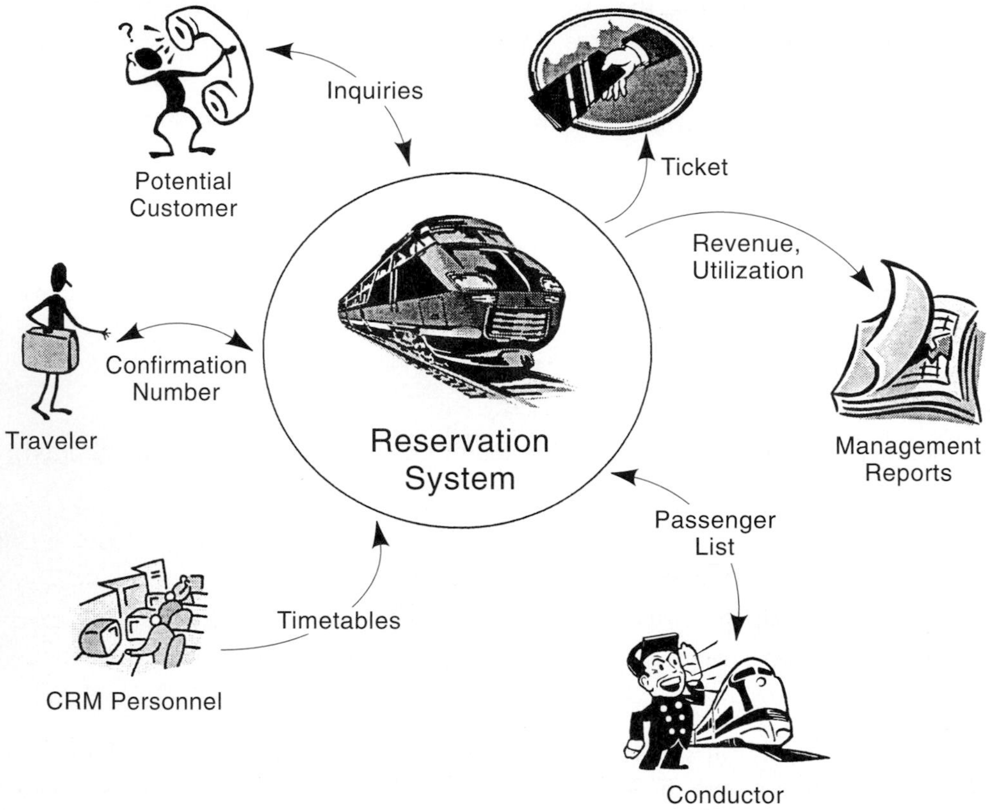

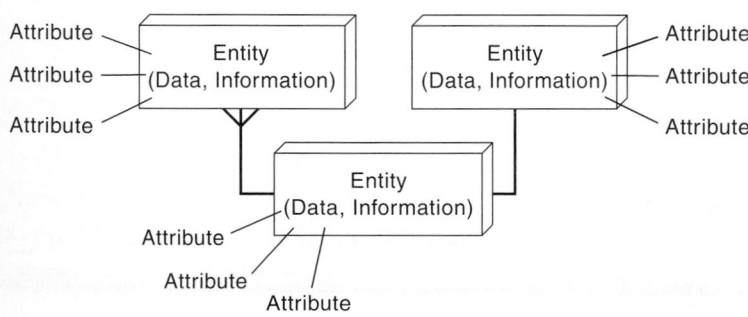

FIGURE 16–6
Example of a Partial Data Context Diagram (DCD)

FIGURE 16–7
Example of a Global Data Model

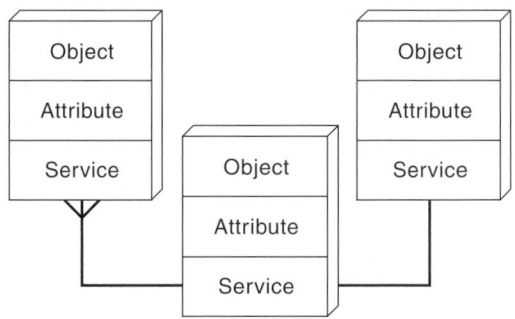

FIGURE 16–8
Example of a High-Level Object Model

Possible Issues with JAD   No method is perfect, and while the JAD technique has been used successfully for several decades, there are a few recognized issues.

For example, participants funnel their ideas through a facilitator and/or a scribe. Precautions must be taken to avoid misinterpretation of the collected data. The use of automated tools during the session and the review of the session deliverables by all participants reduces this risk.

JAD sessions have dealt primarily with IT systems, which emphasize data elements and screen design. The success of JAD used with real-time systems requirements elicitation has not been well documented.

A three-day JAD session with representatives of all stakeholder groups, all having decision-making authority, is an expensive proposition. Three days is only an average—a complex embedded real-time system, or a system upon which human life is dependent, could easily take longer. If the length of the session is "until we are done," a measure of "doneness" could be that no more use cases can be identified.

User Scenario and Use Case Development Sessions

As with so many other topics in this survey of practical methods, all things object-oriented constitute a huge body of knowledge. And, as we indicate with almost all of the subjects in this book, we are barely able to scratch the surface. We describe the basics of what a software project manager needs to know in terms of balanced, useful project, product, and people skills and give references for digging deeper into each area. Here, we have space to briefly mention use cases as a requirements elicitation technique. Object models will be addressed in Chapter 22, "Analysis and Design Methods."

Requirements elicitation is a combination of textual and graphical models used to represent the intended system, detect inconsistencies, errors, omissions, and ambiguities. The text and pictures improve understanding of the requirements, bridging gaps in language and vocabulary. There are many software project managers who believe strongly that creating use case scenarios and diagrams during requirements gathering sessions (JAD, FAST) is a key to definition, user-system interaction, and a basis for validation.

Definition of a Use Case

The use case model is about describing what (not how) our system will do at a high level and with a user focus for the purpose of scoping the project and giving the application some structure. Use cases are scenarios that identify a particular thread of system usage—a written narrative. The terms *use case*, *use case scenario*, and *use case diagram* are often interchanged, but in fact they are different. Use cases are structured outlines or templates for the description of user requirements, modeled in a structured language (English). Use case scenarios are unstructured descriptions of user requirements. Neither is limited to object-oriented methods, but that is the arena in which they are usually discussed. Use case diagrams are graphical representations that may be decomposed into further levels of abstraction. In order to describe them, their components will be described first.

Actor
An *actor*, or external agent, lies outside of the system model, but interacts with it in some way. An actor can be a person, machine, or an information system that is external to the system model; an actor is not part of the system itself. Customers, client application, external systems (e.g., legacy systems, accounting systems), and external devices (e.g., fault monitors) could all be actors.

Use Case
A *use case* is narrative text describing the sequence of events of an actor, using a system. They are "stories" of how a system is used, illustrating and implying requirements. They are transactions (atomic sets of activities) that yield identifiable value to the actor. They represent a description of the courses of events that will be carried out by the system. A use case is a static model of functionality, having static relationships, implying no temporal sequencing.

Use Case Diagram
A *use case diagram* visually represents what happens when an actor interacts with a system. The system is shown as a rectangle with the name of the system (or subsystem) inside; the actors are shown as stick figures (even the nonhuman ones), the use cases are shown as solid-bordered ovals labeled with the name of the use case, and relationships are lines or arrows between actors and use cases and/or between the use cases themselves. Actors appear outside of the rectangle since they are external to the system. Use cases appear within the rectangle, providing functionality. A relationship or association is a solid line between an actor and each use case in which the actor participates—the involvement can be any kind, not necessarily

one of the actor initiating the use case functionality. Figure 16–9 shows an example of a use case diagram.

Richter tells us that the use case models system functions by describing how an actor uses the system. It represents a function that would make sense to an actor. Ask what interactions with the system the actor initiates, and what interactions with the actor the system initiates. A paragraph or more of text describes each use case, also known as a specification. First identify the system's actors and use cases, then combine the information into a use case diagram—a static model of functionality with static relationships, implying no temporal sequencing. It contains no information about the dynamics of these functions. Activity diagrams, which are described in Richter's book, *Designing Flexible Object-Oriented Systems with UML*, provide a solution to these deficiencies, depicting a workflow view of activities.[16]

Benefits of Use Case   The use case model can be a key tool in understanding the requirements of the business, as well as a way of ensuring that everyone who uses the system

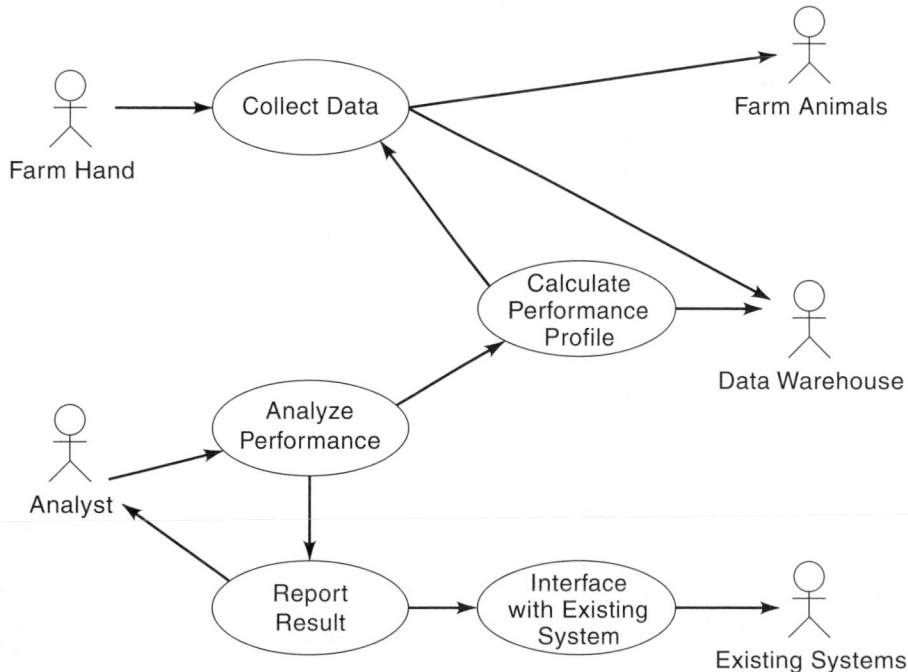

FIGURE 16–9
Use Case Example

or works with it can agree on how the model will look. The following list identifies some of the benefits:

- Having consistent names for the different use cases facilitates communication and avoids errors caused by different people, or groups of people, thinking they are referring to the same thing when they really mean something different.
- Use case diagrams can provide a documented model that accurately describes the existing business, as well as the system under development.
- Use case models are understandable to managers, users, and developers, with no need for specialized training.
- Use cases and scenarios can provide validation as well as implementation testing.
- Use cases can be used to produce business rules.
- Use cases define the process by which the customer interacts with the group.
- Use cases may be easily transformed into object models.
- Use cases provide traceability for functions.
- Use cases provide the basic information needed for creating prototypes.
- Use cases reduce the occurrence of the "orphan function"—one that sounds good but is not a direct contributor to the system goals.
- Use cases show the courses of events that can be performed.

Guidelines for Creating Use Cases   As use cases are developed during require-
ments elicitation sessions, a few guidelines may be helpful:

- Allow each use case to tell a story about how the user interacts with the system under development to satisfy a discrete goal (the conceptual dialog).
- Assign project champions who are actual users for each user class to serve as the primary interface between users and developers.
- Avoid design strategies at this point, including user interface design.
- Avoid duplication across use cases.
- Avoid creating too many use cases too quickly.
- Don't record data definitions in use cases (data attributes belong in class diagrams, logical data models, and the project data dictionary).
- Record the following about each use case:
    1. a unique ID
    2. a concise name
    3. history—the originator, creation date, updater, last update date
    4. the actor(s)
    5. a brief description
    6. pre- and post-conditions

7. priority

8. frequency of use

9. a detailed description of the user actions and system responses under normal, expected conditions

10. alternative courses

11. error conditions and system response

12. includes (other use cases that may be called)

13. special requirements

14. assumptions

15. comments

- There should be more functional requirements than use cases.

During an elicitation session like FAST or JAD, the session leader may use the following steps to get the use case definition process started (see Figure 16–10):

1. Identify who will use the system directly, for example, hitting keys on the keyboard—these are the actors.

2. Pick one of those actors.

3. Define what that actor wants to do with the system; each of these major activities become a use case.

4. For each use case determine the "basic course," what normally happens. Describe that basic course in the description for the use case.

5. Describe it as "Actor does something, system does something; actor does something, system does something," but keep it at a high level. This is not the time to discuss user interface design. Describe only system functions that the actor would be aware of and what the actor does that the system would be aware of.

6. Once you're happy with the basic course, consider the alternates (they will be added as extending use cases, described thoroughly in all of the referenced object-oriented literature).

7. Review each use case description against the descriptions of the other use cases. Where commonality exists, document only one "used" use case to avoid duplication.

8. Repeat Steps 2 through 7 for each actor.

The last piece of advice we will leave for the use case modeler is to "keep it simple."

Guidelines for Writing Quality Requirements _____

Requirements, usually gathered via several different means, will become specifications when they are tightened up and formatted according to the SRS template, or "container." Clarity

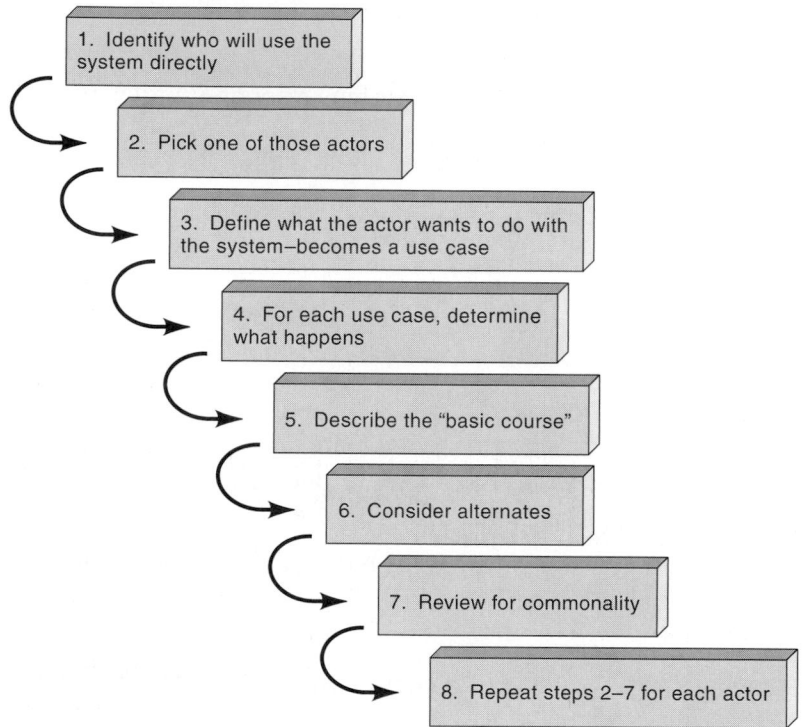

FIGURE 16–10
Steps in Creating a Use Case

that can be imbued at this point will be appreciated later. There is not as much precision in the "rules" for requirements as there are for specifications, but the following guidelines will help with the transformation of one to the other:

- Define the term "requirements" in the context of your project, because it often means different things to different people. Requirements are statements of functionality and quality believed by the stakeholders to be needed in the system, but they are not yet "specifications." Requirements may include high-level functional, behavioral, and informational models (data flow diagrams, entity relationship models, object models, control models), but they are *not* detailed user interface designs that will be used by developers.
- Keep in mind that there are different types of requirements (functional, nonfunctional, quality, performance, business, user, constraints, etc.).
- Address international issues.
- Identify time-critical functions.
- Consider safety and security issues.

- Write requirements that can be traced to specifications (provide the source for specifications' backward trace).
- Trace software requirements back to system requirements, use cases, or elicitation workshop session documentation.
- Create a requirements identification scheme (for forward and backward traceability).
- If meaningful error messages can be determined at this time, document them.
- Communicate, communicate, communicate. It isn't fair to any stakeholder group for developers to make requirements decisions, especially not to developers. Often, when an answer is not forthcoming and schedule pressures mount, a developer will attempt to fill the void by making a decision without adequate information and perspective. No "user class" should be left out. Individual product champions may represent user classes, collecting input from the class members.
- Reduce ambiguity in requirements as early as possible. An ambiguous requirement may have two or more contradictory interpretations or it may be compound, having multiple independent requirement candidates in the same statement. A compound requirement is likely to include the term "and" or "with"—watch for these red flags. An unambiguous requirement will be "primitive," meaning it is clear, concise, and testable. Primitive requirements are cohesive; they represent one and only one thing.
- Explore the need for derived and conditional requirements. A requirement may be derived, obtained as a necessary or precursor condition for another requirement; or conditional, having other (derived) requirements as necessary or precursory conditions. A function that cannot be implemented until a certain version of an operating system is installed is an example of a conditional requirement. Backward compatibility to other system components is also a conditional requirement.
- Avoid using intrinsically subjective and ambiguous words when you write requirements. Terms like *always, sometimes, often, minimize, maximize, optimize, rapid, quick, user-friendly, easy, simple, normal, usual, large, intuitive, robust, state-of-the-art, improved, efficient, support* and *flexible* are particularly dangerous. Most of these terms are not verifiable.
- Write test cases against the functional requirements.
- Consider developing prototypes.
- Begin a data dictionary.
- Keep sentences and paragraphs concise, and keep requirements at a consistent level of granularity (one test case's worth of functionality).
- Avoid redundant requirements.

These guidelines, used along with frequent stakeholder reviews, will provide the proper foundation for the SRS.

Challenges in Eliciting Requirements _____

> The hardest single part of building a software system is deciding precisely what to build. No other part of the conceptual work is as difficult as establishing the detailed technical requirements, including all the interfaces to people, to machines, and to other software systems. No other part of the work so cripples the resulting system if done wrong. No other part is more difficult to rectify later. Therefore, the most important function that the software builder performs for the client is the iterative extraction and refinement of the product requirements.
>
> —Fred Brooks[17]

Challenges in eliciting software requirements are basically the reverse of the guidelines, and there are many of them. Based on Brooks' counsel, we'll take a brief look at the challenges experience tells us to be wary of:

- Accommodating valid requirements changes.
- Achieving requirements completeness without unnecessarily constraining system design.
- Analysts' lack of knowledge of problem domain; user and analyst speaking different languages.
- Changing requirements over time.
- Conflicting views of necessary requirements.
- Considering environmental factors (e.g., the certainty of the system's interfaces to other systems).
- Developing prototypes that are not too expensive, and are understood to be part of requirements elicitation techniques, not implementable components.
- Ease of omitting "obvious" information.
- Emphasizing the computing aspects of the system instead of ways in which the system will change the way of doing business.
- Expressing the requirements in a form that allows the developers to determine if they are implementable and testable.
- Identifying domain experts (application and development).
- Identifying similar systems from which to learn or borrow.
- Ill-defined system boundaries.
- Inadequate understanding of computer capabilities and limitations on the part of stakeholders.
- Incomplete understanding of needs on the part of the users.
- Involving all major stakeholder communities (customers, sponsors, users, developers, quality engineering, analysts, developers).

- Iterating in order to rework requirements in the light of increased knowledge.
- Keeping documentation in electronic form and up-to-date (i.e., if flip chart paper is used during a brainstorming session, it must be entered into a word processing document, spreadsheet, or database, and made available to all stakeholders).
- Keeping the emphasis on methodology instead of technique—there is a danger in being "technique-oriented," so that the problem situation will be distorted to fit the technique; we need rather to be problem- and user-oriented.
- Keeping the level of requirements at the level of "what," and leaving the "how" to later phases, such as design (e.g., What data does the system produce and consume? What functions must the system perform? What interfaces are needed? What constraints apply?).
- Lack of understanding of the mission of the system within the organization it will be placed.
- Maintaining "completeness" by resolving TBDs (to be done issues).
- Managing conflicting goals, views, and interests.
- Modeling large quantities of data.
- Obtaining authorizations.
- Obtaining wish lists for each stakeholder, across multiple levels of authority (i.e., managers should not influence users).
- Partitioning the system to reduce complexity.
- Personnel resistance to the development of a new system (e.g., fear of losing a job because functionality will be automated).
- Prioritizing the requirements; determining the critical functions.
- Producing the appropriate amount of information—enough to move on to the SRS and design, but not too much, as is required by some methodologies.
- Saving unnecessary design information given by the stakeholders until the appropriate phase.
- Stakeholder's backgrounds are so varied that a common language for requirements is difficult to achieve.
- Staying within cost and schedule constraints imposed by the sponsor.
- Tailoring the requirements elicitation methods for what is appropriate to the project; integrating flexibility into the methodology.
- Tracing requirements backward and forward.
- Uncovering design constraints.
- Understanding requirements for large and/or complex systems.
- Validating that requirements are in agreement with project goals.

- Working within nonwaterfall life cycle models where design may be taking place concurrently with requirements gathering—requirements are seldom "frozen" at the end of the requirements phase.

None of these challenges have a pat answer or an easy solution, but the methods discussed here will help to offset, if not overcome, them. The software project manager would do well to assess the project's specific challenges and translate them into risks that are documented, tracked, and controlled.

Requirements and Quality Function Deployment _____

Quality function deployment (QFD), also commonly known as a way to represent the "voice of the customer," is a process for capturing customer requirements and translating them into requirements that can be used by designers, producers, and suppliers. As with many other topics mentioned in this chapter, there are numerous books, articles, consulting services, software, and Web sites devoted to QFD; it will be discussed further in this book in Chapter 30, "Software Quality Assurance." It deserves mention in the context of requirements elicitation because the very first step in QFD is to "identify the customer's vital requirements for the product and translate them into design requirements." At this point in our software life cycle, we are not ready to translate customer requirements into design requirements—that comes later, after the SRS is written and analysis modeling occurs—but we are very interested in all methods of stakeholder requirements elicitation and capture.

The process of QFD can be found within methods of brainstorming, FAST, and JAD. With QFD, sharing of information is achieved through the efforts of a cross-functional team from various stakeholder groups such as marketing, sales, service, distribution, product engineering, process engineering, procurement, production, and of course, the end-user of the software system. A second QFD characteristic found throughout the requirements elicitation process has to do with capturing the requirements information in one place, in a compact form. Lastly, with QFD and other requirements elicitation methods, there is support for consensus and decision making, especially when complex relationships and trade-offs are involved to achieve the best overall solution. Such support is imperative, as we almost always deal with conflicting requirements when all stakeholders are represented.

The QFD method begins with these steps, which clarify the relationship with requirements elicitation:

1. Identify the communities affected by the proposed system, e.g., customers, users, and developers. Also identify any initial constraints identified by the customer that affect requirements development.

2. Create high-level requirements from customer input, considering different viewpoints. Requirements are expressions of what the system will do, which is both perceptible and of value to customers. Because the needs or wishes are mostly thought of in customer language, developers often must help in adjusting them to be testable and measurable.

3. Assign a value, indicating a degree of importance rating, to each requirement. The customer determines if the requirement is: very important (5 points), important (4 points), not important, but nice to have (3 points), not important (2 points), or unimportant (1 point).

Some goals of QFD are parallel to the goals for requirements elicitation:

- Both endeavor to educate management on the importance of the elicitation phase and the benefits of promoting communication during this phase.

- Both strive to capture the "voice of the customer," allowing subsequent design decisions to be traced back to customer needs; the user community's views may be captured through the use of mock-ups and prototypes, as well as brainstorming, FAST, and JAD.

- Both promote group work to achieve the common goal of producing quality requirements and sharing ownership in them.

Advantages of using QFD during requirements elicitation include:

- Cross-functional communication and teamwork result in a more usable product.

- Prioritized requirements allow high-priority items to be undertaken early, and enhances resource allocation throughout the development cycle.

- QFD documentation preserves knowledge and promotes reuse, ultimately shortening development time.

- Customer-focused activities lead to increased satisfaction with the product.

Quality function deployment reminds us that, in addition to functional and nonfunctional requirements, there are also: "normal" requirements that satisfy the customer; "expected" requirements that may not be explicitly stated by the customer, but their absence will cause significant dissatisfaction; and "exciting" requirements that go beyond the customer's expectations and prove to be very satisfying when present. Figure 16–11 points out that the range is from spoken requirements that please the customer when present, to unspoken requirements that displease the customer when absent.

However, requirements elicitators are not allowed to rest on their laurels. Over time, "delighting" requirements become "expected" requirements, and the customer will become dissatisfied if they are not present, spoken or otherwise (see Figure 16–12).

Prioritize Requirements

A theme throughout this book, emphasized in Chapters 10 and 11 on software sizing and estimating, is that there are only so many degrees of freedom when planning and developing

Requirement	Spoken	Unspoken (Functional)	Unspoken (Delights)
If present	Customer is pleased	Customer expects it to be there—takes it for granted	Customer is pleasantly surprised
If absent	Customer is dissatisfied	Customer is dissatisfied	Customer is unaffected

FIGURE 16–11
Spoken and Unspoken Customer Requirements

a software product. We can have fixed quality, fixed schedule, or fixed cost, but not all three. Most of the time, something has to give. Neither managers nor customers appreciate extended schedules or increasing costs, therefore we often plan for incremental deliveries, with only the most important features to be delivered first. (Of course, quality could be sacrificed, but that would rarely be a good idea.) This point in the product development cycle, when the

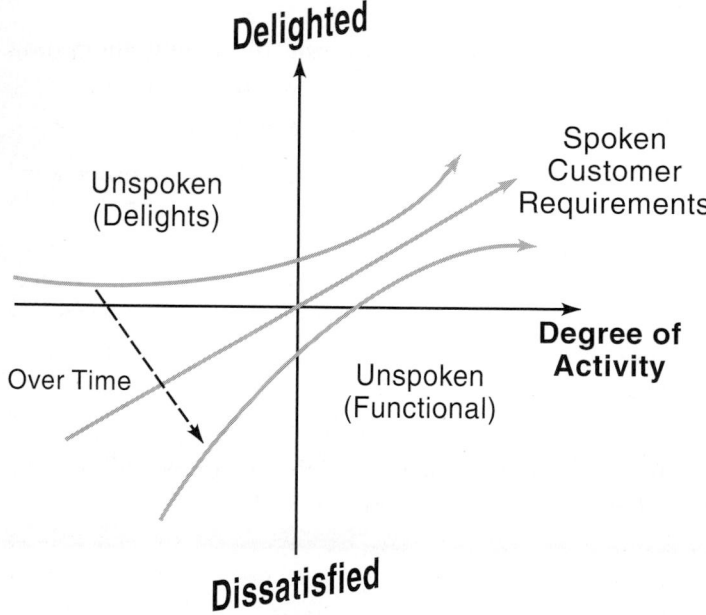

FIGURE 16–12
Keeping the Customer Delighted

requirements have been freshly gathered, is an ideal time to prioritize them. After this stage, deleting a requirement causes more consternation the further down the development process we travel. It is always expensive to develop software in a volatile requirements environment, but the worst dilemma of all is that the stakeholder's expectations will not be met.

When all stakeholder classes are identified and represented, as advised here, there are bound to be different, sometimes incompatible, goals for the project. Frequent communication with the customer and prioritization of the product's requirements will reduce project risk. As long as the important functions (so critical to mission success that they cannot be compromised) are delivered first, all functions are scheduled to be delivered at an agreed upon date, and the prioritization scheme is communicated to all stakeholders, there is diminished project angst.

Requirements prioritization can be a boon to many organizations relying on fiscal-year funding and can use remaining funds to acquire a scaled-down version of the product, as opposed to the optimal version, to meet budget constraints. The dialogue between stakeholders and developers should not stop at finding the topmost requirements, but continue to explore all meaningful options. When features of the product can be estimated for cost and schedule, stakeholders will have additional knowledge to aid decision-making.

Stakeholders will have their own unique set of criteria for determining the "importance," or value, of a requirement. It will be based on cost/benefit analysis particular to the project, and sets of requirements called feature sets. The importance of quality (the "-ilities") and constraints should be in the mix of requirements under consideration.

The process is to first group system functionality into feature sets, which are sets, or categories, of logically related requirements. The next step is for stakeholders to evaluate each requirement within each feature set to determine its value. A simple but often used scheme is:

3 = mission critical (very important, absolutely necessary)

2 = important, but not absolutely necessary

1 = nice to have, but optional

The third step is for developers and stakeholders to determine, for all of the requirements: if it is possible to achieve now; if it should be deferred, and why; or if it is impossible and should be dropped from consideration.

The evaluation process is not always an easy one—if a feature was not attractive to someone, then it probably wouldn't be on the list in the first place. More sessions in the mind mapping, JAD, or focus group format may be necessary to prioritize the requirements once they have been drawn out of the stakeholders' conscious and unconscious needs and desires. Those ranking the requirements are encouraged to remember intangible benefits (e.g., improved customer goodwill) as well as tangible benefits (e.g., increased sales).

Use cases may be helpful in the prioritization process by looking for the anticipated frequency or volume of usage, satisfying most favored user classes, implementation of core business processes, functions required by law, and so on. Critical success factors may be recalled to help determine "what must go right" in order for this application to be successful.

Table 16–1 shows a straightforward approach to documenting agreements for how and when prioritized requirements will be rolled out. It's simplified for the sake of example, but the format can work for any number of levels of priority (three in the example) and any number of feature sets (also three in the example). Once the requirements have been ranked by level of importance, they are grouped into cohesive feature sets. Combinations of the two may be released as versions of the software.

TABLE 16–1
An Example of Releasing Feature Sets by Version

Feature Sets	Feature Set 1	Feature Set 2	Feature Set 3	
Version #				
1	Implement all requirements with priority 3	Implement all requirements with priority 3	Implement all requirements with priority 3	Minimal Version
2	Retain all requirements with priority 3	Retain all requirements with priority 3	Retain all requirements with priority 3; implement all requirements with priority 2	
3	Retain all requirements with priority 3	Retain all requirements with priority 3; implement all requirements with priority 2	Retain all requirements with priority 3 and 2	
4	Retain all requirements with priority 3; implement all requirements with priority 2	Retain all requirements with priority 3 and 2	Retain all requirements with priority 3 and 2	

(Continues)

TABLE 16–1 (Continued)
An Example of Releasing Feature Sets by Version

Feature Sets	Feature Set 1	Feature Set 2	Feature Set 3	
5	Retain all requirements with priority 3 and 2	Retain all requirements with priority 3 and 2	Retain all requirements with priority 3 and 2; implement all requirements with priority 1	
6	Retain all requirements with priority 3 and 2	Retain all requirements with priority 3 and 2; implement all requirements with priority 1	Retain all requirements with priority 3 and 2; implement all requirements with priority 1	
7	Retain all requirements with priority 3 and 2; implement all requirements with priority 1	Retain all requirements with priority 3 and 2; implement all requirements with priority 1	Retain all requirements with priority 3 and 2; implement all requirements with priority 1	Maximal Version

Summary

Requirements elicitation, the most difficult and yet the most crucial activity in software development, occurs throughout the life cycle, although the more that can be done prior to writing the software requirements specification, the better. Gathering requirements draws on almost all of the 34 competencies that a software project manager needs to know, and is so fundamental to the maturity of an organization that the SEI has deemed it a key process area in maturity Level 2.

Requirements are difficult to determine for several reasons, including the fact that we may simply not know what we want until we are presented with it. Almost all software systems of any size have multiple stakeholders and stakeholder classes such as sponsors, customers, users, developer, and quality assurance. So many people with so many points of view are bound to suffer conflicting goals. The establishment of a collaborative customer-developer partnership for requirements development and management becomes essential. Techniques shown by experience to help the project manager with the process include: understanding the critical success factors of the system, involving and communicating with all stakeholder classes, being aware of the types of software requirements, knowing the characteristics of a well-written requirement, and using proven meeting methods for gaining consensus (interviewing, brainstorming, mind mapping, FAST, JAD, and use cases).

We turn to several software engineering authorities for guidance. Weinberg, Pressman, and Boehm have: mapped out a series of useful steps, and given us criteria for what makes a "good" requirement (concise, unambiguous, testable); taught us to understand the problem before creating the analysis model, and ways to use prototyping in that understanding; helped us know the importance of traceability and modeling data, function, and behavior; and helped us to remember that we can't do everything at once, so requirements must be prioritized.

Problems for Review

1. Review the following requirements statements and determine their "goodness."

The summary window shall display the time each order was placed and the number of items ordered.

The summary window shall display the buyer identification.

The order window will allow the user to save a partial order and to add to, or edit, a partial order.

The order window will require the user to enter the order protocol.

Delivered defects must be less that 5.7 sigma.

The accounts window shall display the customer accounts, with the account number first and customer name second.

The interface will be user-friendly.

The forms shall require a minimal number of keystrokes for the order information to be entered by the user.

Error messages shall display in a window following incorrect user entry.

The date will be in standard format.

User entry errors shall be reversible or correctable.

Installation must be completed in 45 minutes.

Error messages shall be provided for operational errors and to indicate system processing or software failures.

The system will have high functionality.

Operational errors will be reversible or correctable.

Error messages shall provide error descriptions within pop-up windows.

Certain operational error messages shall provide diagnostic instructions.

Messages about errors shall provide error recovery instructions and procedures.

2. Examine the control flow diagram in Figure 16–6. In the context of the case study, evaluate this diagram. Is it correct? Complete?

Visit the Case Study

Mr. Lee, your corporation's China sales executive, has contacted Ms. Patel to discuss the sales plan and his commission and quota structure for the next fiscal year. He is tasked with selling a complete new radio, paging, and cellular infrastructure system to a major Chinese ministry. Since he has relatives at the CRM, this will be his target. The culture of our corporation is that the sales executive with the largest open proposal owns the account. He has requested to Ms. Patel that she stay out of the account and have no contact except through him. He wants to meet Mr. Lu and will filter all communication to us from Mr. Lu.

You have four weeks to complete the requirements collection phase. It is supposed to begin in three days when you leave for Beijing to meet with Ms. Patel and collect requirements through Mr. Lu and his reservations team.

Produce a new plan for collecting requirements given the sales situation.

Citations

[1]Gause, Donald C., and Gerald M. Weinberg (1989). *Exploring Requirements: Quality Before Design.* Dorset House. p. 95.

[2]Pressman, Roger S. (2001). *Software Engineering: A Practitioner's Approach*, 5th ed. Boston, MA: McGraw-Hill.

[3]Boehm, Barry, et al. (1997). "Developing Multimedia Applications with the Win Win Spiral Model." *Proceedings, ESEC/FSE 97 and ACM Software Engineering Notes*, November. New York, NY: Association for Computing Machinery.

[4]Paulk, Mark C., Charles V. Weber, Bill Curtis, and Mary Beth Chrissis (1994). *The Capability Maturity Model: Guidelines for Improving the Software Process.* Reading, MA: Addison-Wesley SEI Series in Software Engineering. p. 126.

[5]IEEE 610.12-1990 (1990). "IEEE Standard Glossary of Software Engineering Terminology." *Software Engineering Standards Collection.* New York, NY: Institute of Electrical and Electronics Engineers.

[6]Wiegers, Karl E. (1999). *Software Requirements.* Redmond, WA: Microsoft Press.

[7]von Mayrhauser, Anneliese (1990). *Software Engineering: Methods and Management*. Boston, MA: Academic Press.

[8]*www.m-w.com/cgi-bin/dictionary.*

[9]*www.yourdictionary.com/cgi-bin/mw.cgi.*

[10]See note 1.

[11]Osborn, Alex F. (1983). *Applied Imagination*. Buffalo, NY: Creative Education Foundation.

[12]Buzan, Tony, and Barry Buzan (1996). *The Mind Map Book: How to Use Radiant Thinking to Maximize Your Brain's Untapped Potential*. New York, NY: Penguin Putnam.

[13]See note 2.

[14]Wood, Jane, and Denise Silver (1989). *Joint Application Design: How to Design Quality Systems in 40% Less Time*. New York, NY: John Wiley & Sons.

[15]*www.thebeenet.com/bluebird/jaddoc.htm.* Bill Jennerich (1999). "Joint Application Design: Business Requirements Analysis for Successful Re-engineering." Berwyn, PA: Bluebird Enterprises.

[16]Richter, Charles (1989). *Designing Flexible Object-Oriented Systems with UML*. Indianapolis, IN: Macmillan Technical Publishing.

[17]Brooks, Frederick P. (1986). "No Silver Bullet: Essence and Accidents of Software Engineering." *IEEE Computer*, 20(4):10–19.

Suggested Readings

Akao, Y., ed. (1990). *Quality Function Deployment*. Cambridge, MA: Productivity Press.

Buzan, Tony (1991). *Use Both Sides of Your Brain*, 3rd ed. New York, NY: Penguin Putnam.

Buzan, Tony, Tony Dottino, and Richard Israel (1999). *The Brainsmart Leader*. Burlington, VT: Gower Pub.

Dorfman, M., and R.H. Thayer, eds. (1997). *Software Engineering*. Los Alamitos, CA: IEEE Computer Society Press.

Doyle, Michael, and David Straus (1982). *How to Make Meetings Work: The New Interaction Method*. New York, NY: Penguin Putman.

Gorden, Raymond L. (1998). *Basic Interviewing Skills*. Prospect Heights, IL: Waveland Press.

Guinta, Lawrence R., and Nancy C. Praizler (1993). *The QFD Book*. New York, NY: Amacom Books.

Haag, Stephen, M.K. Raja, and L.L. Schkade (1996). "Quality Function Deployment Usage in Software Development." *Communications of the ACM*, 39(1):41–49.

Hammer, Theodore F., Leonore L. Huffman, and Linda H. Rosenberg (1998). "Doing Requirements Right the First Time." *Crosstalk, Journal of Defense Software Engineering*. December.

Hauser, John R., and Don Clausing (1988). "The House of Quality." *The Harvard Business Review*, May–June(3):63–73.

Hunter, Michael R., and Richard D. Van Landingham (1994). "Listening to the Customer Using QFD." *Quality Progress*, 27(4):55–59.

IEEE 1233 (1998). "Guide for Developing System Requirements Specifications." *Software Engineering Standards Collection*. New York, NY: Institute of Electrical and Electronics Engineers.

IEEE 830-1998 (1998). "IEEE Recommended Practice for Software Requirements Specifications." *Software Engineering Standards Collection*. New York, NY: Institute of Electrical and Electronics Engineers.

Jacobson, Ivar, et al. (1992). *Object-Oriented Software Engineering: A Use Case Driven Approach*. Reading, MA: Addison-Wesley.

Jazayeri, A. Ran, and F. van der Linden (2000). *Software Architecture for Product Families*. Reading, MA: Addison-Wesley.

Keil, Mark, and Erran Carmel (1995). "Customer-Developer Links in Software Development." *Communications of ACM*, 38(5):33–44.

Koltzblatt, Karen, and Hugh R. Beyer (1995). "Requirements Gathering: The Human Factor." *Communications of ACM*, 38(5):30–32.

Marqulies, Nancy (1991). *Mapping Inner Space: Learning and Teaching Mind Mapping*. Tucson, AZ: Zephyr Press.

Metzler, Ken (1996). *Creative Interviewing: The Writer's Guide to Gathering Information by Asking Questions*. New York, NY: Allyn & Bacon, Pearson Education.

Ogren, Ingmar (2000). "Requirements Management as a Matter of Communication." *Crosstalk, Journal of Defense Software Engineering*, 13(4).

Playle, Greg, and Charles Schroeder (1996). "Software Requirements Elicitation: Problems, Tools, and Techniques." *Crosstalk, Journal of Defense Software Engineering*, 9(12).

Plsek, Paul E. (1997). *Creativity, Innovation, and Quality*. New York, NY: McGraw-Hill.

Rumbaugh, James (1994). "Getting Started: Using Use Cases to Capture Requirements." *Journal of Object Oriented Programming*, September.

Somerville, Ian, and Gerald Kotonya (1997). *Requirements Engineering: Processes and Techniques*. New York, NY: John Wiley & Sons.

Strehlo, Kevin (1996). "Catching Up with the Joneses and 'Requirement' Creep." *InfoWorld*, July 29.

Thayer, Richard H., Merlin Dorfman, and Sidney C. Bailin, eds. (1997). *Software Requirements Engineering*, 2nd ed. Los Alamitos, CA: IEEE Computer Society Press.

Thayer, Richard H., ed. (1997). *Software Engineering Project Management*. Los Alamitos, CA: IEEE Computer Society Press.

Walters, Stan B. (1995). *Principles of Kinesic Interview and Interrogation*. Boca Raton, FL: CRC Press.

Wiegers, Karl E. (1999). "Writing Good Requirements." *Software Development*, May.

Wycoff, Joyce (1991). *Mindmapping: Your Personal Guide to Exploring Creativity and Problem-Solving*. New York, NY: Berkley Books.

Web Pages for Further Information

edweb.sdsu.edu/triton/guides/Brainstorming.html.

members.ozemail.com.au/~caveman/Creative/Techniques/brainstorm.htm.

www.acq-ref.navy.mil/wcp/qfd.html. QFD.

www.brainstorming.co.uk. Infinite Innovations Ltd, Brainstorming.

www.brainstorming.org.uk/tutorials/usenewpeople.html.

www.dhutton.com/samples/sampqfd.html. QFD.

www.directedcreativity.com. Brainstorming.

www.humansource.com/trendspotting/19990201.htm. Interviewing.

www.inspiration.com/. Mind Mapping.

www.mcli.dist.maricopa.edu/authoring/studio/guidebook/brain.html. Brainstorming.

www.methods-tools.com/.

www.mindjet.com/. Mind Mapping.

www.nauticom.net/www/qfdi/. The QFD Institute.

www.ozemail.com.au/~caveman/Creative/Mindmap/. Features a selection of mind-mapping related sites.

www.qfdi.org/. Quality Function Deployment Institute.

www.sdmagazine.com/documents/s=758/sdm9905c/9905c.htm.

www.zoo.co.uk/~z0001039/PracGuides/pg_use_cases.htm. Use Cases, Edward Kenworthy.

Developing the Software Requirements Specification

Getting the requirements correct is perhaps the most important part of a software development project. Once a software development team begins to collect the project requirements, it is critical that the project have a consistent format for maintaining and presenting them. This chapter describes the construction of the software requirements specification (SRS), used for the ongoing maintenance and presentation of the project requirements. The SRS is critical to the entire software development life cycle. Not only is it the derivative document for the software design specification, but also it is the base document for generating the validation and acceptance tests. Validation is the determination of whether or not we as project managers have built the right product. Satisfying the requirements determines successful validation. The SRS is the mechanism for capturing those validation criteria—the system requirements.

Barry Boehm defined the economics of software engineering in 1981.[1] Figure 17–1 shows that it costs more to fix a bug the later it is found in a project's life cycle. Most bugs in the later portions of the life cycle are caused by unclear or missing requirements. We cannot change the economics but we can lower the number of bugs that escape from the requirements phase of our life cycle by developing a complete SRS. This chapter describes recommended approaches for the specification of software requirements.

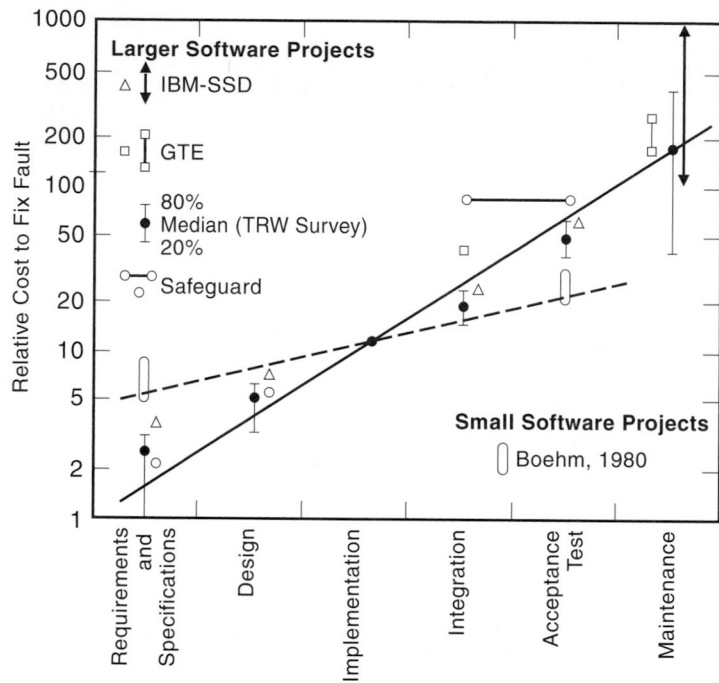

FIGURE 17–1
Defects Found Late in the Life Cycle Cost More to Correct

Where We Are in the Product Development Life Cycle

We have finished with concept and system exploration. At this point in the project we should have an understanding of where the project's ultimate product fits within the system environment. The system environment is important because this is where the software lives. We are now in the requirements phase of the project life cycle and, as shown in Figure 17–2, the one deliverable from the phase is the software requirements specification.

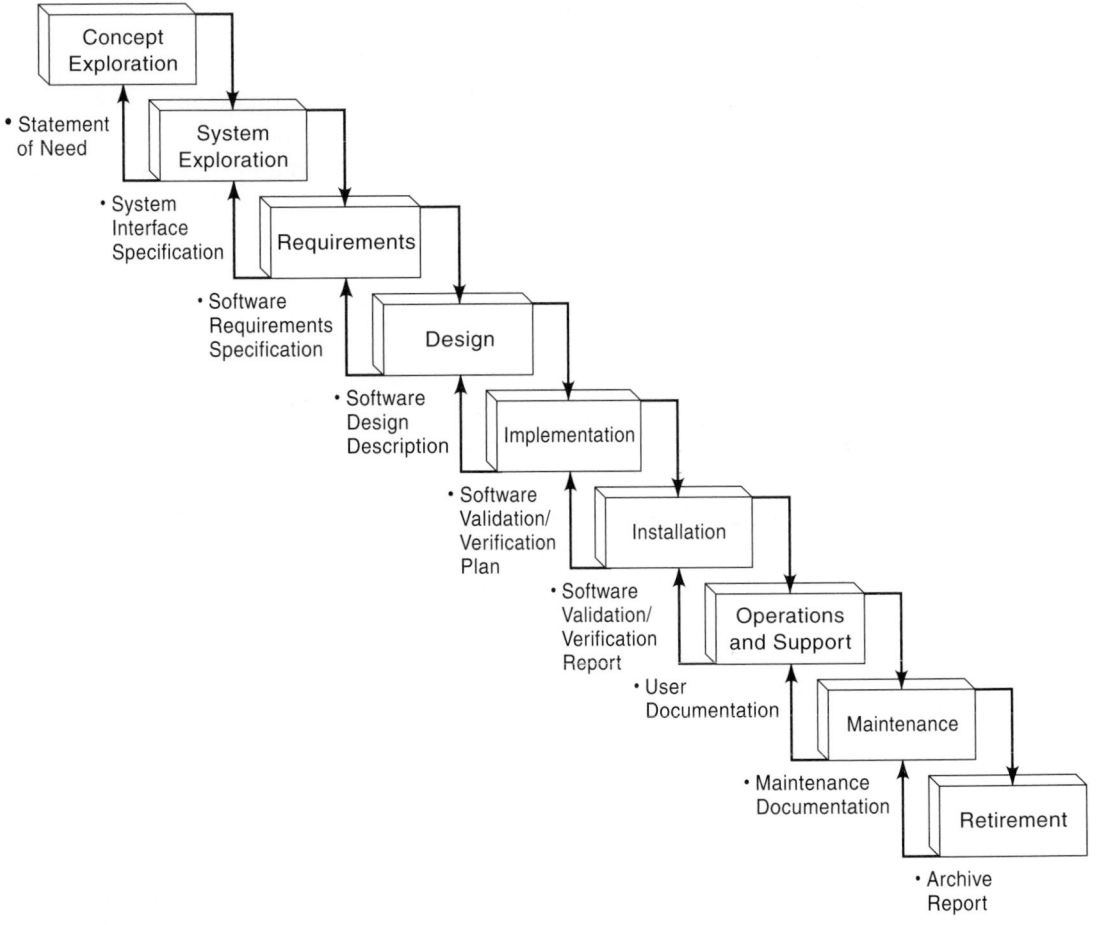

FIGURE 17–2
Where the Development of the Software Requirements Specification Occurs in the Product Development Life Cycle

Chapter 17 Relation to the 34 Competencies _____

A project manager's ability to successfully manage requirements, coupled with documenting and presenting those requirements, is critical to a quality SRS. Estimating effort and developing schedules from these requirements is a major part of the project manager's job in this phase of the software development life cycle.

The competencies that will be addressed in this chapter include:

Product Development Techniques

5. **Managing requirements**—Managing and defining correct requirements is perhaps the most important part of a software development project. This chapter describes the construction of the SRS document itself, beginning with the exploratory activity of helping the customer determine his or her true wants and needs.

Project Management Skills

13. **Documenting plans**

15. **Estimating effort**

People Management Skills

25. **Holding effective meetings**

31. **Presenting effectively**

And, as with almost all activities that depend on customer interaction and result in a project deliverable, people management skills 26—interaction and communication, 27—leadership, 28—managing change, 29—negotiating successfully, and 34—teambuilding, are always in play.

Learning Objectives for Chapter 17 _____

At the completion of this chapter, the reader will be able to:

- Develop a complete SRS for a software development project;
- Evaluate an SRS with respect to critical quality factors;
- Plan and estimate the task of developing an SRS during the requirements phase of a project;
- Lay the groundwork for acceptance and validation testing.

Questions the SRS Answers for a Project _____

The major question that the SRS addresses concerns the problem domain in which the product will exist. As shown in Figure 17–3, all software products can be viewed from three perspectives: data, process, and behavior.

The data view looks at identifying the primary data objects to be processed by the software system. The definition of each object as well as where it resides is identified. One object's relationship to other objects and the processes that act on them are also part of the data view. For an ATM machine, an important piece of data would be a customer's personal identification number (PIN).

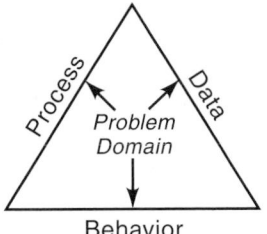

FIGURE 17–3
Three Perspectives of Software Products

As the data within a software system moves, it is modified by a series of transformations. The process view of the problem domain focuses on these data transformations. The transformation of data from inputs to outputs satisfies the business requirements of the system as captured in the SRS. With our ATM, a process would be the validation of the PIN.

The behavior view of the system focuses on the states a system assumes. The state is any externally observable mode of behavior. After a PIN is entered in the ATM, the machine is in the state of validating the PIN. Processes are running and data is being transformed, but the user is only observing a message that may indicate that his or her PIN is being validated.

The SRS is the first step in a project that moves from the recognition and definition of the problem domain to a solution domain. The solution domain fills in the three perspectives with requirements models tailored to capturing data, process, and behavioral characteristics (see Figure 17–4). The development of these individual models will be covered later in this book. The SRS provides the framework for holding the models.

Once we look at the views of our software system, questions arise that lead to the requirements collection. These questions relate to the quality of the SRS produced and to how we eventually validate the completed SRS. Construx Software (*www.construx.com*) provides a series of software development checklists. IEEE 830-1998 provides the set of quality characteristics an SRS exhibits:

1. Correctness
2. Unambiguousness
3. Completeness
4. Consistency
5. Ranking for importance and/or stability
6. Verifiability
7. Modifiability
8. Traceability

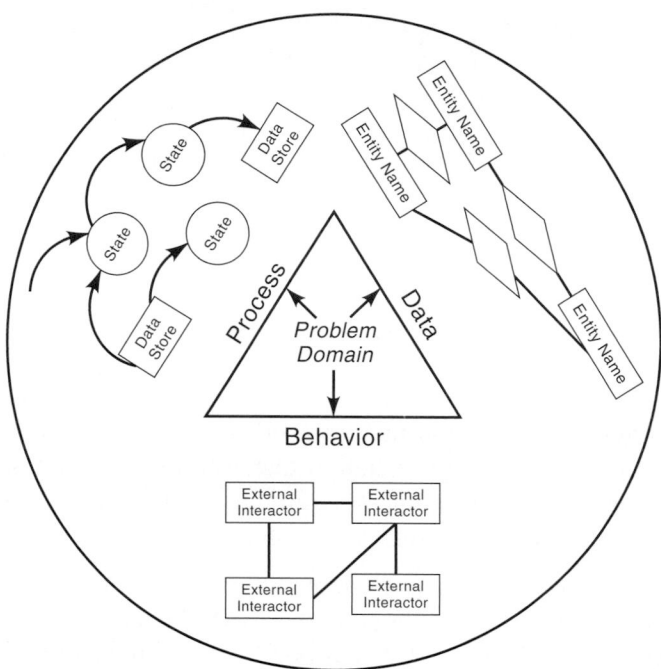

FIGURE 17–4
Process, Data, Behavior

Using the checklist model and the standard, an SRS aids in answering questions for these key characteristics:

1. Correctness

   a. Is the expected response time, from the user's point of view, specified for all necessary operations?

   b. Are other timing considerations specified, such as processing time, data transfer, and system throughput?

   c. Are all the tasks the user wants to perform specified?

   d. Does each task specify the data used in the task and data resulting from the task?

   e. Is the level of security specified?

   f. Is the reliability specified, including the consequences of software failure, vital information protected from failure, error detection, and recovery?

   g. Are acceptable trade-offs between competing attributes specified, for example, between robustness and correctness?

    h. Are external people, software, and hardware interfaces defined?

    i. Is the definition of success included? Of failure?

2. Unambiguousness

    a. Are the requirements clear enough to be turned over to an independent group for implementation and still be understood?

    b. Are functional requirements separated from non-functional?

3. Completeness

    a. Are all the inputs to the system specified, including their source, accuracy, range of values, and frequency?

    b. Are all the outputs from the system specified, including their destination, accuracy, range of values, frequency, and format?

    c. Are all the communication interfaces specified, including handshaking, error checking, and communication protocols?

    d. Where information isn't available before development begins, are the areas of incompleteness specified?

    e. Are the requirements complete in the sense that if a product satisfies every requirement, it will be acceptable?

    f. Is there a sense of unease about any part of the requirements? Are some parts impossible to implement and included just to please a customer or a boss?

    g. Has a complete risk analysis been done with special emphasis on any missing requirements?

4. Consistency

    a. Do the requirements avoid specifying the design?

    b. Are the requirements at a fairly consistent level? Should any requirement be specified in more detail? Should any requirement be specified in less detail?

5. Ranking for importance and/or stability

    a. Is each item relevant to the problem and its solution?

6. Verifiability

    a. Are the requirements written in a language and with a vocabulary the user understands? Do the users agree?

    b. Is each requirement testable? Will it be possible for independent testing to determine whether each requirement has been satisfied?

7. Modifiability

    a. Are all possible changes to the requirements specified including the likelihood of each change?

    b. Is the maintainability of the system specified, including the ability to respond to changes in the operating environment, interfaces with other software, accuracy, performance, and additional predicted capabilities?

8. Traceability

    a. Do all the requirements avoid conflicts with other requirements?

    b. Can each item be traced to its origin in the problem environment?

Benefits of an SRS

Using an SRS model provides a specification process that is unambiguous and delivers a complete specification document. This assists the project manager in communicating clearly with the project stakeholders to ensure that:

1. Software customers accurately describe what they wish to obtain.

2. Software suppliers understand exactly what the customer wants.

3. Individuals accomplish the following goals:

    a. Develop a SRS outline for their project and organization;

    b. Define the format and content of their specific software requirements;

    c. Develop additional local supporting items such as an SRS quality checklist, or an SRS best practices handbook.

A good SRS demonstrates these specific benefits to the project stakeholders:

- The SRS becomes the baseline for agreement between the customers and the suppliers on what the software product is to do. The complete description of the functions to be performed by the software specified in the SRS will assist the potential users to determine if the software specified meets their needs or how the software must be modified to meet their needs.

- It reduces the development effort. The preparation of the SRS forces the various concerned groups in the customer's organization to consider rigorously all of the requirements before design begins and reduces later redesign, recoding, and retesting.

- A careful review of the requirements in the SRS can reveal omissions, misunderstandings, and inconsistencies early in the development cycle when these problems are easier to correct.

- It becomes the basis for estimating costs and schedules. The product description is a realistic basis for estimating project costs. In a public environment where a formal bidding process exists, the SRS is used to obtain approval for bids or price estimates.

- Organizations can develop their validation and verification plans much more productively from a good SRS. As a part of the development contract, the SRS provides a baseline against which compliance can be measured.

- It facilitates the transfer of the software product to new users or new machines. Customers thus find it easier to transfer the software to other parts of their organization, and suppliers find it easier to transfer it to new customers.

- It serves as a basis for enhancement. Because the SRS discusses the product but not the project that developed it, it serves as a basis for later enhancement of the finished product.

Building the SRS

Requirements definition is the most crucial part of the project. The SRS is the mechanism for capturing and containing the project requirements. Incorrect, inaccurate, or excessive definition of requirements will necessarily result in schedule delays, wasted resources, or customer dissatisfaction. Any discussion of requirements analysis methods will quickly become specific to the type of project effort. Many industry areas have specific, proven techniques for obtaining thorough and accurate definition of requirements. Sometimes it is useful to write a draft user's manual as a way to define requirements. While the methods may differ, the principles remain the same across all types and sizes of projects. The requirements analysis should cover the whole scope of the project. It must be comprehensive and thorough. It must consider the views and needs of all the project stakeholders.

It is easy to leave scope out of requirements analysis or to omit necessary clarity or detail thereby making the requirements definition ambiguous. The completed requirements analysis should be reviewed and approved by the customer or project sponsor before work continues. On large projects, the first formal design review is actually a requirements review.

The SRS can take on any reasonable form for specific project needs. It needs to embody the quality characteristics previously described. The following template is based on IEEE 830-1998 with modifications from extensive experience with software project definition. It is a basic SRS outline that accommodates the three views of the project problem domain and is a vehicle for capturing and maintaining project requirements.

Title Page

Identify the document as the software requirements specification, and list the project name and author(s). Place the version/revision control table on either the title page or the following page with the enumeration of the releases of the SRS and other comments as determined by the configuration management process.

Table of Contents

Simply use whatever automated table of contents generator is available with the project documentation tool.

Section 1. Introduction

The following subsections of the SRS should provide an overview of the entire SRS. By itself, Section 1 should stand alone as an executive summary.

1.1 Purpose   Identify the purpose of the SRS and its intended audience. Identify why it has been developed at this point in the product life.

1.2 Scope   In this subsection:

1. Identify the software product(s) produced by name and a one-paragraph description of its function.
2. Explain what the software product(s) will, and will not, do. This is how the product(s) is (are) to be used. Explaining what it will not do removes ambiguity from the SRS.
3. Describe the application of the software being specified. A portion of this should:

   a. Describe the relevant benefits, objectives, and goals as precisely as possible.

   b. Be consistent with similar statements in higher-level specifications if they exist.

1.3 Assumptions and Dependencies   List and describe each of the factors that affect the requirements stated in the SRS. These factors are not design constraints on the software but any changes to them can affect the requirements in the SRS. It is critical that these be enumerated at the front of the SRS. Many times managers and executives read only the introduction (executive summary). Because their job is to facilitate the successful execution of this project, if they are aware of all assumptions and dependencies, they can aid in making the project a success.

An assumption might be that a specific operating system will be available on the hardware designated for the software product. If, in fact, the operating system was not available, the SRS would have to change. Major dependencies like this must be brought to management's attention.

1.4 Overview of the SRS   Describe the rest of the SRS and how it is organized.

Section 2. The General Description

Describe the general factors that affect the product and its requirements. This section does not state specific requirements. Each of the five subsections makes the requirements easier to understand; they do not specify design or express specific requirements. Such detail is provided in Section 3.

2.1 Product Perspective   This subsection of the SRS relates the product to other products or projects.

1. If the product is independent and totally self-contained, it should be stated here.
2. If the SRS defines a product that is a component of a larger system or project:
   a. Describe the functions of each component of the larger system or project, and identify the interfaces.
   b. Identify the principal external interfaces of the software product (not a detailed description).
   c. Describe the computer hardware and peripheral equipment to be used (overview only).

A block diagram showing the major components of the larger system or project, interconnections, and external interfaces is essential for understanding the domain in which this product operates.

2.2 Product Functions   Provide a summary of the functions that the software will perform. Sometimes the function summary can be taken directly from the system specification section that allocates particular functions to the software product. The functions should be organized in a way that makes the list of functions understandable to the customer or to anyone else reading the document for the first time. Block diagrams showing the different functions and their relationships are essential as an effective explanatory tool.

2.3 User Characteristics   Describe those general characteristics of the eventual users of the product that will affect the specific requirements. Many people interact with a system during the operation and maintenance phase of the software life cycle. Some of these people are users, operators, and maintenance and systems personnel. Certain characteristics of these people, such as educational level, experience, and technical expertise impose important constraints on the system's operating environment. This is the audience for the application's user's manual. It is never too early to begin writing the end-user documentation. By the time the SRS is complete, there should be an understanding of how the user interacts with the system. If the user's manual cannot be written at this time, it is an indication of missing requirements.

2.4 General Constraints   Provide a general description of any other items that will limit the developer's options for designing the system. These can include:

1. Regulatory policies
2. Hardware limitations (for example, signal timing requirements)
3. Interface to other applications
4. Parallel operation
5. Audit functions
6. Control functions
7. Higher-order language requirements

8. Signal handshake protocols
9. Criticality of the application
10. Safety and security considerations

Section 3. Specific Requirements

This section of the SRS should contain all the details the software developer needs to create a design. This is typically the largest and most important part of the SRS. It is the section where the three views of the problem domain will be described (please refer to Figure 17–3), along with diagrams and models representing the requirements.

1. Details should be defined as individual specific requirements, keeping in mind the quality characteristics (correctness, unambiguousness, completeness, consistency, rank of importance and/or stability, verifiability, modifiability, and traceability).

2. Specific requirements should be organized in a logical and clear fashion.

3. Each requirement should be stated in such a way that its achievement can be objectively verified by a prescribed method.

4. Sources of a requirement should be identified where useful for understanding of the requirement.

5. One way to classify the specific requirements is as follows:

   a. Functional requirements

   b. Performance requirements

   c. Design constraints

   d. Attributes

   e. External interface requirements

The best organization for this section depends on the application area and the nature of the software product being specified. There are four general classes that the organization can assume:

1. In Figure 17–5, the functional requirements are specified, followed by the four types of interface requirements and the rest of the requirements.

2. Figure 17–6 shows the four classes of interface requirements applied to each individual functional requirement. This is followed by the specification of the rest of the requirements.

3. In Figure 17–7, all of the issues addressed by the functional requirements are specified, followed by the other requirements that apply to them. This pattern is repeated for each of the external interface requirement classifications.

4. In Figure 17–8, the interface requirements and the rest of the requirements are specified as they pertain to each functional requirement.

3. Specific Requirements
  3.1 Functional Requirements
      3.1.1 Functional Requirement 1
            3.1.1.1 Introduction
            3.1.1.2 Inputs
            3.1.1.3 Processing
            3.1.1.4 Outputs
      3.1.2 Functional Requirement 2

     .....
      3.1.n Functional Requirement n
  3.2 External Interface Requirements
      3.2.1 User Interfaces
      3.2.2 Hardware Interfaces
      3.2.3 Software Interfaces
      3.2.4 Communication Interfaces
  3.3 Performance Requirements
  3.4 Design Constraints
      3.4.1 Standards Compliance
      3.4.2 Hardware Limitations

     .....
  3.5 Quality Characteristics
      3.5.1

     .....
  3.6 Other Requirements
      3.6.1 Database
      3.6.2 Operations
      3.6.3 Site Adaptation

     .....

FIGURE 17–5
All Functional Requirements Specified First

The organization of this section of the SRS should be chosen with the goal of properly specifying the requirements in the most readable manner. The template outline that follows uses an organization like Figure 17–5.

3.1 Functional Requirements   This subsection specifies what the product will do, and to what level or requirement it will do it, what inputs should be transformed to what outputs (not how this is done), and what operations are required. Where the rationale for a requirement is not obvious, provide an explanation. Cite any issues that need to be resolved.

3. Specific Requirements
  3.1 Functional Requirements
      3.1.1 Functional Requirement 1
              3.1.1.1 Specification
                    3.1.1.1.1 Introduction
                    3.1.1.1.2 Inputs
                    3.1.1.1.3 Processing
                    3.1.1.1.4 Outputs
              3.1.1.2 External Interfaces
                    3.1.1.2.1 User Interfaces
                    3.1.1.2.2 Hardware Interfaces
                    3.1.1.2.3 Software Interfaces
                    3.1.1.2.4 Communication Interfaces
      3.1.2 Functional Requirement 2
        .....
      3.1.n Functional Requirement n
  3.2 Performance Requirements
  3.3 Design Constraints
  3.4 Quality Characteristics
      3.4.1
      .....
  3.5 Other Requirements
      3.5.1 Database
      3.5.2 Operations
      3.5.3 Site Adaptation
      .....

FIGURE 17–6
Each Interface Requirement Applied to Each Functional Requirement First

For each function, specify requirements on inputs, processing, and outputs. These are usually organized with these four subparagraphs:

1. Purpose of the function: provide rationale to clarify the intent of the function
2. Inputs: sources, valid ranges of values, any timing concerns, operator requirements, special interfaces
3. Operations to be performed: validity checks, responses to abnormal conditions, types of processing required
4. Outputs: destinations, valid ranges of values, timing concerns, handling of illegal values, error messages, interfaces required

3.2 External Interface Requirements   This section of the SRS contains all of the information that the designer needs to adequately develop the interfaces to entities outside of the software being specified. Of critical importance is the specification of the requirements

3. Specific Requirements
  3.1 Functional Requirements
      3.1.1 Functional Requirement 1
           3.1.1.1   Introduction
           3.1.1.2   Inputs
           3.1.1.3   Processing
           3.1.1.4   Outputs
           3.1.1.5   Performance Requirements
           3.1.1.6   Design Constraints
                3.1.1.6.1 Standards Compliance
                3.1.1.6.2 Hardware Limitations

                ....
           3.1.1.7   Attributes
                3.1.1.7.1 Security
                3.1.1.7.2 Maintainability
           3.1.1.8   Other Requirements
                3.1.1.8.1 Database
                3.1.1.8.2 Operations
                3.1.1.8.3 Site Adaptation

      3.1.2   Functional Requirement 2
      .....
      3.1.n Functional Requirement n

  3.2 External Interface Requirements
      3.2.1   User Interfaces
           3.2.1.1   Performance Requirements
           3.2.1.2   Design Constraints
                3.2.1.2.1 Standards Compliance
                3.2.1.2.2 Hardware Limitations

                ....
           3.2.1.3   Quality Characteristics
                3.2.1.3.1

                ....
           3.2.1.4   Other Requirements
                3.2.1.4.1 Database
                3.2.1.4.2 Operations
                3.2.1.4.3 Site Adaptation

                ....
      3.2.2   Hardware Interfaces
      3.2.3   Software Interfaces
      3.2.4   Communications Interfaces

FIGURE 17–7
A Functional Requirement, the Rest of Its Requirements, and All Interface Requirements

for how the end-user will interact with the software system. Where required, specific interfaces to hardware, other software applications, and communication systems are specified in this subsection.

3. Specific Requirements
   3.1 Functional Requirement 1
         3.1.1 Introduction
         3.1.2 Inputs
         3.1.3 Processing
         3.1.4 Outputs
         3.1.5 External Interfaces
              3.1.5.1　User Interfaces
              3.1.5.2　Hardware Interfaces
              3.1.5.3　Software Interfaces
              3.1.5.4　Communications Interfaces
         3.1.6 Performance Requirements
         3.1.7 Design Constraints
         3.1.8 Quality Characteristics
              3.1.8.1
              ....
         3.1.9 Other Requirements
              3.1.9.1　Database
              3.1.9.2　Operations
              3.1.9.3　Site Adaptation
   3.2 Functional Requirement 2
     ....
   3.*n* Functional Requirement *n*

FIGURE 17–8
A Functional Requirement, Its Interface Requirements, and Its Other Requirements

3.2.1 User Interfaces   This should specify:

1. The characteristics that the software must support for each human interface to the software product. For example, if the user of the system operates through a display terminal, the following should be specified:
   a. Required screen formats
   b. Page layout and content of any reports or menus
   c. Relative timing of inputs and outputs
   d. Availability of some form of programmable function keys

2. All the aspects of optimizing the interface with the person who must use the system. This may simply comprise a list of do's and don'ts on how the system will appear to the user.

3.2.2 Hardware Interfaces   Specify the logical characteristics of each interface between the software product and the hardware components of the system. Include such matters as what devices are to be supported, how they are to be supported, and protocols. A block diagram showing the relationship among the hardware blocks and the software functions hosted in each block is essential here.

3.2.3 Software Interfaces   Specify the use of other required software products (for example, a data management system, an operating system, or a mathematical package), and interfaces with other application systems.

For each required software product, the following should be provided:

1. Name
2. Mnemonic
3. Specification number
4. Version number
5. Source

For each interface:

1. Discuss the purpose of the interfacing software as related to this software product.
2. Define the interface in terms of message content and format. It is not necessary to detail any well-documented interface, but a reference to the document defining the interface is required.

3.2.4 Communications Interfaces   Specify the various interfaces to communications, such as local network protocols.

3.3 Performance Requirements   This subsection should specify both the static and the dynamic numerical requirements placed on the software or on human interaction with the software as a whole.

1. Static numerical requirements may include:
   a. The number of terminals to be supported
   b. The number of simultaneous users to be supported
   c. The number of files and records to be handled
   d. The sizes of tables and files
2. Dynamic numerical requirements may include, for example, the numbers of transactions and tasks and the amount of data to be processed within certain time periods for both normal and peak workload conditions.

All of these requirements should be stated in measurable terms, for example, "95 percent of the transactions shall be processed in less than 1 second," rather than, "operator shall not have to wait for the transaction to complete."

  Note: Numerical limits applied to one specific function are normally specified as part of the processing subparagraph description of that function.

3.4 Design Constraints   Design constraints can be imposed by other standards, hardware limitations, and the operating environment.

3.4.1 Standards Compliance
Specify the requirements derived from existing standards or regulations. These might include:

1. Report format
2. Data naming
3. Accounting procedures
4. Audit tracing (For example, this could specify the requirement for software to trace processing activity. Such traces are needed for some applications to meet minimum government or financial standards. An audit trace requirement might state that all changes to a payroll database must be recorded in a trace file with before and after values.)

3.4.2 Hardware Limitations
Identify requirements for the software to operate inside various hardware constraints.

3.5 Quality Characteristics
There are a number of quality characteristics that can apply to software. Pick those most important to the product and develop a section for each one. Figure 17–9 has the definitions of the quality characteristics.

3.5.1 Efficiency
Describe the rationale for including the efficiency characteristic for this product.

Describe how the presence, absence, or level of this characteristic will be measured; identify ways to test the characteristic once the product is complete.

3.5.n Usability
As stated in the instructions, there could be several quality characteristics described in these subsections. Usability is numbered with an "n" prefix to reference the possibility of one or more characteristics.

Describe the rationale for including the usability characteristic for this product.

Describe how the presence, absence, or level of this characteristic will be measured; identify ways to test the characteristic once the product is complete.

3.6 Other Requirements
Certain requirements may, due to the nature of the software, the user organization, and so on, be placed in separate categories such as those below.

3.6.1 Database
This subsection could specify the requirements for any database that is to be developed as part of the product. These might include:

1. Types of information
2. Frequency of use
3. Accessing capabilities

1. *Correctness*—extent to which program satisfies
   specifications and fulfills user's mission objectives
2. *Efficiency*—amount of computing resources
   and code required to perform function
3. *Flexibility*—effort needed to modify operational
   program
4. *Integrity/security*—extent to which access to
   software or data by unauthorized people can
   be controlled
5. *Interoperability*—effort needed to couple one
   system with another
6. *Maintainability*—effort required to locate and
   fix an error during operation
7. *Portability*—effort needed to transfer from one
   hardware or software environment to another
8. *Reliability*—extent to which program performs
   with required precision
9. *Reusability*—extent to which it can be reused
   in another application
10. *Testability*—effort needed to test to ensure
    performs as intended
11. *Usability*—effort required to learn, operate,
    prepare input, interpret output

FIGURE 17–9
Quality Characteristics

4. Data element and file descriptions

5. Relationship of data elements, records, and files

6. Static and dynamic organization

7. Retention requirements for data

If an existing database package is to be used, this package should be named under Subsection 3.2.3., Software Interfaces, and the details of its use specified there.

3.6.2 Operations   This is sometimes specified as part of the User Interfaces section. It could specify the normal and special operations required by the user such as:

1. The various modes of operations in the user organization; for example, user-initiated operations.

2. Periods of interactive operations and periods of unattended operations.

3. Data processing support functions.
4. Backup and recovery operations.

3.6.3 Site Adaptation Requirements   This section could:

1. Define the requirements for any data or initialization sequences that are specific to a given site, mission, or operational mode (for example, safety limits).
2. Specify features that should be modified to adapt the software to an installation.

Section 4. Supporting Information

The supporting information adds to the completeness of the SRS. This section should always be considered part of the formal requirements specification. The SRS remains a "living document" throughout the life cycle of the product, not just its development. Information contained in the document is maintained and placed under version control. It is a critical part of the validation testing and all subsequent regression test suites.

4.1 Definitions, Acronyms, and Abbreviations   Provide the definitions of all terms, acronyms, and abbreviations required to properly interpret the SRS. This information may be provided by reference to an appendix or other document(s).

4.2 References   In this subsection:

1. Provide a complete list of all documents referenced elsewhere in the SRS.
2. Identify each document by title, report number (if applicable), date, and publishing organization.
3. Specify the sources from which the references can be obtained.
4. Use as many Web sources as possible.
5. Include a traceability matrix.

The traceability matrix is one of the key deliverables from the requirements phase and a tool that will be used throughout the life cycle of the product. It is an outgrowth of the numbering scheme for the SRS requirements section and takes on the topology of the layout used.

Table 17–1 shows an example of a requirements traceability matrix with the hardware module in which the requirement is hosted. Traceability matrices can be developed to show any information dimension. Some commonly used ones are:

1. User interface
2. Validation tests
3. Acceptance tests
4. Contract line items
5. Training

6. Design modules
7. Source code
8. Documentation
9. External dependencies
10. Quality factors
11. Errors found

4.3 Appendices   The appendices are considered part of the actual requirements specification, although they may not always be necessary. They might include:

1. Sample I/O formats, descriptions of cost analysis studies, results of user surveys.
2. Supporting or background information that can help the readers of the SRS.
3. A description of the problems to be solved by the software.
4. The history, background, experience, and operational characteristics of the organization to be supported.
5. A cross-reference list, arranged by milestone, of those incomplete software requirements to be completed by specified milestones.
6. Special packaging instructions for the code and the media to meet security, export, initial loading, or other requirements.

4.4 Index   As with the table of contents, simply use the project documentation tool to automatically generate an index for the SRS.

TABLE 17–1
Requirements Traceability Table

Requirement Number and Description	HW Module 1	HW Module 2	HW Module 3	HW Module 4	HW Module 5	HW Module 6	HW Module 7
3.1 Functional Requirements							
3.1.1 Functional Requirement 1							
3.1.1.1 Introduction	X						
3.1.1.2 Inputs		X	X				
3.1.1.3 Processing							

(Continues)

TABLE 17–1 (Continued)
Requirements Traceability Table

Requirement Number and Description		HW Module 1	HW Module 2	HW Module 3	HW Module 4	HW Module 5	HW Module 6	HW Module 7
3.1.1.4	Outputs							
3.1.2	Functional Requirement 2		X		X			
3.1.2.1	Introduction							
3.1.2.2	Inputs			X				
3.1.2.3	Processing		X		X			
3.1.2.4	Outputs							
3.1.n	Functional Requirement n		X					X
3.1.n.1	Introduction							
3.1.n.2	Inputs			X				
3.1.n.3	Processing	X						
3.1.n.4	Outputs	X	X					
3.2	External Interface Requirements	X						
3.2.1	User Interfaces							X
3.2.2	Hardware Interfaces	X	X	X	X			
3.2.3	Software Interfaces		X	X	X	X		
3.2.4	Communications Interfaces				X			
3.3	Performance Requirements							X
3.4	Design Constraints							X
3.4.1	Standards Compliance					X	X	
3.4.2	Hardware Limitations			X	X			

(Continues)

TABLE 17–1 (Continued)
Requirements Traceability Table

Requirement Number and Description		HW Module 1	HW Module 2	HW Module 3	HW Module 4	HW Module 5	HW Module 6	HW Module 7
3.5	Quality Characteristics							
3.5.1	Correctness	X						X
3.5.2	Unambiguousness		X				X	
3.5.3	Completeness			X		X		
3.5.4	Consistency				X			
3.5.5	Ranked for Importance and/or Stability			X		X		
3.5.6	Verifiability		X				X	
3.5.7	Modifiability	X						X
3.5.8	Traceability	X	X	X	X	X	X	X
3.6	Other Requirements							
3.6.1	Database				X	X		
3.6.2	Operations			X				
3.6.3	Site Adaptation		X					

Evaluating the Project SRS _____

During the SRS building process, the project manager must constantly be aware of the quality characteristics of the SRS: correctness, unambiguousness, completeness, and consistency, ranked for importance and/or stability, verifiability, modifiability, and traceability. These characteristics are evaluated as the SRS is being built.

Correctness

An SRS is correct only if every requirement stated therein is one that the software shall meet. There is no tool or procedure that ensures correctness. The SRS should be compared with any applicable superior specification (such as a system requirements specification), with other project documentation, and with other applicable standards, to ensure that it agrees. Alternatively, the customer or user can determine if the SRS correctly reflects the actual needs. Traceability makes this procedure easier and less prone to error.

Unambiguousness

An SRS is unambiguous only if every requirement stated therein has only one interpretation. At a minimum, this requires that each characteristic of the final product be described using a single unique term. In cases where a term used in a particular context could have multiple meanings, the term should be included in a glossary where its meaning is made more specific. An SRS is an important part of the requirements process of the software life cycle and is used in design, implementation, project monitoring, verification and validation, and in training, as described in IEEE Std 1074-1997. The SRS should be unambiguous both to those who create it and to those who use it. However, these groups often do not have the same background and therefore do not tend to describe software requirements the same way. Representations that improve the requirements specification for the developer may be counterproductive in that they diminish understanding to the user and vice versa.

Take note of these specific areas to avoid ambiguity:

1. Natural language pitfalls—Requirements are often written in natural, human language such as English. Natural language is inherently ambiguous. A natural-language SRS should be reviewed by an independent party to identify ambiguous language for correction.

2. Requirements specification languages—One way to avoid ambiguity inherent in natural language is to write the SRS in a particular requirements specification language. Its language processors automatically detect many lexical, syntactic, and semantic errors. One disadvantage of using such languages is the length of time required to learn them. Also, many non-technical users find them unintelligible. Moreover, these languages tend to be better at expressing certain types of requirements and addressing certain types of systems. Thus, they may influence the requirements in subtle ways.

3. Representation tools—Requirements methods and languages and the tools that support them fall into three general categories: object, process, and behavioral. Object-oriented approaches organize the requirements in terms of real-world objects, their attributes, and the services performed by those objects. Process-based approaches organize the requirements into hierarchies of functions that communicate via data flows. Behavioral approaches describe the external behavior of the system in terms of some abstract notion (such as predicate calculus), mathematical functions, or state machines. The

degree to which such tools and methods may be useful in preparing an SRS depends upon the size and complexity of the program. When using any of these approaches it is best to retain the natural language descriptions so that customers unfamiliar with the notations can still understand the SRS.

Completeness

An SRS is complete only if it includes the following elements:

1. All significant requirements, whether relating to functionality, performance, design constraints, attributes, or external interfaces. In particular, any external requirements imposed by a system specification should be acknowledged and treated.

2. Definition of the responses of the software to all realizable classes of input data in all realizable classes of situations. Note that it is important to specify the responses to both valid and invalid input values.

3. Full labels and references to all figures, tables, and diagrams in the SRS and definition of all terms and units of measure.

4. No "To Be Determined" (TBD) labels. If there is a section containing a TBD it must also contain: a description of the conditions causing the TBD (e.g., why an answer is not known) so that the situation can be resolved, a description of what must be done to eliminate the TBD, who is responsible for its elimination, and by when it must be eliminated.

Consistency

Consistency refers to internal consistency. If an SRS does not agree with some higher-level document, such as a system requirements specification, then it is neither consistent nor correct. An SRS is internally consistent only if no subset of individual requirements described in it conflicts. The three types of likely conflict in an SRS are as follows:

1. Conflict among specified characteristics of real-world objects.

   - The format of an output report may be described in one requirement as tabular, but in another as textual.

   - One requirement may state that all lights should be green, while another may state that all lights should be blue.

2. Logical or temporal conflict between two specified actions.

   - One requirement may specify that the program add two inputs, but another may specify that the program should multiply them.

   - One requirement may state that "A" must always follow "B," while another may require that "A and B" occur simultaneously.

3. Two or more requirements may describe the same real-world object but use different terms for that object. For example, a program's request for a user input may be called a "prompt" in one requirement and a "cue" in another. Standard terminology and definitions use promotes consistency.

Ranked for Importance and/or Stability

An SRS is ranked for importance and/or stability if each requirement in it has an identifier that indicates either the importance or stability of that particular requirement. Typically, requirements that relate to a software product are not equally important. Some requirements may be essential, especially for life-saving applications, while others may be desirable. Each requirement in the SRS should be identified to make these differences clear and explicit.

Identifying the requirements in the following manner helps:

1. Have customers give more careful consideration to each requirement, which often clarifies any hidden assumptions they may have.
2. Have developers make correct design decisions and devote appropriate levels of effort to the different parts of the software product.

Degree of Stability

One method of identifying requirements uses the dimension of *stability*. Stability can be expressed in terms of the number of expected changes to any requirement based on experience or knowledge of forthcoming events that affect the organization, functions, and people supported by the software system.

Degree of Necessity

Another way to rank requirements is to distinguish classes of requirements as essential, conditional, and optional.

1. Essential—implies that the software will not be acceptable unless these requirements are provided in an agreed manner.
2. Conditional—implies that these requirements would enhance the software product, but would not make it unacceptable if they are absent.
3. Optional—implies a class of functions that may or may not be worthwhile. This gives the supplier the opportunity to propose something that exceeds the SRS.

Verifiability

An SRS is verifiable only if every requirement stated therein is verifiable. A requirement is verifiable if, and only if, there exists some finite cost-effective process with which a person or machine can check that the software product meets the requirement. In general, any ambiguous requirement is not verifiable. Non-verifiable requirements include statements such as "works well," "good human interface," and "shall usually happen." These requirements cannot be verified because it is impossible to define the terms "good," "well," or "usually." The statement that "the program shall never enter an infinite loop" is non-verifiable because the testing of this quality is theoretically impossible.

An example of a verifiable statement is:

Output of the program shall be produced within 20 seconds of event x 60 percent of the time, and shall be produced within 30 seconds of event x 100 percent of the time. This statement can be verified because it uses concrete terms and measurable quantities. If a method cannot be devised to determine whether the software meets a particular requirement, then that requirement should be removed or revised.

Modifiability

An SRS is modifiable only if its structure and style are such that any changes to the requirements can be made easily, completely, and consistently while retaining the structure and style.

Modifiability generally requires an SRS to:

1. Have a coherent and easy-to-use organization with a table of contents, an index, and explicit cross-referencing.
2. Not be redundant (i.e., the same requirement should not appear in more than one place in the SRS).
3. Express each requirement separately, rather than intermixed with other requirements.
4. Redundancy itself is not an error, but it can easily lead to errors. Redundancy can occasionally help to make an SRS more readable, but a problem can arise when the redundant document is updated. For instance, a requirement may be altered in only one of the places where it appears. The SRS then becomes inconsistent. Whenever redundancy is necessary, the SRS should include explicit cross-references to make it modifiable.

Traceability

An SRS is traceable if the origin of each of its requirements is clear and if it facilitates the referencing of each requirement in future development or enhancement documentation.

The following two types of traceability are recommended:

1. Backward traceability (i.e., to previous stages of development). This depends upon each requirement explicitly referencing its source in earlier documents.

2. Forward traceability (i.e., to all documents spawned by the SRS). This depends upon each requirement in the SRS having a unique name or reference number.

Forward traceability of the SRS is especially important when the software product enters the operation and maintenance phase. As code and design documents are modified, it is essential to be able to ascertain the complete set of requirements that may be affected by those modifications.

Some Final Hints

1. Limit redundancy as much as possible. There will be overlap between sections 2 and 3. Redundancy makes the document harder to maintain.

2. Label each section numerically. This will facilitate traceability and the creation of a traceability matrix.

3. A picture is worth a thousand words. If a requirement is difficult to explain with text, perhaps a diagram (state chart, flow chart, etc.) might make things clearer.

4. It is easier to draw a picture of a dialog box than it is to describe it in text. Use graphics to present user interfaces.

Summary

Getting the requirements correct is the most important part of a software development project. Once a software development team begins to collect the project requirements, it is critical that the project have a consistent format for maintaining and presenting them. This chapter described the construction of the Software Requirements Specification (SRS), used for the ongoing maintenance and presentation of the project requirements. The SRS is critical to the entire software development life cycle. Not only is it the derivative document for the software design specification, but it is also the base document for generating validation and acceptance tests. Validation is the determination of whether or not the project manager built the right product. Satisfying the requirements determines successful validation. The SRS is the mechanism for capturing those validation criteria—the system requirements.

During the SRS building process, the project manager must constantly be aware of the quality characteristics of the SRS: correctness, unambiguousness, completeness, and consistency, ranked for importance and/or stability, verifiability, modifiability, and traceability. The evaluation of these characteristics is a continuous process as the SRS is being built.

Problems for Review

1. The IEEE has a useful set of specifications convertible to templates for software requirements capture and maintenance. Do a Web search and find other templates available from other international standards organizations.
2. How does the WBS created for the project map to the SRS? What changes were made to the WBS based on what was learned from developing the SRS structure?
3. Does the structure of the SRS impact the life cycle processes chosen for the project?
4. How does an incomplete SRS impact the estimating of project schedule and cost?

Visit the Case Study

Because of all the delays in getting the PMP approved, you have only two days to produce the template for your SRS to begin collecting requirements. Since you have mistakenly represented the CMM Level 5 capabilities of the BSD as being able "to save any software schedule," you are not going to be let off the hook for the template deliverable. Indian Independence Day celebrations begin tomorrow and all businesses are closed for four days. How will you recover and get a template for the requirements collection to Ms. Patel and Mr. Lu? What will you use and how will you explain its use to them? Please remember that Ms. Patel has no fondness in her heart for IEEE standards.

Citations

[1]Boehm, Barry W. (1981). *Software Engineering Economics.* Englewood Cliffs, NJ: Prentice-Hall.

References

IEEE Std 830-1998, *IEEE Recommended Practice for Software Requirements Specifications.* IEEE Computer Society.

Pressman, Roger S. (2001). *Software Engineering: a Practitioner's Approach,* 5th ed. New York, NY: McGraw-Hill.

Web Pages for Further Information

sel.gsfc.nasa.gov/website/documents/contents.html. Annotated Bibliography of Software Engineering Laboratory (SEL) Literature, November 1998, National Aeronautics and Space Administration (NASA), Goddard Space Flight Center (GSFC), Greenbelt, MD.

www.atlsysguild.com/GuildSite/Robs/Template.html. This requirements specification template is used as a basis for specifications. The template provides sections for each of the requirements types appropriate to today's software systems. It is intended that the .pdf version be downloaded and adapted to a requirements-gathering process, as well as to requirements tools in use. The template can be used with Requisite, DOORS, Caliber RM, and other popular tools.

www.construx.com/. Construx Software's primary service offering is industry leading consulting, training, software engineering tools, and custom software solutions. Tools include checklists, templates, and estimation software.

www.imappl.org/crest/requirement.html. CREST is grounded in partnership and practicality. As members of the Department of Systems and Computer Science at Howard University, a dedicated group of researchers and students work on the empirical evaluation of software engineering tools, techniques, and resources.

Determining Project Risks

18

Software risk management is the formal process in which risk factors are systematically identified, assessed, and mitigated. The determination of the risk in a project, either due to external or internal causes, is a major part of project management. The PMBOK defines risk as "a subset of project management that includes the processes concerned with identifying, analyzing, and responding to project risk. It consists of risk identification, risk quantification, risk response development, and risk response control."[1] In order to aid the project manager in risk determination and management, this chapter will answer these questions:

- What is risk management all about?
- What are some risk management models?
- How are risks identified?
- How are risks analyzed and quantified?
- How are risk responses developed and risks controlled?
- What are the steps in developing a risk management plan?

Risk management is central to many other areas of project management. Figure 18–1 shows the PMBOK view of where risk management applies in other knowledge areas.

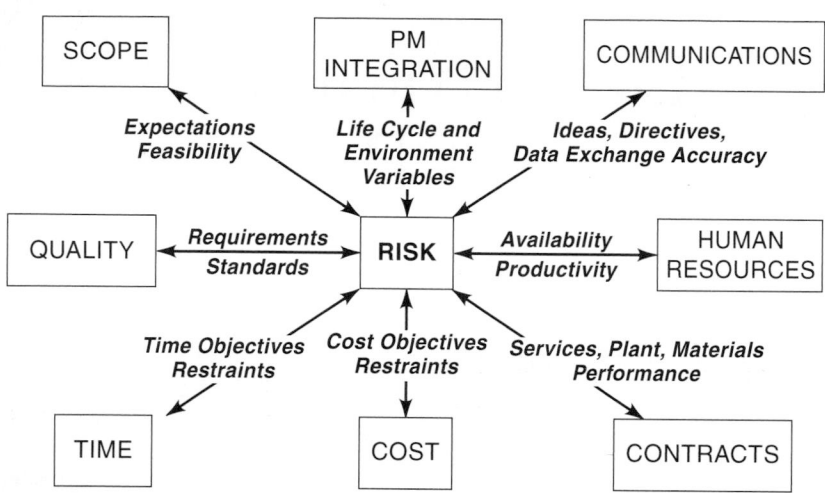

FIGURE 18–1
PMBOK Knowledge Areas Integration with Risk Management

Where We Are in the Product Development Life Cycle _____

Risk management begins with the exploration of the concepts leading up to acceptance of a software development project. A good project manager is a good risk manager. Risk management continues throughout the life cycle until the product is delivered. Risk analysis and contingency planning continue through the implementation stages of the product life cycle. Risks are analyzed and prioritized on no less than a weekly basis and the current "top-ten" risk list is presented at each weekly project status meeting. The only way risk mitigation occurs is through working the risks with the project team. Figure 18–2 shows how risk management fits within the software project management life cycle.

Chapter 18 Relation to the 34 Competencies _____

Although this chapter's focus is to define how a project manager determines risk, the key competency is number 16, managing risk. Handling risks is a key skill for any manager, but it is crucial for software project managers because so much can (and often does) go wrong—software projects are thought of as more complex because the product is intangible, and therefore difficult to test or assess.

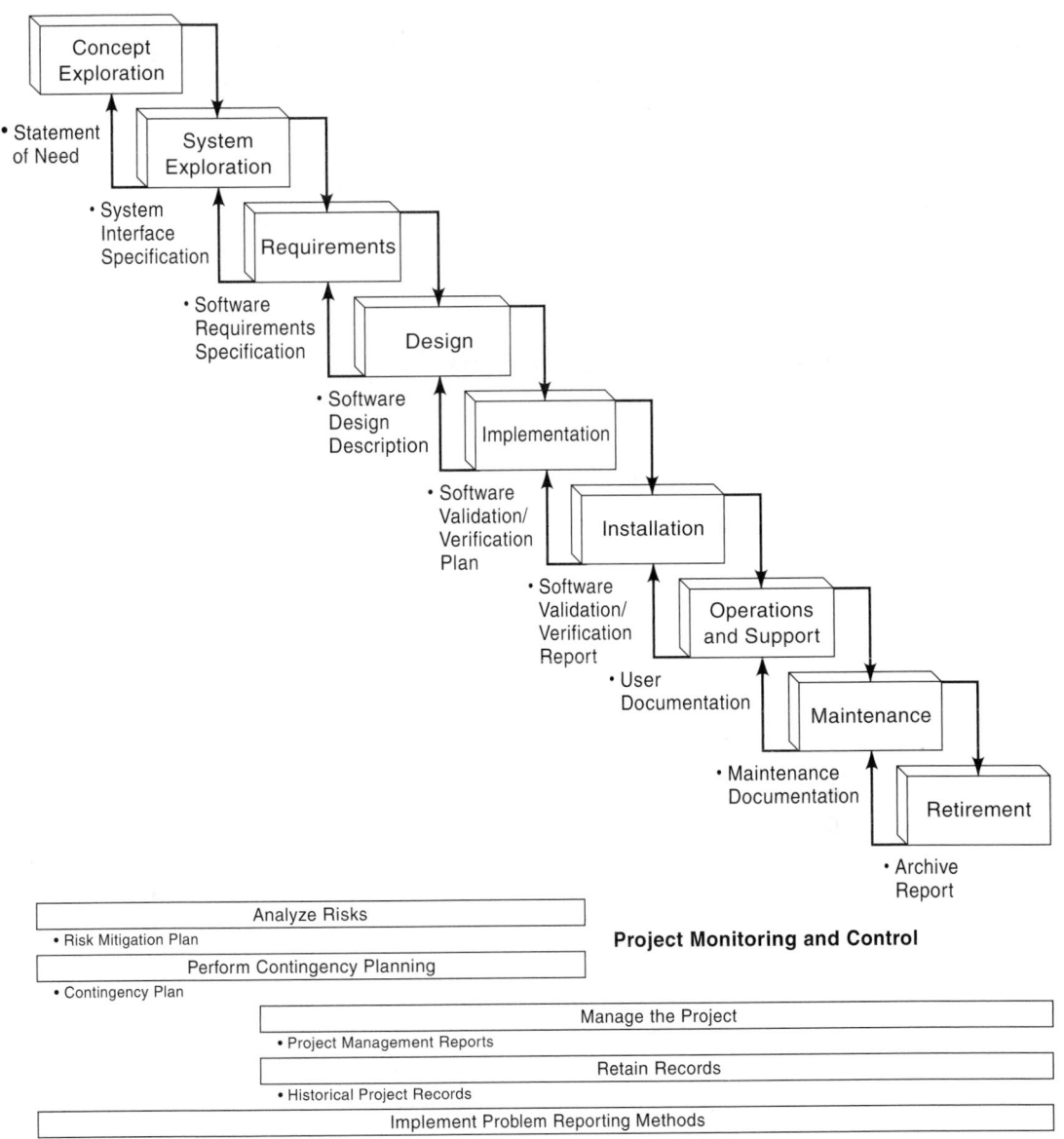

FIGURE 18–2
Where Risk Management Occurs in the Product Development Life Cycle

In order to effectively manage risk, a project manager must also be competent in competencies 7—performing the initial assessment, 18—scheduling, 25—holding effective meetings, and 31—presenting effectively. Determining risk is an integral part of performing the initial assessment. The determined risk profile will affect any scheduling estimated and performed. The main way a project manager determines risk is through interviews and meetings. Meetings and presentations are the most-used communication mechanism for the project manager. As with other project management tasks, determining risk is impacted by several of our 34 competencies.

Learning Objectives for Chapter 18 _____

Upon completion of this chapter, the reader should be able to:

- Describe sources of risk on any software development project;
- Develop a risk categorization table for any software development project;
- Calculate risk exposure for top software development risks.

What Is Risk Management? _____

Risk management is about understanding the internal and external project influences that can cause project failure. Once the project plan is built, a risk analysis should be performed. The result of the initial risk analysis is a risk plan that should be reviewed regularly and adjusted accordingly. *The main purpose of risk management is to identify and handle the uncommon causes of project variation.* This is captured in a formal process in which risk factors are systematically identified, assessed, and provided for.

Within our software domain, the SEI definition is more than adequate: "Risk is the possibility of suffering loss."[2] In a software development project, *loss* describes a negative impact to the project, which could be in the form of the diminished quality of the end product, increased costs, delayed completion, or outright project failure. Risk is uncertainty or lack of complete knowledge of the set of all possible future events. It can be classified as referring either to favorable or unfavorable future events.

Strictly speaking, risk involves only the possibility of suffering harm or loss. Risk can be categorized as:

- Internal, within the control of the project manager;
- External, outside the control of the project manager.

A software development project plan is only the best educated guess that can be made for planned events. Much can happen throughout the life cycle of the project that was not incorporated into the plan. This is *variation*. A good project manager minimizes variation through process management. Figure 18–3 shows the breadth of risk across the project, the classes of risk, and the project artifact where the risks are identified and their mitigation planned.

The project manager deals with risks resulting from three general classes:

1. **Known knowns.** These are risks known to the project team as both a category of risk and a reality of this project. An example of this is not having an executive sponsor for a large project places continued funding at risk. If there is no executive sponsor, this is a known type of risk and it is known to exist on this particular project. A known known risk could also be a category of risk that has been mitigated on this project. These risks are noted and described in the project management plan.

2. **Known unknowns.** These are risks that are known to the project team as a category of risk, but not known as a reality on this project. For example, not having access to the ultimate end-user is a risk in that requirements may not be correctly identified. In this project, if it is unknown whether there is access to the ultimate end-user, this is a known type of risk, but it is unknown whether the risk exists on this project. These risks are described in the risk management plan where they are prioritized and updated on a weekly basis.

3. **Unknown unknowns.** These are risks that are unknown to the project team as both a category of risk and as a reality of this project. Although project managers use broad categories of risk, an unknown unknown can arise in the technology area. An example of this is when a project must use a specific technology solution because it is dictated by the terms of the contract for the project. Even though this in itself is a risk, with no experience in the tool, the project manager cannot know all the potential risks inherent in the tool's use. These can only be addressed in the most general way by setting a budget for contingencies.

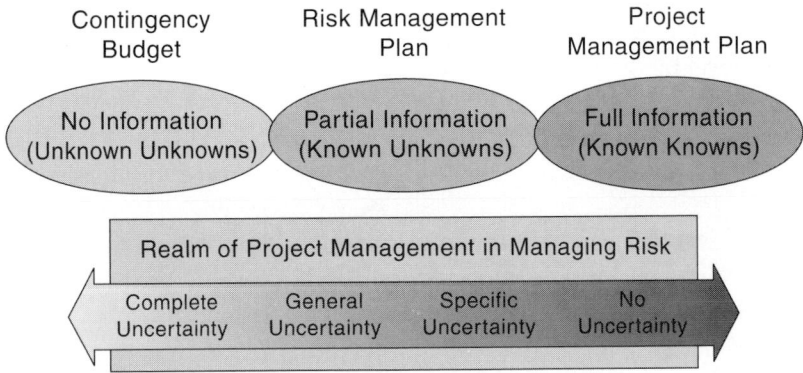

FIGURE 18–3
Risk Uncertainty Spectrum

Using both the project management and risk management plans, the project manager begins to identify contingency budgets. Figure 18–4 shows the relationship between risk and the dollar value of the project over the life cycle. Mapped across the IEEE 1074 project and product life cycle phases, the project investment gradually increases through the end of the requirements phase. Concept and system exploration, along with requirements, are the first three life cycle phases and are the phases where project planning has the greatest impact on risk mitigation. The inherent project risk is highest in these three phases and drops through project execution.

Design, implementation, and installation phases have the highest project execution risk reduction potential. In a world with experienced project managers and well-behaved projects, the risk continues to be reduced and the dollar value of the project investment smoothly increases. The final three phases, operations and support maintenance, and retirement have the lowest software development risk and the highest dollar investment. These three phases derive the highest risk impact from the product market.

The part of the figure labeled "Area of Highest Risk Mitigation Impact" covers requirements, design, implementation, and part of installation. This is the area of the project where the project manager has the most impact on risk mitigation. As long as risks are determined and mitigated, the amount of risk will smoothly decrease and project investment will continue on its predicted path. If risks are not identified and mitigated, the project cost will rapidly increase.

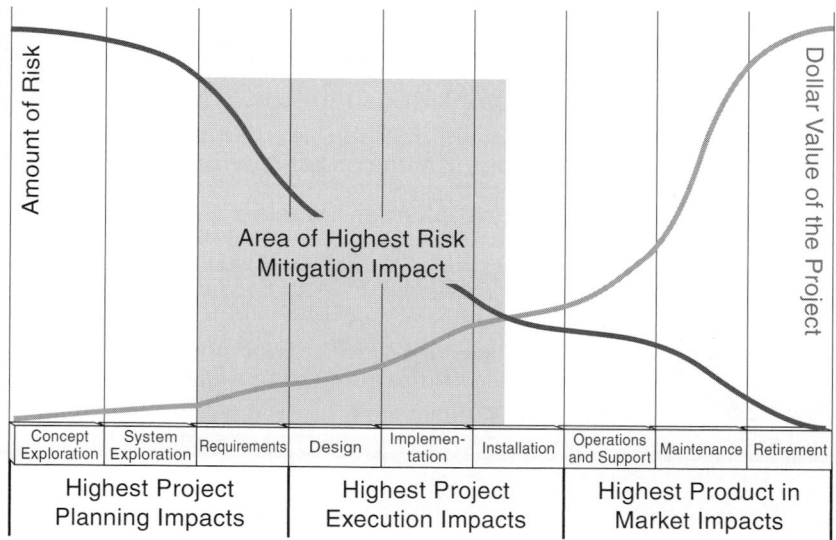

FIGURE 18–4
Project Risks During the Life Cycle

Project managers, as they are identifying the risks within the project life cycle and possible mitigation tactics, need to identify their level of risk tolerance. Varying by individual and organization, Figure 18–5 was derived from comparative responses to alternate-decision acts. A line going from the origin to the upper right corner at a 45 degree angle would represent neutral risk. This line represents the line of equilibrium points between the amount of dollars at stake and the probability of the risk event occurring. Risk-seeking individuals and teams follow the upper curved line, increasing the potential loss due to the risk event occurring. Risk avoiders are below the neutral line. Although risk may be avoided, there is an opportunity cost occurring below the neutral line. As more money is invested over time to avoid risk that will not occur, that money is lost for other investments. The opportunity to invest those monies is lost and the profit that could have been made is the opportunity cost. At a minimum, it is the interest lost by investing the monies in risk-free government bonds.

Business risks must be separated from the project idea of a "pure risk." *Business* or *inherent* risk is the chance for either profit or loss associated with any business endeavor. *Pure* or *insurable* risk only involves the chance for a loss. Examples of these losses are direct property loss, indirect consequential loss, personnel loss, and legal liability. *Direct property losses* include assets insurance, auto collision, fire, and theft. Examples of *indirect consequential loss* include contractor's protection for indirect losses suffered by a third party; removal of debris; and replacement of equipment. *Legal liability* is protection against legal actions for

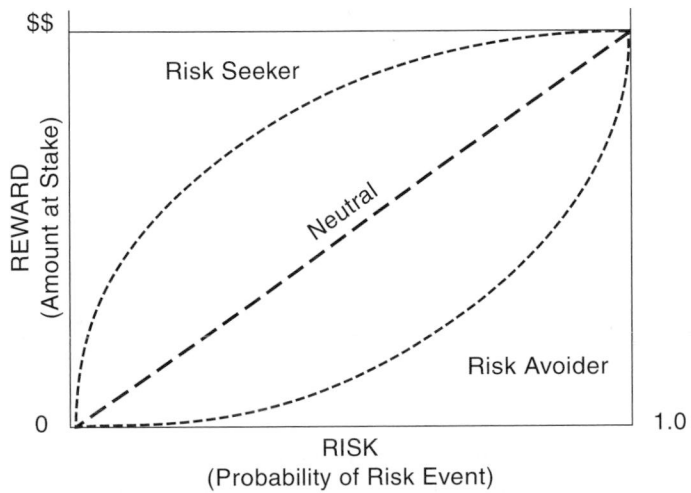

FIGURE 18–5
Variations in Risk Tolerance

design errors, public injury, and project performance failures. Finally, *personnel pure risk* examples are factors such as workman's compensation and employee replacement costs.

Part of what risk management is "all about" is *risk quantification*. Concepts of risk quantification are:

- Risk Event: the precise description of what might happen to the project
- Risk Probability: the degree to which the risk event is likely to occur
- Amount at Stake: the loss if the outcome is unsatisfactory
- Risk exposure: the overall liability potential of the risk; the formula for risk exposure is represented by Figure 18–11

Risk Management Models _____

Several models of risk management, readily usable by project managers, have been identified by the Project Management and Software Engineering Institutes and through the groundbreaking software engineering work of Barry Boehm.

Figure 18–6 shows project risk management made up of:

- Risk identification—developing the sources of risk, identifying potential risk events, and symptoms of risk
- Risk quantification—using qualitative and quantitative analysis, determining the value of the opportunities to pursue versus the threats to avoid, and the opportunities to ignore versus the threats to accept
- Response planning—developing the risk management and contingency plans, identifying reserves required in both dollars and person-hours, and determining how mitigation can occur through contractual means
- Monitoring and control—developing corrective action plans and monitoring their implementation as part of the overall implementation of the risk management plan

Barry Boehm's risk management process was first presented in the tutorial, "Software Risk Management," published by IEEE Computer Society Press in 1989.[3] Figure 18–7 shows the graphic representation of the model. Risk management consists of the two activities of risk assessment and control. Risk assessment is further divided into risk identification, analysis, and prioritization.

Risk identification is accomplished by using checklists, decision-driver analysis, and problem decomposition. For problem domains where the project manager and team have previous experience, checklists can be developed to ensure that all previously "known known" risks are identified for this project. For projects that are in a new domain or a dramatically different technology from the team's experience, decision-driver analysis and problem decomposition

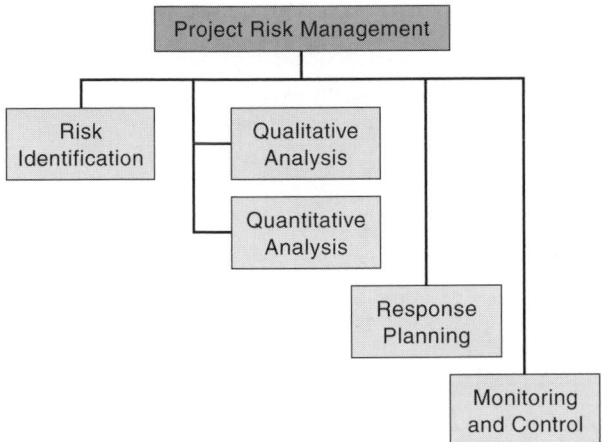

FIGURE 18–6
Project Management Institute Risk Model

are used. With these tools, the project team can take a deeper look into the problem domain for which the software will be developed and decide on the general classes of risk to be faced.

Analysis of the risks identified is done through modeling performance and cost, and analyzing network, decision, and quality factors. Performance and cost models allow the project manager to produce "what-if" scenarios based on performance and cost variables. The values of these variables are estimated based on the inherent knowledge of the problem domain. Advanced Monte Carlo statistical techniques can be added to gain further analysis area coverage. Network, decision, and quality factor analyses provide the team with enhanced views of the information developed during problem decomposition in risk identification.

After the risks have been identified and analyzed, their relative potential for occurrence and impact on the project must be determined. This risk prioritization allows the project team to focus on those critical few risks that will have the greatest potential for causing project failure. The calculation of risk exposure, described later in this chapter, should be done for each high priority risk. *Risk leverage* is a further quantification of risk exposure. First calculate the current risk exposure (RE) and then the RE after completion of mitigation efforts. Calculate the costs of the risk mitigation efforts. Subtracting the RE after mitigation efforts from the RE before and dividing the result by the mitigation cost, derives the measure of the relative cost benefit. Compound risk reduction is simply the decomposition of multi-factored risks into single-factor risks so they can be prioritized within the risk mix.

Risk control consists of risk management planning, risk resolution, and risk monitoring. As with risk assessment, these three components are supported by sets of tools and techniques.

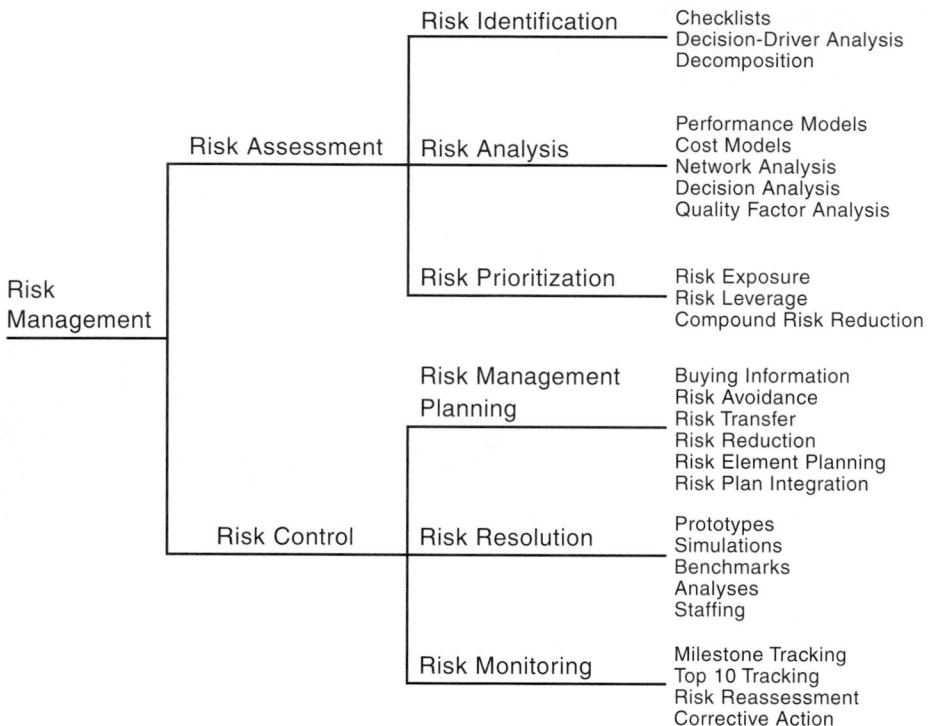

FIGURE 18–7
Boehm's Project Risk Model
Source: Boehm, Barry W. (1989). *Tutorial: Software Risk Management*. Los Alamitos, CA: IEEE Computer Society Press. p. 2.

Risk management planning uses the tools of buying information and risk avoidance, transfer, reduction, element planning, and plan integration. Buying information is another way of saying, "Hire the experts!" It can consist of contracting with subject matter expert consultants, subscribing to databases of topical information, and subscribing to research services.

Risk avoidance is simply finding a way to restructure the project and product to avoid that risk. *Risk transfer* usually involves buying insurance against the occurrence of the risk. It is the actual transfer of responsibility for that part of the project, with the inherent risk, to another organization.

Risk element planning and risk plan integration work together in the structuring of the project plan. By decomposing the risk into its constituent parts, each element of the risk can be separately addressed and resolved. This is the divide-and-conquer strategy to risk mitigation. Risk plan integration takes these separate elements and incorporates their solution into the overall project.

Risk resolution is accomplished through prototypes, simulations, benchmarks, analyses, and staffing. At this point in the risk model, the mapping to Boehm's spiral model of software development becomes very apparent. Prototypes, simulations, and benchmarks usually involve additional tools and capabilities. These tools have tremendous payback in risk reduction and mitigation, but there must be an investment in the tools and training to realize these benefits.

Milestone tracking, top-ten risk tracking, risk reassessment, and corrective action provide the tools for risk monitoring. These tools are all part of the steps that a project manager takes to implement complete risk management. They will be discussed in the section on how to develop a risk management plan.

Project Risk and the SEI

The Carnegie Mellon University's Software Engineering Institute developed a software risk model based on the Shewhart-Deming cycle. The model provides information and feedback, internal and external to the project, on the risk activities, current risks, and emerging risks. Figure 18–8 shows the model's processes:

- Identify—search for and locate risks before they become problems;
- Analyze—transform risk data into decision-making information, evaluate impact, probability, and timeframe; classify risks and prioritize risks;
- Plan—translate risk information into decisions and mitigating actions (both present and future) and implement those actions;
- Track—monitor risk indicators and mitigation actions;
- Control—correct for deviations from the risk mitigation plans.

Communication happens throughout all the functions with common process characteristics being:

- Identification—figure out what the risks are;
- Analysis and quantification—gathering information and prioritizing the risks;
- Response planning—deciding what to do about the risks;
- Tracking and communicating—monitoring the risks and the controlling actions while communicating status.

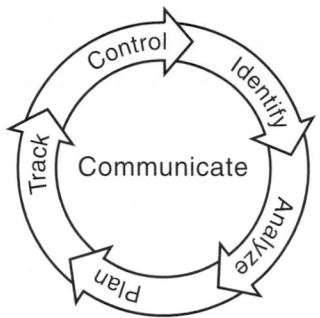

FIGURE 18–8
Software Engineering Institute's Risk Management Model

Identifying Risks

The process of risk identification is accomplished using the same tools as any analysis task. Start out by having the team and the customer brainstorm possible risks to develop "known unknown" lists. Use checklists of problems from prior projects retrieved from the project repository or knowledge-base. Examine all project assumptions in the project plan for the slightest hint of risk. Pay special attention to those that assume a rosy future where everything works. Interview stakeholders for risk identification and quantification.

Take the work breakdown structure and network diagrams from the project management plan and look for precedence bottlenecks. These will show up as tasks that require many other tasks to be completed before they can begin. These are the real choke points in the project planning network and have the highest risk reaction with schedule slips. Sometimes flowcharting a process helps spot risky areas. If the process is not familiar, draw the flow of execution necessary to see all the dependencies to successful completion. Examine the sources of key decisions in the project. Look for decision drivers.

Consider different types of risks:

- Technical
- Operational
- Political
- Legal
- Regulatory
- Market
- Social
- Internal
- External

After the first pass at identifying project risk is made, the project team needs to step back and take a broader look at all the possible risk sources. Figure 18–9 graphically shows that there are three basic risk areas—supportability, technical, and programmatic—that add risk to cost and schedule. Keep in mind that cost and schedule are inherently risky.

Table 18–1 shows possible risks for the three top risk sources. Technical risks are a major part of the software development business since software is the driver of high technology. Programmatic sources arise from the process of trying to manage the software development project. As the software product nears completion, the risks inherent in the software delivery, installation, and maintainability are very real and obvious.

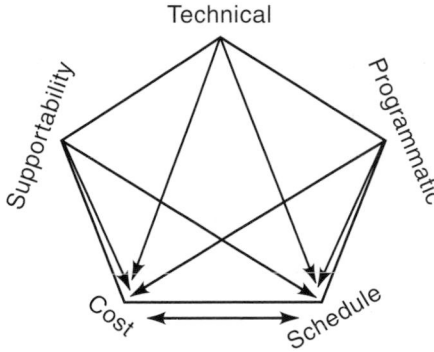

FIGURE 18–9
Risk Sources

TABLE 18–1
Examples of Risks Within Each Source

Technical Sources	Programmatic Sources	Supportability Sources
Physical properties	Material availability	Reliability and maintainability
Material properties	Personnel availability	Training and training support
Radiation properties	Personnel skills	Equipment
Testing and modeling	Safety	Human resource considerations
Integration and interface	Security	System safety

(Continues)

TABLE 18–1 (Continued)
Examples of Risks Within Each Source

Technical Sources	Programmatic Sources	Supportability Sources
Software design	Environmental impact	Technical data
Safety	Communication problems	Facility considerations
Requirements changes	Labor strikes	Interoperability considerations
Fault detection	Requirements changes	Transportability
Operating environment	Political advocacy	Computer resources support
Proven or unproven technology	Contractor stability	Packaging, handling, storage
System complexity	Funding profile	
Unique or special resources	Regulatory changes	

As is obvious from Figure 18–9, cost and schedule are not only impacted by the top three sources of risk, but also impact themselves. Cost risk can further be found in estimating errors and under allocation of overhead, general, and administrative costs. Schedule is made riskier due to increases in the project task degree of concurrency, number of critical path items, and estimating error.

Figure 18–10 shows a simple diagrammatic method for representing the classes and types of risks identified. Risks can easily be grouped into clusters based on scope, quality, schedule, and cost, as well as more coarse divisions of business, technology, and environment. By spending the time to map the clustering and categorize identified risks, the project team can pinpoint areas where risks may remain but have yet to be identified. This process helps discover the "unknown unknowns."

Analyzing and Quantifying Risks _____

There are some old and new risk analysis tools and techniques to use. The previously discussed tools for analyzing the identified risks are:

- Brainstorming
    1. Offer risk analysis ideas without judgment or evaluation

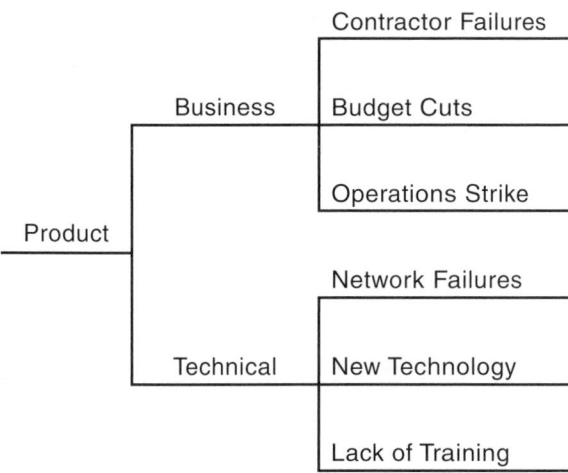

FIGURE 18–10
Risk Clustering

    2. Build on ideas offered

    3. Repeat until all ideas on risk analysis are exhausted

- Delphi method

    1. Select a panel of experts (isolated from each other and unknown to one another)

    2. Prepare and circulate a questionnaire about a risk

    3. Solicit risk handling approaches and opinions

    4. Share all responses and statistical feedback with entire group

    5. Repeat until there is convergence on a consensus approach

New analysis techniques that project managers and teams can use for risk analysis are:

- Sensitivity analysis

    1. Choose a few variables with big impact to the plan

    2. Define a likely range of variation

    3. Assess effect of changing them on project outcome

- Probability analysis

    1. Similar to sensitivity analysis

    2. Adds a probability distribution for each variable, usually skewed to eliminate optimism

- Monte Carlo simulation

    1. Similar to probability analysis

    2. Assign randomly chosen values for each variable

3. Run simulation a number of times to get a probability distribution for the outcome

4. Produces a range of probabilities for the outcome

- Utility theory
    1. Comprehends decision maker's attitude toward risk
    2. Viewed as theoretical
    3. Represented in Figure 18–5
- Decision tree analysis
    1. Graphical method
    2. Forces probability considerations for each outcome
    3. Usually applied to cost and time

The analysis techniques lead directly into the quantification of the risk—assigning a numeric value to an individual, cluster, or class of project risk. The project manager must keep in mind the one, most critical aspect of risk quantification. All of the numeric values are derivatives of best estimates, also known as guesses. Since the time at which these risks are predicted to occur has not yet arrived, there is no certain knowledge of what, if any, impact the risk will really have on the project. The job here is to quantify the relative risk of one compared to many and predict its impact on the project.

Quantification starts with computing the project's exposure to the identified risks through calculation of the risk exposure factor. Figure 18–11 represents the risk exposure formula that is applied to each high-priority risk on your project. The formula can be applied to all risks, but in practice only the highest priority risks need the added attention and quantification of risk exposure calculation.

Probability used in conjunction with decision trees provide a mechanism for quantifying risk of multiple alternatives. For example, if there is a $100,000 bonus for being early with an aggressive schedule (only 18 percent chance of attainment), but a $250,000 penalty for being late with any schedule (being conservative gives a 90 percent chance of being on time or early), should we pursue an aggressive or conservative schedule?

$RE =$

the *risk probability* (P) of an unsatisfactory outcome for the risk event

$\times$

the *amount at stake* (L = loss)

$RE = P \times L$

FIGURE 18–11
Risk Exposure Formula

The decision tree example in Figure 18–12 shows that by choosing an aggressive schedule the potential for risk is a loss of $180,000, while the conservative schedule shows a loss of only $25,000. In this situation the project manager needs to work on reducing the risk further on the conservative schedule.

Developing and Controlling Risks

The following are examples of key engineering development risks and treatments:

1. Unrealistic budget and schedule

   • Track all estimates and actuals; understand the team's performance level;

   • Understand how all team members' time is spent—there are always overhead activities in any organization;

   • Don't allow the client to talk you into an unrealistic estimate.

2. Personnel shortfalls

   • Plan for training in areas needed for the project;

   • Establish a learning pattern for team members throughout the project's life;

   • Cultivate teaming relationships with knowledgeable parties.

3. Developing wrong capabilities

   • Insist on meeting with the customer;

   • Prototype and demonstrate planned approaches.

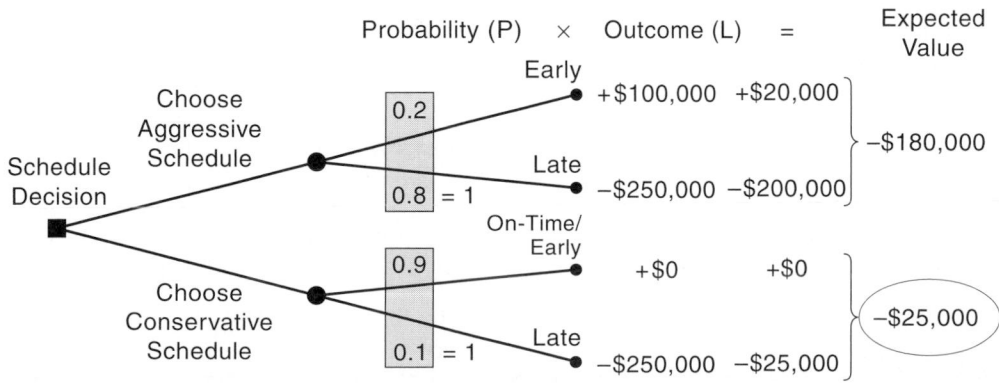

FIGURE 18–12
Decision Tree Example

The project risk management plan will contain all the identified risks and mitigation plans where appropriate. The risk response development can handle identified risks in three ways:

1. Accept—do nothing. Accept consequences in an active or passive fashion.
2. Transfer. Move the loss to a third party through a contract, get a warranty, or buy insurance.
3. Mitigate. Reduce the impact or probability by using contingency planning or a reserve, or eliminate the cause by using alternative software development strategies.

Prepare appropriate responses for each risk item by answering these questions:

1. Who is responsible for the action?
2. When is the action due?
3. What is the metric to watch?
4. What is the metric trigger value?

Table 18–2 shows a risk response table for the top ten project risks. Each risk has an identifier and a description. The metric value to watch is shown along with the trigger. For each risk, the value exceeds or is equal to the trigger. This type of table should be reviewed on no less than a weekly basis.

TABLE 18–2
Risk Response Table

ID	Risk Item	Trigger	Value	Risk Exp.	Resolution Approach	Who	Date
1	Too few engineering experts	10	12	630	Contract now for more	PM	1/15
2	Design schedule tight	25	28	450	Enforce Delphi estimates	PM	ongoing
3	Report function weak	20	25	180	Review with customer	Project Leader	2/15
4	Interface too different	10	20	150	Review with customer	Project Leader	2/15
5	New requirements	5	5	150	Review cost each time	PM	ongoing

(Continues)

TABLE 18–2 (Continued)
Risk Response Table

ID	Risk Item	Trigger	Value	Risk Exp.	Resolution Approach	Who	Date
6	"Goldplating" threat	15	15	120	Hold to requirements document	Project Leader	ongoing
7	Unknown quality	3	6	60	Get second supplier	PM	2/1
8	Wall unstable	10	6	60	Investigate braces	Engineer	2/15
9	Timing problems	5	6	30	Simulate and test	Engineer	ongoing
10	New technology risky	5	8	10	Review with chief scientist	Project Leader	by stage

Risk response management requires a regular review of all risks for changes. The top ten risks are reviewed on at least a weekly basis. They may be the same as the risks on the response table, as shown in Table 18–3. The difference in the two tables is that probability and loss are shown as the components of the risk exposure.

TABLE 18–3
Top Ten Software Project Risks

ID	Risk Item	Prob	Loss	Risk Exp.	Resolution Approach	Who	Date
1	Too few engineering experts	70	9	630	Contract now for more	PM	1/15
2	Design schedule tight	50	9	450	Enforce Delphi estimates	PM	ongoing
3	Report function weak	20	9	180	Review with customer	Project Leader	2/15
4	Interface too different	25	6	150	Review with customer	Project Leader	2/15

(Continues)

TABLE 18–3 (Continued)
Top Ten Software Project Risks

ID	Risk Item	Prob	Loss	Risk Exp.	Resolution Approach	Who	Date
5	New requirements	30	5	150	Review cost each time	PM	ongoing
6	"Goldplating" threat	30	4	120	Hold to requirements document	Project Leader	ongoing
7	Unknown quality	10	6	60	Get second supplier	PM	2/1
8	Wall unstable	10	6	60	Investigate braces	Engineer	2/15
9	Timing problems	5	6	30	Simulate and test	Engineer	ongoing
10	New technology risky	5	2	10	Review with chief scientist	Project Leader	by stage

Risk Categories

The project risk management plan models 12 categories of potential risk to any specific project:

1. **Mission and goals.** Any project accepted must fit within the organization's mission and goals. Projects accepted that do not fit within the organization create tensions that affect all projects. For example, assume an organization exists whose mission is to develop software for internal corporate manufacturing and whose goal it is to produce the most effective, custom software for the organization's factories. If the organization were to accept a project to build a general-purpose software package to be sold commercially, this would be extremely risky because it goes against their current mission and goals.

2. **Organization management.** Any project chosen must be buildable within the current or planned organization. A disorganized or non-existent organization cannot succeed in delivering a software project. An example of this risk is a sales organization that closes a development project with no input from the executing organization. The project is "thrown over the wall" to a development organization that has no team available and no process for building the type of system sold.

3. **Customer.** All projects must have a strong customer commitment to its success. A software development project requires extensive input from the customers and end-users. Without this input, the best development process will only produce a system that works well but may not meet the end-users' real needs. The risk here is that it assigns inexperienced people to the development team who do not have adequate problem domain experience to guide the technical trade-offs needed for the software developers.

4. **Budget/cost.** This category is the one that usually gets the most attention and is affected by all other categories. Project managers focus on the budget and cost because these are the most widely used measurements of a project's success. Understanding project size, having good historic information on similar projects, and completely understanding the external influences, such as technology, are the main ways to reduce this category's risk.

5. **Schedule.** The greatest risk here is that schedule dates are imposed externally from the development team. If the development team does not have any input into the completion and delivery dates for the project, there is very little chance that the schedule will be met. Software development teams must be a part of developing and modifying the project schedules.

6. **Project content.** All projects generate artifacts that are in addition to the final and contracted for deliverables. One of the major components is documentation of requirements, design, and the target system in which the software will reside. If this information does not exist, is in error, or is inconsistent the risk is very high that project knowledge will be lost and the schedule or product content will greatly suffer.

7. **Performance.** These risk factors are related not to specific, delivered system execution times, but to key software development criteria. Some of the major risk areas here are related to performance of the system during testing. The ability to do complete coverage testing of all modules and their interfaces is critical. Inadequate testing is a contributor to project failure.

8. **Project management.** This category relates to both the management processes for the project and to the project manager. Risk exists not only in the lack of, or inadequacy of, management processes, but in the experience level of the project manager. It is not true that a good project manager can manage any project. Project managers need domain experience and understanding of project management processes.

9. **Development process.** This category focuses on the processes that reduce overall risk and improve delivered-product quality. Development processes are not concerned with specific tools such as programming languages, tool builders, or code generators. They focus on configuration management processes, quality assurance practices, and analyses of alternatives.

10. **Development environment.** This category focuses on the physical environment of facilities, hardware platforms, and software development tools. Risk is present in not only the lack of adequate tools, but in inadequate facilities. Not having a colocated team, or not

having adequate meeting space, customer interviewing space, and workrooms greatly increases risk. Teams need face-to-face contact on a regular basis.

11. Staff. This category is one area where risks can be greatly reduced by having an experienced and proven high-productivity software development team. A highly productive team can be 10 to 25 times more productive than an average team. Not being sure of the abilities of the team or its experience with the problem domain necessitates a very conservative approach to the risk factors in this category.

12. Maintenance. This final category attempts to quantify software risk after the product is delivered. The project development team is often responsible for software maintenance for a period of time after delivery. If this is not the case, project risk increases from having inexperienced people try to fix bugs in the software. Tools used for development need to be available for maintenance. Vendor support after delivery is a risk issue if there has been no plan or budget for continued tool-maintenance support.

Steps in Developing a Risk Management Plan _____

Developing a risk management plan is simply a matter of following the following five steps. By beginning with the previously defined 12 risk categories, the analyst ranks and sorts the risks into a manageable set. The plan then is a direct result of the risk identification, categorization, and prioritization processes.

Step 1

Using these categories, construct a risk categorization table. A project team might use this table to review categories of risk for their project. It also provides the team with a set of factors to consider, and provides slots for them to decide which factors are relevant and what evidence they have. As the organization learns more about its performance it may decide on ways to compare ratings on a given project with its prior history. It may determine a total-rating count, or number of risks, or some combination of number and level of impact that predict project failure or success. This table is the starting point for identification of specific risks on each project.

Step 2

Rank the risk to the project for each category:

- Risk factors and areas—Under each category, this column lists category risk factors.
- Low risk evidence (L)—This column has characteristics of this factor when it can be considered low risk to the project.

- Medium risk evidence (M)—This column has characteristics of this factor when it provides a medium risk.
- High risk evidence (H)—This column has characteristics of this factor when it should be considered high risk.
- Rating—Select the level of risk (example: H, M, L or 3, 2, 1) applicable to this project.
- Comments—Provide information about project specifics that support the rating choice.

Note that in some cases, evidence in one category for high risk may be evidence for low risk in another. For example, support for organization goals or use of new technologies may be taken either way, depending on the situation.

Table 18–4 shows the risk factors and categories with their respective evidence of low, medium, and high risk. This table is a template used as a starting point for any software development project. Categories, factors, and evidence can easily be modified within this framework for any project.

Step 3

Sort the risk table in order of risk with high-risk items first. For the top ten risks and all risks rated "high" if more than ten, calculate the risk exposure. These are your key risks. Identify means to control each key risk, establish ownership of the action, and the date of completion. Integrate the key risks into the project plan and determine the impacts on schedule and cost.

Step 4

Establish a regular risk report format for weekly project status meetings. At a minimum, show the status of the top ten (Table 18–3), the ranking of each from the previous week, and the number of weeks on the list. Show the risk response report (Table 18–2) and the risk change report. Table 18–5 shows this report with the change in rankings and the resolution progress.

Step 5

The final step is to ensure that risk management is an ongoing process within your project management. Monitoring and control of the risk list must be done on a regular basis. The project manager and team must be aware of the identified risks and the processes for resolving them. New risks must be identified as soon as possible, prioritized, and added-on to the risk management plan. High-priority risks must be worked on with respect to the overall project plan.

TABLE 18–4
Risk Categorization Table

Risk Factors and Categories	L—Low Risk Evidence	M—Medium Risk Evidence	H—High Risk Evidence	Rating (HML)	Comments
Mission and Goals Factors					
Project fit	directly supports organization mission and/ or goals	indirectly impacts one or more goals	does not support or relate to organization mission or goals		
Work flow	little or no change to work flow	will change some aspect or have small effect on work flow	significantly changes the work flow or method of organization		
Organization Management Factors					
Organization stability	little or no change in management or structure expected	some management change or reorganiza- tion expected	management or organiza- tion structure is continually or rapidly changing		
Development team stability	team chosen, little or no change expected	team chosen but members may change	team not chosen, no decision as to members		
Policies and standards	development policies and standards are defined and carefully followed	development policies and standards are in place, but are weak or not carefully followed	no policies or standards, or they are ill- defined and unused		
Management support	strongly committed to success of project	some commitment, not total	little or no support		

(Continues)

TABLE 18-4 (Continued)
Risk Categorization Table

Risk Factors and Categories	L—Low Risk Evidence	M—Medium Risk Evidence	H—High Risk Evidence	Rating (HML)	Comments
Performance objectives	verifiable performance objectives, reasonable requirements	some performance objectives, measures may be questionable	no established performance requirements or requirements are not measurable		
Executive involvement	visible and strong support	occasional support, provides help on issues when asked	no visible support, no help on unresolved issues		
Customer Factors					
Customer involvement	end-users highly involved with project team, provide significant input	end-users play minor roles, moderate impact on system	minimal or no end-user involvement, little end-user input		
Customer experience	end-users highly experienced in similar projects, have specific ideas of how needs can be met	end-users have experience with similar projects and have needs in mind	end-users have no previous experience with similar projects, unsure of how needs can be met		
Customer acceptance	end-users accept concepts and details of system, process is in place for end-user approvals	end-users accept most of concepts and details of system, process in place for end-user approvals	end-users do not accept any concepts or design details of system		

(Continues)

TABLE 18–4 (Continued)
Risk Categorization Table

Risk Factors and Categories	L—Low Risk Evidence	M—Medium Risk Evidence	H—High Risk Evidence	Rating (HML)	Comments
Customer training needs	end-user training needs considered, training in progress or plan in place	end-user training needs considered, no training yet or training plan is in development	requirements not identified or not addressed		
Customer justification	end-user justification complete, accurate, sound	end-user justification provided, complete with some questions about applicability	no satisfactory justification for system		
Contract fit	contract with customer has good terms, communication with team is good	contract has some open issues which could interrupt team work efforts	contract has burdensome document requirements or requires extra work for compliance		
Benefits defined	benefits well-defined, with identified measures and baselines	some questions remain about benefits, or baseline is changing and measures doubtful	benefits not defined, no baseline established, unattainable or un-measurable		
Budget/Cost Factors					
Project size	small, non-complex, or easily decomposed	medium, moderate complexity, decomposable	large, highly complex, or not decomposable		

(Continues)

TABLE 18–4 (Continued)
Risk Categorization Table

Risk Factors and Categories	L—Low Risk Evidence	M—Medium Risk Evidence	H—High Risk Evidence	Rating (HML)	Comments
Hardware constraints	little or no hardware-imposed constraints or single platform	some hardware-imposed constraints, several platforms	significant hardware-imposed constraints, multiple platforms		
Technology	mature, existent, in-house experience	existent, some in-house experience	new technology or a new use or under development, little in-house experience		
Reusable components	components available and compatible with approach	components promised, delivery dates unsure	components projected, but not available when needed		
Supplied components	components available and directly usable	components work under most circum-stances	components known to fail in certain cases, likely to be late, or incompatible with parts of approach		
Budget size	sufficient budget allocated	questionable budget allocated	doubtful budget is sufficient		
Budget constraints	funds allocated without constraints	some questions about availability of funds	allocation in doubt or subject to change without notice		

(Continues)

TABLE 18–4 (Continued)
Risk Categorization Table

Risk Factors and Categories	L—Low Risk Evidence	M—Medium Risk Evidence	H—High Risk Evidence	Rating (HML)	Comments
Economic justification	completely justified and cost effectiveness proven	justification questionable or effectiveness not completely established	not justified or cost effectiveness demonstrated		
Cost controls	well-established, in place	system in place, weak in areas	system lacking or nonexistent		
Schedule Factors					
Delivery commitment	stable commitment dates	some uncertain commitments	unstable, fluctuating commitments		
Development schedule	team projects that schedule is acceptable and can be met	team finds one phase of the plan to have a schedule that is too aggressive	team projects that two or more phases of schedule are unlikely to be met		
Project Content					
Requirements stability	little or no change expected to approved set (baseline)	some change expected against approved set	rapidly changing or no agreed-upon baseline		
Requirements complete and clear	all completely specified and clearly written	some requirements incomplete or unclear	some requirements only in the head of the customer		
System testability	system requirements easy to test, plans underway	parts of system hard to test, or minimal planning being done	most of system hard to test, or no test plans being made		

(Continues)

TABLE 18–4 (Continued)
Risk Categorization Table

Risk Factors and Categories	L—Low Risk Evidence	M—Medium Risk Evidence	H—High Risk Evidence	Rating (HML)	Comments
Design difficulty	well-defined interfaces; design well-understood	unclear how to design, or aspects of design yet to be decided	interfaces not well-defined or controlled, subject to change		
Implementation difficulty	algorithms and design are reasonable for this team to implement	algorithms and/or design have elements somewhat difficult for this team to implement	algorithms and/or design have components this team will find very difficult to implement		
System dependencies	clearly defined dependencies of the software effort and other parts of system	some elements of the system are well-understood and planned, others are not yet comprehended	no clear plan or schedule for how the whole system will come together		
Documents stability	documents will be available on time and will contain few errors	some documents may be late and contain minor errors	little chance of getting documents on time, many corrections and changes expected		

Performance Factors

Risk Factors and Categories	L—Low Risk Evidence	M—Medium Risk Evidence	H—High Risk Evidence	Rating (HML)	Comments
Test capability	modular design allows for easy coverage test planning and execution	modular design aids developing test harnesses for unit test	no modular design or ability to easily establish test coverage planning		

(Continues)

TABLE 18–4 (Continued)
Risk Categorization Table

Risk Factors and Categories	L—Low Risk Evidence	M—Medium Risk Evidence	H—High Risk Evidence	Rating (HML)	Comments
Expected test effort	good estimate available, readily fits system acceptance process	rough estimate of test time, may be a bottleneck in the process	poor or no estimate of test times, definite chance of bottleneck		
Functionality	highly functional, meets all customer needs	good functionality, meets most customer needs	little functionality, many customer needs not met		
External hardware or software interfaces	little or no integration or interfaces needed	some integration or interfaces needed	extensive interfaces required		

Project Management Factors

Risk Factors and Categories	L—Low Risk Evidence	M—Medium Risk Evidence	H—High Risk Evidence	Rating (HML)	Comments
Approach	product and process planning and monitoring in place	planning and monitoring need enhancement	weak or nonexistent planning and monitoring		
Communication	clearly communicates goals and status between the team and rest of organization	communicates some of the information some of the time	rarely communicates clearly to the team or to others who need to be informed of team status		
Project manager experience	project manager very experienced with similar projects	project manager has moderate experience or has experience with different types of projects	project manager has no experience with this type of project or is new to project management		

(Continues)

TABLE 18–4 (Continued)
Risk Categorization Table

Risk Factors and Categories	L—Low Risk Evidence	M—Medium Risk Evidence	H—High Risk Evidence	Rating (HML)	Comments
Project manager attitude	strongly committed to success	willing to do what it takes	cares very little about project		
Project manager authority/ support	complete support of team and of management	support of most of team, with some reservations	no visible support, manager in name only		

Development Process Factors

Risk Factors and Categories	L—Low Risk Evidence	M—Medium Risk Evidence	H—High Risk Evidence	Rating (HML)	Comments
Alternatives analysis	analysis of alternatives complete, all considered, assumptions verifiable	analysis of alternatives complete, some assumptions questionable or alternatives not fully considered	analysis not completed, not all alternatives considered, or assumptions faulty		
Quality assurance approach	QA system established, followed, effective	procedures established, but not well followed or effective	no QA process or established procedures		
Commitment process	changes to commitments in scope, content, schedule are reviewed and approved by all involved	changes to commitments are communicated to all involved	changes to commitments are made without review or involvement of the team		
Development documentation	correct and available	some deficiencies, available	nonexistent		

(Continues)

TABLE 18–4 (Continued)
Risk Categorization Table

Risk Factors and Categories	L—Low Risk Evidence	M—Medium Risk Evidence	H—High Risk Evidence	Rating (HML)	Comments
Use of defined engineering process	development process in place, established, effective, followed by team	process established, but not followed or is ineffective	no formal process used		
Early identification of defects	peer reviews are incorporated throughout	peer reviews are used sporadically	team expects to find all defects with testing		
Change control for work products	formal change control process in place, followed, effective	change control process in place, not followed, or is ineffective	no change control process used		
Defect tracking	defect tracking defined, consistent, effective	defect tracking process defined, but inconsistently used	no process in place to track defects		
Development Environment Factors					
Physical facilities	little or no modification needed	some modifications needed, some existent	major modifications needed, or facilities nonexistent		
Hardware platform	stable, no changes expected, capacity is sufficient	some changes under evolution, but controlled	platform under development along with software		
Tools availability	in place, documented, validated	available, validated, some development needed (or minimal documentation)	invalidated, proprietary, or major development needed, no documentation		

(Continues)

TABLE 18–4 (Continued)
Risk Categorization Table

Risk Factors and Categories	L—Low Risk Evidence	M—Medium Risk Evidence	H—High Risk Evidence	Rating (HML)	Comments
Configuration management	fully controlled	some controls in place	no controls in place		
Security	all areas following security guidelines, data backed up, disaster recovery system in place, procedures followed	some security measures in place, backups done, disaster recovery considered, but procedures lacking or not followed	no security measures in place, backup lacking, disaster recovery not considered		
Vendor support	complete support at reasonable price and in needed time frame	adequate support at contracted price, reasonable response time	little or no support, high cost, and/or poor response time		
Staff Factors					
Staff availability	in place, little turnover expected, few interrupts for fire fighting	available, some turnover expected, some fire fighting	high turnover, not available, team spends most of time fighting fires		
Mix of staff skills	good mix of disciplines	some disciplines inadequately represented	some disciplines not represented at all		
Product knowledge	very experienced at developing this type of product	some experience in developing this type of product	no experience in developing this type of product		
Software development experience	extensive experience with this type of project	some experience with similar projects	little or no experience with similar projects		

(Continues)

TABLE 18–4 (Continued)
Risk Categorization Table

Risk Factors and Categories	L—Low Risk Evidence	M—Medium Risk Evidence	H—High Risk Evidence	Rating (HML)	Comments
Training of team	training plan in place, training ongoing	training for some areas not available or training planned for future	no training plan or training not readily available		
Team spirit and attitude	strongly committed to success of project, cooperative	willing to do what it takes to get the job done	little or no commitment to the project, not a cohesive team		
Team productivity	all milestones met, deliverables on time, productivity high	milestones met, some delays in deliverables, productivity acceptable	productivity low, milestones not met, delays in deliverables		
Maintenance Factors					
Complexity	structurally maintainable (low complexity measured or projected)	certain aspects difficult to maintain (medium complexity)	extremely difficult to maintain (high complexity)		
Change implementation	team in place can be responsive to customer needs	team experiences delays, but acceptable to customer	team is unable to respond to customer needs		
Support personnel	in place, experienced, sufficient in number	missing some areas of expertise	significant discipline or expertise missing		
Vendor support	complete support at reasonable price and in needed time frame	adequate support at contracted price, reasonable response time	little or no support, high cost, and/or poor response time		

TABLE 18–5
Weekly Risk Change Report

Risk Item	Rank This Week	Last Rank	Number of Weeks on List	Resolution Approach
Too few engineering experts	1	1	2	Contract under discussion
Design schedule tight	2	2	2	Enforcing Delphi estimates
Report function weak	3	5	3	On agenda with customer
Interface too different	4	4	3	On agenda with customer
New requirements	5	3	4	Review each new one for cost
"Goldplating" threat	6	6	4	Reviewing each phase
Unknown quality	7	8	3	No second supplier found yet
Wall unstable	8	new		Contract for braces in process
Timing problems	9	new		Plan to simulate in March
New technology risky	10	10	4	Reviewed requirements

Summary

Software risk management is the formal process in which risk factors are systematically identified, assessed, and mitigated. The determination of the risk in a project either due to external or internal causes is a major part of project management. Risk management consists of risk identification, risk quantification, risk response development, and risk response control. To aid the project manager in risk determination and management, this chapter answered these questions:

- What is risk management?
- What are some risk management models?

- How are risks identified?
- How are risks analyzed and quantified?
- How are risk responses developed and risks controlled?
- What are the steps in developing a risk management plan?

Risk management is central to all areas of project management.

Problems for Review _____

1. The elevator control project manager has used a Delphi technique to get a response to the question: "Should formal methods be used to prove that the safety features of the embedded control system are adequate?" The results of the fifth round are shown in Figure 18–13.

   a. What do these results mean to the project manager?

   b. How many more rounds are needed on the Delphi?

   c. Could the question be re-worded for better effect?

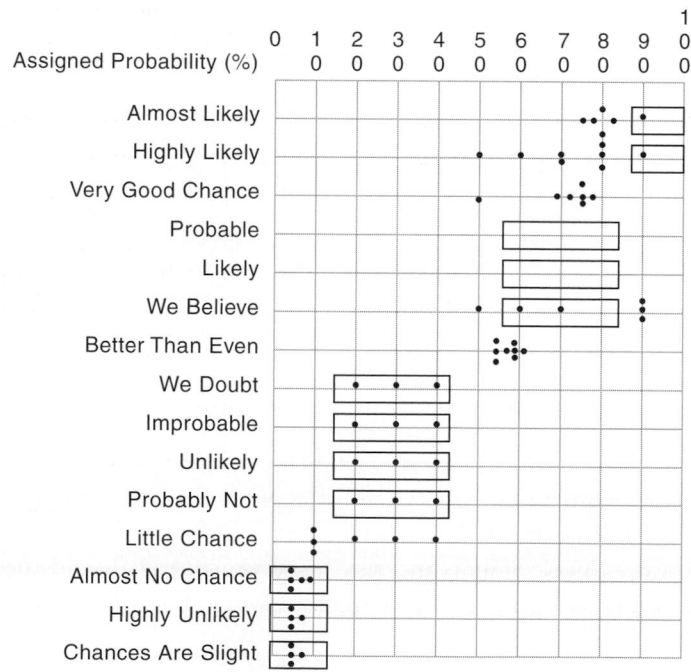

FIGURE 18–13
Fifth Round Delphi Problem Diagram

2. Should the elevator control project spend $500,000 with an independent software auditor to find critical errors if there is an $18 million penalty for letting a critical error slip through to customers? The probability of finding a critical error without an audit is 0.3, of not finding a critical error is 0.1, and of finding no critical error is 0.6. With an audit, the probability of finding a critical error increases to 0.36, while not finding a critical error decreases to 0.04. Build a decision tree for this risk quantification.

3. How would you map the recognition of technical, programmatic, and supportability risk sources to when they could be expected to be identified within the IEEE 1074 life cycle model? Where in the spiral model?

4. How can Delphi and Monte Carlo techniques be used in the risk identification of the elevator problem in Appendix G?

Visit the Case Study

Mr. Adams went to a conference sponsored by your corporation's government products group. They reported on a tool provided by the Software Project Managers Network (*www.spmn.com*) called Risk Radar™. This freeware tool is a risk management database for assisting project managers in identifying, prioritizing, and communicating project risks in a flexible and easy-to-use form. Standard database functions to add and delete risks, as well as specialized functions for prioritizing and retiring project risks, are provided. Each risk has a user-defined risk management plan and a log of historical events.

Mr. Adams has convinced Dr. Harita that this is a mature process tool that will complement the estimating and sizing tools currently used at BSD. Dr. Harita has committed his support to trying it on a small project under his management. Guess what? It is ARRS!

Dr. Harita cannot get access to the Web site through the BSD firewall and has asked you to download it and make a first pass at developing a set of standard short- and long-form reports to share ARRS risk information with the development team. He would like to cover this at the next weekly teleconference. When you go back to the responsibilities matrix you see that you are responsible for the ARRS risk analysis.

Citations

[1]PMI Standards Committee, William R. Duncan, Director of Standards (1996). *A Guide to the Project Management Body of Knowledge*. Newtown Square, PA: Project Management Institute. p. 8.

[2]*www.sei.cmu.edu/programs/sepm/risk/*.

[3]Boehm, Barry W. (1989). *Tutorial: Software Risk Management*. Los Alamitos, CA: IEEE Computer Society Press.

Web Pages for Further Information _____

www.baz.com/kjordan/swse625/intro.html. K. Jordan (1997). Introduction to Software Risk & Risk Management.

www.eas.asu.edu/~riskmgmt/intro.html. Raymond Miller (1997). Quality and Risk Management.

www.sei.cmu.edu/publications/documents/97.reports/97hb002/97hb002abstract.html. Brian Gallagher, Christopher Alberts, and Richard Barbour. Software Acquisition Risk Management Key Process Area (KPA)—A Guidebook Version 1.0.

www.sei.cmu.edu/publications/documents/97.reports/97hb002/97hb002abstract.html. James S. Collofello. Software Risk Management.

Risk Management Tools _____

Risk Radar MS Access-based risk tracking. *www.spmn.com/rsktrkr.html*.

Risk Tool Summary. *www.incose.org/tools/tooltax/riskmgt_tools.html*.

Risk+ Add-on for MS Project. *www.cs-solutions.com/riskplus.htm*.

@Risk Add-on for Excel or MS Project. *www.palisade.com/html/risk.html*.

References _____

Boehm, Barry W. (1989). *Tutorial: Software Risk Management*. Los Alamitos, CA: IEEE Computer Society Press.

Karolak, Dale (1996). *Software Engineering Risk Management*. Los Alamitos, CA: IEEE Computer Society Press.

Pritchard, Carl (1997). *Risk Management*. Arlington, VA: ESI International.

Introduction to Software Engineering

Software engineering is *not* computer science nor is it merely rendering an idea into an abstract computer programming language. First coined in 1968, software development is the youngest recognized branch of engineering: "The phrase 'software engineering' was deliberately chosen for being provocative in implying the need for software manufacture to be based on the types of theoretical foundations and practical disciplines that are traditional in the established branches of engineering."[1] At the same conference, Fritz Bauer defined software engineering as: "the establishment and use of sound engineering principles in order to obtain economically software that is reliable and works efficiently on real machines."[2] Throughout this chapter there will be other definitions of software engineering for the practitioner software project manager to contemplate.

The Project Management Institute's Project Management Body of Knowledge (PMBOK) defines five project management process groups: initiating processes, planning processes, executing processes, controlling processes, and closing processes. This chapter introduces the software engineering executing processes of the software development project. The executing processes are where the estimated and scheduled resources are applied to carry out the project plan. Figure 19–1 shows the relative amount of effort expended in each process.

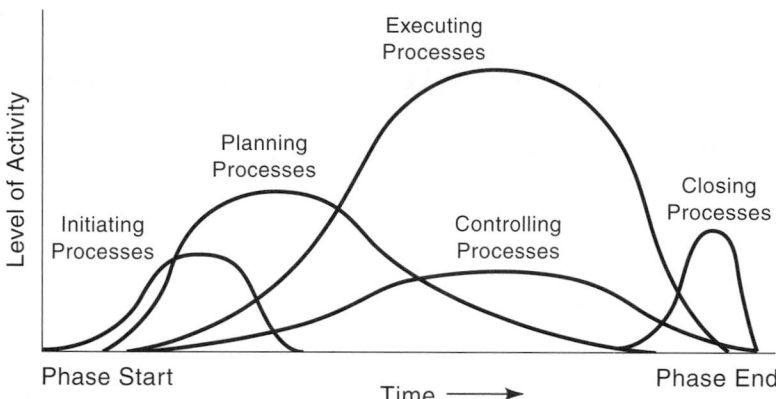

FIGURE 19–1
Project Management Processes

Executing processes will take the largest amount of the project budget because of the level and amount of activity required to engineer quality software.

This chapter does not offer complete coverage of all areas of software engineering. Texts such as Roger Pressman's *Software Engineering, A Practitioner's Approach*,[3] offer greater depth in the engineering areas and are a complement to this book. Software project managers must understand the processes for building high-quality software. This chapter exposes them to the existence of these concepts.

Where We Are in the Product Development Life Cycle

The planning and initiating phases have been completed, as well as the first pass at the software requirements specification. A project manager may have already had a prototype developed for proof-of-concept or feasibilities studies. This is the point at which all software engineering practices must be considered. From completion of all the requirements models to be included in the SRS through to the final delivery and installation, software engineering methods, techniques, and tools support the project executing processes. This period is shown in Figure 19–2.

The IEEE Computer Society and ACM Software Engineering Coordinating Committee have joined together to produce the Software Engineering Body of Knowledge (SWEBOK).[4] The support processes of the project life cycle are covered in the SWEBOK. This will be used to frame the life cycle in Figure 19–1 with the discipline of software engineering.

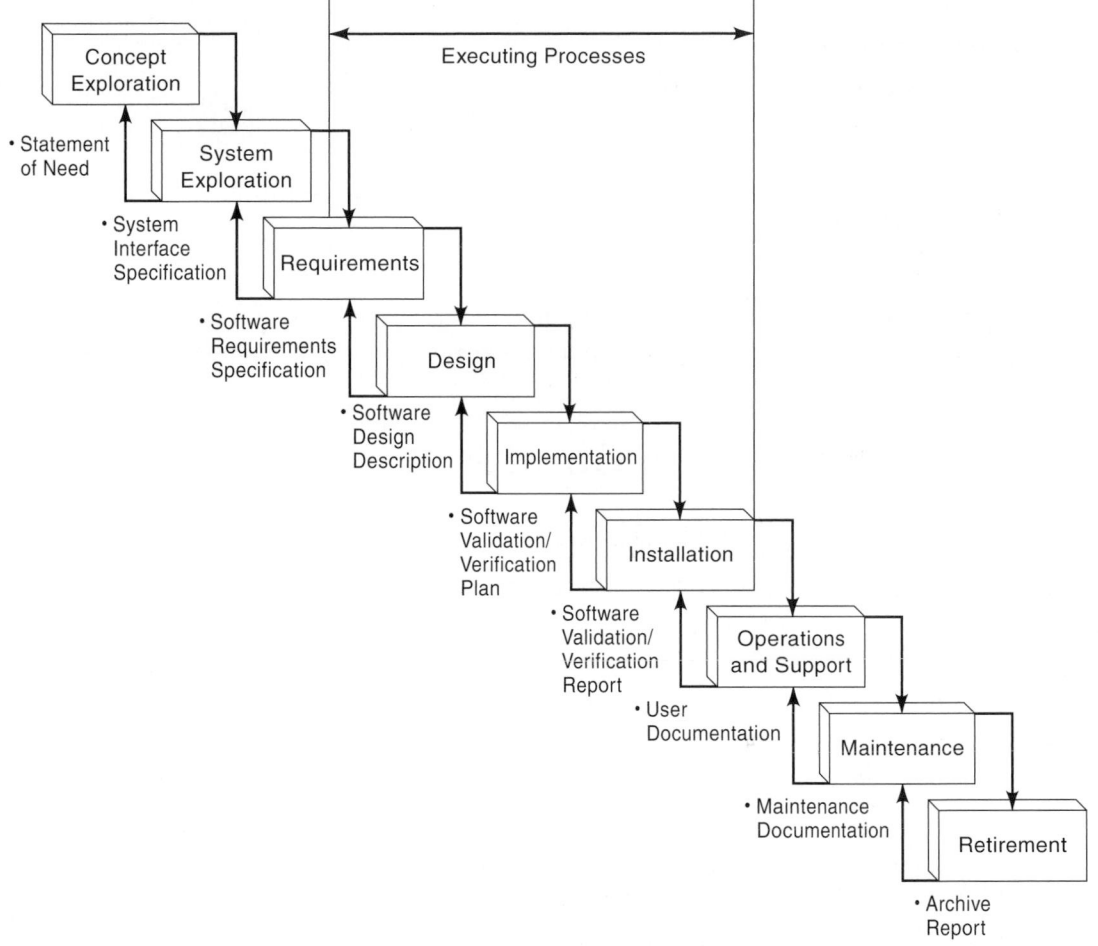

FIGURE 19–2
Where the Executing Processes Occur in the Product Development Life Cycle

Chapter 19 Relation to the 34 Competencies _____

Software engineering relates most closely to several product management skills and to one project management skill. This is the point in the overall project management process where the project manager moves from planning and initiating the project to executing. The competencies that now apply fit most clearly with the active processes of developing software.

Product Development Techniques

1. **Assessing processes**
4. **Evaluating alternative processes**
8. **Selecting methods and tools**
9. **Tailoring processes**

Project Management Skills

17. **Monitoring development**

A project manager's ability to successfully guide the use of software engineering methods, techniques, and tools contributes greatly to the project reaching its development goals.

Learning Objectives for Chapter 19 _____

By the end of this chapter, the reader should be able to:

- Discuss where software engineering occurs in the software development project life cycle;
- Explain which of the 34 product, process, and people competencies support software engineering;
- Describe how the Software Engineering Institute's capability maturity model employs software engineering in quality processes;
- Define *software engineering*.

Software Engineering Defined in the SEI CMM

The CMM is a model of software process developed by a broad base of the software community. As a model it is, necessarily, a simplification of the actual engineering process. Being normative, the CMM identifies what should be expected of an organization at a given maturity level. Organizations that use it as a process measurement and improvement mechanism must apply a reasonable interpretation of the knowledge process areas in light of business objectives. With use as a process evaluation and measurement tool, the CMM becomes a road map to successful process improvement. Overall, the CMM is a grouping of sound engineering and management concepts based on proven principles of quality (e.g., TQM, Deming, Crosby). Software, embodied knowledge to be protected and valued, deserves such quality processes (Box 19–1).

The CMM is *not* prescriptive. It does not specify how an organization should achieve the process attributes. Neither is it a guarantee of instant success. Improvement takes time and sustained effort within the entire organization. It especially requires buy-in from executive management and a committed budget. The CMM is not a "one size fits all" methodology. The first step in its use is to customize the application of the maturity levels to a specific

Box 19–1

Software Is Embodied Knowledge

Source: Howard, Baetjer, Jr. (1997). *Software As Capital: An Economic Perspective on Software Engineering.*
Los Alamitos, CA: IEEE Computer Society.

> Because software, like all capital, is embodied knowledge, and because that knowledge is initially dispersed, tacit, latent, and incomplete in large measure, software is a social learning process. The process is a dialogue in which the knowledge that must become the software is brought together and embodied in the software. The process provides interaction between users and designers, between users and evolving tools, and between designers and evolving tools [technology]. It is an iterative process in which the evolving tool itself serves as the medium for communication, with each new round of the dialogue eliciting more useful knowledge from the people involved.

organization and project mix. SEI has developed other focused maturity models for organizational personal, software acquisition, systems engineering, integrated product development, and a personal software process.

One of the keys to using the CMM is to define what a mature process means. A mature software process has these attributes:

- Defined—There is an established "way to do business."
- Documented—It is written down so it can be known and used.
- Trained—Training is based on the documentation.
- Practiced—It is used, not "shelf-ware."
- Supported—It is available, revised, and improved.
- Controlled—Changes are approved by "stakeholders."
- Verified—The process is executed correctly.
- Validated—The intended process is executed.
- Measured—Performance is measured as a basis for control and improvement of the process.
- Able to be improved—It is flexible and able to be changed.

The benefits of a mature process become obvious with analysis. Schedules and budgets are based on historical performance and are realistic. Expected results for costs, schedule, and functionality are usually achieved. All participants understand the value of following a disciplined process consistently. Infrastructure exists to support the process (software engineering and its business aspects) and managers monitor the quality of software products and the process that produces them. The focus is on the process not the people.

Software product engineering is a key process area for Level 3, "Defined."

> The purpose of Software Product Engineering is to consistently perform a well-defined engineering process that integrates all the software engineering activities to produce correct, consistent software products effectively and efficiently.

Software Project Engineering involves performing the engineering tasks to build and maintain the software using the project's defined software process and appropriate methods and tools. The software engineering tasks include analyzing the system requirements allocated to software, developing the software requirements, developing the software architecture, designing the software, implementing the software in the code, integrating the software components, and testing the software to verify that it satisfies the specified requirements.

> Paulk, Weber, Curtis, and Chrissis, *The Capability Maturity Model:*
> *Guidelines for Improving the Software Process.*[5]

Goals

Goal 1. The software engineering tasks are defined, integrated, and consistently performed to produce the software.

Goal 2. Software work products are kept consistent with each other.

Activities

Activity 1. Appropriate software engineering methods and tools are integrated into the project's defined software process.

Activity 2. The software requirements are developed, maintained, documented, and verified by systematically analyzing the allocated requirements according to the project's defined software process.

Activity 3. The software design is developed, maintained, documented, and verified according to the project's defined software process to accommodate the software requirements and to form the framework for coding.

Activity 4. The software code is developed, maintained, documented, and verified according to the project's defined software process to implement the software requirements and software design.

Activity 5. Software testing is performed according to the project's defined software process.

Activity 6. Integration testing of the software is planned and performed according to the project's defined software process.

Activity 7. System and acceptance testing of the software are planned and performed to demonstrate that the software satisfies its requirements.

Activity 8. The documentation that will be used to operate and maintain the software is developed and maintained according to the project's defined software process.

Activity 9. Data on defects identified in peer reviews and testing are collected and analyzed according to the project's defined software process.

Activity 10. Consistency is maintained across software work products, including the software plans, process descriptions, allocated requirements, software requirements, software
design, code, test plans, and test procedures.

Software engineering is "the application of a systematic, disciplined, quantifiable approach
to the development, operation, and maintenance of software; that is, the application of engineering to software."[6] Figure 19–3 is not a life cycle that can be followed and still engineer a
project's software, but traditionally this is the model that has been followed. Developers take
the incomplete requirements from a shortened requirements phase and write code until they
have a program they think the user wants. It is usually a closed-loop system with the only
feedback being self-referential within the developer group.

Software, Engineering, and Software Engineering ____

Defining software requires some historical context. The term software engineering (see Box 19–2,
Box 19–3, and Box 19–4) was not coined until 1968, 18 years after the mid-point of the twentieth
century, and one year before a human walked on the moon.

What was the first software developed? If we use the IEEE Standard 610 definition of software as all of those objects, "that control the functioning of the hardware and direct its operation,"[7] then the first *software, per se*, was created in 1804. Joseph Marie Jacquard's inspiration

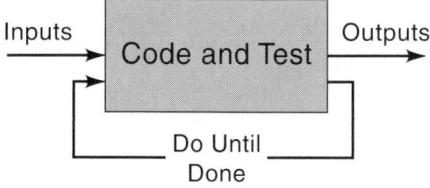

FIGURE 19–3
Do Not Use This Life Cycle

BOX 19–2
Definition of Software Engineering
Source: Boehm, Barry W. (1976). "Software Engineering." *IEEE Transactions on Computers.* Los Alamitos, CA:
IEEE Computer Society.

> Software Engineering is the *practical* application of scientific knowledge in the design and
> construction of computer programs and the associated *documentation* required to develop,
> operate, and maintain them. It is also known as *software development* or *software production*.

Box 19–3
Definition of Software
Source: *Webster's College Dictionary* (1992). New York, NY: Random House.

> **soft·ware (*n*. sôft´-wâr)**   Date: 1960
>
> 1. the programs, routines, and symbolic languages that control the functioning of the hard-
> ware and direct its operation.

Box 19–4
Definition of Engineering
Source: *Webster's Dictionary of the English Language* (1997). New York, NY: Lexicon Publications.

> **en·gi·neer·ing (n)**
>
> 1. the science of applying knowledge of the properties of matter and the natural sources of
> energy to the practical problems of industry.

of 1804 revolutionized patterned textile waving. For the first time, fabrics with big, fancy designs could be woven automatically by one man working without assistants. Jacquard never obtained a patent for this device. His 1801 patent, issued for an improved draw loom, is often mistaken for the punched card controlled device that bears his name. Working in Lyon, France, Jacquard created his machine by combining two earlier French inventors' ideas: he applied Jean Falcon's chain of punched cards to the cylinder mechanism of Jacques Vaucanson; then he mounted his device on top of a treadle-operated loom. This was the earliest use of punched cards programmed to control a manufacturing process.[8]

Box 19–5 lays out the historic perspective for computing engines and software.

Box 19–5
Software Engineering Historical Timeline
Source: *worldhistorysite.com/culttech.html*. Thistlerose Publications, copyright 2000.

Calculators and Computers: Dates in the History of Cultural Technologies	
1617	John Napier shows how to multiply and divide using rods or bones.
1642	Blaise Pascal invents adding machine.
1671	G.W. von Leibniz invents adding machine with geared wheels.

(Continues)

Box 19–5 (Continued)
Software Engineering Historical Timeline

1801(sic)	Joseph Jacquard uses card-controlled looms to weave designs into cloth.
1820	Charles X. Thomas introduces commercial calculating machine.
1835	Charles Babbage invents "Analytic Engine," foreshadowing computers.
1859	George Boole publishes treatise on binary algebra.
1867	Charles Sanders Peirce applies Boolean logic to electric circuits.
1872	Lord Kelvin develops analog computer to predict tides.
1886	Herman Hollerith conceives idea of using punched cards for calculations.
1890	Hollerith's ideas successfully applied to work of the U.S. Census.
1911	Hollerith forms company, which later becomes IBM.
1937	George Stibitz creates electrical circuit to apply Boolean algebra.
1939	IBM engineers and Howard Aiken of Harvard start on the Mark I computer.
1943	Alan Turing's "Colossus" computer breaks the German Enigma code.
1946	Electronic Numerical Integrator and Calculator (ENIAC) computer is built.
1946	Von Neumann, Goldstine, and Burks publish paper on computer concepts.
1949	ILLIAC I built at University of Illinois employing the Von Neumann design.
1951	UNIVAC I machine installed at U.S. Census Bureau.
1956	Computer beats human player in chess game.
1957	IBM unveils FoRTRAN programming language.
1959	Jack St. Clair Kilby of Texas Instruments invents integrated circuits.
1960	Livermore Advanced Research Computer (LARC) built with transistors.
1969	U.S. Department of Defense creates ARPANET computer network.
1971	Engineers at Intel invent the microprocessor.
1972	Nolan Bushnell introduces "Pong" video game.
1972	Ray Tomlinson sends first E-mail using @ in address.

(Continues)

BOX 19–5 (Continued)
Software Engineering Historical Timeline

1974	First personal computers introduced.
1974	First time that a bar code scanned groceries at a supermarket.
1976	Cray Research sells first supercomputer.
1977	A glove device to facilitate computer interaction is patented.
1977	George Lucas' computer effects in Star Wars revolutionize filmmaking.
1979	Pac-Man video game first sold in Japan.
1980	Dan Bricklin and Dan Flystra write software for VisiCalc spreadsheet.
1981	IBM introduces personal computer, using Microsoft operating system.
1982	French postal and telegraph service hooks up nation on Minitel network.
1983	Internet emerges as ARPANET splits civilian from military networks.
1984	Apple Computer introduces its Macintosh machine including a mouse.
1985	Microsoft introduces its first version of Windows.
1991	World Wide Web begins.
1992	Michelangelo computer virus detected in the United States.
2000	Widespread computer glitch, Y2K, expected with new millennium.

The first widespread introduction of software came in 1890 when Herman Hollerith's 1886 invention of punch-cards was used in the U.S. census. This was also the first cost overrun due to "computers." U.S. census results were tabulated for the first time with significant mechanical aid: the punch-card tabulators of Herman Hollerith (1860–1929) of MIT, Cambridge, Massachusetts. This was the start of the punch-card industry. The cost of the census tabulation was 98% higher than the previous one, in part because of the temptation to use the machines to their fullest and tabulate more data than formerly possible. However, the tabulation was completed in a much shorter time. Another precedent is that the cards were read electrically.[9]

Software has been in use since the beginning of the 19th century. The earliest records of "engineering" have been around since 2550 B.C.

The first engineer known by name and achievement is Imhotep, builder of the Step Pyramid at Saqqarah, Egypt, probably in about 2550 B.C. Imhotep's successors—Egyptian, Persian, Greek, and Roman—carried civil engineering to remarkable heights on the basis of empirical methods aided by arithmetic, geometry, and a smattering of physical science. The Pharos (lighthouse) of Alexandria, Solomon's Temple in Jerusalem, the Colosseum in Rome, the Persian and Roman road systems, the Pont du Gard aqueduct in France, and many other large structures, some of which endure to this day, testify to their skill, imagination, and daring. Of many treatises written by them, one in particular survives to provide a picture of engineering education and practice in classical times: Vitruvius' De architectura, published in Rome in the 1st century A.D., a 10-volume work covering building materials, construction methods, hydraulics, measurement, and town planning.[10]

Software Engineering Body of Knowledge

The software engineering *body of knowledge* is an all-inclusive term that describes the sum of knowledge within the profession of software engineering. Since it is usually not possible to put the full body of knowledge of even an emerging discipline, such as software engineering, into a single document, there is a need for a guide to the software engineering body of knowledge. This guide will seek to identify and describe that subset of the body of knowledge that is generally accepted, even though software engineers must be knowledgeable not only in software engineering, but also, of course, in other related disciplines. The SWEBOK project team established the project with five objectives:[11]

1. Characterize the contents of the software engineering discipline.
2. Provide topical access to the software engineering body of knowledge.
3. Promote a consistent view of software engineering worldwide.
4. Clarify the place—and set the boundary—of software engineering with respect to other disciplines, such as computer science, project management, computer engineering, and mathematics.
5. Provide a foundation for curriculum development and individual certification material.

Figure 19–4 is a diagram of the topology of the SWEBOK. Box 19–6 is another view of the definition of software engineering.

Box 19–6
A Definition Different from the IEEE

Software Engineering is the study of the *principles* and *methodologies* for developing and maintaining software systems.

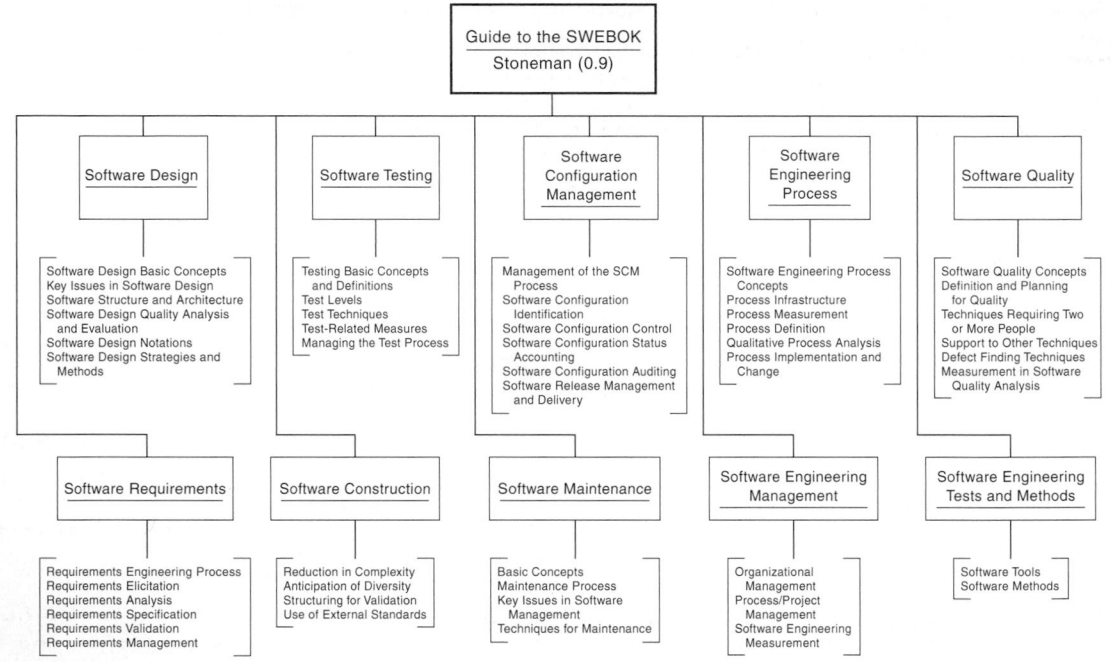

FIGURE 19–4
SWEBOK Taxonomy of Knowledge Areas

SWEBOK Taxonomy of Knowledge Areas covers these knowledge areas. Capital roman numerals denote the major areas:

I. Software Requirements
  a. Requirements engineering process
  b. Requirements elicitation
  c. Requirements analysis
  d. Requirements specification
  e. Requirements validation
  f. Requirements management

II. Software Design
  a. Software design basic concepts
  b. Key issues in software design
  c. Software structure and architecture
  d. Software design quality analysis and evaluation
  e. Software design notations
  f. Software design strategies and methods

III. Software Construction
   a. Reduction in complexity
      i. Linguistic construction methods
      ii. Formal construction methods
      iii. Visual construction methods
   b. Anticipation of diversity
      i. Linguistic construction methods
      ii. Formal construction methods
      iii. Visual construction methods
   c. Structuring for validation
      i. Linguistic construction methods
      ii. Formal construction methods
      iii. Visual construction methods
   d. Use of external standards
      i. Linguistic construction methods
      ii. Formal construction methods
      iii. Visual construction methods

IV. Software Testing
   a. Testing basic concepts and definitions
   b. Test levels
   c. Test techniques
   d. Test-related measures
   e. Managing the test process

V. Software Maintenance
   a. Basic concepts
   b. Maintenance process
   c. Key issues in software maintenance
   d. Techniques for maintenance

VI. Software Configuration Management
   a. Management of the SCM process
   b. Software configuration identification
   c. Software configuration control
   d. Software configuration status accounting
   e. Software configuration auditing
   f. Software release management and delivery

VII. Software Engineering Management

 a. Organizational management

 b. Process/project management

 c. Software engineering measurement

VIII. Software Engineering Process

 a. Software engineering process concepts

 b. Process infrastructure

 c. Process measurement

 d. Process definition

 e. Qualitative process analysis

 f. Process implementation and change

IX. Software Engineering Tools and Methods

 a. Software tools

  i. Software requirements tools

  ii. Software design tools

  iii. Software construction tools

  iv. Software testing tools

  v. Software maintenance tools

  vi. Software engineering process tools

  vii. Software quality tools

  viii. Software configuration management tools

  ix. Software engineering management tools

  x. Infrastructure support tools

  xi. Miscellaneous tools issues

 b. Software methods

  i. Heuristic methods

  ii. Formal methods

  iii. Prototyping methods

  iv. Miscellaneous methods issues

X. Software Quality

 a. Software quality concepts

 b. Definition and planning for quality

 c. Techniques requiring two or more people

 d. Support to other techniques

 e. Testing special to SQA or V&V

f. Defect-finding techniques

g. Measurement in software quality analysis

This comprehensive outline of the body of knowledge needed for software engineering is constantly being improved. It is important to note that this is not computer science. Computer science is related to software engineering in the same fashion that the laws of physics are related to electrical engineering. Science has as its goal the extension of our knowledge of the laws of nature. Engineering's goal is to build useful artifacts based on those laws and the constraints of the product environment.

SWEBOK and the SEI CMM

Other chapters in this book refer to the SEI CMM, particularly with regard to the way that model supports the chapter topic—life cycles, peer reviews, metrics, etc. The CMM is divided into five maturity levels. They are well-defined evolutionary plateaus aimed toward achieving a mature software process. The maturity levels each indicate a level of process capability and those capabilities are decomposed into several key process areas. The levels can be thought of as layers in the foundation for continuous process improvement. These layers comprise sets of process goals that, when satisfied, stabilize an important component of the software process. As these levels of the maturity framework are reached, different components in the software process are more effectively used, resulting in an increase in the process capability of the organization. Organizations cannot skip levels. All key process areas (KPAs) from a lower level must be satisfied before progressing to a higher level. A KPA is a specific process area on which the organization must focus to move to the next maturity level. They are explained for each CMM level in the following paragraphs.

The five maturity levels are shown in Figure 19–5 with their key process areas. Level 1, "Initial," has no KPAs. All organizations start out at a Level 1 when first evaluated. A Level 1 organization typically has no stable environment for developing and maintaining software. During a crisis, projects typically abandon planned procedures and revert to coding and testing. Success depends entirely on having an exceptional manager and a seasoned and effective software team. The software process is constantly changed as the work progresses. Schedules, budgets, functionality, and product quality are generally unpredictable. Performance can be predicted only by individual rather than organizational capability.

Level 2, "Repeatable," has these KPAs:

1. Requirements management

2. Software project planning

3. Software project tracking and oversight

4. Software subcontract management

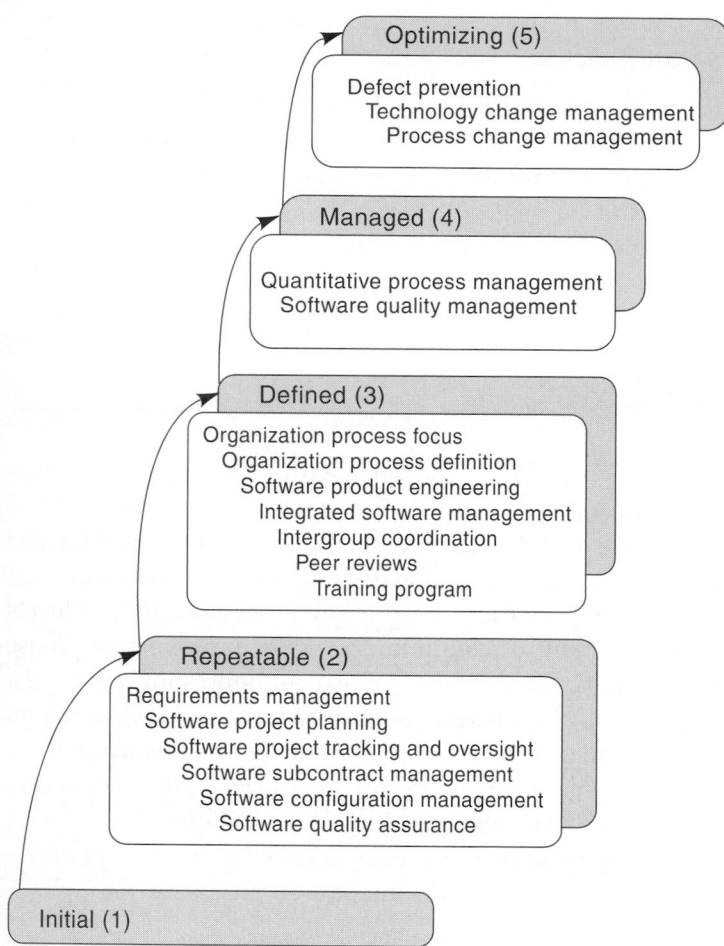

FIGURE 19–5
SEI CMM Key Process Areas by Maturity Level

5. Software configuration management

6. Software quality assurance

At Level 2, the process of building software as a series of black boxes with defined checkpoints (milestones) is in place. As shown in Figure 19–6, requirements come into the process and flow through a series of process black boxes. Outputs result from each box, and milestones and checkpoints are used to monitor the progress of the product through the process. Policies, standards, and procedures are followed. Planning, estimating, and managing new projects are based on experience with similar projects. This experience is quantified in a rudimentary project metrics system. Projects are controlled through formal project management practices. Software costs, schedules, and functionality are tracked. Software requirements and work products are baselined, and their integrity is controlled through a configuration management system. Projects have a strong customer-supplier relationship and the software process capability is disciplined.

At Level 3, "Defined," the standard process for developing and maintaining software across the organization is documented and consistently used (see Figure 19–7). Projects tailor the organization's standard software process to develop their own defined software process. Software engineering and management processes are integrated into a coherent whole. An organization-wide training program is implemented. The software process capability is standard and a group is responsible for the organization's software process activities. These are the KPAs for Level 3:

1. Organization process focus
2. Organization process definition
3. Software product engineering
4. Integrated software management
5. Intergroup coordination
6. Peer reviews
7. Training program

At Level 3, software development is done according to a well-defined process. Roles and responsibilities in the process are understood. The production of the software product is visible throughout the software process.

Level 4 (see Figure 19–8) is the "Managed" level with two KPAs: quantitative process management and software quality management. Detailed measures of the software process and product quality are collected through an extensive metrics system. Both the software process and products are quantitatively understood and controlled. Management has an objective basis for making decisions and is able to predict performance within quantified bounds.

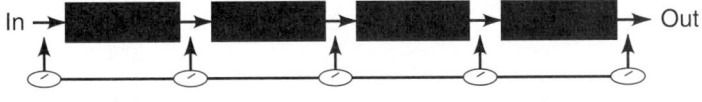

FIGURE 19–6
Level 2 Process

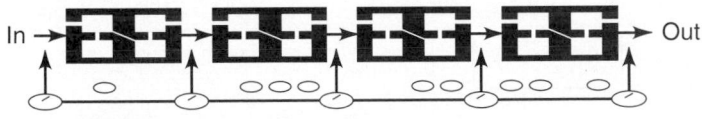

FIGURE 19–7
Level 3 Process

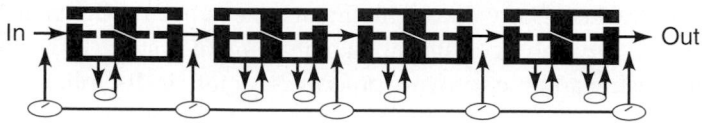

FIGURE 19–8
Level 4 Process

Level 5, "Optimizing," focuses on the KPAs of (a) technology change management, (b) process change management, and (c) defect prevention. Continuous process improvement is enabled by quantitative feedback from the process. At this level, the organization is able to test innovative ideas and technologies to improve product quality. See Figure 19–9.

Disciplined change to the existing process becomes an organizational approach to continuous process improvement. Institutionalizing this change is critical because:

1. The organization outlives those who leave it.
2. The organization culture must convey the process.
3. Management must nurture the culture.
4. Culture is conveyed with role models and rewards.

In summary, the CMM is a road map to success in process improvement. It should be interpreted and used with a view toward business objectives. Today, the CMM is the most widely accepted method (by a broad cross-section of business domains and countries) for process improvement in a software development organization. It is normative, not prescriptive, and is a living model, developed and maintained by a broad base of the software community.

The SWEBOK may be mapped to the SEI CMM key process areas, as shown in Tables 19–1 and 19–2.

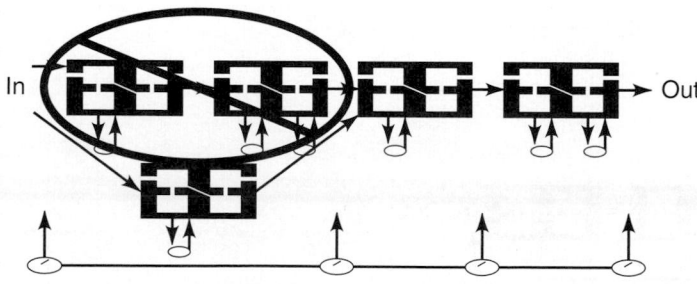

FIGURE 19–9
Level 5 Process

TABLE 19–1

Map of CMM Levels to SWEBOK Knowledge Areas (Part 1 of 2)

SWEBOK Knowledge Areas	Capability Maturity Model Levels																	
	Repeatable (2)						Defined (3)							Man- aged (4)		Optimizing (5)		
	Requirements management	Software project planning	Software project tracking and oversight	Software subcontract management	Software configuration management	Software quality assurance	Organization process focus	Organization process definition	Software product engineering	Integrated software management	Intergroup coordination	Peer reviews	Training program	Quantitative process management	Software quality management	Technology change management	Process change management	Defect prevention
Software Requirements																		
Requirements engineering process	√																	
Requirements elicitation	√																	
Requirements analysis	√																	
Requirements specification	√																	
Requirements validation					√													
Requirements management	√																	
Software Design																		
Software design basic concepts	√																	
Key issues in software design									√									
Software structure and architecture										√								
Software design quality analysis and evaluation															√			

(Continues)

SWEBOK Knowledge Areas	Repeatable (2)						Defined (3)							Managed (4)		Optimizing (5)		
	Requirements management	Software project planning	Software project tracking and oversight	Software subcontract management	Software configuration management	Software quality assurance	Organization process focus	Organization process definition	Software product engineering	Integrated software management	Intergroup coordination	Peer reviews	Training program	Quantitative process management	Software quality management	Technology change management	Process change management	Defect prevention
Software design notations																	√	
Software design strategies and methods																	√	
Software Construction																		
Reduction in Complexity:																		
Linguistic construction methods									√									
Formal construction methods																√		
Visual construction methods																√		
Anticipation of Diversity:																		
Linguistic construction methods									√									
Formal construction methods																√		
Visual construction methods																√		

(Continues)

SWEBOK Knowledge Areas	Capability Maturity Model Levels																	
	Repeatable (2)						Defined (3)							Managed (4)		Optimizing (5)		
	Requirements management	Software project planning	Software project tracking and oversight	Software subcontract management	Software configuration management	Software quality assurance	Organization process focus	Organization process definition	Software product engineering	Integrated software management	Intergroup coordination	Peer reviews	Training program	Quantitative process management	Software quality management	Technology change management	Process change management	Defect prevention
Structuring for Validation:																		
Linguistic construction methods									√									
Formal construction methods																	√	
Visual construction methods																	√	
Use of External Standards:																		
Linguistic construction methods									√									
Formal construction methods																	√	
Visual construction methods																	√	
Software Testing																		
Testing basic concepts and definitions						√												
Test levels									√									
Test techniques									√									

(Continues)

SWEBOK Knowledge Areas	Repeatable (2)						Defined (3)							Managed (4)		Optimizing (5)		
	Requirements management	Software project planning	Software project tracking and oversight	Software subcontract management	Software configuration management	Software quality assurance	Organization process focus	Organization process definition	Software product engineering	Integrated software management	Intergroup coordination	Peer reviews	Training program	Quantitative process management	Software quality management	Technology change management	Process change management	Defect prevention
Test-related measures														√				
Managing the test process															√			
Software Maintenance																		
Basic concepts		√																
Maintenance process									√									
Key issues in software maintenance										√								
Techniques for maintenance										√								
Software Configuration Management																		
Management of the SCM process					√													
Software configuration identification					√													
Software configuration control					√													

(Continues)

SWEBOK Knowledge Areas	Capability Maturity Model Levels																	
	Repeatable (2)						Defined (3)							Managed (4)		Optimizing (5)		
	Requirements management	Software project planning	Software project tracking and oversight	Software subcontract management	Software configuration management	Software quality assurance	Organization process focus	Organization process definition	Software product engineering	Integrated software management	Intergroup coordination	Peer reviews	Training program	Quantitative process management	Software quality management	Technology change management	Process change management	Defect prevention
Software configuration status accounting															√			
Software configuration auditing															√			
Software release management and delivery					√													

TABLE 19–2

Map of CMM Levels to SWEBOK Knowledge Areas (Part 2 of 2)

SWEBOK Knowledge Areas	Capability Maturity Model Levels																	
	Repeatable (2)						Defined (3)							Managed (4)		Optimizing (5)		
	Requirements management	Software project planning	Software project tracking and oversight	Software subcontract management	Software configuration management	Software quality assurance	Organization process focus	Organization process definition	Software product engineering	Integrated software management	Intergroup coordination	Peer reviews	Training program	Quantitative process management	Software quality management	Technology change management	Process change management	Defect prevention
Software Engineering Management																		
Organizational management							√											
Process/project management		√	√	√														
Software engineering measurement														√				
Software Engineering Process																		
Software engineering process concepts							√											
Process infrastructure								√										
Process measurement									√									
Process definition								√										
Qualitative process analysis														√				
Process implementation and change																	√	

(Continues)

SWEBOK Knowledge Areas	Repeatable (2)						Defined (3)							Managed (4)		Optimizing (5)		
	Requirements management	Software project planning	Software project tracking and oversight	Software subcontract management	Software configuration management	Software quality assurance	Organization process focus	Organization process definition	Software product engineering	Integrated software management	Intergroup coordination	Peer reviews	Training program	Quantitative process management	Software quality management	Technology change management	Process change management	Defect prevention
Software Engineering Tools and Methods																		
Software Tools:																		
Software requirements tools	√																	
Software design tools									√									
Software construction tools									√									
Software testing tools									√									
Software maintenance tools									√									
Software engineering process tools									√									
Software quality tools						√												
Software configuration management tools					√													
Software engineering management tools														√	√			

(Continues)

SWEBOK Knowledge Areas	Capability Maturity Model Levels																		
	Repeatable (2)						Defined (3)							Managed (4)		Optimizing (5)		
	Requirements management	Software project planning	Software project tracking and oversight	Software subcontract management	Software configuration management	Software quality assurance	Organization process focus	Organization process definition	Software product engineering	Integrated software management	Intergroup coordination	Peer reviews	Training program	Quantitative process management	Software quality management	Technology change management	Process change management	Defect prevention
Infrastructure support tools										√	√							
Miscellaneous tools issues																		√
Software Methods:																		
Heuristic methods														√				
Formal methods																√	√	
Prototyping methods	√								√									
Miscellaneous methods issues																√	√	
Software Quality																		
Software quality concepts						√												
Definition and planning for quality						√												
Techniques requiring two or more people								√										
Support to other techniques																		√
Testing special to SQA or V&V										√								

| SWEBOK Knowledge Areas | Capability Maturity Model Levels | | | | | | | | | | | | | | | | | |
| | Repeatable (2) | | | | | | Defined (3) | | | | | | | Managed (4) | | Optimizing (5) | | |
	Requirements management	Software project planning	Software project tracking and oversight	Software subcontract management	Software configuration management	Software quality assurance	Organization process focus	Organization process definition	Software product engineering	Integrated software management	Intergroup coordination	Peer reviews	Training program	Quantitative process management	Software quality management	Technology change management	Process change management	Defect prevention
Defect-finding techniques						√												
Measurement in software quality analysis														√				

SWEBOK and the 34 Software Project Management Competencies

The SWEBOK is focused on the body of knowledge specifically for software engineering. The 34 competencies for the software project management certification program emphasize the management of software development projects. As can be seen from the six segments presented in Table 19–3, the 34 competencies are very focused on the PMBOK aspects.

The mappings, in total, of the 34 competencies to SWEBOK may be found in Tables 19–4 through 19–9.

TABLE 19–3

Map of 34 Competencies to SWEBOK Segments

Segment Number	SWEBOK Sections	Competencies
1	Software Requirements Through Configuration Management	Product Competencies 1–11
2	Software Engineering Management Through Software Quality	Product Competencies 1–11
3	Software Requirements Through Configuration Management	Project Competencies 12–22
4	Software Engineering Management Through Software Quality	Project Competencies 12–22
5	Software Requirements Through Configuration Management	Management Competencies 23–34
6	Software Engineering Management Through Software Quality	Management Competencies 23–34

TABLE 19–4

Map of 34 Competencies to SWEBOK Knowledge Areas (Part 1 of 6)

SWEBOK Knowledge Areas	34 SWPM Competencies										
	Product (Software) Competency										
	1. Assessing processes	2. Awareness of process standards	3. Defining the product	4. Evaluating alternative processes	5. Managing requirements	6. Managing subcontractors	7. Performing the initial assessment	8. Selecting methods and tools	9. Tailoring processes	10. Tracking product quality	11. Understanding development activities
Software Requirements											
Requirements engineering process							√				
Requirements elicitation											

(Continues)

SWEBOK Knowledge Areas	34 SWPM Competencies										
	Product (Software) Competency										
	1. Assessing processes	2. Awareness of process standards	3. Defining the product	4. Evaluating alternative processes	5. Managing requirements	6. Managing subcontractors	7. Performing the initial assessment	8. Selecting methods and tools	9. Tailoring processes	10. Tracking product quality	11. Understanding development activities
Requirements analysis											
Requirements specification											
Requirements validation											
Requirements management					√						
Software Design											
Software design basic concepts											
Key issues in software design											
Software structure and architecture											
Software design quality analysis and evaluation											
Software design notations											
Software design strategies and methods											
Software Construction											
Reduction in Complexity:											
Linguistic construction methods											
Formal construction methods											
Visual construction methods											
Anticipation of Diversity:											
Linguistic construction methods											
Formal construction methods											

(Continues)

SWEBOK Knowledge Areas	34 SWPM Competencies										
	Product (Software) Competency										
	1. Assessing processes	2. Awareness of process standards	3. Defining the product	4. Evaluating alternative processes	5. Managing requirements	6. Managing subcontractors	7. Performing the initial assessment	8. Selecting methods and tools	9. Tailoring processes	10. Tracking product quality	11. Understanding development activities
Software Construction (Continued)											
Visual construction methods											
Structuring for Validation:											
Linguistic construction methods											
Formal construction methods											
Visual construction methods											
Use of External Standards:											
Linguistic construction methods											
Formal construction methods											
Visual construction methods											
Software Testing											
Testing basic concepts and definitions											
Test levels											
Test techniques											
Test-related measures											
Managing the test process											
Software Maintenance											
Basic concepts											
Maintenance process											
Key issues in software maintenance											

(Continues)

SWEBOK Knowledge Areas	34 SWPM Competencies										
	Product (Software) Competency										
	1. Assessing processes	2. Awareness of process standards	3. Defining the product	4. Evaluating alternative processes	5. Managing requirements	6. Managing subcontractors	7. Performing the initial assessment	8. Selecting methods and tools	9. Tailoring processes	10. Tracking product quality	11. Understanding development activities
Techniques for maintenance											
Software Configuration Management											
Management of the SCM process											
Software configuration identification											
Software configuration control											
Software configuration status accounting											
Software configuration auditing											
Software release management and delivery											

SWEBOK Knowledge Areas	34 SWPM Competencies										
	Product (Software) Competency										
	1. Assessing processes	2. Awareness of process standards	3. Defining the product	4. Evaluating alternative processes	5. Managing requirements	6. Managing subcontractors	7. Performing the initial assessment	8. Selecting methods and tools	9. Tailoring processes	10. Tracking product quality	11. Understanding development activities
Software Engineering Management											
Organizational management						√					
Process/project management			√								
Software engineering measurement											
Software Engineering Process											
Software engineering process concepts		√									
Process infrastructure											√
Process measurement											
Process definition									√		
Qualitative process analysis	√										
Process implementation and change				√							
Software Engineering Tools and Methods								√			
Software Tools:											
Software requirements tools											
Software design tools											
Software construction tools											
Software testing tools											
Software maintenance tools											
Software engineering process tools											
Software quality tools											

(Continues)

SWEBOK Knowledge Areas	34 SWPM Competencies										
	Product (Software) Competency										
	1. Assessing processes	2. Awareness of process standards	3. Defining the product	4. Evaluating alternative processes	5. Managing requirements	6. Managing subcontractors	7. Performing the initial assessment	8. Selecting methods and tools	9. Tailoring processes	10. Tracking product quality	11. Understanding development activities
Software configuration management tools											
Software engineering management tools											
Infrastructure support tools											
Miscellaneous tools issues											
Software Methods:											
Heuristic methods											
Formal methods											
Prototyping methods											
Miscellaneous methods issues											
Software Quality											
Software quality concepts											
Definition and planning for quality											
Techniques requiring two or more people											
Support to other techniques											
Testing special to SQA or V&V											
Defect-finding techniques											
Measurement in software quality analysis										√	

SWEBOK Knowledge Areas	34 SWPM Competencies										
	Project Competency										
	12. Building a work breakdown structure	13. Documenting plans	14. Estimating cost	15. Estimating effort	16. Managing risk	17. Monitoring development	18. Scheduling	19. Selecting metrics	20. Selecting project management tools	21. Tracking process	22. Tracking project progress
Software Requirements											
Requirements engineering process											
Requirements elicitation											
Requirements analysis											
Requirements specification											
Requirements validation											
Requirements management											
Software Design											
Software design basic concepts											
Key issues in software design											
Software structure and architecture											
Software design quality analysis and evaluation											
Software design notations											
Software design strategies and methods											
Software Construction											
Reduction in Complexity:											
Linguistic construction methods											
Formal construction methods											
Visual construction methods											

(Continues)

SWEBOK Knowledge Areas	34 SWPM Competencies										
	Project Competency										
	12. Building a work breakdown structure	13. Documenting plans	14. Estimating cost	15. Estimating effort	16. Managing risk	17. Monitoring development	18. Scheduling	19. Selecting metrics	20. Selecting project management tools	21. Tracking process	22. Tracking project progress
Anticipation of Diversity:											
Linguistic construction methods											
Formal construction methods											
Visual construction methods											
Structuring for Validation:											
Linguistic construction methods											
Formal construction methods											
Visual construction methods											
Use of External Standards:											
Linguistic construction methods											
Formal construction methods											
Visual construction methods											
Software Testing											
Testing basic concepts and definitions											
Test levels											
Test techniques											
Test-related measures											
Managing the test process											
Software Maintenance											
Basic concepts											

(Continues)

SWEBOK Knowledge Areas	34 SWPM Competencies										
	Project Competency										
	12. Building a work breakdown structure	13. Documenting plans	14. Estimating cost	15. Estimating effort	16. Managing risk	17. Monitoring development	18. Scheduling	19. Selecting metrics	20. Selecting project management tools	21. Tracking process	22. Tracking project progress
Maintenance process											
Key issues in software maintenance											
Techniques for maintenance											
Software Configuration Management											
Management of the SCM process											
Software configuration identification											
Software configuration control											
Software configuration status accounting											
Software configuration auditing											
Software release management and delivery											

SWEBOK Knowledge Areas	34 SWPM Competencies										
	Project Competency										
	12. Building a work breakdown structure	13. Documenting plans	14. Estimating cost	15. Estimating effort	16. Managing risk	17. Monitoring development	18. Scheduling	19. Selecting metrics	20. Selecting project management tools	21. Tracking process	22. Tracking project progress
Software Engineering Management											
Organizational management											
Process/project management											
Software engineering measurement											
Software Engineering Process											
Software engineering process concepts											
Process infrastructure											
Process measurement						√				√	
Process definition											
Qualitative process analysis											
Process implementation and change											
Software Engineering Tools and Methods											
Software Tools:											
Software requirements tools											
Software design tools											
Software construction tools											
Software testing tools											
Software maintenance tools											
Software engineering process tools	√	√	√	√					√		
Software quality tools											

(Continues)

SWEBOK Knowledge Areas	34 SWPM Competencies										
	Project Competency										
	12. Building a work breakdown structure	13. Documenting plans	14. Estimating cost	15. Estimating effort	16. Managing risk	17. Monitoring development	18. Scheduling	19. Selecting metrics	20. Selecting project management tools	21. Tracking process	22. Tracking project progress
Software configuration management tools											
Software engineering management tools											
Infrastructure support tools											
Miscellaneous tools issues											
Software Methods:											
Heuristic methods											
Formal methods											
Prototyping methods											
Miscellaneous methods issues											
Software Quality											
Software quality concepts											
Definition and planning for quality											
Techniques requiring two or more people											
Support to other techniques											
Testing special to SQA or V&V											
Defect-finding techniques											
Measurement in software quality analysis											

SWEBOK Knowledge Areas	34 SWPM Competencies											
	Management (People) Competency											
	23. Appraising performance	24. Handling intellectual property	25. Holding effective meetings	26. Interaction and communication	27. Leadership	28. Managing change	29. Negotiating successfully	30. Planning careers	31. Presenting effectively	32. Recruiting	33. Selecting a team	34. Teambuilding
Software Requirements												
Requirements engineering process												
Requirements elicitation												
Requirements analysis												
Requirements specification												
Requirements validation												
Requirements management												
Software Design												
Software design basic concepts												
Key issues in software design												
Software structure and architecture												
Software design quality analysis and evaluation												
Software design notations												
Software design strategies and methods												
Software Construction												
Reduction in Complexity:												
Linguistic construction methods												
Formal construction methods												
Visual construction methods												
Anticipation of Diversity:												
Linguistic construction methods												

(Continues)

SWEBOK Knowledge Areas	34 SWPM Competencies											
	Management (People) Competency											
	23. Appraising performance	24. Handling intellectual property	25. Holding effective meetings	26. Interaction and communication	27. Leadership	28. Managing change	29. Negotiating successfully	30. Planning careers	31. Presenting effectively	32. Recruiting	33. Selecting a team	34. Teambuilding
Formal construction methods												
Visual construction methods												
Structuring for Validation:												
Linguistic construction methods												
Formal construction methods												
Visual construction methods												
Use of External Standards:												
Linguistic construction methods												
Formal construction methods												
Visual construction methods												
Software Testing												
Testing basic concepts and definitions												
Test levels												
Test techniques												
Test-related measures												
Managing the test process												
Software Maintenance												
Basic concepts												
Maintenance process												
Key issues in software maintenance												
Techniques for maintenance												

(Continues)

SWEBOK Knowledge Areas	34 SWPM Competencies											
	Management (People) Competency											
	23. Appraising performance	24. Handling intellectual property	25. Holding effective meetings	26. Interaction and communication	27. Leadership	28. Managing change	29. Negotiating successfully	30. Planning careers	31. Presenting effectively	32. Recruiting	33. Selecting a team	34. Teambuilding
Software Configuration Management												
Management of the SCM process												
Software configuration identification												
Software configuration control												
Software configuration status accounting												
Software configuration auditing												
Software release management and delivery												

SWEBOK Knowledge Areas	34 SWPM Competencies											
	Management (People) Competency											
	23. Appraising performance	24. Handling intellectual property	25. Holding effective meetings	26. Interaction and communication	27. Leadership	28. Managing change	29. Negotiating successfully	30. Planning careers	31. Presenting effectively	32. Recruiting	33. Selecting a team	34. Teambuilding
Software Engineering Management												
Organizational management			√	√	√		√	√	√	√	√	√
Process/project management	√	√										
Software engineering measurement	√											
Software Engineering Process												
Software engineering process concepts												
Process infrastructure												
Process measurement												
Process definition												
Qualitative process analysis												
Process implementation and change						√						
Software Engineering Tools and Methods												
Software Tools:												
Software requirements tools												
Software design tools												
Software construction tools												
Software testing tools												
Software maintenance tools												
Software engineering process tools												
Software quality tools												

(Continues)

SWEBOK Knowledge Areas	34 SWPM Competencies											
	Management (People) Competency											
	23. Appraising performance	24. Handling intellectual property	25. Holding effective meetings	26. Interaction and communication	27. Leadership	28. Managing change	29. Negotiating successfully	30. Planning careers	31. Presenting effectively	32. Recruiting	33. Selecting a team	34. Teambuilding
Software configuration management tools												
Software engineering management tools												
Infrastructure support tools												
Miscellaneous tools issues												
Software Methods:												
Heuristic methods												
Formal methods												
Prototyping methods												
Miscellaneous methods issues												
Software Quality												
Software quality concepts												
Definition and planning for quality												
Techniques requiring two or more people												
Support to other techniques												
Testing special to SQA or V&V												
Defect-finding techniques												
Measurement in software quality analysis												

SWEBOK and Quality Software Project Management

The final mapping that is required to establish software engineering in the project management arena is the SWEBOK mapped to the chapters in this practitioner's guide. It may be seen in Tables 19–10 through 19–13.

TABLE 19–10
Map of SWEBOK to Quality Software Project Management (Part 1 of 4)

SWEBOK Knowledge Areas	1. Introduction	2. A Case in Point	3. Process Overview	4. Selecting Software Development Life Cycles	5. Managing Domain Processes	6. Selecting a Project Team	7. Defining the Goal and Scope of the Software Project	8. Creating the Work Breakdown Structure	9. Identifying the Tasks and Activities	10. Software Size and Reuse Estimating	11. Estimating Duration and Cost	12. Assigning Resources	13. Choosing an Organizational Form	14. Considering Dependencies	15. Scheduling the Work	16. Eliciting Requirements	17. Developing the Software Requirements Specification	18. Determining Project Risks
			Initiating				**Planning**											
Software Requirements																		
Requirements engineering process			•	•	•	•	•	•	•	•	•	•	•	•	•	•	•	•
Requirements elicitation				•			•									•	•	•
Requirements analysis				•			•	•	•	•	•	•	•	•	•	•	•	•
Requirements specification				•			•					•	•	•		•	•	

(Continues)

SWEBOK Knowledge Areas	1. Introduction	2. A Case in Point	3. Process Overview	4. Selecting Software Development Life Cycles	5. Managing Domain Processes	6. Selecting a Project Team	7. Defining the Goal and Scope of the Software Project	8. Creating the Work Breakdown Structure	9. Identifying the Tasks and Activities	10. Software Size and Reuse Estimating	11. Estimating Duration and Cost	12. Assigning Resources	13. Choosing an Organizational Form	14. Considering Dependencies	15. Scheduling the Work	16. Eliciting Requirements	17. Developing the Software Requirements Specification	18. Determining Project Risks
			Initiating				Planning											
Requirements validation				•	•		•										•	•
Requirements management			•	•	•	•	•	•	•	•	•	•	•	•	•	•	•	•
Software Design																		
Software design basic concepts			•	•	•		•	•	•	•	•	•	•	•	•	•	•	•
Key issues in software design							•			•					•			•
Software structure and architecture				•	•		•			•					•			•
Software design quality analysis and evaluation				•			•		•	•	•	•	•		•	•		•
Software design notations				•			•			•					•		•	
Software design strategies and methods				•			•	•	•	•	•	•	•	•	•	•	•	•
Software Construction																		
Reduction in Complexity:																		

SWEBOK Knowledge Areas	QSPM Chapters																	
				Initiating			Planning											
	1. Introduction	2. A Case in Point	3. Process Overview	4. Selecting Software Development Life Cycles	5. Managing Domain Processes	6. Selecting a Project Team	7. Defining the Goal and Scope of the Software Project	8. Creating the Work Breakdown Structure	9. Identifying the Tasks and Activities	10. Software Size and Reuse Estimating	11. Estimating Duration and Cost	12. Assigning Resources	13. Choosing an Organizational Form	14. Considering Dependencies	15. Scheduling the Work	16. Eliciting Requirements	17. Developing the Software Requirements Specification	18. Determining Project Risks
Linguistic construction methods				•		•		•	•		•	•			•	•		•
Formal construction methods				•		•		•	•		•	•		•	•			•
Visual construction methods				•		•		•	•		•	•		•	•			•
Anticipation of Diversity:																		
Linguistic construction methods				•		•		•	•		•	•		•	•			•
Formal construction methods				•		•		•	•		•	•		•	•			•
Visual construction methods				•		•		•	•		•	•		•	•			•
Structuring for Validation:																		
Linguistic construction methods				•		•		•	•		•	•		•	•			•

SWEBOK Knowledge Areas	1. Introduction	2. A Case in Point	3. Process Overview	4. Selecting Software Development Life Cycles	5. Managing Domain Processes	6. Selecting a Project Team	7. Defining the Goal and Scope of the Software Project	8. Creating the Work Breakdown Structure	9. Identifying the Tasks and Activities	10. Software Size and Reuse Estimating	11. Estimating Duration and Cost	12. Assigning Resources	13. Choosing an Organizational Form	14. Considering Dependencies	15. Scheduling the Work	16. Eliciting Requirements	17. Developing the Software Requirements Specification	18. Determining Project Risks
				Initiating			Planning											
Formal construction methods				•		•	•	•			•	•		•	•			•
Visual construction methods				•		•	•	•			•	•		•	•			•
Use of External Standards:																		
Linguistic construction methods				•		•	•	•			•	•		•	•			•
Formal construction methods				•		•	•	•			•	•		•	•			•
Visual construction methods				•		•	•	•			•	•		•	•			•
Software Testing																		
Testing basic concepts and definitions				•	•	•	•	•	•	•	•	•	•	•	•	•	•	•
Test levels				•		•	•	•	•	•	•					•		•
Test techniques				•		•	•				•					•		•
Test-related measures				•			•				•					•		•

(Continues)

SWEBOK Knowledge Areas	1. Introduction	2. A Case in Point	3. Process Overview	4. Selecting Software Development Life Cycles	5. Managing Domain Processes	6. Selecting a Project Team	7. Defining the Goal and Scope of the Software Project	8. Creating the Work Breakdown Structure	9. Identifying the Tasks and Activities	10. Software Size and Reuse Estimating	11. Estimating Duration and Cost	12. Assigning Resources	13. Choosing an Organizational Form	14. Considering Dependencies	15. Scheduling the Work	16. Eliciting Requirements	17. Developing the Software Requirements Specification	18. Determining Project Risks
				Initiating			Planning											
Managing the test process				•		•	•	•				•	•	•	•		•	•
Software Maintenance																		
Basic concepts			•	•		•	•	•	•	•	•	•	•	•	•	•	•	•
Maintenance process				•			•					•		•				•
Key issues in software maintenance				•			•					•		•				•
Techniques for maintenance				•			•					•		•				•
Software Configuration Management																		
Management of the SCM process			•	•	•	•	•	•	•			•	•		•			•
Software configuration identification																		•
Software configuration control																		•

(Continues)

SWEBOK Knowledge Areas	QSPM Chapters																	
			Initiating			Planning												
	1. Introduction	2. A Case in Point	3. Process Overview	4. Selecting Software Development Life Cycles	5. Managing Domain Processes	6. Selecting a Project Team	7. Defining the Goal and Scope of the Software Project	8. Creating the Work Breakdown Structure	9. Identifying the Tasks and Activities	10. Software Size and Reuse Estimating	11. Estimating Duration and Cost	12. Assigning Resources	13. Choosing an Organizational Form	14. Considering Dependencies	15. Scheduling the Work	16. Eliciting Requirements	17. Developing the Software Requirements Specification	18. Determining Project Risks
Software configuration status accounting																		•
Software configuration auditing																		•
Software release management and delivery																		•

SWEBOK Knowledge Areas	1. Introduction	2. A Case in Point	3. Process Overview	4. Selecting Software Development Life Cycles	5. Managing Domain Processes	6. Selecting a Project Team	7. Defining the Goal and Scope of the Software Project	8. Creating the Work Breakdown Structure	9. Identifying the Tasks and Activities	10. Software Size and Reuse Estimating	11. Estimating Duration and Cost	12. Assigning Resources	13. Choosing an Organizational Form	14. Considering Dependencies	15. Scheduling the Work	16. Eliciting Requirements	17. Developing the Software Requirements Specification	18. Determining Project Risks
			Initiating				Planning											
Software Engineering Management																		
Organizational management			•	•	•	•	•	•	•	•	•	•	•	•	•	•	•	•
Process/project management			•	•	•		•											•
Software engineering measurement			•	•	•		•							•				•
Software Engineering Process																		
Software engineering process concepts			•	•	•	•	•	•	•	•	•	•	•	•	•	•	•	•
Process infrastructure				•	•								•	•		•		•
Process measurement					•				•	•	•	•			•	•		•
Process definition				•										•	•			•
Qualitative process analysis													•					•

SWEBOK Knowledge Areas	1. Introduction	2. A Case in Point	Initiating				Planning											
			3. Process Overview	4. Selecting Software Development Life Cycles	5. Managing Domain Processes	6. Selecting a Project Team	7. Defining the Goal and Scope of the Software Project	8. Creating the Work Breakdown Structure	9. Identifying the Tasks and Activities	10. Software Size and Reuse Estimating	11. Estimating Duration and Cost	12. Assigning Resources	13. Choosing an Organizational Form	14. Considering Dependencies	15. Scheduling the Work	16. Eliciting Requirements	17. Developing the Software Requirements Specification	18. Determining Project Risks
Process implementation and change			•				•						•					•
Software Engineering Tools and Methods																		
Software Tools:																		
Software requirements tools			•						•		•	•				•	•	•
Software design tools			•						•		•	•				•		•
Software construction tools			•						•		•	•				•		•
Software testing tools			•						•		•	•				•		•
Software maintenance tools			•						•		•	•				•		•
Software engineering process tools			•				•	•	•	•	•	•				•	•	•
Software quality tools			•						•		•	•				•		•

(Continues)

SWEBOK Knowledge Areas	QSPM Chapters																	
			Initiating			Planning												
	1. Introduction	2. A Case in Point	3. Process Overview	4. Selecting Software Development Life Cycles	5. Managing Domain Processes	6. Selecting a Project Team	7. Defining the Goal and Scope of the Software Project	8. Creating the Work Breakdown Structure	9. Identifying the Tasks and Activities	10. Software Size and Reuse Estimating	11. Estimating Duration and Cost	12. Assigning Resources	13. Choosing an Organizational Form	14. Considering Dependencies	15. Scheduling the Work	16. Eliciting Requirements	17. Developing the Software Requirements Specification	18. Determining Project Risks
Software configuration management tools				•					•		•	•			•			•
Software engineering management tools				•					•		•	•			•			•
Infrastructure support tools				•					•		•	•			•			•
Miscellaneous tools issues				•					•		•	•			•			•
Software Methods:																		
Heuristic methods				•	•	•	•	•	•		•	•		•	•			•
Formal methods				•	•	•	•	•	•		•	•		•	•			•
Prototyping methods				•	•	•	•	•	•		•	•		•	•			•
Miscellaneous methods issues				•	•	•	•	•	•		•	•		•	•			•
Software Quality																		
Software quality concepts			•	•	•	•	•	•	•	•	•	•	•	•	•	•	•	•

(Continues)

SWEBOK Knowledge Areas	Initiating						Planning											
	1. Introduction	2. A Case in Point	3. Process Overview	4. Selecting Software Development Life Cycles	5. Managing Domain Processes	6. Selecting a Project Team	7. Defining the Goal and Scope of the Software Project	8. Creating the Work Breakdown Structure	9. Identifying the Tasks and Activities	10. Software Size and Reuse Estimating	11. Estimating Duration and Cost	12. Assigning Resources	13. Choosing an Organizational Form	14. Considering Dependencies	15. Scheduling the Work	16. Eliciting Requirements	17. Developing the Software Requirements Specification	18. Determining Project Risks
Definition and planning for quality			•	•	•	•	•	•		•	•	•	•	•	•	•	•	•
Techniques requiring two or more people			•			•	•		•		•	•	•	•	•			•
Support to other techniques			•						•									•
Testing special to SQA or V&V			•						•						•	•		•
Defect-finding techniques			•						•									•
Measurement in software quality analysis			•	•					•									

TABLE 19–12

Map of SWEBOK to Quality Software Project Management (Part 3 of 4)

QSPM Chapters

SWEBOK Knowledge Areas	Executing						Controlling		Closing		Company-Wide Support					Appendices						
	19. Introduction to Software Engineering	20. Reliability	21. Software Metrics	22. Analysis and Design Methods	23. Validation and Verification	24. Use of Tools	25. Project Tracking and Control	26. Continuous Process Improvement	27. Project Termination	28. Post Performance Analysis	29. Reporting and Communication	30. Software Quality Assurance	31. Software Configuration Management	32. Legal Issues in Software	33. Summary	A. Supporting Organizations	B. Real World Projects	C. Creating the Business Plan	D. Understanding Systems Engineering	E. Distance Project Management	F. Project Artifact Templates	G. Joint Application Design in Use
Software Requirements																		•	•	•	•	•
Requirements engineering process	•	•	•	•	•	•	•	•	•	•	•	•	•	•	•							
Requirements elicitation	•					•					•	•	•									•
Requirements analysis	•	•	•	•	•	•					•	•	•									•
Requirements specification	•	•	•	•	•	•	•	•		•	•	•	•	•	•							

(Continues)

TABLE 19-12 (Continued)
Map of SWEBOK to Quality Software Project Management (Part 3 of 4)

SWEBOK Knowledge Areas	QSPM Chapters																					
	Executing						Controlling		Closing		Company-Wide Support					Appendices						
	19. Introduction to Software Engineering	20. Reliability	21. Software Metrics	22. Analysis and Design Methods	23. Validation and Verification	24. Use of Tools	25. Project Tracking and Control	26. Continuous Process Improvement	27. Project Termination	28. Post Performance Analysis	29. Reporting and Communication	30. Software Quality Assurance	31. Software Configuration Management	32. Legal Issues in Software	33. Summary	A. Supporting Organizations	B. Real World Projects	C. Creating the Business Plan	D. Understanding Systems Engineering	E. Distance Project Management	F. Project Artifact Templates	G. Joint Application Design In Use
Requirements validation	•	•	•		•	•					•	•	•					•	•	•	•	•
Requirements management	•	•	•	•	•	•	•	•	•	•	•	•	•	•	•							
Software Design																						
Software design basic concepts	•	•	•			•		•	•	•	•	•	•		•				•	•	•	•
Key issues in software design	•		•			•		•			•											
Software structure and architecture			•			•		•	•	•	•	•	•									

(Continues)

TABLE 19–12 (Continued)

Map of SWEBOK to Quality Software Project Management (Part 3 of 4)

SWEBOK Knowledge Areas	Executing						Controlling		Closing		Company-Wide Support					Appendices						
	19. Introduction to Software Engineering	20. Reliability	21. Software Metrics	22. Analysis and Design Methods	23. Validation and Verification	24. Use of Tools	25. Project Tracking and Control	26. Continuous Process Improvement	27. Project Termination	28. Post Performance Analysis	29. Reporting and Communication	30. Software Quality Assurance	31. Software Configuration Management	32. Legal Issues in Software	33. Summary	A. Supporting Organizations	B. Real World Projects	C. Creating the Business Plan	D. Understanding Systems Engineering	E. Distance Project Management	F. Project Artifact Templates	G. Joint Application Design In Use
Software design quality analysis and evaluation	•	•	•	•	•	•		•			•	•										
Software design notations			•			•	•	•			•										•	
Software design strategies and methods	•	•	•	•	•	•	•	•			•	•									•	
Software Construction																						
Reduction in Complexity:																						

(Continues)

TABLE 19-12 (Continued)
Map of SWEBOK to Quality Software Project Management (Part 3 of 4)

SWEBOK Knowledge Areas	19. Introduction to Software Engineering	20. Reliability	21. Software Metrics	22. Analysis and Design Methods	23. Validation and Verification	24. Use of Tools	25. Project Tracking and Control	26. Continuous Process Improvement	27. Project Termination	28. Post Performance Analysis	29. Reporting and Communication	30. Software Quality Assurance	31. Software Configuration Management	32. Legal Issues in Software	33. Summary	A. Supporting Organizations	B. Real World Projects	C. Creating the Business Plan	D. Understanding Systems Engineering	E. Distance Project Management	F. Project Artifact Templates	G. Joint Application Design In Use
		Executing					Controlling		Closing		Company-Wide Support					Appendices						
Linguistic construction methods		•			•	•						•	•									
Formal construction methods		•			•	•						•	•									
Visual construction methods		•			•	•						•	•									
Anticipation of Diversity:																						
Linguistic construction methods		•			•	•						•	•									

(Continues)

TABLE 19–12 (Continued)
Map of SWEBOK to Quality Software Project Management (Part 3 of 4)

SWEBOK Knowledge Areas	QSPM Chapters — Executing						Controlling		Closing		Company-Wide Support					Appendices						
	19. Introduction to Software Engineering	20. Reliability	21. Software Metrics	22. Analysis and Design Methods	23. Validation and Verification	24. Use of Tools	25. Project Tracking and Control	26. Continuous Process Improvement	27. Project Termination	28. Post Performance Analysis	29. Reporting and Communication	30. Software Quality Assurance	31. Software Configuration Management	32. Legal Issues in Software	33. Summary	A. Supporting Organizations	B. Real World Projects	C. Creating the Business Plan	D. Understanding Systems Engineering	E. Distance Project Management	F. Project Artifact Templates	G. Joint Application Design In Use
Formal construction methods		•			•	•						•	•									
Visual construction methods		•			•	•						•	•									
Structuring for Validation:																						
Linguistic construction methods		•			•	•						•	•									
Formal construction methods		•			•	•						•	•									

(Continues)

SWEBOK Knowledge Areas	Executing						Controlling		Closing		Company-Wide Support					Appendices						
	19. Introduction to Software Engineering	20. Reliability	21. Software Metrics	22. Analysis and Design Methods	23. Validation and Verification	24. Use of Tools	25. Project Tracking and Control	26. Continuous Process Improvement	27. Project Termination	28. Post Performance Analysis	29. Reporting and Communication	30. Software Quality Assurance	31. Software Configuration Management	32. Legal Issues in Software	33. Summary	A. Supporting Organizations	B. Real World Projects	C. Creating the Business Plan	D. Understanding Systems Engineering	E. Distance Project Management	F. Project Artifact Templates	G. Joint Application Design In Use
Visual construction methods		•			•	•						•	•									
Use of External Standards:																						
Linguistic construction methods		•			•	•						•	•									
Formal construction methods		•			•	•						•	•									
Visual construction methods		•			•	•						•	•									

(Continues)

TABLE 19-12 (Continued)
Map of SWEBOK to Quality Software Project Management (Part 3 of 4)

SWEBOK Knowledge Areas	Executing						Controlling		Closing		Company-Wide Support					Appendices						
	19. Introduction to Software Engineering	20. Reliability	21. Software Metrics	22. Analysis and Design Methods	23. Validation and Verification	24. Use of Tools	25. Project Tracking and Control	26. Continuous Process Improvement	27. Project Termination	28. Post Performance Analysis	29. Reporting and Communication	30. Software Quality Assurance	31. Software Configuration Management	32. Legal Issues in Software	33. Summary	A. Supporting Organizations	B. Real World Projects	C. Creating the Business Plan	D. Understanding Systems Engineering	E. Distance Project Management	F. Project Artifact Templates	G. Joint Application Design In Use
Software Testing																						
Testing basic concepts and definitions	•	•	•		•	•	•	•	•			•	•	•							•	
Test levels		•	•		•	•						•	•								•	
Test techniques		•	•		•	•						•	•								•	
Test-related measures		•	•		•	•		•				•	•								•	
Managing the test process	•		•	•	•	•	•		•	•	•	•	•	•							•	
Software Maintenance																						

(Continues)

TABLE 19–12 (Continued)
Map of SWEBOK to Quality Software Project Management (Part 3 of 4)

SWEBOK Knowledge Areas	Executing						Controlling		Closing		Company-Wide Support					Appendices						
	19. Introduction to Software Engineering	20. Reliability	21. Software Metrics	22. Analysis and Design Methods	23. Validation and Verification	24. Use of Tools	25. Project Tracking and Control	26. Continuous Process Improvement	27. Project Termination	28. Post Performance Analysis	29. Reporting and Communication	30. Software Quality Assurance	31. Software Configuration Management	32. Legal Issues in Software	33. Summary	A. Supporting Organizations	B. Real World Projects	C. Creating the Business Plan	D. Understanding Systems Engineering	E. Distance Project Management	F. Project Artifact Templates	G. Joint Application Design In Use
Basic concepts	•	•	•	•	•	•	•		•	•	•	•	•	•								
Maintenance process		•		•	•	•						•	•									
Key issues in software maintenance		•			•	•						•	•									
Techniques for maintenance		•			•	•		•				•	•									
Software Configuration Management																						
Management of the SCM process	•	•	•	•	•	•	•	•	•	•	•	•	•	•							•	

(Continues)

TABLE 19-12 (Continued)
Map of SWEBOK to Quality Software Project Management (Part 3 of 4)

SWEBOK Knowledge Areas	QSPM Chapters — Executing						Controlling		Closing		Company-Wide Support					Appendices						
	19. Introduction to Software Engineering	20. Reliability	21. Software Metrics	22. Analysis and Design Methods	23. Validation and Verification	24. Use of Tools	25. Project Tracking and Control	26. Continuous Process Improvement	27. Project Termination	28. Post Performance Analysis	29. Reporting and Communication	30. Software Quality Assurance	31. Software Configuration Management	32. Legal Issues in Software	33. Summary	A. Supporting Organizations	B. Real World Projects	C. Creating the Business Plan	D. Understanding Systems Engineering	E. Distance Project Management	F. Project Artifact Templates	G. Joint Application Design In Use
Software configuration identification		•	•			•		•			•	•	•								•	
Software configuration control		•	•			•		•			•	•	•								•	
Software configuration status accounting		•	•			•		•		•	•	•	•								•	
Software configuration auditing		•	•			•		•			•	•	•								•	
Software release management and delivery		•	•			•		•		•	•	•	•								•	

TABLE 19–13
Map of SWEBOK to Quality Software Project Management (Part 4 of 4)

SWEBOK Knowledge Areas	19. Introduction to Software Engineering	20. Reliability	21. Software Metrics	22. Analysis and Design Methods	23. Validation and Verification	24. Use of Tools	25. Project Tracking and Control	26. Continuous Process Improvement	27. Project Termination	28. Post Performance Analysis	29. Reporting and Communication	30. Software Quality Assurance	31. Software Configuration Management	32. Legal Issues in Software	33. Summary	A. Supporting Organizations	B. Real World Projects	C. Creating the Business Plan	D. Understanding Systems Engineering	E. Distance Project Management	F. Project Artifact Templates	G. Joint Application Design In Use
	Executing						Controlling		Closing		Company-Wide Support					Appendices						
Software Engineering Management																						
Organizational management	•	•	•	•	•	•	•	•	•	•	•	•	•	•	•	•						
Process/project management			•		•	•					•	•	•	•	•	•						
Software engineering measurement			•			•	•	•			•	•	•			•						

(Continues)

TABLE 19-13 (Continued)
Map of SWEBOK to Quality Software Project Management (Part 4 of 4)

SWEBOK Knowledge Areas	Executing						Controlling		Closing		Company-Wide Support					Appendices						
	19. Introduction to Software Engineering	20. Reliability	21. Software Metrics	22. Analysis and Design Methods	23. Validation and Verification	24. Use of Tools	25. Project Tracking and Control	26. Continuous Process Improvement	27. Project Termination	28. Post Performance Analysis	29. Reporting and Communication	30. Software Quality Assurance	31. Software Configuration Management	32. Legal Issues in Software	33. Summary	A. Supporting Organizations	B. Real World Projects	C. Creating the Business Plan	D. Understanding Systems Engineering	E. Distance Project Management	F. Project Artifact Templates	G. Joint Application Design In Use
Software Engineering Process	•																					
Software engineering process concepts	•	•	•	•	•	•	•	•	•	•	•	•	•	•		•						
Process infrastructure	•																					
Process measurement	•		•			•	•	•														
Process definition	•	•	•	•	•	•	•	•	•	•	•	•	•	•	•							

(Continues)

TABLE 19-13 (Continued)
Map of SWEBOK to Quality Software Project Management (Part 4 of 4)

SWEBOK Knowledge Areas	19. Introduction to Software Engineering	20. Reliability	21. Software Metrics	22. Analysis and Design Methods	23. Validation and Verification	24. Use of Tools	25. Project Tracking and Control	26. Continuous Process Improvement	27. Project Termination	28. Post Performance Analysis	29. Reporting and Communication	30. Software Quality Assurance	31. Software Configuration Management	32. Legal Issues in Software	33. Summary	A. Supporting Organizations	B. Real World Projects	C. Creating the Business Plan	D. Understanding Systems Engineering	E. Distance Project Management	F. Project Artifact Templates	G. Joint Application Design In Use
	QSPM Chapters → Executing						Controlling		Closing		Company-Wide Support					Appendices						
Qualitative process analysis	•						•	•														
Process implementation and change	•										•	•	•	•								
Software Engineering Tools and Methods																			•			
Software Tools:																						
Software requirements tools				•		•					•		•							•	•	

(Continues)

TABLE 19-13 (Continued)
Map of SWEBOK to Quality Software Project Management (Part 4 of 4)

SWEBOK Knowledge Areas	QSPM Chapters — Executing						Controlling		Closing		Company-Wide Support					Appendices						
	19. Introduction to Software Engineering	20. Reliability	21. Software Metrics	22. Analysis and Design Methods	23. Validation and Verification	24. Use of Tools	25. Project Tracking and Control	26. Continuous Process Improvement	27. Project Termination	28. Post Performance Analysis	29. Reporting and Communication	30. Software Quality Assurance	31. Software Configuration Management	32. Legal Issues in Software	33. Summary	A. Supporting Organizations	B. Real World Projects	C. Creating the Business Plan	D. Understanding Systems Engineering	E. Distance Project Management	F. Project Artifact Templates	G. Joint Application Design In Use
Software design tools				•		•					•		•							•	•	
Software construction tools				•		•					•		•							•	•	
Software testing tools				•		•					•		•							•	•	
Software maintenance tools				•		•					•		•							•	•	
Software engineering process tools				•		•				•	•	•	•			•				•	•	

(Continues)

TABLE 19-13 (Continued)
Map of SWEBOK to Quality Software Project Management (Part 4 of 4)

SWEBOK Knowledge Areas	QSPM Chapters																					
	Executing						Controlling		Closing		Company-Wide Support					Appendices						
	19. Introduction to Software Engineering	20. Reliability	21. Software Metrics	22. Analysis and Design Methods	23. Validation and Verification	24. Use of Tools	25. Project Tracking and Control	26. Continuous Process Improvement	27. Project Termination	28. Post Performance Analysis	29. Reporting and Communication	30. Software Quality Assurance	31. Software Configuration Management	32. Legal Issues in Software	33. Summary	A. Supporting Organizations	B. Real World Projects	C. Creating the Business Plan	D. Understanding Systems Engineering	E. Distance Project Management	F. Project Artifact Templates	G. Joint Application Design In Use
Software quality tools				•		•					•		•							•	•	
Software configuration management tools				•		•					•		•							•	•	
Software engineering management tools				•		•					•		•							•	•	
Infrastructure support tools				•		•					•		•							•	•	
Miscellaneous tools issues				•		•					•		•							•	•	

(Continues)

TABLE 19–13 (Continued)
Map of SWEBOK to Quality Software Project Management (Part 4 of 4)

SWEBOK Knowledge Areas	QSPM Chapters — Executing						Controlling		Closing		Company-Wide Support					Appendices						
	19. Introduction to Software Engineering	20. Reliability	21. Software Metrics	22. Analysis and Design Methods	23. Validation and Verification	24. Use of Tools	25. Project Tracking and Control	26. Continuous Process Improvement	27. Project Termination	28. Post Performance Analysis	29. Reporting and Communication	30. Software Quality Assurance	31. Software Configuration Management	32. Legal Issues in Software	33. Summary	A. Supporting Organizations	B. Real World Projects	C. Creating the Business Plan	D. Understanding Systems Engineering	E. Distance Project Management	F. Project Artifact Templates	G. Joint Application Design In Use
Software Methods:																						
Heuristic methods		•				•		•				•										
Formal methods		•				•		•				•										
Prototyping methods		•				•		•				•										
Miscellaneous methods issues		•				•		•				•										
Software Quality																						
Software quality concepts	•	•				•	•	•			•	•	•									

(Continues)

TABLE 19–13 (Continued)
Map of SWEBOK to Quality Software Project Management (Part 4 of 4)

SWEBOK Knowledge Areas	Executing						Controlling		Closing		Company-Wide Support					Appendices						
	19. Introduction to Software Engineering	20. Reliability	21. Software Metrics	22. Analysis and Design Methods	23. Validation and Verification	24. Use of Tools	25. Project Tracking and Control	26. Continuous Process Improvement	27. Project Termination	28. Post Performance Analysis	29. Reporting and Communication	30. Software Quality Assurance	31. Software Configuration Management	32. Legal Issues in Software	33. Summary	A. Supporting Organizations	B. Real World Projects	C. Creating the Business Plan	D. Understanding Systems Engineering	E. Distance Project Management	F. Project Artifact Templates	G. Joint Application Design In Use
Definition and planning for quality	•	•				•	•	•			•	•	•									
Techniques requiring two or more people	•	•			•	•	•	•			•	•	•									
Support to other techniques	•	•				•	•	•			•	•	•									
Testing special to SQA or V&V	•	•			•	•	•	•			•	•	•									
Defect-finding techniques	•	•				•	•	•			•	•	•									
Measurement in software quality analysis	•	•	•			•	•	•			•	•	•									

Summary

As pleasurable and creative as the activity might be, individuals can no longer single-handedly build robust software applications. Software has become too pervasive and too critical in our lives and lifestyles to trust it to undisciplined processes or to developers working in isolation. Writing software has more often been referred to as an art or a craft than as a science or a discipline. While this has served in the past, the notion of developing software systems without a process today is as illogical as building a bridge without blueprints. Software engineering, the systematic, disciplined, quantifiable approach to development, is the body of knowledge that will guide developers to the level of quality necessary to sustain the thousands of applications that will be written and maintained in the future—applications upon which our lives literally depend. The model of code-test-repeat is insufficient for all modern systems—manufacturing, communications, medical—all categories of projects.

While software is a long way from achieving the status of the laws of physics, it is not so far away from mirroring the discipline of engineering. Software engineering processes may be found in the recently derived IEEE software engineering body of knowledge (SWEBOK), the Software Engineering Institute's capability maturity model (SEI CMM), and the 34 competencies of quality software project management.

Problems for Review

1. List five specific software engineering tasks you can perform to move from CMM Level 1 to Level 2.
2. When, in the CMM maturity levels, is an organization ready for CASE tools?
3. Where in the SWEBOK would you account for determination of your project's life cycle model?
4. How does the SWEBOK map to IEEE 1074?
5. How does client mix and product market area impact your organization's moving to higher maturity levels in the software development process?

Visit the Case Study

xTRemeObjectMaker has been adopted by the BSD as its CASE tool of choice for building all new software systems. Everyone views this as great news. Mr. Lu and Ms. Patel came to an agreement that the CRM will get a five-year, no-cost license to use xTRemeObjectMaker if the CRM accepts your corporation as the final developer of ARRS. In order to clinch this deal, Ms. Patel has committed that she will send one of your U.S.-based team members to

Beijing to install the tool, train the CRM developers, and help them decide on the first program to build.

What is the impact on your schedule for providing this resource?

What are the chances of success in the CRM using xTRemeObjectMaker? Be very specific because if there is a *failure* it will *not have been caused by either the tool or marketing*.

Citations

[1]Software Engineering Conference sponsored by the NATO Science Committee, Peter Naur, ed., p. 13, Oct. 1968.

[2]Bauer, Fritz L. (1972). "Software Engineering." *Information Processing*.

[3]Pressman, Roger S. (2001). *Software Engineering: A Practitioner's Approach*, 5th ed. McGraw-Hill.

[4]*www.SWEBOK.org*.

[5]See note 1.

[6]IEEE Std 610.12-1990, *IEEE Standard Glossary of Software Engineering Terminology.*

[7]See note 6.

[8]*history.acusd.edu/gen/recording/notes.html*. Steve Schoenherr (2001). *Recording Technology History*.

[9]*www.best.com/~wilson/faq/*. alt.folklore.computers, List of Frequently Asked Questions.

[10]Bourque, Pierre, et al. (1999). "The Guide to the Software Engineering Body of Knowledge." *IEEE Software*, November/December, pp. 35–44.

[11]See note 10.

Web Pages for Further Information

mingo.info-science.uiowa.edu/soft-eng/. A World Wide Web virtual library of software engineering.

sel.gsfc.nasa.gov/. The Software Engineering Laboratory (SEL) is an organization sponsored by the National Aeronautics and Space Administration/Goddard Space Flight Center (NASA/GSFC) and created to investigate the effectiveness of software engineering technologies when applied to the development of applications software.

sourceforge.net/. SourceForge is a free service to Open Source developers offering easy access to the best in CVS, mailing lists, bug tracking, message boards/forums, task management, site hosting, permanent file archival, full backups, and total web-based administration.

sunset.usc.edu/. The Center was founded in June 1993 by Dr. Barry W. Boehm for the purpose of providing an environment for research and teaching in the areas of large-scale software design and development processes, generic and domain-specific software architectures, software engineering tools and environments, cooperative system design, and the economics of software engineering.

www.cs.queensu.ca/Software-Engineering/. These are the World-Wide Web archives for the USENET newsgroup comp.software-eng, including the Frequently-Asked Questions (FAQ) postings.

www.cs.umd.edu/projects/SoftEng/tame/. The Experimental Software Engineering Group (ESEG) of the University of Maryland views the study of software engineering as a laboratory science. Specific research projects are centered on formalizing various aspects of the quality improvement paradigm (QIP), the experience factory (EF), and the goal/question/metric approach (GQM). The QIP is aimed at building descriptive models of software processes, products, and other forms of experience, experimenting with and analyzing these models in order to build improvement-oriented, packaged, prescriptive models. The EF is an organizational approach for packaging reusable software experiences and supplying them to projects and building core competencies in software.

www.sei.cmu.edu/. The Software Engineering Institute (SEI) was established in 1984 by Congress as a federally-funded research and development center with a broad charter to address the transition of software engineering technology. The SEI is sponsored by the U.S. Department of Defense (DoD) through the Office of the Under-Secretary of Defense for Acquisition, Technology, and Logistics [OUSD (AT&L)]. The SEI has established itself as a trusted partner with industry organizations and government agencies in the development, acquisition, and support of software-intensive systems.

www.spmn.com/. SPMN Mission: To seek out proven industry and government software best practices and convey them to managers of large-scale DoD software-intensive acquisition programs. Applying extensive "in the trenches" experience, the SPMN enables program managers to achieve project success and deliver quality systems on schedule and on budget.

Suggested Readings

Albrecht, Allan J., and John E. Gaffney (1983). "Software Function, Source Lines of Code, and Development Effort Prediction: A Software Science Validation." *IEEE Transactions of Software Engineering,* SE-9(6):639–648.

Basili, Victor R. (1984). "A Methodology for Collecting Valid Software Engineering Data." *IEEE Transactions on Software Engineering,* SE-10(6):728–738.

Basili, Victor R. (1990). "Viewing Maintenance as Reuse-Oriented Software Development." *IEEE Software,* January, pp. 19–25.

Basili, Victor R., and R.W. Selby (1987). "Comparing the Effectiveness of Software Testing Strategies." *IEEE Transactions on Software Engineering,* SE-13(12):1278–1296.

Bowan, Jonathan P., and Michael G. Hinchley (1995). "Ten Commandments of Formal Methods." *Computer,* 28(4):56–63.

Brooks, Fred P. (1987). "No Silver Bullet: Essence and Accidents of Software Engineering." *IEEE Software,* April, pp. 10–19.

Dart, Susan A., et al. (1987). "Software Development Environments." *IEEE Computer,* 20(11):18–28.

Denning, Peter J. (1992). "What is Software Quality?" *Communications of the ACM,* January, pp. 13–15.

Fagan, Michael E. (1976). "Design and Code Inspections to Reduce Errors in Program Development." *IBM Systems Journal*, 15(3):185–211.

Fagan, Michael E. (1986). "Advances in Software Inspections." *IEEE Transactions on Software Engineering*, SE-15(7):744–751.

Hall, Anthony (1990). "Seven Myths of Formal Methods." *IEEE Software*, September, pp. 11–20.

Humphrey, Watts S., and W.L. Sweet (1987). "A Method for Assessing the Software Engineering Capability of Contractors." *Technical Report # CMU/SEI-87-TR-23*, Software Engineering Institute, Carnegie Mellon University, September 1987.

Kitchenham, Barbara, and Shari Lawrence Pfleeger (1996). "Software Quality: The Elusive Target." *IEEE Software*, January, pp. 12–21.

McCabe, Tom (1976). "A Complexity Measure." *IEEE Transactions on Software Engineering*, SE-2(4):308–320.

McFarlan, Warren F. (1974). "Portfolio Approach to Information Systems." *Harvard Business Review.* (1,2):142–150.

Manley, John H. (1984). "CASE: Foundation for Software Factories." *COMPCON Proceedings*, September, pp. 84–91.

Mills, Harlan (1976). "Software Development." *IEEE Transactions on Software Engineering*, SE-2(4):265–273.

Mills, Harlan D., et al. (1987). "Cleanroom Software Engineering." *IEEE Software*, IEEE, 5(5):19–24.

Neumann, Peter G. (1986). "On Hierarchical Design of Computer Systems for Critical Applications." *IEEE Transactions on Software Engineering*, SE-12(9):905–920.

Parnas, David L. (1972). "On the Criteria to Be Used on Decomposing Systems into Modules." *Communications of the ACM*, 12(12):1053–1058.

Paulk, Mark C. (1994). "A Comparison of ISO 9001 and the Capability Maturity Model for Software." *Technical Report # CMU/SEI-94-TR-012*, Software Engineering Institute, Carnegie Mellon University, July 1994.

Pressman, Roger S. (1998). "Can Internet-Based Applications Be Engineered?" *IEEE Software*, September, pp. 104–110.

Symons, Charles R. (1988). "Function Point Analysis: Difficulties and Improvements." *IEEE Transactions on Software Engineering*, 14(1).

Tomayko, James E. (1986). "Support Materials for Software Configuration Management." SEI-SM-4-1.0, Software Engineering Institute, Carnegie Mellon University, September 1986.

Wasserman, Anthony I. (1982). "Rapid Prototyping of Interactive Information Systems." *Software Engineering Notes*, 7(5):171–180.

Wing, Janet M. (1990). "A Specifier's Introduction to Formal Methods." *Computer*, 23(9):8–24.

Wirth, Nicholas (1971). "Program Development by Stepwise Refinement." *Communications of the ACM*, 14(4):221–227.

Wohlin, Claes and Per Runeson (1994). "Certification of Software Components." *IEEE Transactions on Software Engineering*, 9(6):494–499.

Reliability

Software reliability has been listed as a key quality measure for as long as software engineering has been defined. Figure 20–1 represents the quality factor topology as presented by McCall, Richards, and Walters in their 1977 work.[1] Throughout the chapters in this practitioner's guide, these factors are discussed. Particular attention is paid to software reliability because of its high visibility to the end-user. Product revision and transition quality factors are important to the software development and maintenance teams. Product operation factors are customer-facing and cause the most customer pain when they are deficient.

Using the IEEE Standard Glossary of Software Engineering Terminology, *software reliability* is defined as the ability of a system or component to perform its required functions under stated conditions for a specified period of time.[2] Software reliability is also an important factor affecting system reliability. It differs from hardware reliability in that it reflects the design perfection of the product, rather than manufacturing perfection. The high complexity of software is the major contributing factor of software reliability problems. Software reliability is not a function of time, as the industrial and manufacturing reliability modelers show with their traditional bathtub curves as in Figure 20–2. Measurement of software reliability is still in its infancy, but without adequate measurement the data does not exist to execute the extensive statistical models required of real reliability analysis. No good quantitative methods

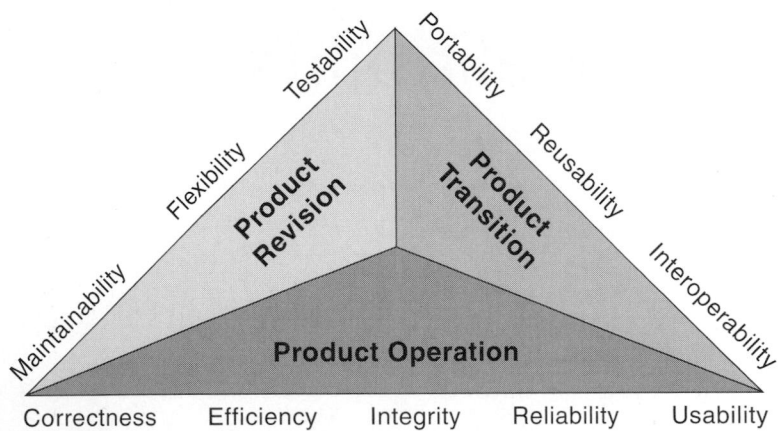

FIGURE 20–1
Software Quality Factors

have been developed to represent software reliability without excessive limitations. Various approaches can be used to improve the reliability of software, however, it is hard to balance development time and budget with the perceived high cost of software reliability.

Unlike hardware, software doesn't "wear out," but is delivered "broken." Determining and planning for the "bugs" that will inevitably be released in the software product are discussed in Chapter 23, "Validation and Verification," Chapter 26, "Continuous Process Improvement," and Chapter 30, "Software Quality Assurance." Figure 20–3 shows this representation of the notional software bathtub curve. The defects never spike as much as for hardware, but they never go to zero. The project manager must understand how much to invest in reliability.

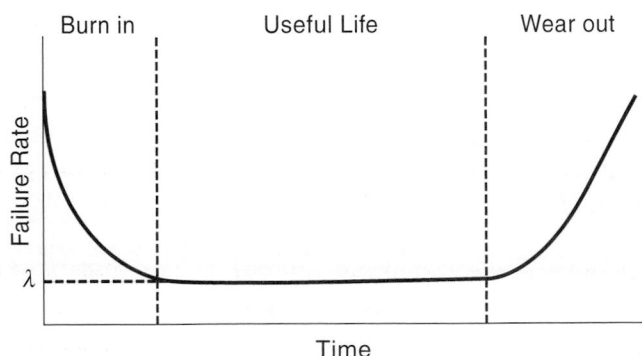

FIGURE 20–2
Hardware Reliability Bathtub Curve

The methods for determining how much is enough were discussed in Chapter 18, "Determining Project Risks." Risk and reliability must be addressed together. Cost-effective application of the principles of software reliability engineering are directed by what risks reliability engineering mitigate. If the use of reliability is not a mitigating risk, there is no reasonable purpose for incurring the additional project cost.

The majority of software reliability problems are not life threatening like the Therac-25[3] or the Patriot Missile[4] problems. The majority of reliability problems that affect the greatest number of people are in the area of scoring standardized tests. "The testing industry is coming off its three most problem-plagued years. Its missteps have affected millions of students who took standardized proficiency tests in at least 20 states."[5] The impact of a hard-to-find software error can have lasting effects on students, teachers, and administrators when standardized tests are involved. It is not only the test scoring that is at risk, but the more subjective calculations of equating—the process that allows test scores to be compared year after year.

> As it turned out, CTB—despite its assurances to Indiana and others—had done an incomplete job of reviewing test data. When a much larger sample was reviewed, a programming error surfaced.
>
> The error had—erroneously—made the current test appear easier than the previous year's. To make the tests equal in difficulty, the computer had then compensated by making it harder for some students to do as well as they had last time. The error did not change students' right and wrong answers, but it did affect their comparative percentile scores.[6]

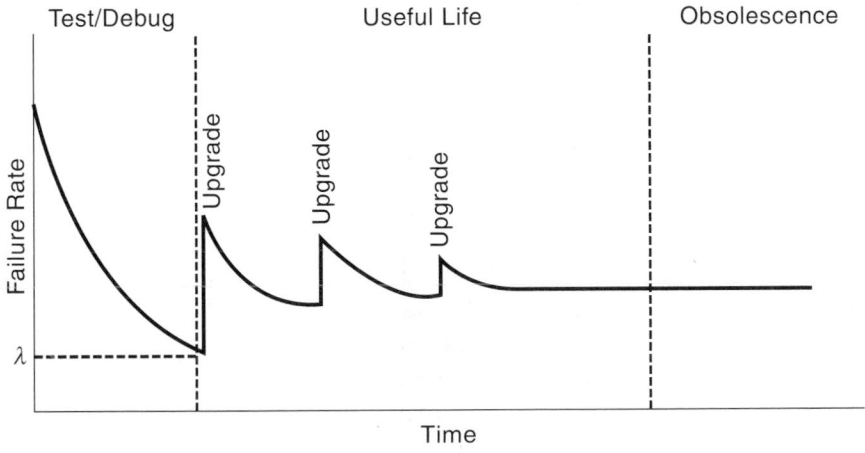

FIGURE 20–3
Software Reliability Bathtub Curve

This lack of software reliability caused administrators to be fired, 40,000 students to have to go to summer school, hundreds of thousands of dollars earmarked for education improvement to be misspent and hundreds of students not promoted to the next grade-level because of perceived low reading skills.

This chapter will focus on four approaches to achieving highly reliable software:

1. Fault forecasting—reliability models, historic data analysis, failure data collection, operational environment profiling
2. Fault prevention—formal methods, software reuse, construction tools
3. Fault removal—formal inspections, verification, and validation
4. Fault tolerance—monitoring techniques, decision verification, redundancy, exception

Where We Are in the Product Development Life Cycle

Software reliability must be planned for in the initial project phases establishing the project environment and planning the project management activities. The process of determining the reliability of the software under construction requires large amounts of data to be gathered from the project metrics system. Chapter 21 of this guide, "Software Metrics," describes the activities of metrics collection and analysis. Metrics are generated throughout the life cycle by all of the engineering activities. The four software reliability approaches are executed across the life cycle phases as shown by the heavy lines in Figure 20–4. Fault forecasting occurs through system exploration and requirements. Fault prevention occurs through requirements, design, and implementation. Fault removal occurs through design, implementation, and installation. Fault tolerance begins at implementation and extends through final product retirement.

Table 20–1 is a further mapping of the four reliability approaches to the life cycle phase activities. These activities will be discussed in detail in each approach subsection of this chapter.

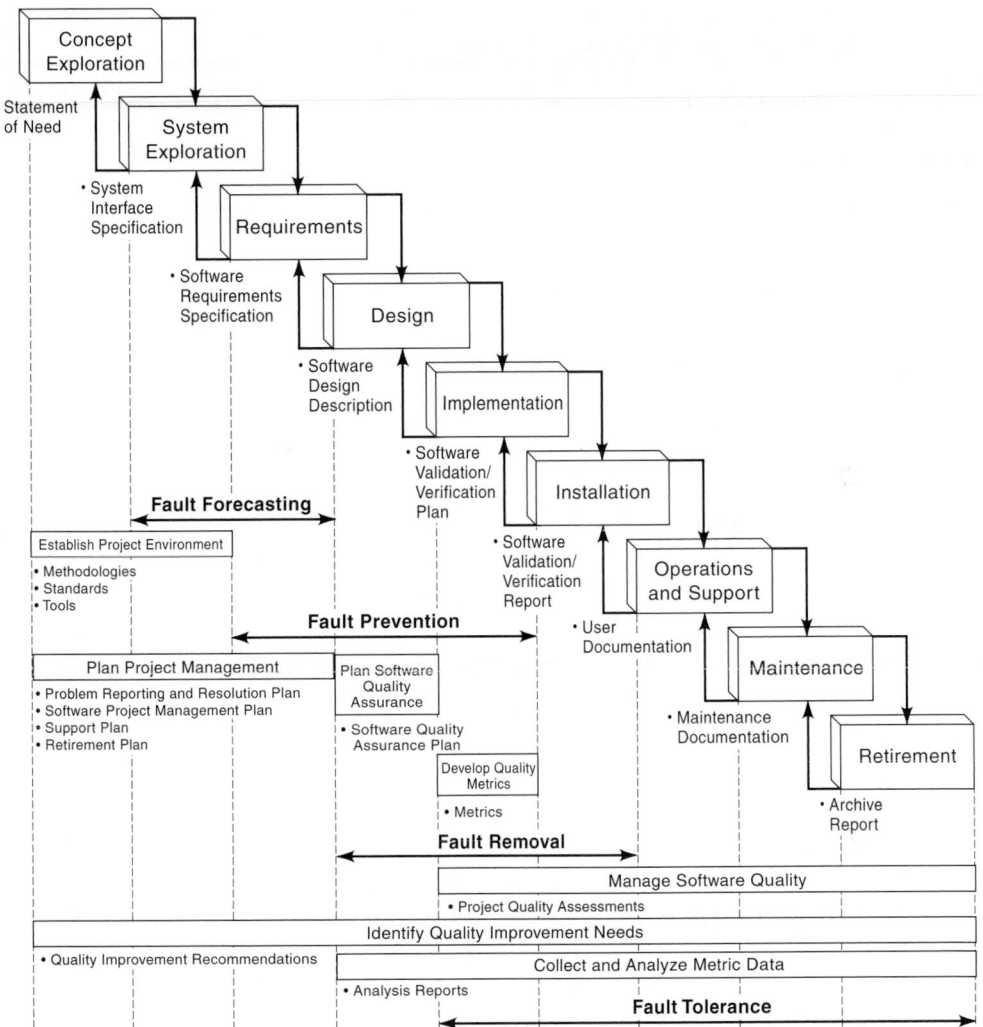

FIGURE 20–4

Software Reliability in the Product Development Life Cycle

TABLE 20–1
Software Reliability Approaches Mapped to Life Cycle Phase Activities

	Forecasting	Prevention	Removal	Tolerance
System Exploration and Requirements				
Determine functional profile	X	X		
Define and classify failures	X	X		
Identify customer reliability needs	X	X		
Conduct trade-off studies	X	X		
Set reliability objectives	X	X		
Design and Implementation				
Allocate reliability among components		X	X	X
Engineer to meet reliability objectives		X	X	X
Focus resources based on functional profile		X	X	X
Manage fault introduction and propagation		X	X	X
Measure reliability of acquired software		X	X	X
Installation				
Determine operational profile			X	X
Conduct reliability growth testing			X	X
Track testing progress			X	X
Project additional testing needed			X	X

(Continues)

TABLE 20–1 (Continued)
Software Reliability Approaches Mapped to Life Cycle Phase Activities

	Forecasting	Prevention	Removal	Tolerance
Certify reliability objectives are met			X	X
Operations, Support, and Maintenance				
Project post-release staff needs				X
Monitor field reliability versus objectives				X
Track customer satisfaction with reliability				X
Time new feature introduction by monitoring reliability				X
Guide product and process improvement with reliability measures				X

Chapter 20 Relation to the 34 Competencies _____

The following three of the 34 competencies described in this practitioner's guide apply especially to software reliability:

Product Development Techniques

1. **Assessing processes**—Specifically assesses the reliability goals of the risk management plan and the processes within the product development life cycle. This adds to the overall organization's approach to continuous process improvement.

Project Management Skills

16. **Managing risk**—The only reason to invest in the high cost of software reliability processes is to mitigate risk.

19. **Metrics selection**—The use of the reliability tools described in this chapter require a well-designed and reliable set of project, process, and product metrics.

Learning Objectives for Chapter 20 _____

Upon completion of this chapter, the reader should be able to:

- Apply basic software reliability concepts;
- Define the benefits of software reliability engineering for specific projects;
- Define the specific data needed to use valid statistical techniques in software reliability engineering;
- Incorporate reliability with an overall organization and project metrics program;
- Calculate expected failures given historic error information;
- Select tools for statistical analysis of reliability data;
- Use the operational profile in calculating reliability.

Software Reliability Terminology_____

Software engineering terminology has become very much like Alice in Lewis Carroll's *Through the Looking Glass*:

> "When I use a word," Humpty Dumpty said, in a rather scornful tone, "it means just what I choose it to mean—neither more nor less."
>
> "The question is," said Alice, "whether you can make words mean so many different things."

Software engineers and project managers have used and misused the terms for *fault, error, problem*, and others. With respect to software reliability, the following terms with definitions will be used. They are standard and accepted throughout the industry.

Defect is a problem found in a later phase or process than when it was introduced.

Error is a problem found in the current phase or process.

Fail-safe is the property of avoiding damage during a failure.

Fault-tolerant is the property of being able to recover from certain errors and keep operating.

Problem is a deviation from specifications or expected results.

Process error is an incorrect output of a process and is, therefore, a resulting incorrect state or condition.

Process failure is an event whereby a faulty resource used by the process produces an error in its output, which is eventually observed.

Process fault resides in the resources used in a process and is viewed as an input to a process. It represents an incorrect state or condition of the system to which the process belongs.

Robustness is the property of being tolerant of bad inputs.

Software failures originate with design defects/errors (system and software), coding defects/errors, clerical mistakes, debugging inadequacies, and testing mistakes.

Fault Forecasting

Fault forecasting is the predictive approach to software reliability engineering. Forecasting is a front-end product development life cycle exercise. It is done during system exploration and requirements definition. Mature development organizations use fault forecasting as part of their front-end project/product evaluation process. The only way to have even a slight amount of accuracy in the predictive models is through access to appropriate historic data. Reliability models, historic data analysis, failure data collection, and operational environment profiling are key activities in this approach. Table 20–2 identifies the steps in fault forecasting.

TABLE 20–2
Fault Forecasting Life Cycle Activities

	Forecasting
System Exploration and Requirements	
Determine functional profile	X
Define and classify failures	X
Identify customer reliability needs	X
Conduct trade-off studies	X
Set reliability objectives	X

The first step in fault forecasting is to determine the functional profile. By keeping track of the state of transitions from module to module and function to function we may learn exactly where a system is fragile. This information coupled with the functional profile will tell us just how reliable the system will be when we use it as specified. Programs make transitions from module to module as they execute. These transitions may be observed. Transitions to program modules that are fault-laden will result in an increased probability of failure. We can model these transitions as a stochastic process. Ultimately, by developing a mathematical description for the behavior of the software as it transitions from one module to another driven by the functionalities that it is performing, we can describe the reliability of the functionality. The software system is the sum of its functionalities. If we can know the reliability of the functionalities and how the system apportions its time among these functionalities, we can then know the reliability of the system.

The next step is to *define* and *classify* failures. As defined previously, software failures originate with design defects/errors (system and software), coding defects/errors, clerical mistakes, debugging inadequacies, and testing mistakes. The definition of failures involves the failure source. The classification of failures provides the severity level. A classification developed by Boris Beizer has an appropriate granularity:[7]

1. **Mild**—Symptoms offend us aesthetically.
2. **Moderate**—Outputs are misleading or redundant.
3. **Annoying**—It causes dehumanizing system behavior (e.g., money machine refuses to cash your paycheck).
4. **Very serious**—Instead of losing your paycheck, the system credits it to another account.
5. **Extreme**—The problem is not limited to a few users.
6. **Intolerable**—Long-term, unrecoverable corruption of database occurs.
7. **Catastrophic**—The decision to shut down is taken out of our hands; the system fails.
8. **Infectious**—It corrupts other systems even though it does not fail itself.

Once the matrix of failure sources and classification is completed, the metrics of failure data should be tracked as in Table 20–3. In each cell of the table are the totals of the failures from historic information for similar projects and products.

TABLE 20–3
Failure Sources and Class

Class	Design defects/ errors	Coding defects/ errors	Clerical mistakes	Debugging inadequacies	Testing mistakes
Mild					
Moderate					
Annoying					
Very serious					
Extreme					
Intolerable					
Catastrophic					
Infectious					

Identifying customer reliability needs is the next step. These needs would have been previously identified and documented in the SRS, as described in Chapter 16 of this guide. The reliability needs for the customer must be stated in measurable terms. Although all requirements should be measureable and testable, reliability requirements absolutely, positively, must have numbers attached. The following are examples of adequate reliability requirement statements:

1. The launch system mission reliability shall be at least 0.999 at 95 percent confidence from launch commit to payload separation.

2. The satellite system mission reliability shall be at least 0.999 at 95 percent confidence for a period of 15 years from payload separation.

3. The avionics system will have 500 mean flight hours between critical failures.

4. A built-in self-test will detect an inoperable missile at a 60 percent probability.

5. A built-in self-test will mistake operable for inoperable at a less than 1 percent probability.

6. Mean-time to repair operational software is 30 minutes or less.

7. Mean-maximum-corrective-time is 60 minutes at the 90th percentile.

8. Built-in self-test maximum completion time is 20 seconds.

9. Mean-time to load full software and execute full internal self-test is 10 minutes.

10. Median-time to update one online page of documentation is 30 minutes.

Conduct trade-off studies is Step 4 in fault forecasting. Using the client functional profile and the failure classification information from previous systems, the specified requirements are analyzed to determine whether the historic data supports the goals. Trade-offs are analyzed to determine the probability of reaching the reliability goals specified in the requirements. If there is no historic data for like products and no analogous systems to analyze, the probability of reaching an artificially set reliability level is extremely low. At this point the project manager needs to develop extensive system models to determine the probable reliability ranges for the new product. Tools such as formal methods would be applied to the reliability requirements for a mathematical proof of the most critical subsystems. This is a very expensive process and should only be used when there is no source of historic reliability data.

Step 5 is to set reliability objectives based on the results of the trade-off studies. This final set of reliability objectives is fed back into the requirements process to modify the requirements. This step allows the information gathered and the analyses made to feed back into the requirements specification process. The reliability objectives/requirements will be used to validate the system reliability and gain user acceptance.

Fault Prevention

Fault prevention includes iterative refinement of the system requirements and engineering software specifications with modeling, verifiable design techniques, and best-of-breed coding practices. Prevention occurs during the product development phases of a project where the requirements, design, and implementation are occurring. At this point in the product development the project team has finished exploring and initially planning, and the team is now executing. Fault prevention is an active part of the development process, not a mere passive recording effort. The first section of fault prevention is system exploration and requirements, as described previously. The initial steps are required for analysis of the reliability requirements and objectives no matter which approach is taken for reliability.

The second major piece of fault prevention approach is design and implementation. Focusing on design and implementation first causes the project team to allocate reliability among components. Chapter 22, "Analysis and Design Methods," discusses several methods for allocation of quality attributes to components. The design process is where the components to be built are identified. Techniques of reducing coupling and increasing cohesion within and between modules are ways to increase reliability of components. Best practices in design, whether structured or object-oriented, must be adopted to have any hope of building reliable software products.

During the early phases of the software development life cycle, reliability objectives focus on prevention. Table 20–4 shows the subprocesses of the major front-end life cycle phases that support prevention.

TABLE 20–4
Fault Prevention Life Cycle Activities

	Prevention
System Exploration and Requirements	
Determine functional profile	X
Define and classify failures	X
Identify customer reliability needs	X
Conduct trade-off studies	X
Set reliability objectives	X
Design and Implementation	
Allocate reliability among components	X
Engineer to meet reliability objectives	X
Focus resources based on functional profile	X
Manage fault introduction and propagation	X
Measure reliability of acquired software	X

The reliability objectives that were previously set and documented in the reliability plan must be engineered into the modules during design. Engineering, like quality, can neither be tested in, nor added on. The project manager must focus resources based on the functional profile. During the system exploration and the justification for using costly reliability methods, a functional profile of the system under development was completed. This profile needs to be used and validated during the design process.

The only way to actively prevent faults is through the management of fault introduction and propagation. Reviews and inspections are the traditional way of actively reducing errors generated in one phase from escaping as defects into the next phase. Another critical activity is to measure the reliability of acquired software. As more Internet-based tools are used and shared libraries are made accessible, software of uncertain pedigree (SOUP) begins to become part of the product. The project team needs a process for verifying, validating, accepting, and measuring the reliability of SOUP components. This must be a formal process with the same level of tracking and configuration present for built-from-scratch software product components. Software reuse provides dramatic increases in developer productivity. It also can be a minefield of defects and hidden problems.

Fault Removal

The old adage "an ounce of prevention is worth a pound of cure" is nowhere more true than in fault removal. Isolating a fault once it is incorporated into a delivered system is from 10 to 100 times more costly than preventing it in the first place. It has been the authors' experience that on a commercial, multimedia software product included as part of Microsoft® Windows™, the cost to isolate and remove a fault consisting of three lines of assemble code is $60,000. The cost to have prevented this fault was one code inspection lasting two hours with four participants. Eight person-hours would have cost less than $1,000. The cost to prevent was determined from the time it took to isolate the fault once discovered in the released operating system and analyzing the development process of the driver code at fault. The final code level inspection was skipped because of time pressures for this driver release to Microsoft®.

Fault removal begins at the first opportunity that faults injected into the product are discovered. At the design phase, requirements phase products are passed to the design team. This is the first opportunity to discover faults in the requirements models and specifications. Fault removal extends into implementation and through installation. For a product being developed for use by an internal client, such as a new human resources system or an electronic commerce Web page, the installation may be just one point in time. For commercial products, the installation occurs every time a new purchaser breaks the shrink-wrap and begins the installation process on their personal computer or company server. The project and product manager must be aware of the temporal nature of the installation phase and gauge their reliability efforts accordingly.

The first portion of fault removal is design and implementation, as described previously in the section on fault prevention. The second portion, installation, begins with work that should have been done during the requirements phase. Realistically, project managers do not need an operational profile defined until there is a partially functioning system to operate. This can be done earlier in the product development life cycle through the use of prototypes.

Building on work done in functional profiling, the next step in the installation portion is to conduct *reliability growth testing*. This is also referred to as load testing. Based on the functions to be performed, functional profile, the way those functions are executed, and operational profile, a set of testing scenarios are defined and executed that progressively push the system past its defined operational regime. The goal of reliability growth testing is to determine the mix of loads at which the system will break. This is a formal process where tracking of testing progress is critical. The results of the tests are analyzed and used to recalibrate the models used in reliability forecasting early in the project. One of the duties of a project manager is to support continuous process improvement. Taking data from one project and using it to refine the tools and techniques for future projects supports the organization's ability to learn.

During the middle phases of the software development life cycle, reliability efforts focus on defect removal. Table 20–5 shows the subprocesses of the major design, implementation, and installation life cycle phases that support defect removal.

TABLE 20–5
Fault Removal Life Cycle Activities

	Removal
Design and Implementation	
Allocate reliability among components	X
Engineer to meet reliability objectives	X
Focus resources based on functional profile	X
Manage fault introduction and propagation	X
Measure reliability of acquired software	X
Installation	
Determine operational profile	X
Conduct reliability growth testing	X
Track testing progress	X
Project additional testing needed	X
Certify reliability objectives are met	X

The projection of additional testing needed is a result of the analysis of the testing data. Load or stress testing may not be adequate to certify that all reliability objectives are met. Some modules may have to go through white- or black-box testing again. Regression testing may have to be increased and expanded. At the end of the fault removal, the project manager must be satisfied with the results and certify that reliability objectives have been met.

Fault Tolerance

Fault tolerance is the intrinsic ability of a software system to continuously deliver service to its users in the presence of faults. This approach to software reliability addresses how to keep a system functioning after the faults in the delivered system manifest themselves. The implementation of software fault tolerance is dramatically different from that of hardware. In a hardware fault tolerant system, a second or third complete set of hardware is running in parallel, shadowing the execution of the main processor. All of the mass-storage and mass-memory devices are mirrored so that if one fails, another immediately picks up the application. This is addressing the faults shown in the bathtub curve—hardware wearing out.

Trying to address software fault tolerance in the same fashion—parallel operation of the same software on a different processor—only results in the second copy of the exact same software failing a millisecond after the first copy. Simply running a separate copy of the application does nothing for software fault tolerance.

From the middle phases of the software development life cycle through product delivery and maintenance, reliability efforts focus on fault tolerance. Table 20–6 shows the subprocesses of the major design, implementation, installation, delivery, and maintenance life cycle phases that support fault tolerance.

Fault tolerance begins at the implementation product development phase and extends through installation, operations and support, and maintenance to final product retirement. As long as the software is running in a production mode, the fault tolerance approach to reliability is useful.

Design and implementation and installation have been discussed in the fault removal approach to software reliability. In fault tolerance, *operations, support,* and *maintenance* are added to complete this approach to software reliability. Fault tolerance is a follow-on to fault removal. All of the processes used in fault removal are used in this approach. The differences are in the focus on the product life cycle after installation. The projection of post-release staff needs can only be done with reference to historic information from previous products. The organization needs to have an available database of faults that were discovered in other products after installation. This database of faults and the effort taken to manage and repair them is used to estimate how much post-release effort will be required on the just-released product. Using the historic metrics on faults discovered by the development phase and the

TABLE 20–6
Fault Tolerance Life Cycle Activities

	Tolerance
Design and Implementation	
Allocate reliability among components	X
Engineer to meet reliability objectives	X
Focus resources based on functional profile	X
Manage fault introduction and propagation	X
Measure reliability of acquired software	X
Installation	
Determine operational profile	X
Conduct reliability growth testing	X
Track testing progress	X
Project additional testing needed	X
Certify reliability objectives are met	X
Operations, Support, and Maintenance	
Project post-release staff needs	X
Monitor field reliability versus objectives	X
Track customer satisfaction with reliability	X
Time new feature introduction by monitoring reliability	X
Guide product and process improvement with reliability measures	X

relative size of the new product compared to others, a quick estimate can be made of faults remaining and effort required to fix the new product.

In order to provide a set of data for future products, the project or product manager must monitor field reliability versus reliability objectives. This is tied into the tracking of customer satisfaction with reliability objectives. The end-user is the best source of reliability information on the software product. This is where fault tolerance predictions meet the reality of the real world. End-users can neither be predicted nor directed. Therefore, estimates and assumptions made early in fault forecasting can only be validated through the fault tolerance approach to reliability.

The project/product manager must time new feature introduction by monitoring reliability. It is not a good idea to release new features to customers while known faults still reside in the software product. Combining the release of new feature sets with fault-fixes is an appropriate practice for software product organizations. Guiding product and process improvement with reliability measures feeds the information gathered from customer experience back into product fault removal and continuous development process improvement. Reliability measures are expensive to institute. Their results must be captured and fed back into the learning organization.

Reliability Tools

The basis of all reliability tools is statistical analysis—any tools with the ability to analyze data sets and rudimentary statistical techniques. Each of the software reliability approaches has an appropriate tool set:

Fault forecasting—reliability models, historic data analysis, failure data collection, functional profiling, operational environment profiling;

Fault prevention—formal methods, software reuse, construction tools;

Fault removal—formal inspections, verification and validation;

Fault tolerance—monitoring techniques, decision verification, redundancy, exception conditions.

The goal of this chapter is not to be a tool guide to reliability engineering. Michael Lyu's 1996 book, *Handbook of Software Reliability Engineering*, is the definitive guide to this field.[8] The goal here is to enumerate the skills needed on a project team in order to successfully use the tools available. A project manager needs to either have these statistical skills or have an experienced team member available before attempting to use commercially available reliability models and statistical methods:

1. Notations
   - Discrete random variables
   - Continuous random variables
   - Conditional probabilities
   - Conditional probability density functions
   - Stochastic processes

2. Reliability theory
   - Time-to-failure relationships
   - Failure rate
   - Mean-time-to-failure
   - Failure intensity
3. Analytical methods
   - Combinatorial models
   - Markov models
   - Markov reward analysis
   - Birth-death process
   - Poisson processes
4. Statistical techniques
   - Parameter estimation
   - Point estimation
   - Interval estimation
   - Distribution characterization
   - Empirical distribution
   - Distribution function fitting
   - Chi-square test
   - Kolmogorov-Smirnov test
   - Multivariate analysis
   - Correlation analysis
   - Factor analysis
   - Cluster analysis

Software Reliability Plan

The following is a simple outline for a software reliability plan derived from sets of plans published by IEEE, SEI, and ISO. The plan is kept to a minimum and is used as a companion to the project software risk plan. Software reliability is expensive to institute in a software development organization. Therefore, the reliability plan must address the specific risks mitigated and the cost of this mitigation. The impact on the project's return on investment must be identified and fed forward into the overall software project plan.

1. Executive summary of product reliability needs
2. Reliability definitions, acronyms and abbreviations, and references
3. Relationship to risk management plan
    a. Specific risk(s) mitigated
    b. Project budget savings
    c. Product reliability impact
    d. Description of reliability approach applicability
        1. Fault forecasting
        2. Fault prevention
        3. Fault removal
        4. Fault tolerance
4. Fault forecasting approach
    a. Functional profile definition
    b. Fault definitions
    c. Fault failure classification scheme
    d. Customer reliability needs
    e. Trade-off studies
    f. Defined product reliability objectives
5. Fault prevention approach
    a. Functional profile definition
    b. Fault definitions
    c. Fault failure classification scheme
    d. Customer reliability needs
    e. Trade-off studies
    f. Defined product reliability objectives
    g. Reliability allocation among design components
    h. Engineering process to meet reliability objectives
    i. Resources plan based on functional profile
    j. Fault introduction and propagation management plan
    k. Acquired software reliability measurement plan
6. Fault removal approach
    a. Reliability allocation among design components
    b. Engineering process to meet reliability objectives

    c. Resources plan based on functional profile

    d. Fault introduction and propagation management plan

    e. Acquired software reliability measurement plan

    f. Operational profile defined

    g. Reliability growth testing plan

    h. Testing progress tracking plan

    i. Additional testing plan

    j. Reliability objectives certification process

7. Fault tolerance approach

    a. Reliability allocation among design components

    b. Engineering process to meet reliability objectives

    c. Resources plan based on functional profile

    d. Fault introduction and propagation management plan

    e. Acquired software reliability measurement plan

    f. Operational profile defined

    g. Reliability growth testing plan

    h. Testing progress tracking plan

    i. Additional testing plan

    j. Reliability objectives certification process

    k. Project post-release staff needs

    l. Monitor field reliability versus objectives

    m. Track customer satisfaction with reliability

    n. Time new feature introduction by monitoring reliability

    o. Guide product and process improvement with reliability measures

8. Reliability plan approval process

Summary

Software reliability has been listed as a key quality measure for as long as software engineering has been defined. Throughout the chapters in this practitioner's guide the authors have focused on the "-ilities" of software: maintainability, flexibility, testability, portability, reusability, and so on. This chapter paid particular attention to software reliability because of its high visibility to, and immediate impact on the end-user. Product revision and transition quality factors are important to the software development and maintenance teams. Product operation factors are customer-facing and cause the most customer pain when they are deficient.

Unlike hardware, software doesn't "wear out." But, it is delivered "broken." Determining and planning for the toleration of "bugs" that will inevitably be released in the software product are discussed in Chapter 23, 26, and 30. The project manager must understand how much to invest in reliability. The methods for determining how much is enough were discussed in Chapter 18. Risk and reliability are inseparable and must be addressed together. Cost-effective application of the principles of software reliability engineering are directed by what risks reliability engineering can potentially mitigate. If the use of reliability is not mitigating risk, there is no reasonable purpose for incurring the additional project cost.

This chapter focused on four approaches to achieving highly reliable software:

1. Fault forecasting
2. Fault prevention
3. Fault removal
4. Fault tolerance

Where these approaches fit within the product development life cycle was shown. Using the approaches and life cycle as a guide, an outline was presented for a software reliability plan as linked to the project risk plan. When faced with the necessity of using software reliability engineering techniques, a project manager can apply the concepts in this chapter to incorporate these approaches into the overall project.

Problems for Review _____

1. A system has various software modules with the relative probability of use and failure rates shown in Table 20–7.

TABLE 20–7
Probability of Use and Failure Rates for Software Modules

	Probability of use	Failures/1000 hrs
Module 1	0.4	0.6
Module 2	0.3	1
Module 3	0.2	1.2
Module 4	0.09	2
Module 5	0.01	4

   a. What is the overall system failure rate?

   b. You have an opportunity to cut the failure rate in half for any two modules. Which modules should be selected to provide the greatest reduction in failure rate?

2. Assume that a program is estimated to experience 100 failures over its lifetime. This was determined from gathering data during the early phases of the project. It has now experienced 50. The initial failure intensity was 10 failures/CPU hr. What is the current failure intensity?

3. Assume that the initial failure intensity is 10 failures/CPU hr. The failure intensity decay parameter is 0.02/failure. Assume that 50 failures have been experienced. What is the current failure intensity?

4. For the basic model, with v_o = 100 failures, initial failure intensity = 10 failures/CPU hr, μ_p = 50, determine the expected number of failures that will be experienced between a present failure intensity of 3.68 failures/CPU hr and the objective failure intensity of 0.000454 failures/CPU hr.

5. For the logarithmic Poisson model, find the expected number of failures experienced between a present failure intensity of 3.33 failures/CPU hr and an objective of 0.476 failure/CPU hr. Assume that the initial failure intensity is 10 failures/CPU hr, and the failure intensity decay parameter is 0.02/failure.

Visit the Case Study

One of the techniques that your team recommended to lower the overall cost of ownership to the CRM of the final ARRS was the extensive use of "commercial-off-the-shelf" (COTS) software products. Mr. Lu has expressed great pleasure emanating from the CRM in being able to use proven software and reduce their overall cost. On the other hand, Dr. Zhou has pointed out that a serious problem with COTS products is that they often lack the guarantee of good development practice and the extensive documentation of it, which are traditionally the basis for accepting and certifying software for critical applications.

   Dr. Zhou can be convinced to use COTS products if you can demonstrate how fault tolerance will be built into the ARRS. From your previous work in the aerospace industry, you know that one approach is fault tolerance via design diversity. This is attractive because it may be applied without requiring access to the internals of the COTS item. The system can be protected against its COTS components by additional components that either monitor it for deviations from its specified behavior, or for violations of a known "safety envelope" of behaviors that do not endanger the rest of the system.

   Mr. Lu needs you to address the project impact of adopting fault tolerant procedures for the COTS software. He has already committed to the CRM that they will save money with your solution. Dr. Zhou, the niece of the Chinese People's Republic Transportation Minister, must be convinced.

Citations

[1]McCall, John, et al. (1977). "Factors in Software Quality," three volumes, NTIS AD-A049-014, 015, 055, November 1977.

[2]IEEE Std 610.12-1990, IEEE Standard Glossary of Software Engineering Terminology (ANSI).

[3]Leveson, Nancy, and Clark S. Turner (1993). "An Investigation of the Therac-25 Accidents." *IEEE Computer*, 26(7):18–41.

[4]*www.ima.umn.edu/~arnold/455.f96/disasters.html*. Two disasters caused by computer arithmetic errors.

[5]*www.nytimes.com/2001/05/02/business/20EXAM.html*. "Right Answer, Wrong Score: Test Flaws Take Toll."

[6]*www.nytimes.com/2001/05/21/business/21EXAM.html*. "When a Test Fails the Schools, Careers and Reputations Suffer."

[7]Beizer, Boris (1990). *Software Testing Techniques*, 2nd ed. New York, NY: Van Nostrand Reinhold. p. 28.

[8]Lyu, Michael (1996). *Handbook of Software Reliability Engineering*. New York, NY: McGraw-Hill.

Standards

IEEE Std 730.1-1995, IEEE Guide for Software Quality Assurance Planning, IEEE Computer Society, 1996.

IEEE Std 730-1998, IEEE Standard for Software Quality Assurance Plans, IEEE Computer Society, 1998.

IEEE Std 982.1-1988, IEEE Standard Dictionary of Measures to Produce Reliable Software, IEEE Computer Society, 1989.

IEEE Std 982.2-1988, IEEE Guide for the Use of IEEE Standard Dictionary of Measures to Produce Reliable Software, IEEE Computer Society, 1989.

IEEE Std 1228-1994, IEEE Standard for Software Safety Plans, IEEE Computer Society, 1994.

Web Pages for Further Information

members.aol.com/JohnDMusa/. Musa, J.D. (1998). More Reliable Software Faster and Cheaper (Software Reliability Engineering).

rac.iitri.org/. The mission of the Reliability Analysis Center (RAC) is to provide technical expertise and information in the engineering disciplines of reliability, maintainability, supportability and quality and to facilitate their cost-effective implementation throughout all phases of the product or system life cycle.

www.asq-rd.org/. American Society of Quality, Reliability Division.

www.cs.cmu.edu/~koopman/des_s99/sw_reliability/. Software Reliability, Carnegie Mellon University, 18-849b Dependable Embedded Systems, Spring 1999.

www.ieee.org/organizations/society/rel.html. IEEE Reliability Society is concerned with the problems involved in attaining reliability, maintaining it through the life of the system or device, and measuring it.

www.salon.com/tech/feature/2000/12/06/bad_computers/index.html. Cheryll Aimée Barron, High tech's missionaries of sloppiness, Computer companies specialize in giving consumers lousy products—it's the American way of techno-capitalism, 2001, Salon.com.

www.sre.org/. Society of Reliability Engineers.

Tools

www.sre.org/sresoft.htm. The Reliability Test Planner (RTP) software simplifies the construction of statistical reliability test plans for the exponential and binomial distributions. By specifying test parameters (length, failures, consumers or producers risks), the OC Curves and risks can be quickly calculated. The test plans may then be modified and tailored to meet your needs. The user has the option of choosing from the test plans in MIL-HDBK-781 or creating original test plans, either fixed length or sequential (PRST).

Suggested Readings

Lyu, Michael (Editor) (1996). *Handbook of Software Reliability Engineering*. New York, NY: McGraw-Hill.

Musa, John D. (1998). *Software Reliability Engineering: More Reliable Software, Faster Development and Testing*. New York, NY: McGraw-Hill.

Musa, John D., et al. (1987). *Software Reliability: Measurement, Prediction, Application*. New York, NY: McGraw-Hill.

Tierney, James (1997). "SRE at Microsoft." *Keynote speech at 8th International Symposium on Software Reliability Engineering*, November 1977, Albuquerque, NM.

Software Metrics

In software engineering circles, we are fond of repeating Lord Kelvin's statement about measurement, "When you can measure what you are speaking about, and express it into numbers, you know something about it; but when you cannot measure it, when you cannot express it in numbers, your knowledge is of a meager and unsatisfactory kind: It may be the beginning of knowledge, but you have scarcely in your thoughts advanced to the stage of science."[1]

Kelvin is joined by rapidly growing ranks of software engineers and managers who realize that measurement is an indispensable tool. Setting goals and measuring achievement toward them leads to understanding of software and the software process, which in turn, can lead to control of the process—continuing to nudge it in the direction of goals. As Tom DeMarco so aptly paraphrased Lord Kelvin, "You can't control what you can't measure."[2] Metrics allow project managers to understand where they stand (gives them a baseline), so they can guide software process improvement. PMs want measures of how well they are doing at achieving goals like these:

Improving the accuracy of software project costs and schedules;

Improving productivity and efficiency;

Improving customer satisfaction and confidence due to higher product quality.

Software engineers strive to turn their practice into a science, thereby advancing it as Lord Kelvin suggested, but it hasn't been easy. In 1977, Maurice Halstead published one of the first attempts, a method for counting software statements (operators and operands) and relating the number to programmer productivity. He called his work a software science metric. In this century, we continue to aspire to the same illusive goal, although we *have* made progress with the development of some exceptionally useful metrics for the software team. Contemporary experts like Bill Curtis have kept up the campaign.

> Rigorous scientific procedures must be applied to studying the development of software systems if we are to transform programming into an engineering discipline. At the core of these procedures is the development of measurement techniques and the determination of cause effect relationships.[3]

Where We Are in the Software Life Cycle

Software measurement occurs throughout the entire life cycle, as shown in Figure 21–1. The integral task, "develop quality metrics," under the project monitoring and control umbrella and, "collect and analyze metric data," under verification and validation, are, by their very names, obvious places where metrics activities occur. Yet, each of the other integral tasks produces one or more project deliverables that also require measurement. Metrics activities occur in all integral phases (support processes) in the software development life cycle.

Project Initiation and Planning

Establish project environment—This often includes the collection mechanisms for measurement data.

Plan project management

The problem reporting and resolution plan contains methods for counting the number and types of internally/externally found issues, pre- and post-deployment.

The software project management plan contains estimates of size, effort, schedule, and cost, all numbers to be continually reworked and compared to actuals.

Project Monitoring and Control

Manage the project—Project management reports often consist almost entirely of metrics: managers need to see, at any given time, what progress has been made and how it tracks with the estimates. Reports including information like earned value are especially useful.

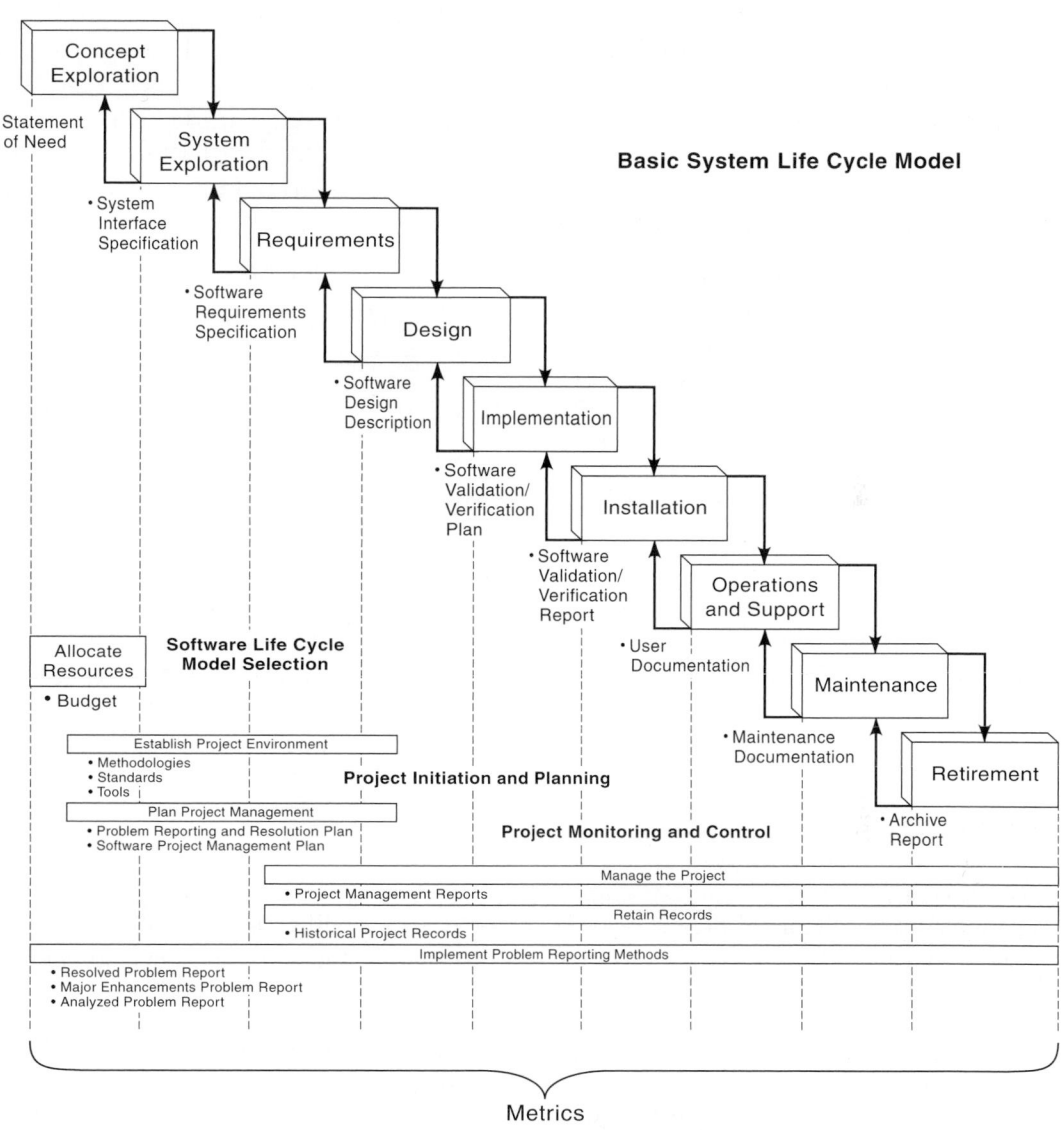

FIGURE 21–1

Where Metrics Occur in the Life Cycle

(Continues)

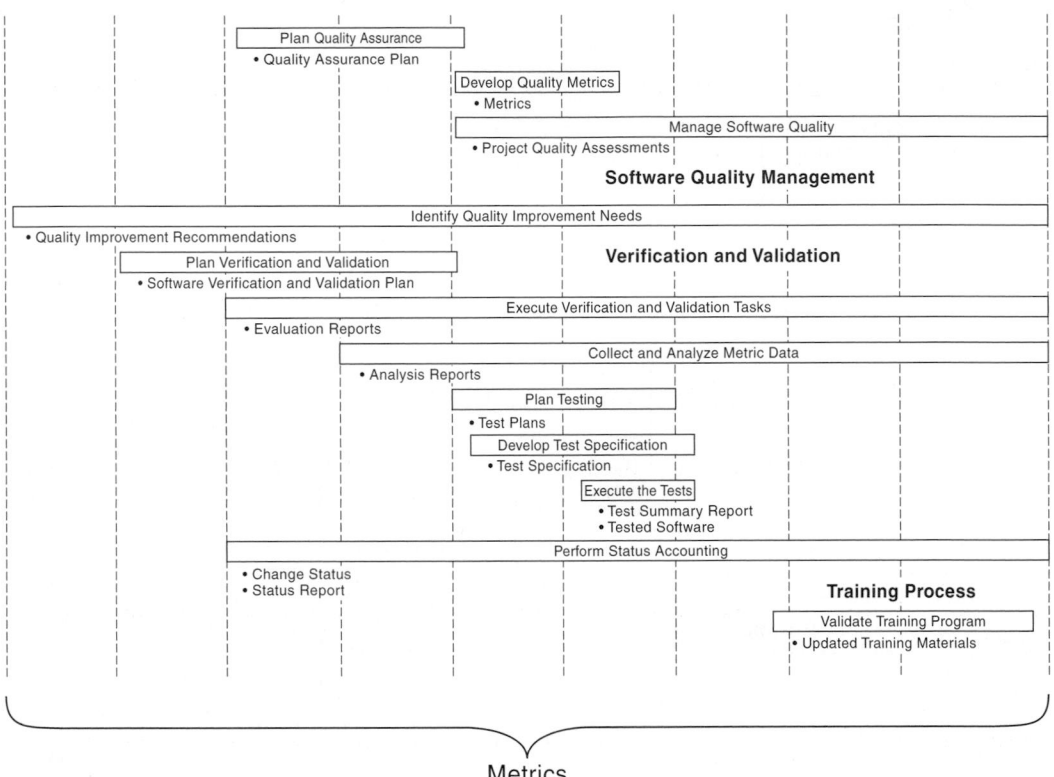

FIGURE 21–1 (Continued)
Where Metrics Occur in the Life Cycle

Retain records—Historical project records are metrics that will be invaluable to future projects, particularly in the area of sizing and estimating the software, development effort, schedule, and cost.

Implement problem reporting—Resolved problem reports, major enhancements problem reports, and analyzed problem reports will be a rich source of metrics data, supplying information such as how long it took to fix the problem, what type of problem it was, where in the life cycle it was introduced, and where in the system it occurred.

Plan quality assurance—Quality assurance plans define quality in quantifiable terms, such as low system complexity or a threshold for the number of errors that must be found pre-delivery.

Develop quality metrics—Goals for the project/organization are established and metrics that will quantify progress toward the goals are defined.

Manage software quality—Project quality assessments frequently take the form of SEI CMM assessments that quantify the maturity level.

Software Quality Management

Identify quality improvement needs—Quality improvement recommendations are usually in a form that can be measured, such as continuous improvement toward an SEI CMM maturity level, a reduced number of delivered defects, or an improved training plan.

Plan verification and validation—The software verification and validation plan is heavily dependent upon metrics to determine the number and type of test cases; which system pathways to execute; test coverage; the number of hours to test, and so on.

Verification and Validation

Execute verification and validation tasks—Evaluation reports should include metrics in graphs, charts, and tables that show the results of executing the test plan.

Collect and analyze metric data—Analysis reports contain data that help project managers make decisions such as how well the project is progressing, and its level of quality. They provide information on processes, the project, and resources via direct observation and by calculations.

Plan testing—Test plans are based, in part, on testing metrics from previous projects.

Develop test specification—Test specifications quantify exactly what must be tested.

Execute the tests—Test summary reports contain metrics on test results.

Perform status accounting—Change status and status reports contain information about the state of the system and its components (configuration items).

Training Process

Validate training program—Updated training materials will result from metrics captured by student evaluation of courses, attendance records, follow-ups on the usefulness of the material, and so on.

Chapter 21 Relation to the 34 Competencies _____

A software metrics program involves almost all of the product, project, and people skills in the 34 competencies, as shown in Figure 21–2. There are alternative processes to define, gather, analyze, and report metrics; this chapter explores only one process with the Basili goal/question/metric paradigm. The steps in the metrics process outlined here may certainly be tailored, as can the types of metrics gathered and the manner in which they are presented.

Software
Product

1. **Assessing processes**
2. Awareness of process standards
3. Defining the product
4. **Evaluating alternative processes**
5. Managing requirements
6. **Managing subcontractors**
7. Performing the initial assessment
8. **Selecting methods and tools**
9. **Tailoring processes**
10. **Tracking product quality**
11. Understanding development activities

Project
Project

12. Building a work breakdown structure
13. **Documenting plans**
14. **Estimating cost**
15. **Estimating effort**
16. Managing risks
17. **Monitoring development**
18. **Scheduling**
19. **Selecting metrics**
20. **Selecting project management tools**
21. **Tracking process**
22. **Tracking project progress**

Management
People

23. **Appraising performance**
24. **Handling intellectual property**
25. **Holding effective meetings**
26. **Interaction and communication**
27. Leadership
28. **Managing change**
29. **Negotiating successfully**
30. Planning careers
31. **Presenting effectively**
32. **Recruiting**
33. Selecting a team
34. Teambuilding

FIGURE 21–2
Metrics Relationship with the 34 Competencies

There are tools that will aid the collection of data, such as automated "timesheet" systems and code complexity analysis packages. Metrics are essential in managing contractors (how they are faring with the schedule and the quality), and in tracking product quality (whether the product is reliable, functional). Effort estimation, cost estimation, scheduling, monitoring development, and tracking processes/progress all depend on the numbers obtained empirically or by derivation. In order to recruit qualified project staff, most organizations rely on databases containing skills measurement. Team selection may use personality typing indicators and scores from skills exams. Presentations are frequently used in reporting to project stakeholders—for the dissemination of information via metrics data.

Learning Objectives for Chapter 21 _____

At the end of this chapter, the reader should be able to:

- Explain the benefits of software-related metrics;
- List categories of metrics and give examples of each;
- Describe where metrics occur in the software life cycle;
- Name the steps in software measurement;
- Identify a good software metric;
- Explain the basic concepts of the Basili goal/question/metric paradigm (GQM);
- Describe a "starter set" of software metrics;
- Define quality-related software metrics.

Chapter 21 will describe a few software metrics and attempt to persuade the hitherto unconvinced reader of the value of going to the trouble to define, gather, analyze, and report metrics. The chapter will define software measurement and describe the characteristics of a "good" (useful) metric. Examples will be given of widely used software metrics and how they were developed using the Basili goal/question/metric paradigm. For those who haven't the time, budget, or inclination to establish a properly customized metrics program for their organization or project, we offer a "starter set" that describes three simple, but very rich, sources of metric data.

What Is a Metric?

A *metric* is a quantifiable measurement of software product, process, or project that is directly observed, calculated, or predicted.

Dr. Barry W. Boehm, the software engineering expert to whom we refer so often in this book, tells us that the value of a metric is dependent upon the degree to which it helps us make a decision. Keeping this statement in mind will help the software project manager gather useful, meaningful metrics instead of collecting them willy-nilly and winding up with a bushel-full of inappropriate data.

> Software measurement is the continuous process of defining, collecting, and analyzing data on the software development process and its products in order to understand and control the process and its products, and to supply meaningful information to improve that process and its products.
>
> —Barry Boehm[4]

> Software measurement is the quantitative assessment of any aspect of a software engineering process, product, or context; it aims to enhance your understanding and to help you control, predict, and improve what you produce and how you produce it.
>
> —Shari Lawrence Pfleeger[5]

We'll keep these definitions in mind as we explore an array of metrics that are in use in various organizations.

Classes of Software Entities that May Be Measured

What can be measured with respect to software? This is a little hard to determine—being abstract, software defies the physical measuring tape. "Observable" entities, such as the number of lines of code, are easily measurable, although we cannot actually see the code—we can only see the representation of code on our computer screen or printout. However, this representation provides something to count—not so different from a thermometer measuring an invisible temperature. There are many other, less obvious characteristics of software development projects that provide useful information. Code complexity, for example, is a useful metric, although somewhat more difficult to quantify. Examples of other product attributes include functionality, modularity, reuse, redundancy, and "structuredness," such as module coupling and cohesiveness (discussed in Chapter 22, "Analysis and Design Methods").

Processes may be thought of as collections of software-related activities. To make decisions about the processes in use, we need to know their level of efficiency and effectiveness—a current baseline. *Products* are any artifact, deliverable, or document that results from a process activity. The project manager must know if these internal or external products are of high quality. *Resources* are entities required by a process activity. The project manager must know about his resources, especially people—are they productive, satisfied, and properly trained?[6]

Table 21–1 shows examples of types of metrics (directly observed, predicted, or calculated) within software categories of product, process, project, and people.

Metrics may also be objective or subjective, where subjective measures involve human, subjective judgment, such as the weighting value on a function point input or output.

Measurable attributes may be internal or external. *Internal* attributes of an entity can be measured in terms of the entity itself, separate from its behavior. *External* attributes are measured with respect to how the entity relates to its environment. Examples of internal attributes are LOC, the duration of an activity, effort, number of test case failures, cost, complexity, and modularity. Examples of external attributes are execution time (requires a program and a computer), usability and understandability (requires an application and a user), reliability, efficiency, testability, reusability, portability, and interoperability.

Measurement Scales

This chapter will describe the steps in software measurement and will offer some observed, predicted, and calculated metrics that are widely used. A concept about measurement of any type that is useful to keep in mind for software metrics programs is this: metrics programs typically start out using directly observable attributes, on an absolute scale or a nominal scale. With an *absolute scale*, measurement consists of counting something, like the number of lines of code in a program. The *nominal scale* groups elements into classes with no implied order (often binary), like "A peer review was held on this program design" (1 = yes) and "No peer review was held on this program design" (2 = no).

Ordinal, interval, and ratio scales are typically added to the repertoire as the metrics process matures. The *ordinal* scale augments the nominal scale with information about an ordering of categories. An example would be post-release defects attributed to errors that escaped from the requirements phase or the design phase, with those that escaped from the former being more expensive to fix than those that escaped from the latter—this represents an ordering of

TABLE 21–1

Types of Software Metrics

	Directly Observed	Predicted	Calculated (Indirect)
Examples	*Direct measurement* of an attribute of an entity involves no other attribute or entity. Direct measurement is assessment of something existing.	A *prediction system* consists of a mathematical model together with a set of prediction procedures for determining unknown parameters and interpreting results.	*Indirect measurement* means calculation involving other attributes or entities by using some mathematical model (always contains a calculation of at least two other metrics).
Product	Number of lines of code; Number of test cases; Number of unresolved customer-reported defects; Test coverage; Number of defects, severity; Number of action items; Number of system components; Component coupling metrics	Number of lines of code; Software quality; Occurrence of software defects; Distribution and characteristics of defects remaining (based upon data from peer reviews and/or tests); Reliability; Number of defects, severity	Efficiency—system behavior over time; Efficiency—system resources; Psychological complexity; Defect density = defects/KLOC; Reliability measures (e.g., mean time to failure)
Process	Adherence to process (yes or no); SEI level; Coverage and efficiency of peer reviews; Effectiveness of training	SEI level	Estimation accuracy = estimate/actual (goal is 1.0); Productivity = LOC/staff-month; Peer review coverage; Test or verification coverage; Rate of closure on action items; Effectiveness of trainers; Risk—probability; Review metrics; Requirements analysis; Maintenance metrics
Project	Project cost; Product development time; Consumption of resources other than people	Project duration; Project cost	Adherence to schedule = earned value (e.g. actual cost of work performed/budgeted cost of work performed); Schedule performance index
People and Other Resources	Number of staff members; List of skills, effort; Programming experience;	Resource loading; Effort	Productivity = LOC/month; Hardware availability; Hardware reliability

the classes. Another example is the intermediate COCOMO cost drivers (Chapter 11), where attributes like analyst capability (ACAP) or modern programming practices (MODP) are measured as very low, low, nominal, high, very high, and extra high, but the actual values for each rating are different for each attribute. The difference between *high* and *very high* is not the same as the difference between *low* and *very low,* for any given cost driver, even though the values are ordered. For example, values for the cost driver (effort multiplier) of analyst capability are: very low = 1.46, low = 1.19, high = 0.86, and very high = 0.71. The difference between very low and low is 0.27, while the difference between very high and high is 0.15. The distances between points on an ordinal scale are not meaningful.

With interval and ratio scales, values can be ranked and distances between points on the scale are meaningful. On an *interval* scale, one unit on the scale represents the same magnitude on the trait or characteristic being measured across the whole range of the scale. Equal distances on the scale represent equal differences in the attribute, but one data point cannot be multiplied or divided by another—only addition and subtraction are supported. For example, the difference between 50 and 55 lines of C++ code is five lines, and the difference between 50 and 60 lines of COBOL code is 10 lines. But, one cannot say that 10 additional lines of COBOL represent twice the program complexity as five additional lines of C++.

On a *ratio* scale, both intervals between values and ratios of values are meaningful. There is an absolute zero point, meaning absence of the attribute. When number of LOC of a C++ program and number of LOC of a COBOL program are translated into equivalent lines of assembly language code, then a change in the number of LOC in either is also equivalent. After each language has been translated to assembly language equivalent LOC, the addition of 10 lines is twice as great as the addition of five lines.

For our purposes here, we'll just keep in mind that starting off with simple metrics makes a lot of sense, be they observed or calculated, internal or external, process or product, objective or subjective.

The Importance of Metrics to Software Projects

In the broadest terms, the objectives of software measurement are to allow managers and practitioners to make timely, data-driven decisions; to track an organization's progress toward its improvement goals; and to assess the impact of process changes. In addition to using software metrics to measure specific attributes of a software product, process, or resource, the project manager can use them to:

- Analyze product errors and defects;
- Assess status;

- Derive a basis for estimates;
- Determine product complexity;
- Establish baselines;
- Experimentally validate best practices;
- Predict quality, schedule, effort, and cost;
- Track project progress;
- Understand when a desired state of quality, in a product or in a process, has been achieved.

Again, paying homage to Boehm: In short, software metrics help us to make better decisions.

Who benefits from measurement? Fortunately, everyone! All stakeholders—any person or group that has a vested interest in the successful outcome of the project, even if they are only peripherally involved, can derive value from metrics. The list would include customers, sponsors, end-users, high-level managers, project managers, domain experts, architects, analysts, designers, developers, software quality engineers, software process engineers, coders, and testers. Project managers are far from being the only group who can profit from having metrics to guide decisions—different groups and different roles will rely on different items to be measured. Consider the potential benefit to the tester, who can examine metrics from previous projects, search for indications of typical error categories, then target extra testing where the biggest payoff is expected on the current project.

Organizations may look back to the measurements taken during the previous projects and ask questions like, "Were most of the problems involved in the message passing control structures?" or "Did we discover, during integration tests, indications that interface specifications based on incorrect parameter passing caused a large percentage of the overall difficulties encountered?" or "Review notes clearly indicated that the functional needs did not survive the transition from logical analysis to physical implementation." Analysis of historical data, including separation of the *vital few* project "gotchas" from the *trivial many* aids the project manager in knowing where to concentrate project control.

While project managers use metrics as an aid in determining how to manage projects, how to improve software performance and reliability, and how to evaluate changes for improving the software development process, development teams use them to:

- Set achievable requirements analysis, design, construction, testing, and implementation goals;
- Demonstrate their potential to meet these goals;
- Track progress toward their goals;
- Adjust processes to correct out-of-control limits conditions. For example, if reviews are deemed to be important, but the team doesn't want to spend an inordinate amount of time on them, they may be tracked on a control chart as shown in Figure 21–3.

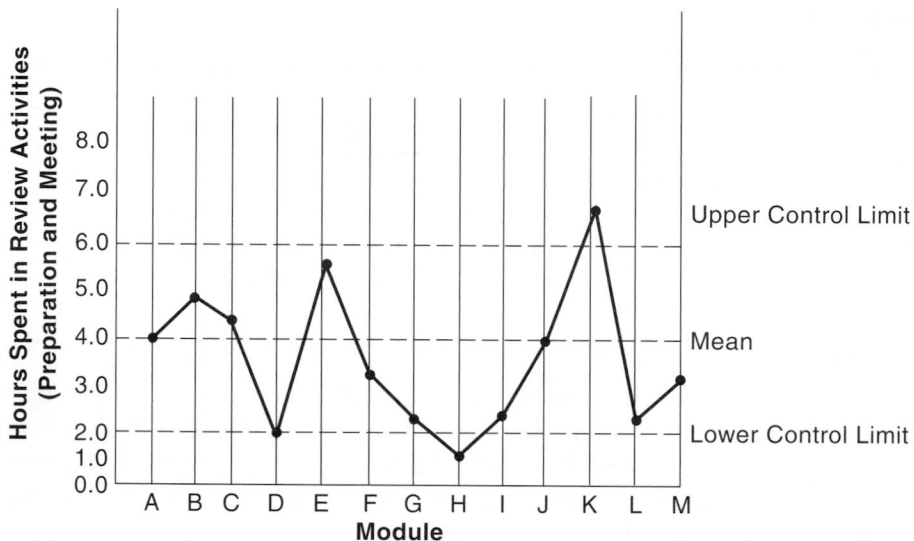

FIGURE 21–3
Example of a Control Chart Used by a Development Team

Metrics that have been collected, synthesized, analyzed, reported to, and studied by the inter-ested parties will gradually be calibrated to be meaningful within a given organization or environment. They may not, and probably will not, be pertinent in another organization. If they are used without resetting goals and recalibrating models, they should be very carefully interpreted. However, as metrics become validated in one environment and added to a repository of knowledge, they will become increasingly valuable in predicting future trends and in improving the software process, particularly in that same or similar environment.

Metrics and the SEI CMM

Measurement and analysis are an integral part of the SEI's software maturity model.

Implications of measurement, as organizations advance through CMM levels, may be seen in Table 21–2.

Metrics also permeate the CMM because every key process area within each maturity level has a measurement and analysis component. *Measurement and analysis* describes the basic measurement practices necessary to determine status related to the process. These mea-surements are used to control and improve the process.

Figure 21–4 shows an example of measurement and analysis for Level 2, "Repeatable," and key process area software requirements management, with examples of measurement.

TABLE 21–2
Metrics Appear in All SEI CMM Levels of Maturity

	SEI CMM				
	Level 1	**Level 2**	**Level 3**	**Level 4**	**Level 5**
Measurement	Data collection and analysis are *ad hoc*	Planning and management data used by individual projects	Data are collected and used in all defined processes	Data definition and collection are standardized across the organization	Data are used to evaluate and select process improvements
			Data are systematically shared across projects	Data are used to understand the process quantitatively and stabilize it	

Metrics also appear directly as an activity within the KPA software product engineering, and as an individual KPA in Level 4, "Quantitative Process Management." A brief look at the metrics-specific goals and activities helps to set the stage for the remainder of our suggestions in this chapter.

**SEI CMM Level 2: Repeatable
Key Process Area:
Software Requirements Management**

Measurement and Analysis

Measurements are made and used to determine the status of the activities for managing the allocated requirements.

Examples of measurements include:

- Status of each of the allocated requirements
- Change activity for the allocated requirements
- Cumulative number of changes to the allocated requirements, including total number of changes proposed, open, approved, and incorporated into the system baseline.

FIGURE 21–4
Every KPA in Every SEI CMM Level Has a Measurement and Analysis Component

SEI CMM Level 2: Repeatable _____

Key Process Area: Software Requirements Management

Measurements are made and used to determine the status of the activities for managing the allocated requirements.

Examples of measurements include:

- Status of each of the allocated requirements;
- Change activity for the allocated requirements;
- Cumulative number of changes to the allocated requirements, including total number of changes proposed, open, approved, and incorporated into the system baseline.

Key Process Area: Software Project Planning

Measurements are made and used to determine the status of the software planning activities.

Examples of measurements include:

- Completions of milestones for the software project planning activities compared to the plan;
- Work completed, effort expended, and funds expended in the software project planning activities compared to the plan.

Key Process Area: Software Project Tracking and Oversight

Measurements are made and used to determine the status of the software tracking and oversight activities.

Examples of measurements include:

- Effort and other resources expended in performing the tracking and oversight activities;
- Change activity for the software development plan, including changes to size estimates of the software work products, software cost estimates, critical computer resource estimates, and schedule.

SEI CMM Level 3: Defined _____

Key Process Area: Training Program

Measurements are made and used to determine the status of the training program activities.

Examples of measurements include:

- Actual attendance at each training course compared to the projected attendance;
- Progress in providing training courses compared to the organization's and project's training plans;
- Number of training waivers approved over time.

Measurements are made and used to determine the quality of the training program.

Examples of measurements include:

- Results of post-training tests;
- Reviews of the courses from the students;
- Feedback from the software managers.

Key Process Area: Software Product Engineering

Goal 1. The software engineering tasks are defined, integrated, and consistently performed to produce the software.

Activity 9. Data on defects identified in peer reviews and testing are collected and analyzed according to the project's defined software process.

Measurements are made and used to determine the functionality and quality of the software products.

Examples of measurements include:

- Numbers, types, and severity of defects identified in the software products tracked cumulatively and by stage;
- Allocated requirements summarized by category (e.g., security, system configuration, performance, and reliability) and traced to the software requirements and system test cases.

Measurements are made and used to determine the status of the software product engineering activities.

Examples of measurements include:

- Status of each allocated requirement throughout the life of the project;
- Problem reports by severity and length of time they are open;
- Change activity for the allocated requirements;
- Effort to analyze proposed changes for each proposed change and cumulative totals;
- Number of changes incorporated into the software baseline by category (e.g., interface, security, system configuration, performance, and usability);
- Size and cost to implement and test incorporated changes, including initial estimate and actual size/cost.

SEI CMM Level 4: Managed

Quantitative process management (QPM) is a key process area for Level 4, "Managed" (see Figure 21–5). It involves establishing goals for the performance of the project's defined software process (described in the integrated software management key process area), taking measurements of the process performance, analyzing these measurements, and making adjustments to maintain process performance within acceptable limits. When the process performance is stabilized within acceptable limits, the project's defined software process, the associated measurements, and the acceptable limits for the measurements are established as a baseline and used to control process performance quantitatively.

Homing in on the two activities that are specifically related to our interests in this chapter, we'll look at Activity 4 and Activity 7.

Activity 4, QPM states: The measurement data used to control the project's defined software process quantitatively are collected according to a documented procedure.

SEI CMM Level 4: Managed
Key Process Area:
Quantitative Process Management

Goal 1: The quantitative process management activities are planned.
Goal 2: The process performance of the project's defined software process is controlled quantitatively.
Goal 3: The process capability of the organization's standard software process is known in quantitative terms.

Activity 1: The software project's plan for quantitative process management is developed according to a documented procedure.
Activity 2: The software project's quantitative process management activities are performed in accordance with the project's quantitative process management plan.
Activity 3: The strategy for the data collection and the quantitative analyses to be performed are determined based on the project's defined software process.
Activity 4: The measurement data used to control the project's defined software process quantitatively are collected according to a documented procedure.
Activity 5: The project's defined software process is analyzed and brought under quantitative control according to a documented procedure.
Activity 6: Reports documenting the results of the software project's quantitative process management activities are prepared and distributed.
Activity 7: The process capability baseline for the organization's standard software process is established and maintained according to a documented procedure.

FIGURE 21–5
SEI CMM Level 4, "Managed," KPA QPM

Examples of measurement data include:

- Estimated/planned versus actual data on software size, cost, and schedule;
- Productivity data;
- Quality measurements as defined in the software quality plan;
- Coverage and efficiency of peer reviews;
- Effectiveness of training;
- Test coverage and efficiency;
- Software reliability measures;
- Number and severity of defects found in the software requirements;
- Number and severity of defects found in the software code;
- Number and rate of closure on action items.

Activity 7, QPM states: The process capability baseline for the organization's standard software process is established and maintained according to a documented procedure.

Examples of using capability trends include:

- Predicting the occurrence of software defects and comparing the predictions to actuals;
- Predicting the distribution and characteristics of defects remaining in a product based on the data from peer reviews and/or testing.

Metrics play an important role in the Capability Maturity Model Integrated (CMMI). In this model, an additional KPA, measurement and analysis, has been added to maturity Level 2. A synopsis of that KPA may be found in Chapter 26, "Continuous Process Improvement," CMMI-SE/SW Version 1.02 (Staged) Maturity Level 2, KPA: Measurement and Analysis.

Useful Metrics

Metrics should not be collected because they are prescribed in the literature or because they are recognized as popular in some companies, but because they are useful in decision-making on a particular project or within a given organization.

A useful metric is precisely defined (i.e., measurable or quantifiable). Terms like "always," "complex," "efficient," or "user-friendly" are not measurable without further definition. A useful metric is independent of the conscious influence of project personnel. The Hawthorne Effect is evidence that the act of taking measurements will, in and of itself, affect the quality of a product, usually in a favorable way. The Hawthorne Effect is briefly described in the glossary.

A useful metric is accountable. Raw metric data and control data (date of observation, identity of the observer, etc.) should be saved along with an audit trail of the metric analysis process. Conclusions may then be reconstructed from the data if further defense or interpretation is required. In addition, the retained raw data will allow reanalysis at a later date in the light of new theories.

A useful metric is precise, as indicated with a range, an explicit tolerance, or a stated rationale or method for collection (for example, a satisfaction index). It also helps indicate whether an organization is achieving software goals.[7]

Useful metrics are also *usable* metrics that are:

- simple and easy to understand.
- inexpensive to use.
- robust.
- consistent and used over time.
- unobtrusively collected.
- easily accessible online by all stakeholders.

Useful metrics must be accompanied by data that is correct (collected according to the rules of the definition of the metric), accurate, exact, and consistent (no large differences in value occur, even if the person or measuring device changes). Most data is associated with a particular activity or time period. It should be annotated and date-time stamped for knowledge of exactly where and when it is collected. The measurement procedure must be described clearly enough for someone else to be able to replicate the measurement.

The Basili Goal/Question/Metric Paradigm _____

A widely used and well-respected approach for determining which metrics will offer the most to project control and decision-making is the "Goal, Question, Metric" (GQM) paradigm authored by Dr. Victor Basili. The GQM requires that goal-setting take place prior to metrics collection. Facilitated brainstorming sessions are common forums for gaining consensus among the members of a project team as to the specific project goals. Of course, organizational goals may be set by upper management or by stakeholders within the entire organization. Dr. Basili was instrumental in founding the Software Engineering Laboratory (SEL), a consortium including the Computer Science Department of the University of Maryland, the Software Engineering Branch of NASA's Goddard's Flight Dynamics Division, and the Software Engineering Operation of Computer Sciences Corporation. Work at the SEL resulted in a seven-step process for systematically applying measurements to software. As shown in Figure 21–6, the steps are: develop a set of goals; develop a set of questions that characterize the goals; specify the metrics needed to answer the questions; develop mechanisms for data collection and analysis; collect, validate, and analyze the data, and take corrective action; analyze in a postmortem fashion and feed forward; and provide feedback to stakeholders. The first three steps of the GQM framework are crucial:

Step 1. Develop a set of goals. Develop a set of corporate, division, or project (development or maintenance) goals for productivity and quality of product or process (e.g., customer satisfaction, on-time delivery, improved quality, develop reusable objects, reuse experiences). Goals are frequently determined by brainstorming problems and requirements from each of the stakeholders' perspectives. They may then be prioritized and grouped into software improvement areas.

Step 2. Develop a set of questions that characterize the goals. Derive from each goal the question that must be answered to determine if the goals are being met. These questions characterize the goals, evaluate progress toward the goals, predict achievement of the goals, or motivate movement toward the goals.

Step. 3. Specify the metrics needed to answer the questions. Decide what must be measured in order to be able to answer the questions adequately.

Each of the seven GQM steps will be described in the following pages.

GQM Step 1: Develop a Set of Goals

To aid in generating the goals, questions, and metrics, Basili and Rombach provide a template for recording the purpose, perspective, and environment that will add structure to the goal.[8] See Table 21–3 for an overview.

Purpose—to (characterize, evaluate, predict, motivate, etc.) the (process, product, model, metric, etc.) in order to (understand, assess, manage, engineer, learn, improve, etc.) it.

- *Understanding* or *characterizing* implies building a model of the object in which collected data will provide insight.

- *Evaluation* implies an existing pattern of data that will allow the development of a consistent model based upon available (or reasonably estimated) factors.

- *Motivation* or *improvement* implies an existing accurate model that represents a true understanding of the object or positive quality.

Example: To *evaluate* the maintenance process in order to *improve* it.

Perspective—Examine the (cost, effectiveness, correctness, defects, changes, product measures, etc.) from the viewpoint of the (developer, manager, customer, etc.).

- Point of view determines such things as when the information should be available, its level of granularity, and its acceptable accuracy.

Example: Examine the *cost* from the viewpoint of the *manager*.

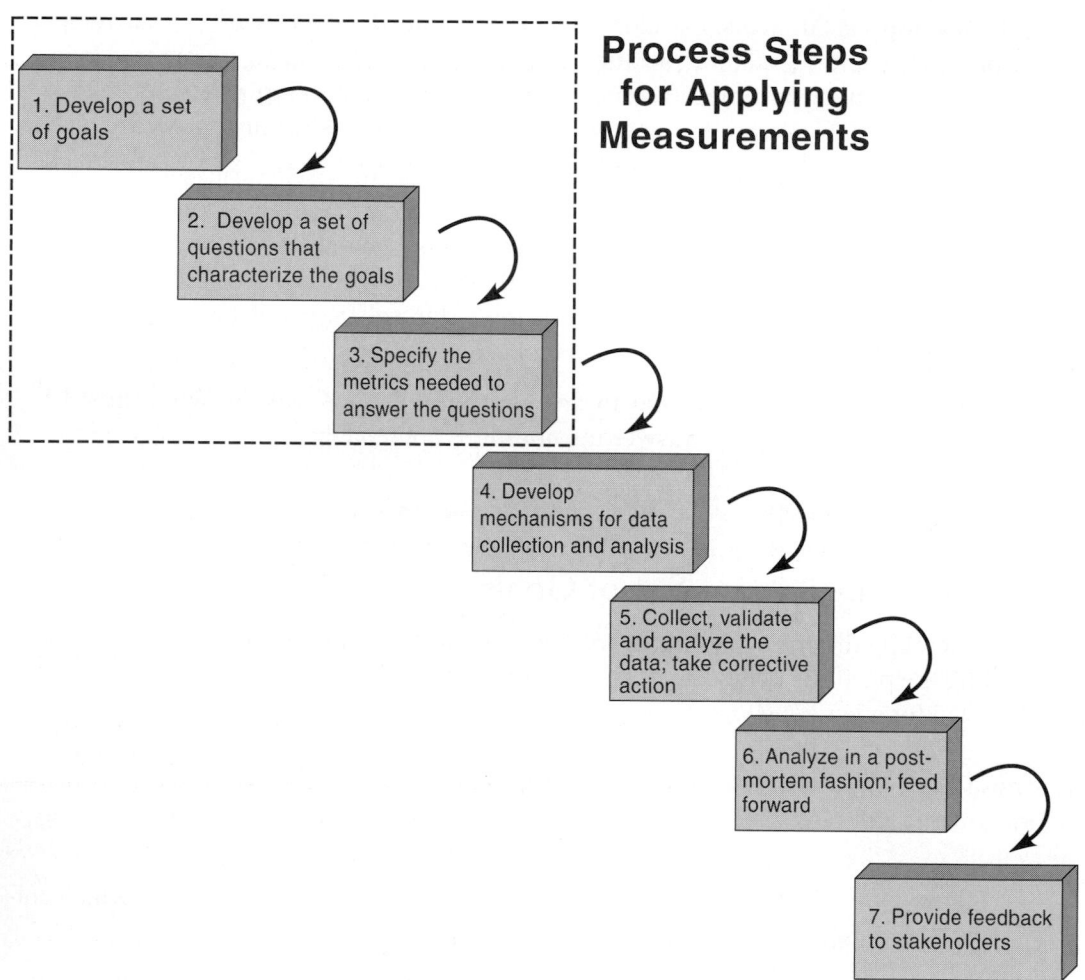

FIGURE 21–6
Basili 7-Step Goal/Question/Metric Approach

Environment—The environment defines the context in which the study is being performed. It helps to classify the current project with respect to a variety of characteristics and distinguish the relevant project environment for the current project, finding the class of projects with similar characteristics and goals to be used as a basis for comparison. The environment consists of process, people, problem factors, methods, tools, and constraints.

- *People factors* could be about the number of people, level of software engineering expertise, group organization issues, application domain experience, process experience, and tool expertise.

TABLE 21–3
Basili GQM Goal Format

	Analyze (what)	The object under measurement—process, product, model, metric, and so on
Purpose	For the purpose of (why)	Characterizing, evaluating, predicting, motivating, improving, understanding, assessing, managing, engineering, learning about, or controlling
	With respect to (focus)	The quality focus of the object that the measurement focuses on—cost, effectiveness, correctness, defect removal, changes, product measures, reliability, user friendliness, and so on
Perspective	From the viewpoint of (perspective—what aspect and who)	The people that measure the object— software developers, top level managers, customers, project managers, the corporation, and so on
Environment	In the context of (characteristics)	The environment in which measurement takes place—resource factors, process factors, people factors, problem factors, methods, tools, constraints, and so on

- *Process factors* could be about the choice of development life cycle model, methods, techniques, tools, and programming languages.

- *Product factors* could be about internal deliverables, system size, and required quality (e.g., reliability, portability).

- *Resource factors* could be based on the similarity of target and development machines, calendar time, budget, and existing software available for reuse.

Example: The development programmers believe their productivity is limited by lack of access to tools.

An example of an entire goal would be:

Analyze the delivered product for the purpose of assessing it with respect to interface complexity from the viewpoint of the project team, in the context of the object-oriented design used on Project ABC.

Goals should be measurable and driven by models of the business. In addition to the GQM paradigm, there are other mechanisms for defining measurable goals, such as the quality function deployment approach (QFD) and the software quality metrics approach (SQM).

As described with GQM, goals may be defined for any object, for a variety of reasons, with respect to various models of quality, from various points of view, relative to a particular environment.

Strategic Goals   *Strategic goals*, usually set by management, often include: providing a baseline for measurement, providing a vehicle for communication, providing insight into the development process, and drawing from a historical base to plan future projects. An example of a metric used to determine progress toward a strategic goal is the SEI CMM (or CMMI) level of maturity.

Tactical Goals   Typical *tactical goals* of project teams and software organizations are to: minimize software engineering effort and schedule, minimize costs, maximize customer satisfaction, minimize defects, and manage quality and testing.

Examples of metrics used to determine progress toward the tactical goal of minimizing defects and managing quality testing include:

- Average time to fix a service request;
- Cumulative defects found;
- Defect analysis by code module;
- Defect fix times, estimated versus actual;
- Defects identified/defects remaining open;
- Distribution of defect origins;
- Mean time between defects;
- Pattern of cyclomatic complexity;
- Project defect status.

Both tactical and strategic goals may be expressed on a graph as a "stretch goal" line showing a quantitative level achieved over time. The progress toward that goal is then graphed on the same chart, as shown in the example in Figure 21–7.

Once the goals are set, the GQM process moves on to the determination of how to measure progress toward them.

GQM Step 2: Develop a Set of Questions that Characterize the Goals

Goals are defined on an abstract level, but questions are aimed at an operational level. By answering the questions, we should be able to determine whether or not a goal has been reached.

For example, the *process* goal, "improve responsiveness to customer problems by reducing cycle time for analysis and correction of the problems," might evoke these questions:

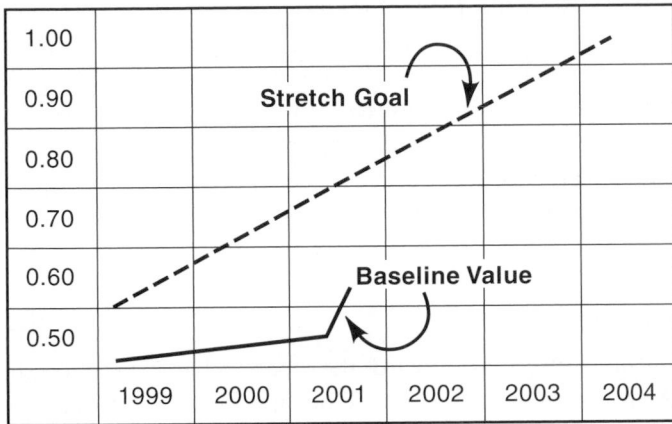

FIGURE 21–7
Example of a Stretch Goal

- Is there a documented process for fixing problems?
- Are the fixes reviewed and tested?
- Are the estimates for problem correction accurate?
- Is there a change control mechanism with which all developers are familiar?
- What is the average elapsed time spent in finding a problem?
- What is the average elapsed time spent in fixing a problem?
- What is the average amount of effort spent in finding and fixing a problem?
- What percentage of fixed customer problems requires additional rework?

If the goals involve *product* improvement issues, the questions will be product-oriented. For example, the goal "reduce the complexity of the software system" might evoke these questions:

- How many program modules are there?
- What is the degree of coupling between modules?
- What is the average McCabe cyclomatic complexity measure?
- What was the development time by module?
- Was each module reviewed?
- What was the number of errors discovered for each module?
- What is the size of each module?
- Are the modules cohesive?
- Are the modules documented with a program abstract?
- Are the modules traceable to the requirements?

Management may require answers to principal questions such as these:

- Can we do it?
- How long will it take?
- How much will it cost?
- How many people will it take?
- What is the risk?
- What are the trade-offs?
- How many errors will there be?
- Can we measure process improvement?

Once the questions needed to determine progress toward the goals have been thought through, the next step in the GQM process is to determine what metrics will answer the questions.

GQM Step 3: Specify the Metrics Needed to Answer the Questions

GQM Step 3 is to specify the metrics needed to answer the questions and track *process* and *product* conformance to the goals. Typically, metrics needed to answer the question will be easily derived from key words in the question. The phrase "average effort spent" appearing in the question, "What is the average effort spent in fixing customer problem reports?" implies the obvious metrics to be collected. They are: effort in staff-weeks/months, and number of customer problem reports closed in a week's/month's period.

Another example would be:

Goal: Characterize the final product with respect to defect classes.

One question might be: What is the error distribution by class within phase of defect insertion?

A metric would then be: requirements errors—number and classification

An example, adapted from van Solingen and Berghout is the following (note that the example has been generalized and simplified from their case study).[9]

Goal: Analyze the delivered product for the purpose of understanding, with respect to the effectiveness of reuse, and from the viewpoint of the software development team in the context of Project A.

Questions and their metrics: What is the percentage of modules that were not developed from scratch (i.e., some portion is reused [overall and per subsystem])?

Metric 1. For each software module: Developed from scratch (yes, no)?

Metric 2. For each software module: Name of subsystem it belongs to

What is the percentage of completely reused code (overall and per subsystem)?

Metric 1. For each software module: Code reused (yes, no)?

Metric 2. For each software module: Name of subsystem it belongs to

For software modules where code is reused: What is the distribution of modules among reuse modification classes (overall and per subsystem)?

Metric 1. Degree of code modification (unchanged, mainly deletions, less than 20 percent of lines changed, more than 20 percent of lines changed)

Metric 2. Name and version of the original reused module

Metric 3. Name and version of the released reusing module

Metric 4. Name of subsystem it belongs to

What is the relationship between module reuse and reliability?

Metric 1. For all modules: What is the level of reuse?

Metric 2. For top faulty modules: What is the level of reuse?

Metric 3. For top non-faulty modules: What is the level of reuse?

Metric 4. For all modules: What is the fault density?

Metric 5. For reused modules: What is the fault density?

Metric 6. For non-reused modules: What is the fault density?

After data was gathered on modules with some degree of reuse, some conclusions were:

- Reusing large parts of a module that is already fixed results in significantly lower faults than if developed from scratch; and
- Faults in reused modules are detected more before delivery because reused modules are reviewed and tested more intensively than newly developed modules.

Metrics provide all of the quantitative information to answer the questions in a satisfactory way.

One metric may be able to answer several questions. For example, the "Age of Open Problems" may answer the question, "Are sufficient resources being allocated to problem resolution?" as well as the question, "How long do problems remain open?"

Several metrics may be required to answer one question. For example, both the "Age of Open Problems" and the "Age of Closed Problems" are needed to answer the question, "How can we determine our responsiveness to our customers who report problems?"

Once the goals, questions, and metrics have been determined, mechanisms for collecting the actual metrics data must be in place in an organization or project environment.

GQM Step 4: Develop Mechanisms for Data Collection

It is important to keep sights set on the goal. Collection of data that is unrelated to the measurement of the goal just isn't useful. Ideally, collected data reside in an organizational repository for sharing across projects.

- **Who should collect the metrics?** Those who are "closest" to the data. For example, development staff effort is best reported by individual staff members—analysts, designers, and programmers. In addition to being the most knowledgeable about the circumstances and in the best position to provide accurate data, the developers are not usually the same people who will be reporting the measurements—a good idea to maintain objectivity.

- **When should the data be collected?** That depends on what it is and how it will be used, but "early and often" is not a bad maxim. If effort data is desired, then once per day is optimal, but once per week is realistic. A once per month schedule is too infrequent for effort data, because it is too difficult to recall where time was spent.

- **How can the data be collected most accurately as well as efficiently?** Through the use of automated tools. Data collection mechanisms must be unobtrusive to be used. Use of Web-enabled data collection married to a modern object/relational database accommodates the modern distributed organization and project team. Flexible systems allow change with lessons learned.

- **Who will be the audience for the metrics?** That depends on the "viewpoint," or perspective, described in the goal statement. However, no matter who receives the reports, those who input the data must know how it was interpreted and who will see it. Otherwise, there will be no motivation to ensure accurate data.

The collection of metrics data must not interfere with the business of software. They must be unobtrusive and easy to use. When the data collection and analysis process is goal driven, automated, and integrated into the software process, it is worth the investment. As mentioned earlier, care must be taken so that the measurement process itself doesn't skew the data. The possibility of the Hawthorne Effect, described in the Glossary, should be taken into consideration.

GQM Step 5: Collect, Validate, and Analyze the Data in Real Time to Provide Feedback to Projects for Corrective Action

Manual recording is subject to bias, error, omission, and delay. Automatic data capture is therefore desirable whenever possible. In planning collection, those involved in a metrics program should:

- Keep procedures simple.
- Avoid unnecessary recording.
- Train staff in the need to record data and in the procedures to be used.
- Provide the results promptly and in useful form to those in charge.
- Validate all data collected at a central collection point.

Analysis may take a number of forms and use a variety of reporting tools. Graphical portrayal of metrics data almost always enhances understanding of the analysis. Control charts, histograms, Ishikawa diagrams, Pareto charts, and scatter diagrams are common graphical vehicles.

An example of an Ishikawa (cause and effect, fishbone) diagram is shown in Figure 21–8.

Combining the goal, the question, the metric, and the graphical analysis in one place (on one "page") is a powerfully descriptive way to report metrics to stakeholders. A major electronics company used the following set of questions and metrics to track progress toward one of their software improvement goals.

Goal: Improve Customer Service

Question 1: What is the number of new problems that were opened during the month?

Metric 1: New Open Problems (NOP) = Total new post-release problems opened during the month

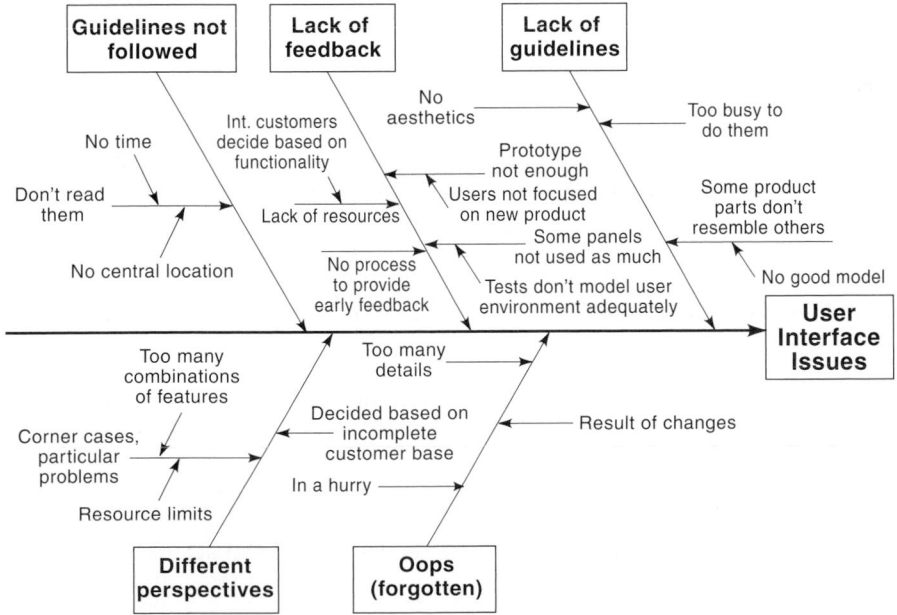

FIGURE 21–8
Step 5: Collect, Validate, and Analyze the Data: An Example of an Ishikawa Diagram

Question 2: What is the total number of open problems at the end of the month?

Metric 2: Total Open Problems (TOP) = Total new post-release problems that remain open at the end of the month

Question 3: What is the mean age of open problems at the end of the month?

Metric 3: Mean Age of Open Problems (AOP) = (Total time post-release problems remaining open at the end of the month have been open)/(Number of open post-release problems remaining open at the end of the month)

Question 4: What is the mean age of the problems that were closed during the month?

Metric 4: Mean Age of Closed Problems (ACP) = (Total time post-release problems closed within the month were open)/(Number of open post-release problems closed within the month)[10, 11]

The Goal, Question 3, Metric 3, Question 4, Metric 4, and an example of graphed results for analysis appear in Figure 21–9.

GQM Step 6: Analyze the Data in a Postmortem Fashion to Assess Conformance to the Goals and Make Recommendations for Future Improvements

Raw metrics are typically too difficult to plow through. For example, if we received an error log consisting of 150 entries with "fields" labeled date, time, error code, it would be difficult to interpret. However, if the occurrence of each type of error were counted for a given time period, some sense could be made of the data and then it can be used to make a decision about reaching a goal. Figure 21–10 shows how the error code can be labeled with a meaningful name, and the count of each type of error graphed as a histogram.

GQM Step 7: Provide Feedback to Stakeholders

Providing feedback is a very important, yet often forgotten step in the measurement process. Affected stakeholders—all of them, particularly data providers—must be able to see the fruits of their labor. Why gather data when you never know what happens to it, or how it might affect you?

For example, if developers and testers have information about the defect density of inspected modules, they may be able to draw some conclusions, or at least ask the next set of questions such as: Why were so many defects discovered in Module 1? Were the reviewers new to the process and doing a conscientious job? Did a programmer who didn't understand the language or the application domain write the module? Figure 21–11 shows a simple graph that may stimulate action toward process improvement. If, however, the developers

Goal: *Improve customer service*

Question:
What is the mean age of open problems at the end of the month?

Metric:
Age of open problems = total time post-release problems remaining open at the end of the month have been open / # of open post-release problems remaining open at the end of the month

Question:
What is the mean age of the problems that were closed during the month?

Metric:
Age of the closed problems = total time post-release problems closed within the month were open / # of post-release problems closed within the month

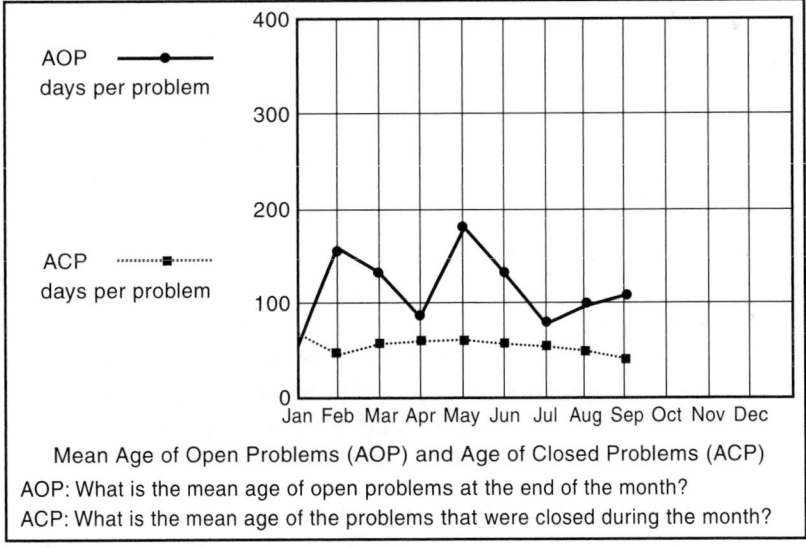

Mean Age of Open Problems (AOP) and Age of Closed Problems (ACP)
AOP: What is the mean age of open problems at the end of the month?
ACP: What is the mean age of the problems that were closed during the month?

FIGURE 21–9
An Example of a Goal/Question/Metric and Analysis Graph on One "Page"

and testers who collected the data from reviews and tests never see the results, they will not only miss an opportunity to discuss process improvement, they will probably lose motivation to supply accurate data. As mentioned, a powerful way to present feedback is to show, on one "page," the goal, the question(s), the metric(s), and the graphed results, as was shown in Figure 21–9. Other examples of graphical feedback mechanisms are shown in Figures 21–12 through 21–16.

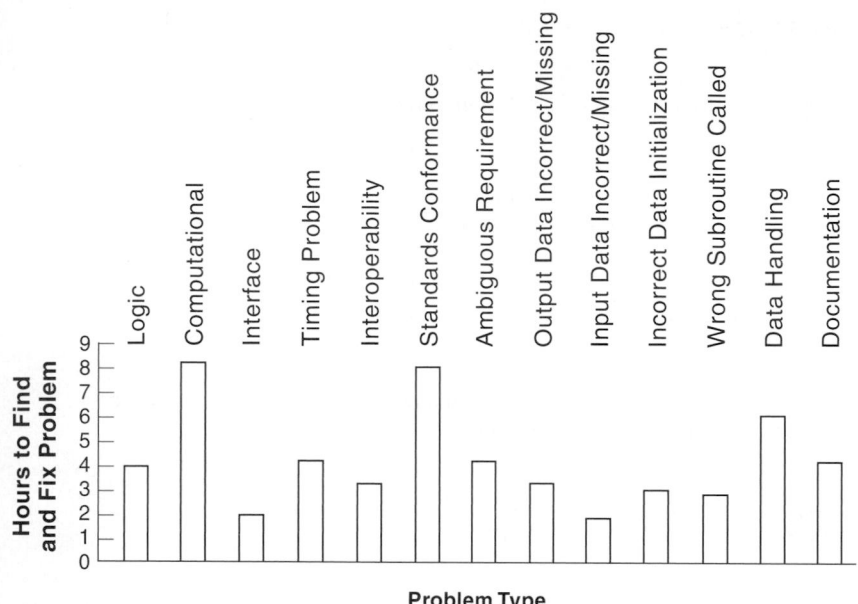

FIGURE 21–10
GQM Step 6: An Example of Feeding Data Forward Via Histogram

Knowledge of defect density is useful because it helps us single-out the modules with the most problems for further analysis, often beginning with root-cause analysis. Were there a lot of defects because the module was complex? Was the developer inexperienced in the programming language or in the application domain? Were there many cases of a certain type of error (e.g., initialization errors) that a certain programmer is prone to make? If so, does he or she need to go to "initialization school?" If we were planning one of these modules to be heavily reused in the future, but its defect density is high, should we rethink those plans?

If we know the average time to correct a major defect and we have some historical data to clue us in on how many defects to expect, we then know something about how much to budget for the effort to correct problems. If the effort to correct major defects is increasing, rather than decreasing, as shown in Figure 21–12, then something is wrong—perhaps we are adding complexity through entropy of structure, rather than making the component "cleaner."

In a test environment, we are finding errors, fixing errors, and running regression tests at a fast pace. Each time the regression suite is executed, we would expect fewer errors to surface, as shown in Figure 21–13. If the failure rate is increasing rather than decreasing, we may be part of the problem rather than the solution. The PM may decide to stop testing and analyze the trend. If the failure rate decreases, and the remaining errors are of low severity, the PM and the customer may agree to release the product. This sort of trend analysis does not have

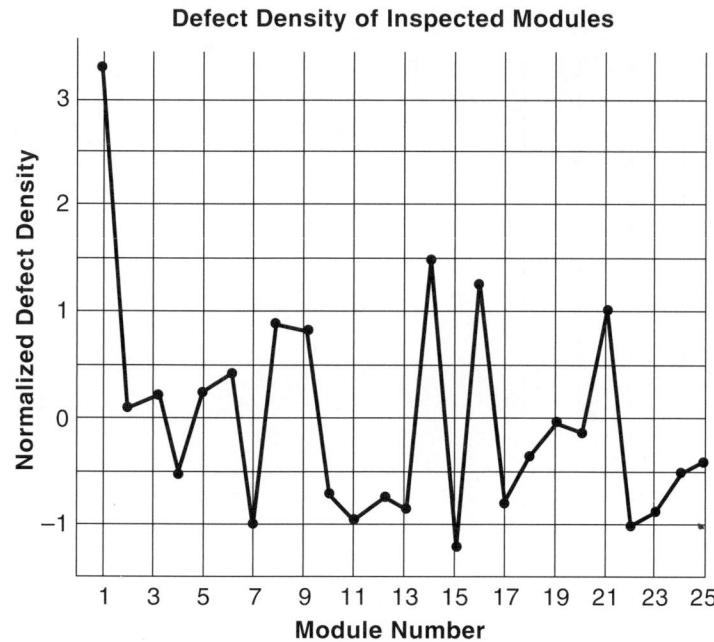

FIGURE 21–11
GQM Step 6: Knowledge of Defect Density May Be Used in Future Planning

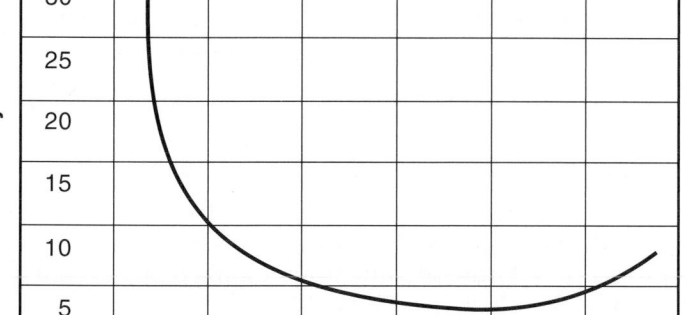

FIGURE 21–12
GQM Step 7: Average Time to Correct a Major Defect

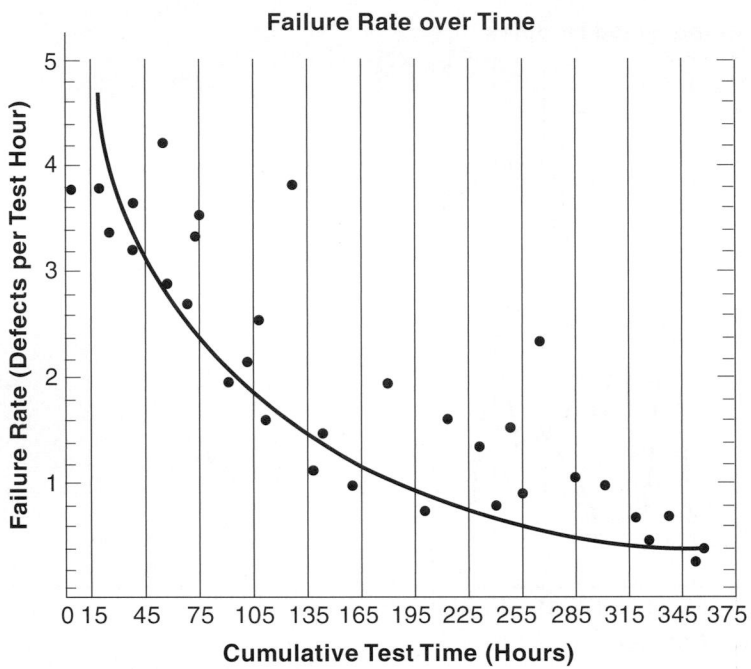

FIGURE 21–13
GQM Step 7: Failure Rate Over Time

to be limited to the testing phase. As shown in Figure 21–14, defect tracking may begin with the first static reviews early in the project.

"Pareto charts," like the one in Figure 21–15 can assist the project manager in determining where to spend resources. If it's true what we've always heard, that "80 percent of the problems occur in 20 percent of the code," then we want to know which 20 percent. The Pareto, an ordered histogram, is perfect to help make that decision. Once the "vital few" have been distinguished from the "trivial many," further analysis can take place where it is needed the most.

When we know where in the product life cycle defects are inserted into the product, then special attention can be paid to that phase. Perhaps more reviews or inspections can be held. Perhaps senior analysts can be assigned to the task. Results from one project may be viewed as an anomaly, but when several projects point out the same troublesome phase, as in Figure 21–16, the PM has some strong indicators on which to base decisions.

In the unfortunate event that planning for a metrics program, using a method such as GQM, must be postponed, there are a few measurements that are reliable. A basic metrics "starter set," described in the next section, lists a few.

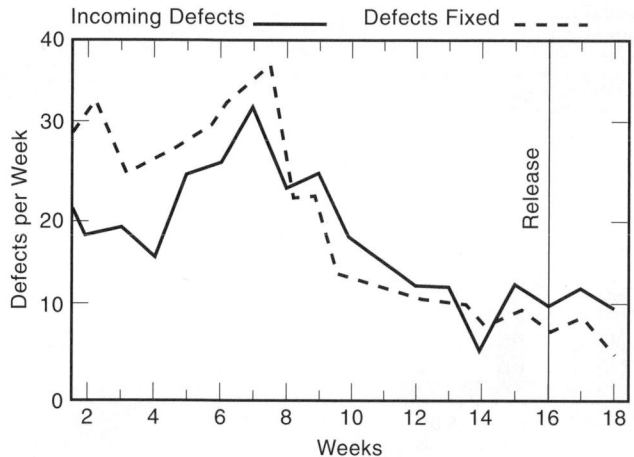

FIGURE 21–14
GQM Step 7: Defects Discovered and Fixed Over Time

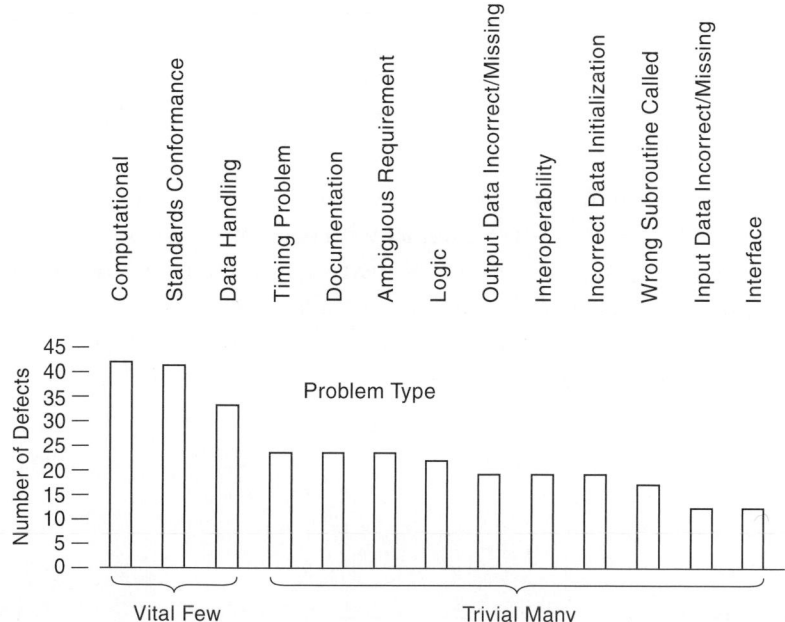

FIGURE 21–15
GQM Step 7: Pareto of Types of Defects

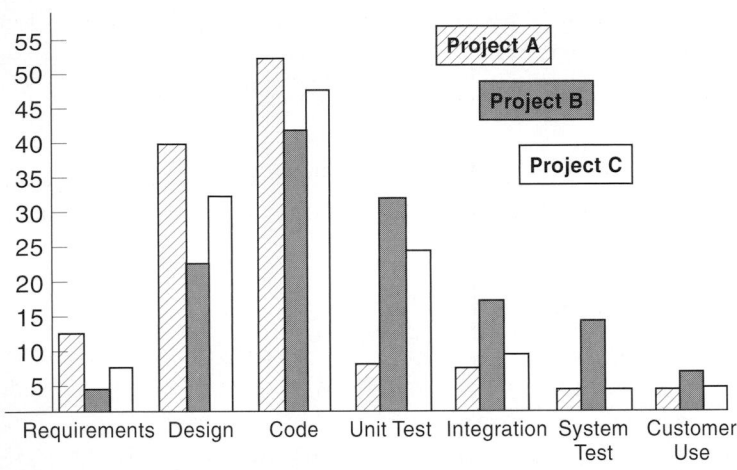

FIGURE 21–16
GQM Step 7: Phase in which Defects Are Inserted

A "Basic Metrics" Starter Set

The best metrics programs almost always begin with goal-setting, as per the Basili G/Q/M method. However, there are a few metrics that the project manager may feel safe in collecting, even before a proper metrics program is in place. These simple measures can do no harm and provide a practical way to get started.

There are three very rich sources of data for use in controlling software projects. These three basics, like a three-legged stool (Figure 21–17), interact with each other to form a solid foundation and may be used as a first step in a practical metrics system. They are: effort expended against a WBS, peer review data, and change request data.

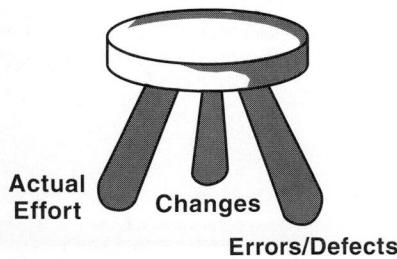

FIGURE 21–17
Basic Metrics Have Three Sources

First, control requires knowledge of exactly how much effort is expended against the project and the characteristics of that effort expenditure.

Second, control requires knowledge of the number and type of errors and defects discovered during the review process.

Third, control requires knowledge of requested changes, whether the request is to change the original system requirements or to change a delivered artifact due to a discovered defect.

Three Basic Metrics: Effort

Effort is one of the most telling of the resources expended in the production of software. Hardware, telecommunications, software tools, and other assets are certainly not dismissed, yet they are rarely the bulk of the software budget. The budget, used to acquire assets, is almost always spent primarily on salaries for knowledge workers. Software requires relatively low-priced production machinery, no fabrication facilities, no storage warehouses; software costs are essentially people-based. Knowledge of where the project staff, this most prized commodity, spends time provides a handle on valuable information about the pace of the project, the progress of the project, how to budget for the remainder of the project, how to improve the process for this and future projects, the productivity of the development staff, and how to predict the cost of future projects.

Effort data will provide, among other things, a phase distribution of effort to be used in future project estimates. One can speak from an individual level to discuss meaningful measures of productivity, such as "number of hours (or days) per object class," which might be defined as the amount of time required, on average, to fully develop all of the services and attributes of an object.

Effort collection is not only invaluable in estimating the next similar project, but it will help project managers with many decisions. For example, knowing how much effort is involved in finding and fixing defects reported against an installed base, will aid in deciding whether it is too complex to proceed.

Was time spent in reviews accounted for correctly? Were process improvement activities expected? If so, were they contributed by the staff, or considered part of the project? Was an object-oriented learning curve in play because it was the first time the project team used OO methods? Was rework honestly reported?

The only way to really know the exact cost of software is to accurately keep track of the amount of human effort spent on each task involved in the software development and maintenance process. And, as has been documented since the beginnings of project planning, the best way to properly identify which tasks are involved is to produce a work breakdown structure (WBS) and associate effort spent with a task or activity.

Effort Data: Barriers to Collection   In many technical environments, the idea of keeping track of engineering time is pure anathema. The activity itself is perceived as time-consuming, wasteful, and inconvenient—and usually, just plain annoying. The data collected is perceived as inaccurate and useless. In the wrong hands, it can be used as a brickbat for beating up "non-productive" workers. Needless to say, this can lead to bogus data being entered by the technical staff to conceal activities that could be construed as nonessential. A downward spiral then results, where "bad" data (such as that entered by developers who see no value in doing it) leads to bad decisions (such as managers assuming that because no overtime was reported, none was worked, so they then schedule the next project on that assumption), which leads to more bad data. Understanding of how much effort is really expended on each task becomes increasingly difficult, as does the prospect of improving the accuracy of future estimates. Workdays are often reported as an inflated eight hours of productive work (overtime is often unreported or underreported), and new projects are estimated on this norm. The true level of productivity remains unknown; the expectation is that it is as high as reported and that this unrealistic level will be sustained.

The most damning case against keeping track of time is the belief that it is a "non-professional" activity. Many organizations have "exempt" versus "non-exempt" employees. The former are exempted from reporting time, including overtime. The supposition is that a fixed salary will be paid to a professional in exchange for the responsibilities of a defined position. There is a certain degree of respect and trust that accompanies the position—the organization will pay on a periodic basis and the professional will get the job done. While this may suffice in some research organizations, it can become problematic in product organizations that live and die based on promised schedules. Unmet deadlines may erroneously infer that marketers and salespeople are untruthful, that managers are unreasonably demanding, that engineers are incompetent, or just lazy. In fact, we know that in this fast-paced, hard-working, competitive industry where technological innovations occur at a rate unparalleled in history, creative talent abounds and precious few are "lazy." We are not poor managers or workers, but we are frequently poor estimators. Lack of an historical foundation upon which to base estimates (no correctly reported effort) is the bane of our existence.

Effort Data: Successful Collection   The way in which effort data is collected is crucial. More than any other data, the collection must be non-invasive and non-threatening. The WIIFM (What's In It For Me) syndrome is understandably in play. Why should technical individuals report exactly what they do if the information is, from their perspective, fed into a black hole? Why should they report accurately and honestly when they may be criticized for inefficiencies? Management that gives feedback to the suppliers and praise for accuracy can expect much cleaner data.

When educating staff on the benefits of effort reporting, managers often explain that stakeholders will gain:

- knowledge of which phases require the most effort (many people are surprised that the bulk of the effort is typically not in the coding phase).
- knowledge of how much time is spent in integral or support tasks like configuration management or reviews.
- knowledge of how much overtime is required to get the job done.
- knowledge of how much non-productive overhead is common and often necessary (most people are surprised that so few productive hours are actually spent on the assigned project).

When the development staff is enlightened and reassured that honest information is the goal, they are usually willing to provide accurate data and can envision how it will help them. No developer can argue that estimating a project based on a four-hour day instead of an eight-hour day isn't to his or her benefit (having first determined that the average day for the organization is four hours). Some managers are so sensitive to the concerns of the staff that they require effort data to be submitted anonymously.

How should technical individuals or teams report effort? The modern equivalent of time cards (or time sheets) remains the best source. An engineer spending hours working on one or more project tasks, as identified in the WBS, has a category to which time may be reported. Any number of reporting fields is acceptable—the type of project dictates the life cycle phases, activities, and deliverables. When the management, development, and support (integral) tasks have been defined in a WBS, the staff may accurately and honestly charge time to any activity that contributes to the completion of the project.

The effort reporting system should be automated and require only a few minutes for an employee to complete a periodic time report. It is unreasonable to expect that software engineers, accustomed to the latest technology, should be required to input data about themselves using a manual system. An easily accessible interactive dialog should utilize the latest multimedia technology and be Web-enabled. Any category to which time may be charged must be capable of appearing on a staff member's screen and only the relevant categories should appear. In the event that a totally new activity becomes necessary, a facility for adding it to the WBS should be allowed. In the truly modern organization, the engineer's workstation would collect effort information via speech synthesis software.

Three Basic Metrics: Reviews

The second of the three important types of measurement data is collected during peer reviews. The number of errors, the type of each error, the phase in which it originated, and the phase in which it is detected are some of the pertinent data recorded during a review.

One very useful metric for controlling projects is the amount of time spent in the review of each product. If reviews are encouraged and time is accurately tracked, it will be possible for staff members from other projects to contribute their expertise to this and vice versa, accomplishing cross-training for backup and maintenance support, as well as achieving a higher-quality product. Recording time spent in reviews helps to test the theory that heavily reviewed products require less rework. It is expected that reviews will save money and improve quality in the long run, but by how much? Only metrics data on quality built-in (time spent in reviews) versus quality delivered (changes requested due to bugs in the product, post-release) can answer the question. In the same manner, other activities can be measured and their correlation to product quality determined.

It is important to know where problems are found for several reasons. One reason is that problems discovered during the latter phases of the life cycle translate into higher costs due to increased rework. Problems discovered after release, typically found by the customer, are the most expensive (it is difficult to put a price tag on the cost of customer satisfaction). Reviews provide information about what kinds of problems occur, so that whole categories of problems may be eliminated or reduced. In-process reviews identify problems that can be corrected relatively early and inexpensively.

Reviews: Errors and Defects   It is useful to separate problems into errors and defects. An *error* is classified as a problem that is found in the phase in which it is inserted (phase of origin). A *defect* is a problem, or error, that escapes the phase in which it is inserted and is not discovered until some later phase in the life cycle. Therefore, a high-level design problem that is found and fixed in the high-level design phase is considered an error. A high-level design problem that is found and fixed in the low-level design phase, or the system-testing phase (or any phase subsequent to high-level design), is considered a defect. Errors are expensive, but not as expensive as defects. The most expensive defects are those introduced early in the life cycle, particularly during the requirements specification phase, and those found late in the life cycle, particularly during the system-testing phase.

Inspection, peer reviews, and structured walk-throughs produce measurements of defects (for convenience we'll call them "reviews"). Finding defects early in development, using reviews, is a valuable contribution that the intelligent organization will reward handsomely.

Like effort data, review data may be underreported and distrusted by technical developers, designers, and testers. As will be discussed in Chapter 23, "Validation and Verification," a successful review is one that uncovers problems so they can be fixed early on. The author of a defect should never be reproved, lest it becomes increasingly difficult to find defects in that organization. Defect statistics should be associated with the review, but not with the reviewed.

What to review? Review everything—every *type* of project artifact (but not necessarily each and every artifact; it would be impossible to review every code module in a large system).

What to record? Record when the review was held, who attended, what was reviewed, agreed-upon errors and defects, agreed-upon types of error or defect, phase of origin for defects, suggestions, the severity level of the error or defect, and whether or not the product is accepted, conditionally accepted, or should be re-reviewed.

How to collect review data? Collect it on review meeting "forms"—whether manual or online (preferred), the review scribe will ensure that the information is placed in the proper database.

Reviews: What Review Data Alone Can Show

- Who's contributing to the review (i.e., quality) process?
- In which phases are the largest numbers of problems being created?
- In which phases are the most problems found?
- What types of errors/defects are occurring? Which ones occur most often? Upon completion of the project, the types of problems (both errors and defects) may be studied. If, for example, the largest number of problems falls into the type, "interface errors," then that is a likely target for improvement. Pareto analysis is a popular method of graphing and studying categories of occurrences. The "vital few" are easily distinguished from the "trivial many."
- Which areas of a system are the most difficult (take the longest) to repair?
- Which types of faults are the most difficult (take the longest) to repair?

Phase Containment Effectiveness   Defects discovered after product deployment can cost up to 100 times as much to fix as defects discovered in early phases of the life cycle. Many experts believe that there is a cost increase of a factor of 10 for every phase boundary where a defect continues to exist. Once defects are distinguished from errors, phase containment effectiveness (PCE) may be calculated using the formula shown in Box 21–1.

Box 21–1
Phase Containment Effectiveness

$$PCE_i = E_i / (E_i + D_i)$$

Where:
E_i is the number of errors caught in phase i
D_i is the number of errors that were introduced in phase i but not caught until phase $i + n$

(i represents life cycle phases such as analysis, design, code, test, etc.)

Initially, project control is interested in driving the defect count to zero, so that PCE = 1. The PCE graph identifies which phases are the problematic ones. The problem that has to be solved is why so many errors of a certain type escape their phase of origin. A second problem can then be tackled: Why are so many errors of a certain type occurring? The number of errors is not an insignificant metric by itself, but the more serious problems require knowledge of the life cycle in order to be solved. Error data, captured on review forms, can be classified, analyzed, and reported via Pareto charts. For example, a Pareto chart may show that 153 interface errors were detected, compared to 11 variable-name errors, indicating where improvements should be concentrated. An example of using the GQM approach with phase containment is shown in Figure 21–18.

Analysis of causes of errors lends itself to root-cause analysis and continuous process improvement. For example, if user-interface defects surface as a frequent problem uncovered via the review process, a cause and effect diagram may help discover the reason—no reviews or ineffective reviews may be a cause.

If enough defects discovered are pegged to early phases of the project, then often a "stop the presses" attitude is appropriate to clean up the earlier problems and ensure the quality of

Goal: *Increase defect containment*

Question:
What is the currently known containment effectiveness of defects introduced during each constructive phase of software development?

Metric:
Phase containment effectiveness for a constructive phase. The figure demonstrates the reliance of PCE on errors found in reviews conducted during that phase (E) and number of defects that escaped the reviews of the phase such that:

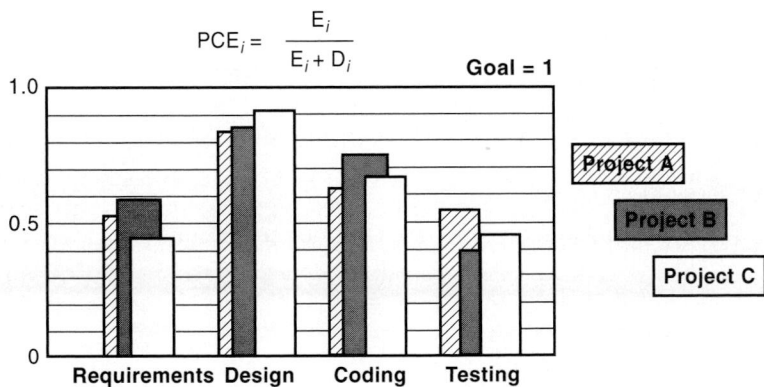

$$PCE_i = \frac{E_i}{E_i + D_i}$$

Goal = 1

Project A

Project B

Project C

FIGURE 21–18
Phase Containment Effectiveness GQM

interim rework. At a minimum, defects and errors are classified, published, and studied for process improvement.

What good will this review data do besides improving the process for some future project? Review results produced during development are analogous to "bug reports" after product delivery. Those bug reports, which will be called "change requests" here, are important to the quality of the system and customer satisfaction with it. They indicate what needs to be fixed and why. They can be prioritized, weighted as to severity, tracked for status, and used as lessons learned for maintainers of this system and developers of future systems. Review results work the same way. Simple errors can be placed in the trust of the author to correct; severe errors can be published and searched for in other places in the emerging system. Review data can also help project managers to predict schedule changes.

Reviews: Review Data Plus Effort Data   When coupled with the amount of time spent reworking a type of problem, even better decisions may be made about where to make improvements. There may have been a large number of interface problems, but they may have been corrected relatively quickly and painlessly, whereas there may have been fewer problems in the category of "incorrect initialization," but they each took much longer to fix and required more extensive rework. The rework data will originate not from the error/defect collection, but from the collection of effort data.

One way to determine if reviews are worth the time and effort put into them is to compare the cost of the review with the number of problems found, then estimate the cost of finding the problem at a later time. The number of hours spent in reviews and preparing for reviews is available on the peer review form, as is the number and severity of problems.

When review data is coupled with effort data, we are able to determine which deliverables took the most effort to develop, including review time, the correlation between fewer defects and more reviews, and the correlation between less effort spent in rework and more effort spent on reviews.

Three Basic Metrics: Change Requests

The third important type of measurement data is collected during software system change. Change request processes are routine in most software organizations and provide a rich source for useful metrics. Once software has been deployed, tracking systems commonly record problems encountered, or changes requested, along with the effort required to satisfy them. Borrowing from the National Institute of Standards and Technology (NIST), problems are of these types:

- Corrective: correcting a fault (error or defect);
- Adaptive: adapting software to system change, accommodating a changed environment (external circumstances) without enhancing or perfecting;

- Preventive: maintenance with the aim of discovering faults before they become failures;
- Perfective: maintenance for easing future maintenance.[12]

Changes to existing systems may entail *enhancements*—new or refined features for an existing system; and changes may occur to pre-release products during *development* of a new system.

In a mature organization, changes to project artifacts during development are also recorded.

Problems are not only found in the maintenance phase after product release, they may also be found during the enhancement and development phases. They are found in reviews (static tests), executed tests (dynamic tests), or observed some other way, typically through developer observation or user problems.

The need for change is commonly initiated by a user of the system, but may be reported by any observer.

Information typically accompanying a need for change includes:

- Who is reporting the need for change;
- A description of the problem or need (the IEEE Standard on Software Anomalies contains a thorough list of problem categories);[13, 14]
- When and where a problem occurred; whether there was an error message; other consequences/results; the environment (preceding events); indications of the cause;
- The name of the system or subsystem (if known);
- The criticality of the need (based upon predefined severity levels);
- Whether the change is corrective, perfective, adaptive, preventative, or enhancing;
- The impact of the change.

The response to the request for change will be accompanied by information such as:

- Where within the system the change will occur, or where the problem location is;
- If there is a problem, the phases of development it was created in;
- The sort of testing required;
- The estimated amount of effort (hours) to make the change;
- When, in calendar time, the change is expected to be completed.

Upon completion of the change, the final set of information relates to finding and fixing the problem, or making the enhancement:

- When was the change complete?
- How much actual effort was required?
- Where, within the system, did the change occur?
- What were the test results?

An example of a change request with slightly different data to be collected is shown in Figure 21–19. After product release it is imperative that we collect information such as that appearing in the list above and on the form in Figure 21–19. Should the same information be collected for a pre-release product? Some organizations find that a less formal and shorter form, in a convenient (online) reporting system is sufficient. Organizations with the highest levels of maturity generally use the same form thoughout.

With new or refined features, having a problem fixed, to perfect or adapt it, becomes increasingly complex—quality and effectiveness may deteriorate. Frequently modified code must, therefore, be continually reevaluated for quality. The application of perfective maintenance when software is undergoing other types of changes, is usually a wise approach.

Typical goals for changing software include:

- Reducing cycle time for response to requests for changes to the product;
- Reducing the number of changes needed by increasing quality.

Questions frequently needed to determine progress toward the goals include:

- What is the nature of the requested changes?
- Are the changes to fix bugs or make enhancements?
- What are the problematic components?
- How often do requirements change?
- How long do problems stay open?
- How many reported problems are severe?
- How fast is the response to problems?
- Which phase(s) contributed to the need for change?

Changes: What Change Request Data Alone Can Show

- Type of changes (i.e., problems) on a histogram or Pareto chart;
- Whether changes reflect problems or enhancements;
- Number of "patches" to a module (or subsystem), where to look for complexity;
- Requirements volatility;
- How many reported problems are severe;
- "Age of Open Problems";
- A way to prioritize problems;
- How many high-priority items remain unresolved;
- "Age of Closed Problems" (How fast are we responding?);
- Which modules or tables undergo the most frequent changes;
- Estimated versus actual effort;
- What phases contributed to the need to change.

Client:		Date:	
System:		Subsystem:	
SYSTEM REVISION CONTROL FORM			
Change request number:		Change request title:	
Problem or enhancement:	Severity:		Priority:
Description of problem/enhancement:			
Description of resolution:			
Phase in which the defect was injected		Phase in which the defect was corrected	
Assessment of impact			
Tables affected:	Programs affected:		Documentation affected:
Change control			
Identified by:	Estimated effort:		Assigned to:
Phase identified:	Impact on schedule:		Version released:
Approved by date:	Actual effort:		Date completed:

FIGURE 21–19

Example of a Change Request Form

Changes: Change Request Data Plus Effort Data

When coupled with effort data, change requests can show:

- Estimated versus actual effort;
- Who is overworked;
- Which parts of the system are the most costly.

Combinations of data provide the basic tracking mechanisms needed to control a project. Reliability, or a mean time to failure (MTTF), is another example of control information. It helps answer the question, "Are we finished testing?"

Combinations of data also provide the historical baseline needed to improve a process. Examples of such information include:

- Cycle time;
- Defects per unit of measure (LOC);
- Earned value;
- Estimation accuracy;
- Productivity;
- Quality;
- Total defect containment effectiveness (TDCE).

Measuring Aspects of Software Quality _____

Chapter 30, "Software Quality Assurance," will discuss the process of building excellence into software. Because much of that effort involves setting quality goals and measuring performance toward them, we will describe a few commonly used quality metrics here.

Most software engineering scholars credit McCall with the first published definition of software quality. In 1977, he identified the attributes of correctness, efficiency, flexibility, integrity, interoperability, maintainability, portability, reliability, reusability, testability, and usability as ways to describe aspects of product quality.[15] Boehm's list of what has become known as the "-ilities" was published in 1978.[16] Table 21–4 lists some ways that different people and organizations focus on the characteristics that are important for their product environment.

It remains a challenge as to how to turn these quality goals into questions and metrics *à la* Basili GQM. Here are some popular approaches.

There is a general belief that architectures and modules with higher *complexity* measures are more difficult to understand, have a higher probability of defects, are more expensive to maintain, and are harder to reuse than those with smaller complexity values. But, if "quality" is defined in terms of "complexity," how is complexity defined? Some of the definitions provide aspects to measure, such as:

- Logical (cyclomatic) complexity—the number of linearly independent test paths;[17]
- Data complexity—the number of data types and counts of parameters passed between modules;
- Calling complexity—the number of called modules, or the number of calling modules;
- Go To usage—the number of "Go To" statements;[18]
- Functional complexity—operators and operands;[19]
- Nesting levels—the depth of nesting of conditional statements.

A study conducted at Los Alamos National Laboratory concluded that complexity might also be exacerbated by the size of a module and by "meaningless" variable names.[20]

Approaches toward architecture can increase or decrease complexity. Imprecise specifications, concurrency of construction, large numbers of design elements, such as functions and classes, are all measurable characteristics that can be tracked and controlled.[21]

Japanese companies use a quality factor for systems called *spoilage*, defined as the time needed to fix post-release defects/total development time.

Usability of a software product is the extent to which the product is convenient and practical to use. This is another quality attribute that is difficult to measure—it must be decomposed into more fundamental attributes, each of which must be assessed by the user for the product in question.

Customer satisfaction has been measured on a five-point scale: very satisfied, satisfied, neutral, dissatisfied, very dissatisfied. The percent found in each category is then published in a graphical format, such as a pie chart.

Backlog index is the number of problems closed during the month/the number of problem arrivals during the month × 100%.

Schedule estimation accuracy is the actual project duration/the estimated project duration (shown in Figure 21–7).

Effort estimation accuracy is the actual project effort/estimated project effort (shown in Figure 21–7).

Failure rate is the number of failures/execution time.

Software productivity is the size/the effort.

TABLE 21-4
Quality Criteria/Goals

Criteria/Goals	McCall 1977[a]	Boehm 1978[b]	Hewlett-Packard FURPS Functionality, Usability, Reliability, Performance, Serviceability[c]	IBM CUPRIMDSO Capability, Usability, Performance, Reliability, Installability, Maintainability, Documentation, Service, Overall[d]	Allen 2000[e]
Accuracy					X
Adaptability					X
Clarity		X			X
Correctness	X	X			
Documentation		X		X	
Economy		X			
Efficiency	X	X			
Flexibility	X	X			X
Functionality			X	X (capability)	
Generality		X			

[a]McCall, J.A., et al. (1977). "Metrics for Software Quality Evaluation and Prediction." *Proceedings of Second Summer Software Engineering Workshop,* Greenbelt, MD, September 19, 1977. [b]Boehm, Barry, et al. (1978). *Characteristics of Software Quality.* Amsterdam: North-Holland Pub. Co.; New York, NY: American Elsevier. [c]Grady, Robert B. (1992). *Practical Software Metrics for Project Management and Process Improvement.* New York, NY: Prentice Hall. [d]Radice, R.A., et al. (1985). "A Programming Process Study." *IBM Systems Journal,* 24(2):91–101. [e]Allen, Paul (2000). *Realizing e-Business with Components.* Reading, MA: Addison-Wesley.

(Continues)

TABLE 21-4 (Continued)
Quality Criteria/Goals

Criteria/Goals	McCall 1977[a]	Boehm 1978[b]	Hewlett-Packard FURPS Functionality, Usability, Reliability, Performance, Serviceability[c]	IBM CUPRIMDSO Capability, Usability, Performance, Reliability, Installability, Maintainability, Documentation, Service, Overall[d]	Allen 2000[e]
Installability				X	
Integrity	X	X			
Interoperability	X				X
Maintainability	X	X		X	X
Modifiability		X			
Overall				X	
Performance			X	X	X
Portability	X	X			
Reliability	X	X	X	X	
Replaceability					X
Resilience		X			

[a]McCall, J.A., et al. (1977). "Metrics for Software Quality Evaluation and Prediction." *Proceedings of Second Summer Software Engineering Workshop*, Greenbelt, MD, September 19, 1977. [b]Boehm, Barry, et al. (1978). *Characteristics of Software Quality*. Amsterdam: North-Holland Pub. Co.; New York, NY: American Elsevier. [c]Grady, Robert B. (1992). *Practical Software Metrics for Project Management and Process Improvement*. New York, NY: Prentice Hall. [d]Radice, R.A., et al. (1985). "A Programming Process Study." *IBM Systems Journal*, 24(2):91–101. [e]Allen, Paul (2000). *Realizing e-Business with Components*. Reading, MA: Addison-Wesley.

(Continues)

TABLE 21-4 (Continued)
Quality Criteria/Goals

Criteria/Goals	McCall 1977[a]	Boehm 1978[b]	Hewlett-Packard FURPS Functionality, Usability, Reliability, Performance, Serviceability[c]	IBM CUPRIMDSO Capability, Usability, Performance, Reliability, Installability, Maintainability, Documentation, Service, Overall[d]	Allen 2000[e]
Reusability	X	X			X
Scalability					X
Service			X (serviceability)	X	
Testability	X				
Understandability		X			
Usability	X	X	X	X	
Validity		X			

[a]McCall, J.A., et al. (1977). "Metrics for Software Quality Evaluation and Prediction." *Proceedings of Second Summer Software Engineering Workshop*, Greenbelt, MD, September 19, 1977. [b]Boehm, Barry, et al. (1978). *Characteristics of Software Quality*. Amsterdam: North-Holland Pub. Co.; New York, NY: American Elsevier. [c]Grady, Robert B. (1992). *Practical Software Metrics for Project Management and Process Improvement*. New York, NY: Prentice Hall. [d]Radice, R.A., et al. (1985). "A Programming Process Study." *IBM Systems Journal*, 24(2):91–101. [e]Allen, Paul (2000). *Realizing e-Business with Components*. Reading, MA: Addison-Wesley.

The Metrics Plan

Organizations that operate with meaningful metrics usually begin by treating the metrics process as if it were a project in and of itself. This means, of course, having a plan. A metrics plan would do well to follow the Basili GQM paradigm. It covers the "who, what, where, when, how, and why" of metrics.

Planning means to decide which products to measure, place the product under configuration control, determine which attributes to measure, design automated data-collection mechanisms, establish procedures for handling the collected data, analyzing the data and reporting the results, documenting all procedures, and training all stakeholders in their use.

Summary

What is not measurable make measurable.

—Galileo Galilei (1564–1642)

Software project managers have been advised by everyone from Galileo to DeMarco to measure in order to understand and control their projects. Yet, managers must resist having their measures become empty copycat platitudes—metrics must be meaningful, useful, accurate, and placed in the hands of the right people in the right format.

Measurements can and should take place during the entire life cycle. Measurements may be taken during:

- Requirements specifications (How do they rate for testability? How volatile are they?);
- Design documentation (What are the fan-in and fan-out ratios of the structure charts? What is the measure of coupling and cohesion?);[22]
- Coding (How many errors were found in each module? How many defects? In what phase were defects introduced? Where were defects found? What kinds of errors are occurring?);
- Testing (How many errors were found in each module? How many paths were tested? What is the cyclomatic complexity?);
- Integral phases (project tracking, for example—how do the estimates of effort, cost, and schedule compare with the actuals?).

Metrics are important to software project managers because they help in decision-making. Has the product been "wrung out" enough during machine testing (have enough problems been found?) to release it? Is it worth the cost to make reviews mandatory? Have the requirements changed so much that they no longer represent the product that we contracted to build?

The importance of metrics is stressed in the SEI CMM and CMMI. Measurement is a component of every key process area—how else would the organization know their baseline or if they are making progress toward the KPA goals?

The Basili goal/question/metric paradigm consists of seven steps, which, if followed, will make metrics meaningful for an organization. It defines a process that is sufficient to form the foundation of the metrics plan, either for a given project, or for an entire organization. An important strength of GQM is that it begins with goal-setting, which prevents the collection of measurements that will not benefit the organization or project.

There are a few metrics that are so basic and so useful that their collection and analysis may be begun prior to a GQM-type plan, if necessary. They are effort data, reviews data, and change request data. Alone and married to each other, they allow management to answer all sorts of questions and then make decisions based on the answers. Where is effort being spent? Is it in coding when it would be better spent in requirements gathering? What kinds of problems is the project experiencing? Is the staff unskilled in the tools? Are most of the faults introduced in the early stages of projects? Are certain modules more error-prone than others? Are the errors being contained in the phase in which they were introduced?

Quality metrics have been debated and collected since the mid-1970s. High-quality software is almost always a goal for project managers, but it isn't easy to define. Borrowing from time-tested publications of trusted authors, a standard set of attributes may be assumed, but even when they are adopted ("usability," for example), they must be decomposed further to be measurable. A standard set of measures, such as defect density, has been defined in the literature and usually serves as a good foundation.

To be successful, a metrics process must *never* be used against a person. It must be simple and straightforward enough to have minimal disruption of the working habits of those reporting the data (automated), collected data must be placed in a database for manipulation and analysis, and the analyzed (preferably graphed) measurements must be fed back to the data collectors and other stakeholders.

All stakeholders are encouraged to understand that software measurement is a means to an end, not an end in itself.

Problems for Review _____

1. Why do you think the 34 competencies people skills of appraisal, negotiation, and managing change were listed as skills involving metrics?
2. In addition to those listed, are there other metrics that can be derived from a combination of effort, review, and change request data?

3. What is your definition of quality? Complexity?

4. Why are the authors so adamant about not using measurements to "judge" people?

Visit the Case Study

You have been presenting the metrics based on your project's life cycle and the work done at BSD. This is only one piece of the effort. Mr. Lu wants to know the impact of the CRM personnel on the project. He wants a report on how effective they are in respect to BSD. Also, since you are making maximum use of COTS software, how does that distort the metrics being reported? For the ARRS project you need to look at the format of a metrics plan and adapt that to take into account the specifics of ARRS. Ms. Patel canceled your metrics plan as "process for the sake of process." Unfortunately, you now need to produce it. Luckily, Mr. Lu is going on annual vacation so you have until next month's status meeting to complete this plan.

Citations

[1]Kelvin, W.T. (1891–1894). *Popular Lectures and Addresses.*

[2]DeMarco, Tom (1982). *Controlling Software Projects.* Upper Saddle River, NJ: Prentice Hall.

[3]Curtis, Bill (1980). "Measurement and Experimentation in Software Engineering." *Proceedings of the IEEE,* 68(9):1144–1157.

[4]Boehm, Barry W. (1981). *Software Engineering Economics.* Englewood Cliffs, NJ: Prentice Hall.

[5]Pfleeger, Shari Lawrence (2000). "Use Realistic, Effective Software Measurement." *Constructing Superior Software.* Macmillan Technical Publishing.

[6]Torn, Aimo: Professor, Department of Computer Science Abo, Akademi University; Faculty member Turku Centre for Computer Science (TUCS) Turku, Finland.

[7]See note 6.

[8]Basili, Victor R., et al. (1994). "Goal/Question/Metric Paradigm." *Encyclopaedia of Software Engineering,* volume 1. New York, NY: John Wiley and Sons. pp. 528–532.

[9]van Solingen, Rini, and Egon Berghout (1999). *The Goal/Question/Metric Method: A Practical Guide for Quality Improvement of Software Development.* New York, NY: McGraw-Hill.

[10]Daskalantonakis, Michael K. (1992). "A Practical View of Software Measurement and Implementation Experiences Within Motorola." *IEEE Transactions on Software Engineering,* 18(11):998–1010.

[11]Kan, Stephen H. (1995). *Metrics and Models in Software Quality Engineering.* Reading, MA: Addison-Wesley.

[12]National Institute of Standards and Technology (1992). NBS Special Publication 500-106, "Guidance on Software Maintenance." Roger J. Martin and Wilma M. Osborne.

[13]IEEE (1993). "IEEE 1044 Standard Classification for Software Anomalies." *IEEE Software Engineering Standards Collection.* New York, NY: Institute of Electrical and Electronics Engineers.

[14]IEEE (1995). "IEEE 1044 Standard Classification for Software Anomalies." *IEEE Software Engineering Standards Collection.* New York, NY: Institute of Electrical and Electronics Engineers.

[15]McCall, J.A., et al. (1977). "Metrics for Software Quality Evaluation and Prediction." *Proceedings of Second Summer Software Engineering Workshop,* Greenbelt, MD, September 19, 1977.

[16]Boehm, Barry, et al. (1978). *Characteristics of Software Quality.* Amsterdam: North-Holland Pub. Co.; New York, NY: American Elsevier.

[17]McCabe, Thomas (1976). "A Complexity Measure." *IEEE Transactions of Software Engineering,* SE-2(4):308–320.

[18]Dijkstra, Edsger Wybe (1976). *A Discipline of Programming.* Englewood Cliffs, NJ: Prentice Hall.

[19]Halstead, Maurice H., (1977). *Elements of Software Science.* Amsterdam: North-Holland Pub. Co.; New York, NY: American Elsevier.

[20]Connell, John, and Linda Shafer (1986). "Reducing Software Maintenance Costs." *Computer Programming Management,* Auerbach Publishers.

[21]Jazayeri, Medhi, et al. (2000). *Software Architecture for Product Families.* Reading, MA: Addison-Wesley.

[22]Stevens, W.P., Glenford J. Myers, and Larry L. Constantine (1974). "Structured Design." *IBM Systems Journal,* No. 2, pp. 115–139.

Suggested Readings

Abreu, F.B. (1993). "Metrics for Object-Oriented Environment." *Proceedings of the Third International Conference on Software Quality,* Lake Tahoe, NV. pp. 67–75.

Albrecht, A.J. (1979). "Measuring Applications Development Productivity." *Proceedings of IBM Application Development Joint SHARE/GUIDE Symposium,* Monterey, CA. pp.83–92.

Albrecht A.J., and S.H. Gaffney (1983). "Software Function, Source Lines of Code and Development Effort Prediction: A Software Science Validation." *IEEE Transactions on Software Engineering,* 9(6):639–648.

Bache, Richard, and Gualtiero Bazzana (1994). *Software Metrics for Product Assessment.* New York, NY: McGraw-Hill.

Baker, A.L., et al. (1990). "A Philosophy for Software Measurement." *The Journal of Systems and Software,* 12(3):277–281.

Barns, Michael G. (1993). "Inheriting Software Metrics." *Journal of Object-Oriented Programming,* November–December, pp. 27–34.

Basili, Victor, and D. Hutchens (1983). "An Empirical Study of a Complexity Family." *IEEE Transactions on Software Engineering,* 9(6):664–672.

Basili, Victor, and Barry T. Perricone (1984). "Software Errors and Complexity: An Empirical Investigation." *Communications of the ACM,* 27(1):42–52.

Basili, Victor, and D. Weiss (1984). "A Methodology for Collecting Valid Software Engineering Data." *IEEE Transactions on Software Engineering*, SE-10(6):728–738.

Becker, Shirley, and Mitchell Bostelman (1999). "Aligning Strategic and Project Measurement Systems." *IEEE Software*, 16(3):46–51.

Boegh, Jorgen, et al. (1999). "A Method for Software Quality Planning, Control, and Evaluation." *IEEE Software*, 16(2):69–77.

Boloix, Germinal, and Pierre Robillard (1988). "Inter-Connectivity Metric for Software Complexity." *Information Systems and Operation Research*, 26(1):17–39.

Briand, Lionel C., Sandro Morasca, and Victor R. Basili (1996). "Property-Based Software Engineering Measurement." *IEEE Transactions on Software Engineering*, 22(1):68–86.

Card, David N., and Robert L. Glass (1990). *Measuring Software Design Quality.* Englewood Cliffs, NJ: Prentice Hall.

Chapin, Ned (1979). "A Measure of Software Complexity." *Proceedings of the AFIPS National Computer Conference,* Spring 1979, pp. 995–1002.

Charette, Robert N. (1990). *Applications Strategies for Risk Analysis.* New York, NY: McGraw-Hill.

Chen, J.Y., and J.F. Lu (1993). "A New Metric for Object-Oriented Design." *Journal of Information and Software Technology,* 35(4):232–240.

Chidamber, Shyam R., David P. Darcy, and Chris F. Kemerer (1998). "Managerial Use of Metrics for Object-Oriented Software: An Exploratory Analysis." *IEEE Transactions on Software Engineering,* 24(8):629–639.

Christensen, K., G.P. Fitsos, and C.P. Smith (1981). "A Perspective on Software Science." *IBM Systems Journal,* 20(4):372–387.

Conte, S.D., H.E. Dunsmore, and V.Y. Shen (1986). *Software Engineering Metrics and Models.* Menlo Park, CA: Benjamin/Cummings.

Cook, Jonathan E., Lawrence Votta, and Alexander L. Wolf (1998). "Cost-Effective Analysis of In-Place Software Processes." *IEEE Transactions on Software Engineering,* 24(8): 640–649.

Curtis, Bill (1979). "In Search of Software Complexity." *Proceedings of the Workshop on Quantitative Software Models for Reliability,* pp. 95–106.

DeMarco, Tom (1982). *Controlling Software Projects: Management, Measurement and Estimation.* Englewood Cliffs, NJ: Prentice Hall.

Dutoit, Allen H., and Bernd Bruegge (1998). "Communication Metrics for Software Development." *IEEE Transactions on Software Engineering,* 24(8):615–628.

Fairley, Richard E. (1985). *Software Engineering Concepts.* New York, NY: McGraw-Hill.

Fenton, Norman E., and Shari Lawrence Pfleeger (1997). *Software Metrics—A Rigorous and Practical Approach,* 2nd ed. Boston, MA: PWS Publications.

Fenton, Norman E., and Martin Neil (1999). "Software Metrics: Successes, Failures and New Directions." *Journal of Systems and Software,* 47(2–3):149–157.

Fenton, Norman (1991). *Software Metrics: A Rigorous Approach.* New York, NY: Chapman & Hall CRC Press.

Fenton, Norman, and Martin Neil (1999). "A Critique of Software Defect Prediction Models." *IEEE Transactions on Software Engineering,* 25(5):55–67.

Hall, Tracy, and Norman Fenton (1997). "Implementing Effective Software Metrics Programs." *IEEE Software*, 14(2):55–67.

Gilb, Tom (1977). *Software Metrics*. Cambridge, MA: Winthrop Publishers.

Goodman, Paul (1992). Practical Implementation of Software Metrics. New York, NY: McGraw-Hill.

Grable, Ross, et al. (1999). "Metrics for Small Projects: Experiences at the SED." *IEEE Software*, 16(2):21–29.

Grady, Robert B., and Deborah L. Caswell (1987). *Software Metrics: Establishing a Company-Wide Program.* Englewood Cliffs, NJ: Prentice Hall.

Grady, Robert B. (1987). "Measuring and Managing Software Maintenance." *IEEE Software*, 4(4):35–45.

Halstead, Maurice H. (1977). *Elements of Software Science*. New York, NY: Elsevier.

Harrison, Warren, and Kenneth Magel (1981). "A Complexity Measure Based on Nesting Level." *ACM SIGPLAN Notices*, 16(3):63–74.

Humphrey, Watts S. (1989). *Managing the Software Process*. Reading, MA: Addison-Wesley.

IEEE STD 982.2-1988 (1988). "IEEE Guide for the Use of IEEE Standard Dictionary of Measures to Produce Reliable Software." New York, NY: The Institute of Electrical and Electronics Engineers.

IEEE STD 1061-1992 (1992). "IEEE Standard for a Software Quality Metrics Methodology." New York, NY: The Institute of Electrical and Electronics Engineers.

IEEE STD 1045-1992 (1992). "IEEE Standard for Software Productivity Metrics." New York, NY: The Institute of Electrical and Electronics Engineers.

Ince, Darrel (1989). "Software Metrics." *Measurement for Software Control and Assurance*, Barbara Kitchenham and B. Littlewood, eds. New York, NY: Elsevier Applied Science.

Jackson, Michael (1998). "Will There Ever Be Software Engineering?" *IEEE Software*, 15(1):36–39.

Jensen, Howard A., and K. Vairavan (1985). "An Experimental Study of Software Metrics for Real-Time Software." *IEEE Transactions on Software Engineering*, SE-11(2):231–234.

Jones, Capers (1978). "Measuring Programming Quality and Productivity." *IBM Systems Journal*, 17(1).

Jones, Capers (1991). *Applied Software Measurement: Assuring Productivity and Quality.* New York, NY: McGraw-Hill.

Kan, Stephen H. (1995). *Metrics and Models in Software Quality Engineering*. Reading, MA: Addison-Wesley.

Kafura, Dennis (1985). "A Survey of Software Metrics." *Proceedings 1985 Annual Conference of the ACM*, Denver, CO, October 14–16, ACM Press, pp. 502–506.

Kearney, Joseph K., et al. (1986). "Software Complexity Measurement." *Communications of the ACM*, 29(11):1044–1050.

Kitchenham, Barbara, and B. Littlewood, eds. (1989). *Measurement for Software Control and Assurance.* New York, NY: Elsevier Applied Science.

Kitchenham, Barbara, Shari Lawrence Pfleeger, and Norman Fenton (1995). "Towards a Framework for Software Measurement Validation." *IEEE Transactions on Software Engineering*, 21(12):929–944.

Lakshmanan, K.B., S. Jayaprakash, and P.K. Sinha (1991). "Properties of Control-Flow Complexity Measures." *IEEE Transactions on Software Engineering*, 17(12):1289–1295.

Landsbaum, Jerome B., and Robert L. Glass (1992). *Measuring and Motivating Maintenance Programmers.* Englewood Cliffs, NJ: Prentice-Hall.

Lind, Randy K., and K. Vairavan (1989). "An Experimental Investigation of Software Metrics and Their Relationship to Software Development Effort." *IEEE Transactions on Software Engineering,* 15(5):649–653.

Marciniak, John J., ed. (1994). *Encyclopedia of Software Engineering.* New York, NY: John Wiley and Sons, pp. 131–166.

McCabe, T., and Charles W. Butler (1989). "Design Complexity Measurement and Testing." *Communications of the ACM,* 32(12):1415–1424.

Mendonta, Manoel G., and Victor R. Basili (2000). "Validation of an Approach for Improving Existing Measurement Frameworks." *IEEE Transactions on Software Engineering,* 26(6):484–499.

Miller, George A. (1956). "The Magic Number Seven, Plus or Minus Two." *Psychological Review,* 63, pp. 81–97.

Moller, K.H., and D.J. Paulish (1993). *Software Metrics: A Practitioner's Guide to Improved Product Development,* 1st ed. New York, NY: Chapman & Hall.

Nielsen, Jakob (1996). "Usability Metrics: Tracking Interface Improvements." *IEEE Software,* 13(6):12–13.

Offen, Raymond J., and Ross Jeffery (1997). "Establishing Software Measurement Programs." *IEEE Software,* 14(2):45–53.

Oviedo, Enrique I. (1980). "Control Flow, Data Flow and Programmers Complexity." *Proceedings of COMPSAC 80,* Chicago, IL, pp.146–152.

Park, Robert E. (1992). "Software Size Measurement: A Framework for Counting Source Statements." *Software Engineering Institute Technical Report SEI-92-TR-020.* Pittsburg, PA: SEI, Carnegie Mellon University.

Patel, Sukesh, William Chu, and Rich Baxter (1992). "A Measure for Composite Module Cohesion." *Proceedings of the 14th International Conference on Software Engineering,* Melbourne, Australia, pp. 38-48. New York, NY: Association for Computing Machinery.

Perlis, Alan, Frederick Sayward, and Mary Shaw, eds. (1981). *Software Metrics: An Analysis and Evaluation.* Cambridge, MA: MIT Press.

Pfleeger, Shari Lawrence, and J.C. Fitzgerald (1991). "Software Metrics Tool Kit." *Support for Selection, Collection and Analysis. Information and Software Technology,* 33(7):477–482.

Pfleeger, Shari Lawrence, Ross Jeffery, Bill Curtis, and Barbara Kitchenham (1997). "Status Report on Software Measurement." *IEEE Software,* 14(2):33–43.

Pressman, Roger S. (2001). *Software Engineering: A Practitioner's Approach,* 5th ed. Boston, MA: McGraw-Hill.

Putnam, Lawrence H., and Ware Myers (1992). *Measures for Excellence: Reliable Software on Time, Within Budget.* Englewood Cliffs, NJ: Yourdon Press.

Putnam, Lawrence H. (1978). "A General Empirical Solution to the Macro Software Sizing and Estimating Problem." *IEEE Transactions of Software Engineering,* SE-4 (4):345–361.

Rifkin, Stan (2001). "What Makes Measuring Software So Hard?" *IEEE Software,* 18(3):41-45.

Rising, Linda, and Frank W. Callis (1992). "Problems with Determining Package Cohesion and Coupling." *Software Practice and Experience*, 22(7):553–571.

Sawyer, Pete, Ian Sommerville, and Stephen Viller (1999). "Capturing the Benefits of Requirements Engineering." *IEEE Software*, 16(2):78–85.

Schneidewind, Norman F. (1991). "Setting Maintenance Quality Objectives and Prioritizing Maintenance Work by Using Quality Metrics." *Proceedings of the Conference on Software Maintenance* (CSM91), October.

Schneidewind, Norman F. (1999). "Measuring and Evaluating Maintenance Process Using Reliability, Risk, and Test Metrics." *IEEE Transactions on Software Engineering*, 25(6):769–781.

Schneiderwind, Norman F. (1997). "Software Metrics Model for Quality Control." *Proceedings of the 4th International Software Metrics Symposium* (Metrics '97), Albuquerque, NM.

Shepperd, Martin, ed. (1993). *Software Engineering Metrics—Volume I: Measures and Validations*. New York, NY: McGraw Hill, International Series in Software Engineering.

Shepperd, Martin, and Darrel Ince (1993). *Derivation and Validation of Software Metrics*. New York, NY: Oxford University Press.

Shooman, Martin L. (1983). *Software Engineering: Design, Reliability, and Management*. New York, NY: McGraw-Hill.

Sommerville, Ian (2000). *Software Engineering*, 6th ed. New York, NY: Addison Wesley.

Tervonen, Iikka (1996). "Support for Quality-Based Design and Inspection." *IEEE Software*, 13(1): 44–54.

Von Mayrhauser, Anneliese (1990). *Software Engineering: Methods and Management*. Boston, MA: Academic Press.

Walston, C.E., and C.P. Felix (1977). "A Method of Programming Measurement and Estimation." *IBM Systems Journal*, 16(1):54–73.

Wasserman, Anthony I. (1996). "Toward a Discipline of Software Engineering." *IEEE Software*, Vol. 13, No. 6, November 1996.

Web Pages for Further Information

hissa.ncsl.nist.gov/. Center for High Integrity Software Systems Assurance—NIST International Software Metrics Symposium.

irb.cs.uni-magdeburg.de/sw-eng/us/index.shtml. Software Measurement Laboratory.

satc.gsfc.nasa.gov/support/STC_APR96/qualtiy/stc_qual.html. 8th Annual Software Technology Conference, Utah, April 1996.

sel.gsfc.nasa.gov/website/documents/contents.htm#1. Software Engineering Laboratory—Section 6, Software Measurement.

stsc.hill.af.mil/. U.S. Air Force's Software Technology Support Center (search "software metrics").

www.software.org. Software Productivity Consortium.

www.acm.org. Association for Computing Machinery.

www.cmg.org. Computer Measurement Group, Inc.

www.iese.fhg.de/ISERN/. International Software Engineering Research Network (ISERN).

www.ifpug.org. International Function Point Users' Group.

www.incose.org. International Council on Systems Engineering.

www.instmc.org.uk. The Institute of Measurement and Control.

www.nist.gov/. National Institute of Standards and Technology.

www.psmsc.com. Practical Software and Systems Measurement Support Center.

www.ssq.org. Society for Software Quality.

Analysis and Design Methods

The process of documenting software requirements calls for elicitation, analysis, specification, and verification. During each of these activities, requirements models may be constructed to ensure correctness and to ease the transition into physical software. Software project managers are unlikely to become involved in the details of lower-level modeling and design, but they are very likely to be drawn in during creation of high-level models and when these models are presented to sponsors for approval. A project manager benefits from familiarity with and an appreciation for the modeling process because this knowledge contributes to accuracy with staffing and in effort and schedule estimation.

Design is important because it also assists with the estimation of tasks, helps in tracking the project during implementation, and helps the project manager speak the same language as the developers and know what questions to ask and when.

Analysis and design models enable software engineers to better understand performance issues as well as the software system's interface with other system components. Software analysts build data, functional, and behavioral models that are passed to designers who build data structure, architectural, interface, and procedural models. These models have often been called the blueprints for building the software. As the complexity of the system increases, the models also increase in importance.

Analysis and design may be accomplished with the use of a number of different models, but the two most accepted are structured analysis/structured design (SA/SD) and object-oriented analysis/object-oriented design (OOA/OOD) using the Unified Modeling Language (UML). Dozens of excellent and detailed works already exist on these subjects, so there is no intent to duplicate them here. We will only name the major models used with each method, give a brief example of each, and list some aspects of quality to be incorporated into them. Armed with an understanding of this material, the software project manager will be in a better position to support the project's analysts and designers.

Where We Are in the Product Development Life Cycle

Analysis and design occur after system exploration, and before implementation in the software product development life cycle. The high-level analysis modeling may begin in tandem with requirements elicitation and specification; detailed analysis typically occurs afterward but before the software design description (SDD) is created. Analyses models often appear within the SRS document, and design models often appear in the SDD. Various integral tasks not shown in Figure 22–1 are always active to support the software product development phase activities.

Chapter 22 Relation to the 34 Competencies

Like most of the responsibilities performed with software processes, analysis and design activities are supported by many of the product, project, and people skills.

Product Development Techniques

2. **Awareness of process standards**—As will be seen in this chapter, there are standards that accompany every analysis and every design method. Data flow diagrams, for example, must adhere to the laws of balancing and leveling between parent and child diagrams to be a valid model.

3. **Defining the product**—Requirements become analysis models that, in turn, become design models upon which the code is built. Analysis and design project artifacts, in this sense, *are* the product.

5. **Managing requirements**—Requirements models are often reviewed and even partially created by customers, users, and other nondevelopment stakeholders. Their approval of the models, which become the product, is a huge help in managing requirements and containing volatility to early stages of the project.

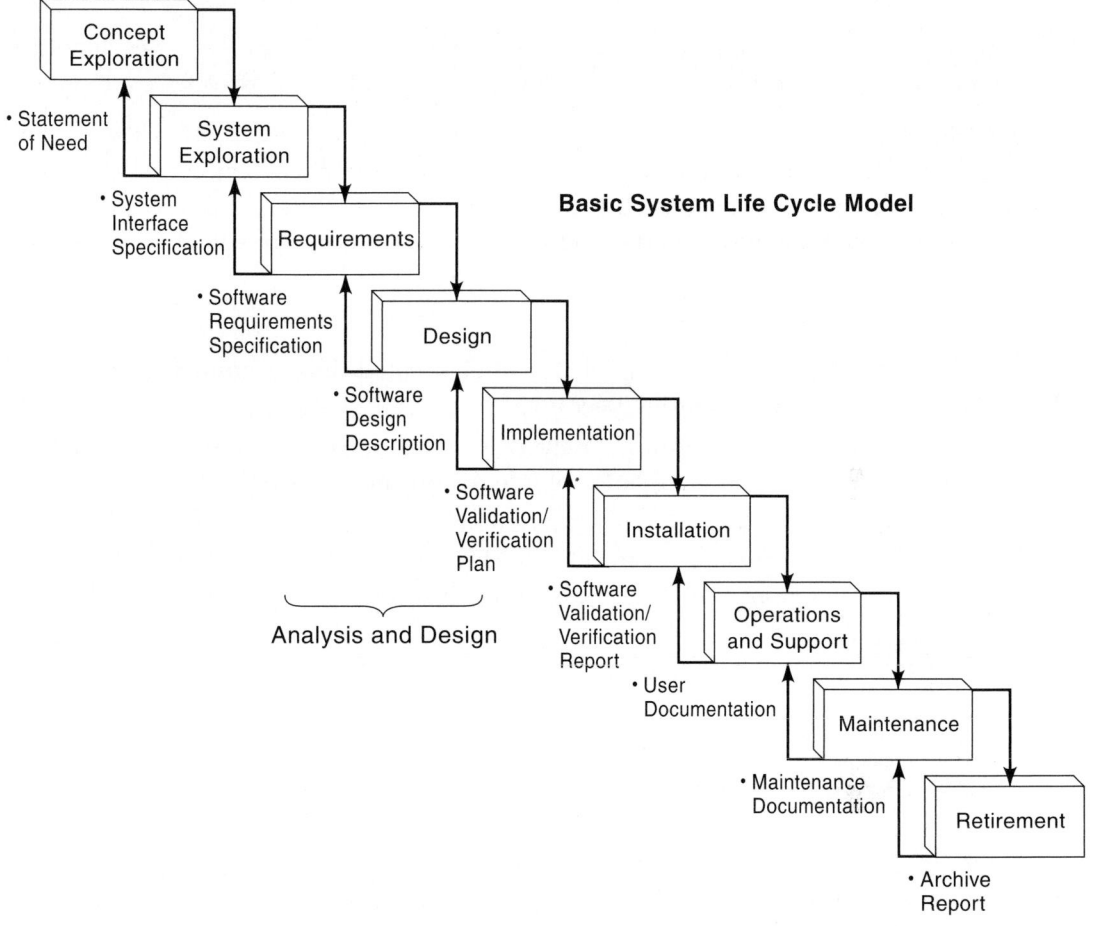

FIGURE 22–1
Analysis and Design Occur in the Early Middle of the Software Product Development Life Cycle

8. **Selecting methods and tools**—Analysis and design may be accomplished by a number of different processes. Here, we will look at two major ones: structured analysis/design and object-oriented analysis/design. The project manager will play a role in the determination of what method is the most appropriate for the project.

11. **Understanding development activities**—Some managers still think of "development" as producing code. The enlightened PM knows that analysis and design activities are critical to the development process. Although he probably will not be the actual modeler, it is important that the PM build adequate amount of time into the schedule for these activities.

Project Management Skills

14. **Estimating cost** and 15. **Estimating effort**—Analysis and design activities should be built into all cost, effort, and schedule estimates, especially the early ones.

16. **Managing risks**—Careful construction of quality analysis and design models reduces risk because they aid in pinning down requirements, generally the greatest risk factor in a software project.

17. **Monitoring development**—Analysis and design deliverables may be used in the computation of progress toward schedule milestones.

People Management Skills

25. **Holding effective meetings**—Models are often created during brainstorming or JAD sessions and are reviewed during peer reviews.

26. **Interaction and communication**—Analysis is an extension of requirements elicitation activities and requires the same skills for interaction and communication.

29. **Negotiating successfully**—As seen in requirements elicitation and the creation of the SRS, not all desired functions can be delivered at once. Creation of feature sets and phased delivery options continues during modeling and requires negotiating skills.

31. **Presenting effectively**—Models are communication devices used to present requirements, and progress toward meeting them, to management and sponsors.

Learning Objectives for Chapter 22 _____

Upon completion of this chapter, the reader should be able to:

- Describe the ways in which structured analysis/structured design (SA/SD) and object-oriented analysis/object-oriented design (OOA/OOD) models represent software requirements;

- Create the artifacts of structured analysis: data context diagram (DCD), data flow diagram (DFD), process specification (PSPEC), data dictionary (DD), entity relationship diagram (ERD), control context diagram (CCD), control flow diagram (CFD), control specification (CSPEC—state transition diagram);

- Describe the quality implications of modeling data in third normal form;

- Describe the transformation of structured analysis models into structured design models;

- Describe architecture diagrams and their usefulness in modeling system requirements;

- Create the artifacts of structured design: structure chart and Chapin chart;

- Create the artifacts of object-oriented analysis/design (OOA/OOD): class model, object model, use case, activity diagram, collaboration diagram, sequence diagram, interaction diagram;

- Compare and contrast the processes for SA/SD versus OOA/OOD;
- Compare and contrast the benefits of SA/SD versus OOA/OOD;
- Recognize the quality aspects of SA/SD and OOA/OOD models.

Analysis and Design and the SEI CMM

Quality software project management is based upon three interlaced bodies of knowledge: the Project Management Institute's Body of Knowledge (PMBOK), IEEE standards and processes, and the SEI capability maturity model. Discussions of the CMM are threaded throughout the book, particularly in Chapter 4, "Selecting Software Development Life Cycles," and in Chapter 26, "Continuous Process Improvement." Software project managers are strongly urged to operate at maturity Level 2, the repeatable level, at a minimum. As an organization moves up the maturity ladder, visibility into the software process improves with each level, as does the improvement of control, predictability, and effectiveness. Level 3, the defined level, should be a goal for all software-producing organizations currently operating below it. At Level 3, integrated management and engineering processes are used across the organization.

A key process area within Level 3 is software product engineering (SPE). This KPA involves performing the engineering tasks to build (and maintain) the software using the project's defined software process and appropriate methods and tools—those methods may be based on SA/SD or OOA/OOD.

According to Paulk, goals of SEI CMM KPA SPE are these:

Goal 1: The software engineering tasks are defined, integrated, and consistently performed to produce the software.

Goal 2: Software work products are kept consistent with each other.

Activities performed include:

Activity 1: Appropriate software engineering methods and tools are integrated into the project's defined software process.

Activity 2: The software requirements are developed, maintained, documented, and verified by systematically analyzing the allocated requirements according to the project's defined software process. The individuals involved in developing the software requirements review the allocated requirements to ensure that issues affecting the software requirements analysis are identified and resolved. Software requirements cover the software functions and performance, the interfaces to both hardware and software, and other system components (e.g., humans). Examples of methods for requirements analysis include functional decomposition, object-oriented decomposition, trade-off studies, simulations, modeling, prototyping, and scenario generation.

Activity 3. The software design is developed, maintained, documented, and verified, according to the project's defined software process, to accommodate the software requirements and to form the framework for coding.

1. Design criteria are developed and reviewed. Examples of design criteria include verifiability, adherence to design standards, ease of construction, simplicity, and ease of planning.

2. Effective methods are used to design the software. Examples of software design methods include prototyping, structural methods, design reuse, object-oriented design, and essential systems analysis.

3. The software architecture is developed early, within the constraints of the software life cycle and technology being used.[1]

The software architecture establishes the top-level software framework with well-defined internal and external interfaces.

In this chapter, we present the specific methods of functional decomposition (data flow diagrams, control flow diagrams), object-oriented decomposition (classes, objects, interaction diagrams, activity diagrams), and scenario generation (use cases). We also present structural methods (structure charts, Chapin charts), object-oriented design (classes, objects, interaction diagrams, activity diagrams, use cases), and essential systems analysis.

The "bottom line" is that the PM who follows the suggestions in this chapter will satisfy the requirement for KPA software product engineering at SEI CMM Level 3. Chapter 16, "Eliciting Requirements," presented high-level generic templates for data modeling in the form of entity relationship diagrams (ERDs), process modeling in the form of data flow diagrams (DFDs and use cases), and process/data modeling (object models). These representations of software requirements are useful during interviewing, brainstorming, and JAD sessions as communication devices. They are not detailed enough, however, to serve as the blueprint for coding and implementation. There are more steps in the development-by-stepwise-refinement process to get the models to that state. The analogy of home construction is frequently used. High-level analysis models are analogous to the drawings that an architect shows to the homeowner—the "look and feel" of the structure. Should there be two bedrooms or three? Should there be one bath or two? Should the garage appear at the front or rear of the home? Lower-level analysis and design models, while available to the homeowners, are not nearly as interesting to them—these documents show where the electrical circuitry and plumbing are to be placed, analogous to the contractors working with a blueprint. In this analogy, software analysis and design transition the product from "architectural renderings" to the final, detailed electrical, structural, and mechanical blueprints.

Structured Analysis/Structured Design (SA/SD) _____

Structured analysis and structured design result in graphical representations of the software system under development. The artifacts are usually a combination of some of the following: a data context diagram (DCD), data flow diagrams (DFD), process specifications (PSPEC), a data dictionary (DD), entity relationship diagram (ERD), a control context diagram (CCD), control flow diagrams (CFD), decision trees, state transition diagrams, and architecture flow diagrams (AFDs). As with OOA/OOD, there are so many possible models that the names and initialisms can be confusing. An overview table is provided in Table 22–1.

TABLE 22–1
Structured Analysis/Structured Design Models

Data, Function, Behavior	Type of Model	Description	Elements
		Phase: Structured Analysis	
Function	Data Context Diagram (DCD)	A picture of the system and its interfaces to external entities or systems. It shows the boundary between the system and its environment, in perspective to the real world, with all net inputs and outputs identified. Having only one process, the system as a "black box" at this point, it represents all of the transformations performed by the system.	External entities (boxes), one process (the system—circle/bubble), named data flows (arched arrows).

(Continues)

TABLE 22–1 (Continued)
Structured Analysis/Structured Design Models

Data, Function, Behavior	Type of Model	Description	Elements
Function	Data Flow Diagrams (DFDs)	A DFD is a picture of the system as a network of functional processes connected to each other by "pipelines" of data (data flows) and "holding tanks" of data (data stores). The processes transform the data. The diagram partitions the system into its component parts.	Labeled process bubbles, named data flows, data stores. Note that external entities do not show on a DFD, but data stores do. The terminators from the DCD are dropped; only the information flowing into and out of the system (the data flow) will be retained, and the one major process circle will be decomposed into several more refined process circles.
Function	Process Specifications (PSPECs)	Description of a function or process at the lowest level of decomposition—one is written for every functional primitive process. It captures the transformation to be performed within each process—that is, what happens to each input to produce the desired output.	PSPECs can be in the form of structured language (pseudocode), decision tables, equations, charts, mathematical equations, block diagrams, or other graphics.
Data	Entity Relationship Model (ERD)	Enables a software engineer to identify data objects and their relationships using a graphical notation. In the context of structured analysis, the ERD defines all data that is input, stored, transformed, and produced within an application. It is a picture of data organized into meaningful groups, and it shows the relationships between the groups.	Entities (boxes), attributes, relationships (directed lines), cardinality (crow's feet = many, bar = one, circle = zero).

TABLE 22–1 (Continued)
Structured Analysis/Structured Design Models

Data, Function, Behavior	Type of Model	Description	Elements
Behavior	Control Context Diagram (CCD)	Like the DFD, the CCD has only one process, shows inputs and outputs from and to external entities, and is broken down into components that end with specifications. The difference is that the data that appears on a CCD or a control flow diagram (CFD) is control data that causes a system state change, resulting in activation and deactivation of transforms.	External entities, one process (the system), named control flows. The elements and symbols on a CCD are the same as for a DCD, except that control data is represented by a dotted line to distinguish it from all other data and allow for clear behavioral modeling.
Behavior	Control Flow Diagrams (CFDs)	Model control flows instead of data flows. Share the naming, numbering, leveling, and balancing properties of DFDs.	Labeled process bubbles, named control flows (dotted lines), data stores, control bars for CSPEC.
Behavior	Control Specifications (CSPECs)	Indicated by a bar on a CFD; may change the state of the system.	State transition diagrams—state, transition, event/action.
Phase: Structured Design			
Data	Enhanced Entity Relationship Diagram (ERD)		Entities, attributes, relationships, cardinality.
Function/ Behavior	Architecture Context Diagrams (ACD)	Establishes information boundary between system and environment. Shows physical allocation of the requirements model's data (DFD) and control (CFD) processing. Assigns processes of the requirements model to physical modules that constitute the system and establishes the relationship between them.	Module = rectangle with rounded corners; regrouped process bubbles. Information flow vector = arrow (data)/dashed arrow (control); bundles of data and control flows.

(Continues)

TABLE 22–1 (Continued)
Structured Analysis/Structured Design Models

Data, Function, Behavior	Type of Model	Description	Elements
Function/ Behavior	Architecture Flow Diagram (AFDs)	The process bubbles from DFDs are rearranged according to more physical properties, such as which process bubbles must be organized together to accomplish the user interface.	Decomposed ACDs. Modules, inputs, outputs, user interface, maintenance, and self-help.
Function/ Behavior	Structure Charts	Structure charts organize systems that have been partitioned into black boxes into hierarchies. Structure charts show temporal sequence vertically but not horizontally.	Module boxes, control, data.
Function	Chapin Charts	Structured flow charts. Single entry, single exit.	Four processing constructs: simple sequence, do while/do until, if-then-else, do case.
Behavior	Architecture Interconnect Diagrams	Representation of the communication channels that exist between architecture modules. Shows the physical means by which modules communicate. Examples are radio signals, electrical bus, mechanical line, and optical link.	Same as AFD, with the addition of communication channels. Multiple channels are lanes (or units).

These methods have been in use since the 1970s and are, therefore, "tried and true." They work with any type of application and may be implemented on any sort of platform. Although numerous contributions to refining the method have been made over the years, a few outstanding individuals deserve credit for "inventing" or popularizing the concept. To recognize but some of these authorities and their seminal works, we salute Peter Chen, E.F. Codd,

Larry Constantine, C.J. Date, Tom DeMarco, Derek J. Hatley, Michael Jackson, James Martin, Stephen J. Mellor, Meilir Page-Jones, Imtiaz A. Pirbhai, P.J. Plauger, Douglas Ross, Paul T. Ward, Jean Dominique Warnier, and Edward Yourdon.

The goals of SA/SD are to improve software quality, reduce the risk of failure, and build in reliability, flexibility, maintainability, and effectiveness. The resulting system benefits from these quality considerations as the method keeps the focus on the system's underlying purpose, insists on documentation at every step of development, and creates a map of the system that is useful to all of the developers and managers involved with the project, in addition to future maintainers of the system.

Although originally viewed as a process-driven approach, SA/SD has always recognized data and behavior. In the 1980s the importance of data was openly recognized and data modeling was embraced. So, where does the analyst start? With the data model or the process model? It doesn't really matter. There are analysts who believe that data drives the system and those who believe it is process. We will start with data modeling and will consider behavior as an element of process.

SA/SD—Structured Analysis: Data Models

Data modeling is a way of describing the way data is to be stored in a system, at a high level of abstraction. It is different from process modeling because it does not model the functions performed by the system, nor does it model the time-dependent behavior of the system—the data model is a static model.

There are several ways to model data, but none as popular as the entity relationship diagram (ERD), which prepares the data to be physically stored in a number of formats; the most compatible is a relational database.

There are systems that control the world (e.g., radio transmission control) and systems that model the world (e.g., company personnel system). Both benefit from data modeling, but for systems that model the world, a data model is essential. It can help answer questions such as these:

- What data is needed to solve the business problem?
- How are the data items related to each other?
- Who owns the data?
- Who may access data?

Data models aid in the construction of an efficient database system with three essential functions: transaction consistency (transactions behave as if they are applied serially), data integrity over time (data is not lost or corrupted during faults in hardware or software hosts), and data independence (data is not constrained by the physical implementation).

The American National Standards Institute (ANSI) Standards Planning and Requirements Committee (SPARC) has described ways in which the data in a system may be viewed. Considering the different viewpoints aids the analyst and designer construct a complete model.

ANSI/SPARC describes a conceptual view of data: the logical organization of all application data managed by the system, the synthesis of the external models, and how different views are integrated via a common language and structure. The external view is a specific subset of the conceptual view data, representing users' view. The logical view is based on the conceptual model, taking into account the type of database management system that will be used, such as hierarchical, relational, network, or object-oriented. The internal view is toward the specific physical organization of storage devices; the organization of data on physical media.[2]

Here, we will be concerned with modeling only the conceptual view of data. We think in terms of a data model for the entire database, known as the "global conceptual scheme." Commonly, different users have different data requirements, so the data model may be partitioned for subclasses of users.

Which comes first, the relational database system (RDBS) from which the ERD may be drawn to represent the way data is stored, or the ERD, which drives the way the RDBS is constructed? We will create the model (the ERD) first, although familiarity with relational database management systems (RDBMS) does not hurt the analyst, designer, or project manager. E.F. Codd, a scientist with IBM, originally proposed the relational data model in the late 1960s. With it, he introduced the idea of data independence and mathematical set concepts as the foundation for database architecture. Up to that point, database applications directly accessed the data files to manipulate them and data was stored in records consisting of fields of individual data items. The relational data model is described in detail in various textbooks, such as *The Theory of Relational Databases* (Maier).

The relational data model provides a very simple construct for representing data structures, a tabular structure called a *relation* consisting of columns called *attributes*, where each attribute is atomic (nondecomposable) and single-valued. The rows of the table are records, where each contains the same set of attributes. Certain fields may be designated as keys, which means that searches for specific values of that field will use indexing to speed them up. The relational data model also provides a large range of integrity *constraints*.

Entity Relationship Diagrams   The entity relationship diagram (ERD) enables a software engineer to identify data objects and their relationships using a graphical notation. In the context of structured analysis, the ERD defines all data that is input, stored, transformed, and produced within an application. It is a picture of data organized into meaningful groups, and it shows the relationships among the groups.

The attributes of each entity noted in the ERD are described in a data dictionary. The set of attributes that is appropriate for a given data object is determined through an understanding of the problem context. These attributes map to identifiers and keys in database management systems. We will leave most of those issues to database analysts and administrators (DBAs). This chapter is a cursory overview, intended to help the project manager understand the complexities involved in data modeling when staffing and scheduling the project. The project manager needs an appreciation of what it takes to develop the various incarnations of the product, but he is unlikely to be the hands-on creator of analysis and design models. Because this is not a database design book or even a strictly software engineering book, the intricacies of ERD design will not be plumbed here, nor will issues such as optional relationships, associative entities, dangling associative entities, derived relationships, or referential integrity be fully addressed. These are all important topics, but the project manager may not "have a need to know," and the developer can find excellent information in existing texts. As evidenced by the listings under the "References" section there are many outstanding texts on structured analysis and data modeling to which the analysts/designers may refer. Some of them are "must haves" in every software engineer's library.

Entities

An ERD is composed of boxes showing entities and lines showing relationships between them. The basic notation is shown in Figure 22–2.

An entity is something in the real world about which we need to store data. In the analysis of the system under development, *nouns* (files, data stores, items that are manufactured, functional roles people adopt, things used to make or deliver or control other things, etc.) give clues to entities. Events or activities may also be entities: "Visual inspection," for example, is a step in a process that could be an entity.

As we will discuss later in this chapter, an entity is not an "object" as used in object-oriented analysis. An object encapsulates both data and function; it consists of data and the methods (procedures, functions, operations) that can act upon the data. An entity is a representation of data only. Nor is an entity the same as an instance of the entity. "Author" is an entity; "Bob Futrell" is an instance of author. An instance usually becomes one row in a table of a relational database. Characteristics of entities include:

- Each entity in the system must be identified. It is an object that exists and is distinguishable from other objects. It can be concrete, such as states in the United States, books in a library, or automobiles. It may be abstract, such as an event (making a purchase, celebrating a holiday). It is represented by a set of attributes, or characteristics.

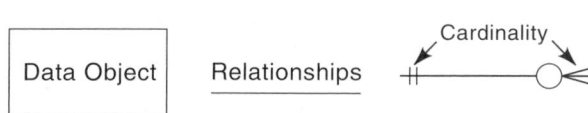

FIGURE 22–2
Basic Notation for Entity Relationship Diagrams

- There must be some way of differentiating among individual instances of the entity. Entities have attributes that differ among instances.
- At least one attribute or combination of attributes must uniquely identify each instance of the entity. (This will become the "primary key" in a relational database.)
- Each entity must play a necessary role in the system. If the system could function without it, it does not belong in the ERD.
- When it is important to show the attributes of an entity, they are shown as a list headed by the entity name. The primary key attributes are asterisked, as shown in Figure 22–3.

Attributes
An attribute is a unique characteristic of an entity. For instance, the entity "Customer" might have such attributes as "Customer Name," "Customer Address," "Customer Zip Code," "Customer Identification Number," and so on.

Relationships
Relationships are connections between entities. Each relationship represents an association between two entities. Cardinality means the number of relationships between instances of the two entities. Examples of cardinality are listed here:

- One-to-one
- One-to-many
- Zero (optional)
- Many-to-many

Cardinality is indicated by the symbols on the line connecting the two entities.

As shown in the top box of Figure 22–4, a one-to-many relationship indicates that each order contains one or more line items. Each line item is contained in one order.

The middle box illustrates a one-to-one relationship. Each manager manages one department; each department is managed by one manager.

The bottom box shows a many-to-many relationship. Each supplier supplies one or more products. Each product is supplied by one or more suppliers.

Order
* Order_ID
Customer
Date

FIGURE 22–3
Entity Relationship Diagram—Example of an Entity

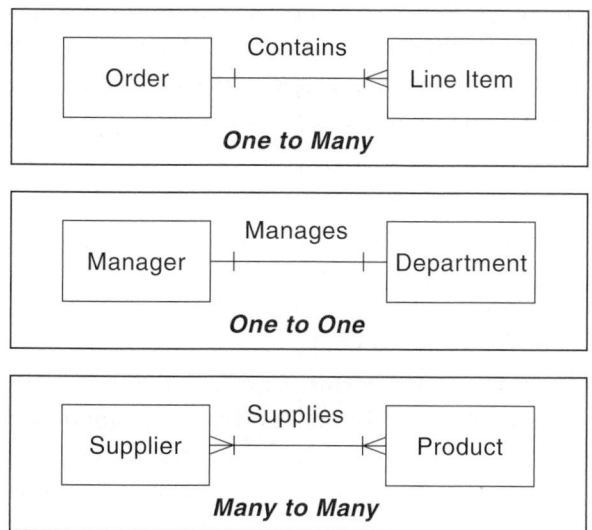

FIGURE 22–4
Entity Relationship Cardinality

Determining entities, their relationships, and their attributes is not an exact science, but a skill that improves with experience. A good way to begin is to interview the users, invite them to brainstorming sessions, search for nouns in written documents and in existing reports, and as always, use your analytical skills to understand the user's application.

As entities and attributes are discovered, they should be immediately placed in a data dictionary. Even if the definition is not crystal clear, the name should become an entry in the DD and should serve as a placeholder until further information can be gathered.

Normalization

Software project managers need to be aware of the importance of normalization, even though they may not be doing the work themselves. It may take an analyst more time during the modeling phase to consider future physical storage of data, but the up-front thinking is an effort-saver in the end. Normalization means to restructure data to remove redundancies and inconsistent dependencies and to increase flexibility of the model. Redundant data wastes disk space and creates maintenance problems. If data that exists in more than one place must be changed, the data must be changed in exactly the same way in all locations.

The underlying ideas in normalization are pretty straightforward. Through normalization, we want to design for our relational database a set of files that contain all the data necessary for the purposes that the database is to serve, have as little redundancy as possible, accommodate multiple values for types of data that require them, permit efficient updates of the data in the database, and avoid the danger of losing data unknowingly.[3]

In addition to removing redundancies and increasing flexibility, normalization reduces the risk of update anomalies (identical data stored in different places that may become out of synch), insertion anomalies (new data doesn't get stored in all of the places it needs to be), and delete anomalies (deleting data that is not associated with the data being deleted; a failure to remove information when it is time).

Before getting started with data normalization, the analyst may want to clean up the global data model. Some entities may not be needed and can be removed from the model. Look for entities that consist of only one identifier, entities for which there is only a single instance, entities with dangling associative entities (those that have only one choice), and derived relationships (those that can be calculated) are candidates for removal.

There are five degrees of normalization, called normal forms. The first three are very important; the last two are more esoteric. The models can be understood as the result of successive transformations of data. Analysts usually agree that if an ERD is constructed correctly and implemented as a relational database, then the database will automatically be in third normal form (not bad for the majority of operations). However, analysts may not always be able to start with a clean slate. Often, legacy data or manual forms already exist in the environment of the system under construction. This data is typically unnormalized, containing disparate data items not clearly related to each other and repeating groups, and it must be reconstructed into normal forms before the new or enhanced database can be designed.

To illustrate the progression of unnormalized data from first through fifth normal forms, an often-used example is the Daisy Hill Puppy Farm, which originated with Marc Retting when he was the technical editor of *Database Programming & Design* magazine.[4] The puppy farm has a number of puppies in residence. Each puppy has been taught or is learning a number of tricks. The owners of the farm need to easily locate a puppy that can perform a certain trick so that it may be shown to prospective clients (circuses, Hollywood agents, etc.). The current system relies on the use of the puppy record form as shown in Figure 22–5. There is a form for each puppy—if the puppy knows more than four tricks, the trick information is penciled in on the back of the form. The unnormalized data, or data in its "raw" form, is puppy (name, number, breed), kennel (code, name, location), and trick (name, costume, where learned, skill level).

When the file was first set up, it was thought that no puppy could possibly learn more than 12 tricks before graduation. But one puppy, a standard poodle named Boulette de Viande, learned more than 20 tricks. This forced a restructuring of the file, but it also left most of the file filled with meaningless spaces because the average puppy learned only four of the possible 20 tricks. In addition, more of the Hollywood agents are asking for puppies that know specific tricks. Before normalization, the entire file of 697 puppies must be searched to find a match.

A global ERD of the puppy farm information might look like Figure 22–6.

Daisy Hill Puppy Farm: A Puppy's Record

Number: *(ID Number of Puppy)*   Name: *(Name of Puppy)*   Breed: *(Breed of Puppy)*

_____   _____   _____

Kennel Code: _____   Kennel Name: _____   Kennel Location: _____

Trick (ID, Name, Description)	Costume (ID, Name, Description)	Where Learned (Name of Kennel)	Skill Level (1–10, Where 10 Is Highest)
_____	_____	_____	_____
_____	_____	_____	_____
_____	_____	_____	_____
_____	_____	_____	_____

FIGURE 22–5
Puppy Farm Unnormalized Form Example

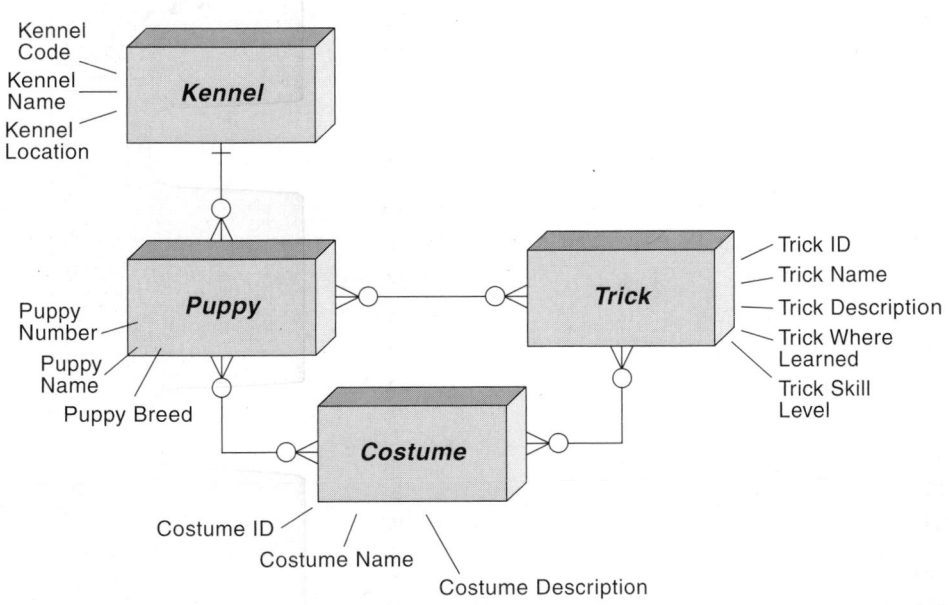

FIGURE 22–6
Global ERD for the Puppy Farm Example

Rule 1. First normal form (1NF) means that there are no duplicated rows in the table, each cell is single-valued (no repeating groups or arrays), and entries in a column are of the same kind. To get to 1NF, eliminate repeating groups.

Suppose that information from the index cards has been entered into some sort of database. To move it to 1NF, we would make a separate table for each set of related attributes and give each table a primary key, without using multiple fields in a single table to store similar data. The order of rows and the order of columns is immaterial. The requirement that there be no duplicated rows in the table means that the table has a key (although the key might be made up of more than one column). Note that the data may still contain disparate data items not clearly related to each other and that the dangers of update and delete anomalies may still exist.

The elimination of repeating groups is illustrated in Figure 22–7 and Figure 22–8. There will now be two tables, a puppy table and a trick table. The trick table has a primary key that is a multivalued, or "composite," key, consisting of both the puppy number and the trick ID.

Unnormalized Data Items for Puppies
- ◇ Puppy Number
- ◇ Puppy Name
- ◇ Kennel Code
- ◇ Kennel Name
- ◇ Kennel Location
- ◇ Puppy Tricks
  - ○ Trick ID 1
  - ○ Trick Name 1
  - ○ Trick Where Learned
  - ○ Skill Level 1
  - ○ Trick ID 2
  - ○ Trick Name 2
  - ○ Trick Where Learned 2
  - ○ Skill Level 2
  - ○
  - ○
  - ○
  - ○ Trick ID *n*
  - ○ Trick Name *n*
  - ○ Trick Where Learned *n*
  - ○ Skill Level *n*

In the original list of data, each puppy's description is followed by a list of tricks that the puppy has learned. Some might know 10 tricks, and some might not know any. To answer the question, "Can Fifi roll over?" we need to first find Fifi's puppy record and then scan the list of tricks associated with the record. This is awkward, inefficient, and extremely untidy.

FIGURE 22–7
ERD Puppy Example Before Rule 1 Is Applied

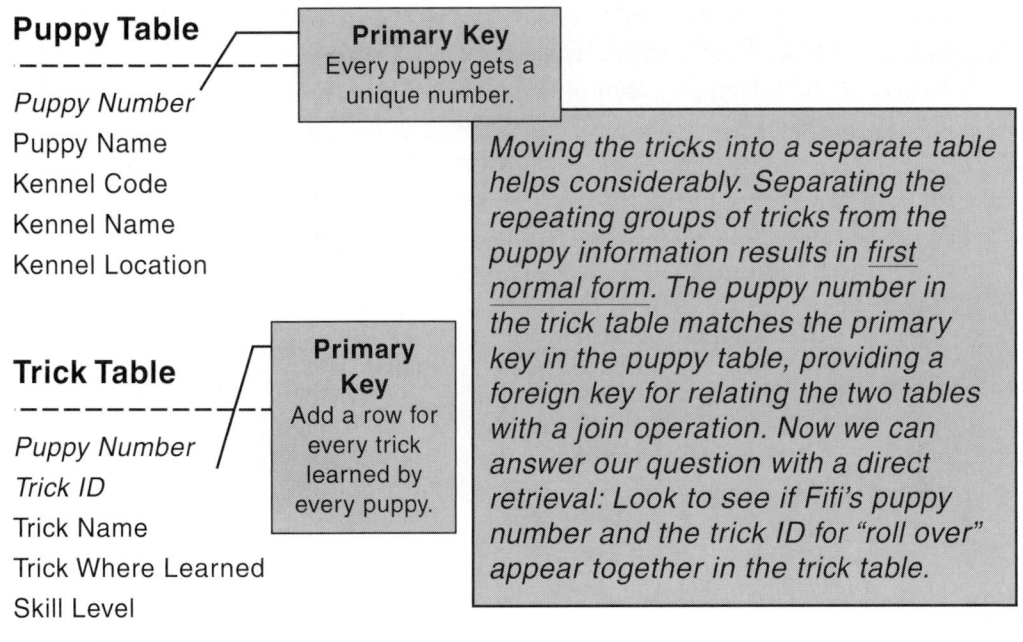

Puppy Table

Primary Key
Every puppy gets a
unique number.

Puppy Number
Puppy Name
Kennel Code
Kennel Name
Kennel Location

*Moving the tricks into a separate table
helps considerably. Separating the
repeating groups of tricks from the
puppy information results in <u>first
normal form</u>. The puppy number in
the trick table matches the primary
key in the puppy table, providing a
foreign key for relating the two tables
with a join operation. Now we can
answer our question with a direct
retrieval: Look to see if Fifi's puppy
number and the trick ID for "roll over"
appear together in the trick table.*

Trick Table

Primary Key
Add a row for
every trick
learned by
every puppy.

Puppy Number
Trick ID
Trick Name
Trick Where Learned
Skill Level

FIGURE 22–8
ERD Puppy Example After Rule 1 Is Applied

Rule 2. Second normal form (2NF) means that a table is in 1NF and all nonkey attributes are dependent on all of the key. To get to 2NF, eliminate redundant data.

If an attribute depends on only part of a multivalued key, remove it to a separate table. A nonkey field must provide a fact about the whole key. Relate tables with a foreign key. Note that fields that describe key data describe only the key and describe the whole key (whole means that it may be compound). All nonkey items are fully functionally dependent on the primary key. Data in a table may describe nonkey data items in that table, and the danger of update and delete anomalies still exists.

Refer to Figure 22–9. In the trick table, the primary key is made up of the puppy number and the trick ID. This makes sense for the Where Learned and Skill Level attributes because they will be different for every puppy/trick combination. But the trick name depends only on the trick ID. The same name will appear redundantly every time its associated ID appears in the trick table.

Suppose that you want to reclassify a trick—give it a different trick ID. The change has to be made for every puppy that knows the trick! If you miss some, you'll have several puppies with the same trick under different IDs. This is an update anomaly.

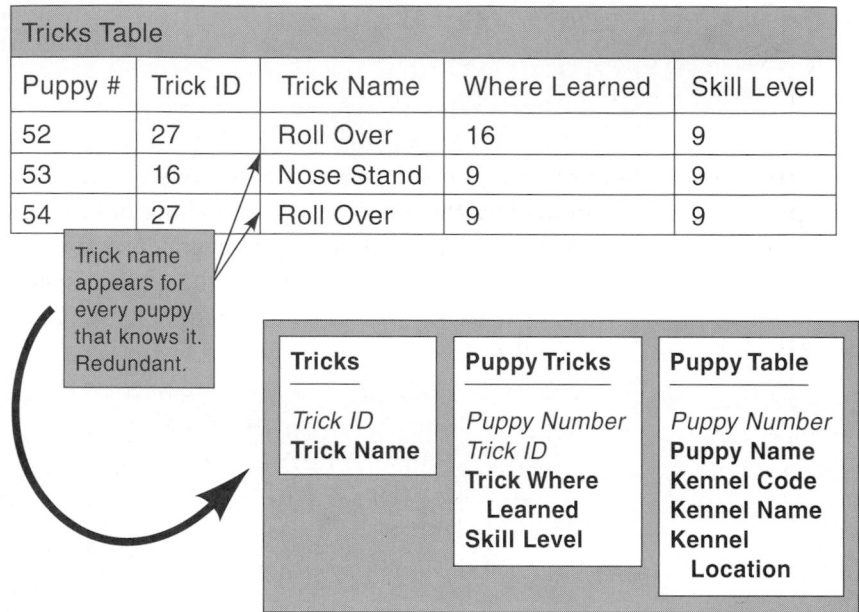

FIGURE 22–9
ERD Puppy Example Rule 2

Or, suppose that the last puppy knowing a particular trick gets adopted and moves to L.A. His records will be removed from the database, and the trick will not be stored anywhere. This is a delete anomaly. To avoid these problems, we need second normal form.

To achieve this, separate the attributes depending on both parts of the key from those depending only on the trick ID. This results in two tables: a tricks table, which gives the name for each trick ID, and a puppy tricks table, which lists the tricks learned by each puppy.

The tricks table is a single-theme table. The puppy tricks table is a single-theme table because it pairs puppies and their tricks—that is, it deals with the relationships between individual puppies and the tricks they know. In the puppy tricks table, the trick Where Learned attribute is clearly dependent on both parts of the key because the attribute is based not only on which particular trick is being referred to, but also on where the particular puppy learned that trick. The same is true of the Skill Level attribute because this attribute is based not only on which particular trick is being referred to, but also on the particular puppy's level of skill on that trick.

Now we can reclassify a trick in a single operation: look up the trick ID in the tricks table and change its name. The result will instantly be available throughout the application.

It would help to have all the trick data in a separate table. This would decrease the table size because every puppy that knows trick 15 would have its name carried. If the last puppy to know trick 15 moves to Los Angeles, her record will be removed and all knowledge of trick 15 will be lost.

Rule 3. A table is in third normal form (3NF) if it is in 2NF and if it has no transitive dependencies. To get to 3NF, eliminate columns not dependent on the key.

If attributes do not contribute to a description of the key, remove them to a separate table. A nonkey column must provide a fact about the key, the whole key, and nothing but the key. If a field does not describe the key at all, move it to a separate table. In general, any time the contents of a group of fields may apply to more than a single record in the table, consider placing those fields in a separate table. This is sometimes stated as removing transitive dependencies—that is, data that describes a field that, in turn, describes the key.

Note that all nonkey items are fully functionally dependent on the primary key and are independent of each other. Typically, third normal form (3NF) is adequate for an efficient database structure. If the database is derived from an accurate ERD, it is likely to automatically be in 3NF.

Refer to Figure 22–10. The puppy table satisfies first normal form—it contains no repeating groups. It satisfies second normal form because it doesn't have a multivalued key. But the key is the puppy number, and the kennel name and kennel location describe only a kennel, not a puppy. To achieve third normal form, they must be moved into a separate table. Because they describe a kennel, the kennel code becomes the key of the new kennels table.

The motivation for this is the same as for second normal form: We want to avoid update and delete anomalies. For example, suppose that no puppies from the Bed 'n Biscuit Puppy Farm currently were stored in the database. With the previous design, there would be no record of its existence!

The kennels table is a single-theme table. The puppies table is close to a single-theme table, in that it concentrates on puppies and their numbers. If the real-life situation is that any given puppy can be identified with one and only one kennel, then we can consider the puppies table to be a single-theme table. But if puppies sometimes start life in one kennel and are then transferred as puppies to another kennel, we would not be able to consider the puppies table to be single-theme because we would have to make further modifications to handle the mixed origins.

Rule 4. A table is in fourth normal form (4NF) if it is in 3NF and if every determinant is a candidate key (also known as Boyce-Codd Normal Form—BCNF), and if it has no multivalued dependencies. To get to 4NF, isolate independent multiple relationships.

Third normal form is sufficient for most situations. But for some purposes, it isn't normal enough, in which case we proceed to Rule 4: No table may contain two or more 1:*n* or *n*:*m* relationships that are not directly related. 4NF isolates independent multiple relationships. If two different facts are stored in a table, each describing the key, the whole key, and nothing but the key, but they bear no meaningful relation to each other, split them into separate tables.

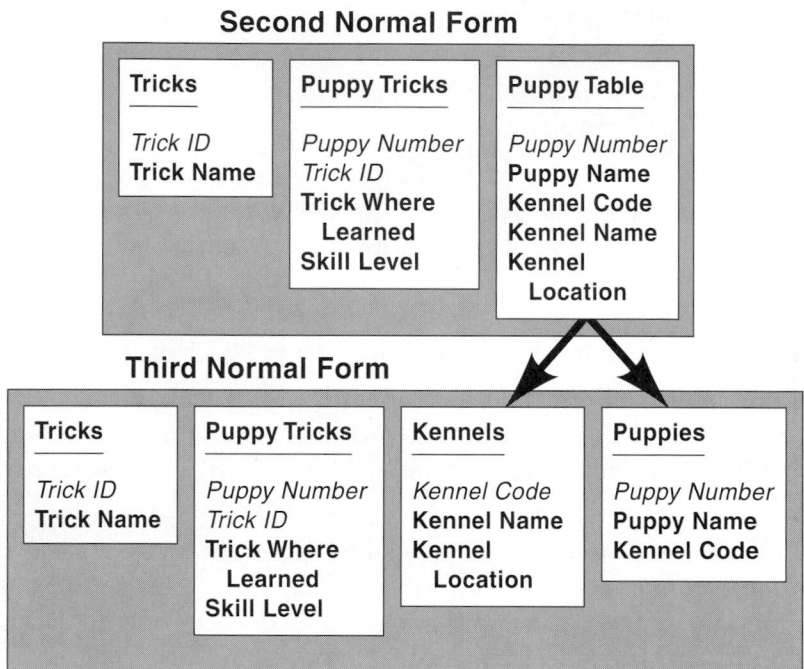

FIGURE 22–10
ERD Puppy Example Rule 3

This applies only to designs that include one-to-many and many-to-many relationships. An example of one-to-many is that one kennel can hold many puppies (Figure 22–11). An example of a many-to-many relationship is that a puppy can know many tricks, and several puppies might know the same trick.

Suppose that we want to add a new attribute to the puppy trick table, Costume (Box 22–1). This way, we can find puppies who can "balance on a ball" while wearing a Regis Philbin mask. The two need not relate.

Fourth normal form dictates against this. The two attributes do not share a meaningful relationship. A puppy may be able to walk upright, and it may be able to wear a wet suit. This doesn't mean that it can do both at the same time. How will you represent this if you store both attributes in the same table?

Here, the puppy number specifies a well-defined set of trick IDs and a well-defined set of costumes. Thus, there is a multidependency. How do we prevent anomalies in this case? Split the puppy tricks table into two tables, for puppy tricks and puppy costumes.

The 4NF in the example consists of the 3NF tables plus two new tables, for costumes and puppy costumes. Note that the puppy costumes table has a composite primary key that is

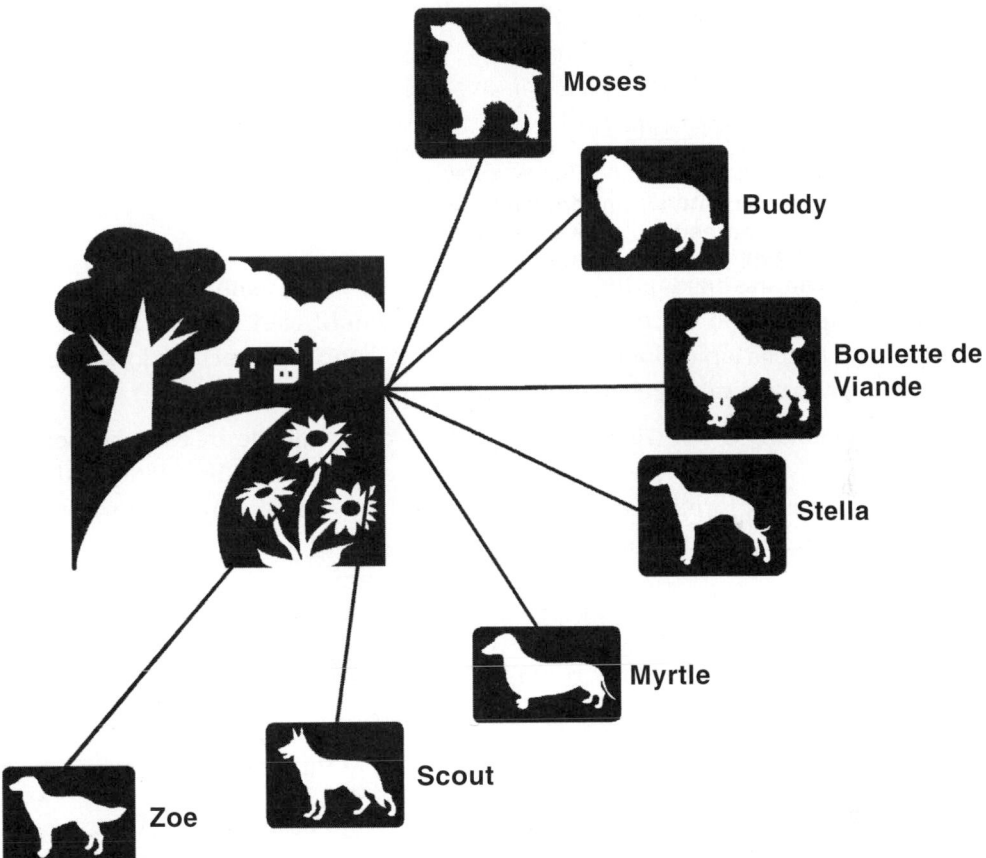

FIGURE 22–11
One-to-Many Relationship Puppy Farm Example

BOX 22–1
ERD Rule 4 Example

Puppy Tricks
Puppy Number
Trick ID
Trick Where Learned
Skill Level
Costume

made up of two foreign keys, from the puppies and costumes tables, respectively, as shown in Figure 22–12.

Rule 5. A table is in fifth normal form (5NF) if it is in 4NF and if every join dependency in the table is a consequence of the candidate keys of the table. To get to 5NF, isolate semantically related multiple relationships.

There may be practical constraints on information that justify separating logically related many-to-many relationships.

Usually, related attributes belong together. For example, if we really wanted to record which tricks each puppy could do in which costume, we would want to keep the Costume attribute in the puppy tricks table. But there are times when special characteristics of the data make it more efficient to separate even logically related attributes.

Imagine that our database will record which breeds are available in each kennel and which breeder supplies dogs to those kennels. This suggests a kennel–breeder–breed table that satisfies fourth normal form. As long as any kennel can supply any breed from any breeder, this works fine. See Figure 22–13 for an example of a 5NF table.

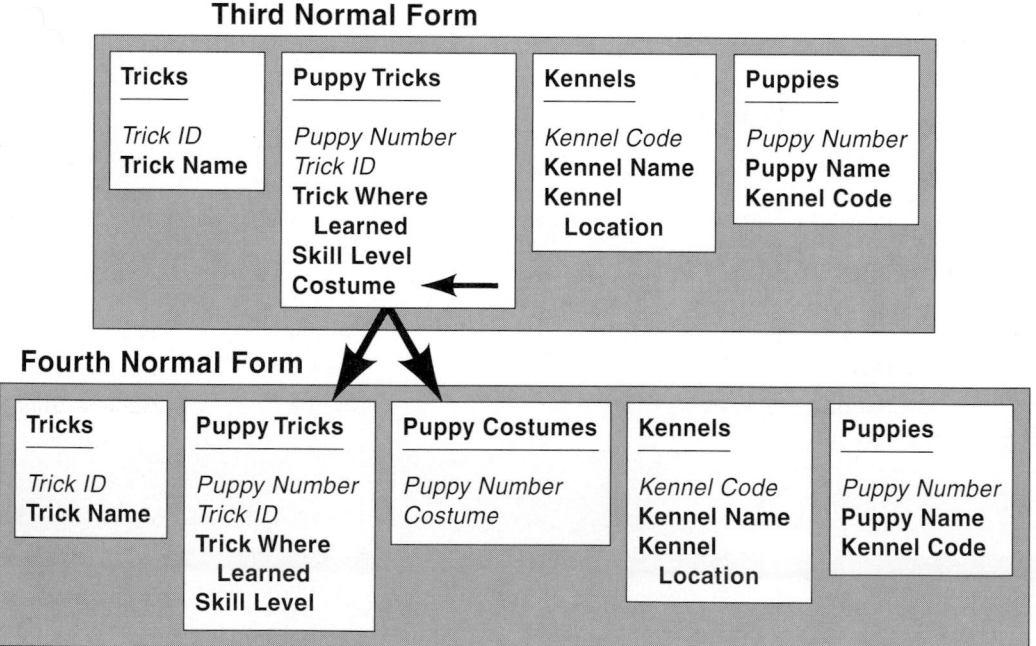

FIGURE 22–12
ERD Puppy Example Rule 4

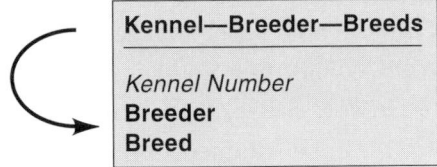

FIGURE 22–13
ERD 5NF Puppy Example

Now suppose that a law is passed to prevent exclusive arrangements: A kennel selling any breed must offer that breed from all breeders it deals with. In other words, if Khabul Khennels sells Afghans and wants to sell any Daisy Hill puppies, it must sell Daisy Hill Afghans. The need for fifth normal form becomes clear when we consider inserts and deletes. Suppose that a kennel decides to offer three new breeds: Spaniels, Dachshunds, and West Indian Banana-Biters. Suppose further that it already deals with three breeders that can supply those breeds. This will require nine new rows in the database, one for each breeder/breed combination. Refer to Figure 22–14.

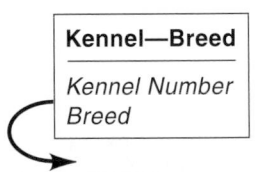

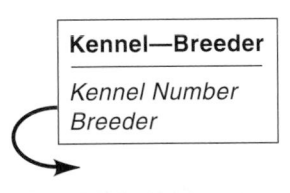

Kennel—Breed

Kennel #	Breed
5	Spaniel
5	Dachshund
5	Banana-Biter

Kennel—Breeder

Kennel #	Breeder
5	Acme
5	Puppy Factory
5	Whatapuppy

Breeder—Breed

Breeder	Breed
Acme	Spaniel
Acme	Dachshund
Acme	Banana-Biter
Puppy Factory	Spaniel
Puppy Factory	Dachshund
Puppy Factory	Banana-Biter
Whatapuppy	Spaniel
Whatapuppy	Dachshund
Whatapuppy	Banana-Biter

FIGURE 22–14
ERD Puppy Example Rule 5

Breaking up the table reduces the number of inserts to six. Here are the tables necessary for fifth normal form, shown with the six newly inserted rows in bold type. If an application involves significant update activity, fifth normal form can mean important savings. Note that these combination tables develop naturally out of entity-relationship analysis.

The rules leading to and including the third normal form can be summed up in a single statement. Each attribute must be a fact about the key, the whole key, and nothing but the key.

To quickly summarize, data modeling is a data view of the three system views (data, function, and behavior) in structured analysis/structured design methods. The most widely used data model is the entity relationship diagram. ERDs are frequently constructed so that, when used as a design document, data structures built from them are normalized at once. However, most software analysts and designers don't have the luxury of starting from scratch and must consider existing data, automated or manual, which is typically unnormalized. When placed into 1NF, then 2NF, and then 3NF, it will reap benefits such as these:

- Consistency—prevents update or deletion anomalies;
- Ease of use—ease of understanding;
- Flexibility;
- Precision—relational algebra and relational calculus;
- Easily implemented security controls;
- Attributes from different entities/files/databases easily related;
- Ease of implementation;
- Data independence;
- Clarity.

The data analyst/designer follows the process of finding and normalizing existing data (manual or automated), modeling it via an ERD for the system under development and then adding "new" data. The model is fleshed out gradually, beginning with major entities only, then adding relationships, then adding keys, then adding attributes, and then adding more entities.

SA/SD—Structured Analysis: Process Models

As information moves through software, it is modified by a series of transformations. A data flow diagram (DFD) is a graphical technique that depicts information flow and the transforms that are applied as data moves from input to output. Used to model the system graphically, the pictures encapsulate details and show the overall structure easily; with very little training, users can participate in the creation of the graphics.

Process modeling is a way of describing the functions performed by the system. Although it describes the data flowing through the system, it does not describe the static relations among stored data in the system, as does an ERD. Nor does it describe the time-dependent behavior of the system, as does a control flow diagram or a state transition diagram. A process model describes the transformations of the data in the system, taking the functional view of the three system viewpoints (data, function, behavior).

Data Context Diagram (DCD)

The data context diagram (DCD) is the top-level data flow diagram—a picture of the system and its interfaces to external entities or systems. It shows the boundary between the system and its environment, in perspective to the real world, with all net inputs and outputs identified. Having only one process, the system as a "black box" at this point, it represents all of the transformations performed by the system. Notation for the DCD is shown in Figure 22–15. It consists of boxes (entities outside the system), labeled data flow, and "the system."

External Entity (or Terminator)

A square or rectangle shows an entity or system external to the system under study. An external entity may be another computer system, a person, an organization, or a physical device that remains outside of the context of the system definition. Each of these special entities represents a source transmitting data or a destination receiving data. Although it is important to identify all of the entities that interact with the system, care should also be taken to include *only* those that interact with the system. It appears only on the DCD, not on the DFDs, as the system model undergoes stepwise refinement.

An external entity can be a source for the data received by the system, a sink for data produced by the system, or both. The name must be a noun and must identify an entity with which the system communicates. The name will not signify any processing

Data flows between an entity external and the system are representations of the interfaces between the system and its environment. External entities are not under control of the system—they cannot be manipulated in any way by the modeler. Relationships between terminators may exist, but they are not modeled on a DCD because our only interest is in bounding the system under development and the entities with which it interacts.

Process

A circle (bubble) shows a process that transforms data inputs into data outputs. The symbol is a circle with a name and a number. The name of the process represented by the circle should sum up all of the processing that occurs within it. The name must be a verb, acting on

FIGURE 22–15
Data Context Diagram Notation

a specific object or group of objects (a noun). The name is a verb-object phrase. The process represents the actions that the system takes. Data can be transformed only by passing through processes.

Data Flow
A curved line shows the flow of data into or out of a process or data store. A data flow is a "pipeline" through which packets of data flow. A data flow indicates data in motion. The symbol is a curved line with a name. The name must be a noun and must not imply any processing. The name represents the contents of the flow, which can be a single data element or a group of elements. More than one data element name may appear on a flow. The flow carries only one type of information, as indicated by the flow name. If you need to model the flow of two different types of information (for instance, customers and invoices), draw two data flows. Every data flow must appear in the requirements dictionary and must be defined down to its primitive elements.

A classic instructive example is the elevator problem, as described in Box 22–2.

Box 22–2
The Elevator Problem

A product is to be installed to control elevators in a building with three floors. The problem concerns the logic required to move elevators between floors according to the following constraints:

- Each elevator has a set of three buttons, one for each floor. These illuminate when pressed and cause the elevator to visit the corresponding floor. The illumination is canceled when the elevator visits the corresponding floor.

- Each floor, except the first floor and the top floor, has two buttons, one to request an up-elevator and one to request a down-elevator. These buttons illuminate when pressed. The illumination is canceled when an elevator visits the floor and then moves in the desired direction.

- When an elevator has no requests, it remains at its current floor with its doors closed.

The DCD for the elevator problem is shown in Figure 22–16. The external entities are the user and the elevator; the data flows are the button push, the illuminated button, the elevator command, and the elevator location. There is only one process, "the system," the control elevator.

Data Flow Diagrams (DFDs)   A DFD is a picture of the system as a network of functional processes connected to each other by "pipelines" of data (data flows) and "holding

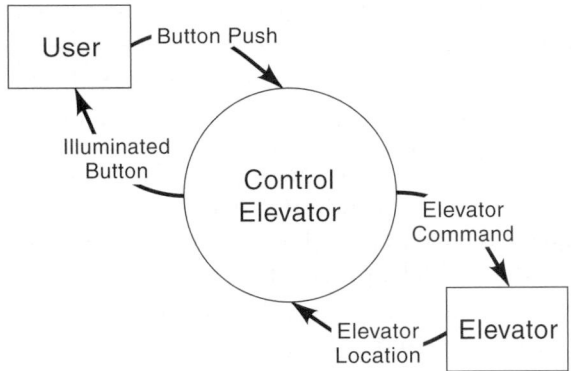

FIGURE 22–16
Data Context Diagram for the Elevator Example

tanks" of data (data stores). The processes transform the data. The diagram partitions the system into its component parts.

The DFD makes use of symbols for processes, data flows, and data stores. Note that external entities do not show on a DFD, but data stores do. The terminators from the DCD are dropped; only the information flowing into and out of the system (the data flow) will be retained, and the one major process circle will be decomposed into several more refined process circles. DFD notation is shown in Figure 22–17.

A circle (bubble) shows a process that transforms data inputs into data outputs. A curved line shows the flow of data into or out of a process or data store. A set of parallel lines shows a collection of data items at rest, a place where data resides. A data store indicates that the data is stored somewhere to be used at a later time or by the other processes in a different order. The data store can contain single elements or a group of elements. The name must be a noun that indicates the content of the data store. It must not imply any processing. It should be the plural of the data packets that go into and out of the store. The data stores on the DFD correspond to the entities on the entity relationship diagram. Typically, the name on the DFD is plural and the name on the ERD is singular. Every data store must appear in the requirements dictionary and must be defined down to its primitive elements.

FIGURE 22–17
Data Flow Diagram Notation

Data Stores and Data Flows

A data flow into or out of a data store shows the net inflow or outflow of data. If the flow to or from a store contains the same information as the store, then it may go unnamed. This indicates that an entire instance of a data packet flows into or out of the store. For example, if an update to the Customers store adds or replaces an entire customer record, the input flow may remain unnamed.

If the flow to or from a store contains a subset of the information in the store, the flow must be named. For example, if the system retrieves only the phone number of a customer or all the names in a certain Zip code, the data flows must be named. The data dictionary defines the data store and all of the elements that flow in and out.

Data flows travel from bubble to bubble. At a lower level DFD, data that flows out of the bubble is shown as a flow with no terminator. Data that flows into a bubble is shown at lower-level DFDs as data flowing in with no source. Of course, there are terminators and sources; they simply appear on higher-level DFDs.

The only area where redundancy is deliberately introduced is with data stores. A data store is shown at the highest level where it is first used as an interface between processes (it should not be shown at levels higher than that), and then the same data store is shown again at every lower-level diagram that further partitions the interface bubbles using it.

Data flows can split or combine. A split can indicate the entire contents of a flow (duplicate copies of the packets) going to more than one place. In this case, the split flows do not need a separate name. A split can also indicate a division into elements or subgroups. This shows that a complex packet of data is being split into several more elementary data packets. In this case, each subgroup must be named. Data that is combined is shown like the data that splits, but with the arrows going the other way. The same naming rules apply. Data flow splits and divides are shown in Figure 22–18.

The top-level DFD for the elevator example is shown in Figure 22–19. In this figure, the processes are Parse Button Push, Create Elevator Command, and Illuminate Buttons; the data store is Elevator Commands; and the data flows are Button Push, Floor Selection, Elevator Location, Elevator Command, Elevator Commands, and Illuminated Button. Because the data flows between the data store and the process Create Elevator Command are not labeled, we can assume that the entire data store is made available. The data flow Floor Selection could be drawn as a divided data flow. The net inputs and outputs match those of the DCD.

Functional Decomposition (Leveling)

The DFD represents the system as a network of processes. It is used to decompose the system functionally into its constituent processes. For all but the most trivial of systems, it would be very difficult to picture all of the constituent processes at once. Consider the example shown in Figure 22–20.

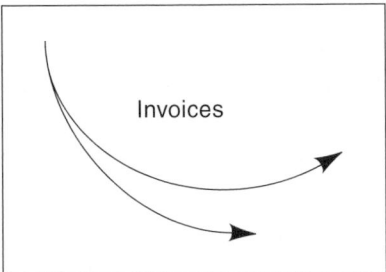

The entire contents of a flow goes
to more than one place.

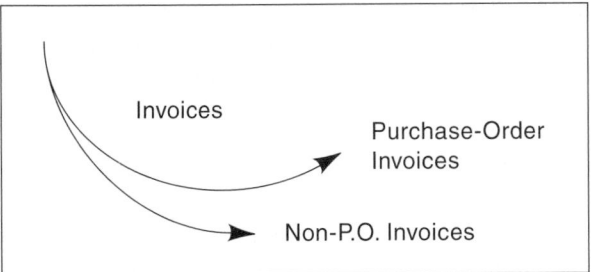

Complex packets of data may be split into several more
elementary data packets.

FIGURE 22–18
Data Flows May Split and Divide

This is far too much detail for the mind to grasp at once, let alone to fit on a single page. The solution is to divide and conquer. Do a top-down analysis and partition the system into subsystems. If the subsystems are still too large, divide them into sub-subsystems and continue the process until you have something reasonable at each level.

At each level of abstraction (except the lowest), there are one or more process circles. Each circle (parent) decomposes into a lower-level DFD (child), showing the contents of the parent.

The top level is the context flow diagram, showing net inputs and outputs to the system. It has only one function, to delineate the domain and boundaries of the system. Except at the very lowest level, the contents of the child are more circles and data flows. Each lower level shows more detail about the level immediately above it. At the lowest level, where a circle cannot be decomposed into any more constituent processes, a PSPEC is an appropriate tool to describe the functionality.

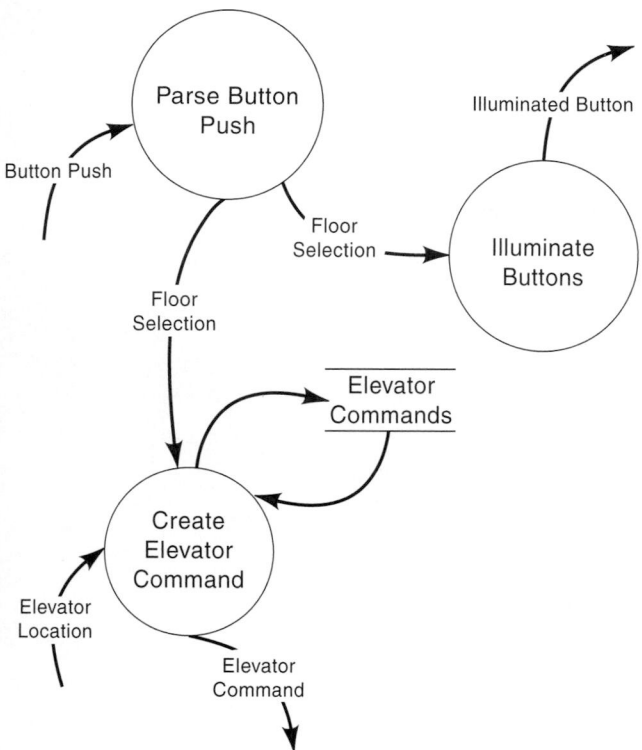

FIGURE 22–19
DFD 0 for Elevator Example

Decomposing DFDs and Labeling the Diagrams
Figure 22–21 shows a partially leveled decomposition. The way in which the DCD, DFDs, and process bubbles on DFDs should be labeled is also shown.

The highest level of the DFD (not to be confused with the DCD) is DFD 0. Its title is the name of the processing bubble in the DCD. Its bubbles are numbered 1, 2, 3, and so on. The numbers do not represent any sort of sequence of execution or sequential processing.

Bubble 3 in DFD 0 is decomposed into lower level DFD 3. The bubbles in DFD 3 are numbered 3.1, 3.2, and so on. Bubble 3.2 in DFD 3 is decomposed into DFD 3.2. That DFD's bubbles are numbered 3.2.1, 3.2.2, and so on.

The general rule is that a DFD's number is the number of its parent bubble, and its name is the name of its parent bubble. The bubbles within it are numbered with the number of the DFD, plus a decimal point and an additional digit: *n*.1, *n*.2, *n*.3, and so on. This numbering convention continues to each lower level.

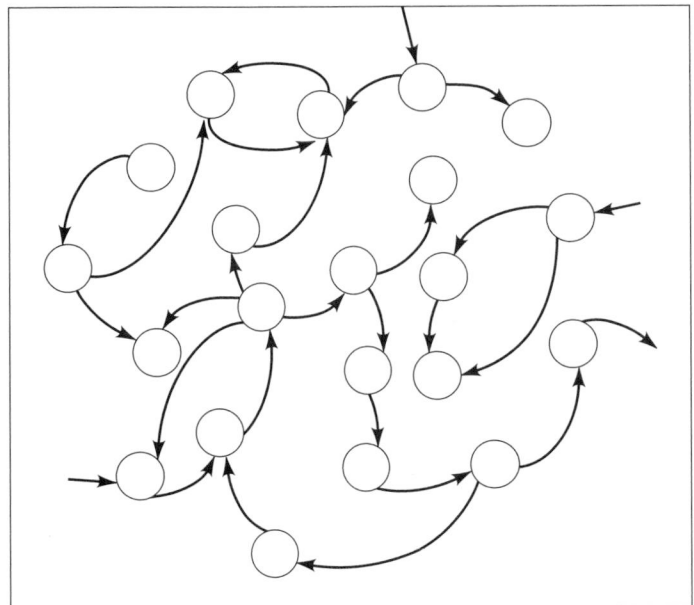

FIGURE 22–20
A DFD Should Not Have Too Many Bubbles

The number of the DFD is not the same as its level. In the example, DFD 0 is at level 1; DFD 3 is at level 2 (and so are DFDs 1 and 2, not shown); and DFD 3.2 is at level 3 (as are DFDs 3.1, 3.3, etc., as well as DFDs 1.*n*, 2.*n*, etc.). The level of a DFD may be determined by counting the number of digits in the bubble numbers inside of it. The parent of a DFD may be found by removing the last digit of its number: DFD 3.2's parent is DFD 3.

Thoughts of good design begin with the analysis models. Guidelines for constructing DFDs, which will carry through to design and on to code, include: Group related functions together, separate unrelated functions, eliminate redundant functions, keep each bubble cohesive (doing one and only one thing), limit the number of processes on a single DFD to about seven plus or minus two (5–9), don't model initialization or termination, and use an automated tool.

Internal Consistency (Balancing)
Balancing is a way of making sure that the requirements are internally consistent. The inputs and outputs of each DFD must agree with the inputs and outputs of its parent bubble.

At the lowest level, the inputs and outputs of a process specification (PSPEC) must agree with the inputs and outputs of its parent, the functional primitive bubble that it describes.

Every data flow and every data store must be defined in the requirements dictionary, and each must be decomposed into its primitive elements. The issue of consistency is particularly

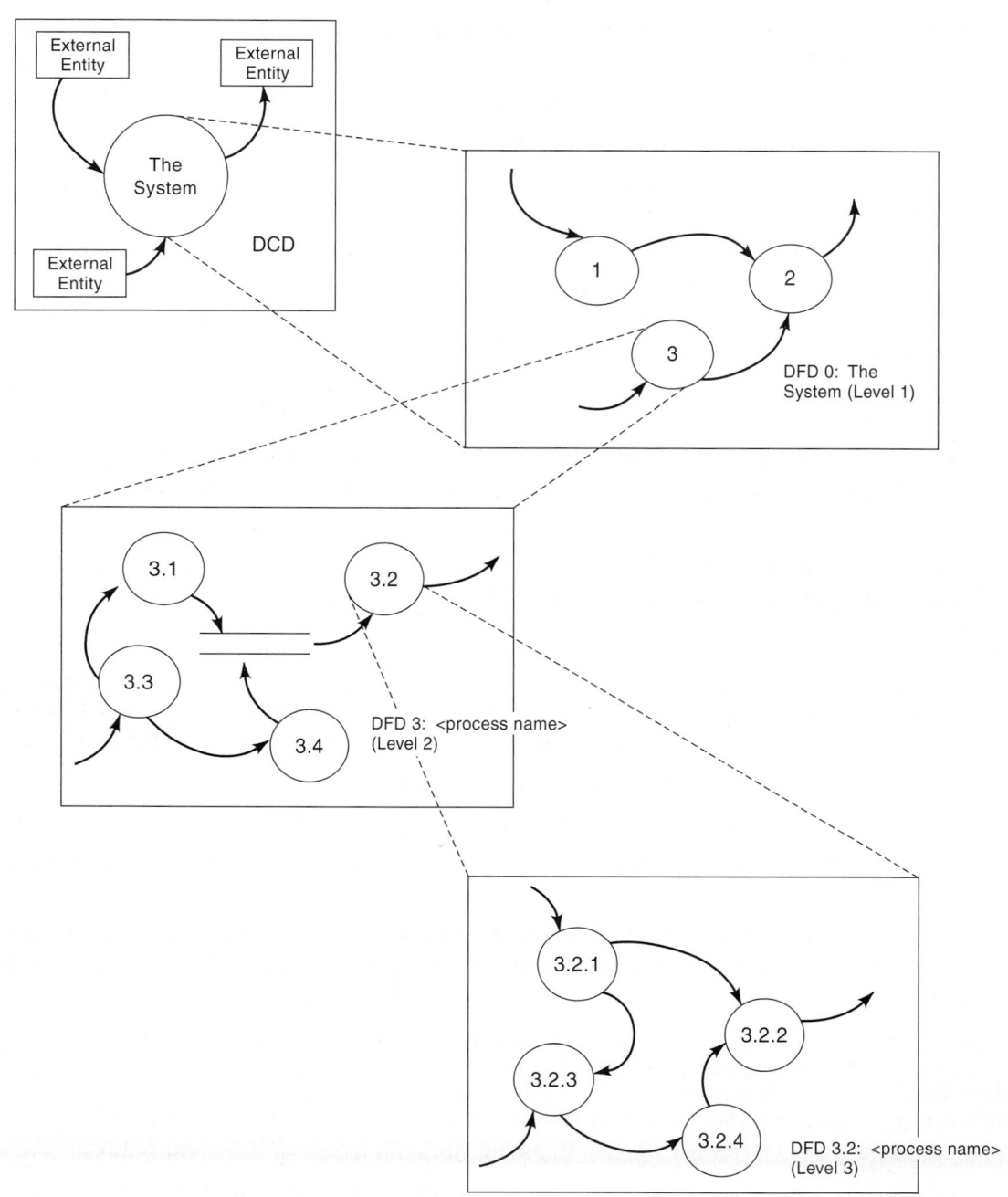

FIGURE 22–21
DFD Decomposition

important on large projects, where different people may be analyzing and modeling different parts of the system.

The following list includes guidelines for creating DFDs:

1. Avoid "black holes," bubbles that have inputs but no outputs.
2. Avoid "spontaneous generation" bubbles, those that have outputs but no inputs. A process rarely "magically" creates new data.
3. Label all flows and processes. Unlabeled flows are allowed only if the flow contains an entire instance of the data in the store it is going to or coming from. If naming a process seems difficult, then perhaps it is not cohesive or more clarification from the user is needed.
4. Watch for read-only and write-only stores. Legitimate read-only and write-only stores are rare.
5. Don't be too concerned if parent processes don't have the same number of children. DFDs will decompose to different levels because some processes are more complex than others.
6. Make sure that all of the data input to a process is really used.
7. Look for "transformation sense." Can the outputs be generated from the inputs?

Leveling DFDs
Know when to stop. Decomposition must come to an end at some point. In the example in Figure 22–21, DFD 3.2 is a likely candidate for a lowest-level DFD, assuming that bubbles 3.2.1, 3.2.2, and 3.2.3 have no further decomposition. There would then be four PSPECs associated with it, one for each bubble. General rules for when to stop decomposing are listed here:

- When the insides of a lowest-level bubble can be described in a PSPEC of one page or less.
- When there is only one input data flow and one output. (Bubble 3.2 appears to violate this rule—it isn't ironclad.)
- When there are clean one-to-one or many-to-one relationships among data flow. If a bubble needs to transform, say, three inputs into two outputs, it can probably be decomposed further.

Bottom-level processes are called functional primitive processes. Instead of being decomposed further, they are described by the PSPEC.

Advantages of Leveled DFDs
The specifications may be read top-down. Managers can get the big picture by looking at the high-level diagrams. Users and implementers can find the details that they need without being bothered by details in other parts of the system. Each diagram is a functional unit that fits on a single page.

Many automated tools on the market support drawing, balancing, and leveling. Although the tools do not eliminate the need for peer reviews, they do make the process less labor-intensive.

Process Specifications (PSPECs)

A PSPEC is a description of a function or process at the lowest level of decomposition—one is written for every functional primitive process. It captures the transformation to be performed within each process—that is, what happens to each input to produce the desired output. PSPECs can be in the form of structured language (pseudocode), decision tables, equations, charts, mathematical equations, block diagrams, or other graphics. Like the process bubbles that it represents, a PSPEC transforms input data into output data, states what must happen to create the outputs, and detects data conditions that indicate system state changes. Processes that are not primitive are broken down into more detailed DFDs and do not have PSPECs. A sample of a PSPEC using pseudocode is shown in Box 22–3.

Rules for PSPECs

Data names must be identical to those used in the requirements dictionary and DFDs. The PSPEC must be numbered the same as the bubble that it represents. For example, the PSPEC for bubble 4.3.3.1 would be labeled "PSPEC 4.3.3.1."

Guidelines for the creation of PSPECs include:

- Create a PSPEC for each functional primitive.
- Don't provide PSPECs for higher-level processes.
- Write PSPECs to describe rules governing the transformation of input data flows into output data flows.
- Balance the PSPEC to its parent. Its inputs and outputs must agree with the inputs and outputs of the functionally primitive bubble that it describes.
- Write the PSPEC to be clear, unambiguous, and concise.
- Remember that the PSPEC describes the requirements but does not impose a specific design or implementation decision.

Control Models
Many time-dependent (real-time), process-intensive, or interrupt-driven systems developers choose to model control in addition to all other data because of its importance to the operation of the system.

Control Context Diagram (CCD)

Like the DFD, the control context diagram (CCD) has only one process, shows inputs and outputs from and to external entities, and is broken down into components that end with specifications. The difference is that the data that appears on a CCD or a control flow diagram (CFD) is control data that causes a system state change, resulting in activation and deactivation of transforms. The basic notation of control diagrams is shown in Figure 22–22.

Box 22–3
Example of a PSPEC

```
Enter
Initialize
Do Until no more transactions or
terminal-error
        Get a transaction
        If      Transaction present
        Then    If add or update or
                delete
                Then    Call Process-Transaction
                        If      Return code = 0
                        Then    Move "unsuccessful" to error-msg
                                Call error message routine
                        Else    Move "successful" to screen-msg
                                Call post screen message routine
                                If      Status code = space
                                Then    Move "yes" to terminal-
                                        error
                                Endif
                        Endif
                Else    Move Invalid transaction type to error-msg
                        Call error message routine
                Endif
        Else Set no more transactions to true
        Endif
Enddo
Exit
```

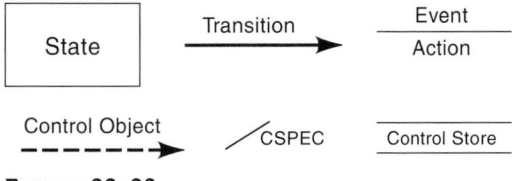

FIGURE 22–22
Basic Notation for Control Models

The elements and symbols on a CCD are the same as for a DCD, except that control data is represented by a dotted line to distinguish it from all other data and to allow for clear behavioral modeling. A CCD for the elevator example is shown in Figure 22–23.

Control Flow Diagrams (CFDs)
CFDs are just like DFDs, except that they model control data flows (control flows) instead of data flows. CFDs share the naming, numbering, leveling, and balancing properties of DFDs. Processes and data stores appear just as they do on a DFD. The differences are that control flows are shown as a dotted line, and a bar symbol is added to represent the control specification (CSPEC) that may change the state of the system. Just as with DCDs and DFDs, CCDs do not show data stores and CFDs do not show external entities. The top-level CFD (CFD 0) for the elevator example is shown in Figure 22–24.

State Transition Diagrams
The state transition diagram (STD) represents the behavior of a system by depicting its observable states and the events that cause the system to change state.

The STD and the CFD serve as the basis for behavior modeling. Additional information about control aspects of the software is contained in the control specification (CSPEC). The primary purpose of the CSPEC is to modify the response of the data processor according to past and present conditions both within and outside the system.

Decision tables, STDs, state transition tables, state event matrices, and state charts are all models of finite state machines that describe the behavior of a system.

STDs show the states of a system or subsystem, the transitions between states, the events that cause a change in state, and the action that the system may take to move to a new state.

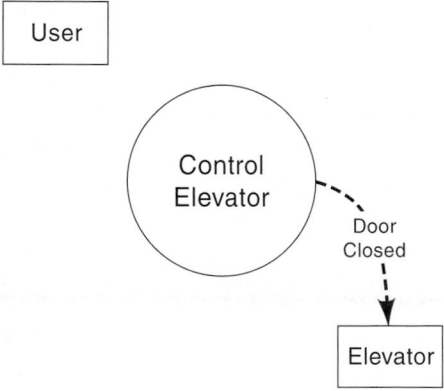

FIGURE 22–23
Control Context Diagram for the Elevator Problem

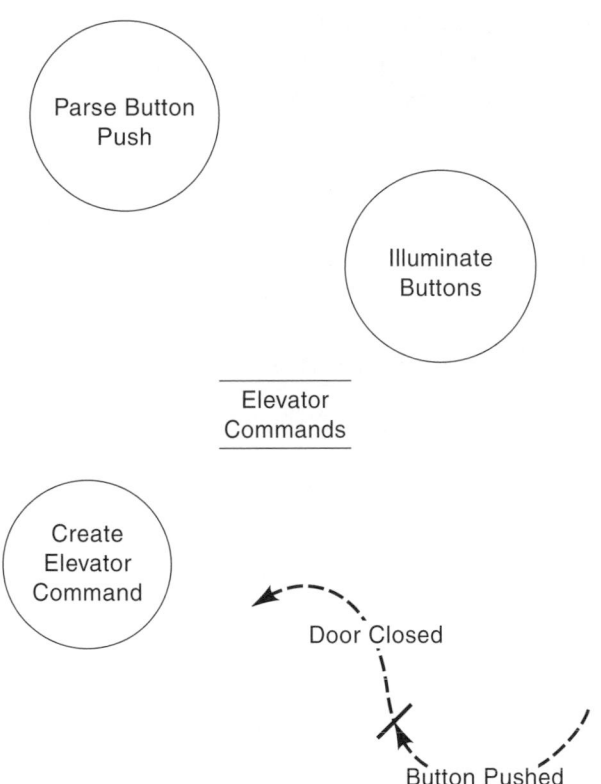

FIGURE 22–24
Level 0 Control Flow Diagram for the Elevator Problem

Typically, the analyst/designer defines all possible states first and then defines the initial state and all transitions. STDs, like all internal project deliverables, are subject to "rules" of verification and completeness: All possible states, including errors, must be defined, all states must be reachable, and all states except the final state must have a successor. As related to DFDs, STDs represent PSPECs or CSPECs, where the conditions are represented by the afferent (incoming) control flow(s) and the actions (reactions) are represented by the efferent (outgoing) control flow.

STDs provide detail for implementation and excellent documentation for time-dependent aspects of the system. While they are necessary for control systems, they are not always necessary for more data-oriented types of applications. A large design effort is required to construct and review STDs and they can become overly complex. Even for real-time systems, only a portion may need to be modeled at this level of detail.

An STD for the elevator problem is illustrated in Figure 22–25.

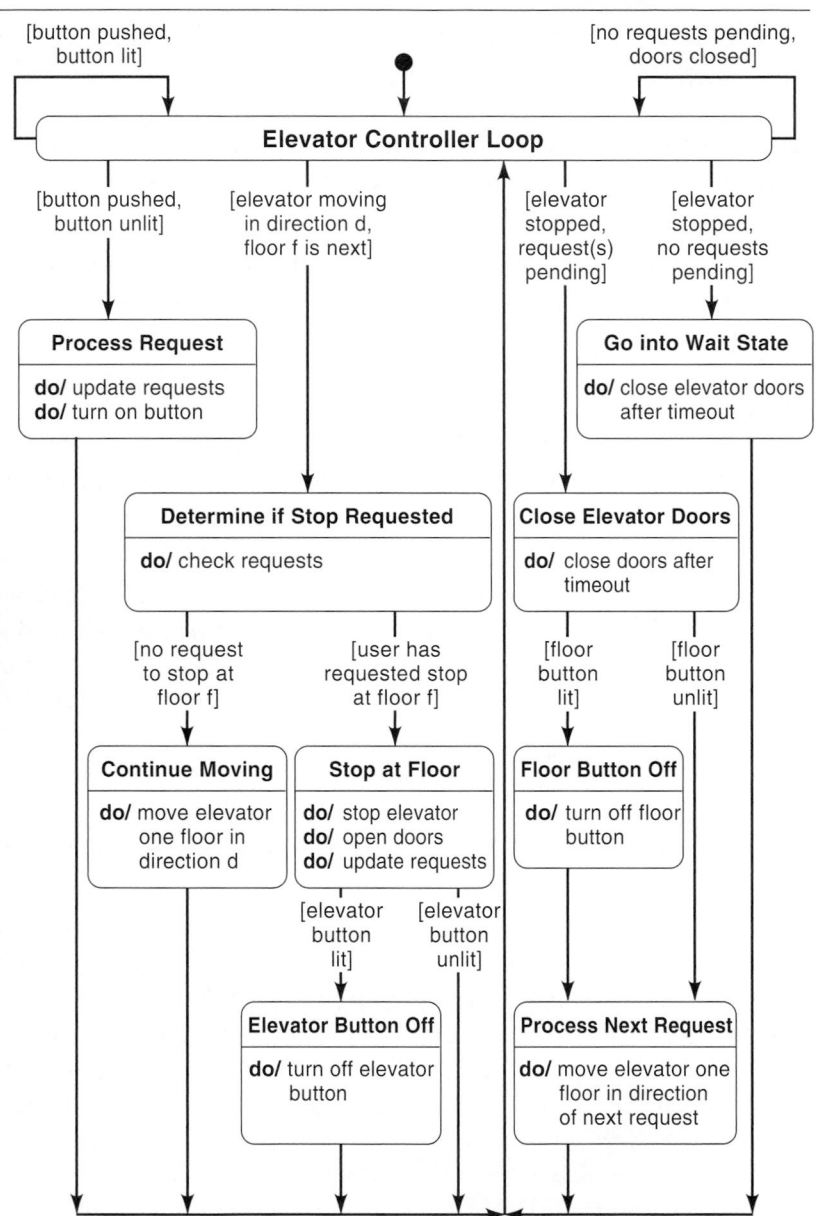

FIGURE 22–25
State Transition Diagram (Finite State Machine) for the Elevator Problem

Data Dictionaries (Requirements Dictionaries)

At the core of the structured analysis model is the data dictionary. This is a repository that contains descriptions of all data objects consumed or produced by the software. The data dictionary (DD) is an organized listing of all the elements in the system. It enhances all system analysis and design efforts, whether SA/SD or OOA/OOD, because it contains precise, rigorous, and unambiguous definitions. "Data dictionary" is a bit of a misnomer because it may contain descriptions of things other than pure data.

The DD shows the composition of every aggregate or group item, describes the meaning of the data elements as comments, and specifies relevant values and units of elementary items. It includes definitions of terminators and external data/control flows, on DCDs and CCDs; definitions of data flows, control flows, and data stores shown on DFDs and CFDs; entities, attributes, and relationships on ERDs; names of PSPECs and CSPECs on DFDs and CFDs; and information about elements of structure charts. If OOA/OOD methods are employed, the DD will contain similar elements, although they will be referred to by OO terminology, such as classes, methods, messages, and so on.

Typically, the DD contains, for each data element, name, representation, units/format, precision/accuracy, range, where used, how used, and other descriptive information. The DD does not contain information about the processing of data (it goes into the PSPEC) or the routing of data, which goes between processes on the DFD. Fortunately, this repository is supported by almost all computer aided software engineering (CASE) tools on the market.

Software Architecture   *Software architecture* is a term that is used in different ways, with different meanings. To avoid confusion, we will present some classic definitions and then briefly describe the Hatley-Pirbhai view of software architecture used with real-time systems.

Architecture is the organizational structure and associated behavior of a system. An architecture can be recursively decomposed into parts that interact through interfaces, relationships that connect parts, and constraints for assembling parts—parts that interact through interfaces.[5] An architecture is the set of significant decisions about the organization of a software system, the selection of the structural elements and their interfaces by which the system is composed, together with their behavior as specified in the collaborations among those elements, the composition of these structural and behavioral elements into progressively larger subsystems, and the architectural style that guides this organization—these elements and their interfaces, their collaborations, and their composition.[6]

A software system architecture comprises:

- a collection of software and system components, connections, and constraints;
- a collection of system stakeholders' need statements; and

- a rationale, which demonstrates that the components, connections, and constraints define a system that, if implemented, would satisfy the collection of system stakeholders' needs statements.[7]

Software architecture is loosely defined as the organizational structure of a software system, including components, connections, constraints, and rationale. Components can be small pieces of code, such as modules, or larger chunks, such as standalone programs like database management systems. Connections in an architecture are abstractions for how components interact in a system (e.g., procedure calls, pipes, and remote procedure calls). An architecture has various constraints and rationales associated with it, including the constraints on component selection and the rationale for choosing a specific component in a given situation.[8]

Whether modeling the software system via SA/SD or OOA/OOD, it is wise to create a view of the overall architecture for certain types of systems, primarily real-time systems. This activity typically falls in between analysis and design. An architecture flow diagram (AFD) is a network representation of a system's physical configuration.

An AFD shows the physical allocation of the requirements model's data and control processing and flows into the physical entities (subsystems) that will perform the allocated tasks. It shows the physical partitioning of the system into its component pieces and the information flow between them. Its main purpose is to allocate the functional processes of the requirements model to physical units of the system and to add more processes as needed to support the new physical interfaces. The definition of the physical modules adds more perspectives to the two (functional and control processing) addressed by the requirements model. They are input processing, output processing, user interface processing, and maintenance or self-test processing. The template for an AFD is shown in Figure 22–26.

The user interface block is a special case of the input- and output-processing blocks. It needs to be separated from the input and output blocks because there are many special considerations, such as human factors, that affect the definition of user interface.

Just as with data context and control context diagrams, there is an architecture control diagram (ACD) that represents the highest level. The elements that make up the ACD are one architecture module, representing the system; terminators that represent entities in the environment with which the system communicates; and information flow vectors that represent the communications that take place between the system and those entities.

The AFD is decomposed to show the next level of system architecture definition, as shown in Figure 22–27, in which AM is used to signify an architecture module and IF is used to represent information flow. An architecture interconnect diagram (AID) is a representation of the communication channels that exist between the architecture modules; it shows the physical means by which the modules communicate. An architecture interconnect specification captures the characteristics of the channels by which information follows between the modules.

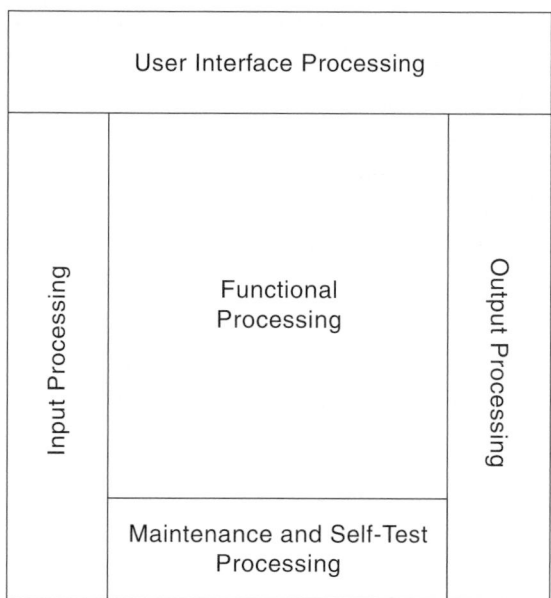

FIGURE 22–26
Architecture Flow Diagram Template

The decomposition of the architecture model is not the same as the functional decomposition of the system. It is a decomposition in the sense that the architecture template is applied successively to each of the modules in the parent AFD to create the next level of AFDs. This process then continues to be applied to successive layers until the system is completely structured. It is different from the functional view in that the users, people, or other automated systems require specific interfaces that have physical properties. In addition to covering the functional requirements, the fully integrated system specification also covers the physical design with an AFD.

Because AFDs describe physical characteristics of systems (timings of events, etc.), we will consider it a "low-level" task (occurring late in the analysis/design process—a low level of decomposition). The software project manager would rarely become involved with such designs, although for complex or real-time systems where control must be modeled, it is important that plenty of time is built into the schedule for their construction.

SA/SD—Structured Design: Structure Charts

Portions of software that can be seen to predictably follow a given procedure can be viewed as hierarchies. That portion of the system that can be seen to act in a "data triggered" sense

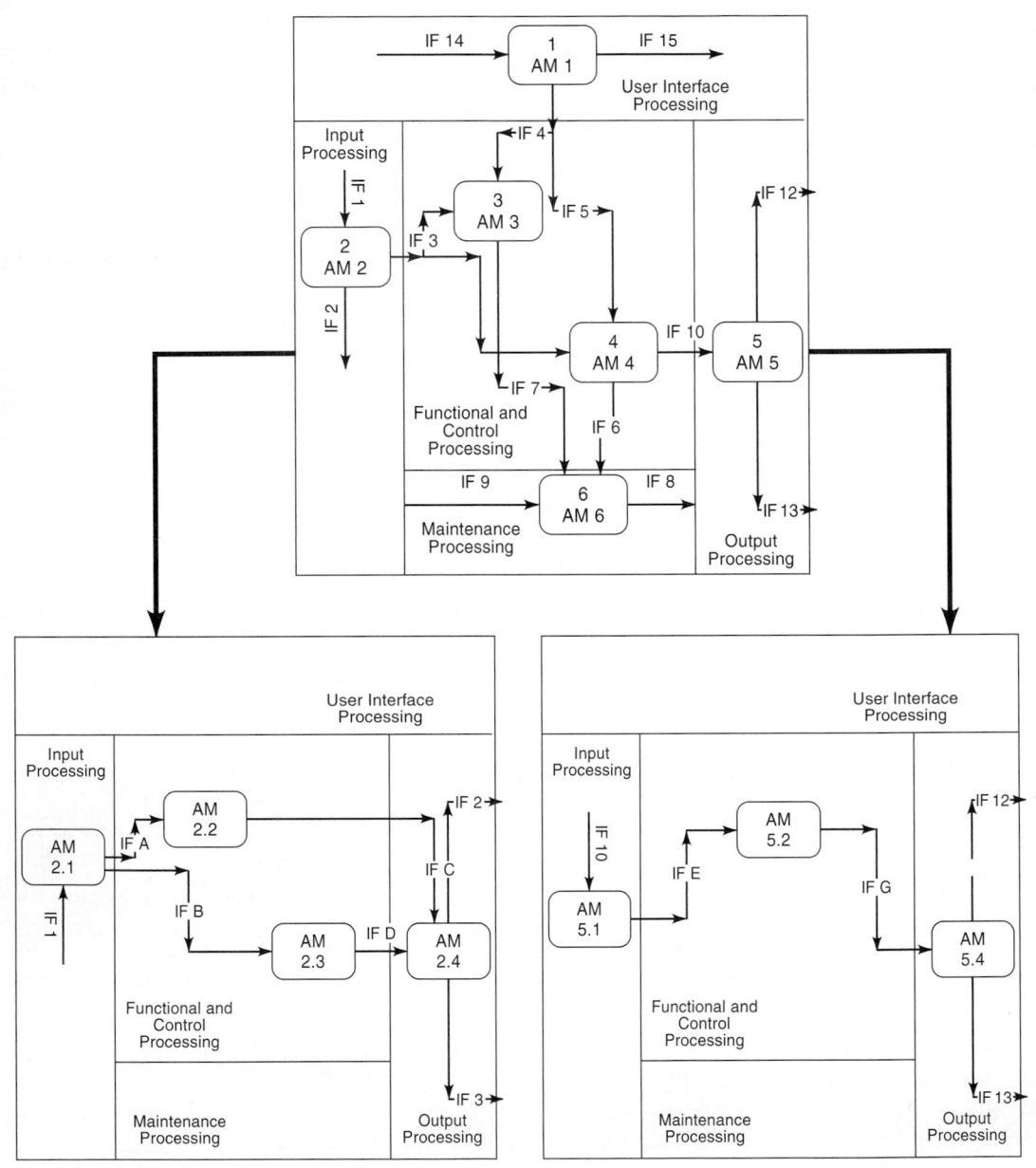

FIGURE 22–27
Decomposed AFD

can be viewed as a network (AFDs). A structure chart is a tool to help define a hierarchical, modularized implementation model for a software system. In the 1960s, the structure chart was the main analysis and design tool, providing an overall view for both developers and designers. It is still a useful tool in the design phase, although we now realize that "structured design," like "structured code," doesn't occur early enough in the overall life cycle to prevent many quality problems. This realization led us to concepts of structured analysis and object-oriented analysis.

Assuming that either SA or OOA has taken place, structured design proceeds with detailed descriptions of modules, input-output routines, low-level functions, mechanics, and internal data. The symbols used in structure charts are shown in Figure 22–28.

Structure charts partition a system into black boxes. A black box means that the user knows the function but not the actual internal operations. Black-box concepts reduce complexity because it is hidden from those who have no need (or desire) to know. A black box receives the inputs that it expects and gives back outputs, but it does not require that the user understand how it carries out its functions. Black-box systems are easy to construct, easy to test, easy to correct, easy to understand, and easy to modify. Structure charts organize systems that have been partitioned into black boxes into hierarchies, as shown in Figure 22–29.

Structure charts are composed of modules. A module is a collection of problem statements encompassing input, output, function, mechanics, and internal data. Mechanics are the procedural code or logic by which a module carries out its function; internal data is the module's private workspace. On a structure chart, named boxes represent modules. Modules have connections to other modules: One module may call (invoke, perform) another and then resume processing. When a module calls another, it views the called module as a black box, passing parameters needed for the called module's functionality and receiving answers. The structure chart notation, such as DFDs and CFDs, distinguishes control data. "Regular" data passed between modules on a structure chart appears on a labeled directed arrow with an open circle on the end (opposite the arrow head). Control data (flags) have a filled-in circle. Structure charts show temporal sequence vertically but not horizontally. In Figure 22–29, the modules on the top level execute before the called modules below. However, if multiple modules are called, there is no indication of the order in which they will execute.

Modules may be described by module specifications (MSPECs). They are typically written in pseudocode, like PSPECs and CSPECs, but they are in a lower level of detail (closer to what will become the actual code). MSPECs, like the others, make use of the basic constructs:

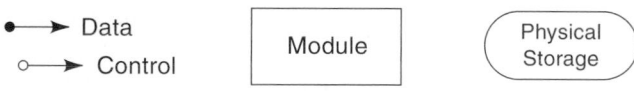

FIGURE 22–28
Structure Chart Notation

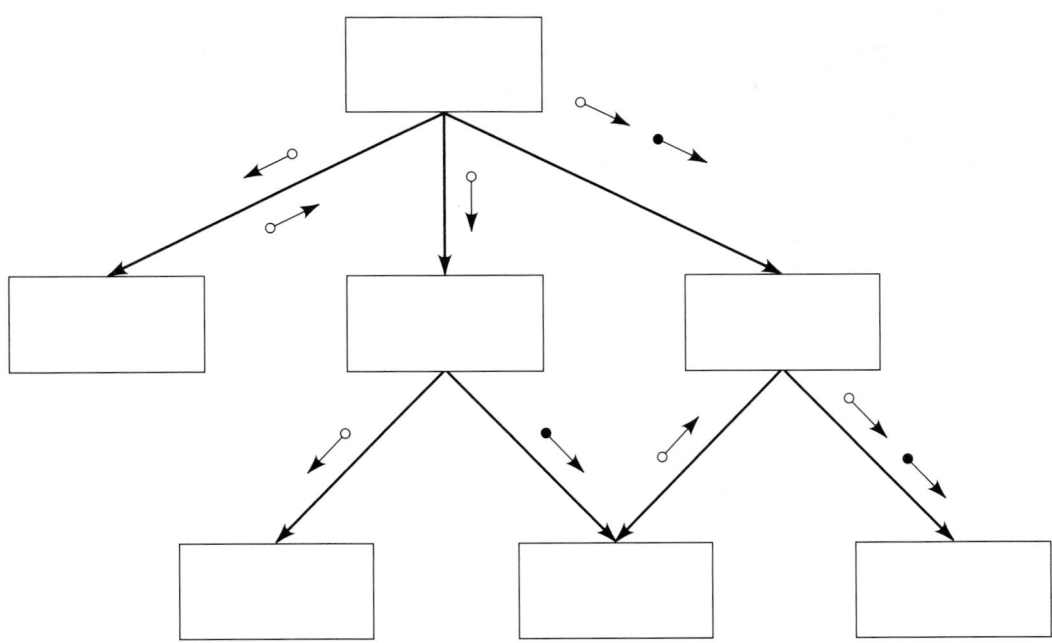

FIGURE 22–29
Structure Chart Template

simple sequence, decision (if-then-else), selection (do case), and repetition (do while, do until). These constructs will be discussed later, in the section on Chapin charts. Decision tables, decision trees, and state transition diagrams may also be used in MSPECs (as with other SA and OOA/OOD dynamic diagramming.)

Structure Chart Quality—Coupling
One way to measure quality in the design of a structure chart is to explore its coupling, the degree of interdependence between two modules. The objective is to minimize coupling, making modules as independent as possible. Low coupling indicates a well-partitioned system and may be obtained by eliminating unnecessary relationships or reducing the number of necessary relationships, and by reducing the "tightness" of necessary relationships. Low coupling minimizes the "ripple effect" (a bug in one module appears as a symptom in another) and minimizes the impact of change (changing one module doesn't require changing several); when involved with one module, the details of others are of little or no concern. Coupling is illustrated in Figure 22–30. Page-Jones has described coupling as falling on a spectrum of good (loose) to bad (tight), depending on the type (see Table 22–2).

Looking at the coupling between two modules, you can see that normal coupling is good. Two modules, A and B, are *normally coupled* if A calls B, B returns to A, and all information

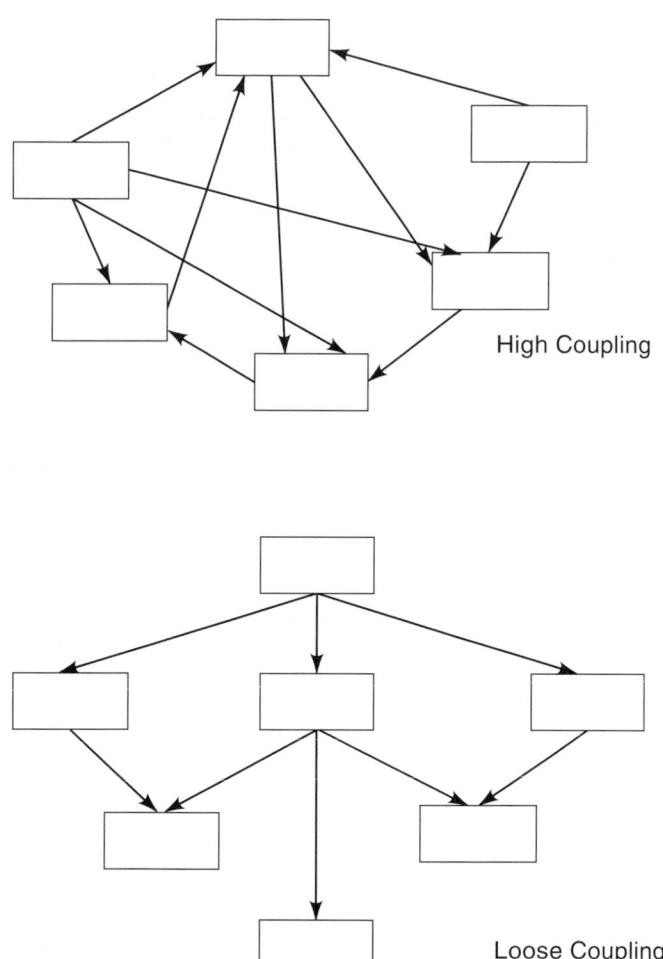

High Coupling

Loose Coupling

FIGURE 22–30
Coupling: Degree of Interdependence of Modules

passed between them is by means of parameters presented with the call itself. Normal coupling is also known as data coupling: Another caller can use the called module because it need know nothing about the module calling it.

Stamp coupling is not bad, but it is not as good as data coupling. Two normally coupled modules are *stamp coupled* if one passes to the other a composite piece of data (meaningful internal structure). When an entire data structure is passed, although only a subset of it is really needed, the unnecessary elements are known as "tramp" data. The more modules a piece of tramp data travels through, the more likely that it will be accidentally altered or that it will spread a defect. The moral is, don't pass records containing many fields to modules

TABLE 22–2
Types of Coupling

Type	Example	Quality
Normal: Data	Arguments are passed	Best
Normal: Data Structure (Stamp)	Whole structures are passed (e.g., tables)	
Normal: Control	Information, status	
Common	Data shared through global data structure	
Content	Content sharing	Worst

that need only one or two of them. Dependencies between otherwise unrelated modules may result from the unnecessary use of stamp coupling.

Control coupling is in the center of the good-to-bad range. Two modules are *control coupled* if one passes to the other a piece of information intended to control the internal logic of the other. If a control flag passes downward from a "boss" module to a subordinate, the boss must know something of the internals of the subordinate—then the subordinate is not a black box. If the control flag heads upward from subordinate to boss, then the hierarchy is disrupted. Avoid control couples that contain specific orders or make a decision for the receiver. Acceptable control couples are information flags or status flags. If the receiver is given maximum freedom in utilizing that information strive to maintain the "black-boxishness" of the modules—don't increase their dependency upon each other.

Common coupling is bad. Modules are *common coupled* if they share data by referring to a global data structure (the data was not passed as parameters). A defect in any module using a global area may show up in any other module using that area because global data doesn't reside in the protective haven of a module. Problems associated with data that is globally accessed include: A change in the common definition requires that all modules referring to that common definition be recompiled; all data elements in the common environment may be accessed and potentially corrupted; and once a module has referenced a common environment, it is no longer a black box. Global data is hard for maintenance programmers to understand and debug. It may be hard to know what data a particular module is using. If a module picks up a piece of bad data, it may be hard to track where it came from.

Content coupling is very bad and very tight. Two modules exhibit *content coupling* if one refers to the inside of the other in any way—for instance, if one branches or falls through into another, if one module refers to (or changes) data within another, or if one module alters a statement in another. Two modules are *content coupled* if one module jumps into another module, one module modifies the statements inside another module, one module references the internal data of another module or modifies that data, or the modules share the same contents. Content coupling is a hazardous practice.

The Structure Chart—Cohesion   Cohesion is a measure of the strength of functional association of elements within a module. It may also be measured on a scale of good to bad (best to worst) for quality purposes. The higher the relationships are among the elements of a module, the greater the strength of that module is, as shown in Table 22–3. "Elements" in this context means a software statement, a group of statements, or a module.

TABLE 22–3
Types of Cohesion

Levels of Cohesion	Brief Description	Maintainability
Functional	"Look down" at the next level	Best—Black Box
Informational	Shares data or data structure(s)	
Sequential	Order of events is important	
Communicational	Processes inputs/outputs	
Temporal	Based on time	
Procedural	Program procedure (iteration, decision, etc.)	
Logical	Requires control	
Coincidental	No constructive relationships	Worst—White Box

Functional cohesion is the best. Every element of the module is an integral part of the performance of a single function—there are no unrelated elements. A *functionally cohesive* module contains elements that all contribute to the execution of one and only one problem-related task. Examples include mathematical functions such as sine/cosine.

Modules with a strong, single-minded purpose are the easiest, and thus the cheapest, to maintain. A functionally cohesive module is very "black-box."

Sequential cohesion is not too bad, but not quite so black-box. A *sequentially cohesive* module is one whose elements are involved in activities such that output data from one activity serves as input data to the next. Here is an example:

Clean cobwebs from grandmother's desk

Fill in holes in wood

Sand desk surfaces

Apply varnish

Wax desk

These five activities cannot be summed into a single function, yet they make a good module called refinish_desk.

Communicational cohesion is about the same strength as sequential cohesion. A *communicationally cohesive* module is one whose elements contribute to activities that use the same input or output data. Here is an example:

Find date the movie was made

Find the actors in the movie

Find director of the movie

Find out if Blockbuster has the movie

These activities are related because they all work on the same input data: a given movie title. If appropriate, the module could be split up into four very maintainable and cohesive functions.

Procedural cohesion is more of a gray box than a black box. A *procedurally cohesive* module is one whose elements are involved in different and possibly unrelated activities in which control flows from each activity to the next (note: control, not data, as with sequential cohesion). The control flow applies to only one instance, not by a single, problem-related function. Here is an example:

Walk dogs

Take shower

Check email

Go to cleaners

Write thank-you notes

Although this may be a reasonable flowchart for a given individual on a given day, it is over-the-top for factoring. The order could be scrambled on another day.

Temporal cohesion is also gray box. A *temporally cohesive* module is one whose elements are involved in activities that are related in time. Here is an example:

Turn off alarm

Throw on shorts

Walk dogs

Brush teeth

Take shower

Make coffee

These activities all happen early in the morning, but they are also caused by "flowchart thinking," especially the old, initialization, housekeeping, and termination procedures. This module would be better split up by function.

Logical cohesion is the worst in terms of maintainability. It is white- or transparent-box instead of black-box. A *logically cohesive* module is one whose elements contribute to activities of the same general category in which the activity or activities to be executed are selected from outside the module.

If you were planning a dinner, you might consider the following scenarios:

Informal buffet outside

Formal buffet inside

Sit down at tables inside

But, for any occasion, you would choose only one plan. A logically cohesive module contains a number of activities of the same general kind. To use the module, we pick out just the piece(s) we need. The activities, although different, share the one and only interface to the module and should be split into separate functions.

Coincidental cohesion is the most difficult to maintain. A *coincidentally cohesive* module is one whose elements contribute to activities with no meaningful relationship to one another. Here is an example:

Make coffee

Bake cake

Walk dog

Apply to medical school

Wax the desk

Have an informal buffet outside

The calling module must send a flag to tell the called module what to do, violating the principle of independent black boxes.

Figure 22–31 shows questions that a designer might ask to determine the cohesiveness of a module.

It isn't always easy to create a cohesive module. One way, offered by Page-Jones, to "test" cohesiveness is to write a short sentence that accurately and fully names the module and describes its function. If the name can be expressed by a precise verb-object combination, with a strong, imperative verb and a specific singular direct object, then cohesion is probably high. "Assign airline seat" is an example.

Creating Structured Design Models from Structured Analysis Models

Structured analysis calls for one type of model (DFD, CFD), while structured design calls for another (structure chart). The conversion of one to the other is usually accomplished via "transform analysis" or "transaction analysis." Balanced systems—whose structure charts have transformations in between afferent modules (those sending information up to bosses) and efferent modules (those sending information down to subordinates)—are easier to develop and cheaper to maintain than poorly formed ones. Figure 22–32 shows a generic software model of a DFD (top), where no temporality is implied, to its transformation into a structure chart (below), where a hierarchy is shown and data/control are passed.

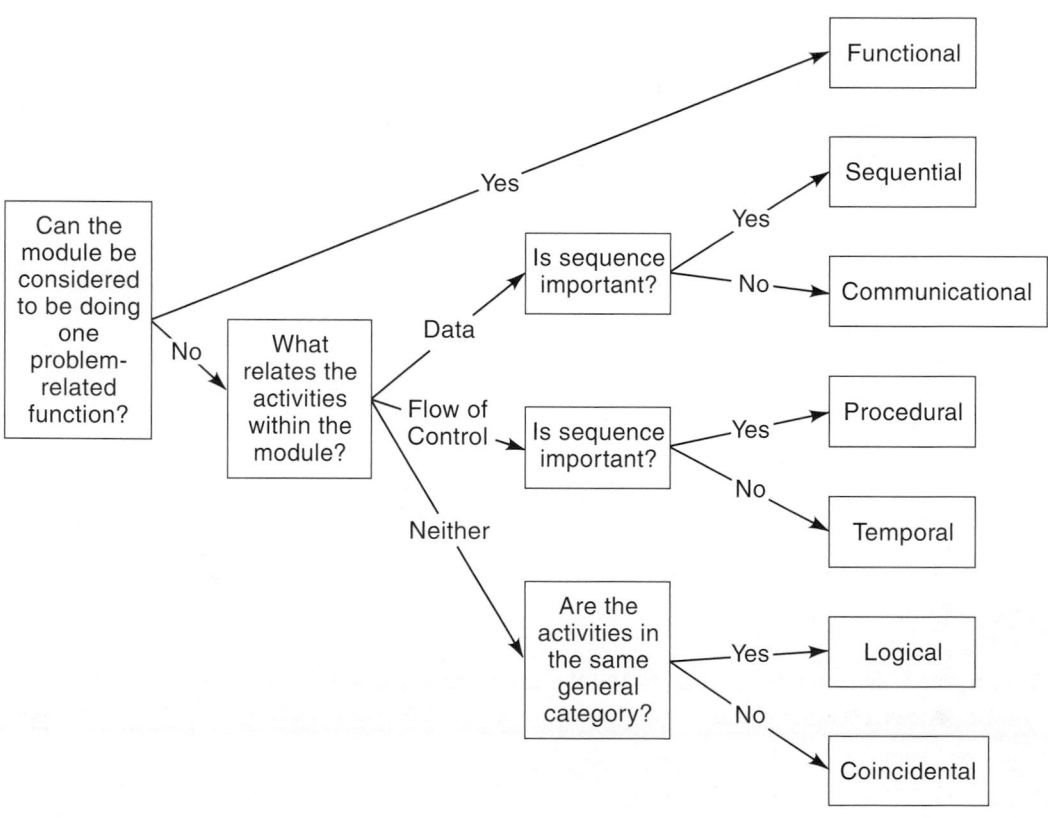

FIGURE 22–31
Summary of Cohesion

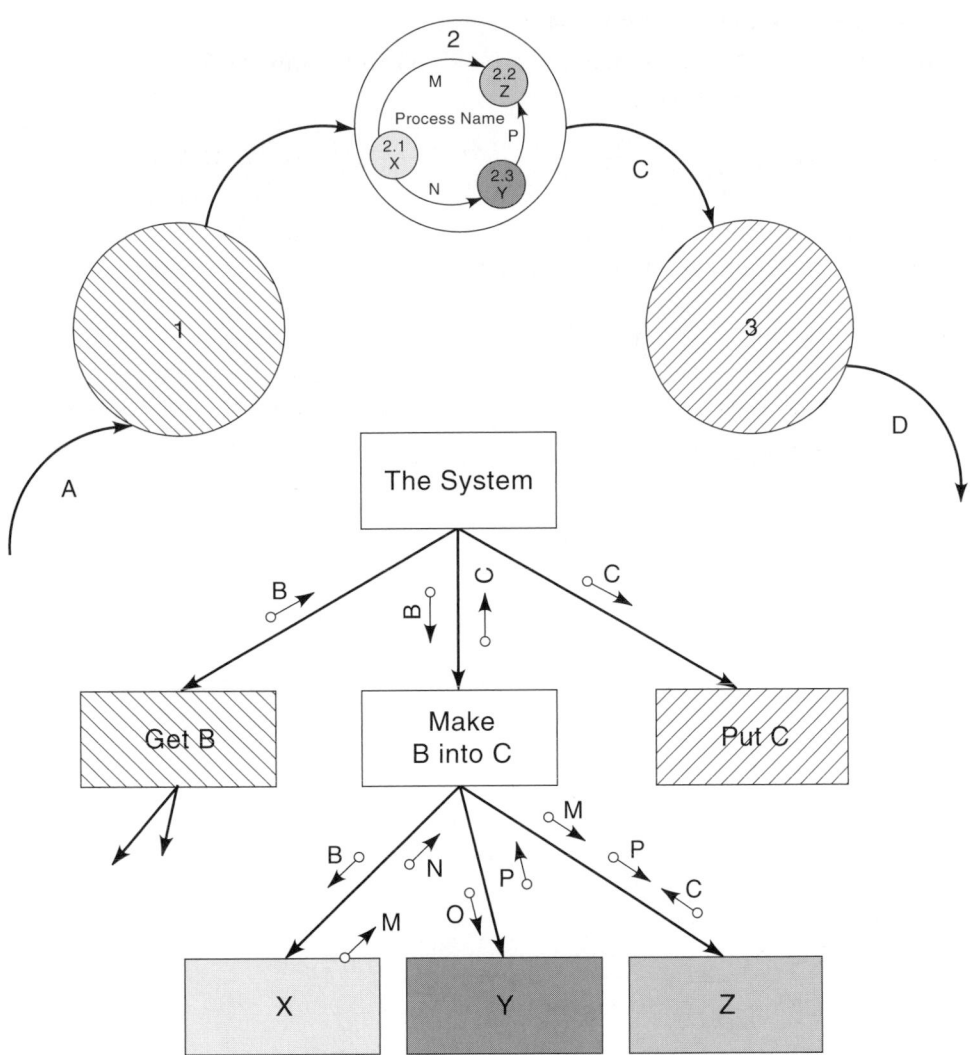

FIGURE 22–32
Transformation of DFD into Structure Chart

Transform Analysis: A Strategy for Converting DFDs to Structure Charts
The steps for converting analysis models into design models are the following:

1. Draw a data flow diagram.
2. Identify the central transform (essential functions)—may be "eyeballed," as in Figure 22–33.
3. Identify afferent and efferent branches (input and output streams).

4. Prune off the branches, as in Figure 22–34.
5. Build a draft structure chart, as shown in Figure 22–33 and Figure 22–34.
6. Refine and balance the structure chart.
7. If the central DFD topology is a network, as in Figure 22–35, then hire a boss; if the central DFD topology is hierarchical, as in Figure 22–36, then promote a boss.

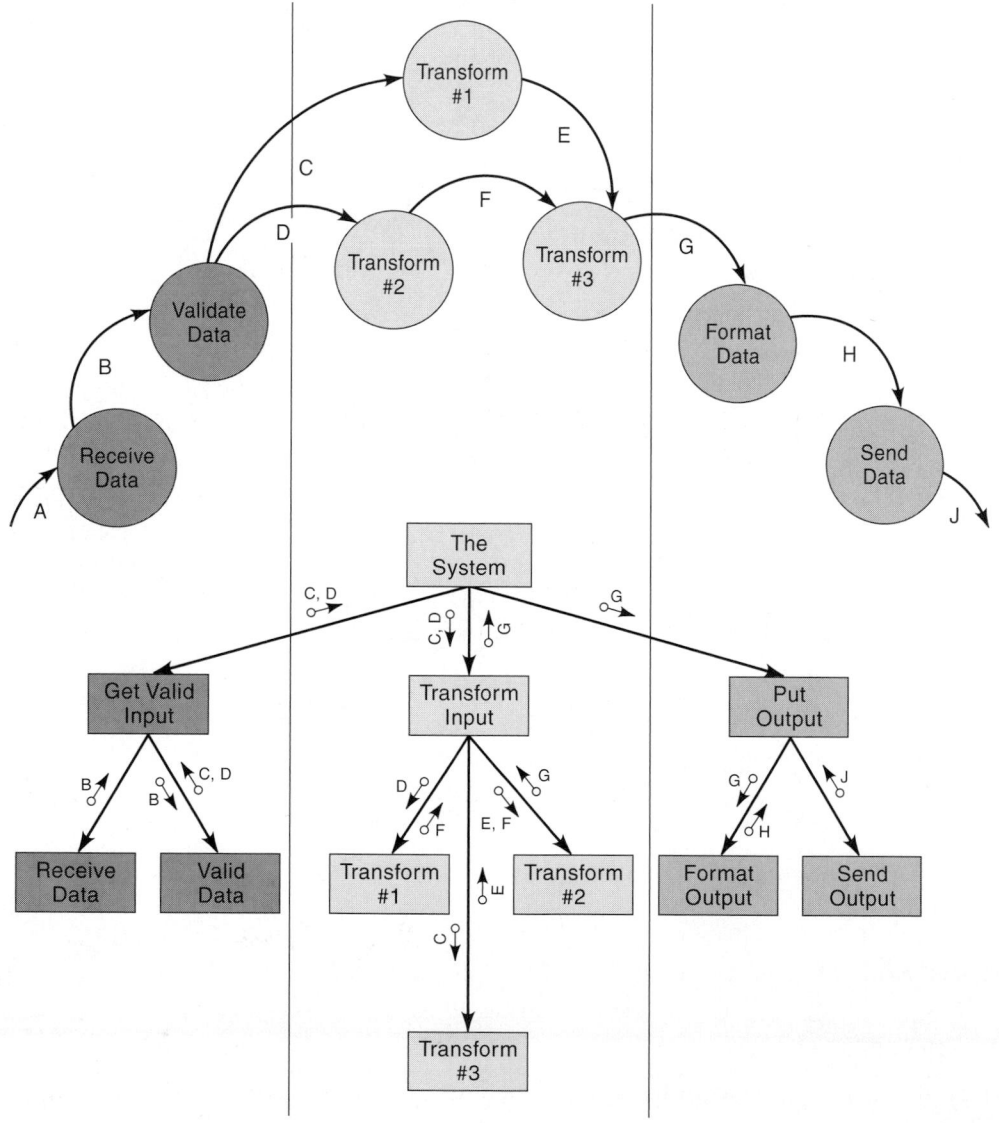

FIGURE 22–33
Identify (Eyeball) Central Transform

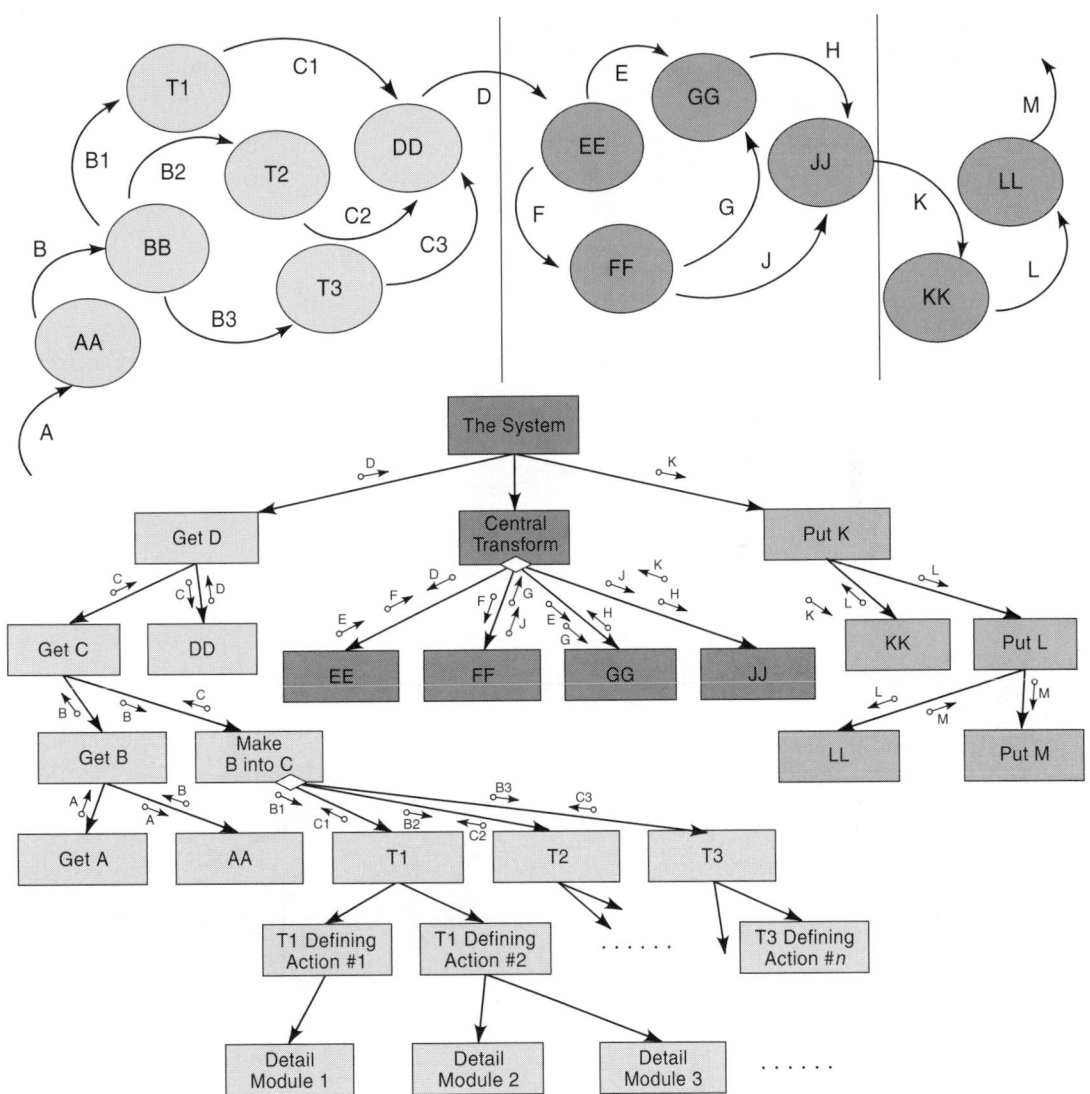

FIGURE 22–34
"Prune to" Central Transform

Transaction Analysis
For systems that process transactions, DFDs may need to be broken into smaller pieces—perhaps one for each transaction processed by the system. The small DFDs may then be converted to small structure charts. It is often easy to recognize transaction centers and processing bubbles on a DFD.

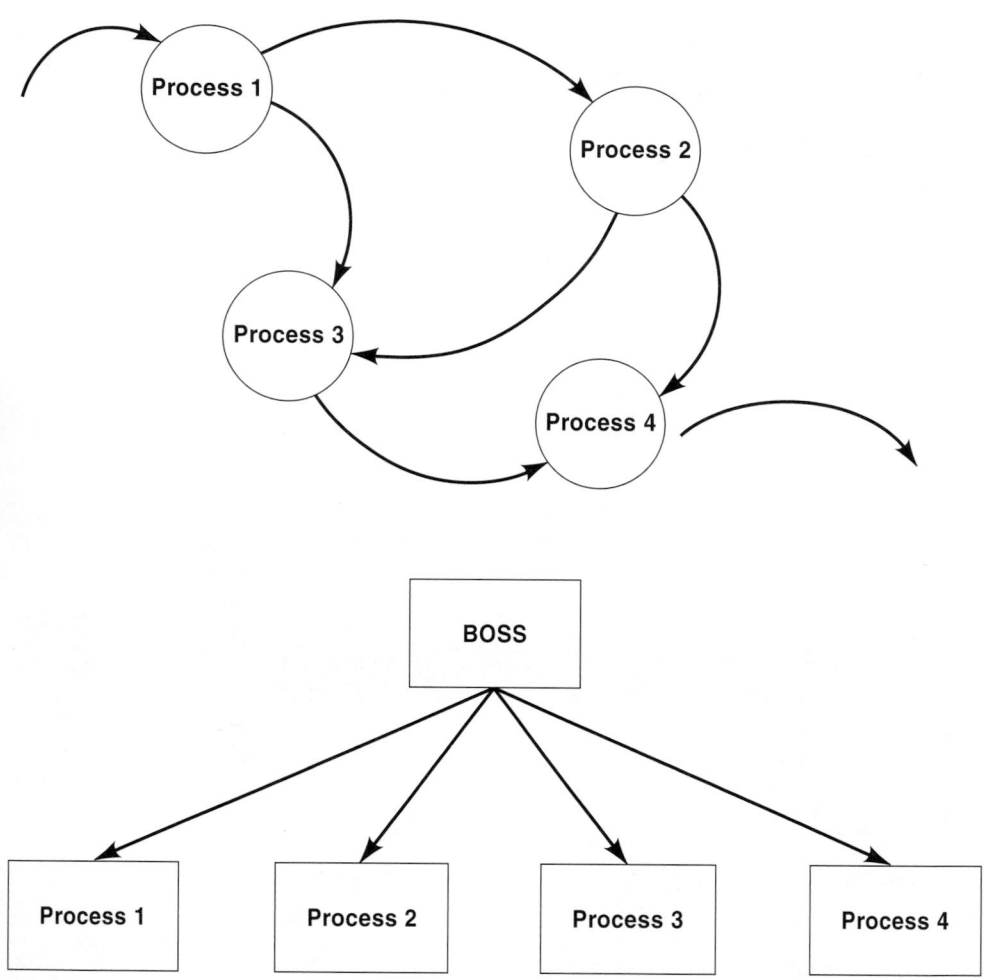

FIGURE 22–35
Transform Analysis: Hire a Boss

The transaction center is a portion of a system that can obtain a transaction stimulus, analyze it to determine its type, dispatch it in the way appropriate to its type, and complete the processing of the transaction activity, as shown in Figure 22–37.

With transaction analysis, it is best to keep data flows separate, using both the "divide and conquer" strategy (break processing into subsystems) and intelligent fan-in to shared modules.

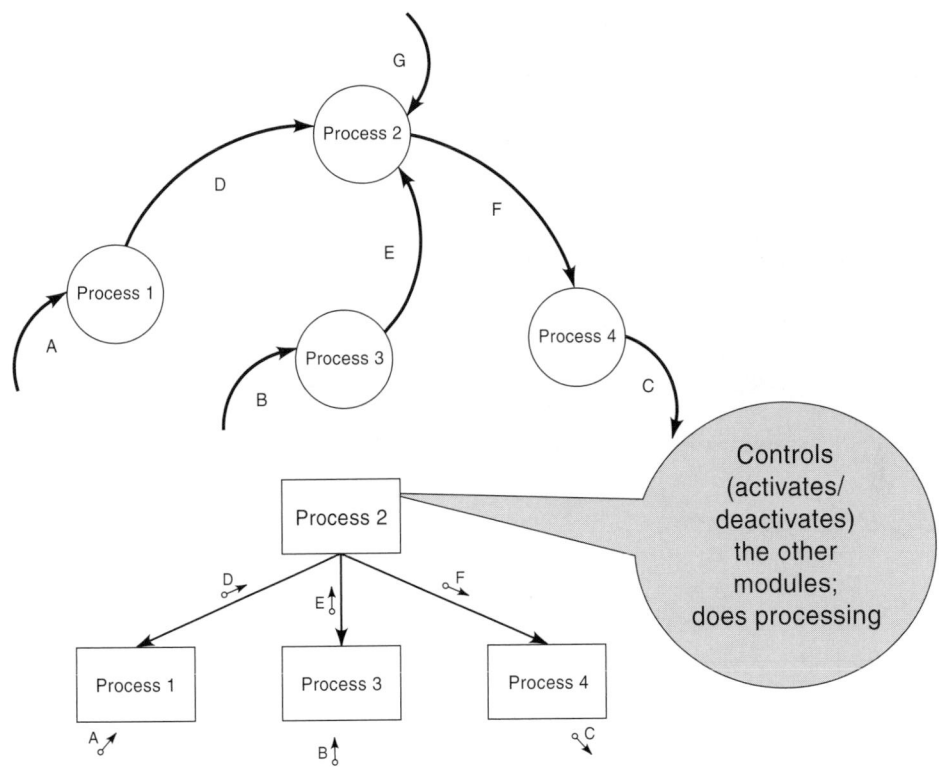

FIGURE 22–36
Transform Analysis: Promote a Boss

Shape and Organization of the Structure Chart

Fan-In/Fan-Out
The fan-in to a module is the number of immediate bosses that it has. High fan-in is good, indicating reuse and eliminating duplicate updating of modules during maintenance. It just makes sense that modules with fan-in must have high cohesion (functional, or at least, sequential or communicational), and low coupling (loose, such as data or stamp). Fan-in/fan-out is illustrated in Figure 22–38.

The fan-out from a module is the number of immediate subordinates to that module, also known as span of control. To avoid "pancaking" (too many subordinates on one level), limit the number of fan-out to the old rule of 7 +/− 2, and install more intermediate levels in the hierarchy. Restructuring of modules, as shown in Figure 22–39, resolves high fan-out.

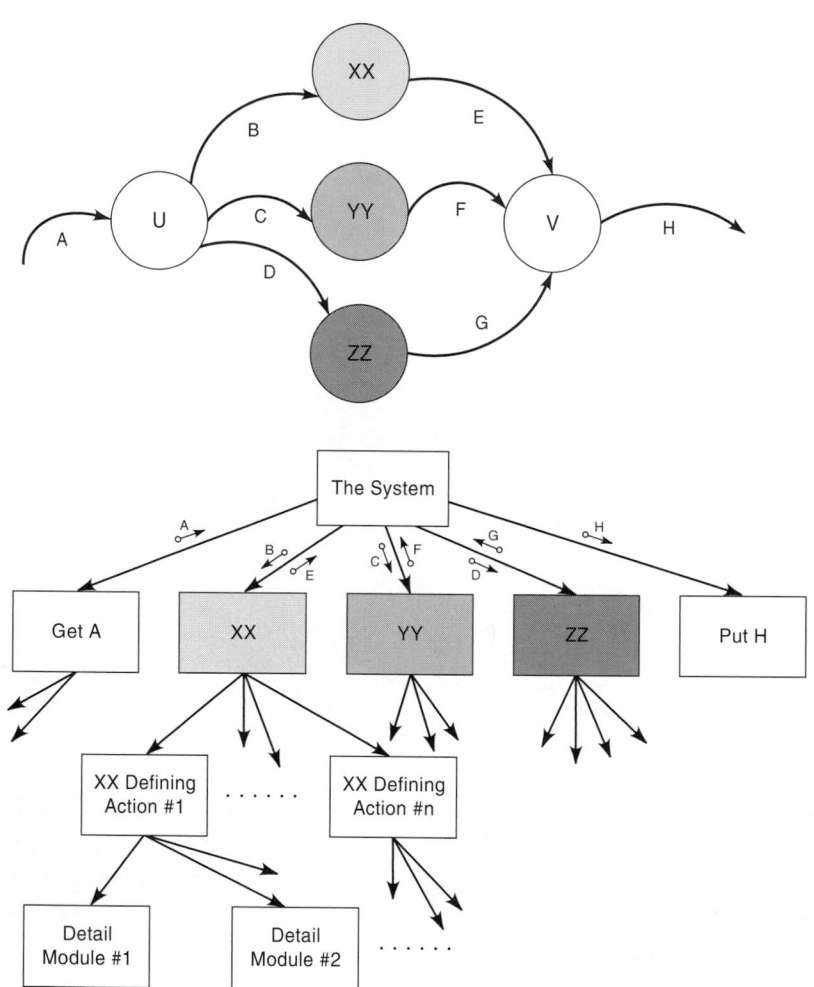

FIGURE 22–37
Transaction Analysis

Scope of Control
The scope of control of a module is the module itself and all of its subordinates, as shown in Figure 22–40.

Module Connections
It is desirable for module connections to be normal, where data and control are passed downward and data is passed upward. When the movement is not clearly up and down the hierarchy, or when one module branches into the center of another, or modifies "hidden

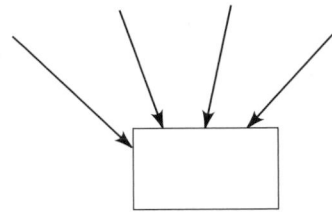

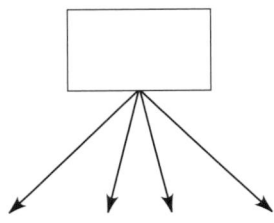

FIGURE 22–38
Fan-in, Fan-out

data" in another, the connections are called "pathological." As shown in Figure 22–41, normal connections are desired as they are easy to understand and easy to maintain.

A Balanced Structure Chart
A balanced hierarchical system has control structure at the top, function structure underneath, and then data management structure, supported by the abstract interface structure. When the designer looks at the rendering of the structure chart and sees something quite different from Figure 22–42, it is an indication that restructuring is in order.

The Chapin Chart: A Model for Low-Level Design

Chapin charts (also known as Nassi-Schneiderman diagrams) describe the procedures used to receive, process, and transmit information, much like a PSPEC or CSPEC. The charts provide all the logic necessary for programmers to immediately write structured programs in any language to support a specific function. A blueprint for a computer program to be written in any language, it is derived from process specifications and module descriptions that were created during data flow diagramming and design activities.

Only five basic structures are used in Chapin charts, with each symbol corresponding to a particular computer programming structure, providing easy translation into computer code. As shown in Figure 22–43, the constructs are sequence, if-then-else, do-while, do-until, and do-case. These visual representations serve as a set of program building blocks that allow only single-entry and single-exit to and from a process, and strictly limit branching. Arbitrary

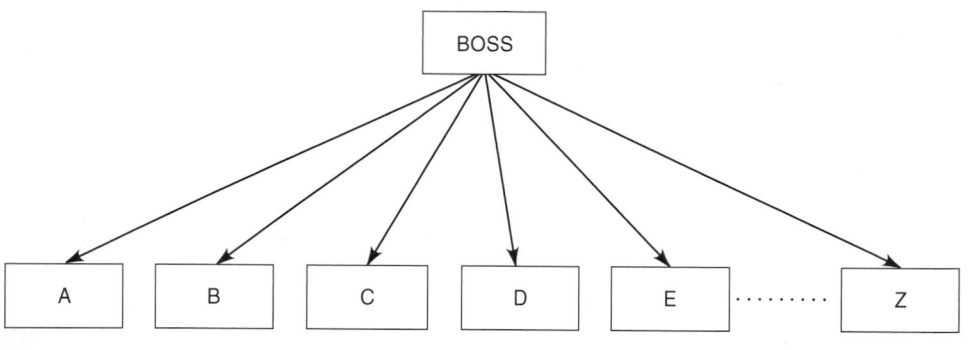

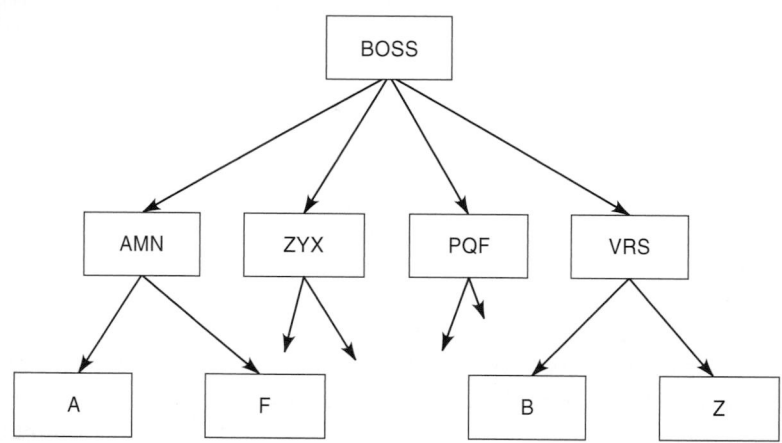

FIGURE 22–39
High Fan-Out

transfers of control are impossible when programs are based strictly on well-designed Chapin charts.

Chapin charts perform the same function as traditional flowcharts. The advantage of Chapin charts is that they read like a printed page; there are no complex arrows to follow all over the diagram. There is a hierarchical flow to the instructions and choices, which forces logic on the procedures. They are compact and required to fit on a single page. Like traditional flowcharts, they can be nested to show successively more complex levels of detail.

It is important for the software project manager to realize that the bulk of all software costs go toward maintaining the product, either before or after release to the customer. If a program is easy to code, to modify, and to read and understand, then there is a direct link to

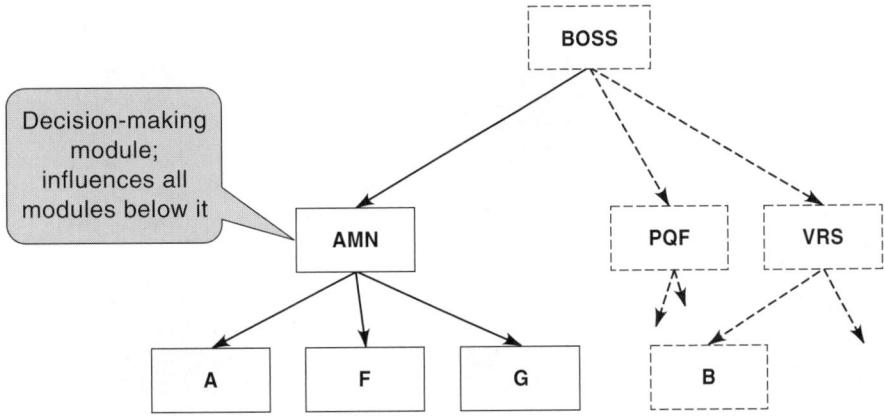

FIGURE 22–40
Module Connections

savings. Well-designed programs just fall out naturally from well-designed Chapin charts. Some simple "rules" include these:

- The start of an NS chart is always at the top.

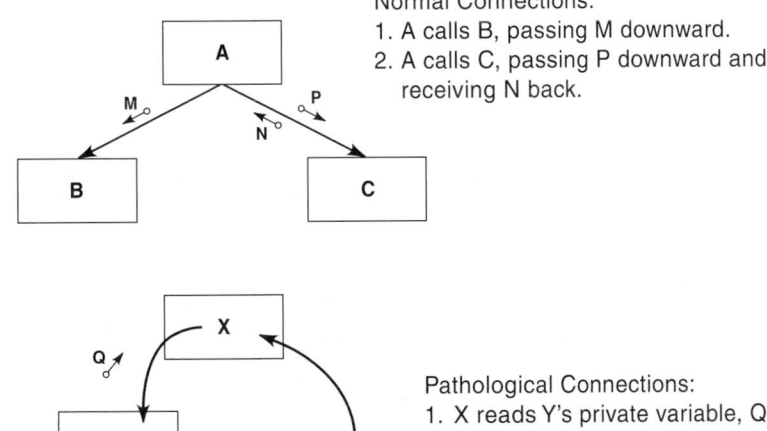

FIGURE 22–41
A Balanced Structure Chart

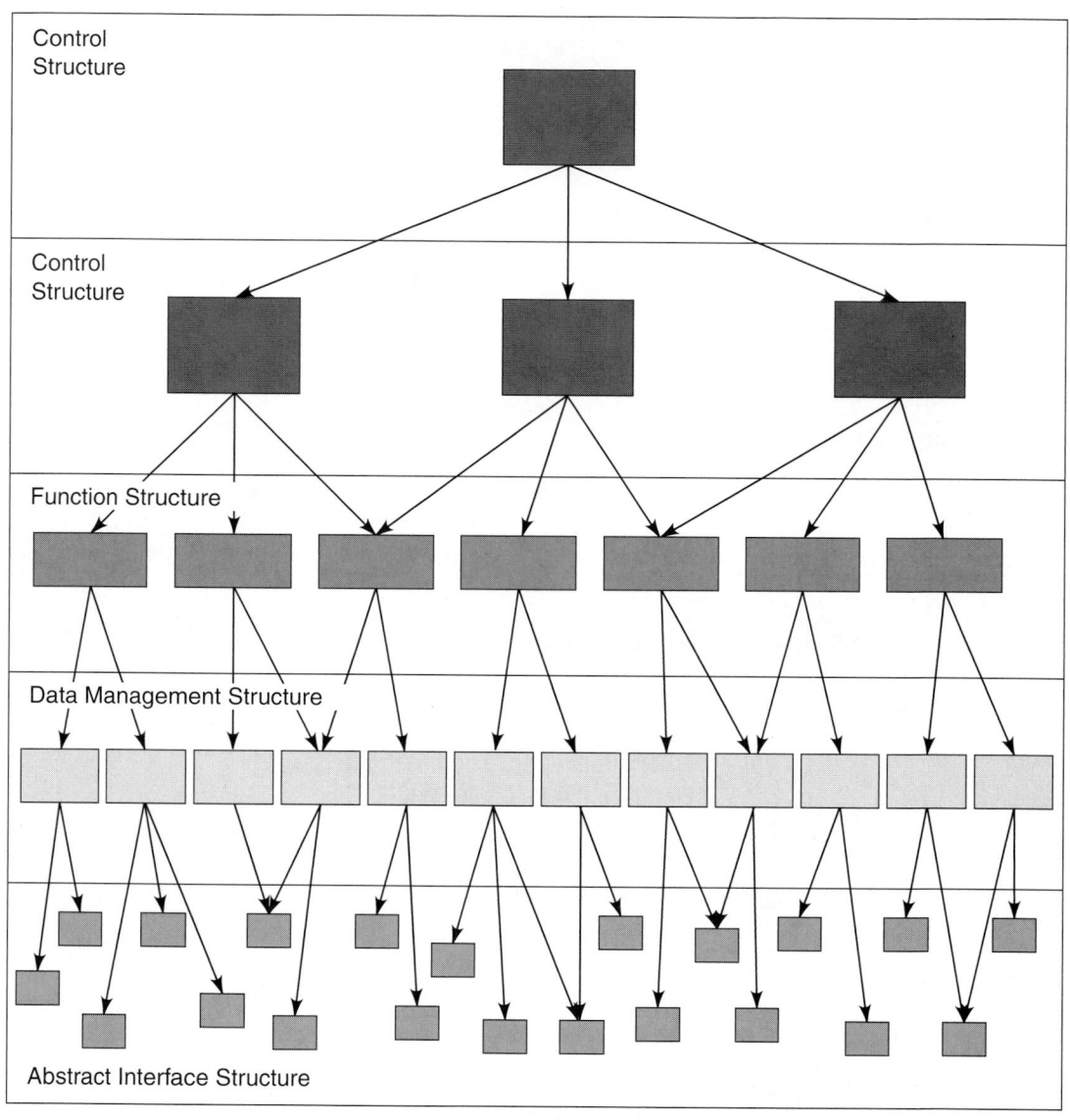

FIGURE 22–42
Scope of Control

- Progress through a chart is always from top to bottom, except at the lower limit of a loop structure (the L-shape and upside-down L-shape frames). If the end of a loop is reached but no exit condition has been satisfied, then progress resumes at the top of the same loop box. Loops may be exited only at the horizontal bar of the L-shape frame.
- Vertical lines are never crossed.

The Basic Constructs

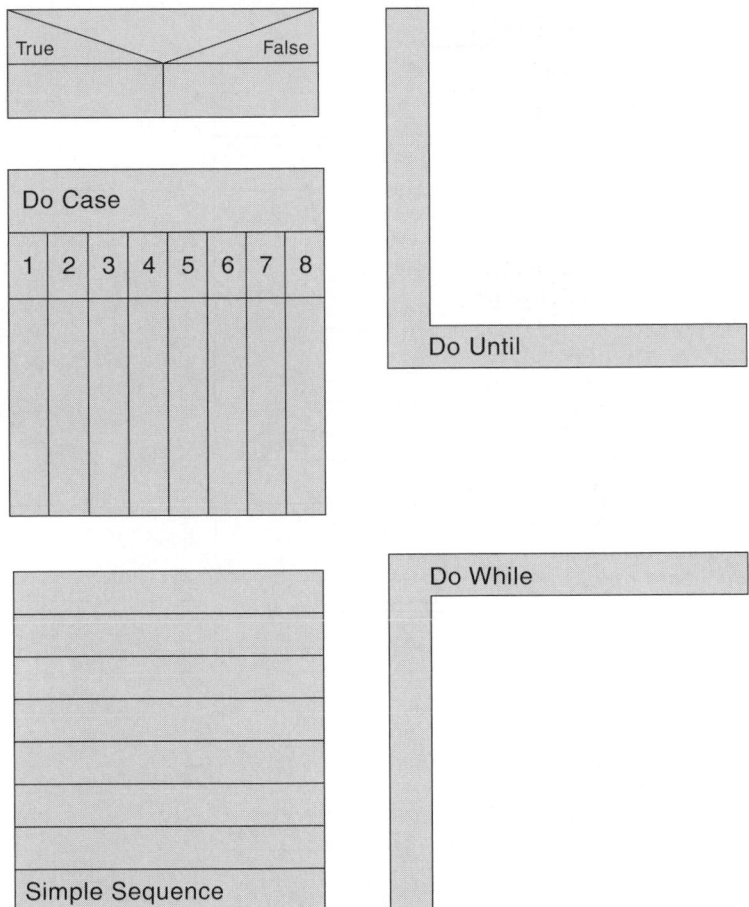

FIGURE 22–43
Chapin Chart: Four Constructs

- A rectangle may be exited at any given time in one direction only, at the bottom. If a rectangle contains a decision (if-then-else or do-case), then it must be exited in the direction of the rectangle directly under the currently appropriate decision outcome.
- Null means that the decision condition falls through at the bottom of the rectangle.
- Any rectangle that contains no other lines is either a single (possibly empty) action or *another* chart.

The way a Chapin chart provides a go-to-less map that graphically depicts program logic is illustrated in Figure 22–44. This type of document is an excellent one to be "walked through"

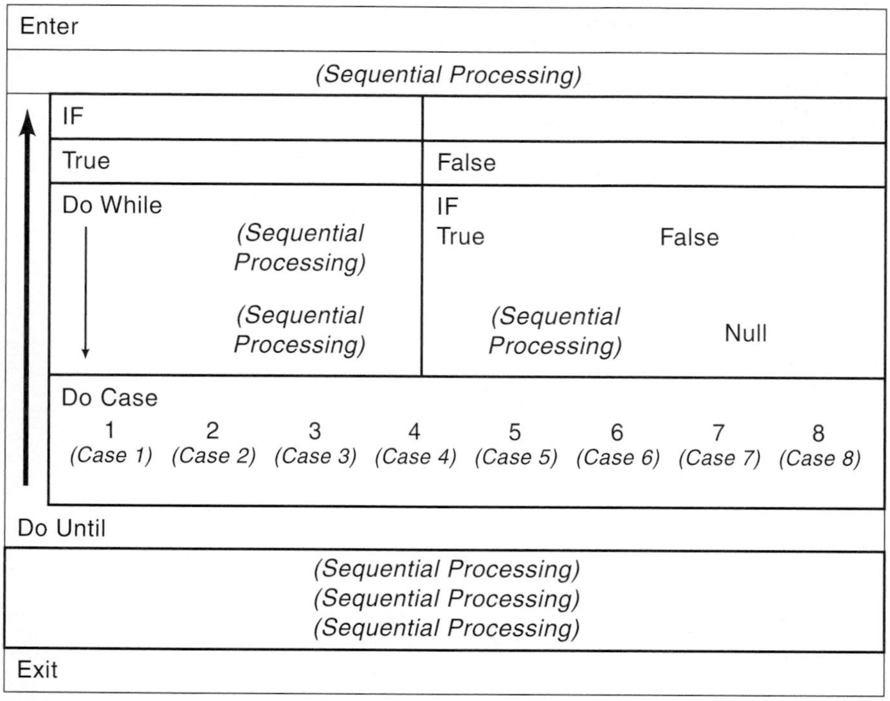
Enter
(Sequential Processing)
IF
True
False
Do While
(Sequential Processing)
(Sequential Processing)
IF
True
False
(Sequential Processing)
Null
Do Case
1 (Case 1)
2 (Case 2)
3 (Case 3)
4 (Case 4)
5 (Case 5)
6 (Case 6)
7 (Case 7)
8 (Case 8)
Do Until
(Sequential Processing)
(Sequential Processing)
(Sequential Processing)
Exit

FIGURE 22–44
Chapin Chart Example Template

during static testing. Figure 22–45 shows a more realistic example that could be taken to a visual inspection or walk-through.

The models described in the preceding sections represent the major ones used in structured analysis/structured design. There are those who believe that it is not, in concept, very different from object-oriented analysis/object-oriented design. We will describe some of the major OOA/OOD models, provide a few pros and cons of each of the two approaches, and describe some of their similarities at the end of the chapter.

Object-Oriented Analysis/Object-Oriented Design (OOA/OOD)

SA/SD has long been used in the industry as a method for process, data, and behavioral modeling. In this methodology, the emphasis is on specifying and decomposing system functionality. Data flow diagrams, control flow diagrams, a data dictionary, state transition diagrams,

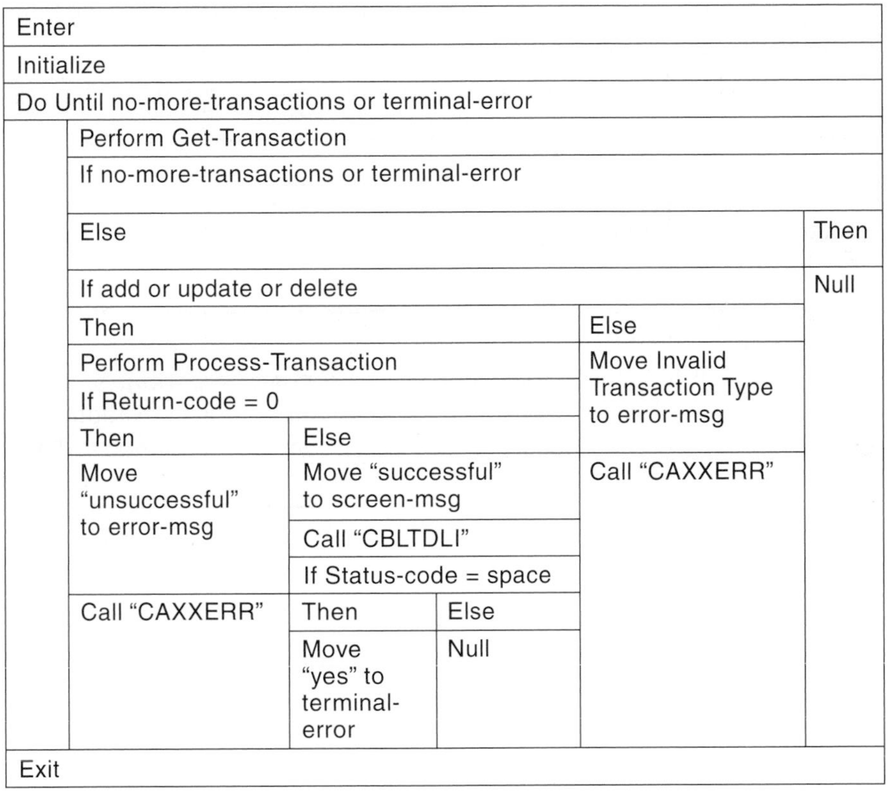

Enter				
Initialize				
Do Until no-more-transactions or terminal-error				
	Perform Get-Transaction			
	If no-more-transactions or terminal-error			
	Else			Then
	If add or update or delete			Null
	Then		Else	
	Perform Process-Transaction		Move Invalid Transaction Type to error-msg	
	If Return-code = 0			
	Then	Else	Call "CAXXERR"	
	Move "unsuccessful" to error-msg	Move "successful" to screen-msg		
		Call "CBLTDLI"		
		If Status-code = space		
	Call "CAXXERR"	Then	Else	
		Move "yes" to terminal-error	Null	
Exit				

FIGURE 22–45
Chapin Chart Example

and entity relationship diagrams are used to accomplish both functional decomposition and data structuring.

DFDs and CFDs model the transformation of the data/control data as it moves through the system. The data dictionary defines the data flows and data stores in the system. Entity relationship diagrams illustrate the relationships between data stores. This approach, while time tested, has shown weaknesses, especially when functional requirements change, often requiring restructuring of the model.

An OO model organizes a system around real-world objects, or conceptual objects, that exist in the user's world, as opposed to functions and data that are split apart. A real-world object, an entity that exists within the application domain, is defined in terms of its responsibilities (behavior), its data (attributes), and its relationships to other objects. All functions of the object are encapsulated (hidden) in the details of the object itself. Therefore, when functional changes are required, they are made within the object, causing little or no disruption to the rest of the model. To utilize the modified or added functions in an object, the remaining objects in the model can be provided with an interface.

As shown in Table 22–4, OO developers typically employ both static and dynamic models.

TABLE 22–4
Object-Oriented Models

Data, Function, Behavior	Type of Model	Description	Elements
Phase: Object-Oriented Analysis			
Static Models; Data, Function	Class Diagrams	A graph of classes connected by static relationships.	Classes (attributes, operations), relation-ships (associations), data types (operations may be described by DFDs or pseudocode, as with SA/SD).
	Object Diagrams	A graph of instances of classes, including objects and data values. Shows a snapshot of the state of a system at a point in time.	Objects (attributes, methods), links, values.
Dynamic Models; Function, Behavior	Use Case	A model of the way an actor interacts with the system.	Actors (stick figures), system functions (ovals), <<uses>>, <<extends>>, arrows.
	Scenario	An instance of a use case; a single execution path through a use case, showing actions and interactions of objects (not classes).	Actors, system functions.
	Activity Diagram	A graphical model of a use case, showing control flow. A set of activities that must be carried out, including temporal sequencing and conditions. No classes or objects are shown.	A flowchart, activities (capsule), sequence (labeled arrows), conditions (diamonds), end of workflow (bulls eye) synchronization bars (parallel activities).

(Continues)

TABLE 22–4 (Continued)
Object-Oriented Models

Data, Function, Behavior	Type of Model	Description	Elements
		Phase: Object-Oriented Design	
Static Model	Enhanced Class Diagram	Elaboration on model.	
Dynamic Models	Interaction Diagrams— Collaboration Diagrams	Spatial graphs with emphasis on objects and links between objects. How a use case is realized in terms of cooperating objects, defined by classes inside the entity, can be specified with a collaboration. A use case of an entity may be refined to a set of use cases of the elements contained in the entity. How these subordinate use cases interact can also be expressed in a collaboration.	Objects (boxes), links (arrows) with sequenced messages, returned references or data.
	Interaction Diagrams— Sequence Diagrams	Graphs showing temporal sequencing, with the focus on the order of messages.	Actors, swimlanes (lifelines) headed by objects, links (arrows), messages positioned vertically.
	State Transition Diagrams	Tied to one class—the states through which an instance of a class may pass.	Event, state, transition triggered by event.

The goal of a good object-oriented model is to have self-sufficient objects. This type of object is capable of initiating itself and possesses the intelligence to manage itself through several states, to provide its functional responsibility in the model.

As with structured methods, OO will be treated in a very cursory fashion in this book. A plethora of books on OO contain in-depth treatment of every aspect of the approach. We would like the software project manager to be aware of the difference between SA/SD and OOA/OOD so that he can select the analysis and design methods that will complement the chosen life cycle and needs of a specific project.

We believe that the use of OO methods should be strongly considered because the benefits have been well documented:

- Productivity of developers is increased due to a shift from low productivity code/debug to high productivity analysis/design.
- The real world is modeled through concentration on classes, not algorithms.
- System components are easy to change and reuse.
- Requirements are easy to trace.
- Iterations between phases are easy to handle.
- Prototyping is promoted.
- Development is a seamless process; there is representational continuity (the same diagram types are used in both analysis and design).
- Powerful tools support the modeling activities.

Of course, OOA/OOD is not a panacea. "Enemies of analysis and design" that have always been with us continue to exist—communications issues, schedule and budget reductions, lack of domain expertise, and so on. OO *does* attempt to do battle with them in innovative ways:

- Reduction of complexity can lead to incomprehensibility.
    - The function and workings of a well-written object can be easily understood.
    - The focus can remain on interactions and allow more elegant design.
    - Divide and conquer—encapsulation and modularity.
- Dynamic and static analysis models describe the what and how of requirements.
- The same dynamic and static models describe the "how" of object interaction in design.
- Encapsulation hides the internal workings of an object, allowing the developer to focus on how objects are used (their essential, inherent characteristics); permits the division of state, function, behavior; and restricts access to variables internal to an algorithm.
- Aggregation allows the creation of a large object from small, simpler objects, allowing for handling of complex states.
- Modularity partitions states into functional blocks.
- Inheritance encourages reuse.
- Polymorphism allows every object knowledge of how to perform its own operations.

Recall that, just as with SA/SD, "analysis" is the phase of the software product development process whose primary purpose is to formulate a model of the problem domain. It focuses on *what* to do, now *how* to do it, which is left to design.

The Unified Modeling Language

In the late 1990s, an open standard emerged for OO, in the form of the Unified Modeling Language (UML). It combines the works of Grady Booch, Ivar Jacobson, and James Rumbaugh, three of the most revered names in the industry. UML is not a programming language, nor is it a "method," because it doesn't address an overall process, prescribe approaches, or include design guidelines. It is a single, common, and widely usable "modeling language" that unifies at least 10 standards for "specifying, visualizing, constructing, and documenting the artifacts of software systems, as well as for business modeling and other non-software systems." The UML "represents a collection of the best engineering practices that have proven successful in the modeling of large and complex systems." UML provides a metamodel for a class diagram and a set of semantic and syntactic rules that define the core elements and relationships. The model is supported by a number of automated tools, including Rational Software's Rose, Computer Associates' Paradigm Plus, Rösch Consulting's Very Quick Modeling (VQM), Secant products, and Microsoft's Visual Modeler. Languages in which OO designs are implemented are typically Java, C++, and Visual Basic.

The primary design goals of the UML are as follows:

- To provide users with a ready-to-use, expressive visual modeling language to develop and exchange meaningful models;
- To furnish extensibility and specialization mechanisms to extend the core concepts;
- To support specifications that are independent of particular programming languages and development processes;
- To provide a formal basis for understanding the modeling language;
- To encourage the growth of the object tools market;
- To support higher-level development concepts such as components, collaborations, frameworks, and patterns;
- To integrate best practices.

A not-for-profit group, the Object Management Group (OMG™) drove the standardization efforts and the rapid adoption of UML; OMG™ continues to maintain these standards, with the help of more than 800 contributing members. The complete UML open standards can be downloaded from the Object Management Group's Web site: *www.omg.org*.

The UML must be applied in the context of a process, but the authors did not dictate a specific one, by design. They realized that different organizations and different projects require very different process steps (e.g., transaction processing vs. real-time embedded applications). UML *does* promote a development environment that is use case–driven, architecture-centric, iterative, and incremental.

The authors of UML also realize that, even with today's outstanding technology, we still have those "same old enemies" when it comes to requirements gathering, analysis, and design. We continue to battle inadequate, unstable requirements and imperfect communications with customers.

Use cases are proposed for specifying dynamic requirements and a providing a clearer understanding of expected behavior. Use cases allow functional enhancements to be captured and addressed in a disciplined way. Classes and objects in UML show flexibility and control through static and dynamic unambiguous descriptions. To combat poor team communication, OO allows for an integrated program team approach with a common vocabulary and a common language; encapsulation of data and algorithms allow team members to work on components in parallel. Encapsulation also helps to limit the impact of requirements volatility; inheritance of functions and attributes allows for efficient addition of functionality.

Object-Oriented Analysis

OOA consists primarily of the creation of class/object diagrams, use cases/use case scenarios, and activity diagrams (see Table 22–4). Just as with SA/SD, debate continues over where to begin. And, just as with SA/SD, it doesn't really matter. Some analysts are more comfortable beginning with the construction of class diagrams, while others like to start with use cases. Charles Richter points out that it matters less with OOA/OOD because of the representational continuity—the actual elements appearing in analysis models continue to exist throughout the development process. With OO, the analysis *becomes* the design because OO development is the process of refinement through elaboration.[9]

Object-Oriented Analysis Static View: Class Diagram   The static model of OO is the class diagram (and the object diagram to represent a specific instance of a class), which includes components of attributes, services, and relationships, and concepts of hierarchy, abstraction, encapsulation, inheritance, and polymorphism. Identifying class responsibilities and then proceeding "upward" to use case scenarios for validation is called the "bottom-up" approach. It is a fine way to proceed, but so is "top-down," which begins with use cases and works down through scenarios to identify classes. When beginning with classes, you may want to first identify them through abstraction or looking for noun phrases in existing documentation, and then list the responsibilities of each class, identify attributes, identify operations (behavior—again through abstraction or looking for verb phrases), and, lastly, employ use case scenarios to validate the class diagram. But first, here's a description of class diagrams.

Classes
A class is an abstraction of something in the application domain, generally stated as a noun. It can be conceptual or physical; it reflects the capabilities of a system to keep information about it, interact with it, or both. A class consists of attributes (data that describes the object and that the system needs to store about the object), relationships with other classes, and operations (behavior of the object, which describes its responsibilities). A class diagram portrays contents of classes (a collection of declarative, static, model elements) in relationship to each other.

A class serves as a type and defines the interfaces of its instances. Although classes are abstract, instances of a class are specific. An object is a single (particular) instance of a class. All objects instantiated from a class will have attribute values matching the attributes of the full class descriptor and will support the operations found in the full class descriptor. For example, a telephone is a class; Susan's telephone is an object, and Wallace's telephone is an object.

Objects

Objects are instances of a class and share the properties (attributes and operations) of the class. Each object has its own identity and its own set of values for the attribute. An object is an entity that encapsulates both state and behavior. State is represented by attributes and links; operations and state machines represent behavior. A state stores the effects of the operations of the entity. An object diagram shows objects and their associations/relationships (links) at a point in time. Object diagrams may be portrayed as collaboration diagrams because the relationships that "link" objects are shown.

A class can be "abstract," meaning that it is used to define subclasses that may be instantiated, but it will not be directly instantiated itself.

Classes have behavior, which is also called operation, service, function, or method. We will use the terms found in the OMG UML specification, "operation" for class and object and "method" for an implementation of an operation. When an operation is invoked, behavior is affected.

Classes must have identity, have well-defined responsibilities, and carry out system functions by collaborating with other objects via messages.

Classes are described by attributes (data, properties), operations (services, functions, behavior, process, methods), a life cycle (state, identity, independent existence), and associations (relationships, links, connections). Classes have properties, structure, behavior, and an independent existence.

An object (just like an entity) may be:

- a tangible thing (or person),
- a role being played,
- an event (e.g., visit to the doctor),
- an interaction (contract),
- an operational procedure (a review),
- an organizational unit (SQI),
- a place (the bank), or
- a structure (the Eiffel Tower).

Definitions are always helpful: An *interface* is a named set of operations that characterize the behavior of an element. A *message* is a specification of the conveyance of information from one instance to another, with the expectation that activity will ensue (a message may specify the raising of a signal or the call of an operation). A *method* is the implementation of an operation (it specifies the algorithm or procedure associated with an operation). A *stimulus* is the passing of information from one instance to another, such as raising a signal or invoking an operation; to receive a message means handling a stimulus passed from a sender instance. A *receiver* (object) is the object handling a stimulus passed from a sender object. A *relationship* is a semantic connection among model elements (examples of relationships include associations and generalizations). *Responsibility* is a contract or obligation of a classifier; to send a message means passing a stimulus from a sender instance to a receiver instance. A *sender* (object) is the object passing a stimulus to a receiver object.

And more: An *object* is an instance that originates from a class—it is structured and behaves according to its class. All objects originating from the same class are structured in the same way, although each of them has its own set of *attribute links*. Each attribute link references an instance, usually a data value. An object may have multiple classes (i.e., it may originate from several classes). In this case, the object will have all the features declared in all of these classes, both the structural and the behavioral ones. Moreover, the set of classes (i.e., the set of features that the object conforms to) may vary over time. New classes may be added to the object and old ones may be detached. This means that the features of the new classes are dynamically added to the object, and the features declared in a class that is removed from the object are dynamically removed from the object.[10]

Attributes
An attribute is a description of a range of values that may be held by the instances of the class. This information is internal to the object. It has also been described as a characteristic, and as:

- a property of an object, conveying information,
- usually a noun,
- describing the object in real-world terms,
- perhaps a state indicator,
- having a data type,
- the same for objects of the same class (may differ in value, but not in kind), and
- able to take on a value defined by an enumerated domain (set of specific values).

Operations
An operation is a service that can be requested from an object to effect behavior. Operations have been described as:

- encapsulated by an object;
- a response to a stimulus (message);
- possibly an action performed on the object by the object;
- perhaps a transformation that the object undergoes; and
- a verb, the "how."

Per UML, the method is the specific implementation of an operation.

An operation (method) is a means by which an object can perform its responsibility. The operation of an object is invoked through a message, which is sent from another object. It may be called a service, behavior, or responsibility. All objects have methods to handle their initialization (birth), and release (death) in the model, as well as "getting" and "putting" its attributes.

Associations

A relationship (association) declares a "meaningful and interesting" connection (link) between "concepts" or classes (objects). It consists of at least two association ends. The multiplicity property of an association end specifies how many instances may be associated with a single instance of the class at the other end.

Messages

Each object has interfaces required for it to fulfill its responsibilities. These interfaces are the means by which objects interact—messages that will be sent to each object by the other objects. The interfaces are considered public methods because they will be referred to by other objects. It is helpful to define these interfaces early in the life cycle. This allows the programming team to be divided across object boundaries rather than functional boundaries. As long as the interfaces and responsibilities have been clearly defined, they can work independently and come together later in the cycle for testing of the model.

The interfaces can provide for the setting of an attribute, the return of the value of an attribute, and a request for the object to perform an operation.

Methods are the way in which objects interact with each other, passing messages to invoke (stimulate) some activity (behavior) within the receiving object. In SA/SD, this would be accomplished by adding a foreign key to each of the objects referencing the other objects. In object technology, the object ID is the alternative approach to foreign keys. It is created and maintained by the OO system. To make the connection between the objects, the object ID is simply included in the definition of the attributes of the target object.

Messages contain a destination object (containing the operation to be performed), the name of operation to be performed, and parameters needed to complete the operation.

Encapsulation (Information Hiding)

Encapsulation consists of the separation of the external aspects of an object from the internal implementation details of the object. Another term for encapsulation is *information hiding*. The external aspects of an object are accessible by other objects through methods of the object, while the internal implementations of those methods are hidden from the external object sending the message. Encapsulation is essential to obtaining the power or maintainability of an object-oriented model. Because the implementation details are hidden from the other objects, thus self-contained within the object, the impact of changes in the implementation of a method is minimal to the overall model. Encapsulation applies to both attributes and operations.

Inheritance
Inheritance is the sharing of attributes and behavior of objects within a hierarchical structure (superclasses and subclasses). Each subclass inherits or incorporates all the properties (attributes and operations) of the superclass (ancestor) and adds its own unique properties. A class contains a description of all of the attributes, associations, and operations that the object contains: It is a generalization of the object. Each class has a set of inheritable features—attributes, operations, and associations. These data structures and algorithms are immediately available for subclass descendants. A class may have children (subclasses, subtypes) where the child is a specialization of the parent. Children inherit (incorporate) the structure and behavior of their more general parents, while being capable of adding attributes and operations of their own. This relationship is also known as generalization. Inheritance/specialization/generalization is an advantage of OOA because it promotes reuse of classes. Through the use of these concepts, the properties of the superclass need not be repeated in each object of the subclass, thus providing a high reuse factor. Changes to attributes or operations are immediately inherited by all subclasses.

Polymorphism
Polymorphism means "many forms." In OO terms, it means the ability of different objects to respond differently to the same message. If the message "go" is sent to different objects, the selection of the reaction is based on the type of a single object. This way, different operations can have the same name; "go_boat" might mean "unfurl the sails" to a sailboat but "start the motor" to a motorboat. Objects are more independent with polymorphism.

Designing Classes
When designing the classes in terms of their responsibilities, it is wise to consider the object as an entire entity. It is tempting to think about only the data that it will need to store or the methods that it will perform, but to do so causes thinking in procedural terms rather than object terms.

To consider the object as an entire entity, try to determine how it would carry out all of the duties for which it is responsible as a self-managing entity. This approach is a responsibility-driven approach as opposed to a data approach. Using the results of the walk-through, which defined and clarified the roles of the candidate objects, determine what each object should know about itself.

Superclasses and Subclasses
A set of classes can be structured hierarchically through the use of superclasses and subclasses. A superclass is a higher level grouping of similar classes (subclasses) with the common attributes and methods contained within this class.

Abstract Classes
An abstract class is a superclass that has no instances and is introduced to give structure to existing classes. The main purpose of this type of class is to group classes and to capture information that is common to the group.

Finding Candidate Objects

The process of identifying candidate objects is often begun by looking for the nouns in the definition of the business cycle, similar to techniques used in the requirements analysis phase of SA/SD. The analyst will consider criteria such as these:

Does the system need to remember anything about the object?

Does an object need to provide some behavior or function?

Does the object have a responsibility?

Does the object have multiple attributes?

Does the object have special cases, which may lead to an inheritance structure?

Does the object share properties with other potential objects? (This may imply that the object is part of a potential inheritance structure of another object.)

Does the object contain things that are already defined as objects?

If the analyst has chosen to produce use case diagrams before class diagramming, then the use case scenarios provide a source for class identification.

Finding Attributes

Once the class/object has been defined, attributes may clarify what the object means, in the context of the problem space. The study of processing narratives or the statement of scope for the problem can lead to the selection of terms that define an object. When working with attributes, do the following:

- Refine object attributes, including derived attributes (the value can be completely determined by the values of other attributes).
- Discard unneeded attributes such as objects, internal identifiers, internal states, and inappropriate levels of detail.
- Remember that attributes are usually nouns followed by possessive phrases.
- Remember that adjectives can be specific enumerated values of the attribute.
- Keep in mind that, just as with SA/SD, the attributes are housed in a data dictionary.

Finding Operations

Study processing narrative or statement of scope for the problem and perform grammatical parse for verbs. Consider the communication that occurs between objects. Remember that operations define the behavior of an object, change one or more attribute values, must have knowledge of the object's attributes, must have the ability to manipulate the data structures, and may manipulate data, perform a computation, or monitor an object for the occurrence of a controlling event.

For developers without domain experience, there are three stages, from highly abstract to less abstract class diagrams, using noun extraction: concise definition, informal strategy, and formal strategy. The following is an example using the classic elevator problem, as described in Box 22–2.

"Create a concise definition" means to define the product as a succinct single sentence, if possible. It might look something like this, "Buttons in elevators and on floors are to be used to control motion of *n* elevators in a building with *m* floors."

"Create an informal strategy" means to incorporate constraints, preferably expressed in a single paragraph. Perhaps the following would work for the elevator problem: "Buttons in elevators and on floors control movement of *n* elevators in a building with *m* floors. Buttons illuminate when pressed to request elevator to stop at specific floor; illumination is canceled when request has been satisfied. If elevator has no requests, it remains at its current floor with its doors closed."

"Formalize the strategy" means to identify the nouns in the informal strategy and use them as candidate classes. Nouns in our example are *button, elevator, floor, movement, building, illumination*, and *door*. The nouns *floor, building*, and *door* are outside the problem boundary (outside of our control). The nouns *movement* and *illumination* are abstract nouns that will be excluded for now but kept in mind for potential attributes. This leaves us with candidate classes *elevator* and *button*. Subclasses appear to be *elevator button* and *floor button*.

Class-Responsibility-Collaboration (CRC)
Proposed about 1989, CRC (class, responsibility, collaboration) "cards" have proved to be a cost-effective and useful way to identify classes. This seems to work particularly well when used during brainstorming sessions with domain experts present. The CRC approach is for participants to fill out "cards" containing the name of a potential class, along with its functionality (responsibility) and a list of classes that it invokes (collaboration). Teams can then use the cards to act out scenarios. Because it is physically easy to change, it becomes a powerful tool for highlighting missing or incorrect items via teamwork. Table 22–5 shows what a CRC card might look like for the elevator problem. The CRC may then be worked into a class diagram, as shown in Figure 22–46.

In this diagram, the classes are Elevator, Elevator Controller, Door, and Button. Elevator Button and Floor Button are subtypes of Button—they inherit the attributes and operations of Button. Button is a generalization of Elevator Button and Floor Button; Elevator Button and Floor Button are specializations of Button.

Object-Oriented Analysis Static Views: Use Case Diagrams   Use case diagrams depict a static, or organizational, view of system functions and their static relationships both with external entities and with one another. A use case is a narrative document that describes the sequence of events of an actor (an external agent) using a system to complete a process. They are stories or cases of using a system that illustrate and imply requirements in the stories they tell. The term originated with Jacobson to describe how an actor (an entity outside of the system that interacts with the system) uses the system. The system, subsystem, or class

TABLE 22–5
Elevator Problem CRC

Class: Elevator Controller	
Responsibilities	**Collaborations**
Turn on elevator button	Elevator button
Turn off elevator button	Elevator button
Turn on floor button	Floor button
Turn off floor button	Floor button
Open elevator doors	Elevator door
Close elevator doors	Elevator door
Move elevator one floor up	Elevator
Move elevator one floor down	Elevator

provides a coherent unit of functionality manifested by sequences of messages exchanged among the system components and one or more outside actors, as shown in Figure 22–47. An actor may play a separate role with regard to each use case with which it communicates.

Use cases define the behavior of an entity, such as a system or subsystem, without specifying (revealing) its internal structure. Each use case specifies a sequence of actions that the entity can perform interacting with the actors of the entity. Instances of use cases and instances of actors *interact* when the services of the entity are used.

Class diagrams show the static structure of the object, their internal structure, and their relationships.

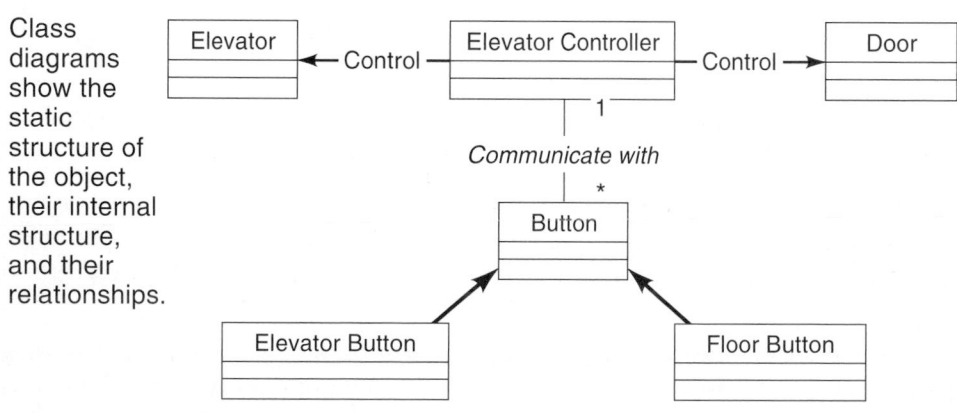

FIGURE 22–46
Elevator Problem Class Diagram

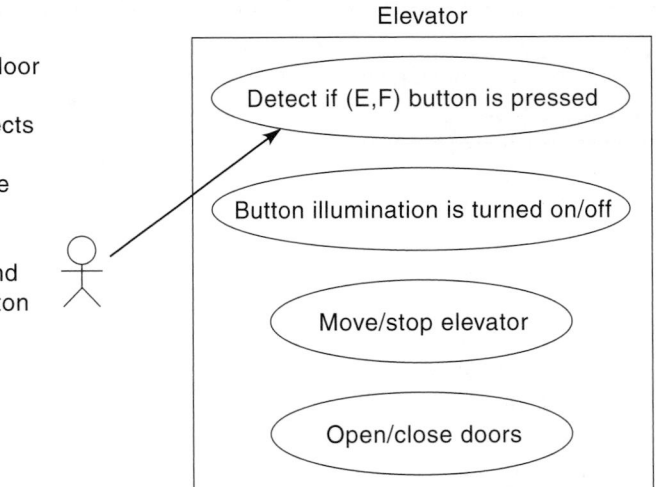

1. Passenger pressed floor button
2. Elevator system detects floor button pressed
3. Elevator moves to the floor
4. Elevator doors open
5. Passenger gets in and presses elevator button
6. Elevator doors close
7. Elevator moves to required floor
8. Elevator doors open
9. Passenger gets out
10. Elevator doors close

FIGURE 22–47
Elevator Problem Example of Use Case/Use Case Scenario

Use case diagrams show actors and use cases together with their relationships. The use cases represent functionality of a system, subsystem, or class, as manifested to external actors with it. Actors communicate with the entity by sending and receiving messages to and from use cases. Associations between the actor and the use case or class show this message passing.

A few definitions may help keep the terminology straight: A use case (class) is the specification of a sequence of actions that a system (or other entity) can perform, interacting with actors of the system. A use case diagram is a diagram that shows the relationships among actors and use cases within a system. A use case instance is the performance of a sequence of actions being specified in a use case. A use case model is a model that describes a system's functional requirements in terms of use cases. A scenario is a specific sequence of actions that illustrates behavior (a scenario may be used to illustrate an interaction or the execution of a use case instance).

An instance of a use case may be augmented by the behavior specified in another by an "extends relationship." An instance of a use case may always contain the behavior of another by an "includes relationship."

A use case can specify the external requirements on an entity as well as specify functionality offered by an already realized entity. It may be described in plain text, using operations together with attributes, in activity graphs, by a state machine, or other behavior description techniques.

When an actor initiates a message, the use case performs a sequence of actions as a response. Use cases, like data flow diagrams, do not imply temporal sequencing. Functions may occur in any order.

Object-Oriented Analysis Dynamic View—Activity Diagram   Activity diagrams impart a dynamic, or behavioral, view of system functions. It may be thought of as an abstract workflow view of activities. Much like the flowcharts of the 1960s, there are a limited number of constructs: One activity must follow another (simple sequence), one activity conditionally follows another (decision or if-then-else), or one activity is followed by many possible instantiations or invocations of another activity (do-while or do-until or do case). The difference between a flowchart and an activity diagram is that activities between synchronization bars may occur in any order or in parallel.

Communication between objects is modeled as events. When a sender generates an event that is delivered to a receiver, it may be asynchronous (the sender continues executing) or synchronous (the sender suspends execution until the receiver handles the sent event). Figure 22–48 shows an activity diagram for the elevator example.

Object-Oriented Design

Recall that, just as with SA/SD, "design" is the phase of the software product development process whose primary purpose is to decide *how* the system will be implemented. During design, strategic and tactical decisions are made to meet the required functional and quality requirements of a system. During design, model elaboration is in play more than the creation of wholly new models. It includes the generation of interfaces and implementations that allow repositories to be instantiated and populated based on the existing models.

Object-Oriented Design Static View—Class Diagram   During the OOD phase, the class/object diagrams are refined via elaboration. If peer reviews and inspections are held using the elevator problem, a more detailed class diagram might look like the one shown in Figure 22–49.

Object-Oriented Design—Interaction Diagrams

Interaction Diagrams
Interaction diagram is a generic term that applies to several types of diagrams emphasizing object interactions. These include collaboration diagrams and sequence diagrams. Collaboration diagrams show the relationships among instances and aid in understanding all the effects on a given instance. Sequence diagrams show the explicit sequence of stimuli and aid in the understanding of real-time specifications and complex scenarios. An interaction diagram describes the dynamic interactions of classes, describes how objects interact in a particular scenario, and indicates what object methods are called in which order in that particular scenario. It does not describe what an object does internally or how it may change over time.

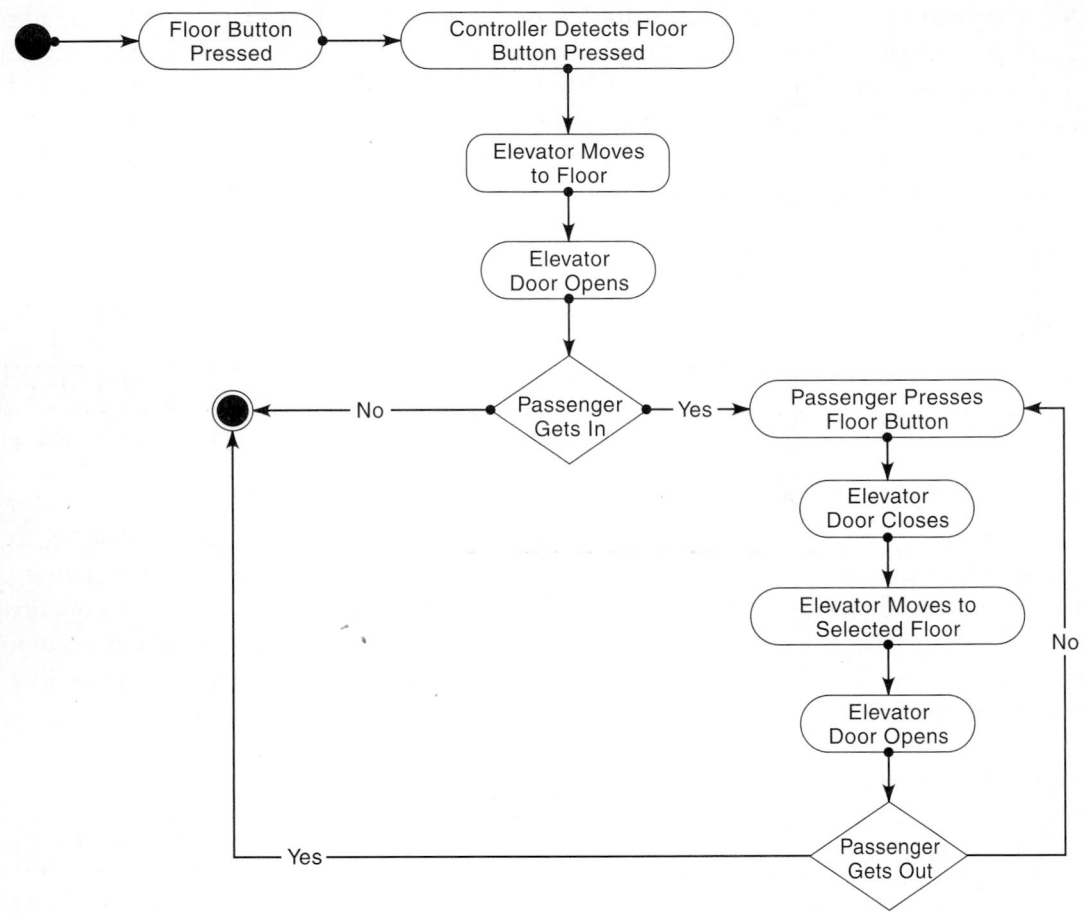

FIGURE 22–48
Activity Diagram for the Elevator Problem

Object-Oriented Design Static View—Interaction Diagrams and Collaboration Diagrams
A collaboration diagram shows interactions oriented spatially around the structure of a model, using classes and associations (instances and links.) A collaboration diagram shows the relationships among the instances. Sequence diagrams and collaboration diagrams express similar information but show it in different ways.

Behavior is implemented by sets of objects that exchange stimuli within an overall interaction to accomplish a purpose. To understand the mechanisms used in a design, it is important to see only those objects and their interaction involved in accomplishing a purpose or a related set of purposes, projected from the larger system of which they are part for other purposes.

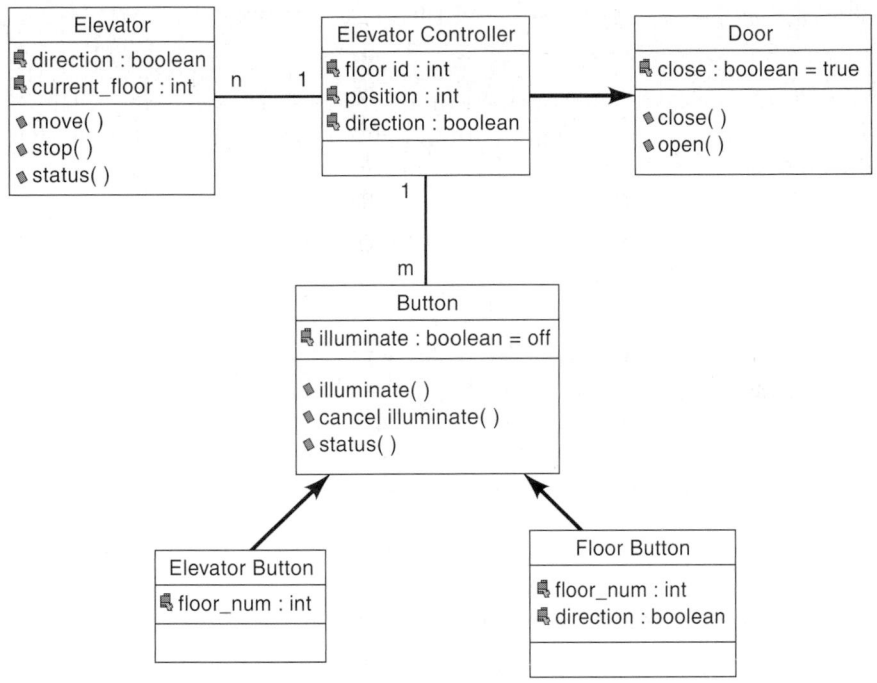

FIGURE 22–49
Detailed Class Diagram

A collaboration defines a specific way to use the model elements in a model. It describes how different kinds of classes and their associations are to be used in accomplishing a particular task. The collaboration defines a restriction of or a projection of a collection of classes (i.e., what properties instances of the participating classifiers must have when performing a particular collaboration).

A set of instances and links conforming to the participants specified in the collaboration cooperate when the specified task is performed.

The purpose of a collaboration is to specify how a use case is realized. The collaboration defines a context in which the behavior of the realized element can be specified in terms of interactions between the participants of the collaboration. Thus, while a model describes a whole system, a collaboration is a slice, or a projection, of that model. A collaboration defines a usage of a subset of the model's contents. A collaboration may be presented at two different levels: specification level or instance level. A diagram presenting the collaboration at the specification level will show class roles and association roles, while a diagram at the instance level will show instances and links conforming to the roles in the collaboration. In a collaboration, it is specified what properties instances must have to be able to take part in the collaboration (i.e., each participant specifies the required set of features that a conforming instance must have).[11]

Examples of collaboration diagrams for the elevator problem are shown in Figure 22–50.

Object-Oriented Design Dynamic View—Interaction Diagrams and Sequence Diagrams
A *sequence diagram* shows an interaction arranged in time sequence. In particular, it shows the instances participating in the interaction by their "lifelines" and the stimuli they exchange arranged in time sequence. Unlike a collaboration diagram, a sequence diagram includes time sequences but does not include object relationships. A sequence diagram can exist in a generic form (describes all possible scenarios) and in an instance form (describes one actual scenario). Sequence diagrams and collaboration diagrams express similar information but show it in different ways.

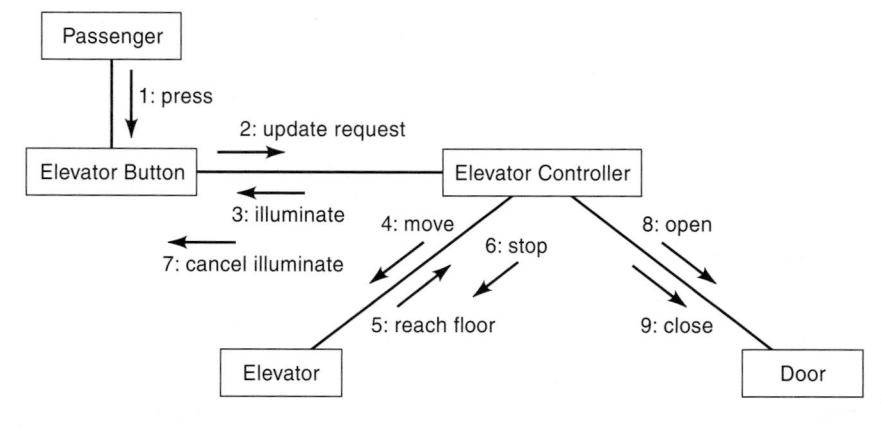

A collaboration
diagram shows
the relationships
between objects.

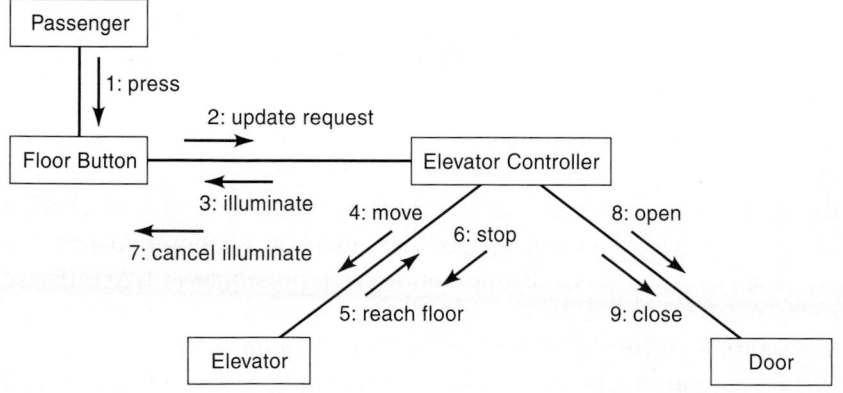

FIGURE 22–50
Elevator Problem: Elevator Button Versus Door Button Collaboration Diagram Example

A sequence diagram has two dimensions:

1. The vertical dimension represents time.
2. The horizontal dimension represents different objects.

Normally, time proceeds down the page. (The dimensions may be reversed, if desired.) Usually only time sequences are important, but in real-time applications, the time axis could be an actual metric. There is no significance to the horizontal ordering of the objects. Objects can be grouped into "swimlanes" on a diagram.[12] Figure 22–51 shows a sequence diagram for the elevator example.

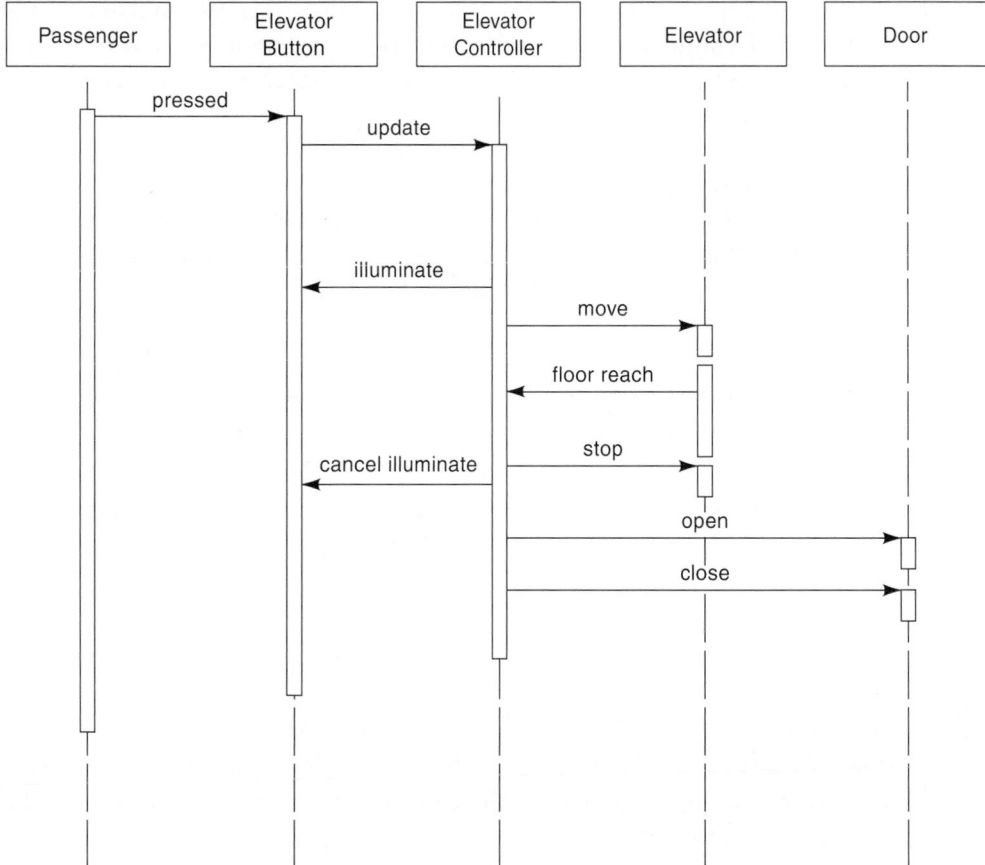

A sequence diagram shows the explicit sequence of messages suitable for modeling a real-time system.

FIGURE 22–51
Sequence Diagram for the Elevator Problem

Object-Oriented Design Dynamic View—State Transition Diagrams
A state transition diagram (STD) describes the state-based behavior of a class of instances across all scenarios. Usually, only classes with objects that are expected to pass through a series of states are modeled.

Definitions include these: A *state* is a condition or situation during the life of an object during which it satisfies some condition, performs some activity, or waits for some event. A *state chart diagram* is a diagram that shows a state machine (behavior that specifies the sequences of states that an object or an interaction goes through during its life in response to events, together with its responses and actions).

The state machine specifies a set of concepts that can be used for modeling discrete behavior through finite state-transition systems. Event instances are generated as a result of some action either within the system or in the environment surrounding the system. An event is then conveyed to one or more targets. The means by which event instances are transported to their destination depend on the type of action, the target, the properties of the communication medium, and numerous other factors. In some cases, this is practically instantaneous and completely reliable, while in others it may involve variable transmission delays, loss of events, reordering, or duplication. No specific assumptions are made in this regard. This provides full flexibility for modeling different types of communication facilities. An event is *received* when it is placed on the event queue of its target. An event is *dispatched* when it is dequeued from the event queue and delivered to the state machine for processing. At this point, it is referred to as the *current event*. Finally, it is *consumed* when event processing is completed. A consumed event is no longer available for processing. No assumptions are made about the time intervals between event reception, event dispatching, and consumption. This leaves open the possibility of different semantic models such as zero-time semantics.

A state can be active or inactive during execution. A state becomes *active* when it is entered as a result of some transition, and it becomes *inactive* if it is exited as a result of a transition. A state can be exited and entered as a result of the same transition (e.g., self-transition).

State chart diagrams represent the behavior of entities capable of dynamic behavior by specifying its response to the receipt of event instances. Typically, it is used for describing the behavior of classes. A state is a condition during the life of an object or an interaction during which it satisfies some condition, performs some action, or waits for some event. Conceptually, an object remains in a state for an interval of time. However, the semantics allow for modeling "flow-through" states that are instantaneous, as well as transitions that are not instantaneous.[13] Figure 22–25 shows a state machine for the elevator problem. It is the same as the finite state machine from structured analysis.

Strengths of OO Modeling
Object-oriented modeling keeps the focus on real-world entities, directly maps the problem domain and system responsibilities into a mode, defers definition of implementation details to later in the design phase, and minimizes impacts of functional requirements changes.

Commonalities of SA/SD and OOA/OOD

Structured analysis/structured design has much in common with object-oriented analysis/object-oriented design. Of course, there are differences, too, but sometimes newer methods have their roots in older ones. Here are a few places where commonalities exist:

- Both model data, function, and behavior.

- Both benefit from an overall architectural viewpoint.

- Both require a data dictionary or information repository that names and describes the elements of the model, both composite and atomic.

- Both rely on state transition diagrams to portray real-time behavior.

- Both look for system boundaries and outside entities that interact with the system (DCDs, CCDs, and use cases/use case scenarios).

- Both start with existing documentation and written requirements specifications to identify noun phrases for data elements and verb phrases for function or behavior elements.

- Both suggest an iterative process—the need to return to the analysis phase during the design phase.

- Both stress the virtues of low coupling and high cohesion—SA/SD in structure chart creation (modules are highly cohesive and interfaces exhibit low coupling) and OOA/OOD in class creation (methods are highly cohesive and objects reflect low coupling—they should know little about each other).

- Both strive for modular systems, where like things are grouped together.

A major advantage of OOA/OOD is the enabling of design by refinement, or elaboration, through what Richter calls representational continuity. The same kinds of diagrams are drawn throughout the development process, and the actual elements appearing in the analysis models continue to exist throughout the design process. The class diagram, thought of as an analysis tool, has properties that will appear throughout the design and in the implementation of the system. Analysis becomes design. This strength of OO may be contrasted with SA/SD where DFDs and CFDs become structure charts through transform or transaction analysis—the analysis models are very different forms than the design models.

A major advantage of SA/SD is that many find it simple and straightforward. Data is traced through the system in a way that is very attractive to the data advocates of the world. Many analysts/designers feel that if you can show them the data, its structure, and its transformations, you have just described the salient points of the system.

Without taking sides here, we suggest that an approach (mixing and matching is okay) be decided upon by the project manager and project team early in the game. When that approach is documented, analysts and designers are trained to speak the same language, and everyone sticks with it.

Summary

Much has been covered in terms of model creation in this chapter, and a large number of models have been presented. The summary will consist of a short review of the steps and the resulting project artifacts of each method.

Review: Steps in Structured Analysis and Structured Design

During both structured analysis and structured design, the PM needs to know:

What tasks are being done?

What artifacts should I expect?

How long it will take?

What process is being used?

What method is being used—pure structured methods or a combination with OO?

How should the organization be structured to support the process?

What tools, automated or manual, should be employed to support the process?

A "big picture" of SA/SD is shown in Figure 22–52. Reading from the top downward, this picture shows, at the top, that data (static) models may include entity relationship diagrams or class models, that functional models are data context diagrams, control context diagrams, data flow diagrams, and control flow diagrams. At the top, or beginning, of SA/SD is also a good time to begin a data dictionary and to flesh out process specifications and control specifications (which are often represented as state transition diagrams).

In the center of the picture, architecture context diagrams, architecture flow diagrams, and architecture interconnect diagrams are represented. This is the phase in which requirements models are parsed out into one of five boxes (core system, user interface, input, output, maintenance and self-help), data flows are bundled, and then the system is decomposed again. For most projects, this is a necessary part of particularly complex real-time or control systems only.

The bottom third of the picture shows how repositioned functional modules undergo transform or transaction analysis to form a series of structure charts, decomposed to their lowest level. At the lowest level, where each black-box module on a structure chart is identified, the modules may be designed for internal structure (white box). These designs, known as Chapin charts or Nassi-Schneiderman diagrams, are used in the construction of actual program code.

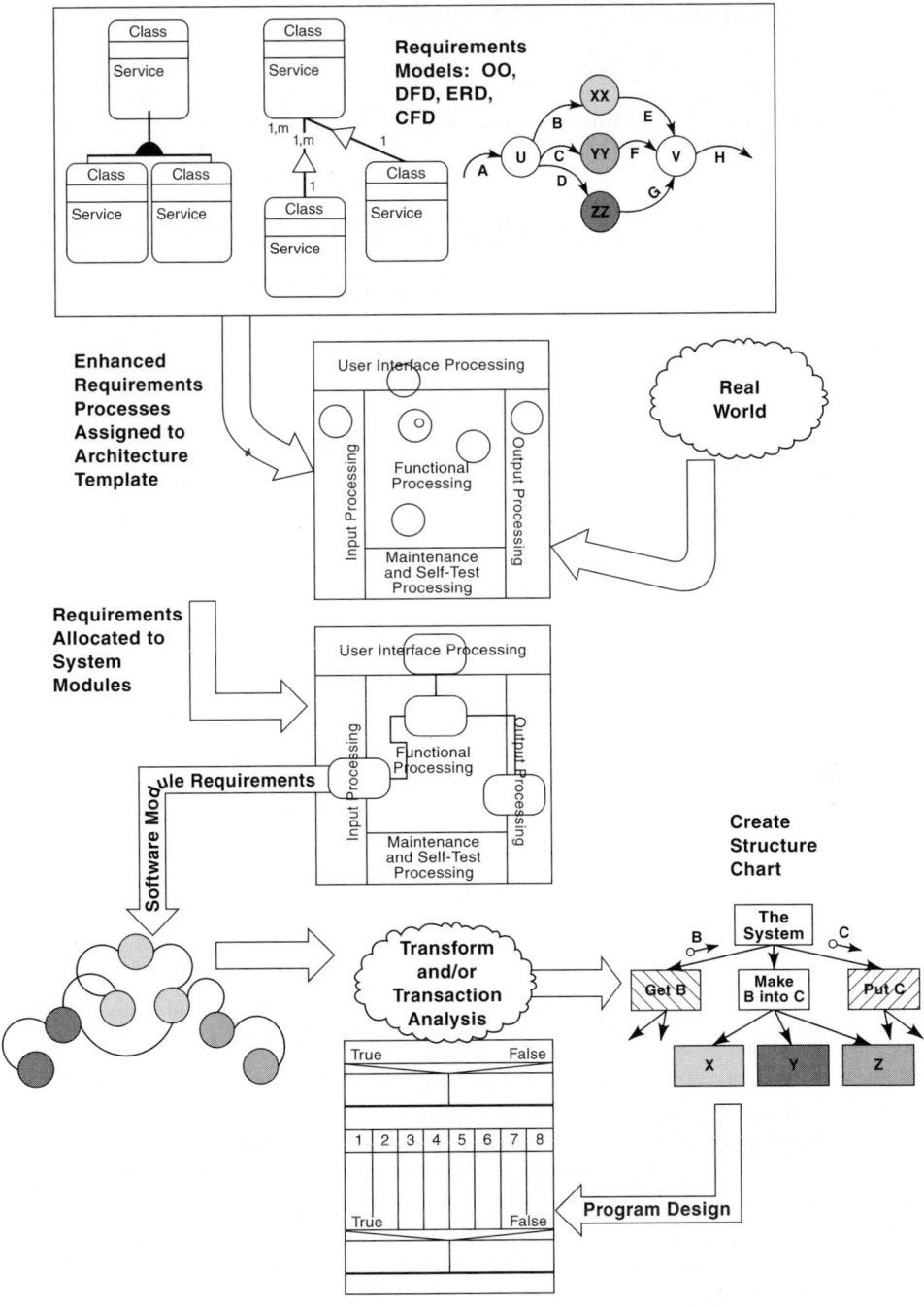

FIGURE 22–52
The Big Picture of Analysis and Design

Review: Steps in Object-Oriented Analysis and Object-Oriented Design

The questions that a PM wants to answer are the same as for SA/SD methods. They can mostly be answered by deciding upon which of the OOA/OOD models will be used and if any will be used in combination with SA/SD models.

There are several ways to create, use, and refine OO models of use case diagrams/scenarios, activity diagrams, class/object diagrams, collaboration diagrams, interaction diagrams, state transition diagrams, data context diagrams, and the data dictionary. Some are thought of as top-down, some as bottom-up, and all are iteratively refined through elaboration. Derived from writings of Richter and Larman, two approaches are listed here.

One sequence of steps would involve something like this:

1. Identify actors and identify their interactions with the system. Create use cases, working on high-level ones first and deferring their expansion until the design phase or when it is their turn to be developed.

2. Create high-level class/object models quickly, emphasizing obvious roles, things, and concepts. Make use of noun phrases from a problem specification. Analyze the life cycles of each class, considering what use cases cause an instance of each class to be created, changed, or destroyed.

3. Document the flow of messages between instances and the invocation of methods via collaboration diagrams. Analyze the action-oriented verb phrases in a problem specification.

4. Use collaboration diagrams to determine how objects interconnect and what methods belong to each class.

An alternative approach is this:

1. Write the problem statement, or use narrative descriptions from SRS documents.

2. Identify objects. Beginning with nouns, select only entities and concepts that are relevant to the project. Defer aggregation and generalization until a later iteration. Concentrate on objects and the most obvious attributes—they can be expanded later. Create a data context diagram and prune terminators and actors. Begin a data dictionary.

3. Select classes. Eliminate redundant classes or those that should be something else (an attribute or an operation); eliminate implementation constructs. Clarify vague classes. Heavily involve domain experts.

4. Construct the data dictionary. Create an entry for each object class and define scope, assumptions, associations, attributes, operations, and methods.

5. Create the class diagram. Iterate models and diagrams, begun early in the project, with domain experts and users.

6. Identify associations and aggregations. Eliminate associations that are irrelevant or redundant, or that are implementation-specific. Begin the estimation of multiplicity for

each association, and then reduce it where possible. Clarify ambiguous associations. Decompose higher-order associations.

7. Identify attributes.

8. Simplify using inheritance. Search classes for similar attributes, associations, or operations, and assign them to a superclass. Refine existing classes into specialized subclasses (define subclasses where a class is treated differently in the application). Avoid complexity—too much detail, deeply nested generalizations.

And, as always, iterate, iterate, iterate.

Problems for Review _____

1. Given this set of unnormalized data, as depicted on the form in Figure 22–53, transform it to 1NF, then 2NF, and then 3NF.

   Order number

   Customer number

   Customer name

   Customer address

   Customer discount

   Customer type

   Order date

   Delivery date

   Parts (occur more than once, each composed of the following)

   > Part number

   > Part description

   > Price

   > Quantity

   > Total cost

2. What questions would you ask your team concerning the concept of coupling? What possible effects would tight coupling have on the success or failure of your project?

3. What phases of your project may be impacted by poor cohesion within the system? How could you help as a project manager to remedy the situation?

Example Company				
Customer Order				

Order #:			Date:	
Customer #:				
Discount:				
Type:				
Delivery Date:				

ITEM #	PRICE	DESCRIPTION	QUANTITY	COST

Customer Name:	Total:
Customer Address:	

FIGURE 22–53
Normalization Problem Form

4. What do you think the level of coupling is for these examples? Is it "good"?
   a. Call SQRT
   b. Call SQRT (number, squareroot, status)
   c. Call SQRT (number, squareroot)
   d. Call SQRT (number)
   e. Call SQRT (Param(3))

5. Determine the cohesion for these examples:

   a. If flag=1, compute square root; if flag=2, sort array.

   b. Get new data, read the sensor, get the system status, build new position matrix.

   c. Open files, obtain first transaction and first master record, and print page headings.

   d. From an electrical connection matrix, produce a circuit diagram.

   e. After input, add control items and verify totals.

   f. Compute FICA, tax withholding, and deductions.

   g. Determine ship position.

   h. Compute the square root using Newton's method.

   i. Update current credit record and update database.

6. Consider the following two designs for the elevator problem.

   a. The elevator control system, acting as a controller, assigns an elevator to an incoming request by iterating through the elevators, asking each elevator for its current location, direction, and so on (state). It then uses that information to determine which elevator is closest and assigns the request to that elevator.

   b. The elevator control system asks each elevator to compute its proximity to a request. Using its location, direction, and so on (state variables), each elevator makes its own determination of the proximity of a request and returns that measure.

7. Which design is more flexible? Suppose that you want to extend this system to work in a building in which some elevators cannot stop on all floors. Which will be the easiest to modify? Suppose that the system must be extended to handle elevators that are out of service. Which design is the most accommodating?

Visit the Case Study

The prototype has been completed and delivered. Information on your corporation being the only bidder was correct, and you have been awarded the contract to build the entire ARRS. All of the CRM resources are assigned to a single project manager, Mr. Sung. A service-level agreement was drawn up between Mr. Lee, Ms. Patel, and Mr. Lu. You were not included because, as Mr. Lee remarked, "This is a sales and marketing issue, not a software programming problem." They will send you a hard copy once all the official signatures are affixed—about three months. The only thing that you need to be concerned about is that you are the overall project manager, and Dr. Harita and Mr. Sung report to you.

   Because you now have a working prototype, the minister of the CRM feels that the project must be close to completion. He wants a plan showing the delivery dates for the final software and an installation plan. He wants it now. You, as the project manager, need to go back over all of the existing project artifacts and update them to show the new project after this prototype. The minister is very busy and impatient. Better get started!

Citations

[1]Paulk, Mark C., Charles V. Weber, Bill Curtis, and Mary Beth Chrissis (1994). *The Capability Maturity Model: Guidelines for Improving the Software Process*. 1st ed. Reading, MA: Addison-Wesley SEI Series in Software Engineering.

[2]Connolly, Thomas, Carolyn Begg, and Anne Strachan (1998). *Database Systems—A Practical Approach to Design, Implementation, and Management*. Reading, MA: Addison-Wesley.

[3]Wyllys, R.E. (2001). "Overview of Normalization: Introduction." LIS 384K.11, *Database-Management Principles and Applications*. The University of Texas at Austin Graduate School of Library and Information Science.

[4]The Daisy Hill Puppy Farm Normalization Exercise, created by Marc Retting, is now widely used in the public domain. Examples of its usage may be found in the following places:

- *fiat.gslis.utexas.edu/~l384k11w/rw38411.html*. R.E. Wyllys (2001). "Overview of Normalization." LIS 384K, "Database-Management Principles and Applications." The University of Texas at Austin Graduate School of Library and Information Science

- *ola.aacc.cc.md.us/csi122/norm/datanorm.html*. Kari Siner (2001). "Personal Computer Database Management System with Microsoft® Access 2000." CSI 122. Arnold, MD: Anne Arundel Community College.

- Pheatt, Chuck (2000). Computer Science CS 444. Emporia State University, Emporia, KS.

- Retting, Marc (1992). "Five Rules of Data Normalization." Poster for *Database Programming & Design*, San Francisco, CA: Miller Freeman Publications.

- *stein.cshl.org/genome_informatics/sql1/lecture_notes.html*. Robert Peitzsch (1999). Genome Informatics, SQL and Relational Database Section, Genomic Informatics Class, CSHL. Stein Laboratory, Cold Spring Harbor Laboratory, Cold Spring Harbor, NY.

- Wiorkowski, Gabrielle, and David Kull (1992). *DB2: Design and Development Guide*, 3rd ed. Reading, MA: Addison-Wesley.

- *www.baldwinw.edu/~gbouw/courses/csc280/puppy.html*. Gerardus Bouw (2001). Department of Math and Computer Science, CSC 280. Baldwin-Wallace College, Berea, OH.

- *www.support.lotus.com/simsold.nsf/*. Lotus Customer Support Technote (1998). "The Five Rules of Database Normalization." Number 127782.

[5]*www.omg.org*. Object Management Group (OMG) (2000). *Unified Modeling Language (UML) Specification*, Version 1.3, March.

[6]Booch, Grady, James Rumbaugh, and Ivar Jacobson (1999). *The UML Modeling Language User Guide*. Reading, MA: Addison-Wesley.

[7]Gacek, Cristina, Ahmed Abd-Allah, Bradford Clark, and Barry W. Boehm (1995). "On the definition of software system architecture." *Proceedings of the First International Workshop on Architectures for Software Systems*, Seattle, WA.

[8]*www.sei.cmu.edu/architecture/definitions.html*. Software Engineering Institute (2001). "How Do You Define Software Architecture?"

[9]Richter, Charles (1999). *Designing Flexible Object-Oriented Systems with UML*. Indianapolis, IN: Macmillan Technical Publishing.

[10]See note 5.

[11]See note 5.

[12]See note 5.

[13]See note 5.

Suggested Readings

Bass, Len, et al. (1997). *Software Architecture in Practice*. Reading, MA: Addison-Wesley.

Bass, Len, Paul Clements, and Rick Kazman (1998). *Software Architecture in Practice: The SEI Series*. New York, NY: Addison-Wesley.

Batini, Carlo, et al. (1991). *Conceptual Database Design: An Entity-Relationship Approach*. Reading, MA: Addison-Wesley.

Booch, Grady (1994). *Object Oriented Design with Applications*. Reading, MA: Addison-Wesley.

Booch, Grady, et al. (1998). *Unified Modeling Language User Guide*. Reading, MA: Addison-Wesley.

Cantor, Murray R. (1998). *Object-Oriented Project Management with UML*. New York, NY: John Wiley & Sons.

Cassel, Paul, and Pamela Palmer (1999). *Sams Teach Yourself Access 2000 in 21 Days*. Indianapolis, IN: Sams.

Chapin, Ned (1974). "A New Format for Flowcharts." *Software—Practice and Experience*, 4(4):341–357.

Chapin, Ned (1985). "Software Maintenance: A Different View." *Proceedings of the 1985 National Computer Conference*. AFIPS Press, pp. 507–513.

Chen, Peter (1977). *The Entity-Relationship Approach to Logical Database Design*. Wellesley, MA: Q.E.D. Information Sciences.

Coad, Peter, and Edward Yourdon (1991). *Object Oriented Analysis*. New York, NY: Prentice Hall Yourdon Press Computing Series.

Coad, Peter, et al. (1996). *Object Models: Strategies, Patterns and Applications*, 2nd ed. New York, NY: Prentice Hall Yourdon Press Computing Series.

Codd, E.F. (1970). "A Relational Model of Data for Large Shared Data Banks." *Communications of the ACM*, 13(6):377–387.

Codd, E.F. (1990) *The Relationship Model for Database Management*, Version 2. New York, NY: Addison-Wesley.

Connell, John, and Linda Shafer (1995). *Object-Oriented Rapid Prototyping*. New York, NY: Prentice Hall Yourdon Press Computing Series.

Date, C.J. (1995, 1999). *An Introduction to Database Systems,* 6th and 7th eds. New York, NY: Addison-Wesley.

DeMarco, Tom (1979). *Structured Analysis and Systems Specification*. New York, NY: Prentice Hall Yourdon Press Computing Series.

DeMarco, Tom, and P.J. Plauger (1985). *Structured Analysis and System Specification*. New York, NY: Prentice Hall Yourdon Press Computing Series.

Eriksson, Hans-Erik, and Magnus Penker (1998). *The UML Toolkit*. New York, NY: John Wiley & Sons.

Flavin, Matt (1981). *Fundamental Concepts of Information Modeling*. New York, NY: Prentice Hall Yourdon Press Computing Series.

Harmon, Paul, and David A. Taylor (1993). *Objects in Action: Commercial Applications of Object-Oriented Technologies*. Reading, MA: Addison-Wesley.

Hatley, Derek J., and Imtiaz A. Pirbhai (1988). *Strategies for Real-Time System Specification*. New York, NY: Dorset House

IEEE (1993). IEEE 1016.1-1993 "Guide to Software Design Descriptions." New York, NY: The Institute of Electrical and Electronics Engineers.

IEEE (1998). IEEE 1016-1998 "Recommended Practice for Software Design Descriptions." New York, NY: The Institute of Electrical and Electronics Engineers.

IEEE (1998). IEEE 1320.1-1998 "Standard for Functional Modeling Language—Syntax and Semantics for IDEF0." New York, NY: The Institute of Electrical and Electronics Engineers.

IEEE (1998). IEEE 1320.2-1998 "Standard for Conceptual Modeling Language Syntax and Semantics for IDEF1X97 (IDEFobject)." New York, NY: The Institute of Electrical and Electronics Engineers.

IEEE (2000). IEEE 1471-2000 "Recommended Practice for Architectural Description of Software Incentive Systems." New York, NY: The Institute of Electrical and Electronics Engineers.

Jacobson, Ivar (1994). *Object-Oriented Software Engineering: A Use Case Driven Approach*. Addison-Wesley Object Technology Series.

Jacobson, Ivar, Grady Booch, and James Rumbaugh (1999). *The Unified Software Development Process*. Reading, MA: Addison-Wesley.

Kruchten, Philippe (1996). "A Rational Process." *CrossTalk*, 9(7):11–16.

Kruchten, Philippe (2000). *The Rational Unified Process: An Introduction*. Reading, MA: Addison-Wesley.

Larman, Craig (1998). *Applying UML and Patterns: An Introduction to Object-Oriented Analysis and Design*. Reading, MA: Addison-Wesley.

Maier, David (1983). *The Theory of Relational Databases*. Rockville, MD: Computer Science Press.

Martin, James (1981). *An End-User's Guide to Data Base*. Englewood Cliffs, NJ: Prentice Hall.

Martin, James (1982). *Computer Database Organization*. Englewood Cliffs, NJ: Prentice Hall.

McConnell, Steve C. (1993). *Code Complete: A Practical Handbook of Software Construction*. Redmond, WA: Microsoft Press.

McMenamin, Stephen M., and John Palmer (1984). *Essential Systems Analysis*. New York, NY: Prentice Hall Yourdon Press Computing Series.

Mellor, Stephen J., and Paul T. Ward (1989). *Structured Development for Real-Time Systems: Implementation Modeling Techniques*. New York, NY: Prentice Hall Yourdon Press Computing Series.

Nassi, I., and B. Shneiderman (1973). "Flowchart Techniques for Structured Programming." *ACM SIGPLAN Notices*, 8(8):12–26.

Page-Jones, Meilir (1988). *The Practical Guide to Structured Systems Design*, 2nd ed. Englewood Cliffs, NJ: Prentice Hall.

Pratt, Philip J., and Joe Adamski (2000). *Concepts of Database Management*, 3rd ed. Boston, MA: Course Technology.

Pressman, Roger S. (2001). *Software Engineering: A Practitioner's Approach*, 5th ed. Boston, MA: McGraw-Hill.

Rob, Peter, and Carlos Coronel (1999). *Database Systems: Design, Implementation, and Management*, 4th ed. Cambridge, MA: Course Technology.

Royce, Walker, Jr. (1998). *Software Project Management, a Unified Framework*. Reading, MA: Addison-Wesley.

Rumbaugh, James, et al. (1991). *Object-Oriented Modeling and Design*. Englewood Cliffs, NJ: Prentice Hall.

Schach, Stephen R. (1999). *Classical and Object-Oriented Software Engineering: with UML and Java*, 4th ed. New York, NY: McGraw-Hill.

Shlaer, Sally, and Stephen Mellor (1988). *Object-Oriented Systems Analysis: Modeling the World in Data*. New York, NY: Prentice Hall Yourdon Press Computing Series.

Taylor, David A. (1990). *Object-Oriented Technology: A Manager's Guide*. Reading, MA: Addison-Wesley.

Taylor, David A. (1992). *Object-Oriented Information Systems: Planning and Implementation*. New York, NY: John Wiley & Sons.

Ullman, Jeffrey (1982). *Principles of Database Systems*. Rockville, MD: Computer Science Press.

Ward, Paul T., and Stephen J. Mellor (1986). *Structured Development for Real-Time Systems: Essential Modeling Techniques*. New York, NY: Prentice Hall Yourdon Press Computing Series.

Wiorkowski, Gabrielle, and David Kull (1992). *DB2: Design and Development Guide Book*, 3rd ed. Reading, MA: Addison-Wesley.

Wirfs-Brock, Rebecca, et al. (1990). *Designing Object-Oriented Software*. New York, NY: Prentice Hall.

Yourdon, Edward (1989). *Modern Structured Analysis*. New York, NY: Prentice Hall Yourdon Press Computing Series.

Yourdon, Edward (1994). *Object-Oriented Systems Design: An Integrated Approach*. New York, NY: Prentice Hall Yourdon Press Computing Series.

Yourdon, Edward, and Larry Constantine (1975). *Structured Design*. New York, NY: Prentice Hall Yourdon Press Computing Series.

Web Pages for Further Information _____

www-4.ibm.com/software/data/db2/udb/. DB2 Universal Database.

www.lotusnotes.com. Lotus Notes Software.

www.omg.org. The Object Management Group, Inc. (OMG), is an international organization supported by more than 800 members, including information system vendors, software developers, and users. Founded in 1989, the OMG promotes the theory and practice of object-oriented technology in software development. The organization's charter includes the establishment of industry guidelines and object management specifications to provide a common framework for application development. Primary goals are the reusability, portability, and interoperability of object-based software in distributed, heterogeneous environments. Conformance to these specifications will make it possible to develop a heterogeneous applications environment across all major hardware platforms and operating systems. OMG's objectives are to foster the growth of object technology and influence its direction by establishing the Object Management Architecture (OMA). The OMA provides the conceptual infrastructure upon which all OMG specifications are based. OMG's adoption of the UML specification reduces the degree of confusion within the industry surrounding modeling languages. It settles unproductive arguments about method notations and model interchange mechanisms, and allows the industry to focus on higher leverage, more productive activities. Additionally, it enables semantic interchange between visual modeling tools.

www.oracle.com/. Oracle Corporation.

www.rational.com/index.jsp. Rational Software.

www.open.org/~prslkg/sy_chap.htm. Paul R. Seesing and ARMA International (1993). Basic Systems Analysis Tools for Computer Users.

www.sybase.com/. Sybase.

Validation and Verification

Software verification and validation (V&V) is the process of ensuring that software under development or change will satisfy functional and other requirements (validation) and that each step in the process of building the software yields the right products (verification). It is a systematic and technical evaluation of software and associated products of the development and maintenance process. Reviews and tests are done at the end of each phase of the development process to ensure that software requirements are complete and testable, and that design, code, documentation, and data satisfy those requirements.[1]

Verification evaluates a system or component to determine whether the product of a given life cycle phase satisfies the conditions imposed at the start of the phase. It typically involves review meetings to evaluate documents, plans, code, requirements, and specifications, using checklists, issues lists, standards, and organizational conventions. Verification (are we building the system right?) takes place during every phase of the software development life cycle.

Validation typically involves actual testing and takes place after verifications are completed. Validation occurs at the end with user acceptance testing (are we building the right system?). However, this question about "the right system" may also be thought of as occurring during the entire life cycle because requirements traceability matrices will allow for continuous evaluation.

Software practitioners use the term V&V to refer to all of the activities that are aimed at making sure the software will function as required.

All software has bugs, known and unknown. Although the most stringent V&V processes cannot find all system faults, they go a long way toward increasing product quality. Each and every V&V activity increases the chances that the project team will find problems instead of the customer finding them. And each and every problem found decreases embarrassment, ill will, expense, and the likelihood of losing the customer altogether.

The two major V&V activities are *peer reviews* and *testing*.

Reviews, Inspections, and Walkthroughs

Static *peer review* is the process of trying to uncover problems in project deliverables via manual review of each system component product—it finds problems by direct examination. Reviews are conducted during and at the end of each phase of the life cycle, to determine whether established requirements, design concepts, and specifications have been met. They consist of the presentation of material to a review team.

An especially useful technique for finding errors is *formal inspection*, developed by Michael Fagan when he was at IBM. Inspections involve the line-by-line evaluation of the product under review. A team, each member of which has a specific role, does the reviewing. A moderator, who is formally trained in the process, leads the team. The team includes a reader, who leads the team through the item; one or more reviewers, who look for faults in the item; a recorder, who notes the faults; and the author, who helps explain the item being inspected.

This formal, highly structured inspection process has been extremely effective in finding and eliminating errors. It can be applied to any product of the software development process, including documents, design, and code. One of its important side benefits has been the direct feedback to the developer/author and the significant improvement in quality that results.

Reviews are also called *walkthroughs*, or inspections, although many practitioners made a distinction between the formal and informal aspects of each. For our purposes, we will use the term *review* throughout, meaning it to be a formal process, roughly synonymous with *inspection*.

Testing

Dynamic testing is the process of creating executable test cases used to physically test the functioning of the system. It is the detection of things that can go wrong—things that happen when they shouldn't and things that don't happen when they should. Separate individual units such as program modules are tested for functionality, as are integrated combined units such as subsystems. Testing finds product faults, and the symptoms are used in a debugging effort to reveal the underlying code defects.

To test software means to operate it with real or simulated inputs, both normal and abnormal, under controlled conditions. If the product does not satisfy requirements, the specific differences between expected and actual results are identified. There are varied levels of software tests, ranging from unit or element testing through integration testing and performance testing, up to software system and acceptance tests.

Testing differs from quality assurance in that QA is focused on processes that *prevent* defects, while testing focuses on *detection* of errors and defects. Testing differs from reviews in that reviews may be held on any project artifact, while testing is on the software system only (i.e., code, interface languages, job control language), often to find problems related to execution, timing, traffic, transaction rates, and system interactions.

Informal tests are done by the developer to measure the development progress. "Informal" in this case does not mean that the tests are done in a casual manner—just that the customer is not formally involved, that witnessing of the testing is not required, and that the prime purpose of the tests is to find errors. Unit, component, and subsystem integration tests may all be informal tests.

Formal testing demonstrates that the software is ready for its intended use. A formal test should include an approved test plan and procedures, quality assurance witnesses, a record of all discrepancies, and a test report. Formal testing is always requirements-driven, and its purpose is to demonstrate that the software meets its requirements.

Each software development project, no matter how small, should have at least one formal test, the acceptance test that concludes the development activities and demonstrates that the software is ready for operation. In addition to the final acceptance test, other formal testing may be done on a project. For example, if the software is to be developed and delivered in increments or builds, there may be incremental acceptance tests. Any contractually required test is usually considered a formal test.

After acceptance of a software product, all changes to the product should be accepted only after another formal test. Post-acceptance testing includes regression testing, which involves rerunning previously used tests to ensure that the change did not disturb functions that have already been accepted.

Both static review and dynamic testing are part of V&V and are thought of as integral tasks—crucial to providing a quality product, but not directly contributing to the construction of it. We will begin with a discussion of the static peer review because it is more encompassing than dynamic testing, may be begun earlier in the life cycle, may be performed on more products, and has been shown to be more effective than dynamic testing in some instances. This is not to discredit the importance of dynamic testing, which is an absolutely necessary part of system development, but to recommend that static peer reviews be given equal weight to improve the effectiveness of dynamic testing and shorten that phase of the life cycle.

Dynamic *testing* requires that compiled code exists and that test cases have been constructed. Static peer reviews require only that a work product (project deliverable) has been created. A *review* may be conducted on a software project management plan (SPMP), a data flow diagram (DFD), an object-oriented model (OOM), an architecture flow diagram (AFD), a state transition diagram (STD), a structure chart, a program abstract, pseudocode, a Chapin (Nassi-Schneiderman) chart, compiled code, or any other project artifact, internal or external, manually produced or machine-based. Because reviews do not require an artifact created with an automated tool, they may begin very early in the life cycle.

Independent verification and validation (IV&V) is a process in which the products of the software development life cycle phases are independently reviewed, verified, and validated by an organization that is neither the developer nor the sponsor of the software. The IV&V agent should have no stake in the success or failure of the software, only an interest in making sure that the software is thoroughly tested against its complete set of requirements. The IV&V activities duplicate the V&V activities step by step during the life cycle, with the exception that the IV&V agent does no informal testing. If there is an IV&V agent, the formal acceptance testing may be done only once, by the IV&V agent. In this case, the developer will do a formal demonstration that the software is ready for formal acceptance.

Where We Are in the Product Development Life Cycle

A V&V plan is necessary for the software PM to estimate the cost, schedule, and complexity of the project and provide adequate test capabilities. When the V&V concept receives proper attention from the beginning, it can be practiced during the entire life cycle, as shown in Figure 23–1. Every phase has internal or external deliverables, and each deliverable should undergo some sort of examination:

- During the software concept exploration phase and the system exploration phase, the concept of how the system is to be reviewed and tested should be included. All planning documents, such as the statement of need, the system interface specification, the SPMP, and the risk management plan, require review.

- During the software requirements phase, developers need to make sure that the software requirements are consistent with and are within the scope of system requirements. Each requirement needs to be testable and capable of being satisfied, so this is the time to be thinking about what tests will determine satisfaction (an acceptance plan). The SRS will require review.

- During the software design phase, informal reviews and walkthroughs or inspections of the software architecture (design) take place. This may include preliminary software, low-level software models, and database design. The SDD and acceptance test plan will require review.

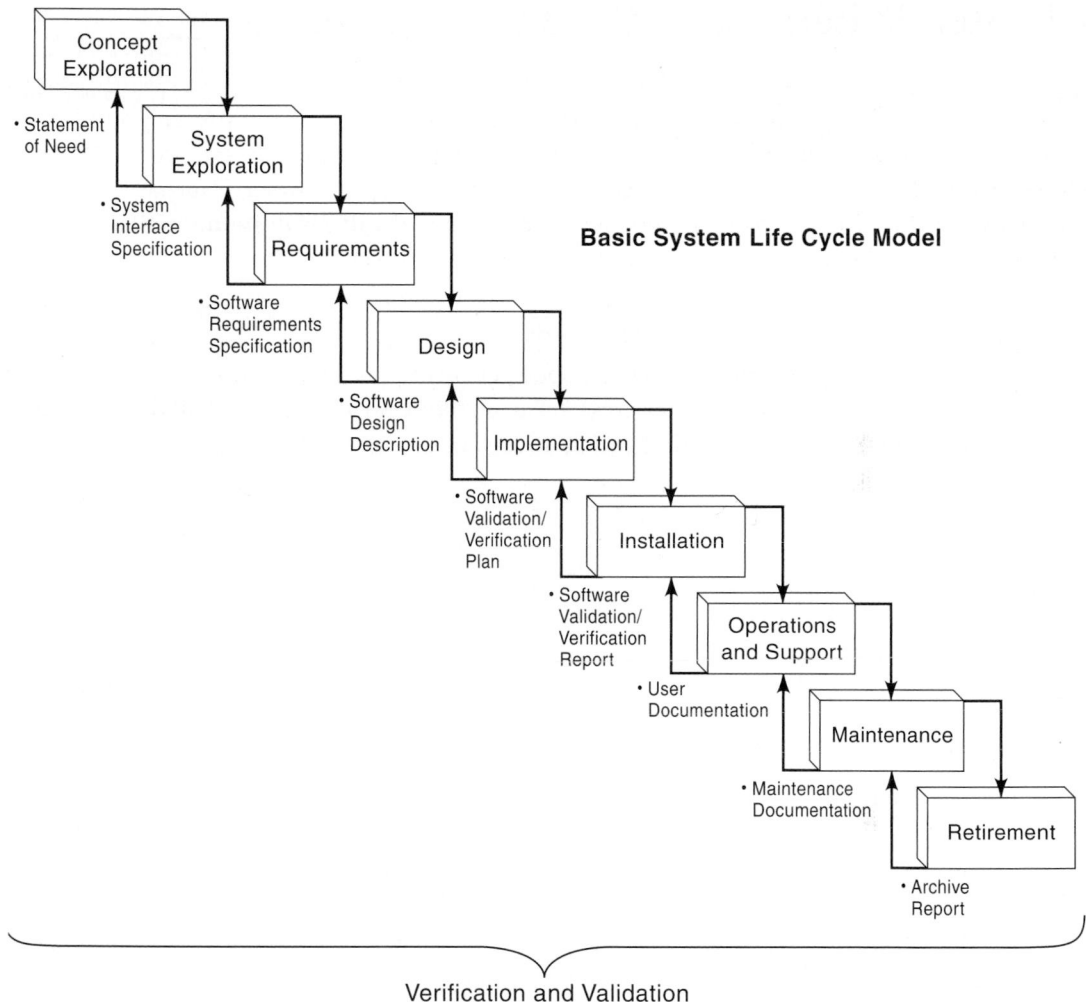

Basic System Life Cycle Model

Verification and Validation

FIGURE 23–1
Validation and Verification Occurs Throughout the Product Development Life Cycle

- During the implementation phase, the software V&V plan itself will require review, and code inspections will occur along with unit testing and integration testing. Test performance, test completion, and test results will be reported.
- The implementation phase sees software acceptance and delivery, once test, analysis, and inspection demonstrate that the developed system meets its functional, performance, and interface requirements.
- During operations and support, all of the V&V activities that occur during development reoccur on a smaller scale during changes to the software.

Chapter 23 Relation to the 34 Competencies _____

As with so many of the topics in this book, V&V relies upon multiple product, project, and people skills. Very briefly, those skills include:

Product Development Techniques

1. **Assessing processes**—Both static and dynamic testing rely heavily upon written organizational procedures.
2. **Awareness of process standards**—Peer reviews examine work products to determine their adherence to organizational standards.
10. **Tracking product quality**—V&V is all about ensuring quality, including the concept of building it in rather than "tacking it on." The goal of peer reviews and all dynamic tests is to find and remove defects that equate to lack of quality.

Project Management Skills

14. **Estimating cost**—The software PM is encouraged to consider the return on investment (ROI) with effective peer review and testing processes.
15. **Estimating effort**—To achieve the quality goals and savings potential, effort must be expended toward V&V early in the life cycle.
16. **Managing risks**—The risk of not delivering a software product with acceptable quality levels is one that must be managed throughout the product development life cycle, beginning in the early phases.
19. **Selecting metrics**—Metrics are used heavily in V&V, providing the PM with knowledge of quality levels and their effect on cost and schedule.
20. **Selecting project management tools**—Dynamic testing is an area with tremendous automated tool support.
21. **Tracking process**—Both review and testing processes must be tracked for compliance. Tracking information not only aids the PM on the current project, but it provides valuable information to feed forward into process improvement (see Chapter 26, "Continuous Process Improvement").

People Management Skills

23. **Appraising performance**—Performance goals are a bit unusual for peer reviews in that team members are rewarded for attending, participating, contributing, and finding flaws. They are never, ever "punished" for inserting them.
25. **Holding effective meetings**—Peer review meetings must be short and controlled because they are focused, intense efforts. Moderators (facilitators) need to be well trained.
26. **Interaction and communication**—Individual developers create small, modular work products; teams make sure that they are complete and correct and that they interface with the rest of the system.

27. **Leadership**—Peer review leaders (moderators, facilitators) and testing team leaders are indispensable members of the project team.

Learning Objectives for Chapter 23 _____

Upon completion of this chapter, the reader should be able to:

- Discuss where V&V fits within the software product development life cycle;
- Describe which of the people, product, and process skills are the most relevant to V&V;
- Compare and contrast static and dynamic testing;
- Explain the importance of V&V to the software project;
- Reason with those who feel that software reviews, inspections, and walkthroughs are not economically feasible;
- Describe the salient aspects of static testing: why, what, who, when, and how;
- Explain the purpose of testing;
- Describe the major types of dynamic tests: unit, subsystem (integration), system, alpha, beta, user acceptance, regression;
- Compare and contrast white-box and black-box testing;
- Describe usability testing;
- Explain how a manager knows when it is time to stop testing.

Static Testing: Reviews _____

Reviews have long been known to be the most effective hedge against rework. Conducted properly, they can also be quite an effective means for controlling software projects. Fairley says that rework consumes 30–50% of all project costs, a significant amount![2] Because rework is the software equivalent of manufacturing "scrap" (waste that can't be used and must be reproduced), and because we have so much of it, the software project manager has a clear motivation to promote reviews.

Reviews and testing go hand in hand as V&V activities. Testing is the last activity before product release, so all schedule slippage preceding it gets taken out of the allotted test time. Even when original overall project estimates are produced as accurately as possible, early project stages often consume longer time than anticipated, squeezing the later stages, particularly testing. It is difficult to know how much testing is "enough" under any circumstances; therefore, testing typically occupies whatever space is left between coding and release. It may seem counterintuitive that reviews will relieve the squeeze on testing time by adding even more activities to the phases that precede test. In fact, reviews are testing's best friend because they find so many defects early in the game that dynamic testing can become almost a formality.

Peer Reviews and the SEI CMM

In the SEI CMM, peer reviews are a key process area for the defined level, Level 3. The goals are that peer review activities are planned and that defects in the software work products are identified and removed.

The purpose of peer reviews is to remove defects from the software work products early and efficiently. An important corollary effect is to develop a better understanding of the software work products and of defects that might be prevented. Peer reviews involve a methodical examination of software work products by the producer's peers to identify defects and areas where changes are needed.

The activities that must be performed to satisfy this KPA are these:

- Peer reviews are planned, and the plans are documented.
- Peer reviews are performed according to a documented procedure. This procedure typically specifies that peer reviews are led by trained moderators, review materials are distributed in advance, reviewers have assigned roles, readiness and completion criteria are specified and enforced, and actions are tracked through resolution.
- Data on the conduct and results of the peer reviews is recorded. Examples of data include software work product identifier, size of the work product, size and composition of the review team, preparation time per reviewer, length of the review meeting, types and number of defects found and fixed, and rework effort.

Commitment to perform is a written organizational policy specifying, in part, that peer reviews are led by trained moderators, they focus on the software work product being reviewed and not on the author, and the results of the peer reviews are not used by management to evaluate the performance of individuals.

As we will show in the following paragraphs, we wholly support the goals of this SEI CMM KPA.

Static Testing Definitions

Static testing terms are used inconsistently in the software community, so for the sake of good communication, a few definitions are in order.

Architectural design refers to the high-level software system design. It should meet approved requirements, interface with all necessary components, describe the general function(s) of each module, include required fault detection and recovery, employ reusable components where possible, and trace to the requirements.

Defect classification is the process in which all defects identified during an inspection are classified by severity and type.

Defect is a term for a problem that is not detected during the phase in which it was introduced but that was found in a later phase. It is any occurrence in a software product that is determined to be incomplete or incorrect relative to the software requirements or program standards. Defects become manifest in the end product, but most of them are injected during development of the requirements, the design, and coding, or by insertion of changes. According to Fagan, a defect is an instance in which a requirement is not satisfied. A requirement is any agreed-upon commitment. It is not only the recognizable external product requirement, but it can also include internal development requirements (e.g., the exit criteria of an operation) that must be met to satisfy the requirements of the end product. Examples would be the requirement that a test plan completely verifies that the product meets the agreed-upon needs of the user, or that the code of a program must be complete before it is submitted to be tested. According to Boehm, a defect violates quality standards such as intrinsic code quality, freedom from problems in operation, usability, installability, documentation for intended users, portability, maintainability and extendability, or fitness for use (implicit conventional user needs are satisfied).

Error is a term for a problem found during the phase in which it was introduced. It is a discrepancy between a computed, observed, or measured value or condition and the true, specified, or theoretically correct value or condition.

Formal reviews are conducted at the end of each life cycle phase. They are held when the author believes that the product is error-free. A formal review follows a published process. The findings of the review are documented. The acquirer of the software appoints the formal review panel or board, who may make or affect a go/no-go decision to proceed to the next step of the life cycle. Formal reviews include the SRS review, the SDD review, and the software test readiness review. We do not distinguish a formal review from an inspection.

Informal reviews are conducted on an as-needed basis. They may be held at any time, serving the purpose of a brainstorming session and following no set agenda. No documentation of the meeting is necessary. The developer chooses the reviewers and provides or presents the material to be reviewed. The material may be as informal as a computer listing or handwritten documentation.

Inspections are detailed examinations of a product on a step-by-step or line-of-code basis, following a rigorous set of rules. The purpose of conducting inspections is to find errors. The group that does an inspection is composed of peers from development, test, and quality assurance.

A *peer* is someone who does not have control over the performance assessment of another (i.e., has no direct decision-making authority over the financial merit increase of another).

Presentations may involve individuals other than peers and do not generally elicit feedback, nor are they conducted for the purpose of finding problems. The purpose of a presentation is to describe the state of the system to stakeholders.

Problem is a term for an error or defect.

Requirements (software requirements) are the software functions, inputs and outputs, states and modes, response time requirements, and interfaces desired by the customer. Specified requirements include those for error detection and recovery, reliability, maintainability, performance, and accuracy. They should trace to higher-level documents, such as a concept statement. They should provide a sufficient base for the software design and should be measurable, consistent, and testable.

Requirements (system requirements) are the high-level requirements for the software system. They should properly allocate all functions to software, firmware, hardware, and operations. Their external usage interfaces should be validated. System requirements break functions into identifiable configuration items and identify interfaces between them. They should be verifiable.

Reviews are methodical examinations of software work products by the producers' peers to identify defects and places where changes are needed. People get together to work toward quality and technical correctness. They are an assumed part of the software development, enhancement, and maintenance process. The terms *review* and *inspection* are sometimes viewed as two different things, where a review is considered less formal than an inspection. Here, we treat an inspection as a type of formal review.

Traceability is the degree to which a relationship can be established between two or more products of the development process, especially products having a predecessor-successor or master-subordinate relationship to one another; for example, the degree to which the requirements and design of a given software component match (IEEE Standard 610.12-1990). Traceability is the characteristic of a system that allows identification and control of relationships between requirements, software components, data, and documentation at different levels in the system.

The definition of *walkthrough* depends on who you ask. Some people say that a walkthrough is an informal review; others say that it is a formal one. We'll stick with the latter, but we'll use the term *review* instead.

Many of these definitions of project artifacts (i.e., architectural design) may be used as a checklist in a peer review of the product. Keeping these definitions in mind, we'll proceed to the why, what, when, who, and how of static testing, which we will refer to as *reviews*.

Why Review?

When money and time are spent up front on reviews and repairs, many times the investment will be saved later, in testing, maintenance, and customer support. The initial investment may be substantial, but organizations that have instituted effective review programs and kept track of their return on investment report that the payoff is well worth the effort. The benefits of conducting reviews extend well beyond the financial bottom line.

A code defect that leaks into testing may require multiple test executions to confirm the error and additional executions to obtain debug information. Once a leaked defect has been detected, the producing programmer must put aside the task at hand, refocus attention on correcting the defect and confirming the correction, and then return to the task at hand. The economics of software quality largely concern the costs of defect detection, prevention, and removal. According to Watts Humphrey, the cost of finding and fixing a defect includes the costs of each of the following elements:

- Determining that there is a problem
- Isolating the source of the problem
- Determining exactly what is wrong with the product
- Fixing the requirements as needed
- Fixing the design as needed
- Fixing the implementation as needed
- Inspecting the fix to ensure that it is correct
- Testing the fix to ensure that it fixes the identified problem
- Testing the fix to ensure that it doesn't cause other problems
- Changing the documentation as needed to reflect the fix[3]

The only way to reduce the cost of finding and fixing defects is to eliminate them—don't inject defects into the product in the first place. Reviews find in-process errors before they become defects.

Economics of Reviews   All manner of claims have been made about the effectiveness of reviews. Assertions that early defect detection minimizes overall project cost and minimizes effort have been circulating for years. Reviews are said to find 60–90% of all defects. Reviews are said to be from 2 to 10 times as efficient in defect removal as dynamic testing. According to Fagan, reviews can catch errors in one-fourth the time that it takes to discover them using dynamic machine testing techniques.[4] Notational graphs, such as the one in Figure 23–2, where reviews are shown as actually shrinking overall effort and accelerating delivery schedules, are favorites among the process faithful.

Oddly enough, reviews are often a "hard sell." Few dispute the value of nonmonetary benefits, such as dissemination of information, but these rewards are frequently forgotten in the hurly-burly of schedule crunches. Software project managers are often like bankers in their lack of emotionality when considering an investment—the payback must be described in cold, hard, factual, financial terms. Any activity that is even remotely perceived as lengthening the schedule is anathema to managers, and platitudes about reviews from earlier days in computing hardly cut it anymore.

Happily, data has been collected over the last two decades to justify static testing. Early studies conducted in the 1970s and 1980s have been corroborated in recent years. Contemporary data, supplied by the SEL and by Watts Humphrey (SEI), among others, are beginning to prove what our intuition has told us all along. A strong contributor to the data bank is the Software Engineering Laboratory (SEL), an organization sponsored by the National Aeronautics and Space Administration/Goddard Space Flight Center (NASA/GSFC) and created to investigate the effectiveness of software engineering technologies when applied to the development of applications software. The SEL was created in 1976 and has three primary organizational members: NASA/GSFC, Software Engineering Branch; University of Maryland, Department of Computer Science; and Computer Sciences Corporation, Space and Earth Technology Systems.[5]

It has often been quoted that, for procedural software produced using a sequential life cycle approach, defects discovered after product deployment can cost up to 100 times as much to fix as defects discovered in early phases of the life cycle. The factors causing this phenomenon include cumulative analysis, design, and coding rework, plus a magnified ripple effect throughout a completed system. We now know that these statements are not the stuff of urban myth. Studies by Watts Humphrey found that early defect detection not only minimizes time and cost, but does so drastically. An average error-correction time ratio of 1 hour during the requirements phase translates to 3–6 hours for defects that escape to the design

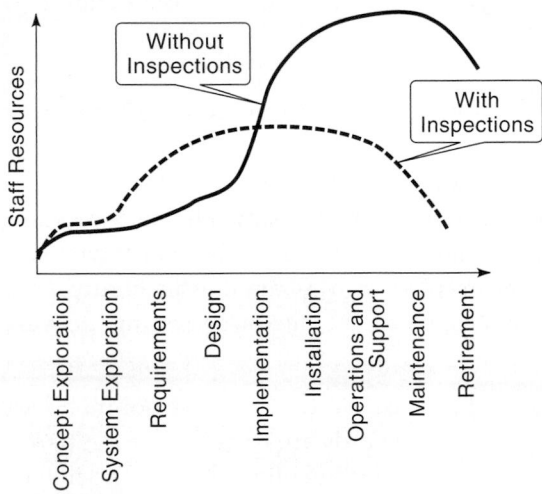

FIGURE 23–2
Reviews Result in Less Effort

phase, 10 hours for the coding phase, 15–40 hours in the development testing activity, 30–70 hours during acceptance test, and 40–1,000 during operation! Furthermore, research shows that an average cost per defect ranged from $90–$120 in inspections to $10,000 in testing. Companies that used an early inspection system reported a tenfold reduction in the number of defects found in testing and up to an 80% reduction in test costs, including the cost of the inspections.

The National Software Quality Experiment benchmarks the state of software product quality and measures progress toward an objective to improve cycle time. It is a mechanism for obtaining core samples of software product quality from industry, government, and military services. This data provides the means to benchmark and measure progress toward the objective, containing data from 1992 through 1997. The experiment reveals that the return on investment (net savings/detection cost) for software reviews ranges from 4 to 8, independent of the context of usage.

> Through 1997 there have been 112 inspection labs in which 2317 participants were trained and conducted inspection sessions.... [The study found] a return on investment of 4.48. Managers are interested in knowing the return on investment to be derived from software process improvement actions. The software inspections process gathers the data needed to determine this.... The return on investment for software inspections is defined as:
>
> Savings/Cost
>
> Where:
>
> Savings = (Major Defects × 9) + Minor Defects
>
> Cost = (Minutes of Preparation Effort + (Minutes of Conduct Time × 4))/60
>
> This model for return on investment bases the savings on the cost avoidance associated with detecting and correcting defects earlier rather than later in the product evolution cycle. A major defect that leaks into later phases may cost ten hours to detect and correct. Ten hours to fix later minus one hour to fix now results in the constant nine (9) applied to major defects. A minor defect may cost two hours to fix later minus one hour to fix now resulting in a constant of one (1) applied to minor defects. To convert the minutes of conduct time to effort, the average number of participants (4) is applied. The constant 60 minutes is applied to convert minutes to hours. Results showing the return on investment for each organization participating in the National Software Quality Experiment suggest that the return on investment for software inspections ranges from 4:1 to 8:1. For every dollar spent on software inspections, the organization can expect to avoid 4–8 dollars on higher cost rework.
>
> Don O'Neill, "National Software Quality Experiment,
> A Lesson in Measurement: 1992–1997."[6]

In addition to cost savings, the adopting organization benefits by improved predictability in cost and schedule performance, reduced defects in the field, increased customer satisfaction, and improved morale among practitioners.

Figure 23–3 is adapted from a study conducted by IBM, "Software Product Assurance." The idea is that some defects may be found and fixed with relative ease, while others have a "ripple" effect where multiple project artifacts are affected. In the example shown, six errors were introduced in the early stages of concept and system exploration of a project. They went undetected, without a review, and passed to the requirements specification phase, where four of them had a ripple effect (albeit, not a bad one). In this phase, 9 more errors were added to the 6 defects so that a total of 15 defects were passed to the design phase. The design phase saw 8 of those defects having a ripple effect of 3.5 (making the effect $8 \times 3.5 = 28$) and introduced 30 new errors. Now, a total of 55 defects $(7 + 28 + 20)$ are passed to the coding phase. In the coding phase, 15 of the 55 defects had a ripple effect of 5 (things are getting worse), for an effect of 75. The total number of defects passed to unit testing is now 145 $(40 + 75 + 30)$. If unit tests catch and correct half of them, then 72 defects will be passed to system testing. If system testing catches and corrects half of those, then 36 defects will be passed to user acceptance test. If user acceptance testing catches and corrects half, then 18 defects will be delivered to the customer—an unacceptable level.

Compare this same scenario to one in which reviews are conducted during each phase. In Figure 23–4, the same six errors are introduced during concept and system exploration. But this time, instead of going undetected, a review was held, and half of the errors were caught and corrected, so only three became defects passed to the next phase. In requirements, two of the three defects had a ripple effect, and the same nine errors were introduced. Because half of them were caught in a review, only six defects were passed to the next phase. In design, 2 of the 6 incoming defects had the same ripple effect of 3.5, and the same 20 errors were introduced. However, because a review was held and caught about half of the problems, only 15 defects were passed to the coding phase. Applying the same math with the same number of errors as before yields 28 defects passed to unit testing. Each of the three testing phases catches half of the defects that they receive, resulting in 3.5 defects being passed to the customer. Not good enough, perhaps, but certainly better than the 18 in the previous scenario.

Many other studies have been conducted, not only to determine whether reviews should be embraced, but to also determine how to go about conducting them. For example, some organizations have reported that the "right-sized" chunks of product are important to the success of reviewing. If the article under review is too small, time is wasted; if too large, defect prevention effectiveness suffers. The notional chart in Figure 23–5 shows that about 150 lines of code is the right amount to take to a review. Raytheon studied historical data to find that the ideal preparation and review rates for design inspections were less than 250 source lines of code (SLOC) per hour, and the ideal review rate for code inspections was less than 300 SLOC per hour. As the review rate decreased, the number of errors found tended to increase in both design and code inspections. As preparation speed decreased, the number of

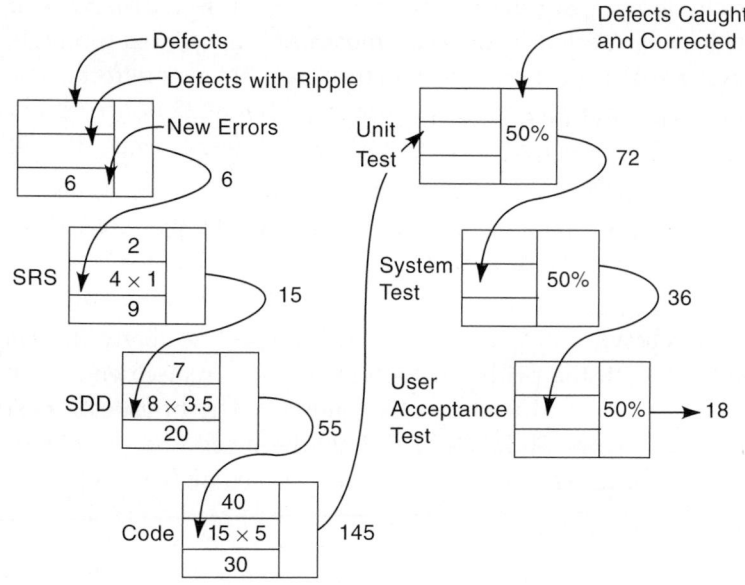

FIGURE 23–3
Ripple Effect Without Reviews

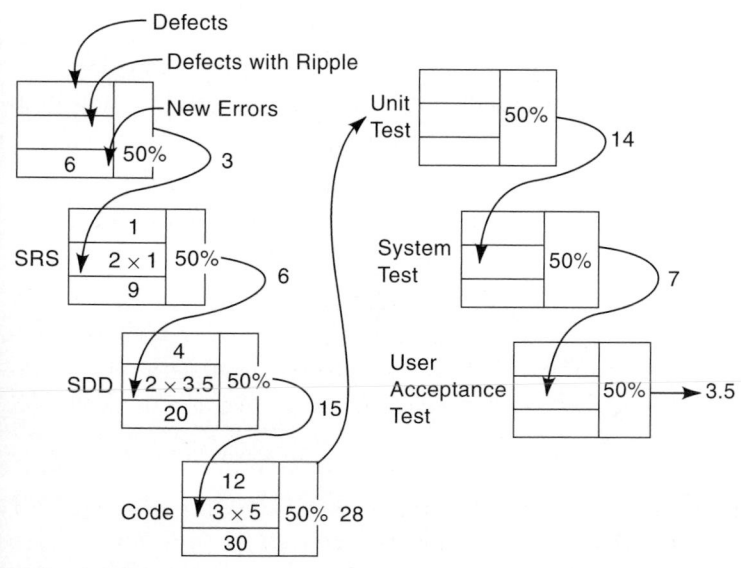

FIGURE 23–4
Ripple Effect with Reviews and Testing

errors found tended to increase in design inspections.[7] A similar study at IBM also showed that excessive size of materials to be inspected leads to a preparation rate that is too high, which contributes to an excessive rate of inspection, which in turn, causes fewer defects to be found and leads to rework. This study indicates that an average of about 125 noncomment LOC per hour is a reasonable rate for review preparation, and an average of about 90 non-comment LOC per hour is a reasonable rate for the review meeting itself.[8]

We will discuss the positive payback for reviews later, in the section "Risks of Not Conducting Reviews."

Nonmonetary Benefits of Reviews   Do developers really inject so many defects into their products? Well, yes. Even with the pride that accompanies a creative endeavor, software development is complex and is produced by mere mortals. The brightest, most experienced software engineer injects errors. Some studies show the defect density ranges from 49.5 to 94.6 per thousand lines of code, while other studies reveal even higher estimates.

Reviews help counteract the humanness of the task:

- Reviews may find extraneous parts, whereas testing cannot. Reviews may follow all execution paths. Testing cannot test all paths, often leaving errors in infrequently traveled paths.
- Diverse mind sets, personalities, and life experiences help in catching all sorts of problems that are elusive to only one perspective.
- Developers are free to be more creative when they know that their peers are there to act as a safety net and to offer a dose of reality if inspired thoughts get out of hand.
- Work is separated from the worker, freeing reviewers to concentrate on finding problems.
- Because an appropriate "chunk" of work must be taken to a review, developers begin to think in terms of modularity and draw upon their knowledge of low coupling and high cohesion (refer to Chapter 22, "Analysis and Design Methods").

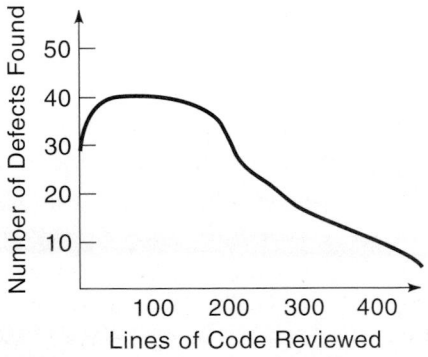

FIGURE 23–5
Right-Size the Amount of Material Reviewed

- Dissemination of information and training occur when developers meet under review circumstances. People quickly pick up and spread the good ideas that they see in the work of others. According to some industry experts, such as Gerald Weinberg, this is the most important result of a review program.[9]
- Consistency across teams and projects is increased. *De facto* group norms become established, making software products easier for all to understand and maintain.
- Project managers can know the real status of products. Sometimes developers take it upon themselves to work on what they deem important (although usually with no malicious intent, such behavior may sabotage the project).
- Everyone makes mistakes and unknowingly inserts faults into products. When reviewers are rewarded for finding errors, it becomes "safe" to see them and more are uncovered.

Ultimately, reviews improve the product by:

- Finding problems while they are still relatively easy and inexpensive to correct, and confirming parts of products that have no problems.
- Finding problems as near to their point of origin as possible.
- Inspecting the output of a phase to see if it satisfies the output requirements or exit criteria.
- Preventing future problems from occurring by publishing solutions to frequently discovered problems.
- Disseminating information about the project and contributing to the manageability of the project.
- Spreading good organizational procedures and practices, and achieving more uniform technical work.
- Teaching developers how to avoid injection of defects in future work.
- Preventing injection of defects in the current product because the process of getting materials ready for inspection forces clarification of requirements and design.
- Training and mentoring new project members.
- Giving management reliable milestones and estimates.
- Helping with project discipline and providing objective, measurable feedback.

Among other advantages, reviews have the time-tested fringe benefit of providing a training ground for new hires, domain novices, and fresh-outs. Anything that can be done to improve domain expertise is useful, especially because almost all software problems begin with requirements. Bill Curtis has noted that up to 70% of the swing in required effort depends on developers' experience in the application arena and expertise with development tools.[10] As always, when members of other organizations attend the review, a cross-pollination effect occurs. In the spirit of achieving the Software Engineering Institute's Maturity Level 2, the repeatable level, reviews provide a communication vehicle to allow backup or repeatability, in that at least one other person has been exposed to the material. Some companies, including Motorola, suggest that the presenter in a review session be someone other than the author, thereby strengthening the quality of repeatability through insistence that the presenter become completely familiar with the product.

Review results produced during development are important to the quality of the system and customer satisfaction with it. They indicate what needs to be fixed and why. Problems found can be prioritized, weighted as to severity, tracked for status, and used as lessons learned for maintainers of this system and developers of future systems. Simple errors can be placed in the trust of the author to correct; severe errors can be published and searched for in other places in the emerging system.

Experience has shown that inspections have the effect of slightly front-end-loading the commitment of people resources in development, adding to requirements and design. While greatly reducing the effort required during testing and for rework of design and code, the result is an overall net reduction in development resource and usually in schedule, too.[11]

What Gets Reviewed?

The nature and format of deliverables change with each software product development phase. Despite their differences, each deliverable will be reviewed in a standard type of review session. Each will become output or "exit criteria" from the associated phase. Items for review are as follows:

- Any software artifact (deliverable)
- Anything that can be created and described
- A deliverable that is particularly complex
- A cross-functional product
- Deliverables that need to be taught to someone else

Potential articles for undergoing a review are listed in Box 23–1.

Deliverables from some modern software projects will be different from those of the past. The waterfall phases are often replaced with object-oriented rapid prototyping life cycles containing phases such as "define preliminary requirements," "design, develop requirements prototype," "iterate and refine requirements definition and prototype," and "performance tuning, acceptance testing, and maintenance." However, the standard "roles" and "rules" of reviews continue to serve. What might be different on a prototyping or an OO project would be the analysis/design documents (e.g., class models vs. ERDs), and standards that serve as review criteria (standards for a DFD are not the same as those for a use case diagram). Whatever development methodology and resulting manifestation of plans and models, all project artifacts, internal and external, are candidates for review.

When Do Reviews Occur?

Early and often! Reviews can and should occur in each phase of the project, before exiting a phase, and upon completion of a project deliverable.

Box 23–1
Potential Articles for a Review

- Proposal

- Contract

- Schedule

- Budget

- Software project management plan (SPMP)

- Feasibility statement

- Software quality assurance plan (SQAP)

- Software requirements specification (SRS)

- Software configuration management plan (SCMP)

- Project test plan

- Logical model—DCD, DFD, ERD, class model, object model, PSPEC, CSPEC, AFD

- Activity diagram, use case

- Data dictionary

- Traceability matrix

- Software design document

- Structure chart

- Chapin (Nassi-Schneiderman) chart

- State transition diagram, use case scenario, interaction diagram

- Pseudocode, decision table, decision tree

- Integration test plan

- Conversion plan

- System test plan

- Software baseline

- Acquisition plan

- Transition plan

(Continues)

Box 23–1 (Continued)
Potential Articles for a Review

- User's guide/manual

- Operating documentation

- Test report

- Training plan

- Preacceptance checklist

- Installation plan

- Acceptance test plan

- Operational system

- Acceptance test report

- Maintenance plan

Informal reviews may be held at any time and may be quickly set up because there is no required agenda or documentation of the meeting. The focus is on general direction and feasibility.

Formal reviews are held when the author believes the product to be error-free. They follow a published process; their findings are documented. The focus is on final product approval.

Who Is Involved in Reviews?

Software project managers are involved in peer reviews to the extent that they are supportive of the process. They provide the facilities such as meeting rooms or global collaboration tools. They review the metrics and make decisions based upon them. Most importantly, software PMs allow the process to occur unimpeded. Enough time is built into the schedule for reviews, and all team members are trained on the process. Once the foundation is formed and management expectations are set ("we believe in peer reviews" comes from the top), then managers are well served to turn the job over to the team. Peer reviews are just that— reviews by the peers of the developers; managers need not apply.

Peers are drawn from all stakeholder categories: customers and sponsors for early, high-level articles such as contracts; requirements gatherers; specification analysts; modelers; designers; SQA; SQE; coders; network experts; database administrators; and so on.

Peers play defined roles. Each role carries with it the specific behaviors, skills, and knowledge needed to achieve the expert practice of software reviews. These roles are listed here:

- Author
- Moderator (facilitator, review leader)
- Presenter (reader)
- Scribe (recorder
- Inspector(s)/reviewer(s)

These roles will be discussed in more detail in the section "Roles Played in the Review Meeting." Here is an overview:

The *author* is ultimately responsible for updating the work product after the review. This is usually the person who originally constructed the work product.

The *moderator* (facilitator or review leader) ensures that the other review team members perform their roles to the best of their ability. He leads the meeting and keeps it on track while maintaining neutrality (has no vested interest in the outcome).

The *scribe* (recorder or documenter) ensures that review documentation includes where the error or defect was found and makes sure that every error or defect is assigned a severity level, category, and type. All the error/defect data is recorded on a software review form, including suggestions. The recorder completes the review results report.

Each member of the team acts as a *reviewer*, independent of other roles assigned. The reviewer role is responsible for detecting errors/defects within the work product. Reviewers find problems, suggest minor improvements (without solving the problem), and retain professional demeanor toward the other members of the review team.

How Are Reviews Conducted? What Is the Process?

As shown in Figure 23–6, the review process is one of planning, preparing, meeting, and following up. Rework may be necessary if the product has been submitted for review but is not really ready, or if the reviewed product is rejected or conditionally accepted. For simplicity, we'll think in terms of prereview, review, and post-review.

Prereview   In getting ready for a review, a selected moderator ensures that reviewers are invited, are available, and have been assigned roles, and that only peers of the author are invited, not management. Why not management? They may not have fully internalized that the purpose of a review is to uncover errors. Perhaps they feel, consciously or otherwise, that the discovery of many errors is an indictment of the author. Managers have been known to use reviews as a means of solidifying attitudes toward favored/unfavored employees. Perhaps most importantly, attendees may be swayed by a manager's opinion.

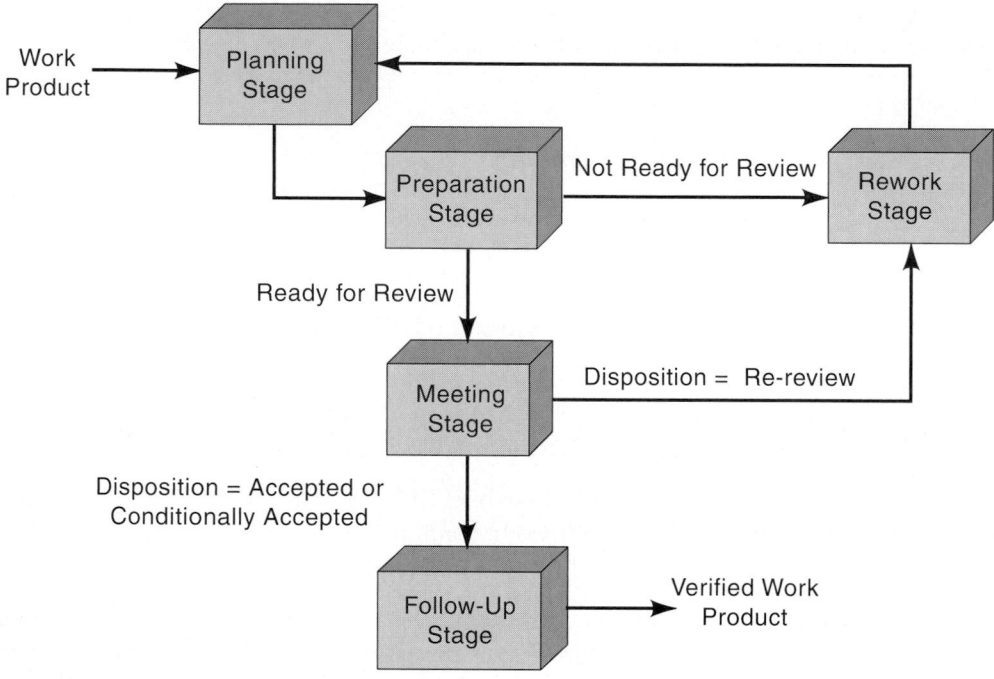

FIGURE 23–6
The Review Process

In addition to inviting reviewers, the moderator reserves meeting space if proximity permits or sets up a collaboration via a chat facility or other automated tool for remote reviewers.

The moderator ensures that the material to be reviewed meets the entry criteria:

- The author cannot find any more problems.
- The author has studied ranked distribution of defect types.
- The author has complied with standards.

If entry criteria are not met, the work product is not ready for review and is returned to the author for rework. Box 23–2 lists standard entry criteria.

The moderator distributes the material in advance, typically between 24 and 72 hours before the review meeting:

- The necessary background information is also distributed.
- Traceability matrices are distributed, where appropriate.

The moderator checks with the reviewers to make sure that they are prepared and agree that the product is indeed ready to be reviewed.

Box 23–2
Standard Entry Criteria for a Work Product to Undergo a Review

- Clarity: Are the requirements clear and unambiguous?

- Standards: Have all requirements standards been followed?

- Completeness: Are all the requirements complete?

- Level of detail: Are the requirements free from design?

- Consistency: Are requirements consistent? Are data structures and functions named and used consistently?

- Functionality: Are functions correctly specified? Are inputs and outputs clearly specified? Are functions logically independent and highly cohesive?

- Performance: Are the performance requirements for timing, memory, and resource utilization clearly defined?

- Testability: Are requirements testable and verifiable?

- Feasibility: Can each item be implemented with the available techniques, tools, resources, and personnel and within the specified cost and schedule constraints?

- Traceability: Are the requirements uniquely identified so that they will be able to be traced back from the SRS and SDD and be coded?

- Modifiability: Are the requirements uniquely structured so that any necessary changes to the requirements can be made easily, completely, and consistently?

- Any other "-ilities" that are appropriate for the work product to be reviewed.

The Review Meeting   The review meeting is attended by the moderator, the scribe, the presenter, the author, and the reviewers.

Roles Played in the Review Meeting
The *moderator* (facilitator, review leader) chairs the meeting and keeps it productive—he keeps the meeting on track and ensures that it does not exceed two hours in length. The choice of the moderator is an important one because it should be an individual who is capable of keeping the meeting impersonal and on the subject. The purpose of holding a review is to uncover errors in the phase of introduction (a requirements error is caught in the requirements phase) and to catch defects as soon after the phase of introduction as possible

(a requirements error is caught in the preliminary design phase rather than the unit test of services phase). The moderator should be qualified and trusted to uphold the philosophy of utmost importance—it is the product under review, never the author. The moderator must also be adroit at the art of gaining consensus and would do well to have been trained in the areas of successful negotiating and conducting effective meetings. Important issues for which the moderator is responsible include verifying the work product's readiness for review, verifying that the entry criteria is met, assembling an effective review team, keeping the review meeting on track, and verifying that the exit criteria is met.

The *scribe* (recorder) records errors and defects, severity and classification of errors and defects, suggestions, action items, and review meeting disposition (hold another review? conditionally approved? approved?).

The *presenter* paraphrases and summarizes each section of the material, expressing functionality as best he can. If possible, the presenter should be different from the author. There is debate about this in the literature, but we believe that there are advantages to having the roles separate, if project resource staffing allows such a luxury. When someone other than the author must present a product, that person is forced to learn it thoroughly (as anyone who has ever taught from someone else's prepared material will attest). In addition, when at least two individuals know a deliverable intimately, the chances of having a repeatable process are greatly enhanced. Lastly, when someone other than the author presents a work, the author may relax from defending the product and concentrate on offering clarification. The risk of an author who also happens to be a good salesperson and can sway the reviewers is diminished.

The *author* clarifies material, answers questions with facts, and does not paraphrase. This person will address specific questions that arise concerning the content of the work product and will use his special knowledge to help identify and detect errors/defects in the work product.

Reviewers (inspectors) find problems. Reviewers may have the following roles on the project team or may assume a role for the review: client, customer, sponsor, functional analyst, prototyper, high-level designer, low-level designer, tester, maintainer, database administrator, network analyst, software quality engineer, software quality assurance (SQA ensures adherence to standards), or other project stakeholders. Table 23–1 is an example of different reviews for different work products. A reviewer may be anyone with good domain knowledge or superior technical skills. The creator of the product from the previous level of abstraction and the receiver of the product from this phase are excellent candidates for attending a review. For example, if the product under review is a service (method) design, the presence of an object modeler would add to the productivity of the review (did the intent of the requirements or design object model translate into the service design correctly?), as would the presence of a coder (is the service design rigorous enough to be understood and translated into service scripts without further clarification from the designer?).

TABLE 23-1
Reviewer Roles and the Product Under Review

Example Reviewer (Stakeholder)	Example Work Product Under Review								
	Project Plan	Risk Management Plan	SRS	SDD	Test Plan	Code	Unit Test	System Test	User Acceptance Test
Project Leader	X	X							
Sponsor	X	X							X
Analyst			X	X					
Designer			X	X	X				
Database Administrator				X					
Network Administrator									
SQA		X	X	X	X	X	X	X	X
Testers		X			X	X	X	X	X
Users								X	X
Programmers						X	X		

There is typically a relationship between the number of reviewers or participants and the level of effort that was required to create the artifact. Large, complex, or critical products may warrant more reviewers. A manageable number of reviewer participants ranges between three and seven. Small teams may require doubling up on roles. The scribe may also be a reviewer, such as QA; the presenter may also be the moderator. Other combinations are always possible, but it is usually preferable to find a reviewer from another project (then return the favor) rather than slimming down the process too much.

Rules of the Review Meeting
As with any meeting, it is wise to follow a predefined agenda to make proper use of time and effort. The following is a recommended agenda:

- Introduce the review meeting.
- Establish the preparedness of the inspectors.
- Review the work product, and identify the errors and defects (presenter, author, reviewers).
- Record the errors and defects (scribe)—a form like the one shown in Figure 23–7 may be used for data collection.
- Determine the work product disposition.
    - Accept (no changes)
    - Conditionally accept (trust the author to make suggested changes)
    - Rework and rereview

There are additional "rules" that many published supporters of the process feel should be inviolable:

- Reviewers review the product, not the person.
- Reviewers uncover problems but do not solve them (the author can do this—he just didn't catch the problem).
- Reviewers search for deviations from product specifications and deviations from quality goals based on published product requirements (outputs from the previous phase), the reviewer's expertise, and organizational standards.
- Reviewers determine:
    - Which items are errors?
    - Which items are defects?
    - What was the phase of origin of the defect?
    - What is the severity level of each error or defect?
        - Trivial to fix—The author will simply make the correction.
        - Somewhat difficult to fix—A reviewer will be assigned to verify the correction.
        - Difficult to fix—Another review will be held following the correction.

Peer Review Defect Log

								Baseline		Review Date:		
Element								Module				
#	Page	Line	Defect Category	Defect Severity	Defect Type	Defect Type	Assigned To	Module or Procedure	Due Date	Date Closed	# Hours to Fix	Defect Description	Response (Include Root Cause)
1													
2													
3													
4													
5													
6													
etc.													

Defect Category: Data, Documentation, Interface, Logic, Maintainability, Performance, Standards, Incomplete, Inconsistent, Unverifiable

Defect Severity: Major, Minor

Defect Type: Missing, Wrong, Extra

Defect Origin: Requirements, Design, Code, Unit Test, Integration, Maintenance

Please indicate Error (originated in this phase) or Defect (originated in a previous phase)

FIGURE 23–7
Review Meeting Data Collection Form

- Are there any suggestions that will improve the efficiency or effectiveness of the product? Make it easier to understand? Make it easier to maintain? Make it use less memory? Produce a more user-friendly product? Adhere to anticipated future standards?

- Is there anything, besides a difficult fix or unresolved research items that would require another review?

• If there are no further reviews necessary, the reviewers take ownership of the product as a team, with the rights to claim credit for the quality and the responsibility to address any undiscovered problems.

• Limit the review session to one or two hours.

• Set an agenda and maintain it.

• Limit debate and rebuttal.

• Enunciate problem areas, but don't attempt to solve every problem noted.

• Take written notes.

• Limit the number of participants and insist upon advance preparation.

- Allocate resources and time schedule for follow-up meetings on issues uncovered.
- Conduct meaningful training for all reviewers.
- Review the review process.
- Eliminate management from the meeting.
- Use the preparation review checklists to help identify errors and defects.
- Allow a minimum of two days' lead time for the preparation.
- Review a reasonable amount of material (e.g., 20 pages of text, or 150–250 SLOC maximum).
- Allow the author to be present for clarification only.
- Never, ever use review metrics or any other aspect of the review process to judge individual performance.
- Assign research when agreement cannot be reached.
- Reviewers may make suggestions that are not critical (e.g., style).
- If reviewers participate too little or too much, rotate comments.
- All attendees charge preparation time and meeting attendance time to an appropriate WBS effort-charge code.
- The author charges effort spent in correction to an appropriate WBS effort-charge code.
- Reviews are not brainstorming sessions.

Post-Review   After the review meeting, the moderator follows up. The author corrects problems (errors and defects) and considers incorporating suggestions. Revisions made by the author in the rework stage must be formally verified (the author may have injected new defects in attempts to correct the previously identified defects), so the moderator must ensure that problems are fixed and must schedule any follow-up reviews. If the product disposition was conditionally accepted, then the moderator will verify the revisions. If the product disposition was rework and rereview, then a full review process is performed but is focused toward the revisions and their interdependencies. The review leader (moderator) obtains approvals and submits the document to configuration management. The scribe records post-review activities, publishes review meeting notes to all review attendees (perhaps to the entire project team), publishes a summary report to management, and incorporates meeting data into metrics repository.

Review Metrics

Chapter 21, "Software Metrics," described how review metrics, coupled with effort data and change request (rework) information, can form a powerful foundation from which the software project manager can make decisions. If data collected in the review meeting includes that collected on forms (databases) such as the one in Figure 23–7, then many useful management reports may be produced. Refer to the figures in Chapter 21 to see how phase containment effectiveness may be charted along with Pareto charts that show which types of errors should be focused on for elimination.

Review data may be product-based or process-based. Information about the product will include number, types/severity, and phase of origin of errors/defects in each work product under review. Information about the review process may include the number of hours spent in preparing for a review and the number of defects found—data needed to calculate the ROI. People metrics come into play as well—managers may want to reward team members who consistently contribute by volunteering to be review moderators or reviewers. Review metrics that are gathered at the time of the review may be recorded on a simple form such at the one in Figure 23–7, or a more thorough form, if additional data is deemed useful. The following data elements may provide further insight into how to manage the project and, therefore, belong in the review metrics database:

- Prior inspection date, if not the first review
- Names and roles of inspectors, excluding the author
- Time spent in planning by author and moderator
- Duration of the review (hh:mm)
- Time spent in planning by each reviewer
- Time spent in rework
- Time spent in follow-up
- Disposition—accept, conditionally accept, rereview
- Target date for rereview
- Number and type of major defects found
- Number and type of minor defects found
- Number of major defects corrected since last review
- Number of minor defects corrected since last review
- Authorized deviations list
- Inspection close date

Reviews and Trend Analysis

Graphs and charts are great management devices because they allow trends to be spotted quickly. Software PMs generally like to see whether the numbers are going up or down for these items:

- Defects by phase
- Total defects (major/minor) by delivery/release ID
- Total defects (major/minor) by delivery/release ID by type
- Defect density of products (number of major/minor defects per lines/pages)

- Defect density of defect types sorted by type and by type and application
- Labor hours (planning, preparation, review, follow-up, and rework) versus number of defects found, lines/pages reviewed
- Effective rates for preparation, inspection, number of lines/pages inspected per inspection
- Number of inspections complete versus planned for each product

Again, a useful management graph, where the data is collected from reviews, focuses on phase containment effectiveness (PCE), as described in Chapter 21.

Risks of Not Conducting Reviews

When Phillip Crosby said, "Quality is free," he didn't mean that there is no investment. His statement had more to do with "you can have it all"—quality, contained cost, and reasonable schedule—with careful planning and adherence to effective processes. We know that reviews are an expensive proposition, especially when so much project talent is focused on one work product at a time. Rollout and operating costs associated with software reviews include the initial training of practitioners and managers, the ongoing preparation and conduct of review sessions, the ongoing management and use of measurement data for defect prevention, and return on investment computations.

Considering the preparation and conduct of review sessions alone seems off-putting in financial terms. There is the preparation effort of each participant before the session and the conduct effort of participants in the review session. Typically five people participate, and each expends one to two hours of preparation and one to two hours of conduct. This is a cost of 10 to 20 hours of total effort per session! Yet, the effort typically results in the early detection of 5 to 10 defects in 250–500 lines of new development code or 1,000–1,500 lines of legacy code.

Can the software project manager afford not to conduct reviews? Hardly. Let's look at risk exposure, as we taught in Chapter 18, "Determining Project Risks."

Risk exposure is defined by the relationship:

$$RE = P(UO) \times L(UO)$$

where RE is the risk exposure, P(UO) is the probability of an unsatisfactory outcome, and L(UO) is the loss to the parties affected if the outcome is unsatisfactory.

"Unsatisfactory" for software projects may mean budget overruns and schedule slips, products with the wrong functionality, user-interface shortfalls, performance shortfalls, reliability shortfalls, poor quality of structure, and so on.

The example in Figure 23–8 is a potentially risky situation where the software is under development by a team that understands the problem domain but is inexperienced in and somewhat casual about software development. As a result, the manager estimates that there is a probability P(UO) of 0.4 that the developers' software will have a critical error, one that will wipe out the entire experiment and cause an associated loss L(UO) of the total $20 million investment in the experiment.

The manager identified two major options for reducing the risk of losing the experiment:

1. **Do IV&V.** Hiring a contractor to independently verify and validate (IV&V) the software. This costs an additional $500,000; based on the results of similar IV&V efforts, the manager estimates that this will reduce the error probability P(UO) to 0.04.

2. **Don't do IV&V.** Convincing and helping the development team to apply better development methods. This incurs no additional cost, and, from previous experience, the manager estimates that this will reduce the error probability P(UO) to 0.1.

The decision tree in Figure 23–8 shows, for each of the two major decision options, the possible outcomes in terms of the critical error (CE) existing or being found and eliminated, their probabilities, the losses associated with each outcome, the risk exposure associated with each outcome, and total risk exposure (or expected loss) associated with each decision option. In this case, the total risk exposure associated with the experiment-team option is only $2 million.

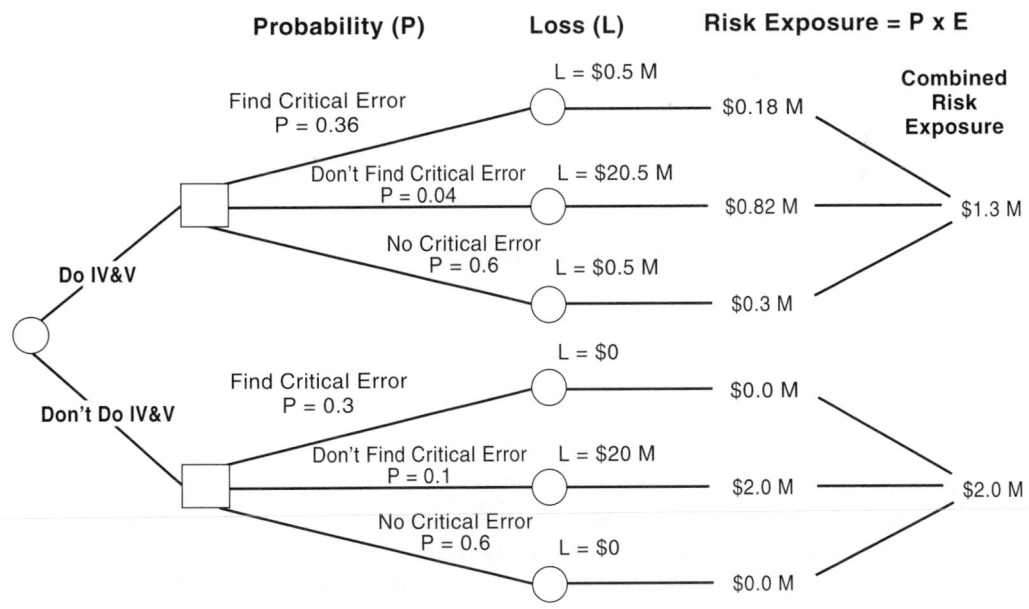

FIGURE 23–8
Risk Assessment of Independent Verification and Validation
Source: Adapted from Barry W. Boehm (1991). "Software Risk Management: Principles and Practices." *IEEE Software*, January.

For the IV&V option, the total risk exposure is only $1.3 million, so it represents the more attractive option.

If there is doubt that reviews, thorough testing, or IV&V activities are worth the investment on any given project, a similar risk assessment may be constructed by the software PM.

Software Inspection Quality

Fagan, regarded as the originator of code inspection techniques, created the software inspection process at IBM and published his studies in the *IBM Systems Journal*.[12] He defines "quality of inspection" as its ability to detect all instances in which the product does not meet its requirements. Studies, evaluations, and the observations of many people who have been involved in inspections over the past decade provide insights into the contributors to inspection quality. The relationships between contributors must be understood to isolate and deal with initiating root causes of problems. The Ishikawa or Fishbone Cause/Effect Diagram shown in Figure 23–9 shows these main contributors to inspection quality:[13]

- Product inspectability (Is the product ready to be reviewed? Has the proper size product subset been chosen for a review? etc.)

- Inspection process (Is it published, understood, followed? Are the developers trained for their roles? etc.)

- Managers (Do they understand the process? Support it? Allow time for it? Believe that it reduces effort and enhances quality? etc.)

- Programmers (Do they work as a team? Are they motivated to care about quality? etc.)

Issues with Reviews

Now that we've extolled the virtues of reviews, it's only fair to remember what Brooks said about "no silver bullet" (there isn't one...).[14] Not all quality problems can be solved by reviews, and even when they *are* used there is controversy about *how* to use them.

There are arguments over whether an author should be a presenter, over the degree of formalism, over whether any review is better than no review, over the wisdom of reviewers on a small project assuming multiple roles, over the very definition of the term—to equate a "walkthrough" to an "inspection" is enough to make some software engineers' blood boil. The savvy PM can minimize such disagreements by defining the meanings of terms and the process rules for a specific project, based on the organization's standards. In the past, one of the greatest challenges to the adoption of the review process was the concept of ego-less programming. It can be difficult to critique a single-author work product, such as a software program, without denigrating the creator. Why would anyone open himself up to such criticism? Fortunately, in many modern organizations, this is no longer an issue. The enlightened establishment follows the guidelines from the SEI CMM and IEEE standards. When the team

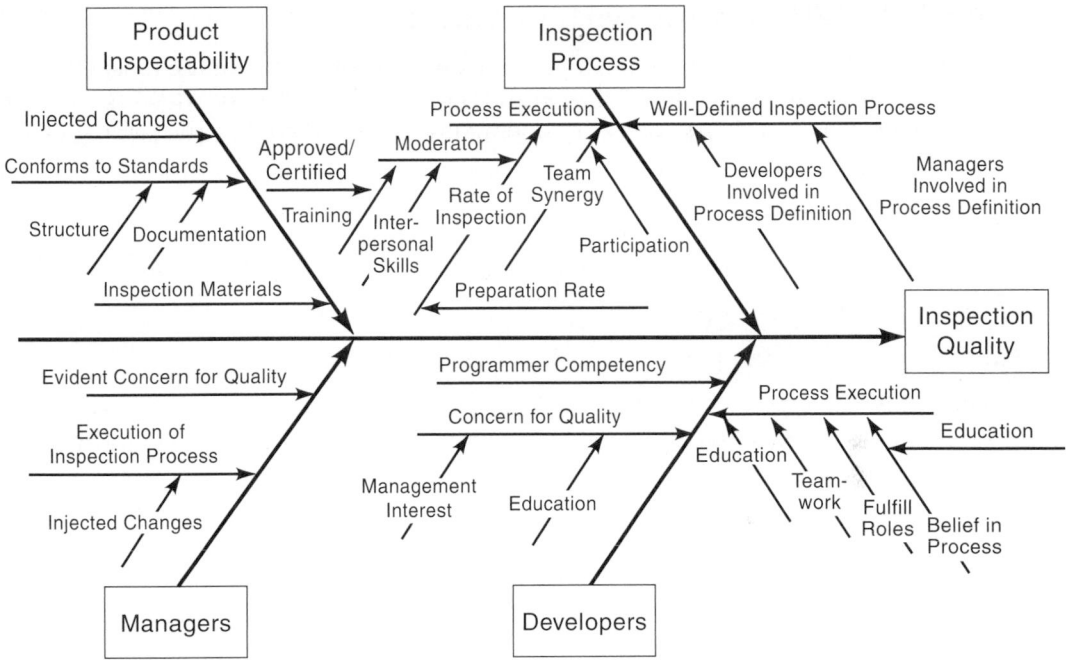

FIGURE 23–9
Ishikawa Diagram for Quality Inspections

shares the philosophy that "the product is under review, not the producer," egotism fades to the background.

A related issue that *does* remain a problem in many organizations is the way in which management handles the review data. Sometimes managers use it to make decisions but forget to feed the outcomes back to the team. Sometimes they use it as input to performance evaluations. In the first case, the project team will be casual about the accuracy of the data, assuming that no one really cares about it. In the second case, the team members will fudge the data to look good. Or, an "honest" author who has put aside his ego to have a work product reviewed will not receive helpful feedback—peers will be reluctant to find defects if they know that the information will be used against the co-worker. Because the software project manager wants to use peer review metrics to improve the quality of the system under development as well as future ones, accuracy is particularly important. It is possible to fix these issues with constant feedback and ownership of each product by the entire team after acceptance upon review.

The only way in which a project manager may use review data in a performance evaluation is to reward the person who willingly participates in reviews. Assuming any role in a review is a time-consuming proposition, and those who volunteer to be moderators or scribes, especially for other projects, do a service for the organization that deserves positive recognition.

Summary of Static Testing with Reviews

No process will find all software faults, but peer reviews constitute one of the most effective tools known. Reviews will help eliminate errors and omissions from a software work product. But reviews do more than just help to produce a quality product. On a macro level, reviews can provide the information needed for process improvement. Over time, fewer errors will be inserted in the first place.

Formal reviews place demands on management for support, resources, and team member training, but they are well worth the effort because they produce a high rate of return on the investment. They are part of V&V processes espoused by ISO and IEEE, they are a key process area within the SEI CMM, and they are crucial to a metrics program.

There are different types of reviews, but a formal meeting in which the participants assume specific roles, the material under review is studied beforehand, the rules of the meeting (e.g., review the product, not the person; no management participation) are set forth, review data is collected, and so on will produce the best results. Reviewers are recruited to serve on the review team from a diverse stakeholder base. Each reviewer brings a unique perspective to the process—an SQA may be able to find an error or defect that a network administrator cannot, and vice versa. Table 23–1 shows how stakeholder roles may play into the reviews of various documents from different life cycle phases.

Review metrics, such as the number of errors/defects uncovered, their type and severity, and where they originated and were found, provide valuable information for the project manager. From them, decisions may be made about training, process improvements, organization, and how to estimate and plan future projects.

There are several challenging aspects to instantiating a review process, including how to convince upper management that reviews are good for the bottom line, and how to convince developers that reviews are tremendous opportunities for learning.

Dynamic Testing

This chapter began with a definition: V&V consists of two major activities—*reviewing* a software project work product and *testing* one. The former is static, meaning that it does not require a computer and may be applied to any project artifact. The latter is dynamic, meaning that it *does* require execution on a computer and is therefore limited to certain project artifacts. With modern analysis and design tools, dynamic testing has moved up the life cycle, to earlier and earlier phases—an analyst can now "test" an object model or a data flow diagram. However, most developers view testing as the activity of executing software code to see how it performs.

The Purpose of Testing

The goal of testing is to uncover and fix as many errors as possible, within the bounds of diminishing returns—it may be thought of as a filter for removing nonquality characteristics. Testing strives to uncover problems that contribute to the fragility of the system so that they may be corrected before release of the product, when they become many times more expensive and displeasing to customers. The purpose of testing is not to "test in quality" but to confirm built-in quality. Will the software do what it is supposed to do consistently, reliably, and accurately during long-term production use? Glenford Myers tells us that a "successful" test is one that detects an as-yet undiscovered error.[15] Pressman reminds us that although testing cannot show the absence of defects, it can show that defects are present.[16] We can never test long enough or hard enough to be 100% certain that no defects will be delivered to the customer. This leaves us with the option of testing "smart," to best utilize this rather expensive phase in the software product development life cycle. One example of smart testing is to identify the particularly risky areas of the product, such as the ones that are the most complex or heavily used, and concentrate on finding their faults.

Developers and Destruction

Testing is a destructive process, a factor that can cause a fair amount of psychological difficulty for software developers accustomed to only creative behaviors. Creating a software system is bliss to the productive mind; software "inventors" are proud of their product and want to believe that it is of high quality (i.e., error-free). The goal of testing, however, is not to prove that the product works, nor to demonstrate that errors are not present. Software, built by imperfect human beings, is destined to contain errors. If we knew what they were, we would fix them. The goal of testing is to uncover these errors that have been injected into the product during the construction phase.

It is difficult for developers to test their own products because they are required to change perspectives, or attitude, from creator to critic. The developer has a fundamental understanding of how the software works, making it hard to discover scenarios where it won't work. It has been pointed out that it is much more difficult to find errors in one's own code than in somebody else's. The reason for this is called cognitive dissonance, a phenomenon that makes conscious acknowledgment of one's own mistakes more difficult. In addition, the creator may have a fundamental misunderstanding of the problem statement or specification, which means that no amount of searching by him could uncover the root of error. For these reasons, it is recommended that developers do not test their own products.

Of course, each developer should self-test his creations as thoroughly as possible before passing the work product on to an independent tester, usually a peer. Testing requires learning to live with the humanness of practitioners. Many software developers don't really like to test their software thoroughly, finding it boring or even depressing to watch the application failing under stress. Others don't mind and do a first-rate job at it. Popular or not, we know that there exists a strong correlation between the thoroughness of test activities and the number of residual defects in delivered software. Even though there is a good chance that testing by an independent party will produce a more thoroughly tested program, the individual developer still has a responsibility to deliver as clean a product as possible to the next stage of V&V.

Debugging

Testing is not debugging, nor vice versa. The process of program debugging can be described as the activity that one performs after executing a successful test case. (Remember, a successful test case is one that finds a bug.) Describing it in more concrete terms, debugging is a two-part process; it begins with some indication of the existence of an error (e.g., the results of a successful test case), and it is the activity of determining the exact nature and location of the suspected error within the program and fixing or repairing the error.[17]

Testing and debugging are important to quality because all software has bugs, no matter how many reviews we do or how hard we try not to insert bugs in the first place. The reasons that bugs defy us and get inserted anyway are pretty well documented in this book and dozens of others—basically, they are the common risk factors that were discussed in Chapter 18. For a quick review, the bases for injected defects are rooted in the following:

- Incomplete or incorrect requirements specifications, largely due to miscommunication between developers and customers. Requirements that are too general, unclear, unattainable or untestable.
- Requirements volatility.
- Goldplating or "featureitis."
- Complexity of the modern environment, including Windows-type interfaces, client/server and distributed applications, data communications, large relational databases, and large applications.
- Human error in requirements specification, design, and coding.
- Schedules that are too short due to misestimating or market/customer pressure. Inadequate time for test planning, testing, debugging, and retesting. Too much work crammed into too little time generates additional human error.
- Desire to please, optimism, or ego on the part of the developer.
- Lack of documentation or poor documentation, particularly in code.
- Overdependence on tools (visual aids, class libraries, compilers, etc.) that are poorly documented or inadequately tested themselves.

Testing Is Never Complete

Every program operates on a finite number of inputs. A complete functional test would consist of subjecting the program to all possible input streams. For each input, the routine either accepts the stream and produces a correct outcome, accepts the stream and produces an incorrect outcome, or rejects the stream. Consider a 10-character input string (each character is composed of 8 bits; each bit may be 0 or 1). There are 2^{80} possible input streams and corresponding outcomes. Complete functional testing is impractical (actually impossible) because at one test per microsecond, it would take twice the current estimated age of the universe.[18] Because it is impossible to test every single combination and permutation of data inputs and interfaces that cause a system to react, we have another reason to "test smart" and not "test hard." This means determining the ways in which the system is most likely to be used, searching out the probabilities of each type of use, and creating tests to exercise the system in a sensible manner.

The V-Shaped Software Product Development Life Cycle Supports Testing

Chapter 4, "Selecting Software Development Life Cycles," described a number of ways that a software project could be approached in terms of the organization of its phases, activities, and deliverables. It was pointed out that whatever is the most appropriate for the project at hand is the "correct" approach, even if that means the formation of a wholly new software product development life cycle or a combination of existing ones. One life cycle, called the V-shaped model, was declared to be particularly useful for projects that require a high degree of reliability. The V-shaped model may stand alone or may be used in combination with others, such as incremental release.

As we said in Chapter 4, the V-shaped model places a strong emphasis on the verification and validation activities of the product. It illustrates that the testing of the product is discussed, designed, and planned in the early phases of the development life cycle. The customer acceptance test plan is developed during the planning phase, the system integration test plan is developed during the analysis and design phase, and so on. This test plan development activity is represented by the dotted lines between the rectangles of the V.

The V-shaped model, reproduced here in Figure 23–10, emphasizes the relationship between the analytical and design phases that precede coding with the testing phases that follow coding. The dotted lines indicate that these phases should be considered in parallel.

Phases in the V-shaped model typically include these:

- Project and requirements planning.
- Product requirements and specification analysis.
- Architecture or high-level design.
- Detailed design.
- Coding.
- Unit testing—checks each coded module for errors.

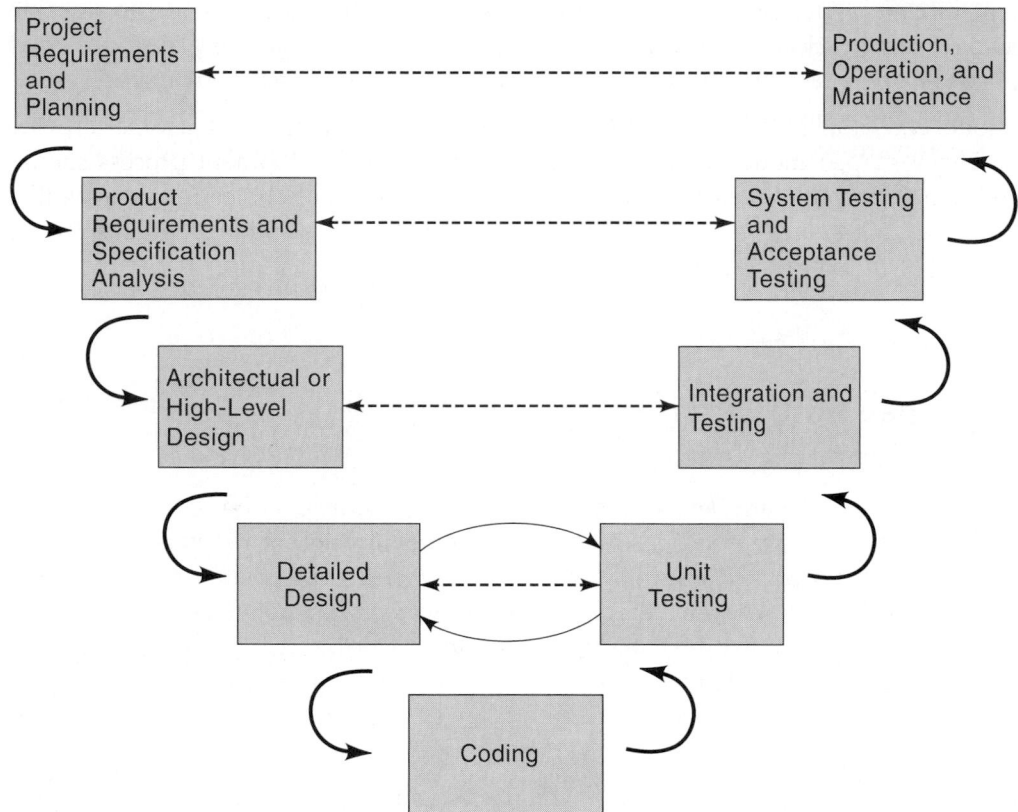

FIGURE 23–10
The V-Shaped Model for a V&V Life Cycle

- Integration and testing—interconnects the sets of previously unit-tested modules to ensure that the sets behave as well as the independently tested modules did during the unit-testing phase.
- System testing—checks whether the entire software system (fully integrated) embedded in its actual hardware environment behaves according to the software requirements specification.
- Production, operation, and maintenance—puts software into production and provides for enhancing and corrections.
- Acceptance testing—allows the user to test the functionality of the system against the original requirements. After final testing, the software and its surrounding hardware become operational. Maintenance of the system follows.

When applied to a project for which it is well suited, the model emphasizes planning for V&V of the product in the early stages of product development. Emphasis is placed on testing by matching the test phase or process with the development process. The unit testing phase validates detailed design. The integration and testing phase validates architectural or high-level design. The system testing phase validates the product requirements and specification phase.

The model encourages V&V of all internal and external deliverables, not just the software product. The V-shaped model defines the products that the development process should generate; each deliverable must be testable, so this is an excellent choice for systems that require high reliability, such as hospital patient control applications and embedded software for air-bag chip controllers in automobiles.

Dynamic Testing Definitions

As with static testing, dynamic testing comes with multiple definitions and numerous terms. The following definitions describe popular use of many of them:

Acceptance testing is final testing based on specifications of the end-user or customer, or based on use by end-users/customers over some limited period of time.

Ad-hoc testing is similar to exploratory testing, but it often is taken to mean that the testers have significant understanding of the software before testing it.

Alpha testing refers to testing of an application when development is nearing completion; minor design changes may still be made as a result of such testing. Typically this is done by end-users or others, not by programmers or testers.

Beta testing means testing when development and testing are essentially completed and final bugs and problems need to be found before final release. Typically this is done by end-users or others, not by programmers or testers.

Black-box testing is not based on any knowledge of internal design or code. Tests are based on requirements and functionality.

Bug means a defect, problem, or fault.

Certification extends the processes of verification and validation to an operational environment; it confirms that the system is operationally effective and is capable of satisfying requirements under specified operating conditions, and it guarantees its compliance with requirements in writing. Certification usually implies the existence of an independent quality control group for the acceptance testing of the overall system. Acceptance testing may be accomplished by doing operational testing or laboratory testing, or placing the system in simulated operation. Certification is the formal demonstration of system acceptability to obtain authorization for its operational use.

Code refers to module source code. It should meet approved requirements, be technically accurate and complete with respect to requirements, implement the detailed design, satisfy all required/applicable standards, trace to approved requirements, and trace to detailed design.

Comparison testing is comparing software weaknesses and strengths to competing products.

Compatibility testing means testing how well software performs in a particular hardware/software/operating system/network environment.

Design refers to the software component or module design at either the high or the detailed level. It should meet the approved requirements; be complete with all required logic algorithms, data structures, and calls; trace to the approved requirements; and follow all required and applicable standards.

End-to-end testing is similar to system testing, the "macro" end of the test scale. It involves testing a complete application environment in a situation that mimics real-world use, such as interacting with a database, using network communications, or interacting with other hardware, applications, or systems, if appropriate.

Error (or fault) seeding, as described in the 1970s by Harlan Mills, suggested this approach: First, inject (seed) X representative faults into the program, then run a test suite; you will probably find X–Y faults, but not all of X; you probably found roughly the same proportion of unseeded "native" faults as well. The estimated effectiveness is expressed as (X–Y)/X. Inserting faults is not as easy as it sounds because it requires a usable taxonomy of fault types, knowledge of their relative chances of occurring, and an understanding of how their placement affects visibility as failures. The wrong proportions of the wrong kinds of faults seeded in the wrong places can befuddle estimates.

Exploratory testing is often taken to mean a creative, informal software test that is not based on formal test plans or test cases; testers may be learning the software as they test it.

Failure is the behavior of the software or system component when a fault is encountered, producing an incorrect or undesired effect of a specified severity.

Fault is a manifestation of an error in software. If encountered, a fault may cause a failure.

Functional testing is black-box type of testing geared to functional requirements of an application; this type of testing should be done by testers. This doesn't mean that the programmers shouldn't check that their code works before releasing it (which, of course, applies to any stage of testing).

Good enough testing refers to knowing when to stop. Most errors occur because of the (il)logical decisions that the software makes, based on input values encountered. A complete functional test would consist of subjecting the program to all possible input streams. Complete functional testing is impractical because of the very large number of possible permutations of input data. It is impossible to test every single combination and permutation of data inputs and interfaces that cause a system to react. The most practical means of testing is to determine the ways in which the system is most likely to be used, searching out the probabilities of each type of use, and then creating tests to exercise the system within those scenarios.

Guerrilla testing is the nastiest test cases that can be thought up, executed "on the fly." The test may include boundaries, error handling, challenges for module interactions—anything that the tester thinks is likely to expose a bug is fair game.

Incremental integration testing means continuous testing of an application as new functionality is added; it requires that various aspects of an application's functionality be independent enough to work separately before all parts of the program are completed, or that test drivers be developed as needed. It is done by programmers or by testers.

Install/uninstall testing is testing of full, partial, or upgrade install/uninstall processes.

Integration testing is testing of combined components of an application to determine whether they function together correctly. The components can be code modules, individual applications, client and server applications on a network, and so on. This type of testing is especially relevant to client/server and distributed systems.

Load testing means testing an application under heavy loads, such as testing of a Web site under a range of loads to determine at what point the system's response time degrades or fails.

Module—see *program*.

Mutation testing is a method for determining whether a set of test data or test cases is useful by deliberately introducing various code changes (bugs) and retesting with the original test data/cases to determine if the bugs are detected. Proper implementation requires large computational resources.

Performance testing is a term often used interchangeably with *stress* and *load* testing. Ideally, performance testing (and any other type of testing) is defined in requirements documentation or QA or test plans.

Program, unit, or module is often described as an invokable, executable section of code with a single entry point and a single exit point that performs a single function (it is cohesive).

Recovery testing means testing how well a system recovers from crashes, hardware failures, or other catastrophic problems.

Regression testing is retesting after fixes or modifications of the software or its environment. It can be difficult to determine how much retesting is needed, especially near the end of the development cycle. Automated testing tools can be especially useful for this type of testing.

Sanity testing is typically an initial testing effort to determine whether a new software version is performing well enough to accept it for a major testing effort. For example, if the new software is crashing systems every five minutes, bogging down systems to a crawl, or destroying databases, the software may not be in a "sane" enough condition to warrant further testing in its current state.

Security testing is testing how well the system protects against unauthorized internal or external access, willful damage, and so on; it may require sophisticated testing techniques.

Stress testing is a term often used interchangeably with *load* and *performance* testing. It is also used to describe tests such as system functional testing while under unusually heavy loads, heavy repetition of certain actions or inputs, input of large numerical values, large complex queries to a database system, and so on.

Subsystem testing—see *integration testing*.

System testing means a black-box type of testing that is based on overall requirements specifications and that covers all combined parts of a system. System tests involve running the system in the environment in which it is expected to execute and looking for environmental factors or inputs that could cause the system to fail or produce an unexpected response. System testing can begin before all components are finished.

Test case describes an input, action, or event and an expected response, to determine whether a feature of an application is working correctly. A test case should contain particulars such as test case identifier, test case name, objective, test conditions/setup, input data requirements, steps, and expected results. A test case specification might include a test-case specification identifier, test items, input/output specifications (values, tolerances, constant tables, transaction files, databases, terminal messages, operating system flags), environmental needs, and procedural requirements.

A *test plan* is a document prescribing the approach for testing activities. A software project test plan describes the objectives, scope, approach, and focus of a software testing effort. The plan typically identifies the items to be tested, the testing to be performed, test schedules, personnel requirements, reporting requirements, evaluation criteria, the level of acceptable risk, and any risk requiring contingency planning. The process of preparing a test plan is a useful way to think through the efforts needed to validate the acceptability of a software product. Ultimately, the plan should ensure that all new and modified software functions operate correctly within the intended environment and according to approved requirements, that all new and modified interfaces will be verified, and that each requirement will be tested. It may also need to specify intercase dependencies—what test cases must be executed before this one. Some questions for software PMs to ask about a software test plan include these:

- Have major test phases properly been identified and sequenced?
- Has traceability to validation criteria/requirements been established as part of software requirements analysis?
- Are major functions demonstrated early?
- Is the test plan consistent with the overall project plan?
- Has a test schedule been explicitly defined?

- Are test resources and tools identified and available?
- Has a test record-keeping mechanism been established?
- Have test drivers and stubs been identified, and has work to develop them been scheduled?
- Has stress testing for software been specified?

A *test procedure* is the detailed instructions for the setup, operation, and evaluation of results for a given test. A set of associated procedures is often combined to form a test procedure document. A test procedure should include a complete and accurate description of its purpose, a description of how it executes, and all expected results. Each test procedure should identify which requirement(s) it is testing and the required hardware and software configurations.

Unit—see *program*.

Unit testing is the smallest scale of testing. It tests the internal workings (functions) of a program, unit, or module without regard to how it is invoked. It is typically done by the programmer and not by testers because it requires detailed knowledge of the internal program design and code. It is not always easily done unless the application has a well-designed architecture with tight code, and it may require developing test driver modules or test harnesses.

Usability testing is testing for "user-friendliness," from the user's point of view. This is subjective and will depend on the targeted end-user or customer. User interviews, surveys, video recording of user sessions, and other techniques can be used. It may include ergonomic considerations, screen design, and so on.

User acceptance testing is testing to determine whether software is satisfactory to an end-user or customer.

White-box testing is based on knowledge of the internal logic of an application's code. Tests are based on coverage of code statements, branches, paths, and conditions.

Many of these definitions of project artifacts (i.e., test plan, code) may be used as a checklist in a peer review of the product.

Types of Tests

Very often, the chronological order of testing follows this scenario:

1. Individual program units are built and tested (white-box tests).
2. Those units are hooked together as subsystems and are tested (black-box tests).
3. Those subsystems are then hooked together in a complete system and are tested (integration tests).
4. That system is placed in its real environment and tested (system tests).

5. Those system tests are preserved, to be rerun when changes are made (regression tests).

There are other types of tests, but this is typically the minimal set. White-box, black-box, system, and regression testing will be described in more detail.

White-Box Testing   Referring to the V-shaped model in Figure 23–10, testing is thought to begin with unit tests (read the V down the left side and then up the right side). Our slightly more detailed discussions of the main types of tests will then begin with white-box, also known as clear-box, unit, module, bottom-up, or structural, tests. It tests the internal workings of a program, unit, or module without regard to how it is invoked. A program, unit, or module is often described as an invokable, executable, bounded section of code with a single entry point and a single exit point, that performs one and only one primary function. Sometimes test drivers must be built to cause a unit-box test module to execute.

Having a module design is critical to successful unit testing. Examples of module design include these:

Flowchart

Pseudocode

Chapin (Nassi-Schneiderman) chart

PSPEC

CSPEC

Decision table

State transition diagram

Hierarchical-input-process-output (HIPO) charts

Prose

Flow graphs

Chapin charts will be revisited here (they were described in Chapter 22), and flow graphs will be discussed for the first time. Design-driven or white-box testing is the process in which the tester examines the internal workings of code. Design-driven testing is done by selecting the input data and other parameters based on the internal logic paths that are to be checked. The goals of design-driven testing include ascertaining correctness of:

- all paths through the code. (For most software products, this can be feasibly done only at the unit test level.)
- bit-by-bit functioning of interfaces.
- size and timing of critical elements of code.

As shown in Figure 23–11, harnesses must be devised to provide the input necessary for white-box testing of program modules.

Usually, test drivers or "harnesses" must be built to cause a white-box test to execute.

Following unit testing, on the right side of the V in Figure 23–10, is integration testing. This is also known as black-box testing.

Black-Box Testing   Black-box testing is also known as interface, top-down, or functional testing. It assumes that individual units may be treated as "black boxes," or components that function properly. The unit is expected to process, or transform, inputs into correct and expected outputs. The test, in this case, is to find errors in inputs to the black boxes, to test the parameters that are passed or the interfaces between the boxes.

To test subsystems, you must have a "map" to the way in which the individual units in the subsystem are expected to interface and function together. A good design specification will contain such a map. For OO software, this might be a combination of object class models and object interaction diagrams for a subject area or object collection. Subsystem testing is often referred to as integration testing. In an object-oriented paradigm, several objects pertaining to a topic (subject area) are grouped together and subjected to testing.

Informal testing may be requirements-driven or design-driven. Requirements-driven or black-box testing is done by selecting the input data and other parameters based on the software requirements and observing the outputs and reactions of the software. Black-box testing

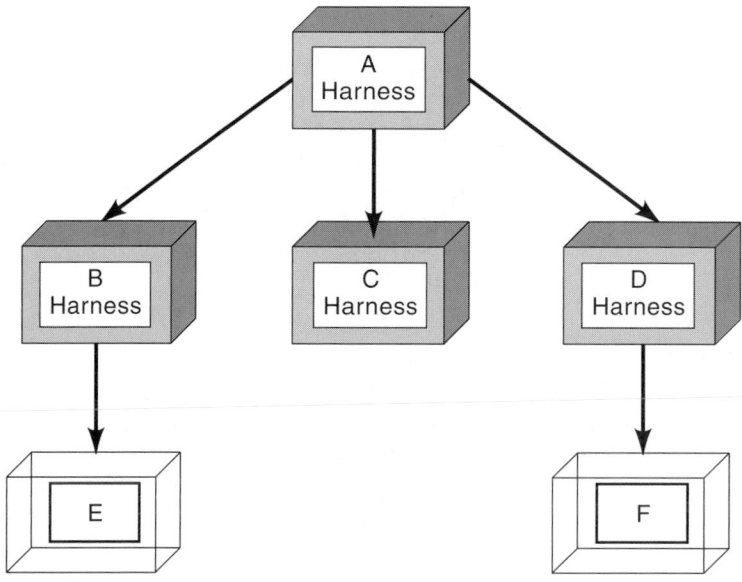

FIGURE 23–11
Harnesses Drive White-Box Testing

can be done at any level of integration. In addition to testing for satisfaction of requirements, some of the objectives of requirements-driven testing are to ascertain:

- Computational correctness.
- Proper handling of boundary conditions, including extreme inputs and conditions that cause extreme outputs.
- State transitioning as expected.
- Proper behavior under stress or high load.
- Adequate error detection, handling, and recovery.

Having a "map" to the way in which the individual units are expected to fit together is critical to successful interface testing. A widely used approach, to mapping components and their interfaces is the structure chart (described in Chapter 22).

Sometimes, stubs or "no-ops," or responders ("intelligent stubs"), as shown in Figure 23–12, must be built to allow for black-box testing. Testers build a skeleton of the software product to ensure that all functions can be accessed. The responders simply indicate that the test traversed the path to where a given capacity occurs.

Once individual modules have been tested via white-box tests, they may be grouped into subsystems that are subjected to other kinds of tests. Equivalence partitioning and boundary

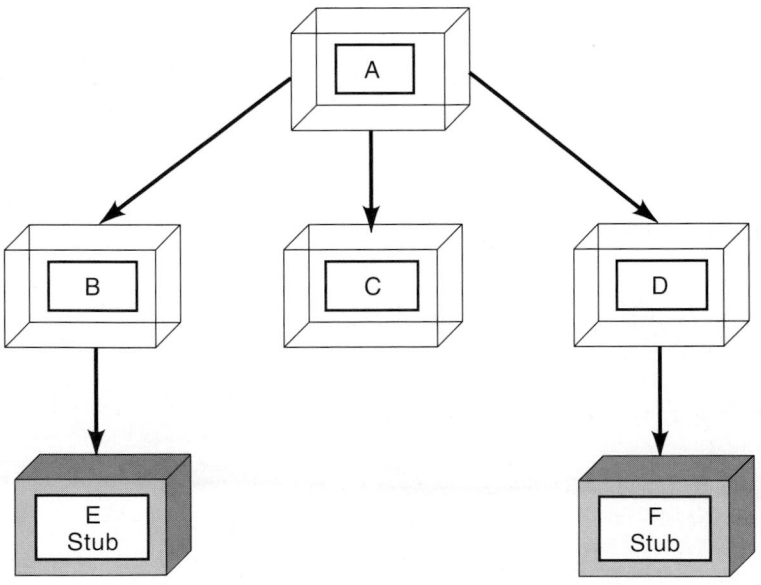

FIGURE 23–12
Stubs Support Black-Box Testing

value analysis, described next, may certainly be used during white-box testing, but they are more often used as very effective tests for subsystems. Distinct units, considered to be "working" independently as "black boxes" (we no longer need to know what goes on inside), are placed in logical groupings and are subjected to black-box tests. We discuss the four most prominent ones here.

Equivalence Partitioning   The input domain of a program or subsystem may be partitioned into a finite number of equivalence classes. You can assume (although not be absolutely sure) that a test of a representative value of each class is equivalent to a test of any other value. A blood test is an example of an equivalence test—a drop drawn from the finger is, for many tests, equivalent to testing any drop of blood in the body. Equivalence partitioning is the determination of how all possible input states may be carved up into a much smaller number of equivalence classes.

Equivalence partitioning is a useful technique that can increase the efficiency of testing. The key to the technique lies in the fact that many input states are very similar to one another, differing in only a few aspects. For example, two deposit transactions in a banking program may differ only in the amount of the deposit. If one functions correctly, it is extremely (but not perfectly!) likely that the other will also. You can perform a grouping or equivalence partitioning of the input space. You select only one input state from each group, with a probability equal to the total probability of occurrence of all states in the group. This drastically reduces the number of input states that you must select from and speeds up testing because input states that are unlikely to expose new failures are not executed.[19] The following is a checklist for performing simple equivalence class partitioning.

1. Divide any input space into at least two classes: *valid values* and *invalid values*. Make sure that at least one invalid value is input for each test; frequently, several valid values will be input for each test.

2. If the input space covers an ascending or descending *range of values* (i.e., 2, 3, 4, 5, 6), select from the valid inputs the first value in the range (2), the last value in the range (6), and a "nominal" value from the center of the range (3 or 4) as input for the test. Select from the invalid inputs a value below (or above) the first value that falls outside of the valid range (say, 0), and a value above (or below) the last value that falls outside of the valid range (say, 10).

3. If the input space covers a specific number or *enumeration of values* (i.e., 2, 4, 12, 17, 19), select from the valid inputs the minimal value (2), the maximum value (19), and a nominal value (17). Select from the invalid inputs a value below the set range (say, 0), above the set range (say, 25), and within the set range, but not a member of the set (say, 8).

4. If the input space covers a set of input values—such as ((2, 3, 4, 5), (B, C, D, E), (73, 106))—select from the valid subset inputs the minimal (2, B), maximum (5, E, 106), and nominal values (3, C, 73). Select from the invalid subset inputs values below (0, A),

above (say, 17, Q), within but not a member (say, 100), and below (say, 0) and above (say, 110) the entire set.

5. If the input space contains a mandatory value ("the first character must be an X or a Z"), select one valid set for correct characters (say, Zoo), and one invalid set to represent all other characters (say, Apple).

Boundary-Value Analysis

Boundary-value analysis differs from equivalence partitioning in two respects:

1. Rather than selecting any element in an equivalence class as being representative, boundary-value analysis requires that one or more elements be selected so that each edge of the equivalence class is the subject of a test.

2. Rather than just focusing attention on the input conditions (input space), test cases are also derived by considering the result space (i.e., output equivalence classes).

General guidelines for boundary value analysis are:

1. If an input condition specifies a range of values (i.e., 2, 3, 4, 5, 6), write test cases for the ends of the range (2, 6) and write invalid-input test cases for situations just beyond the ends (1, 7).

2. If an input condition specifies a number of values (i.e., 2, 4, 12, 17, 19), write test cases for the minimum (2) and maximum (19) values, and one beneath (1) and beyond (20) these values.

3. Use guideline 1 for each output condition. If possible, generate test cases that will result in values outside the expected range. For example, if a program computes the monthly FICA deduction and the minimum is $0.00 and the maximum is $3,055.37, write test cases that cause $0.00 and $3,055.37 to be deducted. Also, see if it is possible to invent test cases that might cause a negative deduction or a deduction more than $3,055.37.

4. Use guideline 2 for each output condition. For example, if an information-retrieval system displays the most-relevant abstracts based on an input request, but never more than four, write test cases so that the program displays zero, one, and four abstracts, and write a test case that might cause the program to erroneously display five abstracts.

5. If the input or output of a program is an ordered set, focus attention on the first and last elements of the set.[20]

Integration Tests

Integration tests are also black-box tests, but the black boxes are typically larger than just one unit. Often, units have been grouped into components (integrated aggregates) or programs with several subroutines, or even subsystems. In an object-oriented paradigm, several objects pertaining to a topic (subsystem) may have been grouped together and subjected to black-box testing, and then the topic grouping is combined with other topic groupings (subsystems) to form a whole system that is then subjected to an integration test (see Figure 23–13.)

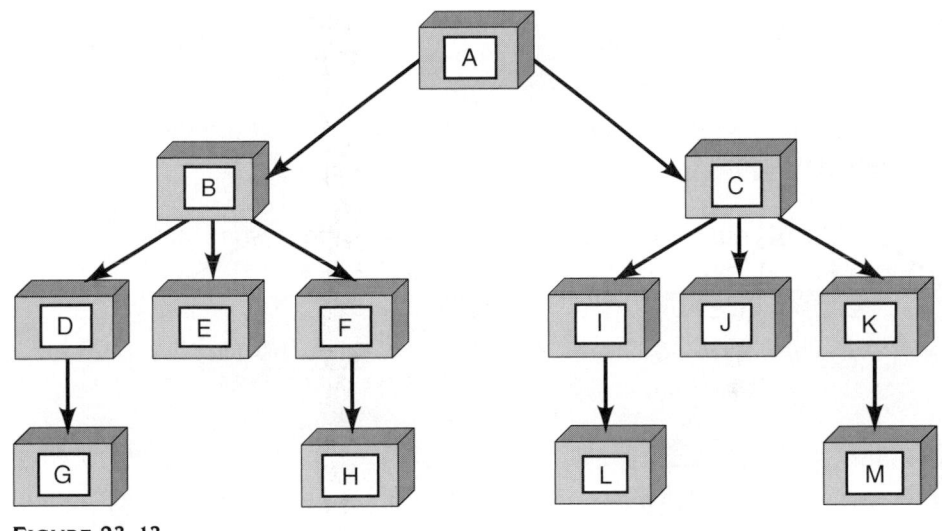

FIGURE 23–13
Integration Testing

Structure charts, described in Chapter 22, are also helpful in integration testing. At this level of testing, the original work breakdown structure (WBS), created during the planning phase, may also provide the way to how major subsystem components fit together.

System Tests   System tests involve placing the system in the environment (see Figure 23–14) in which it is expected to execute and searching out all environmental factors or inputs that could cause the system to fail (produce an unexpected response). Placing the software-based product in the environment means putting it in front of the customer. System testing is the verification and validation of all the system requirements derived from customers to build the product.

System testing often begins before all of the components are created. Some of the major functions, also known as the system "backbone" are built, combined, and subjected to a "smoke test." Knowing that system testing will and must occur before the final system is completed, developers must plan for these tests. A test plan template may be found in Appendix F, "Project Artifact Templates."

One method to plan and execute the system test strategy is profiling. John Musa, one of the most well-known experts in the testing arena, describes the use of these profiles in the context of software reliability engineering.[21]

Operational Profile   Use of profiles should begin early in the requirements collection phase of the project. Profiles extend from the "customer profile" developed by marketing/sales, through the actual test scenario selection used to support black/white-box testing. Figure 23–15 shows this profiling continuum.

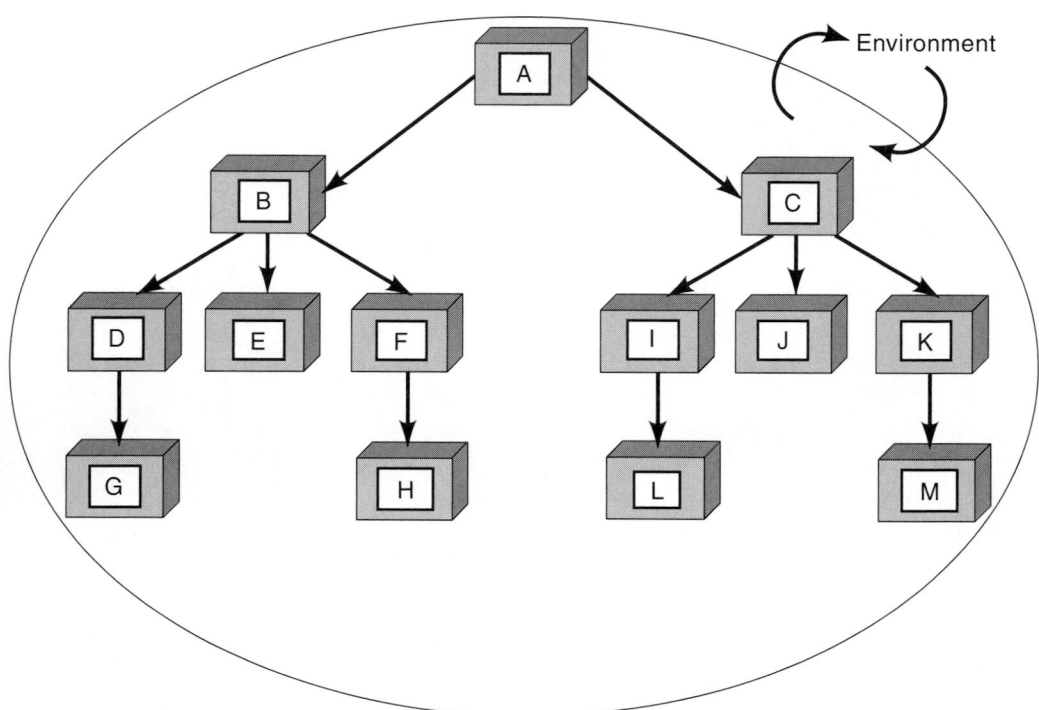

FIGURE 23–14
System Testing

As shown in Figure 23–15, developing an operational profile to guide system testing involves a minimum of five steps. Table 23–2 shows the step, responsibility, perspective, and project phase where it initially occurs. Each profile before the operational has a user or customer perspective, while the operational profile has a system perspective. This system perspective can be thought of as an inside-out view of how the product is to perform. As a paradigm for system testing, the operational profile provides the actual usage scenarios, the precise input provided by the user, the exact resultant outputs or responses from the system, the internal partitioning of processing space, and the probabilities of these scenarios occurring.

Regression Tests   Regression testing is the re-execution of a subset of tests that have already been conducted, to ensure that recent changes to the software have not propagated unintended side effects. Regression tests repeat the input states or test cases used in system tests. This repetition is necessary because systems are rarely stable—just as freshly developed code is imperfect, so is changed code. Changes can unintentionally introduce erroneous functionality or additional errors. Whenever software is changed, a battery of regression tests is run to ensure that it still runs like it did, except for the changes made.

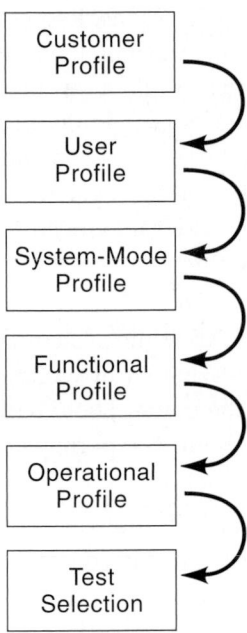

FIGURE 23–15
Operational Profile

TABLE 23–2
Operational Profile/Responsibility/Perspective/Project Phase

Step	Profile	Responsibility	Perspective	Project Phase
1	Customer	Marketing	User	Requirements Gathering
2	User	Marketing/ Analysts	User	Requirements Gathering
3	System-Mode	User/Marketing/ Analysts	User	Requirements Gathering
4	Functional	User/Analysts/ Designers	User	Requirements Analysis
5	Operational	Designers/ Testers	System	Design

Once a system has been placed in use, it can be the basis for testing modifications. Regression tests ensure that production systems do not have errors introduced during the maintenance phase when enhancements are made or bugs are fixed. A regression test is simply a test that was run during the system's development, together with a fixed test bed of data known to exercise the software's limits, thresholds, and rules. When the regression test suite is run and the results produce the expected output, confidence in the reliability of the system is improved. When major enhancements are made, the regression test suite itself may need to be modified, to correctly and completely test all functionality, old and new.

Alpha and Beta Testing   Alpha testing typically refers to the first time the system is turned on, at the developer's site, to be tested by the user. Clearly, involvement of willing customers can be a benefit to a new release of software at this point in the game. There will almost certainly be some programming changes to be made following the tests—perhaps a few design changes, but hopefully no requirements changes.

Beta testing follows alpha testing and is also tested by "friendly users," but at the customer's site. Customers validate their usage of the product through normal, everyday use. At this point, the system should be stabilizing, but a few program changes may be needed.

Alpha and beta testing may produce growing confidence in the product and success stories, as well as lessons learned and refinements to the system. The completion of these tests is a natural progression into user acceptance testing.

Rex Black tells us that system testing can *begin* when the problem/test tracking systems are in place; all components are under formal configuration and release management control; target hardware components and subsystems have been configured; the development team has unit tested all features scheduled for release; a minimum number (agreed upon by sales, marketing, and customer service) of high-priority bugs are still open, and a target date has been set for their fix; the test team completes a "smoke test"; and the project management team agrees to proceed into the system testing phase (all entry criteria are met). System testing *continues* as long as release notes are written, bug reports accompany all changes, the open-bug backlog (quality gap) remains less than the minimum number of high-priority bugs, and the daily and rolling closure periods remain less than two weeks. System test *ends* when no changes have occurred in the past three weeks, no crashes have occurred, the development team has resolved all high-priority bugs, the test team has closed or deferred all issues in the bug tracking system verified by regression testing, and an open/close curve indicates product stability and reliability.[22]

Now that the standard repertoire of tests have been listed and briefly defined, let's return to white-box testing.

White-Box Testing with Chapin Charts and Directed Flow Graphs   There are many ways to depict the design of a software unit so that structural testing is simplified. The graphical design of the program is usually created and tested in a static peer review before coding. Upon acceptance of the design, the code is written, compiled, and sometimes inspected via another static peer review. At this point, the design will ensure a modular, structured, maintainable (easy to fix errors), modifiable (easy to make changes), readable unit and will also point out the places where a structural test should take place.

Chapin charts, also known as Nassi-Scheiderman charts, were described in Chapter 22. These charts are an excellent design tool for eliminating arbitrary transfers of control, which lead to complex "spaghetti code" and for understanding how many test cases are necessary and where they should be applied.

The philosophy is that only five basic constructs can make up a software unit, no matter what type of application, real-time embedded space station or information-intensive payroll, and no matter what programming language. The constructs are: simple sequence, if-then-else, do-while, do-until, and do-case.

Figure 23–16 is a simple example of how the structures are put together to form the design of a program, which may be reviewed, coded from, and used to place test cases.

Note that each block has a single entry point and a single exit point, forcing the structure of the entire program to avoid unnecessary branching (transfer of control or "GOTO") and reducing complexity. As long as the program design follows this building-block approach, nested iteration and decision symbols will cause the blocks to become increasingly smaller.

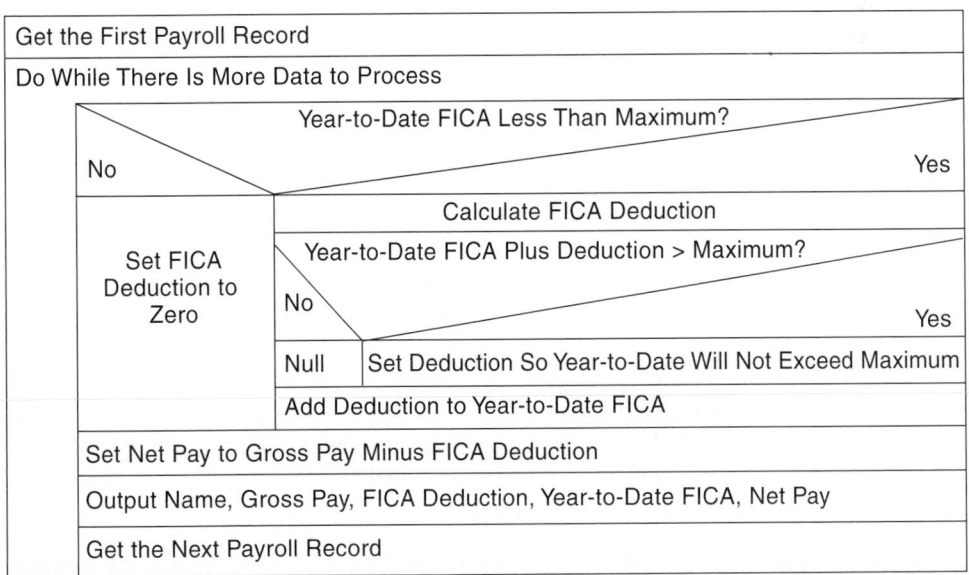

FIGURE 23–16

Example of a Chapin Chart Used to Pinpoint Test Placement

To ensure a properly sized "chunk" of processing suitable to become one program unit, a good rule of thumb is to contain the Chapin chart to one 8×11-inch page.

Programmers who first learn to design programs with these symbols never develop the bad habits that other flowchart notation systems permit. No more than fifteen or twenty symbols can be drawn on a single sheet of paper, so the programmer must modularize this program into meaningful sections. The temptation to use off-page connectors, which lead only to confusion, is eliminated. Finally, the ease with which a structured flowchart can be translated into a structured program is pleasantly surprising.[23]

The N-S chart can be used as a guide while testing the module. The number of test cases that will be required may be readily determined by counting decision blocks (count two per decision) and iteration blocks (count two or three per loop, depending on boundary conditions of the loop). The precise test cases needed and data required may be developed directly from the charts, and the tested paths may be checked off on the charts as tests are executed.[24]

If a module is complex, it may call for another step to refine the program design. The Chapin chart used in Figure 23–16 would suffice for a design review, a document from which to code, and a document from which the test cases could be produced. If complexity is a factor, then a more precise Chapin chart would be more appropriate for coding and testing activities. The complexity of the chart is usually directly related to the risk assumed with the software product—the reliability of mission-critical systems where human lives are at stake necessitates more complexity.

Directed Flow Graph: McCabe Cyclomatic Complexity Analysis

Thomas McCabe devised another widely used approach to graphically mapping the design of a module so that test points may be identified. Just as Nassi, Schneiderman, and Chapin concentrated on basic constructs, McCabe referred to his "graph theory" as edges (connections) between nodes (executable instructions or pseudocode). Similar to Chapin, McCabe calls the constructs: sequence, if-then-else, if-then, do-while, case, and repeat-until.

The constructs are shown in Figure 23–17.

Thomas McCabe devised a method of graphically mapping the design of a module so that test points may be identified. McCabe referred to his graph theory as edges (connections) between nodes (executable instructions or pseudocode). Similar to Chapin charts, McCabe's method utilizes the five basic constructs shown in Chapter 22.

McCabe calls his measure a complexity metric, which serves the function of establishing a value of complexity for an individual unit. Organizations may determine an acceptable threshold of complexity, rate each unit, and peg the more complex ones to receive extra

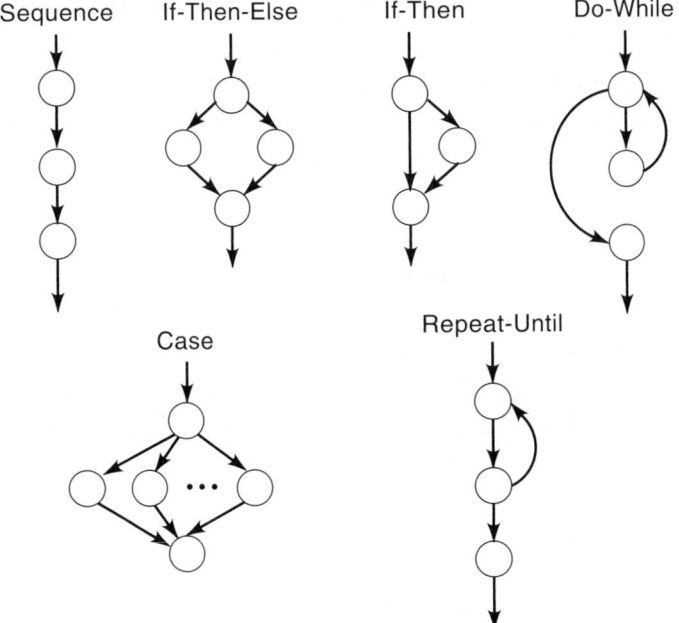

FIGURE 23–17
Graph Theory Constructs

review and testing attention. For example, if an organization determines that the complexity metric for each unit on a specific project, using Java, should be 30 for an understandable, maintainable Java system, and if there are five JavaScripts that exceed 90, then those five might be candidates to be split into smaller modules, to receive more documentation, or to undergo extra peer reviews. McCabe metrics for an entire system are often displayed, Pareto style, to develop a monotonically decreasing histogram of module complexity values. Then it becomes easy to identify the 20% of the system that is the most complex and will probably cause 80% of the problems, and take corrective action. Studies have shown that there is a direct relationship between the complexity of a system and the cost to maintain and enhance that system, making worthwhile the time spent in identification and correction.[25]

Although the complexity metric is useful in pointing out areas of concern, it is also useful in producing test cases. To calculate a complexity metric, a flow graph must be produced. Once the flow graph exists, the paths through the program become apparent; those paths provide the knowledge of variable settings required to execute them. In this material, flow graph theory will be presented and methods of calculating complexity metrics by manual means will be discussed. These are just simplified examples, of course. For large projects, automated tools are available to perform the calculations. For small projects, probably only a small number of modules, suspected to be complex, would be manually examined. The thoroughness of testing depends on the quality and reliability requirements of the system. Figure 23–18 shows a simple flow graph.

There are three ways to determine the index or complexity metric of a flow graph:

1. Edges – nodes + 2
2. Count of regions
3. Predicate nodes + 1

To calculate this index manually on a large program would be a daunting task. Fortunately, there are automated tools that will compute McCabe's complexity metric by analyzing existing source code.

The complexity metric is not only useful in pointing out areas of concern, but it is also useful in producing test cases. Once the flow graph exists, the paths through the program become apparent and provide the knowledge required to execute them in a test.

Edges – Nodes + 2

The number of edges are the vectors or arrows in Figure 23–19, which is 9. The dotted-line edge branching back to the beginning of the program or entry node is added because the graph is "strongly connected"; there is a path joining any pair of arbitrary distinct vertices. In other words, the program is re-entrant and may always be started over. This tenth edge is not included in the basic count.

Applying McCabe's process to Figure 23–19:

C (complexity) = edges – nodes + 2

The number of nodes is the number of circles, or 6 (a, b, c, d, e, f).

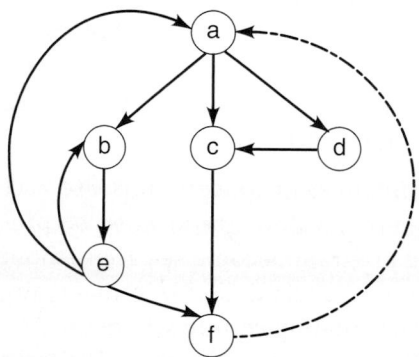

FIGURE 23–18
A Simple Flow Graph

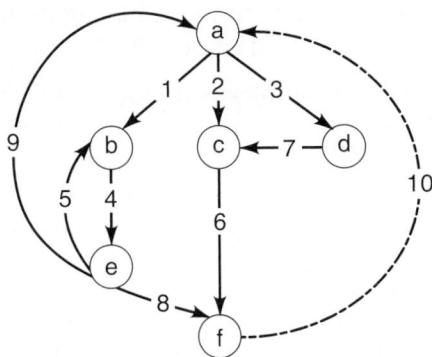

FIGURE 23–19
McCabe: Complexity—Nodes and Edges

The number 2 is added because the graph is planer (two dimensions).

The complexity is then $9 - 6 + 2 = 5$.

Count of Bounded Regions

In Figure 23–20, the regions are counted. A region is a bounded area, with the tenth vector included. Again, the complexity metric is 5.

Predicate Nodes + 1

As shown in Figure 23–21, a predicate node is defined as one having two or more exit points. A sum of (number of exit points minus 1) for each predicate node, plus 1, will also provide the

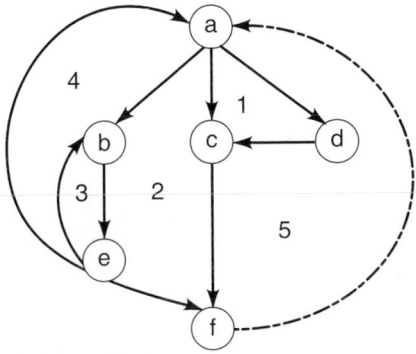

FIGURE 23–20
McCabe: Complexity—Regions

complexity metric. In this example, the nodes a and e are predicate nodes, each having three exit points. Exit points minus 1 results in the value of 2 for both a and e. Thus, $C = 2 + 2 + 1 = 5$.

What does all this mean for testing? It is valuable because the complexity metric, C, which may be derived any of three different ways, indicates the number of test cases that will test all paths through the module. All possible paths through the module should be tested to uncover errors or unexpected results for complex modules or modules of high importance (perhaps human life is at stake, such as software controlling hospital equipment). C may be derived from existing code in any language, or it may be calculated from a design document such as a Chapin chart or a flow graph.

Module design via Chapin charts or flow graphs has a side benefit in that nonstructured modules are discovered. Unstructured units may have their C calculated by the edges – nodes + 2 formula (it is usually a high number), but they become "nonplaner" and cannot be assessed by a count of regions. Figure 23–22 shows an unstructured flow graph. Work by McCabe relies on "essential complexity which collapses regions of nodes and edges, with single-entry and single-exit points, into larger abstract nodes. Ultimately, a well-structured module may be collapsed into one giant node." [26] Figure 23–23 shows such a module.

Figure 23–23 shows a structured module that is complex (C = 20), but the essential complexity (EC) = 1. Figure 23–24 shows a smaller module with a lower complexity metric (C = 18), fewer nodes and edges, but a high essential complexity (EC = 17). Clearly, the module in Figure 23–24 will not only be easier to completely test, but it will also be easier to modify when fixing bugs or making enhancements.

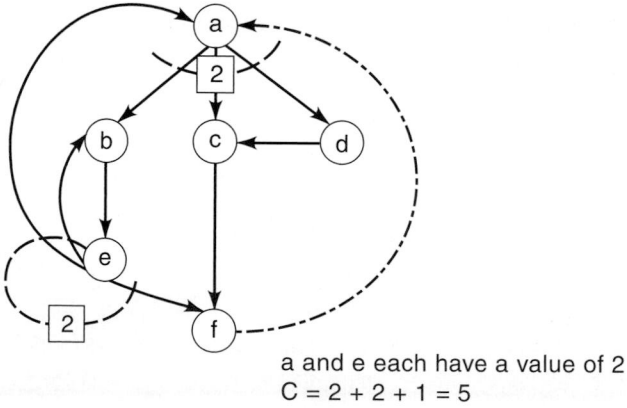

a and e each have a value of 2
C = 2 + 2 + 1 = 5

FIGURE 23–21
McCabe: Complexity—Predicate Nodes

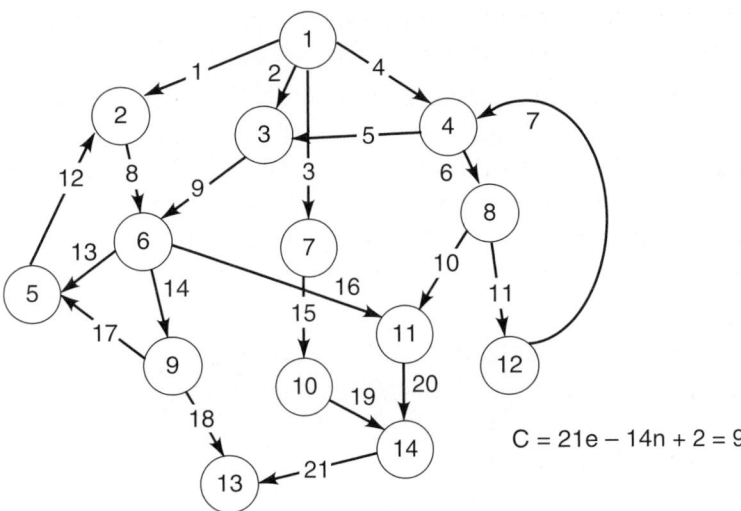

$$C = 21e - 14n + 2 = 9$$

FIGURE 23-22
An Unstructured Flow Graph

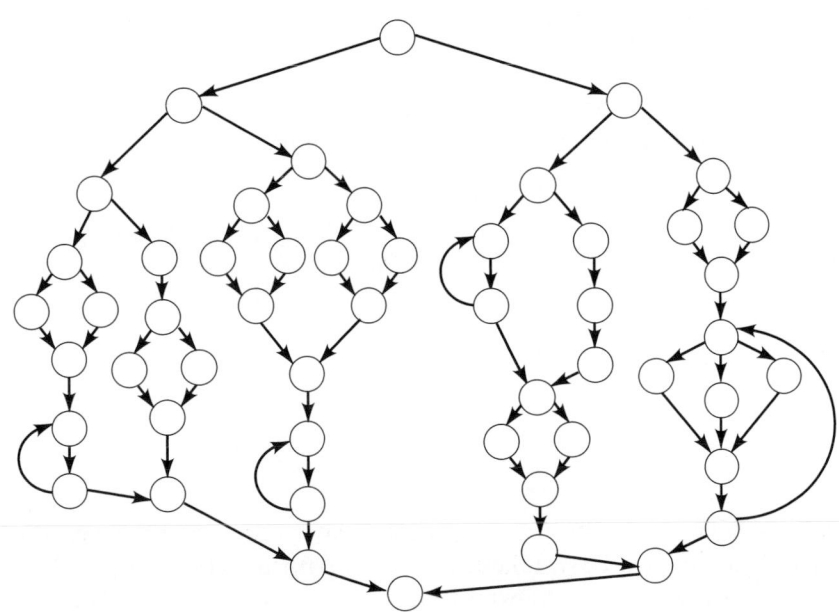

FIGURE 23-23
A Structured Flow Graph with EC = 1

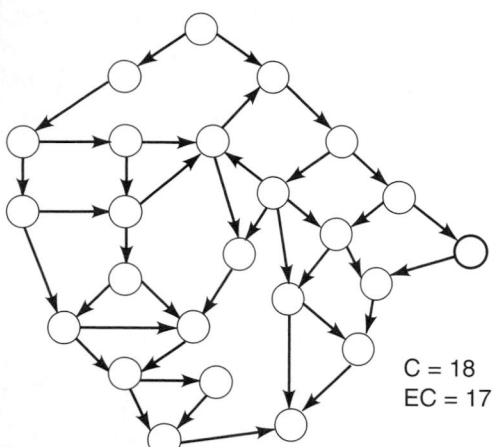

C = 18
EC = 17

FIGURE 23–24
An Unstructured Flow Graph with EC > 1

If each path through the programs is followed at least once, a certain quality assurance level may be reached. This minimal number of independent paths does not represent all possible test scenarios; testing them will by no means guarantee or prove the software, but it can surface more bugs and improve the quality.

Test data can be used with various values that will force the program to follow each path at least once, providing that a good minimal quality assurance level may be reached.

In Figure 23–18, the paths through the module are:

a,c,f,a (the shortest path)

a,d,c,f,a

a,b,e,f,a

a,b,e,b,e,f,a

a,b,e,a,c,f,a

Together, these paths are known as the "basis set." An easy way to construct this set is to flip the switches on the predicate nodes: First, take the shortest path through the program. Next, from the bottom, work backward to the most recent predicate node and take another exit. Do until all exits have been taken. Finally, repeat the whole process, shifting emphasis from the control flow to data flow.

Now the emphasis shifts from the issue of control flow to data flow—it is data behavior that either precludes or makes realizable the execution of any particular control path.

It is often difficult, if not impossible, to obtain 100% path coverage on all modules. If there are many modules with many paths, testing will take too long this way. Other types of white-box or structural testing that will exercise a module less stringently but still provide some confidence in reliability are the statement coverage, decision coverage, condition coverage, decision/condition, and multiple condition.

Statement Coverage

Every statement in the module is executed in the test environment at least once.

This short sample segment of pseudocode

```
        IF A AND B
                Then GO TO 10
        ENDIF
5       X = Y + Z
        IF C = 3
        .
        .
        .
```

must be tested such that:

1. (A and B) is evaluated as true at least once:
   A = true, B = true, and

2. (A and B) is evaluated as false at least once:
   One of the following:
   A = true, B = false or
   A = false, B = true.

Decision Coverage

Statement coverage is satisfied, and each branch of each decision is taken at least once.

This short sample segment of pseudocode

```
IF A OR B THEN
        X = Y + Z
ELSE
        X = U + V
```

```
ENDIF
     .
     .
     .
```

must be tested such that:

1. (A or B) is evaluated as true at least once:
   A = true, B = true, or
   A = true, B = false, or
   A = false, B = true, and
2. (A or B) is evaluated as false at least once:
   A = false, B = false.

Condition Coverage

Decisions are executed so that each condition takes on every possible value at least once.

This short sample segment of pseudocode

```
IF  A  AND  B  AND  C  THEN
        X  =  Y  +  Z
ELSE
        X  =  U  +  V
ENDIF
        .
        .
        .
```

must be tested with each condition (A,B,C) true once and false once:

A true once and A false once, and

B true once and B false once, and

C true once and C false once.

Any one of these four sets of tests would be sufficient:

A = true, B = true, C = true

A = false, B = false, C = false

A = true, B = true, C = false

A = false, B = false, C = true

A = true, B = false, C = true

A = false, B = true, C = false

A = true, B = false, C = false

A = false, B = true, C = true.

Decision/Condition Coverage

Condition coverage is satisfied, and each decision takes on all possible outcomes at least once.

This same sample segment of pseudocode

```
IF A AND B AND C THEN

     X = Y + Z

ELSE

     X = U + V

ENDIF

     .

     .

     .
```

must be tested such that:

1. (A and B and C) is evaluated as true at least once:
   A = true, B = true, C = true, and
2. (A and B and C) is evaluated as false at least once:
   One of the following:

   A = true, B = true, C = false

   A = true, B = false, C = true

   A = true, B = false, C = false

   A = false, B = true, C = true

   A = false, B = true, C = false

   A = false, B = false, C = true

   A = false, B = false, C = false

Note that, for this simple example, only two tests—A = true, B = true, C = true, and A = false, B = false, C = false—will satisfy statement, decision, condition, and decision condition coverage. This is not always the case.

Multiple-Condition Coverage

Decision coverage is satisfied, and each decision is executed so that all possible combinations of conditions are exercised.

This same sample segment of pseudocode

```
IF A AND B AND C THEN
        X = Y + Z
ELSE
        X = U + V
ENDIF
        .
        .
        .
```

must be tested with all of the following:

A = true, B = true, C = true

A = true, B = true, C = false

A = true, B = false, C = true

A = true, B = false, C = false

A = false, B = true, C = true

A = false, B = true, C = false

A = false, B = false, C = true

A = false, B = false, C = false

In summary, suppose that our example had been the following:

```
IF (A AND B AND C) GO TO 110
        X = Y + Z
DO CASE . . .
```

Table 23–3 shows the difference in the number and type of test cases to achieve different levels of coverage, depending on quality requirements.

TABLE 23–3
Types of Tests to Achieve Levels of Coverage

	100 IF (A AND B AND C) GO TO 110	
	X = Y + Z	
	110 DO CASE . . .	
Type of Coverage	Guidelines for Achieving the Coverage	Test Cases That Would Achieve the Coverage
Statement	Exercise all statements at least once	A = true, B = true, C = false
Decision	1. Statement coverage is satisfied	1. A = true, B = true, C = true
	2. Exercise all possible outcomes of decisions at least once	2. A = true, B = true, C = false
Simple Condition	Conditions take on all possible values at least once	1. A = false, B = true, C = true
		2. A = true, B = false, C = false
Decision Condition	1. Simple condition coverage is satisfied	1. A = true, B = true, C = true
	2. Conditions take on all possible values at least once	2. A = false, B = false, C = false
	3. Decisions take on all possible outcomes at least once	
Multiple Condition	Decision condition coverage is satisfied	1. A = true, B = true, C = true
		2. A = true, B = true, C = false
		3. A = true, B = false, C = true
		4. A = true, B = false, C = false
	Conditions assume all possible combinations	5. A = false, B = true, C = true
		6. A = false, B = true, C = false
		7. A = false, B = false, C = true
		8. A = false, B = false, C = false

Again, two tests—A = true, B = true, C = true, and A = false, B = false, C = false—would satisfy the first four types, while a multiple condition requires eight tests.

The order in which they appear represents the weakest to the strongest coverage.

User Acceptance and Usability Testing

User acceptance testing (UAT), considered to be the last step before final product release, has been in play for many years. Sometimes it becomes synonymous with beta testing, which is also conducted at the user site. UAT reaches a wide audience of users, allowing the development team to get feedback on how well the system really meets user expectations and how readily the users take to it.

Usability testing, which often precedes UAT, is a relatively new concept. It was introduced as a formal procedure in the late 1980s and began to achieve widespread use in the mid-1990s. Usability testing is typically conducted in a laboratory where users perform normal tasks and usability specialists record observations. It is a technology-driven approach in that screen images of the application under evaluation are videoed, as are the user's body language and hand movements. Users also provide feedback in the form of satisfaction ratings and comments/suggestions on an evaluation form.

One of the toughest aspects of usability testing is how to define and measure "usability." An accepted definition is the perception of the user of the ease, speed, and pleasantness of the application. *Ease* refers to effortlessness of learning and of use; *speed* means that the users don't feel that they waste time waiting for the system to respond; *pleasantness* is just that—if the tool gets in the way or is frustrating, then the experience of using it isn't very pleasant. Even though the software is feature-rich and of high quality, poor usability will discredit it. And rightly so—software with low usability marks makes the user unproductive and error-prone. Of course, we cannot simply say, "The software must have high usability ratings," because that is not a testable requirement. Adding specificity to the term, so that we know what and how to test, the attributes that make software "usable" are something like the following: Users feel that their actions are natural; dialog flow is intuitive and quick, providing adequate feedback; screen context and organization is well designed, including attention to layout and menu names; and user documentation is readily available and thorough. Working our way toward measurability and testability, the next step in usability testing is to define even more specific goals. The term *quick* in the attribute description above might become, "Average time for users to complete <name of task> should be less than 30 seconds."

Once goals are set, usability tests are constructed—test scenarios for the users to follow. The testing laboratory is prepared to support the systematic study of human-computer interaction. It will include a test section where the users sit; a control section for the usability specialists, who may choose to mix the video sources from screen images and those from body language videos; and the observation section, where usability specialists and perhaps other observers, such as members of the development team, watch the test, usually through a one-way glass.

Usability Requirements

Some usability requirements that the testing team may want to focus on as goals, once they are defined in measurable terms, include these:

- Keep users informed about what is going on, through appropriate and timely feedback.
- Speak user-familiar language.
- Provide a way to exit an unwanted state arrived at by mistake; support undo and redo.
- Keep the screen "clean" by hiding rarely used functions or moving them to a separate screen.
- Follow operating system platform naming conventions.
- Make objects, actions, and options visible—don't expect the user to remember information from one part of the dialog to another.
- Design dialog boxes to be usable, with clear choices.
- Make instructions for use of the system visible or easily retrievable.
- Allow the expert user to tailor frequent actions via "accelerators."
- Make all dialogs succinct.
- Express error messages in plain language—don't use codes that are meaningless to the user.
- Constructively suggest a solution when a problem is encountered.
- Provide help and documentation in an easily searchable form that is pertinent to the user's task, listing concrete steps.

Users Talk Back

The following statements illustrate actual usability feedback from users:

- "When a test application bombs, a red window requests that I close the application for the process to continue. This window has only a close box in the upper-right corner. So I close the window and, before I can barely move the pointer, another window of the same type opens—so now I have to close this one, too. I have found that the only way to continue is to employ the 'Vulcan Death Grip' (Ctrl-Alt-Del)."
- "Please tell what it is supposed to do! Make it a standard that appears in both the Help Index and in the About section. There are always plenty of instructions on how to install software, and sometimes there are adequate instructions on how to use it, but there is almost never a description of what it is and why it will help you."
- "The latest released version of the application has many more features, but the newer ones just seem to have been affixed to the previous version of the program without any thought as to the increased confusion they bring to the user interface."

Entire books exist on how to avoid eliciting bad impressions from the user. Many of them are listed in the reference section.

Usability testing fits nicely within a software prototyping environment, as described in Chapter 4. Prototyping encourages the tests to begin quite early, allowing problems to be found and fixed long before the system or UAT phases.

The Ideal Test Coverage

If V&V could be perfected on a software project, all technical quality characteristics would be met. It would mean that each of those characteristics could be defined in testable, measurable terms (not a simple task, as we have seen). In fact, when three of the most respected viewpoints are considered together, they cover dozens of attributes, as shown in Table 23–4.

TABLE 23–4
Software Quality Characteristics

Quality Characteristic	ISO/IEC 9126-1991	IEEE Standard 1061-1992	FURPSI (Krasner [1999]/Grady [1992])
Efficiency			
Time Behavior	X	X (Time Economy)	
Resource Utilization	X	X (Resource Economy)	
Functionality			
Accuracy	X		
Adequacy			X
Compatibility		X	
Completeness		X	
Compliance	X		
Correctness		X	X
Customizability			X
Evolvability			X
Extensiveness			X
Interoperability	X	X	

(Continues)

TABLE 23–4 (Continued)
Software Quality Characteristics

Quality Characteristic	ISO/IEC 9126-1991	IEEE Standard 1061-1992	FURPSI (Krasner [1999]/Grady [1992])
Security	X	X	
Suitability	X		
Value/Satisfaction			X
Integratability			
Applicability			X
Compatibility			X
Evolvability			X
Expressability			X
Integrity			X
Openness			X
Quality of the Parts			X
Requirements Enabler			X
Special Topics			X
Maintainability			
Analyzability	X		
Changeability	X		
Correctability		X	
Expandability		X	
Stability	X		
Testability	X	X	
Performance			
Time-Constrained			X
Resource-Constrained			X
Portability			
Adaptability	X		
Installability	X	X	
Conformance	X		

(Continues)

TABLE 23–4 (Continued)
Software Quality Characteristics

Quality Characteristic	ISO/IEC 9126-1991	IEEE Standard 1061-1992	FURPSI (Krasner [1999]/Grady [1992])
Hardware Independence		X	
Software Independence		X	
Reusability		X	
Replaceability	X		
Reliability			
Availability		X	X
Failure Rate	X		
Fault Tolerance	X	X	X
Maturity			X
Nondeficiency		X	
Recoverability	X		X
Supportability			
Maintainable			X
Reusable			X
Support Response			X
Testable			X
Usability			
Understandability	X	X	X
Learnability	X	X	X (Easy to Learn and Use)
Communicativeness		X	X
Operability	X	X	X (Easy to Operate)

These quality factors, which we would like to test as if they are firm requirements, include ISO 9126, the IEEE Standard 1061, and FURPS (Functionality, Usability, Reliability, Performance, Supportability, and Integratability), from Grady,[27] later expanded by Krasner[28] to be

FURPSI (Integratability was added). They are fundamentally based on the McCall quality model from 1977,[29] which was organized around three types of quality characteristics:

- Factors (to specify): They describe the external view of the software, as viewed by the users.
- Criteria (to build): They describe the internal view of the software, as seen by the developer.
- Metrics (to control): They are defined and used to provide a scale and method for measurement.

As the need for one recognized standard quality model became important, many gravitated to the ISO/IEC 9126 standard. As with McCall's, this is also based on three levels:

- Characteristics (functionality, reliability, usability, efficiency, maintainability, portability)
- Subcharacteristics
- Metrics

Each characteristic is refined to a set of subcharacteristics, and each subcharacteristic is evaluated by a set of metrics. Halstead[30] and McCabe have also contributed to the field of software measurement, and many of the metrics for code analysis comes from their studies.

Examples of subcharacteristics and corresponding metrics follow:

- **Analyzability**—Cyclomatic complexity number; number of statements; comments rate; number of calls
- **Changeability**—Number of GOTOs; number of nested levels; average size of statement; number of variables
- **Stability**—Number of parameters referenced; number of global variables; number of parameters changed; number of called relationships
- **Testability**—Number of noncyclic paths; number of nested levels; cyclomatic complexity index; number of module-call-paths

A study by Shafer and Connell at Los Alamos National Laboratory showed that program complexity contributed directly to high maintenance costs and that the most expensive complexity characteristics were GOTOs, number of calls, meaningless variable names, and sheer size.[31]

A project called the "Software Assessment and Certification Programme in Europe" (SCOPE) defined an evaluation process, parts of which found their way to ISO 14598. They selected evaluation levels of software risks to be of four major types: Level D, small damage to property, no risk to people; Level C, damage to property, few people disabled; Level B, threat to human lives; and Level A, many people killed. As risks increase due to nonconformity of the product to a quality characteristic, a more stringent level is selected. The levels are selected independently for each relevant quality characteristic and show what testing mechanisms can be used for each. As can be seen in Table 23–5, we cover many of the techniques that a PM needs to know about in this chapter, but there are many more and more stringent ones available.[32]

TABLE 23–5
SCOPE Evaluation

	Level D	Level C	Level B	Level A
Functionality	Functional testing (black box)	Review (check lists)	Component testing (glass box)	Formal proof
Reliability	Programming language facilities	Fault tolerance analysis	Reliability growth model	Formal proof
Usability	User interface inspection	Conformity to interface standards	Laboratory testing	User mental model
Efficiency	Execution time measurement	Benchmark testing	Algorithmic complexity	Performance profiling analysis
Maintainability	Inspection of documents (checklists)	Static analysis	Analysis of development process	Traceability evaluation
Portability	Analysis of installation	Conformity to programming rules	Environment constraints evaluation	Program design evaluation

In a perfect world, all tests would be executed. In the real world, the project manager must select the appropriate ones, thereby testing "smart."

The Testing Process

Testing should begin only when certain activities are complete and the foundation has been laid.

Preparing for Testing   The following items are indicators of testing readiness:

- Requirements (SRS), functional design (SDD), and internal design (Chapin charts, flow graphs) specifications are complete, approved, and available.
- Budget and schedule requirements are published; schedule estimates, timelines, and milestones have been set.
- The test plan has been written, reviewed, and approved.
- Standards and processes (such as release and change processes) are documented.

- The project team has been assembled, had their responsibilities assigned, and been trained on standards and processes.
- The high-risk aspects of the system have been identified.
- Priorities and the scope and limitations of tests have been determined.
- Test approaches and methods have been identified—how will the test be conducted, by whom, and when, for unit (white box), integration (black box), functional, system, usability, and so on.
- Test environment requirements have been satisfied (hardware, operating systems, configuration management, communications, etc.).
- Supporting software requirements (i.e., coverage analyzers, problem tracking, record/ playback tools) have been determined.
- Test input data requirements have been determined; test input data has been obtained.
- Input equivalence classes, boundary value analysis, and error classes have been determined.
- Test cases have been written, reviewed, and approved.

Static testing (reviews) can be used in preparing for dynamic testing. For example, a software test procedure might be reviewed using the following as a partial checklist:

- Have both white- and black-box tests been specified?
- Have all the independent logic paths been tested?
- Have test cases been identified and listed with their expected results?
- Is error handling to be tested?
- Are boundary values to be tested?
- Are timing and performance to be tested?
- Has an acceptable variation from the expected results been specified?

Testing   During the testing activity itself, the tests are performed and the results are evaluated and reported; test cases, bugs, and fixes are tracked and managed; bugs are characterized and isolated; retesting occurs, where needed; and documents are maintained (test plans, test cases, the test environment, testing software). A test execution and release schedule is established, and processes for installing a new build and removing a bad build are documented.

When a bug is found during testing, the debugging process begins separate from testing. A problem identified by a test must be recorded and communicated to (assigned to) developers so that it can be removed from the software. The developer locates the problem, isolates it, resolves it, and submits it to the test team to be retested. Retesting includes regression testing to ensure that the fix didn't cause a problem elsewhere in the software. (Remember that low coupling and high cohesion reduce this "ripple" or "domino" effect.)

Careful record keeping via a problem reporting system should take place in every step. Information recorded usually includes when the bug was discovered, where and how it was found (what test case), and how it can be reproduced; its severity is recorded by the tester. This data is typically recorded in an automated bug tracking system and includes: an identifier; status (newly discovered bug, released for retest, etc.); the system/application name, identifier, and version; the subsystem/module where the problem was found; a description of the environment; the test case name, number, and identifier; a full description; how to reproduce it; additional information that might help the developer, such as screen shots and error messages; estimate of severity; and tester name, test date, and report date.

Post-Testing   Information recorded when the problem is resolved includes the name of the developer, the cause of the problem, a description of the fix, the component of the system where changes were made, the date, and the version of the system.

Information recorded when the problem is retested includes the name of the tester, the retest date, the retest results, regression tests, and regression test results.

Testing Teams

Organizing for testing is another area where the software project manager must make decisions. There has been a long-standing debate over the best way. Some experts advocate an independent test group to perform IV&V functions using employees rather than contractors. Others feel that the test team needs to be a part of the project team.

In selecting a testing organizational model, there is a skills-based approach, in which a tester with specific skills works for a test manager who assigns the tester to one or more projects in a matrix organization. This has advantages in that the tester has the opportunity to become a true specialist in one area and make that expertise available across projects. The disadvantages are that the tester may be uncertain about where to spend time, and project managers may be wary about getting "their share" of the resource.

Another organizational model is the project-based model, which assigns a testing team to each project. This approach allows the testing team to share in the project vision and become dedicated to its success. In terms of team building, this is a better choice. A potential risk with the project-based model is that the testers may become too close to the developers and succumb to compromising stringent testing principles.

There is an anecdote about a testing team at IBM that became known as "the Black Team" because they wore black capes, grew moustaches (which they twisted), and reveled in their reputation as evil destroyers of software. Not only did they have a lot of fun, but the competition between them and the developers was a boon to project quality. Developers strove to produce a product that the Black Team could not break, and the team was intent on preserving its standing. It would be great if all teams could develop into such "performing" groups. Doubtless, having a shared vision of the mission is a cornerstone of team building.

In selecting test engineers for either organizational approach, the PM will be looking for basic testing skills, an attention to detail, a curious mind, as well as a commitment to testing as a respected professional specialty. The more domain knowledge a tester possesses, the more effective he can be. The project manager would do well to keep in mind that a successful test is one that finds a defect and should not become discouraged or look disparagingly upon the tester who brings "bad news" (don't shoot the messenger). The failures that are uncovered are still within a safe environment and are really "good news" in that they have not yet reached the customer.

Test Documentation

This chapter has presented a sampling of widely used techniques for testing. It is by no means comprehensive. Many other types of testing may be performed, including cause and effect, error guessing, conversion, security, recovery, performance (stress), and more. All testing items are also configuration items that should be managed under configuration control. For example, regression test cases must be archived with the software version that they were built to test. What's more, there should exist a full set of test documentation that is kept in synch with the software. How do these tests get executed? Where are they stored? How is the test environment set up? IEEE offers standards for software test documentation and suggests that the basic documents include these:[33]

- A test plan to prescribe the scope, approach, resources, and schedule of the testing activities to identify the items being tested, the features to be tested, the testing tasks to be performed, the personnel responsible for each task, and the risks associated with this plan
- A test design specification to specify refinements of the test approach and to identify the features to be tested by its design and its associated tests
- A test case specification to define a test case identified by a test-design specification
- A test procedure specification to specify the steps for executing a set of test cases or, more generally, the steps used to analyze a software item to evaluate a set of features
- A test item transmittal report to identify the test items being transmitted for testing
- A test log to provide a chronological record of relevant details about the execution of tests
- A test incident report to document any event that occurs during the testing process that requires investigation
- A test summary report to summarize the results of the designated testing activities and to provide evaluations based on these results.

Dynamic Testing: Measurement, Reporting, and Decision Making _____

Some of the reports delivered to the software project manager during the testing phase include these:

- Defect find-and-close rates by week, normalized against the level of effort (are we finding defects, and can developers keep up with the number found and the ones necessary to fix?)
- Number of tests planned, run, passed by week (do we know what we have to test, and are we able to do so?)
- Defects found per activity compared to the total defects found (which activities find the most defects?)
- Schedule estimates versus the actuals (will we make the dates, and how well do we estimate?)
- People on the project, planned versus actual by week or month (do we have the people we need when we need them?)
- Major and minor requirements changes (do we know what we have to do, and does it change?)

Project managers have to make a couple of particularly tough decisions during testing: what to do if there isn't enough time for thorough testing and how to know when it is time to stop testing.

There never seems to be enough time to test as thoroughly as we would like. Back to the concept of "testing smart, not hard," knowing where to expend testing time is best governed by risk analysis. The PM may consider which functionality is most important to the project's intended purpose, is most visible to the user, has the biggest safety impact, and has the largest financial impact on users. All aspects of the application that can be tested early in the development cycle via prototyping, reviews, or usability testing should be. Focus should be placed on the parts of the system that are the most complex (have the most complex interfaces or algorithms). If any parts of the system were developed in a hurry, they are likely to be error-prone and should undergo testing. According to Pareto analysis of previous projects, concentrate testing on the troublesome areas. According to maintenance (change request) logs, find which aspects of similar or related projects had high maintenance expense, and go after those areas. Ask the developers for their opinion of what the highest risk areas might be. Employ tests that serve double duty by covering multiple functionalities.

It can be difficult to determine when to stop testing. The decision may be driven by deadlines or the testing budget, of course, but it is better to stop testing when reliability, functionality, and quality standards have been met. The PM who set goals early on, in the SPMP and in the test plan, will know when the required test cases have been executed and the required number has been passed, when the desired code coverage has been achieved, and when the bug rate falls below the acceptable level; the goals will be quantified.

Testing Metrics

As was discussed in Chapter 21, software measurements are the key to project management tracking and control. Here are some data that the PM will most likely be interested in tracking:

- How many faults are found in each phase?
- What type of faults are they?
- How many faults are defects? Errors?
- How many bug reports have been opened versus the number that has been closed? The cumulative opened curve flattens, and the cumulative closed curve converges to the cumulative open curve as the system under test stabilizes, the test system finds the identifiable bugs, and the quality gap closes.
- What does root cause analysis reveal about injected defects? What causes them, and how can the process be changed?

When tests fail, the problem may be with the test rather than with the software. Reviews of test plans, test cases, and test scenarios are as important as reviews of design documents.

As with review data, test information is gathered at the time of the event. Both severity and priority is recorded, just as it is for errors and defects discovered during a review.

Severity refers to the impact on the system under test. A typical enumerated data set for severity follows:

1. Data loss, hardware damage, or safety risk
2. Loss of functionality without workaround
3. Loss of functionality with workaround
4. Partial loss of a function or a feature set
5. A cosmetic error

Priority refers to marketing importance, likely loss of revenue. A typical enumerated data set for priority is as follows:

1. System practically unusable/unsaleable
2. Serious impact on ability to sales, maintenance
3. Release date may be more important than fixing
4. Release date is more important than fixing
5. Fix when possible

Testing Decisions

Often, the decision made repeatedly by the PM is weighing whether the risk of fixing a bug exceeds the risk of shipping it. With help from the development and testing teams, the software project manager asks these questions:

- What are the testing implications of fixing the bug—should it be isolated and fixed alone, or grouped with other bugs?
- How much will making the fix cost? What about testing it?
- Are the resources available to do it?
- What regression tests will need to be rerun, and how long will they take?
- Will any new tests have to be written?
- What is the rate of success for bug fixes in this system (subsystem)?

Object-Oriented Testing _____

In Chapter 4, we discussed how most prototyping and object-oriented (OO) projects proceed according to a life cycle that is quite different from the waterfall model. In Chapter 22, we discussed OO modeling techniques, which are distinct from more traditional structured analysis/structured design techniques. It only makes sense that with these differences in place, testing would assume different characteristics as well.

In traditional terms, the smallest testable item is the unit, or module, which can be tested with white-box tests. In OO, this functional item is not separated from its class, where it is encapsulated with its methods. This means unit testing is basically replaced with class testing. However, we don't stray too far from our roots in that each object class method (operation or service) could be considered a "small unit" and tested alone, before test sequences, with white- and black-box tests. Individual object classes may continue to employ black-box concepts as well.

Object classes need to be exercised in all possible states, meaning that all events that cause a state change in the object should be simulated.

In traditional terms, units are put together into subsystems and are subjected to integration tests. With OO, testing a structure chart from the top down and bottom up doesn't apply because we are never sure "who's in control" or what class will be called upon next by the user. Integration tests are replaced with thread-based testing, which tests the set of classes required to respond to one input or system event, or use-based testing, which describes one mode of use of the system based on use case scenarios.

Object interaction testing follows "method message" paths to trace a sequence of object interactions that ends only when the last object has been invoked (it doesn't send a message to or call upon the services of any other object.)

System, alpha, beta, usability, and user acceptance testing change very little because the OO system will undergo user-based tests just as traditionally developed systems. This means that V&V are essentially the same. Showing that a system conforms to requirements specifications and is of an acceptable quality level is always the goal of V&V.

Summary of Dynamic Testing

Test management includes estimating for the testing effort, defect tracking, reporting the results, hiring and leading a team, and providing a career path for testers in the organization. Planning for testing includes lining up all necessary resources, such as networks, test tools, data lines, and the test engineers. A test plan prescribes the scope, approach, resources, and schedule of the testing activities. It identifies the risks, the features to be tested, the testing tasks to be performed, and the testers responsible for each task. Test documentation belongs under configuration management and is kept in synch with the software; regression test cases are archived with the software version they were build to test.

Test reports provide a chronological record of relevant details about the execution of tests, documenting events that require investigation.

Testing, related to quality, is one way to measure quality through the "-ilities" such as these:

- Operability
- Observability
- Controllability
- Decomposability
- Simplicity
- Stability
- Understandability

Summary

Verification is the process of verifying that what has been built is correct according to internal specifications. Validation is the process of validating that user requirements are met via the internal specifications. In the vernacular, verification ensures that we are building the system right; validation ensures that we are building the right system. Although it is often thought that static testing constitutes verification and dynamic testing represents validation, in actuality, V&V occur throughout the software product development life cycle. Verification, referring to the set of activities that ensure that software correctly implements a specific function, can occur in both static and dynamic testing. Validation, referring to the set of activities that ensure that the software products are traceable to customer requirements, may also occur in both static and dynamic testing.

Static testing (peer reviews) constitute one of the most effective tools known to increase software product quality. They require no automated tool purchase, and they are easy to understand and to use. All project artifacts should undergo reviews, beginning with those produced very early in the software product development life cycle (e.g., the software project management plan). Peer reviews are recognized by the SEI CMM as being essential in a defined level of maturity. The rewards for conducting reviews are great and well documented—they include financial reward as well as organizational rewards, such as cross-training. Peer reviews are held according to strict "rules," and specific "roles" must be filled. Reviewers are recruited from many sources, depending on the phase in which the review occurs and the product under review.

Dynamic testing refers to a set of test procedures and test cases that operate on program code. When the system is tested "bottom up," units (program modules) are tested according to white-box concepts, units are connected into subsystem components and tested according to black-box concepts, and subsystems are combined into systems and subjected to a variety of tests. Object-oriented systems require a different approach at the beginning but have the same system tests from the user's viewpoint.

A software PM may be leading a project that is large enough to have a separate test manager (preferred), but even a small project where the PM does double duty as the project and the test manager requires certain minimum activities.

This chapter left many important testing issues begging because there is so much existing software engineering literature that covers formal methods, stress testing, safety assurance and assessment, and more. Its intent is to give the software project manager a flavor of the complexity of the tasks performed by a testing team, to encourage the PM to support a review process, to suggest to the PM the importance of hiring and nurturing capable test engineers and organizing for their productivity, and to plan for all testing activities based on predetermined quality criteria and then follow the plan.

Problems for Review

1. Why can't most programs be tested completely?
2. Why shouldn't the software developer take responsibility for finding and fixing his own errors?
3. Why does testing take up such a large percentage of technical effort in the software development process? Should it? What could be done to change the situation?
4. What is the objective of testing?

5. Why is configuration control such an important enabler of testing?

6. What sort of review and testing metrics does the software PM need to manage by?

Visit the Case Study

xTRemeObjectMaker was designed to produce a complete requirements matrix to be used as the foundation of the validation and acceptance testing. Unfortunately, you have just discovered while doing a tool output verification that a correct requirements traceability matrix has never been built. There was a mismatch among the Java compiler, the Java Swing library version used, and the build process for the EJBs. Based on your expanded SRS for the complete product, you must now develop a comprehensive traceability matrix to drive the validation effort. Mr. Lu had mentioned during the prototyping effort that a complete acceptance test plan would not be needed until a final vendor was selected. Ms. Patel got the entire test plan process canceled for the prototype, so Dr. Harita has done no work. Based on the problem with your CASE tool, you are no longer comfortable with the in-process tool verification done. The entire ARRS test process must be re-evaluated and a plan must be done. Ms. Patel is on annual leave and will not return for two more weeks. This is an ideal time to complete those plans and have them waiting for her.

Citations

[1]National Aeronautics and Space Administration (1993). *Software Formal Inspections Guidebook*, NASA-GB-A-302, Office of Safety and Mission Assurance, National Aeronautics and Space Administration.

[2]Fairley, Richard E. (1992). "Recent Advances in Software Estimation Techniques." *IEEE 14th International Conference on Software Engineering*, Los Alamitos CA, IEEE Computer Society Press, pp. 382–391.

[3]Humphrey, Watts (1995). *A Discipline for Software Engineering*. Reading, MA: Addison-Wesley, SEI Series in Software Engineering.

[4]Fagan, Michael (1976). "Design and Code Inspection to Reduce Errors in Program Development." *IBM Systems Journal*, 15(3).

[5]*sel.gsfc.nasa.gov/website/index.htm*. Software Engineering Laboratory.

[6]*stsc.hill.af.mil/CrossTalk/1998/dec/oneill.asp*. Don O'Neill (1998). "National Software Quality Experiment A Lesson In Measurement: 1992–1997." *CrossTalk: Journal of Defense Software Engineering*, December.

[7]Haley, Tom, et al. (1995). "Raytheon Electronic Systems Experience in Software Process Improvement." *Software Engineering Institute Technical Report*. CMU/SEI-95-TR-017, November.

[8]Buck, F.O. (1981). "Indicators of Quality Inspections." *IBM Corporation Technical Report*. IBM TR21, 802, September.

[9]Freeman, Daniel, and Gerald Weinberg (1990). *Handbook of Walkthroughs, Inspections, and Technical Reviews*, 3rd ed. New York, NY: Dorset House.

[10]Curtis, Bill (1996). Personal communication.

[11]Fagan, Michael E. (1986). "Advances in Software Inspections." *IEEE Transactions on Software Engineering*, 12(7): 744–751.

[12]See note 4.

[13]Ishikawa, K. (1976). *Guide to Quality Control*. Tokyo, Japan: Asian Productivity Organization.

[14]Brooks, Fredrick P. (1987). "No Silver Bullet: Essence and Accidents of Software Engineering." *IEEE Computer*, 20(4):10–19.

[15]Myers, Glenford J. (1979). *The Art of Software Testing*. New York, NY: John Wiley & Sons.

[16]Pressman, Roger S. (2001). *Software Engineering: A Practitioner's Approach*, 5th ed. Boston, MA: McGraw-Hill.

[17]See note 15.

[18]Beizer, Boris (1990). *Software Testing Techniques*, 2nd ed. New York, NY: Van Nostrand Reinhold.

[19]See note 15.

[20]Boehm, Barry, et al. (1978). *Characteristics of Software Quality*. Amsterdam: North-Holland; New York, NY: American Elsevier.

[21]Musa, John D. (1999). *Software Reliability Engineering: More Reliable Software, Faster Development and Testing*. New York, NY: McGraw-Hill.

[22]Black, Rex (1999). *Managing the Testing Process*. Redmond, WA: Microsoft Press.

[23]Yoder, Cornelia M., and Marilyn L. Schrag (1983). "Nassi-Schneiderman Charts: An Alternative to Flowcharts for Design." White Paper, IBM Corporation, System Products Division, Endicott, NY.

[24]Nassi, I., and Ben Schneiderman (1973). "Flowchart Techniques for Structured Programming." *SIGPLAN Notices of the ACM*, 8(8):12–26.

[25]McCabe, Thomas J. (1976). "A Complexity Measure." *IEEE Transactions on Software Engineering*, SE-2(4):308-320.

[26]McCabe, Thomas (1994). "Quality Metrics, Reverse Engineering, Client Server—the Synergy." Presentation at the Quality Assurance Association of Maryland, Baltimore, MD, April 19, 1994.

[27]Grady, Robert (1992). *Practical Software Metrics for Project Management and Process Improvement*, New York, NY: Prentice Hall.

[28]Krasner, Herb (2001). "Implementing Software Quality." Session 32, *Software Project Management Certificate Program Sequence XI*, Software Quality Institute, The University of Texas at Austin.

[29]McCall, James A., et al. (1977). "Metrics for Software Quality Evaluation and Prediction." *Proceedings of Second Summer Software Engineering Workshop*, Greenbelt, Maryland, September 19.

[30]Halstead, Maurice H. (1977). *Elements of Software Science*. New York, NY: Elsevier.

[31]Shafer, L., and John Connell (1982). "Deriving Metrics for Relating Complexity Measures to Software Maintenance Costs." *Proceedings of the 1982 Computer Measurement Group International Conference*, pp. 134–141.

[32]Bache, Richard, and Gualteiro Bazzana (1994). *Software Metrics for Product Assessment*. New York, NY: McGraw-Hill.

[33]IEEE (1983). IEEE 829-1983, "IEEE Standard for Software Test Documentation." New York, NY: The Institute of Electrical and Electronics Engineers.

Suggested Readings

Baber, Robert Laurence (1991). *Error-Free Software: Know-how and Know-why of Program Correctness*. New York, NY: Wiley.

Beizer, Boris (1984). *Software System Testing and Quality Assurance*. New York, NY: Van Nostrand Reinhold.

Beizer, Boris (1995). *Black Box Testing: Techniques for Functional Testing of Software and Systems*. New York, NY: Wiley.

Berard, E.V. (1993). *Essays on Object-Oriented Software Engineering*, vol.1. Reading, MA: Addison-Wesley.

Bias, Randolph G., and Deborah J. Mayhew, eds. (1994). *Cost-Justifying Usability*. Boston, MA: Academic Press.

Binder, Robert (1993). "Scenario-Based Testing for Client/Server Systems." *The Software Testing Forum*, 1(2):12–17.

Binder, Robert V. (1999). *Testing Object-oriented Systems: Models, Patterns and Tools*. Reading, MA: Addison-Wesley.

Bush, Marilyn (1990). "Improving Software Quality: The Use of Formal Inspections at the Jet Propulsion Laboratory." *Proceedings, 12th International Conference on Software Engineering*, Nice, France, March 26-30, pp. 196–199.

Carmel, E. (1995). "Cycle Time in Packaged Software Firms." *Journal of Product Innovation Management*, 12(2):110–123.

DeMarco, Tom (1995). *Why Does Software Cost So Much? And Other Puzzles of the Information Age*. New York, NY: Dorset House.

Devor, Richard E., et al. (1992). *Statistical Quality Design and Control*. New York, NY: Prentice Hall.

Dumas, Joseph S., and Janice C. Redish (1999). *A Practical Guide to Usability Testing*, rev. ed. Portland, OR: Intellect Books.

Dyer, Michael (1992). *The Cleanroom Approach to Quality Software Development*. New York, NY: Wiley.

Ebenau, Robert G., and Susan H. Strauss (1994). *Software Inspection Process*. New York, NY: McGraw-Hill.

Florac, William A. (1992). "Software Quality Measurement: A Framework for Counting Problems and Defects." CMU/SEI-92-TR-22. Pittsburgh, PA: Software Engineering Institute, Carnegie Mellon University.

Florac, William A., et al. (1996). "Practical Software Measurement: Measuring for Process Management and Improvement," CMU/SEI-97-HB-003. Pittsburgh, PA: Software Engineering Institute, Carnegie Mellon University.

Friedman, Michael A., and Jeffrey M. Voas (1995). *Software Assessment: Reliability, Safety, Testability.* New York, NY: Wiley.

Gilb, Tom, and Dorothy Graham (1993). *Software Inspection.* Reading, MA: Addison-Wesley.

Grady, Robert (1997). *Successful Software Process Improvement.* Englewood Cliffs, NJ: Prentice Hall.

Grady, Robert B., and Deborah L. Caswell (1987). *Software Metrics: Establishing a Company-wide Program.* Englewood Cliffs, NJ: Prentice Hall.

Hetzel, William C. (1988). *The Complete Guide to Software Testing*, 2nd ed. Wellesley, MA: QED Information Sciences.

Hetzel, William C. (1993). *Making Software Measurement Work: Building an Effective Measurement Program.* Boston, MA: QED Pub. Group.

Humphrey, Watts S. (1989). *Managing the Software Process.* Reading, MA: Addison-Wesley.

IEEE (1987). IEEE 1008-1987, "IEEE Standard for Software Unit Testing." New York, NY: The Institute of Electrical and Electronics Engineers.

IEEE (1983). IEEE 729-1983, "IEEE Standard Glossary of Software Engineering Terminology." New York, NY: The Institute of Electrical and Electronics Engineers.

IEEE (1988). IEEE 982.1-1988, "IEEE Standard Dictionary of Measures to Produce Reliable Software." New York, NY: The Institute of Electrical and Electronics Engineers.

Jones, T. Capers (1986). *Programming Productivity.* New York, NY: McGraw-Hill.

Kan, Stephen H. (1995). *Metrics and Models in Software Quality Engineering.* Reading, MA: Addison-Wesley.

Kaner, Cem, et al. (1993). *Testing Computer Software*, 2nd ed. New York, NY: Van Nostrand Reinhold

Knight, J.C., and E.A. Meyers (1993). "An Improved Inspection Technique." *Communications of the ACM*, 36(11):51–61.

Lyu, Michael R., ed. (1996). *Handbook of Software Reliability Engineering*, New York, NY: McGraw-Hill.

Marick, Brian (1995). *The Craft of Software Testing.* Englewood Cliffs, NJ: Prentice Hall.

Martin, James, and Carma McClure (1983). *Software Maintenance: The Problem and Its Solution.* Englewood Cliffs, NJ: Prentice Hall.

McConnell, Steve (1996). *Rapid Development: Taming Wild Software Schedules.* 1st ed. Redmond, WA: Microsoft Press.

Miller, Ann (1992). *Engineering Quality Software: Defect Detection and Prevention.* Reading, MA: Addison-Wesley, Motorola University Press Six Sigma Research Institute Publications.

Mosley, Daniel J. (1993). *The Handbook of MIS Application Software Testing: Methods, Techniques, and Tools for Assuring Quality through Testing.* Englewood Cliffs, NJ: Prentice Hall.

Musa, John D., et al. (1987). *Software Reliability: Measurement, Prediction, Application.* New York, NY: McGraw-Hill.

Musa, John. D. (1993). "Operational Profiles in Software Reliability Engineering." *IEEE Software,* 10(2):14–32.

Nielsen, Jakob (1993). *Usability Engineering,* Boston, MA: Academic Press.

Nielsen, Jakob, and Robert L. Mack, eds. (1994). *Usability Inspection Methods.* New York, NY: John Wiley & Sons.

Offutt, A. Jefferson (1992). "Investigations of the Software Testing Coupling Effect." *ACM Transactions on Software Engineering and Methodology,* 1(1).

O'Neill, Don (1997). "Setting Up a Software Inspection Program." *CrossTalk, The Journal of Defense Software Engineering,* 10(2).

Perry, William E. (1986). *How to Test Software Packages.* New York, NY: John Wiley & Sons.

Porter, A.A., et al. (1997). "An Experiment to Assess the Cost-Benefits of Code Inspection In Large Scale Software Development." *IEEE Transactions of Software Engineering,* 23(6):329–346.

Rae, A.K., et al., eds. (1995). *Software Evaluation for Certification: Principles, Practice and Legal Liability.* New York, NY: McGraw-Hill.

Royer, Thomas C. (1993). *Software Testing Management: Life on the Critical Path.* Englewood Cliffs, NJ: Prentice Hall.

Shneiderman, Ben (1997). *Designing the User Interface: Strategies for Effective Human-Computer Interaction.* Reading, MA: Addison-Wesley.

Shooman, Martin L. (1983). *Software Engineering Design, Reliability, and Management.* New York, NY: McGraw-Hill.

Sommerville, Ian (2001). *Software Engineering,* 6th ed. Reading, MA: Addison-Wesley.

Voas, Jeffrey M., and Gary McGraw (1998). *Software Fault Injection: Inoculating Programs Against Errors.* New York, NY: Wiley.

Watson, Arthur H., and Thomas J. McCabe (1996). "Structured Testing: A Testing Methodology Using the Cyclomatic Complexity Metric." *National Institute of Standards and Technology Special Publication 500-235.* Gaithersburg, MD: NIST.

Weinberg, Gerald M. (1971). *The Psychology of Computer Programming.* New York, NY: Van Nostrand Reinhold.

Weinberg, Gerald M. (1992). *Quality Software Management, vol. 1, Systems Thinking.* New York, NY: Dorset House.

Weinberg, Gerald M. (1997). *Quality Software Management, vol. 4, Anticipating Change.* New York, NY: Dorset House.

Weller, E.F. (1993). "Lessons Learned from Two Years of Inspection Data." *IEEE Software,* 10(5):38–45.

Wheeler, David A., Bill Brykczynski, and Reginald N. Meeson, Jr., eds. (1996). *Software Inspection, An Industry Best Practice.* New York, NY: IEEE Computer Society Press.

Wiklund, Michael E., ed. (1994). *Usability in Practice: How Companies Develop User-Friendly Products.* Boston, MA: Academic Press.

Yamaura, Tsuneo (1998). "How to Design Practical Test Cases." *IEEE Software,* 15(6):30–36.

Yourdon, Edward (1989). *Modern Structured Analysis*. Englewood Cliffs, NJ: Prentice Hall.

Yourdon, Edward (1997). "Metrics for Death-March Projects." *Proceedings of Symposium: Eighth International Conference On Applications of Software Measurement*, Atlanta, GA, October.

Web Pages for Further Information_____

satc.gsfc.nasa.gov/fi/fipage.html. NASA's Formal Inspections Process.

world.std.com/~jr/Papers/QW96.html. Rothman, Johanna (1996). "Measurements to Reduce Risk in Product Ship Decisions." *Proceedings of the Ninth International Quality Week*, Software Research, San Francisco, CA.

www.chasmgroup.com/.

www.cse.dcu.ie/. Centre for Software Engineering, Ltd., Dublin City University Campus, Dublin Ireland.

www.geraldmweinberg.com. Gerald M. Weinberg's Home Page.

www.geraldmweinberg.com/shape.html. The SHAPE forum (Software as a Human Activity Practiced Effectively).

www.ics.hawaii.edu/~johnson/FTR/. Formal Technical Review Archive.

www.ics.hawaii.edu/~siro/. Software Inspections and Review Organization.

www.io.com/~wazmo/qa/. Software Testing Hotlist, Brett Pettichord, ed.

www.iso.ch/iso/en/ISOOnline.openerpage. International Organization for Standardization (ISO).

www.jrothman.com.

www.kaner.com/. Dr. Kaner is the senior author of *Testing Computer Software*.

www.kaner.com/coverage.htm. Kaner, Cem (1996). "Software Negligence and Testing Coverage," *STAR 96 Proceedings*, May.

www.mtsu.edu/~storm/. Software Testing Online Resources.

www.nist.gov/. National Institute of Standards and Technology (NIST).

www.nstl.com/. National Software Testing Labs.

www.softwareqatest.com/TOP. The Software QA/Test Resource Center, maintained by Rick Hower.

www.ondaweb.com/sti/. The Software Testing Institute.

www.ondaweb.com/sti/stivend.htm. A Professional Software Tester's Resource Guide.

www.qaiusa.com/. Quality Assurance Institute.

www.satisfice.com/articles/good_enough_quality.pdf. James Bach (1997). "Good Enough Quality: Beyond the Buzzword" (Software Realities column). *IEEE Computer*, August.

www.satisfice.com/articles/software_reality.pdf. James Bach (1999). "What Software Reality is Really About" (Software Realities column). *IEEE Computer*, December.

www.satisfice.com/articles/test_automation_snake_oil.pdf. James Bach (1996). "Test Automation Snake Oil." *Windows Tech Journal*, October.

www.softwareqatest.com/WEB_SECURITY. Testing of worldwide Web sites.

www.spmn.com. Software Program Managers Network.

www.sqe.com/index.asp. Software Quality Engineering.

www.stlabs.com/~marick/root.htm.

www.stqemagazine.com/featured.asp?stamp=1129125440. James Bach (1999). "Risk-Based Testing." *Software Testing and Quality Engineering Magazine*, 1(6).

www.stqemagazine.com/webinfo_detail.asp?id=102. Brian Marick (1999). "Web Watch: Automating Testing." *Software Testing and Quality Engineering Magazine*, 1(5), Sep/Oct.

www.stsc.hill.af.mil/CrossTalk/1998/dec/oneill.asp.

www.stsc.hill.af.mil/SWTesting/gilb.html. Tom Gilb documents.

www.testing.com/writings/automate.pdf. Brian Marick (1988). "When Should a Test be Automated?" *Proceedings of International Quality Week*, May.

www.testing.com/writings/classic/mistakes.html. Brian Marick (1997). "Classic Testing Mistakes." *Proceedings of STAR 97*, Software Quality Engineering, Jacksonville, FL.

www.testing.com/writings/coverage.pdf. Brian Marick (1999). "How to Misuse Code Coverage." *International Conference and Exposition on Testing Computer Software*, June.

www.testing.com/writings/effective.pdf. Brian Marick (1998). "Working Effectively With Developers." *STAR West Conference*, October.

www.testing.com/writings/experience.pdf. Brian Marick (1991). "Experience with the Cost of Different Coverage Goals for Testing." *Pacific Northwest Software Quality Conference*, October.

www.testing.com/writings/purpose-of-testing.htm. Brian Marick. "The Testing Team's Motto."

www.testingcraft.com/exploratory-pettichord.html. Bret Pettichord (1999). "An Exploratory Testing Workshop Report," July.

www.useit.com/.

www.zdnett.com/pcmag/pctech/content/17/17/tu1717.001.html. Neil Randall, "Making Software Easier Through Usability Testing: Software companies take a rigorous approach to determining how easy their products are to use." PC Magazine Online.

Use of Tools

Project managers use two drivers in the use of tools: the life cycle and the model for process improvement. As discussed in Chapter 19, "Introduction to Software Engineering," the IEEE Computer Society and ACM Software Engineering Coordinating Committee have joined together to produce the Software Engineering Body of Knowledge (SWEBOK). The software engineering and development tools that support the project life cycle are covered in the SWEBOK. Table 24–1 shows the SWEBOK tools with the addition of the design tools for verification and optimization.

Table 24–2 shows the relationship among the five process maturity levels of the Software Engineering Institute's Capabilities Maturity Model and the individual tools identified in the SWEBOK. A subset of this table is presented in each tool category to identify the maturity level of the software development organization with the tools. Software project managers must understand the maturity level of the organization developing the software product. Providing tools to an immature organization merely allows the developers to produce the wrong product faster. Power tools require maturity to be used effectively.

TABLE 24–1
Software Engineering Tools Categorization

Tool Class	Specific Tool Type
• Software requirements tools	Requirements modeling Traceability
• Software design tools	Design verification Design optimization
• Software construction tools	Program editors Compilers Interpreters Debuggers
• Software testing tools	Test generators Test execution frameworks Test evaluation Test management Performance analysis
• Software maintenance tools	Comprehension Re-engineering
• Software engineering process tools	Process modeling Process management Integrated CASE environments Process-centered software engineering environments
• Software quality tools	Inspection Static analysis
• Software configuration management tools	Defect, enhancement, issue and problem tracking Version management Release-and-build
• Software engineering management tools	Project planning and tracking Risk management Measurement
• Infrastructure support tools	Interpersonal communications Information retrieval system Administration and support
• Miscellaneous tools issues	Tool integration techniques Meta tool Tool evaluation

TABLE 24–2
SWEBOK Tools and the CMM

Level	Focus	Key Process Areas	SWEBOK Tools
5 **Optimizing**	Continuous process improvement	1. Defect prevention 2. Technology change management 3. Process change management	1. Comprehension 2. Re-engineering 3. Process-centered software engineering environments
4 **Managed**	Product and process quality	1. Quantitative process management 2. Software quality management	1. Design verification 2. Design optimization 3. Process management 4. Integrated CASE environments 5. Static analysis
3 **Defined**	Defined engineering process	1. Organization process focus 2. Organization process definition 3. Integrated software management 4. Software product engineering 5. Intergroup coordination 6. Training program 7. Peer reviews	1. Design modeling 2. Performance analysis 3. Process modeling 4. Inspection 5. Tool integration techniques 6. Tool evaluation
2 **Repeatable**	Project management commitment process	1. Requirements management 2. Software project planning 3. Software project tracking 4. Software subcontractor management 5. Software quality assurance 6. Software configuration management	1. Requirements modeling 2. Traceability 3. Test evaluation 4. Test management 5. Defect, enhancement, issue and problem tracking 6. Version management 7. Release and build 8. Project planning and tracking 9. Risk management 10. Measurement

(Continues)

TABLE 24–2 (Continued)
SWEBOK Tools and the CMM

Level	Focus	Key Process Areas	SWEBOK Tools
2 **Repeatable** (Continued)	Project management commitment process (Continued)		11. Information retrieval system 12. Administration and support
1 **Initial**	Heroes		Program editors Compilers Interpreters Debuggers Test generators Test execution frameworks Interpersonal communications Meta tool

Where We Are in the Product Development Life Cycle

Tools are necessary throughout the software development life cycle, as shown in Figure 24–1. There is never a perfect mapping between the category of the tool and the life cycle phase. For example, requirements tools are necessary from the very beginning of the project. The ability for easy elicitation and recording must be available from the concept exploration onward to the end of requirements. Design tools overlap the requirements and implementation phases. Construction tools overlap design and installation. Test tools are not just for the implementation, coding, and test phases. The concept of validation and acceptance testing is driven by the requirements gathered and agreed to by the client. White- and black-box testing is driven by design considerations. All of verification testing is driven by both design and the tools used to build the final product.

Maintenance tools are a combination of all the previously used tools in the life cycle. The most realistic way to approach maintenance is as a separate life cycle that used techniques and tools from earlier development phases. Configuration management tools are needed from the instant that the first project artifact is created.

Infrastructure, quality, and engineering process and management tools are used across all phases of the development life cycle. These tools span projects and products. They are the glue that holds together the software development organization.

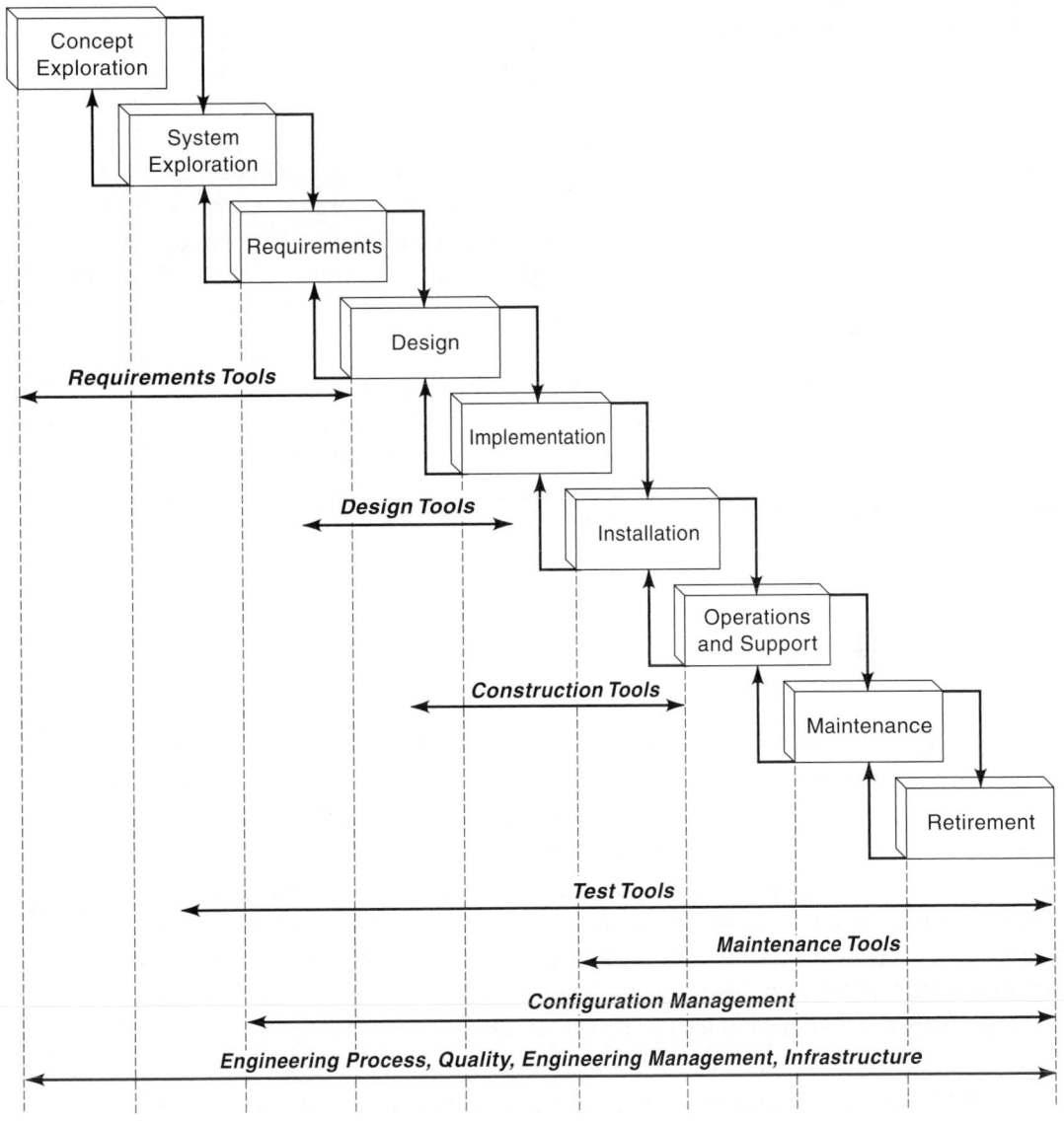

FIGURE 24–1
Tool Use in the Product Development Life Cycle

Learning Objectives for Chapter 24 _____

Upon completion of this chapter, the reader should be able to:

- Describe the classes and types of tools for each CMM maturity level;
- Plan for tools used on a software development project;
- Select specific tools based on a repeatable process.

The following discussions of the tools used throughout the software development life cycle will be mapped to the CMM level in Figure 24–2 appropriate for using the specific tool. Tools are there to aid in the construction of quality systems. They are not used to create the wrong system faster. Automating a Level 1 chaotic and *ad hoc* organization results in speeding up chaos. A development organization's maturity level must be considered before tools are selected. There is no "silver bullet" with respect to merely buying tools for fixing a lack of process.[1]

No lists of recommended tools are contained within these descriptions. The volatility of the software tools market makes such an enumeration impractical. To begin a search for existing tools and suppliers, use an Internet search engine such as Copernic (*www.copernic.com*). As an example, searching for "software requirement modeling" returns 106 Web pages after validating that the found links are all active. Using this initial search information along with the tool evaluation techniques presented later provides the starting point for automated tool investigation and selection.

Software Requirements Tools _____

Tools dealing with eliciting, capturing, using, and maintaining software requirements fall into the two general categories of modeling and traceability. There is finer granularity that could be accomplished in the categorization but that has been found to be unnecessary because most tools fall into one of these categories.

Figure 24–2 shows the parts of the life cycle covered by requirements tools. Not just the requirements phase, but also the preparatory phases of concept and system exploration require the use of requirements tools. These tools aid in the development of the functional requirements that will eventually be enumerated in the software requirements specification (SRS) discussed in detail in Chapter 17, "Developing the Software Requirements Specification."

Requirements Modeling—CMM Level 2 and Above

Tools used for eliciting, recording, analyzing, and validating software requirements are in this category. They are traditionally classified as either structured or classical requirements

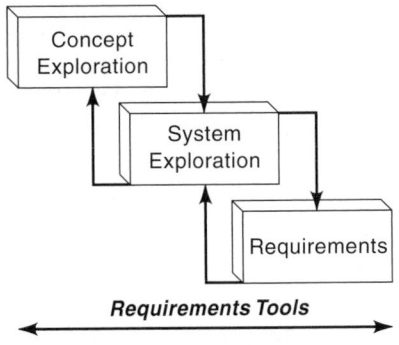

FIGURE 24–2
Requirements Tools Life Cycle Coverage

modeling, or object-oriented requirements analysis and modeling. All of these tools have three basic components. The first is a rules engine that contains that modeling rules of the methodology being used. The second is a drawing/graphics engine that maintains the icons that are legal for the methodology described by the rules and the legal ways of connecting the icons. The last component that is required is a textural requirements description tool that describes the functional requirement, data elements required, and other requirements-specific information.

The most simple requirements modeling tool kit to construct in the Microsoft Windows environment is to use Visio as the drawing tool and Access for textural information capture. Although Visio has many plug-ins for supporting various software development methodologies, it is not a CASE tool. Much of the "rules engine" must be in the user's head.

Traceability—CMM Level 2 and Above

As the complexity of software systems increases, requirements traceability tools are crucial to requirements representation throughout the product life cycle. Traceability begins with capturing the product requirements in a textural description tool. The output from that tool is a uniquely numbered requirement, along with a short description. Those two pieces of information can be input to a spreadsheet program such as Excel for the rightmost columns in the sheet. Across the top row of the spreadsheet can then appear those artifacts to be traced. This may be a list of acceptance tests, design objects, code modules, or risk areas. What is important at this minimal level of automation is that the requirements are captured and maintained in one place and used throughout the life cycle.

Software Design Tools

Because of the diversity of notation and methods, this section categorizes the variety of design tools into verification and optimization categories. Much of the diversity is due to the evolution from classical, structured modeling methods to methods based on the Unified Modeling Language (UML). Figure 24–3 shows that design tools are first used in the middle parts of the requirements phase and are not finished being used until the middle parts of the implementation phase. This overlap is due to the fact that some product features move from requirements into design before the phase is completed. Some design activities are still ongoing during implementation. Therefore, the design tools cover more than just the design phase.

Design Modeling—CMM Level 3 and Above

Tools used in design modeling are tightly tied to the product development methodology adopted. The actual modeling requires the same set of tools as the requirements modeling does. The major difference is that the graphics and rules engines are expanded to account for the design objects and rules for tying them together.

Design Verification—CMM Level 4 and Above

Design verification occurs after the software design, or an increment of the software design, has been completed. The verification tasks of traceability, evaluation, and interface analysis provide assurance that software requirements are not misrepresented or incorrectly implemented. By verifying that the software design meets its software requirements, the software design verification activity also supports validation that the software design meets system requirements. There may be several instantiations of the software requirements and software

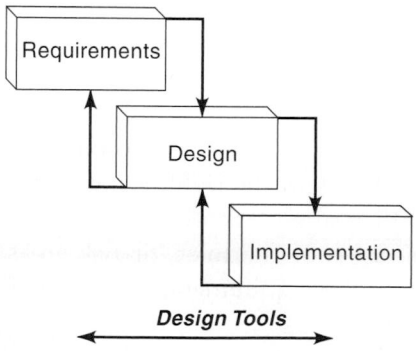

FIGURE 24–3
Design Tools Life Cycle Coverage

design verification before the entire system is verified. Traceability matrices and some auto-mated components of the design modeling tools assist in the design verification.

Design Optimization—CMM Level 4 and Above

Design optimization tools are not only methodology-specific, but they're domain-specific as well. Some CASE tools can do first-order design optimization. These simply measure design attributes as fan-in, fan-out, coupling, and cohesion based on the module structures. For object-oriented projects, design complexity is looked at in relation to inheritance, poly-morphism, and encapsulation shown in the design model. For in-depth optimization, the domain for the product must be known and optimum design topologies must be defined. These types of tools are built within mature organizations and become part of the "secret sauce" in their products.

Software Construction Tools

Software construction tools are tools that convert the requirements and design models into a language suitable for execution on a set of computer hardware. Figure 24–4 shows where in the life cycle software construction tools are mainly used. Construction tools are begun to be used in the middle of the design phase. This occurs because some product capabilities may need to be implemented before the design phase is complete. Also, some of the features of the construction tools may need to be exercised to ensure that they function seamlessly with the design tools. Construction tools are used until the end of the installation phase because of the need to do bug fixes, modifications, and simple customizations. In reality, the construc-tion tools are always used after installation. If the organization is responsible for mainte-nance of the installed software, a set of the construction tools will be used for that maintenance.

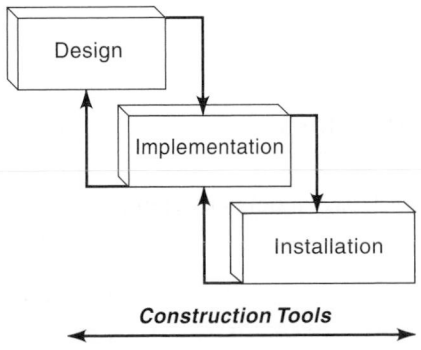

FIGURE 24–4
Construction Tools Life Cycle Coverage

Program Editors—CMM Level 1 and Above

These tools are used for creation and modification of computer programs and associated documentation. Editors can be general-purpose or can be tailored for a specific programming language. These are human-controlled development tools. These are the "power" tools of the CMM Level 1 organizations. All organizations, no matter what their maturity level, eventually have to render the product in code. Level 1 organizations look at this as the only tool set needed. Level 5 organizations look at this as the last tool kit to use.

Compilers—CMM Level 1 and Above

Traditionally, compilers have been noninteractive translators of a stream of source code. There is a trend to integrate program editors with specific language compilers to provide a basic development environment. Preprocessors, linker/loaders, and code generators also fit in the compiler category.

Interpreters—CMM Level 1 and Above

These tools provide an emulation of the runtime environment. Usually slower in execution time than compiled code, interpreters provide a more controlled and observable environment for program execution.

When looking at the use of either a compiler or an interpreter tool for software construction, these comparisons are important[2]:

1. Writing "some" programs in a scripting language (Perl, Python, Rexx, Tcl) takes no more than half as much time as writing in C, C++, or Java. The resulting code is only half as long.

2. No clear differences in program reliability exist among languages.

3. A typical script program consumes twice the memory of C or C++. Java consumes three to four times the amount of memory.

4. When reading a 1MB file and creating a 70k-entry internal table at initialization, C and C++ are twice as fast as Java and 5 to 10 times faster than scripting.

5. Doing an internal data structure search, C and C++ are twice as fast as Java. Scripting programs are also faster than Java.

6. For all languages and programs, any variability among languages is overshadowed by the skill-level variability of the programmers.

Debuggers—CMM Level 1 and Above

These tools work in concert with the other software construction tools to assist in problem isolation and correction of complex systems. Debuggers are runtime extensions to the construction tools that allow the insertion of break points of simple print statements to look at how the code is executing.

Software Testing Tools

Categorization of testing tools is by their general function within the software development life cycle. As shown in Figure 24–5, testing tools must be used from the very beginning of the development life cycle to test assumptions, turn collected requirements into test cases, verify designs, test code, and regress maintenance changes. Highly integrated test environments add to delivered product quality.

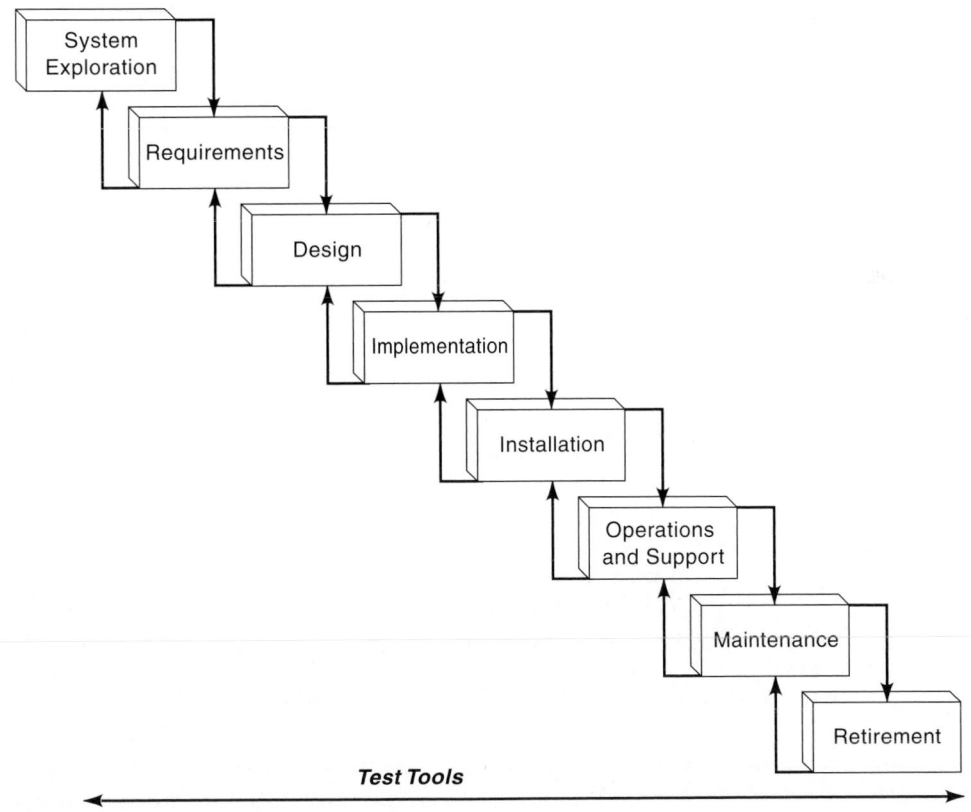

FIGURE 24–5
Testing Tools Life Cycle Coverage

Test Generators—CMM Level 1 and Above

These tools assist in the development and generation of test cases and the associated data sets against which to test. Test case design techniques to identify test data values that will be constructed are the heart of test generators. The developers will be responsible for designing unit testing test cases. The test team will aid developers in use of the techniques. For integration, system, and regression testing, the test team will apply the techniques themselves. The test case description either can be documented manually or can be stored in the test repository of an automated testing tool suite. If the test cases are documented automatically, the format and content will be limited to what the input forms and test repository can accept. Each tool vendor will probably store a different set of descriptive elements. Whether manual or automated, the test case description should minimally contain the elements illustrated in the sample output document listed here. The test data *must* include a description of the expected behavior for each test case.

At Level 1, the developers manually generate the test cases and data sets for testing. As the organization increases in maturity, more automation is added. The easiest set of initial automation is to use a simple database application such as Access to generate test cases from the requirements and data sets from random data sets generated from the requirements model's data dictionary.

Test Execution Frameworks—CMM Level 1 and Above

A framework for the execution of test cases in a controlled environment is critical for the observation of the object being tested. Without a framework, the concept of software unit being tested is not implementable. A test execution framework develops the test harnesses to execute the levels of testing from unit test through integration, to system and finally validation and acceptance testing. There are multiple software generation activities in any new project: The first is concerned with the production of code that will form the final product, and the others are concerned with suites of test harnesses that will be used to demonstrate correct operation. This also means that when any function is designed, testability must be built in from the start.

The sophistication of the test framework increases with the organization's CMM maturity level. In the early maturity levels, the framework can be tied together with scripts that check data in Access, Excel, and simple data-capture and case-generation programs.

During the maintenance phase of a software project, any run-time–optimized version of the function can be retested with the original harness suite so that subtle errors can be spotted before re-installation in the main body of software. The new project overhead for any software section involves the generation of a test harness to accompany it. Before any new function is entered into main system software, all relevant harnesses must be run and signed off as correct, and the relevant paperwork must be added to the system documentation.

Test Evaluation—CMM Level 2 and Above

Test evaluation tools answer the question, "Did the observed product behavior match the expected product behavior?" Unless the entire process is automated, this question ends up being answered in a manual fashion. Excel can be used as an extension to the entire analysis work. Depending on where the project is in the life cycle, the evaluation could consist of validation, verification, acceptance, or unit, integration, or system testing. Any automated tool needs to account for the temporal positioning in the life cycle and the activity being executed.

Test Management—CMM Level 2 and Above

These tools provide management of all the subprocesses of the overall testing process. The most important objective of test management is the maintenance of all the test artifacts for regression testing. The primary goal of regression testing is to ensure that everything that has been fixed in past versions is still fixed. More broadly stated, regression testing refers to the process of executing a set of test cases designed to validate as much of the functionality of the application as possible. While the timing of a particular pass through the test cases may be tied to releasing new functionality or fixing a certain bug, if the tests are restructured to focus on only those elements, then the process would more properly be called functional or unit testing. Regression testing should be as broad as possible in coverage and as consistent as possible in application so that the results are comparable from one pass to the next. The main tool for test management is the configuration management system.

Performance Analysis—CMM Level 3 and Above

As shown in Figure 24–6, performance analysis is only one of the pieces of performance management for a software system. Starting with a service-level agreement (SLA), the upper ring, including the help desk, reporting, and process change activities, are all user-facing activities. The bottom ring, beginning with the performance lab, monitoring systems, analysis, and optimization activities, are the technology and inward-facing activities. Once the help desk is running and the monitoring systems are monitoring, someone has to look at the data that results, or much of its value will be lost. This analysis and reporting does not require expensive tools or complex procedures. What is important is that someone takes the time to look at the data on a regular basis and follow up on any trends or exceptional conditions.

The simple analysis tool could be a built-in report from the help desk, a chart from the network monitor, an *ad hoc* reporting tool, or even just Excel. The goal is to see trends in the data and then drill down to find out the causes of those trends. If the CPU was high last week, has a root cause analysis been done to understand why? Was it because of some business cycle that will occur again, or was it a one-time event? Was the load as high when this cycle last occurred? By choosing metrics well and watching them regularly, it is possible to tell what is normal and what is not. In some cases, the same metrics that are being

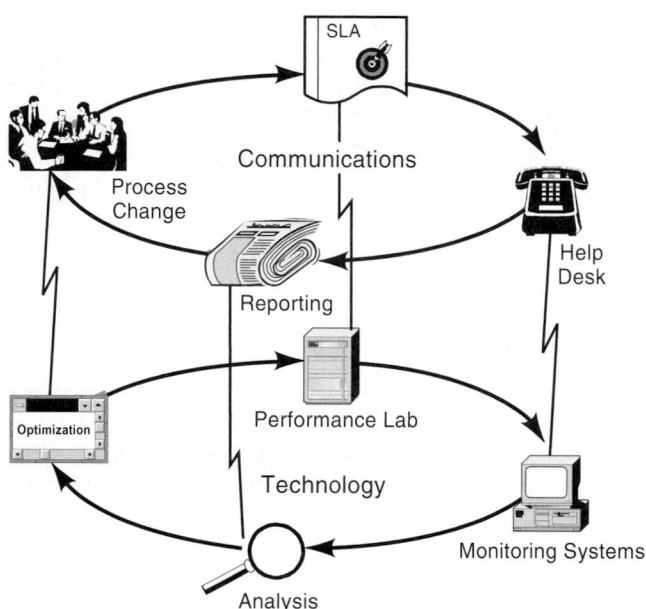

FIGURE 24–6
Performance Management Cycle
Source: *stealthis.athensgroup.com/presentations*. Athens Group, Inc. (2001). *The Business Case and Methodology for Performance Management*.

reported to users will be sufficient. For more complex systems, special reports may be needed to make the data easier to deal with.

If the performance test designer was thorough, there would be a series of scenarios adding Web servers until the database limit was reached (e.g., the database can support 1,500 users). Now we know that no more than six Web servers should be attached to this level of database server. Perhaps another test measures the network activity and gives the average figure of 10Kbps per user. Now when the managers tell us that some of our users will be moving off-site, we have a model for determining the size of network pipe needed—in this case, a T1 (1500Kbps) for each 150 users.

A prudent project manager will have models ready for all of the critical resources loads that the system requirements' use cases describe. These use cases require managing processor time, bandwidth on the wide area network, and disk space in the database. Each model should show how the use of that resource depends on the top two or three factors that affect it. A model for a network pipe might need to consider the size of the pipe, the number of users at the far end, and perhaps the amount and type of activity that those users perform.

Aside from validating project choices of performance goals and metrics reporting, system performance analysis can show users the impacts of the requirements levied on the system before it goes into production. Analysis points out cycles and trends that otherwise would not be visible. If the users know that the system is very busy on the last day of each month, they might do certain noncritical work at other times, or might be more careful of abusive practices such as rerunning a large report just to change one number. Even if the users can't or won't change their habits, they will know what to expect, which might avoid a few support calls. At a minimum, regular system performance analysis should remind the users that one slow response is not the norm and should demonstrate that the project planned for the occurrence of these issues.

Software Maintenance Tools

Software maintenance is represented as a modified version of the organization's software development life cycle. There are differences in the amount of emphasis spent on each phase's activities. All phases are touched, and the tools used initially to build the software product must be used for the maintenance of the product. The value of the tools used lies in the amount of development information that is maintained and can be reused during the maintenance phase. This development information reuse is especially important in the testing area, where regression testing must be done to verify that no additional problems were introduced in the product by fixing the ones that were apparent and that necessitated the fix.

Figure 24–7 shows the portion of the life cycle touched by these specific maintenance tools. Use of comprehension and re-engineering tools begins at installation and continues through operations and support and maintenance to retirement. Keep in mind that parts of all the other tools described in this chapter are used in the maintenance process for existing legacy software systems.

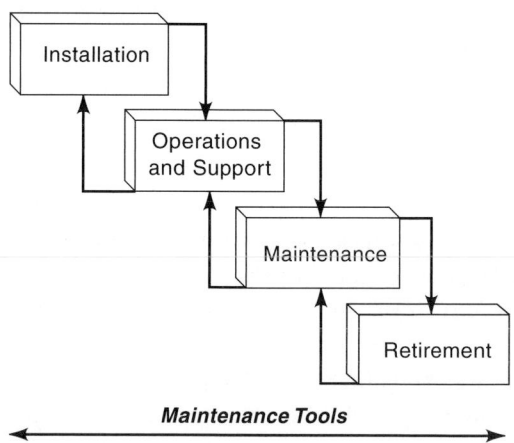

Maintenance Tools

FIGURE 24–7
Maintenance Tools Life Cycle Coverage

Comprehension—CMM Level 5

This topic concerns tools to assist in human comprehension of programs. Cross-reference tools are some of the first to consider in comprehending the running systems that are under maintenance. These tools scan and extract information from the source code, creating a program database. At the same time, they provide a query interface for a software engineer to access the extracted information. Within the Microsoft development environment, Visual Studio's Visual C++ development environment has these tools built in. Cross-reference tools assist in understanding some global aspects of the source and help trace threads of interaction. They are limited in not providing an overview of structural interactions, they have an inability to get a clear sense of design, and they contribute to information overload by displaying too much data in the cross-referencing.

Software visualization is the next set of tools grouped into the comprehension category. These tools analyze the dynamic behavior of software and allow the user to visualize all program data through an integrated graphical user interface. Visualization tools automate the tasks of determining code coverage, selecting code to cover that will increase coverage rapidly, finding a minimized test set, debugging, identifying what part of the software implements a specific feature, profiling program performance, and finding static program relationships. These tools provide an overview of structural information, can overlay different structural relations, and provide a "direct and precise" view of the source information. As with the cross-reference tools, the output can be voluminous and hard to analyze because of the lack of abstracted viewing layers, and it is still hard to derive the inherent software design.

Re-engineering—CMM Level 5

Re-engineering tools allow translation of an existing program to a new programming language, or a database to a new format. Reverse-engineering tools assist the process by working backward from an existing product to create abstract artifacts such as design and specification descriptions, which then can be transformed to generate a new product from an old one. The combination of reverse-engineering the design and then forward- or re-engineering a new product is also labeled round-trip engineering by many tool vendors.

The intent of reverse-engineering tools is to create high-level model(s) of a system from the information in the source. The source information can be from a program database created by software visualization tools. The benefits to re-engineering tools are in creating an overview of the system structure along with a sense of the system design. The software engineer doesn't need much knowledge about the system because the re-engineering tools typically provide a precise view based on their internal methodology of interpreting and deriving inherent design from source code. The limitations are the same as with the comprehension tools, in that there can still be information overload and the tool may not create the view that the software engineer can really use.

Software Configuration Management Tools— CMM Level 2 and Above

The minimum features for SCM tools are closely related to the task of handling the different product deliverables produced within the project software engineering process. Tool requirements and selection criteria are based on a series of features that provide a consistent look and feel with state-of-the-art software development environments. An SCM tool must have multiuser support, an intuitive graphic user interface, conformity to the organization's development environment, scalability, flexibility in integrating other software development tools, ease of setup, modifiable models, process management, extensive support for the development phase, and management of nondevelopment objects. Figure 24–8 shows the SCM life cycle coverage.

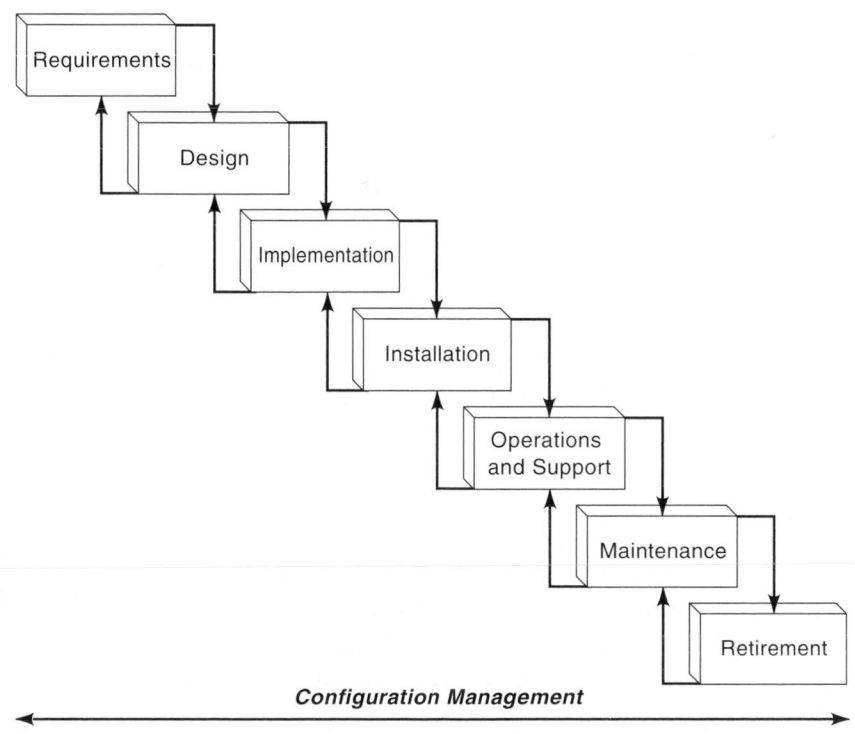

FIGURE 24–8
Configuration Management Tools Life Cycle Coverage

Configuration is categorized in these three areas:

1. Defect, enhancement, issue, and problem tracking
2. Version management
3. Release and build

Chapter 31, "Software Configuration Management," has complete information in software configuration management.

Software Engineering Life Cycle Process Tools _____

As shown in Figure 24–9, software engineering life cycle process tools handle the tasks associated with software engineering process, quality, engineering management, and infrastructure. These tools are used throughout the life cycle in all the phases.

Software Engineering Process Tools _____

Process-centered software engineering tools model the environment in which the software product is being developed. A process-centered software engineering environment recognizes the importance of the defined software development process and its dynamic nature. It supports the activity of defining a process for a development project and the subsequent process monitoring and support during execution. Some tool sets support the dynamic modification of the process as it is being executed. This type of process change during a project execution is akin to changing the tire on a moving car. It can be done, but control is difficult to maintain.

Process Management—CMM Level 4 and Above

Process management is the activity undertaken by project managers before they can begin any project. This activity lays out the framework against how they will act and measure their progress on their projects. Process management ensures the correct execution of the organization's procedures, policies, and life cycle model. Process management controls the software development activities. For example, it might check to ensure that a change request existed and had been approved for fixing and that the associated design, documentation, and review activities have been completed before allowing the code to be "checked in" again. The tools for process management include the process model and interpersonal communication tools, as described later.

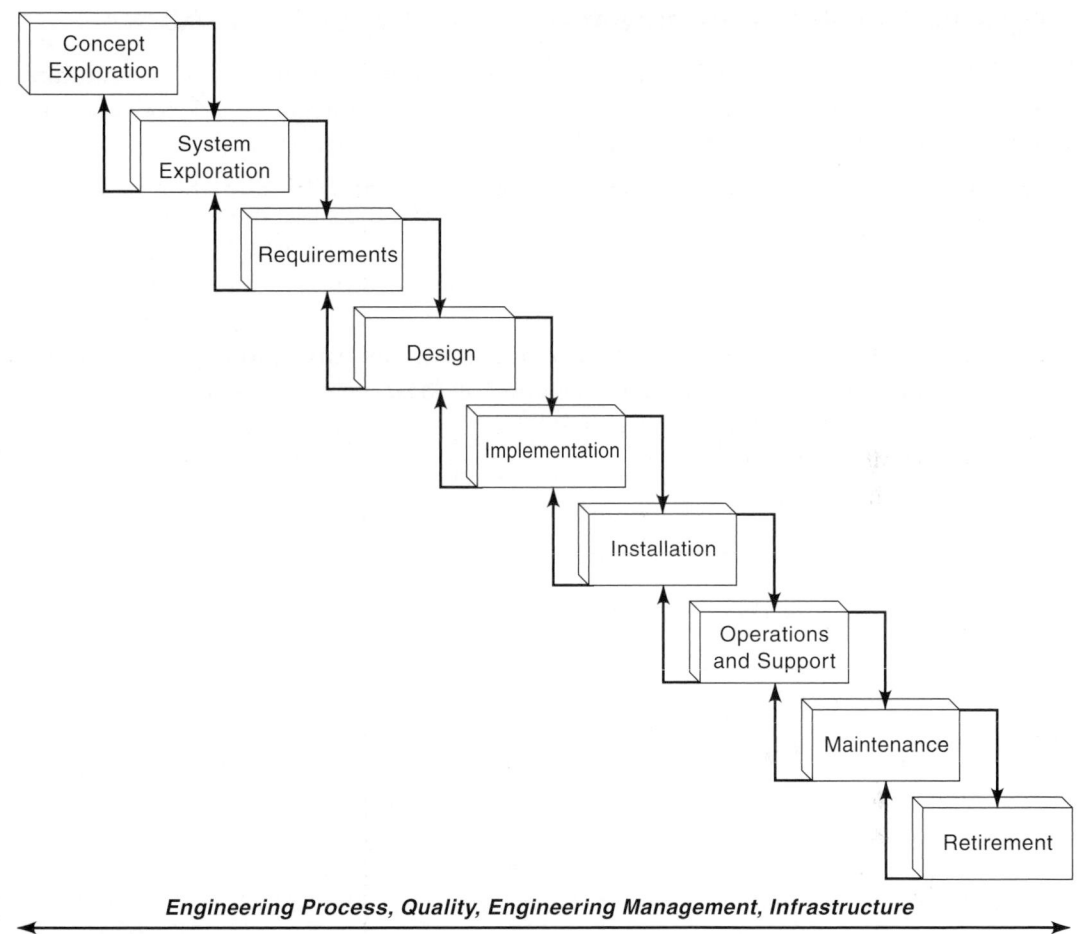

FIGURE 24–9
Software Engineering Process Tools Life Cycle Coverage

Process Modeling—CMM Level 3 and Above

The model for the process being managed is developed and documented by a process-modeling tool. Many process-modeling tools are available, and a Web search is one place to begin. If the development organization is not at Level 3, modeling the process would not gain any appreciable end product quality. This activity also cannot begin until there is a defined development life cycle with clearly understood and documented entry and exit criteria. All of this can easily be initially documented with a tool such as Visio. A tool selection process should be followed with a strong return-on-investment business case made before a full featured, expensive commercial tool is purchased.

Integrated CASE Environments—CMM Level 4 and Above

Computer-aided software engineering (CASE) tools or environments that cover multiple phases of the software development life cycle reside in this category. Such tools perform multiple functions and, hence, potentially interact with the software process that is being managed and modeled. CASE tools are further subcategorized into upper CASE tools that model the requirements and design phases, and lower CASE tools that are more code generators for the implementation phase. In the Microsoft development world, Visual Studio qualifies as both an upper and lower CASE development environment. As long as the product is targeted at an environment supported by Visual Studio, the tools are completely integrated. In the Linux development environment, tools such as AnyJ and ArgoUML provide the same level of coverage when they are integrated by the developing organization.

Some CASE tools available incorporate process modeling and management capabilities. These integrated tools focus on a specific methodology, such as information engineering, or techniques, such as object-oriented. In most environments, the project manager must adopt the internal process model of the tool to be successful. These tools must be selected with care and a strong proof of positive return on investment. Since making their debut in the early 1980s, CASE tool suites and packages have become a famous shelfware.

Process-Centered Software Engineering Environments— CMM Level 5 and Above

This type of software development environment manager is a combination of all the previously described tools. The software development process model and the integrated CASE environment are combined with all of the process management functions of reporting, analyzing, maintaining, and evolving. This is the automation of the CMM Level 5 continuous process improvement. This tool set provides for the process improvement feedback to be acquired and implemented by the process itself. The complexity of this type of end-to-end software development process manager cannot be underestimated. It should be considered only by a Level 5 organization after in-depth analysis and best practices interviews of other organizations using these kinds of tools.

Software Quality Tools

Inspection and static analysis tools are appropriate to use in CMM organizations with a maturity Level 3 and greater. Software quality can be measurably improved through use of tools in mature organizations.

Inspection—CMM Level 3 and Above

Inspections and reviews are a critical part of the software development process. Fortunately, only the most basic of tools are required to support them: email, word processing, and a spreadsheet. The notification and results tracking from reviews and inspections can be an elaborate work flow–oriented process, but exotic tools are not needed. The basics are to notify team members of the activity, collect the results for metrics purposes, and publish the minutes of the sessions.

Static Analysis—CMM Level 4 and Above

A basic tool that can be used in either Windows or the Linux environment for basic, static source code analysis is Resource Standard Metrics (RSM).[3] Resource Standard Metrics is a source code metrics and quality analysis tool for ANSI C, ANSI C++, and Java for use on all Windows and Unix operating systems. RSM supports the language syntax of ANSI C, ANSI C++, and Java. RSM is designed to analyze compiled source code. Source code that will not compile will not correctly pass through the RSM parser. RSM may miss functions and or code constructs if the source code cannot be compiled according to the specific grammar of the source language. RSM is a shell-based tool, meaning that you must use a command shell or any Unix shell or Xterm that you desire to run RSM. This allows RSM to integrate into Visual Studio, Kawa, and other IDEs. RSM creates HTML reports for metrics that interact with source code hyperlinks and comma-separated value format for direct input to Excel or other spreadsheets.

Software Engineering Management Tools _____

Software engineering management tools support the foundation processes of project planning, risk management, and metrics. These are critical processes, but the tools required to implement them are neither difficult to use nor hard to find. The critical portion of these tools is the plan that they must follow.

Project Planning and Tracking—CMM Level 2 and Above

The very first project planning and tracking tool that a project manager should pick up is a spreadsheet. Unless the project has more than 100 individually tracked subtasks and more than five team members, and has other task dependencies, there is no need to go to a commercial project management tool. The project manager needs to keep in mind that the objective is to deliver a successful, quality software product within budget and on schedule. The project manager's objective should not be to become the world's best mouse driver for a project management software tool.

Risk Management—CMM Level 2 and Above

Chapter 18, "Determining Project Risks," covers the management of risk and provides templates for use. These templates are easily implemented in a spreadsheet tool. The only tools needed for risk management are the risk management plan and a spreadsheet.

Measurement—CMM Level 2 and Above

Chapter 21, "Software Metrics," covers the planning and analyzing of software development project metrics. The only tools needed for measurement are the metrics plan and a spreadsheet.

Infrastructure Support Tools _____

This section covers tools that provide interpersonal communication, information retrieval, and system administration and support. These tools, such as email, databases, Web browsers, and file-backup tools, are generally specific neither to a particular life cycle stage nor to a particular development method.

Interpersonal Communications—CMM Level 1 and Above

Communications are the most important task that the project manager has to make successful. Software development is a process requiring many specialists to understand the entire product under construction. The key to communication is that it absolutely, positively must be reliable. Email, Web-based document-sharing schemes, chat rooms, and online meeting applications must work all the time, every time. Without reliable communications any project will fail.

Information Retrieval—CMM Level 2 and Above

As software development organizations become more mature they begin to generate more data about the process of building products. This data in the form of metrics about the process and product needs a home. Although the initial use of a spreadsheet is adequate, it takes a very short amount of time to overload the capabilities of Excel. Moving to a simple database management application is essential. A tool with the capabilities of Microsoft Access is more than adequate for the data collection, analysis, and reporting. This information will be used to populate and drive the tools used for process-centered software engineering environments. This will be the key organizational repository for information on process improvement and process activity. Started early in the organization maturation process, this tool will aid in reaching the higher maturity levels sooner.

System Administration and Support—CMM Level 2 and Above

This category of tools should be prefaced with the word *formal*. Even an individual developer spends time administering the operating system and supporting network connections. Moving to higher levels of process maturity requires a formal process within the development organization for system administration and support. Standardizing on operating system types, releases, service package installations, security precautions, and basic tools saves time and effort when integrating developers into a standard production environment. Providing a constant and expected level of support is important so that individuals do not have to debug and fix the same system issue just alleviated by a co-worker on a machine. Providing a consistent tool kit here saves time and increases individual productivity.

Miscellaneous Tools Issues _____

The final category of software development tools is that famous catchall of "miscellaneous." In here are grouped tools that support the integration of other tools, tools for building tools, and the techniques of tool evaluation.

Tool Integration Techniques—CMM Level 3 and Above

Tool integration is important for making individual tools cooperate with others in the software development environment. This category overlaps with software engineering environments in which integration techniques are part of the tool set. For a tool to be acceptable for use within a state-of-the-art software development environment, the tool must have some defined application programming interface (API). Without a way to interface and, therefore, integrate with a tool, the information and output of the tool is worthless in a comprehensive environment. No tools should be treated as black boxes. To get to a CMM Level 5, all tools have to be open for continuous process improvement.

Tools are integrated using the scripting language of the overall environment. If the development environment is Microsoft-based, then the scripting language of choice is probably Visual Basic. If the environment is based on Web technologies, the scripting language probably will be Perl. Domain-specific environments such as semiconductor manufacturing would use Tcl/Tk as the integrating scripting language.

Meta Tools—CMM Level 1 and Above

Developers use tools to make the process of software product building easier, more robust, and repeatable. Throughout the life cycle, tools are acquired and built. Tools are much broader than the traditional YACC (Yet Another Complier Compiler) of Unix fame. Any tool that provides a mechanism through an API for customization can be transformed from a general-purpose to a special-purpose tool. Taking applications such as presentation managers and developing an interactive graphical user interface demonstration or a spreadsheet and customizing it into a metrics collection and analysis tool are some examples. All database management applications have customizable data collection front ends and reporting output. These can be customized to serve as prototyping platforms and process integration tools. In the early maturity levels of an organization, it is a good ides to try out new processes and tools through customizing general-purpose tools to the project's specific needs. As the organization matures, investments can be made in extending the homegrown tools, or they can be used as the specifications for purchasing a commercial tool.

Tool Evaluation—CMM Level 3 and Above

Tool evaluation requires only a spreadsheet application, the list of tool requirements, a weighting factor for each requirement, and some potential vendors. The vendor response to each requirement is entered into a spot on the spreadsheet. The response could be binary 1 or 0, indicating that it does or doesn't exist. When vendors almost meet the requirements or exceed them, a rating of from 0 to 5 could be used. Here, 0 indicates that the requirement is not met, 3 denotes that it meets the requirement, and 4 and 5 are used for a level of exceeding the requirement. Ratings 1 and 2 are used for gradations of almost meeting the requirement.

Table 24–3 is an example of evaluating a code-complexity tool. The requirements section begins with the "Must Have Requirements." If any of these are missing from the evaluated tool, the tool cannot be selected. In the case of Vendor B, it failed the operating system and source code escrow requirement. The next requirements are the "Should Have Requirements," with individual weighting factors that are multiplied by the vendor score to get a weighted score. As can be seen from Vendor B, the "Must Have Result" also multiplies the weighted score. Where the must have is 0, the entire score is 0. Finally the "Nice to Have Requirements" are listed and are all weighted at one.

Once the spreadsheet does all the calculations, it is obvious that Vendor D scores the highest. This tool can be used to re-evaluate and change scoring and weighting. If a mistake is made in the mandatory requirements, changing from 0 to 1 or 1 to 0 changes the scoring of the vendor. This type of evaluation can be used for any type of software development tool.

Minimal Tool Sets

Table 24–4 contains a collection of the minimal tool sets applicable to the previous tool category descriptions. There are only two categories, Microsoft Windows and Linux. Most of the Linux tools will also work on other flavors of Unix. What make these minimal are cost and capability. All mentioned tools have limitations that may make them unsuitable for developing mission-critical or industrial-strength software. The project manager must take the maturity

TABLE 24–3
Complexity Tool Evaluation

Requirement	Weight Factor	Vendor A		Vendor B		Vendor C		Vendor D	
		Score	Weighted	Score	Weighted	Score	Weighted	Score	Weighted
Must Have Requirements									
Operate in a Linux Environment	1	1	1	0	0	1	1	1	1
API for Data Extraction	1	1	1	1	1	1	1	1	1
Escrow Source Code	1	1	1	0	0	1	1	1	1
Must Have Result			1		0		1		1
Should Have Requirements									
Function Metrics Per Function:									
LOC Lines of Code	5	3	15	5	0	3	15	3	15
eLOC (Effective LOC)	5	3	15	5	0	2	10	4	20
lLOC (Logical Statements LOC)	5	2	10	5	0	1	5	4	20
Comments Lines	5	4	20	5	0	1	5	4	20
Blank Lines	5	5	25	5	0	2	10	5	25
Physical Lines	5	2	10	5	0	3	15	5	25
Number of Input Parameters	4	1	4	4	0	2	8	5	20
Number of Return Points	4	1	4	4	0	1	4	3	12
Interface Complexity (Parameters + Returns)	4	0	0	4	0	1	4	3	12
Cyclomatic Complexity Logical Branching	4	0	0	4	0	3	12	3	12
Functional Complexity (Interface + Cyclomatic)	4	2	8	4	0	3	12	3	12

(Continues)

TABLE 24–3 (Continued)
Complexity Tool Evaluation

Requirement	Weight Factor	Vendor A		Vendor B		Vendor C		Vendor D	
		Score	Weighted	Score	Weighted	Score	Weighted	Score	Weighted
Quality Per Function:									
Function Parameters	4	1	4	3	0	1	4	5	20
Cyclomatic Complexity	5	5	25	3	0	1	5	5	25
Functional Complexity	5	2	10	3	0	1	5	5	25
Total Quality Profile	4	5	20	5	0	1	4	5	20
Class Metrics	3	5	15	5	0	2	6	4	12
Template Type	3	3	9	5	0	3	9	4	12
Inheritance	5	3	15	5	0	1	5	4	20
Depth of Inheritance Tree	5	3	15	4	0	1	5	4	20
Number of Derived Child Classes per Base Class	2	3	6	4	0	2	4	4	8
Interface Complexity (Parameters + Returns)	2	0	0	4	0	2	4	5	10
Class Complexity (Interface + Cyclomatic)	2	2	4	4	0	3	6	5	10
All Classes Information:									
Total Number of Classes	3	3	9	5	0	3	9	5	15
Inheritance Tree	3	3	9	3	0	3	9	5	15
Number of Base Classes	3	3	9	4	0	3	9	5	15
Number of Derived Classes	3	3	9	5	0	2	6	5	15
Derived/Base Class Ratio	3	3	9	3	0	2	6	5	15
Maximum and Average Inheritance Depth	3	3	9	4	0	1	3	5	15

(Continues)

TABLE 24–3 (Continued)
Complexity Tool Evaluation

Requirement	Weight Factor	Vendor A		Vendor B		Vendor C		Vendor D	
		Score	Weighted	Score	Weighted	Score	Weighted	Score	Weighted
Maximum and Average Number of Child Classes	3	3	9	5	0	1	3	5	15
Nice to Have Requirements									
Namespace or Package Metrics:									
Per Namespace	1	5	5	2	0	1	1	3	3
Number of Classes	1	5	5	3	0	1	1	4	4
Number of Functions	1	5	5	1	0	1	1	3	3
Average Functions per Class	1	5	5	3	0	2	2	4	4
Number of Public, Private, Protected Data Attributes	1	5	5	2	0	2	2	3	3
Number of Public, Private, Protected Methods	1	5	5	1	0	2	2	3	3
Number of Input Parameters	1	5	5	2	0	2	2	3	3
Number of Return Points	1	5	5	2	0	2	2	4	4
Interface Complexity (Parameters + Returns)	1	5	5	4	0	2	2	4	4
Total			342		0		217		511

and robustness of the tools into account when risk mitigation is done. The tools mentioned in this chapter are merely starting points. An example is for project planning and scheduling. Other industrial-strength tools are described in this handbook. But if the project manager does not know the basics of developing a work breakdown structure or estimating, or if the development organization is a CMM Level 1, automation is not an issue. The project manager will be merely automating chaos.

All of the Linux tools listed are either freeware or shareware. Although there are freeware and shareware versions of some tools for Windows platforms, most users of the Windows operating system families are not disposed to the Open Source movement, as are Linux aficionados.

TABLE 24–4
Minimal Tool Sets

Tool Class	Specific Tool Type	Microsoft® Windows Tools	Linux Tools
Software Requirements Tools	Requirements Modeling	Visio® Access	Dia QuickList
	Traceability	Excel	abs
Software Design Tools	Design modeling	Visio® Access	ArgoUML
	Design verification	Visio® Excel	ArgoUML abs
	Design optimization	Visual Studio	ArgoUML
Software Construction Tools	Program editors	Visual Studio	Emacs
	Compilers	Visual Studio	AnyJ
	Interpreters	Visual Studio	Perl
	Debuggers	Visual Studio	AnyJ
Software Testing Tools	Test generators	Access	QuickList ArgoUML
	Test execution frameworks	Visual Studio	Perl
	Test evaluation	Excel	abs
	Test management	Visual Source Safe	CVS
	Performance analysis	Excel	abs
Software Maintenance Tools	Comprehension	Visual Studio	Cxref
	Re-engineering	Visual Studio	ArgoUML

(Continues)

TABLE 24–4 (Continued)
Minimal Tool Sets

Tool Class	Specific Tool Type	Microsoft® Windows Tools	Linux Tools
Software Engineering Process Tools	Process management	email, Web, word processor	email, Web, word processor
	Process modeling	Visio®	Dia
	Integrated CASE environments	Visual Studio	AnyJ
	Process-centered software engineering environments		
Software Quality Tools	Inspection	email, word processor, Excel	email, word processor, abs
	Static analysis	RSM	RSM
Software Configuration Management Tools	Defect, enhancement, issue and problem tracking	Visual Source Safe	CVS
	Version management	Visual Source Safe	CVS
	Release and build	Visual Source Safe	CVS
Software Engineering Management Tools	Project planning and tracking	Excel	abs
	Risk management	Excel	abs
	Measurement	Excel	abs
Infrastructure Support Tools	Interpersonal communications	email, Web chat	email, Web chat
	Information retrieval system	Access, Web	QuickList, Web
	Administration and support	email, Web	email, Web
Miscellaneous Tools Issues	Tool integration techniques	Visual Basic, Perl, Tcl/Tk	Perl, Tcl/Tk
	Meta tool	Access, Excel	Dia, abs
	Tool evaluation	Excel	abs

Summary

The project's life cycle and the organization's model for process improvement are both used by project managers to frame the selection of tools. As previously discussed, the software engineering and development tools that support the project life cycle are covered in the SWEBOK. Table 24–1 shows the SWEBOK tools with the addition of the design tools for verification and optimization. All investigations of tools for project and software engineering development organization use should begin here.

The relationship among the five process maturity levels of the Software Engineering Institute's capability maturity model and the individual tools identified in the SWEBOK ensures that the project is not investing in automation beyond the organization's maturity level. Providing tools to an immature organization merely allows the developers to produce the wrong product faster. Powerful tools require maturity to be used effectively.

The volatility of the software tools market makes listing specific tools impractical. To begin a search for existing tools and suppliers use an Internet search engine such as Copernic (*www.copernic.com*). As an example, searching for "software requirement modeling" returns 106 active Web pages. Using this initial search information along with the tool evaluation techniques presented provides the starting point for automated tool investigation and selection.

Problems for Review

1. Find an existing C, C++, or Java program of no less than 500 source code lines. Download RSM from *www.m2tech.net/rsm/default.htm* and install it on your computer system. Answer the following questions about your source code:

   a. Total LOC, eLOC, ILOC, comment, blanks, lines

   b. Total function metrics

   c. Total class metrics

   d. Total namespace metrics

   e. Inheritance tree and metrics

   f. Language keywords, constructs, and metrics

   g. Quality profile

   h. Metric estimation factors for software estimates

   i. Total C, C++, and header files

   j. Total Java files

   k. Total number of files

2. A configuration management tool is needed for a Microsoft Windows NT operating system C++ development environment. Build an evaluation tool, and use it to rank four configuration management tools.

3. Map the SWEBOK tool categories to the Boehm Spiral Model for software development.

4. Describe a process and specific tools to use in taking an existing C language, command-line stock portfolio analysis system and converting it to Java to run in a Web browser.

Visit the Case Study

On March 20, 2001, China's government said that it would invest in Red Flag Software, China's largest Linux software developer, to try to curb Microsoft's dominance of the country's software market. Chinese ministries are encouraging government institutions and state-owned companies to use Red Flag Linux software to trim Microsoft's dominance in the market. Because of this, Mr. Lu has directed that you deliver with the ARRS software a Linux development and maintenance environment. Because you are already developing in Java, Mr. Lu remembered your presentations, where Java is a "write once, run everywhere," portable software.

The project will build and deliver a Java software engineering development environment with these requirements:

1. Must run on any Pentium 1–based hardware or better.

2. Must run on a machine with hard drive of less than 4GB.

3. Must load from CD-ROM(s).

4. Machine will have access to the Internet.

5. Must load into a green-field machine.

6. Must include the entire software system.

7. Must cost less than 200 Chinese Renminbi for the end-user delivered software system.

8. Must *not* include hardware in the system cost.

9. Must use all browser-based documentation.

10. Must provide licenses with all software.

11. Must use tools that cover the entire software life cycle.

12. Must implement all project support processes.

13. Must support team development environment.

14. Must deliver full system and user documentation.

15. xTRemeObjectMaker does have a Linux version. You need to get this incorporated into your plans because it will change your ultimate deliverables and acceptance.

Citations

[1]Brooks, Fred P. (1986). "No Silver Bullet: Essence and Accidents of Software Engineering." *Information Processing*, pp. 1069–1076.

[2]Prechelt, Lutz (2000). "An Empirical Comparison of Seven Programming Languages." *IEEE Software*, October, pp. 23–29.

[3]*www.m2tech.net/rsm/default.htm.* Resource Standard Metrics, known as RSM, is a source code metrics and quality analysis tool unlike any other on the market today. RSM provides a standard method for analyzing C, ANSI C++, and Java source code across operating systems. The unique ability of RSM to support virtually any operating system provides your enterprise with the ability to standardize the measurement of source code quality and metrics throughout your organization. RSM provides the fastest, most flexible and easy-to-use tool to assist in the measurement of code quality and metrics.

Tools

argouml.tigris.org/. The goal of the ArgoUML project is to build an object-oriented design tool that is a joy to use, actually helpful to designers when they are making design decisions, completely Open Source Java, leading-edge (supports the latest UML specifications), modular, and extensible, integrated with the Web and other Tigris tools.

cvshome.org/. CVS is the Concurrent Versions System, the dominant Open Source network-transparent version control system. CVS is useful for everyone from individual developers to large, distributed teams: Its client/server access method lets developers access the latest code from anywhere there's an Internet connection. Its unreserved check-out model to version control avoids artificial conflicts common with the exclusive check-out model. Its client tools are available on most platforms.

sourceforge.net/foundry/tcl-foundry/. Foundry for Tcl (Tool Command Language): a cross-platform (Unix/Windows/Macintosh/and more) scripting language that was created by John Ousterhout in 1988 and that is used by companies and organizations worldwide. The tcl SF (SourceForge) project has the main Tcl source code, and the tktoolkit project has the Tk source code ("tk" was too short). An informal survey shows more than 100 more Tcl-related projects. Some are Tcl extensions, and some are applications built with Tcl. If your project is not listed, please contact one of the Foundry guides.

www.gedanken.demon.co.uk/cxref/. Cxref is a program that will produce documentation (in LaTeX, HTML, RTF, or SGML), including cross-references from C program source code. It has been designed to work with ANSI C, incorporating K&R, and most popular GNU extensions. The documentation for the program is produced from comments in the code that are appropriately formatted. The cross-referencing comes from the code itself and requires no extra work.

www.gnu.org/software/emacs/. GNU Emacs is an advanced, self-documenting, customizable, extensible real-time display editor Emacs. It is a display editor because normally the text being edited is visible on the screen and is updated automatically as you type your commands. It is called a real-time editor because the display is updated very frequently, usually after each character or pair of characters that you type. This minimizes the amount of information that you must keep in your head as you edit. GNU Emacs provides facilities that go beyond simple insertion and deletion: filling of text; automatic indentation of programs; viewing two or more files at once; and dealing in terms of characters, words, lines, sentences, paragraphs, and pages, as well as expressions and comments in several different programming languages.

www.lysator.liu.se/~alla/dia/dia.html. Dia is a gtk+–based diagram creation program released under the GPL license. Dia is designed to be much like the commercial Windows program Visio. It can be used to draw many different kinds of diagrams. It currently has special objects to help draw entity relationship diagrams, UML diagrams, flowcharts, network diagrams, and simple circuits. It is also possible to add support for new shapes by writing simple XML files, using a subset of SVG to draw the shape.

www.microsoft.com/ms.htm.

www.netcomputing.de/html/main.html. AnyJ is a cross-platform Java IDE and source code engineering solution. AnyJ includes various browsers and analyzing tools, a Java Beans–compliant Visual GUI-Builder (JFC, Swing), a source-level debugger, and a very powerful, intelligent, and fast editor.

www.perl.com/pub. Perl is an interpreted language optimized for scanning arbitrary text files, extracting information from those text files, and printing reports based on that information. It's also a good language for many system management tasks. The language is intended to be practical (easy to use, efficient, complete) rather than beautiful (tiny, elegant, minimal). It combines (in the author's opinion, anyway) some of the best features of C, sed, awk, and sh, so people familiar with those languages should have little difficulty with it.

www.ping.be/bertin/abs.shtml. abs is a standalone state-of-the-art spreadsheet designed to run on any Unix platform. abs comes with the ABVisual macro language (compatible with Microsoft Visual Basic). abs can exchange data with Microsoft Excel through Visual Basic. All data, formats, drawings, controls, and charts are exportable to Microsoft Excel. abs is distributed with source code under General Public License. It is under development but is already stable enough to be used.

www.quicklist.org/. QuickList is a free (GPL) gtk+ program for any UNIX system with gtk+ 1.2 or better that allows novice and experienced users to keep track of "things" without any help from a system administrator. "Things" can be anything, including bug lists, phone lists, restaurants, team members, calendars, cool Urls, checkbooks, fishing holes, CDs, bunjee-jumping cool sites, and so on. It is completely flexible. QuickList can list things in column format, much as they would appear in a spreadsheet. It is planned to show things in a one per page in "forms" format. The data can be edited in either list form or "form" form. QuickList can sort lists of things, search from them, and print reports from them.

Web Pages for Further Information

search.kachinatech.com/index.shtml. SAL (Scientific Applications on Linux) is a collection of information and links to software that will be of interest to scientists and engineers. The broad coverage of Linux applications will also benefit the whole Linux/Unix community. There are currently 3,017 entries in SAL.

www.construx.com/. The "Software Engineering Tools" page lists software development resources provided by Construx and other organizations. The "Software Estimation Tools, including Construx Estimate" page provides access to a free software project estimation program. It also provides links to other estimation programs and estimation resources on the Internet. The "Software Development

Checklists" page provides links to more than two dozen checklists covering all aspects of software development, including requirements definition, architecture, design, coding, and subcontract management. The "Document Templates" page discusses one of the major obstacles to more effective technical and technical-management work: simply not knowing what the relevant software documents are supposed to look like. This page contains sample requirements documents, design documents, coding standards, and many other documents. It also contains source code in various languages. The "Survival Guide Web site" is related to the Software Project Survival Guide, written by Construx Software's chief software engineer, Steve McConnell. "Links to Other Resources" provides links to resources provided by other organizations.

www.cs.queensu.ca/Software-Engineering/. These are the World Wide Web archives for the USENET newsgroup comp.software-eng, including the frequently asked questions (FAQ) postings. Please read our disclaimers. This archive is mirrored at the University of Technology Vienna, Austria; the master copy is at the Department of Computing and Information Science of Queen's University at Kingston, Canada.

www.li.org/. Linux International is a nonprofit association of groups, corporations, and others that work toward the promotion of growth of the Linux operating system and the Linux community.

www.qucis.queensu.ca/Software-Engineering/tools.html. The CASE tool index is a good starting point to do Web research. Due to the volatile nature of these companies, many of the Web links are no longer active.

www.spmn.com/. SPMN's Mission is to seek out proven industry and government software best practices and convey them to managers of large-scale DoD software-intensive acquisition programs. Applying extensive "in the trenches" experience, the SPMN enables program managers to achieve project success and deliver quality systems on schedule and on budget.

www.swebok.org/. In spite of the millions of software professionals worldwide and the ubiquitous presence of software in our society, software engineering has not reached the status of a legitimate engineering discipline and a recognized profession. Since 1993, the IEEE Computer Society and the ACM have been actively promoting software engineering as a profession, notably through their involvement in the IEEE Computer Society and ACM Software Engineering Coordinating Committee.

References

Garg, Pankaj K., and Mehdi Jazayeri (1999). *Process-Centered Software Engineering Environments*. IEEE Computer Society Press.

Project Tracking and Control

Many projects burn energy but don't get anywhere. A key project management skill is to know how to track real progress, not just effort. This chapter introduces methods and tools for tracking progress. It is about project tracking and control, and it shows how to use tools to assess the real progress being made by the project team. The case study uses few progress tracking techniques, so the people involved think they are 90 percent complete all the time. They could have use earned value analysis and other tracking techniques to assess time-based progress toward milestones.

Where We Are in the Product Development Life Cycle

Where are we in the basic software life cycle model that serves as our map? As shown in Figure 4–1 and in Figure 25–1, we are primarily focused on the execution-oriented parts of the life cycle rather than the planning parts. These would include all the product development steps through installation. Tracking progress requires a plan to track against, and real measurement doesn't begin until a software development plan is approved by sponsorship.

In the project process framework shown in Figure 25–2, we are in the *do it* step: The SPMP has been approved, and the team is now being measured against the plan and schedule. At every review, all parts of the triple constraint will be checked.

Chapter 25 Relation to the 34 Competencies _____

Tracking a project's activities requires product skills in subcontractor management and quality tracking. The project management skills needed are selecting and monitoring development, and tracking process and project progress. The people management skills involved include

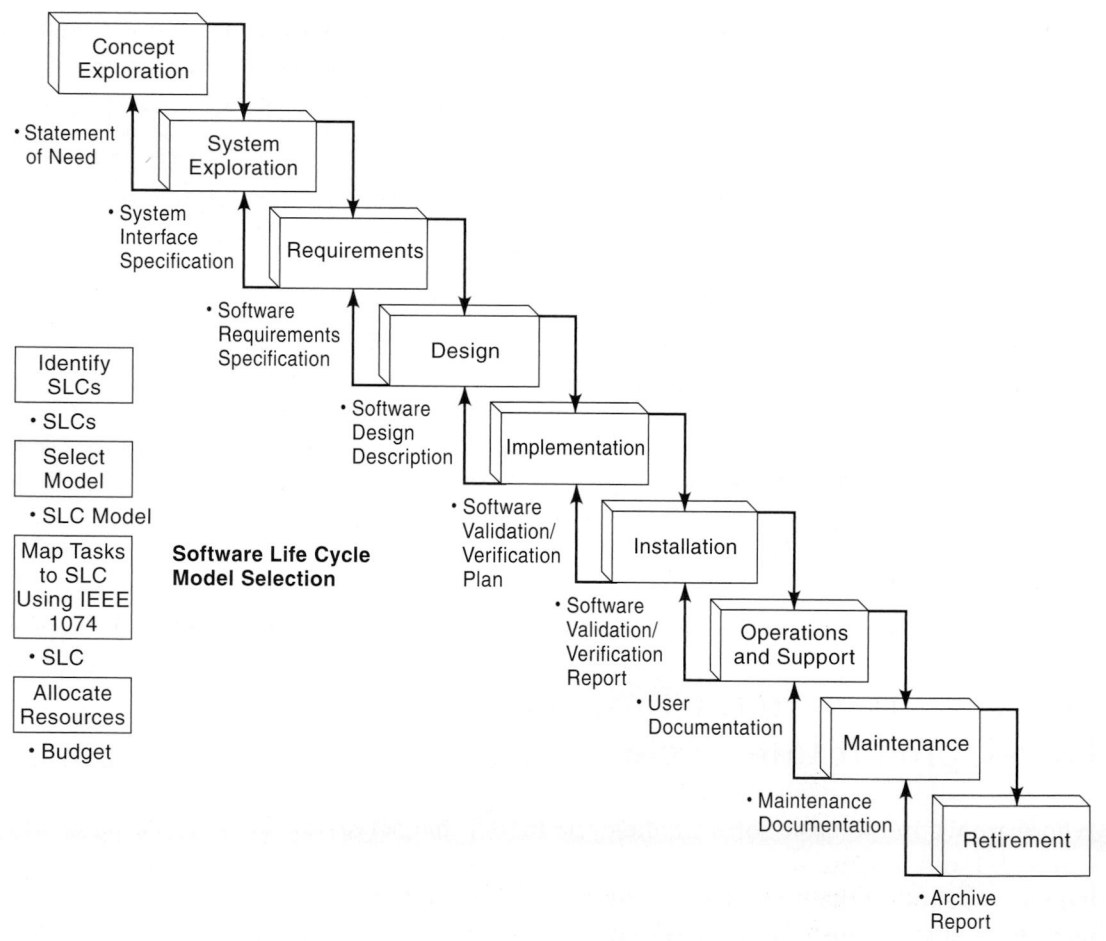

FIGURE 25–1
Product Process Framework

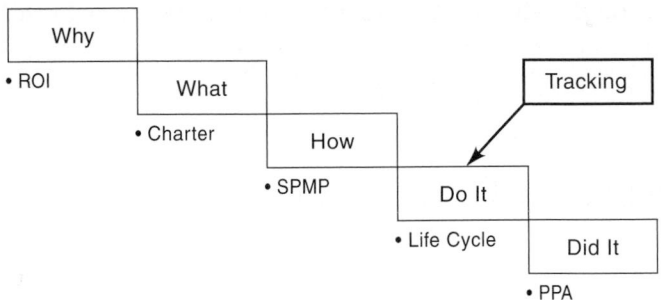

FIGURE 25–2
Project Process Framework

making performance appraisals for team members and managing change in the organization. Throughout the project, interacting and communicating with developers, upper management, and other teams is always required. These competencies are shown next.

Product Development Techniques

6. **Managing subcontractors**—Planning, managing, and monitoring performance
10. **Tracking product quality**—Monitoring the quality of an evolving product

Project Management Skills

17. **Monitoring development**—Monitoring the production of software
19. **Selecting metrics**—Choosing appropriate metrics
21. **Tracking process**—Monitoring compliance of project team
22. **Tracking project progress**—Monitoring progress using metrics

People Management Skills

23. **Appraising performance**—Evaluating teams to enhance performance
26. **Interaction and communication**—Dealing with developers, upper management, and other teams
28. **Managing change**—Being an effective change agent

Learning Objectives for Chapter 25 _____

Upon completion of this chapter, the reader should be able to:

- Describe several different ways of tracking and monitoring project activities;
- Demonstrate the ability to crash a project schedule;

- Explain the difference between earned value management and critical chain buffer management;
- Calculate the measurements of earned value management;
- Describe the requirements for a change control system for a project;
- Explain the use of a flexibility matrix.

Control Systems

To be effective, a software development project manager must have a control system in place for the project. What is a control system? Generally, it is a process that can monitor and control other processes. Your household thermostat is a control system designed to keep your house temperature within a certain range of comfort. All control systems have the general structure illustrated in Figure 25–3.

The important part is the *feedback loop* from the output to the input. This provides the ability to control and correct. For project control, this usually means data collection, validation, analysis, summarization, and reporting in a *timely* manner.

Timely is important here. It has been said that running a project by reading the monthly or quarterly reports is like trying to drive your car down the road by following the yellow stripe in your rearview mirror. You want data that allows you to *anticipate* what is ahead and react accordingly. Advanced thermostats for homes have an anticipation feature, which gradually adjusts the temperature to a new setting well in advance of its programmed time. In your incoming data about project parameters, look for *indicators* of outcomes that are reasonable predictors of what will occur before you have complete data. An example indicator to look for in a software development project is inspection metrics, the statistics about how much time was spent and how many defects were found in formal inspection data-logging meetings. This data is available almost instantly, as soon as the meeting is concluded. It can

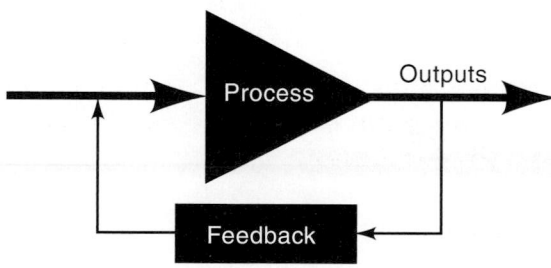

FIGURE 25–3
Generic Control System

be a good predictor of the quality of the resulting work product downstream because too few defects found per hour of inspection in a design phase (compared to that expected in a Rayleigh distribution) mean that the team members are not finding enough problems and that real errors will probably be found later (e.g. by the customer) when they are *much* more costly to correct. Other indicators are accelerating overtime use or extra hours to complete activities. Sometimes the informal metric for this is how many cars are still in the parking lot after dark! All of these are elements of a control system.

Process Control, Management, and Reporting

Fundamental to any project, but not necessarily obvious, is that a project must define a set of processes to be followed to execute the project. Some of these get defined in the SPMP, while others get defined in the risk, quality, or communications plans. When operating inside a larger organization, the project usually adopts the standard and well-known processes of the parent organization, where applicable, often without explicitly referencing them—they are simply part of the culture. It is important for the project to institutionalize these processes into the project's culture for these reasons:

- The project organization outlives those who leave it. (You don't want the know-how to leave with any departing members of the team.)
- The project's organizational culture is the conveyance of the process to new members. (Attitudes determine attention to detail and quality.)
- Management must nurture the culture. (The project manager must actively promote an understanding of the processes and procedures to be observed.)
- Culture is conveyed with role models and rewards. (An organization adopts the character of its leader; you get the behavior you reward.)

When the project must organize and staff from scratch, clear, simple processes (what to do) and procedures (how to do them) must be established for all to follow. These would certainly include, but not be limited to:

- configuration management and change control procedures;
- information reporting procedures;
- quality control procedures;

So, to control a project, a set of processes and procedures must be defined. But that is not all. A proper control system, as described earlier, must be established as well. See Chapter 3, "Process Overview," for more information on process management.

Project Management Information System

Every project has sources of information that a project manager should tap. Lots of metrics about code-related items are available in most configuration management and development tool environments. Meeting minutes and notices often contain valuable data. Issue logs contain indicators of project problems. Defect logs contain quality information. There are many ways to construct a useful project management information system (PMIS) from these sources. The core PMIS for your organization may be just an extension of your engineering management infrastructure, or you may have to build your own. Whichever it is, it must provide timely feedback on at least the elements in the triple constraint diagram, shown in Figure 1–4, repeated in Figure 25–4.

At every project review, management and the customer (and the project team, too) will want to know where the project is relative to the triple constraint parameters of scope, schedule, cost, and quality. It is the project manager's job to figure out where they are and report it as accurately as possible. Therefore, we will be looking at issues and methods related to these four parameters in the rest of this chapter. Several other chapters, such as Chapter 29, "Reporting and Communicating," Chapter 26, "Continuous Process Improvements," Chapter 23, "Validation and Verification," Chapter 30, "Software Quality Assurance," and Chapter 31, "Software Configuration Management," have other specific information useful for a project management information system. Also, most of the chapters on core software engineering topics (requirements, design, analysis, etc.) have useful methods and tools for monitoring software development project performance, product compliance, and quality achievement.

Scope Management

> If a project is allowed to change freely, the rate of change will exceed the rate of progress.
>
> —Unknown

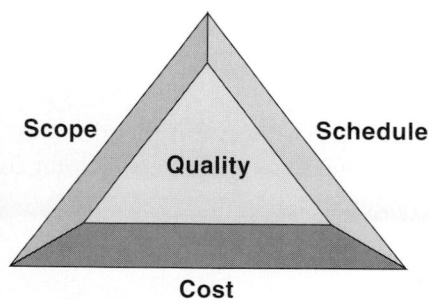

FIGURE 25–4
The Project Triple Constraint

Every project needs change control; otherwise, things will get out of control rather quickly. One of the worst things that can happen to a project is "scope creep," where the requirements seem to balloon out of control, usually slowly, until the balloon bursts and they exceed the capacity of the team and the time available to satisfy them. So, you need a scope control system to keep things under control. A scope control system is just a change control system focused on scope management. The basic elements of a change control system are:

- a means of identification and nomenclature—figuring out a plan for naming things, to avoid confusion;
- a process for managing baselines and processing changes, to keep versions straight and owners identified;
- a way to report the current status of any or all items, for handling inquiries about items or summaries; and
- a periodic audit or review process, to ensure integrity of the data you have.

A software development configuration management system usually has these basic parts of a control system (see Chapter 31 for a discussion of configuration management systems). Indeed, IEEE 1042 describes these items very well. But a scope control system is more than a configuration management system. A configuration management system is a subset of a project's scope control system. And the CM tool is just a subset of the CM system, as illustrated in Figure 25–5.

The change control process's central idea is that all changes start as "requests" that must go through a predefined control point, usually a change control board (CCB) of some kind. This can be a single part-time person for a small project or a large department for a major defense contract. However it is handled, there is always some kind of official repository for the official versions of anything important to the project. For software products, the CM system is the project's work product library. Changes to anything in there are not permitted until the

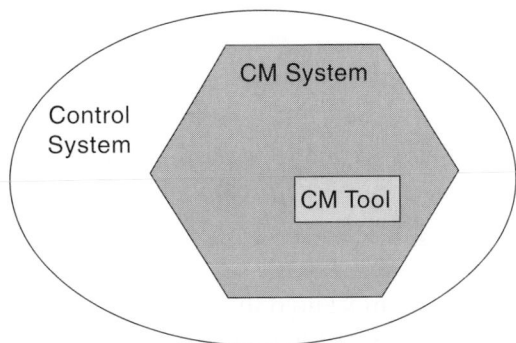

FIGURE 25–5
Relationship of Configuration Management to a Project Control System

change request can be evaluated for impact on other areas of the project, such as scope, schedule, cost, and quality. This is the function of the CCB.

Versions are tracked in the secured repository through some kind of check-out/check-in process that prevents multiple simultaneous changes to work products from occurring. Also, every work product should have an owner identified (and kept up-to-date). Obviously, the first items usually put under change management are the charter and the SPMP. If there is a request for proposal (RFP) involved, it is usually a good idea to put that under change management as well.

Successful *project* control is good *change* control. Some guidelines to follow are listed here:

- All project contracts or agreements must include a description of *how* changes to it will be handled.
- All change orders must be *approved* by the appropriate signature authority.
- All project artifacts must be amended with the *impact* of approved changes.
- Any change to a project artifact requires a captured *change control request* or *change order*.
- For each change order:
  - Review all changes for product and process impact.
  - Identify all activities and work-package impacts.
  - Translate impacts to performance, cost, and schedule.
  - Evaluate benefits and costs of changes.
  - Identify alternatives that may do the same thing.
  - Accept or reject on merit.
  - Communicate changes to all parties.
  - Summarize all changes in next reporting period.

Flexibility Matrix

It is also useful for change management control to prepare a decision-making matrix beforehand so that decisions can be made regarding trade-offs when they occur. This is often called a flexibility matrix, and it helps the team choose more effectively. It is best to discuss which of the three main items in the triple constraint are most flexible and least flexible with regard to the conditions on this particular project. A simple matrix can be presented as shown in Figure 25–6.

Notice that only one X is permitted in each row and column. For the sample matrix in the figure, the least flexible parameter is the schedule. The team must hold to the schedule. However, the team can hold to it by increasing resources, if necessary, and possibly by reducing scope. Deciding how to decide for the project at the beginning of the project can make for fewer arguments later.

	Flexibility		
	Least	Moderate	Most
Scope		X	
Schedule	X		
Cost			X

FIGURE 25–6
A Sample Flexibility Matrix

Schedule Management

Controlling the schedule is what project management seems to be all about. Commitments are made, and people try to perform to meet them. Yet the industry's track record isn't very good on this. Let's look at some ways to help keep things on track.

Milestone Lists

Milestone lists are simple lists of achievable milestones that the project planners have defined as signposts indicating progress toward the goals of the project. Milestones were defined and discussed in Chapter 8, "Creating the Work Breakdown Structure." Milestone lists are derived from the WBS and make a very handy checklist for the project. After the WBS data is loaded, milestone lists are easily generated from most project scheduling tools. Figure 25–7 shows a sample milestone list.

Crashing and Fast Tracking

Occasionally, a well-crafted plan must be changed due to circumstances beyond the team's control. Most often this means accelerating a due date. This becomes nearly impossible and unrealistic if the cost and quality sides of the triple constraint must remain unchanged. However, if it is important enough and additional resources *are* made available to achieve the acceleration, then the existing schedule can be collapsed to achieve an earlier finish date than currently planned. This process is called "crashing." Let's see how it works.

Crashing a project means to collapse the schedule, to shorten the total project time. This is also known as fast-tracking. Presumably, there is some major benefit to doing so, such as achieving a bonus for being early or avoiding a penalty for being late. The first place to look for crashing possibilities is on the critical path. Taking actions such as adding help to certain

WBS Code	Milestone	Expected Date	Actual Date
3.5.1	Plan and Develop Midlevel Architecture	11/19/2001	11/14/2001
4.2.6	Develop Phase I of the System	2/25/2002	2/12/2002
5.4.4	System Engine Component Built	3/25/2002	
6.9.2	Web Interface Component Completed	3/25/2002	
7.4.5	Network Traffic Study Completed	4/19/2002	

FIGURE 25–7
A Sample Milestone List

teams to accelerate their progress does nothing if those teams weren't working on anything on the critical path. Here's the process that we'll follow to find which activities to shorten. Table 25–1 is an example matrix problem set up to help solve crashing and fast-tracking.

Four Steps to Crash a Project   Although collapsing a schedule appears to be a complex task, these are the four basic steps in crashing the project:

1. Build a precedence network.
2. Find all activities on the *critical path* (check to see if it changes).
3. Find the activity or activities with the most favorable cost-time trade-offs.
4. Crash the activity *by 1 unit of time* until the project cannot be crashed anymore.

Crashing Example Setup   Let's consider an example problem. Here's the setup:

As requested, Heather sent an email to her boss, Jack, Director of Projects, saying that her team had estimated that the eX project would require 13 months for completion. Heather realized that the customer wanted the job completed in less time. To meet market windows, the contract has a $50,000 bonus for every month earlier, down to six months of total project time, and Jack would like to invest more resources into the project, for maximum return. Heather and her team collected the information shown in Table 25–2. What is the minimum

TABLE 25–1

Example Problem Statement

WBS Information		Initial Project Estimate		Crash Project Parameters	
Activity	Precedence	Time (Months)	Cost ($K)	Additional Cost of Resources per Month ($K)	Total # Months That Could Be Saved by Adding Resources to This Activity
A	—	3	60	30	1
B	A	5	120	20	1
C	A	5	160	50	2
D	A	4	80	10	2
E	C, D	2	60	15	1
F	B, E	3	140	40	2
			Cost Total: 620		

number of months that Heather and Jack should predict to the customer, and at what net benefit to their company?

Set Up the Problem Workspace

To solve this problem, do Step 1 to initially draw the network diagram and find the critical path. This is done for you and is shown in Figure 25–8.

Next, for convenience, lay out the problem like the solution table in Table 25–2, with columns for your work.

Then look over the network and enter the initial project length in the Project Length column for Step 0 (the initial condition). Enter the critical path for that project length (given initially as ACEF). Leave the rest on that line blank; they don't mean anything until you begin crashing the schedule.

Crash Process

Next, look over the Cost to Crash column in the problem table and choose the cheapest one that is an activity on the critical path. That is the first activity to crash, and it should be entered as the activity to crash at Step 1. Write what it costs to crash that activity in the Cost to Crash column, and mark it as being used from the Total Crash Time Available column in the problem statement table. Then calculate the net project savings from that single crash step (benefit minus cost to crash). The problem statement says that each crash gives a benefit of $50,000. Because the crashing shortens the critical path by total crash

TABLE 25–2
Example Problem Solution

Step	Activity to Crash	Cost to Crash	Net Project Savings	Project Length	Critical Path	Comments
0	—	—	—	13	ACEF	Initial State
1						
2						
3						
...						

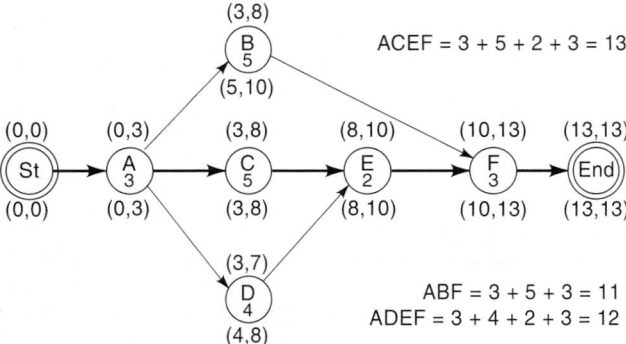

FIGURE 25–8
Example Crashing Problem Network Diagram

time available for that activity (calculate the new project length by subtracting the total crash time available from the project length in the previous step (Step 0 initially). Then check the network diagram to see if the critical path has changed. You need to know that for your next choice of activity to crash.

It is convenient to mark up the network diagram values for each change as you make them (the network shape won't change—only its values will). Then, to check the critical path, look at each node and compare the top numbers to the bottom numbers. If they are equal, there is no slack there and that activity is on the critical path. You want to crash activities only that are on the critical path; otherwise, you are wasting money.

Check If Done   Repeat the process for each activity until there is no more benefit to be gained by crashing, or until the total crash time available on the problem statement is exhausted for activities on the critical path. Always remember to make sure that you know what the critical path is when you make your choice of activity to crash for the next step. Record the critical path at each step as a string of letters, such as ACEF.

Example Problem Solution   The solution to the problem is shown in Table 25–3. Each step shows the time remaining for each node and its remaining cost and time available to crash. The current critical path and its length are shown in the box in italics. Notice that when you get to Step 8, all paths are critical, yet you can crash it one more time because there is time available for Activity D. However, it won't shorten the total project time.

Crashing is a computationally intensive exercise, like building a network, but it is a skill that all project managers should have.

Cost Management _____

Controlling costs is one of the most important things for any project. In software development projects, costs are almost entirely composed of labor because it is an intellectual activity. We usually try to control labor costs by minimizing the hours needed to do an activity and by reducing or avoiding rework.

To properly understand the costs for a project, though, you need to see how they add up over the life cycle of the project. In Chapter 8 you saw the WBS relationship to cost control in Figure 8–3. If cost accounts are being set up and managed for the project according to the WBS, they will provide the basis for cost measurement for the project. If no costs are being directly collected by activity, perhaps an indicator measurement such as hours (or even days) can be collected and extrapolated to costs based on the wages and overhead of an average software engineer on the project. Finance or human resources professionals in your organization usually can provide these numbers for you.

Cost Baseline

For any project, whether measured in hours or currency, a cost baseline curve can be built to show how resources will be spent over the life of the project.

The cost baseline is the time-phased budget that will be used to monitor progress on the project. It is usually represented as an "S" curve, showing the cumulative costs of the project over time. The "S" shape comes from the typical distribution of costs in a project: smaller at the beginning and end, and larger in the middle, as shown in Figure 25–9. When summed cumulatively, they form the familiar "S" curve representing the cost baseline for the project, shown in Figure 25–10.

The cost baseline represents your forecast of costs against time for the whole project. It says that you are planning to finish the project at time x using y dollars or hours. This is where z is in Figure 25–10. The cost baseline is a very useful representation, as you will see later when you study earned value management.

TABLE 25-3
Worksheet for Example Crashing Problem

Step 0	Activity	Precedence	Time Remaining	Cost Remaining	Add'l Cost to Crash	Total Crash Time Avail.	Network Path	New Length
Initial	A	—	3	60	30	1	ABF	11
	B	A	5	120	20	1	*ACEF*	*13*
	C	A	5	160	50	2	ADEF	12
	D	A	4	80	10	2		
	E	C, D	2	60	15	1		
	F	B, E	3	140	40	2		
				620				

Step 1	Activity	Precedence	Time Remaining	Cost Remaining	Add'l Cost to Crash	Total Crash Time Avail.	Network Path	New Length
	A	—	3	60	30	1	ABF	11
	B	A	5	120	20	1	*ACEF*	*12*
	C	A	5	160	50	2	ADEF	11
	D	A	4	80	10	2		
	E	C, D	*1*	*45*	15	*0*		
	F	B, E	3	140	40	2		
				605				

(Continues)

TABLE 25-3 (Continued)
Worksheet for Example Crashing Problem

Step 2	Activity	Precedence	Time Remaining	Cost Remaining	Add'l Cost to Crash	Total Crash Time Avail.	Network Path	New Length
	A	—	2	*30*	30	*0*	ABF	10
	B	A	5	120	20	1	*ACEF*	*11*
	C	A	5	160	50	2	ADEF	10
	D	A	4	80	10	2		
	E	C, D	*1*	*45*	15	*0*		
	F	B, E	3	140	40	2		
				575				

Step 3	Activity	Precedence	Time Remaining	Cost Remaining	Add'l Cost to Crash	Total Crash Time Avail.	Network Path	New Length
	A	—	2	*30*	30	*0*	ABF	9
	B	A	5	120	20	1	*ACEF*	*10*
	C	A	5	160	50	2	ADEF	9
	D	A	4	80	10	2		
	E	C, D	*1*	*45*	15	*0*		
	F	B, E	2	*100*	40	*1*		
				535				

(Continues)

TABLE 25-3 (Continued)

Worksheet for Example Crashing Problem

Step 4	Activity	Precedence	Time Remaining	Cost Remaining	Add'l Cost to Crash	Total Crash Time Avail.	Network Path	New Length
	A	—	2	30	30	0	ABF	8
	B	A	5	120	20	1	ACEF	9
	C	A	5	160	50	2	ADEF	8
	D	A	4	80	10	2		
	E	C, D	1	45	15	0		
	F	B, E	1	60	40	0		
				495				

Step 5	Activity	Precedence	Time Remaining	Cost Remaining	Add'l Cost to Crash	Total Crash Time Avail.	Network Path	New Length
	A	—	2	30	30	0	ABF	8
	B	A	5	120	20	1	ACEF	8
	C	A	4	110	50	1	ADEF	8
	D	A	4	80	10	2		
	E	C, D	1	45	15	0		
	F	B, E	1	100	40	0		
				485				

(Continues)

TABLE 25–3 (Continued)

Worksheet for Example Crashing Problem

Step 6 Activity	Precedence	Time Remaining	Cost Remaining	Add'l Cost to Crash	Total Crash Time Avail.	Network Path	New Length
A	—	2	*30*	30	*0*	*ABF*	*8*
B	A	5	120	20	1	*ACEF*	*8*
C	A	4	*110*	50	*1*	ADEF	7
D	A	3	70	10	*1*		
E	C, D	1	45	15	*0*		
F	B, E	1	*100*	40	*0*		
			475				

Step 7 Activity	Precedence	Time Remaining	Cost Remaining	Add'l Cost to Crash	Total Crash Time Avail.	Network Path	New Length
A	—	2	*30*	30	*0*	ABF	7
B	A	4	*100*	20	*0*	*ACEF*	*8*
C	A	4	*110*	50	*1*	ADEF	7
D	A	3	70	10	*1*		
E	C, D	1	45	15	*0*		
F	B, E	1	*100*	40	*0*		
			455				

(Continues)

TABLE 25-3 (Continued)
Worksheet for Example Crashing Problem

Step 8								
Activity	Precedence	Time Remaining	Cost Remaining	Add'l Cost to Crash	Total Crash Time Avail.	Network Path	New Length
A	—	2	30	30	0	*ABF*	7
B	A	4	100	20	0	*ACEF*	7
C	A	3	60	50	0	*ADEF*	7
D	A	3	70	10	1		
E	C, D	1	45	15	0		
F	B, E	1	100	40	0		
			405				

Step 9								
Activity	Precedence	Time Remaining	Cost Remaining	Add'l Cost to Crash	Total Crash Time Avail.	Network Path	New Length
A	—	2	30	30	0	*ABF*	7
B	A	4	100	20	0	*ACEF*	7
C	A	3	60	50	0	*ADEF*	6
D	A	2	60	10	0		
E	C, D	1	45	15	0		
F	B, E	1	100	40	0		
			395				

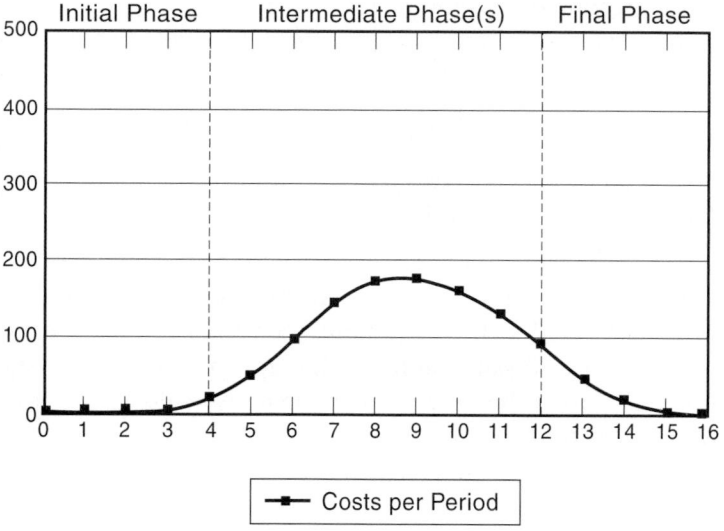

FIGURE 25–9
Costs per Period

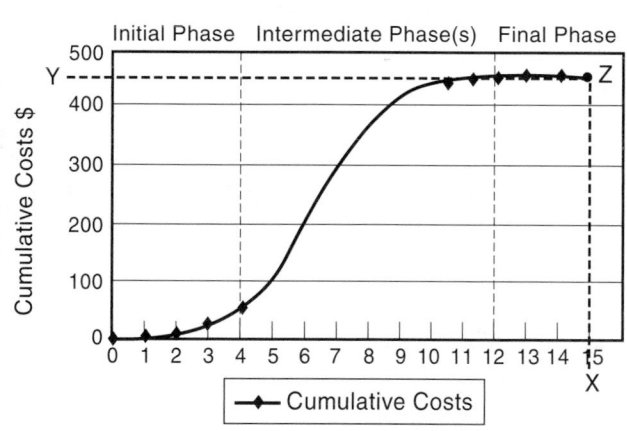

FIGURE 25–10
Cumulative Costs = Cost Baseline

Building the Cost Baseline

When leveling is completed, you can turn your attention to costing. At this point, your schedule has realism, and you can assign costs to the various resources you need. When aggregated by period, you may find that another round of leveling is needed, this time based on cash flow. If so, perform it again as before.

For each resource used, assign resource costs for the following:

- Standard rates—usually $/hour
- Overtime rates—usually $$/hour
- Per use costs—usually a lump fee for using an item (often consumable)

For longer duration activities, you may allocate resource costs at the start of the activity, pro-rated over the duration of the activity, or at the end of the activity.

The point at which you plan to record the resource costs when tracking the project is really a matter of choice for how conservative you want to be in representing the cost of your project. If all resource costs are allocated at the beginning, then the project appears to be incurring costs more rapidly. If cost are allocated at the end, it appears to be incurring costs more conservatively. Prorating costs over the duration may be more realistic, but it usually requires more administrative work to track.

You can build a budget, item by item, against your WBS so that you understand the costs for each major work activity, phase, or other WBS grouping. These can then be allocated to departments or costs centers, as appropriate, for budgeting and tracking purposes. Usually, each cost center is assigned a different charge-out number, and any resource working on a particular activity charges its time to the cost center budget for that activity. This cost information can be aggregated and summarized to show how the project is performing to its planned budget. The mapping of WBS items to the cost accounts is shown in Figure 25–11.

When you've mapped all the resource costs to the cost accounts based on the WBS, you can create the performance measurement baseline (PMB) for the project by plotting the costs over time. You will usually get a curve similar to Figure 25–11. For large, long-duration projects, the detail cost accounts for work packages are created for only a few milestones ahead. Later funds are lumped together into planning packages for larger WBS groups, shown in the middle of Figure 25–11. These will be detailed out to costs centers as the project progresses.

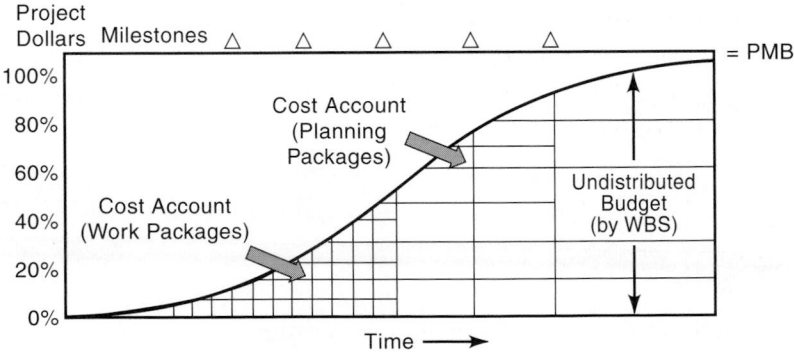

FIGURE 25–11
Cost Accounts in the Cost Baseline
Source: Fleming, Quentin, and Joel Hoppelman (1996). *Earned Value Project Management*. PMI.

Cost control on a project involves control of the assets and human resources. It also involves tracking the money flows. You don't have to be an accountant to be a project manager, but it helps to understand accounting principles. Some of the more useful basics are listed here:

- Time value of money—The concept of interest; a dollar today is worth more than a dollar tomorrow.

- Two sides to every transaction—The double-entry accounting system; for every asset, there is probably an equal and opposite liability.

- The chart of accounts—Description of what cost centers are available to collect costs and revenues.

- The difference between financial and cost accounting—Financial's focus is external; cost's is internal.

- The differing views of costs by different groups—Project managers worry about the commitments, accountants worry about the invoices, and treasurers worry about the cash flow to pay the invoices.

Quality Management _____

Every software development project should have several quality metrics identified as key indicators of the quality of the product that the team is producing. See Chapter 20, "Reliability," Chapter 21, "Software Metrics," and Chapter 26, which have much information on quality measurements for software development. Most of this book concerns areas of software engineering and management that will help you with measuring quality on any project.

Central to good process management is a good set of tools. Many in use today are from the statistical process control (SPC) world and have been developed through total quality management (TQM) activities in recent years. Often, these tools are used by quality assurance to track and improve software development processes (or any organizational process, not just on a project). Your project may benefit from using the seven famous quality tools to monitor process compliance and incremental improvements. As has been said, "If you can't measure it, then you can't manage it." The seven quality tools are:

1. Process flowcharts
2. Cause-and-effect analysis
3. Data-collection arrays
4. Pareto charts
5. Histograms
6. Scatter plots
7. Run charts

You should know how to use each one of these to identify process improvement areas, analyze collected data, and create an action plan for improvement.

Progress Management

Of course, you want to know how the project team is doing on the planned activities. But you saw in Chapter 15, "Scheduling the Work," that there are some inherent problems with estimating that tend to give a false picture of where you are. Trying to cover for the student syndrome can cause people to report on their activity status that they are "90 percent done" for a long, long time. Let's investigate two ways to measure the real progress of a project. The first method is called earned value management (EVM), and it has been around since the 1950s. The second method was developed more recently, in 1997, by Eliyahu Goldratt, and it relies on the buffer management approach of critical chain scheduling. Either or both can be used to measure project progress.

Earned Value Management

Earned value is a cost control concept developed to measure how much *real* progress is being made on a project, not just how much *effort* is being expended. Your PMIS should define how costs and time (labor costs) will be collected and reported. But that is only half the problem (effort). You also need to know what was *accomplished* with that effort (milestones) to measure *progress* (which is what you *really* care about).

The basic concept in EVM is that it combines effort metrics with milestone achievement to measure *real* progress, as illustrated in Figure 25–12. It shows what you got for what you spent. It can compute both budget and schedule variance. It doesn't matter whether you are tracking currency or hours, but you have to be tracking something. EVM systems require some sort of timesheet accounting system input to track the effort component.

Earned value was derived from concepts developed by industrial engineers in the late 1800s to measure factory performance. It was enhanced to be included in PERT/Cost in the early 1960s, and it was established by the U.S. Department of Defense (DOD) as the Cost/Schedule Control System Criteria (C/SCSC) in 1967. The original C/SCSC defined 35 criteria that were necessary to have an earned value system. In 1995, DOD adopted 32 of the original C/SCSC criteria as the Earned Value Management System (EVMS). Today, only five criteria are needed for commercial use to qualify as an earned value management system in the private sector. The five criteria are:

1. Define the project scope (use WBS).
2. Plan and schedule the project (CPM).
3. Form cost account plans and budget them to specific functions (cost accounts).

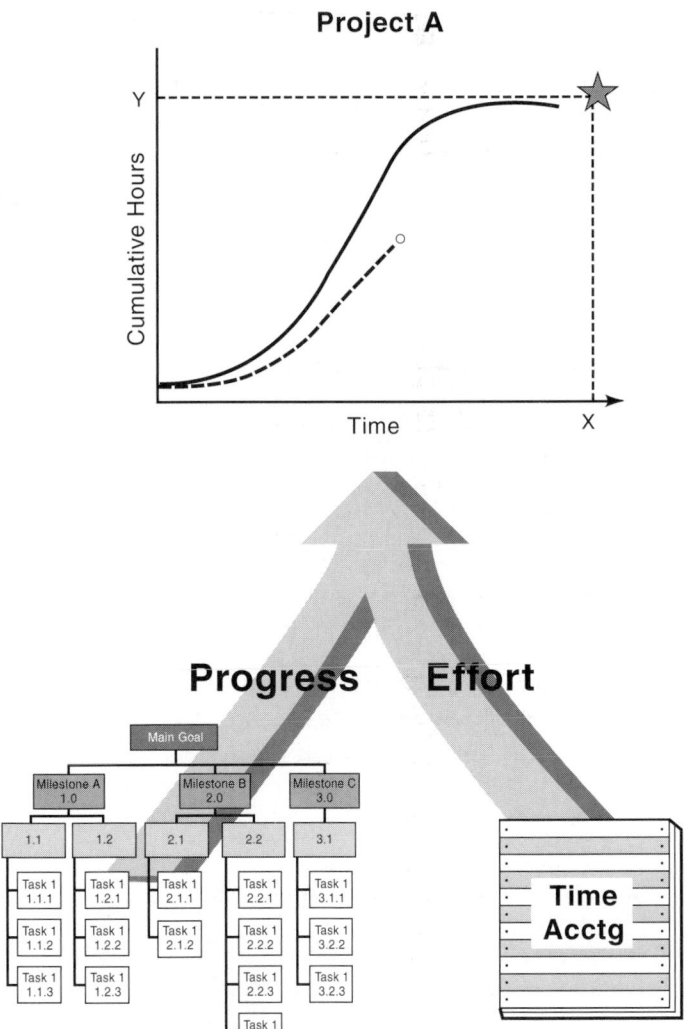

FIGURE 25–12
EVM Marries Progress and Effort to Compute Real Earned Value

4. Establish and maintain a performance measurement baseline (cost baseline).

5. Monitor project performance and forecast the final results (earned value analysis).

The key to understanding EVM is to understand its three major components, because most everything else is computed from them. Their acronym, meaning, and concept are:

- BCWS—Budgeted cost of work scheduled ("yearned")
- BCWP—Budgeted cost of work performed ("earned")
- ACWP—Actual cost of work performed ("burned")

Let's look at what each of these really means.

BCWS   The budgeted cost of work scheduled is what the project "yearns" for. It is the cost baseline, as seen in Figure 25–10. It answers the question, "How much work *should* be done?" It is the planned work for the project plotted at each time period.

BCWP   The budgeted cost of work performed is what the project really "earned" at a point in time along the cost baseline. It answers the question, "How much work *is* done?" This is what the project really accomplished.

ACWP   The actual cost of work performed is what the project spent or "burned" to accomplish what it did. It answers the question, "How much *did* the *is done* work cost?" This is what the project spent in terms of currency or hours.

From these three components, many measures can be computed. Two of the most useful are the cost variance and the schedule variance. Cost variance is computed with the formula:

$$CV = BCWP - ACWP$$

It compares the actual costs to the budgeted costs to get a variance. The variance is expressed in currency or hours, but it does not provide a comparison of work planned to work done. It compares deviations from budget only. The schedule variance is computed with the formula:

$$SV = BCWP - BCWS$$

It compares planned work to completed work to get a variance. The variance is expressed in either currency or hours, but *not* dates. This seems confusing at first because we are so used to thinking of schedules as dates. But this is about the work, not the time.

Some additional measures can be computed from the basic three, and their derivatives. The budget at completion (BAC) is the planned total cost for the project. It is point Z on the cost baseline in Figure 25–10.

The estimated cost at completion (ECAC) is a forecast of the total cost when the project is completed. It is computed with the formula:

$$ECAC = BAC \times (ACWP/BCWP)$$

This is just the BAC adjusted by the ratio of the actuals and the work that was done. If the actuals are less than the budget at the point in time where the measurements are being made, the ratio will be less than 1 and it will reduce the BAC figure. If the actuals are more than the budget, the ratio is greater than 1 and it will increase the BAC figure.

The estimated time at completion uses the same ratio approach to forecast the estimated end date of the project. But this time, you compare the work that was planned to the work that was scheduled. It is computed with the formula:

$$ETAC = Original\ Time \times (BCWP/BCWP)$$

Two other very useful measures are the cost performance index (CPI) and the schedule performance index (SPI). These are both ratios that boil cost and schedule adherence into a ratio value, suitable for plotting and tracking on a control chart. The cost performance index compares the budget with the actual costs and is computed with the formula:

$$CPI = (BCWP/ACWP)$$

If the CPI ratio is less than 1, the project is over budget because actuals exceed those budgeted. If the CPI ratio is greater than 1, the project is under budget because the actuals are less than budgeted.

The schedule performance index compares the budget with the plan and is computed with the formula:

$$SPI = (BCWP/BCWS)$$

If the SPI ratio is less than 1, the project is ahead of schedule because the budgeted work completed was less than the work that was planned. If the SPI ratio is greater than 1, the project is behind schedule because the budgeted work is more than what was planned.

Using the CPI and SPI, a single number can be plotted on a control chart to represent the whole project's performance. This is the critical ratio (CR) and is just the product of the CPI and the SPI. The formula for the critical ratio is:

$$CR = SPI \times CPI$$

If both the schedule and cost indices are 1, the CR is 1, indicating that everything is on track. But if either the CPI or the SPI strays from 1, the CR begins to move away from 1, indicating a problem. Some rules of thumb are that if the CR is between 0.9 and 1.2, then the project is moving along okay. But if the CR is either between 0.8 and 0.9, or between 1.2 and 1.3, the project bears looking into because either the costs or the schedule are starting to drift. If the CR is less than 0.8 or more than 1.3, there is definitely something wrong, and action should be taken. A plot of the CR on a control chart becomes a good way to monitor the progress of a project. This is illustrated in Figure 25–13.

Recognize that EVM metrics require some form of effort input to be computed properly. Garbage in, garbage out. If your project has only two milestones, both due at the end of the project, you really don't have very good EVM measures, even if you track hours closely, because you can't "earn" anything until the milestones are completed. Your CR control chart will look very out of whack until the very end of the project. It is better to make many smaller milestones so that you have incremental progress to measure. This will give you smoother curves to view. In Figures 25–14 through 25–18, a sequence of EVM calculations and graphs against the cost baseline are shown to illustrate how EVM parameters change over time.

Plotted as curves over time, these EVM measures can tell you a lot about the condition of the project. Figures 25–19 and 25–20 show a project that is ahead of schedule or budget. The slope of the plotted curve at the time of the calculation indicates whether things are better or worse. Figures 25–21 and 25–22 show a project that is behind cost or schedule, with similar indications.

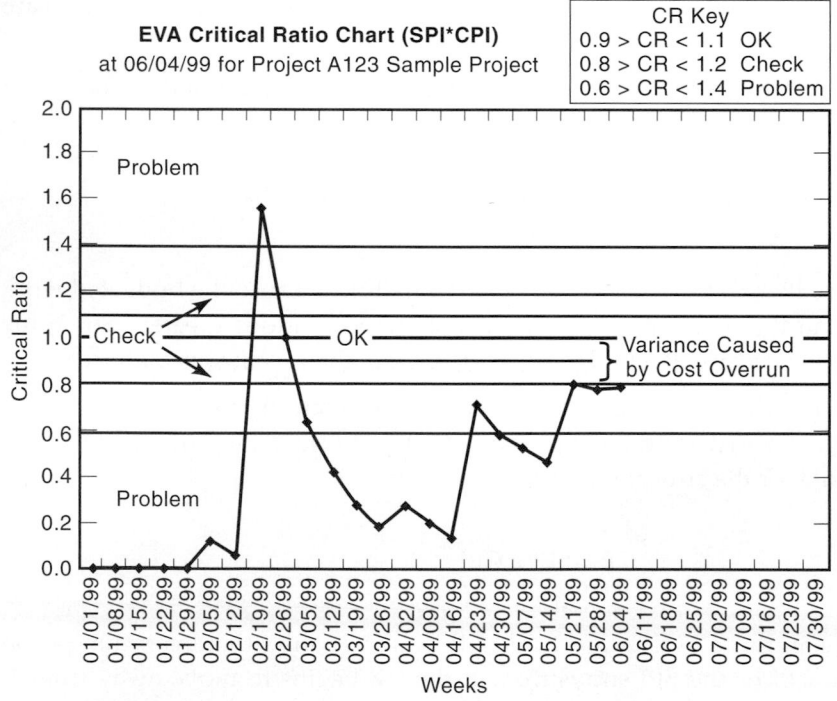

FIGURE 25–13
A Project Control Chart Using the Critical Ratio (CR)

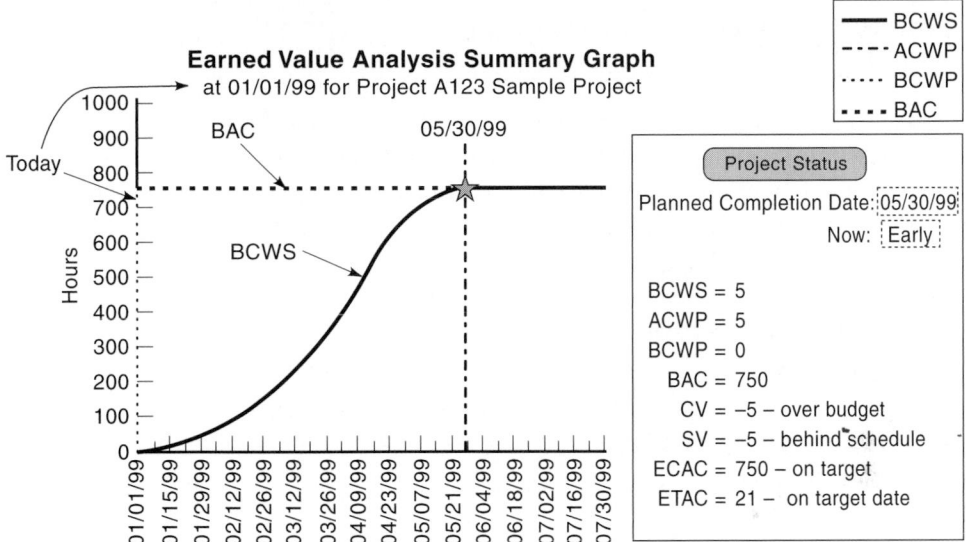

FIGURE 25–14
Example Project at January 1 Showing Planned Cost Baseline

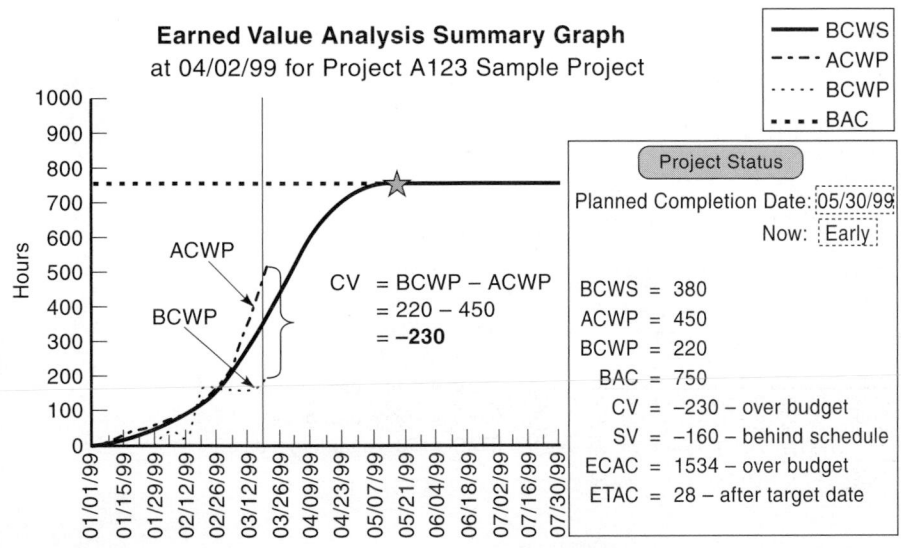

FIGURE 25–15
Example Project at April 2 Showing Cost Variance Calculations

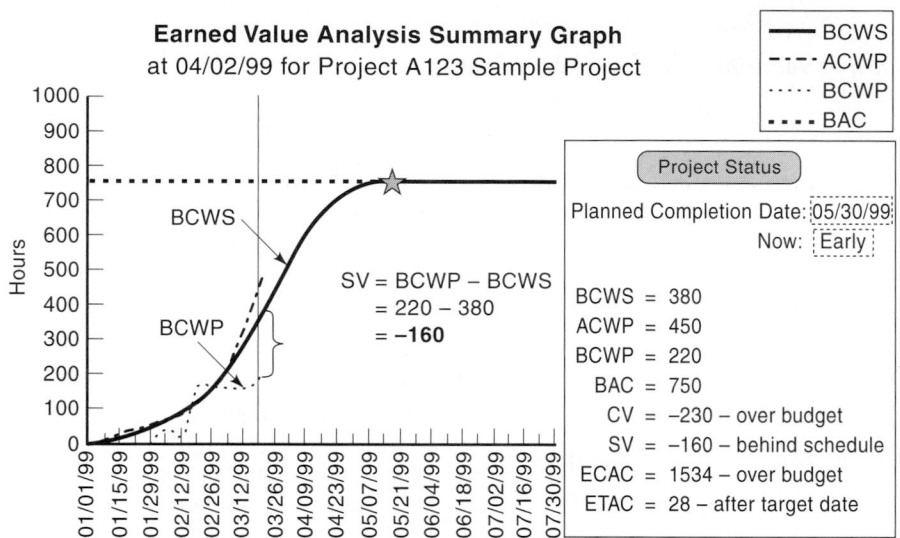

FIGURE 25–16
Example Project at April 2 Showing Schedule Variance Calculations

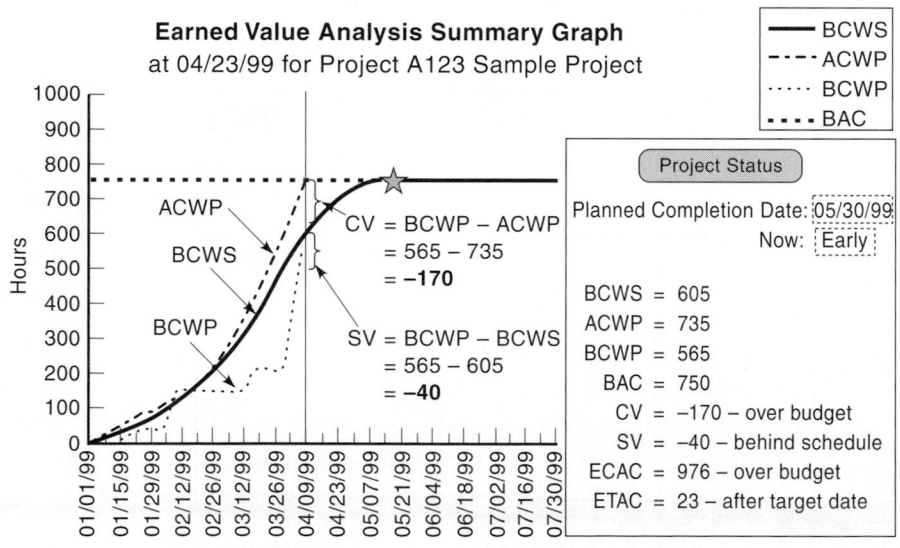

FIGURE 25–17
Example Project at April 23 Showing All EVM Calculations

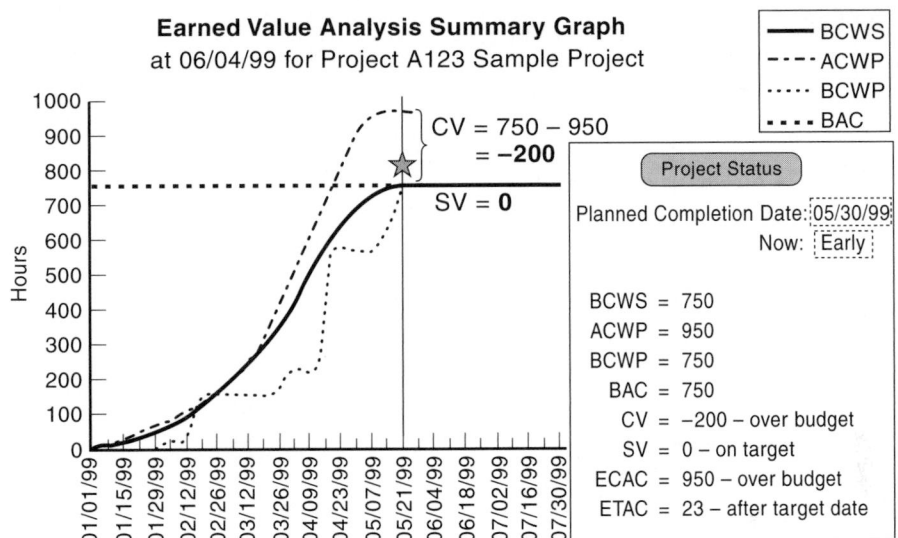

FIGURE 25–18
Completed Example Project at June 4 Showing On Schedule but Over Budget

In the sequence of Figures 25–14 through 25–18, note how "bumpy" the BCWP is. This is a result of not earning the milestones until they were completed. If there were more milestones in the project or they were recognized differently, the BCWP curves would be smoother.

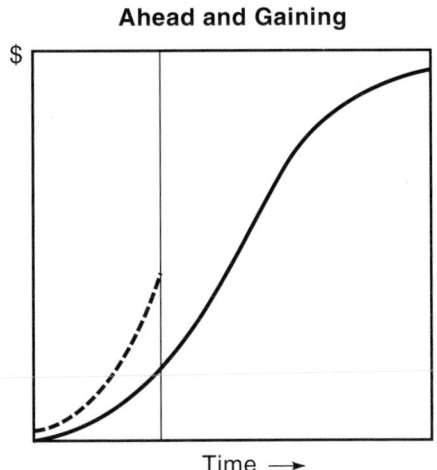

FIGURE 25–19
Project Is Ahead and Gaining

Ahead but Losing

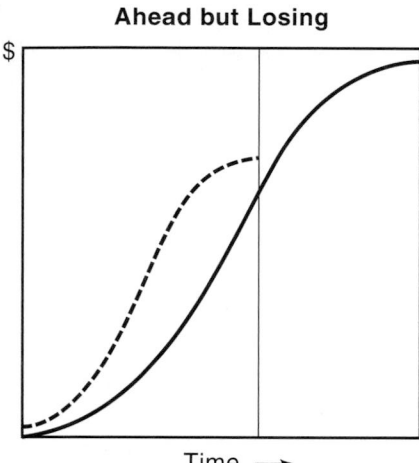

FIGURE 25–20
Project Is Ahead but Losing

Behind and Losing

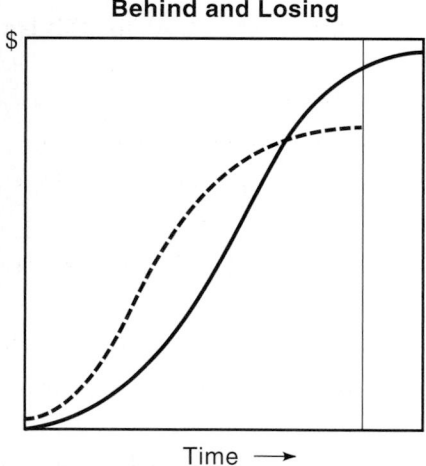

FIGURE 25–21
Project Is Behind and Losing

This raises the question, how do you recognize "done"? That is, what rule do you follow to count something as "done" for EVM calculations? Fleming and Hoppelman cite several common rules for doneness, organized into two types: those for recurring activities and those for nonrecurring activities. The ones typically used for nonrecurring activities are listed here:

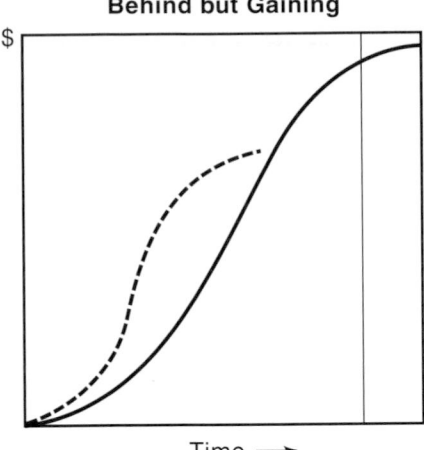

FIGURE 25–22
Project Is Behind but Gaining

- Weighted milestone—Each milestone is weighted by its value to the project.
- Fixed formula (0/100, 25/75, 50/50)—First number is earned upon start, and last number is earned upon finish.
- Percent complete estimates—Subjective estimate of activity performed.
- Percent complete and milestone gates—Subjective estimate plus milestone completion.
- Equivalent units—Awards whole-unit equivalents for collections of fractional completions.
- Earned standards—Measured against a historical standard.
- Apportioned relationship to discrete work (percent of a larger effort)—To allocate overhead activities.
- Level of effort (not recommended)—Constant cost, more time-driven than activity-driven.

To be conservative, you should choose a rule like the fixed formula 0/100. Nothing is earned for the project's EVM calculations until it is completely done.

As an example in calculating EVM measures, let's look at the next problem and see how to interpret the data given to you as a project manager. Here's the situation:

The project has been running since January 1 now, completing milestones A and B ahead of schedule and under budget. Milestone C was completed on budget, although slightly late. The cost and schedule data for each milestone is shown in Table 25–4.

Today is May 1. The project has come to the point in time where milestone D should have been completed but is only 50 percent done. This project follows the procedure that only completed milestones are counted for earned value calculations. As project manager, you are asked to provide the EVA parameters in Table 25–4 for the monthly project review.

TABLE 25–4

Monthly Review EVA Parameters

Project Data:	Completion Date		Cost	
WBS Milestone	Planned	Actual	Planned	Actual
A	2/1	1/20	15,000	10,000
B	3/1	2/28	20,000	15,000
C	4/1	4/5	25,000	25,000
D	5/1		20,000	10,000
E	6/1		15,000	
F	7/1		5,000	
Totals			100,000	60,000

Milestone D isn't complete yet, so costs for work on it can't be counted in the ACWP (by rule in the problem description). So, you cannot count BCWP for it either. At 5/1, the three main EVA parameters would be (all figures expressed in $K for simplicity):

1. BCWS = 15 + 20 + 25 + 20 = 80
2. BCWP = 15 + 20 + 25 = 60
3. ACWP = 10 + 15 + 25 = 50

Now that you have the main three measures calculated, the rest fall out easily.

4. CV = BCWP – ACWP = 60 – 50 = 10 (favorable)
5. SV = BCWP – BCWS = 60 – 80 = –20 (unfavorable)
6. CPI = BCWP / ACWP = 60 / 50 = 1.2 (favorable)
7. SPI = BCWP / BCWS = 60 / 80 = 0.75 (unfavorable)
8. CR = CPI × SPI = 1.2 × 0.75 = 0.9 (marginal)

What does this tell you about the condition of the project? The project is marginally okay and should probably be looked at more closely. It seemed to be off to a good start, but it is now beginning to fall behind. The trend is unfavorable.

The trick in performing EVM on a project is to see when to recognize what. Once you can recognize the "yearned," "earned," and "burned," the remainder of the measures comes easily.

Critical Chain Measurement

In Chapter 15 we looked primarily at the critical path method (CPM) of scheduling activities in a project plan, but we also investigated the use of buffer management and resource-driven schedules. EVM is a companion to CPM and is widely used to track project progress. Here, we will look at how to use buffer management to track the progress of a project, and then we'll compare it to EVM.

Recall that the critical chain approach tries to remove uncertainty from the activity estimates and to put it into a set of buffers so that it can be monitored and managed at the project level, as illustrated in Figure 25–23. Activity estimates are desired to be at about a 50 percent probability of achieving the estimated duration.

The project manager can then watch what happens to the buffer as time is consumed on the project and make adjustments as necessary. This becomes a simple calculation and plot to see how fast the buffer is being consumed relative to the milestones achieved. A chart similar to the one shown in Figure 25–24, by Rob Newbold, can be built to plot progress.

As milestones are achieved, the percentage completed is plotted against the uncertainty buffer consumed to achieve the milestone, and a dot is placed on the chart. If the dots are in the green zone, the project is okay. If they drift into the yellow zone, some action should be contemplated, such as adding staff to the project or rearranging team members to help those on critical chain activities. If it drifts into the red zone, you should take action to correct the

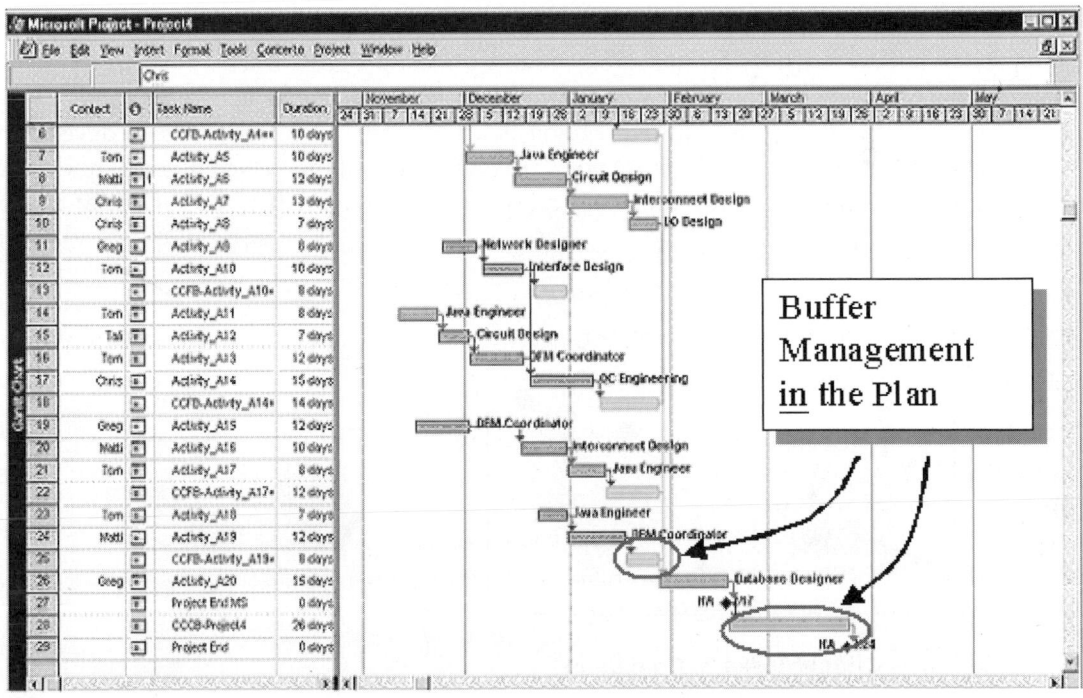

FIGURE 25–23
Example of Buffer Management in the Project Schedule

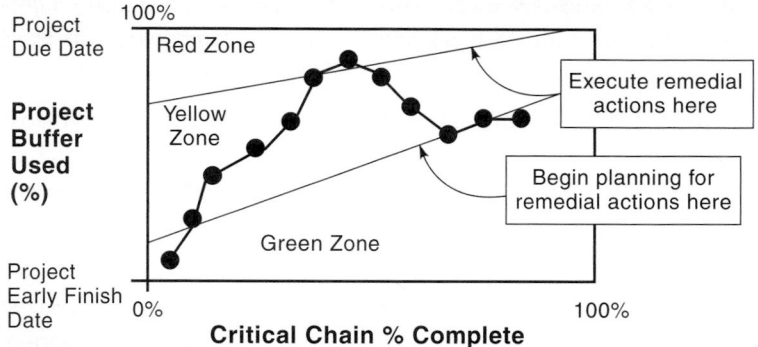

FIGURE 25–24
Example of Progress Measurement Using Buffer Management

project. The goal is to finish somewhere at or below the upper-right corner because that would mean that the project has finished on time or early.

This same technique can just as easily be applied at the portfolio level, where many projects are being tracked. Using the same chart, a dot can be placed for where each project is now. This will yield a chart like the one shown in Figure 25–25.

The use of critical chain buffer management and project progress tracking has a couple of advantages. EVM can be complicated to administer. Critical chain can be simple. EVM requires an effort metric such as hours worked on an activity, and the question for the developer on an activity is, "What percent done are you?" In critical chain, the "percent done" question is unnecessary because the more important question is, "What's left to do?" Critical chain

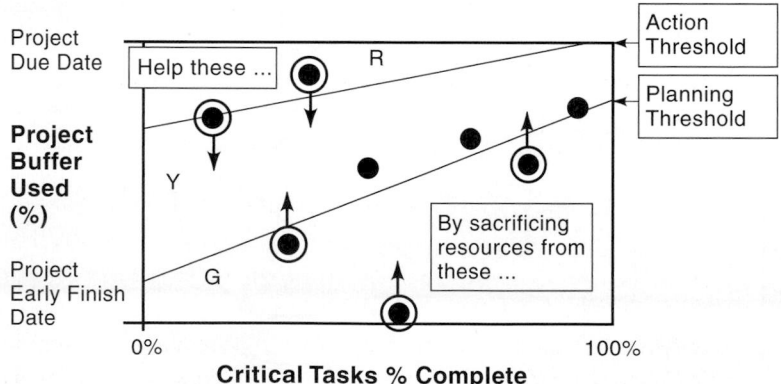

FIGURE 25–25
Example of Progress Measurement Using Buffer Management for a Collection of Projects

emphasizes constant re-estimation at the activity level, where the work is being done. Half-way through an activity, the developer will know far more about the problem being worked on than was known months ago when it was first estimated and laid into a Gantt chart. This means that the focus of critical chain is largely forward-looking, whereas EVM is largely backward-looking.

This means that the critical chain buffer management approach may help the project manager keep his eyes on the road, instead of staring into the rear view mirror too much.

Risk Management

Tracking a project implies that risk management principles are being followed. Any project review should include a treatment of the risks in the project, from many sources. At minimum, the project's top 10 risk items for the reporting period should be presented and reviewed for action, as should the risk tracking chart showing the rise and fall of new and old risks.

Chapter 18, "Determining Project Risks," gives thorough treatment to the subject of risks.

Summary

In this chapter, we covered the tools and techniques for tracking and monitoring a software development project after it has been planned and baselined. We focused on the elements of the triple constraint as a framework for tracking. We looked into some methods for control of scope, schedule, and cost, and also touched briefly on quality and risk that are covered in depth in other chapters.

Good software development project management breaks the problem into two parts, planning and tracking. Much of this book is about planning a project, but here we have focused primarily on the tracking processes needed for every development project.

Problems for Review

1. Would you agree or disagree that the cost of accelerating a project rises exponentially, especially as the project nears completion? Explain your reasoning.
2. Should a different set of schedules and charts be maintained for outside as well as inside the organization for reporting? Should separate schedules be made for different levels of management? Is there a more effective way to ease these types of problems? Discuss your reasoning.

3. Do you really think that something as simple as the critical ratio can represent the current state of a complex project? Why or why not?

Visit the Case Study

The downturn in the semiconductor industry has impacted your corporation. Although you are part of a business unit that is making a profit on the software and systems being produced, you have to trim 10 percent off your budget for the fiscal year. There are only nine months left in the year so you have to do some real cutting to get to a cumulative 10 percent reduction. Your preliminary plan is due in two days. Once that is approved, you have 10 days to implement the plan. Prepare and present the plan as soon as possible.

Suggested Readings

Ahuja, H. (1976). *Construction Performance Control by Network.* John Wiley & Sons.

Burrill, C.W., and L.W. Ellsworth (1980). *Modern Project Management.* Burrill-Ellsworth Associates.

Cleland, David I., and William R. King, Editors (1983). *Project Management Handbook.* Van Nostrand.

Kerzner, H. (1995). *Project Management: A Systems Approach to Planning, Scheduling, and Controlling,* 5th ed. Van Nostrand Reinhold.

Lewis, James P. (1995). *Project Planning, Scheduling, and Control: A Hands-On Guide to Bringing Projects in on Time and on Budget.* McGraw-Hill.

Meredith, Mantel (1995). *Project Management: A Managerial Approach,* 3rd ed. John Wiley & Sons.

Paulk, Mark C., et al. (1994). *The Capability Maturity Model: Guidelines for Improving the Software Process.* Addison-Wesley. Section 7.2, "Software Project Planning," and Section 7.3, "Software Project Tracking and Oversight."

Pressman, Roger S. (2001). *Software Engineering: A Practitioner's Approach,* 5th ed. McGraw-Hill. Chapter 5, "Software Project Planning," and Chapter 7, "Project Scheduling and Tracking."

Rea, Kathryn P., and Bennet P. Lientz, Editors (1998). *Project Management for the 21st Century.* Academic Press.

Snyder, James R. (1998). "How to Monitor and Evaluate Projects." *Field Guide to Project Management.* John Wiley & Sons.

Stuckenbruck, Linn C. (1981). *The Implementation of Project Management.* Addison-Wesley.

Walpole, Ronald E. (1974). *Introduction to Statistics,* 2nd ed. Macmillan.

Wysocki, Robert K., et al. (2000). *Effective Project Management,* 2nd ed. John Wiley & Sons.

Web Pages for Further Information _____

stsc.hill.af.mil/crosstalk/1999/apr/smith.asp. "Gaining Confidence in Using Return on Investment and Earned Value," by Larry W. Smith, Software Technology Support Center A. Todd Steadman, TRW Avionics Systems Division.

stsc.hill.af.mil/crosstalk/1998/jul/value.asp. "PM GMT Earned Value Project Management A Powerful Tool for Software Projects," by Quentin W. Fleming and Joel M. Koppelman, Primavera Systems, Inc.

www.pmi.org/publictn/pmboktoc.htm. PMI's *A Guide to the Project Management Body of Knowledge* (*PMBOK® Guide*), Chapter 10.

Continuous Process
Improvement

Success as a software project manager is judged by delivering quality products on time and with the resources budgeted. Quality is determined by the customer and comes from improving the product development process. Continuous process improvement is the mechanism that an organization uses to ensure products that are less costly, more capable of meeting customer requirements, and more reliable. This mechanism also reduces cost and eliminates waste within the existing development processes, thus allowing project execution on time and within resources.

Continuous process improvement begins with an awareness of the process maturity within the project development organization. Although continuous improvement could be done by a single project, the benefit is not realized until the next project. Continuous improvement is an organization-wide initiative. It must be supported by the entire organization and must extend over all projects. Documented case studies of software process improvement indicate that significant improvements in both quality and productivity are a result of the improvement effort.[1] When the organizational investment is made, the return on investment is typically between 5:1 and 8:1 for successful process improvement efforts.[2]

The first step in a successful process improvement effort is to understand the process maturity level of the development organization. The authors' recommended approach is to use the Software Engineering Institute's Capability Maturity Model, first discussed in Chapter 4, "Selecting Software Development Life Cycles." The maturity of an organization's software process helps to predict a project's ability to meet its goals. Figure 26–1 represents the model's maturity levels. These five maturity levels are:

1. **Initial**—The software process is characterized as ad hoc and chaotic. Few processes are defined, and success depends on individual effort and heroics.

2. **Repeatable**—Basic project management processes are established to track cost, schedule, and functionality. The necessary process discipline is in place to repeat earlier successes on projects with similar applications. New types of products revert back to Level 5 characteristics.

3. **Defined**—There is a standard software process for the organization. All projects use an approved, tailored version of the organization's standard software process for developing and maintaining software.

4. **Managed**—Detailed measures of the software process and product quality are collected. Both the software process and the products are quantitatively understood and controlled.

5. **Optimizing**—Continuous process improvement is enabled by quantitative feedback from the process and from using new ideas and technologies.

Level 5 is where continuous process improvement is enabled. The culture of process improvement must be instantiated within the organization long before Level 5 is reached. This chapter will present the process characteristics of each maturity level and the amount of continuous process improvement that can be instituted.

Chapter 3, "Process Overview," of this guide discussed process and the part it plays in project management. It discussed the classical Deming/Shewhart/Ishikawa plan-do-check-act cycle and showed how that cycle evolved into the software development process front end represented in Figure 26–2. The six outer processes are used to guide the required steps in process improvement efforts. Between the processes are specific tasks that must be completed from process to process. Within the central core of the model are the organization's information repositories for past and current projects. This chapter will take this model, develop a format for its use in process improvement, and apply it to a real-world development organization.

Where We Are in the Product Development Life Cycle

Continuous process improvement is fed by project-focused quality improvement needs. Because of that, the information presented in Chapter 30, "Software Quality Assurance," will

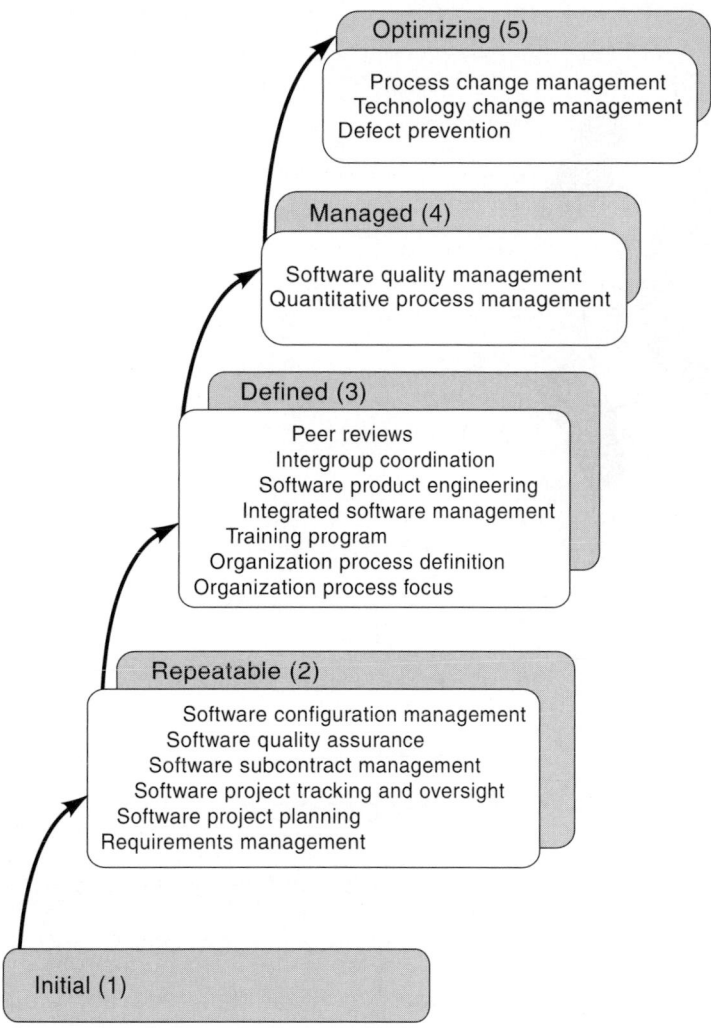

FIGURE 26–1
Software Engineering Institute's Capability Maturity Model

detail the software quality assurance process on a project-by-project basis. Continuous process improvement focuses not only on the entire project, but also on the improvement goals of the entire organization. As the project manager moves from an individual project to a family of projects to the whole organization view, process improvement broadens into organizational maturity advancement. See Figure 26–3.

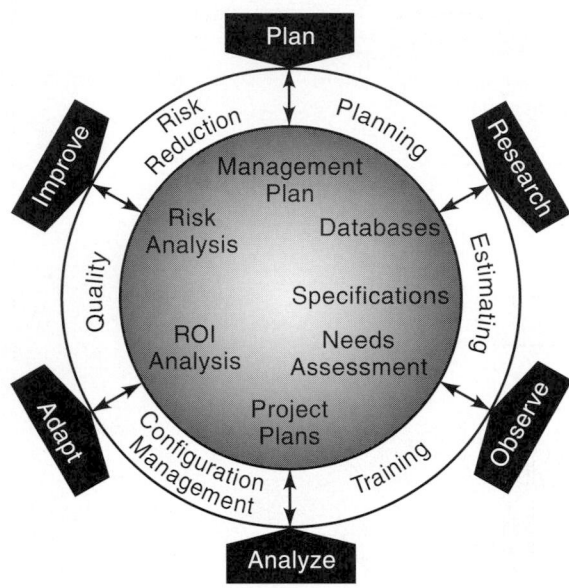

FIGURE 26–2
Six-Step Software Development Process Improvement Model

Chapter 26 Relation to the 34 Competencies _____

The following seven of the 34 competencies described apply especially to continuous process improvement:

1. **Assessing processes**—This involves specifically assessing the continuous process improvement goals of the CMM Level 5 and the processes within the product development life cycle. This leads directly into the overall organization's approach to continuous process improvement.

17. **Monitoring development**—Implementing continuous process improvement requires monitoring the product development processes for non–value-added effort.

19. **Selecting metrics**—Project managers can neither manage nor improve that which is not measured. Choosing the appropriate metrics for the project and organization is critical in an improvement effort that requires a systems view.

21. **Tracking process**—Throughout the project, continuous process improvement acts as the glue binding an individual project process to the overall organization structure for quality.

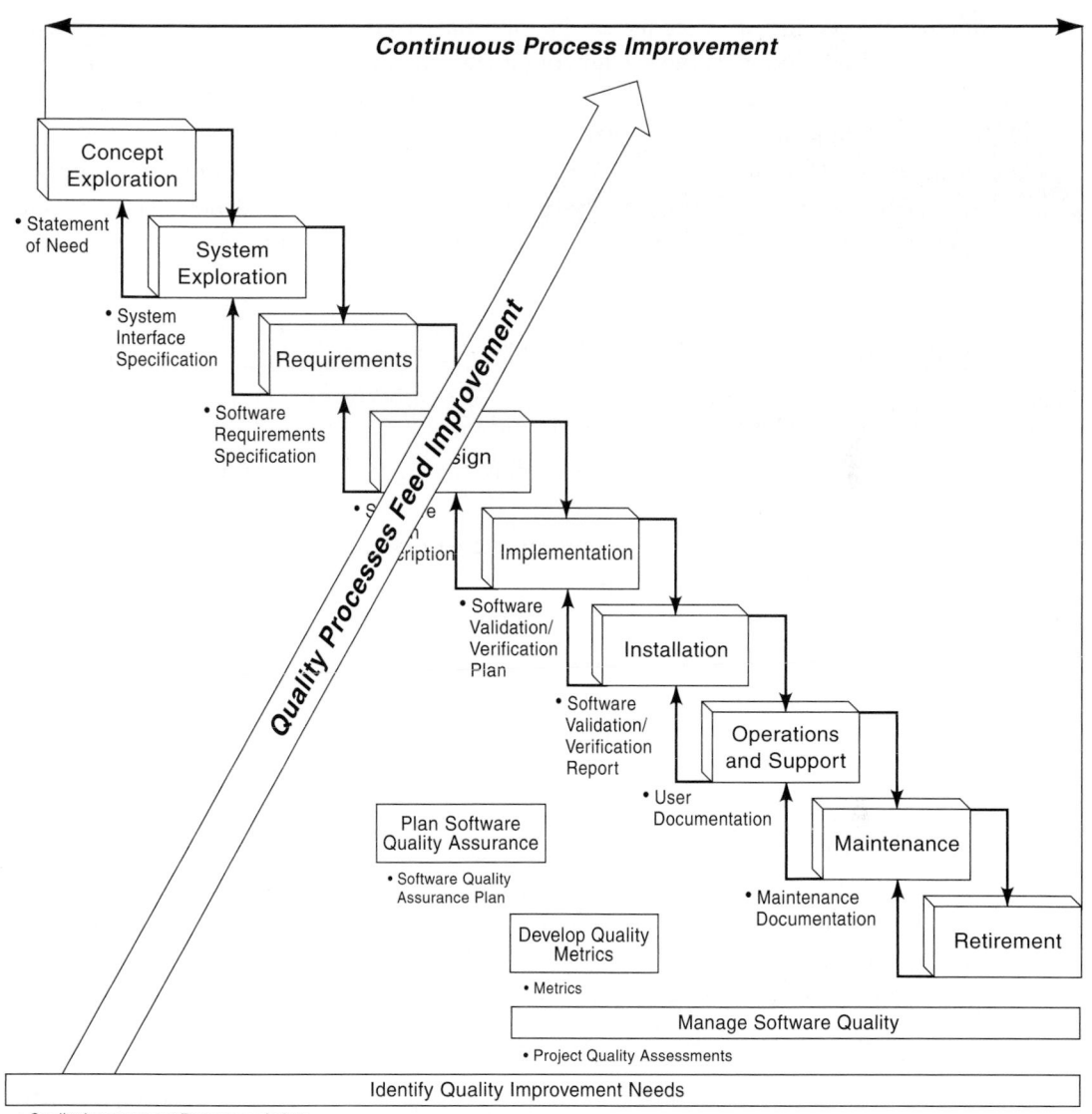

FIGURE 26–3

Continuous Improvement in the Product Development Life Cycle

22. **Tracking project progress**—This is done within the framework of the metrics chosen for collection and the organizational goals of continuous process improvement.

27. **Leadership**—Coaching project teams for optimal results is critical when the narrow project focus is expanded to the system, organization, and customer view. Project leadership is challenged when continuous process improvement adds that extra effort to improve the next project, not just the one on which the team is currently working.

34. **Teambuilding**—This is critical to the organizational success of continuous process improvement in the long run. Process improvement benefits the next project. Team members must be able to think strategically and perform tactically.

Learning Objectives for Chapter 26 _____

Upon completion of this chapter, the reader should be able to:

- Develop a continuous process improvement plan for an organization that is not at Level 5 CMM maturity;
- Define the method for introduction of continuous process improvement in an organization;
- Produce a step-by-step plan for focusing on process improvement through removing organizational waste;
- Define value for the organization's customers;
- Recognize non–value-added work, waste, for which customers are being charged;
- Define the organization's metrics needed to support continuous process improvement.

Maturity Level Process Characteristics _____

The first step to introducing continuous process improvement in an organization is to understand the process maturity level of that organization. The distribution of the resources required to complete a project and the probability of hitting the target for each level is represented in Figures 26–4 through 26–8. Chapter 10, "Software Size and Reuse Estimating," and Chapter 11, "Estimating Duration and Cost," describe how to arrive at the target numbers. These distributions are based on historic project information gathered by the Software Engineering Institute. They represent a broad range of software development types, organizations, and industries. The statistical distribution shapes are accurate representations for predicting where a project will land under the curve for each maturity level. For continuous process improvement, a project manager can consider any project that lands more than one standard deviation from the target a high opportunity for waste removal.

Level 1: Schedule and Cost Targets Are Regularly Overrun

Projects in Level 1 organizations experience wide variations in achieving cost, schedule, functionality, and quality targets. Level 1 organizations often miss their originally scheduled delivery dates by a wide margin, illustrated in Figure 26–4 by how much of the area under the curve lies to the right of the target line.

It is not feasible to begin process improvement initiatives in a Level 1 organization. The ad hoc, chaotic nature of this level of maturity works against any process definition or improvement effort. Do not try to implement any continuous process improvement in a Level 1 software development organization.

Level 2: Plans Based on Past Performance Are More Attainable

As development process maturity increases, the variability of actual results around targeted results decreases. As shown in Figure 26–5, the distribution of the project results is now around the target and no longer is displaced to the right of the target line. In a Level 2 organization, processes are in place that allow repeatable results of projects of a similar domain. To

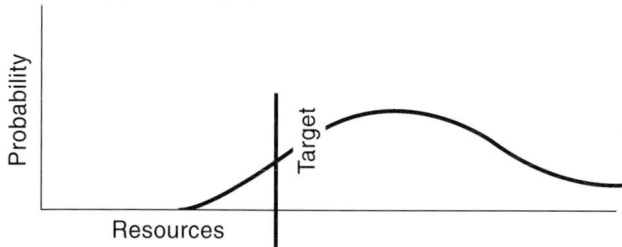

FIGURE 26–4
Maturity Level 1 Resource Distribution

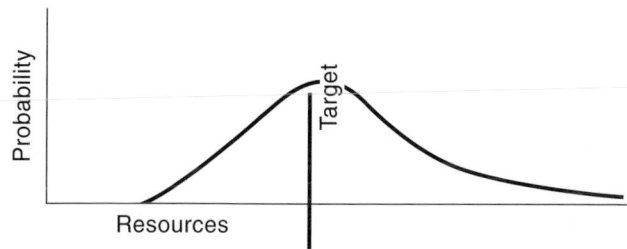

FIGURE 26–5
Maturity Level 2 Resource Distribution

reach Level 2, an organization has begun project and process tracking. This requires the building of an initial, rudimentary metrics system. This is the point in the march toward higher maturity levels that the organization can begin to plan for continuous process improvement. Minimal metrics need to be collected, as discussed in Chapter 1, "Introduction." The project manager must keep in mind that continuous process improvement cannot begin in an organization until there is a history of completed projects upon which to improve. All those projects need a consistent set of metrics. The question arises, "How many is enough?" The authors' experience has shown that a minimum of five projects done by the organization is a good starting point for the improvement analysis process to begin. Individual organizations vary in the time it takes to do five end-to-end projects.

Level 2 organizations can begin the continuous improvement process by defining the metrics to be gathered and establishing the collection and reporting facilities. This is the earliest phase of continuous process improvement. No real institutionalized process improvement efforts can begin in a Level 2 organization. Targets of opportunity to remove waste will become obvious and should be taken. But a project manager should not mistake serendipitous process improvement opportunities for an internalized, organization-wide continuous process improvement process.

Level 3: With Well-Defined Processes, Performance Improves

As the development organization reaches maturity Level 3, targeted results improve, as shown by the narrowed distribution curve around the target in Figure 26–6. The probability of hitting the estimated cost and schedule targets for projects increases rapidly, while costs and development time decrease.

At Level 3, an organization can begin a continuous process improvement initiative. Level 5 is where the institutionalization of continuous process improvement occurs, with the optimized process changes being fed back into the development process. The initiative must

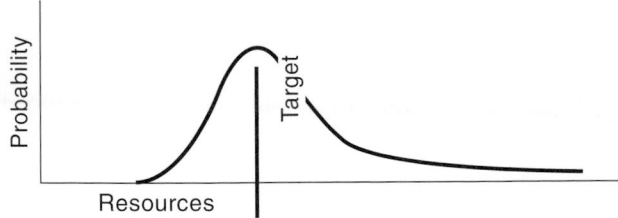

FIGURE 26–6
Maturity Level 3 Resource Distribution

begin long before the organization reaches Level 5. It can begin no sooner than at Level 3 of maturity, and it should begin no later than Level 4.

Level 4: Performance Continues to Improve Based on Quantitative Understanding of Process and Produce

A Level 4 organization demonstrates a managed software development process. The process is quantitatively managed, changing, and adapting to meet relevant current and projected business objectives. The Level 4 process focuses on continually improving the process performance through both incremental and innovative technological improvements. Process improvements are identified through the use of well-collected and analyzed metrics. These metrics address common causes of process variation. Management measurably improves the organization's processes through improvements based on a quantitative understanding of their expected contribution to achieving the organization's process improvement objectives versus the cost and impact to the organization.

As shown in Figure 26–7, the area under the distribution curve has gotten much smaller from Level 3. The probability that estimates will equal actuals in software development projects is again greatly improved. The organization is not on process improvement autopilot. It still requires active management of the processes to continue driving waste and improving quality. But, at Level 4, all processes are in place, especially a superb metrics system, for creating that process improvement autopilot.

Level 5: Performance Continuously Improves

At Level 5, Figure 26–8 shows another dramatic decrease in the area under the resource distribution curve around the project estimate target. A critical distinction between the Level 4 (quantitatively managed) and the Level 5 (optimizing) process is that the software development

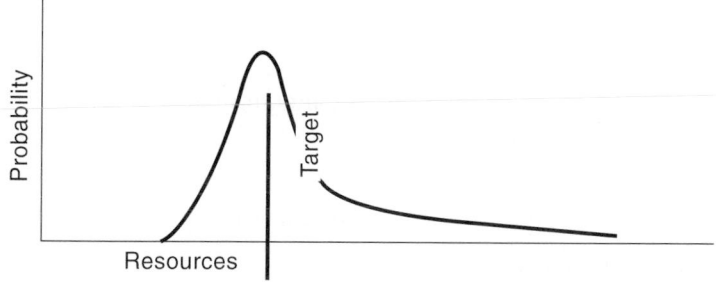

FIGURE 26–7
Maturity Level 4 Resource Distribution

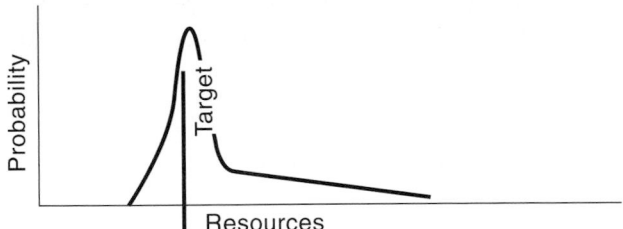

FIGURE 26–8
Maturity Level 5 Resource Distribution

process is continuously improved. This improvement is in response to the statistical controls placed on the system in response to past experience, current customer quality initiatives, and future technology innovations. The whole reason for the process is to deliver quality products to the end customer. At Level 5, this constant quality improvement is addressed through continuous process improvement as an automatic feedback into the process mechanics. The process improves itself through statistical feedback and customer interaction.

Continuous product and process improvement have become vitally important to the long-term success of today's companies. Software is the mechanism to gain the necessary competitive edge. Companies have to integrate and harmonize their automated production and nonproduction process systems rather than just one or the other. Therefore, a mature software process system must be used to continuously improve quality and reduce process waste. Developing and maintaining software is very complex, time-consuming, risky, and costly to a company if managers and process engineers do not have the proper knowledge and skills to analyze, design, implement, and continuously improve their software development and maintenance processes. Understanding the organization's maturity level is critical before embarking on a continuous process improvement initiative. Do not begin until Level 3 is reached. Begin no later than the earliest stages of Level 4.

Waste in the Software Development Organization ____

Value-added work is judged from the customer's perspective. All other work, as far as the customer is concerned, is waste. A software development organization has value-added tasks, essential non–value-added tasks, and nonessential non–value-added tasks. The customer is interested in paying only for value-added effort but is charged for all effort.

Value-added work is defined as any part of the software development process that:

1. in some way positively changes the product.
2. makes the product more desirable.
3. is performed correctly the first time.

This is a very precise and limited definition. In software development, project managers believe that many activities are value-added. Remember, continuous process improvement takes the view of the customer. Customers do *not* believe that these activities add value:

- activities unrelated to the producing the product;
- features that the engineer thinks are nice but that the customer doesn't care about;
- management;
- moving a product from one place to another;
- repairing mistakes;
- tests and inspections; and
- all other activities that project team members think are "necessary" or "desirable."

Of all the tasks that the customer would deem non–value-added, some are costs for tasks performed because the process is not perfectly efficient:

- peer reviews;
- evaluations, inspections, verification, and validation;
- metrics collection, storage, and analysis;
- extra reviews and verifications required by customer or company policy;
- certain overhead costs (benefits, support activities); and
- project management costs.

The final category of non–value-added and not essential to the project consists of:

- costs for tasks performed because you have always done it that way with inefficient tools and processes.
- excessive paperwork.
- waits for test equipment.
- costs resulting from bugs in software development tools.
- costs for activities unrelated to the process.

Table 26–1 shows a layout of value-added versus non–value-added tasks within a software development project. This table can be used as a guide to customize for specific projects, products, and customers. Not all customers see value in the same light. Many do believe that this is a close model of what they see as real value in a software development process.

Using Table 26–1 as a template, Table 26–2 is an example of a spreadsheet that can be used to calculate perceived value versus real cost to the customer. Some simple but important ratios are shown on this template. The ratio of value- to non–value-added activities is usually an eye-opening value. Essential to nonessential non–value-added is also a good ratio to monitor for projects. The nonessential, non–value-added activities are the prime targets for elimination as waste. A final ratio is the value-added plus essential costs divided by the nonessential

TABLE 26–1
Task Values in a Software Product

Value-Added	Non–Value-Added	
	Essential	Nonessential
Design	Acceptance Testing	Bottlenecks
Documentation	Moving Data Between Steps	Correction
Implementation	Planning	Delays
Installation	Setup	Error Analysis
Requirements	Some Process	Expediting
Shipping	Training	Extra Paperwork
Upgrading		Extra Unwanted Features
		Installing Software Tools
		Management
		Metrics
		Modification
		Process Improvement
		Recall
		Retest
		Rework

costs. If this number is less than 1, it is critical to begin eliminating waste in the software development process.

Table 26–3 shows the spreadsheet template completed for elevator system control software. The units in the spreadsheet are hours. As long as the units are consistent, they can be whatever unit of effort is collected in the organization's metrics system: hours, dollars, days, or something else.

Performing a customer view, value-based analysis of the project costs shows that only 46.1% of the entire project cost is viewed as value-added by the customer. Almost one third (32.6%) of the entire project cost would be viewed as not only non–value-added, but also nonessential. This set of activities can be the first to be targeted for waste reduction.

TABLE 26–2
Spreadsheet Template for Value Calculation

Project Identifier:					
Value-Added		**Non–Value-Added**			
		Essential		**Nonessential**	
Design		Acceptance Testing		Bottlenecks	
Documentation		Moving Data Between Steps		Correction	
Implementation		Planning		Delays	
Installation		Setup		Error Analysis	
Requirements		Some Process		Expediting	
Shipping		Training		Extra Paperwork	
Upgrading				Extra Unwanted Features	
				Installing Software Tools	
				Management	
				Metrics	
				Modification	
				Process Improvement	
				Recall	
				Retest	
				Rework	
Total Value Added:	0	Total Essential:	0	Total Nonessential:	0
Project Value to Total:	0.0%				
Percent Essential to Nonessential:	0.0%			Percent Nonessential to Total:	0.0%
Percent Value Plus Essential to Total:	0.0%				

TABLE 26–3
Elevator Control Software Value Analysis

Project Identifier: Elevator Control System Software					
Value-Added		**Non–Value-Added**			
		Essential		**Nonessential**	
Design	1000	Acceptance Testing	600	Bottlenecks	80
Documentation	550	Moving Data Between Steps	0	Correction	975
Implementation	360	Planning	600	Delays	124
Installation	500	Setup	240	Error Analysis	40
Requirements	1200	Some Process	200	Expediting	20
Shipping	40	Training	40	Extra Paperwork	80
Upgrading	0			Extra Unwanted Features	120
				Installing Software Tools	60
				Management	400
				Metrics	10
				Modification	90
				Process Improvement	20
				Recall	40
				Retest	400
				Rework	120
Total Value Added:	3650	Total Essential:	1680	Total Nonessential:	2579
Project Value to Total:	46.1%				
Percent Essential to Nonessential:	65.1%			Percent Nonessential to Total:	32.6%
Percent Value Plus Essential to Total:	67.4%				

Six-Step Software Development Process Improvement Model

Figure 26–9 is the model used for process improvement analysis. The six steps are an evolution of the classical Deming/Shewhart/Ishikawa plan-do-check-act cycle for process improvement. This model is geared for software development organizations. This model is especially useful in any maturity level organization for the front-end activities of a software development process, before doing the requirements elicitation. This model can also be used to drive problem analysis efforts in any organization. Continuous process improvement initiatives should be started only in organizations of Level 3 maturity or above.

Plan

This first step involves completing the process improvement worksheet for the plan phase. Figure 26–10 shows the worksheet template. The phase to which it applies is circled—in this case, plan. Enter the name of this improvement project manager and a description of the project. The description needs to be longer than 25 words, but not so long that it takes pages to describe. Remember, this is a process improvement project that needs to eliminate waste and improve quality. It does not need to contribute to next month's nonessential, non–value-added total of company hours.

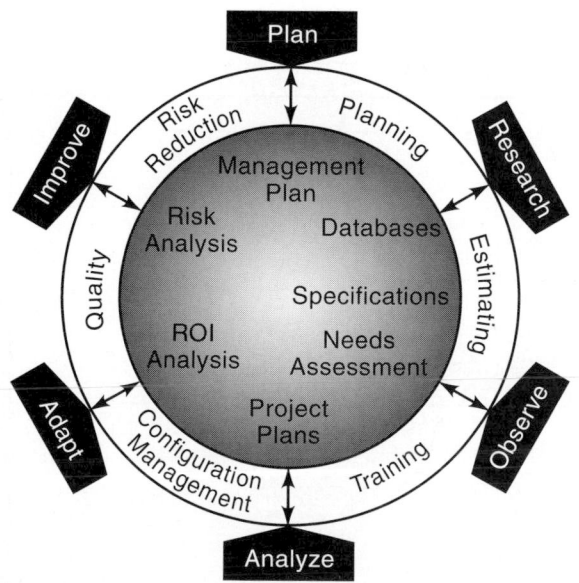

FIGURE 26–9
Six-Step Software Development Process Improvement Model

Process Improvement Worksheet for Circled Phase

(**Plan**)   **Research**   **Observe**   **Analyze**   **Adapt**   **Improve**

Process Improvement Project Manager: _____

Step 1: Describe the improvement project:

Step 2: Complete the effort estimates:

Process Phase	Estimate at Plan			Estimate at Research			Actuals		
	Start Date	End Date	Hours	Start Date	End Date	Hours	Start Date	End Date	Hours
Plan									
Research									
Observe									
Analyze									
Adapt									
Improve									
Total		0	0		0	0		0	0

Step 3: List personnel resources needed by phase:

Process Phase	Resource 1		Resource 2		Resource 3		Resource 4		Total Hours
	Start Date	Hours	Start Date	Hours	Start Date	Hours	Start Date	Hours	
Plan									0
Research									0
Observe									0
Analyze									0
Adapt									0
Improve									0
Total		0		0		0		0	0

Step 4: List other resources and tools needed for this phase:

Step 5: Describe the deliverable from this improvement project phase:

FIGURE 26–10

Process Improvement Planning Worksheet

Step 2 on the worksheet is for tracking the effort estimates and actuals. The mechanisms must be in place to continuously improve. Especially in the area of estimating tasks, software developers can never get enough practice. This worksheet has the first set of estimates done at the planning phase, and then they are revised after the research is completed on the project. The actual hours are recorded here as well. It is assumed that in a Level 3 organization, all hours will be tracked as part of the metrics system.

Listing the specific personnel resources and when they are required for each phase is the next step. There are only four resource slots. Process improvement projects are small, tightly focused efforts. Large teams do not get results. This is a small team effort. If the project being defined needs more than four personnel resources plus the project manager, break it into multiple projects.

Step 4 is a spot to list other resources and tools needed for this project. If this is the first process improvement project, statistical analysis tools may be needed. Depending on the internal databases being used, some data-scrubbing and characterization tools might decrease the amount of analysis time.

Step 5 describes exactly what the deliverable is to be from this process phase. It is very important that for internal process improvement projects, management knows exactly what it is getting. Instituting continuous process improvement is an expensive and politically dangerous exercise. A project manager of internal projects is only as good as the amount of money the last project returned to the bottom line.

All the information about each one of these process improvement phases should fit on one sheet of paper. Process improvement projects must be short and to the point. Major projects that have the overall goal of improving all the organization's processes at once look like an exercise in boiling the ocean. For the overall process improvement initiative to be continued, process-focused projects must show early, successful results. It is extremely easy for management to cancel internal projects that look neither successful nor able to contribute to the economic bottom line.

Research

At the end of the research phase, the project manager re-estimates the effort for all subsequent phases. The actuals for the plan and research phases are put in the Estimate at Research column entries, and new estimates made for the remaining four phases. The research phase is where the project manager identifies all the data sources that are required for the project and secures access to them. The data sources are usually organization metrics and performance data files, project files, and customer deliverables. Depending on the types of information required, outside data sources may have to be accessed. For a process improvement project focused on one aspect of the development process, the project manager may find all current projects in that process phase.

Observe

When all the information sources are identified, this phase gathers all the information required into a format usable by the process improvement project. Where there are development processes under analysis, the project manager may want to observe those processes being executed. For example, a process improvement effort focused on code inspections would require benchmarking how they were done today and the observable results of an inspection meeting. All recorded observations are gathered and forwarded on to the next phase for analysis.

Analyze

In process improvement projects, this is the phase where statistical analysis and data-visualization tools are used. This chapter is not going to discuss the myriad of statistical tools and techniques that can be used to manipulate the observed data. It is up to the discretion and training of the project manager and the receptivity of the management audience for the project recommendations that determine how the data is cooked for presentation.[3, 4, 5, 6]

Adapt

The adapt phase takes the information derived from the data analysis and produces the recommendations to adapt the existing process. These recommendations are based on analysis of the organization's process metrics. Each adaptation recommendation needs a description, risk of implementation analysis, and cost-benefit justification. Each recommendation for adaptation may be approved individually and could result in a separate project.

Improve

This final step is the execution of the adaptation recommendations made in the previous phase. For complex process improvements, this could become a separate project. An example is the justified need to acquire a new framework for code development. This could require an entire COTS tools-selection life cycle.

Applying the Software Development Process Improvement Model

A 50-person software development organization is our example of applying the six-step software process development model. For purposes of this example, the company will be called Atlanta Elevator Company (AEC). AEC has three years of project metrics in its database and is performing at CMM Level 3 maturity. It is a standalone business unit of a major elevator hardware manufacturer that develops software only to generate revenue. There are no product sales to cloud the revenue stream. Full financials have been analyzed to arrive at the revenue numbers used for costing. In the last three years of project record-keeping, the organization billed $15,000,000 at an average hourly rate of $165.00.

The total number of billed hours was 90,900. AEC uses a timesheet system to track all billable and nonbillable work broken out into projects. Each project has a series of phases that also can be tracked. AEC wants to begin a continuous process improvement initiative and will use the current set of metrics to baseline the entire organization and look for waste targets of opportunity to begin the improvement process. This is not a cost-accounting exercise. The continuous process improvement initiative must look at AEC from the customer's perspective. Areas that may need more business financial information are recommended to the internal business practices re-engineering task force.

Plan

AEC needs to baseline the software development process over the last three years. There is no established categorization of value- versus non–value-added tasks done on a project-by-project basis or organization-wide. This project will set that baseline through the use of a value-analysis worksheet. This worksheet will cover the past three years of data. The adapt phase will focus on recommending changes to the current metrics system to collect information not currently gathered for completing customer-based value analysis. The improve phase will implement those collection changes.

The AEC project manager, Mr. Lifté, will develop estimates based on past history with process improvement efforts. There are a minimum number of internal resources that can assist on these projects. They are reserved for software developers between projects who have a couple of days or, at most, a week to commit to an internal project. See Figure 26–11.

Research

The basic AEC information needed for the value analysis was available in two easy-to-access databases. The systems admin merely directed Mr. Lifté to the correct share and charged nothing to the process improvement project because the effort took less than five minutes. The information required has been collected in a consistent format for the past three years. It requires no special access, and it looks like there will be little modification needed in the next phase. See Figure 26–12.

Observe

The project manager copied all of the data found in the research phase into a separate database to be used for analysis. This took a total of five hours. There were no problems in accessing the data. The financial information needed was on a report generated monthly for the organization business manager. One of the interesting occurrences of data collection for process

Process Improvement Worksheet for Circled Phase					
⬭ Plan ⬭	Research	Observe	Analyze	Adapt	Improve

Process Improvement Project Manager: Jorge Lifte

Step 1: Describe the improvement project:
AEC needs to baseline the software development process over the last three years. There is no established categorization of value versus non–value-added tasks done on a project by project basis or organization-wide. This project will set that baseline through the use of a value analysis worksheet. This worksheet will cover the past three years of data.
The adapt phase will focus on recommending changes to the current metrics system to collect information not currently gathered for completing customer-based value analysis. The improve phase will implement those collection changes.

Step 2: Complete the effort estimates:

Process Phase	Estimate at Plan			Estimate at Research			Actuals		
	Start Date	End Date	Hours	Start Date	End Date	Hours	Start Date	End Date	Hours
Plan	2-Jul-01	2-Jul-01	8						
Research	3-Jul-01	6-Jul-01	25						
Observe	9-Jul-01	13-Jul-01	44						
Analyze	16-Jul-01	18-Jul-01	24						
Adapt	19-Jul-01	31-Jul-01	24						
Improve	6-Aug-01	27-Aug-01	40						
Total		55	165		0	0		0	0

Step 3: List personnel resources needed by phase:

Process Phase	System Admin		Financial Analyst		Resource 3		Resource 4		Total Hours
	Start Date	Hours	Start Date	Hours	Start Date	Hours	Start Date	Hours	
Plan									0
Research	3-Jul-01	1							1
Observe			9-Jul-01	4					4
Analyze									0
Adapt									0
Improve									0
Total		1		4		0		0	5

Step 4: List other resources and tools needed for this phase:
This will be an analysis project. Tools to be used already exist in the organization. The value analysis template will be used to present the analysis results.

Step 5: Describe the deliverable from this improvement project phase:
This phase will produce the process improvement project plan for approval.

FIGURE 26–11
AEC Process Improvement Plan Phase Worksheet

Process Improvement Worksheet for Circled Phase					
Plan	(Research)	Observe	Analyze	Adapt	Improve

Process Improvement Project Manager: Jorge Lifte

Step 1: Describe the improvement project:
AEC needs to baseline the software development process over the last three years. There is no established categorization of value versus non–value-added tasks done on a project by project basis or organization-wide. This project will set that baseline through the use of a value analysis worksheet. This worksheet will cover the past three years of data.
The adapt phase will focus on recommending changes to the current metrics system to collect information not currently gathered for completing customer-based value analysis. The improve phase will implement those collection changes.

Step 2: Complete the effort estimates:

Process Phase	Estimate at Plan			Estimate at Research			Actuals		
	Start Date	End Date	Hours	Start Date	End Date	Hours	Start Date	End Date	Hours
Plan	2-Jul-01	2-Jul-01	8	2-Jul-01	2-Jul-01	2	2-Jul-01	2-Jul-01	2
Research	3-Jul-01	6-Jul-01	25	3-Jul-01	5-Jul-01	8	3-Jul-01	5-Jul-01	8
Observe	9-Jul-01	13-Jul-01	44	5-Jul-01	6-Jul-01	12			
Analyze	16-Jul-01	18-Jul-01	24	9-Jul-01	11-Jul-01	16			
Adapt	19-Jul-01	31-Jul-01	24	12-Jul-01	17-Jul-01	24			
Improve	6-Aug-01	27-Aug-01	40	23-Jul-01	13-Aug-01	40			
Total		55	165		41	102		3	10

Step 3: List personnel resources needed by phase:

Process Phase	System Admin		Financial Analyst		Resource 3		Resource 4		Total Hours
	Start Date	Hours	Start Date	Hours	Start Date	Hours	Start Date	Hours	
Plan									0
Research	3-Jul-01	0							0
Observe			5-Jul-01	4					4
Analyze									0
Adapt									0
Improve									0
Total		0		4		0		0	4

Step 4: List other resources and tools needed for this phase:
This will be an analysis project. Tools to be used already exist in the organization. The value analysis template will be used to present the analysis results.

Step 5: Describe the deliverable from this improvement project phase:
This phase produced the revised project effort estimate that reduced the effort by 43 hours and brought in the overall schedule by 63 days.

FIGURE 26–12
AEC Process Improvement Research Phase Worksheet

improvement is that there exists a lot of data that is not being used. Even in relatively young organizations, data collections activities, once begun, never seem to end. Megabytes of data are there just for the asking. Waste is not that difficult to find. See Figure 26–13.

Analyze

The analyze phase took the database developed in the previous phase and did simple statistical analyses using Microsoft Excel. Using the value-analysis template (Table 26–2), the information developed from the AEC metrics data was entered into the template. Figure 26–14 shows the process improvement phase worksheet for the analyze phase. Note that the estimate was 16 hours, but the actual was 20. The data analysis required the project manager to use four hours of a financial analyst's time to complete the statistical study.

Table 26–4 shows the results of the analysis. These results will be further analyzed in the adapt phase to produce process improvement recommendations.

Adapt

Based on the three-year value analysis of Table 26–4, a set of information visualization graphics needs to be prepared to lay the foundation for the adaptation recommendations. Figure 26–15 shows a gross distribution of the value-analysis data. This chart represents the total hours recorded in the metrics system for the past three years:

- **Value-added**—What the customer really wants and sees as quality—69,300 hours
- **Essential**—What the customer will accept as necessary, but is not willing to really pay for—18,025 hours
- **Nonessential**—What the customer will readily admit is overhead—83,700 hours
- **Hours billed**—What the customer really paid for—90,900 hours

Analyzing how the hours were broken out in the value analysis versus what was paid for by the customer, this pattern emerges:

1. The customer paid for all value-added work.
2. The customer paid for all non–value-added essential work.
3. The customer paid for 3,575 hours of non-value added, nonessential hours.
4. The customer paid for 131% of what is considered value work.

Process Improvement Worksheet for Circled Phase

Plan   Research   (Observe)   Analyze   Adapt   Improve

Process Improvement Project Manager: Jorge Lifte

Step 1: Describe the improvement project:

AEC needs to baseline the software development process over the last three years. There is no established categorization of value versus non–value-added tasks done on a project by project basis or organization-wide. This project will set that baseline through the use of a value analysis worksheet. This worksheet will cover the past three years of data.

The adapt phase will focus on recommending changes to the current metrics system to collect information not currently gathered for completing customer-based value analysis. The improve phase will implement those collection changes.

Step 2: Complete the effort estimates:

Process Phase	Estimate at Plan			Estimate at Research			Actuals		
	Start Date	End Date	Hours	Start Date	End Date	Hours	Start Date	End Date	Hours
Plan	2-Jul-01	2-Jul-01	8	2-Jul-01	2-Jul-01	2	2-Jul-01	2-Jul-01	2
Research	3-Jul-01	6-Jul-01	25	3-Jul-01	5-Jul-01	8	3-Jul-01	5-Jul-01	8
Observe	9-Jul-01	13-Jul-01	44	5-Jul-01	6-Jul-01	12	5-Jul-01	6-Jul-01	5
Analyze	16-Jul-01	18-Jul-01	24	9-Jul-01	11-Jul-01	16			
Adapt	19-Jul-01	31-Jul-01	24	12-Jul-01	17-Jul-01	24			
Improve	6-Aug-01	27-Aug-01	40	23-Jul-01	13-Aug-01	40			
Total		55	165		41	102		0	15

Step 3: List personnel resources needed by phase:

Process Phase	System Admin		Financial Analyst		Resource 3		Resource 4		Total
	Start Date	Hours	Start Date	Hours	Start Date	Hours	Start Date	Hours	Hours
Plan									0
Research	3-Jul-01	0							0
Observe			5-Jul-01	1					1
Analyze									0
Adapt									0
Improve									0
Total		0		1		0		0	1

Step 4: List other resources and tools needed for this phase:

This will be an analysis project. Tools to be used already exist in the organization. The value analysis template will be used to present the analysis results.

Step 5: Describe the deliverable from this improvement project phase:

This phase retrieved 61,379 records with 24 attributes each. The data were then conditioned to match the available financial reporting periods. The observation phase also took five fewer hours of effort than estimated because of the rapid availability of financial information.

FIGURE 26–13
AEC Process Improvement Observe Phase Worksheet

Process Improvement Worksheet for Circled Phase					
Plan	**Research**	**Observe**	⟨ **Analyze** ⟩	**Adapt**	**Improve**

Process Improvement Project Manager: Jorge Lifte

Step 1: Describe the improvement project:
AEC needs to baseline the software development process over the last three years. There is no established categorization of value versus non–value-added tasks done on a project by project basis or organization-wide. This project will set that baseline through the use of a value analysis worksheet. This worksheet will cover the past three years of data.
The adapt phase will focus on recommending changes to the current metrics system to collect information not currently gathered for completing customer-based value analysis. The improve phase will implement those collection changes.

Step 2: Complete the effort estimates:

Process Phase	Estimate at Plan			Estimate at Research			Actuals		
	Start Date	End Date	Hours	Start Date	End Date	Hours	Start Date	End Date	Hours
Plan	2-Jul-01	2-Jul-01	8	2-Jul-01	2-Jul-01	2	2-Jul-01	2-Jul-01	2
Research	3-Jul-01	6-Jul-01	25	3-Jul-01	5-Jul-01	8	3-Jul-01	5-Jul-01	8
Observe	9-Jul-01	13-Jul-01	44	5-Jul-01	6-Jul-01	12	5-Jul-01	6-Jul-01	5
Analyze	16-Jul-01	18-Jul-01	24	9-Jul-01	11-Jul-01	16	9-Jul-01	11-Jul-01	20
Adapt	19-Jul-01	31-Jul-01	24	12-Jul-01	17-Jul-01	24			
Improve	6-Aug-01	27-Aug-01	40	23-Jul-01	13-Aug-01	40			
Total		55	165		41	102		0	35

Step 3: List personnel resources needed by phase:

Process Phase	System Admin		Financial Analyst		Resource 3		Resource 4		Total
	Start Date	Hours	Start Date	Hours	Start Date	Hours	Start Date	Hours	Hours
Plan									0
Research	3-Jul-01	0							0
Observe			5-Jul-01	1					1
Analyze			9-Jul-01	4					4
Adapt									0
Improve									0
Total		0		5		0		0	5

Step 4: List other resources and tools needed for this phase:
Simple Microsoft Excel™ spreadsheets will be used to analyze the data. The value analysis template will be used to present the analysis results.

Step 5: Describe the deliverable from this improvement project phase:
This phase delivered the value analysis table for the three years of AEC data.

FIGURE 26–14
AEC Process Improvement Analyze Phase Worksheet

TABLE 26–4
AEC Three-Year Value Analysis

Project Identifier: AEC Baseline Historic Value Analysis					
Value-Added		**Non–Value-Added**			
		Essential		**Nonessential**	
Design	14250	Acceptance Testing	7200	Bottlenecks	
Documentation	2500	Moving Data Between Steps		Correction	700
Implementation	28000	Planning	9250	Delays	
Installation	850	Setup	200	Error Analysis	
Requirements	19500	Some Process	625	Expediting	
Shipping	3000	Training	750	Extra Paperwork	
Upgrading	1200			Extra Unwanted Features	
Value-Added		**Non–Value-Added**			
		Essential		**Nonessential**	
				Installing Software Tools	11000
				Management	62500
				Metrics	
				Modification	
				Process Improvement	9500
				Recall	
				Retest	
				Rework	
Total Value Added:	69300	Total Essential:	18025	Total Nonessential:	83700
Project Value to Total:	40.5%				
Percent Essential to Nonessential:	21.5%			Percent Nonessential to Total:	48.9%
Percent Value Plus Essential to Total:	51.1%				

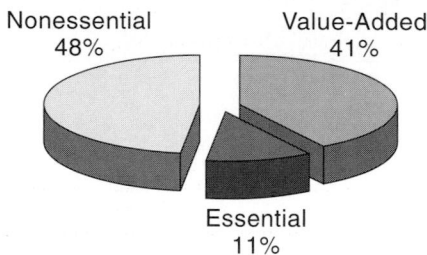

FIGURE 26–15
Gross Distribution from Value Analysis

Going back to the purpose of this first, the organization-wide process improvement project was intended to define the baseline for continuous process improvement. This baseline has now been set, and the following questions arise for further analysis:

1. If this organization's customers are billed and are paying for hours that are traditionally viewed as non–value-added, what is their satisfaction level with the product received?

2. Forty-eight percent of all hours recorded for the past three years were non–value-added, nonessential. Figure 26–16 shows the distribution of where those hours were recorded. The easy target is the enormous chunk of 62,500 hours in management. What is really in this bucket, and how can the waste be driven out?

3. Looking again at the nonessential portion of the value analysis, why are there no recorded values for the categories bottlenecks, delays, error analysis, expediting, extra paperwork, extra unwanted features, metrics, modification, recall, retest, and rework?

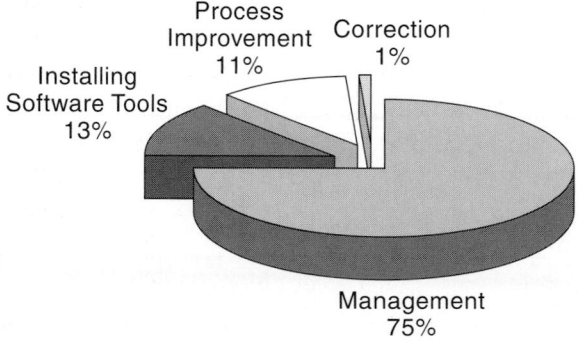

FIGURE 26–16
Non–Value-Added, Nonessential Hours Distribution

Using all the information presented for AEC, it is left to the reader and student to complete the recommendations in Table 26–5. This should be done as either an individual homework assignment or an in-class team exercise. See Figure 26–17.

TABLE 26–5
Adaptation Recommendation

ID	Description	Implementation Risk	Cost Benefit
1	Customer Satisfaction Analysis		
2	Waste in Management		
3	Missing Metrics Data		
4			
5			

Improve

Based on the individual or teamwork done in the previous section, complete Figure 26–18 for the improve phase. This can be done as individual homework or in-class team exercises.

Summary

The main question that organization executives and project managers ask is, "But, does it really work?" Documented case studies of software process improvement indicate that significant improvements in both quality and productivity are a result of the improvement effort.[7] When the organizational investment is made, the return on investment is typically between 5:1 and 8:1 for successful process improvement efforts.[8] Continuous process improvement begins with an awareness of the process maturity within the project development organization. Although continuous improvement could be done by a single project, the benefit is not realized until the next project. Continuous improvement is an organization-wide initiative. It must be supported by the entire organization and must extend over all projects. For an organization like AEC, in which the average billable rate is $165 per hour, a 5:1 improvement would be a net $825 for each process improvement hour invested.

Success as a software project manager is judged by delivering quality products on time and with the resources budgeted. Quality is determined by the customer and comes from improving the product development process. Continuous process improvement is the mechanism that an organization uses to ensure that products that are less costly, more capable of

Process Improvement Worksheet for Circled Phase

Plan　　　Research　　　Observe　　　Analyze　　　(Adapt)　　　Improve

Process Improvement Project Manager: ___Jorge Lifte___

Step 1: Describe the improvement project:

AEC needs to baseline the software development process over the last three years. There is no established categorization of value versus non–value-added tasks done on a project by project basis or organization-wide. This project will set that baseline through the use of a value analysis worksheet. This worksheet will cover the past three years of data.

The adapt phase will focus on recommending changes to the current metrics system to collect information not currently gathered for completing customer-based value analysis. The improve phase will implement those collection changes.

Step 2: Complete the effort estimates:

Process Phase	Estimate at Plan			Estimate at Research			Actuals		
	Start Date	End Date	Hours	Start Date	End Date	Hours	Start Date	End Date	Hours
Plan	2-Jul-01	2-Jul-01	8	2-Jul-01	2-Jul-01	2	2-Jul-01	2-Jul-01	2
Research	3-Jul-01	6-Jul-01	25	3-Jul-01	5-Jul-01	8	3-Jul-01	5-Jul-01	8
Observe	9-Jul-01	13-Jul-01	44	5-Jul-01	6-Jul-01	12	5-Jul-01	6-Jul-01	5
Analyze	16-Jul-01	18-Jul-01	24	9-Jul-01	11-Jul-01	16	9-Jul-01	11-Jul-01	20
Adapt	19-Jul-01	31-Jul-01	24	12-Jul-01	17-Jul-01	24	12-Jul-01	18-Jul-01	28
Improve	6-Aug-01	27-Aug-01	40	23-Jul-01	13-Aug-01	40			
Total		55	165		41	102		0	63

Step 3: List personnel resources needed by phase:

Process Phase	System Admin		Financial Analyst		Reviewers		Resource 4		Total
	Start Date	Hours	Start Date	Hours	Start Date	Hours	Start Date	Hours	Hours
Plan									0
Research	3-Jul-01	0							0
Observe			5-Jul-01	1					1
Analyze			9-Jul-01	4					4
Adapt					17-Jul-01	8			8
Improve									0
Total		0		5		8		0	13

Step 4: List other resources and tools needed for this phase:

None

Step 5: Describe the deliverable from this improvement project phase:

This phase delivered the attached set of process adaptation recommendations.

FIGURE 26–17

AEC Process Improvement Adapt Phase Worksheet

Process Improvement Worksheet for Circled Phase

Plan   Research   Observe   Analyze   Adapt   (Improve)

Process Improvement Project Manager: Jorge Lifte

Step 1: Describe the improvement project:

AEC needs to baseline the software development process over the last three years. There is no established categorization of value versus non–value-added tasks done on a project by project basis or organization-wide. This project will set that baseline through the use of a value analysis worksheet. This worksheet will cover the past three years of data.

The adapt phase will focus on recommending changes to the current metrics system to collect information not currently gathered for completing customer-based value analysis. The improve phase will implement those collection changes.

Step 2: Complete the effort estimates:

Process Phase	Estimate at Plan			Estimate at Research			Actuals		
	Start Date	End Date	Hours	Start Date	End Date	Hours	Start Date	End Date	Hours
Plan	2-Jul-01	2-Jul-01	8	2-Jul-01	2-Jul-01	2	2-Jul-01	2-Jul-01	2
Research	3-Jul-01	6-Jul-01	25	3-Jul-01	5-Jul-01	8	3-Jul-01	5-Jul-01	8
Observe	9-Jul-01	13-Jul-01	44	5-Jul-01	6-Jul-01	12	5-Jul-01	6-Jul-01	5
Analyze	16-Jul-01	18-Jul-01	24	9-Jul-01	11-Jul-01	16	9-Jul-01	11-Jul-01	20
Adapt	19-Jul-01	31-Jul-01	24	12-Jul-01	17-Jul-01	24	12-Jul-01	18-Jul-01	28
Improve	6-Aug-01	27-Aug-01	40	23-Jul-01	13-Aug-01	40			
Total			55	165		41	102	0	63

Step 3: List personnel resources needed by phase:

Process Phase	System Admin		Financial Analyst		Resource 3		Resource 4		Total Hours
	Start Date	Hours	Start Date	Hours	Start Date	Hours	Start Date	Hours	
Plan									0
Research	3-Jul-01	0							0
Observe			5-Jul-01	1					1
Analyze			9-Jul-01	4					4
Adapt					17-Jul-01	8			8
Improve									0
Total		0		5		8		0	13

Step 4: List other resources and tools needed for this phase:

Step 5: Describe the deliverable from this improvement project phase:

FIGURE 26–18

AEC Process Improvement Improve Phase Worksheet

meeting customer requirements, and more reliable. This mechanism also reduces cost and eliminates waste within the existing development processes, thus allowing project execution on time and within resources.

This chapter looked at continuous process improvement as a process in and of itself. It is not a collection of statistical tools. It is a process of analysis and picking the highest payback improvement targets to add quality and eliminate waste.

Problems for Review

1. What does the area under the curve look like for your organization's probability of hitting resource estimate targets for past and current projects? If your organization has not had a formal CMM assessment, estimate your maturity level.

2. Using the value-analysis template, modify it for your organization. What information are you missing from your metrics system to complete the value analysis?

3. Focusing on a project on which you are currently working, how would you institute process improvement on that individual project?

4. Define *value* for your organization's customers.

5. Using the six-phase process improvement model, design a continuous process improvement plan for your class project team.

Visit the Case Study

Dr. Harita has been promoted out of the BSD to the corporate offices of software research and standardization. In his new role, he will be responsible for introducing automated software development tools into organizations throughout the corporation. The first thing he will have to do is to reinstate the SEI CMM, international corporate internal evaluations. Several years ago, interest waned in the CMM after the majority of the software organizations reached Level 3 and business unit vice presidents no longer had that as a line item on their annual bonus performance measures.

The corporation has acquired a number of software product organizations and now has a substantial portfolio of productivity tools. Dr. Harita wants to use a small but visible software project as the "poster child" for corporate software tool use. ARRS is it!

This provides you, as the project manager, and Ms. Patel, as the marketing manager, with visibility and an opportunity for promotion. The first thing you need to do is have an outside evaluation of the project to set the SEI maturity level. Before an outside team can come in, Ms. Patel wants you to do an internal evaluation. She will not be happy unless the project is a 4 or 5. And why shouldn't it be? You are using BSD, which is a Level 5. Prepare the evaluation scoring for a review by Friday.

Citations

[1] *www.utexas.edu/coe/sqi/archive/krasner/spi.pdf.* Krasner, Herb (1997). *Accumulating the Body of Evidence for The Payoff of Software Process Improvement.*

[2] Paulk, Mark C., et al. (1993). "Capability Maturity Model, Version 1.1." *IEEE Software*, 10(4):18–27.

[3] Brassard, Michael, and Diane Ritter (1994). *The Memory Jogger™ II.*

[4] Brassard, Michael, et al. (1995). *The Team Memory Jogger™.*

[5] Brassard, Michael, et al. (2000). *The Problem Solver Memory Jogger™.*

[6] *www.man.deakin.edu.au/rodneyc/XLStats.htm.* XLStatistics is a set of Microsoft Excel (version 5+) workbooks for statistical analysis of data designed to replace and enhance the tools provided with Excel's Data Analysis Toolbox add-in. The workbooks are designed to implement a step-by-step guide to the statistical analysis of data (this guide appears commonly as a flow chart in many texts).

[7] See note 1.

[8] See note 2.

Tools

silver.sdsmt.edu/~fmatejci/kcqc~1.htm. Sound motivation from practice and theory are presented to support the use of ancient tools (a triangle, a ruler, and a few geometric properties) for teaching statistical process control. Detailed examples of ancient tools approaches for computing means, standard deviations, X-bar charts, R charts, and S charts are included. Applicability of ancient tools approaches to other statistical applications is demonstrated, and special tables for confidence interval calculations are included. Listings of short XLISP-STAT programs to make the plots in the paper are included. Statistical process control was taught to a work group at Landstrom's Black Hill's Gold using a novel approach: Diagrams served as an alternative to formulas, and calculations were done using ancient tools. The results of that trial are described in this paper.

www.stat.umn.edu/~luke/xls/xlsinfo/xlsinfo.html. Lisp-Stat is an extensible statistical computing environment for data analysis, statistical instruction, and research, with an emphasis on providing a framework for exploring the use of dynamic graphical methods. Extensibility is achieved by basing Lisp-Stat on the Lisp language, in particular on a subset of Common Lisp. Lisp-Stat extends standard Lisp arithmetic operations to perform element-wise operations on lists and vectors, and it adds a variety of basic statistical and linear algebra functions. A portable window system interface forms the basis of a dynamic graphics system that is designed to work identically in a number of different graphical user interface environments, such as the Macintosh operating system, the X Window system, and Microsoft Windows. A prototype-based object-oriented programming system is used to implement the graphics system and to allow it to be customized and adapted. The object-oriented programming system is also used as the basis for statistical model representations, such as linear and nonlinear regression models and generalized linear models. The S language motivated many aspects of the system design.

Web Pages for Further Information

www-bcf.usc.edu/~madachy/spmsd/spmsd.html. Draft version 4/01, Software Process Dynamics, Raymond J. Madachy, Barry W. Boehm, IEEE Computer Society Press.

www.qualitydigest.com/apr99/html/excel.html. William A. Levinson, P.E., Using Excel Control Charts with Varying Sample Sizes—Spreadsheets can actually exceed the capabilities of many commercially available SPC packages.

www.qualitydigest.com/mar01/html/ci.html. Craig Cochran, Two Hidden Gems of Continual Improvement—With a pair of basic actions, you can lead your organization to true long-term improvement.

www.qualitydigest.com/mar99/html/itech.html. Douglas L. Swanson, Ph.D.; Richard A. Esposito; and Jean Jester, Ph.D., Managing Quality for Information Technology—Performance can be substantially improved by ensuring that tactical decisions to develop and support IT emphasize quality.

www.qualitydigest.com/may99/html/ci.html. "The Road to Continuous Improvement," Lee C. Bravener.

www.qualitydigest.com/jul/contimp.html#anchor112080. Reengineering and Continuous Improvement. J. Chris White—In a complex system, relations dominate and primarily determine the success of the system.

www.qualitydigest.com/june97/html/cover.html. "Essential Tools for Quality Managers, Or, What I Wish I Knew Before I Took This Job," J. Michael Crouch.

www.qualitydigest.com/pdfs/2001src-software.pdf. 2001 Software Quality and Calibration Guide—Separate sections for calibration software and services, document control, flowcharting and process simulation, and ISO 9000 software.

Suggested Readings

Fowler, P., and S. Rifkin (1990). *Software Engineering Process Group Guide.* Software Engineering Institute.

Gabor, Andrea (1992). *The Man Who Discovered Quality.* Penguin Books.

Gause, Donald C., and Gerald M. Weinberg (1989). *Exploring Requirements: Quality Before Design.* Dorset House Publishing.

Humphrey, W.S., and W.L. Sweet (1987). *A Method for Assessing the Software Engineering Capability of Contractors.* Software Engineering Institute.

Humphrey, W.S. (1987). "Characterizing the Software Process: A Maturity Framework." *IEEE Software,* 5(2):73–79.

Humphrey, W.S., D.H. Kitson, and J. Gale (1991). "A Comparison of U.S. and Japanese Software Process Maturity." *Proceedings of the 13th International Conference on Software Engineering,* Austin, TX, 13–17 May 1991, pp. 38–49.

Humphrey, W.S. (1989). *Managing the Software Process*. Reading, MA: Addison-Wesley.

Kitson, D.H., and S. Masters (1992). *An Analysis of SEI Software Process Assessment Results: 1987–1991*. Software Engineering Institute.

Paulk, M.C., et al. (1991). *Capability Maturity Model for Software*, Software Engineering Institute.

Paulk, M.C., et al. (1993). *Capability Maturity Model for Software*, Version 1.1. Software Engineering Institute.

Paulk, M.C., et al. (1993). *Key Practices of the Capability Maturity Model*, Version 1.1. Software Engineering Institute.

Walton, Mary (1986). *The Deming Management Method*. Putnam Publishing Group.

Weber, C.V., et al. (1991). *Key Practices of the Capability Maturity Model*. Software Engineering Institute.

Williams, Karl (1994). *Continuous Improvement and Reengineering*. Harvard Quality Associates.

Project Termination

Do we really need a chapter on project termination? Isn't this a foregone conclusion? By definition, don't all projects end? These are some of the questions that pop into mind when the subject is mentioned. Surprising as it may seem, many projects become the Thing That Wouldn't Die.

In this chapter, we explore the reasons for termination and some of the ways it happens.

Where We Are in the Product Development Life Cycle

Where are we in the basic software life cycle model that serves as our map? As shown in Figure 27–1, we could be anywhere along the product path, but usually termination occurs toward the middle or end of the life cycle. Termination during the operations and maintenance phases of the product life cycle is considered cessation of operation. Project termination would occur during the software development project life cycle to build the product as shown in Figure 27–2.

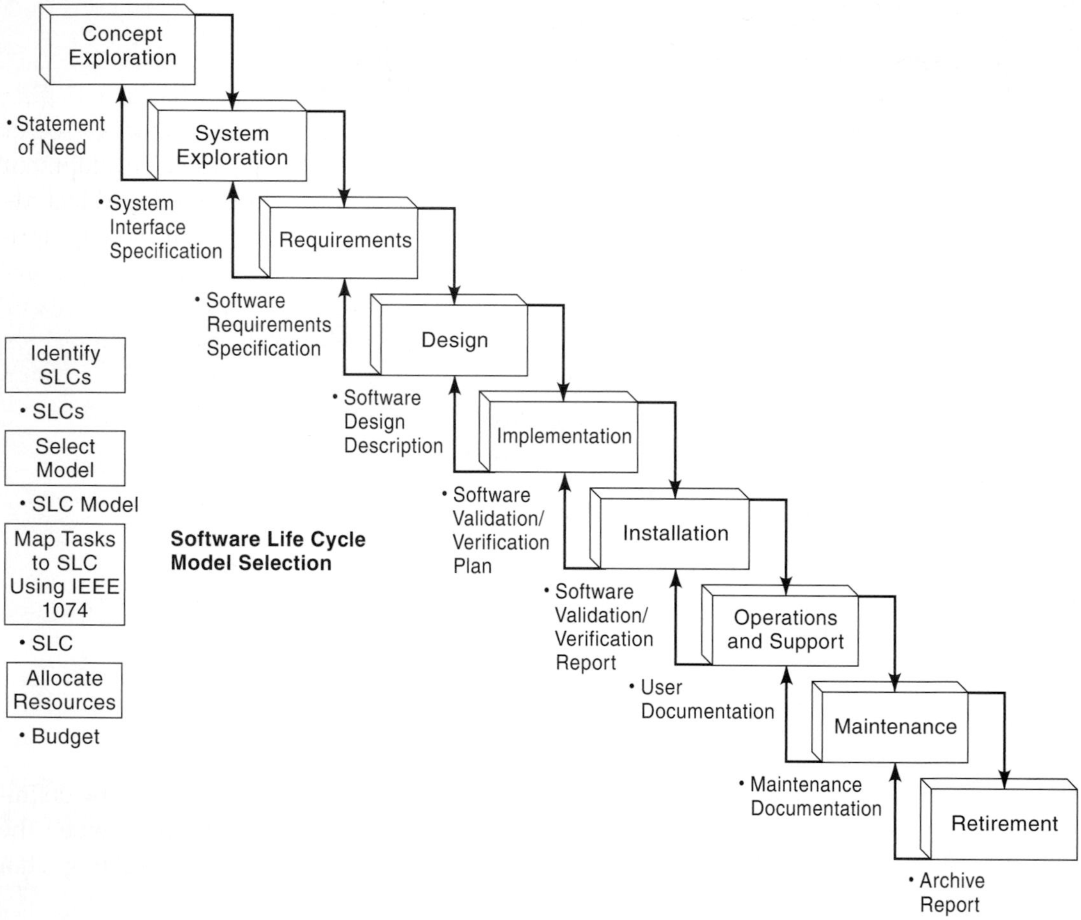

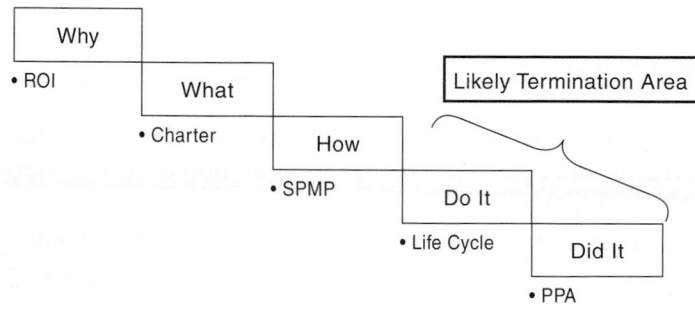

FIGURE 27–1
Product Process Framework

FIGURE 27–2
Project Process Framework

Chapter 27 Relation to the 34 Competencies _____

The product development techniques used in project termination include understanding development activities and assessing and tailoring processes to perform project close-out activities properly. It is critical that the project manager know what product development steps are needed upon project termination. The project management skills employed include tracking process compliance by the team and project progress toward the goals using appropriate metrics. The most important people skill required is managing change because project termination is a pretty big change to manage. It is also necessary to assess team members' performance and help them plan career moves as they transition off the project to other things. And it is critical to handle and dispose of any project intellectual property in a proper manner. "Good housekeeping" is needed with all intellectual property associated with the project.

Product Development Techniques

1. **Assessing processes**—Defining criteria for reviews
9. **Tailoring processes**—Modifying standard processes to suit a project
11. **Understanding development activities**—Learning the software development cycle

Project Management Skills

21. **Tracking process**—Monitoring compliance of project team
22. **Tracking project progress**—Monitoring progress using metrics

People Management Skills

23. **Appraising performance**—Evaluating teams to enhance performance
24. **Handling intellectual property**—Understanding the impact of critical issues
28. **Managing change**—Being an effective change agent
30. **Planning careers**—Structuring and giving career guidance

Learning Objectives for Chapter 27 _____

Upon completion of this chapter, the reader should be able to:

- Describe seven different ways to terminate a project;
- List the steps necessary to terminate a project;
- Cite at least one reason from each part of the triple constraint for why a project may be terminated;
- Explain why termination is important to humans.

Why Terminate?

Just as a software development project may start for a variety of reasons (new product development, repair or maintenance, systems integration or consolidation, etc.), it may end for a variety of reasons. Obviously, a project will terminate if it reaches its objectives (by definition). But there are a lot of other reasons one might end. Let's look at them in the framework of the triple constraints of scope, schedule, and cost, with special considerations for quality, technology, and business.

Business Reasons

Even if the project was well launched, with great sponsor, team, and stakeholder support, and has been well executed to date, management may decide to terminate the project prematurely. One of the reasons may be that the project no longer is consistent with the business strategy or organizational goals. There may be better uses for scarce funds, or it may be subcontracted more effectively than done internally.

Much of upper management's job is to balance a portfolio of activities to achieve goals. Something to realize is that the language of management is money, and, at some level, all projects are looked at as simply an economic return. They may also be balanced with nonmonetary considerations such as strategic value, but it is always a good idea to have some kind of return on investment (ROI) computed for your software development project. This tells you how important the project is to your organization financially. It is possible that an ROI computed at the start of a project may be acceptable enough to gain sponsorship and approve a charter to get started. But over time, the cost of keeping the project going might exceed the projected ROI, making it a candidate for termination. This situation can develop because businesses get money to fund projects from several sources:

- Bank loans (at prevailing interest rates)
- Stock (common and preferred)
- Earnings (money earned from earlier periods and retained for internal use)

Each of these has some cost associated with it, usually expressed as an interest rate. Financial people in the organization compute something called a weighted average cost of capital (WACC) during their capital budgeting process that represents how much it costs the organization to fund the labor and equipment for any project, whether it is for doing software development, paving the parking lot, or deploying cell phones to every sales representative. The organization's treasurer may compute an ROI measure, such as the internal rate of return (IRR), as a way to put into numbers facts about a diverse set of potential projects, with varying durations and scale, for ease of comparison. The resulting list may look something like Figure 27–3.

Treasurers Compare the Returns of Many Projects

Project	Cost ($K)	Inflows ($K)	Project Life	IRR
Enhance Sales Force	1750	5245	2	12%
Your Project	1550	4820	4	15%
Add New Bldg Wing	22000	35000	35	18%
Another SW Project	3515	7905	6	17%

FIGURE 27–3
Comparing Diverse Projects Using IRR

Obviously, if it appears to cost more to fund the project (WACC) than the project is expected to return (ROI), then it doesn't look like a good deal to management and may pop up on their radar screen for termination. This situation is illustrated in Figure 27–4, where your project (the shaded one) was once showing a positive ROI but is now showing a negative ROI because the cost to get money (interest rate) has gone way up. Your project's ROI is considerably lower than the ROIs for project 4 or for the new project 7 that has just started. This may lead management to want to terminate your project and shift resources to project 4 or 7. Part of your job as project manager is to stay tuned to the project environment, so this becomes important to you.

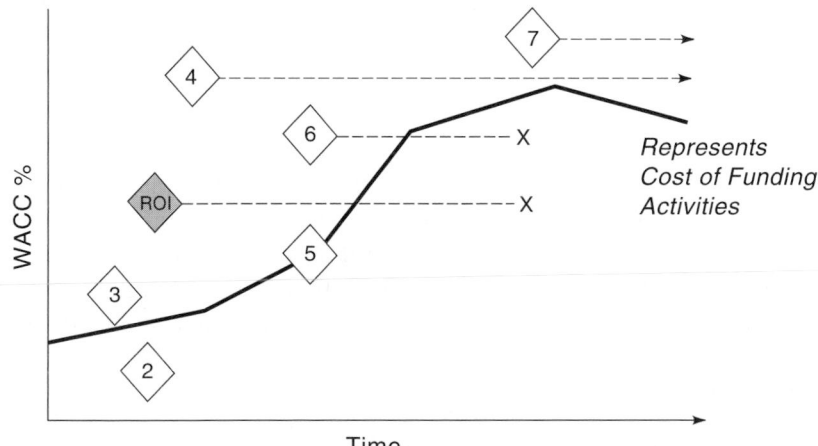

Represents Cost of Funding Activities

FIGURE 27–4
Comparing Diverse Projects Against WACC

Some other business reasons that a software development project might be terminated are:

- The customer no longer wants the product.
- The customer changed his mind and now wants a dramatically changed outcome.
- The new product will scavenge the company's present software product revenue.
- The resulting product is not likely to be a commercial success.

Technical Reasons

In a world traveling at Internet speed, technology can change very rapidly. This can lead to hardware platforms and software bases that are no longer supported or that are otherwise not viable for performing software development. If the project team cannot make adjustments quickly enough, the project may terminate prematurely. For example, a software product being developed as an application for the Palm or Windows CE operating system for small handheld computing devices may be completely superceded by the advent of a new technology based on cellular phone standards. This might cause termination of the development project but may spawn a completely new project with different goals using different technical experts.

The technology selected for a given project may turn out to be immature and not ready for prime time yet. Many projects incorrectly estimate the maturity of technology bases selected for development and get into trouble with schedules and functionality because they can't get the new technology to work properly for them. This often ties into termination for cost or schedule reasons because of the incorrect estimation. New technology is generally risky, but because risk and reward are usually related, the project's ROI may be very high and may justify continuation. But if too much time elapses while the technology is debugged and learned, the situation depicted in Figure 27–4 may occur.

It could also be that the technology for the project is just too old to be viable anymore. It is a popular notion that the difference between hardware and software is that hardware wears out but software doesn't. That's true if nothing ever changes the software. But as the world changes, so must most software code to accommodate the changes. This is called software maintenance. If patched too much, by too many different people, applications can become very complex and difficult to maintain. Complexity metrics, such as the McCabe cyclomatic complexity metric (see Chapter 21, "Software Metrics"), can help determine when code has become too complex to maintain. When this happens, using it as a basis for development can become quite risky. Sometimes the hardware or software base for a project becomes unsupported by the manufacturer during the project, thereby killing the viability of the project's product.

Some other reasons that a project might be terminated are:

- The resulting product will not offer a big enough advance over current technology or methods.
- The project cannot be done with the current state-of-the-art technology.

- The risk-reducing technical experiments did not pan out.
- New advances have made the project unnecessary or noncompetitive.
- Environmental changes have made the project obsolete.

Scope Reasons

One of the keys to software development project success is getting the requirements right (see Chapter 16, "Eliciting Requirements," and Chapter 17, "Developing the Software Requirements Specification"). Once documented in the software requirements specification (SRS), a good change-control system can monitor the changes that occur from increasing knowledge about the problem space and additional customer requests. However, it is entirely possible for the scope of the project to change so much, due to large or frequent requirements changes, that the project should be terminated and another new project should be begun. It is a judgment call when too much change is too much, but this kind of change would result in termination due to scope change. It is also possible that the need for the product has just disappeared or that the project results to date point to a better way to achieve the customer's needs.

Schedule Reasons

The most common reason for schedule-based termination is that the project just ran out of time. Many software development projects have a due date given to them as part of the requirements. This is just another constraint to be factored into the project planning. If the project misses the due date, it doesn't matter whether the project completes.

An example might be a project to produce a Y2K date-changing tool. If the project runs past its due date, then its product may become obsolete because the Year 2000 rollover due date of midnight on January 1 cannot slip. This is often related to missing a market window for a commercial software product. In the Internet world, market windows for software products have become extremely small.

Cost Reasons

Related to schedule slippage and changing ROIs is cost-based termination. Projects can be terminated for simply exceeding budgets or available funds. There becomes no money left to pay anyone working on the project. This leads a software development project manager to closely monitor costs, which, for software projects, are most directly related to labor effort. Using techniques such as earned value management, project managers can track costs relative to schedules and can avoid surprises. Any ROI calculations made at the beginning of the project should be revisited periodically to see if they have changed enough to impact the project.

When you are considering costs as a reason to terminate work on a project, be sure to consider only the relevant costs to the decision. Those would be the costs that you have yet to incur and that are still under your control to change. Sunk costs are those that are already committed to or that have been spent and that are out of your control. Therefore, a decision to terminate cannot change them. Termination decisions should be based on looking to the future, not looking to the past. This keeps you away from throwing good money after bad using the logic, "We've spent so much money already on this, I think we should keep going instead of stopping." This kind of thinking leads to an ever-increasing spiral of costs.

Quality Reasons

Termination has happened to many software projects because their product just didn't work well enough to satisfy the customer or was so buggy that it wasn't worth fixing. These are often associated with mismanaged requirements or development processes. If the failure rate (defects per test hour) in Figure 21–13 is increasing rather than decreasing, there would appear to be a significant quality problem that could lead to project termination. The same might be true for increasing phase containment effectiveness metrics (see Figure 21–18). Whatever quality metrics the project team is tracking, having them go in the "wrong" direction makes the project a candidate for termination, or at least serious management attention.

Politics

Ugly as it has to be, project terminations are sometimes the results of organizational politics. Often a project will be terminated when it should be continued or will be continued when it should be terminated, purely because doing so will enhance someone's career or satisfy a need for exerting power. This kind of situation cannot be quantified, but it usually can be recognized. Corporate management is often dripping with politics as more people try to rise to fewer available power positions. Being associated with "winners" or "losers" is one way to climb the organizational ladder. Recognizing these situations is the first step to dealing with them. Then using your negotiating skills to find a suitable win-win solution usually gets the right thing to happen. Sometimes, just "naming the game" is enough to flush out the politics and get everyone focused on the customer again. Putting it on the table for all to see makes it harder to execute the stealthy moves that characterize organizational politics.

Types of Termination

The most important part of termination is making the decision to terminate. This can be very hard and troublesome because killing a project usually impacts a lot of people and has serious career and economic consequences. However, the decision must be made, or the project may drag on interminably. Note the key part of the word *decide* is *-cide*, which means "to kill" (as in herbicide, pesticide, homicide, etc.). It is important to kill the lingering question and make a choice (to *decide*).

Humans have a need for closure. We feel incomplete when something is left open and the end point is uncertain. This is basically what funeral services are for, to provide closure for those remaining after the deceased has already moved on. It is your responsibility to bring closure to the project and let everyone move on. Hopefully, though, it won't be your funeral. Another important reason to explicitly close a project is to avoid Parkinson's and Murphy's laws. The longer a project remains open and active, the more changes and problems can occur. Any activities left open are works in process (WIPs) and are subject to the uncertainties of life. Closing the project allows everyone to clear their desktops of WIPs and move on to something else.

Once the decision to terminate has been made, there are a number of ways to look at termination of the software project. We can see them as positive or negative, successful or unsuccessful, normal or premature, or we can categorize them by the way they end.

We like to have projects that end normally, when all the objectives have been met and the products have been delivered to the customer. They might be ended prematurely, though, for reasons discussed earlier. Research by the Standish Group suggests that normal successful termination occurs only in about one out of three information technology projects.[1] Success means that the project achieved all its original objectives on time and within budget (the triple constraint). But there are also degrees of success. A project may have achieved enough of its goals to be useful to the customer. Indeed, many contracts are worded so that if the work is "substantially complete" or the customer has "put the product into use," the developer should be paid.

Pritchard divides terminations into positive and negative types.[2] The positive ones occur when the project has a positive outcome and there is an upbeat relationship with the customer. The negatives ones close, but there are less-than-positive feelings between the customer and the project team. Because project management has a lot to do with managing relationships and expectations, a negative outcome indicates a lack of good project management practice.

Meredith and Mantel classify project terminations into four categories: extinction, addition, integration, and starvation.[3] Extinction means that the project really comes to a clear end. It doesn't drag on (this is good thing). Extinctions occur when the project is terminated because it is successful, unsuccessful, superceded, or murdered. As soon as the decision to terminate is made, work on the *substance* of the project ceases. Administrative work such as cost reporting, vendor payments, equipment disposition, or post-performance reports may continue for a while, but software development ceases. Extinctions should be handled by an explicit written order, to allow everyone concerned to execute closure activities. Successful projects meet all their objectives, and unsuccessful projects don't. Superceded projects are those that get replaced by (usually) larger, more comprehensive projects. Murdered projects are done in by politics of some kind.

Termination by addition means that the project was successful and was merged into operations by making the project team the operations department for the new software product.

This is common for internal projects in large information technology departments that have introduced a new technology to the organization.

Termination by integration is similar to termination by addition and means that the project ends successfully and that its assets and people are among the existing elements of the parent organization. This is the most common form of extinction for successful projects. When the project concludes, the project manager is responsible for seeing that the people, equipment, processes, and products are integrated into the parent organization's departments.

Termination by starvation means that the resources for work on the project have been slowly decreased to the point where nothing substantive can happen anymore. Work has essentially stopped, but there are nothing but "no progress" reports from the project. Some internal projects get into this position as a result of the startup of higher priority projects in the organization that drain all the technical resources away. The advice here is to kill them mercifully, but kill them. Declare them done or suspended, and release their obligations. This will allow those concerned to bring closure to it and concentrate on more productive activities.

What to Do upon Project Termination

When a project terminates, there are a number of things to take care of—and there are some special considerations, depending on what type of organization the project was operating within. The first thing to take care of is the official announcement, in writing. This starts the closure process. Even a simple email announcement such as "The Widget Project is closed" allows people to begin tidying things up for closure. If appropriate, a closure event may be planned to mark the passage. The larger the project is, the larger and more formal the announcement and event should be.

One of the big things to consider is how people will react to the closure of a project. In Chapter 13, "Choosing an Organizational Form," we discussed a number of organizational forms: functional, matrixed, and projectized. Project termination in a largely functional organization is not too worrisome because everyone knows that they will stay in the functional organization. When the Widget Project is over, the software engineers will remain in the engineering department and will just move on to the next assignment. However, in the matrixed and projectized environments, there is less security because the organization's *raison d'etre* was the project. When the project is over, the people may need to find other jobs. The project manager should recognize this and take actions toward the end of the project to see that the team is taken care of properly. The type of organization may also influence the disposition of any equipment that the project bought or was using. It may need to be integrated into the parent organization or sold or scrapped.

The project manager must also consider costs. When a project ends, the development work ceases, but the administrative work continues. You should consider the timing of costs.

As a software project manager, you are concerned about when you *commit* to incur a cost for the project. When it is actually invoiced and paid is usually the concern of someone in accounts payable or finance, but you may need to be involved administratively. For example, with approval, you committed to the cost of an object-oriented development environment tool for your team early in the project, in January. But the invoice did not arrive until the product was installed and running on March 15, and the invoice was not fully paid until May 1 because the terms were net 45. This means that for months (or even quarters!) after a project closes, there may be administrative issues to handle regarding the "closed" project. This situation is illustrated by the cumulative cost baseline curves in Figure 27–5. The solid line represents the costs commitments by the project manager. The large dashed line represents when the invoice arrives, and the small dashed line represents when the invoice gets paid. This same cost shifting may occur for other items such as refunds, travel expense reconciliation, or payments to you for work performed.

Depending on the project, there may be special items needing disposition at the end of the project. Such items should be identified in the software project management plan (SPMP), describing what their disposition should be. For example, a project to develop operating software for an automated teller machine (ATM) may have required a loaner device from the customer (an ATM manufacturer) for development and testing. The equipment is to be returned at the conclusion of the project. There may also be special considerations for the removal of information from disks of borrowed computers before they are returned.

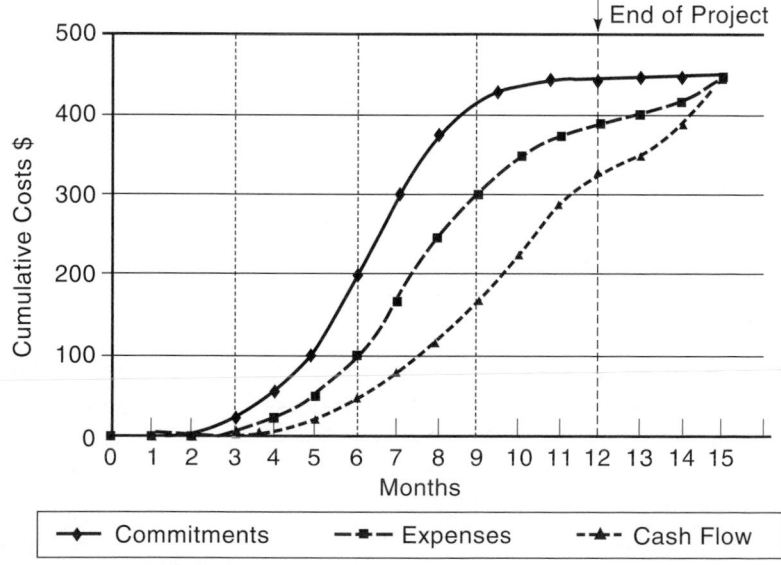

FIGURE 27–5
Shifted Timing of Project Costs

Termination Process

Once the termination decision has been made, the process begins. The steps for project closure will vary with project and organization, but there are generally a few that will always be done:

1. Make the decision to terminate.
2. Communicate the decision to all concerned.
3. Identify final team activities that need to be completed.
4. Get sponsor and customer approvals.
5. Perform a post-performance analysis (PPA). (See Chapter 28, "Post-Performance Analysis.")
6. Schedule and hold a closure event (usually a celebration).
7. Release and reassign staff as needed.
8. Publish the final report, including lessons learned and recommendations for process improvements.
9. Disposition equipment, software, documentation, and any other materials.
10. Perform financial administrative closure.

The message here is to plan for the closure and shutdown of a project rather than to just let it happen. A checklist can be very useful for closure activities in an organization. There may be different checklists according to the size or nature of the project, just as there are different customized life cycles for different types of software development. An example checklist for a typical software development project is shown in Table 27–1.

Summary

In this chapter, we have talked about the often-overlooked subject of project termination. We looked at some common reasons for terminating a project in the framework of the triple constraints of scope, schedule, and cost, with special considerations for quality, technology, and business. We explored some taxonomy for classifying terminations. They could be successful or unsuccessful, positive or negative, normal or prematurely ended, or they could just be ended by extinction, addition, integration, and starvation.

We discussed the importance of making the decision to terminate, to avoid dragging out projects interminably. Finally, we looked at the termination process and the approach of using a checklist to guide closure activities.

TABLE 27–1
Example Project Closure Checklist

Description	Needed? Y / N	Due Date	Responsible	Done
Communicate decision				☐
Identify remaining work				☐
Deliver released software				☐
Get customer approvals				☐
Publish release documentation				☐
Perform personnel evaluations				☐
Perform post-performance analysis				☐
Hold closure event				☐
Release or reassign team				☐
Close outstanding work orders				☐
Review final configuration management audit				☐
Return or release vendor or customer materials				☐
Return all borrowed equipment				☐
Publish final report				☐

Problems for Review _____

1. Prepare a closure checklist for the case study project.
2. What is the relationship of project closure to continuous process improvement? How does it relate to the SEI CMM v1.1? ISO 9000? Malcolm Baldrige Award for Performance Excellence?
3. On termination of a project, what happens to the lessons learned? How does the next project leader find them to benefit from your project's experiences?

Visit the Case Study _____

Requirements and design phases have proceeded smoothly. You have done a second prototype that successfully included yet another railway line. The team is ready to begin the implementation phase.

Mr. Lu is concerned that the delivery will not go smoothly. In fact, he is concerned that delivery is impossible because of the differences among the sophistication in each railway station. Although the CRM was responsible for training and rollout, Mr. Lu does not have the staff to do either training or on-site installation. He has heard from many of his colleagues in this and other ministries that the "out-of-the-box" Linux experience is suboptimal for managers with no formal education past high school.

Mr. Lu has come to you to request a change in the delivery. He wants the ARRS to be delivered totally over the Web. He wants to ship Web-enabled computers to each railway station and let them automatically come up on the CRM network. You have grown to like working with the CRM and want to help them turn out with a product that will be useful and make the Peoples' Railway System the most efficient on the Asian continent. Within three days, you will deliver a preliminary proposal and project plan to Mr. Lu.

Citations _____

[1]*standishgroup.com/visitor/chaos.htm*. Standish Group, *Chaos Report*.

[2]Pritchard, Carl (1998). "Project Termination: The Good, the Bad, the Ugly." *Field Guide to Project Management*. John Wiley & Sons.

[3]Meredith, Jack R., and Samuel J. Mantel, Jr. (1995). *Project Management, A Managerial Approach*, 3rd ed. New York, NY: John Wiley & Sons.

Suggested Readings _____

Adams, John (1997). *Principles of Project Management*. Project Management Institute.

Cleland, David I. (1999). *Project Management, Strategic Design and Implementation*, 3rd ed. McGraw-Hill.

Kerzner, Harold (1998). *Project Management, A Systems Approach to Planning, Scheduling, and Controlling*, 6th ed. John Wiley & Sons.

Lewis, James P. (1995). *Project Planning, Scheduling, and Control*, revised edition. Chicago, IL: Irwin Professional Publishing.

Meredith, Jack R., and Samuel J. Mantel, Jr. (1995). *Project Management, A Managerial Approach*, 3rd ed. New York, NY: John Wiley & Sons.

Project Management Institute (2000). *A Guide to the Project Management Body of Knowledge*.

Web Pages for Further Information _____

dijest.editthispage.com/stories/storyReader$91. Phil Wolff's collection of forms and templates.

www.pmforum.org/library/glossary/PMG_P12.htm. PM Forum's glossary of project management terms.

Post-Performance
Analysis

"How are we doing?" "Are we doing the best that we can do?" "How should we change what we are doing to do it better?" At key points in the execution of a project plan, it is crucial to look back and evaluate how you got where you are. Techniques such as buffer management and earned value management can tell you about the real progress you are making on the product development front, but a periodic formal assessment of your operating processes, called a post-performance analysis (PPA), can tell you what corrections to implement for the next stage in your project plan. It also provides a breather of sorts for your team and allows closure for the stage just completed. Of course, doing this at the end of the project allows your team to reflect on the entire product development process, accumulate lessons learned, and leave a legacy of organizational learning for the next project team to benefit from. This is an investment in continuous improvement.

The SEI CMM v1.1 calls for such investment in the quantitative process improvement key process area at the managed level (Level 4). The focus there is on identifying special causes of variation within a measurably stable process and correcting the circumstances that caused them.

Where We Are in the Product Development Life Cycle

Where are we in the basic software life cycle model that serves as our map? As shown in Figure 28–1, we are either in the middle of execution of the project or at the end. PPAs typically occur from system exploration right up through installation and maintenance. In Figure 28–2, PPAs fit in the *do it* and *did it* steps. There may be many PPAs performed during a software development project because most of the product development framework (concept exploration through implementation) is done in the *do it* step, providing many opportunities for studying the processes being followed.

Chapter 28 Relation to the 34 Competencies

The PPA uses the product development techniques of assessing processes and evaluating different approaches for improvements, which requires an awareness of process standards. The standards may be tailored to suit the needs of the project, and special tools and methods may be needed to fulfill project needs. Of course, it is important to understand the details of the software development life cycle being used. The project management skills needed are primarily those for monitoring development activities and for tracking the compliance of the team to the processes prescribed in the project plan. The most important people skill needed is the ability to manage change because the ultimate purpose of the PPA is to find and implement corrections to the development and management processes being used.

Product Development Techniques

1. **Assessing processes**—Defining criteria for reviews
2. **Awareness of process standards**—Understanding process standards
4. **Evaluating alternative processes**—Evaluating various approaches
8. **Selecting methods and tools**—Defining selection processes
9. **Tailoring processes**—Modifying standard processes to suit a project
11. **Understanding Development Activities**—Learning the software development cycle

Project Management Skills

17. **Monitoring development**—Monitoring the production of software
21. **Tracking process**—Monitoring compliance of project team

People Management Skills

28. **Managing change**—Being an effective change agent

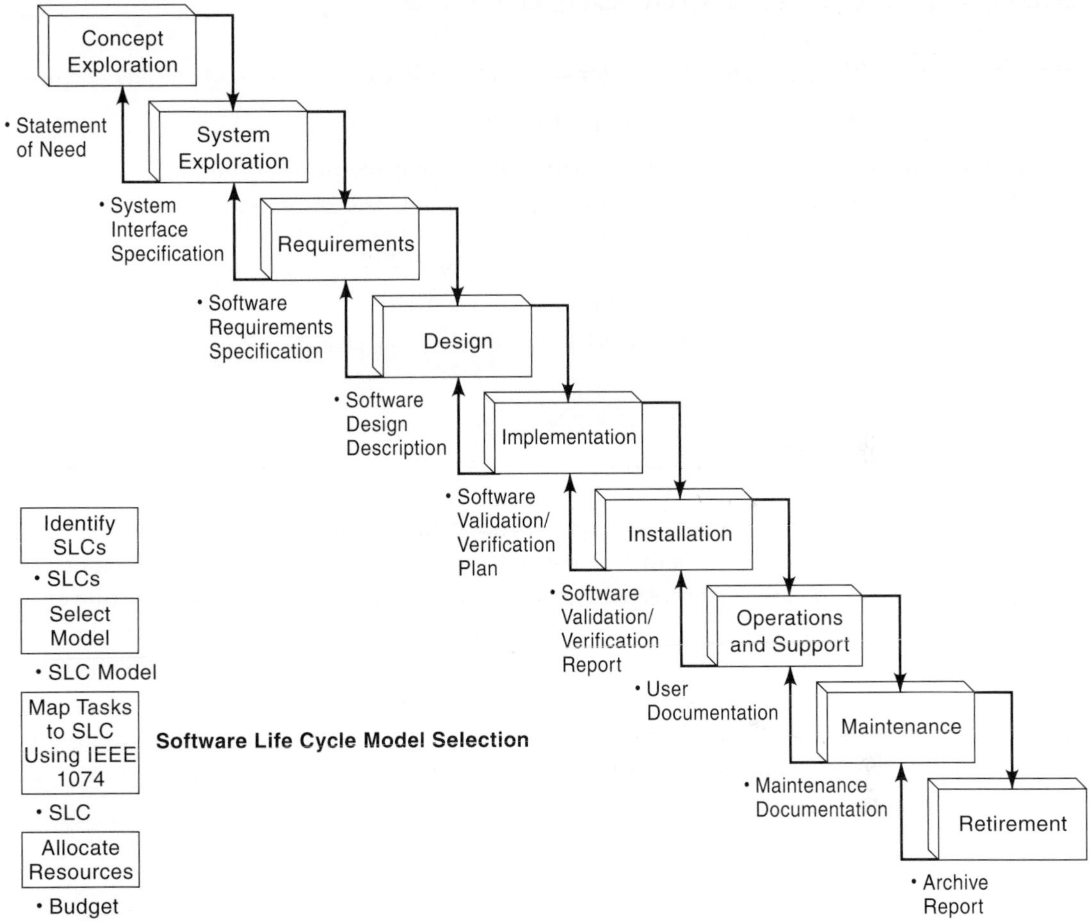

Concept
Exploration

- Statement
  of Need

System
Exploration

- System
  Interface
  Specification

Requirements

- Software
  Requirements
  Specification

Design

- Software
  Design
  Description

Implementation

- Software
  Validation/
  Verification
  Plan

Installation

- Software
  Validation/
  Verification
  Report

Operations
and Support

- User
  Documentation

Maintenance

- Maintenance
  Documentation

Retirement

- Archive
  Report

| Identify SLCs |
| • SLCs |

| Select Model |
| • SLC Model |

| Map Tasks to SLC Using IEEE 1074 |
| • SLC |

| Allocate Resources |
| • Budget |

Software Life Cycle Model Selection

FIGURE 28–1
Product Process Framework

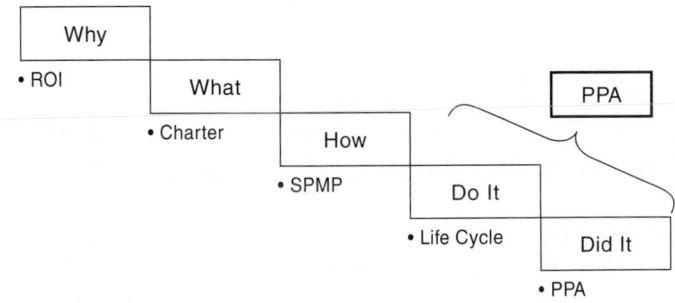

Why

- ROI

What

- Charter

How

- SPMP

Do It

- Life Cycle

Did It

- PPA

PPA

FIGURE 28–2
Project Process Framework

Learning Objectives for Chapter 28 _____

Upon completion of this chapter, the reader should be able to:

- Cite several common names for a post-performance analysis;
- Compose a list of questions for a post-performance analysis questionnaire;
- List the steps in the post-performance analysis process;
- Conduct a post-performance analysis data-gathering meeting;
- Prepare a post-performance analysis report;
- Explain how to use the outputs of a post-performance analysis.

What's in a Name? _____

We call the process of implementing continuous process improvement as described in Chapter 26, "Continuous Process Improvement," a post-performance analysis (PPA). When done only at the very end of the project when most of the important development activities are completed, you may hear it called the post-phase analysis, post-project analysis, or sometimes the post-mortem. *Postmortem* has a morbid ring to it, implying that the project died (which it may have). In the predominately low CMM maturity organizations in the world, this is probably appropriate. However, for higher maturity organizations, post-performance analysis is preferred. This term is appropriate for any place in the product development cycle where predefined processes are performed.

Purpose of a PPA

What's the purpose of a PPA? As described in Chapter 26, we want to use the PPA process to collect measures for our process metrics and to define strategies that would tune the processes for better performance. The project team should be employing the six-step process improvement model described in Figure 26–9. Because projects are, by definition, unique, there will always be something new involved and, therefore, new data and lessons learned. These should be captured while the memories are still fresh in the team members' minds. And they should be applied to product development processes frequently, after major phases and milestones are completed, while they can still have an impact on the current product being developed. The "big bang" approach of waiting until the very end of the project, when the team is burned out from the push to meet deadlines, has little impact to organizational learning. By then, most of the reasons for decisions made along the way have been forgotten, and most of the decision makers have moved on to something else. This is especially true for large, long software development projects. Just as it is important for progress measurement to define many smaller milestones along the product development life cycle path (see Chapter 8, "Creating the Work Breakdown Structure"), it is important also to continue process improvement to use some of those milestones as points to review the process just followed. When planning the project, it may be useful to group several milestones together as a phase marker to provide convenient points to perform PPAs and to celebrate progress. Psychologically, this is good for the team. They begin to associate PPAs with positive events such as celebrations, not with negative events such as affixing blame.

PPA Focus

PPAs should be focused on the process, not the people. By the time a PPA is performed, most of the people on the team know what has happened (the email grapevine is very fast), and there is no need for finger pointing. It is not a witch hunt. PPA meetings should be structured data-gathering sessions, not a courtroom. It is often a challenge for a software development project manager to control this environment. This is where skill as a negotiator and a change agent is very useful. It helps to start preparing the team for PPAs at the beginning of the project. Even as early as the project kickoff, inform the members of the project processes that you want to follow, and give them some guidance on what will be collected for measurement. Some of it will seem foreign to them at first, but it will not be as much a shock as being asked to collect a bunch of data at the end of the project. This results in team reaction to the PPA process as time wasted because the members see no direct benefit to what they are doing now. It is seen as having some benefit only for the current project manager (completing a management checklist item) or for the manager of the next project, which they may not be around for.

Another advantage to doing several smaller PPAs during the course of a software development project rather than one "big bang" PPA at the end of the project is that the amount of time required for each is far smaller. The "big bang" PPA requires sifting through mountains of data accumulated over a long period of time and seems to benefit only others.

The PPA at the end of the project is still important, though, because it is the place where lessons learned can be captured and passed on to posterity for organizational memory and improvement. This implies that the organization has a place to keep organizational memory. Many low-maturity organizations do not. SEI CMM–based assessments, ISO 9000 audits, and Malcolm Baldrige Award for Performance Excellence examinations will all be looking for documented evidence of a focus on continuous improvements. Each development organization should have a process library defined, where templates of tailorable processes can be found, logs of improvements are kept, and lessons learned can be researched. Part of the start-up process for any new development project should be to research this library and should apply any appropriate lessons to the next project. This is continuous improvement in action.

What Does a PPA Produce?

The primary output of a PPA is the PPA report. These reports could have any number of formats and are quite organization-specific. The key things that they must have are a summary of data for process metrics and process change recommendations that are driven from lessons learned on the project. They need not be lengthy tomes that no one wants to read. They are more useful as crisp summaries of the best of what comes out of the PPA meetings.

How to Conduct a PPA

The first step in conducting a PPA is to prepare. This begins at the start of the project, when planning is taking place. Let's look at the details of the PPA process and consider some interesting questions that you may want to ask the team in the data-gathering portion.

Post-Performance Analysis Process

This is an outline for the PPA process, whether it is done at the end of the project or for an interim milestone. Be sure to make the team members aware of this process at the very beginning of the project so that they will know what to be collecting during the course of product development.

1. Send a memo to the team calling a PPA meeting. Include instructions to assemble all available data for collection and archiving. This includes:

   - dimensional data for all work products (how many, how big, what frequency, etc.);

   - lessons learned (check risk logs, issue logs, and internal memos);

   - change requests (to anything, such as specifications, the project plan, etc.);

   - time and effort data (hours or dollars for each WBS item, compared to estimates); and

   - anything else you deem useful to characterize the project.

2. The benefit of this data-collection step, done individually by team members, is that it allows the quieter, more analytical people to develop their responses to the questions without being interrupted by the more outgoing, vocal types who might otherwise dominate in the face-to-face meeting. Also, it allows everyone the time to create more thoughtful responses.

3. Assemble the team for a PPA meeting, keeping the meeting short and focused on data collection and learning from the past. It is wise to make a short speech to set the stage and avoid a finger-pointing session. By this time in a project, most everyone knows what has happened and why. The purpose of the meeting is not to affix blame, but to learn ways to improve the process next time. The other purpose is to clean up all the

loose ends from the project and archive all data and materials properly. It is *not* a project review meeting.

4. Get everyone to supply information or materials from their knowledge or experiences on the project.

5. Categorize the data and material as appropriate. It is useful to separate the information into process data and product data. The process data can be used to tune the project processes by going onto the project initiation checklist for the next project, and the product data can be used to improve the product, perhaps going on the backlog list for enhancements to the product (potentially a follow-up project).

6. Archive or dispose of all the data and material, as appropriate. This is just good housekeeping.

7. Publish a PPA report summarizing the findings in a short memo. Make it available for reference by future PMs doing similar work by publishing. This can be invaluable for future project estimating. For interim PPAs, publish only locally, to the team. For the end of project PPA, publish the findings in the organization's process library.

Figures 28–3 and 28–4 show an example of data-gathering questionnaires for a PPA meeting. Figure 28–3 shows the questionnaire for a team leader, and Figure 28–4 shows the questionnaire for a team member. It is possible for some people to perform multiple roles. This example should be modified to fit your development environment and perhaps should be Web-automated for ease of data collection.

At the PPA meeting, stay focused on the process data-gathering function of the meeting. Keep it structured, lest it deteriorate into a finger-pointing contest. *Do not* make it a basis for gathering personnel review information. If the team gets any whiff of this purpose, then the value of it as an organizational improvement tool vanishes. Mostly, you want to pile all the data that the team has gathered on the table and sort through it for useful information. Aggregate the data into metrics that help define your team's process performance. Figure 28–5 shows an example data-gathering template. This is the summary information that you want to collect to feed your process metrics (defined at the beginning of the project during life cycle selection). Some of this information may be available in an automated way from some of the development support systems in your organization. Use those if you can, instead of asking the team members for it. Try to minimize the effort that they must expend to collect data. Of course, subjective items such as identifying key things done right must be supplied by the team members. To minimize personality issues, use the nominal group technique described in Chapter 14, "Considering Dependencies" (see Box 14–2).

Post-Performance Analysis Questionnaire for Development Team Leaders

As you review the following annotated template, note that portions of the document in nonbold italics are meant to be deleted. They are explanatory information.

In this first section, give the boilerplate information about the project, perhaps leaving open the project description for them to identify what element of the project they worked on.

Project Information

    Name of project: _____
    Contract number: _____
    Customer name: _____
    Start date: _____
    Finish date: _____

Type of project (select one of the following: data processing, systems software, applications software, test software, simulation, prototype):

    Short project description:

    Internal contact name: _____
    Phone: _____
    Customer contact:_____
    Phone:_____
    Project status: _____

Gather information about the respondent to be able to statistically identify the classes of people with summary information later. Keep this information on a sheet separate from the responses to the questions that follow so that you can remove it for data analysis, if needed. Note that we ask the role question twice so that you can correlate responses to classes of roles.

Background Information of Analysis Respondent

    Name: _____
    Phone: _____

    Team or Organization: _____
    Address: _____
    Email: _____

Add or remove roles here as appropriate to your environment.

Role(s) I played in this project (check all that apply):

_____ Process engineer
_____ Quality assurance
_____ Configuration management
_____ User documentation development
_____ Requirements analysis
_____ Designer

FIGURE 28–3
Example Post-Performance Analysis Data-Gathering Questionnaire for a Team Leader

(Continues)

_____ Implementation/test
_____ Integration
_____ System test
_____ Build
_____ Team leader
_____ Project manager
_____ Other (specify): _____

Questionnaire for Project Manager and Team Leads

Add or remove items here as appropriate to your environment.

1. Identify the organizations involved during the development project.

_____ System engineering
_____ Hardware engineering
_____ Software engineering
_____ IT/MIS
_____ Software quality assurance
_____ Software configuration management
_____ Software test
_____ Independent verification and validation
_____ Other (identify): _____

Add or remove items here as appropriate to your environment.

2. Mark the standards used for the development project.

_____ IEEE requirements specification
_____ IEEE design specification
_____ IEEE test documentation specification
_____ Organization programming standards and style guidelines
_____ Other (identify): _____

Add or remove items here as appropriate to your environment.

3. Identify the development paradigm used for the project.

_____ Spiral development
_____ Classic waterfall development
_____ Incremental development from a prototype
_____ Prototyping
_____ Other (identify): _____

Add or remove items here as appropriate to your environment.

4. Identify the method used for the project.

_____ Information engineering
_____ Structured analysis and structured design
_____ Booch object-oriented
_____ Coad/Yourdon object-oriented
_____ Rumbaugh object-oriented
_____ Schlaer/Mellor object-oriented
_____ Other (identify): _____

FIGURE 28–3 (Continued)
Example Post-Performance Analysis Data-Gathering Questionnaire for a Team Leader

(Continues)

Add or remove items here as appropriate to your environment.

5. Mark the types of management reviews that were held.

_____ Monthly project reviews
_____ Weekly team status meetings
_____ Team status meetings based on need
_____ Regular project reviews, not monthly; specify period: _____
_____ Milestone reviews; specify milestones at which they occurred: _____

Add or remove items here as appropriate to your environment.

6. Mark the types of technical reviews that were held.

_____ Customer input review (request for proposal, statement of work, other)
_____ Software requirements review
_____ Requirements inspections
_____ Preliminary design review
_____ Critical design review
_____ Phased detailed design reviews
_____ Design walkthroughs
_____ Design inspections
_____ Code readings
_____ Code walkthroughs
_____ Code inspections
_____ System test readiness review
_____ Test case reviews
_____ Test case inspections
_____ Other (identify): _____

Add or remove items here as appropriate to your environment, matching to the cover page changes.

7. Other roles I played in this project (check all that apply):

_____ Project manager
_____ Team leader
_____ Process engineer
_____ Quality assurance
_____ Configuration management
_____ User documentation development
_____ Requirements analysis
_____ Designer
_____ Implementation/test
_____ Integration
_____ System test
_____ Build master
_____ Other (specify): _____

Be sure there is enough space for people to answer completely.

8. For this project, identify the key things that were done right, in your opinion.

FIGURE 28–3 (Continued)
Example Post-Performance Analysis Data-Gathering Questionnaire for a Team Leader

(Continues)

9. For this project, identify the key things that were done wrong, in your opinion.

10. What unusual environmental influences (which might have either adversely or favorably affected the project) should be kept in mind when examining the history of this project?

11. For this project, how would you do things differently, if you could start over again?

12. Describe one thing you could have done personally to improve the quality of the product produced by this project.

FIGURE 28–3 (Continued)
Example Post-Performance Analysis Data-Gathering Questionnaire for a Team Leader

Post-Performance Analysis Questionnaire for Development Team Members

As you review the following annotated template, note that portions of the document in nonbold italics are meant to be deleted. They are explanatory information.

In this first section, give the boilerplate information about the project, perhaps leaving open the project description for them to identify what element of the project they worked on.

Project Information

      Name of project: _____
      Contract number: _____
      Customer name: _____
      Start date: _____
      Finish date: _____

Type of project (select one of the following: data processing, systems software, applications software, test software, simulation, prototype):

      Short project description:

      Internal contact name: _____
      Phone: _____
      Customer contact: _____
      Phone: _____
      Project status: _____

Gather information about the respondent to be able to statistically identify the classes of people with summary information later. Keep this information on a sheet separate from the responses to the questions that follow so that you can remove it for data analysis, if needed. Note that we ask the role question twice so that you can correlate responses to classes of roles.

Background Information of Analysis Respondent

      Name: _____
      Phone: _____

      Team or Organization: _____
      Address: _____
      Email: _____

Add or remove roles here as appropriate to your environment.

Role(s) I played in this project (check all that apply):

_____   Project manager
_____   Team leader
_____   Process engineer
_____   Quality assurance
_____   Configuration management
_____   User documentation development
_____   Requirements analysis
_____   Designer

FIGURE 28–4

Example Post-Performance Analysis Data-Gathering Questionnaire for a Team Member

(Continues)

_____ Implementation/test
_____ Integration
_____ System test
_____ Build master
_____ Other (specify): _____

Rate the following characteristics for the environment for the project being reviewed. Use a scale of 1 to 5, where 1 is the lowest rating and 5 is the highest. If the item does not apply, mark an X.

Add or remove items here as appropriate to your environment.

_____ 1. Clarity of customer requirements
_____ 2. Support software availability
_____ 3. Support hardware availability
_____ 4. Team analysis capability
_____ 5. Team design capability
_____ 6. Team implementation capability
_____ 7. Team test capability
_____ 8. Team analysis capability
_____ 9. Team design capacity
_____ 10. Team implementation capacity
_____ 11. Team test capacity
_____ 12. Team experience with project domain area
_____ 13. Team experience with project process
_____ 14. Team experience with project methods
_____ 15. Team experience with the language or implementation medium
_____ 16. Timely availability of externally furnished software components
_____ 17. Quality of externally furnished software components
_____ 18. Degree of reuse (in all phases)
_____ 19. Use of software tools
_____ 20. Use of appropriate methods
_____ 21. Use of risk analysis
_____ 22. Stability of organizational environment
_____ 23. Appropriateness of technology used to build product
_____ 24. Configuration management
_____ 25. Quality assurance

For the following, use a rating of 1 to 5, where 1 indicates a low level of the factor and 5 a high level.

_____ 26. Product complexity
_____ 27. Requirements volatility
_____ 28. Reliability requirements
_____ 29. Efficiency requirements
_____ 30. Maintainability requirements
_____ 31. Portability requirements
_____ 32. Performance requirements
_____ 33. Degree of security requirements
_____ 34. International requirements
_____ 35. Complexity of project organization
_____ 36. Schedule aggressiveness
_____ 37. Number and types of technical reviews
_____ 38. Number and types of management reviews
_____ 39. Amount of integration and test
_____ 40. Customer acceptance testing

FIGURE 28–4 (Continued)
Example Post-Performance Analysis Data-Gathering Questionnaire for a Team Member

(Continues)

41. Role(s) I played in this project (check all that apply):

—— Process engineer
—— Quality assurance
—— Configuration management
—— User documentation analysis
—— Requirements analysis
—— Design
—— Implementation/test
—— Integration
—— System test
—— Build
—— Team leader
—— Project manager
—— Other (specify): _____

Be sure there is enough space for people to answer completely.

42. For this project, identify the key things that were done right, in your opinion.

43. For this project, identify the key things that were done wrong, in your opinion.

44. What unusual environmental influences (which might have either adversely or favorably affected the project) should be kept in mind when examining the history of this project?

45. For this project, how would you do things differently, if you could start over again?

46. Describe one thing you could have done personally to improve the quality of the product produced by this project.

FIGURE 28–4 (Continued)
Example Post-Performance Analysis Data-Gathering Questionnaire for a Team Member

Post-Performance Analysis Data-Gathering Template

Project Name:	Survey Date:
Start Date:	
Finish Date:	

Requirements Specified

WBS Element Name or ID	Count	Units	% Reuse	# Staff-days
Totals				

Design Elements Completed

WBS Element Name or ID	Count	Units	% Reuse	# Staff-days
Totals				

Implementation Units Completed (include code and unit tests as separate line items)

WBS Element Name or ID	Count	Units	% Reuse	# Staff-days
Totals				

Other Project Activities (please identify)

WBS Element Name or ID	Count	Units	% Reuse	# Staff-days
Totals				

Quality Data

Item	Reqmts	Design	Implementation	Integration
Error Count by Phase				
Element Count in Phase				
Error Density by Phase				
Time in Phase (hours)				
Productivity by Phase (units/day)				

FIGURE 28–5
Example Post-Performance Analysis Data-Gathering Template

Additional Questions to Ask

You are encouraged to create your own questionnaire questions, for best effect in your organization. Choose questions that match the level of maturity of your organization. Increase the level of detail according to the CMM maturity of your organization. Michael Greer, the New Grange Center for Project Management, and others have compiled lists of questions to stimulate your thinking.[1, 2] Some selected ideas that might be useful for software development projects are listed here:

- Did you learn anything from this project? If you did learn anything from this project, what was it?
- Are you proud of our finished deliverables (project work products)? If yes, what's so good about them? If no, what's wrong with them?
- How could we have improved our work process for creating deliverables?
- How did the team perform as a whole? What did we do well?
- What was the most gratifying or professionally satisfying part of the project?
- Describe any early warning signs of problems that occurred later in the project? How should we have reacted to these signs? How can we be sure to notice these early warning signs next time?
- Do you think the project was managed well?
- What would you change in the management of the project?
- Were you informed about what was expected from you on the project?
- Were the deliverables specifications, milestones, and specific schedule elements/dates clearly communicated? If not, how could we improve this?
- Were roles of the team members clearly defined?
- Do you think the communication process among all involved was efficient?
- Were the issues, action, and change logs useful? If not, how could they be made better?
- Were you properly informed on the project progress?
- Were stakeholders properly informed on the project progress?
- Do you think the communication process among all involved was efficient?
- Were the meetings useful and efficient? How could the meetings be more effective? How could agendas/minutes be improved?
- Could we have completed this project without one or more of our vendors/contractors? If so, how?
- Were there any difficulties setting up vendor paperwork (purchase orders, contracts, etc.) or getting the vendor started? How could these have been avoided?
- Did our requirements analysis identify all the deliverables or work products that we eventually had to build? If not, what did we miss and how can we be sure that our future analyses don't miss such items?

- Did our requirements analysis identify unnecessary deliverables or work products? If so, how can we be sure that our future analyses don't make this mistake?
- How can we improve our requirements process?
- Which of our methods or processes worked particularly well?
- Which of our methods or processes were difficult or frustrating to use?
- How accurate were our original estimates of the size and effort of our project? What did we over- or underestimate? (Consider deliverables, work effort, materials required, etc.)
- How could we have improved our estimate of size and effort so that it was more accurate?
- Did all the important project players have creative input into the creation of the design specifications? If not, whom were we missing and how can we assure their involvement next time?
- Did those who reviewed the design specifications provide timely and meaningful input? If not, how could we have improved their involvement and the quality of their contributions?
- Were the members of our test audience truly representative of our target audience? If not, how could we ensure better representation in the future?
- Did the test facilities, equipment, materials, and support people help to make the test an accurate representation of how the deliverables will be used in the "real world"? If not, how could we have improved on these items?
- Did we get timely, high-quality feedback about how we might improve our deliverables? If not, how could we get better feedback in the future?
- Was our implementation strategy accurate and effective? How could we improve this strategy?
- Did our hand-off of deliverables to the user/customer/sponsor represent a smooth and easy transition? If not, how could we have improved this process?
- Did we do the best that we could do?
- How should we change what we are doing to do it better?
- What unusual environmental influences (which might have either adversely or favorably affected the project) should be kept in mind when examining the history of this project?
- Describe one thing you could have done personally to improve the quality of the product produced by this project.

Summary

In this chapter, we have described the why, what, when, and how for performing post-performance analyses for software development projects. They are called variously by some organizations (varying by maturity) post-phase analysis, post-project analysis, or sometimes postmortem. We've seen how they can influence the organizational learning needed by some CMM KPAs, and how they might be useful for ISO 9000 and Malcolm Baldrige Award for Performance Excellence assessments. PPAs should be performed throughout the project life cycle at appropriate points (not too many, but not too few, either). More but smaller sprinkled throughout is preferred to the big bang approach at the end for performing PPAs.

We explored some useful questions to ask in collecting post-performance analysis questionnaires. These should be tailored to the individual organization as appropriate for the type of project and the maturity level of the performing organization.

We also described the process for conducting a post-performance analysis for a software development project. How the meeting is run is extremely important to prevent the perception that the information will be used in personnel reviews.

Problems for Review _____

1. Should a post-performance analysis be performed after completion of every work package? Why or why not?
2. Lessons learned from previous projects are significant because they:
   a. are needed to meet requirements of organizational policies and procedures.
   b. show why certain people were selected as the project manager and team members over others.
   c. show why certain projects were selected by the organization over others.
   d. show the causes of variances and the reasons certain corrective actions were taken.

Visit the Case Study _____

Your proposal for the automatic railway reservation terminal has been accepted by the CRM. Unfortunately, it did not go through Mr. Lee, the China corporate sales executive. Even though it means more budget for your project, it might not be in the interest of the entire corporation for you to make this enhancement for total Web delivery. You must now take the proposal and develop a complete project plan, addressing all contingencies and interfaces to any other corporate products. This has to be presented in two days at the Asia Pac strategy meeting in Kuala Lumpur.

Citations

[1]*www.michaelgreer.com/postmortem.htm*. Greer, Michael, Project "Post Mortem" Review Questions.

[2]*www.newgrange.org/*. New Grange Center for Project Management.

Suggested Readings

www.4pm.com/articles/pmtalk8-2-00.pdf. PMTalk Newsletter, Post-Project Reviews: Lessons Never Learned.

Web Pages for Further Information

allpm.com/. This PM resource provides details of resources available on project management.

info.nrel.gov/esh/manual/esh-27.shtml. NREL Lessons Learned Program. The NREL Lessons Learned Program has been developed to provide a means of communicating internal and external experiences that can potentially reduce risk, improve efficiency, and enhance the cost effectiveness of the laboratory.

www.4pm.com/. The Project Managers Watch Tower has PM resources and information.

www.hq.nasa.gov/office/hqlibrary/ppm/ppmbib.htm. The NASA PPM Library has program/project management resource lists originally written for the NASA project management community. Their purpose was to promote the use of the NASA Headquarters Library Program/Project Management Collection funded by NASA Headquarters Code FT, Training & Development Division, by offering introductions to the management topics studied by today's managers.

www.lanl.gov/orgs/ism/lessons.html. Los Alamos/DOE Lessons Learned. This is a bit more than project post-performance analysis, but it is interesting reading. Thanks to the Society for Effective Lessons Learned Sharing.

www.mapnp.org/library/prog_mng/prog_mng.htm. Dr. McNamara's Program Management Library is a community resource to be shared and contributed to by the public. The overall goal of the library is to provide basic, how-to management information to managers—particularly those with very limited resources. Items in the library are relevant to both for-profit and nonprofit organizations, unless otherwise marked at the top of the item.

www.michaelgreer.com/postmortem.htm. Consultant Michael Greer's PM Resources Web site.

www.newgrange.org/. The New Grange Center for Project Management is a non-profit professional organization whose focus is on a hands-on, practical approach to project management. It sponsors an active email news and discussion service.

www.pmforum.org/. The WWW Project Management Forum is a nonprofit resource for information on international project management affairs dedicated to development, international cooperation, promotion, and support of a professional and worldwide project management discipline.

www.project-manager.com/. The Project Manager Web site contains PM resources and information.

Reporting and Communicating

The project manager is the spokesperson for the project, both formally and informally. It is his responsibility to communicate with all stakeholders, including subordinates, peers, managers, and clients.

Communications management, the application of the concepts of communicating to specific project needs, may be formalized and transformed into a communications management plan (CMP). The CMP may be a standalone document or a part of the software project management plan. But communications on software projects are much more than the formal CMP. Ideas and work products cannot be shared without constant attempts to get into the heads of others. Lacking clairvoyance, we turn to visual and auditory transmission mechanisms. The larger a project team is, the harder it must try to maintain communications—imagine parallel development, concurrent engineering, or a large integration effort without almost constant communication. And informal communications are every bit as important as formal ones.

This chapter will address some of the many forms of communication on a software project, including the formal reporting that occurs via a communications management plan. Communication takes place within the project team as well as between it and outside entities, such as upper management, customers, other project teams, and sponsors. Revisiting some of the concepts, such as team building and personality typing, presented in Chapter 6,

"Selecting a Project Team," will provide a bit more depth. Intrateam communication relies on a functioning team—one that is motivated, is able to negotiate and handle conflict, and knows how to exchange information in written form (formal reports, graphs, charts, email, etc.) and verbally (in-person meetings, virtual meetings, phone calls, pager, water-cooler chats, coffee klatch conclave, soda machine scuttlebutt, cube-farm broadcast, etc.). Therefore, the methods that may be used by a PM to help the team reach a high level of maturity are important to communications overall.

Where We Are in the Product Development Life Cycle

Reporting and communication occur throughout the software product development life cycle, as can be seen in Figure 29–1. Communication can and must occur continuously; reporting may occur on a time frequency such as weekly or semimonthly, or on an event-driven basis, such as upon the completion of a milestone.

Chapter 29 Relation to the 34 Competencies

Communication is an absolute necessity, to be used with every product and project skill. During planning, the specific time, cost, and resource commitments required to complete a project and how the goals are to be attained must be communicated to all stakeholders. In organizing, how the human and physical resources will be organized so that the project is complete within the specified constraints of time, money, and performance requirements must be communicated to the project team and reported to upper management. Leading (or directing and motivating) the team involves influencing the project team to behave in a manner that will facilitate attaining the goals of the project—all communication skills. While controlling, plans are followed and progress is evaluated in relation to time schedules, cost allocations, and performance requirements—all are reported to the appropriate stakeholders.

Specific people skills that are involved in reporting and communicating include:

25. **Holding effective meetings**
26. **Interaction and communication**
27. **Leadership**
29. **Negotiating successfully**
31. **Presenting effectively**
34. **Teambuilding**

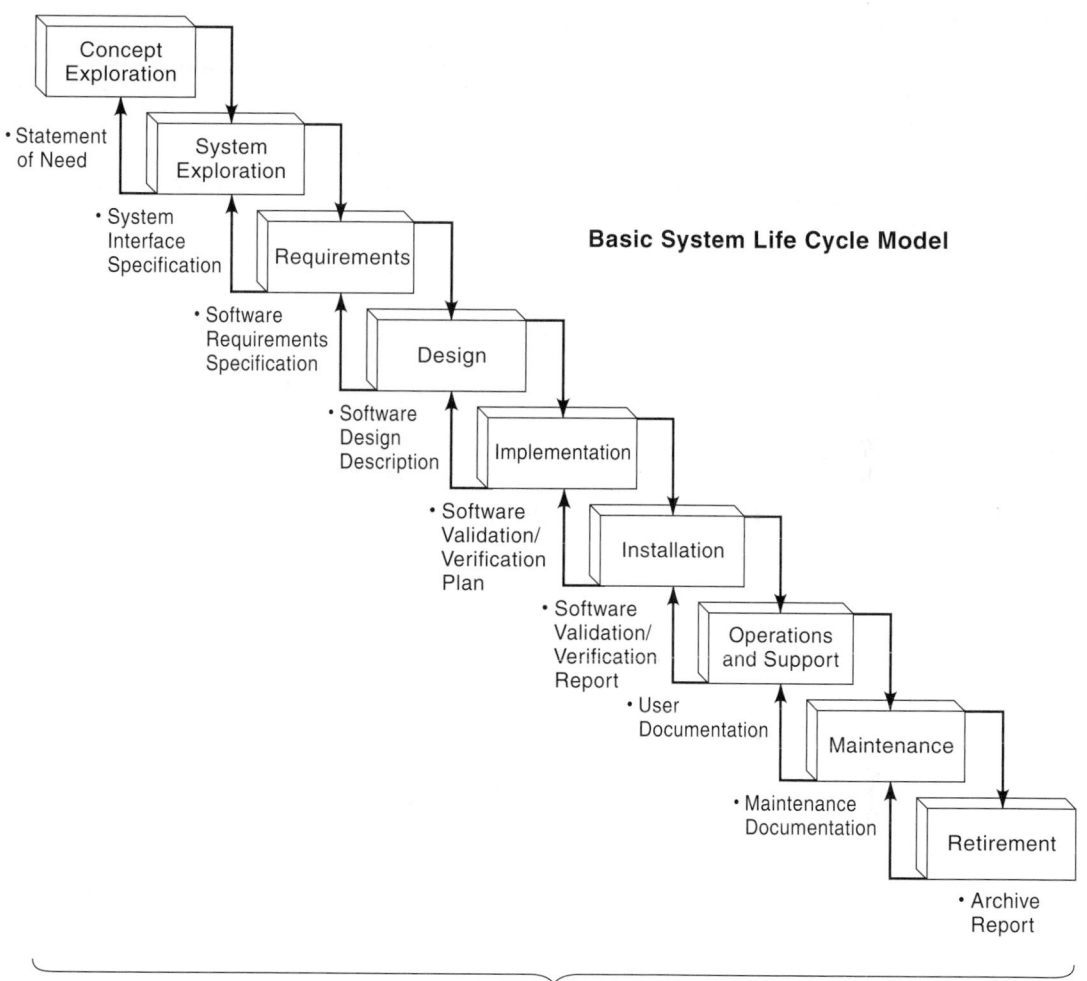

Basic System Life Cycle Model

FIGURE 29–1
Reporting and Communicating Occur Throughout the Product Development Life Cycle

Learning Objectives for Chapter 29 _____

Upon completion of this chapter, the reader should be able to:

- Assess the importance of communication on a software product development team;
- Describe some of the difficulties in achieving "true" communication;

- Define "frame of reference" and discuss how it affects communication;
- Explain why teams and team building activities are so important to communication;
- Name some team motivators;
- Explain why motivated teams are better able to communicate;
- Describe Maslow's Hierarchy of Needs and explain how it applies to motivation and communication;
- Describe Herzberg's two-factor theory and differentiate motivators from dissatisfiers;
- List the characteristics that high achievers prefer in a job;
- Compare and contrast management Theories X, Y, Z, and W;
- Name the MBTI dimensions of preference and describe how each affects communication in the sender and the receiver;
- Weigh the effect of situational leadership on communication;
- Summarize the types of goals that increase performance;
- Clarify the key relationships in expectancy theory and equity theory, and explain how each could impact team motivation and, therefore, communication;
- Explain how the contemporary theories of motivation complement each other;
- Differentiate between the kind of communication that occurs in meetings and the kind that occurs during negotiation;
- Contrast bargaining with negotiating;
- Analyze the types of communication that occur with change;
- Apply communication tips provided by Dr. Edward Tufte;
- Distinguish types and frequency of project reports;
- Employ a communications management plan.

Effective Communication _____

Communications are not something done "to" somebody, but something done "with" somebody.

   We often mistakenly think of a project manager as immersed in technical activities such as updating Gantt charts and calculating earned value. In fact, automated tools make the technical aspects of the job much easier than the nontechnical ones. The effective PM is almost constantly communicating—describing the project to others, motivating the team, listening to team and product issues (technical and otherwise), and making sure that the left hand knows what the right is doing. As shown in Figure 29–2, up to 75–90% of a PM's time is spent in communications. The ability to speak well is certainly a plus, but the PM's ability to listen is critical to project success.

Project Managers spend roughly 75–90% of their work time communicating.

"One's effectiveness is determined by one's ability to reach others through the spoken or written word ... perhaps the most important of skills."

—Peter Drucker

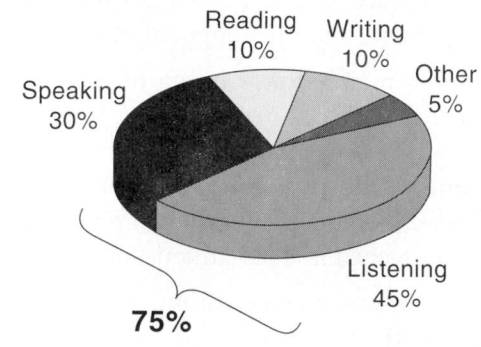

FIGURE 29–2

Project Managers Spend Most of Their Time Communicating

Source: Bob Futrell (2001). Presentation material for Motorola and for the Software Quality Institute at The University of Texas at Austin.

As with so many topics in *Quality Software Project Management*, only the very surface level of the subject of communications is touched. It is a psychological discipline in and of itself, with dozens of full-length texts devoted to it. In this brief space, what can be said is that nothing about communications should be taken for granted. A person (sender) with an idea may simply want to transmit it to another, but the process is really quite complex. As shown in Figure 29–3, the first step is for the sender to get it out of his head and through his mouth—a process of encoding. Assuming that the medium presents no distortion, there is still a formidable filter through which the idea must pass—attitudes, beliefs, and emotions put their mark on the message, during both encoding and decoding at the other end. Each and every one of us operates within a filtered view of the world—our own personally ground lens. If the sender has an opportunity for feedback from the receiver, a helpful check is thereby provided. The noise inside the decoding and encoding filters tends to get worn away with iteration.

These lenses, or frames of reference, originate as a result of both our nature and our experiences. Some are natural (genetic), others are learned, and many revolve around the nature/nurture influence on how we see the world and its events. The most common frame of reference is each person's way of observing, interpreting, and acting in the world. But there are gaps in our perception, knowledge, experience, and ability to process information and report accurately on what we have seen or heard. We may be affected by prejudice or a momentary distraction, or by some previous encounter with what looks much like the current situation but, in fact, is different. The fact that we use a frame of reference, with all its limitations, as the basis for decisions and actions, is important to the project manager.

Any number of other frames are used, such as time, codes of conduct, and professions.

The past, present, and future affect our way of looking at things. Youth frames the world in optimistic terms; in middle age, people become more realistic and come to terms with the way things are. In later years, we tend to take a short-term view. In the absence of a crisis, we may be inclined to procrastinate and miss opportunities.

A code of conduct, or a moral-ethical frame of reference, is influential. Such rules of behavior may incline us to see things in our terms of right and wrong, good and bad, and acceptable or not acceptable. Codes of conduct are often affected by larger questions of values, culture, religion, and ethnic contexts. With the proliferation of global project teams, we must take care that this expanded, homogenized frame of reference doesn't confuse team members from other nations that are steeped in the traditions, mores, and practices of their countries.

At a professional level, certain frames are introduced for participation in such fields as medicine, the military, law, the political environment, or software engineering. Professions give still another set of lenses through which to view the world.[1]

The way in which we send and receive information may be vastly different between the sender and the receiver. As we will see with the Myers-Briggs Type Indicator (MBTI) discussion in this chapter and alluded to in Figure 29–4, a great deal about whether we prefer to be specific and ordered in dispensing data, or general and scattered about proposing ideas depends on our personality type. There are no judgments, no right or wrong, only preferences.

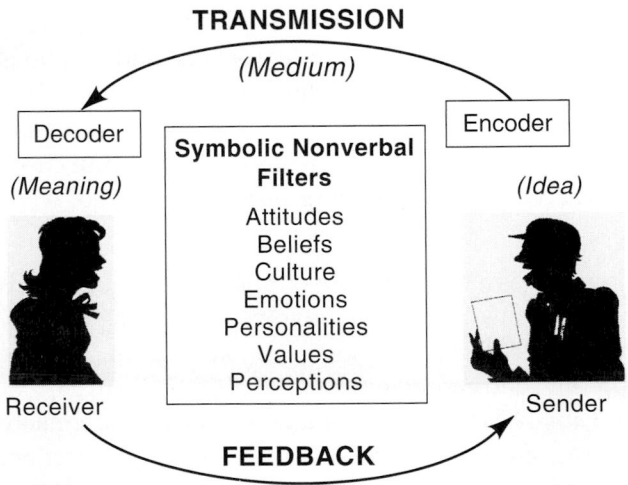

FIGURE 29–3
Communication Is Through Filters

Concrete versus Abstract

Sequential versus Random

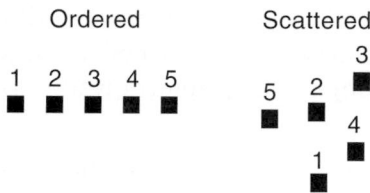

FIGURE 29–4
Communicating Styles: Speaking/Communicating Dimensions

When it is important that the sender is certain that the message has been internalized in its purest form, he may want to observe whether it has been acted upon. If I tell you, "Please submit the report," and you look up and nod, you have received the message. If you say, "Yes, I have the milestone report right here," you doubtless understood the message. If you submit the report, communication has truly occurred. Figure 29–5 illustrates these three levels of acknowledgement.

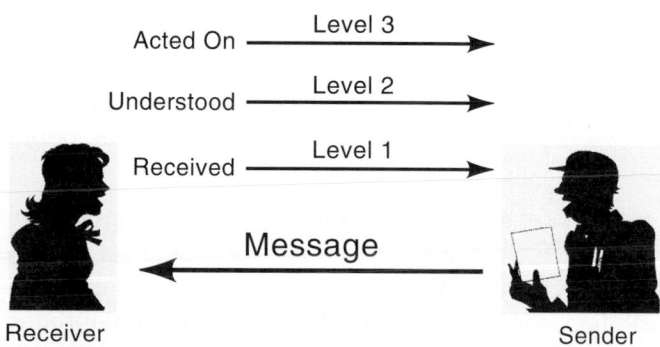

FIGURE 29–5
Three Steps of an Acknowledgement

Communication Techniques _____

Fundamental to any project's success, yet often taken for granted, is free flow of information among the stakeholders of a project. In small projects using existing staff within a larger organization, this is often taken for granted as part of the office culture. However, with larger projects, external operations, or special needs, a formal communications plan must be devised.

To design a workable plan, however, you must first understand the basics of how information passes from one person to another and the resulting potential for misinterpretation. All of us have experienced misinterpretations sometime in our careers, sometimes with disastrous effects. It's amazing how much "parachutes" sounds like "pair of shoes" around the roar of the airplane engine, when the jumpmaster runs down the equipment readiness checklist ("Do you have your _____ ready?").

As more people are added to a work on a project, the number of different communication paths increases rapidly, according the formula $n(n-1)/2$ where n is the number of people on the project team. This explosion of communication paths was illustrated in Figure 6–4 in Chapter 6.

Communicating with Teams _____

Talk of intra- and interteam communications requires a "jelled" team, not just a group of people. A team is an organization of diverse individuals having different disciplinary background and experience that enjoys working together and helping one another, shares a common goal, and makes a commitment to achieve the goals and objectives of the project. An effective team is any group of people who must significantly relate with each other to accomplish shared objectives.[2]

Team dynamics, discussed in Chapter 6, are such that the individuals selected pass through various stages of learning how to work together and then doing it. Figure 29–6 shows the stages and associated activities and characteristics.[3]

Obviously, the goal is to get to the "performing" stage as soon as possible—productivity will likely suffer until then. Figure 29–7 would hopefully enjoy a much longer period between norming and adjourning.

Chapter 6 warns the project manager to be on the lookout for teams that are about to commit teamicide, a word coined by Tom DeMarco. Sometimes teams are not able to get past the storming stage and members revert to the roots of their personalities. Observable symptoms of bad teamwork in general include frustration, conflict and unhealthy competition, unproductive meetings, lack of trust or confidence in the PM, excessive wheel-spinning, unimplemented

Stage	Activity	Characterized by
Forming	Members find out: • what they will be doing, • the styles of acceptable leadership, and • possible kinds of interpersonal and task relationships.	• Courtesy • Confusion • Caution • Commonality
Storming	• Members begin resisting the influence of the group. • There is conflict over competing approaches to reaching the group's goals.	• Tension • Criticism • Confrontation
Norming	Resistance is overcome as the group: • establishes its rules and standards, • develops intragroup cohesiveness, and • delineates task standards and expectations.	• Cooperation • Collaboration • Cohesion • Commitment
Performing	• The group is ready to focus attention on task accomplishment. • Issues of interpersonal relations, member status, and division of tasks are settled.	• Challenge • Creativity • Group consciousness • Consideration of members
Adjourning	• The group has fulfilled its purpose or died.	• Compromise • Communication • Consensus • Closure

Forming   Storming   Norming   Performing   Adjourning

FIGURE 29–6
Team Dynamics

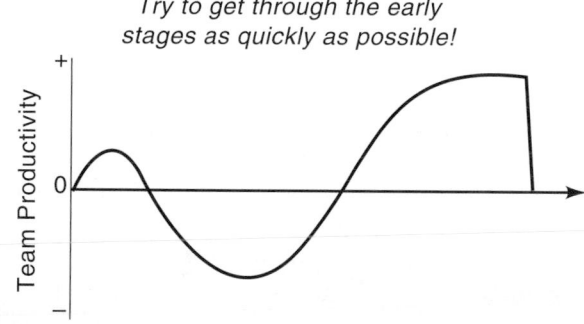

Try to get through the early stages as quickly as possible!

Team Productivity

Stage: Forming Storming Norming Performing Adjourning

FIGURE 29–7
Team Dynamics—Productivity

decisions, detrimental surprises, unresponsive or apathetic team members, or team members who withdraw into their own areas of responsibility, avoiding cooperation with the team.[4] When PMs observe those symptoms, they should watch for likely causes: defensive management, bureaucracy, unnecessary physical separation of team members, fragmentation of people's time, quality reduction of the product, phony deadlines, and clique control.[5] Sometimes the team may get unstuck from the storming stage, but, left unchecked, a group of people are unlikely to mature into a team.

Goals of Team Building

The goals of team building are to obtain effective team member characteristics: be interdependent, have a reason to work together, be committed to working together; be accountable as a functioning unit, have a moderate level of competition and conflict; ensure that every team member is going in the same direction and recognizes the same project goals and objectives; and identify and obtain consensus on project goals and objectives.[6]

Of course, teams have attributes of all groups—the team itself has status, each team member plays a role, and the team develops norms and, unfortunately, sometimes falls prey to groupthink and or "social loafing."

The actual team development is, "The process of planned and deliberate encouragement of effective working practices while diminishing difficulties or blockages which interfere with the team's competence and resourcefulness."[7] Team development is essential for bringing diverse individuals together to work effectively, and it can be the most important aspect of the project manager's job. Team development must be a simple, practical method of achieving a feeling of team membership and a unified team spirit, and it must be integrated into the everyday activities of the project.[8] There are all sorts of teams, ranging from quality control circles, voluntary problem-solving groups committed to improving quality and reducing costs, to self-managed teams, high-performance teams that assume traditional managerial duties such as staffing and planning.

Some Tools and Techniques for Team Development

When the Software Quality Institute Advisory Board at The University of Texas at Austin created the list of "34 skills that every software project manager needs to know," interaction and communication, leadership, selecting a team, and teambuilding were chosen as essential people skills. Chapter 6 discussed general management skills needed by a leader, including teambuilding activities. Project managers must be cognizant of reward and recognition systems and take formal action that promote or reinforce desired behavior. They must consider cultural differences, even when teams enjoy the benefits afforded a collocated team. The experienced PM knows the value of technical training, as well as process and "soft skills" training such as negotiation. Almost all training will enhance the skills, knowledge, and capabilities of the project team.

When to Use Team Building

Team building strategies are especially important on projects requiring multidisciplinary teams of diverse backgrounds and capabilities. They are nearly always required to attain a unity of purpose for the team. A kick-off meeting where everyone attends (even those who must travel, if at all affordable) is a powerful team building technique to use at the start of every new project. Team building is crucial in a matrix organization. Team building is not something done once and then forgotten—it must be reinforced continuously. The PM is responsible for monitoring team effectiveness and taking corrective action when needed.[9]

Benefits of Team Building

When teams "jell," people come together to solve mutual problems, synergy develops, job satisfaction increases for the team members, conflicts are more easily resolved, and creativity is stimulated. As team members become motivated, they acquire a collective strength.[10]

Limitations of Team Building

For all of its benefits, team building, like technical tools, is no silver bullet. The best team cannot fix a project that has a faulty concept or lacks management support. It cannot rectify inept team members or project managers. It cannot always fix an inherited project that is already in trouble.[11]

Motivation in Teams

Motivation is defined as the force that energizes, directs, and sustains behavior. It is the willingness to exert high levels of effort toward organizational goals, conditioned by the effort's ability to satisfy some individual need. Motivating a team is similar to motivating an individual. And individuals work best when they respond to intrinsic motivation, something that "turns them on." It is rare that extrinsic motivation, such as money, works in the same way—someone may perform a task that is loathsome to get money for some pleasurable pursuit, but that person still won't like the task. Instead of expecting that teams can be bribed into being motivated, it is wiser for the PM to realize that some tasks have to be done, but no one will like them. Yet, there are plenty of other tasks that are intrinsically motivating (and will therefore be done extremely well). The trick is in matching the person (team) to the task.

Motivation is behaviorally specific—that is, it is more appropriate to think in terms of an individual's motivation to excel in a particular job requirement or even to carry out a specific behavior than it is to think about an individual's overall motivation. What is the best way to determine what motivates someone? Ask, but do so in a way that allows that person to tell you. Lewis says that it is hard for many people to answer such a direct question, but indirect questions will allow you to determine a motivating pattern of activity. He suggests questions such as, "Tell me about some job you've had, during the past six months to a year, that you really enjoyed" (or "during your entire career"), "Tell me about some hobbies, sports, or other outside interests that you like to spend time with," and "Tell me—is there anything you've always wanted to do but never got to do, maybe because you didn't have the time or money, or your family responsibilities prevented it?" Most of the time, a pattern of activities will appear in the responses. Some people are motivated by a pattern of activity that indicates that they enjoy troubleshooting (fixing things); some are motivated by innovating, and some by helping. Michael Maccoby lists five types (Innovator, Helper, Expert, Defender, Self-Developer), and Lewis believes there are more. Everyone likes a challenge, but the definition of "challenge" is different for each individual. Knowing the pattern of activity that motivates a person will allow you to assign challenging tasks that require those activities. If there are no such jobs on the project, this is useful information as well because the individual needs to be reassigned.[12]

Maslow's Hierarchy of Needs and Herzberg's Motivation-Hygiene factors are models that have been in use for decades. While they may be of limited use to the modern software project manager, they are important as a foundation.

Before turning to a brief description of motivation per Maslow and Herzberg, a few definitions are in order.

Intrinsic process motivation refers to individuals being primarily motivated by intrinsic process and engaging only in activities that they consider fun. These individuals are often diverted from tasks that are relevant to goal attainment to pursue tasks that are intrinsically more enjoyable. Intrinsic rewards have been noted to include: challenge, the ability to take responsibility and direct one's own work, variety, creativity, the ability to use one's own talent, and opportunity for feedback. As long as team tasks are enjoyable, these individuals will be motivated to continue working effectively in the context of the team. Because they are relatively indifferent to task and social feedback, such feedback will not serve to motivate continued performance on the part of the intrinsically motivated person.

Instrumental motivation refers to rewards as a motivating source when individuals believe that their behaviors will lead to certain outcomes such as pay or praise. The basic assumption is that individuals and organizations constitute an exchange relationship. Expectancy and equity theories, discussed later, are currently accepted models of motivation based on exchange relationships. Extrinsic rewards have been noted to include the ability to develop relationships with colleagues and supervisors, pay, promotion, fringe benefits, and job security.

External self-concept motivation is externally based when the individual is primarily other-directed. In this case, adopting the role expectations of reference groups derives the ideal self. The individual attempts to meet the expectations of others by behaving in ways that will elicit social feedback consistent with self-perceptions. When positive task feedback is obtained, the individual finds it necessary to communicate these results to members of the reference or peer group. The individual behaves in ways that satisfy reference group members, first to gain acceptance and then to gain status.

Internal self-concept–based motivation will be internally based when the individual is primarily inner-directed. Internal self-concept motivation takes the form of the individual setting internal standards that become the basis for the ideal self. The individual attempts to first reinforce perceptions of competency and later achieve higher levels of competency. The motivating force for individuals who are inner-driven and motivated by their self-concept is task feedback. It is important to these individuals that their efforts are vital in achieving outcomes and that their ideas and actions are instrumental in performing a job well. It is not important that others provide reinforcing feedback, as is true for other-directed individuals.

Goal internalization behavior is motivated by goal internalization when the individual adopts attitudes and behaviors because their content is congruent with his value system. The individual believes in the cause and, as such, is willing to work toward the goals of an organization supporting this cause.

Inducement systems are those aspects of an organization that act to energize, direct, or sustain behavior. Common inducement systems are reward, task, managerial, and social inducement. Reward is typically the compensation system and the promotional system. Task inducement is involved with the motivational aspects of job and task design. Managerial inducement is born of leadership style. The motivational impact of the work group or the organization as a social system defines the social inducement system.

The sources of motivation model explains the hierarchy of motives behind work behavior. It argues that there are five basic sources of motivation and five motivational inducement systems, as described in Table 29–1.

The motivational properties of the reward inducement system are tied to the expectation that increased effort will lead to greater pay and the instrumental value of pay to the individual.

The task inducement system describes a way to enhance internal work motivation (i.e., the individual does the work because it interests or challenges him).

The managerial inducement system energizes, directs, and sustains behavior through a number of sources. Under the social inducement system, instrumentally motivated individuals respond to norms and sanctions enforced by the work group or organization. These norms and sanctions provide both rewards and punishments that direct and sustain behavior.[13]

TABLE 29-1
Sources of Motivation and Motivational Inducement Systems

Sources of Motivation Conditions for Motivation	Motivational Driver	Motivational Inducement Systems			
		Reward System Pay and Promotion	**Managerial System** Leadership Style	**Task System** Job Design	**Social System** Culture
Intrinsic Process	Enjoyment		*Laissez-faire* Leadership	Job Rotation	• Social Activities • Quality of Work Life Programs
Instrumental Increased pay and/or promotion is linked to high performance. (ERB)	Increases in Pay and Promotion	• Merit Pay • Commissions • Incentive Pay • Gainsharing • Profit Sharing • Bonuses • Promotion			
Self-Concept: External Increased status, recognition and external validation are associated with high performance. (ERB)	• Group Acceptance • Individual Worth • Group Status • Group Influence	Promotion	• Recognition • Empowerment • Positive Reinforcement	Job Enlargement	• Peer Recognition • Customer Recognition • Team Building

(Continues)

TABLE 29–1 (Continued)
Sources of Motivation and Motivational Inducement Systems

Sources of Motivation	Motivational Driver	Motivational Inducement Systems			
		Reward System Pay and Promotion	Managerial System Leadership Style	Task System Job Design	Social System Culture
Conditions for Motivation					
Self-Concept: Internal Skills, abilities and values are validated through high performance. (ERB)	• Achievement • Validation of Competencies		• Empowerment • Participation in Problem Solving • Linking Skills to Mission	• Job Enrichment • Knowledge of Results	
Goal Identification High performance (ERB) is essential in the accomplishment of important goals or benefits to others.	Accomplishment		• Vision Creation • Goal Setting • Empowerment in Mission Development	• Alignment Activities • Knowledge of Results	

Source: *www.cba.uri.edu/Scholl/Papers/Self_Concept_Motivation.HTM.* Nancy H. Leonard et al. (1995). "A Self Concept-Based Model of Work Motivation." *Proceedings of the Academy of Management Annual Meeting,* Vancouver, B.C.

Expectancy Theory

Expectancy theory suggests that the strength of a tendency to act in a certain way (motivation) depends on the strength of an expectation that the act will be followed by a given outcome (the perceived likelihood of getting something) and on the attractiveness of that outcome to the individual. The theory focuses on three relationships:

- Effort-performance relationship, or the probability perceived by the individual that exerting a given amount of effort will lead to performance

- Performance-reward relationship, or the degree to which the individual believes that performing at a particular level will lead to the attainment of a desired outcome

- Rewards-personal goals relationship, or the degree to which organizational rewards satisfy an individual's personal goals or needs, and the attractiveness of those potential rewards for the individual

The theory assumes that motivational *strength* is determined by perceived probabilities of success—one's belief or expectation that one thing will lead to another. It deals with the direction of motivation—once behavior is energized, individuals pursue certain behavioral alternatives. Of course, they select the option with the greatest motivational forces.

Motivational Forces = Expectancy × Instrumentality × Valance

Expectancy (E) (effort-to-performance) is the belief that one's effort will result in attainment of desired performance goals—the probability that effort will lead to performance. This belief or perception is generally based on an individual's past experience and self-confidence (often termed self-efficacy), and the perceived difficulty of the performance standard or goal. The team member might ask, for example, "If I work harder and validate more requirements, will I produce a higher quality software product?"

Instrumentality (I) (performance-to-outcome expectancy) is a perception about the probability that performance will lead to the outcome. Instrumentality is the belief that if one does meet performance expectations, he will receive a greater reward. This reward may come in the form of a pay increase, a promotion, recognition, or a sense of accomplishment. "If I produce a higher quality software product, will I get a bigger raise? A faster promotion? A chance to work on the next killer app?"

Valence (V) (perceived performance-reward probability) is the degree of attractiveness or unattractiveness of a particular outcome. An outcome is anything that results from performing a particular behavior. It is the desirability of an outcome to an individual—the value that the individual personally places on the rewards. This is a function of his needs, goals, and values. "Do I really want a bigger raise, faster promotion, or position on the next project team? Is it worth the extra effort?"

An individual will act in a certain way based on the expectation that the act will be followed by a given outcome and on the attractiveness of that outcome to the individual.

Effort leads to performance (How hard will I have to work?). Performance leads to reward (What is the reward?).

For workers to be motivated to perform desired behaviors at a high level valence must be high, instrumentality must be high, and expectancy must be high.

$$\text{EFFORT} = V \times I \times E$$

Effort $\to$ performance $\to$ reward expectations determine whether motivation will be high or low.

Employees tend to work harder when they believe that they have a good chance of getting personally meaningful rewards.[14]

The Equity Theory

The equity theory is based on the relatively simple premise that people in organizations want to be treated fairly.

Equity implies that we are being treated fairly in relation to others. Inequity implies that we are being treated unfairly in relation to others. Equity (or inequity) is a psychological state residing within an individual. It creates a feeling of dissonance that the individual attempts to resolve in some manner.

Individuals compare their job inputs and outcomes with those of others and then respond so as to eliminate inequities. Equity theory recognizes that individuals are concerned not only with the absolute amount of rewards for their efforts, but also with the relationship of this amount to what others receive. Historically, equity theory has focused on distributive justice or the perceived fairness of the amount and allocation of rewards among individuals. However, equity should also consider procedural justice or the perceived fairness of the process used to determine the distribution of rewards.

Equity is a social comparison process, resulting when individuals compare their outcomes (usually pay) to those of others. There is no "rational" or single "equitable pay rate" for any given job or individual. Equity is a subjective evaluation, not an objective one. Based on the comparison that individuals use, each individual is likely to develop different perceptions of equity.

The comparisons that individuals use tend to fall into five classes of comparison:

Job equity—Individuals compare their pay to the pay of other individuals in the same position that they hold within their organization.

Company equity—Individuals compare their pay to the pay of other individuals holding the different positions within their organization.

Occupational (market) equity—Individuals compare their pay to the pay of other individuals holding the same position in other organizations.

Cohort equity—Individuals compare their pay to the pay of others in similar cohort groups, generally those based on age and education.

Self-equity—Individuals compare their pay to the pay that they received at another point in time.

People in organizations form perceptions of the equity of their treatment through a four-step process:

Step 1: A person evaluates how he is being treated by the organization.

Step 2: The person forms a perception of how a comparable other is being treated.

Step 3: The person compares his own circumstances with those of the comparable other.

Step 4: On the strength of this feeling, the person may choose to pursue one or more alternatives.

The software project manager can determine the primary outcome that each employee wants, decide what levels and kinds of performance are needed to meet organizational goals, make sure that the desired levels of performance are possible, link desired outcomes and desired performance, analyze the situation for conflicting expectations, make sure that the rewards are large enough, and make sure that the overall system is equitable for everyone.

Equity theory describes the equity comparison process in terms of an input-to-outcome ratio. Individuals determine equity by comparing their contributions (job inputs) and their rewards (job outcomes) to those of their comparisons. This comparison takes the form of the following ratio:

$$\frac{\text{Self}}{\begin{array}{c}\text{Contributions}\\\text{Rewards}\end{array}} : \frac{\text{Comparison}}{\begin{array}{c}\text{Contributions}\\\text{Rewards}\end{array}}$$

When this ratio is in balance, the individual perceives equity. Inequity is experienced when the ratio is out of balance. Thus, when the individual perceives that his contributions are equal to the comparison and his rewards are lower, or his contributions are greater and rewards are equal, inequity is felt.

Equity theory offers managers these messages: Everyone in the organization needs to understand the basis for rewards (for example, if people are to be rewarded more for high-quality work than for quantity of work, that fact needs to be clearly communicated to employees); people tend to take a multifaceted view of their rewards (they perceive and experience a variety of rewards, some tangible and others intangible); and people base their actions on their perceptions of reality.

A team member will be motivated to reduce inequity. Their choices are as follows:

1. Change inputs, reduce performance
2. Change outcomes, attempt to increase one's pay
3. Alter perceptions of self, rationalize or perceptually alter reward or contributions
4. Alter perceptions of others, attempt to reduce the performance of others
5. Change comparisons
6. Leave situation, leave the organization

What do individuals view as relevant contributions? Given the perceptual nature of equity, the answer varies with each individual, but contributions fall into a number of categories:

- Job contributions include the factors that differentiate one job from another. They typically include responsibility, effect, skills, education, and working conditions required by the job itself (e.g., individuals working in jobs requiring greater levels of responsibility generally expect higher levels of pay).

- Personal contributions include attributes that the individuals bring to the organization that they believe differentiate them from others, such as experience, longevity, and extra education (e.g., individuals with greater seniority often expect higher levels of pay).

- Performance contributions include the extra effort and results that differentiate one employee from another (e.g., individuals who perceive that their performance is better than others with whom they work often believe that they are entitled to higher levels of pay).

Managers generally define pay-related problems in terms of their behavioral consequences (turnover or performance). Therefore, inequity itself is not generally viewed as a management problem unless it appears to be related to turnover or reduced performance. Because the links between turnover and pay are often much clearer than those between pay and extra role behavior, turnover often becomes the only managerial focus. Therefore, typical management interests relate to keeping the employees whom it deems valuable.

From the employee perspective, the perception of inequity is a problem in itself. Low morale is often a consequence of inequity. Even when low morale is not manifested in turnover, reduced performance, and reluctance to take on extra duties, it is still viewed as a problem from the employee perspective. From the perspective of interest-based bargaining, we should be attempting to develop solutions that meet the interests of both parties.[15]

The challenge is how to resolve issues in which the limits to our creativity do not allow us to satisfy both sets of interests entirely.

Goal Setting Theory

Goal setting is the process of improving individual or group job performance with formally stated objectives, deadlines, or quality standards. Goals are able to motivate by directing attention, encouraging effort, encouraging persistence, and fostering goal-attainment strategies and action plans. The goals must be specific, difficult, and participatively set.

The theory is that specific and difficult goals lead to higher performance. Goals tell an employee what needs to be done and how much effort will need to be expended. Specific goals increase performance; difficult goals, when accepted, result in higher performance than do easy goals; and feedback leads to higher performance than does nonfeedback. Specific hard goals produce a higher level of output than does the generalized goal of "do your best"—the specificity of the goal itself acts as an internal stimulus.

Behavioral theory has been around for decades, but some "old favorites" continue to be corroborated by modern studies, so they are worthwhile for the software PM to know. Notably, Maslow's Hierarchy of Needs and Herzberg's Hygiene Factors are part of every PM's vocabulary.

Maslow's Hierarchy of Needs

In 1954, Maslow first published *Motivation and Personality*, which introduced his theory about how people satisfy various personal needs in the context of their work. He postulated, based on his observations as a humanistic psychologist, that there is a general pattern of needs recognition and satisfaction that people follow in generally the same sequence. He also theorized that a person could not recognize or pursue the next higher need in the hierarchy until his currently recognized need was substantially or completely satisfied, a concept called prepotency. Maslow's hierarchy of needs is shown in Figure 29–8.

According to literature on motivation, individuals often have problems consistently articulating what they want from a job. Therefore, employers have ignored what individuals say that they want, instead telling employees what they want based on what managers believe most people want under the circumstances. Frequently, these decisions have been based on Maslow's needs hierarchy, including the factor of prepotency. As a person advances through an organization, his employer supplies or provides opportunities to satisfy needs higher on Maslow's pyramid.

Maslow seemed to sense that, aside from the people with emotional limitations and problems, there were times when man was at his best. One of Maslow's most important contributions to psychology was his theory of human needs, developed in the late 1960s. This theory explains that human needs are hierarchical in nature. He believed that people are not merely controlled by mechanical forces (the stimuli and reinforcement forces of behaviorism) or unconscious instinctual impulses of psychoanalysis, but that they should be understood in

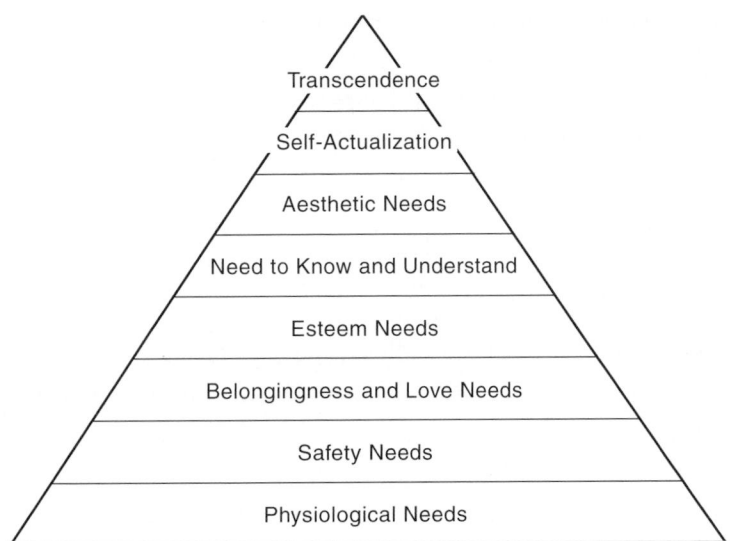

FIGURE 29–8
Maslow's Hierarchy of Needs
Source: Abraham Harold Maslow (1954). *Motivation and Personality,* 1st ed. New York, NY: Harper.

terms of human potential. He believed that humans strive to reach the highest levels of their capabilities. People seek the frontiers of creativity and strive to reach the highest levels of consciousness and wisdom. Other psychologists labeled people at this level and below as "fully functioning" or possessing a "healthy personality." Maslow called the people who were at the top "self-actualizing" persons.

Maslow set up a hierarchical theory of needs. The animal or physical needs were placed at the bottom, and the human needs were at the top. This hierarchic theory can be seen as a pyramid, with the base occupied by people who are focused not on values, but on just staying alive. A person who is starving dreams about food and thinks about food and nothing else. According to Maslow, an individual is ready to act upon the growth needs if and only if the deficiency needs are met.

Maslow's Hierarchy of Needs (rephrased) includes eight levels:

1. **Physiological needs**—Biological needs include oxygen, food, water, warmth/coolness, protection from storms, and so forth. These needs are the strongest because if deprived, the person could or would die. They come first in a person's search for satisfaction.

2. **Safety needs**—When all physiological needs are satisfied and are no longer controlling thoughts and behaviors, the needs for security can become active. These are felt by adults during emergencies, periods of disorganization in the social structure (such as

widespread rioting). They are felt more frequently by children who often display signs of insecurity and their need to be safe.

3. **Love, affection, and belongingness needs**—When the needs for safety and for physiological well-being are satisfied, the next class of needs for love, affection, and belongingness can emerge. These include the needs to escape loneliness and alienation and give (and receive) love, affection, and the sense of belonging.

4. **Esteem needs**—When the first three classes of needs are satisfied, the needs for esteem can become dominant. These include a need for a stable, firmly based, high level of self-respect and respect from others to feel satisfied, self-confident, and valuable. If these needs are not met, the person feels inferior, weak, helpless, and worthless.

5. **Need to know and understand**—These are cognitive needs to know, to understand, and to explore.

6. **Aesthetic needs**—These include symmetry, order, and beauty.

7. **Self-actualization needs**—When all of the previous needs are satisfied, then and only then are the needs for self-actualization activated. These are needs to find self-fulfillment and realize one's potential—to do that which a person was "born to do." Maslow describes self-actualization as an ongoing process.

> Self-actualizing people are ... involved in a cause outside their own skin. They are devoted, work at something, something very precious to them—some calling or vocation, in the old sense, the priestly sense. When you select out of a careful study, very fine and healthy people, strong people, creative people, saintly people, sagacious people ... you get a different view of mankind. You ask how tall can people grow, what can a human being become?
>
> Abraham H. Maslow (1943). "A Theory of Human Motivation."
> *Psychological Review,* July. pp. 370–396.

Maslow also describes self-actualization as a person's need to be and do that which the person was born to do. It is his "calling." "A musician must make music, an artist must paint, and a poet must write." If these needs are not met, the person feels restlessness, on edge, tense, and lacking something. Lower needs may also produce a restless feeling, but here it is much easier to find the cause. If a person is hungry, unsafe, not loved or accepted, or lacking self-esteem, the cause is apparent. It is not always clear what a person wants when there is a need for self-actualization.

8. **Transcendence**—To help others find self-fulfillment and realize their potential. Maslow believed that as one becomes more self-actualized and transcendent, one becomes more wise (develops wisdom) and automatically knows what to do in a variety of situations.

Maslow believes that the only reason that people would not move through the needs to self-actualization is because of the hindrances placed in their way by society. For example, education is often a hindrance with imposed ideas of the culture. On the other hand, respectful teaching promotes personal growth. Maslow indicated that the educational process could take some of these steps listed below to promote personal growth:

We should teach people to be authentic, to be aware of their inner selves, and to hear their inner-feeling voices.

We should teach people to transcend their own cultural conditioning and become world citizens.

We should help people discover their vocation in life, their calling, fate, or destiny. This is especially focused upon finding the right career and the right mate.

We should teach people that life is precious, that there is joy to be experienced in life. If people are open to seeing the good and joyous in all kinds of situations, it makes life worth living.

We must accept each person and help everyone learn their inner nature. From real knowledge of aptitudes and limitations, we can know what to build upon and what potentials are really there.

We must see that each person's basic needs are satisfied. That includes safety, belongingness, and esteem needs.

We should refreshen consciousness, teaching each person to appreciate beauty and the other good things in nature and in living.

We should teach people that controls are good and that complete abandon is bad. It takes control to improve the quality of life in all areas.

We should teach people to transcend the trifling problems and grapple with the serious problems in life. These include the problems of injustice, pain, suffering, and death.

We must teach people to be good choosers. They must be given practice in making choices, first between one good and another.[16]

The MBTI type preferences of introversion and extroversion may have an impact on the way different personalities follow the Maslow hierarchy. An introvert might be more concerned with his own perceptions of being included in a group, whereas an extrovert would pay more attention to how others value that membership.

Herzberg's Theory of Motivators and Dissatisfiers

Fredrick Herzberg constructed a two-dimensional paradigm of factors affecting people's attitudes about work (the two-factor theory.) He recognized that work characteristics generated by dissatisfaction are quite different from those created by satisfaction. He stated that two entirely different dimensions contribute to an employee's behavior at work. He called one set of factors "motivators" and the other "dissatisfiers" (or "hygiene factors"). Motivators influence satisfaction based on fulfillment of higher-level needs. He concluded that such factors as company policy, supervision, interpersonal relations, working conditions, and salary are hygiene factors rather than motivators. According to the theory, the absence of hygiene factors can create job dissatisfaction, but their presence does not motivate or create satisfaction.

Motivators are elements that enrich a person's job; five factors in particular are strong determiners of job satisfaction: achievement, recognition, the work itself, responsibility, advancement, and growth. These motivators (satisfiers) are associated with long-term positive effects in job performance, while the hygiene factors (dissatisfiers) consistently produce only short-term changes in job attitudes and performance, which quickly fall back to previous levels.

In summary, satisfiers describe a person's relationship with what he does, many related to the tasks being performed. Dissatisfiers, on the other hand, have to do with a person's relationship to the context or environment in which he performs the job. Dissatisfiers include work conditions, pay, and interpersonal relationships. When hygiene factors are poor, work is dissatisfying. When hygiene factors are good, work improves.

The satisfiers relate to what a person does, while the dissatisfiers relate to the situation in which the person does what he does. Simply removing the dissatisfiers is not enough. Unless people can fulfill higher needs, motivation will not be successful.

Motivation Through Rewards

Rewards are the material and psychological payoffs for working. Extrinsic rewards are payoffs granted to the individual by other people (e.g., money, benefits, recognition, praise); intrinsic rewards are self-granted and internally experienced payoffs (e.g., a sense of accomplishment).

To improve performance with extrinsic rewards, the rewards must satisfy individual needs, and employees must believe that effort will lead to reward. In addition, the rewards must be equitable and must be linked to performance.

Keys to successful employee participation programs include a profit-sharing or gain-sharing plan, a long-term employment relationship with good job security, a concerted effort to build and maintain group cohesiveness, and protection of the individual employee's rights.

Communication and Motivation Skills of a Software Project Manager

In addition to the planning, organizing, leading, and controlling skills required for the management of a software project, other general skills are required of any manager. None is more important than another, so, in alphabetical order, they include the ability to do the following:

Affect an emotional reaction in others

Affect behavioral change in others, contrary to their effect (influence)

Control anger

Develop a strong self-concept that is not continually dependent on external validation

Draw upon emotional intelligence skills

Facilitate team problem solving

Give credit to others, self-diagnose your own style, and place the good of the group ahead of your own

Make personnel decisions that are not totally overshadowed by feelings

Motivate yourself when feeling negative

Override emotions in your own behavior

Place little dependency on external validation

Read the self-concept of others and determine their needs for validation

Resolve conflicts in win-win way

Sell an idea, program, plan, or problem solution

Understand and control your own emotions (self-awareness)

Understand and predict your own "hot" buttons (triggers to emotional reactions)

Understand the source of motivation of others (empathy)

Understand why certain things annoy or please.[17]

Project Manager's Role in Team Development

After the project team has been formed, the PM must perform management as well as demonstrate leadership. What's the difference? Leaders set direction and do the right thing; managers follow process and do things right. Effective project control entails understanding organizational behavior as well as individual behavior (this begins with your own behavior).

The software project manager is responsible for guiding, motivating, and controlling the project team, as well as the product created by the team. The PM behaves as technical director, system integrator, project planner, project administrator, decision maker, the team's communication expeditor and climate creator, and the negotiator and mender of relationships. He constantly works to draw upon the abilities of the total team, develop commitment and ownership within each team member, and develop a collective culture and trust. Qualifications for the role of PM have been said to be: ability to work well with others, good salesperson traits, experience in the area of expertise, supervisory experience, profit-oriented outlook, ability to accurately present the company's position, and a personal style of management.

The software project manager is responsible for job design, which may entail fitting people to jobs, fitting jobs to people, or both. Fitting people to jobs requires realistic job previews, job rotation, limited exposure, and contingent time off—rewarding people with early time off when they get the job done.

Fitting jobs to people requires "job enlargement," combining two or more specialized tasks to increase motivation (also called horizontal job loading), and job enrichment, redesigning jobs to increase their motivating potential (also called vertical job loading). Job enrichment may include consideration of skill variety, task identity, task significance, autonomy, and feedback from the job.

To the extent that a PM becomes involved with the Human Resources department (maybe there isn't one—project HR represents the entire HR), he must ensure that individuals are cultivated for growth and development. Activities include giving appraisals and performance reviews, making appointments, giving promotions, and retaining good people.

Situational Leadership

Situational leadership was introduced in Chapter 6; in Figure 29–9, it is shown how performance drives performer readiness, which determines the performer's maturity, from which leadership styles are selected. Then the cycle of performance begins again. Leaders have a "basic" style of participating, selling, delegating, or telling, but the results of their style, fed through the team, may influence it. If the team performs in a mature, willing, and able fashion, then the PM is comfortable delegating.

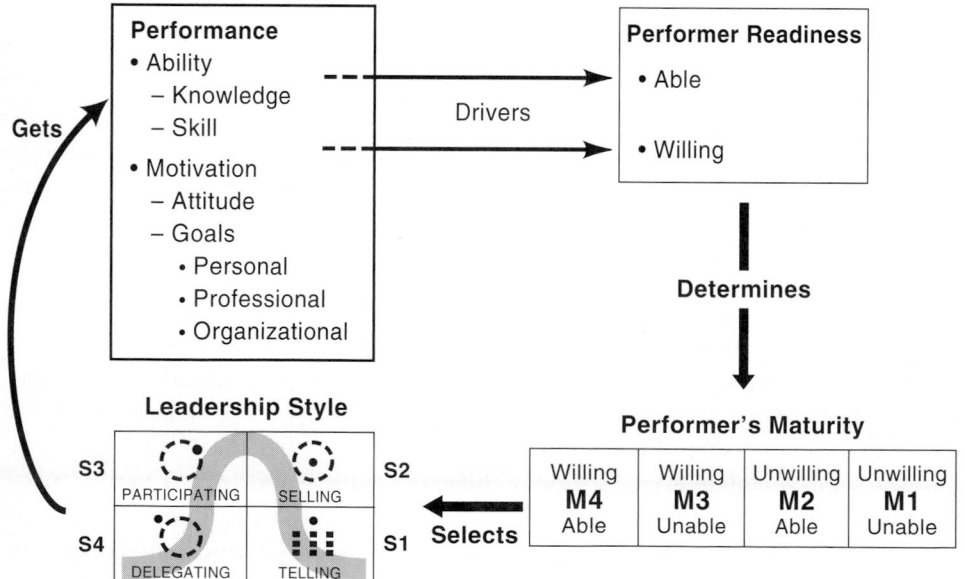

FIGURE 29–9
How Situational Leadership Works

Figure 29–10 shows selection of an appropriate style, chosen according to the maturity of the team.

After a team is selected and the team building activities have occurred, the PM's job is not over. The team must continue to be motivated both as a team and as individuals, as shown in Figure 29–11. When the performer's maturity is high (willing and able) and the team's maturity is high (performing), delegating is appropriate. As with Figure 29–7, the project would be far better off if forming (requiring a telling management style), storming (requiring a selling management style), and norming (requiring a participating management style) were crunched up toward the left end of the x-axis.

Methods of Group Decision Making

Project managers and their teams may draw on a variety of approaches when making decisions. With the autocratic or directive style of problem solving, the leader defines the problem, diagnoses the problem, and generates, evaluates, and chooses among alternative solutions. The autocratic style may allow group information input where the leader defines the problem and then invites the group to be an information source in obtaining data to determine cause. Using his list of potential solutions, the leader may once again obtain data from the group in evaluation of these alternatives and make a choice among them.

A step in further involving the group is autocratic with group's review and feedback, where the leader defines the problem, diagnoses its causes, and selects a solution. The leader then presents his plan to the group for understanding, review, and feedback.

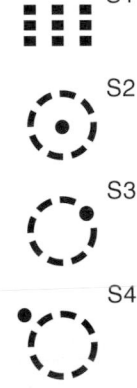

Forming
– Members are polite, guarded, businesslike
– Lead with <u>directive behavior</u>

Storming
– Members are confrontational and struggle for control
– Lead with <u>highly directive and supportive behavior</u>

Norming
– Members confront issues and become team-oriented
– Lead with <u>high support and low direction</u>

Performing
– Members display open and productive effort, trust, flexibility, mature cohesiveness; are self-directed
– Lead with <u>low direction and support</u>; coach and support as needed

FIGURE 29–10
How to Lead During Team Stages
Source: Vijay K. Verma (1996). *Managing the Project Team: the Human Aspects of Project Management*. Upper Darby, PA: Project Management Institute.

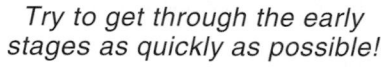

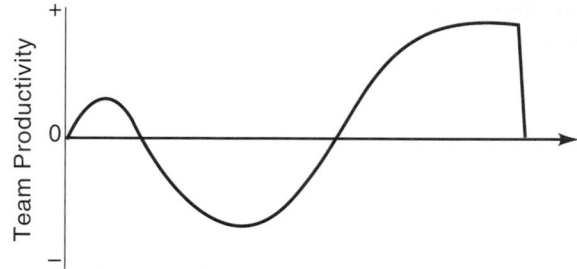

FIGURE 29–11
Team Dynamics, Stages, and Styles

With the individual consultative style, the leader defines the problem and shares this defini-tion with individual members of the work group. The leader solicits ideas regarding problem causes and potential solutions. The leader may also use these individuals' expertise in evalua-tion of alternative solutions. Once this information is obtained, the leader makes the choice of which alternative solution to implement.

The group consultative style adds to the individual consultative style in that the leader shares his definition of the problem with the group as a whole. The PM may use the group decision style by sharing his definition of the problem with the work group. The group them proceeds to diagnose the causes of the problem. Following diagnosis, the group generates, evaluates, and chooses among solutions.

With the participative style, the group as a whole proceeds through the entire decision making process. The group defines the problem and performs all other functions as a group. The role of the leader is that of process facilitator.

The most autonomous arrangement for the team is the leaderless team, where the group has no formal leader but rather is assembled as a leaderless team. If no substitute for task leadership or process leadership is present, a process leader often emerges. This person may change from problem to problem. The group generates its own problem definition, performs its own diagnosis, generates alternatives, and chooses among alternatives.[18]

Group Problem Solving

Groups solve problems in fairly standard ways, whether including the PM, as with the partici-pative style, or without a PM, as in the leaderless team style.

Strategy or planning meetings are to determine the future direction of the organization or unit. Generally the issues of the appropriateness of the mission and current strategies for achieving it are discussed—the current direction of the organization is assessed. If it is discovered that changes in the environment render the current mission or strategy inappropriate, a new strategic plan is developed.

When a specific problem emerges, usually manifesting itself in the form of some type of response from a dissatisfied stakeholder, a problem solving meeting is held. These meetings take one of two general forms:

1. Solve the immediate problem. The focus of this type of meeting is to determine how to satisfy the immediate concerns of the dissatisfied stakeholder. For example, if a specific customer has received a version of software with serious defects, the issue might be, how do we fix the software without introducing any new problems and get another version to the customer quickly?

2. Solve the long-range problem. The focus of this type of meeting is to reduce the likelihood of a given type of problem surfacing in the future by diagnosing the cause(s) of this recurring problem and developing a solution consistent with these causes that solves the problem. The problem might be defined as, how do we conduct more effective reviews, better categorize defects, create more meaningful reports with better Pareto charts, and get the reports to the right individuals?

Make operational decisions such as staffing, purchase, or work method decisions. The issue here is the establishment of a set of criteria (derived from the goal of the decision) by which to evaluate alternatives.

Evaluation meetings are held to evaluate a new process, structural modification, new program, and so on. Once again, the important issue is to establish a set of evaluative criteria based on the goals of the new program or process.

Why group decision making? To integrate the team, especially if it consists of subgroups of specialized, functional expertise. Arguably, groups produce superior decisions. As group membership increases, there is a likelihood that more stakeholders will be represented, and their interests can be incorporated into the criteria used in the decision process. By including individuals with specialized expertise, we tend to increase the likelihood that more accurate cause/effect assumptions (theory) will be used in the decision making process. Groups tend to develop a greater number of potential options and more creative options. Individuals contributing to a decision tend to feel greater ownership to the decision, especially when their identities are tied to it. Resistance to change and motivation to ensure that the decision is implemented properly can be increased through participation.

The first step for the software PM is to define his style, which may change as appropriate for the occasion. It can range from completely autocratic to full participation. If the leader opts for some form of group problem solving, it is important that one individual be assigned as the process leader or facilitator. This individual has the responsibility of guiding the group through the problem solving process. The leader should decide whether he wants to take an advocacy role for a particular solution. If so, he should have someone else facilitate the problem solving process. The leader must decide whether he has the skills to facilitate the process. If not, once again, someone else should take on this role. Sometimes a process leader (facilitator) emerges as the process progresses. It is important for the leader to turn over the process reigns explicitly (if it is his wish to do so) rather than leave group members confused as to who is in charge of the process.

When groups make decisions, members of the group attempt to arrive at a decision that is satisfactory to each group member—that is, one that satisfies their individual interests. There is no need or expectation of a common group goal or focus. The only issue is that the decision satisfies the interest of the members acting as individuals or representatives of stakeholder groups. However, when teams make decisions, there is an overriding group goal independent of the goals and interests of the individual members. When the team operates effectively, each member focuses on the unifying team goals, placing individual interests subservient to the group goal.

What motivates an individual to adopt "group goals"? The individual has internalized the group goals as his own (goal identification). The individual sees some extrinsic personal gain when the group is successful (group goal-based bonus, gain sharing plan, etc.). The individual social identity is tied to the group; when the group is viewed as successful, the individual believes that he is viewed as successful by his reference group (external self-concept). The individual believes that members of his reference group will attribute group success to his competencies. The individual sees group success as a reinforcement or validation of his internally held self-perception of competencies. Therefore, when the group is successful, this success is validation of the individual competencies. This requires that the individual perceive that the role that he performs has significant impact on group success. (This is the fundamental logic behind job enrichment and participative management.)

Keep Team Members Satisfied—Avoiding Turnover

Individuals have great impact on other individuals, on groups of workers, on the organization as a whole, and on the environment. Project managers who are concerned with keeping their staff motivated, satisfied, and committed will find that morale for supervisors and staff improves as well, there are fewer accidents, efficiency and effectiveness are increased, absenteeism and tardiness are decreased, turnover is lower, employees become more promotable and trainable, conflict is reduced, and the negative effects of turnover are reduced.

Turnover is expensive, increasing costs with separation costs, exit interviews, administrative activities, and separation pay. Turnover also involves replacement costs such as advertising, recruiting and interviewing, training, and orientation. There is loss of productivity of the worker just before leaving, and usually loss of the productivity of other team members as well. Often the morale of the entire team is lowered when a person leaves—the perception may be that something is wrong with the organization itself. Other team members begin to wonder if they should be looking for jobs as well.

The effective PM knows the value of motivating the team to be willing to work hard and to be committed to the goals through satisfaction. Job satisfaction is understood in terms of the relationship between the worker and his work environment—satisfaction residing in the interaction. Some aspects of the worker affect his perception of the job, such as the worker's values, expectations, and needs, and other aspects identify actual working conditions and how these conditions meet the worker's values, expectations, and needs.

> A job is not an entity, but an abstraction referring to a combination of tasks performed by an individual in a certain physical and social context for financial (and other) remuneration. Because a job is not perceived or experienced as such, it cannot initially be evaluated as a single unit. Overall job satisfaction is the sum of the evaluations of the discriminable elements of which the job is composed....
>
> Job satisfaction is the pleasurable emotional state resulting from the appraisal of one's job as achieving or facilitating the achievement of one's job values. Job dissatisfaction is the unpleasurable emotional state resulting from the appraisal of one's job as frustrating or blocking the attainment of one's job values or as entailing disvalues. Job satisfaction and dissatisfaction are a function of the perceived relationship between what one wants from one's job and what one perceives it as offering or entailing.
>
> —Edwin Locke (1969). "What is Job Satisfaction?"

A value is something that a person actually seeks to gain or keep, or that he considers beneficial. A value presupposes awareness, at some level, of the object or condition sought. (This is in contrast to a need, which may not be known.) Values contain content, pertaining to what the person wants to gain, and intensity, pertaining to how much the person wants to gain or keep it.

Frequently mentioned satisfiers or motivators include the customer, team members, variety in the work, flexibility and autonomy in getting the job done, problem solving, learning, and a sense of accomplishment.

Typical stressors include customers, heavy workloads, tight schedules, demanding supervisors and management, lack of positive feedback, dissatisfied coworkers, lack of information, lack of training, poorly functioning technology and equipment, physical facilities, bureaucratic procedures and red tape, unchallenging work, failure and uncertainty, change, lack of budget and resources, feelings of inadequacy, lack of positive feedback, fragmentation, poor communication, and having no input into decisions.

As managers and scholars attempt to explain why individuals within an organization often exhibit similar patterns of behavior, they have turned to the concepts of organizational structure and organizational culture. The term *organizational culture* is often used both as a description of existing patterns of behavior with an organization and as an explanation for these patterns of behavior.

The list of patterns of behavior influenced by culture is long. To name but a few: innovation versus stability (judging vs. perceiving), strategic versus operational focus—attention to detail (intuition vs. sensing), outcome versus process orientation (intuition vs. sensing), task versus social focus (concern for people, concern for relationships, concern for task accomplishment at all costs), team versus individual orientation (individual vs. collective decision making, individual vs. group rewards), customer focus versus cost control (service orientation), internal versus external orientation (adaptiveness and learning), source of motivation (instrumental orientation, status orientation, internal standard orientation, goal orientation), conformity versus individuality, "ad hockery" versus planning, centralized versus decentralized decision making, and cooperation versus competition.

Mechanisms that actually create consistent patterns of behavior include social norms, social identities, shared values, and mental models (shared assumptions/beliefs).

Cultures may be strong or weak. In strong cultures, core values are intensely held and widely shared. Culture will "happen" whether we want it to or not. There are many positive aspects of keeping culture alive—it defines roles and provides identity, generates commitment to something larger than one's self-interest, and controls by reducing formalization and increasing shared meaning. The liabilities may be that strong cultures can become barriers to change and diversity. Cultures are self-sustaining, often reinforced through stories, myths, rituals, symbols, and symbolic actions.

What else can a software project manager do to improve communications with team members and to find out their needs, desires, motivators, and dissatisfiers? Keep a long list of potential motivators handy—perhaps a "plateaued" employee would appreciate attending conferences and workshops, participation in professional organizations, cross-training, job rotation, more participation in decision making, or the opportunity to serve as a mentor (or have one).

Watch out for these danger signs: low, inappropriate skills, low need for growth (not valuing advancement), lack of intrinsic motivation, lack of extrinsic reward, stress and burnout, slow organizational growth, and slow economic growth. Provide stress-management training and encourage professional networking. Build job commitment: Hire people whose goals match those of the organization and people who place a high value on work in general. Orient employees to realistic job expectations. Be aware of each member's career goals and aspirations. Provide interesting tasks early in the tenure of the employee. Provide opportunities for job satisfaction—achievement, autonomy, recognition, interesting tasks.

Provide unlimited opportunity for communication and feedback: Make sure that jobs are clear, make sure that people know their jobs are important, use performance review as a coaching and training tool, set difficult and challenging goals, respond to problems in a timely manner, talk with employees and listen, be fair and objective, be open to new ideas, provide constructive and timely feedback, give enough time for employees to perform their required work, and promote trust.

Create a pleasant work environment: Provide tasks that have variety and that are interesting and challenging, provide opportunities for social bonds, hire pleasant coworkers, provide opportunities for positive feedback from customers, promote trust in coworkers, give respect to departments and work groups, and have a clean, healthy, and safe work environment.

Involve staff in the decision-making processes and recognize good work with titles, promotions, desks, offices, and support staff. Provide the necessary resources. Provide job security. Provide promotional opportunities. Have a good performance review and evaluation program, and provide coaching as a performance tool.

Promote confidence that the administration will solve problems, provide for fair pay and benefits, show no favoritism, promote new ideas, remain loyal to workers, provide channels for staff development, and provide access to information.

If the project manager and the organization do their best to achieve these goals, employees will respond by believing that they are responsible for the outcome of their work, believe that their work is meaningful, remain loyal to the organization, use their capabilities, and feel a sense of importance to the organization.

A key phrase to remember is, "Motivate through rewards and recognition." When management takes action to promote or reinforce desired behavior, clearly link performance and reward, make them both specific to the project, and consider cultural difference, they are following the number one rule of management: You get the behavior you reward![19]

Behavioral Theory and Motivation_____

When someone says, "It's not the money, it's the principle," it's the money! Well, maybe, maybe not. Behavioral theories differ in what motivates us humans, whether as individuals or as teams, at work or at play.

Theories X and Y

In his 1960 work, *The Human Side of Enterprise,* Douglas McGregor suggested various management styles, based on the manager's goals, how they deal with subordinates, and notions of human behavior. Now commonly referred to as the "carrot and the stick," the theories are a bit dated (Table 29–2) but still are important to the foundation concepts of modern organizational psychology. He called the two theories X and Y.

Theory X is a control strategy or control-oriented approach. The goal of control human resource systems is to reduce direct labor costs or improve efficiency by enforcing employee compliance with specified rules and procedures and basing employee rewards on some

TABLE 29–2
Past Versus Present Ideas on Work

	Past (Traditional)	Present (for the Future)
Principle	(McGregor's X theory) Work is a burden that people will avoid unless driven by some external need. They also do not like responsibility.	(McGregor's Y theory) People like work; it is a form of self-fulfillment. People will take responsibility.
Manifestation	The setting of targets/budgets and subsequent monitoring of effort relative to those targets, the ready use of rewards/punishment to encourage effort and compensate for the pain of hard work. The vast majority of decisions and innovations come from senior management. Little thought is given to job satisfaction. Morale is not seen as a major contributor to productivity, cost-effectiveness, and profit.	The principal recognition is that the vast majority of us come to work intent on doing a good job—we want to take pride in our work. Furthermore, the creativity of every employee is recognized and there are established structures within the organization to capture everybody's ideas. Innovation and the development of opportunities are seen as an integral part of the long-term survival strategy of the company. These ideas come from the total intelligence of the employees of the firm. From this basis, the organization can develop a feeling of mutual trust and full commitment to the aims of the enterprise.
Losses vs. Gains	Morale is damaged in the long term. A jaundiced view of the supervised, and conversely the supervisors, becomes inbred until the limited perception of human capabilities becomes self-fulfilling. We upward-delegate our responsibility. We become risk-averse. Compliance rather than innovation is seen as a successful survival strategy. The responsibility for maintaining discipline is seen as an external function—inspection, audit, and so on, which adds to overhead cost. As soon as possible, employees start to look forward to retirement, with the subsequent decline in their commitment. Once retired, their knowledge, instead of contributing to the economy, becomes a drain on our resources.	Greatly improved morale and, hence, productivity. The majorities are aligned to the aims and objectives of the organization. A good proportion of employees' thinking time is devoted to improving the work situation. A momentum for continual improvement can be established. Far less need for supervision; increased sense of responsibility; the development of self-discipline; the recognition and nurturing of pride. Far less pressure on the "boss."

measurable output criteria. Assumptions are that people are lazy; follow the path of least resistance; inherently dislike work; are motivated by money, position and punishment; must be coerced or controlled to do work to achieve objectives; and prefer to be directed.

Theory Y is a commitment strategy. Commitment human resource systems shape desired employee behaviors and attitudes by forging psychological links between organizational and employee goals. In other words, the focus is on developing committed employees who can be trusted to use their discretion to carry out job tasks in ways that are consistent with organizational goals. It implies a humanistic and supportive approach to managing people. Assumptions are that people view work as being as natural as play and rest; will exercise self-direction and self-control toward achieving objectives to which they are committed; meet high performance expectations if motivated; are creative, imaginative, and ambitious; are self-disciplined and desire responsibilities; and are motivated by Maslow's higher levels of needs.[20]

Theory Z

In 1978, William G. Ouchi published a seminal work on a radical new approach to management. For decades, managers subscribed to either Theory X or Theory Y, often with little in between. Theory Z became the secret to motivation and productivity in Japan, as a special way of treating people with trust, confidence, and commitment to workers on the part of management. Theory Z reflects the central assumptions of the human resources frame: that individuals want their productive time to be a rewarding experience, that they want to contribute to the success of whatever enterprise they may be associated with, and that if the structure is engineered appropriately, they will be able to achieve those goals. Theory Z suggests that humanized working conditions not only increase productivity and profits to the company, but also enhance self-esteem for employees. Cultural values that characterize Japanese organizations are lifetime employment, slow promotions and infrequent evaluations, nonspecialized career paths, and collective decision making and responsibility. Theory Z became a keystone in the Japanese philosophy, as Japan led the world to higher quality in the 1970s and 1980s.[21]

Project Manager Behavior That Motivates_____

Leadership, a complicated and expansive subject, has dozens (or hundreds) of books devoted to its rules, laws, and principles. There is no single set of principles or behaviors of leadership—the most effective leadership style in a given situation is a function of the task, the organization's culture, the leader's team, and the leader's own attributes.

Management is largely about:

- **Decision making**—Creating a vision, developing and deciding among competing strategies, operational planning and resource allocation

- **Coaching/development**—Developing the skills and competencies of the members of the group
- **Influence**—Motivating extra role behavior of group members, directing behavior of group members, eliciting behaviors consistent with group's mission and strategy, eliciting behavior outside the preference zone of the group members

Management effectiveness is measured in terms of how effectively the group accomplishes its goals. Leadership homes in on the influence function of management. Leadership effectiveness is measured in terms of how successful the leader is in motivating behavior:

What motivational approaches are available?

What does a leader actually do to align mission, inspire, and so on?

What basis of influence can a leader use?

Leaders can tap into all five sources of motivation: intrinsic, instrumental, external self-concept, internal self-concept, and goal identification.

Force-Field Analysis

Kurt Lewin (1890–1947), a German psychologist and pioneer in the field of social science, wrote about forces affecting a desired organizational change in a manner that is still relevant today.

Force-field analysis is a management technique for diagnosing situations. It may be useful when looking at the variables involved in determining effectiveness of planning and implementing a change management program and is of use in team building efforts.

Lewin assumes that in any situation, there are both driving and restraining forces that influence any change that may occur. Driving forces are those forces affecting a situation that are pushing in a particular direction; they tend to initiate a change and keep it going. In terms of improving productivity in a work group, pressure from a supervisor, incentive earnings, and competition may be examples of driving forces. Restraining forces are forces acting to restrain or decrease the driving forces. Apathy, hostility, and poor maintenance of equipment may be examples of restraining forces against increased production. Equilibrium is reached when the sum of the driving forces equals the sum of the restraining forces.

The force-field analytic problem solving model has been widely used as technique for encouraging groups of people to tackle organizational issues that previously seemed too complex or too deeply rooted to approach. Community groups, governmental agencies, business teams, and many other organizations have successfully applied the model to their problems.

Many work groups do not have a systematic strategy for solving problems, so a simple model such as this one can provide a fresh and innovative approach to a perennial problem. The Lewin model operates as follows:

In any problem situation, the existing condition (status quo) has been reached because of a number of opposing forces. Some of these forces (drivers) push toward a solution to the problem. Other forces (restrainers) inhibit improvement or solution of the problem. When the strength of the drivers is approximately equal to the strength of the restrainers, a balance or status quo is apparent, as shown in Figure 29–12. Until the relative strength of the forces is changed, the problem will continue to persist. To apply the model to any problem, follow these steps:

Step 1: Carefully and fully specify the problem (status quo). A problem may be defined as the difference between what currently exists and what should be.

Step 2: Define your objectives. What will the situation be like when it is solved?

Step 3: Brainstorm (without initial analysis) the driving forces and the restraining forces that contribute to the problem.

Step 4: Analyze these forces more fully. Develop a strategy for strengthening the driving forces under your control and weakening the restraining forces that you can realistically do something about.

Step 5: Consider your strategy against your objectives. Will your problem solving strategy promote a change in the status quo?[22]

Change is characterized as a state of imbalance between driving forces (e.g., new personnel, changing markets, new technology) and restraining forces (e.g., individuals' fear of failure, organizational inertia). To achieve change toward a goal or vision, three steps are required.

First, an organization has to unfreeze the driving and restraining forces that hold it in a state of quasi-equilibrium. Second, an imbalance is introduced to the forces to enable the change to take place. This can be achieved by increasing the drivers, reducing the restraints, or both. Third, once the change is complete, the forces are brought back into quasi-equilibrium and are refrozen.

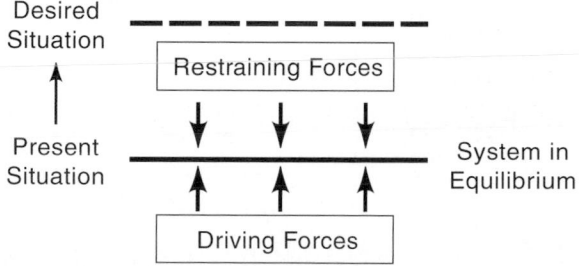

FIGURE 29–12
Lewin's Force-Field Analysis

All change is disruptive. But, if done well, it leads to better results (see Figure 29–13).

Team/organizational change begins with individual attitude adjustment and progresses through to knowledge. The stages of organizational change are shown in Figure 29–14:

1. **Awareness**—People are familiar with the terms that represent an initiative or new process and have a perception of the accompanying issue.
2. **Questioning/understanding**—People have an understanding of what the change or initiative is and appreciate its implications and importance to their organization.
3. **Acceptance**—People have the knowledge needed to be intellectually prepared and understand how the initiative affects their job or functional organization and how they can contribute to the success/failure.
4. **Ownership**—People are personally committed to making the initiative successful in their department and at their job.

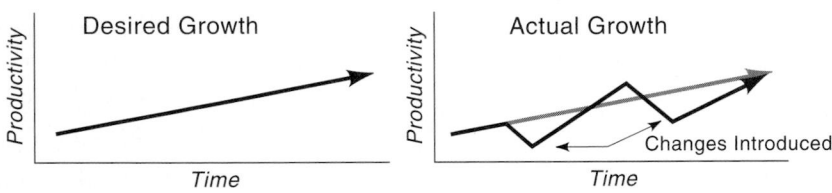

FIGURE 29–13
Implementation of Change

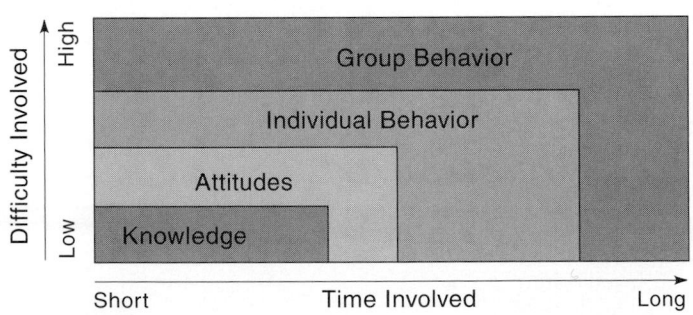

FIGURE 29–14
Four Levels of Change

Communication with Help from Understanding of Personality Types

True communication can be greatly improved when the sender/receiver and encoder/decoder have an understanding of how the other "thinks" based on personality type or certain preferences. About 150 different personality models have been defined since Carl Jung's theory of "psychological types" appeared in the 1930s. A popular model is the Myers-Briggs Type Indicator (MBTI), as discussed in Chapter 6. Because it is so helpful in the area of communication, we'll offer a quick review of MBTI here.

MBTI is based upon the empirical work of Kathryn Briggs and Isabel Myers Briggs. It measures preference, not intelligence, ability, or "deep personality." Preference is like being left- or right-handed—there is no "right or wrong."[23]

MBTI measures four scales or dimensions, as shown in Figure 29–15.

The MBTI extrovert (E)/introvert (I) dimension describes the source and direction of one's energy.

For those preferring extroversion (E), energy comes from the external world of people, activities, or things. E's "plug into" the energy of others and represent 50% of the U.S. population.

For those preferring introversion (I), energy comes from the internal world of ideas, emotions, or impressions. I's are drained of energy by being around others and represent about 50% of the U.S. population.

A few terms describing an extrovert include: external, outside thrust, blurt it out, breadth, involved with people and things, interaction, action, and do-think-do. Some terms that are

Scale	Refers to	Key Activity
• Extroversion/ Introversion	• How a person is energized	• Energizing
• Sensing/iNtuition	• What a person pays attention to	• Attending
• Thinking/Feeling	• How a person decides	• Deciding
• Judging/Perceiving	• Lifestyle a person adopts	• Living

FIGURE 29–15
The Four Scales Measured by MBTI
Source: Richard Grant (2000). The University of Texas at Austin, Software Quality Institute Certificate Program. Sequence XI, Session 3.

associated with an introvert include: internal, inside pull, keep it in, depth, work with ideas and thoughts, concentration, reflection, and think-do-think.

Introversion/extroversion relates to people's styles in interacting and engaging in conversation. Extroverts "think out loud." They want to be included in all communications, to talk through issues, and to develop their thoughts through interaction with others. Their style is speak, listen, speak, speak, listen, speak, speak—then perhaps reflect. In contrast, introverts prefer written communication so that they can think through issues before commenting on them. In verbal communication, they reflect on what's being said and then wait for an opening to speak. The introvert's style is listen, reflect, listen, reflect, reflect, reflect—then perhaps speak.

A message for the PM is to provide both written communication before face-to-face conversations and also opportunities for face-to-face discussion, questions, and expression of opinions and ideas.

The MBTI sensing (S)/intuition (N) dimension describes a method of information reception. This is an important scale in the realm of communication.

S's believe mainly in information received directly from the external or real world, with the input of primary senses, and notice what is actual. This group represents about 68% of U.S. population.

N's believe mainly in information received from the internal or imaginative world, grab onto the "connections" between things and ideas, use their "sixth sense," and notice what might be. They comprise 32% of the U.S. population.

Terms describing S's include: the five senses, what is real, practical, present orientation, facts, using established skills, utility, and step-by-step. Terms describing N's include: sixth sense, hunches, what could be, theoretical, future possibilities, insights, learning new skills, novelty, and leap around.

Sensing/intuition influences the kinds of information that people focus on when speaking, listening, or writing. Sensing types want to focus on specific details, the "real" who, what, where, when, and why. They need and give relevant information and examples. In contrast, intuitive thinkers want to move communication to a bigger context, to connections and wider meanings. They are great brainstormers and are able to offer different perspectives.

The MBTI thinking (T)/feeling (F) dimension is a way of information processing. T's make decisions according to their intelligence and thoughts, and decide in a logical, objective way. They must disconnect to be objective. About 60% of U.S. males and 40% of U.S. females are T's.

F's make decisions according to feelings of harmony or "everybody's prosperity" and decide in a personal, value-oriented way. They must connect to be related. About 40% of U.S. males and 60% of U.S. females are F's.

Terms describing T's include: head, logical system, objective, justice, critique, principles, reason, and firm but fair. Terms describing F's include: heart, value system, subjective, mercy, compliment, harmony, empathy, and compassionate.

Thinking/feeling relates most directly to the individual's decision to participate or to tune out. Thinkers appreciate logical structure and clarity in communication and want it to focus on the work. They disengage when too much time is spent on things they view as irrelevant, such as personal emotions. "Rambling" can drive them to distraction. Feelers, on the other hand, *want* communications to have a personal edge. F's will tune out when there is no connection to people or if there is interpersonal tension.

A message to the PM is to engage everyone in communication; both task and people focuses are important.

The MBTI judging (J)/perceiving (P) dimension is a way of realizing and living with processed information.

J's organize all life events and act strictly according to their plans. They focus on goals, planning, strategy, and control, and they prefer to live a planned and organized life. Fifty-eight percent of the U.S. population are J's.

P's are inclined to improvisation and seek different alternatives. They focus on adapting, positioning, and troubleshooting, and they prefer to live a spontaneous and flexible life. P's represent 42% of the U.S. population.

Terms describing J's include: planful, regulate, control, settled, run one's life, set goals, decisive, and organized. Terms describing P's include: spontaneous, flow, adapt, tentative, let life happen, gather information, open, and flexible.

Judging/perceiving impacts the structure and style of communications. J's want written and verbal communication to be goal-oriented and to the point: Introduce the topic, finish it, and then move on to the next point. P's are likely to veer off into interesting digressions, suggest additional information that would be helpful, and leave the topic open.

PMs should be careful about leaving the P's out of the loop. Most organizational cultures support the J-style of email, memo, and meeting communication. It's okay to keep agendas tight and memos short and sweet, but an invitation to P's, perhaps through a "Comments" section on written correspondence and surveys, will retain their valuable contributions. A problem solving model using types is shown in Figure 29–16.

As Kummerow, Barger, and Kirby point out, we can't *not* communicate. The question is not whether we do it, but how effectively we do it.[24]

Keirsey Temperament Sorter

The Keirsey Temperament Sorter is a variant of the MBTI. It measures temperament based on MBTI types, and, therefore, is also based loosely on Jung. It is based on observable, extroverted patterns or clusters of behavior; it describes differences in people noticed and documented throughout history by the Greeks and other cultures; and it has 4 variations, not 16, so it may be easier to grasp and remember.[25]

Keirsey grouped the types for interpretation based on dimensions of communication, goal implementation, primary skill, and self-image: sensing/judging (SJ) guardians; sensing/perceiving (SP) artisans; intuitive/feelers (NF) idealists; and intuitive/thinkers (NT) rationals.

He found the guardian SJ types to be supervisors (ESTJ), inspectors (ISTJ), providers (ESFJ), and protectors (ISFJ). They are concrete in communicating, are cooperative in implementing goals, and can become highly skilled in logistics. Guardians base their self-image on reliability, service, and respectability.

Keirsey found artisan SP types to be promoters (ESTP), crafters (ISTP), performers (ESFP), and composers (ISFP). They are concrete in communicating, are utilitarian in implementing goals, and can become highly skilled in tactical variation. Artisans base their self-image on graceful action, bold spirit, and adaptability to circumstance.

Idealist NF types are often teachers (ENFJ), counselors (INFJ), champions (ENFP), and healers (INFP). They are abstract in communicating, are cooperative in implementing goals, and can become highly skilled in diplomatic integration. Idealists base their self-image on empathy, benevolence, and authenticity.

Rational NT types make good field marshals (ENTJ), masterminds (INTJ), inventors (ENTP), and architects (INTP). They are abstract in communicating, are utilitarian in implementing goals, and can become highly skilled in strategic analysis. Rationals base their self-image on ingenuity, autonomy, and willpower.

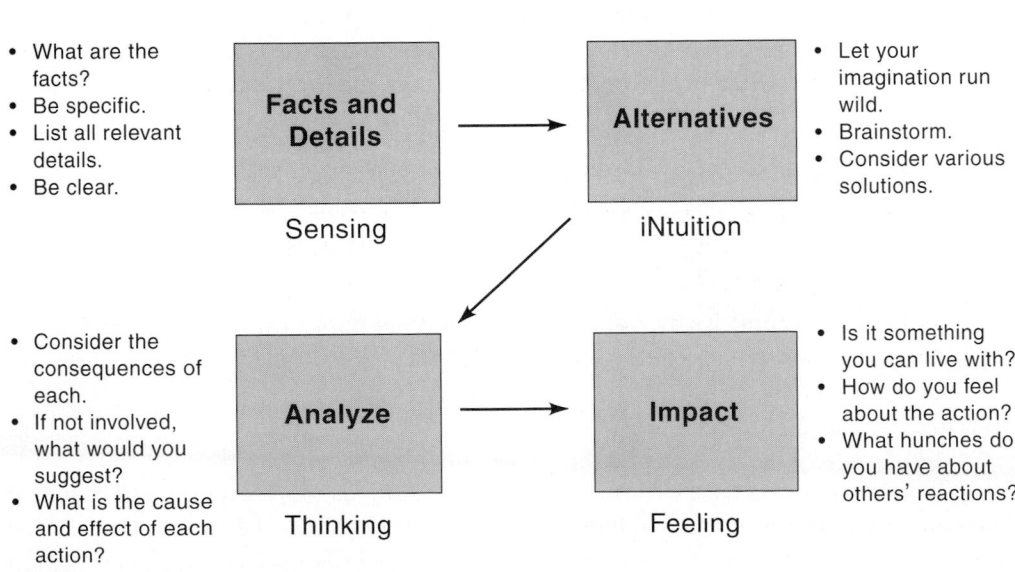

FIGURE 29–16
Problem Solving Model Using Type

Implications for engineering projects are that 60% of individuals in high-tech are Myers-Briggs ISTJ (introvert, sensing, thinking, judging). In Keirseyian terms, they are guardian inspectors who are reliable, respectable, and service-oriented.

When the Team Is Not Collocated

Some major differences exist between dispersed and collocated team members, including physical separation (virtual project team), control of the communication process, and methods for project communications.

A virtual project team may be described by geographical separation of team members, skewed working hours, temporary/matrix reporting structures, and multiorganizational teams.

While there are definite advantages from the software project manager's point of view (a richer talent pool, broader reach, 24 × 7 workforce, less expense), the team member's view may be quite different because he may experience isolation, a toolset mismatch, more freedom, and time flexibility. Each member may experience issues of dispersement, a low frequency of communication corresponding to the length of the distance apart, and infrastructure differences at each local organization.

Collocated teams do not have this difference in the manager's view versus the member's view, nor do they have the cultural variation or differences in infrastructure and communication control. A comparison of control levels is shown in Figure 29–17.

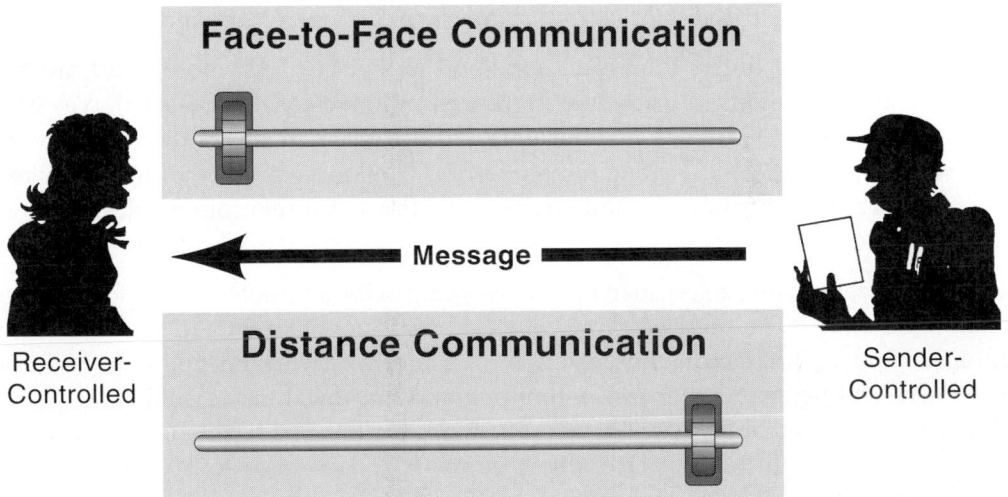

FIGURE 29–17
Comparison of Control Levels

Project communications may take the form of face-to-face meetings (regularly scheduled and special), electronic bulletin boards and newsgroups, Web pages, intranet folders, source control systems, document control systems, formal reports (word processor documents), pager calls, phone calls, voice mail, email, videoconferencing (desktop and studio), document conferencing (whiteboards, discussion groups, chats, teleconferencing, and voice over IP) in conference rooms, as well as desktop collaboration applications.

Communications may be "push" or "pull." Pushed information refers to the team member receiving an interrupt, such as face-to-face meetings, pager calls, phone calls, unprioritized email, and unprioritized voice mail. Pulled information refers to the team member actively seeking information from electronic bulletin boards, Web pages, intranets, source control systems, and document control systems.

Success with virtual teams may be improved by understanding basic communicating principles, applying those principles to available tools and media, learning how to do remote team building, and managing a remote team differently from a collocated team. Communications must be utilized appropriately, both synchronous and asynchronous. If on a telephone call, spatial context may be lost and need to be replaced—watch out for words such as *here*, *this*, *that*, and so on, as well as visual context such as body language, gestures, and references. And, when using audio, as in a telephone conversation, be sure to identify the speaker ("John speaking, and this is for Karen..."). Language differences, especially where translators are involved, require speaking slowly.

The remote team deserves to know responsibility for prioritization—push versus pull, urgent, important, and so on. Availability standards for their teammates should be published—project team Web pages with photos, personal information, best ways to be reached, expected availability, response time to expect for various channels of communication, and so on.

Remote team building differs from local team building in that a bit more effort must go into activities such as building a team identity (choosing a name is a good start), creating a shared vision (have a synchronous kick-off event), selecting team members for a good fit (not everyone works best remotely), creating remote rewards (tailor rewards to culture and likes/dislikes, and be careful with humor), and creating an infrastructure (ground rules, common tools, timetables, etc.).

There are issues for the project manager in working with a remote team. How do you know that the members are really working? How do you know that they're working on the right things? How do you handle time delays and transfers of work products? In addition, the remoteness will demand better task estimating and improved task visibility. The work must be partitioned equitably, a shared development process must be adopted, and mentoring and training must continue to take place, albeit remotely. Collaboration tools exist to support the virtual team—email, calendar, newsgroups, networking services, Netmeeting, videoconference centers, and other Web tools. The communications management plan (CMP), described later in this chapter, describes the flow of communication. The CMP may be a standalone document or part of the SPMP. A linear responsibility matrix, described in Chapter 6, "Selecting a Project Team," and Chapter 12, "Assigning Resources," describes roles of project personnel for the production of project artifacts. It, too, may be standalone or part of the SPMP.

The communications management plan template appears in Figure 29–32. It defines a distribution structure for information flow; ways for gathering and storing information; procedures for handling corrections and updates; format, content, and detail of information to be disseminated; and a process for producing each communication.

The CMP contains sources, sinks, and timing for standard project information such as the weekly/monthly status reports; the milestone achievement reports and issues; action items; risks; and requests for change to any project artifact. It lists the types of information to be managed, such as oral, paper, or electronic; specifications, reports, schedules, minutes, plans, and changes; and performance data such as costs, schedule, and quality. The CMP outlines reporting frequency—interval-based such as daily, weekly, or monthly, and event-based, such as milestone, stage, or phase.

Communicating in Meetings

Team members spend from 25% to 75% of their time in meetings. These are often not popular activities. ("If I didn't have to go to so many meetings, I could get my work done.") In extreme cases, they are considered a major time-waste. But we know that we have to have them because meetings are a necessary part of business and the business of communication.

Although we recognize meetings as a necessity, the PM doesn't need to feel obligated to attend all of them. A project manager's most productive time is spent working on tasks that are "important but not urgent," as shown in Figure 29–18.

For times when meetings are the right answer, we will discuss some ways to optimize this "necessary evil." Research on meetings indicates that whenever two or more people gather to "do business," there are only about five basic "products" they are after: information exchange, problem solving, decision making, planning, and evaluation.

Information exchange is just that—sharing with each other what you know. Problem solving is inventing ways to get from where we are to where we want to go. Decision making is deciding which of the invented ways will be tried first. Planning is a statement of who is going to do what to whom and when. Evaluation is determining how well the team carried out the plan, thereby generating new information for the group as the process recycles.

Meeting Roles

Meeting roles include the client or customer, the meeting manager, the participants, and perhaps a coach.

URGENCY

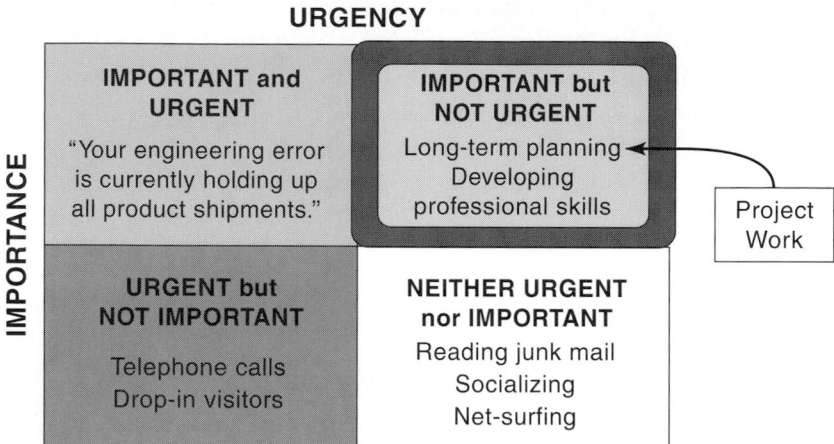

FIGURE 29–18
Time Management Matrix
Source: Stephen Covey (1989). *The 7 Habits of Highly Effective People.* New York, NY: Simon & Schuster.

The meeting client/customer is the one with "the issue," so he calls the meeting, supplies the data and background information, receives the group's input and manages the content, and takes responsibility for deciding or acting. This person is needed in meetings that address problem solving, decision making, and evaluating.

The meeting manager, or facilitator, is selected for "neutrality" and lack of vested interest in meeting content, but this is usually not the person with seniority or position power. He keeps the group "on track," manages the process, records the content of the meeting on a surface that all can see, summarizes a discussion, but stays out of the content of the meeting. The meeting manager has been likened to an air traffic controller, who regulates the pace of the meeting, observes the agenda, and keeps time commitments ("polices the use of air-time"). Such a person is needed in information sharing, problem solving, decision making, planning, and evaluation meetings and may be called upon to deal with emotions raised during a meeting.

If affordable, a scribe, separate from the meeting manager, can assist by assuming these duties: writing on a flip chart, whiteboard, or blackboard; organizing the information; keeping a history of group thoughts; remembering what is recorded; hanging flip-chart sheets and doing other helpful logistical tasks; taking care not to change meanings; recording all items, even unpopular ones; and writing a summary of the work.

Meeting participants are the people who have the expertise to offer suggestions, ideas, options, alternatives, insight, experience, and energy. They work for the meeting client and are the "resource people" of the meeting, selected for their potential contribution. They play an active, responsible role needed in information sharing, problem solving, decision making, planning, and evaluation meetings.

A coach is an optional meeting participant who takes notes of behaviors that made the meeting go well and offers suggestions of what might be done differently at the next meeting. He offers ongoing guidance during a meeting to help keep it going well, stays out of the content of the meeting, and offers alternate procedures if the meeting reaches an impasse. The coach, selected for neutrality and lack of vested interest in meeting content, works for the meeting manager. He is needed in problem solving and decision making meetings.

Meeting "Rules"

Every meeting must have an agenda, published before the meeting. The agenda will list time/place, participants/roles, prework, topics, time limits, proposed process (time-boxed, drill-down), and expected outcomes. Figures 29–19 through 29–21 show the progression of a sample meeting agenda from "poor" to "better," to "thorough."

Decision Making Meetings

We often speak of "decision making" as if there was a single process that we use for that activity. Actually, there are many ways that we "decide" issues or priorities. A few of those are commonly seen: discussion—focused or rambling; consensus—the sense of the group; compromise—give and take; questioning—exploration of the issue; argument—conflict on or off the issue; voting—and often, revoting; comparison; dictatorship; minority rule; majority rule; emotions—use or avoidance of; analysis—research and study; attrition—wearing down; filibustering—dominating air time; threats—coercion, guilt, intimidation; proposals to review; and challenging convention and tradition.

Topics:

    I.   Orientation Program

    II.   Q.W.L Report

    III.   Communication with Another Department

    IV.   Department Goals

    V.   Equipment Installation

    VI.   Flex-time Policy

FIGURE 29–19
A Sample Agenda (Poor)

MEETING LOCATION _____ CALLED BY _____

MEETING TIME _____

TOPICS	PROCEDURES/ PRODUCTS	TIME	CLIENT	MEETING MANAGER	RESOURCES NEEDED

FIGURE 29–20

A Sample Agenda (Better)

TOPICS	PROCEDURES/ PRODUCTS	TIME	CLIENT	MEETING MANAGER	RESOURCES NEEDED
I. Prioritize department goals from list developed by goals task force	Decision	15 minutes	V.P. of Accounting	Rep. from meeting manager cadre	Handout A— Departmental Goals
II. Q.W.L. team II recommendations on how to eliminate duplication of work on reports to executive management	Decision	20 minutes	Q.W.L. team leader	V.P. of Accounting	Handout B— minutes from last meeting
III. Installation of new personal computer equipment in Accounts Receivable by Office Services Dept.	Planning	30 minutes	Office Services rep. Computer rep. Mgr. of Accts. rep.	V.P. of Accounting	Handout C
IV. New employee orientation report from personnel	Information	5 minutes	V.P. of Accounting	Mgr. of _____	Handout D
V. New corporate flex-time policy	Information Problem solving	5 minutes 15 minutes	V.P. of Accounting	Mgr. of _____	
VI. How to keep Engineering Department informed and trained regarding all accounting policy changes	Problem solving Decision	30 minutes	V.P. of Accounting	Rep. from meeting manager cadre	

FIGURE 29–21

A Sample Agenda (Thorough)

Typical Meeting Outputs

It's easy to get a group of people together, brainstorm, and then walk away—and this is the necessary and creative part of developing software. But, for a formal meeting, there needs to be accountability.

Output from meetings are the minutes—discussions, decisions, and a checklist of agenda items—and the action items—who, when, and what for each action ("when" is sometimes postponed until the assignee can estimate the work). These outputs must be published to the common project space, typically a Web space or configuration management tool or a collaboration tool.

Personality Types and Communication in Meetings

When meetings recognize and support individual differences, they are more productive. To address the needs of both introverts and extroverts, these hints are helpful:

- Provide an agenda ahead of time.
- Give advance notice to anyone who will be asked to speak.
- Ask each attendee for input before leaving a topic.
- Allow time for extroverts to "think out loud," but don't allow them to dominate all of the air time.
- Allow opportunities for introverts to communicate their ideas—give them an opening.

To address the needs of both sensing and intuitive types, follow these tips:

- Give intuitives the overview (table of contents) at the beginning.
- Keep the meeting focused for the sensors, but allow intuitives a short, timed period to theorize.
- Allow time at the end of the meeting to clarify and identify the specific decisions made and steps that will be taken.

To address the needs of both thinking and feeling types, do the following:

- Designate a specific time for thinking concerns and another for feeling perspectives.
- Allow feeling types to take the risk of speaking out about supporting people.
- Curtail, or at least label, "T humor," which can be sarcastic and focused on one-upmanship, because this can be uncomfortable or offensive for F's.
- Recognize the contributions that F's make to team relationships, which keep it functioning.

  To address the needs of both judging and perceiving types, do this:

- Try to accommodate both J and P sense of timing—J's know when they've heard enough information; P's are good about knowing when too little information is present to make a decision.
- Try to keep the interactions from taking on a parent/teacher (J) to child/student (P) quality, residual patterns that don't belong in adult team situations.

Communicating via Negotiation _____

> Partnering is a business culture that fosters open communication and mutually beneficial relationships in a supportive environment built on trust. Partnering relationships stimulate competitive quality improvement and a reduction in the total-cost-of-ownership (life cycle cost).
>
> —Mike Oswald, Manager, Partnering Programs, Sematech

Negotiation skills are key skills for *any* manager. By definition, a PM manages a project through the actions of others. Negotiation is the key skill to accomplish this.

What Is Negotiation?

Negotiation is the process of getting two people from the point where they have a problem or conflict to the point where they have a solution or agreement. Figure 29–22 shows some basic approaches to negotiation.

Negotiation versus Bargaining

Bargaining is not negotiation because it is more about winning and losing than it is about finding an agreeable solution. Frankly, bargaining shouldn't be done in the workplace unless absolutely necessary. But, sometimes, it is ….

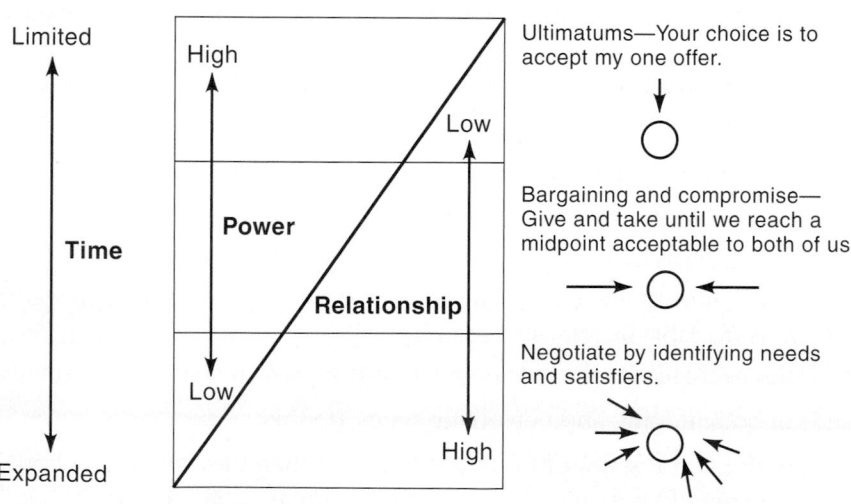

FIGURE 29–22
Basic Approaches to Negotiation

When is bargaining appropriate? Bargaining comes into play when competitiveness or suspicion pervade, ideologies/values conflict, use of power or threat is the norm, the relationship is short term or formal, haggling is expected or appropriate, or an impasse exists.

Basic principles of bargaining include: be prepared (soften up the other party); let the other party do the work; apply your power gently at first; make the other side compete; leave yourself room to bargain; listen, don't talk; keep contact with their hopes; let them get used to your big ideas; and maintain your integrity.

There are two basic stances in bargaining: dominance (when you've got power), where inferiority is generated in the other party and criticism is fierce, and subservience (when they've got power), where flattery and withdrawal are useful techniques.

Basic preparation for bargaining differs for buying and selling.

When buying, ask:

What is the maximum amount I am willing to pay?

What is the minimum amount I can offer and not be laughed out of the room?

When selling, ask:

What is the minimum amount I will accept?

What is the maximum amount I can ask for and not be laughed out of the room?

Negotiation Is a Process

Negotiation is the process in which two or more parties with both common and conflicting interests have a need or a mandate to reach an agreement that divides or allocates resources or resolves differences. It is a process of offer and counteroffer, of discussion and concession, through which the parties reach a point that both understand is the best (for them) that can be achieved.

Negotiating involves conferring with others to come to terms or reach an agreement. Principles of negotiation include: Separate personalities from issues, focus on shared interests, generate possible solutions reflecting common interests, and base results on project objectives and success criteria. Methods of negotiation are to plan, execute and agree, critique, and follow up.

Planning the Negotiation   Planning is the key to the negotiation process. Most professional negotiators consider it the single most important factor. Planning requires an investment of time in gathering information on issues and people and in thinking about how to use that information. It's really a lot of hard work.

The process involves two or more individuals or organizations with common interests/ needs and a need or mandate for settlement. The considerations are our needs and resources (our position) versus their needs and resources (their position).

A planning form, shown in Figure 29–23, is helpful in keeping the planning activities focused.

In addition to "their" needs and resources and "our" needs and resources, negotiation planners should answer the following questions:

- What are the issues to be negotiated? (List them all.)
- Who are the parties? Are they heterogeneous or homogeneous?
- What are the deadlines, and how flexible are they?
- What has been your experience with the other party in previous negotiations (strategies, tactics, style, needs)?
- What additional information would you like from the other party? (What questions would you like answers to?)
- Are we going to bargain or win-win negotiate?
- What criteria might we establish to arrive at a mutually wise decision?
- What is our best alternative to a negotiated agreement (BATNA)?
- What environmental concerns should we be aware of? (Place, time, physical arrangements of room and environmental issues, such as equipment and amenities needed, etc.)
- What "ground rules" or "principles" do we want to negotiate before we negotiate the issues?

Their Needs		Our Needs	
A	B	A	B
Their Satisfiers		Our Satisfiers	
10	10	10	10
9	9	9	9
8	8	8	8
7	7	7	7
6	6	6	6
5	5	5	5
4	4	4	4
3	3	3	3
2	2	2	2
1	1	1	1

FIGURE 29–23
Negotiation Planning Form

- How will we "open" the negotiations?
- What concerns or resistances is the other party liable to have, and how will we respond?
- How will we practice for the negotiation?

While planning, be aware of the types of negotiations:

Distributive (win-lose)—Traditional; one party's gain is another party's loss

Integrative (win-win)—Beneficial to both sides; mutually acceptable

Lose-lose—Both parties take an extreme position; no satisfactory agreement

Executing the Negotiation   Some basic principles and guidelines include these:

- Sit in some arrangement other than across from each other.
- Have some means for visibly recording data, positions, concessions, needs, resources, and "minutes."
- Be sure to negotiate the negotiation before negotiating the issues.
- Seek common ground and mutual understanding and agreement on easy issues first.
- Match the pace of concessions; do not let them get unbalanced.
- Do not attack "unfair tactics." Call time out and take a break; come back and describe the issues and renegotiate the negotiation.
- Don't ever just "walk out." Signal the possibility not as a threat, but as an appropriate option.
- Do not use the word *deadlines*. Talk about "time targets" or "time objectives." (*Deadline* is believed by your subconscious and theirs. It leads to bad deals.)
- No deal is better than a bad deal.
- Write the memorandum of agreement (or at least public notes to go into it) as the negotiation event progresses.
- Anything that is the product of a negotiation is negotiable. (It may even be worth the time and effort.)[26]

Win-Win Negotiation   Win/win negotiation is a mutual effort by both parties to use their resources to meet each other's needs. The "enemy" to be defeated is anything that would prevent both parties from getting their needs met.

Some principles of win-win negotiation include these:

Seek some principles on which to base the choice of the wisest option.

Be tough on the issues; be soft on people.

Negotiate the negotiation first. Compromise is *not* the goal; flexibility and synergy are required.

Be open to reason—yield to principles but not to pressure.

A critical strategy for win-win negotiation is shown in Figure 29–24.

Dr. Boehm, whom we have quoted so much in this book in terms of software project size, cost, and schedule estimating, as well as in terms of software risk analysis, has also published a win-win model that can be used when negotiating requirements with customers.[27] He has developed a three-step process:

1. Set win-win preconditions:
   Understand how people want to win.
   Establish reasonable expectations.
   Match people's tasks to their win conditions.
   Provide a supportive environment.
2. Structure a win-win project process:
   Establish a realistic process plan.
   Use the plan to control the project.
   Identify and manage your win-lose or lose-lose risks.
   Keep people involved.

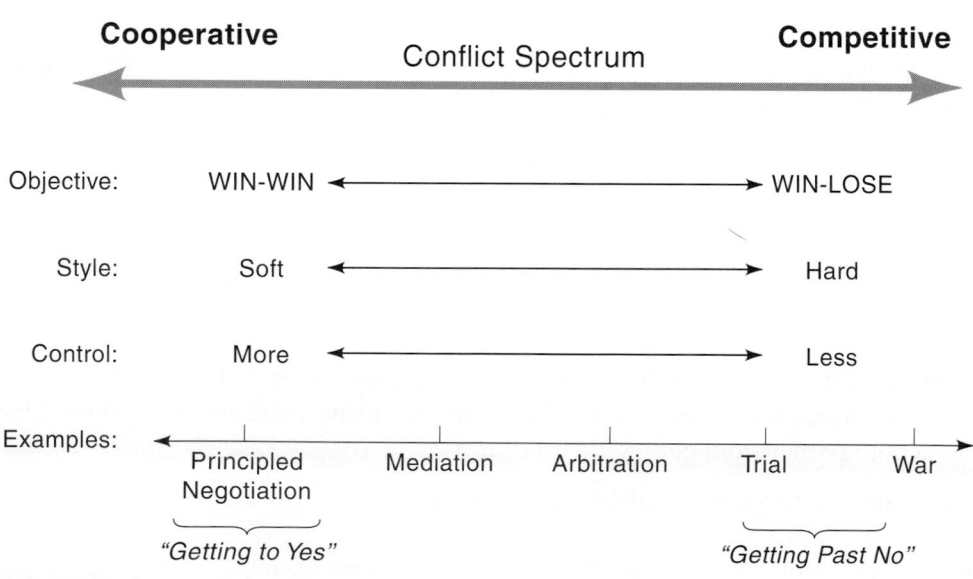

FIGURE 29–24
Negotiation Spectrum

3. Structure a win-win project product:
   Match product to users' and maintainers' win conditions.
   Iterate.

Boehm suggests a new management theory, following Theory X, Y, and Z, which he calls Theory W. He suggests that we understand how people want to win, identify the *key people* and talk to them, *project ourselves* into others' win situations, and get close to our customers. Figures 29–25 and 29–26 illustrate Boehm and his co-author Ross's Theory W as negotiation techniques formulated specifically for software projects.

Principled Negotiation: The Win-Win Approach in General

The generalized win-win negotiating approach is a four-step process:

1. Separate the *people* from the *problem.*

2. Focus on *interests*, not *positions.*

3. Invent options for mutual gain.

4. Insist on using objective criterion.[28]

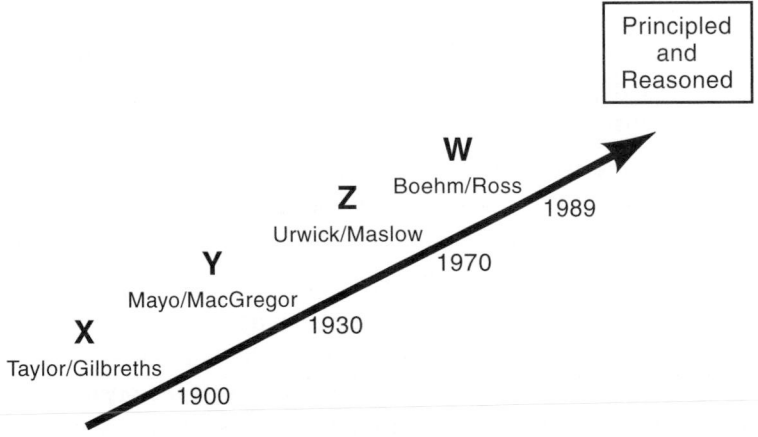

Boehm and Ross's View of Management Theory
(or "How We Got Where We Are Today")

Principled
and
Reasoned

W   Boehm/Ross
Z   1989
Urwick/Maslow
Y   1970
Mayo/MacGregor
X   1930
Taylor/Gilbreths
      1900

Cutthroat
and
Callous

FIGURE 29–25
Theory W (Win-Win)
Source: Adapted from Daniel Wren (1987). *The Evolution of Management Thought.*

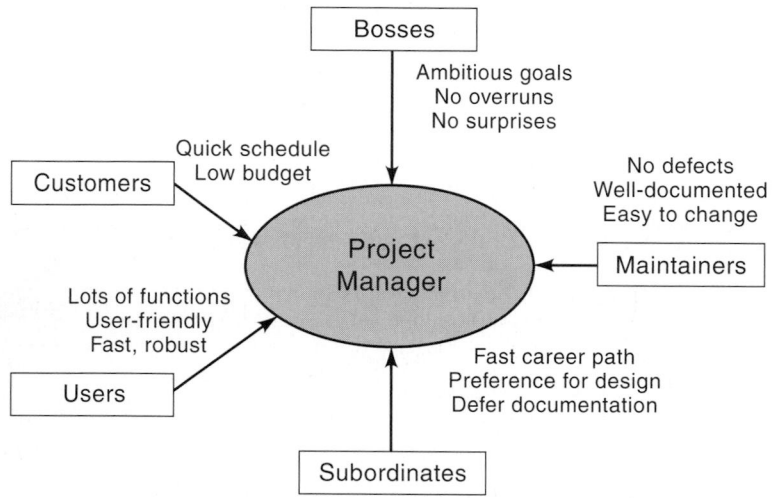

Make Everybody a Winner in the Project
– "Plan the flight and fly the plan."
– "Identify and manage the risks."

FIGURE 29–26
Theory "W-in"
Source: Boehm and Ross (1989). *Theory-W Software Project Management.*

Separating the people from the problem requires being *hard* on the *problem*, but *soft* on the *people*, building a working relationship, dealing with emotions, and, of course, communicating by talking to the other person, listening actively, speaking to be understood, speaking with a purpose, and limiting group size during negotiations.

Focusing on interests, not positions, requires understanding the position, something you have already decided upon, and the interest, what caused you to decide on a position, and then finding common ground. It's okay to start small (even tiny, if necessary!); remember that, often, more than one position can serve your interests.

You may be surprised to learn that you and the other person may have more shared interests than opposing ones. Interests are often unexpressed and intangible. To help identify them, ask "Why?" about each position, and look for the hopes, needs, and fears that the position serves; ask "Why not?" about the decision you want, and look for interests that stand in the way.

Inventing options may call upon the brainstorming techniques described in Chapter 16, "Eliciting Requirements." Remember to brainstorm not only within your own group but also with the other side. When inventing options, the invention comes first, the decision about which one to use comes later. Obstacles to an abundance of options include using premature judgment, searching for a single answer, assuming a "fixed" pie, and thinking that "solving the problem" is the other side's problem. Being open is the best approach, with the understanding that there is a slight risk in exposing your information, to gain understanding of the others' interests. Inviting experts from different areas to analyze proposals may broaden options as well as consideration of change of scope or strength of proposed agreements. Shared interests can lead to areas of mutual gain, and even differing interests can be dovetailed to be low in cost to you and high in benefit to others, or low in cost to others and high in benefit to you. In making the decision, make it easy, fair, legitimate, legal, honest, and honorable.

The use of objective criteria in decision making will help with the fairness. The other side may be asked to suggest standards for criteria, such as IEEE standards or ISO standards, using reason as to which ones are appropriate. Each issue should be framed as a joint search for objective criteria.

In his work *Getting Past No*, William Ury suggests that "competitive negotiation" can overcome the win-lose approach. He calls his techniques "go to the balcony," "step to their side," "reframe the problem," "build them a golden bridge," and "don't escalate—educate."[29]

"Going to the balcony" is an alternative to reacting by striking out, giving in, or breaking off. In fact, it is not reacting at all, at least not immediately. Going to the balcony means distancing yourself from your natural impulses and emotions. This requires some "unnatural" activities, such as pausing and saying nothing, to buy time to think. In thinking about an issue, one tactic is to "name the game," thereby breaking its spell. The "game" may be an attack, a stonewall (take it or leave it), or a trick (misleading figures, pretend lack of authority, or a last minute added-on demand). Once the game is named, it loses its power over you, allowing time to react rationally. Don't ever feel forced into making important decisions on the spot (especially if it's a contract to sign!). Buy time to think by pausing, taking notes, rephrasing and repeating, or simply calling time out.

"Step to their side" means to look at an issue from the other party's perspective. This can be done by listening actively, rephrasing, and repeating; withholding judgment; trying on the opponent's views; acknowledging the other side's point; acknowledging others' feelings; agreeing whenever you can; acknowledging others' authority and competence; building a working relationship; discussing each other's perceptions; creating a favorable climate; avoiding blaming others for your problem; and searching for common ground.

"Reframing the problem" means to change the game by treating the opponent like a partner; directing attention to identifying interests; inventing options; finding fair standards; asking problem solving questions such as why, why not, what if, and what makes that fair; and ignoring stonewalls and attacks.

"Building them a golden bridge" means to find a way for the other side to come to you by identifying obstacles to agreement, such as admittance that it's not their idea, unmet interests, fear of losing face, and too much too fast. It means to involve the other side in devising a solution by asking for and building on ideas, asking for constructive criticism, and offering choices.

"Don't escalate, educate" means avoiding the trap of spiraling emotions by exploring facts on points of contention, pointing out what may be lost if the best alternative to a negotiated agreement (BATNA) is used, and educating the other side on the process.

Negotiating and Culture

Culture is the distinctive and collective set of beliefs of people linked by a common cause, geographic location, religion, or ethnic values by which they lead their lives.

Elements of culture include material culture (tools and skills, language, aesthetics) art, literature, music, education, beliefs and attitudes, social organization, and political life.

Just as with communications in general, where we apply our personal filters to encoding and decoding messages, as PMs, we can't help but allow our own conditions to affect negotiations to some degree.

Conflict

Substantive conflict is defined as a breakdown in the decision-making process: An alternative cannot be chosen, and conflict manifests itself in a disagreement over an alternative (positions). However, conflict has its root causes in one of two types of disagreements: criteria, interests, and goals; or cause/effect beliefs, theories, and assumptions.

While substantive conflict over criteria, interest, and goals may be resolved when a decision is made, emotive conflict over beliefs, theories, and assumptions may still exist. Emotional conflict results in an affective orientation to the other party that is often stored long after the issues are resolved and forgotten. It manifests itself in we/they feelings, distrust, stereotyping, anger, information withholding and distortion, and a general desire to "beat" the other side on future issues. Obviously, the PM wants to take care to manage the emotional conflict as well as the substantive one.

Conflict Management

Conflict, like communication, is simply a fact of life in the workplace. While it can't be avoided, it can be managed. As software project managers invariably face conflict, they must be skilled at recognizing it and dealing with its many different forms. Negotiating skills come in quite handy for this. Communication also makes a huge difference in the amount and intensity of conflict. As Kummerow explains in *Work Types*, "Communication can cause conflict; it's a way to express conflict, and it's a way to resolve or to perpetuate and fuel it. Likewise, conflict can interfere with communication—short-circuit it, change its style, influence the way we listen, and limit what we hear."[30]

Conflict is made up of both the *issue* and the *relationship*. With conflict, as with communication and meetings, personality type preferences come into play. Obviously, thinking types are going to be more concerned with the issue and feeling types with the relationship. Extroverts want to talk about a problem right now; introverts like to think it over first.

Conflict management is the process by which the project manager uses appropriate managerial techniques to deal with inevitable disagreements—both technical and personal—that develop among those working toward project accomplishment. Traditional views of conflict are that it is caused by troublemakers and should be avoided. Contemporary views of conflict are that it is the natural result of change and can be managed. Table 29–3 lists common conflicts in project environments. Figures 29–27 and 29–28 show the best techniques for a PM to use: Withdrawal and smoothing never really resolve the issue; compromise and forcing will provide a resolution (and are sometimes the right choices), but at what price? Solving the problem is almost always the best solution.

TABLE 29–3
Conflict in Project Environments

Sources of Conflict	Definitions
Project Priorities	Views of project participants differ over sequence of activities and tasks.
Administrative Procedures	Managerial and administration-oriented conflicts over how the project will be managed.
Technical Opinions and Performance Trade-offs	Disagreements over technical issues, performance specifications, technical trade-offs.
Human Resource	Conflicts about staffing a project team with personnel from other areas.
Cost	Conflict over cost estimates from support areas regarding work breakdown structures.
Schedule	Disagreements about the timing, sequencing, and scheduling of project-related tasks.
Personality	Disagreements on interpersonal issues.

Source: Nicki S. Kirchof and John R. Adams (1982). "Conflict Management for Project Managers." *Principles of Project Management*. Upper Darby, PA: Project Management Institute. Sylva, NC: PMI Publication Division. p. 19.

Dealing with Conflict

Project Manager Selects the Most Appropriate Mode:

- Withdraw
  - Retreat from disagreements and conflict
- Smooth
  - De-emphasize differences and
    emphasize commonalities
  - Friendly

> **TEMPORARY ONLY,**
> **FAILS TO RESOLVE**

- Compromise
  - Find solutions that bring some degree of
    satisfaction to conflicting parties
  - Neither wins
- Force
  - Exerting one's view at the expense of
    another party
- Solve problem
  - Address disagreement directly
  - Most appropriate alternative selected

> **PROVIDES**
> **RESOLUTION**

FIGURE 29–27

Dealing with Conflict

Source: Nicki S. Kirchof and John R. Adams (1982). "Conflict Management for Project Managers." *Principles of Project Management*. Upper Darby, PA: Project Management Institute. Sylva, NC: PMI Publication Division. pp. 10–11.

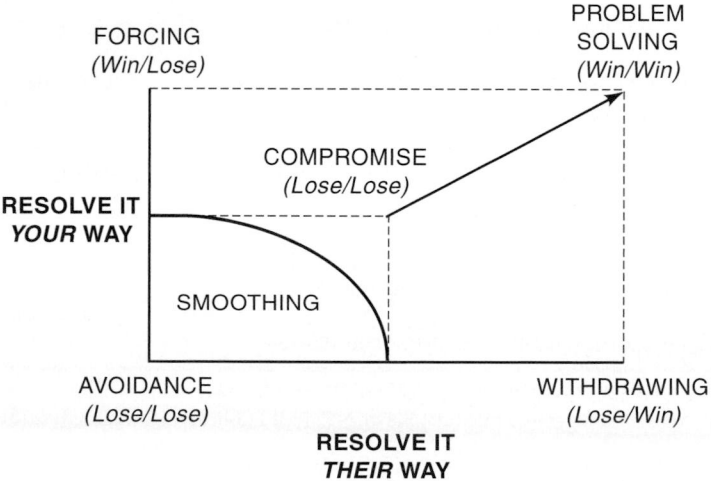

FIGURE 29–28

Possible Conflict Resolutions

Source: Nicki S. Kirchof and John R. Adams (1982). "Conflict Management for Project Managers." *Principles of Project Management*. Upper Darby, PA: Project Management Institute. Sylva, NC: PMI Publication Division. pp. 40–42.

Conflict Management Techniques for the Project Manager

The following are some conflict management principles that will serve as tools for the PM:

We will invest time and energy in creating win-win outcomes.

We will attack problems, not persons.

We commit ourselves to listening to the other party: hearing, understanding, appreciating, valuing, taking responsive action.

It is not appropriate to attack a person behind his back—or even to his face.

We will seek direct, open, trustful communication.

When discussing our problem with a third party, we will tell what we need: listening, training/advice, facilitation, negotiation, arbitration, or intervention.

It is okay to experience and express anger, fear, hurt, inadequacy, and other difficult emotions in a conflict. It is not okay to verbally or physically attack another person in a conflict.

It is okay to have conflicts. We believe that conflict can be useful, helpful, valuable, important, and beneficial. In most cases, it is not okay to keep your problem/conflict hidden.

Each party in a conflict has the responsibility to be clear about its own goals and to ask the other party, "What are your goals?"

Communication skills and techniques that are useful to the PM in conflict situations (listed in alphabetical order) include these:

Accepting anger and sorting angry behaviors

Appreciating

Asking for what you want

Congruity, honesty, and truth-telling without attacking

Hearing

Listening

Moving from gripe to goal (transmitting skill and listening)

Paraphrasing of feelings for acknowledgement, for goals

Pre-calling

Responsively acting

Separating "interests" from "position"

Thinking creatively and synergistically

Understanding

Mike Murray tells us that there are really four conflicts in every conflict, as interpersonal feelings and ground rules and beliefs, in addition to the issue itself, become our frame of reference. The very method that we choose to use for resolution can skew the results. By choosing to look at the other party as a cosolver and aim for an output of synergy, some of the conflicts in the frame can be neutralized (Figure 29–29).

Conflict Resolution

Conflict resolution is a subset of conflict management. Conflicts are usually solved in one of these ways:

- **Forcing**—Conflict is resolved when one party is successful in achieving its own interests at the expense of the other party's interest through the use of high relative power. This is the win-lose approach.

- **Withdrawal**—Conflict is resolved when one party attempts to satisfy the concerns of other by neglecting its own interests or goals.

- **Smoothing**—An unassertive approach: Both parties neglect the concerns involved by sidestepping the issue or postponing the conflict or choosing not to deal with it.

- **Compromise**—An intermediate approach: Partial satisfaction is sought for both parties through a "middle ground" position that reflects mutual sacrifice. Compromise evokes thoughts of giving up something, therefore earning the name "lose-lose."

- **Integrative decision making/problem solving**—Cooperative mode: Attempts to satisfy the interests of both parties. In terms of process, this is generally accomplished through identification of "interests" and freeing the process from initial positions. Once interests

1 Issue	2 Interpersonal Feelings	3 Resolution Methods	4 Ground Rules and Beliefs	Ways to Look at the Other Party	Outcome Options
• Data • Method • Goals • Values • Ego • Interpersonal styles • Right/wrong • Good/bad • Correct/ incorrect • Limited resources	• Anger • Hurt • (Hostility) • Inadequacy • Fear • Guilt	• Reason/ persuade/ convince • Higher authority • Problem- solve • Voting • Chance	• Generated by individuals and organizations	• A problem • An enemy • A resource • A cosolver of conflicts	• Defeat the other party • Agree to disagree • Learn • Synergize–create something new • Maintain other side and use its existence to mobilize yours

FIGURE 29–29
Four Conflicts in Every Conflict

are identified, the process moves into a phase of generation of creative alternatives designed to satisfy of interests (criteria) identified.

Roles in Conflict Resolution

Resolving a conflict may involve more parties than just those having the dispute (the advocates.) An arbitrator and a mediator/facilitator often appear as additional roles.

The arbitrator resolves the conflict by actually making the decision for the parties. Each party may advocate a position or interest to the arbitrator. A group leader may decide to take on this role to resolve intragroup conflict.

The mediator resolves conflict by attempting to refocus the parties from positions to interests. The mediator starts by determining the true reasons (interest) why they are so committed to their given positions. Once the problem is defined in terms of interests, the mediator attempts to engage both parties in the process of generating new alternatives that satisfy the interests of both parties.

The advocate attempts to influence the decision of an individual or group. The advocate argues for either a position (specific alternative) or an interest (ensure that the choice satisfies a specific criterion). The successful advocate either operates from a strong base of power, thus reducing the importance of the specific issues, or uses powers of persuasion to effect the decision. In using persuasion, he either convinces the decision maker that specific criteria should be added or given more weight, or convinces the decision maker to change his theory. Knowledge of the decisionmaker's actual criteria and theories (cause/effect beliefs) are important to the effective advocate.

Task versus Relationship

One way to think about conflict is to think about two dimensions, or outcomes, of a conflict decision. These two dimensions are:

1. **Task**—How important is the accomplishment of the task (goal, value, interest) to you? This can vary from very important (high) to total indifference (low). Low task importance is often the result when you are relatively indifferent to the options being considered.

2. **Relationship**—How important is maintenance of the relationship with the other party to you? A range exists along the relationship importance continuum. If low, the relationship is *conditional*—that is, you are willing to maintain the relationship as long as it is *instrumental* in satisfying your interests. If high, the relationship is *unconditional,* in that you want to maintain it regardless of the short-term exchange and satisfaction derived from it.

Figure 29–30 shows the relationship between task and relationship importance and the type of conflict resolution mechanism likely to be used. Most conflicts are resolved below the red line. This line represents the perceived trade-off between task accomplishment and relationship maintenance. It is only when we operate above the line (in the problem solving zone) that we realize long-term effectiveness. Someone will operate in this zone only when he places both

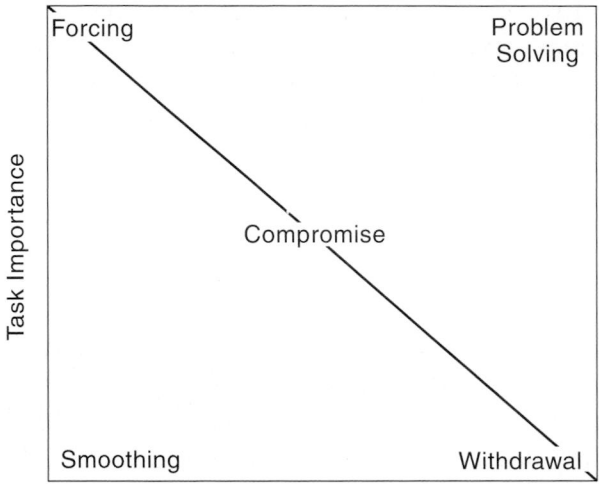

FIGURE 29–30

Tasks Versus Relationship Importance Dictate Conflict Resolution Mechanisms

Source: *www.cba.uri.edu/Scholl/Notes/Conflict.htm.* Richard W. Scholl (2001). "Conflict Resolution." Class notes for students in Management, Organizational Behavior, Labor Relations and Human Resources, School of Management, University of Rhode Island.

high importance on the task and the relationship and is unwilling to sacrifice one for the other. It is through framing the conflict in terms of *interests* rather than *positions* that this increased effectiveness begins to be realized.

Communicating via Visual Expression of Information

Graphical representations of data are commonly found in project documentation. Indeed, the famous Gantt chart is how most PMs communicate schedule information. More than likely, many requirements will be expressed as words or numbers requiring summarization and interpretation. As we know, our spoken language is very ambiguous and our written language is worse. Specifications are often piles of numbers that are summarized into graphical formats, such as bar, pie, and line charts. Most of us learn how to use the graphics available in spreadsheets and drawing programs, but few of us really understand the subtleties of representing information well unambiguously.

A famous book on this subject is *How To Lie with Statistics,* by Darrell Huff. Published in 1949, it is now in its 14th printing because the information is timeless. Although the examples used are dated now (such as houses that cost $3,000), the principles remain the same:

- Carefully chosen measures can disguise or distort any facts that the author wants.
- Casually omitting scale information can make any graph look they way the author wants it to.
- What does "average" really mean? (There are several ways to measure it: mean, median, mode, etc.)
- Using percentages of percentages can make a mountain out of a molehill.

Along those same lines, Prof. Edward Tufte of Yale has been studying the principles of information display for more than 20 years. He has published three very good books on the subject, all from Graphics Press:

- *The Visual Display of Quantitative Information,* 1983
- *Envisioning Information,* 1990
- *Visual Explanations: Images and Qualities, Evidence and Narrative,* 1997

Some of his principles apply very well to any graphically oriented display of quantitative data, for truer understanding. As an example, he uses the documents that Morton Thiokol engineers sent to NASA officials to argue against the launch in cold weather of the ill-fated Challenger Space Shuttle in 1986. In 13 different faxed documents (many handwritten) of tables, calculations, and drawings, they presented the data that cold weather launches had previously resulted in small failures in the O-ring seals on the solid rocket boosters (found after recovery) and that a launch on January 26, 1986, in 20°F weather was ill-advised.

Unfortunately, the data was confusing at best, and the NASA officials decided to launch anyway, with the disastrous effects that we know of today. If summarized and presented correctly, in one scatter chart plotting the history of failures against the ambient air temperature at launch (all data that was contained somewhere in the 13 documents from Thiokol), it would have been obvious that the probability of failure was *very* high. This presentation may have convinced the NASA officials not to launch. Dr. Tufte's summary chart, using the same data that the Thiokol engineers presented in their 13 documents, is shown in Figure 29–31. It is not hard to see that a launch at a temperature as low as 26°F could result in three to four times the expected damage.

Some of Dr. Tufte's principles for information display are summarized in the tips and tricks listed in the next section. Many of his principles of information display have a great significance today as we begin to use the Internet as an information display medium. His principles readily translate to better Web page design and teach us to avoid the "chart junk" of heavy gridlines, excessive labeling, and use of colors that often clutter the information to be displayed. Using the principles of Darrell Huff and Edward Tufte, we should be careful to avoid presenting data in a misleading fashion, and we should be wary of others who do.

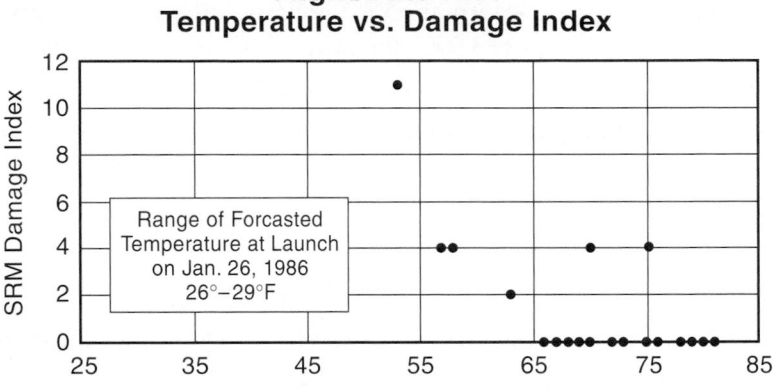

FIGURE 29–31
Tufte's Summary Chart of Thiokol's Launch Information

Tips and Tricks for the Visual Display of Quantitative Information

These tips and tricks are extracted from a seminar by Edward Tufte, Ph.D., of Yale University, in Austin, Texas, July 20, 1998.

Principles for information display:

1. Make comparisons (e.g., difference in a variable over time).
2. Show causality (the process or mechanism by which something changed).
3. Provide multivariable complexity (e.g., show scales, dates, temperatures—more than just one thing that is "happening" at a given time).
4. Integrate text, numbers, figures, and narrative into a seamless presentation (only numbers are boring and hard to make sense of; only pictures may leave the reader guessing, etc.).
5. Focus on the quality, relevance, and integrity of the content (or, garbage-in, garbage-out, as we say in the computer business).
6. Good design is clear thinking made visible (e.g., Excel can produce chart-junk easily without indicating statistical correctness). The design is not the issue; the design is merely the thinking that needs showing.

Principles for data display (financial and other):

1. Assess a change in the numbers, not just the bulk numbers for the sake of completeness.
2. Show averages and variations to them.
3. Massage, standardize, and adjust data before publishing it.

4. Always use footnotes for graphics (place footnotes where they belong—near the thing being explained).

5. Annotate "policy thinking" or causality thinking (use the particular-to-general-to-particular method of explaining).

6. Reuse "solved problems"; borrow strength from experts; work with familiar architectures; don't always invent a new design (e.g., the *New York Times* and *The Wall Street Journal* have already figured out the best font to use for certain displays—copy them).

In designing Web sites and overhead presentations, beware of:

1. Design reproducing hierarchy/bureaucracy (e.g., too many frames and borders)

2. Use of computer language instead of the language of the problem (e.g., geeky language)

3. Requirement of too much navigation to get to meat (e.g., too many nested links)

4. Web sites where the average download time exceeds the time of the average visit

5. George Miller's 7 +/− 2 rule applied to *memory*—not to scanning data, so put a lot of info on each page

6. Operating system imperialism; celebration of the interface (e.g., bright color frames around dull content)

7. Too small percent of terminal screen real estate used for content (e.g., a few small letters in the page center)

8. Marketers and programmers "stealing" from content space (e.g., brightly blinking banner ads)

9. Using the "strip tease" method during overhead presentations

10. "Information denial"—not backing up overhead slide presentations with hard copy (transparency images are fleeting, but paper images remain)

11. Not leaving traces of a presentation for information exchange (e.g., hang charts on wall for reference)

12. Censorship (e.g., if quoting, quote all)

Always follow these tips:

1. Place someone's name on a presentation for ownership.

2. Give presentation attendees at least one piece of paper (compared to a computer screen, paper is a very high-resolution communication device).

3. Marry temporal and causal domains (show time scales and cause-effect).

4. Present cause and effect on the same chart.

5. Ask, "What do I really need to see?"

6. Avoid strictly oral presentations.

7. Order data to reveal trends (not always chronological).

During oral presentations, do the following:

1. Show up early.
2. Tell the problem, who cares, and the solution.
3. Advance the argument through: particular-general-particular.
4. Give everyone at least one piece of paper—a testament, credible detail.
5. Know the audience—what do they read?
6. Back up information on the overhead—it is a low-resolution information device.
7. Respect the audience—they are your colleagues; they care as much about the subject as you. *Dumb* is not a verb (don't "dumb it down"); respectfully tell them what you think (don't shut up); don't patronize them.
8. Use of humor, hyperbole, exaggeration should be relevant and pointed, and should advance the cause (never refer to religion, race, gender, etc.—it will gratuitously lose the audience for you).
9. Don't use strictly masculine pronouns—it's okay to mix singular and plural (*they* is not verboten).
10. Answer questions as best you can—make eye contact. A speaker may be judged solely on question answering abilities.
11. If you ask a question, count to 10 before speaking again. Don't start with, "Have you done the reading?"
12. Let the audience know that you believe in what you're saying. Don't hide behind the podium.
13. Finish early! The audience will remember that.
14. Practice, practice, practice in front of colleagues and in front of a video camera. Watch the video at high speed. Listen to the sound track and pick out "placeholders" (*like, basically,* etc.). Knowing the material cold allows you to think while you're presenting, opening up new communication channels.
15. Drink lots of water; skip alcohol. Flying, staying in hotels, and speaking in front of overheads are the most dehydrating activities in the world....[31]

Reporting Project Status

The first step in reporting the project status is to create the plan for doing so. The communications management plan (CMP) defines a distribution structure for information flow; ways for gathering and storing information; procedures for handling corrections and updates; format, content, and detail of information to be disseminated; and process for producing each communication.

When complete, the software project management plan becomes the baseline from which variation is measured. All changes to the SPMP(s) and requirements must be under change control. The main purpose is to track the project's activities.

The project's communications plan is closely related to and usually relies on the project management information system (PMIS). The PMIS is usually constructed to carry required information to and from the people who need it, in a timely fashion. Today, they are almost always computer-system–based. Think about both of these items at the same time to get the best and most usable results. The project communication matrix in the communications plan will show which information should be reported to whom when. Look at the communications plan template for more information.

Communications Management Plan Template _____

The CMP is usually included as a section in the project management plan. It can be formal or informal, detailed or broad, depending on the needs and context of the project.

It should describe the information flow into, out of, and through the project, at all levels of the organization, to provide the control feedback necessary to run the project. It should cover the needs of all stakeholders. Basically, it describes the PMIS that the project needs to function.

The format provided here is necessarily vague because the communications needs of projects and the tools available vary greatly. Use judgment.

Often, the existing communications paths, patterns, and resources of the parent organization are used to satisfy the needs of project communication. If this is the case, the specific systems features and inputs/outputs need only be referenced here. For completely new or standalone projects, these items must be specified explicitly. That is, who gives what to whom, by when, and why? Other than prose, you may use charts, tables, and lists to describe a communication plan.

Instructions for filling out the plan, as shown in Figure 29–32 are: Items that are intended to stay in as part of your document are in **bold**; explanatory comments are in plain text. The plan fits into the overall project scheme as shown in Figure 29–33, where it is assumed to be part of the project management plan.

Baseline Plans _____

With a baseline plan and control structures in place, the elements of the triple constraint—cost, schedule, and scope (milestones)—can be tracked. The information is used to control and guide the project toward the goals and objectives in the project charter. A variety of techniques

<Name of Project>

1. Introduction
If needed, the introduction should provide any needed overview information of the project for the reader. The project management plan may have everything that is needed here.

2. Stakeholders
Here, list the stakeholders that need information about the project. These are the sources and sinks for most of the data. This information should also be in the charter or PMP.

3. Information
For each of the stakeholders, identify their information requirements in a general sense. Among pertinent items, include:
- Type: Oral, paper, electronic
- Description: Specs, reports, schedule, minutes, plans, changes (to anything)
- Frequency:
    - Time-based: Immediately, hourly, daily, weekly, monthly
    - Event-based: Task start or end, milestone accomplishment, phase end

4. Distribution
For each piece of information needed, describe how it will be communicated to the stakeholder. Include:
- Location: Where it needs to go (home office, field office, customer, supplier)
- Distribution method: Postal, email, Web page, presentation

5. Performance Reporting
Explain how the project will report performance to plan. These usually include the metrics of:
- Cost: Hours or dollars, actual versus budgeted, forecasts, reserves
- Schedule: Progress to plan, slips and pulls, interrelationships
- Quality: Defects, scraps
- Scope: Requirements, deliverables

Where applicable, include:
- Procurement: Contracts, schedules, payments, collections
- Risk: Top 10, changes, issues

6. Approvals
Strengthen your authority by obtaining approvals.

Name	Date	Signature or Authorizing ID

FIGURE 29–32
Communications Plan Template

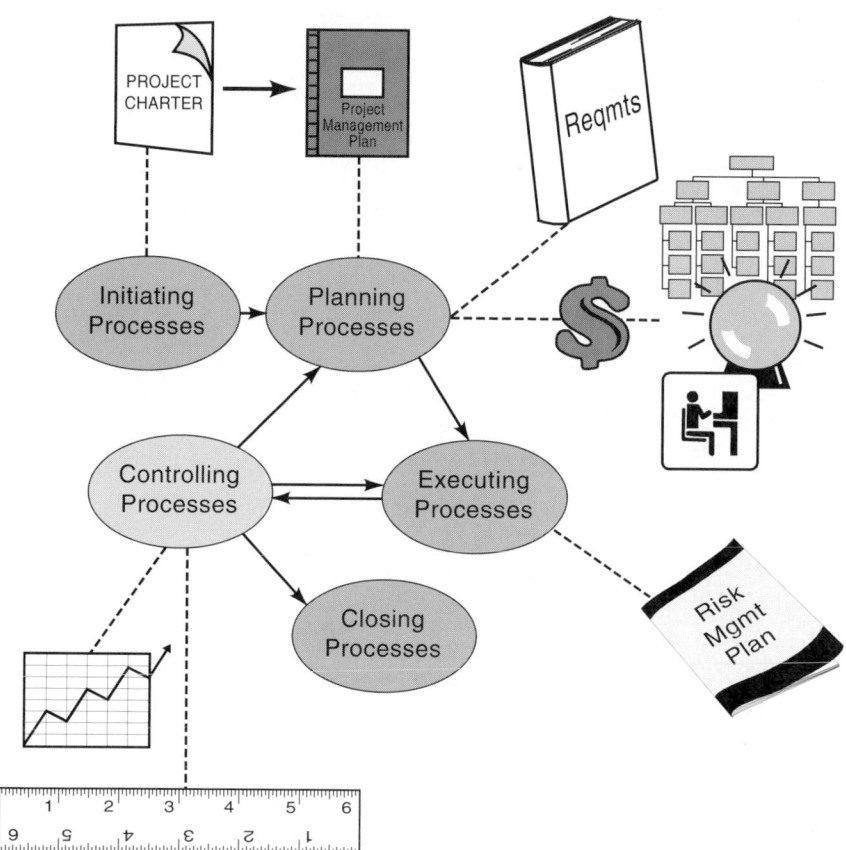

FIGURE 29–33
Project Tracking

may be employed to get the information across, but typical reports are milestone achievements, variances to the plan, and resource actuals versus the budget.

Earned value management (EVM, shown in Figure 29–34) is also useful. It shows the basic concepts—what we got for what we spent, the budget and schedule variance, and effort metrics combined with milestone achievement to measure real progress.

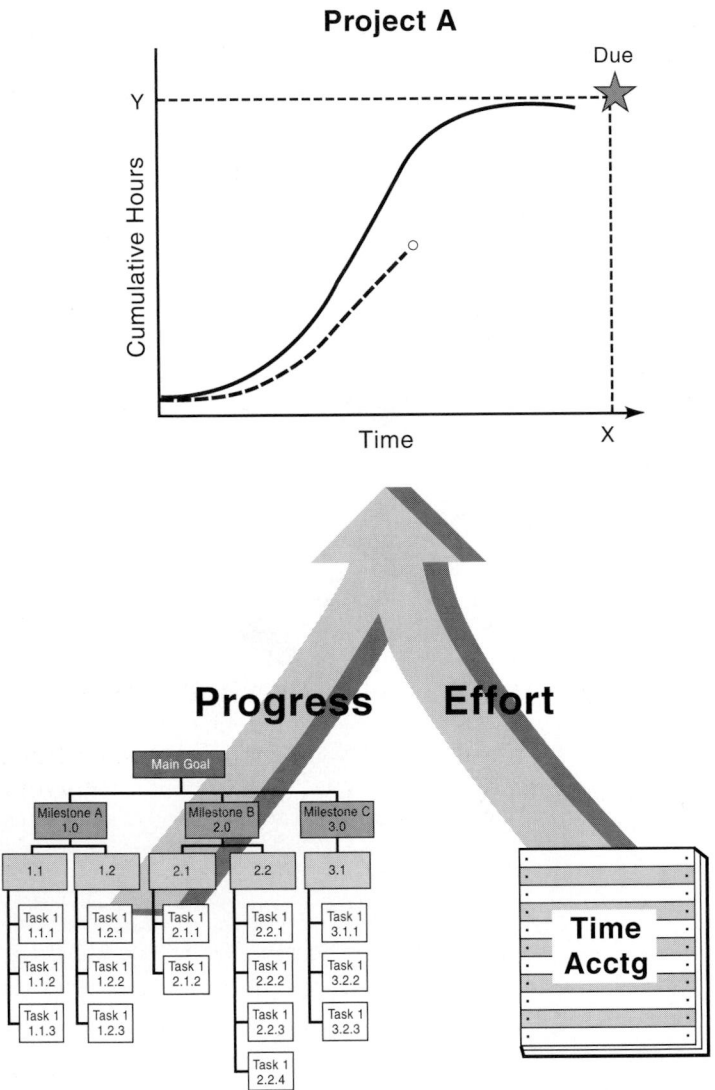

FIGURE 29–34
Earned Value Management

Project Reporting

Project reporting is part of the PMIS. Formats and frequency of reports vary widely—they may be daily, weekly, monthly, or quarterly.

At the end of a phase or major milestone accomplishment, a critical design review is generally held; at the end of a project, a post-project review is held.

Typical content format includes these items:

A brief summary of the project, with descriptions of goal(s), product(s), and major milestones and dates

Accomplishments this period, with the schedule, milestones achieved, a cost summary and EVA, and quality metrics

Plans for the next period, including milestones and cost forecasts

Risk analysis and review

Issues

Actions

Always be sure to say something about each piece of the triple constraint: scope, schedule, and cost. What things need to be reported about every project? When complete, the project plan becomes the baseline from which variation is measured. All changes to the project plan(s) and requirements must be under change control. The main purpose is to track the project's activities and to report controlled information to stakeholders.

Status Reports

Formats and frequency of status reports vary widely. They may be time-based, such as daily, weekly, monthly, or quarterly. Generally, they are event-based, meaning that they are performed at the end of a phase, stage, or major milestone accomplishment such as a phase gate, critical design review, or post-project review.

Project reporting in general may produce other reports, such as meeting minutes, action items, tasks and work packages, resource and workload, costs/EVM, or other custom reports.

Project Control

The project plan is only a roadmap; it is the project manager who must drive the project to completion, making corrections and adjustments where necessary. The main purpose of the plan is to help steer the project's execution in the right direction, as shown in Figure 29–35.

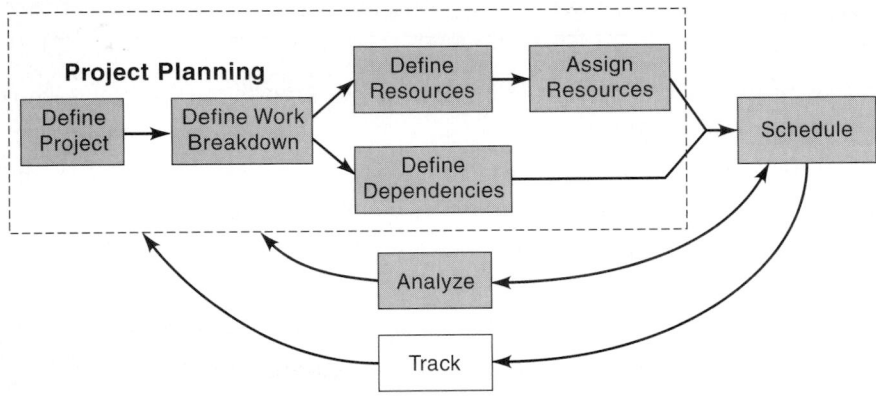

FIGURE 29–35
Project Control

Control System

Because a project is a collection of organized processes, it must have a control system, such as the one shown in Figure 29–36, in place to effectively control the project.

The components of a project control system may be: human resource control—people management skills; physical asset control—"good housekeeping"; and financial resource control—resource management.

Methods to implement control systems include status reports, project reviews, and process improvement programs. These are generally supported by data forms (hopefully online and Web-enabled) such as these:

- Project status report (forward/rearward looking)
- Resource forecast spreadsheet (forward looking)
- Top 10 risk summary (point-in-time view)

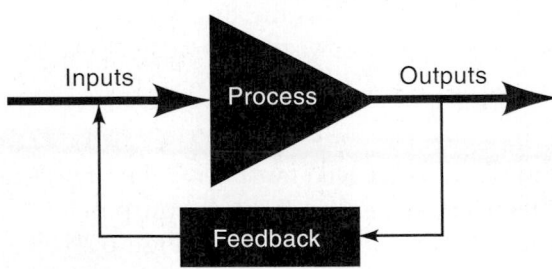

FIGURE 29–36
Control System

- Top 10 risk reporting (changes over time)
- Earned value management (rearward looking)
- Many others possible; must be tailored to organizational maturity and project needs

As with everything else, balance is the key to a good control system. A balanced control system recognizes that costs increase exponentially with the degree of control; too much control dampens innovation; it should be directed toward error correction, not punishment; it should exert only the minimum control necessary for quality; and easy-to-measure factors shouldn't be emphasized over difficult-to-measure factors (intangibles). Some misinterpret control by thinking, "If it's not measured, it doesn't count" or "If you're not keeping score, you're just practicing." The successful software project manager will remember that short-term results don't overshadow long-term goals and that goals and objectives can change over time (often slowly).

Summary _____

Communication is about receiving as well as sending, each of which has a variety of styles. Senders encode messages, and receivers decode them; messages pass through filters made of beliefs, experiences, and values. Communication networks become exponentially more complex with every additional node (person). One of the best things that a software project manager can do to ensure good communications is to create a communications management plan.

A team is not just a group of people, but a group that is motivated and committed to a shared vision. Teams typically pass through several stages of developmental behavior, including forming, storming, norming, performing, and adjourning. "Teamicide" is when the team dies at its own hands when individuals revert to their base personalities.

Leading a team requires both leadership and management skills and qualifications, which are different. The situational leadership model is adaptive to the needs of the team.

Teams may be motivated in several ways. Authors of some of the more well-known behavioral theories include: Maslow (needs), Herzberg (motivators/dissatisfiers), McGregor (Theories X and Y), Ouchi (Theory Z), Lewin (force field), and Boehm (win-win). The PM's ability to motivate a team rests on awareness, questioning, acceptance, ownership, and the number one management rule: People adopt the behavior for which they are rewarded.

The Myers-Briggs Type Indicator (MBTI) is a personality model of preferences. It is a well-researched empirical model based on the work of Carl Jung. A powerful communication tool, it can be used by the PM to understand how to approach people. MBTI measures preferences along four dimensions: introvert/extrovert (I/E), sensing/intuitive (S/N), thinking/feeling (T/F), and judging/perceiving (J/P).

The Keirsey Temperament Sorter is a personality model similar to Myers-Briggs—that is, a personality model of preferences. Keirsey defines four type groups: sensitive/judging (SJ) guardians, sensitive/perceiving (SP) artisans, intuitive/feeling (NF) idealists, and intuitive/ thinking (NT) rationals.

Developing staff into a team requires PM involvement. Collective culture and trust must be developed. The PM must be adroit at recognizing "bad" teamwork, types of groups, and team/group behavior. The PM also must be cognizant of team building activities, benefits and limitations of team building, and the importance of a project framework.

Project reporting is part of the project management information system. Remember to baseline the plan before reporting. The contents and formats vary but usually include accomplishments, plans, risks, issues, and actions. The components of the triple constraint should always be covered. Frequency of project reporting may be time-based (i.e., every other week) or event-based (i.e., with every milestone).

Conflict resolution requires preparation and an understanding of where on the spectrum you are. Apply the appropriate techniques: go to the balcony, step to their side, reframe the problem, build a golden bridge, and don't escalate—educate.

Negotiation promotes partnering for win-win principled negotiations. It involves brainstorming and finding shared interests. Principled negotiations should be pursued first, before other approaches. Negotiations begin by sorting out problems, people, and interests or positions. The idea is to find a basis in objective criteria. When principled negotiations fail, competitive negotiation may ensue. Even so, it is best to think "outside the box" of emotion and build a way for the competitor to come to you.

Planning and handling project communications begins with the preparation of a short communications plan. In the early stages, it may need only a few ground rules, to be elaborated for larger, nonstandard projects. A responsibility matrix is an excellent tool for clarifying roles.

Communications requires the use of appropriate tools and methods, both synchronous and asynchronous.

With spatial-, visual-, and audio-only communications, certain contexts may be lost and need to be replaced.

Communication in meetings requires certain roles. The client/customer, meeting manager, participants, and coach have defined responsibilities. All meetings should have a preassigned leader and a scribe. Meetings are held for information exchange, problem solving, decision making, planning, and evaluation. They work best with preset agendas and may produce a number of different outputs, depending on the type. Project control systems rely on feedback and balance. Their three major components are human resource control, physical asset control, and financial resource control.

Problems for Review _____

1. What are some of the barriers to planning for negotiation that you experience?

2. What could be done to overcome these barriers?

3. Effective negotiators must be able to differentiate between "needs" and "satisfiers" or "resources" for meeting the needs. In some negotiations, what must be separated is "position" from "interest." The following exercise is designed to help you practice this skill. You are currently managing several projects. A member of one of the project teams, who reports to you, has come to you and explained that he must have a significant raise to stay with the company. This person is critical to the project, which is currently behind schedule and over budget. You realize that there may be more here than meets the eye. For several days, people have been talking about what recently happened in another department: A manager at your level obtained a large bonus for a person who is much less competent and who has made much less contribution than the subordinate standing in your office. Your subordinate was visibly upset. The project is over budget. You cannot give your subordinate a raise. You must negotiate. Using the form in Figure 29–23, identify needs and satisfiers (or resources). What are the subordinate's needs? What are *your* primary needs in this situation?

4. What is your MBTI? What is your Keirsey Temperament Sorter type? Do these descriptions seem to fit you?

5. Using the MBTI personality types "communication styles" as a guide, you are preparing a presentation about your current project for a general audience. Considering your four-letter type preference, describe two ways to communicate effectively in your speech with each of the opposite types of your preference. For example, if you are an I-type on extroversion/introversion, describe how you would appeal to an E.

6. Give two reasons why teams are necessary in today's work environment.

7. Name and briefly describe the four stages in a team's life cycle.

8. Why should project managers invest in teambuilding? List four benefits that they might expect to receive.

9. What are the four Keirseyian psychological temperaments, and how can they offer a way to match leadership style to the phases of change in an organization?

10. What are some ways to accommodate introverted style in an extroverted U.S. culture? How can thinking types and feeling types help each other to write balanced letters?

11. Explain why suddenly changing your team from 98% push to 98% pull could result in disaster.

Visit the Case Study

The software integration specification has been under review for two months. An open item from the risk matrix was how security was to be implemented post-prototype. When the project team received this week's status report from Mr. Lu, the members found this section attached:

Security Issues for the Prototype Chinese Railroad Ministry Software System

1. The system must be protected from nonauthorized personnel. The system should be secure at each terminal so that only authorized personnel can operate the system.
2. The system should include protections at the network level to prevent outsiders from breaking into the system.
3. The system should include mechanisms to lock terminals when operators are absent from them.
4. The system should require the changing of passwords from time to time to protect against outsiders using the passwords of authorized personnel.

The system should disallow the use of browsers to access any Internet sites other than those necessary to the software system. Different groups of users of the system should have access to different functions. Currently, the list of user groups, as determined by the CRM, is as follows:

User Group	Authorizations
CRM Administrators	Reporting functions, "overview" functions
System Administrators	All functions
Ticket Sales Managers	Ticket reports, ticketing functions
Ticket Salespeople	Ticketing functions
Train Dispatchers and Conductors	Reports by train, ticket acceptance functions
Ticket Takers	Ticket acceptance functions
Financial	Ticket order reports, ticket purchase reports

Mr. Lu further mentioned that this list might not be complete. For example, the CRM may in the future subdivide the CRM Administrators group to differentiate planners from those tracking potential scalpers. As the project leader, you must now re-evaluate the risk matrix and the SIS for conformance to these new reporting requirements. Of course, the budget and schedule will not be impacted, will it? Does this impact the Web site that you and your team use to communicate the project status and exchange documents with your development group in Bangalore?

Citations _____

[1]*www.ndu.edu/inss/books/strategic/pt1ch5.htm.* (1999). "Chapter 5: Framing Perspectives." *Strategic Leadership and Decision Making.* Washington, DC: National Defense University.

[2]Stuckenbruck, Linn C., and David Marshall (1985). "Team Building for Project Managers." *The Principles of Project Management: Collected Handbooks from the Project Management Institute,* John R. Adams et al., eds. (1997). Sylva, NC: PMI Publication Division. p. 3.

[3]Tuchman, B.W. (1965). "Development Sequence in Small Groups." *Psychological Development Bulletin,* 63(6), and refined by numerous people since.

[4]See note 2. pp. 7–8.

[5]DeMarco, Tom, and Timothy Lister (1987). *Peopleware: Productive Projects and Teams.* New York, NY: Dorset House.

[6]See note 2. pp. 4–5.

[7]Woodcock, Mike, and David Francis (1981). *Organization Development Through Team Building: Planning a Cost Effective Strategy.* New York, NY: Wiley. p. 3.

[8]See note 2. pp. 3, 50.

[9]See note 2. pp. 5–6. Also in: Jack R. Meredith and Samuel Mantel, Jr. (2000). *Project Management: A Managerial Approach,* 4th ed. New York, NY: Wiley.

[10]See note 2. pp. 9–10.

[11]See note 2.

[12]Maccoby, Michael (1988). *Why Work: Leading the New Generation.* New York, NY: Simon & Schuster.

[13]*www.cba.uri.edu/Scholl/Papers/Self_Concept_Motivation.HTM.* Nancy H. Leonard et al. (1995). "A Self Concept-Based Model of Work Motivation." *Proceedings of the Academy of Management Annual Meeting,* Vancouver, B.C.

[14]*www.cba.uri.edu/Scholl/Notes/Motivation_Expectancy.html.* Richard W. Scholl (2001). "Expectancy Theory." Class notes for students in Management, Organizational Behavior, Labor Relations and Human Resources, School of Management, University of Rhode Island.

[15]*www.cba.uri.edu/Scholl/Notes/Equity.html.* Richard W. Scholl (2001). "Primer on Equity." Class notes for students in Management, Organizational Behavior, Labor Relations and Human Resources, School of Management, University of Rhode Island.

[16]Maslow, Abraham Harold (1954). *Motivation and Personality,* 1st ed. New York, NY: Harper. Also: Victor Vroom (1994). *Work and Motivation.* New York, NY: Wiley, Jossey-Bass Management Series.

[17]Lewis, James P. (1995). *Project Planning, Scheduling and Control: A Hands-On Guide to Bringing Projects in on Time and on Budget.* New York, NY: McGraw-Hill.

[18]*www.cba.uri.edu/Scholl/Notes/Group_Problem_Solving.htm.* Richard W. Scholl (2001). "Group Problem Solving." Class notes for students in Management, Organizational Behavior, Labor Relations and Human Resources, School of Management, University of Rhode Island.

[19]Herzberg, Frederick, Bernard Mausner, and Barbara Bloch Snyderman (1993). *The Motivation to Work*. New Brunswick, NJ: Transaction Publishers.
Also: Vijay K. Verma (1997). *The Human Aspects of Project Management*. Upper Darby, PA: Project Management Institute.

[20]McGregor, Douglas (1960). *The Human Side of Enterprise*. New York, NY: McGraw-Hill. pp. 33–34.

[21]Ouchi, William G., and Alfred M. Jaeger (1978). "Type Z Organization: Stability in the Midst of Mobility." *Academy of Management Review*, 3(2):159–168.

[22]*www.sol-ne.org/res/wp/toc*. Edgar H. Schein (2000). "Kurt Lewin's Change Theory in the Field and in the Classroom: Notes Toward a Model of Managed Learning." Society for Organizational Learning.

[23]Grant, Richard (2000). Instructor, University of Texas Software Quality Institute Certificate Program, Sequence XI, Session 3.

[24]Kummerow, Jean M., et al. (1997). *Work Types*. New York, NY: Warner Books.

[25]Keirsey, David, and Marilyn Bates (1984). *Please Understand Me: Character and Temperament Types*. Del Mar, CA: Prometheus Nemesis Book Company.
Also: David Keirsey (1998). *Please Understand Me II: Temperament, Character, Intelligence*. Del Mar, CA: Prometheus Nemesis Book Company.

[26]Murray, Mike (2000). Instructor, University of Texas Software Quality Institute Certificate Program, Sequence XI, Session 22.

[27]Boehm, Barry W., and Rony Ross (1989). "Theory W Software Project Management Principles and Examples." *IEEE Transactions on Software Engineering*, 15(7):902–916.

[28]Fisher, Roger, and William Ury (1991). *Getting To Yes*, 2nd ed. New York: NY: Penguin Books.

[29]Ury, William (1993). *Getting Past No*. New York, NY: Bantam Books.

[30]See note 24.

[31]Tufte, Edward (1983). *The Visual Display of Quantitative Information*. Cheshire, CT: Graphics Press.
Also: Tufte, Edward (1990). *Envisioning Information*. Cheshire, CT: Graphics Press.
Also: Tufte, Edward (1997). *Visual Explanations: Images and Qualities, Evidence and Narrative*. Cheshire, CT: Graphics Press.

Suggested Readings

Ackerman, Phillip L., et al., eds. (1990). *Learning and Individual Differences: Process, Trait, and Content Determinants*. Washington, DC: American Psychological Association Books.

Alderfer, Clayton P. (1972). *Existence, Relatedness, and Growth: Human Needs in Organizational Settings*. New York, NY: Free Press.

Allport, Gordon W. (1960). *Personality and Social Encounter: Selected Essays*. Boston, MA: Beacon Press.

Allport, Gordon W. (1961). *Pattern and Growth in Personality*. New York, NY: Holt, Rinehart and Winston.

Calero, Henry H. (1979). *Winning the Negotiation*. New York, NY: Hawthorn Books.

Cantor, N., and J.F. Kihlstrom (1987). *Personality and Social Intelligence.* Upper Saddle River, NJ: Prentice Hall.

Cohen, Herb (1980). *You Can Negotiate Anything.* Secaucus, NJ: L. Stuart.

Franken, Robert E. (2002). *Human Motivation,* 5th ed. Pacific Grove, CA: Brooks/Cole.

Ilich, John, and Barbara Schindler-Jones (1981). *Successful Negotiating Skills for Women.* Reading, MA: Addison-Wesley.

Karras, Chester L. (1993). *Give and Take: the Complete Guide to Negotiating Strategies and Tactics.* New York, NY: HarperBusiness Publishers.

Katz, Daniel, and Robert L. Kahn (1978). *The Social Psychology of Organizations,* 2nd ed. New York, NY: Wiley.

Kennedy, Gavin (1998). *The New Negotiating Edge: the Behavioral Approach for Results and Relationships.* Sonoma, CA: Nicholas Brealey Publishing.

Lewicki, Roy J., et al. (1996). *Think Before You Speak: the Complete Guide to Strategic Negotiation.* New York, NY: John Wiley & Sons.

Lewicki, Roy J., et al. (1999). *Negotiation,* 3rd ed. Boston, MA: Irwin/McGraw-Hill.

Lewin, Kurt (1975). *Field Theory in Social Science: Selected Theoretical Papers,* Dorwin Cartwright, ed. Westport, CT: Greenwood Press.

Lewin, Kurt (1997). *Resolving Social Conflicts; Field Theory in Social Science.* Washington, DC: American Psychological Association.

Maslow, Abraham H. (1971). *The Farther Reaches of Human Nature.* New York, NY: Viking Press.

Maslow, Abraham H. (1999). *Toward a Psychology of Being,* 3rd ed. New York, NY: John Wiley & Sons.

Maxwell, John C. (1999). *The 21 Indispensable Qualities of a Leader: Becoming the Person that People Will Want to Follow.* Nashville, TN: T. Nelson.

Nierenberg, Gerard I. (1986) *The Art of Negotiating,* 2nd ed. New York, NY: Simon & Schuster.

Nierenberg, Gerard I. (1987). *Fundamentals of Negotiating.* New York, NY: Perennial Library.

Nierenberg, Gerard I. (1991). *The Complete Negotiator.* New York, NY: Berkley Books.

Schein, Edgar H. (1980). *Organizational Psychology,* 3rd ed. Englewood Cliffs, NJ: Prentice-Hall.

Schein, Edgar H. (1992). *Organizational Culture and Leadership,* 2nd ed. San Francisco, CA: Jossey-Bass.

Woolf, Bob (1990). *Friendly Persuasion: My Life as a Negotiator.* New York, NY: Putnam.

Yukl, Gary (2001). *Leadership in Organizations,* 5th ed. Upper Saddle River, NJ: Prentice Hall.

Web Pages for Further Information _____

typelogic.com/. MBTI Type Information.

www.humanmetrics.com/cgi-win/JungType.htm. Abbreviated MBTI test.

www.keirsey.com/. Abbreviated Keirsey Temperament Sorter test.

www.personalitypage.com/info.html. Information About Personality Types.

www.personalitytype.com/. Barbara Barron-Tieger and Paul Tieger, authors of four books on personality type.

Software Quality Assurance

The Software Engineering Institute's Capability Maturity Model (CMM) has listed software quality assurance (SQA) as a key process area since the institute's inception. Figure 30–1 represents the maturity levels; software quality assurance is the bottom key process in Level 2, Repeatable. As a hardware design manager for a major semiconductor manufacturing company asked one of the authors in the mid-1990s: "I've been directed to get to Level 2, and I need a SQAP! What's a SQAP? And where do I get one?" Getting a SQAP (software quality assurance plan) is what this chapter is all about. It is a very basic but often overlooked process that all practitioners need to follow for successful software development projects.

Software quality assurance involves reviewing all delivered software products and the activities within the life cycle that produced them. Auditing can be performed to ensure that the products and processes conform to the internal organization policies and procedures for software development, as well as industry standards. The CMM lists four goals that must be achieved to satisfy this key process area:

Goal 1—Software quality assurance activities are planned.

Goal 2—Adherence of software products and activities to the applicable standards, procedures, and requirements is verified objectively.

Goal 3—Affected groups and individuals are informed of the SQA activities and results.

Goal 4—Senior management addresses noncompliance issues that cannot be resolved within the software project.

Using the *IEEE Standard Glossary of Software Engineering Terminology*, software quality assurance is defined as: (1) a planned and systematic pattern of all actions necessary to provide adequate confidence that an item or product conforms to established technical requirements, and (2) a set of activities designed to evaluate the process by which products are developed

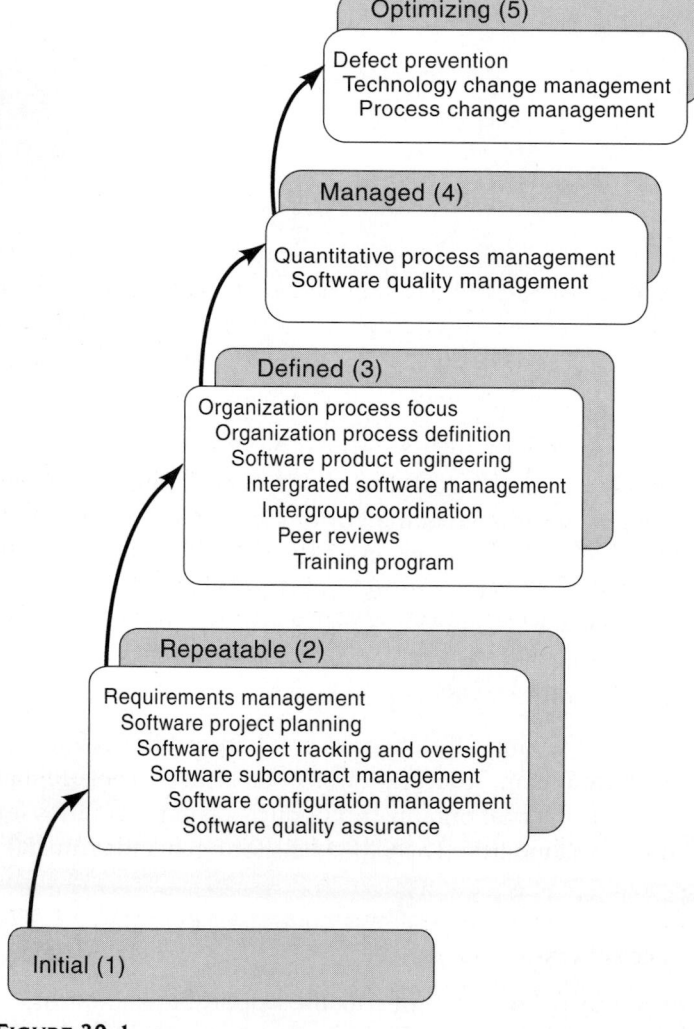

FIGURE 30–1
Capability Maturity Model Maturity Levels

or manufactured. The references at the end of this chapter have complete in-depth information on quality lessons from quality experts, personnel requirements, training plans, organizations for project quality, and ways to calculate the cost of product and project quality. All of these are important quality issues of which professional software project managers should be aware. The focus of this handbook is on tools that practitioners can use. Therefore, this chapter will focus on how to build an adequate SQAP, what checklists to employ, and where to find the information. Please see the references for the theoretical treatments of software quality assurance.

When is it practical to build a SQAP? The authors of this practitioner's guide have found through experience that it is cost-effective to build a software quality assurance plan for any project that is estimated to take more than six person-months of effort to complete.

Where We Are in the Product Development Life Cycle

Software quality assurance begins in the requirements phase of the product development life cycle (see Figure 30–2). The SQAP should be complete when the requirements phase is complete and the software requirements specification is delivered. A mature organization will have a metrics plan for each project. This plan must be reviewed and the metrics specific to quality must be emphasized. Chapter 21, "Software Metrics," in this guide contains detailed information on the determination and measurement of quality metrics.

The implementation of the SQAP begins at its acceptance, usually at the end of the requirements phase, and ends at product retirement. The SQAP must address the entire product life cycle, not just the development phases. Keep in mind that ability of a mature organization to do continuous process improvements results from the SQAP process. The process line extending across the entire life cycle of "Identify Quality Improvement Needs" is where mature organizations implement continuous process improvement.

Chapter 30 Relation to the 34 Competencies

The following five of the 34 competencies described in this practitioner's guide apply especially to software quality assurance:

1. **Assessing processes**—Specifically assessing the quality assurance goals of the CMM and the processes within the product development life cycle. This leads directly into the overall organization's approach to continuous process improvement.
10. **Tracking product quality**—Once the SQAP is completed, it is used for that specific product development life cycle to monitor the quality activities.

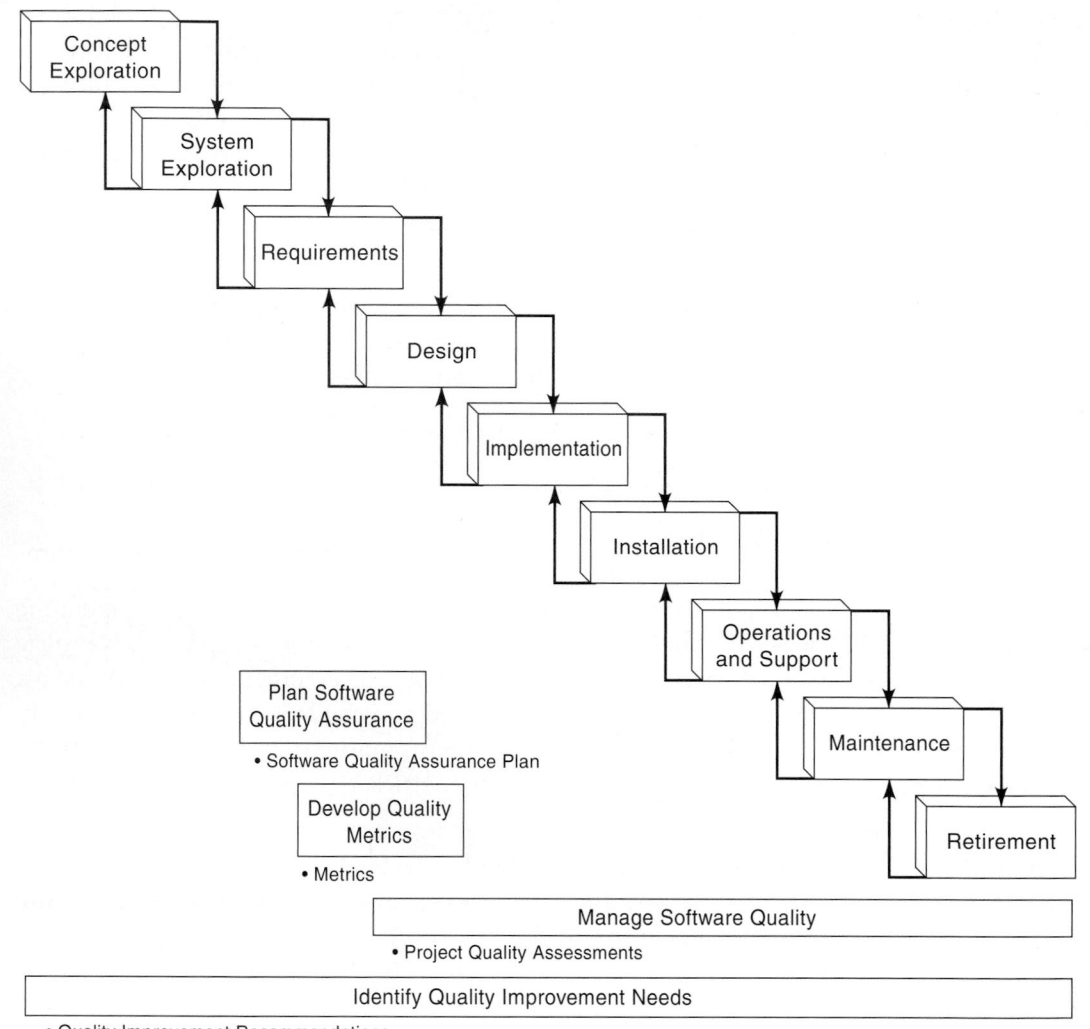

FIGURE 30–2
Software Quality Assurance in the Product Development Life Cycle

13. **Documenting plans**—Building the SQAP is the major plan development activity in software quality assurance.

17. **Monitoring development**—Implementing the SQAP provides for monitoring the product development processes.

21. **Tracking process**—Throughout the project, the SQAP guides the tracking of the software quality processes within the project and development processes.

Learning Objectives for Chapter 30 _____

Upon completion of this chapter, the reader should be able to:

- Develop a software quality assurance plan that complies with the goals of the CMM;
- Define the benefits of software quality assurance for specific projects;
- Develop a complete SQAP for any software development project;
- Modify SQAP checklists for organization-specific projects;
- Incorporate quality assurance with an overall organization and project metrics program.

Building the Software Quality Assurance Plan _____

The sections listed in Table 30–1 are the major parts of the SQAP. These are taken from IEEE 730-1998. This standard is the best general-purpose SQAP template for practitioner use. The information about section content and specific development techniques are derived from the authors' software development experience and do not track with the IEEE standard. The authors have found the framework useful, but not necessarily the total content. This has been modified based on the authors' experience in software product development best practices from the IEEE 730 template.

The remainder of this chapter describes how to build the plan. Each major section has a checklist of what the project manager needs to include and investigate to build that section.

1 Purpose

The purpose of the SQAP frames the part that software quality assurance plays within overall project management. These pieces need to be in this section:

- Definition of the software end use;
- Definition of the criticality of the need for this software solution;
- Block diagram of how it fits with other software systems;
- Intended audience for the SQAP;
- Justification of the project;
- Specific software deliverables covered;
- Description of software life cycle development model used; and
- List of specific COTS software to be used.

TABLE 30–1
Major Sections of the SQAP

Section	Description
1	Purpose
2	Reference documents
3	Management
4	Documentation
5	Standards, practices, conventions, and metrics
6	Reviews and audits
7	Risk management
8	Problem reporting and corrective action
9	Tools, techniques, and methodologies
10	Supplier control
11	Training
12	Records collection, maintenance, and retention

2 Reference Documents

A complete list of all documents such as industry standards and textbooks used to develop the SQAP needs to be produced here. Along with those external references, all organization policy and procedure documents that apply need to be listed. Finally, project documentation that is referenced must be provided. Specific items in this section are:

- List of documents that form the basis of this SQAP;
- Reason for listed documents used;
- List of deviations from standards, policies, and procedures;
- List of software deliverables covered by the SQAP that require additional, more rigorous, or more relaxed practices or procedures; and
- Record of deviations that reflect the criticality presented in the last section and the references that justify those deviations.

3 Management

This section describes the product development organization and the organization's tasks and responsibilities.

3.1 Organization This paragraph depicts the organizational structure that influences and controls the quality of the software. A simple organization chart that shows the development organization's relationship to the greater organization represents it. For a development organization of more than seven people, it is practical to show an organization chart of the development organization itself. These items need to be in the section:

- The organization chart showing all stakeholders and their relationship to the development organization;
- Reporting and approval paths within the organization;
- Conflict-resolution process;
- Issue tracking mechanism; and
- Change control board responsibilities and organization.

3.2 Tasks The items to be included in this paragraph are listed here:

- The specific tasks to be performed in the SQA process, to include auditing, reporting, and reviewing;
- The specific actions to be executed on the specific deliverables;
- The specific points within the software development life cycle where SQA plays an active role; and
- A workflow diagram of the SQA activities for this specific project.

3.3 Responsibilities A table of roles and responsibilities of all members of the development team must be shown.

4 Documentation

This section consists of the deliverable documentation that will be tracked by the SQAP. The documents listed here may be a subset of all the configuration items tracked in the software configuration management plan. But in no case would a document be here listed that is not also a configuration item. All deliverables are configuration items, but not all configuration items are managed within the SQAP. Management of the tracking of the development of each of these documents is described in the earlier section "Tasks."

The section "Documentation Requirements," next, lists the set of documents that would be produced in a project requiring a SQAP. Other documents that are to be included in the project manager's specific development project either can be included here or can be listed in a section titled "Other Documents." From a practitioner's viewpoint, the minimum is enough. If the project requires another document because of contractual reasons, list it in the minimum set. Software development projects never have a resource luxury, so such things are listed in categories with titles containing the words *other, miscellaneous,* or *optional.*

4.1 Documentation Requirements   This list is the minimum set of documents that would be produced on a project requiring a SQAP:

- Project management plan;
- Software requirements specification;
- Software design specification;
- Software test plan;
- Software risk management plan;
- Software configuration management plan; and
- User-deliverable documentation.

5 Standards, Practices, Conventions, and Metrics

Software quality assurance is driven by many industry standards, best-of-breed practices, local organization conventions, and individual project metrics. This section enumerates all of these external and internal factors that will have an impact on the ultimate quality of the software product.

5.1 Purpose   The section "Reference Documents," earlier, listed all the referenced documents that contain standards, policies, and procedures followed on this project. This section describes how specific practices within those documents are to be monitored for successful execution within the project. Remember, the SQA function is a monitoring, review, and auditing function. It is not an execution function. The SQA is the scorekeeper, not the quarterback. These items are included in the purpose:

- Cross-references of all documents to the specific practices to be applied from each;
- Cross-references of monitoring, review, and audit compliance for each; and
- Cross-references of where each occurs in the development life cycle.

5.2 Content   The basic reason for all of the section "Standards, Practices, Conventions, and Metrics" is to provide the baselines against which the project work products are measured. Although the references and the cross-references lay out the big picture of the reason behind and the process of the review, monitor, and audit assurances, this section is the description of the actual content to be reviewed. For example, if the standard calls for using Hungarian Notation in all variable names, Table 30–2 shows the rules to be followed when all code reviews are looking at variable names. Other examples would be the minimum model sets to use in object-oriented analysis with a UML representation.

These items need to be in the content section:

- Product-specific quality measures;
- Web page standards;

TABLE 30–2
Hungarian Notation Standard

Prefix	Type	Example
b	Boolean	`bool bStillGoing;`
c	Character	`char cLetterButton;`
str	C++ string	`string strFirstIdentity;`
si	Short integer	`short siChairs;`
i	Integer	`int iCars;`
li	Long integer	`long liStars;`
f	Floating point	`float fPercent;`
d	Double-precision floating point	`double dMiles;`
ld	Long double-precision floating point	`long double ldLightYears;`
sz	Old-style null-terminated string	`char szIdentity[IDENTITY_LEN];`
if	Input file stream	`ifstream ifIdentityFile;`
is	Input stream	`void fct(istream &risIn);`
of	Output file stream	`ofstream ofIdentityFile;`
os	Output stream	`void fct(ostream &rosIn);`
S	Declaring a struct	`struct SPoint`
C	Declaring a class	`class CPerson`
struct name or abbrev	Declaring an instance of a struct	`SPoint pointLeft; SPoint ptLeft;`
class name or abbrev	Declaring an instance of a class	`CPerson personFound;` `CPerson perFound;`
u	Unsigned	`unsigned short usiStudents;`
k	Constant formal parameter	`void fct(const long kliGalaxies)`

(Continues)

TABLE 30–2 (Continued)
Hungarian Notation Standard

Prefix	Type	Example
r	Reference formal parameter	`void fct(long &rliShafts)`
s	Static	`static char scChoice;`
rg	Array (stands for range)	`float rgfTemp[MAX_TEMP];`
m_	Member variable of a struct or class	`char m_cLetterButton;`
p	Pointer to a single thing	`char *pcButton;`
prg	Dynamically allocated array	`char *prgcButtons;`

- Documentation standards;
- Logic structure standards;
- Coding standards;
- Naming conventions;
- Commentary standards;
- Testing standards and practices; and
- All software quality assurance product and process metrics.

6 Reviews and Audits

Reviews and audits are the SQA activities that provide both a testing mechanism to determine the progress of the project and a feedback loop for the developers to check the quality of the product in progress.

6.1 Purpose   This section will have the following information:

- Definitions of the technical and managerial reviews and audits to be conducted;
- Rules and procedures for the reviews and audits to be accomplished;
- Minimum attendees at reviews and audits in order to proceed;
- Cross-reference of all reviews and audits to the project life cycle;
- Minimum recording standards for all reviews;
- Disposition process for issues uncovered during reviews and audits;
- Use of issue tracking system; and
- Use of change control.

6.2 SQA Required Reviews   These are the reviews required for completing the SQA project activities:

- Project management plan preview;
- Software requirements specification review;
- Software design specification review;
- Software test plan review;
- Software risk management plan review;
- Software configuration management plan review;
- User-deliverable documentation review;
- Functional audit as part of delivery milestone;
- Physical audit for code and documentation internal consistency;
- In-process audits for design to code consistently;
- Managerial reviews to assess process and procedure compliance; and
- Postmortem review for lessons learned at project end.

7 Risk Management

Any project requiring a SQAP also has a risk management plan. The cross-reference to the SQAP is in those specific risks that are mitigated through the use of the SQAP. These items would be included:

- Cross-reference to specific risk mitigation plans aided by SQAP;
- Statement of how SQAP reduced specific classes of risk for this project;
- SQA review cycle, with special emphasis on risk mitigation;
- Cross-reference of periodic risk reviews, with specific SQAP reviews, assessments, and audits; and
- SQAP risk reporting requirements over and above those in the risk management plan.

8 Problem Reporting and Corrective Action

The earlier section "Organization" described the organization that will be implementing the problem reporting, issue tracking, and change control mechanisms. This section lists the specific processes for problem reporting, corrective action, and problem escalation:

- Cross-reference the roles and responsibilities previously listed to their relationship to problem reporting and resolution.
- Describe the process for issue tracking.
- Describe the process for problem reporting.

- Describe the life cycle of issue to problem to resolved problem.
- Cross-reference how these processes interact with the configuration management process.

9 Tools, Techniques, and Methodologies

These are the activities to complete the definition of all tools, techniques, and methodologies used within the SQAP:

- List all tools that are used for SQA on this project.
- List who is responsible for managing the tools.
- Describe the process for securing tool licenses.
- Define all SQA-specific techniques used.
- Provide ROI information on the use of the techniques.
- Define all SQA-specific methodologies used.
- Provide ROI information on the use of the methodologies.
- Define how the SCMP handles code control.
- Define how the SCMP handles the delivery media of the final product.

10 Supplier Control

A major resource saver can be a COTS software product. If COTS products are used on the project, special care must be taken in their quality assurance. Contract programmers, testers, and consultants are put on projects to smooth out resource loading. The quality assurance of these resources is an issue for the project management. These items need to be included in this section:

- All COTS application software included in the final product;
- All COTS application development tools used to build the final product;
- All COTS database products used on the project;
- A specific quality assurance plan for each piece of COTS software used on the project;
- All personnel requirements for nonemployee team members;
- A plan for ensuring the work product quality of contractors on the project team.

11 Training

These are the three steps needed to address SQA training within the SQAP:

- List all baseline SQA training required for project team members.
- List all SQA refresher training required.
- List training requirements for audit, review, and facilitator positions.

12 Records Collection, Maintenance, and Retention

Ownership of all the basic quality records of the project resides in the organization's quality function. The following information must be provided in this section, and it is probably boilerplate from one of the organization's policies:

- Location of the server file system maintaining all the project records;
- Backup schedule of the project information;
- Recovery instructions for the project information repository; and
- Retention periods for project-generated quality records.

Ensuring the SQAP

It is important to ensure that the plan used to ensure quality is itself complete, testable, and usable. The recommended way to do that is to take all the checklists for the SQAP, combine them into one meta-checklist, and add it to the form of the SQAP to show the completeness. This also provides a way to internally check the plan as it is developed and reviewed by the SQA team. This is the meta-checklist based on the recommended SQAP structure:

Purpose

- ☐ Definition of the software end use.
- ☐ Definition of the criticality of the need for this software solution.
- ☐ Block diagram of how it fits with other software systems.
- ☐ Intended audience for the SQAP.
- ☐ Justification of the project.
- ☐ Specific software deliverables covered.
- ☐ Description of software life cycle development model used.
- ☐ Specific COTS software to be used.

Reference Documents

- ☐ List of documents that form the basis of this SQAP.
- ☐ Reason for listed documents used.
- ☐ List of deviations from standards, policies, and procedures.

☐ List of software deliverables covered by the SQAP that require additional, more rigorous, or more relaxed practices or procedures.

☐ Record of deviations that reflect the criticality presented in section 1 and the references that justify those deviations.

Management

Organization

☐ The organization chart showing all stakeholders and their relationship to the development organization.

☐ Reporting and approval paths within the organization.

☐ Conflict resolution process.

☐ Issue tracking mechanism.

☐ Change control board responsibilities and organization.

Tasks

☐ The specific tasks to be performed in the SQA process, to include auditing, reporting, and reviewing.

☐ The specific actions to be executed on the specific deliverables.

☐ The specific points within the software development life cycle where SQA plays an active role.

☐ A workflow diagram of the SQA activities for this specific project.

Responsibilities

☐ A table of the roles and responsibilities of all members of the development team.

Documentation

Documentation Requirements

☐ Project management plan.

☐ Software requirements specification.

☐ Software design specification.

☐   Software test plan.

☐   Software risk management plan.

☐   Software configuration management plan.

☐   User-deliverable documentation.

Standards, Practices, Conventions, and Metrics

Purpose

☐   Cross-reference all documents to the specific practices to be applied from each.

☐   Cross-reference monitoring, review, and audit compliance for each.

☐   Cross-reference where each occurs in the development life cycle.

Content

☐   Product-specific quality measures.

☐   Web page standards.

☐   Documentation standards.

☐   Logic structure standards.

☐   Coding standards.

☐   Naming conventions.

☐   Commentary standards.

☐   Testing standards and practices.

☐   All software quality assurance product and process metrics.

Reviews and Audits

Purpose

☐   Definitions of the technical and managerial reviews and audits to be conducted.

☐   Rules and procedures for the reviews and audits to be accomplished.

☐   Minimum attendees at reviews and audits in order to proceed.

☐   Cross-reference of all reviews and audits to the project life cycle.

☐ Minimum recording standards for all reviews.

☐ Disposition process for issues uncovered during reviews and audits.

☐ Use of issue tracking system.

☐ Use of change control.

SQA Required Reviews

☐ Project management plan review.

☐ Software requirements specification review.

☐ Software design specification review.

☐ Software test plan review.

☐ Software risk management plan review.

☐ Software configuration management plan review.

☐ User-deliverable documentation review.

☐ Functional audit as part of delivery milestone.

☐ Physical audit for code and documentation internal consistency.

☐ In-process audits for design to code consistency.

☐ Managerial reviews to assess process and procedure compliance.

☐ Postmortem review for lessons learned at project end.

Risk Management

☐ Cross-reference to specific risk mitigation plans aided by SQAP.

☐ Statement of how SQAP reduced specific classes of risk for this project.

☐ SQA review cycle with especial emphasis on risk mitigation.

☐ Cross-reference of periodic risk reviews with specific SQAP reviews, assessments, and audits.

☐ SQAP risk reporting requirements over and above those in the risk management plan.

Problem Reporting and Corrective Action

☐ Cross-reference the roles and responsibilities previously listed to their relationship to problem reporting and resolution.

- [ ] Describe the process for issue tracking.
- [ ] Describe the process for problem reporting.
- [ ] Describe the life cycle of issue to problem to resolved problem.
- [ ] Cross-reference how these processes interact with the configuration management process.

Tools, Techniques, and Methodologies

- [ ] List all tools that are used for SQA on this project.
- [ ] List who is responsible for managing the tools.
- [ ] Describe the process for securing tool licenses.
- [ ] Define all SQA-specific techniques used.
- [ ] Provide ROI information on the use of the techniques.
- [ ] Define all SQA-specific methodologies used.
- [ ] Provide ROI information on the use of the methodologies.
- [ ] Define how the SCMP handles code control.
- [ ] Define how the SCMP handles the delivery media of the final product.

Supplier Control

- [ ] List all COTS application software included in the final product.
- [ ] List all COTS application development tools used to build the final product.
- [ ] List all COTS database products used on the project.
- [ ] Provide a specific quality assurance plan for each piece of COTS software used on the project.
- [ ] List all personnel requirements for nonemployee team members.
- [ ] Provide a plan for ensuring the work product quality of contractors on the project team.

Training

- [ ] List all baseline SQA training required for project team members.
- [ ] List all SQA refresher training required.
- [ ] List training requirements for audit, review, and facilitator positions.

Records Collection, Maintenance, and Retention

☐   Location of the server file system maintaining all the project records.

☐   Backup schedule of the project information.

☐   Recovery instructions for the project information repository.

☐   Retention periods for project-generated quality records.

Summary

The Software Engineering Institute's Capability Maturity Model (CMM) has listed software quality assurance (SQA) as a key process area since the institute's inception. Getting a SQAP (software quality assurance plan) is what this chapter presented. This is one of the basic but often overlooked processes all software development practitioners need to follow for successful software development projects. Software quality assurance involves the reviewing of all delivered software products and the activities within the life cycle that produced them. Auditing can be performed to ensure that the products and processes conform to the internal organization policies and procedures for software development as well as industry standards. The CMM lists four goals that must be achieved to satisfy this key process area:

Goal 1—Software quality assurance activities are planned.

Goal 2—Adherence of software products and activities to the applicable standards, procedures, and requirements is verified objectively.

Goal 3—Affected groups and individuals are informed of the SQA activities and results.

Goal 4—Senior management addresses noncompliance issues that cannot be resolved within the software project.

This chapter has presented the mechanism for meeting those CMM goals in a efficient and cost-effective fashion.

In the *IEEE Standard Glossary of Software Engineering Terminology, software quality assurance* is defined as: (1) a planned and systematic pattern of all actions necessary to provide adequate confidence that an item or product conforms to established technical requirements, and (2) a set of activities designed to evaluate the process by which products are developed or manufactured. The references at the end of this chapter have complete in-depth information on quality lessons from quality experts, personnel requirements, training plans, organizations for project quality, and calculating the cost of product and project quality. All of these are important quality issues of which professional software project managers should be aware. The focus of this book is on tools that practitioners can use. Therefore, this chapter discussed how to build an adequate SQAP, what checklists to employ, and where to find the information. Please see the references for the theoretical treatments of software quality assurance.

When is it practical to build a SQAP? The authors of this book have found through experience that it is cost-effective to build a software quality assurance plan for any project that is estimated to take more than six person-months of effort to complete.

Problems for Review

1. Go online to *www.asq.org/cert/types/csqe/studyguide.html*, Software Quality Engineer Certification (CSQE) Study Guide, and take the sample examination.
2. SQA is a key process for reaching Level 2 in the CMM. Is this too early in the organizational maturity for most software developers?
3. How would you modify the SQAP template for use as a general-purpose template in your organization?
4. Is the SQAP template provide in this chapter adequate for an ISO 9001 certification?
5. Has a SQAP been done for your team on the Chinese Railway project?
6. Build a SQAP for the lift problem as detailed in Appendix F, "Project Artifact Templates."

Visit the Case Study

It was a good thing that, as project manager, you had to address re-evaluating your project plan and implementing the 10% cut. Mr. Lu and Dr. Zhou have found a source of funding within the Peoples Railway Ministry that was going to be used for upgrading to the latest Microsoft operating system. Because the ministry is moving to Red Flag Linux, that money is available for other projects. Mr. Lu will provide an additional $500,000 to you if you can bring in the project completion date 90 days. Dr. Zhou said that this is truly possible because her first look at crashing the project says that this is possible. You must respond within five working days, or the funding will go into upgrading the tea service on the soft-seat cars.

References

Clements, Paul C. (1999). *Constructing Superior Software*. Macmillan Technical Publishing.

IEEE 610.12-1990, *IEEE Standard Glossary of Software Engineering Terminology* (ANSI).

IEEE 730.1-1995, *IEEE Guide for Software Quality Assurance Planning*, IEEE Computer Society, 1996.

IEEE 730–1998, *IEEE Standard for Software Quality Assurance Plans*, IEEE Computer Society, 1998.

IEEE 982.1-1988, *IEEE Standard Dictionary of Measures to Produce Reliable Software*, IEEE Computer Society, 1989.

IEEE 982.2-1988, *IEEE Guide for the Use of IEEE Standard Dictionary of Measures to Produce Reliable Software*, IEEE Computer Society, 1989.

IEEE 1228-1994, *IEEE Standard for Software Safety Plans*, IEEE Computer Society, 1994.

Schulmeyer, Gordon C., and James I. McManus (1999). *Handbook of Software Quality Assurance*, 3rd ed. Prentice-Hall.

Web Pages for Further Information

acis.mit.edu/acis/sqap/sqap.r1.html. An SQAP prepared by MIT for NASA.

home.okstate.edu/homepages.nsf/toc/level2.index.html. CMM Level 2 Focus Group.

irb.cs.uni-magdeburg.de/sw-eng/us/. Software Measurement Lab at the University of Magdeburg.

lifelong.engr.utexas.edu/sqi/index.cfm. Software Quality Institute.

qaiusa.com. Quality Assurance Institute.

satc.gsfc.nasa.gov/homepage.html. Software Assurance Technology Center.

seg.iit.nrc.ca/English/index.html. National Research Center of Canada.

standards.ieee.org/index.html. IEEE Standards.

www.acm.org/jacm/. Association for Computing Journal of the ACM.

www.acm.org/sigsoft/. Association for Computing Machinery SIG Software Engineering.

www.acm.org/tosem/. Association for Computing Transactions on Software Engineering and Methodology.

www.adtmag.com/. Application development trends.

www.asq.org. American Society for Quality (ASQ).

www.asq-software.org. ASQ Software Division.

www.computer.org. IEEE Computer Society.

www.cs.uwf.edu/~wilde/gump/sqa.htm. Document that describes the Software Quality Assurance (SQA) plan for the generic software-maintenance process used in the Software Engineering graduate program at the University of West Florida (UWF).

www.esi.es/. European Software Institute.

www.faqs.org/faqs/software-eng/. Software Engineering FAQ.

www.ics.hawaii.edu/~johnson/FTR/. Technical Review Archive.

www.ics.hawaii.edu/~siro/. Software Inspections and Review Organization.

www.ondaweb.com/sti/newsltr.htm. Software Testing Newsletter.

www.psmsc.com. Practical Software Measurement.

www.qfdi.org/. QFD Institute.

www.sei.cmu.edu. Software Engineering Institute.

www.sigmetrics.org/. Association for Computing Machinery SIG Metrics.

www.soft.com/AppNotes/TestWorksIndex/index.html. TestWorks Quality Index.

www.soft.com/News/TTN-Online. Testing Techniques Newsletter.

www.spc.ca/. Software Productivity Centre.

www.sqatester.com. SQAtester.com.

www.sqe.com. Software Quality Engineering.

www.ssq.org/. Society for Software Quality.

wwwsel.iit.nrc.ca/SPN/. Software Process Newsletter.

www-sqi.cit.gu.edu.au/. Australian SW Quality Research Institute.

Software Configuration Management

31

Software engineers usually find coding to be the most satisfying aspect of their job. This is easy to understand because programming is a challenging, creative activity requiring extensive technical skills. It can mean getting to "play" with state-of-the-art tools, and it provides almost instant gratification in the form of immediate feedback. Programming is the development task that most readily comes to mind when the profession of software engineering is mentioned.

That said, seasoned engineers and project managers realize that programmers are part of a larger team. All of the integral tasks, such as quality assurance and verification and validation, are behind-the-scenes activities necessary to turn standalone software into a useful and usable commodity. Software configuration management (SCM) falls into this category—it can't achieve star status, like the latest "killer app," but it is essential to project success. The smart software project manager highly values the individuals and tools that provide this service.

This chapter will answer the following questions about software configuration management.

What Is Software Configuration Management? _____

Software configuration management (SCM) is the organization of the components of a software system so that they fit together in a working order, never out of synch with each other. Those who have studied the best way to manage the configuration of software parts have more elegant responses.

Roger Pressman says that SCM is a "set of activities designed to control change by identifying the work products that are likely to change, establishing relationships among them, defining mechanisms for managing different versions of these work products, controlling the changes imposed, and auditing and reporting on the changes made."[1]

We think that Pressman's description is a better description because we often view SCM as meaning software *change* management.

Wayne Babich describes SCM as "the art of identifying, organizing, and controlling modifications to the software being built by a programming team. It maximizes productivity by minimizing mistakes."[2]

The Software Engineering Institute says that it is necessary to establish and maintain the integrity of the products of the software project throughout the software life cycle. Activities necessary to accomplish this include identifying configuration items/units, systematically controlling changes, and maintaining the integrity and the traceability of the configuration throughout the software life cycle.

Military standards view *configuration* as the functional and/or physical characteristics of hardware/software as set forth in technical documentation and archives in a product. In identifying the items that need to be configured, we must remember that all project artifacts are candidates—documents, graphical models, prototypes, code, and any internal or external deliverable that can undergo change. In SW PM terminology, a configuration item might be a proposal/estimate or bid, project plan, risk management plan, quality assurance plan, CM plan itself, test plan, system requirements specification, system design document, review metric, code, test result, tool (editors, compilers, CASE), and so on. There are basic objects and aggregate objects to be configured. The number of relationships among them reflects the complexity of the configuration task.

Why Is SCM Important? _____

Software project managers pay attention to the planning and execution of configuration management, an integral task, because it facilitates the ability to communicate status of documents and code as well as changes that have been made to them. High-quality released software has been tested and used, making it a reusable asset and saving development costs. Reused components aren't free, though—they require integration into new products, a difficult task without knowing exactly what they are and where they are.

CM enhances the ability to provide maintenance support necessary once the software is deployed. If software didn't change, maintenance wouldn't exist. Of course, changes do occur. The National Institute of Standards and Technology (NIST) says that software will be changed to adapt, perfect, or correct it. Pressman points out that new business, new customer needs, reorganizations, and budgetary or scheduling constraints may lead to software revision.

CM works for the project and the organization in other ways as well. It helps to eliminate confusion, chaos, double maintenance, the shared data problem, and the simultaneous update problem, to name but a few issues to be discussed in this chapter.

Who Is Involved in SCM?

Virtually everyone on a software project is affected by SCM. From the framers of the project plan to the final tester, we rely on it to tell us how to find the object with the latest changes. During development, when iterations are informal and frequent, little needs to be known about a change except what it is, who did it, and where it is. In deployment and baselining, changes must be prioritized, and the impact of a change upon all customers must be considered. A change control board (CCB) is the governing body for modifications after implementation.

How Can Software Configuration Be Implemented in Your Organization?

We used to say, "Make a plan and stick with it—never waffle," and "Requirements must be frozen—how else will we know what to code?" Now, we say, "Plans are living documents— they will be in a continual state of change as project knowledge increases." We now know that requirements are never frozen—they merge, morph, and evolve and become expanded, enhanced, and extended. As long as artifacts of software development can undergo change, we will need some method of managing the change.

Because SCM is such a key tool in improving the quality of delivered products, understanding it and how to implement it in your organization and on your projects is a critical success factor. This chapter will review SCM plan templates and provide you with a composite SCM plan template for use in any of your projects. We will cover the issues and basics for a sound software project CM system, including these:

- SCM principles
- The four basic requirements for an SCM system

- Planning and organizing for SCM
- SCM tools
- Benefits of SCM
- Path to SCM implementation

The concept of configuration is analogous to a bill of materials to assemble any product. Think of the product of an SCM as a system parts list, as in Figure 31–1.

Unlike hardware, software is not physical (tangible), is more complex, is easier to change, propagates change effects, and is data as well as logic.

Where We Are in the Product Development Life Cycle _____

SCM is an integral task, beginning early in the life cycle. Required from the beginning of the system exploration phase, the project software configuration management system must be available for the remainder of the project. Figure 31–2 illustrates the "when" of SCM on our full product development life cycle.

Chapter 31 Relation to the 34 Competencies _____

Software configuration management falls within competency 8, selecting methods and tools, a product development technique. Project managers' application of sound software development methods, techniques, and tools coupled with project management practices, determines organizational success or failure. A critical method in this success is formalized configuration management.

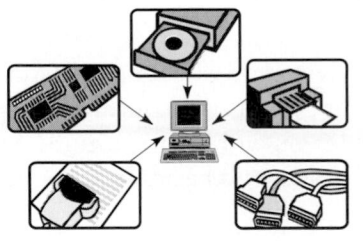

| Parts List |
| 3D Graphics Accelerator—1 |
| SCSI Host Adapter—1 |
| Network Interface Card—1 |
| 32X CR-ROM—1 |
| Tape Backup Unit—1 |
| 32 MB SIMMs—2 |

FIGURE 31–1
SCM Is a "Software Parts List"

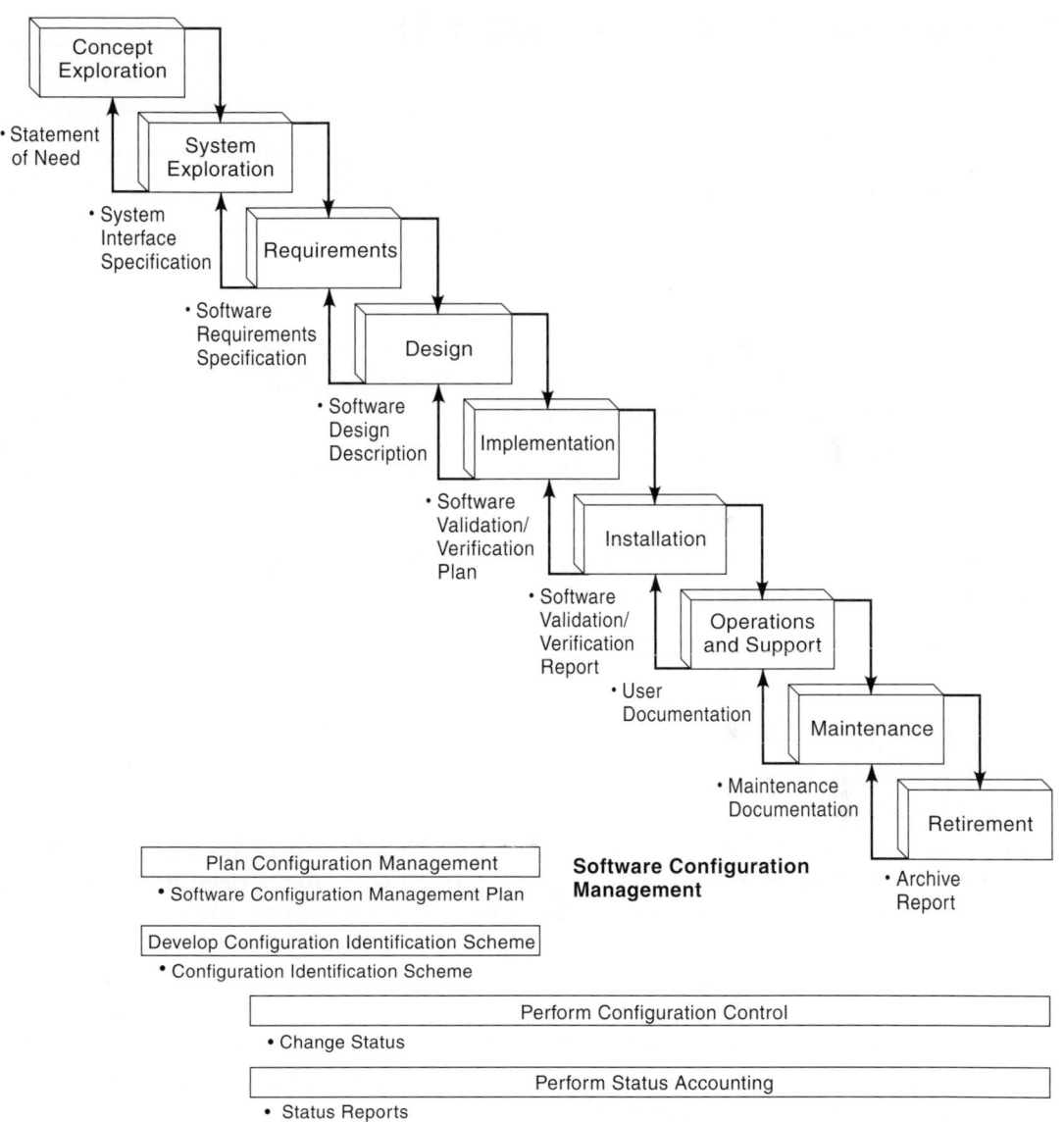

FIGURE 31–2

Configuration Management Occurs Throughout the Product Development Life Cycle

Learning Objectives for Chapter 31 _____

Upon completion of this chapter, readers will be able to perform the following:

- Describe sound software development methods, techniques, and tools coupled with project management practices;

- Apply configuration management tools that support these five areas contributing to software product quality:

  - Design and code inspections,

  - Formal design methods,

  - Configuration management tools,

  - Testing methods, and

  - Prototyping and modern languages;

- Define configuration management processes for use throughout the product development life cycle phases of any organization;

- Evaluate commercial off-the-shelf configuration management and change control tools for use within software development projects.

SCM Principles _____

SCM can be viewed as a pyramid, as shown in Figure 31–3. Let's explore each of the six layers, starting at the bottom and working to the top. Then we'll look at two other faces of the pyramid—the training plan and the transition plan.

Understanding of SCM

An understanding of SCM is critical to the organization attempting to institute any system of product control. Understanding through training is a key initial goal, as shown in the pyramid. Executives and management must understand both the benefits and the cost of SCM to provide the needed support in its implementation. Software developers must understand the basics of SCM because they are required to use the tool in building their software products. Without a total understanding, a partial implementation of SCM with workarounds and back doors will result in disaster for an SCM system.

SCM Plans and Policies

Development of an SCM policy for an organization and the subsequent plans for each product developed is crucial to successful SCM implementation. Putting SCM into an organization is

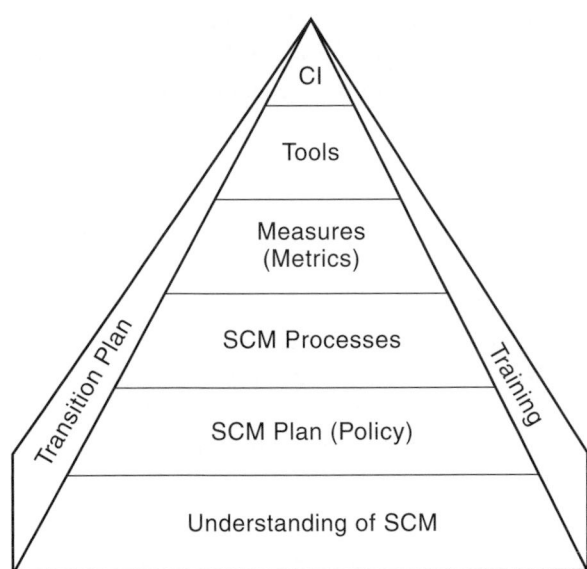

FIGURE 31–3
The Software Configuration Management Pyramid

a project like any other, requiring resources of time and money. There will be specific deliverables and a timeline against which to perform. The policy for the organization lays out in a clear, concise fashion the expectations that the organizational leadership has for its system. It must lay out the anticipated benefits and the method to measure the performance to those benefits.

SCM Processes

The specific processes of SCM are documented for all users to recognize. Not all SCM processes need to be used within an organization or on a product. Yet, it is important to have available, in "plain sight," those processes that are used specifically in your organization. This also maps those processes to how they are implemented.

Metrics

The measures used to show conformance to policy and product plans are important details. These measures show where the organization is along the path to reaping the benefits of SCM.

Tools for SCM

The tools used to implement SCM are the next-to-last item on the pyramid. For too many managers, this is often the first instead of the fifth stem in SCM—many organizations and projects simply buy a tool, plop it in place, and expect magic. Actually, it makes little sense to pick the tools to use in SCM without having done all the previous work. Putting a tool in place without training, policy, or metrics is an exercise in automating chaos. You will simply have an automated way to turn out the wrong product faster.

SCM Configuration Items

The configuration items (CI) are those "things" that represent internal and external project deliverables. They are the final result of all the work done to implement SCM in your organization.

Along one face of the SCM pyramid is the training plan and its execution. A common management mistake is to arbitrarily drop an SCM requirement on a development organization without a corresponding investment in training. The process of SCM and the tools used in its instantiation are complex in concept and execution, making training a true requirement.

Along another face of the pyramid, we indicate the transition plan to get to an effective SCM implementation. The introduction of configuration management is a project in and of itself, requiring a project plan within the context of the organization. Just like planning for development, plans for improving product quality and reducing development time must be followed to reap the benefits.

SCM definitions appear at the end of this chapter. Five of them are covered in part here so that we can begin to use them throughout the chapter.

SCM is the identification scheme for the software components of a system. It controls changes to the configuration and maintains integrity and traceability of the configuration. Software in this context refers to all deliverables: documentation, test scripts, test data files, code, and so on. *Change control* is the management of change as one part of the SCM process. *Version control* is the management of the product versions generated as part of the SCM process. *Release control* is the transformation of configuration items into a deliverable product. A *configuration item* (CI) is a standalone part of the product development that is combined with other CIs into a release. Examples of software CIs include design documents, manuals and tutorials, measurement data, program trouble reports, requirements, source code, and test cases.

SCM Is an SEI CMM Level 2 Key Process Area

In Chapter 30, "Software Quality Assurance," we discussed the Software Engineering Institute (SEI) Capability Maturity Model (CMM) levels of maturity. At Level 2, an organization moves beyond just getting the job done and into an environment where a software project management process is in place, the organization sets expectations via policies, and projects have disciplined phases and milestones. This level is described as the repeatable level, built upon key process areas of requirements management, software project planning, software project tracking and oversight, software subcontract management, software quality assurance, and software configuration management. The goals for SCM at maturity Level 2 are:

- Software configuration management activities are planned.
- Selected software work products are identified, controlled, and available.
- Changes to identified software work products are controlled.
- Affected groups and individuals are informed of the status and content of software baselines.

Questions that assessors might ask include:

- Is a mechanism used for controlling changes to the software requirements?
- Is a mechanism used for controlling changes to the software design?
- Is a mechanism used for controlling changes to the code?
- Is a mechanism used for configuration management of the software tools used in the development process?

The Four Basic Requirements for an SCM System _____

Identification, control, audit, and status accounting are the four basic requirements for a software configuration management system. These requirements must be satisfied regardless of the amount of automation within the SCM process. All four may be satisfied by an SCM tool, a tool set, or a combination of automated and manual procedures.

1. **Identification**—Each software part is labeled so that it can be identified. Furthermore, there will be different versions of the software parts as they evolve over time, so a version or revision number will be associated with the part. The key is to be able to identify any and all artifacts that compose a released configuration item. Think of this as a bill of materials for all the components in your automobile. When the manufacturer realizes that there has been a problem with parking brakes purchased from a subcontractor, it needs to know all the automobile models using that version of the parking brake. It is the same with software. If we are building a multimedia system that has audio MPEG3 drivers for Windows 98, Windows 2000, Windows CE, Linux, and FreeBSD operating systems, how do we find out which releases are impacted when we find an error in the Linux product? You must go back to your SCM system to identify all the common components in all operating system releases that are impacted.

2. **Control**—In the context of configuration management, "control" means that proposed changes to a CI are reviewed and, if approved, incorporated into the software configuration. The goal is to make informed decisions and to acknowledge the repercussions associated with a change to the system. These changes may impact budgets, schedules, and associated changes to other components. If a problem is reported in a released product, software engineers must act quickly to evaluate repercussions—a "fix" for one client's version of the product may be dangerous to another. The control inherent in an SCM system shows each version in which the flawed component appears.

3. **Auditing**—Auditing an SCM system means that approved requested changes have indeed been implemented. The audits allow managers to determine whether software evolution is proceeding both logically and in conformance with requirements for the software. The SCM system should document changes, versions, and release information for all components of each configuration item. When such documentation is in place, auditing becomes a straightforward analysis task.

4. **Status accounting**—Reports and documentation produced by the status accounting function are the auditable entries. All approved parts of a software configuration must be accounted for, and the software parts list must reflect the transition from part CIn to CIn+1. This accounting provides the historic information to determine both what happened and when on the software project. Status accounting enables the auditing requirement of the SCM. As a project manager, the status accounting holds a wealth of information on the amount of effort required throughout the life cycle of the product in its development and maintenance. This is critical to the software project manager in making estimates for new systems based on historic information. The SCM can be used as one of the key components of the project managers' metrics system.

Planning and Organizing for SCM

When planning for SCM in your product development organization, you must first understand the classes of potential problems that can exist. Once the classes are understood, the inherent problems that are causing configuration management issues may be easily identified.

Potential SCM Problem Classes

1. **Multiple developer syndrome**—When you have a project that requires more than one developer, there is the problem with multiple people working on one product base. This could be a test plan, requirements specification, or code. Effort is wasted when two or more people work on the same file and then save it. Without SCM control, the last person to save the file has those changes saved. All the other changes are lost. The simplistic method of locking a file while one person reads it prevents others from simultaneously working on the file.

2. **Multiple releases**—Enhancements to the base product should result in additional releases of the product containing the latest changes. Once the second release is available, some users are on an earlier release. Having an SCM makes managing those releases possible. When bugs are reported, changes must be made across all impacted releases. As new features become available in the product, they must be made available to all current users, no matter what the release date.

3. **Product family**—As products are built that offer the same capabilities across a heterogeneous set of hardware platforms, both the common and the platform-specific software bases must be managed. If a product operates on four versions of Windows, three versions of Unix, Red Hat Linux, and FreeBSD the user manual may be significantly the same. But there is a different installation process for all nine platforms. Without SCM, nine individual manuals must be written and maintained. With SCM, one documentation configuration item with nine versions will suffice, with the differences being only the installation procedure.

4. **Requirements change**—The first law of systems engineering is that no matter where we are in the system life cycle, the system/software will change, and the desire to change it will persist throughout the life cycle. Dealing with this change represents a major management challenge. Having an SCM in place will ease the management of these changes to the requirements of the products that will occur. An SCM allows the easy identification of feature sets that group the requirements satisfied by a release or version of the product. These feature sets are tracked through development to delivery.

5. **Schedule change**—As requirements change, so must the schedule. Mapping the feature sets for release to the schedule allows project managers to more accurately estimate the effort required for generating that next release. Having the SCM in place allows the project manager to look at historic effort levels in getting out releases. This is an enormous aid in estimating the "what if" scenarios that result from taking on new product users or providing customized solutions to other clients.

6. **Software changes**—No product developer has the luxury to write code once and forget about it. Along with requirements and schedules, the software being developed changes in response to those other changes. Software is not static. That is its inherent power. It *can* be changed, so it will be changed. SCM systems track those changes so that, if the wrong change is made, a previous working version is available. This capability alone has saved enormous amounts of time as developers have tried out specific solutions that did not work in the product environment and were able to rapidly back up to a working version.

7. **Staff changes**—In the best of organizations, people get promoted, take other jobs, and leave. When that happens in the midst of a development project, not just the technology knowledge goes out the door. The long-learned knowledge of how things are done is also gone. So when a replacement person is brought on board, they may know the technology, but without a documented SCM process, they will have no real idea how to do product development. SCM provides the framework and knowledge base of what has gone on before in the project. A new staff member has one place to go to understand the "how" of the organization's development process and the "what" of the project to date.

8. **System/user documentation change**—No product developer has the luxury to produce in a technology or tool vacuum. All product developers use hardware microcode, operating systems, tools, and documentation that are not under their control. When a major

operating system change occurs (e.g., the next "best" release of Windows), an SCM will allow tracing all the CIs, components, and subcomponents that are impacted by that change. The change is isolated, and the amount of effort required to respond to the change can be estimated. This provides a responsible schedule for an upgrade based on situations beyond the organization's control.

A template that may be used in the creation of a software configuration management plan (SCMP) appears in Appendix F, "Project Artifact Templates." It includes management issues (organization, responsibility, etc.), SCM activities (configuration item identification, change control, status accounting, audit, and reviews), tools, techniques and methods, supplier control, and standards collection and retention.

SCM Staffing

On any given project, a few engineers or developers specialize in and become your SCM experts. While they are the gurus, everyone on your project will be a user of the product that they select, develop, and maintain. It is better to have a few highly experienced people than a large number of inexperienced people. These experienced few must be able to see congruence between software products and perceive what is missing from a software product.

We can group the characteristics and abilities needed by the four SCM functions: identification, control, auditing, and status accounting.

Identification

1. Ability to see partitions
2. Ability to see relationships
3. Some technical ability
4. System engineering orientation
5. Programming

Control

1. Ability to evaluate benefits versus cost
2. System viewpoint (balance of technical/managerial, user/buyer/seller)
3. An appreciation of what is involved in engineering a software change

Auditing

1. Extreme attention to detail
2. Ability to see congruence
3. Ability to perceive what is missing
4. Extensive experience with technical aspects of system engineering or software engineering

Status Accounting

1. Ability to take notes and record data
2. Ability to organize data
3. Some technical familiarity
4. System engineering orientation
5. Programming

Once the staffing of the SCM function is complete and the overall organization's SCM policy is established, the configuration control board (CCB) is identified. The CCB is the heart of the control function. It infuses sustained visibility into the process of change throughout the system life cycle and traceability into the process of change. The membership in the CCB is not limited to the developers or product line management. All stakeholders in the product must be represented. This includes the end-user usually represented by marketing, subcontractors used in the product development, product development funders, and the product developers. The CCB is the final decision maker as to what bug fixes, enhancements, and feature sets get included in the next product release.

The CCB has periodic meetings, with the results documented. These meetings can be done in a rapid fashion, and doing them online or via email is an adequate way to gain consensus and come to a decision. Important to status accounting is the documentation of CCB meeting minutes. The basic purpose of the minutes is to provide the CCB decision makers with the information needed to make intelligent, informed decisions. The amount of detail varies with the meeting frequency and technical content.

SCM Tools

The minimum features for SCM tools are closely related to the task of handling the different product deliverables produced within the project software engineering process. Tool requirements and selection criteria are based on a series of features that provide a consistent look and feel with state-of-the-art software development environments. An SCM tool must have multiuser support, an intuitive graphical user interface, conformity to the organization's development environment, scalability, flexibility in integrating other software development tools, ease of setup, modifiable models, process management, extensive support for the development phase, and management of nondevelopment objects.

Basic selection criteria includes the following:

- **Multiuser support**—Tools are to be used concurrently by several users. They have to store all acquired information in a central, shared repository, and the SCM tool has to allow controlled parallel work on the different project documents.

- **Intuitive GUI**—Because the tools will be used throughout the project and not only by developers, an intuitive, easy-to-use graphical user interface is considered very important.

- **Conformity to the organization's development environment**—The organization must define up front the hardware and software development platforms used. For example, the project may work on a heterogeneous network of Unix-based workstations (mainly Sun Sparc stations) and PCs. The workstations may be used for some part of the development and as a file server and communication server. The PCs may be using MS Windows 2000 NT. PCs and workstations may be interconnected using the NFS protocol (especially Sun PC-NFSpro on the PCs). The tool has to be able to store its shared repositories on a workstation and has to allow PC clients as well as workstation clients supporting the operating systems and protocols.

- **Scalability**—The tool should work equally well for smaller projects as for larger ones.

- **Flexibility in integrating other software development tools**—The tool must allow the integration of all the other development tools to provide a highly homogeneous environment. Especially the tools for design, implementation, and testing will have to co-operate on the common SCM repository.

- **Ease of setup**—The SCM tool should allow an easy installation and setup, and should be able to run nearly "out of the box." It should contain predefined, immediately usable models describing the types of items, the life cycle, and the roles of the different users. The importance of existing projects and their directory structures should be made as easy as possible.

- **Modifiable models**—Though a working set of models should be predefined, each of these should be modifiable and extensible. This is especially important because project managers and developers want to adapt these models to the software development process as defined for the company. Role models must be adapted to the roles assigned to the different employees on the project. Object-type models must be extensible to reflect different types of objects used in the environment and especially with respect to nondevelopment objects.

- **Process management**—Process management comprises efficient support of object life cycles and object promotion, together with a flexible and extensible approach to life cycle models. Based on a concept of object types, it should be possible to attach different life cycles to different types of objects.

- **Extensive support for the development phase**—During development when checkout and update of objects is frequent, the tool should aid a developer in determining the set of objects that need an update or renewed check-in. Although this requirement seems to be trivial at first, the latest version of the tool you plan to use must be evaluated with emphasis on the environment prior to the first build. These do a good job in change management once the first release has been produced.

- **Management of nondevelopment objects**—SCM tools must manage all artifacts of the project, not just code. These will mainly be documents and their versions and releases. The tool must be able to support that.

- **Permission management**—Everyone should not have access to make changes to different pieces of the software. In many situations, check-in and checkout only will not prevent integration from being broken by multiple people modifying code for their own designs and interfaces.

Many configuration management tools in the market promise to fulfill more or less all of the requirements. Chapter 24, "Use of Tools," presented a general model for the selection of tools to support software development and project management. The keys to any tool selection are to know your project's tool requirements, to understand how tools relate to the project's success factors, and to do a current market search for tools. The following is an example of using that tool selection method for an SCM tool. This is simply an example, and it must be updated with individual key project success factors, tool requirements, and the tools available in the market based on the project's schedule requirements.

A quick search of the market in SCM tools provided the list of potential candidates for the tool as shown in Table 31–1.

TABLE 31–1
SCM Tools

Name of Tool	Description and Company	Internet Address
AllChange 2000 SE	IntaSoft	*www.intasoft.net/*
CCC/Harvest, CCC/ Manager, CCC QuikTrak	Computer Associates (formerly Platinum)	*ca.com/products/ccm/*
ClearCase	Rational (formerly PureAtria)	*www.rational.com/products/ clearcase*
CMVC, now VisualAge Team Connection	Configuration Management and Version Control, IBM	*www-4.ibm.com/software/ad/ teamcon/*
Continuus	Continuus	*www.continuus.com/*
eChange Man	Serena	*www.serena.com/html/echange.htm*
Enabler aqua	Softlab	*www.softlab.com/technology/ frm_tech00.asp*
Endevor	Computer Associates	*www.cai.com/products/ endevor_ws.htm*
Perforce	Perforce Software	*www.perforce.com/*

(Continues)

TABLE 31–1 (Continued)
SCM Tools

Name of Tool	Description and Company	Internet Address
PVCS	MERANT (formed by a combination of MicroFocus and Intersolv)	*www.merant.com/products/pvcs/*
PVCS Dimensions	MERANT (formerly PCMS Dimensions from SQL Software)	*www.merant.com/products/pvcs/* *www.pvcs.synergex.com/*
Razor	Visible Software	
RCE (VRCE)	Revision Control Engine (Visual RCE) DuraSoft GmbH	*wwwipd.ira.uka.de/~RCE/*
Sablime	Lucent Technologies	*www.bell-labs.com/project/sablime/*
SCCS	Source Code Control System	*Comes with most Unix distributions.*
SCLM	Software Configuration Library Manager, IBM	*booksrv2.raleigh.ibm.com/*
SCM	Source Code Manager, UniPress Software, Inc.	*www.unipress.com/cat/scm.html*
SoftBench	HP	*www.devresource.hp.com/softbench/sb_description.html*
Source Integrity	MKS	*www.mks.com/products/scm/si/*
StarTeam	StarBase	*www.starbase.com/products/starteam/*
TeamSite	Interwoven	*www.interwoven.com*
TRUEchange	McCabe and Associates	*www.mccabe.com/products/truechange.htm*
TurnOver	Soft Landing Systems	*www.softlanding.com/turnover.html*
Visual Age TeamConnection	IBM	*www-4.ibm.com/software/ad/teamcon/*
Visual Enabler	Soft Lab	*www.softlabna.com/pages/espages/visenable.htm*
Visual Source Safe	Microsoft Corp. (PC) / Metrowerks (Macintosh)	*www.microsoft.com/ssafe/*

From the list, four were picked as possible commercial products that would meet the project's requirements:

1. **PCMS** is an established product with strong all-round capability to manage the development of complex software projects over a wide range of platforms. Based on information in the public domain, PCMS has shown the greatest level of product development.

2. **ClearCase** is the dominant commercial SCM-tool in Unix development environments and is rapidly moving into NT client/server market development environments. It has achieved this principally by providing developers with transparent tools supporting their work environment and culture. The introduction of ClearTrack extends the all-around capability of the tool set by supporting the management and documentation of changes. After the recent liaison between Rational Software Corporation and Atria Software, Inc., an interesting merge of features between the object-oriented design tool Rational Rose and ClearCase may be expected.

3. **Continuus/CM** toolset is characterized by a strong embedded support for process, and its breadth of SCM coverage. The task-based process model is an intuitive approach to the management of change. Distributed development via direct links or over the Internet is simple to set up and operate. However, working across low-grade communication networks is difficult to set up and administer.

4. **PVCS** is the market-leading system for software configuration management by numbers sold. It is simple to use and has stood the test of time. Intersolv has gradually added functionality to Version Manager with associated products such as Tracker, Configuration Builder, and Gateway, and by integrating PVCS with many third-party tools.

Following an example from SEI, we formed a ranking system for comparing the tools (Figure 31–4). Table 31–2 shows the rating for the considered tools.

The result of this first ranking allows one of the potential tools, PVCS, to be dropped. This would then leave three for the project manager and tool evaluation team to take a more in-depth look. Note that there has been no discussion of price at this time. Once the technical decision has been made, the cost decision should follow. Do not introduce price early in the evaluation. If there is discomfort with the technical capabilities and life cycle coverage of a tool, adding in a cost variable will only further confuse the decision. Many software project tools become less desirable after full life cycle cost is analyzed and estimated. Make the technical decision first.

As a final note on tools, working strictly in a Microsoft development environment with Microsoft tools working under Visual InterDev, Visual Source Safe (VSS) is included as an integral part of the tool suite. VSS is an adequate SCM tool for small commercial product development that is strictly targeted to Microsoft platforms. If you're developing on Microsoft platforms and have delivery targets on Linux or Unix, investigate the use of WinCVS. WinCVS is a shareware package that is very capable in providing large-project, multiplatform SCM. It compares favorably with most and betters some commercial SCM tools.

CRITERIA	IEEE	NASA	DoD
Ease of Use	3	1	1
Completeness	2	1	0
Tailorability	3	1	1
Consistency	3	3	3
Correctness	3	1	1
Life Cycle Connection	1	1	1

RATING KEY

0 = Does not satisfy minimum requirements
1 = Satisfies requirements for average standard
2 = Satisfies requirements for good standard
3 = Satisfies requirements for excellent standard

Ranking CM Plans

These three standards were compared using six criteria. They were: ease of use, completeness, tailorability, consistency, correctness, and life cycle connection. The rating of the three standards is shown in the matrix above. The rating system used was 0–3. A standard received a score of 0 if it did not meet the minimum attributes for a criterion, a score of 1 if it met the minimum attributes, a score of 2 if it met the attributes associated with a good standard, and a score of 3 if it met the attributes associated with an excellent standard.

FIGURE 31–4
SEI Template for Ranking CM Plans
Source: SEI, from *Configuration Management Plans: The Beginning to your CM Solution*.

Benefits of SCM Process and Tools

SCM benefits an organization in four areas: control, management, cost savings, and quality (Figure 31–5). These four benefits are mapped to an organization's overall goals and objectives when the decisions are made to bring a SCM tool in-house. The features of a SCM tool further support these benefits.

TABLE 31–2
Comparison of Four Commercial SCM Tools

	PCMS	ClearCase	Continuus/CM	PVCS
Multiuser support	4	3	3	2
Intuitive GUI	3	4	3	3
Environment conformity	3	4	4	4
Scalability	4	4	4	2
Flexibility in integrating other software development tools	2	3	1	3
Ease of setup	3	3	3	4
Modifiable models	4	3	4	3
Process management	4	2	4	2
Development phase support	4	4	4	3
Nondevelopment objects	4	4	4	4
Total	36	35	34	30

These values are used to indicate ratings: 5 = Excellent; 4 = Good; 3 = Fair, 2 = Unsatisfactory; 1 = Unknown

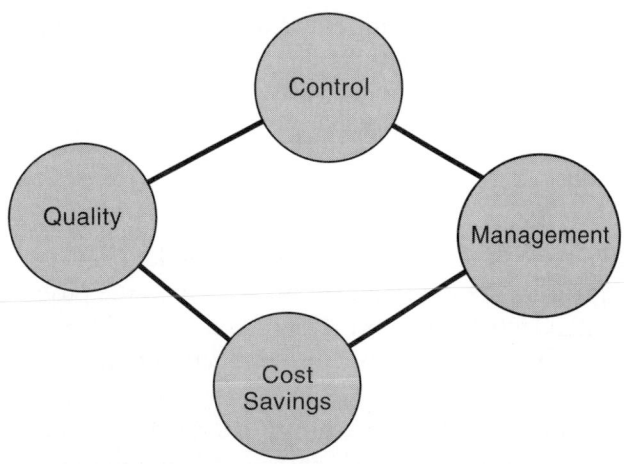

FIGURE 31–5
SCM Benefits the Organization in Four Major Ways

Control

Control in SCM provides the ability to review, approve, and incorporate changes into a configuration item. There must be one controlling SCM tool so that there is only one set of training, license management, installation, and user procedures. All project personnel use the tool. Inherent in the tool is a standardized, measurable process for change. Integrity maintenance of CIs is enforced throughout the product life cycle. The tool permits only controlled change to the baseline CIs, and all changes are tracked.

Management

Management in SCM is concerned with the automation of identifying and guiding configuration items through their life cycle to final assembly as part of product and delivery. Identification of CIs through a unique naming convention allows version, release, update, and full change tracking. Baselining of CIs with the ability to produce product deltas from the baseline satisfies requirement and schedule changes along with product family support. Rapid reviews and audits of CIs are accomplished through the analysis of historic information collected. Project status reporting is accomplished in a clear and consistent format based on SCM collected information on all CIs under configuration management.

Cost Savings

Cost savings are realized across the entire product development life cycle with SCM. Maintaining product integrity through defined, tracked, and audited CIs provides a managed bill of materials for the product released to customers. Cost savings scale with SCM use and application across applications. This scaling is dependent on the depth of control needed for each application product release tree. Deep combinations for product families can be analyzed for risk exposure and cost savings directly impacted by the amount of configuration management applied. Side effects are reduced through controlled change by understanding the impact on all versions and releases. Accurate and repeatable release control is produced in a repeatable fashion over entire product families for all customers and users.

Quality

Software development is a people-intensive activity, and quality must be considered at every person-to-tool interface. Ensuring a high-quality work environment must address the process of building software products in an automated fashion. This must include tracking CIs to the tools that produced them and the clients that ultimately receive the product. Measuring the end product to ensure high quality is done through tracking the changes made to a product throughout its life cycle. Repeatable management and change control in a documented and measured fashion allows accurate estimation of future efforts. Quality is an ongoing process. The lessons learned in one product must be transferred to new, related products and entire product families.

Some Problems with Software _____

Software development has traditionally suffered from producing end products with a definite lack of inherent quality. The symptoms of this quality lack are listed here:

- Software development projects are often delivered late and over budget.
- Often the delivered product does not meet customer requirements and is never used.
- Software products simply do not work right.

As we look into the symptoms of our software development malaise, five principal issues related to software development arise.

Lack of Visibility

Software is conceptual in nature. Unlike a bridge, a building, or another physical structure, it is not easy to look at software and assess how close it is to completion. Without strong project management, "software is 90% complete 90% of the time." Through the adoption of SCM policy and the definition of the configuration management model of the software under development, all CIs, components, and subcomponents are immediately visible for versions, releases, and product families.

Lack of Control

Because software is inherently intangible, it is also more difficult to control. Without an accurate assessment of progress, schedules slip and budgets are overrun. It is hard to assess what has been accomplished and what remains to be done. SCM provides the mechanism for controlling the project through measuring the amount of effort compared to the project management plan and estimating the future effort based on past work.

Lack of Traceability

A lack of linkage between project events contributes to project failures. The main benefit of SCM is providing the traceability among versions, releases, and product families. The value of this traceability is enormous when a problem arises in one release or product family that impacts other client releases and products. Making one change and promoting that through the entire product software base is an incredible cost savings in time, money, and client good will. A lack of linkage between project events contributes to project failures where solving one problem either exacerbates a problem in another area or fails to fix the same problem elsewhere. A traceability thread allows management to examine the chain of events that caused a project to encounter difficulty as an integral process within the auditing capability of SCM. A project becomes a year late one day at a time unless the effort reported on the schedule maps to the actual work being done and traced within the software configuration management system.

Lack of Monitoring

Without traceability and visibility, monitoring of software development projects becomes extremely difficult. Management cannot make informed decisions, and thus schedules slip further and costs continue to exceed budget.

There is no way to monitor a project when the project manager has no tools to look into the actual product development within the project. SCM provides the tools that open up the process to external monitoring. With SCM in place and a policy of traceability and visibility accepted, monitoring of software development projects becomes a simple part of the overall project management task. Management makes informed decisions avoiding schedule slips and budget excesses through the monitoring available with SCM tools and the integral workings of the CCB.

Uncontrolled Change

Software is very malleable; it is idea-stuff, and customers constantly have new ideas for it. People would rarely ask a bridge constructor to make the kinds of changes midproject that software customers tend to request. The impact of such changes can be just as great. All SCM tools, along with the CCB, support a mechanism for appropriate change control.

Figure 31–6 shows the relationship of SCM to another integral task, verification and validation (V&V).

SCM is most important, and most often neglected, during V&V activities, which include software testing. It is employed in tracking which module versions are included in a particular system build, as well as which tests have been run. The results of the tests are tied directly to the modules or subcomponents being tested. Many times there are "action items" resulting from the tests. SCM tracks the action item status, so overall system status can be assessed well before final builds and releases are done.

Verification and validation testing are supported through the four basic SCM processes: identification, control, auditing, and status accounting. Let's look at examples of V&V testing in the context of each of these components.

SCM Identification Benefits to V&V

- Automatic preparation of release notes
- List of changed software modules
- Definition of development baseline
- Generation of incident reports
- Definition of operational baseline
- Control of the configuration item identification

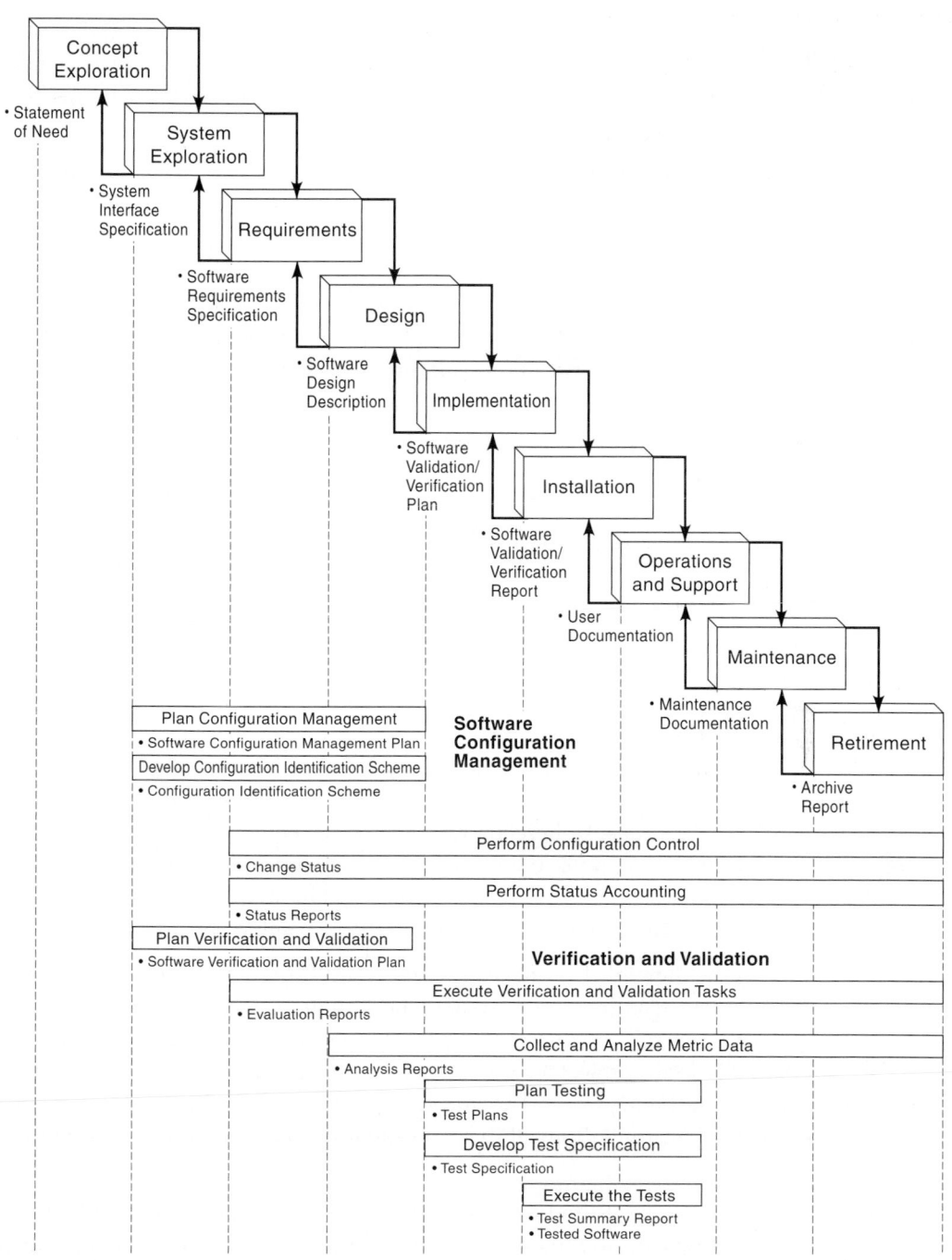

FIGURE 31–6

SCM Interacts with Verification and Validation

- Management of CCB meetings
- Prioritization of test and incident issues
- Establishment of turnover dates
- Approval of audit and test reports
- Approval of incident report resolutions

SCM Auditing Benefits to V&V

- Comparison of new baseline to previous baseline
- Assurance that standards have been met
- Audit trail of the testing process (verification, validation, and acceptance) of the software system
- Documentation of experience with technical aspects of system engineering or software engineering

SCM Status Accounting Benefits to V&V

- Logging and tracking of incident reports
- Publication of CCB minutes

With all of these potential benefits of SCM, project managers must address real-world considerations. Management commitment is the real key to implementing SCM on a specific project in a given organization. By treating the implementation of SCM as a project, the project plan must start at the top to secure commitment to checks and balances. Now is the time to bring out the organization's list of project disasters to draw on management experience with their previous software project difficulties. If there are no historic disasters in the organization, or if it is inappropriate to discuss them, refer to literature articles that provide accounts of project disasters (refer to the Web resources at the end of this chapter). Finally, after putting a notional return-on-investment financial argument in place, explain the intangible benefits of SCM.

One of the major sources intangible benefits is auditing. Auditing can be a heavy consumer of configuration management resources, and management may question the benefit of this kind of expenditure. Auditing pays for itself through the avoidance of larger, unnecessary expenses. Savings of 100:1 (large projects) or 4–6:1 (small projects) are obtained by finding and fixing problems early in the life cycle. The auditing process in SCM uncovers the areas where a little more effort or control will result in higher-quality software products and lower overall project costs.

There can be audit compromises to reduce costs. As a project manager, plan audits based on both the phases of the life cycle and the frequency of builds, versions, releases, and product families. Auditing each baseline in a project while reducing the depth of each audit maintains some traceability with loss of visibility.

Eliminating one or more audits (installation baseline, for example) maintains visibility but slightly impacts traceability.

Summary

As shown in Figure 31–3, SCM is a pyramid consisting of six layers and three faces. The six layers of the pyramid shown on the front face are:

1. Understanding of SCM—Without a total understanding, a partial implementation of SCM with work-arounds and back doors will result in disaster for an SCM system.
2. SCM plans and policies—The policy for the organization lays out in a clear, concise fashion the expectations that the organizational leadership has for its system.
3. SCM processes—The specific processes of SCM are documented for all users to recognize.
4. Metrics—These measures show where the organization is along the path to reaping the benefits of SCM.
5. Tools for SCM—It makes little sense to pick the tools to use in SCM without having completed all the previous layers.
6. SCM configuration items—The configuration items (CI) are those "things" that represent internal and external project deliverables. They are the final result of all the work done to implement SCM in your organization.

The second face of the SCM pyramid is the training plan and its execution while the third is the transition plan to get to an effective SCM implementation. By following this as the process map to SCM, an organization can meet the software configuration management KPA for an SEI CMM Level 2 organization.

In Chapter 30 we discussed the Software Engineering Institute (SEI) Capability Maturity Model (CMM) levels of maturity. At Level 2, an organization moves beyond just getting the job done and into an environment where a software project management process is in place, the organization sets expectations via policies, and projects have disciplined phases and milestones. This level is described as the repeatable level, built upon key process areas of requirements management, software project planning, software project tracking and over-sight, software subcontract management, software quality assurance, and software configuration management. The goals for SCM at maturity Level 2 are:

- Software configuration management activities are planned.
- Selected software work products are identified, controlled, and available.
- Changes to identified software work products are controlled.
- Affected groups and individuals are informed of the status and content of software baselines.

Questions that assessors might ask include:

- Is a mechanism used for controlling changes to the software requirements?
- Is a mechanism used for controlling changes to the software design?
- Is a mechanism used for controlling changes to the code?
- Is a mechanism used for configuration management of the software tools used in the development process?

SCM is a key building block of an organization's development process. Without it, no organization can achieve the quality levels needed for basic customer satisfaction.

Problems for Review

Take the outline for a software configuration management plan, adapted from the IEEE Standard for Software Configuration Management Plans (Std. 828-1990). Tailor this to your needs, removing explanatory comments as you go along. Where you decide to omit a section, you might keep the header but insert a comment saying why you omit the data.

1. What are five barriers to SCM in your work organizations?
2. What are three barriers to SCM in your project's environment?
3. Looking back on projects you have completed or are currently working on, how could SCM have enhanced them? If SCM was used, did it perform to everyone's satisfaction? If not, why?
4. Describe how you would perform SCM on a moderately sized Java implementation using a code development environment in which you had 50 classes and 200 methods.
5. Define the membership of a CCB for your entire organization. Define your product line and your current project.
6. Define 10 characteristics for CIs in your products.
7. Define the process in your organization for selecting an automated tool for SCM. What are the top five benefits to your organization from an automated SCM tool?
8. What SCM is different for developing a Web-based, browser-delivered software application?
9. Where does SCM fit in your product development life cycle? Provide a graphic representation of your life cycle, and identify the processes served by SCM.

Visit the Case Study

The Chinese Railway Ministry central software development group is an all-Microsoft shop. They develop software for DOS, Windows 3.1, Windows NT, and Windows CE. For development, they use the integrated visual development environment with Visual Source Safe (VSS) as the configuration management tool. Their VSS repository reached 5.5 GB in size with the revision branch of one of their train maintenance scheduling programs. At this size, Microsoft advises splitting the repository into two or more pieces. You will no longer be able to rely on the centralized VSS to handle your prototype development needs. As a matter of fact, Mr. Lu has intimated that the ministry may move off of VSS completely.

Mr. Lu requests that the ministry review your configuration management plan for not only the prototype, but for the entire system that you propose. Based on the current conditions at the ministry, you may not use the VSS. You must recommend a solution that will add no software licensing cost to your project and will be usable in a Microsoft development environment. Because your marketing team has already touted the extensive configuration management plan that you produce for each project, Mr. Lu feels that giving you, the project manager, a week to update the plan and recommend a configuration management tool is more than reasonable.

Citations

[1]Pressman, Roger S. (2001). *Software Engineering: A Practitioner's Approach*, 5th ed. New York, NY: McGraw-Hill. p. 225.

[2]Babich, Wayne A. (1986). *Software Configuration Management: Coordination for Team Productivity.* Reading, MA: Addison-Wesley. p. vi.

References

Ayer, S.J., and F.S. Patrinostro (1992). *Software Configuration Management: Identification, Accounting, Control, and Management.* New York, NY: McGraw-Hill.

Berlack, R.H. (1992). *Software Configuration Management.* New York, NY: John Wiley and Sons.

Bersoff, E., V. Henderson, and S. Siegel (1980). *Software Configuration Management.* Prentice Hall.

Buckley, F. (1993). *Configuration Management: Hardware, Software, and Firmware.* IEEE Computer Society Press.

DoD (1985). DoD-STD-2167A, "Military Standard for Defense System Software Development." Department of Defense.

DoD (1986). DI-MCCR-80030A, "Data Item Description for the Software Development Plan." Department of Defense.

DoD (1986). MIL-STD-480, "Engineering Changes, Deviations and Waivers." Department of Defense.

DoD (1986). MIL-STD-483A, "Configuration Management Practices for Systems, Equipment, Munitions, and Computer Programs." Department of Defense.

DoD (1989). MIL-STD-973, "Military Standard for Configuration Management." Department of Defense.

IEEE Std 828-1990, "IEEE Standard for Software Configuration Management Plans." American National Standards Institute, 1990.

IEEE Std 1042-1987, "IEEE Guide to Software Configuration Management." American National Standards Institute, 1987.

NASA D-GL-11, "Software Configuration Management for Project Managers." National Aeronautics and Space Administration, Version 0.2, March 1987.

NASA Sfw DID 04, "Software Configuration Management Plan Data Item Description." National Aeronautics and Space Administration, Version 3.0, October 15, 1986.

Pressman, Roger S. (2001). *Software Engineering: A Practitioner's Approach*, 5th ed. New York, NY: McGraw-Hill.

Whitgift, D. (1991). *Software Configuration Management: Methods and Tools.* England: John Wiley and Sons.

Web Pages for Further Information

sourceforge.net/. SourceForge is a free service to Open Source developers offering easy access to the best in CVS, mailing lists, bug tracking, message boards/forums, task management, site hosting, permanent file archival, full backups, and total Web-based administration.

www.cmtoday.com/yp/configuration_management.html. Welcome to the "Yellow Pages" for configuration management. This page references as many Web pages related to configuration management around the world as possible.

www.dtkhh.de/tsr.htm. European Software and Systems Initiative (ESSI) Process Improvement Experiment (PIE). Improvement of process architecture through configuration and change management, and enhanced test strategies for a knowledge-based test path generator.

www.iac.honeywell.com/Pub/Tech/CM/index.html. Honeywell Inc. IAC manages and updates the frequently asked questions lists for the newsgroup comp.software.config-mgmt. The information contained in these summaries is a consolidation of data obtained from user comments, vendor materials, and a variety of sources around the Internet. It does not represent an official position or opinion of Honeywell, Inc.

www.mks.com/products/scm/si/2134.htm. "Configuration Management and ISO 9001," by Robert Bamford and William J. Deibler II, Software Systems Quality Consulting.

www.sei.cmu.edu/legacy/scm/. The intent of this area is to share the configuration management research done by the SEI between 1988 and 1994 and to provide pointers to other useful sources of information on software configuration management.

www.sei.cmu.edu/legacy/scm/abstracts/abscm_past_pres_future_TR08_92.html. Automated support for configuration management is one aspect of software engineering environments that has progressed over the last 20 years. The progress is seen by the burgeoning interest in CM, many technical papers and conferences involving CM, a large number of CM tool vendors, and new software development environments that incorporate CM capabilities. This paper is about future issues affecting solutions to CM problems.

www.sei.cmu.edu/legacy/scm/papers/CM_Plans/CMPlans.MasterToC.html. The purpose of this document is to give an understanding of the importance of the role of the configuration management plan, to give the results from a set of informal discussions that shows how such plans are used, and to provide an evaluation of three standards.

www.sei.cmu.edu/legacy/scm/scmDocSummary.html. Summary of available CM related documents.

Legal Issues in Software

32

This book has consistently emphasized the 34 competencies needed to be a successful software project manager. Along with the competencies, the idea of the software development life cycle has been consistently presented as a mechanism for framing where the reader is in the overall process of developing quality software. Legal issues in software are divided in the same three competency categories: product development techniques, project management skills, and people management skills.

The legal profession has a multitude of taxonomies for framing specific areas of legal expertise. Simplifying this to the three groups for project management practitioners is more effective in relating to the process of software development. The authors of this practitioners' guide are not attorneys, nor have they had any legal training. In numerous projects since the early 1970s, the authors have had to deal with many of the legal issues described in this chapter. The only way to manage project risk with legal issues is to bring an experienced attorney onto the project team to handle the contracting, intellectual property, or litigation. This is truly an area where the project manager needs to call in the experts.

Figure 32–1 shows the relationships among the three competency categories and technology. Although technology is not called out specifically, it is a major driver in developing software. Technology impacts all aspects of a software project because the product being delivered is composed of implemented pieces of state-of-the-art technology. Developers of computer software are both the builders and the victims of technology.

The ultimate goal of any software development project is to produce a working product. A project manager must use the most critical resource available to deliver the product—people. People and the project and technology all interact and work in a synergistic fashion to complete the product. This model functions in a legal environment. The general categories of the practice of law are listed in Table 32–1. Each has a short description, and this specifies whether they will be considered to directly impact the software project manager as a practitioner. There is no recommended list of national practice areas specified by the American Bar Association. For a specific list in the state in which the software development occurs, see that state's bar association. In a development project, any distraction from the main focus of developing the product will cause a delay in schedule and a budget increase. In Table 32–1, where the practice area is marked with a "no," even if there is not a direct impact on the project, there will be collateral impact if the corporation or business unit responsible for the project is undergoing any kind of legal action.

Table 32–2 is a derivative of the complete list of legal area specialties. It simply lists those that have a direct impact on quality software development project management. The table also shows which of the three competencies' categories the legal practice area impacts. This table will drive the following sections as each impact is explained.

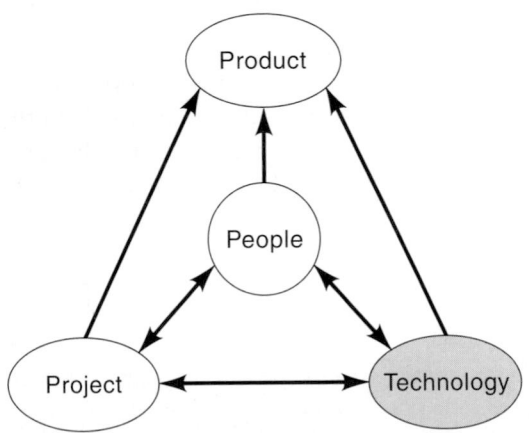

FIGURE 32–1
Product, Project, and People with Technology Influences

TABLE 32–1
Law Specialty Areas for Legal Practice

Legal Practice Area	Description	Applies
Administrative	This category is directly applicable to the administrative procedures of the functioning of state and federal law. It is important for attorneys to understand the procedures within certain courts and jurisdictions.	No
Advertising and Consumer	This category is focused on truth in advertising and product consumer liabilities that are not torts. This is an area of risk, depending on the type of product being developed.	Yes
Alternative Dispute Resolution	The concept of going to arbitration before filing a lawsuit is in many of today's contracts. This is an awareness area for the project manager.	Yes
Antitrust	Unless the organization is Microsoft, this is not an issue.	No
Appellate	Appellate refers to the process of filing appeals to higher courts to protest a lower court finding. If this is an issue on a project, there will already be in place a legal team.	No
Banking	This legal practice area focuses on laws of state, federal, and international banking. Unless the project is developing software directly for banks that require conformance to this body of the law, it is not an issue.	No
Bankruptcy	Unless this is the corporation's exit strategy, if this is a legal factor in the project, the risk factors probably show failure.	No
Civil Procedure	Civil procedure is the process attorneys follow when pleading before civil courts. It is part of the legal process and is not a direct impact on the project management.	No
Communications	Technology impacts the law and the classification of practice areas in many ways. Communications deal with email, the Internet, and the medium itself. This is an impact, and it is distinct from the intellectual property contained in the content.	Yes
Constitutional	The issues specific to the Constitution of the United States of America are covered here.	No

(Continues)

TABLE 32–1 (Continued)
Law Specialty Areas for Legal Practice

Legal Practice Area	Description	Applies
Contracts	This is one of the major areas of impact for project managers. The contracts practice area contains the work done on the Uniform Commercial Code (UCC).	Yes
Corporate and Business	The University of Cincinnati Center for Corporate Law (*www.law.uc.edu/CCL/*) defines this area as: "Although nearly all legal disciplines affect corporations and are therefore of interest to corporate lawyers, the Center for Corporate Law focuses on those issues of central concern to corporate lawyers. Such matters include but are not limited to: formation and capitalization of corporations (including attention to federal and state law regulating the issuance of securities); fiduciary duties of managers; executive compensation; relationships between managers and shareholders; possible fiduciary duties to nonshareholder constituency groups (bondholders, for example); acquisitions, both friendly and hostile; taxation of the corporate enterprise; individual liability for corporate acts; and the relationship of the corporation to the society."	No
Criminal	This practice area has to do with the commission of a crime through intentionally breaking a law. It differs from the tort practice due to the law breaking and intent.	No
Disability/ Handicap	The body of law having to do with the rights of the disabled and handicapped to work are of special interest to project managers. The project, business unit, and corporation cannot discriminate against workers due to disability. The location of software development must be physically accessible.	Yes
Divorce and Family	Software development projects may be the cause of legal activity in this practice area, but it is not an intentional impact.	No
Elder	This practice area has to do mainly with Medicare, Medicaid, and estate and trust planning. The areas that would concern age discrimination are covered in the employment practice area.	No
Employment	The body of law about hiring, termination, legal working hours, and pay are included in the employment practice area. Software development is a labor-intensive business. This is a critical area of law.	Yes

(Continues)

TABLE 32–1 (Continued)
Law Specialty Areas for Legal Practice

Legal Practice Area	Description	Applies
Environmental Law	Software development is not a resource-depleting activity, nor does it, in and of itself, cause environmental damage.	No
Governmental Records	This practice area emphasizes the law surrounding the retention, release, and classification of government records based on actions such as the Freedom of Information Act.	No
Health	Software development is not a health-endangering activity nor does it, in and of itself, cause health damage. Although there is some link to repetitive stress syndrome, that can be accounted for in the risk area of project management.	No
Human Rights	Software development is an intellectual activity wide open to diversity. There are no barriers in the technology. Issues in this practice area are assumed into the employment specialization.	No
Immigration	High technology knows no national boundaries. A large number of highly trained software professionals immigrate to countries around the world. For project management, this is assumed to be under the employment concerns area.	No
Insurance	This legal practice area focuses on laws of the state and federal insurance industry. Unless the project is developing software directly for insurance companies that require conformance to this body of the law, it is not an issue.	No
Intellectual Property	Intellectual property has the greatest impact on the use of technology and the protection of the product developed. This area contains the body of legal work on patents, trademarks, trade secrets, and copyrights.	Yes
International	This practice area focuses on the relationship of United States and foreign countries through the legal system. On an individual project basis, this is an issue only in the team separation. At a corporate level, the international relationships among design centers, software developers, and marketing must be defined outside the project management structure.	No

TABLE 32–1 (Continued)
Law Specialty Areas for Legal Practice

Legal Practice Area	Description	Applies
Internet Regulation	The Internet regulation practice area contains information on the body of law created through efforts by legislators, regulators, and the judiciary to tame the seemingly untamable online universe. It contains the prominent legal cases concerning the liability of online access providers for electronic transmissions. It includes analyses of congressional and state legislative efforts aimed at regulating online activities. The question it attempts to answer is whether the Internet is a proper candidate for regulation, and to what extent our existing framework of laws can be adequately used to prosecute illegal online activities.	Yes
Privacy	Privacy concerns the liabilities of online providers to maintain the confidentiality of information that they capture and transmit. It is also concerned with the encryption laws as they apply to export issues and tort and criminal law.	Yes
Professional Responsibility and Ethics	This practice area is related directly to the attorneys' professional ethics in the practice of law and their responsibilities to clients.	No
Real Estate and Housing	This legal practice area focuses on laws of the state and federal real estate industry. Unless the project is developing software directly for real estate companies that require conformance to this body of the law, it is not an issue.	No
Securities	This legal practice area focuses on laws of the state and federal securities industry. Unless the project is developing software directly for securities companies that require conformance to this body of the law, it is not an issue.	No
Taxation	This legal practice area focuses on state and federal laws as they apply to personal and corporate taxes. Unless the project is developing software directly for taxation reporting that requires conformance to this body of the law, it is not an issue.	No

(Continues)

TABLE 32–1 (Continued)
Law Specialty Areas for Legal Practice

Legal Practice Area	Description	Applies
Tort	From *Black's Law Dictionary*, a *tort* is defined as a wrongful act other than a breach of contract that injures another and for which the law imposes civil liability. The definition continues as a violation of a duty (as to exercise due care) imposed by law; it is distinguished from a contract for which damages or declaratory relief (as an injunction) may be obtained. If the software controls a process that can cause injury if the software fails, the company can be liable for the injury under tort law.	Yes
Wills, Trusts, and Estates	This legal practice area focuses on laws of the state and federal wills, trusts, estates, and probate laws. Unless the project is developing software directly for these specialties, it is not an issue.	No

TABLE 32–2
Law Specialty Areas Mapped to Product, Project, and People

Legal Practice Area	Product	Project	People
Advertising and Consumer	X		
Alternative Dispute Resolution		X	
Communications	X		
Contracts	X	X	X
Disability/Handicap			X
Employment			X
Intellectual Property			X
Internet Regulation	X	X	
Privacy	X	X	X
Tort	X		

Where We Are in the Product Development Life Cycle _____

Legal issues occur throughout the life cycle based on the practice areas identified. Figure 32–2 shows the life cycle model and identifies where the impact of each of the practice areas is greatest. Because legal issues are part of the overall project environment, they can occur at any time in the life cycle. This shows where the most likely opportunity occurs.

Table 32–3 shows a tabular representation of the information in Figure 32–2. This table is useful in tracking the risk impacts at each life cycle phase for the legal issues.

Chapter 32 Relation to the 34 Competencies _____

Just as this book emphasizes the 34 competencies needed to be a successful software project manager, there are impacts on project performance that extend across many competencies. Based on the experience of the authors, legal issues impact many competencies necessary for successful project execution. Legal issues in software project management have been categorized to map the 34 competencies:

1. Product development techniques;
2. Project management skills; and
3. People management skills.

Throughout this chapter, the relationship of the various facets of the legal system to all the 34 competencies will be presented.

Learning Objectives for Chapter 32 _____

Upon completion of this chapter, the reader should be able to:

- Define specific legal issues that can occur within a project;
- Apply the impact of legal issues to product, project, and people aspects of developing quality software;
- Account for legal issues in project risk assessment.

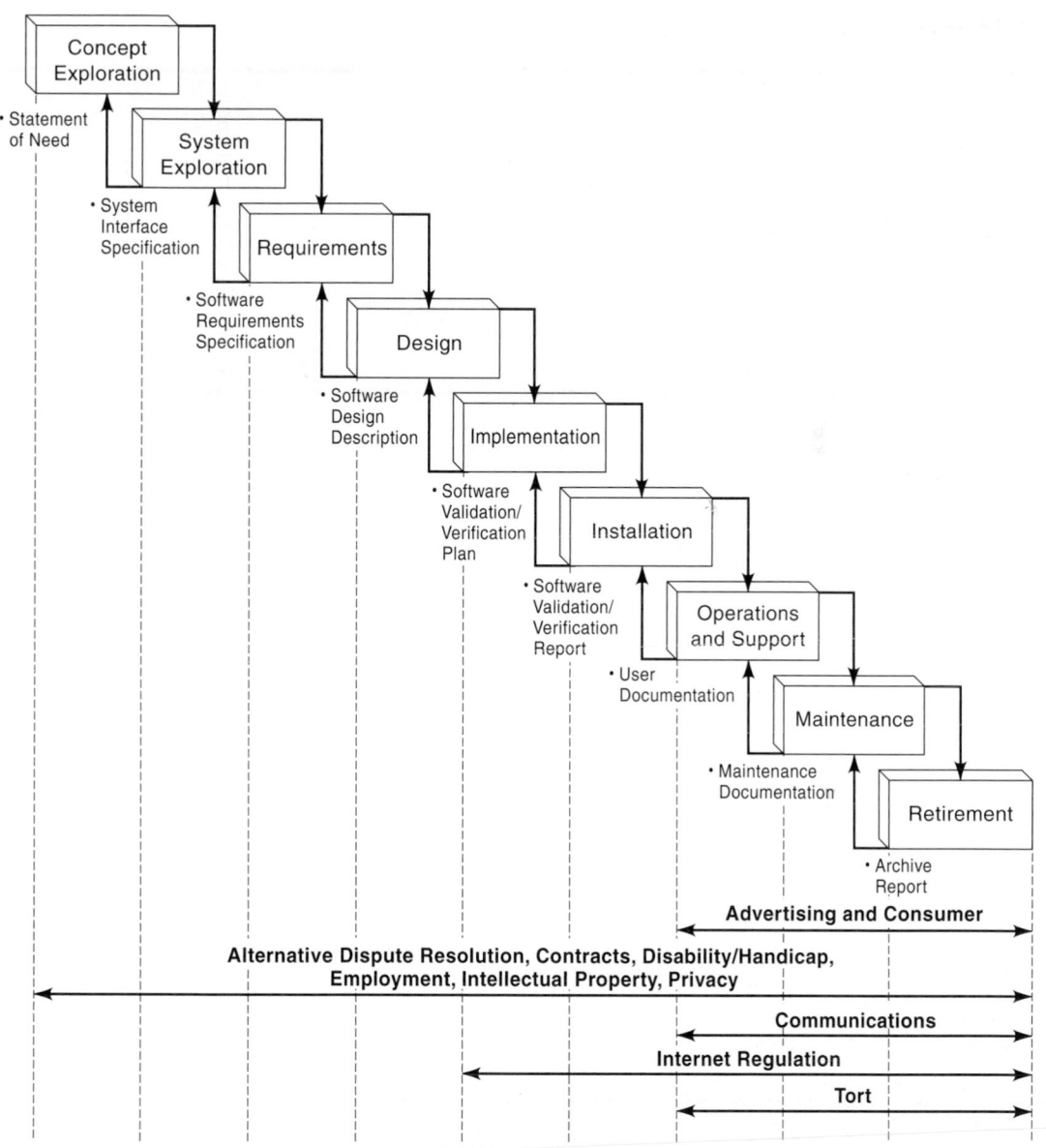

FIGURE 32–2
Legal Issues in the Product Development Life Cycle

TABLE 32–3
Legal Issues in Each Life Cycle Stage

Legal Practice Area	Concept Exploration	System Exploration	Requirements	Design	Implementation	Installation	Operations and Support	Maintenance	Retirement
Advertising and Consumer							X	X	X
Alternative Dispute Resolution	X	X	X	X	X	X	X	X	X
Communications							X	X	X
Contracts	X	X	X	X	X	X	X	X	X
Disability/Handicap	X	X	X	X	X	X	X	X	X
Employment	X	X	X	X	X	X	X	X	X
Intellectual Property	X	X	X	X	X	X	X	X	X
Internet Regulation					X	X	X	X	X
Privacy	X	X	X	X	X	X	X	X	X
Tort							X	X	X

Product Development Techniques

The six legal practice areas that impact product development techniques are shown in Table 32–4. The extent to which any of the six impact the specific project being executed depends on the type of product being developed. Each one of the discussions will start with the types of products impacted most by this practice area.

TABLE 32–4
Legal Practice Areas Impacting Product Development

Legal Practice Area	Product	Project	People
Advertising and Consumer	X		
Communications	X		
Contracts	X	X	X
Internet Regulation	X	X	
Privacy	X	X	X
Tort	X		

Advertising and Consumer

This category is focused on truth in advertising and product consumer liabilities that are not torts. Because of the history of strong enforcement of consumer protection laws by agencies such as the Federal Trade Commission, products developed for sale through a consumer-facing distribution channel must comply with all applicable laws. Online and Internet sales are not treated any differently. When it comes to online ads, three basic principles of advertising law apply:

1. Advertising must be truthful and not misleading. As explained in the FTC's "Deception Policy Statement," an ad is deceptive if it contains a statement—or omits information—that is likely to mislead consumers acting reasonably under the circumstances and that is "material" or important to a consumer's decision to buy or use the product. A statement also may be deceptive if the advertiser does not have a reasonable basis to support the claim.

2. Advertisers must have evidence to back up their claims. Before disseminating an ad, advertisers must have reasonable support for all express and implied objective claims that the ad conveys to consumers. When an ad lends itself to more than one reasonable interpretation, there must be substantiation for each interpretation. The type of evidence needed to substantiate a claim may depend on the product, the claims, and what experts believe is necessary. If an ad specifies a certain level of support for a claim— "tests show x"—the advertiser must have at least that level of support.

3. Advertisements cannot be unfair. According to the FTC's "Unfairness Policy Statement," an advertisement or business practice is unfair if it causes or is likely to cause substantial consumer injury that consumers could not reasonably avoid and that is not outweighed by the benefit to consumers or competition.

Unique features in Internet ads also may affect how an ad and any required disclosures are evaluated. To ensure that products and services are described truthfully in online ads and that consumers get what they pay for, the FTC has enforced and will continue to enforce its consumer protection laws. Many of the general principles of advertising law apply to online ads, but new issues arise almost as fast as technology develops. The FTC continues to evaluate online advertising, using traditional criteria, while recognizing the uniqueness of the new medium. Software project managers must consider these criteria when developing products that will be marketed via online ads. An experienced project team member must be responsible for all consumer law compliance.

Communications

Technology impacts the law and the classification of practice areas in many ways. Communications deal with email, the Internet, and the medium itself. This is an impact, and it is distinct from the intellectual property contained in the content.

The 1934 Communications Act initially set the national policy for segments of the telecommunications industry. In 1982, Judge Harold Greene determined the fate of the telephone companies when he handed down his modified final judgment (MFJ) that decreed the breakup of AT&T. In 1984, the regional Bell operating companies provided local telephone service, and AT&T was in the long-distance business. In 1984, the Cable Communications Policy Act was amended to the 1934 Communication Act to prescribe national policy regarding the cable television industry. The Cable Act of 1984 was changed with the passage of the Cable Television Consumer Protection and Competition Act in 1992, and, in 1994, Congress made an attempt to rewrite the Communications Act of 1934. Although it fell short, the momentum of that effort carried over through 1995 and into 1996.

Each of the industries or technologies being gathered under the umbrella called "telecommunications" is huge. Each one—entertainment, electrical utilities, computers, television, cable TV, radio, telephone, and wireless communications—has manufacturing, sales, and distribution networks with large numbers of employees and almost $1 trillion in annual revenue. All these actions by the law-making branch of the U.S. federal government have enormous impact on the development of computer software.

The new Telecommunications Act has been under construction for several years, causing companies to act cautiously and conservatively until they knew how they fit into the road map for the information superhighway. While it doesn't throw the gates wide open or tear down all the previous restraints, the Telecommunications Act of 1996 does provide a degree of opportunity for change and growth that has been absent since 1934. The communications law area is still a work in progress for software development projects with products targeted to the Internet, with email components or managing audio and video content.

Contracts

Contracts are promises that the law will enforce. The law provides a remedy if a promise is breached. The law recognizes the performance of a promise as a duty. Contracts arise when a duty does or may come into existence because of a promise made by one of the parties. To be legally binding as a contract, a promise must be exchanged for adequate consideration. Adequate consideration is a benefit or detriment that a party receives that reasonably and fairly induces it to enter into the contract. For example, promises that are purely gifts are not considered enforceable because the personal satisfaction that the grantor of the promise may receive from the act of giving is normally not considered adequate consideration. Certain promises that are not considered contracts may, in limited circumstances, be enforced if one party has relied on the assurances of the other party to his detriment.

Contracts are mainly governed by state statutory and common law and private law. Private law principally includes the terms of the agreement between the parties exchanging promises. This private law may override many of the rules otherwise established by state law. Statutory law may require that some contracts be put in writing and executed with particular formalities. Otherwise, the parties may enter into a binding agreement without signing a formal written document. Most of the principles of the common law of contracts are outlined in the *Restatement Second of The Law of Contracts* published by the American Law Institute. The Uniform Commercial Code, whose original articles have been adopted in nearly every state, represents a body of statutory law that governs important categories of contracts. The main articles that deal with the law of contracts are Article 1 ("General Provisions") and Article 2 ("Sales"). Sections of Article 9 ("Secured Transactions") govern contracts assigning the rights to payment in security interest agreements. Contracts related to particular activities or business sectors may be highly regulated by state or federal law.

The reasons for the development of the Uniform Commercial Code include these underlying purposes and policies:

- To simplify, clarify, and modernize the law governing commercial transactions;
- To permit the continued expansion of commercial practices through custom, usage, and agreement of the parties; and
- To make the law uniform among the various jurisdictions.

Contracts are an important tool to be used for the development of software products. They cover the product, project, and people aspects of the development. No project can be done without an awareness of contracts for employment, procuring packaged software, securing contract services, and selling the final product.

Internet Regulation

The Internet regulation practice area contains information on the body of law created through efforts by legislators, regulators, and the judiciary to tame the seemingly untamable online universe. It contains the prominent legal cases concerning the liability of online access providers for electronic transmissions. It includes analyses of congressional and state legislative efforts aimed at regulating online activities. The question it attempts to answer is whether the Internet is a proper candidate for regulation, and to what extent our existing framework of laws can be adequately used to prosecute illegal online activities. The 1996 Communications Act and other legal activities impact the Internet.

Due to the rapid technology changes in the Internet—we now build on "Internet time"—the legal system is sadly left in the dust. Books in the works and some that have already been published discuss all of the legal issues of the Web. For project managers developing projects that have an Internet component, these areas must be analyzed for an impact:

1. Intellectual property rights in content being delivered;
2. Privacy of individuals using the product;
3. Email spam laws;
4. Pornography laws; and
5. Anything to do with First Amendment free speech rights.

Privacy

Privacy concerns the liabilities of online providers to maintain the confidentiality of information that they capture and transmit. It is also concerned with the encryption laws as they apply to export issues and tort and criminal law. Supreme Court Justice Louis Brandeis, in his decision on *Olmstead v. U.S.*, rendered in 1928, said: "The right to be left alone—the most comprehensive of rights, and the right most valued by a free people."

The body of law as it intersects between software and privacy is slowly evolving. A software development project manager must be aware of any privacy issues that have a project impact. These can extend from the simple collection of personal information in a database to the process of selecting a hardware platform that transmits the processor chip ID on the Internet. The internalization of software products raises more privacy issues because different countries have more stringent levels of privacy protection for their citizens. This is another legal specialization area where an experienced attorney is a must for the team if the project faces privacy issues.

Tort

From *Black's Law Dictionary*, a *tort* is defined as a wrongful act other than a breach of contract that injures another and for which the law imposes civil liability. The definition continues as a violation of a duty (as to exercise due care) imposed by law, as distinguished from contract for which damages or declaratory relief (as an injunction) may be obtained. If the software controls a process that can cause injury if the software fails, the company can be liable for the injury under tort law.

Product liability of seller of a product, which causes injury due to a defect, is the area of concern in torts related to computer software development. There are three principal liability theories:

First, negligence arises in the duty of care to the purchaser and the breach of duty that causes personal or property harm. The duty of care of the manufacturer resides in the care to design products in a safe way, the duty to set up reasonably error-free manufacturing procedures, and the duty to inspect and test. Vicarious liability exists if the product incorporates other products creating liability for defects caused by other products.

The reasonableness standard is used to determine whether a person's conduct is negligent—that is, whether it violates the duty of care in any given situation. The standard is usually stated as ordinary care or due care as measured against the conduct of a hypothetical person—the reasonable person. The reasonable person represents a standard of how persons in the relevant community ought to behave. If the person is a skilled professional, such as a doctor, financial consultant, or executive, the standard is that of a reasonably skilled, competent, and experienced person who is a qualified member of that profession. In determining whether a person's conduct was negligent, the question is, what would a reasonable, qualified person have done under the same or similar circumstances? If the conduct was not that of a reasonable person in the eyes of the jury or the judge, the person has failed the reasonableness test and has acted negligently. The reasonableness standard is basic and can be used by project managers to question inappropriate project actions.

Second, warranty is the legal concept that goods are not as they were contracted to be. The warranty can be expressed in writing or can be simply implied. Warranty is covered extensively in the UCC. It must be noted that, to be effective, warranties must be available to customers before the sale.

The third principal of liability is strict liability. This arises when the product is defective and unreasonably dangerous, and causes personal injury or property damage. A product may be considered defective and unreasonably dangerous if no adequate warnings are provided.

Limiting Software Liability

Software defects are rarely lethal. But software is becoming a principal controlling element in many industrial and consumer products. Product liability suits for personal injury and property damage will increase as software becomes more widespread as an embedded control product.

Ways to minimize impact of software liability include:

- strong contracts that limit liability;
- warnings against using the software for applications that may cause injury;
- product liability insurance; and
- use of standards in the software development process.

Software development standards to achieve software process maturity are an effective strategy in liability minimization. Besides offering the ability to dramatically improve productivity, adherence to standards will minimize product liability exposure and implement a rigorous, systematic approach to software development using structured design and development, standard reviews, and uniform and independent testing.

Table 32–5 shows the product development legal issues mapped to the affected life cycle phases. Contracts and privacy cover the entire life cycle because they are so attached to the people aspect of the project. Internet regulation occurs during and after implementation because this is the point at which the product goes "live" if there are Internet components. Advertising, communications, and tort show up as the product is delivered.

TABLE 32–5
Product Development Legal Issues in Each Life Cycle Stage

Legal Practice Area	Concept Exploration	System Exploration	Requirements	Design	Implementation	Installation	Operations and Support	Maintenance	Retirement
Advertising and Consumer							X	X	X
Communications							X	X	X
Contracts	X	X	X	X	X	X	X	X	X
Internet Regulation					X	X	X	X	X
Privacy	X	X	X	X	X	X	X	X	X
Tort							X	X	X

Project Management Skills

The four legal practice areas that impact project management skills are shown in Table 32–6. The extent to which any of the four impact the specific project being executed depends on the type of product being developed. Each one of the discussions will start with the types of products impacted most by this practice area. Because there is a major overlap with the product development techniques set of legal practice areas, only alternative dispute resolution will be discussed in this section.

TABLE 32–6
Legal Practice Areas Impacting Project Management

Legal Practice Area	Product	Project	People
Alternative Dispute Resolution		X	
Contracts	X	X	X
Internet Regulation	X	X	
Privacy	X	X	X

Alternative Dispute Resolution

Arbitration, negotiation, and mediation are forms of alternative dispute resolution (ADR) recognized by the American Arbitration Association (*www.adr.org*). They are mechanisms for resolving contractual differences before going to court. Many contracts have clauses requiring one of these alternatives to be exercised before going to court. This section presents the possible clauses that could be in any type of project and product of contract.

The benefits of taking an ADR approach are listed here:

- It makes clear that all disputes can be arbitrated and that there is no need to have a court action to force preliminary arbitration.
- It is self-enforcing. Arbitration can continue despite an objection from a party, unless the proceedings are stayed by court order or by agreement of the parties.
- It provides a complete set of rules and procedures. This eliminates the need to spell out dozens of procedural matters in the parties' agreement.
- It provides for the selection of a specialized, impartial panel. Arbitrators are selected by the parties from a screened and trained pool of available experts.
- It settles disputes over the location of proceedings. When the parties disagree, the arbitrator makes location determinations, precluding the need for intervention by a court.
- It makes possible administrative conferences to expand the scope of the arbitration and remedies.
- It makes available preliminary hearings. Preliminary hearings can be arranged in large and complex cases to specify the issues to be resolved, clarify claims and counterclaims, provide for a prehearing exchange of information, and consider other matters that will expedite the arbitration proceedings.

- Mediation is made available, if specified in the contract. Mediation conferences can be arranged to facilitate a voluntary settlement without additional administrative cost to the parties.
- The ADR activities are time-boxed with the arbitrator(s) responsible for completion in a timely fashion.
- Arbitration provides for enforcement of the award. The award can be enforced in any court having jurisdiction, with only limited statutory grounds for resisting the award.

Arbitration   The contracting parties can provide for arbitration of future disputes by inserting the following clause into new contracts:

> Any controversy or claim arising out of or relating to this contract, or the breach thereof, shall be settled by arbitration administered by the American Arbitration Association in accordance with its Commercial Arbitration Rules, and judgment on the award rendered by the arbitrator(s) may be entered in any court having jurisdiction thereof.

Arbitration of existing disputes may be accomplished by use of the following:

> We, the undersigned parties, hereby agree to submit to arbitration administered by the American Arbitration Association under its Commercial Arbitration Rules the following controversy: [describe briefly]. We further agree that a judgment of any court having jurisdiction may be entered upon the award.

Negotiation   Negotiation is done before sitting down to formal arbitration. A sample of a clause that provides for negotiation is as follows:

> In the event of any dispute, claim, question, or disagreement arising from or relating to this agreement or the breach thereof, the parties hereto shall use their best efforts to settle the dispute, claim, question, or disagreement. To this effect, they shall consult and negotiate with each other in good faith and, recognizing their mutual interests, attempt to reach a just and equitable solution satisfactory to both parties. If they do not reach such solution within a period of 60 days, then, upon notice by either party to the other, all disputes, claims, questions, or differences shall be finally settled by arbitration administered by the American Arbitration Association in accordance with the provisions of its Commercial Arbitration Rules.

Mediation   The parties may want to attempt mediation before submitting their dispute to arbitration. This can be accomplished by making reference to mediation in the arbitration clause:

If a dispute arises out of or relates to this contract, or the breach thereof, and if the dispute cannot be settled through negotiation, the parties agree first to try in good faith to settle the dispute by mediation administered by the American Arbitration Association under its Commercial Mediation Rules before resorting to arbitration, litigation, or some other dispute resolution procedure.

It is prudent to include time limits on the negotiation and mediation steps before arbitration. Depending on how broadly the ADR clauses are written, the arbitrator has exceptional decision-making latitude.

Table 32–7 shows how all life cycle phases are impacted by legal issues. Except for Internet regulation, the other legal practice areas impact all of the life cycle phases. This is because they deal with people management also. Whenever people management is mapped to a legal risk area, the entire life cycle is impacted. Internet regulation is an issue in the software development life cycle only when the product is ready to go live. But this does not mean to wait until then to consider the legal impacts. A prudent project manager will have recognized any risks early in the project life cycle and will have developed appropriate mitigation strategies.

TABLE 32–7
Project Management Legal Issues in Each Life Cycle Stage

Legal Practice Area	Concept Exploration	System Exploration	Requirements	Design	Implementation	Installation	Operations and Support	Maintenance	Retirement
Alternative Dispute Resolution	X	X	X	X	X	X	X	X	X
Contracts	X	X	X	X	X	X	X	X	X
Internet Regulation					X	X	X	X	X
Privacy	X	X	X	X	X	X	X	X	X

People Management Skills _____

The five legal practice areas that impact people management skills are shown in Table 32–8. The extent to which any of the five impact the specific project being executed depends on the type of product being developed. Each one of the discussions will start with the types of products impacted most by this practice area.

TABLE 32–8
Legal Practice Areas Impacting People Management

Legal Practice Area	Product	Project	People
Contracts	X	X	X
Disability/Handicap			X
Employment			X
Intellectual Property			X
Privacy	X	X	X

Contracts

This was discussed in the "Product Development Techniques" section of this chapter. The major focus on the people for contracting is employment contracts.

Disability/Handicap

The body of law having to do with the rights of the disabled and handicapped to work is of special interest to project managers. The project, business unit, and corporation cannot discriminate against workers due to disability. The location of software development must be physically accessible.

Enacted on July 26, 1990, the Americans with Disabilities Act (ADA) is federal civil rights legislation that protects people with disabilities from discrimination and ensures equal access to employment, privately owned businesses serving the public (public accommodations), programs controlled by state and local governments, and telecommunication systems. The ADA affects employers with 15 or more employees and private businesses of any size that operate facilities accessible to the public. This law has the broadest impact on project management from the legal aspect of disability. To address this legal aspect of project risk, the project manager needs to also be aware of all international, state, and local laws that apply to the project.

Employment

The body of law about hiring, termination, legal working hours, and pay is included in the employment practice area. Software development is a labor-intensive business. This is a critical and comprehensive area of law. Employment law covers rights that employees have with respect to:

- job hunting;
- discrimination;
- sexual harassment;
- fair pay and time off;
- health and safety;
- losing or leaving a job; and
- privacy.

Employment law also addresses the employers' rights and responsibilities with respect to hiring workers, wage and hour laws, and the time when workers leave.

Depending on the size of the company, the state in which the company does work, and the profession of the workers, the project team may be entitled to certain legal protections in the workplace, including these:

- The right not to be discriminated against on the basis of race, national origin, skin color, gender, pregnancy, religious beliefs, disability, or age (and, in some places, marital status or sexual orientation);
- The right to a workplace free of harassment ;
- The right to be paid at least the minimum wage, and an overtime premium for any hours worked more than 40 in one week (or, in some places, more than 8 hours in one day)
- The right to a safe workplace;
- The right to take leave to care for your own or a family member's serious illness, or following the birth or adoption of a child;
- The right to some privacy in personal matters.

A project manager must keep in mind that ignorance of the law is not a defense. It is merely ignorance.

Intellectual Property

Intellectual property has the greatest impact on the use of technology and the protection of the product developed. For software companies, intellectual property (inventions or ideas) is what gives the business value. Patents, copyrights, and trademarks are the means to protect the invention and ideas to increase business valuation.

Patents   Patents protect any new or useful product, process, article of manufacture, composition of matter, or improvement. They legally extend the right to exclude others from making, using, and selling products based on the patent. It is a grant from the federal government based on the United States' Constitution authorization for promotion of "useful arts." Patents protect ideas and are exclusive rights for novel inventions for a limited period of time. The patent protects the underlying concept, not just the implementation, for 20 years from the filing date of the patent application.

Most of the patentable material resulting from software development is new and not obvious. Legal (patentable) inventions often are different from scientific inventions because the standards are legal, not scientific. Invention occurs when a problem is solved in a new way that isn't an obvious solution. Many sources of this inventive inspiration are technical research, professional articles, education, work experience, market awareness, customer and competitor contact, and patent searches in target and related technologies.

Copyrights   Copyrights protect original works of authorship such as writings, software, photos, music, artwork architecture, and sound recordings. Protection is automatic once the original work is fixed in a tangible medium of expression. The © notice no longer is required but is advisable. The copyright is an exclusive right to reproduce the work, prepare derivative works, and publicly perform, display, and distribute the work.

The copyright protects only the expression, not the underlying idea, and there is no protection against independent creation. The difference between a copyright and a patent is as follows:

1. Software copyright protects only the software's expression.
2. Copyright does not protect ideas, discoveries, processes, or methods of operation.
3. Patents protect the underlying ideas, processes, and functionality.
4. Copyright protection is much narrower, in that only copying is prohibited.
5. Patents protect against independent development of software having the same or similar functionality.

With the exception of innovative designs, patents are closely associated with things and processes that are useful in the real world. While it is possible to get a patent on technologies used in the arts, it is copyright that keeps one artist from stealing another artist's creative work.

Trade Secrets   Trade secrets are confidential business information that gives the company competitive advantage. It has value because it is not generally known and reasonable precautions must be in place to safeguard the trade secrets. Customer lists, manufacturing processes, business methods, and source code are examples. The trade secrets are information that does not have to be unique, just not generally known. The major disadvantage of this form of protection is that once it is public, the trade secret is lost.

Examples of reasonable efforts to maintain secrecy are confidentiality agreements, limited access, documents marked as confidential, and the establishment of a secure location.

The proper methods of obtaining trade secrets are through independent discovery, reverse engineering, discovery by observation of public use or display, and discovery through publicly available data.

Trademarks   Trademarks are used to identify goods and distinguish them from goods made or sold by others. It may be a word, name, symbol, design, slogan or color, sound, or other device. Trademarks are often referred to as the company "brand" or "service mark." As a grant from the federal government under the commerce clause of the United States Constitution, it must be used in interstate commerce with ® designating registered with U.S. PTO and ™ designating unregistered trademark. The trademark duration is unlimited if properly used and renewed.

When selecting a trademark, it must have these characteristics:

1. Must identify the source of goods;
2. Must distinguish them from competing goods;
3. Must be distinctive or an invented or coined word that suggests or is associated with the goods sold; and
4. Must not describe the goods or services or be the generic or common name of a product.

Trademark is not concerned with how a new technology is used. It applies to the names, logos, and other devices—such as color, sound, and smell—that are used to identify the source of goods or services and distinguish them from their competition. On the other hand, patents allow those who create inventions to keep others from making commercial use of the inventions without the creator's permission.

Trade Dress   Trade dress is the product's total visual image. This is all factors making up the total image presented to customers extending to a distinctive look and feel. Protection for trade dress expands to software areas or video games and graphic user interfaces. Trade dress creates a visual impression that functions like a word trademark. The U.S. Supreme Court confirmed in *Two Pesos*, 112 S.Ct. 2753, that there is really no difference between a word trademark and a visual trademark except that a word mark may be spoken, while trade dress and color, *per se*, must be seen to make a commercial impression. This is the example of protectable trade dress from the Supreme Court: "… not only that restaurant decor may be protected as trade dress, but also that restaurant—and other trade dresses— may be inherently distinctive and protectable from the moment of adoption." As an example, the plaintiff's trade dress in *Two Pesos* was described as follows:

> A festive eating atmosphere having interior dining and patio areas decorated with artifacts, bright colors, paintings, and murals. The patio includes interior and

exterior areas with the interior patio capable of being sealed off from the outside patio by overhead garage doors. The stepped exterior of the building is a festive and vivid color scheme using top border paint and neon stripes. Bright awnings and umbrellas continue the theme.

While it is possible to invent definitions that draw clear lines between the areas of patent, copyright, and trademark (the three major types of intellectual property protection), there are complications when it comes to certain innovative designs. In some cases, a design may be subject to patent, trademark, and copyright protection at the same time.

Here are the top 10 things to remember about intellectual property:

1. Without a patent, anyone can copy the idea.
2. If the organization doesn't patent and the competitor does, the organization may be out of business.
3. Don't make the mistake of thinking that everything done is "obvious" and not patentable.
4. A very small improvement may be a very valuable one.
5. Look at industry trends—patent what makes the product different.
6. Have a patent strategy.
7. Develop a patent portfolio to protect the organization's market niche.
8. Don't publicly disclose, offer for sale, or sell prematurely because you may lose IP rights.
9. Use nondisclosure agreements.
10. Be alert to IP ownership issues.

Privacy

This was discussed in the "Product Development Techniques" section of this chapter.

Table 32–9 maps the people management legal issues to the development life cycle. As is obvious, people have the greatest impact throughout the life cycle, and the legal practice areas mapped to people impact every phase. People are the project manager's most important resource and risk source. People, legal actions, and risk all go together to add work for a project manager.

TABLE 32–9
People Management Legal Issues in Each Life Cycle Stage

Legal Practice Area	Concept Exploration	System Exploration	Requirements	Design	Implementation	Installation	Operations and Support	Maintenance	Retirement
Contracts	X	X	X	X	X	X	X	X	X
Disability/ Handicap	X	X	X	X	X	X	X	X	X
Employment	X	X	X	X	X	X	X	X	X
Intellectual Property	X	X	X	X	X	X	X	X	X
Privacy	X	X	X	X	X	X	X	X	X

Legal Risk Issues

Chapter 18, "Determining Project Risks," contained the entire table of risk categorizations. Table 32–10 shows just those specific risks that are impacted by legal issues. The columns on risk levels and comments have been replaced, for information purposes only, with a column identifying the specific legal practice area that affects the risk factor. The 10 areas of interest for software project managers are: advertising and the consumer, alternative dispute resolution, communications, contracts, disability/handicap, employment, intellectual property, Internet regulation, privacy, and tort.

In projects where legal issues play a major part, adding a new risk category especially tailored for legal factors would be appropriate. Table 32–11 is an extension to the risk categorization table for legal factors.

TABLE 32–10
Legal Risk Categorization

Risk Factors and Categories	L—Low Risk Evidence	M—Medium Risk Evidence	H—High Risk Evidence	Legal Practice Area Affected
Mission and Goals Factors				
Organization Management Factors				
Organization Stability	Little or no change in management or structure expected	Some management change or reorganization expected	Management or organization structure that is continually or rapidly changing	Contracts, disability/handicap, employment
Development Team Stability	Team chosen; little or no change expected	Team chosen, but members may change	Team not chosen; no decision on members	Contracts, disability/handicap, employment
Policies and Standards	Development policies and standards defined and carefully followed	Development policies/standards in place, but are weak or not carefully followed	No policies or standards, or they are ill-defined and unused	Contracts, intellectual property, privacy, tort
Performance Objectives	Verifiable performance objectives, reasonable requirements	Some performance objectives; measures may be questionable	No established performance requirements, or requirements are not measurable	Contracts, alternative dispute resolution, tort
Customer Factors				
Customer Acceptance	End-users accept concepts and details of system; process is in place for end-user approvals	End-users accept most of concepts and details of system; process in place for end-user approvals	End-users do not accept any concepts or design details of system	Alternative dispute resolution, contracts, tort
Contract Fit	Contract with customer has good terms; communication with team is good	Contract has some open issues that could interrupt team work efforts	Contract has burdensome document requirements or causes extra work to comply	Alternative dispute resolution, contracts, tort

(Continues)

TABLE 32-10 (Continued)
Legal Risk Categorization

Risk Factors and Categories	L—Low Risk Evidence	M—Medium Risk Evidence	H—High Risk Evidence	Legal Practice Area Affected
Budget/Cost Factors				
Project Size	Small, noncomplex, or easily decomposed	Medium, moderate complexity; decomposable	Large, highly complex, or not decomposable	Communications, Internet regulation, privacy, tort
Technology	Mature, existent, in-house experience	Existent, some in-house experience	New technology or a new use under development; little in-house experience	Contracts, communications, Internet regulation, privacy, tort
Reusable Components	Components available and compatible with approach	Components promised; delivery dates unsure	Components projected but not available when needed	Contracts, communications, Internet regulation, privacy, tort
Supplied Components	Components available and directly usable	Components work under most circumstances	Components known to fail in certain cases, likely to be late, or incompatible with parts of approach	Contracts, communications, Internet regulation, privacy, tort
Cost Controls	Well established, in place	System in place, but weak in areas	System lacking or nonexistent	Alternative dispute resolution, contracts, tort
Schedule Factors				
Delivery Commitment	Stable commitment dates	Some uncertain commitments	Unstable, fluctuating commitments	Alternative dispute resolution, contracts, tort
Development Schedule	Team projects that schedule is acceptable and can be met	Team finds one phase of the plan to have a schedule that is too aggressive	Team projects that two or more phases of schedule are unlikely to be met	Alternative dispute resolution, contracts, tort

(Continues)

TABLE 32–10 (Continued)
Legal Risk Categorization

Risk Factors and Categories	L—Low Risk Evidence	M—Medium Risk Evidence	H—High Risk Evidence	Legal Practice Area Affected
Project Content				
System Testability	System requirements easy to test; plans underway	Parts of system are hard to test, or minimal planning is being done	Most of system is hard to test, or no test plans being made	Contracts, communications, Internet regulation, privacy, tort
Design Difficulty	Well-defined interfaces; design well understood	Unclear how to design, or aspects of design yet to be decided	Interfaces not well defined or controlled; subject to change	Contracts, communications, Internet regulation, privacy, tort
Implementation Difficulty	Algorithms and design that are reasonable for this team to implement	Algorithms or design have elements somewhat difficult for this team to implement	Algorithms or design have components that this team will find very difficult to implement	Contracts, communications, Internet regulation, privacy, tort
Performance Factors				
Test Capability	Modular design that allows for easy-coverage test planning and execution	Modular design aids developing test harnesses for unit test	No modular design or ability to easily establish test coverage planning	Contracts, communications, Internet regulation, privacy, tort
Project Management Factors				
Approach	Product and process planning and monitoring in place	Planning and monitoring need enhancement	Weak or nonexistent planning and monitoring	Alternative dispute resolution, contracts, tort

(Continues)

TABLE 32–10 (Continued)
Legal Risk Categorization

Risk Factors and Categories	L—Low Risk Evidence	M—Medium Risk Evidence	H—High Risk Evidence	Legal Practice Area Affected
Development Process Factors				
Quality Assurance Approach	QA system established, followed, and effective	Procedures established, but not well followed or effective	No QA process or established procedures	Alternative dispute resolution, contracts, tort
Use of Defined Engineering Process	Development process in place, established, effective, and followed by team	Process established, but not followed or ineffective	No formal process used	Alternative dispute resolution, contracts, tort
Defect Tracking	Defect tracking defined, consistent, and effective	Defect tracking process defined but inconsistently used	No process in place to track defects	Alternative dispute resolution, contracts, tort
Development Environment Factors				
Physical Facilities	Little or no modification needed	Some modifications needed; some existent	Major modifications needed, or facilities nonexistent	Contracts, disability/handicap, employment
Security	All areas following security guidelines; data backed up; disaster recovery system in place; procedures followed	Some security measures in place; backups done; disaster recovery considered, but procedures lacking or not followed	No security measures in place; backup lacking; disaster recovery not considered	Contracts, communications, Internet regulation, privacy, tort
Vendor Support	Complete support at reasonable price and in needed time frame	Adequate support at contracted price, reasonable response time	Little or no support, high cost, or poor response time	Contracts, communications, Internet regulation, privacy, tort

(Continues)

TABLE 32–10 (Continued)
Legal Risk Categorization

Risk Factors and Categories	L—Low Risk Evidence	M—Medium Risk Evidence	H—High Risk Evidence	Legal Practice Area Affected
Staff Factors				
Staff Availability	In place, little turnover expected; few interrupts for fire fighting	Available, some turnover expected; some fire fighting	High turnover, not available; team spends most of time fighting fires	Contracts, disability/handicap, employment
Maintenance Factors				
Complexity	Structurally maintainable (low complexity measured or projected)	Certain aspects difficult to maintain (medium complexity)	Extremely difficult to maintain (high complexity)	Contracts, communications, Internet regulation, privacy, tort
Change Implementation	Team in place that can be responsive to customer needs	Team experiences delays, but acceptable to customer	Team is unable to respond to customer needs	Contracts, communications, Internet regulation, privacy, tort
Support Personnel	In place, experienced, sufficient in number	Missing some areas of expertise	Significant discipline or expertise missing	Contracts, disability/handicap, employment
Vendor Support	Complete support at reasonable price and in needed time frame	Adequate support at contracted price, reasonable response time	Little or no support, high cost, or poor response time	Contracts, communications, Internet regulation, privacy, tort

TABLE 32-11
Legal Risk Factor Extension to Basic Risk

Risk Factors and Categories	L—Low Risk Evidence	M—Medium Risk Evidence	H—High Risk Evidence	Rating (HML)	Comments
Mission and Goals Factors					
Organization Management Factors					
Customer Factors					
Budget/Cost Factors					
Schedule Factors					
Project Content					
Performance Factors					
Project Management Factors					
Development Process Factors					
Development Environment Factors					
Staff Factors					
Maintenance Factors					
Legal Factors					
Advertising and Consumer	Not a consumer product.	Simple computer product with no warranty needed.	Complex consumer product with warranty required.		

(Continues)

TABLE 32-11 (Continued)
Legal Risk Factor Extension to Basic Risk

Risk Factors and Categories	L—Low Risk Evidence	M—Medium Risk Evidence	H—High Risk Evidence	Rating (HML)	Comments
Alternative Dispute Resolution	Standard arbitration terms written into the contract boilerplate.	Nonstandard arbitration terms written into the contract.	No arbitration in the contract.		
Communications	No electronic communication is done on the project.	Electronic communication is done only for the development of the product.	Electronic communication is an integral part of the delivered product.		
Contracts	UCC has been reviewed for any product and project impacts. No other contracts are needed.	UCC and employment contracts are required.	Project relies heavily on contract development and commercial component integration.		
Disability/Handicap	All facilities are accessible to disabled employees.	Facilities are available separate from the development team.	No facilities are available that meet the minimum Americans with Disabilities Act.		
Employment	Standard employment agreements are in place protecting ownership of intellectual property.	Developers are all contract personnel.	No employment agreements are used.		

(Continues)

TABLE 32-11 (Continued)
Legal Risk Factor Extension to Basic Risk

Risk Factors and Categories	L—Low Risk Evidence	M—Medium Risk Evidence	H—High Risk Evidence	Rating (HML)	Comments
Intellectual Property	Standard process to review for intellectual property are defined points within the project life cycle.	Intellectual property is only an issue at the beginning and end of projects.	No process for recognizing intellectual property.		
Internet Regulation	No Internet access is allowed on the project.	Internet access is done only for the development of the product.	Internet access is an integral part of the delivered product.		
Privacy	No personal information is handled by the product under development.	Personal information is used only for minimal user identification.	This is a personal data-management system or has components that collect and store personal data.		
Tort	The software under development does not control physical devices.	The software underdevelopment controls physical devices that do not present any possibility of human injury.	The software controls hardware functions that could have life-threatening effects if a failure occurred.		

Summary

This book has consistently emphasized the 34 competencies needed to be a successful software project manager. Along with the competencies, the idea of the software product development life cycle has been consistently presented as a mechanism for framing where the reader is in the overall process of developing quality software. Legal issues in software are divided in the same three competency categories: product development techniques, project management skills, and people management skills.

The legal profession has a multitude of taxonomies for framing specific areas of legal expertise. Simplifying this to the three groups for project management practitioners is more effective in relating to the process of software development. The authors of this practitioners' guide are not attorneys, nor have they had any legal training. In numerous projects since the early 1970s, the authors have had to deal with many of the legal issues described in this chapter. The only way to manage project risk with legal issues is to bring an experienced attorney onto the project team to handle the contracting, intellectual property, or litigation. This is truly an area where the project manager needs to call in the experts.

The complex taxonomies of legal expertise were simplified in this chapter to map to the three major software project management competency categories. Legal issues can occur anywhere in the product development life cycle. The project manager must take special care in mitigating the risks imposed by legal impacts.

Problems for Review

1. Using Table 32–11, extend the risk analysis done for the elevator problem in Appendix F, "Project Artifact Templates," to include legal risk due to the following:

   a. A browser interface must be delivered to access the status of all elevators in a building.

   b. A competitor trapped a group of Chinese business people for three hours between the 95th and 96th floors at the Sears Tower because their elevator control software failed to recognize a down selection, floor up, and door open command string while the elevator was moving.

   c. The project's tool vendor has just been served with a notice that its tool violates a Microsoft patent. This tool is integral to building the elevator controller.

2. How would a project manager improve the project life cycle model used in the project plan in Appendix F to include the legal issues?

3. How would a project manager account for the legal issue of privacy on an online data collection project executed over the Internet?

4. The project team marketing representatives have developed the advertising campaign for the next generation of the product scheduled for delivery in two months. The campaign for the new product will be released coincident with the current version release. This next-generation product is all smoke and mirrors to the developers. As the project manager, is there a legal issue here?

5. If copyright exists, is there a copyleft?

Visit the Case Study

The organization's intellectual property and litigation attorneys just walked into your office. They both introduce themselves and remark that they are glad you are sitting down. A major U.S. East Coast computer software company has sued your company for patent, copyright, trademark, and trade secret infringement over xTRemeObjectMaker. It seems that, a year ago, when your company purchased the CASE toolmaker, it had not completed all the intellectual property paperwork to legally cover xTRemeObjectMaker. The company has gotten the Clerk, U.S. District Court, District of Columbia, to issue an injunction under Civil Action 94-1564 (TPJ) against your company to use the CASE tool or any intellectual property associated with xTRemeObjectMaker.

The attorneys inform you that you must stop using the tool *now*. And, you are responsible for stopping all use on your project and collecting all copies and licenses distributed to other design centers and clients. You have 10 working days to personally comply and deliver a report of compliance with the order to the corporate legal office in Chicago. As the project manager, you have three tasks:

- Complete the compliance report.
- Assess the impact of switching to a new tool environment.
- Select the tool environment and redo the project plan.

The first task is due within 10 working days. The other two need to be done in parallel. You need a plan and you need to complete the three tasks.

Web Pages for Further Information

palimpsest.stanford.edu/bytopic/intprop/crews.html. Kenneth D. Crews (1992). "Copyright Law, Libraries, and Universities: Overview, Recent Developments, and Future Issues." Working paper presented to the Association of Research Libraries.

www.411legalinfo.com/. For all your Legal needs.

www.abanet.org/. Welcome to the American Bar Association, the largest voluntary professional association in the world. With more than 400,000 members, the ABA provides law school accreditation, continuing legal education, information about the law, programs to assist lawyers and judges in their work, and initiatives to improve the legal system for the public. The ABA strives to provide you with the knowledge and tools you need to expand your career. From ABA-sponsored workshops, meetings, seminars, and CLE sessions to the widest variety of respected and up-to-date publications, the ABA is your association, dedicated to helping you advance your career and the legal profession.

www.adr.org/. The American Arbitration Association is available to resolve a wide range of disputes through mediation, arbitration, elections and other out-of-court settlement procedures. That the AAA has flourished for nearly 75 years affirms an unparalleled commitment to progressive leadership in alternative dispute resolution (ADR) and the association's facility for change and service innovation. The history, mission and not-for-profit status of the AAA are unique within the ADR industry. It is, however, the Association's ADR resources—its panels, rules, administration, and education and training services—that provide cost-effective and tangible value to counsel, businesses and industry professionals and their employees, customers, and business partners.

www.cni.org/docs/ima.ip-workshop/. Proceedings of a workshop jointly sponsored by the Coalition for Networked Information; the Interactive Multimedia Association; the John F. Kennedy School of Government, Science, Technology & Public Policy Program; and the Massachusetts Institute of Technology Program on Digital Open High-Resolution Systems.

www.dtcwv.org/news.htm. Commission on lawyer specialization and certification report to the West Virginia state bar board of governors. August 1998. West Virginia State Bar Commission on Lawyer Specialization and Certification. This is an HTML report on the status of national recognition of practice areas for attorneys.

www.ed.gov/databases/ERIC_Digests/ed381177.html. Janis H. Bruwelheide (1995). "Copyright Issues for the Electronic Age." ERIC Clearinghouse on Information and Technology. ERIC Digest ED381177.

www.epic.org/. EPIC is a public interest research center in Washington, D.C. It was established in 1994 to focus public attention on emerging civil liberties issues and to protect privacy, the First Amendment, and constitutional values. EPIC works in association with Privacy International, an international human rights group based in London, and is also a member of the Global Internet Liberty Campaign, the Internet Free Expression Alliance, the Internet Privacy Coalition, the Internet Democracy Project, and the Trans Atlantic Consumer Dialogue (TACD).

www.findlaw.com/. FindLaw, the leading Web portal focused on law and government, provides access to a comprehensive and fast-growing online library of legal resources for use by legal professionals, consumers, and small businesses. FindLaw's mission is to make legal information on the Internet easy to find. Visitors to the FindLaw site will find a broad array of features that include Web search utilities, cases and codes, legal news, and community-oriented tools, such as a secure document management utility, mailing lists, message boards, and free email.

www.ilrg.com/. Welcome to the Internet Legal Resource Guide™. A categorized index of more than 4,000 select Web sites in 238 nations, islands, and territories, as well as more than 850 locally stored Web pages and downloadable files, this site was established to serve as a comprehensive resource of the information available on the Internet concerning law and the legal profession, with an emphasis on the United States of America. Designed for everyone, lay persons and legal scholars alike, it is quality controlled to include only the most substantive legal resources online. The selection criteria are predicated on two principles: the extent to which the resource is unique, and the relative value of the information it provides.

www.ldrc.com/cyber6.html. Samuel Fifer and Chad J. Doellinger. "Annotated Bibliography of Materials Concerning First Amendment and Intellectual Property Internet Law Issues."

www.mycounsel.com/. MyCounsel.com uses the power of the Internet to offer a new and better way to meet your legal needs—law that is unexpectedly simple and affordable. It offers you the guidance of leading lawyers from around the country, the Web's largest collection of free, reliable legal information and comprehensive legal services that are guaranteed.

www.nolo.com/index.html. Nolo Press Web site: To help people handle their own everyday legal matters—or learn enough about them to make working with a lawyer a more satisfying experience—this company publishes reliable, plain-English books, software, forms, and this Web site.

www.richmond.edu/jolt/v2i1/caden_lucas.html. Marc L. Caden and Stephanie E. Lucas (1996). *Accidents On the Information Superhighway: Online Liability And Regulation.*

www.usdoj.gov/crt/ada/cguide.htm. A Guide to Disability Rights Laws, from the U.S. Department of Justice.

Suggested Readings

Garner, Bryan A. (2000). *Blacks Law Dictionary,* 7th abridged edition. West Group.

Lemley, Mark A., Peter S. Menell, Robert P. Merges, and Pamel Samuelson (2001). *Software and Internet Law,* Aspen Publishers, Inc.

Reed, Chris (2001). *Internet Law: Text and Materials (Law in Context).* Northwestern University Press.

Summary   33

In the early stages of software project management, the best programmers were promoted to the role of project manager because they demonstrated competence with the tools (programming languages, compilers, etc.) and often displayed knowledge of a domain, such as a scientific, business, or real-time application. They frequently did not succeed in this position because they were unprepared for situations outside of the technical realm. This guide has shown that software development managers need skills far beyond knowing how to code. A working knowledge of software engineering is necessary to succeed, but a good software manager needs to excel in people and project management skills, too.

Throughout this guide, 34 competencies employed by the most successful software project managers have been presented. This list came from the experiences of many practicing software project managers who contributed to the Software Project Management certificate program at the University of Texas at Austin from 1993 to 2001. It represents the Software Quality Institute's body of knowledge for software project management.

This summary chapter will recap all the methods, techniques, and tools presented for software project management use. They will be presented within the framework of the three categories of the 34 competencies: product, project, and people.

Product Development Techniques _____

1. **Assessing processes**—Defining criteria for reviews
2. **Awareness of process standards**—Understanding process standards
3. **Defining the product**—Identifying customer environment and product requirements
4. **Evaluating alternative processes**—Evaluating various approaches
5. **Managing requirements**—Monitoring requirements changes
6. **Managing subcontractors**—Planning, managing, and monitoring performance
7. **Performing the initial assessment**—Assessing difficulty, risks, costs, and schedule
8. **Selecting methods and tools**—Defining selection processes
9. **Tailoring processes**—Modifying standard processes to suit a project
10. **Tracking product quality**—Monitoring the quality of an evolving product
11. **Understanding development activities**—Learning the software development cycle

These first 11 product development competencies focus the project manager, the product development team, and the organization on the external customer. Value and quality are identified and derived from the viewpoint and experience of the customer with the product being developed. Quality and value are not self-referential within an organization. They are measured through client satisfaction, not internally focused process initiatives. The following are specific methods, techniques, and tools described in this guide that support product development competencies.

Process

In defining the process that a project team and software development organization will follow for product development, the project manager needs a method for evaluating process decisions and a template to derive the product development framework. Figure 33–1 is the front-end process model used for evaluating process options. Based on the classical Deming/Shewhart/Ishikawa plan-do-check-act process model, the software front-end model combines historic information and experience with software-specific tasks. The model is useful at the front end of a project to begin the concept exploration phases and during project execution to evaluate process improvement options.

The second part of the process definition is selecting a baseline template for customization to specific projects and organizations. Figure 33–2 is the IEEE 1074–inclusive software development process model framework. This is the starting point for selecting life cycle phases and support processes.

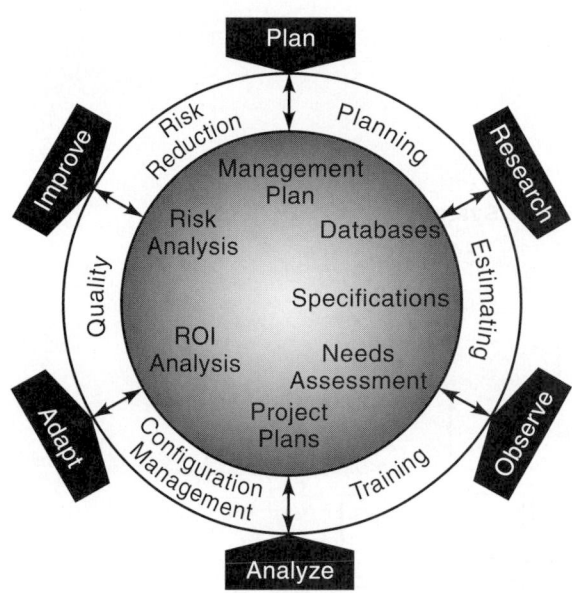

FIGURE 33–1
Software Development Process Front-End Model

Life Cycles

The most important lesson to take from the discussion on life cycles is that Figure 33–3 is *not* the way to develop software. Use this as the measure against which the typical CMM maturity Level 1 organization functions.

Selecting the most appropriate life cycle depends on the project requirements, the experience level of the project ream, the sophistication of the end-user, and the inherent project risk. Matrices are a powerful tool for analysis and data visualization. These three matrices provide that view into the selection criteria for a project's life cycle. The requirements category (Table 33–1) consists of questions related to those things that have been requested by the user for the project. They are sometimes termed as functions or features of the system that will be provided by the project.

Whenever possible, it is best to select the people for the project team before selecting the life cycle model. The characteristics of this team (Table 33–2) are important in the selection process because they are responsible for the successful completion of the cycle and because they can assist in the selection process.

The early project phases can provide a good understanding of the user community (Table 33–3) and the expected relationship with the project team for the duration of the project. This

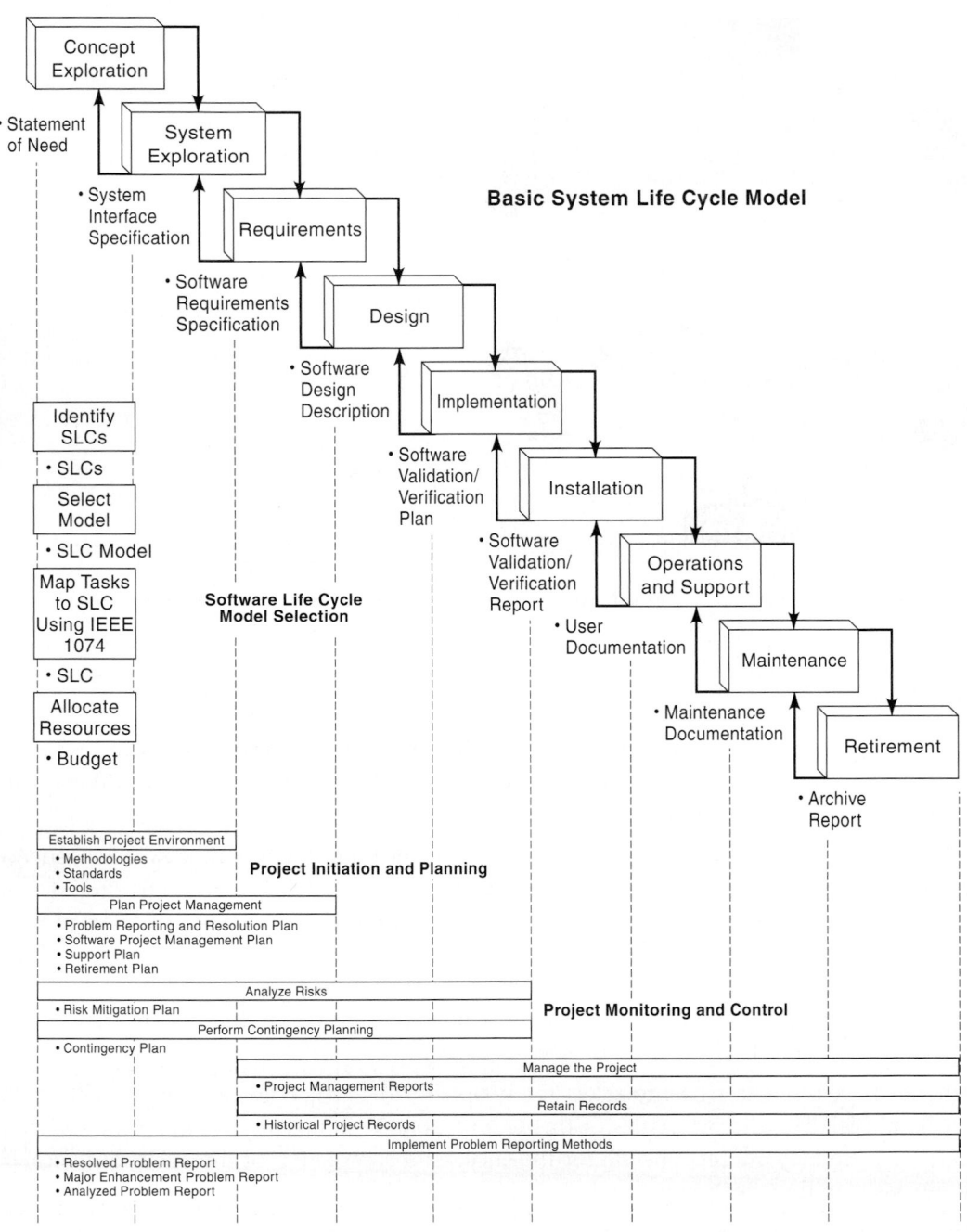

FIGURE 33–2
Software Development Process Framework

(Continues)

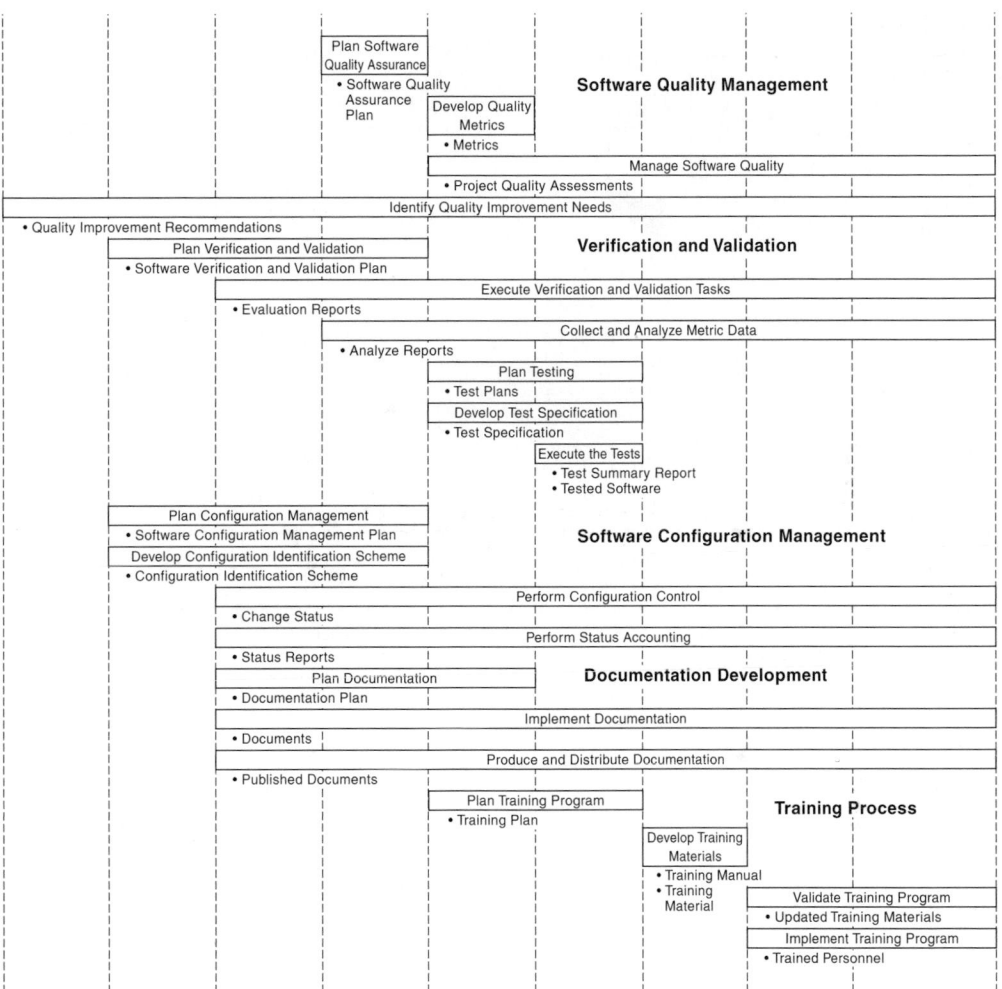

FIGURE 33–2 (Continued)
Software Development Process Framework

understanding will assist you in selecting the appropriate model because some models are dependent on high user involvement and understanding of the project.

Finally, examine the type of project and the risk (Table 33–4) that has been identified to this point in the planning phase. Some models are designed to accommodate high-risk management, while others are not. The selection of a model that accommodates risk management does not mean that you do not have to create an action plan to minimize the risk identified. The model simply provides a framework within which this action plan can be discussed and executed.

What's Wrong with This Process?

FIGURE 33–3
Not This Life Cycle

TABLE 33–1
Software Development Life Cycle Selection Based on Knowledge of Requirements

Requirements	Water-fall	V-Shaped	Proto-type	Spiral	RAD	Incre-mental
Are the requirements easily defined and/or well known?	Yes	Yes	No	No	Yes	No
Can the requirements be defined early in the cycle?	Yes	Yes	No	No	Yes	Yes
Will the requirements change often in the cycle?	No	No	Yes	Yes	No	No
Is there a need to demonstrate the requirements to achieve definition?	No	No	Yes	Yes	Yes	No
Is a proof of concept required to demonstrate capability?	No	No	Yes	Yes	Yes	No
Do the requirements indicate a complex system?	No	No	Yes	Yes	No	Yes
Is early functionality a requirement?	No	No	Yes	Yes	Yes	Yes

TABLE 33–2

Software Development Life Cycle Selection Based on Knowledge of the Project Team

Project Team	Water-fall	V-Shaped	Proto-type	Spiral	RAD	Incre-mental
Are the majority of team members new to the problem domain for the project?	No	No	Yes	Yes	No	No
Are the majority of team members new to the technology domain for the project?	Yes	Yes	No	Yes	No	Yes
Are the majority of team members new to the tools to be used on the project?	Yes	Yes	No	Yes	No	No
Are the team members subject to reassignment during the life cycle?	No	No	Yes	Yes	No	Yes
Is there training available for the project team, if required?	No	Yes	No	No	Yes	Yes
Is the team more comfortable with structure than flexibility?	Yes	Yes	No	No	No	Yes
Will the project manager closely track the team's progress?	Yes	Yes	No	Yes	No	Yes
Is ease of resource allocation important?	Yes	Yes	No	No	Yes	Yes
Does the team accept peer reviews and inspections, management/customer reviews, and milestones?	Yes	Yes	Yes	Yes	No	Yes

TABLE 33–3
Software Development Life Cycle Selection Based on Knowledge of the User Community

User Community	Water-fall	V-Shaped	Proto-type	Spiral	RAD	Incre-mental
Will the availability of the user representatives be restricted or limited during the life cycle?	Yes	Yes	No	Yes	No	Yes
Are the user representatives new to system definition?	No	No	Yes	Yes	No	Yes
Are the user representatives experts in the problem domain?	No	No	Yes	No	Yes	Yes
Do the users want to be involved in all phases of the life cycle?	No	No	Yes	No	Yes	No
Does the customer want to track project progress?	No	No	Yes	Yes	No	No

TABLE 33–4
Software Development Life Cycle Selection Based on Knowledge of the Project Type and Risk

Project Type and Risk	Water-fall	V-Shaped	Proto-type	Spiral	RAD	Incre-mental
Does the project identify a new product direction for the organization?	No	No	Yes	Yes	No	Yes
Is the project a system integration project?	No	Yes	Yes	Yes	Yes	Yes
Is the project an enhancement to an existing system?	No	Yes	No	No	Yes	Yes

(Continues)

TABLE 33–4 (Continued)
Software Development Life Cycle Selection Based on Knowledge of the Project Type and Risk

Project Type and Risk	Water-fall	V-Shaped	Proto-type	Spiral	RAD	Incre-mental
Is the funding for the project expected to be stable throughout the life cycle?	Yes	Yes	Yes	No	Yes	No
Is the product expected to have a long life in the organization?	Yes	Yes	No	Yes	No	Yes
Is high reliability a must?	No	Yes	No	Yes	No	Yes
Is the system expected to be modified, perhaps in ways not anticipated, post-deployment?	No	No	Yes	Yes	No	Yes
Is the schedule constrained?	No	No	Yes	Yes	Yes	Yes
Are the module interfaces clean?	Yes	Yes	No	No	No	Yes
Are reusable components available?	No	No	Yes	Yes	Yes	No
Are resources (time, money, tools, people) scarce?	No	No	Yes	Yes	No	No

Domain Processes

Project managers care about domain processes because this is the intersection with the rest of the world. Dependencies are required with marketing and finance organizations. Figure 33–4 shows the entire product life cycle plotted in months versus thousands of dollars invested. The number of dollars of investment on the left side of the graph and below the zero line is the estimated investment in the product. The dollars above the zero line are the estimated revenue dollars that the product will earn. This type of information is usually developed by

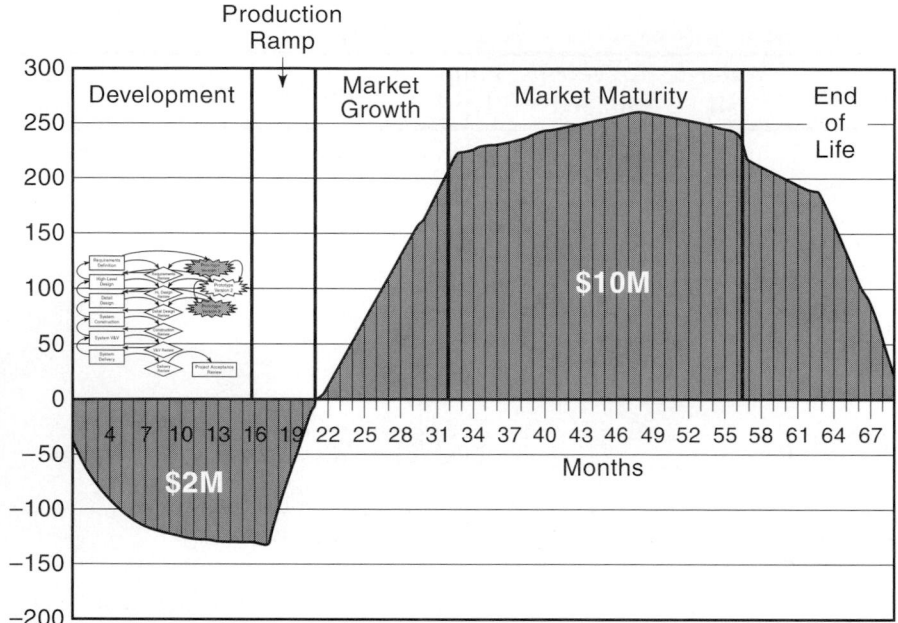

FIGURE 33–4
Software Product Life Cycle

marketing and is a critical part of the return on investment that the product will make. The software development is on the left side of the graph where the investment is taking place.

This relationship is critical to keep in mind as the project manager works through the product development process. In the product world, the product life cycle drives decisions and investment. Only the investment part of the software development life cycle is important to product managers planning product portfolios.

The project manager needs to be aware of how the organization's project portfolio is evaluated from a financial viewpoint. The most widely used economic return model applies financial measures of internal rate of return, net present value, marginal cost of capital, return on investment, assets and invested capital, and weighted average cost of capital (WACC). Figure 33–5 shows how this model is applied in its simplest fashion. Over time, the line that tracks the cost of asset deployment rises and falls with respect to the WACC. Projects that have a return above this moving line are earning a return above the WACC. Those that are below the line need to be evaluated for termination. This model can be used to both track historic trends and predict the future cost of asset deployment. Project managers must know, over time, where their projects are on this chart.

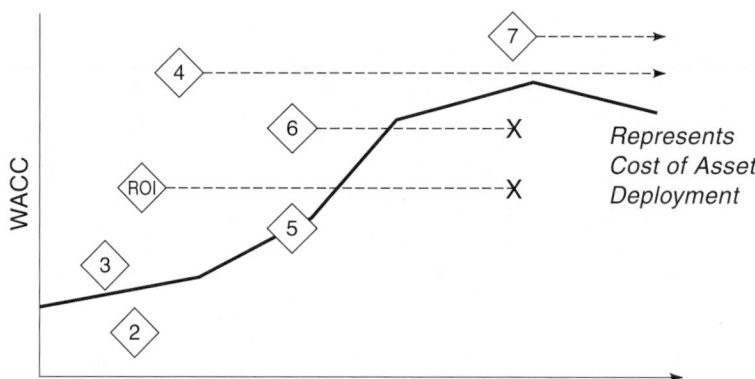

FIGURE 33–5
Economic Return Model Project Selection

Software Requirements Specifications

Figure 33–6 shows the three perspectives that the project team needs to take when analyzing and documenting requirements. The classical process, data, and behavior views of the problem domain work for classical structured methods and object-oriented requirements model representations.

One analysis tool used in developing the software requirements specification is the traceability matrix, Table 33–5. This basic traceability matrix will be used throughout the software development life cycle to map design modules to requirements, tests, and configuration items. This one tool has a long life and is worth taking extra care in its development during requirements.

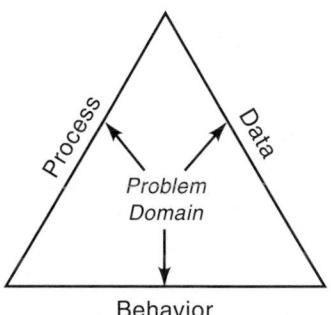

FIGURE 33–6
Three Perspectives of Software Products

TABLE 33–5
Requirements Traceability Matrix

Requirement Number and Description		HW Module 1	HW Module 2	HW Module 3	HW Module 4	HW Module 5	HW Module 6	HW Module 7
3.1	Functional Requirements							
3.1.1	Functional Requirement 1							
3.1.1.1	Introduction	X						
3.1.1.2	Inputs		X	X				
3.1.1.3	Processing							
3.1.1.4	Outputs							
3.1.2	Functional Requirement 2		X		X			
3.1.2.1	Introduction							
3.1.2.2	Inputs			X				
3.1.2.3	Processing		X		X			
3.1.2.4	Outputs							
3.1.n	Functional Requirement n		X					X
3.1.n.1	Introduction							
3.1.n.2	Inputs			X				
3.1.n.3	Processing	X						
3.1.n.4	Outputs	X	X					
3.2	External Interface Requirements	X						
3.2.1	User Interface							X
3.2.2	Hardware Interfaces	X	X	X	X			
3.2.3	Software Interfaces		X	X	X	X		

(Continues)

TABLE 33–5 (Continued)
Requirements Traceability Matrix

Requirement Number and Description		HW Module 1	HW Module 2	HW Module 3	HW Module 4	HW Module 5	HW Module 6	HW Module 7
3.2.4	Communications Interfaces				X			
3.3	Performance Requirements							X
3.4	Design Constraints							X
3.4.1	Standards Compliance					X	X	
3.4.2	Hardware Limitations			X	X			
3.5	Quality Characteristics							
3.5.1	Correctness	X						X
3.5.2	Unambiguousness		X				X	
3.5.3	Completeness			X		X		
3.5.4	Consistency				X			
3.5.5	Ranked for importance or stability			X		X		
3.5.6	Verifiability		X				X	
3.5.7	Modifiability	X						X
3.5.8	Traceability	X	X	X	X	X	X	X
3.6	Other Requirements							
3.6.1	Database				X	X		
3.6.2	Operations			X				
3.6.3	Site Adaptation		X					

Software Engineering

The Software Engineering Institute's Capability Maturity Model has defined how to measure process implementation for all software development organizations. A project manager needs to learn no other process assessment tool. Figure 33–7 shows the model maturity levels and key process areas. The model has been validated and is shown to increase quality and decrease cost in organizations that improve their maturity levels.

Analysis and Design

Software development organizations are subject to internal wars over using structured versus object-oriented analysis and design methods. Some organizations even put together a

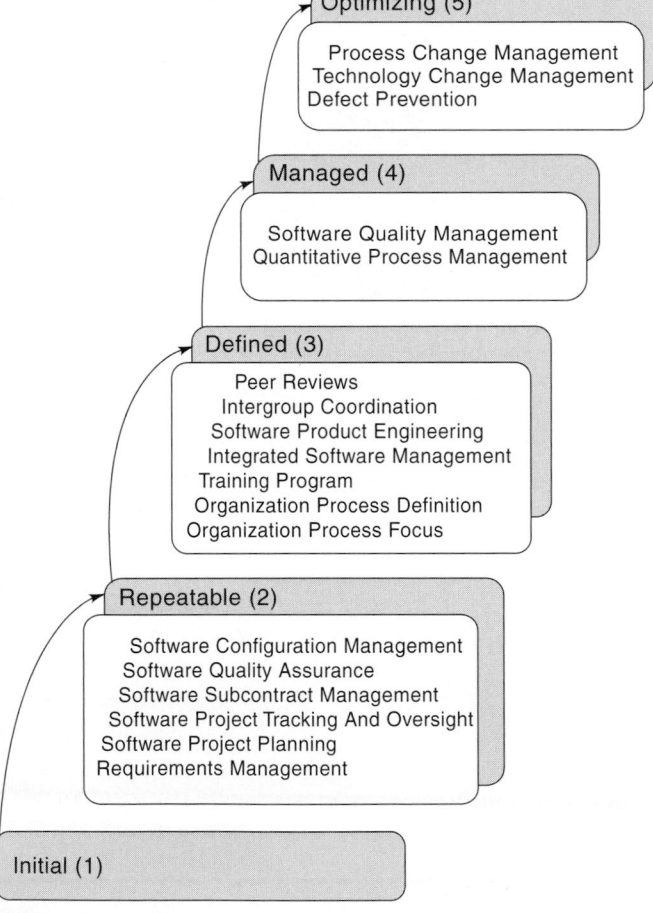

FIGURE 33–7
SEI CMM Key Process Areas

combined set with models from both camps. Tables 33–6 and 33–7 describe the models used for analysis and design for both classical and object-oriented methods. This is an important reference to use in decoding the rhetoric.

TABLE 33–6
Structured Analysis/Structured Design Models

Data, Function, Behavior	Type of Model	Description	Elements
		Phase: Structured Analysis	
Function	Data Context Diagram (DCD)	A picture of the system and its interfaces to external entities or systems. It shows the boundary between the system and its environment, in perspective to the real world, with all net inputs and outputs identified. Having only one process, the system as a "black box" at this point, it represents all of the transformations performed by the system.	External entities (boxes), one process (the System—circle/bubble), named data flows (arched arrows).
Function	Data Flow Diagrams (DFDs)	A DFD is a picture of the system as a network of functional processes connected to each other by "pipelines" of data (data flows) and "holding tanks" of data (data stores). The processes transform the data. The diagram partitions the system into its component parts.	Labeled process bubbles, named data flows, data stores. Note that external entities do not show on a DFD, but data stores do. The terminators from the DCD are dropped; only the information flowing into and out of the system (the data flow) will be retained, and the one major process circle will be decomposed into several more refined process circles.

(Continues)

TABLE 33–6 (Continued)
Structured Analysis/Structured Design Models

Data, Function, Behavior	Type of Model	Description	Elements
Phase: Structured Analysis (continued)			
Function	Process Specifications (PSPECs)	Description of a function or process at the lowest level of decomposition—one is written for every functional primitive process. It captures the transformation to be performed within each process—that is, what happens to each input to produce the desired output.	PSPECs can be in the form of structured language (pseudocode), decision tables, equations, charts, mathematical equations, block diagrams, or other graphics.
Data	Entity Relationship Model/ Diagram (ERD)	Enables a software engineer to identify data objects and their relationships using a graphical notation. In the context of structured analysis, the ERD defines all data that are input, stored, transformed, and produced within an application. It is a picture of data organized into meaningful groups, and it shows the relationships between the groups.	Entities (boxes), attributes, relationships (directed lines), cardinality (crow's feet = many, bar = one, circle = zero).
Behavior	Control Context Diagram (CCD)	Like the DFD, the CCD has only one process, shows inputs and outputs from and to external entities, and is broken down into components that end with specifications. The difference is that the data that appears on a CCD or a control flow diagram (CFD) is control data that causes a system state change, resulting in activation and deactivation of transforms.	External entities, one process (the system), named control flows. The elements and symbols on a CCD are the same as for a DCD, except that control data is represented by a dotted line to distinguish it from all other data and allow for clear behavioral modeling.

(Continues)

TABLE 33–6 (Continued)
Structured Analysis/Structured Design Models

Data, Function, Behavior	Type of Model	Description	Elements
Phase: Structured Analysis (continued)			
Behavior	Control Flow Diagrams (CFDs)	Model control flows instead of data flows. Share the naming, numbering, leveling, and balancing properties of DFDs.	Labeled process bubbles, named control flows (dotted lines), data stores, control bars for CSPEC.
Behavior	Control Specifications (CSPECs)	Indicated by a bar on a CFD; may change the state of the system.	State transition diagrams—state, transition, event/action.
Phase: Structured Design			
Data	Enhanced Entity Relationship Diagram (ERD)	Further iteration of the ERD based on information determined during the design phase.	Entities, attributes, relationships, cardinality.
Function/ Behavior	Architecture Context Diagrams (ACD)	Establishes information boundary between system and environment. Shows physical allocation of the requirements model's data (DFD) and control (CFD) processing. Assigns processes of the requirements model to physical modules that constitute the system and establishes the relationship between them.	Module = rectangle with rounded corners; regrouped process bubbles. Information flow vector = arrow (data)/ dashed arrow (control); bundles of data and control flows.
Function/ Behavior	Architecture Flow Diagram (AFDs)	The process bubbles from DFDs are rearranged according to more physical properties, such as which process bubbles must be organized together to accomplish the user interface.	Decomposed ACDs. Modules, inputs, outputs, user interface, maintenance, and self-help.

(Continues)

TABLE 33–6 (Continued)
Structured Analysis/Structured Design Models

Data, Function, Behavior	Type of Model	Description	Elements
		Phase: Structured Design (continued)	
Function/ Behavior	Structure Charts	Structure charts organize systems that have been partitioned into black boxes into hierarchies. Structure charts show temporal sequence vertically but not horizontally.	Module boxes, control, data.
Function	Chapin Charts	Structured flow charts. Single entry, single exit.	Four processing constructs: simple sequence, do while/do until, if-then-else, do case.
Behavior	Architecture Interconnect Diagrams	Representation of the communication channels that exist between architecture modules. Shows the physical means by which modules communicate. Examples are radio signals, electrical bus, mechanical line, and optical link.	Same as AFD, with the addition of communication channels. Multiple channels are lanes (or units).

Software Development Tools, Including CM

Project managers and team members expend an enormous amount of time in researching, selecting, and learning software engineering tools. The life cycle chosen for the project along with the supporting processes form a framework in which the tools must function. Table 33–8 shows a set of tools covering the entire life cycle. This is a basic toolkit that all experienced software engineers should know how to use. It is a minimal toolkit, but it is more than enough to get started on a development project. Project members need some tools with which to get started. Do not get focused looking at tools when the project needs to define the product.

TABLE 33–7
Object-Oriented Models

Data, Function, Behavior	Type of Model	Description	Elements
Phase: Object-Oriented Analysis			
Static Models; Data, Function	Class Diagrams	A graph of classes connected by static relationships.	Classes (attributes, operations), relationships (associations), data types (operations may be described by DFDs or pseudocode, as with SA/SD).
	Object Diagrams	A graph of instances of classes, including objects and data values. Shows snapshot of the state of a system at a point in time.	Objects (attributes, methods), links, values.
Dynamic Models; Function, Behavior	Use Case	A model of the way an actor interacts with the system.	Actors (stick figures), system functions (ovals), <<uses>>, <<extends>>, arrows.
	Scenario	An instance of a use case; a single execution path through a use case, showing actions and interactions of objects (not classes).	Actors, system functions.
	Activity Diagram	A graphical model of a use case, showing control flow. A set of activities that must be carried out, including temporal sequencing and conditions. No classes or objects are shown.	A flowchart, activities (capsule), sequence (labeled arrows), conditions (diamonds), end of workflow (bulls eye) synchronization bars (parallel activities).

(Continues)

TABLE 33–7 (Continued)
Object-Oriented Models

Data, Function, Behavior	Type of Model	Description	Elements
Phase: Object-Oriented Design			
Static Model	Enhanced Class Diagram	Elaboration on model.	
Dynamic Models	Interaction Diagrams— Collaboration Diagrams	Spatial graphs with emphasis on objects and links between objects. How a use case is realized in terms of cooperating objects, defined by classes inside the entity, can be specified with a collaboration. A use case of an entity may be refined to a set of use cases of the elements contained in the entity. How these subordinate use cases interact can also be expressed in a collaboration.	Objects (boxes), links (arrows) with sequenced messages, returned references or data.
	Interaction Diagrams— Sequence Diagrams	Graphs showing temporal sequencing with the focus on the order of messages.	Actors, swimlanes (lifelines) headed by objects, links (arrows), messages positioned vertically.
	State Transition Diagrams	Tied to one class—the states through which an instance of a class may pass.	Event, state, transition triggered by event.

TABLE 33–8

Minimal Tool Sets

Tool Class	Specific Tool Type	Microsoft® Windows Tools	Linux Tools
Software Requirements Tools	Requirements Modeling	Visio® Access	Dia Quicklist
	Traceability	Excel	abs
Software Design Tools	Design modeling	Visio® Access	ArgoUML
	Design verification	Visio® Excel	ArgoUML abs
	Design optimization	Visual Studio	ArgoUML
Software Construction Tools	Program editors	Visual Studio	Emacs
	Compilers	Visual Studio	AnyJ
	Interpreters	Visual Studio	Perl
	Debuggers	Visual Studio	AnyJ
Software Testing Tools	Test generators	Access	Quicklist ArgoUML
	Test execution frameworks	Visual Studio	Perl
	Test evaluation	Excel	abs
	Test management	Visual Source Safe	CVS
	Performance analysis	Excel	abs
Software Maintenance Tools	Comprehension	Visual Studio	Cxref
	Re-engineering	Visual Studio	ArgoUML
Software Engineering Process Tools	Process management	Email, Web, word processor	email, web, word processor
	Process modeling	Visio®	Dia

(Continues)

TABLE 33–8 (Continued)
Minimal Tool Sets

Tool Class	Specific Tool Type	Microsoft® Windows Tools	Linux Tools
	Integrated CASE environments	Visual Studio	AnyJ
	Process-centered software engineering environments		
Software Quality Tools	Inspection	Email, word processor, Excel	email, word processor, abs
	Static analysis	RSM	RSM
Software Configuration Management Tools	Defect, enhancement, issue, and problem tracking	Visual Source Safe	CVS
	Version management	Visual Source Safe	CVS
	Release and build	Visual Source Safe	CVS
Software Engineering Management Tools	Project planning and tracking	Excel	abs
	Risk management	Excel	abs
	Measurement	Excel	abs
Infrastructure Support Tools	Interpersonal communications	Email, Web chat	Email, Web chat
	Information retrieval system	Access, Web	QuickList, Web
	Administration and support	Email, Web	Email, Web
Miscellaneous Tools Issues	Tool integration techniques	Visual Basic, Perl, Tcl/Tk	Perl, Tcl/Tk
	Metatool	Access, Excel	Dia, abs
	Tool evaluation	Excel	abs

Continuous Process Improvement

Continuous process improvement is one of the most customer-facing activities that an organization can initiate. Developing a definition and constituent parts of what customers believe to be quality in an organization's product drives how value is determined. Table 33–9 gives a method for classifying and calculating value for a customer based on the cost of developing the product. Identifying essential and nonessential non–value-added activities is an enlightening effort for the project manager to lead.

Project Management Skills _____

12. **Building a work breakdown structure**—Building a WBS for a project
13. **Documenting plans**—Identifying key components
14. **Estimating cost**—Estimating cost to complete the project
15. **Estimating effort**—Estimating effort required to complete the project
16. **Managing risks**—Identifying and determining the impact and handling of risks
17. **Monitoring development**—Monitoring the production of software
18. **Scheduling**—Creating a schedule and key milestones
19. **Selecting metrics**—Choosing appropriate metrics
20. **Selecting project management tools**—Knowing how to select PM tools
21. **Tracking processes**—Monitoring compliance of project team
22. **Tracking project progress**—Monitoring progress using metrics

The middle 11 competencies focus on the project management skills needed by software development project managers. They are necessary for the successful initiation, execution, and completion of a software project. The following are specific methods, techniques, and tools that support the project management competencies.

Defining Project Goals

Defining a project's goals brings into play yet another process framework. The project process framework shown in Figure 33–8 looks at the steps and the outputs for goal definition.

A useful technique for defining clear goals and objectives is the S.M.A.R.T. method. S.M.A.R.T. is comprised of the initials for: specific, measurable, achievable, realistic, and time-bound.

For any objective, determine the specific results and performance targets necessary to meet expectations. Are the objectives specific? Do you and your sponsor/customer both agree on the results needed for each of your project's objectives? Are the objectives measurable? How will you know that you are achieving results? What does "meet expectations" mean to

TABLE 33–9
Spreadsheet Template for Value Calculation

Project Identifier:					
Value-Added		**Non–Value-Added**			
		Essential		**Nonessential**	
Design		Acceptance Testing		Bottlenecks	
Documentation		Moving Data Between Steps		Correction	
Implementation		Planning		Delays	
Installation		Setup		Error Analysis	
Requirements		Some Process		Expediting	
Shipping		Training		Extra Paperwork	
Upgrading				Extra Unwanted Features	
				Installing Software Tools	
				Management	
				Metrics	
				Modification	
				Process Improvement	
				Recall	
				Retest	
				Rework	
Total Value Added:	0	Total Essential:	0	Total Nonessential:	0
Project Value to Total:	0.0%				
Percent Essential to Nonessential:	0.0%			Percent Nonessential to Total:	0.0%
Percent Value Plus Essential to Total:	0.0%				

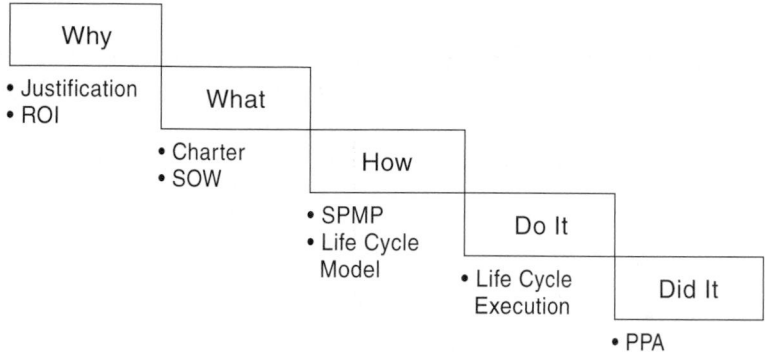

FIGURE 33–8
Project Process Framework

you and your customer for each of the objectives? Are the objectives achievable and attainable? Why or why not? What support would you need to attain them? Are the objectives realistic and relevant? Do they address the customer's requirements and real needs? Do they align with the key success factors for the organization, the business goals, and strategies? Are your objectives time-bound? Are there specific dates that the objectives should be achieved? Is there a clearly understood reason for each of the dates? What is the driver behind the dates (e.g., your customer's customer needs the product then)?

Now that the individual objectives have been identified and the overall project scope is understood and agreed upon, it is time to prepare the project charter. Basically, the project manager will capture the high-level objectives and the scope, and then add other pertinent high-level information so that a sponsor or customer can approve it. Often, the charter is the basic document needed for project selection in the organization's project portfolio management process, where this project would be compared to others in a cost/benefit sense and funded, if selected.

Work Breakdown Structure

At some point in the project life, project managers have to explain to the accounting people how costs are tracked. The ties in many organizations among budgeting, actual monies spent, and cost accounting are arbitrary and capricious. Figure 33–9 can be successfully used to communicate the software development project among the financial and cost accountants.

Identifying Tasks and Activities

For a project manager who has followed the advice in this guide to begin the process and life cycle definition with IEEE 1074, there is a bonus when it comes to identifying tasks and activities. Table 33–10 is a list of the activities mapped to each IEEE 1074 life cycle phase. This is a perfect starter kit.

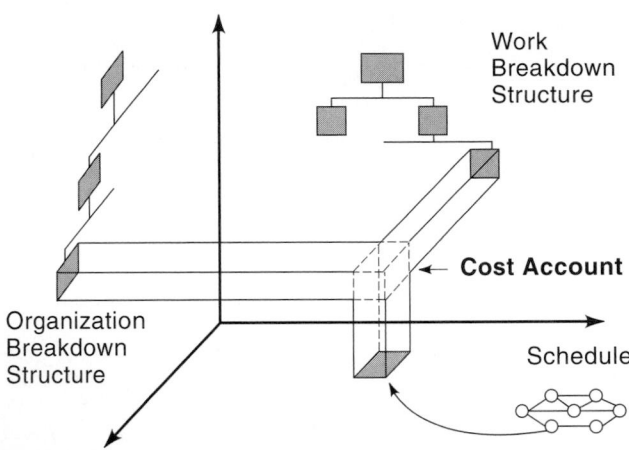

FIGURE 33–9
WBS Relationship to Cost Control
Source: Stuckenbruck, ed. (1981). *The Implementation of Project Management*. Addison-Wesley.

TABLE 33–10
IEEE 1074 Software Development Product Life Cycle Processes and Activities

Development Phase	Life Cycle Processes	Activities
Software Life Cycle Model Planning	1. Map software life cycle model to project needs	1. Identify candidate software life cycle models 2. Select project model
Project Management	2. Project initiation	3. Map activities to software life cycle model 4. Allocate project resources 5. Establish project environment 6. Plan project management
	3. Project monitoring and control	7. Analyze risks 8. Perform contingency planning 9. Manage the project 10. Retain records 11. Implement problem reporting method
	4. Software quality management	12. Plan software quality management 13. Define metrics 14. Manage software quality 15. Identify quality improvement needs

(Continues)

TABLE 33–10 (Continued)
IEEE 1074 Software Development Product Life Cycle Processes and Activities

Development Phase	Life Cycle Processes	Activities
Predevelopment	5. Concept exploration	16. Identify ideas or needs 17. Formulate potential approaches 18. Conduct feasibility studies 19. Plan system transition (if applicable) 20. Refine and finalize the idea or need
	6. System allocation	21. Analyze functions 22. Develop system architecture 23. Decompose system requirements
Development	7. Requirements	24. Define and develop software requirements 25. Define interface requirements 26. Prioritize and integrate software requirements
	8. Design	27. Perform architectural design 28. Design database (if applicable) 29. Design interfaces 30. Select or develop algorithms (if applicable) 31. Perform detailed design
	9. Implementation	32. Create test data 33. Create source code 34. Generate object code 35. Create operating documentation 36. Plan integration 37. Perform integration
Post-Development	10. Installation	38. Plan installation 39. Distribute software 40. Install software 41. Accept software in operational environment
	11. Operation and support	42. Operate the system 43. Provide technical assistance and consulting 44. Maintain support request log

(Continues)

TABLE 33–10 (Continued)
IEEE 1074 Software Development Product Life Cycle Processes and Activities

Development Phase	Life Cycle Processes	Activities
	12. Maintenance	45. Reapply software life cycle
	13. Retirement	46. Notify user(s) 47. Conduct parallel operations (if applicable) 48. Retire system
Integral	14. Verification and validation	49. Plan verification and validation 50. Execute verification and validation tasks 51. Collect and analyze metric data 52. Plan testing 53. Develop test requirements 54. Execute the tests
	15. Software configuration management	55. Plan configuration management 56. Develop configuration identification 57. Perform configuration control 58. Perform status accounting
	16. Documentation development	59. Plan documentation 60. Implement documentation 61. Produce and distribute documentation
	17. Training	62. Plan the training program 63. Develop training materials 64. Validate the training program 65. Implement the training program

Estimating and Sizing

Two important "takeaways" for the project manager in the estimating costs and effort competencies are the traditional estimating accuracy curve represented in Figure 33–10 and the use of function point analysis. As a project manager and a project funder, the best place for estimates is to be on the center line. Being under an estimate can be as bad as being over an estimate. With experience, estimates should improve, but for new project types, the estimate will be at the edges of the curves, not the center line.

Function point analysis requires no more than a simple spreadsheet program and good requirements elicitation techniques. The use of this technique will improve both the project

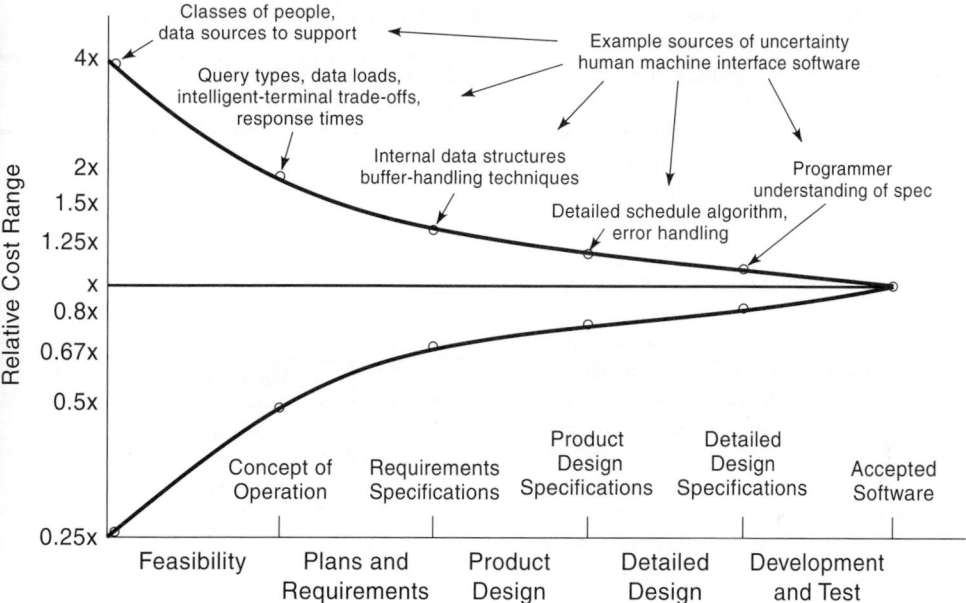

FIGURE 33–10
Estimating Accuracy Versus Life Cycle Phase

manager's estimates and the information about the project. No time is wasted in guessing a "lines of code equivalent" for a project that is only in the planning stages. Figure 33–11 shows an example of a spreadsheet calculation of a function point set.

Project Risk and Quality Assurance

There is nothing more that we can say about risk other than to use Table 33–11 as the project risk template. This template makes project managers *really* think about risk. It is important—do it! For projects that have more than seven high-level risks, do a software quality assurance plan. This will focus risk mitigation on the quality assurance aspects that will improve the probability of project success.

Reliability

Throughout the chapters in this guide, the factors shown in Figure 33–12 have been discussed. Particular attention has been paid to software reliability because of its high visibility to the end-user. Product revision and transition quality factors are important to the software development and maintenance teams. Product operation factors are customer-facing and cause the most customer pain when they are deficient. For project managers, this is the topology of all the "-ilities" that are shown to represent quality.

Measurement Parameter	Count	Simple	Count	Average	Count	Complex	Total
Number of User inputs	16	3	0	4	0	6	48
Number of User Outputs	4	4	3	5	0	7	31
Number of User Inquiries	13	3	0	4	0	6	39
Number of Files	7	7	0	10	0	15	49
Number of External Interfaces	0	5	0	7	0	10	0
							167

Complexity Adjustment Values   0 to 5

1	Does the system require reliable backup and recovery?	5
2	Are data communications required?	5
3	Are there distributed processing functions?	5
4	Is performance critical?	2
5	Will the system run on existing, heavily utilized operational environment?	3
6	Does the system require online data entry?	5
7	Does the online data entry require the input transaction to be built over multiple screens or operations?	5
8	Are the master files updated online?	5
9	Are the inputs, outputs, files, or inquiries complex?	1
10	Is the internal processing complex?	2
11	Is the code designed to be reusable?	0
12	Are conversion and installation included in the design?	0
13	Is the system designed for multiple installations in different organizations?	0
14	Is the application designed to facilitate change and ease of use by the user?	3
	Total	**41**

Legend	
0	No Influence
1	Incidental
2	Moderate
3	Average
4	Significant
5	Essential

$$FP = \text{count total} \times [0.65 + 0.01 \times \sum F_i]$$

Function Point Count = 177.02

FIGURE 33–11
Function Point Analysis Example

Verification and Validation

Software inspections, in-process reviews and formal end-of-phase reviews contribute greatly to product quality and life cycle cost reduction. It has often been quoted that, for procedural software produced using a sequential life-cycle approach, defects discovered after product deployment can cost up to 100 times as much to fix as defects discovered in early phases of the life cycle. The factors causing this phenomenon include cumulative analysis, design, and coding rework, plus a magnified ripple effect throughout a completed system. Requirements, design, and code reviews are the most effective way to reduce testing time because defects get removed before testing occurs. We now know that these statements are not the stuff of urban myth. Studies by Watts Humphrey found that early defect detection not only minimizes time

TABLE 33-11
Risk Categorization

Risk Factors and Categories	L—Low Risk Evidence	M—Medium Risk Evidence	H—High Risk Evidence	Rating (HML)	Comments
Mission and Goals Factors					
Project Fit	Directly supports organization mission and goals	Indirectly impacts one or more goals	Does not support or relate to organization mission or goals		
Workflow	Little or no change to workflow	Will change some aspect or have small effect on workflow	Significantly changes the workflow or method of organization		
Organization Management Factors					
Organization Stability	Little or no change in management or structure expected	Some management change or reorganization expected	Management or organization structure is continually or rapidly changing		
Development Team Stability	Team chosen, little or no change expected	Team chosen but members may change	Team not chosen, no decision about members		
Policies and Standards	Development policies and standards defined and carefully followed	Development policies/standards are in place but are weak or not carefully followed	No policies or standards, or they are ill-defined and unused		
Management Support	Strongly committed to success of project	Some commitment, not total	Little or no support		

(Continues)

TABLE 33–11 (Continued)
Risk Categorization

Risk Factors and Categories	L—Low Risk Evidence	M—Medium Risk Evidence	H—High Risk Evidence	Rating (HML)	Comments
Performance Objectives	Verifiable performance objectives, reasonable requirements	Some performance objectives; measures may be questionable	No established performance requirements, or requirements are not measurable		
Executive Involvement	Visible and strong support	Occasional support, provides help on issues when asked	No visible support; no help on unresolved issues		
Customer Factors					
Customer Involvement	End-users highly involved with project team, provide significant input	End-users play minor roles, moderate impact on system	Minimal or no end-user involvement; little end-user input		
Customer Experience	End-users highly experienced in similar projects, have specific ideas of how needs can be met	End-users have experience with similar projects and have needs in mind	End-users have no previous experience with similar projects; unsure of how needs can be met		
Customer Acceptance	End-users accept concepts and details of system; process is in place for end-user approvals	End-users accept most of concepts and details of system; process in place for end-user approvals	End-users do not accept any concepts or design details of system		

(Continues)

TABLE 33–11 (Continued)
Risk Categorization

Risk Factors and Categories	L—Low Risk Evidence	M—Medium Risk Evidence	H—High Risk Evidence	Rating (HML)	Comments
Customer Training Needs	End-user training needs considered; training in progress or plan in place	End-user training needs considered; no training yet or training plan in development	Requirements not identified or not addressed		
Customer Justification	End-user justification complete, accurate, sound	End-user justification provided, complete with some questions about applicability	No satisfactory justification for system		
Contract Fit	Contract with customer has good terms; communication with team is good	Contract has some open issues that could interrupt team work efforts	Contract has burdensome document requirements or causes extra work to comply		
Benefits Defined	Benefits well-defined, with identified measures and baselines	Some questions remain about benefits, or baseline is changing and measures doubtful	Benefits not defined, no baseline established, unattainable or un-measurable		
Budget/Cost Factors					
Project Size	Small, noncomplex, or easily decomposed	Medium, moderate complexity, decomposable	Large, highly complex, or not decomposable		

(Continues)

TABLE 33–11 (Continued)
Risk Categorization

Risk Factors and Categories	L—Low Risk Evidence	M—Medium Risk Evidence	H—High Risk Evidence	Rating (HML)	Comments
Hardware Constraints	Little or no hardware-imposed constraints or single platform	Some hardware-imposed constraints; several platforms	Significant hardware-imposed constraints; multiple platforms		
Technology	Mature, existent, in-house experience	Existent, some in-house experience	New technology or a new use or under development; little in-house experience		
Reusable Components	Components available and compatible with approach	Components promised; delivery dates unsure	Components projected, but not available when needed		
Supplied Components	Components available and directly usable	Components work under most circumstances	Components known to fail in certain cases, likely to be late, or incompatible with parts of approach		
Budget Size	Sufficient budget allocated	Questionable budget allocated	Doubtful budget is sufficient		
Budget Constraints	Funds allocated without constraints	Some questions about availability of funds	Allocation in doubt or subject to change without notice		

(Continues)

TABLE 33–11 (Continued)
Risk Categorization

Risk Factors and Categories	L—Low Risk Evidence	M—Medium Risk Evidence	H—High Risk Evidence	Rating (HML)	Comments
Economic Justification	Completely justified and cost-effectiveness proven	Justification questionable or effectiveness not completely established	Not justified, or cost-effectiveness not demonstrated		
Cost Controls	Well established, in place	System in place, weak in areas	System lacking or nonexistent		
Schedule Factors					
Delivery Commitment	Stable commitment dates	Some uncertain commitments	Unstable, fluctuating commitments		
Development Schedule	Team projects that schedule is acceptable and can be met	Team finds one phase of the plan to have a schedule that is too aggressive	Team projects that two or more phases of schedule are unlikely to be met		
Project Content					
Requirements Stability	Little or no change expected to approved set (baseline)	Some change expected against approved set	Rapidly changing or no agreed-upon baseline		
Requirements Complete and Clear	All completely specified and clearly written	Some requirements incomplete or unclear	Some requirements only in the head of the customer		

(Continues)

TABLE 33-11 (Continued)
Risk Categorization

Risk Factors and Categories	L—Low Risk Evidence	M—Medium Risk Evidence	H—High Risk Evidence	Rating (HML)	Comments
System Testability	System requirements easy to test, plans underway	Parts of system hard to test, or minimal planning being done	Most of system hard to test, or no test plans being made		
Design Difficulty	Well-defined interfaces; design well understood	Unclear how to design, or aspects of design yet to be decided	Interfaces not well-defined or controlled; subject to change		
Implementation Difficulty	Algorithms and design reasonable for this team to implement	Algorithms or design have elements somewhat difficult for this team to implement	Algorithms or design have components this team will find very difficult to implement		
System Dependencies	Clearly defined dependencies of the software effort and other parts of system	Some elements of the system are well understood and planned; others are not yet comprehended	No clear plan or schedule for how the whole system will come together		
Documents Stability	Documents will be available on time and will contain few errors	Some documents may be late and may contain minor errors	Little chance of getting documents on time, many corrections and changes expected		

(Continues)

TABLE 33–11 (Continued)
Risk Categorization

Risk Factors and Categories	L—Low Risk Evidence	M—Medium Risk Evidence	H—High Risk Evidence	Rating (HML)	Comments
Performance Factors					
Test Capability	Modular design allows for easy test coverage planning and execution	Modular design aids in developing test harnesses for unit test	No modular design or ability to easily establish test coverage planning		
Expected Test Effort	Good estimate available, readily fits system acceptance process	Rough estimate of test time, may be a bottleneck in the process	Poor or no estimate of test times; definite chance of bottleneck		
Functionality	Highly functional, meets all customer needs	Good functionality, meets most customer needs	Little functionality, many customer needs not met		
External Hardware or Software Interfaces	Little or no integration or interfaces needed	Some integration or interfaces needed	Extensive interfaces required		
Project Management Factors					
Approach	Product and process planning and monitoring in place	Planning and monitoring need enhancement	Weak or nonexistent planning and monitoring		

(Continues)

TABLE 33–11 (Continued)

Risk Categorization

Risk Factors and Categories	L—Low Risk Evidence	M—Medium Risk Evidence	H—High Risk Evidence	Rating (HML)	Comments
Communication	Clearly communicates goals and status between the team and rest of organization	Communicates some of the information some of the time	Rarely communicates clearly to the team or to others who need to be informed of team status		
Project Manager Experience	Project manager very experienced with similar projects	Project manager has moderate experience or has experience with different types of projects	Project manager has no experience with this type of project or is new to project management		
Project Manager Attitude	Strongly committed to success	Willing to do what it takes	Cares very little about project		
Project Manager Authority/ Support	Complete support of team and of management	Support of most of team, with some reservations	No visible support; manager in name only		
Development Process Factors					
Alternatives Analysis	Analysis of alternatives complete; all considered assumptions verifiable	Analysis of alternatives complete, some assumptions questionable or alternatives not fully considered	Analysis not completed, not all alternatives considered, or assumptions faulty		

(Continues)

TABLE 33-11 (Continued)

Risk Categorization

Risk Factors and Categories	L—Low Risk Evidence	M—Medium Risk Evidence	H—High Risk Evidence	Rating (HML)	Comments
Quality Assurance Approach	QA system established, followed, effective	Procedures established but not well followed or effective	No QA process or established procedures		
Commitment Process	Changes to commitments in scope, content, schedule are reviewed and approved by all involved	Changes to commitments are communicated to all involved	Changes to commitments are made without review or involvement of the team		
Development Documentation	Correct and available	Some deficiencies, available	Nonexistent		
Use of Defined Engineering Process	Development process in place, established, effective, followed by team	Process established but not followed or is ineffective	No formal process used		
Early Identification of Defects	Peer reviews are incorporated throughout	Peer reviews are used sporadically	Team expects to find all defects with testing		
Change Control for Work Products	Formal change control process in place, followed, effective	Change control process in place, not followed or is ineffective	No change control process used		

(Continues)

TABLE 33-11 (Continued)
Risk Categorization

Risk Factors and Categories	L—Low Risk Evidence	M—Medium Risk Evidence	H—High Risk Evidence	Rating (HML)	Comments
Defect Tracking	Defect tracking defined, consistent, effective	Defect tracking process defined but inconsistently used	No process in place to track defects		
Development Environment Factors					
Physical Facilities	Little or no modification needed	Some modifications needed; some existent	Major modifications needed, or facilities nonexistent		
Hardware Platform	Stable, no changes expected, capacity is sufficient	Some changes under evolution, but controlled	Platform under development along with software		
Tools Availability	In place, documented, validated	Available, validated, some development needed (or minimal documentation)	Invalidated, proprietary or major development needed; no documentation		
Configuration Management	Fully controlled	Some controls in place	No controls in place		
Security	All areas following security guidelines; data backed up; disaster recovery system in place; procedures followed	Some security measures in place; backups done; disaster recovery considered, but procedures lacking or not followed	No security measures in place; backup lacking; disaster recovery not considered		

(Continues)

TABLE 33-11 (Continued)
Risk Categorization

Risk Factors and Categories	L—Low Risk Evidence	M—Medium Risk Evidence	H—High Risk Evidence	Rating (HML)	Comments
Vendor Support	Complete support at reasonable price and in needed time frame	Adequate support at contracted price, reasonable response time	Little or no support, high cost, or poor response time		
Staff Factors					
Staff Availability	In place, little turnover expected; few interrupts for fire fighting	Available, some turnover expected; some fire fighting	High turnover, not available; team spends most of time fighting fires		
Mix of Staff Skills	Good mix of disciplines	Some disciplines inadequately represented	Some disciplines not represented at all		
Product Knowledge	Very experienced in developing this type of product	Some experience in developing this type of product	No experience in developing this type of product		
Software Development Experience	Extensive experience with this type of project	Some experience with similar projects	Little or no experience with similar projects		
Training of Team	Training plan in place, training ongoing	Training for some areas not available, or training planned for future	No training plan, or training not readily available		

(Continues)

TABLE 33–11 (Continued)
Risk Categorization

Risk Factors and Categories	L—Low Risk Evidence	M—Medium Risk Evidence	H—High Risk Evidence	Rating (HML)	Comments
Team Spirit and Attitude	Strongly committed to success of project; cooperative	Willing to do what it takes to get the job done	Little or no commitment to the project; not a cohesive team		
Team Productivity	All milestones met, deliverables on time, productivity high	Milestones met, some delays in deliverables, productivity acceptable	Productivity low, milestones not met, delays in deliverables		
Maintenance Factors					
Complexity	Structurally maintainable (low complexity measured or projected)	Certain aspects difficult to maintain (medium complexity)	Extremely difficult to maintain (high complexity)		
Change Implementation	Team in place can be responsive to customer needs	Team experiences delays, but acceptable to customer	Team is unable to respond to customer needs		
Support Personnel	In place, experienced, sufficient in number	Missing some areas of expertise	Significant discipline or expertise missing		
Vendor Support	Complete support at reasonable price and in needed time frame	Adequate support at contracted price, reasonable response time	Little or no support, high cost, or poor response time		

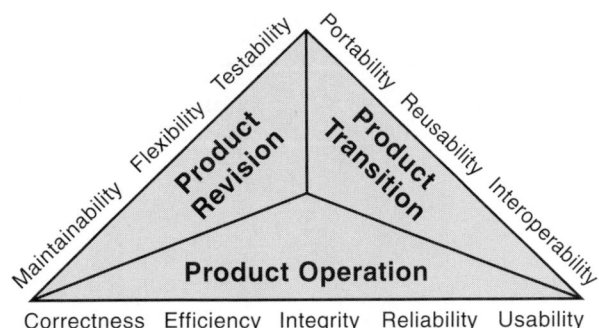

FIGURE 33–12
Software Quality Factors

and cost, but does so drastically. An average error-correction time ratio of 1 hour during the requirements phase translates to 3–6 hours for defects that escape to the design phase, 10 hours for the coding phase, 15–40 hours in the development testing activity, 30–70 hours during acceptance testing, and 40–1,000 hours during operation! Furthermore, research showed an average cost per defect range of $90–$120 in inspections to $10,000 in testing. Companies that used an early inspection system reported a tenfold reduction in the number of defects found in testing and up to an 80% reduction in test costs, including the cost of the inspections.

The National Software Quality Experiment benchmarks the state of software product quality and measures progress toward a national objective to improve cycle time. It is a mechanism for obtaining core samples of software product quality. A national database of product quality is populated by samples from industry, government, and military services. This database provides the means to benchmark and measure progress toward the software quality objective and contains data from 1992 through 1997. The experiment reveals that the return on investment (net savings/detection cost) for software reviews ranges from 4 to 8, independent of the context of usage. These are extremely low-cost techniques to implement. A software development project manager cannot afford to ignore this use.

Project Closure

It is the project manager's job to ensure that all participants learn from the software development experience. All projects in Level 1 organizations end with the traditional beer and pizza lobotomy. All participants celebrate that they lived through one more software project. They may have lived through it, but there were no formal lessons learned. Everything other than the code moved into corporate lore. The formal processes of project termination need a checklist like in Table 33–12.

TABLE 33–12
Example Project Closure Checklist

Description	Needed? Y/N	Due Date	Responsible	Done
Communicate decision				☐
Identify remaining work				☐
Deliver released software				☐
Get customer approvals				☐
Publish release documentation				☐
Perform personnel evaluations				☐
Perform post-performance analysis				☐
Hold closure event				☐
Release or reassign team				☐
Close outstanding work orders				☐
Review final configuration management audit				☐
Return or release vendor or customer materials				☐
Return all borrowed equipment				☐
Publish final report				☐

Beyond the simple checklist is a full post-performance analysis questionnaire. This type of instrument allows for much more complete data gathering for process improvement. Figure 33–13 is an example of this type of questionnaire. Use it to improve the next project.

Post-Performance Analysis Questionnaire for Development Team Members

As you review the following annotated template, note that portions of the document in nonbold italics are meant to be deleted. They are explanatory information.

In this first section, give the boilerplate information about the project, perhaps leaving open the project description for team members to identify what element of the project they worked on.

Project Information

     Name of project: —————————————————————————
     Contract number: —————————————————————————
     Customer name: —————————————————————————
     Start date: —————————————————————————
     Finish date: —————————————————————————

Type of project (select one of the following: data processing, systems software, applications software, test software, simulation, prototype):

     Short project description: —————————————————————————
     —————————————————————————————————————

     Internal contact name: —————————————————————————
     Phone: —————————————————————————
     Customer contact: —————————————————————————
     Phone: —————————————————————————
     Project status: —————————————————————————

Gather information about the respondent to be able to statistically identify the classes of people with summary information later. Keep this information on a sheet separate from the responses to the questions that follow so that you can remove it for data analysis, if needed. Note that we ask the role question twice so that you can correlate responses to classes of roles.

Background Information of Analysis Respondent

     Name: —————————————————————————
     Phone: —————————————————————————

     Team or organization: —————————————————————————
     Address: —————————————————————————
     Email: —————————————————————————

Add or remove roles here as appropriate to your environment.

Role(s) I played in this project (check all that apply):

—————   Project manager
—————   Team leader
—————   Process engineer
—————   Quality assurance
—————   Configuration management
—————   User documentation development
—————   Requirements analysis
—————   Designer

FIGURE 33–13

Example Post-Performance Analysis Data-Gathering Template

(Continues)

_____ Implementation/test
_____ Integration
_____ System test
_____ Build master
_____ Other (specify): _____

Rate the following characteristics for the environment for the project being reviewed. Use a scale of 1 to 5, where 1 is the lowest rating and 5 is the highest. If the item does not apply, mark an X.

Add or remove items here as appropriate to your environment.

_____ 1. Clarity of customer requirements
_____ 2. Support software availability
_____ 3. Support hardware availability
_____ 4. Team analysis capability
_____ 5. Team design capability
_____ 6. Team implementation capability
_____ 7. Team test capability
_____ 8. Team analysis capacity
_____ 9. Team design capacity
_____ 10. Team implementation capacity
_____ 11. Team test capacity
_____ 12. Team experience with project domain area
_____ 13. Team experience with project process
_____ 14. Team experience with project methods
_____ 15. Team experience with the language or implementation medium
_____ 16. Timely availability of externally furnished software components
_____ 17. Quality of externally furnished software components
_____ 18. Degree of reuse (in all phases)
_____ 19. Use of software tools
_____ 20. Use of appropriate methods
_____ 21. Use of risk analysis
_____ 22. Stability of organizational environment
_____ 23. Appropriateness of technology used to build product
_____ 24. Configuration management
_____ 25. Quality assurance

For the following, use a rating of 1 to 5, where 1 indicates a low level of the factor and 5 indicates a high level.

_____ 26. Product complexity
_____ 27. Requirements volatility
_____ 28. Reliability requirements
_____ 29. Efficiency requirements
_____ 30. Maintainability requirements
_____ 31. Portability requirements
_____ 32. Performance requirements
_____ 33. Degree of security requirements
_____ 34. International requirements
_____ 35. Complexity of project organization
_____ 36. Schedule aggressiveness
_____ 37. Number and types of technical reviews
_____ 38. Number and types of management reviews
_____ 39. Amount of integration and testing
_____ 40. Customer acceptance testing

FIGURE 33–13 (Continued)
Example Post-Performance Analysis Data-Gathering Template

(Continues)

41. Role(s) I played in this project (check all that apply):

_____ Process engineer
_____ Quality assurance
_____ Configuration management
_____ User documentation development
_____ Requirements analysis
_____ Design
_____ Implementation/test
_____ Integration
_____ System test
_____ Build
_____ Team leader
_____ Project manager
_____ Other (specify): _____

Be sure there is enough space for people to answer completely.

42. For this project, identify the key things that were done right, in your opinion.

43. For this project, identify the key things that were done wrong, in your opinion.

44. What unusual environmental influences (which might have either adversely or favorably affected the project) should be kept in mind when examining the history of this project?

45. For this project, how would you do things differently if you could start over again?

46. Describe one thing you could have done personally to improve the quality of the product produced by this project.

FIGURE 33–13 (Continued)
Example Post-Performance Analysis Data-Gathering Template

People Management Skills _____

23. **Appraising performance**—Evaluating teams to enhance performance
24. **Handling intellectual property**—Understanding the impact of critical issues
25. **Holding effective meetings**—Planning and running excellent meetings
26. **Interaction and communication**—Dealing with developers, upper management, and other teams
27. **Leadership**—Coaching project teams for optimal results
28. **Managing change**—Being an effective change agent
29. **Negotiating successfully**—Resolving conflicts and negotiating successfully
30. **Planning careers**—Structuring and giving career guidance
31. **Presenting effectively**—Using effective written and oral skills
32. **Recruiting**—Recruiting and interviewing team members successfully
33. **Selecting a team**—Choosing highly competent teams
34. **Teambuilding**—Forming, guiding, and maintaining an effective team

These last 12 competencies focus the project manager, the product development team, and the organization on the major resource used to build software: people. There is nothing in software development that can be done without people in the analysis, design, and development loop. People management is how these competencies are traditionally labeled, but the real competency that makes a project manager successful is not management, but leadership. The following are specific methods, techniques, and tools described in this guide that support people management competencies.

Selecting Project Teams

The key to making project teams work is to understand the personality type of the team members. Table 33–13 recaps the Myers-Briggs personality types. This works for all types of projects. This allows team members to communicate in a fashion not imagined before the understanding of each unique personality. It is worth the time—do it!

Estimating Duration and Cost

Estimating duration and cost, at first blush, appears to be better slotted into product competencies. However, it is totally reliant on people. This is a 100% people-based activity. It has been the authors' experience that excellent software developers are up to 25 times more productive than average developers. These are the resources that project managers must use to make the product. These are not mythical normed numbers in an estimating program. Figure 33–14 shows the steps in estimating.

TABLE 33–13
Myers-Briggs Type Indicator (MBTI)

MBTI Type Dimension	Characteristics
Introvert (I, E) Extrovert	*Source and Direction of Energy:* **I**: From internal concentration (is drained of energy by being around others) **E**: From external contact ("plugs into" the energy of others)
Sensing (S, N) iNtuitive	*Preferred Method of Information Reception:* **S**: Prefers empirical, sensory data **N**: Prefers meaningful patterns and abstractions
Thinking (T, F) Feeling	*Way of Information Processing:* **T**: Makes decisions according to their impersonal logic **F**: Makes a decision according to their personal values
Judging (J, P) Perceiving	*Way of Living Out Processed Information:* **J**: Organizes all life events and acts strictly according to their plans **P**: Inclined to improvisation and seeking different alternatives

Assigning Resources

One of the most useful tools for dealing with resource assignments is the responsibility assignment matrix (RAM). This sometimes appears under other names, such as responsibility matrix, staffing matrix, linear responsibility chart (LRC), or some variation of these names. The RAM clearly identifies an individual's responsibilities and roles for work products and activities. It defines *who* does *what* for the project activities, and it can easily be expanded into a work product progress-tracking sheet. Figure 33–15 shows the template. As with other project management tools, this is a simple matrix that conveys information inverse to the amount of effort to use. Successful project managers use simple tools.

Eliciting Product Requirements

Eliciting the requirements is another 100% people-oriented competency. Once the requirement notes are gathered from interviews, JAD sessions, and inspection of existing systems, the requirements need to be written. Clarity that can be imbued at this point will be appreciated later. There is not as much precision in the "rules" for requirements as there are for specifications, but the following guidelines will help with the transformation of one to the other:

• Define the term *requirements* in the context of your project because it often means different things to different people. Requirements are statements of functionality and quality

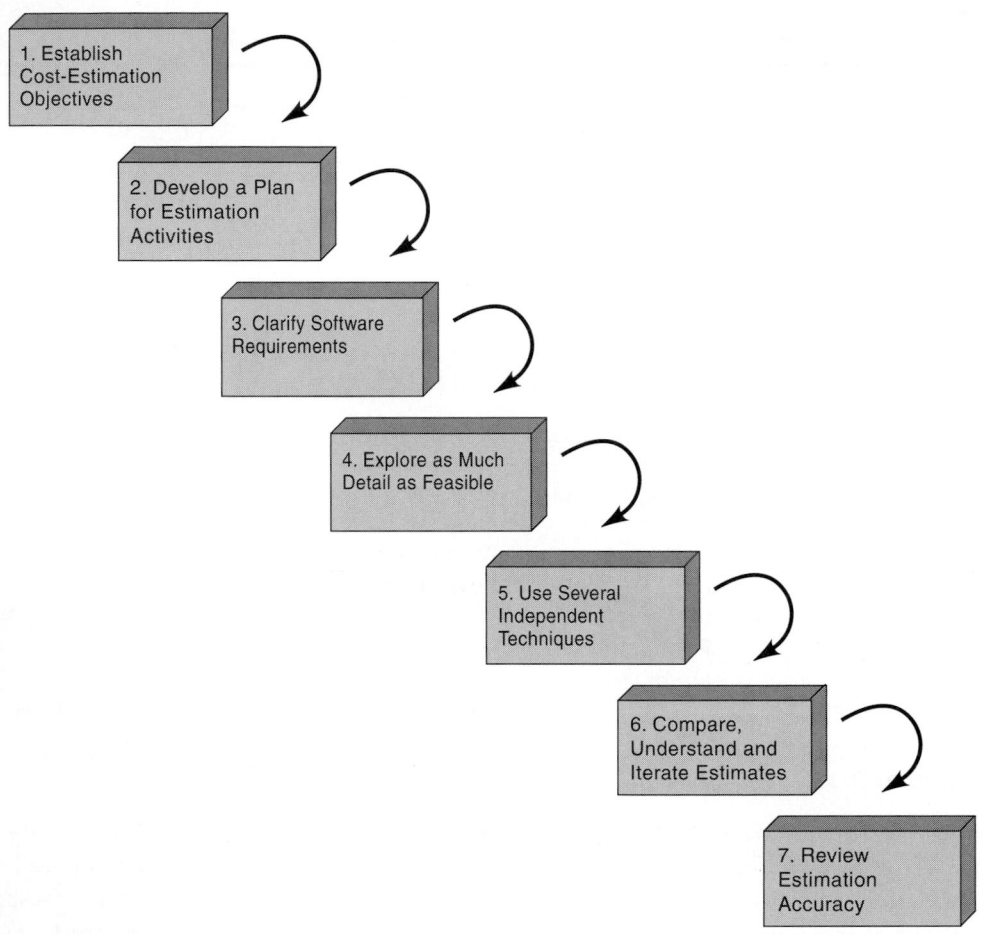

FIGURE 33–14
Steps in Estimating

believed by the stakeholders to be needed in the system, but they are not yet "specifications." Requirements may include high-level functional, behavioral, and informational models (data flow diagrams, entity relationship models, object models, control models), but they are *not* detailed user interface designs that will be used by developers.

- Keep in mind that there are different types of requirements: functional, nonfunctional, quality, performance, business, user, constraints, and so on.
- Address international issues.
- Identify time-critical functions.
- Consider safety and security issues.

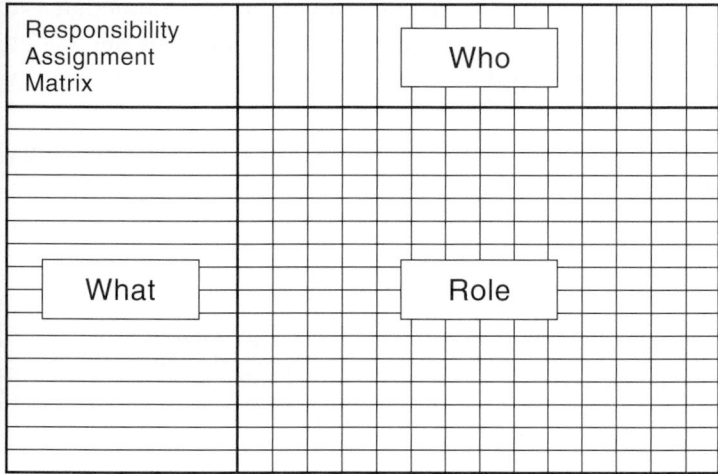

FIGURE 33–15
Responsibility Assignment Matrix

- Write requirements that can be traced to specifications (provide the source for specifications backward).

- Trace software requirements back to system requirements, use cases, or elicitation workshop session documentation.

- Create a requirements identification scheme (for forward and backward traceability).

- If meaningful error messages can be determined at this time, document them.

- Communicate, communicate, and communicate. It isn't fair to any stakeholder group for developers to make requirements decisions, especially not to developers. Often when an answer is not forthcoming and schedule pressures mount, a developer will attempt to fill the void by making a decision without adequate information and perspective. No user class should be left out. Individual product champions may represent user classes, collecting input from the class members.

- Reduce ambiguity in requirements as early as possible. An ambiguous requirement may have two or more contradictory interpretations, or it may be compound, having multiple independent requirement candidates in the same statement. A compound requirement is likely to include the terms *and* or *with*—watch for these red flags. An unambiguous requirement will be "primitive," meaning that it is clear, concise, and testable. Primitive requirements are cohesive; they represent one and only one thing.

- Explore the need for derived and conditional requirements. A requirement may be derived, obtained as a necessary or precursor condition for another requirement, or conditional, having other (derived) requirements as necessary or precursor conditions. A function that cannot be implemented until a certain version of an operating system is installed is an example of a conditional requirement. Backward compatibility with other system components is also a conditional requirement.

- Avoid using intrinsically subjective and ambiguous words when you write requirements. Terms such as *always, sometimes, often, minimize, maximize, optimize, rapid, quick, user-friendly, easy, simple, normal, usual, large, intuitive, robust, state-of-the-art, improved, efficient, support,* and *flexible* are particularly dangerous. Most of these terms are not verifiable.
- Write test cases against the functional requirements.
- Consider developing prototypes.
- Begin a data dictionary.
- Keep sentences and paragraphs concise, and keep requirements at a consistent level of granularity (one test case's worth of functionality).
- Avoid redundant requirements.

These guidelines, used along with frequent stakeholder reviews, will provide the proper foundation for the SRS.

Metrics

This is another people-dependent competency. People define, collect, and analyze metrics. Although much research is done annually on automatic metrics systems, in the real work of software development, people are the automation. A widely used and well-respected approach for determining which metrics will offer the most to project control and decision-making is the goal, question, metric (GQM) paradigm authored by Dr. Victor Basili. The GQM requires that goal setting take place before metrics collections. Facilitated brainstorming sessions are common forums for gaining consensus among the members of a project team on the specific project goals. Of course, organizational goals may be set by upper management or by stakeholders within the entire organization. Dr. Basili was instrumental in founding the Software Engineering Laboratory, a consortium including the Computer Science Department of the University of Maryland, the Software Engineering Branch of NASA Goddard's Flight Dynamics Division, and the Software Engineering Operation of Computer Sciences Corporation. Work at the SEL resulted in a seven-step process for systematically applying measurements to software. As shown in Figure 33–16, the steps are to develop a set of goals; develop a set of questions that characterize the goals; specify the metrics needed to answer the questions; develop mechanisms for data collection and analysis; collect, validate, and analyze the data; take corrective action; analyze in a post-mortem fashion; feed forward; and provide feedback to stakeholders. Figure 33–16 is a graphic representation of the GQM approach.

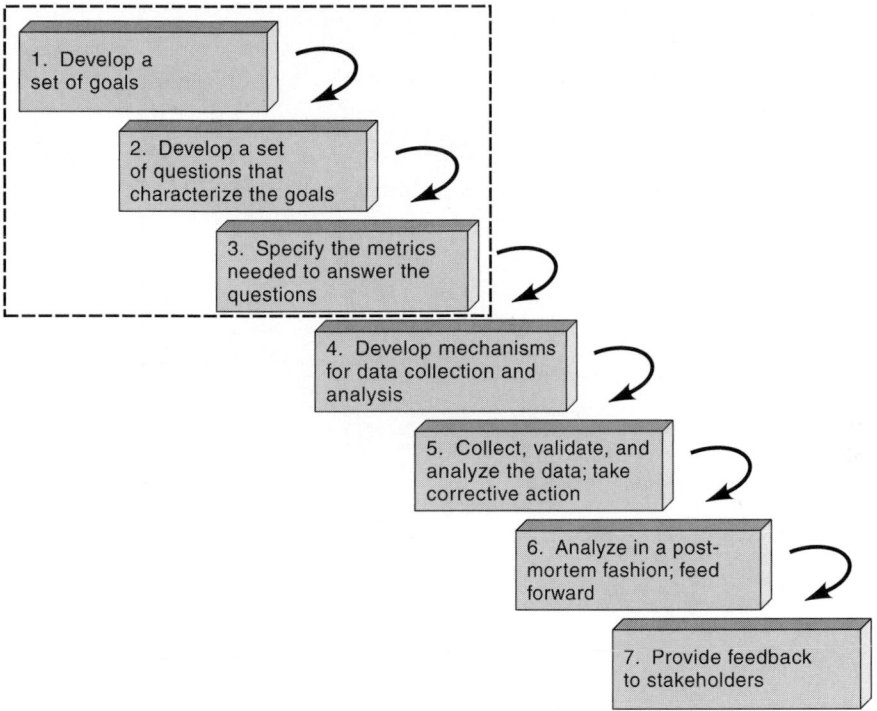

FIGURE 33–16
Basili Seven-Step Goal/Question/Metric Approach

Legal Issues

The legal profession has a multitude of taxonomies for framing specific areas of legal expertise. Simplifying this to the three groups for project management practitioners is more effective in relating to the process of software development. The authors of this guide are not attorneys nor have we had any legal training. In numerous projects since the early 1970s, we have had to deal with many of the legal issues described in this chapter. The only way to manage project risk with legal issues is to bring an experienced attorney on to the project team to handle the contracting, intellectual property, or litigation. This is truly an area where the project manager needs to call in the experts. Table 33–14 is the extension to the risk categorization matrix for projects where there is excessive legal risk.

TABLE 33–14
Legal Risk Factor Extension to Basic Risk

Risk Factors and Categories	L—Low Risk Evidence	M—Medium Risk Evidence	H—High Risk Evidence	Rating (HML)	Comments
Mission and Goals Factors					
Organization Management Factors					
Customer Factors					
Budget/Cost Factors					
Schedule Factors					
Project Content					
Performance Factors					
Project Management Factors					
Development Process Factors					
Development Environment Factors					
Staff Factors					
Maintenance Factors					
Legal Factors					
Advertising and Consumer	Not a consumer product.	Simple computer product with no warranty needed.	Complex consumer product with warranty required.		

(Continues)

TABLE 33-14 (Continued)
Legal Risk Factor Extension to Basic Risk

Risk Factors and Categories	L—Low Risk Evidence	M—Medium Risk Evidence	H—High Risk Evidence	Rating (HML)	Comments
Alternative Dispute Resolution	Standard arbitration terms written into the contract boilerplate.	Nonstandard arbitration terms written into the contract.	No arbitration in the contract.		
Communications	No electronic communication is done on the project.	Electronic communication is done only for the development of the product.	Electronic communication is an integral part of the delivered product.		
Contracts	UCC has been reviewed for any product and project impacts. No other contracts are needed.	UCC and employment contracts are required.	Project relies heavily on contract development and commercial component integration.		
Disability/Handicap	All facilities are accessible to disabled employees.	Facilities are available separate from the development team.	No facilities are available that meet the minimum Americans with Disabilities Act.		
Employment	Standard employment agreements are in place protecting ownership of intellectual property.	Developers are all contract personnel.	No employment agreements are used.		

(Continues)

TABLE 33–14 (Continued)
Legal Risk Factor Extension to Basic Risk

Risk Factors and Categories	L—Low Risk Evidence	M—Medium Risk Evidence	H—High Risk Evidence	Rating (HML)	Comments
Intellectual Property	Standard process to review for intellectual property are defined points within the project life cycle.	Intellectual property is only an issue at the beginning and end of projects.	No process for recognizing intellectual property.		
Internet Regulation	No Internet access is allowed on the project.	Internet access is done only for the development of the product.	Internet access is an integral part of the delivered product.		
Privacy	No personal information is handled by the product under development.	Personal information is used only for minimal user identification.	This is a personal data-management system or has components that collect and store personal data.		
Tort	The software under development does not control physical devices.	The software underdevelopment controls physical devices that do not present any possibility of human injury.	The software controls hardware functions that could have life-threatening effects if a failure occurred.		

Visit the Case Study

The semiconductor industry turned around last month, and your application for an overseas assignment to the European Software Center has been approved. The ARRS project is moving toward its first full code release, and BSD is going "code complete" tomorrow. Mr. Lu has been promoted, and Dr. Zhou is the new software acquisition director for the CRM. Ms. Patel, the new corporate marketing executive for AsiaPac, has protested your reassignment, but your gaining organization has claimed that you are critical to rolling out the next generation of European cellular telephone infrastructure code. Because that represents $1.2 billion a year, Ms. Patel did not get her request honored. But before you can transfer, you have to provide a transition plan for your successor. Your successor has not been picked, and your recommendation of who it will be is part of the transition plan. The more complete the plan is, the sooner you can leave. There is no company-recommended template for this plan, and they are relying on you to define that template and leave it as corporate intellectual property when you leave. Treat this as a miniproject, and complete the plan as soon as possible. The sooner it is done, the sooner you are in Toulouse.

Supporting Organizations

Appendix A

Appendix A Relation to the 34 Competencies _____

The following are the competencies emphasized by the information in this appendix.

Product Development Techniques

1. **Assessing processes**—Defining criteria for reviews
2. **Awareness of process standards**—Understanding process standards
8. **Selecting methods and tools**—Defining the selection processes
9. **Tailoring processes**—Modifying standard processes to suit a project
10. **Tracking product quality**—Monitoring the quality of an evolving product

Project Management Skills

13. **Documenting plans**—Identifying key components
20. **Selecting project management tools**—Learning how to select PM tools

People Management Skills

26. **Interaction and communication**—Dealing with developers, upper management, and other teams
30. **Planning careers**—Structuring and giving career guidance

Key Appendix A Points

To get a firm footing for the principles of software project management, we first need to know where the foundations come from, and how to keep ourselves current with them. In general, the foundations of software project management rest on project management skills and techniques, software engineering processes, and quality systems and measurement.

Although the competencies identified in relation to the 34 competencies have strong relevance here, all 34 competencies in project, process, and people skills permeate all three of the above areas.

Organizations Supporting Software Development Project Management

In this appendix, we look at general information about whom and where the software project management foundation organizations are, and what resources they have to offer to support software project managers. Although the interests of these organizations overlap a bit, each does have a distinct focus.

Table A–1 shows the organizations that will be reviewed in this appendix.

Project Management Institute

The Project Management Institute (PMI) was founded in 1969 in Pennsylvania to help put form to the specialty of management that deals with projects, and to share information about it with practitioners.

PICTURE A–1
PMI Logo

TABLE A–1

Organizations Effecting Quality Software Development

Label	Organiza-tion	Primary Focus	Of Interest for SWPM	URL
PMI®	Project Management Institute	General project management	Project Body of Knowledge (PMBOK™)	*www.pmi.org*
ASQ	American Society of Quality	Quality improvement	Software Quality Engineering Body of Knowledge (CSQE BOK)	*www.asq.org*
IEEE	Institute of Electrical and Electronics Engineers	Engineering standards	Software Engineering Standards Collection	*www.ieee.org*
ISO	International Organization for Standardization	International standards	ISO 9000 Quality Standards; ISO/IEC 12207 IT—software life cycle process standard	*www.iso.ch*
ANSI	American National Standards Institute	National standards for the U.S.	Guide for application of ISO/IEC 12207 to software engineering project management	*www.ansi.org*
NIST	National Institute of Standards and Technology	Technology, measurements, and standards for U.S. industry	Malcolm Baldrige National Quality Award for Performance Excellence (MBNQA)	*www.nist.gov*
SEI	Software Engineering Institute	Software engineering	Capability Maturity Model for Software v.1.1 (CMM™)	*www.sei.cmu.edu*

PMI's Project Management Body of Knowledge   Today's project management body of knowledge was born from the informal practices used by functional managers in the construction, defense, and aerospace industries of the 1960s and 1970s. In 1987, PMI successfully defined a generic body of knowledge that described what managers of projects in any industry needed to know, and published the *Project Management Body of Knowledge*. In 1996, this document was revised and renamed *A Guide to the Project Management Body of Knowledge* (now known as the *PMBOK™ Guide*) to reflect that the actual body of knowledge that a project manager needs to know is HUGE, and can't be adequately represented in just one 176-page book. In 2000, another revision was published to refine and expand the definition of the profession.

In 1998, the American National Standards Association (ANSI) recognized PMI as an Accredited Standard Developer. PMI's *A Guide to the Project Management Body of Knowledge* (*PMBOK® Guide*) was approved by ANSI as an American National Standard in October 1999. In February 1999, the IEEE adopted it as its guide to project management.

The *PMBOK® Guide* defines knowledge in 11 areas as the basis for the body of knowledge. These are illustrated in Figure A–1, and summarized below.

The current *PMBOK® Guide* can be downloaded in its entirety from the PMI Web site *www.pmi.org*.

Project Management Context

- Project phases and life cycle
- Project stakeholders
- Organizational influences
- Key general management skills
- Socioeconomic influences

PICTURE A–2
PMBOK

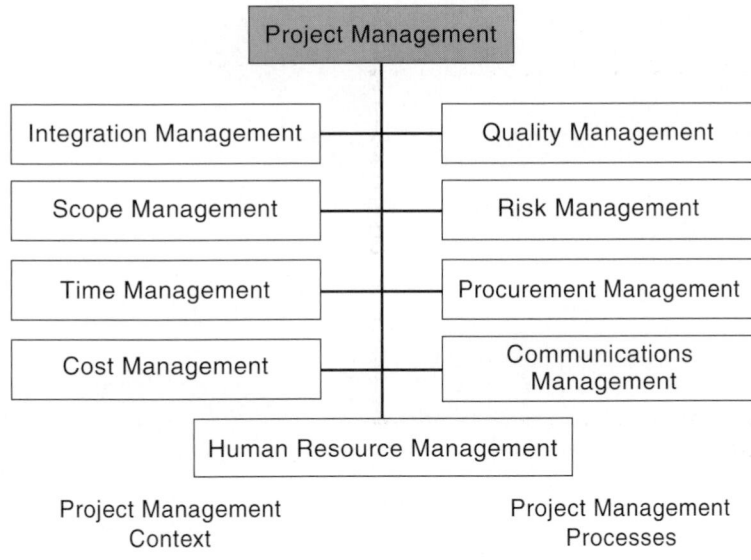

Project Management Context

Project Management Processes

FIGURE A–1
PM Body of Knowledge

Project Management Processes
- Project processes
- Process groups
- Process interactions
- Customizing process interactions

Integration Management
- Project plan development
- Project plan execution
- Overall change control

Scope Management
- Initiation
- Scope planning
- Scope definition
- Scope verification
- Scope change control

Time Management
- Activity definition
- Activity sequencing
- Activity duration estimation
- Schedule development
- Schedule control

Human Resource Management
- Organizational planning
- Staff acquisition
- Team development

Quality Management
- Quality planning
- Quality assurance
- Quality control

Cost Management
- Resource planning
- Cost estimating
- Cost budgeting
- Cost control

Communications Management
- Communications planning
- Information distribution
- Performance reporting
- Administrative closure

Risk Management
- Risk identification
- Risk quantification
- Risk response development
- Risk response control

Procurement Management
- Procurement planning
- Solicitation planning

- Solicitation
- Source selection
- Contract administration
- Contract close-out

PMI's Project Management Professional (PMP®) Certification   Not required to be a software project manager, but certainly helpful in a crowded job market, is professional certification. PMI has certified over 10,000 practitioners internationally as "Project Management Professionals" (PMP®) since 1984. This number is growing rapidly as the profession's importance is becoming more recognized, and the certification process was streamlined in 1999.

PMP® certification requires meeting minimum standards in:

- education—formal education (e.g. Bachelor's degree).
- experience—paid project management work (e.g. 4,500 hours, with a Bachelor's degree).
- service—nonpaid work applying project management principles (e.g. chapter service).

This is in addition to demonstrating knowledge in all areas of the Project Management Body of Knowledge by passing a rigorous professional examination. As requirements for certification are subject to change occasionally, check the PMI Web site *www.pmi.org/certification/* for the current requirements.

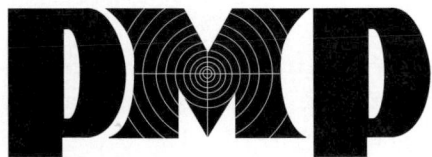

PICTURE A–3
PMP Logo

SIDEBAR A–1
OTHER BOKs

Many organizations define bodies of knowledge (BOK) for project management, and certify project and program managers in them. For the U.S., the predominate organization is the Project Management Institute (PMI®), and it is the one we focus on in this book. However, there are other international organizations that also have defined a BOK, such as the Association for Project Management (APM) in the United Kingdom and the Australian Institute for Project Management (AIPM) in Australia.

American Society for Quality (ASQ)

Founded in 1946 with the merger of several local quality societies scattered across the United States, the ASQ's original focus was to share information about statistical quality control after classes on that subject were taught during World War II to improve and maintain the quality of defense materials.

Since then, ASQ has grown to include more than 1,000 local organizations, with a total membership of over 130,000 individuals. ASQ members initiated most of the quality methods used throughout the world today. These include: statistical process control, cost of quality measurement and control, total quality management, and zero defects.

ASQ's vision is to advance individual and organizational performance excellence worldwide by providing opportunities for learning, quality improvement, and knowledge exchange. There are two key services provided by the ASQ that are of importance to software project managers: administration of the Malcolm Baldrige National Quality Award process for NIST and certification of professionals in Software Quality Engineering.

Administration of the Malcolm Baldrige
National Quality Award Process   The ASQ, through its local chapter's organizations,
recruits, trains, and manages examiners for the Malcolm Baldrige National Quality Award, as a service to NIST. Generally, examiners are quality professionals who have served as examiners for local and state quality organizations, and are selected for national participation after years of service. As the criteria change slightly each year, examiner training and improvement require constant management.

Certification of Professionals in Software Quality Engineering   The ASQ has
been defining the bodies of knowledge, examining, and certifying quality professionals for many years. Among the certifications offered are:

- Certified Quality Improvement Associate (CQIA);
- Certified Quality Auditor (CQA);
- Certified Quality Engineer (CQE);

American Society for Quality

ℚASQ

PICTURE A–4
ASQ Logo

- Certified Reliability Engineer (CRE);
- Certified Quality Technician (CQT);
- Certified Mechanical Inspector (CMI);
- Certified Quality Manager (CQM);
- Certified Software Quality Engineer (CSQE).

Local ASQ sections and international organizations usually conduct examinations twice per year, in June and December. All examinations are open-book. All of these career-enhancing certifications focus on a specialty area of quality. Each certification candidate is required to pass a written examination that consists of multiple-choice questions that measure comprehension of the appropriate body of knowledge. Of interest to software project managers is the CSQE, which defines the body of knowledge for software quality engineering. The Software Quality Engineer examination is a 160-question, four-hour exam and is offered in the English language only.

CSQE Body of Knowledge   The Body of Knowledge for the CSQE covers a broad array of subjects that affect the quality of software produced by the software engineering process. All of these are important to the software project manager, especially the one covering software project management, which includes the planning, tracking, and implementation for a software development project.

The BOK is arranged into eight areas, as illustrated in Figure A–2 and the following table. *www.asq.org/standcert/certification/csqe.html#csqebok* has the CSQE BOK details.

General Knowledge, Conduct, and Ethics

- Standards
- Quality philosophies and principles

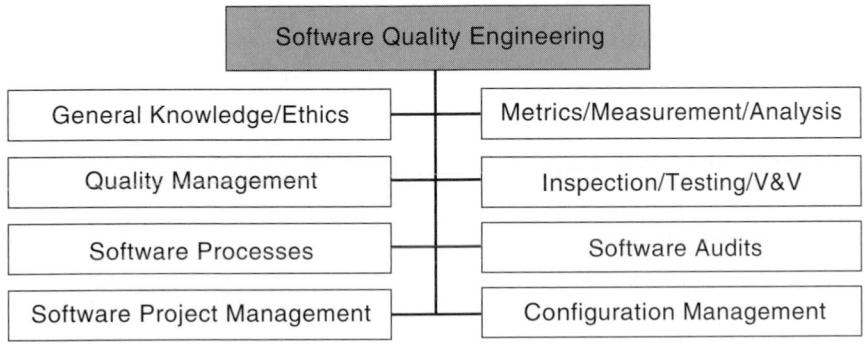

FIGURE A–2
ASQ Body of Knowledge

- Organizational and interpersonal techniques
- Problem solving tools and processes
- Professional conduct and ethics

Software Quality Management

- Planning
- Tracking
- Organizational and professional software quality training

Software Processes

- Development and maintenance methods
- Process and technology change management

Software Project Management

- Planning
- Tracking
- Implementation

Software Metrics, Measurement, and Analytical Methods

- Measurement theory
- Analytical techniques
- Software measurement

Software Inspection, Testing, Verification and Validation

- Inspection
- Testing
- Verification and validation (V&V)

Software Audits

- Audit types
- Audit methodology
- Audit planning

Software Configuration Management

- Planning and configuration identification
- Configuration control
- Status accounting
- Reporting

Another important service of the ASQ is the publication of monthly and quarterly journals for specialized audiences. These include titles such as those below. Of interest to software project managers is the *Software Quality Professional*, which focuses on topics from the CSQE BOK. Table A–2 lists all of the ASQ publications of interest to software project managers.

TABLE A–2
ASQ Software Project Management Publications

Quality Progress	Includes in-depth articles written by quality practitioners describing the application of innovative methods in areas such as knowledge management, process improvement, and organizational behavior
Quality Management Journal	Publishes significant research relevant to quality management practice and provides a forum for discussion of such research by both academics and practitioners
Quality Engineering	Articles provide in-depth examples of the application of the quality sciences to management and operating processes in government, business, and industry
Journal of Quality Technology	Publishes papers that emphasize the practical applicability of new techniques, instructive examples of the operation of existing techniques, and results of historical researches
Software Quality Professional	Provides readers with an understanding of software quality practices as defined by the body of knowledge for ASQ's Certified Software Quality Engineer (CSQE) that have been proven effective in a wide range of industries, applications, and organizational settings
Technometrics	Co-published with the American Statistical Association (ASA), it contributes to the development and use of statistical methods in the physical, chemical, and engineering sciences
The Informed Outlook	A monthly newsletter on standards that provides timely and accurate information on standards, such as ISO 9000, ISO 14000, QS-9000, TL 9000, and AS 9100

Malcolm Baldrige National Quality Award (MBNQA)

In response to the perceived threat of domination by goods produced off-shore with higher quality than could be obtained from domestic companies, the U.S. government decided to do something to focus national attention on quality as a competitive weapon. The Malcolm Baldrige National Quality Award was created when Public Law 100-107 was signed on August 20, 1987, authorizing a new public-private partnership called the Foundation for the

Malcolm Baldrige National Quality Award. Established in 1988, the foundation provides the principal support for the award promotion and competition.

The award is named for Malcolm Baldrige, who served as secretary of commerce from 1981 until his death in a 1987 rodeo accident. His managerial excellence contributed to long-term improvement in the efficiency and effectiveness of government.

ASQ assists NIST with the application review process, preparation of award documents, publicity, and information transfer about quality. Examiners are recruited from the local ranks of quality professionals at the city and state levels, and undergo further training in the criteria before being allowed to examine an award applicant.

The award criteria are divided into seven main areas, with each area subdivided even further. Figure A–3 shows the relationships among the Baldrige Award areas. See *www.quality.nist.gov* for details of the criteria.

Seven Main Areas of the Award Criteria

1. Leadership
2. Strategic planning
3. Customer and market focus
4. Information and analysis
5. Human resource focus
6. Process management
7. Business results

Malcolm Baldrige
1922–1987

PICTURE A–5
Baldrige Pictures

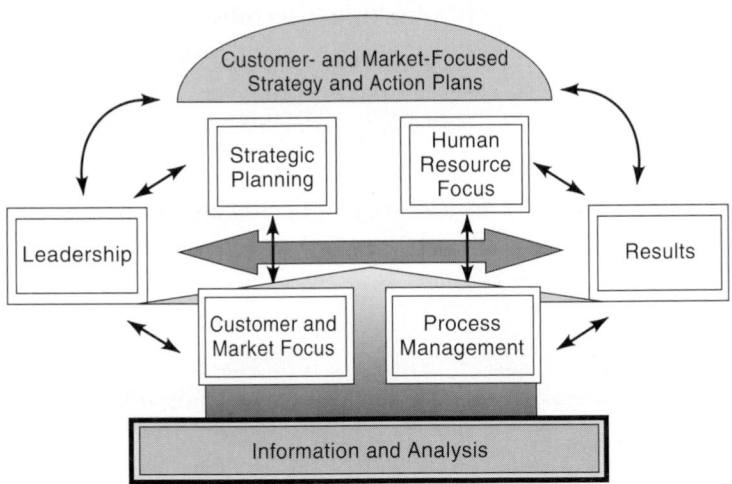

FIGURE A–3
Baldrige Award Areas

These areas are related to each other and form a system that turns leadership into results. Moving from left to right in the figure, "leadership," "strategic planning," and "customer and market focus" constitute the *direction and planning* side of the business, while "human resource focus," "process management," and "results" form the *execution* side of the business. "Information and analysis" supports the other six areas.

All seven areas of the MBNQA embody the core concepts shown below. These are what examiners look for when assessing an application for award.

MBNQA Core Concepts and Values

1. Customer-driven quality
2. Leadership
3. Continuous improvement
4. Full participation of all in company, customers, suppliers
5. Fast response to customers and short cycle time
6. Design quality and prevention of defects
7. Long-range outlook
8. Management by fact
9. Partnership development
10. Public responsibility

Good project management permeates an entire organization (not just software projects), and is reflected in crisp execution and management by fact. Usually, this is reflected in the scoring by examiners.

Scoring and Feedback

Since 1995, the criteria are specialized for business, education, and healthcare industries. The principles are the same, but the criteria use specialized language and shift focus a bit to accommodate the differences, such as:

Business—traditional customer and profit orientation

Healthcare—profit or non-profit, customers are patients and insurance companies

Education—non-profit oriented, customers are students and parents

The MBNQA is designed for diagnosis of organizations' business practices. As such, three dimensions are measured for each item:

Approach—a strategic statement about how the item is addressed;

Deployment—a description of how the strategic statement has been implemented;

Results—evidence that results have been obtained from deployment of the approach.

Scoring for MBNQA is done by examiner team consensus for each item. Strengths and areas for improvement are noted, and a feedback assessment report is prepared for the applicant. Since the MBNQA is an award process and only a small fraction of applicants receive the award, the feedback report is the most valuable output of the process and becomes a valued guide for continuous improvement.

The actual scores are weighted at the front by "Leadership" and at the back by "Results," with everything between being of equal weight. See Table A–3.

State and Local Quality Organizations and Awards

Helping to spread the gospel of quality are numerous state and local quality organizations, many of which offer their own quality awards, usually based on criteria derived directly from the Malcolm Baldrige National Quality Award criteria for performance excellence. These state and local organizations offer companies who are just beginning a quality journey, and an easy way to learn about quality improvement and to compete at a local level with similar organizations.

TABLE A–3
MBNQA 2000 Scoring System

1	Leadership		125
	1.1 Organizational Leadership	85	
	1.2 Public Responsibility	40	
2	Strategic Planning		85
	2.1 Strategy Development	40	
	2.2 Strategy Deployment	45	
3	Customer and Market Focus		85
	3.1 Customer and Market Knowledge	40	
	3.2 Customer Satisfaction	45	
4	Information and Analysis		85
	4.1 Measurement of Organizational Performance	40	
	4.2 Analysis of Organizational Performance		
5	Human Resource Focus		85
	5.1 Work Systems		35
	5.2 Employee Education, Training, and Development		
	5.3 Employee Well-Being and Satisfaction		
6	Process Management		85
	6.1 Product and Service Processes		
	6.2 Support Processes	15	
	6.3 Supplier and Partnering Processes		
7	Business Results		450
	7.1 Customer-Focused Results		
	7.2 Financial and Market Results		
	7.3 Human Resource Results		
	7.4 Supplier and Partner Results		
	7.5 Organizational Effectiveness Results		
Total Points			1000

SIDEBAR A–2
THE STOCK STORY

Quality guru Joseph Juran wondered what would happen to $1,000 if invested in each of the Baldrige winners. As of 1998, NIST found that the group of six whole company winners (as opposed to a suborganization of the larger company) outperformed the S&P 500 by 2.6 to 1, achieving a 460% return on investment, compared to a 175% return for the S&P 500. The message here is that companies focused on quality improvement outdo others in the long run.

Examples of state and local quality organizations are the Quality Texas Foundation (*www.texasquality.org/*) and the Greater Austin Quality Council (*www.gaqc.org/*).

Quality Texas' mission is to involve as many Texas organizations and individuals as possible in a process of continuous improvement, customer satisfaction focus, and performance excellence. The Texas award process, patterned after the Malcolm Baldrige National Quality Award, is the primary tool to carry out this mission. The benefits of participation are in the self-assessment that occurs during application preparation, and in the extensive feedback report that is prepared for the applicant by a team of trained, certified quality examiners who review and analyze the application.

Similar to the Quality Texas Foundation, the Greater Austin Quality Council uses an award process and criteria patterned after the Baldrige Performance Excellence criteria. As one of the more active city programs in the United States, it recognizes dozens of organizations in the Austin, Texas area that have embarked on a quality improvement journey. The GAQC operates under the Austin Chamber of Commerce and has trained hundreds of local examiners on the assessment criteria.

Software project managers who are interested in continuous process improvement should seek out quality organizations at the state and local levels to learn more about how to improve their work quality, and to network with like-minded people in their local community and state.

PICTURE A–6
Texas Quality

**GREATER
AUSTIN
QUALITY**

PICTURE A–7
Austin Quality

International Organization for Standardization (ISO)

The International Organization for Standardization (ISO, pronounced "EYE-so") is a non-governmental organization established in 1947, and headquartered in Geneva, Switzerland. It is a worldwide federation of national standards bodies from about 130 countries whose mission it is to promote the development of worldwide standardization to facilitate the international exchange of goods and services. The American National Standards Institute (ANSI) is the member representing the United States.

ISO promotes cooperation in the spheres of intellectual, scientific, technological, and economic activity, which results in international agreements that are published as international standards.

PICTURE A–8
ISO Logo

ISO is highly decentralized, with over 2,800 active technical committees, subcommittees, and working groups, composed of about 30,000 qualified representatives of industry, research institutes, government authorities, consumer bodies, and international organizations.

Of particular interest to software project managers is the ISO 9000 series of quality standards introduced in 1987. The ISO 9000 series has been adopted as ANSI ASQ series Q90 through

SIDEBAR A–3
ISO NAME

"ISO" is not an acronym, it is a word derived from the Greek isos, meaning "equal," which is the root of the prefix "iso-" found in a host of terms (such as "isometric" meaning "of equal measure or dimensions").

Meaning "equal" and "standard," "ISO" as the name of the organization made a lot of sense as it reflects the mission. Also, "ISO" can be used internationally to denote the organization, thus avoiding all the acronyms that result from the translation of "International Organization for Standardization" into different languages; for example, IOS in English or OIN in French (from Organisation Internationale de Normalisation). Whatever the country or language, the short form of the organization's name is always ISO.

Q94; ISO 9001 is the British standard BS5750 Part 1, and the European Norm standard EN29001. The ISO standards were reviewed in 1994, producing the set most in use today.

The ISO 9000 standards are a set of international quality management standards and guidelines with applicability to a wide range of businesses. Since their initial publication in 1987, they have earned a global reputation as a basis for establishing minimum standards for quality management systems (QMS). Three of the current standards, ISO 9001, 9002, and 9003, have been used extensively as the basis for independent (third party) quality system certification. This has resulted in the certification of over 200,000 organizations worldwide, with many more in the process of setting up and implementing ISO 9000 quality management systems.

The ISO 9000 1994 publication is a set of standards that apply to different kinds of businesses, depending on how much of the production, delivery, and maintenance cycle they participate in. Derivatives of the ISO 9000 standards have been formulated for certain industries, such as the QS 9000 standards for the automotive industry. QS 9000 is basically the same standard, with supplements from the American Industry Automotive Group (AIAG). QS 9000 supersedes previous American Automotive Supplier Quality Standards. All of the applicable ISO standards are shown in Table A–4.

Figure A–4 depicts how the ISO and QS 9000 standards relate to the product development life cycle.

The ISO 9000 standards contain clauses that describe the characteristics a quality management system should have.

Twenty Clauses in the ISO 9001 1996 Quality Systems Standard

4.1   Management responsibility

4.2   Quality system

TABLE A–4
ISO Standards

ISO 9000-1	QM Guidelines and QA Standards Use	Explains the fundamental quality concepts of the standards, and provides guidance for the selection and use of ISO 9001, 9002, 9003, and 9004
ISO 9000-3	Quality Standards Guidelines for Software	Explains how to apply the ISO 9000 standards to software
ISO 9001	Model for QA in Design, Development, Production, Installation, and Service	Standards for businesses involved in all phases of a product's life cycle
ISO 9002	Model for QA in Production, Installation, and Service	Standards for businesses involved in all phases of a product's life cycle, except design and development (e.g. factories)
ISO 9003	Model for QA in Final Inspection and Test	Standards for businesses involved in all phases of a product's life cycle, except design and development, and production (e.g. distributors)
ISO 9004-1	Guidelines for Quality Management and Quality System Elements	

4.3	Contract review
4.4	Design control
4.5	Document and data control
4.6	Purchasing
4.7	Control of customer-supplied product
4.8	Product identification and traceability
4.9	Process control
4.10	Inspection and testing
4.11	Control of inspection, measuring, and test equipment
4.12	Inspection and test status
4.13	Control of non-conforming product
4.14	Corrective and preventive action
4.15	Handling, storage, packaging, preservation, and delivery

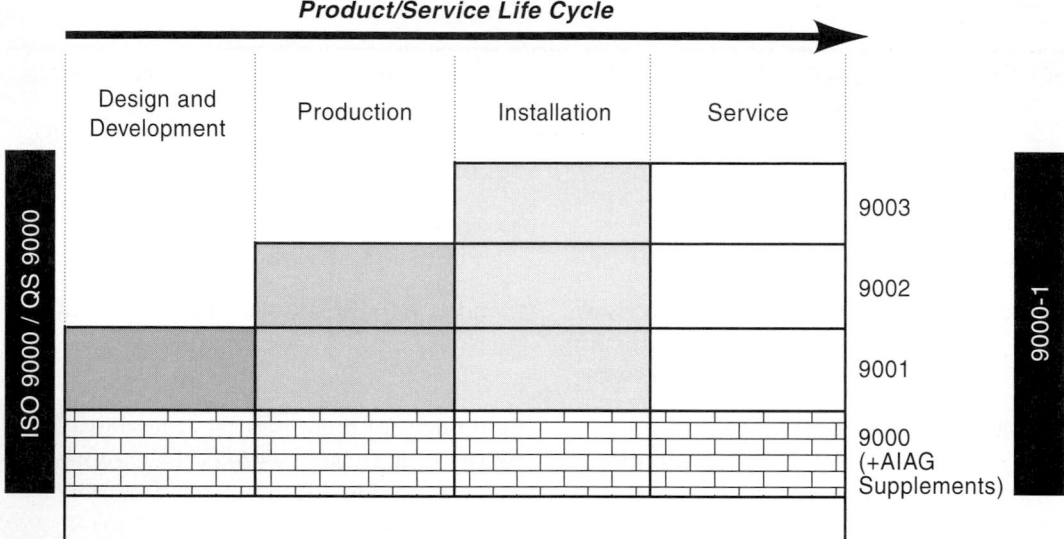

FIGURE A–4
9004-1 Guidelines to Implement QMS Coverage
Adapted from: The Memory Jogger 9000, GOAL/QPC, 1996.

4.16   Control of quality records

4.17   Internal quality audits

4.18   Training

4.19   Servicing

4.20   Statistical techniques

There is another standard often mentioned with ISO 9000: ISO 14000. Whereas ISO 9000 is concerned with quality management, ISO 14000 is primarily concerned with environmental management (what the organization does to minimize harmful effects on the environment). Both of these are concerned about how an organization works (its processes), rather than the quality of what it produces (its products). For example, being ISO 9000-certified means your business *processes* have achieved a *minimum* quality standard. It does not mean that your business produces quality *products*. Note that the Malcolm Baldrige National Quality Award certifies *maximum* achievement of business processes in any given award year.

ISO's Technical Committee TC 176 is revising the 1994 versions of the ISO 9000 family for publication in the year 2000. The current ISO 9000 family will be reduced to three quality

PICTURE A–9
ISO 9000 Certification Logo

management systems standards with a small number of additional standards, technical reports, and/or brochures to address specific issues.

ISO 9000 2000 Quality Systems Standards

ISO 9000:2000   QMS—fundamentals and vocabulary

ISO 9001:2000   QMS—requirements

ISO 9004:2000   QMS—guidance for performance improvement

There will only be one QMS requirement standard—ISO 9001, which will replace the current ISO 9001, ISO 9002, and ISO 9003. ISO 9004 will be the QMS standard that will drive organizations toward business performance improvement and will form a consistent pair with ISO 9001 with the same sequence and numbering.

American National Standards Institute (ANSI)

The American National Standards Institute (ANSI) has served as administrator and coordinator of the United States private-sector voluntary standardization system since 1918. It was founded by five engineering societies and three government agencies, and remains a private, nonprofit membership organization supported by a diverse constituency of private and public sector organizations.

PICTURE A–10
ANSI Logo

ANSI's Mission: Promote U.S. Standardization Policies Globally

Goal: To have global standards that reflect U.S. interests;

To have U.S. standards used abroad;

To have U.S. positions (policy and technical) accepted in international and regional standards organizations;

To have international standards adopted as national standards where these meet the needs of the user community.

ANSI does not itself develop American National Standards. Instead, it promotes its guiding principles of consensus, due process, and openness to facilitate standard development by establishing consensus among qualified standards development groups. ANSI is one of five permanent members to the governing ISO Council (and was a founding member of ISO), and is one of four permanent members of ISO's Technical Management Board.

ANSI's Participation in ISO

ANSI is one of five permanent members to the ISO Management Council of 18.

ANSI has four permanent members to the Technical Management Board of 12.

ANSI and its members participate in 74 percent of technical committees (TC).

ANSI administers 16 percent of TC secretariats.

Of particular interest to software project managers are some of the standards ANSI helps develop with other organizations for software development. See Table A–5 for information on technology standards.

Since there are so many standards available, from so many different organizations, it is difficult for a software project manager to keep up with what they are and which ones are current. It is helpful to subscribe to a service such as the *NSSN: A National Resource for Global Standards*, a good resource to find appropriate standards. NSSN has more than 17,500 standards from organizations, like:

- American National Standards Institute (ANSI);
- International Organization for Standardization (ISO);
- International Electrotechnical Commission (IEC);
- ISO/IEC Joint Technical Committee on Information Technology (JTC 1);
- European Committee for Standardization (CEN);
- European Committee for Electrotechnical Standards (CENELEC);
- Software Engineering Institute (SEI).

TABLE A–5
ANSI Publications for Software Project Managers

Document Number	Document Title
ISO/IEC 12207:1995	Information technology—software life cycle processes
ISO/IEC 12207.0–1996	Standard for information technology—software life cycle processes
ISO/IEC 12207.1–1997	Guide for information technology—software life cycle processes; life cycle data
ISO/IEC 12207.2–1997	Guide for information technology—software life cycle processes; implementation considerations
ISO/IEC TR 16326:1999	Software engineering—guide for the application of ISO/IEC 12207 to project management
ISO/IEC TR 15271:1998	Information technology—guide for ISO/IEC 12207 (software life cycle processes)
IEEE 1012a–1998	IEEE standard for software verification and validation—content map to IEEE 12207.1

SIDEBAR A–4
NSSN: A NATIONAL RESOURCE FOR GLOBAL STANDARDS

When first named, "NSSN" was an acronym for the phrase *National Standards Systems Network*. As global organizations began to contribute data, it became clear that the scope of NSSN went well beyond *national* standards (the service now contains information from more than 600 national, foreign, regional, and international bodies). A survey of users reported that the "NSSN" acronym had a high degree of recognition; the acronym was kept and the tag line "A National Resource for Global Standards" was added.

The Software Engineering Institute (SEI) is a federally-funded research and development institute at Carnegie Mellon University, Pittsburgh, PA. It is sponsored by the U.S. Department of Defense through the Office of the Under-Secretary of Defense for Acquisition, Technology, and Logistics. The SEI contract was competitively awarded to Carnegie Mellon

CarnegieMellon
Software Engineering Institute

PICTURE A–11
SEI Logo

University in December 1984, and the SEI staff has extensive technical and managerial experience from government, industry, and academia.

SEI's mission is to:

- Provide rapid improvement in the quality of mission-critical computer systems.
- Accelerate the practice of modern software engineering techniques and methods.
- Ensure the use of modern techniques in mission-critical software organizations.
- Establish standards of excellence for software.

The SEI also sponsors several special research programs in fields such as:

- Software process, methods, and systems;
- Education;
- Technology transition;
- Ada and STARS support;
- Risk management.

Capability Maturity Model for Software (CMM-S/W v.1.1)   Of interest to software project managers is the highly regarded *Capability Maturity Model for Software (CMM-S/W v.1.1)*. Figure A–5 shows a graphical representation of the five maturity levels. The CMM-S/W provides a good framework to understand what the important processes of software engineering are, and how they relate to the software development capability of an organization. Much of the work done by the SEI in the CMM is focused on software quality improvement.

A continuation of software quality assessment efforts at IBM, the CMM was created in the mid-1980s by a team lead by Watts Humphrey (formerly of IBM) to create a framework for software process improvement. Based on the W. Edwards Deming and Joseph Juran quality improvement concepts of repeatability (stabilize, then improve a process), and the Philip Crosby quality management maturity grid (a five-stage model for management's quality awareness: uncertainty, awakening, enlightenment, wisdom, certainty), Humphrey and his team created a five-level model of organizational software process maturity.

SIDEBAR A–5
THE STORY OF THE FIVE-LEVEL MODEL IDEA

After gathering a series of 150 assessment questions about software capability (and sitting in an airport for a while), Watts said the Deming concepts of quality and the Crosby stage model "clicked" to inspire sorting the CMM assessment questions as we know them today.

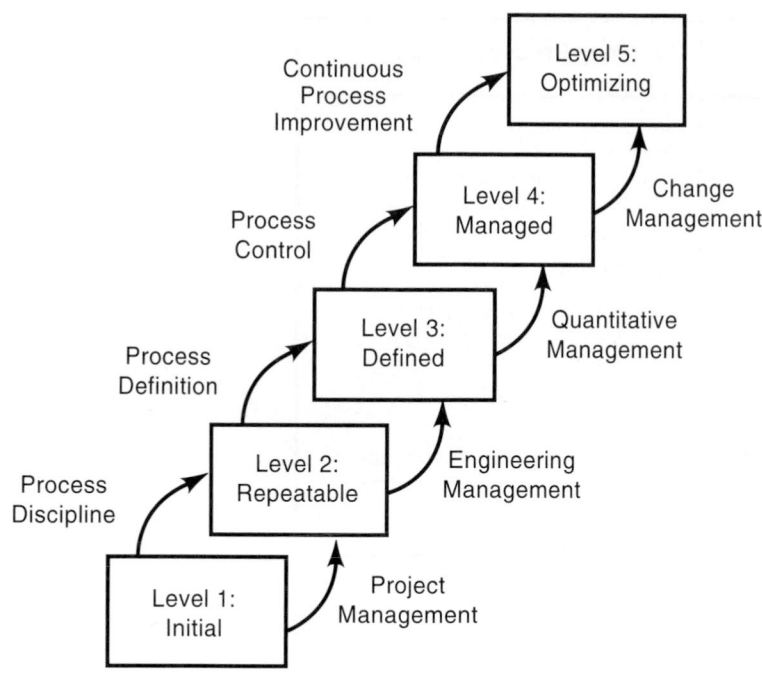

FIGURE A–5
SEI CMM Maturity Levels

Each level indicates a more mature organization, and has a different focus. Demonstrated capability in key process areas (KPAs) must be shown to achieve a higher maturity rating. Figure A–6 shows a tabular representation of the focus and key process areas for each maturity level.

Process Determines Capability

Key to the concepts in the CMM-S/W v.1.1 is the notion that the process maturity in an organization determines the capability of that organization to produce high-quality software products.

Process: set of activities or tasks which are necessary to accomplish a given mission

Capability: the range of results expected from following a given process

The relationship of the maturity levels, key process areas, key practices within those KPAs, and the key indicators of those key practices is depicted in Figure A–7.

Level	Focus	Key Process Areas
5 Optimizing	Continuous process improvement	Defect prevention Technology change management Process change management
4 Managed	Product and process quality	Quantitative process management Software quality management
3 Defined	Defined engineering process	Organization process focus Organization process definition Peer reviews Training program Intergroup coordination Software product engineering Intergrated software management
2 Repeatable	Project management and commitment process	Software project planning Software project tracking Software subcontract management Software quality assurance Software configuration management Requirements management
1 Initial	Heroes	

FIGURE A–6
CMM v.1.1 Levels and KPAs

An example of how the CMM v.1.1 items relate to each other is shown in Figure A–8 for configuration management.

Related Capability Maturity Models® that the SEI is involved in developing, expanding, or maintaining include the following:

CMMI	CMM® Integration
SW-CMM	Capability Maturity Model® for Software
P-CMM	People Capability Maturity Model
SA-CMM	Software Acquisition Capability Maturity Model
SE-CMM	Systems Engineering Capability Maturity Model
IPD-CMM	Integrated Product Development Capability Maturity Model

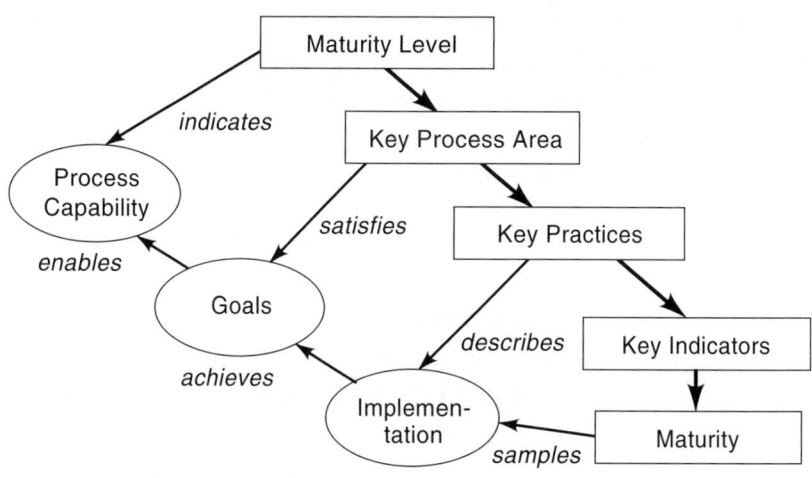

FIGURE A–7
CMM Relationships

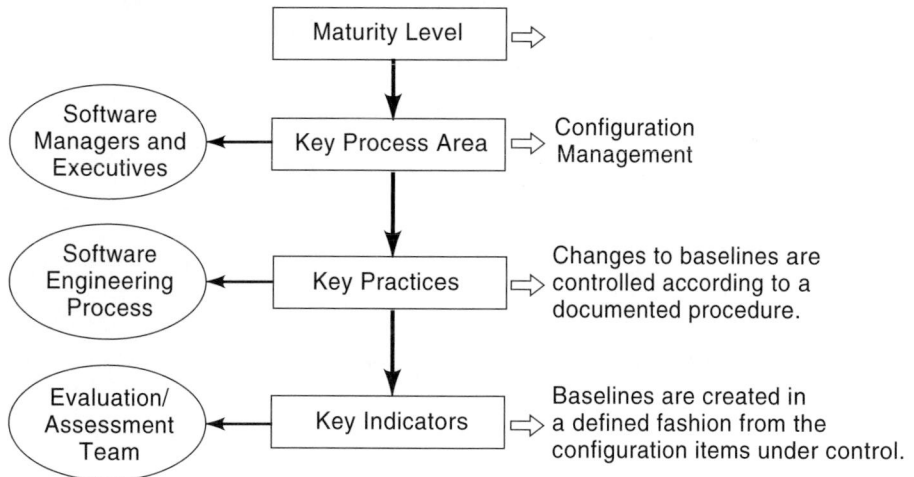

FIGURE A–8
CMM Relationships for Configuration Management

Comparisons of Standards   It is often confusing for a software manager managing one development organization to choose amongst several different software quality standards. ISO 9000, the SEI CMM v.1.1, and the Malcolm Baldrige National Quality Award for Performance Excellence are all good yardsticks to measure an organization with, and serve as a guide for improvement. Some points help make the choices clearer.

ISO 9000 compared to MBNQA:

- Requires annual re-approval to claim compliance, while Baldrige is a one-time assessment;
- Requires more evidence of existence and use of documentation.

ISO 9000 compared to SEI CMM:

- ISO 9000-3 requires elements of SEI Levels 2 and 3;
- ISO 9000 does not address some of the SEI CMM areas of requirements management, tracking, and oversight;
- ISO 9000 sets a minimum bar for quality processes, as do the levels of the SEI CMM v.1.1;
- MBNQA rewards the highest achievement levels in any set of processes;
- MBNQA and ISO are not software specific; SEI CMM v.1.1 is focused only on software development.

Institute of Electrical and Electronics Engineers (IEEE)

Founded in 1884, the IEEE (usually pronounced "eye triple E") is one of the oldest and largest engineering organizations. It promotes the engineering process of creating, developing, integrating, sharing, and applying knowledge about electrical and information technologies and sciences.

The IEEE is involved in the generation and promulgation of standards covering all things electrical, in many industries. With over 320,000 members in 147 countries, it sponsors 35 societies and councils organized into divisions that focus on special interest areas:

Division I—Circuits and Devices

Circuits and Systems Society

Components, Packaging, and Manufacturing Technology Society

Electron Devices Society

Lasers and Electro-Optics Society

Sensors Council

Solid-State Circuits Society

PICTURE A–12
IEEE Logo

Division II—Industrial Applications

Dielectrics and Electrical Insulation Society

Industry Applications Society

Instrumentation and Measurement Society

Power Electronics Society

Division III—Communications Technology

Communications Society

Division IV—Electromagnetics and Radiation

Antennas and Propagation Society

Broadcast Technology Society

Consumer Electronics Society

Electromagnetic Compatibility Society

Magnetics Society

Microwave Theory and Techniques Society

Nuclear and Plasma Sciences Society

Superconductivity Council

Division V—Computer

Computer Society

Division VI—Engineering and Human Society

Education Society

Engineering Management Society

Professional Communication Society

Reliability Society

Society on Social Implications of Technology

Division VII—Energy and Power Engineering

Power Engineering Society

Division VIII—Computer

Computer Society

Division IX—Signals and Applications

Aerospace and Electronic Systems Society

Geoscience and Remote Sensing Society

Oceanic Engineering Society

Signal Processing Society

Ultrasonics, Ferroelectrics, and Frequency Control Society

Vehicular Technology Society

Division X—Systems and Control

Control Systems Society

Engineering in Medicine and Biology Society

Industrial Electronics Society

Information Theory Society

Intelligent Transportation Systems Council

Neural Networks Council

Robotics and Automation Society

Systems, Man, and Cybernetics Society

IEEE Computer Society   The IEEE Computer Society, formed in 1946, covers software engineering and is the largest and fastest growing society. With nearly 100,000 members, the IEEE Computer Society is one of the world's leading organizations of computer professionals.

The society is dedicated to advancing the theory, practice, and application of computer and information processing technology. Through its conferences and tutorials, applications- and research-oriented journals, local and student branch chapters, technical committees, and standards working groups, the society promotes an active exchange of information, ideas, and technological innovation among its members. In addition, it accredits collegiate programs of computer science and engineering in the United States.

Of interest to software project managers is the useful set of templates and guidelines for elements of software engineering and project management. Although IEEE sells all standards separately, those concerning software engineering are offered in the *IEEE Standards Collection for Software Engineering*, which contains about two dozen standards.

Some of the more useful standards for software project managers are:

610	Std Glossary of Software Engineering Terminology
730	ANSI Std for SQA Plans
828	Std for Configuration Mgmt Plans
829	Std for S/W Test Documentation
830	Recommended Practice for S/W Requirements Specs
1042	Guide to S/W Configuration Mgmt
1045	Std for S/W Productivity Metrics
1058	Std for Software Project Management Plans
1074	Guide for Developing S/W Life Cycle Processes
1233	Guide for Developing S/W Requirements Specs
1298	IEEE S/W Quality Management System

It is useful for a software project manager to prepare editable templates tailored for their organization from the information in the standards.

PICTURE A–13
IEEE Computer Society Logo

Visit the Case Study

Mr. Lu shared a document with Mr. Lee on the ISO 9000 efforts being done in Beijing, known as Beijing 9000. He identified these Chinese companies as already having been certified: China No. 1 Automobile Corporation, Gezhouba Construction Group, Zhongyuan Oil Field, Capital Steel and Iron Company, Lufthansa Friendship Shopping Centre, and the Kunming Cigarette Factory. Mr. Lee explained that your corporation is ISO 9000 certified and is "ISO certified in all software areas." Mr. Lu wants you to explain how your ARRS project is ISO 9000 compliant so he can begin the certification process with his minister in the CRM. He said that if you need any help you can use Dr. Zhou.

Web Pages for Further Information

sqp.asq.org/. ASQ Software Quality Professional.

www.ansi.org/. American National Standards Institute.

www.asq.org. American Society of Quality.

www.asq.org/standcert/certification/csqe.html#csqebok. CSQE BOK Information.

www.computer.org/. IEEE Computer Society.

www.gaqc.org/. Greater Austin Quality Council.

www.iso.ch/9000e/execabstract.htm. ISO 9000 Information.

www.iso.ch/9000e/plain.htm. ISO 9000 and 14000 Explained.

www.iso.ch/infoe/intro.htm. ISO Organization Information.

www.nist.gov. NIST (MBNQA).

www.nssn.org. National Standards Systems Network.

www.pmi.org. Project Management Institute.

www.pmi.org/certification/. PMP Certification Requirements.

www.sei.cmu.edu/. Software Engineering Institute.

www.texasquality.org/. Quality Texas Foundation.

Real World Projects

Where the rubber meets the road in software project management is the application of the methods, techniques, and tools presented in this practitioner's guide to real world projects. This appendix will present three case studies of projects with which the authors were personally involved from 1998 to 2001. These are real projects with real customers and deliverables. Although not extensive case treatments of each project, this appendix will highlight the key project issues and look at the impact several of the 34 competencies had on the projects' executions. Client and project names have been changed so as to not reveal proprietary information.

Figure B–1 shows the 34 competencies that software managers need to master to provide a quality deliverable from the development process. This is completely described in Chapter 1 of this book and added here as a reminder of all the competencies. Each case study will emphasize specific competencies that impacted the project success.

Table B–1 maps the 34 competencies to the case study in which they are emphasized. As has been emphasized throughout this guide, the people-focused competencies, 23 through 34, must be addressed in every project. Software development is a people-intensive undertaking. A project manager cannot succeed without people *leadership*, not management skills. All of these projects have an emphasis on the people-focused competencies.

Software   Project   Management

Product

1. Assessing processes
2. Awareness of process standards
3. Defining the product
4. Evaluating alternative processes
5. Managing requirements
6. Managing subcontractors
7. Performing the initial assessment
8. Selecting methods and tools
9. Tailoring processes
10. Tracking product quality
11. Understanding development activities

Project

12. Building a work breakdown structure
13. Documenting plans
14. Estimating cost
15. Estimating effort
16. Managing risks
17. Monitoring development
18. Scheduling
19. Selecting metrics
20. Selecting project management tools
21. Tracking process
22. Tracking project progress

People

23. Appraising performance
24. Handling intellectual property
25. Holding effective meetings
26. Interaction and communication
27. Leadership
28. Managing change
29. Negotiating successfully
30. Planning careers
31. Presenting effectively
32. Recruiting
33. Selecting a team
34. Teambuilding

FIGURE B–1
The 34 Competencies

TABLE B–1
Case Study Mapping to the 34 Competencies

		Case 1: Managing a Client Project Portfolio	Case 2: COTS Software Selection for Information Technology Systems	Case 3: Legacy Software Re-engineering
Product Competencies				
1	Assessing processes			
2	Awareness of process standards			
3	Defining the product	X	X	
4	Evaluating alternative processes	X		X
5	Managing requirements	X	X	X
6	Managing subcontractors		X	

(Continues)

		Case 1: Managing a Client Project Portfolio	Case 2: COTS Software Selection for Information Technology Systems	Case 3: Legacy Software Re-engineering
7	Performing the initial assessment		X	
8	Selecting methods and tools	X		
9	Tailoring processes			X
10	Tracking product quality	X	X	X
11	Understanding development activities		X	
	Project Competencies			
12	Building a work breakdown structure			
13	Documenting plans	X	X	X
14	Estimating cost	X		X
15	Estimating effort	X		
16	Managing risks	X	X	X
17	Monitoring development	X		
18	Scheduling	X	X	
19	Selecting metrics	X	X	
20	Selecting project management tools		X	
21	Tracking process			
22	Tracking project progress	X	X	
	People Competencies			
23	Appraising performance			
24	Handling intellectual property	X		
25	Holding effective meetings	X	X	

(Continues)

TABLE B–1 (Continued)
Case Study Mapping to the 34 Competencies

		Case 1: Managing a Client Project Portfolio	Case 2: COTS Software Selection for Information Technology Systems	Case 3: Legacy Software Re-engineering
26	Interaction and communication	X	X	
27	Leadership	X	X	
28	Managing change	X	X	X
29	Negotiating successfully		X	
30	Planning careers			
31	Presenting effectively	X	X	X
32	Recruiting	X		
33	Selecting a team	X	X	
34	Teambuilding	X	X	
	Total Competencies Emphasized	22	20	9

Case 1: Managing a Portfolio of Client Projects _____

Successful software development groups will execute multiple projects for a single client organization. The authors' experiences have shown that very successful, mature development organizations will have a customer return rate exceeding 85 percent. This portfolio of projects was done for one client by a custom software development organization. When looking at the work done for this client beginning in 1998, the first area to explore is the 34 competencies, followed by a discussion of two projects, and a lessons learned section.

Subset of the 34 Competencies Used

Product Competencies

3. Defining the product
4. Evaluating alternative processes
5. Managing requirements
8. Selecting methods and tools
10. Tracking product quality

Product competencies were, initially, the most important to the client. There was the typical client resistance and ignorance of process. The standard comment was either, "Why are you doing that extra work?" or "I'm not paying for that, am I?" The client had never contracted with an outside development firm to build a deliverable part of a client system. The software development company had to use stealth process to ensure all requirements were captured and modeled, the correct processes were selected in dealing with this *ad hoc*, chaotic client, and that quality tracking was in place.

Project Competencies

13. Documenting plans
14. Estimating cost
15. Estimating effort
16. Managing risks
17. Monitoring development
18. Scheduling
19. Selecting metrics
22. Tracking project progress

It was not until the first project was complete that the client realized the worth of having mature processes in place for software development. Managing risks was especially important in that the software development company began working with the client's clients in gathering implementation and installation requirements. At installation, the software development company's consultants did the on-site installations, customizations, and acceptance testing for the client's clients.

People Competencies

24. Handling intellectual property
25. Holding effective meetings
26. Interaction and communication
27. Leadership

28. Managing change
31. Presenting effectively
32. Recruiting
33. Selecting a team
34. Teambuilding

People competencies were extremely important because of the need to work closely with client hardware and systems development engineers, client's clients, and client marketing managers. These projects were truly made up of interdisciplinary teams. Communication through tele-conferences, face-to-face presentations, and effective meetings was critical. In addition, the client was introducing more capable hardware solutions that allowed sophisticated software designing, creating patent opportunities. The vast amount of client confidential information and patent disclosures made for stressful intellectual property issues.

Project Descriptions

The software development company directed a multi-phase software development and integration program for a client that makes tester hardware for semiconductors and serves large international industry leaders like Motorola, IBM, STMicro, and Intel. Table B–2 shows the amount of work delivered to the hardware tester company to mid-June 2001.

TABLE B–2
Hours for all Hardware Tester Company Projects

	1998	1999	2000	2001	Total
Billed Development	0	1548.85	9270.62	4184.65	15004.12
Nonbilled Support	113.25	165.40	871.68	251.40	1401.73
Total	113.25	1714.25	10142.30	4436.05	16405.85

Of the more than sixteen thousand hours worked, fifteen thousand have been used in developing products for the hardware tester company and their clients, e.g. Motorola, STMicro, IBM, and Intel. More than 360 hours have been spent traveling to Europe and Japan for product definition and installation sessions at the hardware tester company and client offices. More than 15 of the software development company employees have participated in the hardware tester company projects. Chart B–1 shows the annual distribution of billed development versus non-billed direct support to the hardware tester company.

Two major projects will be discussed in subsequent sections. The total amount of non-billed support work almost equals an effective person-year of work. This work included presentations at the hardware tester company user group meetings, patent disclosure meetings,

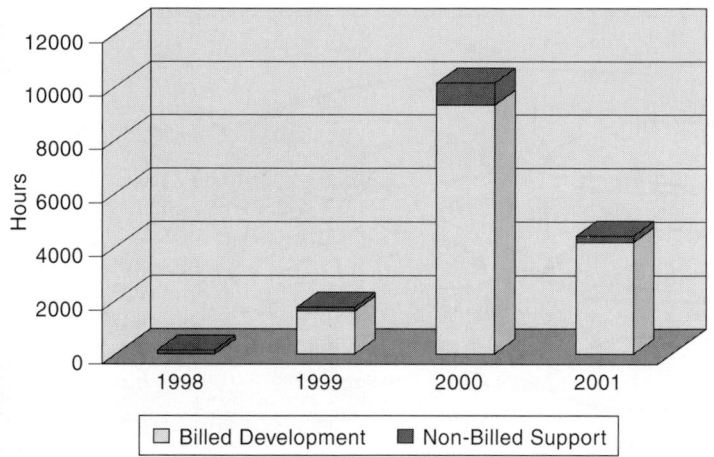

CHART B–1
Annual Distribution of Billed Versus Non-Billed Hours

software project management process transfer, and new product analysis. Some 325 non-billed hours were used to evaluate new low-cost tester architectures, IC test software environments for automatic test code conversion, and new handler technologies for integrated test cells.

The software development company's employee owners together average more than 15 years of experience. That high level of experience has contributed directly to the use of a mature software development process. This process, although changed depending on the nature of the project, is represented in its general model in Figure B–2. In order to make the process as painless as possible for all the software development company consultants to use, the project management support processes are all enabled through a company-wide capabilities team. This team is not billed to any one project, but is a resource for all projects to use.

Due to the metrics kept company-wide, all of these tables and charts can be generated. Across all projects, Table B–3 shows the percentage spent in each process step for all projects done to date for the hardware tester company. This only shows the effort of the software development company consultants. During the requirements and design phases, the hardware tester company engineers were involved to review the Athens designs and requirements specifications. These deliverables were all accessible on a secure client Web site hosted by Athens. The hardware tester company engineers were also part of all validation and acceptance testing of Athens-built products. This testing was completed before any products were installed on the hardware tester company client sites.

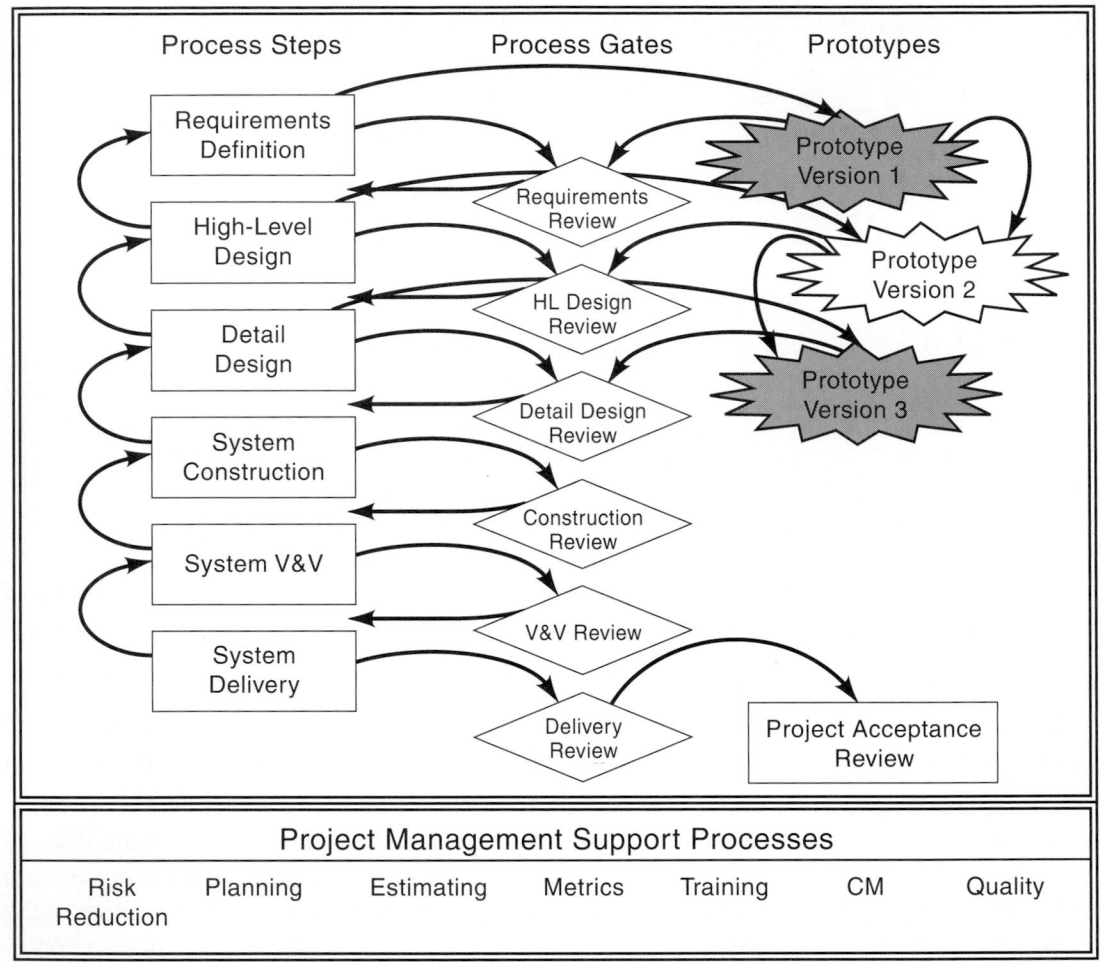

FIGURE B–2
Software Development Life Cycle Model

TABLE B–3
Life Cycle Distribution of Effort

Requirements Definition	High-Level Design	Detail Design	System Construction	System V&V	System Delivery
27%	15%	3%	36%	10%	9%

Hardware Tester Company Projects _____

The first contracted project between the software development company and the hardware tester company began in January 1999. This was the development of the first semiconductor SECS/GEM compliant tester interface software. There are currently four funded projects and one on hold status. Figure B–3 shows the timeline for all funded projects. Chart B–2 shows their respective size. A case study description is included for the SEMICON and the FAB_XFR projects.

SEMICON Project

Background   The SECS/GEM interface is comprised of a hierarchical set of services providing a common way of detecting and reporting factory process equipment events to the factory host control system. "GEM" refers to Generic Equipment Model, a standard model for the communication interface to semiconductor and electronics manufacturing equipment. GEM describes usage of a subset of the "SECS-II" protocol—the Semiconductor Equipment Communication Standard that deals with message content. In creating software for the client's semiconductor testers, the project requirements dictated that the system be:

- Transportable across the client's various platforms, including AIX, HPUX, Solaris, SunOS, Linux, and Windows NT;
- Networkable among heterogeneous hardware environments;

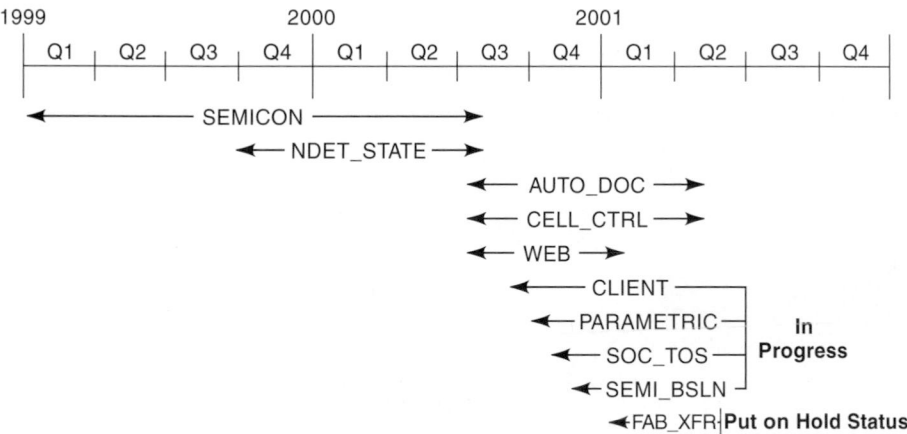

FIGURE B–3
Timeline of All Funded Client Projects

- Scalable with the mini-factory, product line, and secure test cell environment;
- Modular so that only the pieces required at any point in the network need to be purchased.

The project also had to include:

- Evolutionary development to see rapid product delivery and cost tied to functionality delivery;
- Commercial-off-the-shelf (COTS) software as well as state-of-the-art tools and standards;
- Client customizing, on-site, based on unique production and product mix;
- Integrated real-time test suite and tools for SECS/GEM product validation in the client fab.

Solution   In Phase 1, the software development company consultants built the first international standards-compliant software for SECS/GEM on semiconductor testers. The software development company consultants used a COTS, memory resident database package for the heart of the system in combination with an industry accepted programming language. In Phase 2, consultants developed SECS/GEM models for new parametric testers, knitting together the factory and the equipment, and improving availability for the client's customers. The software development company consultants designed the code base to incorporate individual instantiations of hardware into the SECS/GEM engine. The code design was reused in total for a port to using a new Java-based software delivery environment.

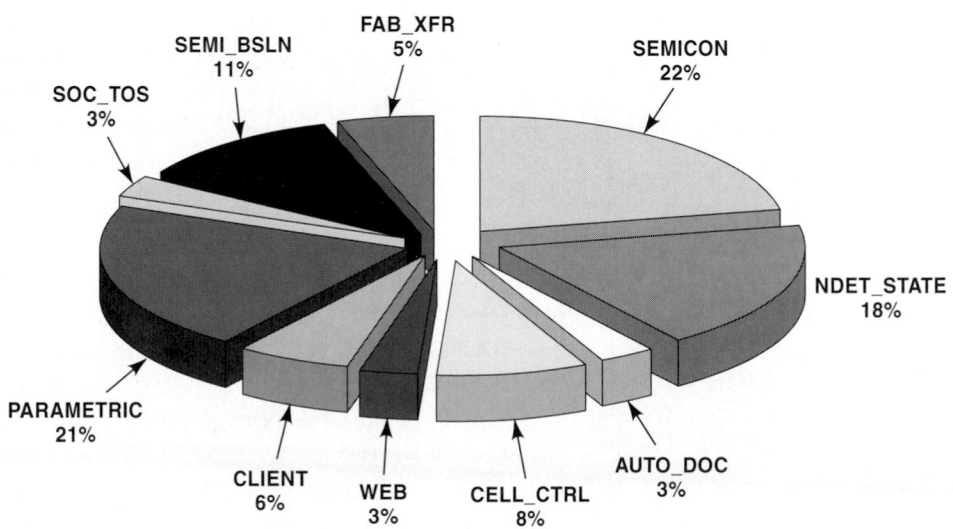

CHART B–2
Client Project Respective Sizes

Project Value   In the future, as the software development company makes steady improvements to the product, it will accommodate all testers and will specify equipment on the semiconductor floor without custom code, which means it will function across a variety of platforms and for multiple manufacturers. The software development company's newest designs will expand the client's marketability by delivering even more advanced capabilities to their customers.

FAB_XFR Project

Background   From January through April of 2001, the software development company provided consulting services to the hardware tester company in the form of analysis, design, and software development for a project known as FAB_XFR. The goal was to automate data collection at one wafer fabrication site and integrate this function with a standard, COTS manufacturing execution system. Data collection was to be implemented using a proprietary software system that was developed at the hardware tester company's software center of excellence. This proprietary system includes a database, statistical process control and design of experiment software, and a separate data representation tool. The fab was evolving from an R&D facility to a production site. They were using a mix of both paper travelers and MS Access application screens used to collect process data. The COTS package had just been implemented in December 2000.

Solution   The first deliverable due was an hour's estimate. Based on the numbers provided by SLIM, an estimating tool, the software development company recommended reducing the scope of the project by implementing the data collection functionality first and postponing the automated dispatching. The team also agreed to focus on three representative products for which template data collection screens would be developed. This would allow the customer team to reduce costs by reusing the templates for subsequent products. The hardware tester company accepted the recommendations and the software development company prepared a project plan.

Development work was conducted from inside the hardware tester company firewall at the hardware tester company offices in Austin, Texas. Using an X-windows emulation tool, the software development company consultants were able to access the statistical system to create several prototype data collection screens. The screens were then opened locally at the fab for review. Weekly teleconference meetings between the software development company and the customer team were held to convey status and review issues.

Project Value   The project was well into the development phase when the software development company was notified that the project would have to be put on hold due to financial reasons. All project work was mothballed using the configuration management system in place within the software development company within eight hours. A final teleconference was held to level-set the customer as to the status of the project and how to access all project records and deliverables on the project Web site.

Lessons Learned

1. Never assume that hardware development companies with mature products and processes know how to apply process to software development.
2. When responsible for delivering to the client's client, there is never enough process or quality that can be built into the final product.
3. When managing a portfolio of projects, metrics that show comparisons among projects are critical for the client's upper management to grasp the breadth of the software development being done.
4. With interdisciplinary teams, effective communication is extremely important.
5. Metrics that show the ROI in process are critical in demonstrating the quality that processes bring to software products.
6. Software configuration management systems are invaluable in snapshoting and mothballing software projects.

Case 2: COTS Software Selection for Information Technology Systems _____

A common software project is the selection and implementation of commercial-off-the-shelf software applications. Application vendors provide almost every type of software package that an organization would need to accomplish their mission. The first activity is insuring that the package meets the organization's requirements and needs. The second is ensuring that the package can be economically implemented in the purchaser's environment. Changes to the environment always involve hardware, software, personnel, and business rules.

Subset of the 34 Competencies Used

Product Competencies

  3. Defining the product
  5. Managing requirements
  6. Managing subcontractors
  7. Performing the initial assessment
 10. Tracking product quality
 11. Understanding development activities

Product definition and requirements management are two of the most critical product competencies in COTS implementation projects. Figure B–5 shows the COTS integration life cycle. The further decomposition of the requirements process for COTS is shown in Figure B–4. Having a requirement's process specifics called out brings their importance to the front of the project team consciousness.

Project Competencies

13. Documenting plans
16. Managing risks
18. Scheduling
19. Selecting metrics

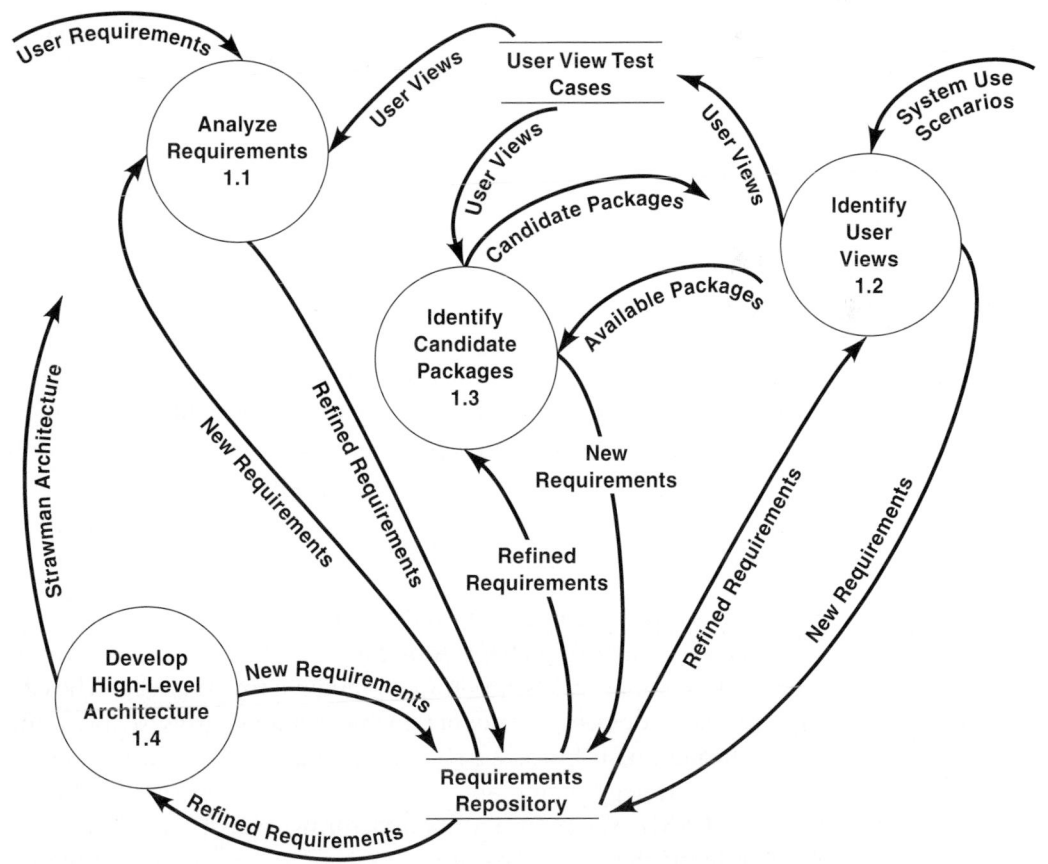

FIGURE B–4
COTS Integration Requirements Process

20. Selecting project management tools

22. Tracking project progress

These process competencies tie into the product competencies of managing subcontractors, tracking product quality, and understanding development activities. The technology consultants leading this project had to be aware of the quality issues inherent in the COTS application selected and the third party contractors that would be employed in the package integration. What holds a group effort project together like this one is pure process. Without the process to make the project function, disaster is the only probable outcome.

People Competencies

25. Holding effective meetings

26. Interaction and communication

27. Leadership

28. Managing change

29. Negotiating successfully

31. Presenting effectively

33. Selecting a team

34. Teambuilding

This subset of the people competencies is fairly consistent across all projects. One of the key competencies required here is negotiating successfully. Although all projects today require a level of consensus building, when dealing with application software suppliers, negotiation is critical. Most enterprise packages cost in the millions of dollars to acquire and implement. Maintenance, training, consulting, and access to developer expertise are important areas to include in any contract. Only through successful negotiation with the vendors can the end-client get an effective and economical system that will meet expected ROI targets.

Project Description

A technology consulting firm assisted with defining the information technology strategy to support the rapid growth of a manufacturing client. Along with the strategy, enterprise software package selection had to be completed to support the company growth targets. The client, a manufacturer of communications devices, was experiencing dynamic growth and wanted to expand its market share through distributor, VAR, international, and end-user sales. The consulting firm developed an IT strategy plan that recommended the selection of both a customer relations management (CRM) system and a manufacturing execution system (MES). These systems would integrate the various needs of their sales force with account management, customer support tools, and manufacturing automation. Figure B–5 shows the COTS life cycle model followed for the package selections.

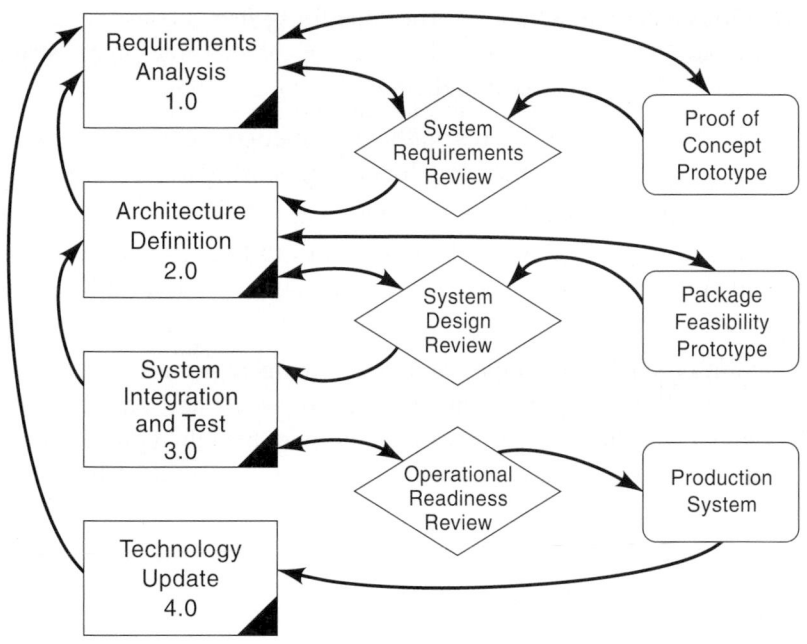

FIGURE B–5
COTS Integration Life Cycle

Background   Significant growth in the client's core business and an impending initial public offering required rapid technology strategy definition and implementation of new systems and processes. The client needed an integrated approach to sales force automation, including:

- Multi-channel sales commissions, reporting, and analysis;
- Support for "disconnected" salespeople in the field;
- Sales pipeline management and pricing tools;
- Account planning and management tools;
- Customer entitlement systems for customer support;
- End-of-quarter sales reporting automation.

Solution   The consulting firm's consultants conducted interviews with the client team and documented the findings with a requirements database and process maps. They then assisted the client with vendor negotiations. The consulting firm's consultants organized a comprehensive technology strategy into a clear, manageable, three-phase structure that directly engaged the client and responded to their goals:

1. The consultants directed requirements gathering, helped define business processes, identified key success factors, including operating cost drivers, evaluated vendor options, and documented a vendor risk analysis.

2. Consultants focused on risk analysis, a detailed analysis of vendor proposals, evaluation of vendor ability to meet the client's requirements, negotiation, and high-level implementation planning.

3. The projects culminated in an implementation management process of the selected packages, which typically integrate commercial-off-the-shelf and custom-build applications. A technology consulting and software development firm then provided the program management of the entire project, including objective oversight of the COTS vendor consultants.

The consulting firm utilized an innovative set of tools to ensure accurate requirements definition, appropriate vendor selection, and client visibility into the process. The tools included a detailed evaluation and risk analysis of selected vendors in both hardcopy format and as an electronic database; and an internal Web site for the client that serves as a repository for project documentation, requirements updates, status, and process maps.

The client is able to use these tools as their needs evolve to keep requirements up-to-date and conduct future evaluations on systems to meet the changing business requirements. The technology consulting and software development firm also assisted the client in negotiations with their selected vendors as well as implementation.

Project Value

The client gained the capability to effectively and quickly evaluate vendor functionality, perform risk analysis, and create a foundation for implementation plans. This project resulted in the implementation of an enterprise resources planning (ERP) system, which is an integrated suite of applications that enables eBusiness transactions between internal business units, customers, suppliers, and partners. A follow-up project supplied the customer with an effective definition of sales force automation and customer support needs, and a selection process to effectively provide for those needs.

The consulting firm's program management oversight of the vendor/client team implementation achieved client needs with lower risk and effective cost containment. Unlike the great majority of ERP implementation projects, this implementation came in on time and on budget. The client is able to utilize process maps and system requirements tools in an online format that will allow them to continually improve their process and relationships with vendors as their needs evolve. Moreover, this process gives senior management insight into the project and coordinates the implementation team.

The project developed and implemented a technology strategy for the client in three specific ways:

1. Minimized the time-to-market for new products, services, and the required technology investments.
2. Minimized the risk to the business of an insufficient/inappropriate technology architecture.
3. Maximized the flexibility of internal systems to enable the business to respond to new service opportunities, changes in the market (maneuverability), and deliver world-class customer support.

Lessons Learned

1. For adequate COTS package comparison and selection, critical client requirements must be captured.
2. Automated tools must be used to map client requirement to COTS package capabilities.
3. Requirements must be used to directly derive acceptance tests for COTS application packages.
4. Communication in the selection and installation of COTS applications must be managed among the client, package providers, and all third-party consultants involved in the application installation.
5. It is critical to understand the client's business domain in order to perform an adequate ROI for package selection.

Case 3: Legacy Software Re-engineering _____

The option of re-engineering an organization's existing code base must always be included as an option to purchasing new COTS applications and building systems from scratch. Most ongoing organizations have a large investment and sunk cost in their automation systems. In many cases, this is the only manifestation of the rules by which the business operates. The system may be the only record of the rules. Even if a new system was to be built, these types of projects occur for the derivation of the current rules for business operations.

Subset of the 34 Competencies Used

Product Competencies

4. Evaluating alternative processes
5. Managing requirements
9. Tailoring processes
10. Tracking product quality

Successful re-engineering of a complex legacy system, on the fly, while the system is still performing mission-critical functions, requires a mature process. The software development process needs to be tailored to the specific aspects of reverse and forward engineering subprocesses. Requirements, many times, become derived from the code base and are added into what the client perceives are the current application requirements. Many times there are real surprises as to what rules the software really follows. Because of the derivative nature of the requirements, the quality of the current and target products must be carefully tracked and measured.

Project Competencies

13. Documenting plans
14. Estimating cost
16. Managing risks

Re-engineering is a balancing act between the cost of delving into every last instruction of the code and the risk of missing an important business rule. One of the most important products of the re-engineering activity is a current set of system documentation. This might be the only time since the system was built that the documentation has a chance of being current with what is executing in the software.

People Competencies

28. Managing change
31. Presenting effectively

Because of the cost and skills involved, re-engineering is done is very small groups. Change to the code base must be managed effectively, usually through an industrial strength configuration management and build process tool set. The small team will, by design, have excellent internal communications, but the team must be able to communicate through presentations to the stakeholders of the present system and whomever remains of the original developers.

Project Description

Re-engineering of legacy systems takes a markedly different life cycle approach. Figure B–6 shows the life cycle process for re-engineering. The goal is to derive business rules and the software design by reverse engineering the legacy code base. Once the design and business rules have been derived, the next step is to forward engineer the derived code back into the application. These steps need to take place within the framework of requirements to design the implementation process steps. All of the attendant support processes such as configuration management, metrics, quality, and documentation must be performed. Although there are tools that can do the mechanics of reverse and forward engineering of a code base, none exist that can derive business rules. Another fatal drawback to most reverse engineering tools is that they only work on the code. Many of the business rules in long-lived legacy systems are incorporated in to make files and database structures. By focusing only on code, part of the picture is seen, but not the critical whole.

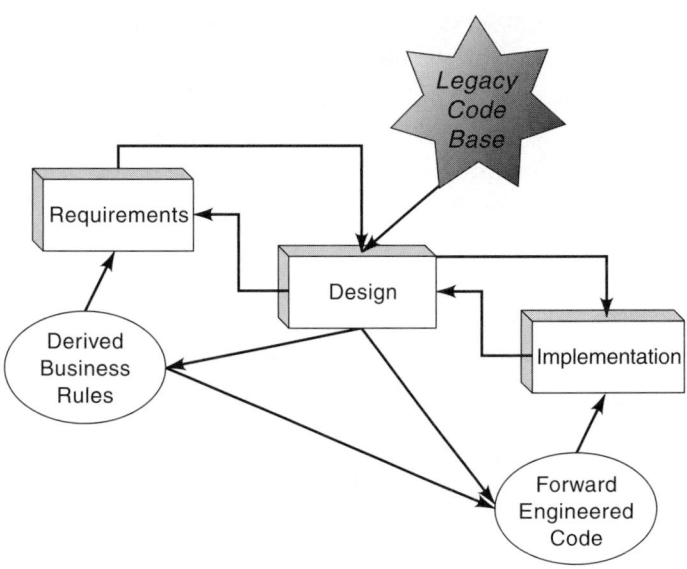

FIGURE B–6
Legacy Code Re-engineering Life Cycle

Senior software consultants, working for a client company that resells communications network connectivity, built a requirements set and reverse-engineered a set of business rules from an existing code structure. They then used this data as the foundation for a Web-enabled knowledge library, which was available to users company-wide.

Background   After a recent merger—of companies, people, and IT departments—this Fortune 500 company found its service-tracking software coming up short on functionality. The company couldn't examine its full range of communications service offerings to determine which were highly utilized, which were underutilized, and the profits and losses associated with both. This led to an inability to quickly and accurately assess overall company profitability. Not being able to share information in a consistent format on a company-wide basis added to the confusion.

Solution   Senior software consultants initiated the analysis project by performing an in-depth examination of the client's existing processes and systems. They also conducted interviews with key client contacts to capture requirements about the additional functionality needed. The project and process proceeded to include the following deliverables:

- Requirements management;
- Business rules capture;
- Problem domain mapping;

- Evaluation, recommendation, and implementation configuration management tools;
- Design and implementation of a Web-based knowledge library.

Senior software consultants reverse-engineered a set of business rules from an existing code structure and built a Web-enabled knowledge library to share new data and information across departments and functions. The consultants brought to this project not only the domain expertise to tackle the technical issues, but also the ability to improve the existing development and analysis processes, and the tools infrastructure.

Project Value   The client is now able to track communications service costs more accurately, and as a result can quickly and easily track overall company profitability.

Lessons Learned

1. Commercial-off-the-shelf reverse and forward engineering tools focus only on code. They miss the critical 20 percent of the application that can only be understood through human analysis.
2. Re-engineering takes more, not less, process.
3. Re-engineering take 15 to 40 percent longer than any best estimate.
4. The developer that knows all about the legacy system just left the client company.
5. Production systems cannot be re-engineered in place. A development system is necessary for complete testing and "what-if" scenario generation.

Problems for Review _____

1. In the first case study, process competencies 12 and 20 were not emphasized. Building a WBS and selecting project management tools seem to be a big part of this practitioner's guide. In your opinion and based on the facts presented, why were they not emphasized?
2. What other metrics could be used in managing a client's project portfolio?
3. What metrics are applicable for a COTS project?
4. What would be the factors of a comprehensive ROI calculation for a COTS package selection?
5. How would you use an automatic code profiler and complexity calculator in a re-engineering project?
6. Would you use the same life cycle in Case 3 if you were porting from one programming language to another?

Visit the Case Study _____

Ms. Patel and Dr. Harita have looked at the University of Texas Software Quality Institute's Web site for the Software Project Management (SWPM) Certification Program (*lifelong.engr.utexas.edu/sqi/swpm/faq.cfm*) and were intrigued by the 34 competencies. As the project manager for the CRM project you have been asked to do a competency-based evaluation of the project as it is functioning today. They want a plan for the competency audit based on the SWPM 34 competencies and a preliminary findings within one week.

Creating the Business Plan

The Technology Business Plan as the Company's Meta-Plan

Technology companies need to develop an overall approach to how the development of products fit within the corporation's accountability process. Having a standard, or at least a template, technology product business plan in one way provides visibility into the business case for a product and identifies the process measures of success. Figure C–1 shows a notional complete life cycle for a successful technology product. A technology business plan covers this entire life cycle.

The portions of the life cycle are:

Development—maps to our software product development life cycle as shown in Figure C–1. It is the heavy investment portion where the product is being built.

Production ramp—the marketing and sales intensive portion of the life cycle. The software product has been released to the set of Beta customers, modifications and initial problems have been fixed, and it is now ready for market release.

Market growth—the time of rapid sales of the product and intense market segment penetration. There may be an increased maintenance activity to rapidly add new features to the product that keep the market momentum moving up and to the right.

Market maturity—growth of product sales slows but continues at a flat rate. The product has a profitable portion of the market and evolutionary development continues to add new features and maintain market share.

End of life—the product is now known as a cash cow. No further investment is made in the product. It is milked for any possible income and planned for retirement.

What Is the Technology Business Plan?

Road Map for a Business, Business Unit, and Product

Using the product life cycle as the foundation, the technology business plan acts as the map to a successful business. It will answer these questions:

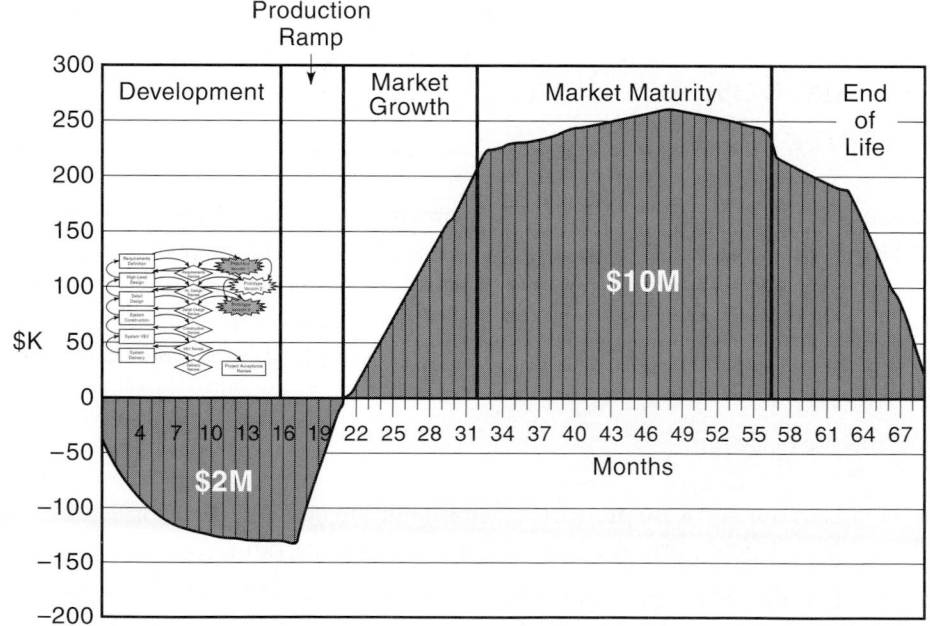

FIGURE C–1
Technology Product Life Cycle

1. Why is this company in business?
2. What are its products or services?
3. How does it plan on merchandising the products?
4. What are the product markets?
5. How are the products channels of distribution?
6. How are sales done?
7. Who is the competition?
8. What kind of advertising is done?
9. Who handles customer relations?
10. How are public relations conducted?
11. What marketing research has been done?

Focusing Mechanism

Doing the technology business plan helps the principles in the company to focus their ideas on what will be the keys to a successful product and company. One of the major problems in technology development is getting lost in the technology and ignoring the other aspects of business, such as marketing. The market is a critical part of the business environment. If the products being developed do not meet a market need, they will fail. It matters not how sophisticated or sexy the technology, without hitting the market needs, the product will fail economically. The purpose of being in business is to make a profit. Without having a product that sells, no profit will be made.

Reality Check

Is this a business or a hobby? If there is no chance to make any money, it is a hobby. Investing the effort up front to develop a business plan provides the reality check necessary to determine if this is a real product. Investigating the mundane aspects of the business such as sales and support after the sale, market research, and identifying competition puts that needed dose of reality into the mystifying aspects of the technology being developed. The business plan allows us the opportunity to really look at the market environment in which we will be operating and determine which of the many needs we fill.

Sales Tool

How do we present our product to the market we have identified? If we are typical technologists we have an enormous problem in separating the benefits of our product and the technology used to build the product. Our business plan will function as a sales tool to our target market. Executing the business plan provides us the necessary market research, market identification, and competitive analysis to describe our product in terms of fulfillment of needs, not technology bells and whistles. Our customers are not buying technology, they are filling a need.

Another use for the business plan is if we are in the process of seeking outside funding for our company. Venture capital firms and other investors require a rigorous planning process and proof of marketability before funds are committed to products and new companies.

Why Build a Technology Business Plan? _____

Clarify What You Want to Do

Taking the time to develop a business plan acts as a focusing mechanism for your technology ideas. You must step out of the technology arena and directly into business. You must make your product plans and goals clear for business people and potential customers to understand.

Communication Mechanism

Communication resides in the receiver not the transmitter. The technology business plan acts as a communication medium for non-technical partners, clients, and the general public who will need to understand the benefits of acquiring and using your product.

Baseline for Your Business

You cannot measure your progress toward a business goal without establishing a baseline. The technology business plan defines your company organization, market, and where your product fits. It identifies your competition and it communicates your goals and objectives.

Move from Talking to Doing

The technology business plan is a catalyst for action. Up to this point you are merely talking about a product or playing with technology. The business plan is the means toward a business end. It puts your ideas into actions that are visible and understandable to others.

Technology Business Plan Contents _____

Company Overview

A. Identification of the company
   1. Name
   2. Signature

3. Trademark

4. Colors, symbols, etc.

5. Slogan

B. Company relationships

C. Company structure

    1. Divisions

    2. Contribution to volume, profit, etc.

    3. International operations

D. Existing plants, branches, warehouses, etc.

E. Company history

F. Historical response to changes in economy, technology, user practices, etc.

G. What is the company's reputation?

    1. What business are we in?

    2. What business will we be in ten years from now?

    3. What is our image?

    4. Significant achievements

    5. Newsworthy facilities

    6. Newsworthy employees

H. Marketing approach

    1. Statement of marketing policy

    2. Formal or informal plan

    3. Market research, conducted or planned

    4. Test marketing, conducted or planned

I. Promotional mix

    1. Personnel selling

    2. Advertising

    3. Public relations

    4. Sales promotion

J. Long-range objectives of the company

K. Plans regarding expansion, diversification, decentralization, acquisitions, etc.

L. Status of our industry

    1. Growth

    2. Profits

M. Legal considerations in our industry

N. Organizational chart, personnel
    1. Chains of authority on operations
    2. Chains of authority on advertising
    3. Chains of authority on administration

O. Policies:
    1. Regarding classified information
    2. With respect to reciprocity, entertainment of buyers, etc.

P. Management consultants, past or planned

Q. Association memberships and services received

R. International or multinational goals, policies, and strategies
    1. Past
    2. Current
    3. Future

S. Financial information

Products or Services

A. Identification
    1. Name
    2. Trademark
    3. Colors, symbols, etc.
    4. Product shape, other characteristics of product or service

B. Lines (including degree of completeness)

C. Types, styles, sizes, price ranges, profitability
    1. Coding
    2. Standards, specials
    3. Product life cycles

D. Usage
    1. Who, when, methods of use
    2. Customer profile, lifestyle

E. Factors in selection of product or service type, including resistances

F. Factors in selection of brand, including resistances

G. Patents, licenses

H. Points of differentiation of product or service

    1. Exclusive and/or superior processes, ingredients, features

    2. Competitive advantages

I. Product or service weakness

J. Packaging, labeling, tagging

    1. Responsibility, types

K. Packing and shipping

L. Accessories, tools, cabinets, dispensers, etc.

M. Warehousing

N. Delivery

    1. Normal

    2. Past, current performance

    3. Product shortages

O. Engineering service

P. Customer services

Q. Reconditioning, repair parts

R. What is the biggest sales problem?

S. New product or service program

    1. Number per year

    2. Responsibility

    3. Testing procedures

    4. Criteria

    5. Success rate

T. New products or services planned

U. Products or services to be dropped

V. Which products or services to promote and where?

W. Inventory

    1. Control methods

    2. Historic levels

    3. Current level

    4. Turns per year

Merchandising

A. Pricing of products or services

B. Allowances, deals

C. Financing

    1. Trade-in

    2. Financing plan

    3. Leasing

    4. Contract

D. Guarantee, warranty

E. Tags, seals, etc.

F. Dispenser, rack, merchandiser, etc.

G. Sampling

H. Trial

I. Premium

J. Servicing policy

    1. Installation

    2. Repair

K. Returned goods policy

Markets

A. Coverage

B. Markets ranked by industry or geography

C. Market trends

    1. Market as a whole

    2. Product or service in market

D. Criteria for determining a market (or prospect) for our products or services

E. Purchasing or specifying influences of our products or services

    1. Direct

    2. Indirect

F. Purchasing factors

    1. Seasonal

    2. How an order develops

    3. Bidding

    4. Importance of price, availability, service

    5. Average order

6. Obsolescence
7. Tax considerations
8. Labor considerations
9. Emotional considerations
10. Freight rate
11. Buy hand-to-mouth or for inventory
12. Reorder cycle
13. Reciprocity

G. Replacement

H. Second-hand market

I. International
1. Exports
2. Subsidiaries
3. Licensing agreements
4. Distribution overseas
5. Competition
6. Objectives, plans for international marketing

J. New markets to exploit

K. Market studies available

L. Markets in which to concentrate promotion

M. Test marketing—Which industries? Which markets?

N. Segmentation—industry, market

Distribution (If Not Direct-to-Buyer)

A. Present channels
1. "Road map" of distribution
2. Percent of sales
3. Trends
4. Adequacy of coverage
5. Quality
6. Desired distribution mix

B. Policies
1. Franchise arrangements
2. Consignment

  3. Stocking

  4. House accounts

  5. Returned goods

  6. Missionary work

  7. Printed policy

C. Importance of line to distributor

D. Discount schedule

E. Average order for inventory

F. Turnover

G. Dealer identification (sign, decal, wall plaque)

H. Deals, allowances, incentives

I. Sales training

J. Sales aids

  1. How are they used?

  2. How are they paid for?

K. Promotion plan

  1. Materials

  2. How is it distributed?

  3. How is it paid for?

L. Cooperative advertising plan

M. Dealer listings

  1. Nationally

  2. Locally

N. Distributor cooperation

O. Communications with distributors

P. Satisfaction level with present distributors

Q. New distributors desired, by market or industry

R. Distribution acquisition plan

Sales Makeup

A. Sales management

B. Salespeople

  1. Number

    2. Type

    3. Qualifications

    4. Characteristics

C. General line or specialists

D. Compensation and incentives

E. Training

F. Sales meetings

G. Communications

H. The sales call

    1. Whom called on?

    2. Frequency, cost, etc.

    3. Team selling

I. Number of accounts per salesperson

J. Prospecting versus servicing accounts

K. Time period, number of calls to make sale

L. Quotas? How are they set?

M. Sales aids (with samples) and degree of usage

N. Seasonal factors in buying

O. Typical resistances

P. Team spirit

Q. System selling

Competition (Direct and Indirect)

A. By divisions

B. By product lines

    1. Breadth of line

    2. Comparisons

        a. Construction

        b. Patents

        c. Features

        d. Price

        e. Packaging

        f. Availability

C. By markets—industry or service
   1. Sales coverage
   2. Share of market
D. Selling effectiveness
E. Engineering service and other facilities
F. Versus second-hand market
G. Versus imports
H. Price-cutting
I. Competitors' positions, strengths and weaknesses
J. Lost-order analysis
   1. Bid/no bid analysis
   2. Lost bid analysis
   3. Lost order analysis

Advertising

A. Ad department personnel, division of work
B. Agency responsibilities
C. Company policies regarding role of advertising and relationship to sales
D. Management's attitude toward advertising
E. Sales organization's attitude toward advertising
F. Positioning
G. Target audiences
H. Copy strategy or creative platform
I. Unique selling proposition
J. Any "sacred cows"
K. Colors, typography, etc.
L. References to subsidiaries, divisions, addresses, etc.
M. Patent registration notice
N. Legal factors
O. Method of setting budget
   1. Items included
   2. Percent of sales, per unit, task method, other

   3. How corporate advertising is paid for

   4. Budget year

   5. When prepared

P. Media being used

   1. Media strategy

   2. Magazines, newspapers, broadcast, outdoor, etc.

   3. Trade or firm

   4. Trade shows

   5. Catalogs, trade directories

   6. Telephone directories

   7. Direct mail

   8. House organ

   9. Other

   10. Any significant changes in emphasis over recent years

Q. Existing contracts

R. Seasonal factors

S. Merchandising to salespeople, distributors, etc.

T. Mailing facilities

   1. Outside services

   2. Lists

U. Inquiry-handling system

V. Competitive advertising

W. Recent and current performance

X. Samples

Y. Recruitment advertising

Z. Statement of marketing objectives

   1. Long-range

   2. Short-range

AA. Statement of advertising objectives

   1. Specific

   2. Measurable

AB. Measurement

   1. Sales increase

   2. Share of market

3. Awareness
4. Preference
5. Sales leads
6. Conversions
7. New customers created
8. Change of mind
9. Cost per incremental unit moved
10. Syndicated service ratings

AC. Pre-testing

Customer Relations

A. Order acknowledgement

B. Engineering service

C. Instruction manual or directions

D. Factory school

E. Complaint handling

F. Repair parts catalog

G. Repair, reconditioning service

H. House organ

Public Relations

A. Structure
1. How PR is handled
2. Policies and procedures
3. Staffing, use of counsel
4. Press relations
5. Management attitude
6. Other considerations

B. Plans
1. Availability of written plans
2. Timetable
3. Measurement
4. Assessment of public, target audiences

C. Product publicity

    1. Relationship to total communications

    2. Ongoing programs

    3. Priorities

    4. Immediate tasks

    5. Internal contacts for briefings, project responsibility

    6. Other

D. Financial

    1. Fact book availability

    2. Management exposure

    3. Research studies available

    4. P/E ratio evaluation

    5. Specific goals of management

    6. External communications

    7. Annual report

E. Special programs

    1. Customers, distributors, trade

    2. Employee, community

    3. Environment, consumerism

    4. External affairs, public affairs

    5. Test marketing

    6. Marketing communications

    7. Institutions

    8. Government

    9. Other

F. Communications audit

    1. Appraisal of all internal publications

    2. External communications

    3. Management appraisals and opinion

    4. Opinion leaders

    5. Media attitudes

    6. Consumer attitudes

    7. Consultants' past recommendations

    8. Other considerations

G. International

H. Anniversaries

 I. Writers

 J. Speakers bureau

K. Clipping service

 L. Merchandising of performance

M. Archives, museums, etc.

N. Industry public relations program

Marketing Research

A. General

    1. Research conducted

    2. Management attitudes

B. Studies pertinent to marketing

C. Advertising research, pre-testing policy

D. Public relations research

E. Trade association resources, studies available

 F. Sales forecasting

G. Biggest unsolved problem that research might help solve now

    1. What will it cost?

Making the Business Case Cost Benefit Analysis in a Technology Business Plan _____

A crucial analysis exercise in technology business plan development is determining the profit to be earned from the products developed. In the business world this is referred to as a cost benefit analysis. Most investments and costs are incurred today. Most returns from the investment or costs are generated in the future. Since money received in the future is worth less than money received today, these returns must be adjusted for the time value of money. Opportunity cost occurs by investing in this project—you sacrificed an investment in the next best alternative. Cost benefit analysis is a set of techniques to analytically compare costs, benefits, and opportunity costs mixed in with the time value of money.

Models for Cost Benefit Analysis

There are a number of different models and techniques used for cost benefit analysis. Some of them are:

- Internal rate of return (IRR)
- Net present value (NPV):
    - Marginal cost of capital (MCC)
- Return on:
    - Investment (ROI)
    - Assets (ROA)
    - Invested capital (ROIC)
    - Equity (ROE)
- Economic value added (EVA):
    - Weighted average cost of capital (WACC)
    - Net operating income (NOI)
    - Earnings before interest and taxes (EBIT)

Benefit/Cost Techniques

Project benefit/cost analysis techniques allow the project manager to:

- Compare project alternatives when some benefits are not tangible (e.g. internal projects, or public projects)
- Provide a calculated benefit for each project divided by cost or relative cost
- Rank projects by the relative benefit-to-cost ratio

Return on Investment (ROI)

Measures how efficiently management uses the average money invested in company assets. A simple return on investment calculation is shown in Figure C–2.

Time Value of Money   This is the most important concept in the financial part of your business plan. Also known as "discounted cash flow," the basic principle is that a dollar today is worth more than a dollar sometime in the future. The key parts:

PV—present value, the value today;

FV—future value, the value at some time in the future;

$$\text{ROI} = \frac{\textbf{Net Profit After Taxes}}{\textbf{Total Assets}}$$

Example:

Income Statement	
Revenue	$1000
Costs	−750
Profits	$250
Taxes (40%)	−100
Profit After Taxes	$150

Balance Sheet			
Assets $800	Liab	$350
	Equity	450
Total $800	Total	$800

$$\text{ROI} = \frac{\$150}{\$800} = 18.75\%$$

FIGURE C–2
ROI Calculation Example

I—interest rate that the money could earn;

N—number of periods (days, months, years) to wait for the future value to be paid;

Pmt—payment or cash flow per period.

Making a Decision with Present Value Techniques

The relationships among the parts of present value calculations are shown in Figure C–3.

Which would a "reasonable and prudent" firm prefer—a $5,000 service contract paid now, or a $7,000 maintenance expense paid in two years, assuming the firm wants a 12 percent return?

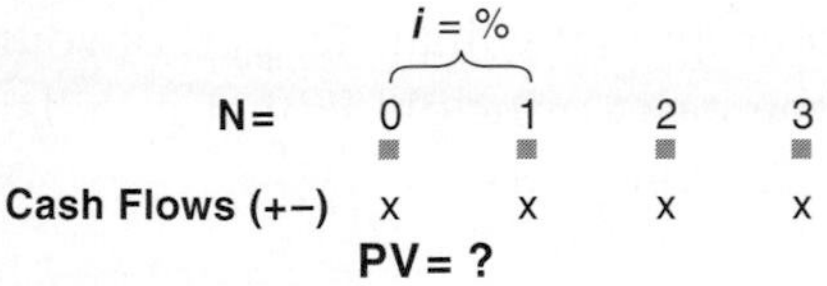

$$i = \%$$

N=	0	1	2	3
Cash Flows (+−)	x	x	x	x
	PV = ?			

FIGURE C–3
Present Value Relationships

$$PV = \$5,000/(1 + 0.12)0 = \$5,000$$
$$PV = \$7,000/(1 + 0.12)2 = \$5,580$$

The firm would prefer to pay the $5,000 now since the present value of the expenditure is lower.

Payback Period

The payback period is the number of periods required to recover the original investment. It is determined when cumulative cash flows reach zero. Figure C–4 shows a graph of a project's payback period plotted in dollars versus months. Figure C–5 shows the cumulative cash flows moving from negative to positive.

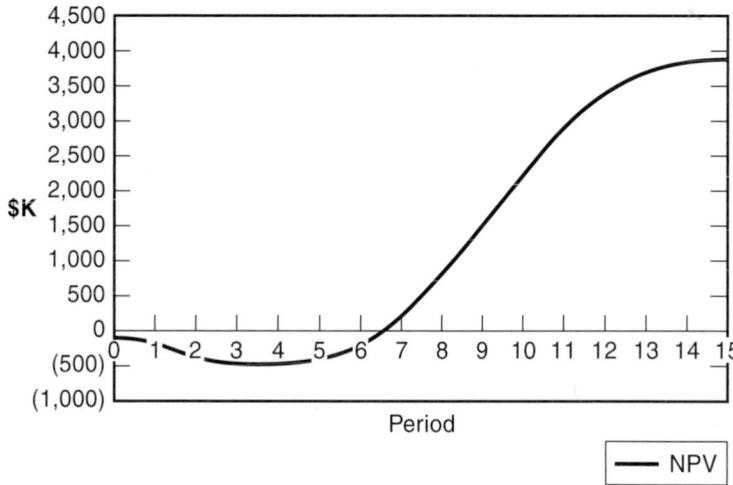

FIGURE C–4
Net Present Value Payback Period

N=	0	i = 5%	1	5%	2	5%	3
Cash Flows (+−)	−500.00		+100		+200		+300
Cumulative CFs	−500		−400		−200		+100

Payback

FIGURE C–5
Cumulative Cash Flow Representation

Net Present Value (NPV)

NPV is the excess value of a project's present value minus its expected costs (investment). Figure C–6 shows the relationship among the parts of the NPV calculation.

Internal Rate of Return (IRR)

IRR measures how much interest must be earned by a project to make the NPV of all future cash flows (+ and –) equal zero. This is the preferred technique instead of using NPV. Figure C–7 shows the IRR calculation.

$NPV = PV - I$
Example: $NPV = \$535.80 - 500 = \$35.80$

N =	0 $i = 5\%$ 1	5%	2	5%	3
	■	■	■		■
Cash Flows (+–)	−500.00	+100		+200	+300
PVs =	95.24				
	181.41				
	+ 259.15				
PV =	$535.80				
NPV =	$35.80				

FIGURE C–6
Net Present Value Calculation

$PV(Inflows) = PV(Outflows)$

N =	0 $i = ?\%$ 1	?%	2	?%	3
	■	■	■		■
Cash Flows (+–)	−500.00	+100		+200	+300
PVs =	xx.xx				
	xxx.xx				
	xxx.xx				
PV =	$500.00				
NPV =	$0				

FIGURE C–7
Internal Rate of Return Calculation

Problems for Review _____

Here are two options for a high technology manufacturing company. Which is the most cost-effective based on the techniques of cost benefit analysis presented? Why?

Option 1

Glenn Computer sells an average of $4 million of computers per day via the Internet.

Its variable cost to produce the made-to-order computers is 78 percent of revenues.

The Web page is up 24 hours per day year round (8,736 hours per year).

Glenn estimates that for each failure, they lose 40 percent of the potential sales during the downtime to competitors.

Their server has an average failure of nine times annually and the proposed maintenance will reduce the failures to four times annually.

The current mean time to repair is four hours and the response time proposed with the service contract is two hours (guaranteed).

The proposed service contract is $75,000 per year.

Option 2

An updated factory control system will cost $800,000 and has an estimated useful life of five years.

The system will require two maintenance personnel, each at $45,000 annually, including benefits.

Maintenance, training, and education is expected to cost $5,000 per year.

Glenn expects to carry $50,000 in spare parts and spend $15,000 in repair parts per year.

This production line is expected to contribute $400,000 in gross margins to the company annually.

Glenn has a cost of capital of 12 percent.

You are offered a maintenance contract that covers parts and labor for five years for $100,000 per year. The preventative maintenance is expected to extend the useful life by one year.

Visit the Case Study _____

You and your team have completed the first draft of the SRS when your receive an urgent email from Ms. Patel and Mr. Adams requesting a conference call including them, you, and your software development manager in Bangalore, Dr. Harita. It seems that Dr. Zhou has gotten Mr. Lu to request that she personally approve all project deliverables that relate to the ARRS. According to your project plan, the SRS is a customer deliverable. Since the initial project meetings, ARRS SRS has turned into more of a product than a custom software development requirements document. Your management does not want the CRM to know that you will be productizing their solution for sale to other Asian railroads. During the conference call, these options are discussed:

- Delay the delivery of the final SRS until delivery of the prototype.
- Re-write the SRS so it addresses only the CRM prototype.
- Announce that for cost-cutting reasons you are not going to produce any other documentation other than that in the prototype code.
- Use xTRemeObjectMaker to generate the code based on the UML requirements model, and throw out all other documents.

During the conference call, Dr. Harita sends you an email saying that the BSD will under no conditions change their development processes. At the end of the conference call, you are asked to make a recommendation based on what's best for the project from the project manager's point of view. You have two days until the SRS is scheduled to be delivered.

Web Pages for Further Information _____

bcentral.com/resource/articles/bizplans/101.asp. Microsoft bCentral Business Plans: C.E. Yandle, "How to Write a Business Plan."

web.mit.edu/entforum/www/Business_Plans/bplans.html. The MIT Enterprise Forum's Business Plan Resource Guide. The guide is a list of resources focused entirely or substantially on writing a business plan. It has been developed to address one of the most frequently asked questions of Forum chapters: "How can I learn about writing a business plan?" The resources on the list are available at most public libraries and bookstores with good business sections.

www.bplans.com/dp/. Developing a business plan is easier than you might think. If you know enough to run a business, you know enough to develop a good business plan. Just take it step by step, and use the tools available to you.

www.sba.gov/starting/indexbusplans.html. "The Business Plan, Road Map to Success," a tutorial and self-paced activity.

www.planware.org/bizplan.htm. White Paper—"Writing a Business Plan."

www.ecofinance.net/bptemplate01.html. New Ventures Investor Forum: Writing your Business Plan.

Understanding Systems Engineering

Systems engineering is an interdisciplinary approach and means to enable the realization of successful systems. It focuses on defining customer needs and required functionality early in the development cycle, documenting requirements, then proceeding with design synthesis and system validation while considering the complete problem:

- Operations;
- Performance;
- Test;
- Manufacturing;
- Cost and schedule;
- Training and support;
- Disposal.

Systems engineering integrates all the disciplines and specialty groups into a team effort forming a structured development process that proceeds from concept to production to operation. It considers both the business and the technical needs of all customers with the goal of providing a quality product that meets the user's needs. System engineering forces the software development project manager to realize that there is more to the product equation than merely software. Software needs a platform on which to operate and a support environment around it.

Systems engineering is focused on the product requirements and where it fits within its market environment. Figure D–1 represents how the environment impacts a product. If we were building a product that operates in the personal computer (PC) environment, our system concerns are impacted by:

Market trends—how the consumer currently defines the PC. The rate of change and adoption of new technologies in the PC will dictate the market window that the product must hit.

Social trends—how the PC is viewed within the context of its use in society. The trend for PCs had been one of toys for geeks. Having a product that emphasizes this view may place it right at the center of the competition. Look to where the market is trending and place the product in its path.

Business trends—how the product is sold within the business community. The greatest number of PCs are sold into businesses. Although the business environment shoots for a state-of-the-art system, a stronger driver may be the lifetime cost of ownership of the equipment. Low-cost upgrading and finding ways of expensing versus capitalizing the cost may be the key in the business area.

Technology—how Moore's law affects this product under development. The cost of computing decreases while the complexity of the hardware increases. The product under development must be at the market fast enough that it is not obsolete at introduction.

Competition—how your product competes in a crowded market. Developing a product with software poses almost no monetary barrier to entry for your competition. As part of the system analysis, the project manager needs to be able to determine where the product protection resides. In most instances, that protection is in securing the earliest and largest market share before a competing product is released.

History—how the product company is perceived in the marketplace. Company history and reputation is important in product introduction and placement. If your company is known as a consumer-oriented, shrink-wrapped, off-the-shelf product company, it will be very difficult to sell into the high-end, corporate enterprise management solution software market. Likewise, if your products have traditionally been high-end with maintenance and service built into the cost structure, releasing a very low-cost product with little support muddies your product line with the high-end clients.

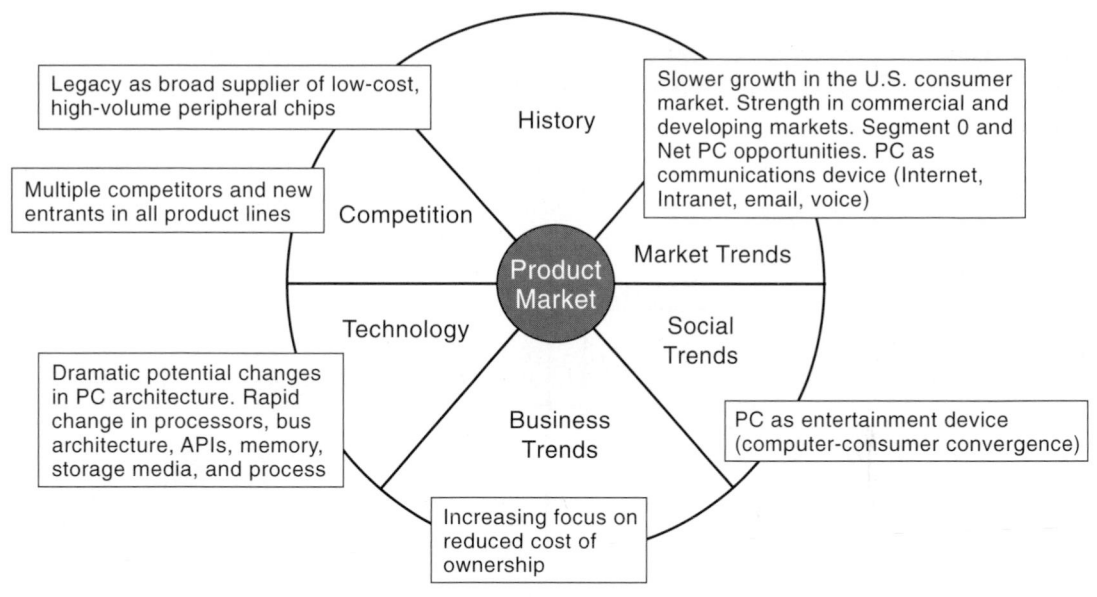

FIGURE D–1
Product Environment Defines the Product Requirements

Where We Are in the Project Management Life Cycle

Systems engineering happens at the "front end" of the life cycle: concept exploration, system exploration, and the beginnings of requirements. Although at the front end of the life cycle, decisions made based on systems engineering impact the entire product life. Figure D–2 shows where systems engineering fits within the IEEE 1074 life cycle model.

Systems engineering impacts the establishment of the project environment and the development of the initial project plan. All of the environmental issues of development platform, ultimate end-user identification, channels of distribution, and total product definition must be accounted for before software development can begin.

The systems environment frames risk analysis and contingency planning. Complete risk identification cannot occur in isolation from the product's ultimate installation environment. Contingency plans cannot be made without an understanding of all the impacts on the final product. Software does not work in isolation. It must have a host and that host must be understood from a system's perspective.

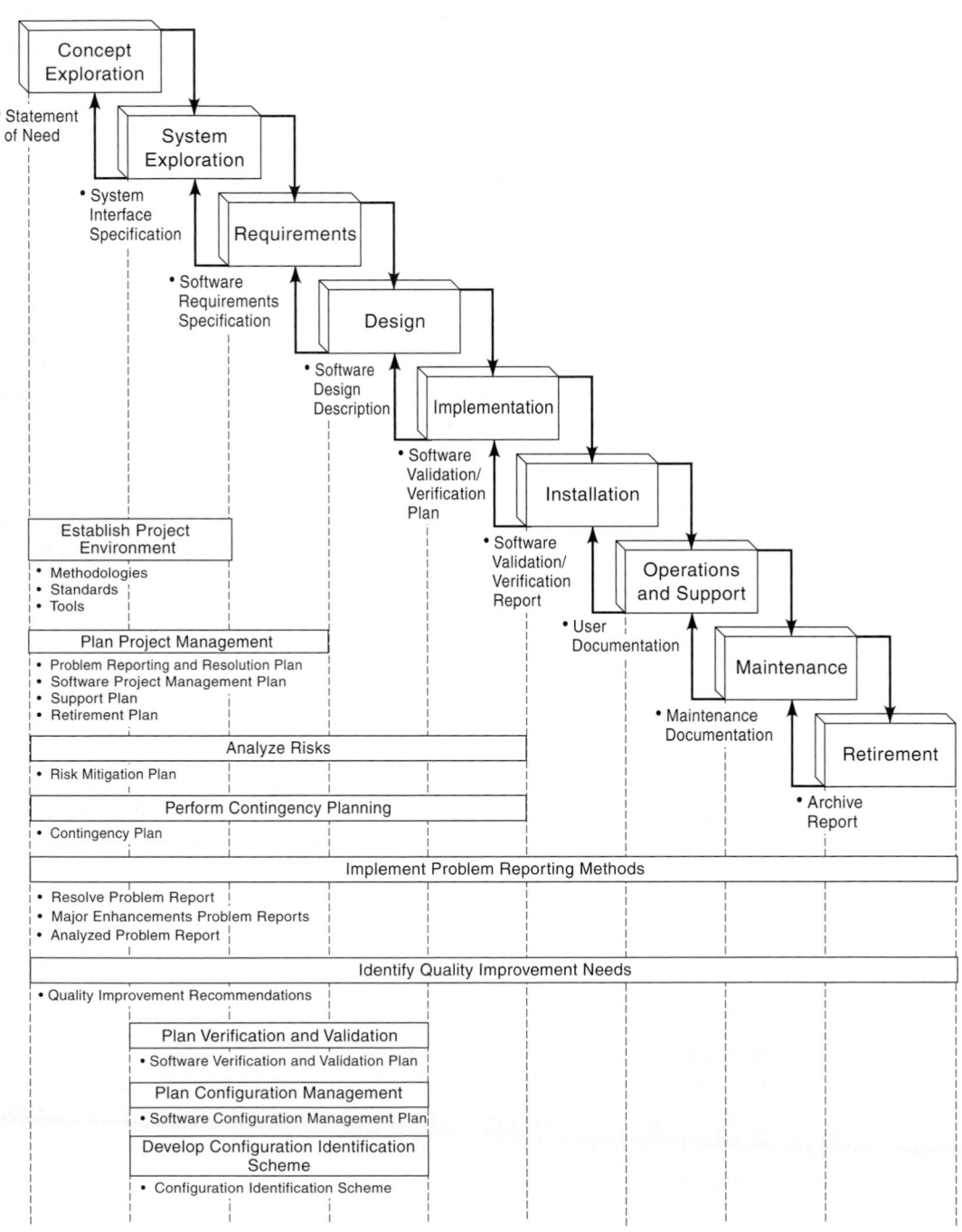

FIGURE D–2

Systems Engineering in the Product Development Life Cycle

Problem reporting and quality improvements are project management processes that occur throughout the product life cycle. Their contribution to the finished product is directly related to the ability to do an adequate systems analysis prior to completing the requirements analysis phase. Requirements engineering, as part of systems analysis, lays the groundwork for a quality improvement and problem feedback process.

The validation and verification plan is a direct result of the effort spent in requirements engineering. Validation answers the question of whether the correct system was built. The only way that question can be answered is from the system and software requirements. Verification answers the question of whether the software was built correctly. The selection of the correct tools, techniques, and methods occurs within the definition of the system and final product.

Configuration management and the identification of the configuration items to be managed must be done with respect to the total system. Looking at managing product deliverables cannot be isolated from the ultimate environment in which the product will operate. That must be defined up front in the life cycle using systems engineering.

The software is not the system. The software is a piece of the system.

Learning Objectives for Appendix D _____

Upon completion of this appendix, the reader should be able to:

- Define the goal of any computer-based system to assist in meeting an organizational goal or objective, to support a business goal, and/or to develop a product that is sold to generate business revenue;
- Define the general parts of a technology product that are more than software;
- Account for hardware, people, data, documentation, and procedures within the development life cycle;
- Define the up-front work that has to be done in systems engineering before the software requirements process can begin.

Classical Systems Engineering Model _____

Figure D–3 shows the classical hardware/software systems development model. Each of the five portions will be separately described. The flow through the model begins with developing an entire system requirements model. From there the system requirements are enhanced and a system architecture model defined with modules of the final system identified. At this point hardware and software partitioning occurs and separate hardware and software requirements models are defined.

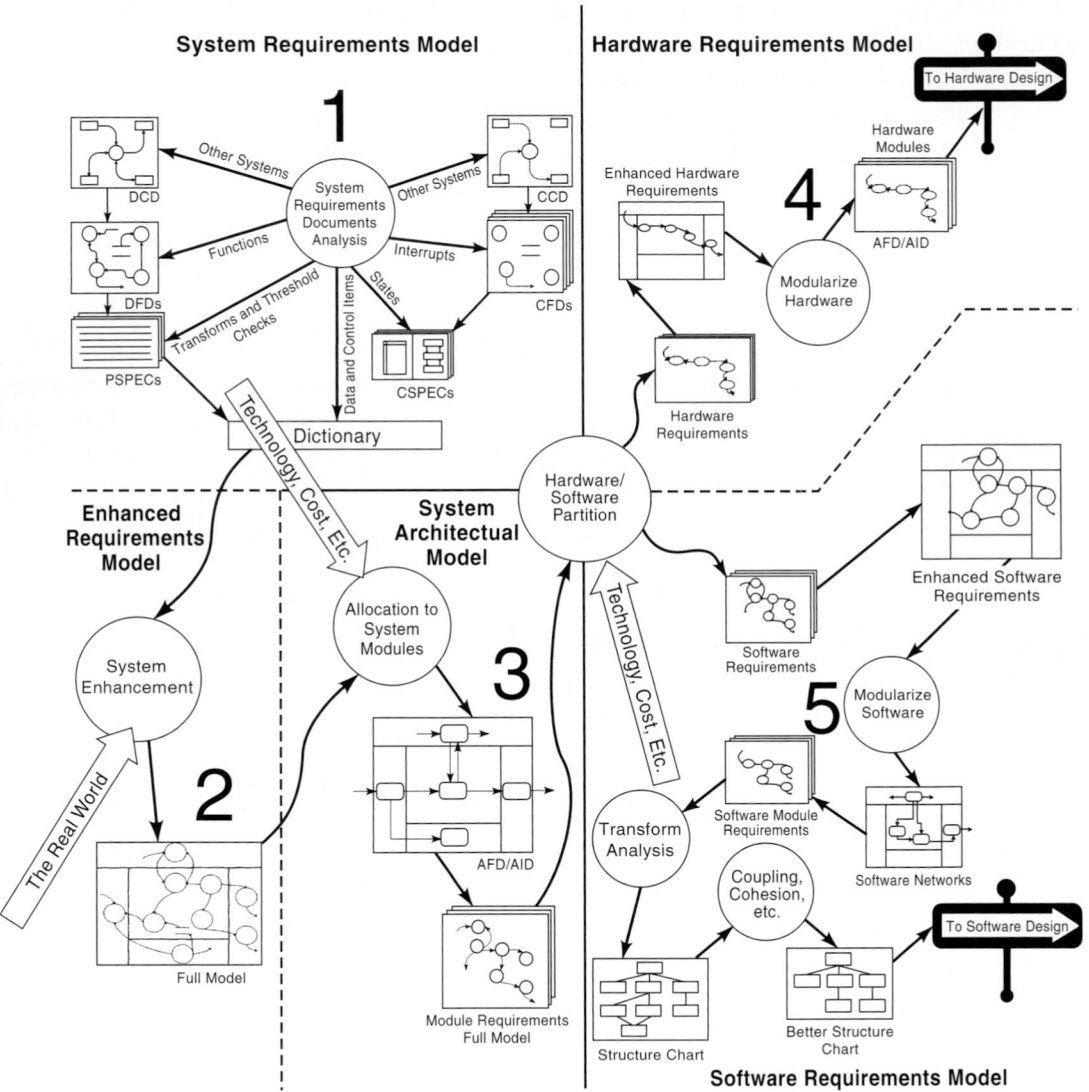

FIGURE D–3
Classical Systems Engineering Front-End Process Model

Having a systems engineering model of the problem domain is an absolute necessity for developing high technology products. The emphasis on requirements gathering and modeling is driven by the complexity of the products being developed and the multifaceted interfaces software must address. Getting the requirements right at the beginning of a project is the single greatest contributor to project success. Software development project managers must always consider moving up the systems engineering food chain to analyze the total system requirement before isolating the software. Figure D–3 is a model of the systems engineering process needed to get to the software partition of the problem.

Derek J. Hatley and the late Imtiaz A. Pirbhai wrote "Strategies for Real-Time System Specification" in 1988. This reference has complete descriptions of all the process and behavior modeling techniques of systems modeling. Developed to model real-time systems, the book contains full examples of the classical systems model for hardware and software systems.

System Requirements Model

Through using an integrated systems model, the system requirements are captured first. Figure D–4 shows the representation of this tri-state problem domain view. The problem domain for the system is analyzed from three aspects:

1. The process aspect takes the functional, information processing view of the problem domain.
2. The system state and control mechanisms are viewed from the behavior aspect.
3. The information modeling or data aspect is the third view of the system.

Figure D–5 shows the system requirements model components.

The information processing view is captured using traditional data flow diagrams and structured methods techniques. Decomposition of the data flows extends to developing process specifications (PSPECs) as the bottom of the requirements model. The behavioral portion is captured with control flow diagrams and a control analog to data flow. Control flow diagrams decompose into control specs (CSPECs) in which truth tables and finite state machines are modeled. This control flow part of the model is the view of how the system really looks to the outside world and user.

The data dimension in classical systems engineering was represented by the data dictionary as the repository of all information about the data and control flows. In systems that are data intensive, a system data model using entity-relationship diagrams should supplement this simple data dictionary.

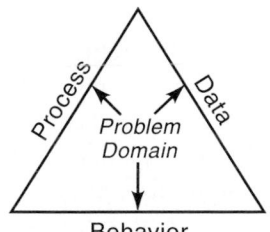

FIGURE D–4
Three Views of the Problem Domain

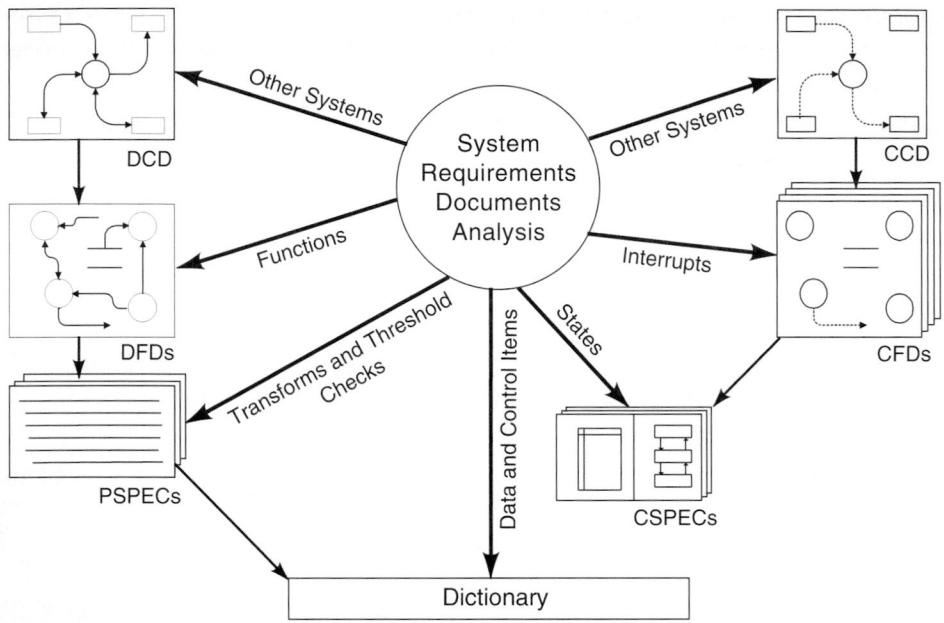

FIGURE D–5
Systems Requirements Model

Enhanced Requirements Model

Building the system requirements model uses all the techniques of analysis previously described in this practitioner's guide. There is a fine line between brainstorming that adds the "sun, moon, and stars" in the system requirements, and sticking to a narrow target market definition. The system requirements modeling should be wide open and collect as many requirements as possible. At the second stage, the process of system enhancement is applied to the system requirements model through the use of the architecture template. Using the template, an introduction of real-world constraints is introduced to the model. Figure D–6 shows the system enhancement of the requirements model.

Figure D–7 represents the architecture template applied in this stage. The systems requirements model is focused solely on the "what" to be developed. Application of the architecture template is the first application of "how" to the model. When the template is completely applied, the model shows the physical allocation of the requirements model's data and control processing flows into the physical entities that will perform the allocated tasks. The definition of the physical modules adds four more processing perspectives: input, output, user interface, and maintenance.

The input and output processing modules represent the additional processing needed beyond that specified in the requirements model. These additional requirements facilitate the

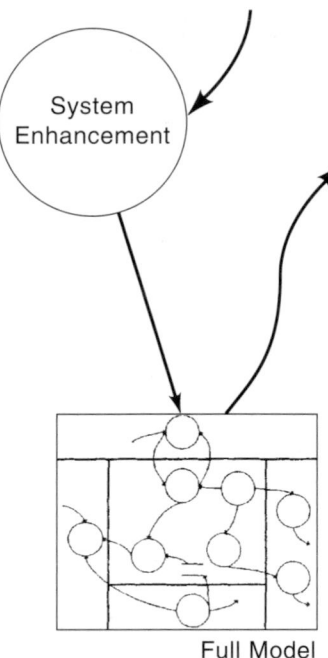

System
Enhancement

Full Model

FIGURE D–6
Enhanced Requirements Model

physical processing of data by getting it into the system and moving it out. For example, the requirements model may simply specify that "a wireless link will be provided to output maps to GSM enabled PDAs." This enhancement will show the WAP drivers necessary for GSM output and the SMS drivers needed for input request processing.

The user interface module is a special case of the input and output modules. It is separated because of graphic user interface, human factors, and final "look and feel" considerations. This is a system area that can suffer greatly from feature creep as users continuously redefine their needs. Prototypes are the most successfully used here to lock down user understanding of their system's interface.

The maintenance module contains the requirements for self-test, audit data collection, redundancy and integrity testing, and requirements for data shadowing and mirroring. The specification for processing concurrency and redundant computing would be addressed here.

The central processes module contains those processes taken directly from the requirements model. These are the targets of your enhancements. System enhancement and requirements modeling are iterative processes. As enhancement proceeds, more requirements will be uncovered, existing requirements dropped, and modifications made to the model based on architecture considerations. This is an extremely valuable exercise in early requirements validation.

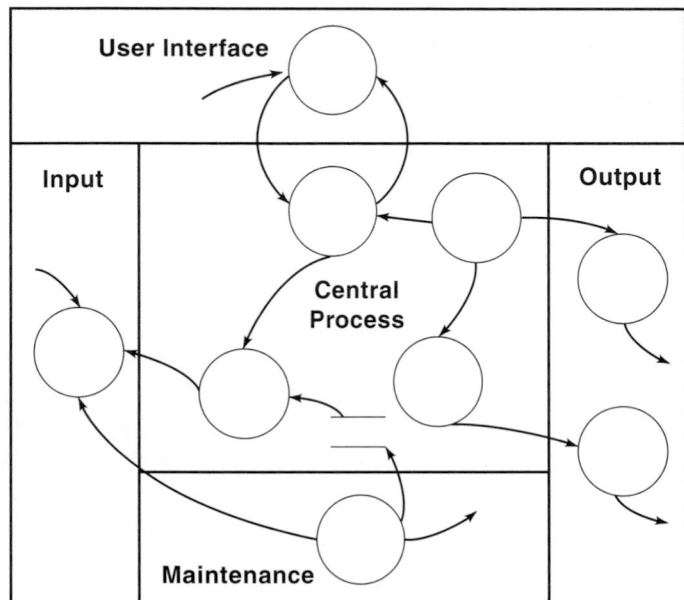

Enhancement Template

FIGURE D–7
Architecture Template

System Architecture Model

Figure D–8 represents the system architecture model as the enhanced requirements model is decomposed into architecture modules using the architecture template. An architecture module is either a basic process entity or a collection of processes into a grouped module. Then the basic entities are grouped, all processes, data and control flows, CSPECs and PSPECs, are grouped into a module. This restructuring is a further enhancement and recomposition of the modeled requirements.

After the grouping into architecture modules is complete, the modules are segregated into hardware and software modules. Investigating each architecture module and its constituent requirements to determine whether the function should be implemented in either hardware of software does this. A system requirement that states "provide touch screen selection input for menu items," has both hardware and software requirements. The hardware portion would describe the screen layout, how the "touch" was identified, the analog signal format before conversion to a digital signal, the physical "wire" connection, and data packet format sent to the data processor. The software components include how the data packets are interpreted, how the screen maps to the menu items, what controls are associated with each screen move, and when the item is selected.

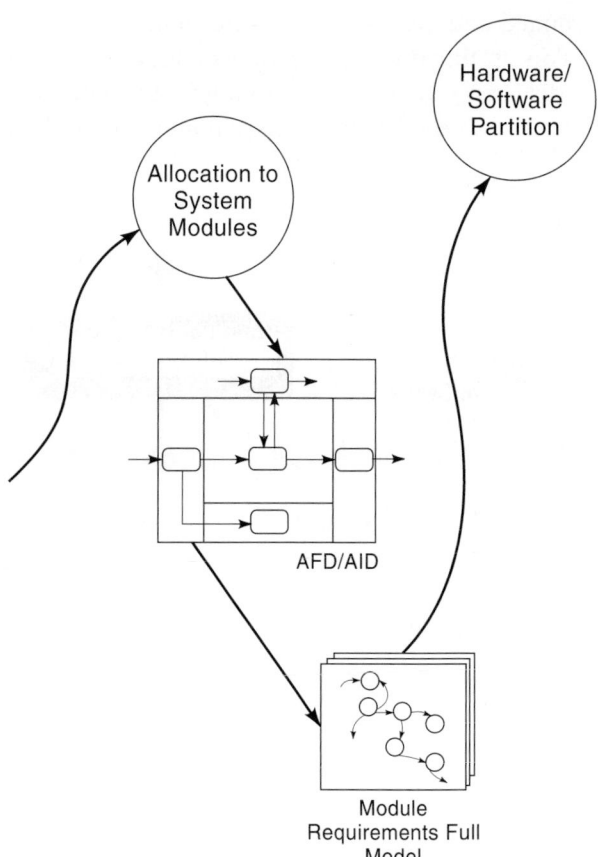

FIGURE D–8
System Architecture Model

Each module goes through this interrogation. It is still part of the iterative process of requirements definition. This portion of the systems model causes a great deal of change in the requirements model. Project managers must be familiar with doing hardware/software implementation trade studies. The economics of implementing functions in hardware versus software must be analyzed. There is also the issue of "firmware," software implemented in hardware. This is yet another dimension that may come out of the partitioning. If firmware is part of the product, the project manager must settle early the decision as to whether firmware is done by the software or hardware team.

Hardware Requirements Model

After hardware/software partitioning is completed, the hardware-focused part of the systems team takes over and further enhances the architecture modules allocated to hardware. Using the architecture template, the modules are arranged and evaluated to ensure all input, output, user interface, and maintenance modules. This is the final application of looking at the "what" of the system. The final architecture model is passed into the beginning for the hardware "how" definition, hardware design. Figure D–9 shows the hardware requirements model on its way to hardware design.

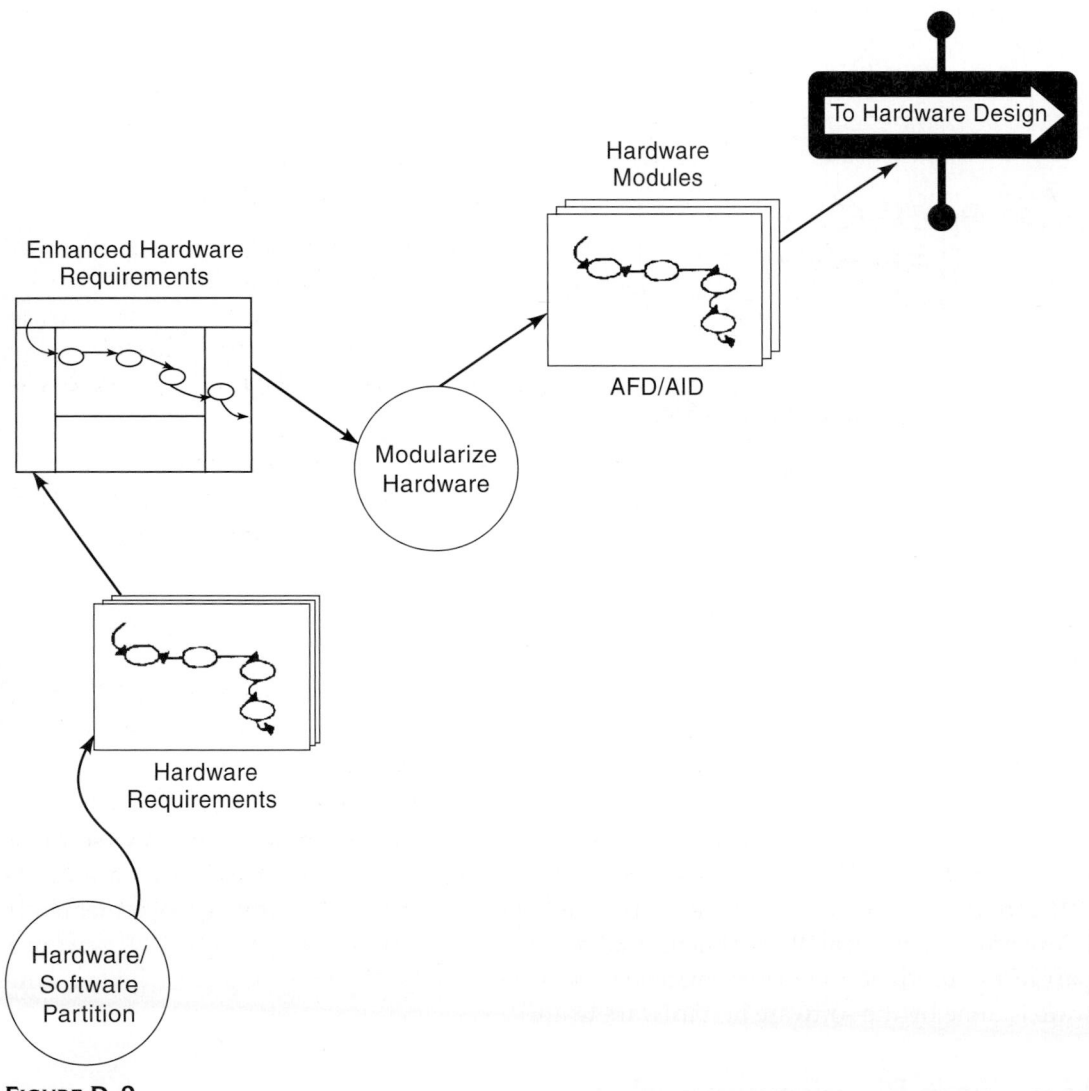

FIGURE D–9
Hardware Requirements Model

Software Requirements Model

The requirements passed along to the software-focused part of the systems team are all of the modules implemented in software. The team first takes the architecture modules and recomposes them back to the requirements model. This is necessary since the requirements model has been sliced and diced to get to the hardware/software partitioning. The job now is to rebuild the model as software-only requirements. Once the requirements model is complete, the architecture template is used to identify any further input, output, maintenance, and user interface requirements.

Once the software has been modularized back into an architecture model, transform analysis is done to convert the architecture modules into a structure chart. Transform analysis is a strategy for getting to the first cut structure chart. Meilir Page-Jones in *The Practical Guide to Structured Systems Design*, written in 1988, covers this strategy in its entirety in Section 10.2.

The last step in the "what" of the system's software requirements modeling is to refine the structure chart derived from transform analysis. Analyzing coupling, cohesion, and implied calling sequences does this. Coupling measures the degree of interdependence between modules. Low coupling is always the goal. Cohesion is the measure of how interrelated the functions grouped within a module are. High cohesion is desired. Figure D–10 shows the final enhanced software requirements model of software design.

Final looks at the structure chart should be used to determine if modules can be broken into smaller parts, and whether the implicit module-to-module communication can be minimized or abstracted away from specific modules. Once this is complete, the software requirements model is ready to be passed off to the software design team.

System Drivers

Once the initial system requirements model is completed, the system team must address the issues imposed by the "real world" as shown by the large, labeled arrows in Figure D–11. The first time this intrudes on the modeling effort is at requirements model enhancement. Application of the architecture template imposed the constraints of defining hard input, output, user interface, and maintenance requirements. The next occurrence of this imposition is at the allocation of system modules. Constraints of technology, cost, schedule, material availability, and personnel resources must be considered. The final hit in the system requirements model process is at hardware/software partitioning. Here the realities of what can be most economically implemented in either hardware or software is determined.

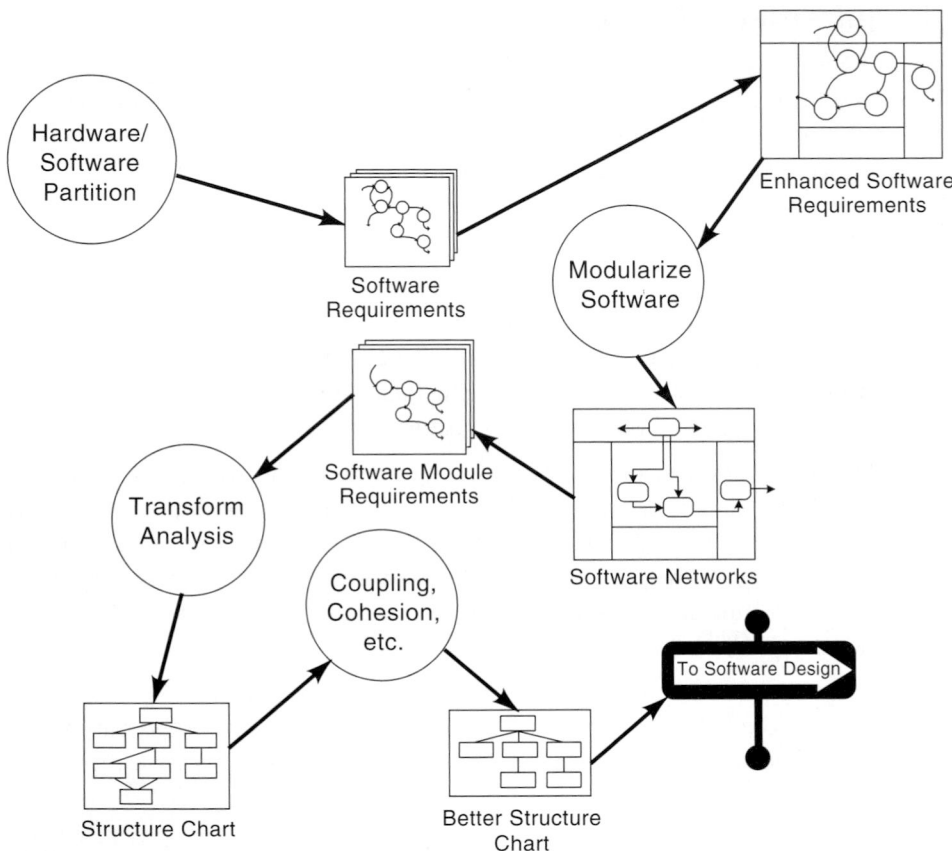

FIGURE D–10
Software Architecture Model

Requirements Engineering _____

Requirements engineering (RE) is one of the most important and yet least understood sub-disciplines of systems and software engineering. The major objective of the set of activities included in RE is defining the purpose of a proposed computer-based system and capturing its external behavior.

RE categories:

1. Requirements elicitation—the process of exploring, acquiring, and reifying user requirements through discussion with the problem owners, introspection, observation of the existing system, task analysis, and so on. Refer to Chapter 16 in this book.

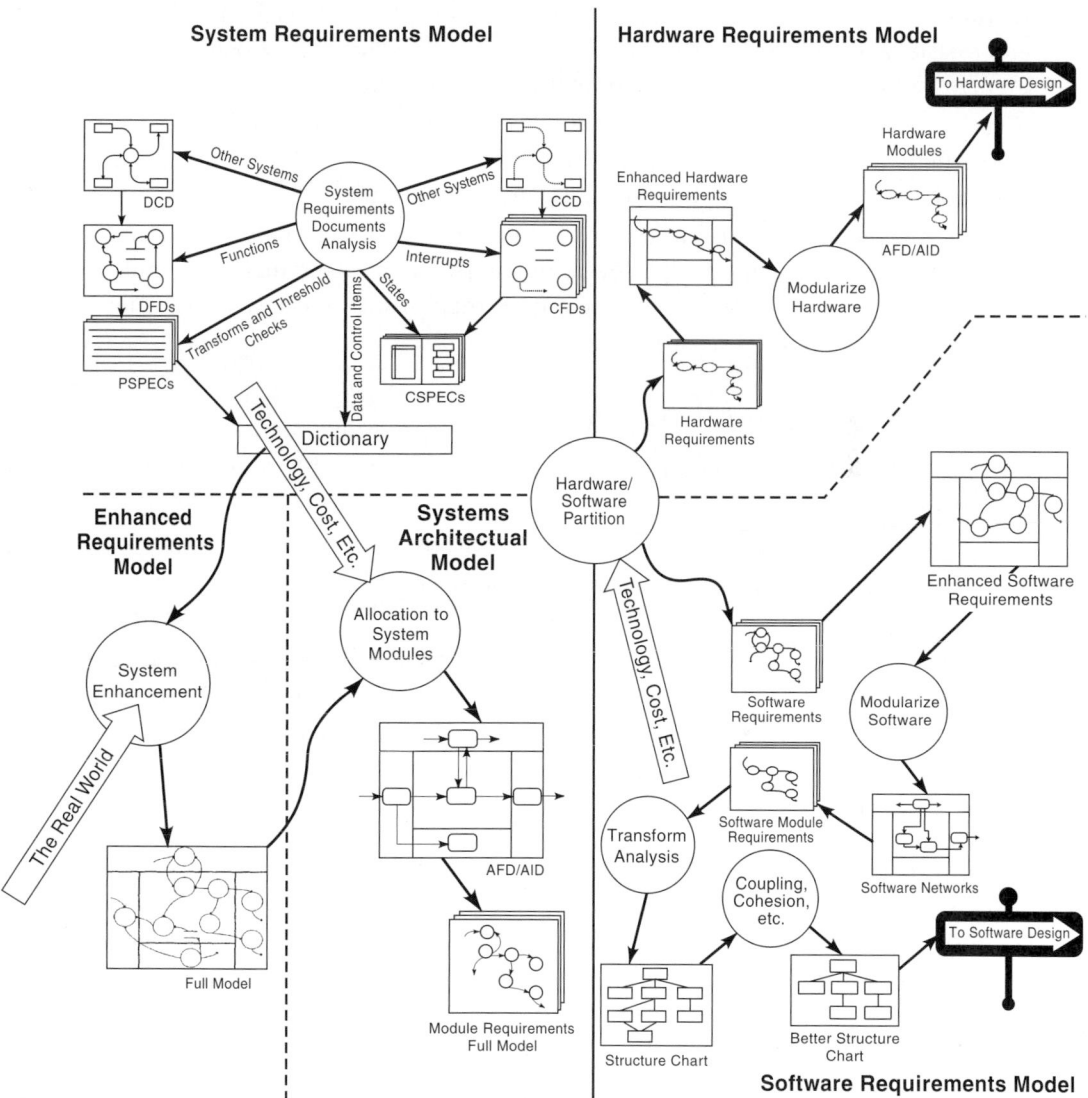

FIGURE D–11
System Model Drivers

2. Requirements modeling—alternative models for the target composite system are elaborated and a conceptual model of the enterprise as seen by the system's eventual users is produced. This model is meant to capture as much of the semantics of the real world as possible and is used as the foundation for an abstract description of the requirements. Refer to Chapter 22 of this book.

3. Requirements specification—various components of the models are precisely described and possibly formalized to act as a basis for contractual purposes between the problem owners and the developers. Refer to Chapter 17 of this book.

4. Requirements validation—specifications are evaluated and analyzed against correctness properties (such as completeness and consistency), and feasibility properties (such as cost and resources needed). Refer to Chapter 23 of this book.

5. Requirements management—a set of procedures that assists in maintaining the evolution of requirements throughout the development process. These include planning, traceability, impact assessment of changing requirements, and so on. Refer to Chapter 19 of this book.

Requirements Engineering Product

The final product of software requirements engineering is normally a document referred to as the software requirements specification (SRS).

This document must be internally consistent; consistent with the existing business practice documents; correct and complete in relation to the users' needs; clear to users, customers, designers, and testers; and capable of serving as a basis for both design and testing procedures.

The SRS, in addition, often acts as a legal document between the customers and the developers. Project managers utilize it for project planning and management. In many circumstances it is also used as the basis of the end-users manual or generally a document that the customers will use to understand how the delivered system fits together.

Types of Product Systems _____

Another valuable tool of systems engineering analysis is to define when the product being developed fits within various product systems. The first dimension to identify is the product domain type. In order to do that, the project team needs to define the type of product being developed. The product is either:

1. New hardware and software product—characterized by developing either new hardware, software, or both. This is a product that has *never* before been built.

2. Re-engineering existing product—the redesign and redevelopment of an existing product. Usually a software product, this may be done to move a successful software application to a new hardware platform.

3. Component integration—usually referred to as best-of-breed commercial-off-the-shelf product development. The prime goal of this product development is to take existing products and integrate them into a new product that meets an unmet market need.

4. Heroic maintenance—the reworking of an existing product without redesign to meet its current market. This is usually done to put a veneer of the "new" on an old product. An example is the tendency to put a "relational-like" front-end on old flat file based data management systems to make them appear technologically state-of-the-art. It is also known as "old dog, new collar."

The second dimension identifies to which of the six product system domains the product belongs:

1. Consumer—commercially available, shrink-wrapped products that can be easily purchased by anyone in the public. In technology products, these are cell phones, digital televisions, personal digital assistants, and pagers.

2. Business—products targeted at business-specific needs. Examples are powerful servers, storage networks, manufacturing execution system software, and customer resource management systems.

3. Industrial—products are ruggedized to work within a factory environment.

4. Real time—products that have critical timing budgets to meet. They can be data collection systems that must operate within nanoseconds of the onset of an occurrence, and operating systems that control multitasking operations like video teleconferencing.

5. Really timely—systems are like automatic teller machines. Users want responses in a short period of time but not against a critical time budget. Time is measured in seconds not nanoseconds.

6. Scientific—products that are used to measure, run, and collect data from scientific operations. These are usually laboratory equipment that measure fine tolerances and automatically collect data on the measurements.

Two projects will be used as examples. The first, represented by an "X" is a set of new software that will allow easy determination of a hiker's location imposed on an area map shown on a PDA. The second, represented by an "O" is a software program used to control scientific metrology equipment within a semiconductor fab. The control information needs to be stored for review along with all measurements taken. Figure D–12 represents the intersection of the product system domain on the X-axis and the product domain type on the Y-axis.

   The product domain type can now be identified. For the map on PDA product, this is identified as a really timely consumer product that includes new hardware/software product and component integration development. The reasoning is that hikers are consumers and their response to a map request needs to be served up in seconds. New software to serve up the maps and navigate on them must be written. GPS hardware to PDA interfaces may have to be built. The component integration is with existing PDA, GPS hardware, and existing map databases.

1. Identify the product domain type	Consumer	Business	Industrial	Real-Time	Really Timely	Scientific
New hardware/software product	X	O	O	O	X	O
Re-engineering existing product		O	O	O		O
Component integration	X				X	
Heroic maintenance						

FIGURE D–12
Product Domain Type

The metrology product has business, industrial, real-time, and scientific attributes, while the development is in new hardware/software and the re-engineering of existing products. The reason for the four domains is that the product will be bought by businesses, installed in a factory, require data collection at sub-millisecond speeds, and operate scientific test equipment. New software has to be built but existing semiconductor fab data collection and equipment control software must be re-engineered to accept the new equipment.

The final dimension is the system component categories:

1. Software—those instructions run on hardware that cause the system to function in the manner defined in the requirements.
2. Hardware—the equipment hosting the software and interfacing with the end-user.
3. People—human resources required to support the product.
4. Database—the tools used to store and manipulate the data required for the product.
5. Documentation—the information on how to make the system function by the end-user.
6. Procedures—the rules on how the system functions internally that are configurable by the end-user.

Having this third dimension, the critical product components can be identified. This matrix, Figure D–13, shows the product intersections of the component categories with the type of product.

2. Identify Critical Product Components	Software	Hardware	People	Database	Documentation	Procedures
New hardware/software product	X O		O	O	X O	O
Re-engineering existing product	X		O	O	O	O
Component integration	X				X	
Heroic maintenance						

FIGURE D–13
Critical Product Components

The PDA for hikers requires software and documentation for both the new software and the components being integrated. This matrix shows that no new hardware is to be developed.

The metrology equipment requires new software and ongoing people, database, documentation, and configurable business rules. Component integration within the factory is done with software and documentation.

Finally, the product domains are linked with the components in Figure D–14. This matrix now shows what domains need which components. For the PDA product, the consumer gets software and documentation for a really timely product. The factory gets industrial business, real time, scientific software with people support, a database, documentation, and configurable business rules.

Combined with system requirements modeling, these matrices provide a high-level look at the product to be developed. As a first step, these matrices help to complete the requirements gathering. They also help to communicate the product characteristics to marketing and customer representatives.

3. Link Product Domains with Components	Software	Hardware	People	Database	Documentation	Procedures
Consumer	X				X	
Business	O		O	O	O	O
Industrial	O		O	O	O	O
Real-Time	O		O	O	O	O
Really Timely	X				X	
Scientific	O		O	O	O	O

FIGURE D–14
Product Domains Linked to Components

Problems for Review _____

1. How much effort would be involved in building a systems requirements model for the Chinese Railway case study? Would the investment be worth it? Please explain your answer.
2. How does requirements engineering differ from object-oriented requirements analysis?
3. Build a set of three product system matrices for the Chinese Railway case study.

Visit the Case Study

Dr. Weng Wei has been named the interface for transportation technology between the CRM and the People's Liberation Army (PLA) Ground Forces. Dr. Wei is a Stanford doctoral graduate in electrical engineering and one of the original developers of PalmOS. China has a massive land territory and the only mode of transporting large numbers of troops and material to the borders is via rail. The old method was to commandeer whole trains for the military. This does not play well in the "kinder and gentler," post-Tianamen People's Republic. Dr. Wei wants you to slightly modify your second prototype in order to meet these simple requirements:

1. Each company commander will have a wireless, personal digital assistant supplied by the CRM.

2. The commander will be able to reserve slots for the entire company and all of its equipment on a regularly scheduled train. A company in the PLA has 500 troops and enough equipment for two freight cars.

3. It is possible to break the company into its five individual platoons and each one of them can go in a separate train. If that is the case, the two freight cars must go with the headquarters and heavy weapons platoon.

4. The company commander also wants a map of all military bases along the train route downloaded to the PDA.

References

Hatley, Derek J., and Imtiaz A. Pirbhai (1988). *Strategies for Real-Time System Specification*. Dorset House Publishing.

Page-Jones, Meilir (1988). *The Practical Guide to Structured Systems Design*. Prentice Hall.

Web Pages for Further Information

www.acq-ref.navy.mil/turbo2/index_ie.html. Turbo Streamliner is a repository of acquisition definitions, principles, best practices, lessons learned, references, sample contractual language, and related Web sites. This tool is organized by acquisition functional areas and associated Request for Proposal (RFP) elements. The purpose of Turbo Streamliner is to assist the acquisition community in applying acquisition reform (AR) principles, concepts, and techniques to acquiring and sustaining Department of the Navy war-fighting capabilities for new requirements and re-procurements.

www.incose.org/. The International Council on Systems Engineering is a not-for-profit membership organization founded in 1990. INCOSE is an international authoritative body promoting the application of an interdisciplinary approach and means to enable the realization of successful systems.

www.seas.smu.edu/disted/sys/r.html. Southern Methodist University School of Engineering Systems Engineering Resource Sites.

www.w3.org. The World Wide Web Consortium (W3C) develops interoperable technologies (specifications, guidelines, software, and tools) to lead the Web to its full potential as a forum for information, commerce, communication, and collective understanding.

Tools

www.stgcase.com/. AxiomSys is a complete, user-friendly implementation of the Structured Analysis method, including the Hatley-Pirbhai Real-Time extensions. It also includes the Hatley-Pirbhai Architecture modeling capabilities. AxiomSys is uniquely suited to both software and systems requirements modeling.

www.turbocase.com/. TurboCASE/Sys for Windows is the first tool to fully automate the system requirements and architecture methods developed by Derek Hatley and the late Imtiaz Pirbhai, including the latest advances in the methods. Other tools have provided some support, most of them partially covering the requirements method only. TurboCASE/Sys fully supports both methods.

Distance Project Management

All of the tools, techniques, and methods presented in this practitioner's handbook are applicable to managing distant projects. This appendix will look specifically at managing projects with dispersed teams. Project teams do not have to be many time zones away from each other; they can be in different buildings in the same campus. The critical piece of dispersed projects is communication. Perhaps most famous was the study by T.J. Allen, who demonstrated that the probability of two people communicating in an organization is a decreasing hyperbolic function of the separation distance.[1] It rapidly decreases to where at 12 meters the chance for a once a week communication is only 5 percent. Figure E–1 shows the results of these studies as they indicate the importance of spatial arrangements of information in a face-to-face context.

Distance project management is more important today because of the virtual nature of project teams. Mergers, acquisitions, downsizing, outsourcing, and telecommuting have made virtual teams both possible and part of the project management landscape. A virtual project team consists of geographically separated team members, skewed working hours, and temporary/matrix reporting structures. The critical issues that must be addressed are

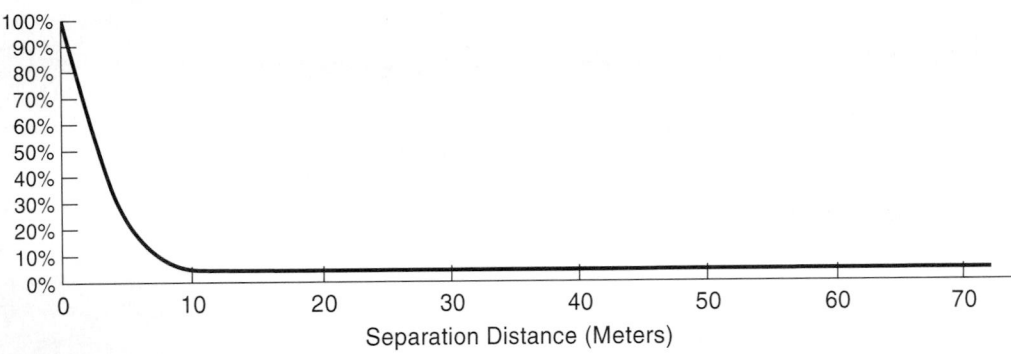

FIGURE E–1
Percent Probability of Weekly Communication Versus Separation Distance

facilities and frequency of communication versus distance apart; infrastructure differences, managers' versus members' views, infrastructure control, and the inherent cultural variation.

Just one warning on the economics of distance project management: Going offshore is *not* less expensive than developing the product within the project corporate sponsor's own country. The only reason to go offshore for product development is if the project cannot get the resources any other way. Experience has shown that the cost of a programmer in Bangalore, Tianjin, Novosibirsk, Bucharest, or Budapest is equal to the cost of a United States programmer. Once travel, infrastructure, and customs are put into the equation, the offshore programmer is an expensive commodity.

Where We Are in the Product Development Life Cycle _____

As Figure E–2 shows, distance project management affects all phases and activities of the project development life cycle.

Distance impacts the establishment of the project environment and the development of the initial project plan. All of the environmental issues of development platform, ultimate end-user identification, channels of distribution, and total product definition are exacerbated by distance and time.

Distance frames risk analysis and contingency planning. Complete risk identification cannot occur in isolation but must extend across all project resources and locations. Contingency plans cannot be made without an understanding of all the spatial impacts on the final product.

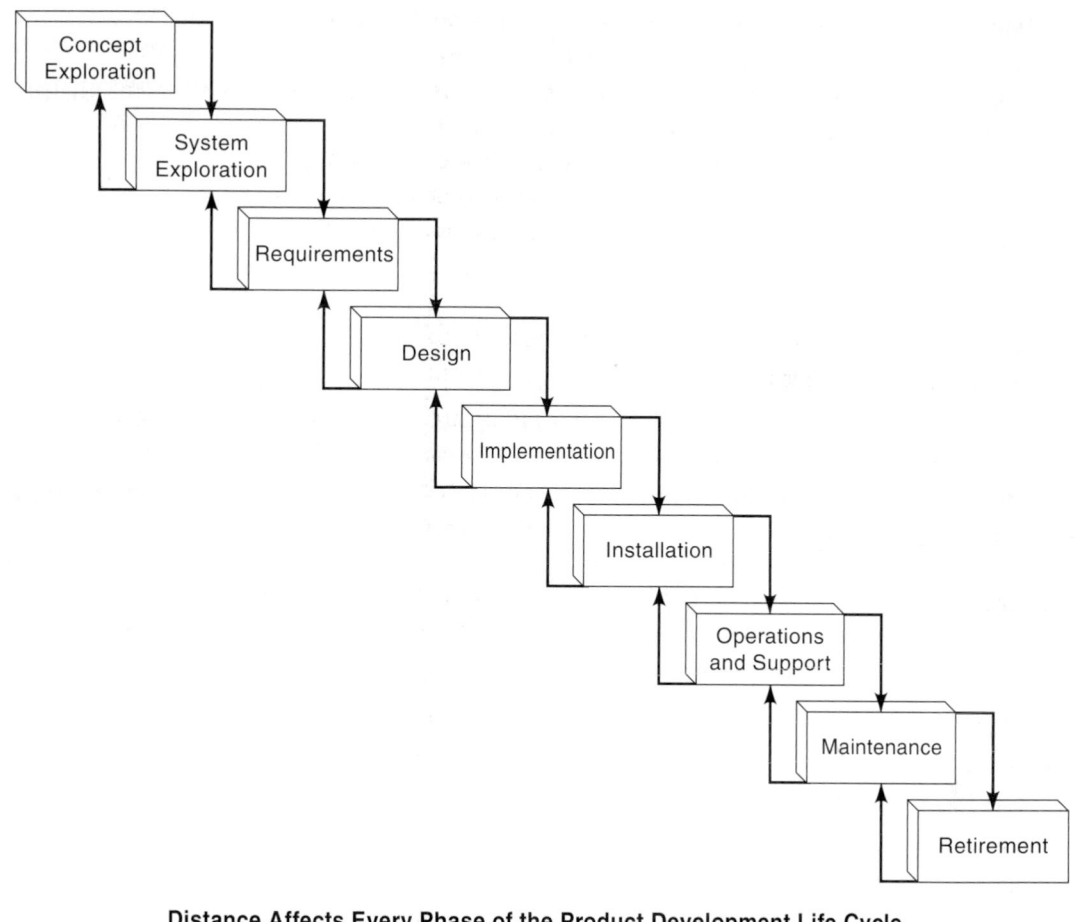

Distance Affects Every Phase of the Product Development Life Cycle

FIGURE E–2

Distance Project Management Can Occur Throughout the Project Development Life Cycle

Problem reporting and quality improvements are project management processes that occur throughout the product life cycle. Their contribution to the finished product is directly related to the ability to adequately communicate through all phases.

Learning Objectives for Appendix E _____

Upon completion of this appendix, the reader should be able to:

• Describe the critical difference between collocated and distributed project teams;

- Define the inherent communication issues of contact frequency versus distance for any project;
- Account for hardware, people, data, documentation, and procedures within the distributed project development life cycle;
- Calculate the number of communication base paths based on the number of communication nodes on a distributed project.

Managing Distance Projects—Communications _____

The techniques to improve success with virtual teams revolve around the two basic areas of communications and team building. The first understanding with communications is that distance reverses the control aspect of communications. Figure E–3 shows the differences. During all the traditional training of managers and presenters the mantra has always been that communication resides in the receiver. Presenters must constantly test for verbal and non-verbal signals that their message is being received and understood by the receiver. For face-to-face communications, this is the model. For distance communication where the transmission medium may be email, teleconference, chat, or a slow video link, the control resides in the sender. The sender has all the control of the message and does not have the clues to the receiver.

For a project manager, this is a critical concept to understand. Peter Drucker said: "One's effectiveness is determined by one's ability to reach others through the spoken or written word ... perhaps the most important of skills." Project managers spend roughly 75 percent of

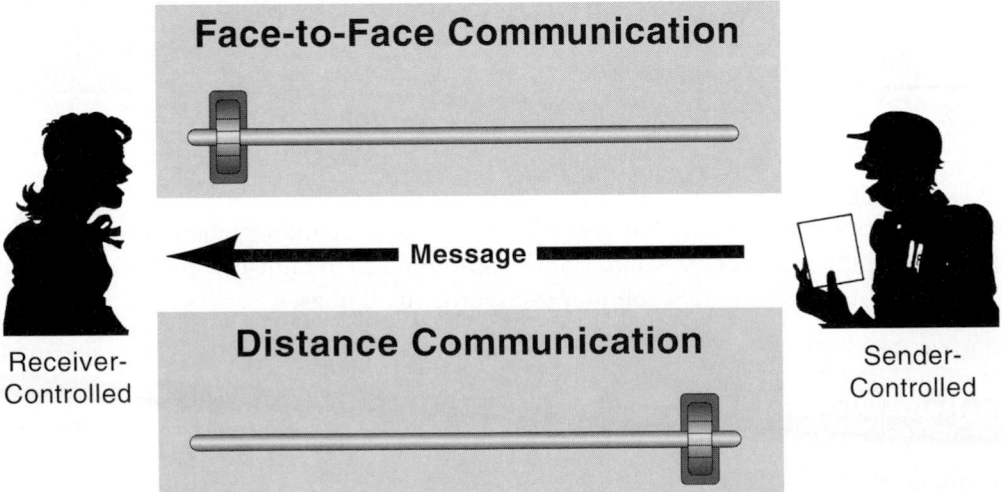

FIGURE E–3
Control Level Comparison

their time communicating as shown in Figure E–4. The ratio remains the same for distance projects but the absolute amount of time increases. Project management is never an eight-hour-a-day job. With projects executing 24 hours a day across 16 time zones, project managers must decide carefully when they sleep.

Understanding the project manager's communication type along with that of all the other project members is vitally important. For distance communication this is an absolute necessity. Remember, the project manager does not have the face-to-face control model from which to work, but the sender-controlled distance model. Figure E–5 shows the communication types encountered.

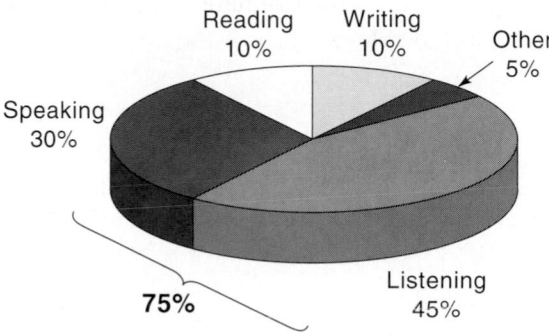

FIGURE E–4
Distribution of Project Management Time

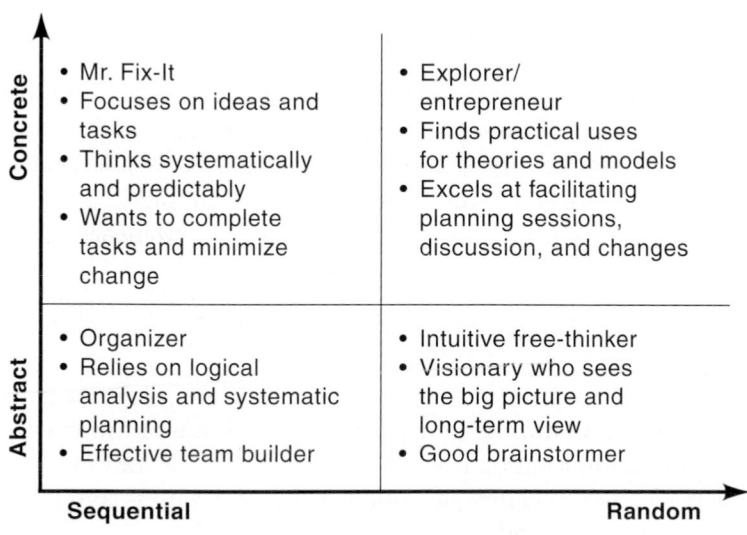

	Concrete	
Concrete	• Mr. Fix-It • Focuses on ideas and tasks • Thinks systematically and predictably • Wants to complete tasks and minimize change	• Explorer/ entrepreneur • Finds practical uses for theories and models • Excels at facilitating planning sessions, discussion, and changes
Abstract	• Organizer • Relies on logical analysis and systematic planning • Effective team builder	• Intuitive free-thinker • Visionary who sees the big picture and long-term view • Good brainstormer
	Sequential	**Random**

FIGURE E–5
Communication Styles

Communication styles fall into four quadrants defined by an abstract–concrete X-axis and a sequential–random Y-axis. The project manager needs to place him or herself in their style continuum and then understand where the remainder of the team falls. The message to the project manager is to not try to use abstract-random communication techniques with the Indian design team when their communication style is concrete-sequential.

Channels of communication increase dramatically with more people involved in the project. Multiplying the number of people in the team by that number minus one and dividing the result by two, calculates the number of communication paths. Therefore, if a project has fifteen people on the team the calculation would be 15 multiplied by 14 and the result, 210, divided by 2. This results in 105 base communication paths in the project person network. Box E–1 shows the formula and calculation. Figure E–6 shows the dramatic increase in communication paths as the number of people on the team increases.

Box E–1
Base Communication Path Formula and Calculation

Let P equal the number of people on the team, and let C equal the number of communication paths, then:

$$(P \times (P–1)) / 2 = C$$

If there are 15 team members, then:

$$(15 \times (15–1)) / 2 = 105$$

The project manager is the formal and informal spokesperson for the project. She must communicate with all stakeholders including subordinates, peers, managers, and clients. Communications management is applying the concepts of communicating to specific project needs and may be incorporated into a formal communications management plan. The communication management plan should be done early in the project life cycle and incorporated into the overall project management plan.

Communicating principles that must be addressed in the communications plan for distance project management are:

1. Synchronous versus asynchronous communication—both the time and order of communications changes with distance and multiple time zones. Most communication ends up being asynchronous and not all information is known at each interface point because of the absence of team members. These synchronous points for asynchronous communications must be defined and well understood.

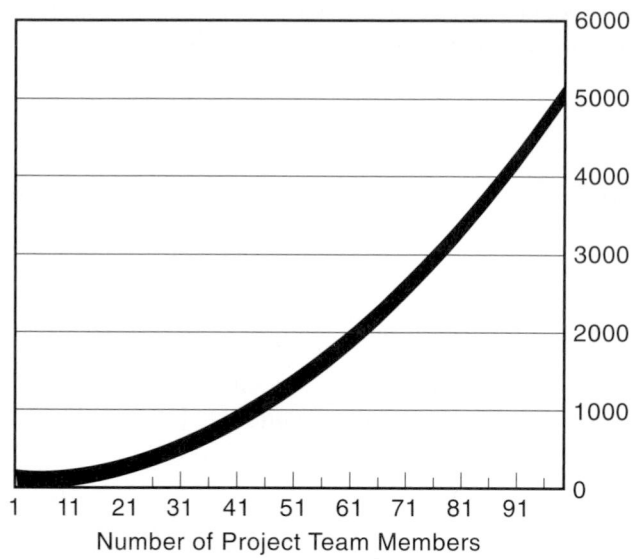

FIGURE E–6
Number of Possible Communication Paths

2. Published availability standards—the time and protocols for communication must be available to all participants. Basic problems of line speed mismatches, server availability, database backup scheduling and repository mirroring must be avoided during the "work day" of each distributed organization.

3. Replacements for lost contexts—addressing the method and medium for replacing the information lost because only three of the eight organizations could participate with full video, and the other five only had audio communications. The lost context of the visual portion of the online meeting must be replaced for those attendees who did not have it available.

4. Responsibility for prioritization—the formal methods for deciding how and who gets diminished communication bandwidth due to communication system problems. This must be understood so that one organization doesn't feel like the technology stepchild when they only have audio connections—or worse, only email.

The communications plan would also address applying these principles to available tools. For email tools, priorities, filters, correct channels, and delays would be defined. Videoconferencing would identify the use of desktop versus studio for meetings and reviews. This is an important distinction because the bandwidth use for a desktop videoconferencing system can adversely impact overall team productivity. The use of document conferencing with whiteboards, discussion groups, and chats needs to be defined, and the project tools identified with necessary installation and use of help files. Finally, the use of basic teleconferencing with telephones or Voice over Internet Protocol (VoIP) needs to be defined. As with desktop videoconferencing, VoIP can adversely impact the overall project productivity by absorbing an inappropriate amount of bandwidth.

Managing Distance Projects— Remote Teambuilding

Creating a shared vision and building team identity are the two main tasks for the project manager in assembling a remote team. Many projects with collocated teams have trouble enumerating the project vision. Where communication is an issue, a shared vision and identity are critical. This is a "leadership" issue for the project manager and has been covered in detail previously in this book.

Selecting team members for remote teams must take into account where the team member is located, a clear definition of the member's role and responsibilities, and the span of influence. Key attributes for remote team members are ability to travel, and flexibility in working hours. Conference calls occur at 7 a.m. and 10 p.m. in the member's home time zone. Project and client meetings can occur half a world away. Being facile with tools is important, but being able to communicate is essential.

Rewarding team members remotely is fraught with cultural and economic overtones. For some remote teams, the ability to travel outside of their home countries is enough of a reward. For others, getting to use state-of-the-art hardware and software is sufficient. In all cases, timely recognition of positive performance and good communication skills is at the top of the reward structure.

Creating the project support infrastructure for the distance team is vital to the project's success. Putting in place an infrastructure that supports planning, analysis, configuration management, risk identification, problem resolution, and issue tracking is vital to the distance project execution. All of the support processes a mature project organization has in place, as previously described in this guide, are absolutely essential on a distributed project team.

Questions that a project manager must answer concerning the remote team are:

1. What is the maturity level of the entire team?
2. How do I know they are really working?
3. How do I know they are working on the right things?
4. How do we estimate distance projects?
5. What can be done to improve task visibility?
6. What can be done for mentoring and training remotely?
7. How are best of breed practices shared?

8. What can be done to fairly partition work?

9. What is the project process for handling time delays?

10. How are deliverables transferred?

This appendix discusses the framework to answer these questions, as does the entire practitioner's guide. There are no cookbook answers here for the project manager. As every project team is different, every distance project team is different on steroids! The project manager needs to answer these questions in the project and communication plans for the overall project.

Managing Distance Projects—Tools

As has been discussed in Chapter 24, "Use of Tools," project managers use two drivers in the use of tools: the life cycle, and the model for process improvement. With distance project management these two drivers take on added importance. Guidelines for supporting tool selection must take into account the technologies of:

- Networking basics and remote access—bandwidth, LANs, WANs, ISDN, xDSL, Frame Relay, Cable Modem, wireless, and so on

- Security and privacy issues—dial back, PAP, CHAP, RADIUS, security cards, firewalls, information handling

- Telecommuting—implementing a program, legal and policy issues, home offices, zoning, reimbursement, and so on

- Teleconferencing—NetMeeting, CU-SeeMe, renting a studio

The spectrums of tools that can assist in distance project management are document collaboration, personal communication, schedulers, and resource planners. Important tool characteristics for virtual team management are:

- Technology base—Web versus proprietary, platforms, database requirements, and so on

- Security—project data inside/outside firewall

- Maturity fit—simple versus Swiss army knife

- Cost—purchase versus ASP, number of seats, number of MBs, and so on

- Vendor—new versus established

There is no silver bullet in tools for distance project management. The references to this appendix list a few to evaluate. One of the most important for a project manager is a simple time zone calculator. The project manager needs to be able to know the time at each of the remote project sites. This is just as important when the project manager is at the home site as when traveling to distance project centers.

A Case in Point—Quorus™

Quorus™ was a video-teleconferencing hardware and software system project done by Motorola in the mid-1990s. Two of the authors of this guide had direct experience on the project. Figure E–7 shows a map of how the project pieces fit together. Here are the major project pieces:

The client was in Martlesham Heath, Suffolk, Great Britain.

The Motorola corporate owner was in Austin, Texas.

The project manager was in the Motorola Corporate Research Laboratories, Schaumberg, Illinois.

The system architect was in Aylesbury, Great Britain.

The software and system managers were in Austin, Texas.

The hardware was done in five locations: Tel Aviv, Israel; Toulouse, France; Martlesham Heath, Great Britain; Schaumberg, Illinois; and Austin, Texas.

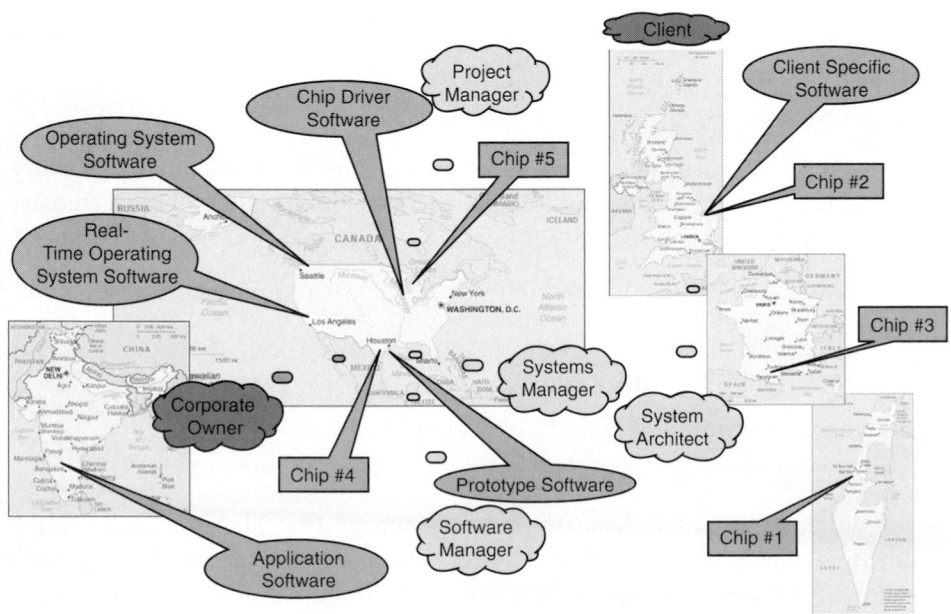

FIGURE E–7
Quorus™ Project Topology

The software operating systems were done in Redmond, Washington, and Santa Barbara, California.

The hardware driver level software was done in Schaumberg, Illinois.

The client specific software was done in Martlesham Heath, Great Britain.

The prototype software and hardware was done in Austin, Texas.

The application software was done in Bangalore, India.

There were 17 distributed project sites and functions for Quorus™. Just communication among the major players caused $(17 \times (17-1))/2$, or 136 base communication paths. Add to that the fact that in a time dimension the project was 12 time zones wide as shown in Figure E–8.

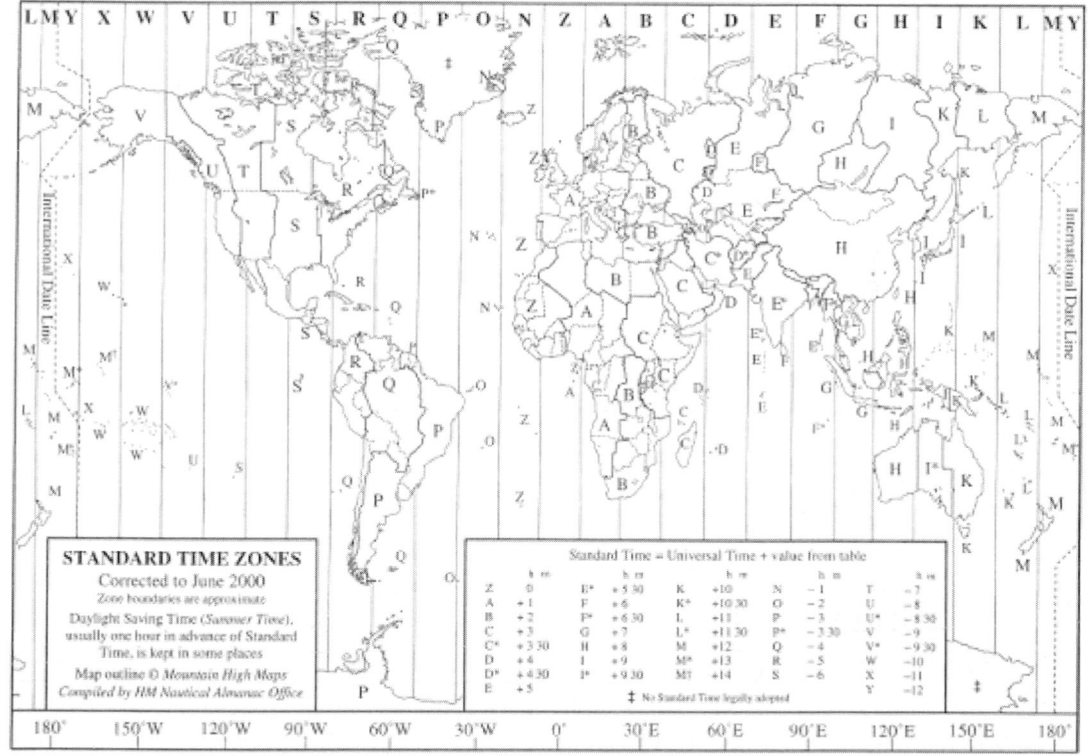

FIGURE E–8

Time Zone Map of the World

Source: *aa.usno.navy.mil/faq/docs/world_tzones.html*. World Time Zones Web Page from the U.S. Naval Observatory, 2001.

As an entire case study, this project would easily consume an entire book. The bottom line on Quorus™ was that the system was never delivered. Parts of the software and a few of the semiconductor chips were completed, delivered, and sold for revenue. Based on 20/20 hindsight, the project failed because there never was a shared vision among all the project sites, and there was no "burning platform" for success. The corporate owner had no threat of adverse career impact due to project failure.

The tools that worked on the project were:

- Email;
- Teleconferencing;
- Face-to-face meetings;
- Minimal project management tool;
- Development life cycle;
- Documentation.

The one tool used that didn't work was the same one the project was attempting to build: video-teleconferencing. The studio versions were incompatible from site to site. There was never enough bandwidth for effective use and the underlying software was not robust. Person-days of managers' time were wasted at each two-hour weekly meeting.

The lessons learned from Quorus™ were:

- No project can survive without a shared vision.
- People cannot "over"-communicate.
- There is no replacement for face-to-face meetings.
- Hardware cannot drive the project.
- Systems engineering must trump the corporate "owner."
- Politics can kill any project.
- Software can be delivered ahead of schedule.
- Software development costs at least 10 times as much as hardware development.

Ten Commandments of Managing a Remote Project Team

The following ten commandments of distance project management sum up the information presented in this appendix. These commandments are based on the authors' experience in managing remote teams in Southeast Asia, India, Russia, Australia, China, Japan, France, Germany, Great Britain, and from coast to coast in the United States. They are simple, intuitive, and do not require any sophisticated tools.

1. The project team must meet, face to face, to get consensus on how the project will be run at a formal project kick-off meeting.
2. The project team must repeat the kick-off face-to-face every time a new remote site becomes part of the project.
3. The project must have an all-hands, face-to-face meeting once a year.
4. The project must have key stakeholders meet face-to-face every calendar quarter.
5. The project must rotate the quarterly face-to-face meeting among all the sites.
6. The project team must have the customer present at all project meetings—*not* just marketing!
7. The project manager must ensure that individual teams have a minimum of weekly status meetings.
8. The project must have a project Web site with all project documentation available for downloading.
9. The project manager must communicate project status early and often.
10. When in doubt, see Commandment 9.

Problems for Review

1. Look at the Chinese Railway Reservation System case study and calculate the number of base communication paths for the distance development sites of your solution. Calculate the number of base paths including all team members.
2. What is an appropriate set of tools for distance project management in your present work environment?
3. How would you incorporate distance project management in one of your existing projects?
4. Determine the return on investment for outsourcing the development of the wireless application protocol software driver stack of your new product to a development group in Budapest. Do the ROI for the same project with the development group in Hanoi.

Visit the Case Study

The Chinese Railway Ministry has for years worked with bordering countries like Vietnam (see the map in Figure E–9) to ensure that railway passengers and freight could travel from country to country without having to change railway stock. Improvements have been made to the Nanjing-Hanoi main line with additional work done to Vinh, Hue, Da Nang, and into Ho Chi Minh City. The Railway Ministry has gone as far as investing in high technology firms in Hanoi. One of them, Glorious Revolution Analysis Software Systems (GRASS), has experience in developing scheduling algorithms for the Vietnamese National Airlines. Mr. Lu's distant cousin, Dr. Giap, runs GRASS and has assured him that the programmers will be top class and will develop the code faster than the Ministry personnel. Because of budget considerations and considerations between governments, you will need to incorporate GRASS into your development plans for ARRS.

FIGURE E–9
Map of Vietnam
Source: *www.odci.gov/cia/publications/factbook/index.html*. 2001, The World Fact Book, CIA.

Citations

[1]Allen, T.J. (1977). *Managing the Flow of Technology.* Cambridge, MA: MIT Press.

Web Pages for Further Information

web.mit.edu/icrmot/. The International Center for Research on the Management of Technology.
www.fek.umu.se/irnop/projweb.html#top. WWW Guide to Project Management Research Sites.
www.infogoal.com/pmc/pmchome.htm. The Project Management Center.

Distance Project Management Tools

iatek.com/WebPM/default.asp. ProjectLab.
timezone50.homepage.com/index.html. Time Zone Calculator.
www.microsoft.com/Office/Project/PRK/2000/Six/70ct.htm. MS Project Central: Collaborative.

Planning Tool for MS Project2000 Users

www.eproject.com. eProject.
www.eroom.com. eRoom: Virtual Team Collaboration Tools.
www.inventx.com. InventX: Web-based Enterprise Project Management.

Project Artifact Templates

This appendix presents the starting templates for a set of software development project artifacts and those templates customized for a single project. All the templates are derived from one of the IEEE standards cited. The IEEE, PMI, and SEI have done an enormous amount of work to provide software project managers with starting points for documenting their projects. No plans have been presented in this practitioner's guide that do not have a base template originally built by one of these organizations. The project manager's goal has to be to turn out the best possible product within the budget provided. Reuse of previous work is an admirable trait in project managers. None need "reinvent the wheel" when it comes to document templates. The templates used are from these chapters:

- Software project management plan—Chapter 7
- Software requirements specification—Chapter 17
- Project risk mitigation plan—Chapter 18
- Software test plan—Chapter 23
- Configuration management plan—Chapter 31

These are only recommended templates—they are not immutable in form or content. Modify them for individual projects and organizations. They are merely a starting point. Project managers need to develop the process and deliverables appropriate to the project at hand. Graphics, tables, and the use of simple database tools for collecting information extend the usefulness of these templates and ensure better understanding and reuse throughout the life of the project.

The example project to be documented is a simplified version of the "lift problem": an elevator control system. The system has been described as follows:

A product is to be installed to control elevators in a building with three floors. The problem concerns the logic required to move elevators between floors according to the following constraints:

1. Each elevator has a set of three buttons, one for each floor. These illuminate when pressed and cause the elevator to visit the corresponding floor. The illumination is canceled when the elevator visits the corresponding floor.

2. The first and third floors have one elevator button, while the second floor has two buttons: one to request an up elevator and one to request a down elevator. These buttons illuminate when pressed. The illumination is canceled when an elevator visits the floor and then moves in the desired direction.

3. When an elevator has no requests, it remains at its current floor with its doors closed.

Where We Are in the Product Development Life Cycle

We are at the front end of the project. The templates in this appendix add significantly to the up-front understanding of the project, its requirements, and management. Figure F–1 shows the location of each plan circled on the IEEE 1074 life cycle model.

Learning Objectives for Appendix F

Upon completion of this appendix, the reader should be able to:

- Customize the software project management plan template for a specific project;
- Customize the software requirements specification template for a specific project;
- Customize the project risk mitigation plan template for a specific project;
- Customize the software test plan template for a specific project;
- Customize the configuration management plan template for a specific project.

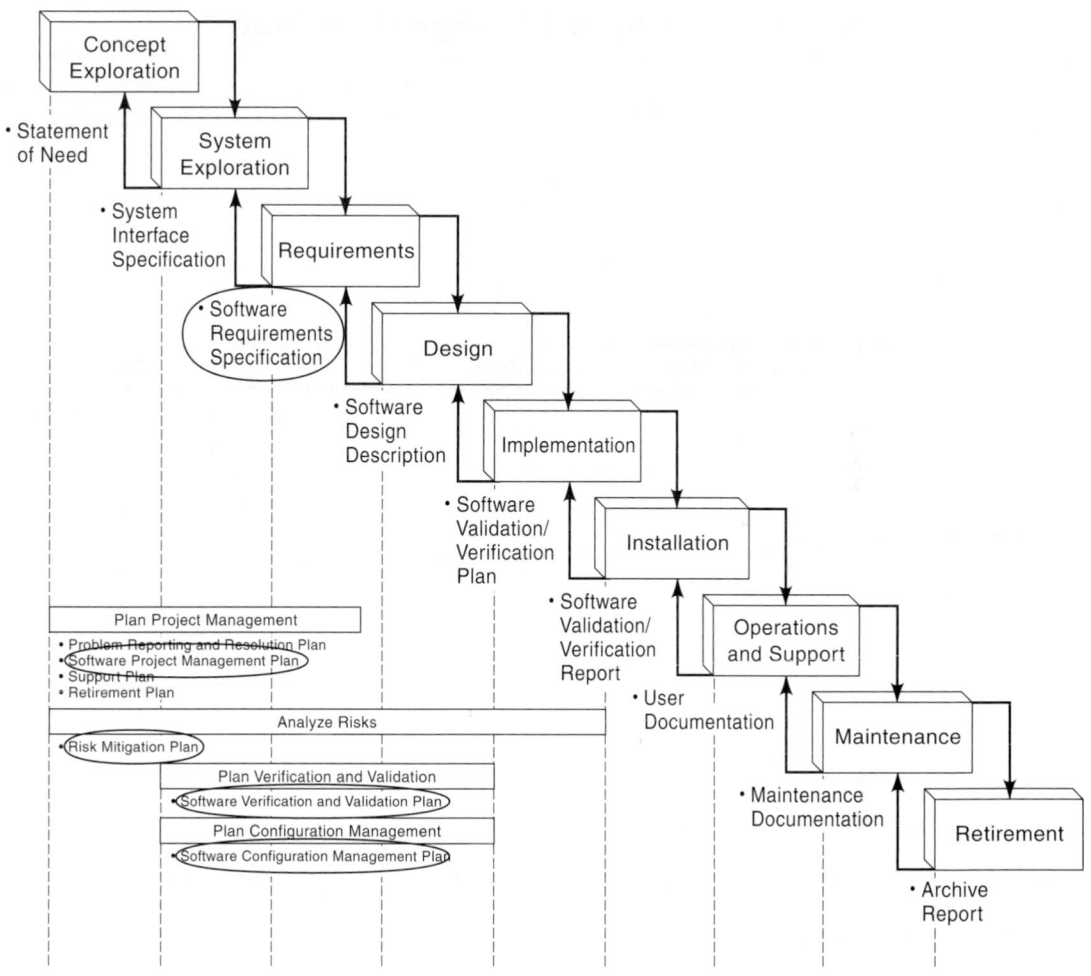

FIGURE F-1
Planning Templates Use in the Life Cycle

Software Project Management Plan (SPMP) _____

The basic template to be used is derived from IEEE Std 1058-1998, "IEEE Standard for Software Project Management Plans." The following is a template for the SPMP. It begins with a cover page that contains the version control and release information. Each section has a description of the information contained within. The SPMP for the elevator project follows the template. Review Chapter 7, "Defining the Goal and Scope of the Software Project," in this practitioner's guide before filling in the SPMP template.

Software Project Management Plan

\<Name of Project\>

\<author\>

\<date\>

Version	Release Date	Responsible Party	Major Changes
0.1			Initial Document Release for Comment

Table of Contents

Build the table of contents here. Insert it when you finish your document.

1. Introduction

This section of the SPMP provides an overview of the project.

1.1 Project Overview   Include a concise summary of the project objectives, major work activities, major milestones, required resources, and budget. Describe the relationship of this project to other projects, if appropriate. Provide a reference to the official statement of product requirements.

1.2 Project Deliverables   List the primary deliverables for the customer, the delivery dates, delivery locations, and quantities required satisfying the terms of the project agreement.

1.3 Evolution of the SPMP   Describe how this plan will be completed, disseminated, and put under change control. Describe how both scheduled and unscheduled updates will be handled.

1.4 Reference Materials   Provide a complete list of all documents and other sources of information referenced in the plan. Include for each the title, report number, date, author, and publishing organization.

1.5 Definitions and Acronyms   Define or provide references to the definition of all terms and acronyms required to properly interpret the SPMP.

2. Project Organization

This section specifies the process model for the project and its organizational structure.

2.1 Process Model   Specify the life cycle model to be used for this project, or refer to an organizational standard model that will be followed. The process model must include roles, activities, entry criteria, and exit criteria for project initiation, product development, product release, and project termination.

2.2 Organizational Structure   Describe the internal management structure of the project and how the project relates to the rest of the organization. It is recommended that charts be used to show the lines of authority. (See Figure F–2.)

2.3 Organizational Interfaces   Describe the administrative and managerial interfaces between the project and the primary entities with which it interacts. A table may be a useful way to represent this. (See Table F–1.)

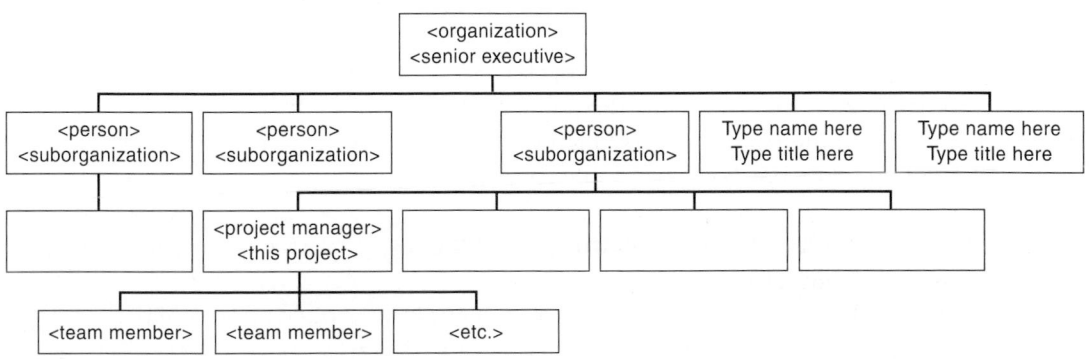

FIGURE F–2
Organization Chart

TABLE F–1
Project Interfaces

Organization	Liaison	Contact Information
Customer: <name>	<name>	<phone, email, etc.>
Subcontractor: <name>		
Software Quality Assurance		
Software Configuration Management		
<etc.>		

2.4 Project Responsibilities   Identify and state the nature of each major project function and activity, and identify the individuals who are responsible for those functions and activities. Tables of functions and activities may be used to depict project responsibilities. (See Table F–2.)

TABLE F–2
Project Responsibilities

Role	Description	Person
Project Manager	leads project team; responsible for project deliverables	<name>
Technical Team Leader(s)	<define as locally used>	<name>
<etc.>	<etc.>	

3. Managerial Process

This section of the SPMP specifies the management process for this project.

3.1 Management Objectives and Priorities   Describe the philosophy, goals, and priorities for managing this project. A flexibility matrix might be helpful in communicating which dimensions of the project are fixed, constrained, or flexible. Each degree of flexibility column can contain only one "X." (See Table F–3.)

3.2 Assumptions, Dependencies, and Constraints   State the assumptions on which the project is based, any external events upon which the project is dependent, and the constraints under which the project is to be conducted. Include an explicit statement of the relative priorities among meeting the functionality, schedule, and budget goals for this project.

TABLE F–3
Flexibility Matrix

Project Dimension	Fixed	Constrained	Flexible
Cost		X	
Schedule	X		
Scope (Functionality)			X

3.3 Risk Management

Describe the process to be used to identify, analyze, and manage the risk factors associated with the project. Describe mechanisms for tracking the various risk factors and implementing contingency plans. Risk factors that should be considered include contractual risks, technological risks, risks due to size and complexity of the product, risks in personnel acquisition and retention, and risks in achieving customer acceptance of the product. The specific risks for this project and the methods for managing them may be documented here or in another document included as an appendix or by reference.

3.4 Monitoring and Controlling Mechanisms

Define the reporting mechanisms, report formats, review and audit mechanisms, and other tools and techniques to be used in monitoring and controlling adherence to the SPMP. Project monitoring should occur at the level of work packages. Include monitoring and controlling mechanisms for the project support functions (quality assurance, configuration management, documentation, and training).

A table may be used to show the reporting and communication plan for the project. The communication table can show the regular reports and communication expected of the project, such as weekly status reports, regular reviews, or as-needed communication. The exact types of communication vary between groups, but it is useful to identify the planned means at the start of the project. (See Table F–4.)

TABLE F–4
Communication and Reporting Plan

Information Communicated	From	To	Time Period
Status Report	Project Team	Project Manager	Weekly
Status Report	Project Manager	Software Manager, Project Team	Weekly
Project Review	Project Team	Software Manager	Monthly
<etc.>			

3.5 Staffing Approach   Describe the types of skills required for the project, how appropriate personnel will be recruited, and any training required for project team members.

4. Technical Process

This section specifies the technical methods, tools, and techniques to be used on the project. It also includes identification of the work products and reviews to be held and the plans for the support group activities in user documentation, training, software quality assurance, and configuration management.

4.1 Methods, Tools, and Techniques   Identify the computing system(s), development method(s), standards, policies, procedures, team structure(s), programming language(s), and other notations, tools, techniques, and methods to be used to specify, design, build, test, integrate, document, deliver, modify, or maintain the project deliverables.

4.2 Software Documentation   Specify the work products to be built for this project and the types of peer reviews to be held for those products. It may be useful to include a table that is adapted from the organization's standard collection of work products and reviews. Identify any relevant style guide, naming conventions, and documentation formats. In either this documentation plan or the project schedule, provide a summary of the schedule and resource requirements for the documentation effort.

To ensure that the implementation of the software satisfies the requirements, the following documentation is required as a minimum:

4.2.1 Software Requirements Specification (SRS)—The SRS clearly and precisely describes each of the essential requirements (functions, performance, design constraints, and attributes) of the software and the external interfaces. Each requirement is defined so that achievement of it is objectively verifiable and can be validated by a prescribed method, for example, inspection, analysis, demonstration, or test.

4.2.2 Software Design Description (SDD)—The SDD describes the major components of the software design, including databases and internal interfaces.

4.2.3 Software Test Plan—The software test plan describes the methods to be used for testing at all levels of development and integration: requirements as expressed in the SRS, designs as expressed in the SDD, and code as expressed in the implemented product. The test plan also describes the test procedures, test cases, and test results that are created during testing activities.

4.3 User Documentation   Describe how the user documentation will be planned and developed. (This may be just a reference to a plan being built by someone else.) Include work planned for online and paper documentation, online help, network accessible files, and support facilities.

4.4 Project Support Functions   Provide either directly or by reference, the plans for the supporting functions for the software project. Examples of these functions are configuration management, software quality assurance, and verification and validation. Plans for project support functions are developed to a level of detail consistent with the other sections of the SPMP. In particular, the responsibilities, resource requirements, schedules, and budgets for each supporting function must be specified. The nature and type of support functions required will vary from project to project; however, the absence of a software quality assurance, configuration management, or verification and validation plan must be explicitly justified in project plans that do not include them.

5. Work Packages, Schedule, and Budget

Specify the work packages, dependency relationships, resource requirements, allocation of budget and resources to work packages, and project schedule. Much of the content may be in appendices that are living documents, updated as the work progresses.

5.1 Work Packages   Specify the work packages for the activities and tasks that must be completed in order to satisfy the project agreement. Each work package is uniquely identified. A diagram depicting the breakdown of project activities and tasks (a work breakdown structure) may be used to depict hierarchical relationships among work packages.

5.2 Dependencies   Specify the ordering relations among work packages to account for interdependencies among them and dependencies on external events. Techniques such as dependency lists, activity networks, and the critical path method may be used to depict dependencies among work packages.

5.3 Resource Requirements   Provide, as a function of time, estimates of the total resources required to complete the project. Numbers and types of personnel, computer time, support software, computer hardware, office and laboratory facilities, travel, and maintenance requirements for the project resources are typical items that should be specified.

5.4 Budget and Resource Allocation   Specify the allocation of budget and resources to the various project functions, activities, and tasks.

5.5 Schedule   Provide the schedule for the various project functions, activities, and tasks, taking into account the precedence relations and the required milestone dates. Schedules may be expressed in absolute calendar time or in increments relative to a key project milestone.

6. Additional Components

Certain extra components may be required and may be appended as additional sections or subsections to the SPMP. Additional items of importance on any particular project may include subcontractor management plans, security plans, independent verification and validation plans, training plans, hardware procurement plans, facilities plans, installation plans, data conversion plans, system transition plans, or the product maintenance plan.

6.1 Index   An index to the key terms and acronyms used throughout the SPMP is optional, but recommended to improve usability of the SPMP.

6.2 Appendices   Appendices may be included, either directly or by reference, to provide supporting details that could detract from the SPMP if included in the body of the SPMP. Suggested appendices include: "Current Top 10 Risk Chart," "Current Project Work Breakdown Structure," and "Current Detailed Project Schedule."

Software Project Management Plan

Lift Controller

Excelsior Elevator Embedded Software Development Team

March 8, 2001

Version 0.9.0	Modification at 2.2	March 8, 2001
Version 0.7.0	Modification at 1.1.1, 1.1.3, 1.2, 1.3.1,2.1, 3.2, 4.1	March 7, 2001
Version 0.6.0	first draft	March 1, 2001

Table of Contents   Page

1. Introduction

1.1 Project Overview   Using formal methods, verify the correctness of the Elevator Problem specification using an Alloy model in Z.

Enumerate the lift problem use cases in English.

Write formal specification.

1. Determine Boolean expressions for the problem
2. Translate use cases into Boolean expressions
3. Write truth table for the Boolean expressions
4. Review formal specification

Code model and assertions into Alloy from Boolean expressions.

Run each assertion and verify that there are no counter-examples for the model.

Refine model until no counter-examples are found.

Final project review preparation and presentation.

Passing each review is a milestone, as it indicates progression to the next phase of development. They are:

1. Use cases completed and reviewed
2. Formal specification completed and reviewed
3. Alloy model completed and proven
4. Final project presentation completed

1.2 Project Deliverables   The deliverable is a product to control and move elevators in a building with three floors according to the following logic:

1. Each elevator has a set of three buttons, one for each floor. These illuminate when pressed and cause the elevator to visit the corresponding floor. The illumination is canceled when the elevator visits the corresponding floor.

2. The first and the third floors have one elevator button, while the second has two: one to request an up elevator and one to request a down elevator. These buttons illuminate when pressed. The illumination is canceled when an elevator visits the floor and then moves in the desired direction.

3. When an elevator has no requests, it remains at its current floor with its doors closed.

Delivery dates:

-   Project plan—March 8
-   Formal specification—March 22
-   Review of first formal proof—April 12
-   Project delivery—May 3

1.3 Evolution of the SPMP   Upon completion, our SPMP will be executed once in order to formally prove the lift problem specification.

Our team Web page will document our timeline and deliverables. Hyperlinks will be created to access the current level of each deliverable item and the date when it was last updated.

To prevent duplication of effort, each team member will have individual assignments. When more than one person is working on the same deliverable, they must coordinate to produce one final document.

Email will be the primary communication vehicle among our team members. Each scheduled update will be set to our team mailing list, so that all members have the updated data. Our Web page administrator will post updates to our team Web page, providing a central location for project status and schedule.

Email will also be used to communicate unscheduled updates throughout the team.

2. Project Organization

2.1 The Process Model

1. Describe the assumptions about the world in which the elevator control will operate.
2. Review assumptions.
3. Describe the requirements that the elevator control is to achieve.

4. Review requirements.

5. Create a design to meet those requirements.

6. Review design.

7. Develop the formal specification.

8. Review formal specification.

9. Run this model with Alloy to prove that it is true.

10. Review Alloy results.

11. Deliver project results.

2.2 Project Responsibilities   See Table F–5.

TABLE F–5
SPMP Project Responsibilities

Subteams	Description	Team Member
Project Manager	Leads project team; responsible for project deliverables	Fernanda
Z/Alloy Team	Responsible for studying Z/Alloy	Ross, Bruce
Use Case Team	Generate use cases	Nikilo, Bruce
Translation Team	Translate English statement of use cases into variables	Khushru, Susanto, Fernanda
Product Delivery/Maintenance Specialist	Updates the Web page	Bruce

3. Managerial Process

3.1 Assumptions, Dependencies, and Constraints   This is a project for a group of six graduate students. The project will be continued unless the following criteria are met:

1. Five of the six members leave the team.

2. The project is canceled.

3. More than 2000 person-hours have been spent on the project.

4. A critical bug or defect in the Alloy software package prevents the continuation of the project.

3.2 Monitoring and Controlling Mechanisms   The initial and final deliverables will be delivered through the team Web page so that the whole team and the client have access to them and can give feedback if necessary.

Each team member is assigned a particular task to avoid redundancy. Tasks assignments can also be found on the team Web page and project plan.

The team Web page will contain the project updates and the schedule for reviews, delivery dates, and other necessary information.

Every week there will be submission of each part of the deliverable produced by the team members to the team's Web site administrator. Submission will be done by group mailing list so that the project manager and team members can provide each other with suggestions and advice and warn of inconsistencies through emails.

Review meetings will be scheduled if necessary. General communications among the team members will be done through group mailing list, phone, email, and during class meetings.

4. Technical Process

4.1 Methods, Tools, and Techniques   Necessary document templates are located on the project Web page. Each member will perform his assigned tasks using those templates as a guide.

Documents will be produced in HTML format for Web page submission; however, the team members may use any editor when necessary to produce their part of the assignment.

Alloy constraint analyzer will be used to perform formal proof on the formal specifications produced by the group.

The overall project will be conducted following the model decided on by the team.

5. Work Packages, Schedule, and Budget

5.1 Work Packages

1. English description of the project. This includes assumptions, and the requirements for the elevator control.
2. A high-level design to meet the requirements.
3. Formal specification in Z.
4. Alloy model of the formal specification.

5.2 Dependencies

1. All the work packages are dependent on the previous work packages. Alloy model depends on formal specification in Z.

2. Formal specification depends on the high-level design.

3. Design depends on assumptions and requirements.

5.3 Schedule   See Table F–6.

TABLE F–6
SPMP Project Schedule

Tasks	Completion Date
Initial Project Plan Submission	February 27, 2001
Project Plan Review and Revision	March 7, 2001
Final Project Plan Submission	March 8, 2001
Initial Formal Specification Submission	March 13, 2001
Formal Specification Review and Revision	March 22, 2001
Final Formal Specification Submission	March 29, 2001
Initial First Formal Proof Submission	April 3, 2001
First Formal Proof Review and Revision	April 11, 2001
Final First Formal Proof Submission	April 12, 2001
Initial Final Project Submission	April 24, 2001
Final Project Review and Revision	May 2, 2001
Final Project Delivered	May 3, 2001

6. Additional Components

6.1 Index

Alloy	1, 3, 4
Deliverable	2
Elevator	1
Formal specification	1, 4
Z	1, 3, 4

Software Requirements Specification (SRS) _____

Review Chapter 17, "Developing the Software Requirements Specification," in this practitioner's guide before filling in the SRS template.

Software Requirements Specification

<Name of Project>

<author>

<date>

Version	Release Date	Responsible Party	Major Changes
0.1			Initial Document Release for Comment

Table of Contents

Build the table of contents here. Insert it when you finish your document.

1. Introduction

The following subsections of the SRS should provide an overview of the entire SRS.

1.1 Purpose   Identify the purpose of this SRS and its intended audience.

1.2 Scope   In this subsection:

1. Identify the software product(s) to be produced, by name.
2. Explain what the software product(s) will, and if necessary, will not, do.
3. Describe the application of the software being specified. As a part of this:
   a. Describe the relevant benefits, objectives, and goals as precisely as possible.
   b. Be consistent with similar statements in higher-level specifications, if they exist.

1.3 Definitions, Acronyms, and Abbreviations   Provide the definitions of all
terms, acronyms, and abbreviations required to properly interpret the SRS. This information
may be provided by reference to an appendix or other document(s).

1.4 References   In this subsection:

1. Provide a complete list of all documents referenced elsewhere in the SRS.
2. Identify each document by title, report number (if applicable), date, and publishing organization.
3. Specify the sources from which the references can be obtained.

1.5 Overview   Describe the rest of the SRS and how it is organized.

2. General Description

Describe the general factors that affect the product and its requirements. This section usually
consists of the five subsections that follow. This section does not state specific requirements—
each of its subsections makes those requirements easier to understand, but they do not specify
design or express specific requirements. Such detail is provided in Section 3.

2.1 Product Perspective   This subsection of the SRS relates the product to other prod-
ucts or projects.

1. If the product is independent and totally self-contained, that should be stated here.
2. If the SRS defines a product that is a component of a larger system or project:
   a. Describe the functions of each component of the larger system or project, and identify interfaces.
   b. Identify the principal external interfaces of this software product (this should not be a detailed description).
   c. Describe the computer hardware and peripheral equipment to be used (overview only).

A block diagram showing the major components of the larger system or project, interconnections, and external interfaces can be helpful.

2.2 Product Functions   Provide a summary of the functions that the software will perform. Sometimes the function summary that is necessary for this part can be taken directly from the section of the higher-level specification (if one exists) that allocates particular functions to the software product. The functions should be organized in a way that makes the list of functions understandable to the customer or to anyone else reading the document for the first time. Block diagrams showing the different functions and their relationships can be helpful. Such a diagram is not a requirement on the design of a product itself, it is simply an effective explanatory tool.

2.3 User Characteristics   Describe the general characteristics of the end-users of the product that will affect the specific requirements.

Many people interact with a system during the operation and maintenance phases of the software life cycle. Some of these people are users, operators, and maintenance and systems personnel. Certain characteristics of these people, such as educational level, experience, and technical expertise impose important constraints on the system's operating environment.

2.4 General Constraints   Provide a general description of any other items that will limit the developer's options for designing the system. These can include:

- Regulatory policies;
- Hardware limitations (for example, signal timing requirements);
- Interface to other applications;
- Parallel operation;
- Audit functions;
- Control functions;
- Higher-order language requirements;
- Signal handshake protocols (for example, XON–XOFF, ACK–NACK);
- Criticality of the application;
- Safety and security considerations.

2.5 Assumptions and Dependencies   List and describe each of the factors that affect the requirements stated in the SRS. These factors are not design constraints on the software, but any changes to them can affect the requirements in the SRS. For example, an assumption might be that a specific operating system will be available on the hardware designated for the software product. If, in fact, the operating system is not available, the SRS would then have to change.

3. Specific Requirements

This is typically the largest and most important part of the SRS. It should contain all the details the software developer needs to create a design:

1. The details within it should be defined as individual, specific requirements, following the guidelines for sound requirements (verifiable, unambiguous, etc.).
2. Specific requirements should be organized in a logical and readable manner.
3. Each requirement should be stated so its achievement is objectively verifiable by a prescribed method.
4. Sources of a requirement should be identified where that is useful in understanding the requirement.
5. One way to classify the specific requirements is as follows:

   a. Functional requirements

   b. Performance requirements

   c. Design constraints

   d. Attributes

   e. External interface requirements

The organization of this section of the SRS should be chosen with the goal of properly specifying the requirements in the most readable manner.

3.1 Functional Requirements
This subsection of the SRS should specify what is to be done by the product, to what level or specific requirement, what inputs should be transformed to what outputs (not *how* this is done), and what specific operations are required. Where the rationale for a requirement is not obvious, provide an explanation. Where issues need to be resolved, cite them.

For each function, specify requirements on inputs, processing, and outputs. These are usually organized with these four subparagraphs:

1. **Purpose of the function:** rationale to clarify the intent of the function
2. **Inputs:** sources, valid ranges of values, any timing concerns, operator requirements, special interfaces
3. **Operations to be performed:** validity checks, responses to abnormal conditions, types of processing required
4. **Outputs:** destinations, valid ranges of values, timing concerns, handling of illegal values, error messages, interfaces required

3.2 External Interface Requirements   This subsection should do the following:

1. List the characteristics that the software must support for each human interface to the software product. For example, if the user of the system operates through a display terminal, the following should be specified:

   a. Required screen formats

   b. Page layout and content of any reports or menus

   c. Relative timing of inputs and outputs

   d. Availability of some form of programmable function keys

2. Specify all the aspects of optimizing the interface with the person who must use the system. This may simply comprise a list of dos and don'ts on how the system will appear to the user.

3. Detail the logical characteristics of each interface between the software product and the hardware components of the system. Include such matters as what devices are to be supported, how they are to be supported, and protocols.

4. Specify the use of other required software products (for example, a data management system, an operating system, or a mathematical package), and interfaces with other application systems. For each required software product, the following should be provided: name, mnemonic, specification number, version number, and source. For each interface discuss the purpose of the interfacing software as related to this software product, and define the interface in terms of message content and format. It is not necessary to detail any well-documented interface, but a reference to the document defining the interface is required.

5. Specify the various interfaces to communications such as local network protocols, and so on.

3.3 Performance Requirements   This subsection should specify both the static and the dynamic numerical requirements placed on the software or on human interaction with the software, as a whole.

   Static numerical requirements may include:

- The number of terminals to be supported;
- The number of simultaneous users to be supported;
- Number of files and records to be handled;
- Sizes of tables and files.

Static numerical requirements are sometimes identified under a separate section entitled "Capacity."

   Dynamic numerical requirements may include, for example, the numbers of transactions and tasks and the amount of data to be processed within certain time periods for both normal and peak workload conditions.

All of these requirements should be stated in measurable terms; for example, "95 percent of the transactions shall be processed in less than 1 second," rather than, "Operator shall not have to wait for the transaction to complete."

Note: Numerical limits applied to one specific function are normally specified as part of the processing subparagraph description of that function.

3.4 Design Constraints

Design constraints can be imposed by other standards, hardware limitations, and so on.

Specify the requirements derived from existing standards or regulations. They might include:

- Report format;
- Data naming;
- Accounting procedures;
- Audit tracing. For example, this could specify the requirement for software to trace processing activity. Such traces are needed for some applications to meet minimum government or financial standards. An audit trace requirement might state that all changes to a payroll data base must be recorded in a trace file with before and after values.

Identify the requirements for the software to operate inside various hardware constraints.

3.5 Quality Characteristics

There are a number of quality characteristics that can apply to software. Pick the ones most important to this product and develop a section for each one. Definitions of the quality characteristics follow.

- Correctness—extent to which program satisfies specifications, and fulfills user's mission objectives
- Efficiency—amount of computing resources and code required to perform a function
- Flexibility—effort needed to modify the operational program
- Integrity/security—extent to which access to software or data by unauthorized people can be controlled
- Interoperability—effort needed to couple one system with another
- Maintainability—effort required to locate and fix an error during operation
- Portability—effort needed to transfer from one hardware or software environment to another
- Reliability—extent to which the program performs with the required precision
- Reusability—extent to which the program can be reused in another application
- Testability—effort needed to test to ensure the program performs as intended
- Usability—effort required to learn, operate, prepare input for, and interpret output of the program

Describe the rationale for including this characteristic for this product. Also, describe how the presence, absence, or level of this characteristic will be measured and identify ways to test the characteristic once the product is complete.

3.6 Other Requirements   This subsection could specify the requirements for any database that is to be developed as part of the product. Certain requirements may, due to the nature of the software, the user organization, or other factors, be placed in separate categories such as the following:

- Types of information;
- Frequency of use;
- Accessing capabilities;
- Data element and file descriptions;
- Relationship of data elements, records, and files;
- Static and dynamic organization;
- Retention requirements for data.

Note: If an existing database package is to be used, this package should be named under "3.2 External Interface Requirements," and the details of using it should be specified there.

This subsection could specify the normal and special operations required by the user, such as:

- The various modes of operations in the user organization; for example, user-initiated operations;
- Periods of interactive operations and periods of unattended operations;
- Data processing support functions;
- Backup and recovery operations.

This subsection could also define the requirements for any data or initialization sequences that are specific to a given site, mission, or operational mode (for example, safety limits) and specify features that should be modified to adapt the software to an installation.

4. Supporting Information

This section includes supporting information; that is, the Table of Contents, the Appendices, and the Index, which make the SRS easier to use. The Appendices are not always considered part of the actual requirements specification and are not always necessary. They might include:

- Sample I/O formats, descriptions of cost analysis studies, and results of user surveys;
- Supporting or background information that can help the readers of the SRS;
- A description of the problems to be solved by the software;

- The history, background, experience, and operational characteristics of the organization to be supported;
- A cross-reference list, arranged by milestone, of incomplete software requirements that are to be completed by specified milestones;
- Special packaging instructions for the code and the media to meet security, export, initial loading, or other requirements.

When Appendices are included, the SRS should explicitly state whether the Appendices are to be considered part of the requirements.

Software Requirements Specification

Lift Controller

Excelsior Elevator Embedded Software Development Team

March 22, 2001

Version	Release Date	Responsible Party	Major Changes
0.1	1 March 2001	Team	Initial Document Release for Commen
1.0	22 March 2001	Team	Version 1.0 Release of Document After Review

Table of Contents

1. Introduction

The following subsections of the SRS should provide an overview of the entire SRS.

1.1 Purpose   Identify the purpose of this SRS and its intended audience.

1.2 Scope   Using formal methods, verify the correctness of the elevator problem specification using an Alloy model in Z.

Enumerate the lift problem use cases in English.

Write formal specification.

1. Determine Boolean expressions for the problem
2. Translate use cases into Boolean expressions
3. Write truth table for the Boolean expressions
4. Review formal specification

Code model and assertions into Alloy from Boolean expressions.

Run each assertion and verify that there are no counter-examples for the model.

Refine model until no counter-examples are found.

Final project review preparation and presentation.

Passing each review is a milestone, as it indicates progression to the next phase of development. They are:

1. Use cases completed and reviewed
2. Formal specification completed and reviewed
3. Alloy model completed and proven
4. Final project presentation completed

The deliverable is a product to control and move elevators in a building with three floors according to the following logic:

1. Each elevator has a set of three buttons, one for each floor. These illuminate when pressed and cause the elevator to visit the corresponding floor. The illumination is canceled when the elevator visits the corresponding floor.

2. The first and the third floors have one elevator button, while the second has two: one to request an up elevator and one to request a down elevator. These buttons illuminate when pressed. The illumination is canceled when an elevator visits the floor and then moves in the desired direction.

3. When an elevator has no requests, it remains at its current floor with its doors closed.

1.3 Definitions, Acronyms, and Abbreviations   None.

1.4 References   No references other than what are mentioned in the project management plan.

1.5 Overview   Describe the rest of the SRS and how it is organized.

2. General Description

A product is to be designed, developed, and installed to control elevators in a building with seven floors. The problem concerns the logic required to move elevators between floors. Figure F–3 shows the context diagram for the product. The external entity for this is only the user of the elevator.

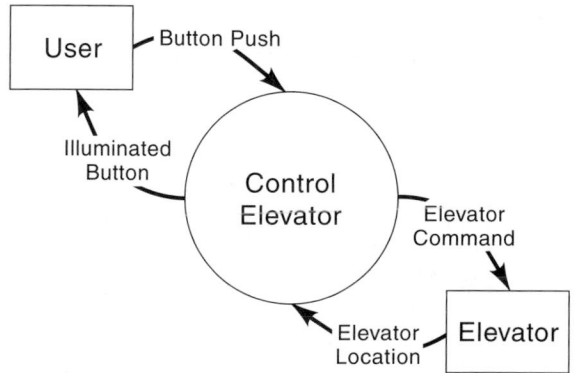

FIGURE F–3
Elevator Control Context Diagram

2.1 Product Perspective   Figure F–4 shows the use case diagram for the control system as a generalized description of how the system will be used. Providing an overview of the intended functionality of the system, the use case diagram enumerates the functions that the user observes being performed by the elevator.

From the use case, this set of common uses can be derived:

1. Passenger presses floor button
2. Elevator system detects floor button pressed
3. Elevator moves to the floor
4. Elevator doors open
5. Passenger gets in and presses elevator button
6. Elevator doors close
7. Elevator moves to required floor
8. Elevator doors open
9. Passenger gets out
10. Elevator doors close

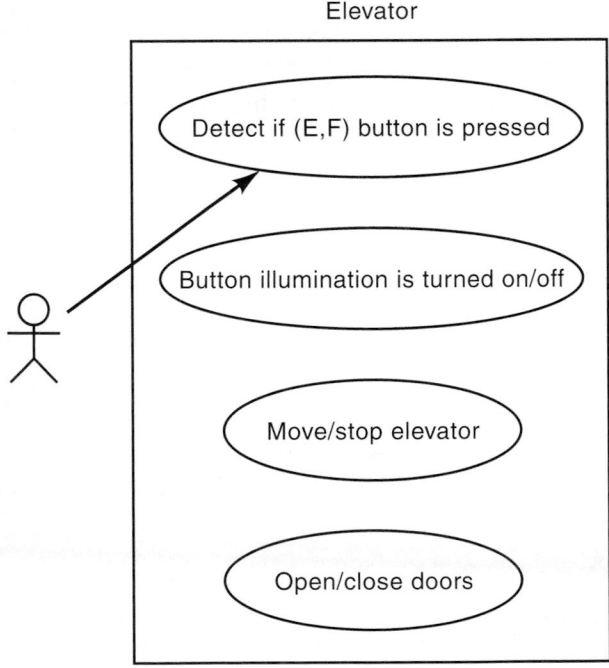

FIGURE F–4
Elevator Control Use Case

2.2 Product Functions   A product is to be installed to control elevators in a building with seven floors. The problem concerns the logic required to move elevators between floors according to the following constraints:

1. Each elevator has a set of seven buttons, one for each floor. These illuminate when pressed and cause the elevator to visit the corresponding floor. The illumination is canceled when the elevator visits the corresponding floor.

2. The first and top floors have one elevator button, while the rest have two: one to request an up elevator and one to request a down elevator. These buttons illuminate when pressed. The illumination is canceled when an elevator visits the floor and then moves in the desired direction.

3. When an elevator has no requests, it remains at its current floor with its doors closed.

2.3 User Characteristics   User characteristics are described by these two use cases:

Use Case #1—Normal Scenario

1. User A presses Up button at floor 2 to request elevator. User A wishes to go to floor 3.
2. Up button is turned on.
3. An elevator arrives at floor 3. It contains User B who has entered the elevator at floor 1 and pressed the elevator button for floor 9.
4. Up button is turned off.
5. Elevator doors open. User A enters elevator.
6. User A presses elevator button for floor 7.
7. Floor 7 button is turned on.
8. Elevator doors close.
9. Elevator travels to floor 7.
10. Floor 7 button is turned off.
11. Elevator doors open to allow User A to exit elevator.
12. Timer starts. User A exits.
13. Elevator doors close after timeout.
14. Elevator proceeds to floor 9 with User B.

Use Case #2—Abnormal Scenario

1. User A presses Up button at floor 3 to request elevator. User A wishes to go to floor 1.
2. Up button is turned on.
3. An elevator arrives at floor 3. It contains User B who has entered the elevator at floor 1 and pressed the elevator button for floor 9.
4. Up button is turned off.

5. Elevator doors open. User A enters elevator.

6. User A presses elevator button for floor 1.

7. Floor 1 button is turned on.

8. Elevator doors close after timeout.

9. Elevator travels to floor 9.

10. Floor 9 button is turned off.

11. Elevator doors open to allow User B to exit elevator.

12. Timer starts. User B exits.

13. Elevator doors close after timeout.

14. Elevator proceeds to floor 1 with User A.

2.4 General Constraints   The general constraint on the control system is to open an elevator door only when the elevator is at the floor at which the door is opening. Do not open an elevator door into the open elevator shaft. In order to ensure the safety of the users, there must be a formal proof approved before design can begin on the project.

The product constraints as enumerated by the user are:

1. Each elevator has a set of seven buttons, one for each floor. These illuminate when pressed and cause the elevator to visit the corresponding floor. The illumination is canceled when the elevator visits the corresponding floor.

2. The first and top floors have one elevator button, while the rest have two buttons: one to request an up elevator and one to request a down elevator. These buttons illuminate when pressed. The illumination is canceled when an elevator visits the floor and then moves in the desired direction.

3. When an elevator has no requests, it remains at its current floor with its doors closed.

2.5 Assumptions and Dependencies   In completing these requirements, the major assumption is that the tool used for generating the formal proof is robust enough to accept all of the variables and conditions of the proof.

3. Specific Requirements

The requirements for the elevator control system will be presented using the three views of the problem domain as expressed in Figure F–5. Process will be represented by a set of data flow diagrams down to the level necessary to express major processes. Data will be expressed with an entity relationship diagram and behavior by a finite state machine model.

3.1 Process Requirements   Figure F–3, previously presented, is the elevator problem context diagram. The next level of decomposition is represented in Figure F–6.

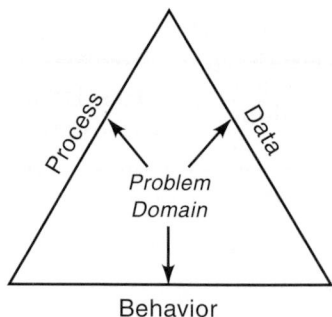

FIGURE F–5
Elevator Problem Domain Requirements Views

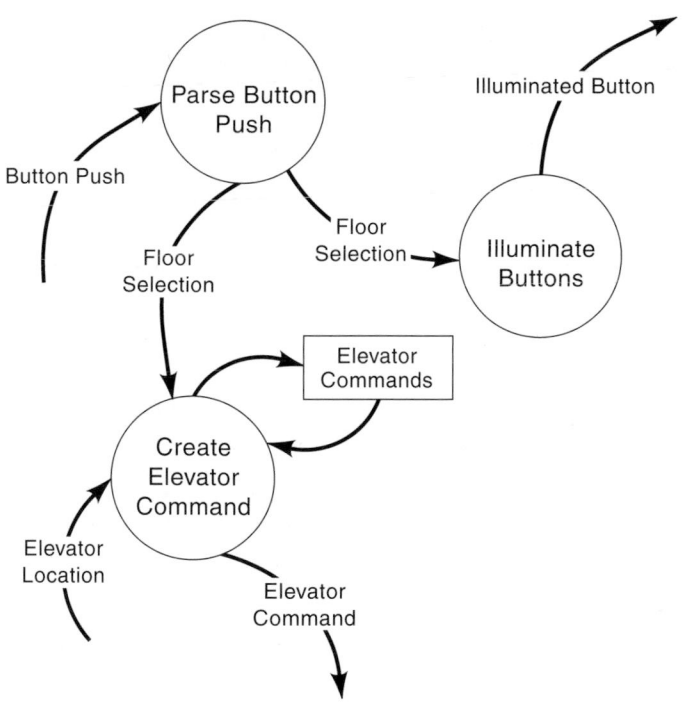

FIGURE F–6
Control Elevator Level 0 Data Flow Diagram

3.2 Data Requirements Data requirements are represented by an entity relationship diagram and a data dictionary, Table F–7. Figure F–7 represents the relationships among the entities and is the starting point for the class view presented in Section 3.4.

TABLE F–7
Elevator Control Data Dictionary

Name	Alias	Where Used/How Used	Content Description	Data (D) or Control (C)
Button Push	none		=0{[QUARTERS ǀ DIMES ǀ NICKELS]}8	Data
Elevator Command	none		=[COINS ǀ SLUGS]	
Elevator Commands	none			
Elevator Location	none			
Floor Selection	none		*U.S. currency coin value with standard weight, size and composition*	
Units: Dollar/4				
Illuminated Button	none			

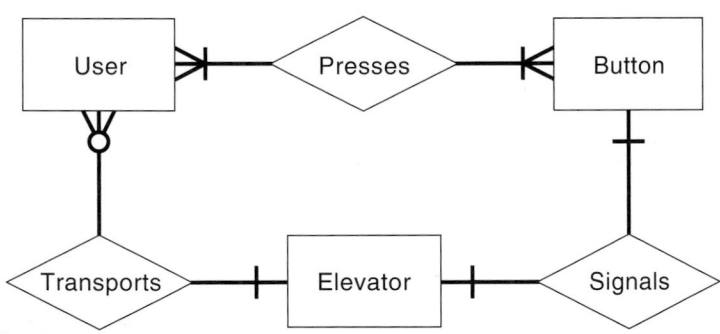

FIGURE F–7
Elevator Control Entity Relationship Diagram

3.3 Behavior Requirements

Use of formal methods to prove that the requirements are complete requires a behavioral representation of the elevator control. The states in the behavior model are mapped to the logic developed for the formal proof. Figure F–8 represents the elevator control behavior.

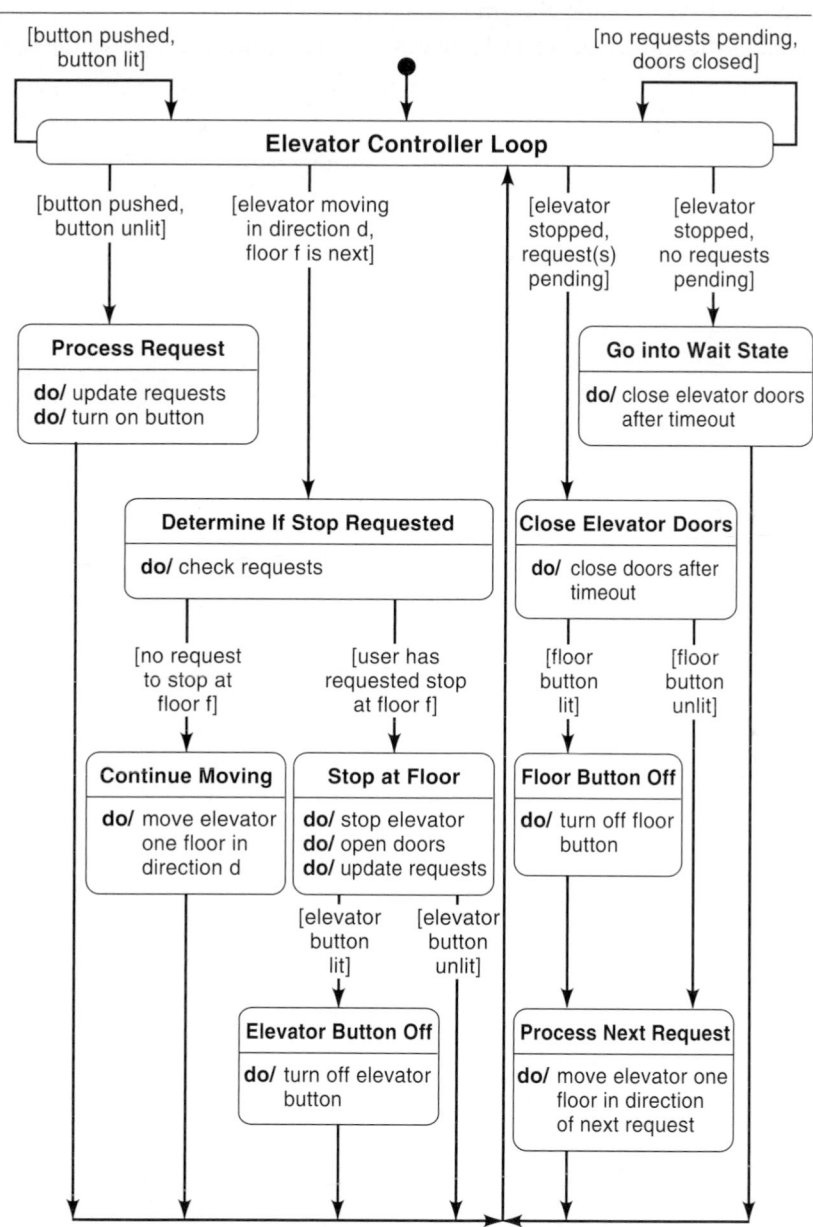

FIGURE F–8
Elevator Control Behavior Model

3.4 Requirements Class View   Using the previous three sections' formal view of the requirements, this section takes that information and derives an object-oriented view of the elevator control.

Class: **Elevator Controller**

Responsibility

1. Turn on elevator button

2. Turn off elevator button

3. Turn on floor button

4. Turn off floor button

5. Open elevator doors

6. Close elevator doors

7. Move elevator one floor up

8. Move elevator one floor down

Collaboration

1. Class Elevator Button

2. Class Floor Button

3. Class Elevator

Figure F–9 shows the static structure of each object, its internal structure, and its relationships.

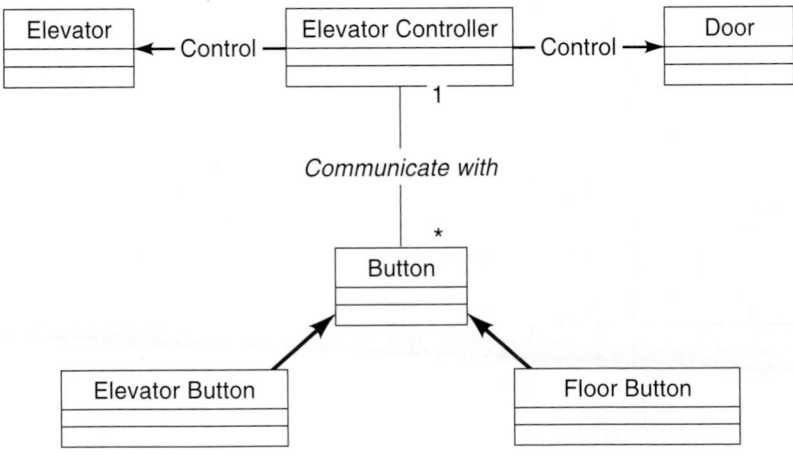

FIGURE F–9
Elevator Controller Class Diagram

Figure F–10 shows the sequence diagram for the elevator buttons. F–11 shows the sequence diagram for the door buttons.

The collaboration diagrams show the relationship between the elevator controller objects. Figure F–12 shows the relationship between the passenger and the floor button. Figure F–13 shows the relationship between the passenger and the elevator button.

The final diagram of the elevator controller object oriented requirements is shown in Figure F–14.

3.5 External Interface Requirements   The user interfaces are the exterior buttons to select up or down and the interior buttons to select a floor.

3.6 Performance Requirements   The elevator control system must respond within the industry-accepted time frame for an elevator/building system of this magnitude.

3.7 Design Constraints   There are no known design constraints.

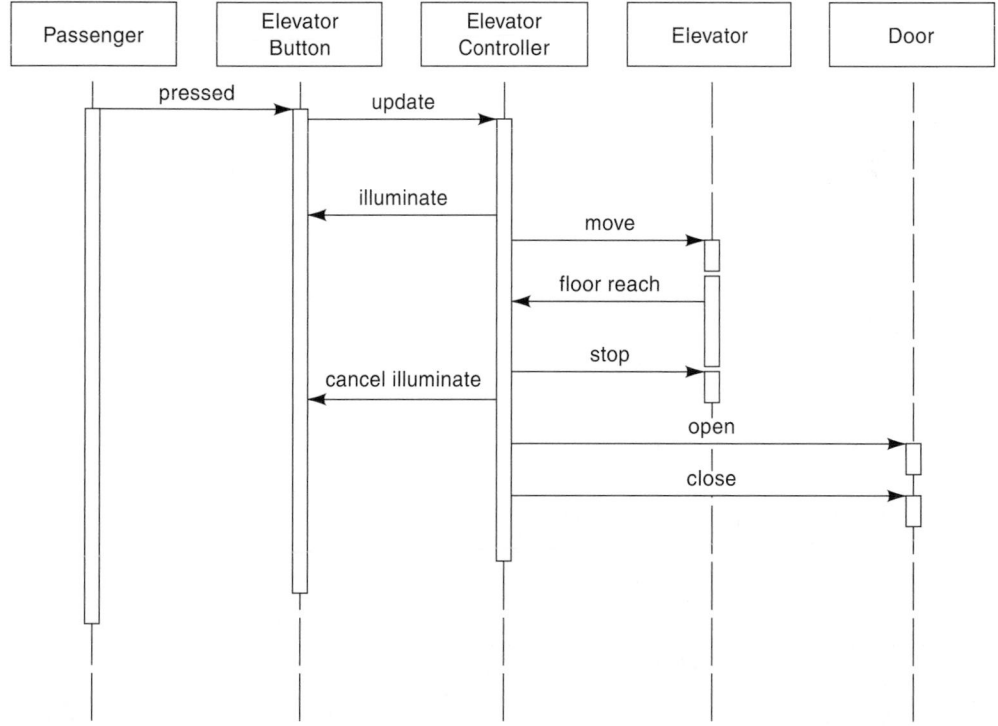

FIGURE F–10
Elevator Button Sequence Diagram

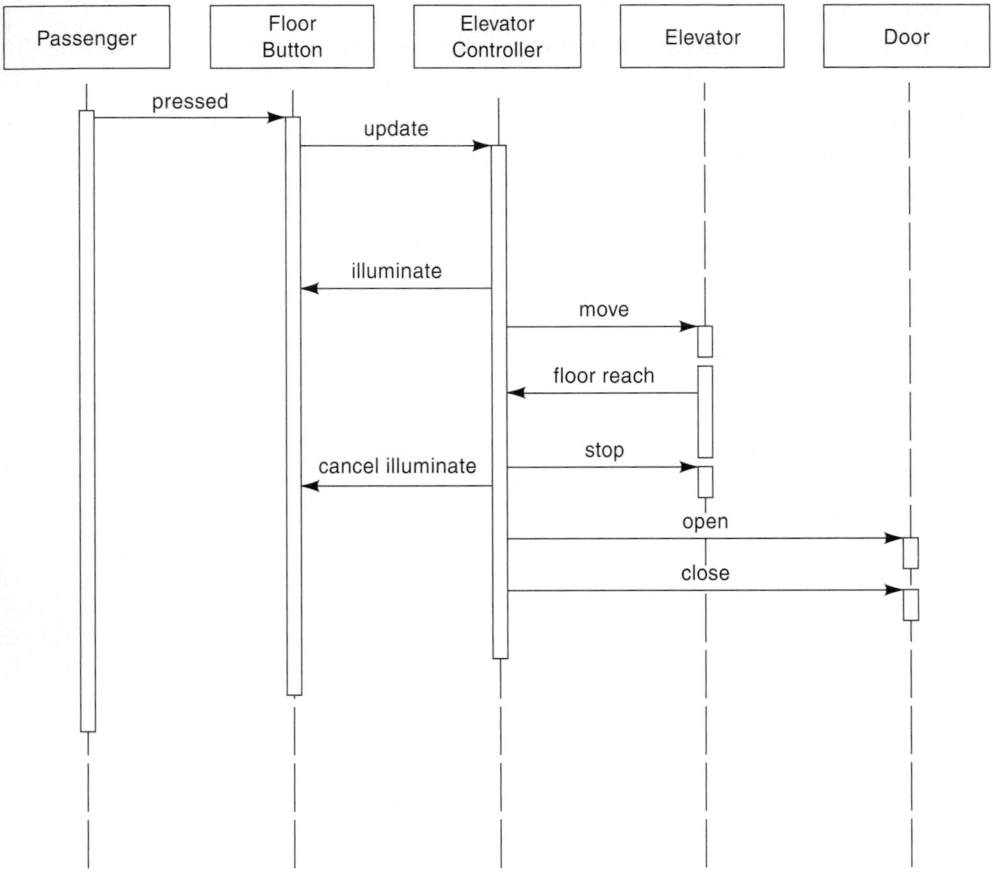

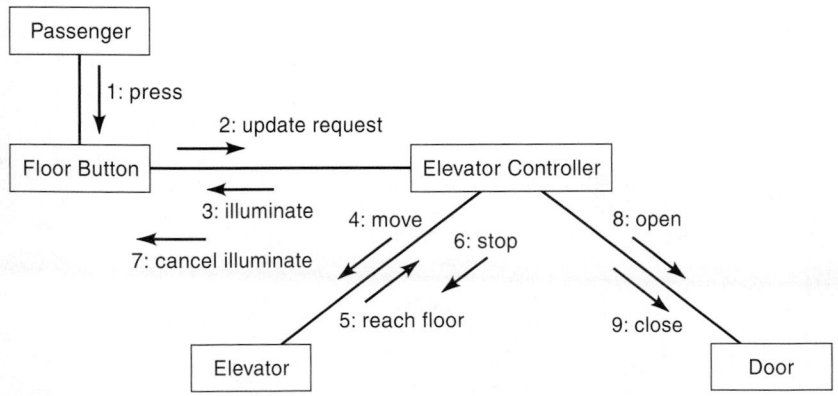

FIGURE F–11
Door Button Sequence Diagram

FIGURE F–12
Passenger–Door Button Collaboration Diagram

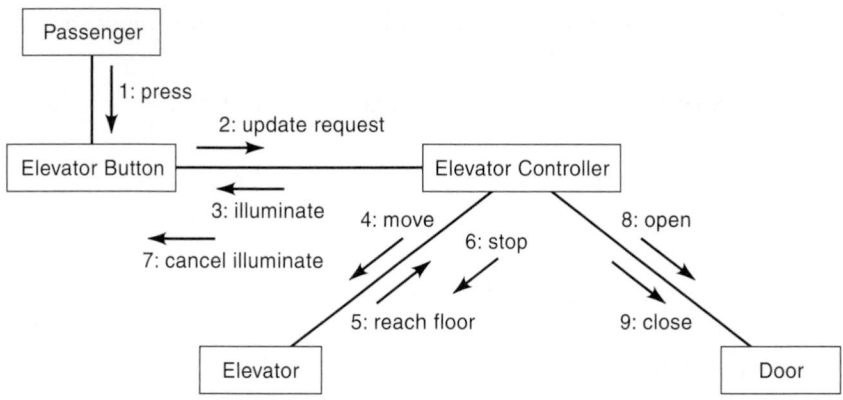

FIGURE F–13

Passenger–Elevator Button Collaboration Diagram

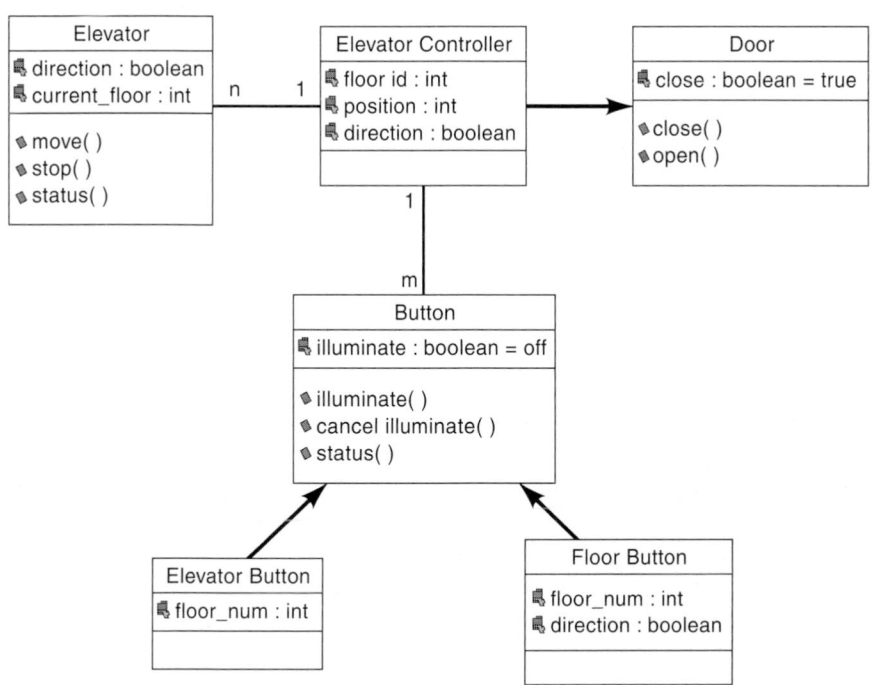

FIGURE F–14

Elevator Controller Detailed Class Diagram

3.8 Quality Characteristics   These three quality characteristics are the most important to the elevator controller software being developed:

- Correctness—extent to which program satisfies specifications and fulfills user's mission objectives
- Reliability—extent to which the program performs with the required precision
- Testability—effort needed to test to ensure the program performs as intended

3.9 Other Requirements   There are no other known requirements.

4. Supporting Information

There is no other known supporting documentation not referenced in the project management plan document.

Project Risk Management Plan _____

Review the twelve categories of risk in Chapter 18, "Determining Project Risks," of this practitioner's guide before completing this software risk management plan.

Software Risk Management Plan

\<Name of Project\>

\<author\>

\<date\>

Version	Release Date	Responsible Party	Major Changes
0.1			Initial Document Release for Comment

Table of Contents

Build the table of contents here. Insert it when you finish your document.

1. Introduction

This section of the risk management plan provides the focus for risk management and mitigation within the project.

2. Risk Categorization Table

A project team might use this table to review the categories of risk for their project. This table provides the team with a set of factors to consider and provides slots for them to decide which are relevant and what evidence they have. As the organization learns more about its performance, it may decide on ways to compare ratings on a given project with its history. It may determine a total rating count, number of risks, or some combination of number and level of impact that predict project failure or success. This table is a starting point for identification of specific risks on each project. Table F–8 is an example of a general purpose risk categorization table.

3. Risk Ranking

Rank the risk to the project for each category:

- Risk Factors and Areas—Under each category, this column lists category risk factors.
- Low Risk Evidence (L)—This column has characteristics of this factor when it can be considered low-risk to the project.
- Medium Risk Evidence (M)—This column has characteristics of this factor when it provides a medium risk.
- High Risk Evidence (H)—This column has characteristics of this factor when it should be considered high-risk.
- Rating—Select the level of risk (example: H, M, L, or 3, 2, 1) applicable to this project.
- Comments—Provide information about project specifics that support the rating choice.

Note that in some cases, evidence in one category for high risk may be evidence for low risk in another. For example, support for organization goals or use of new technologies may be taken either way, depending on the situation.

4. Key Risk Identification

Sort the risk table in order of risk with high-risk items first. For the top ten risks, and all risks rated high if more than ten, calculate the risk exposure. These are your key risks. Identify the means of controlling each key risk, and establish ownership of the action and date of completion. Integrate the key risks into the project plan and determine the impacts on schedule and cost.

TABLE F–8

Risk Categorization Table Template

Risk Factors and Categories	L—Low Risk Evidence	M—Medium Risk Evidence	H—High Risk Evidence	Rating (H/M/L)	Comments
Mission and Goals Factors					
Project Fit	directly supports organization mission and/or goals	indirectly impacts one or more goals	does not support or relate to organization mission or goals		
Workflow	little or no change to workflow	will change some aspect or have small effect on workflow	significantly changes the workflow or method of organization		
Organization Management Factors					
Organization Stability	little or no change in management or structure expected	some management change or reorganization expected	management or organization structure is continually or rapidly changing		
Development Team Stability	team chosen, little or no change expected	team chosen but members may change	team not chosen, no decision as to members		
Policies and Standards	development policies and standards are defined and carefully followed	development policies/ standards are in place, but are weak or not carefully followed	no policies or standards, or they are ill-defined and unused		
Management Support	strongly committed to success of project	some commitment, not total	little or no support		

(Continues)

TABLE F-8 (Continued)
Risk Categorization Table Template

Risk Factors and Categories	L—Low Risk Evidence	M—Medium Risk Evidence	H—High Risk Evidence	Rating (H/M/L)	Comments
Performance Objectives	verifiable performance objectives, reasonable requirements	some performance objectives, measures may be questionable	no established performance requirements or requirements are not measurable		
Executive Involvement	visible and strong support	occasional support, provides help on issues when asked	no visible support; no help on unresolved issues		
Customer Factors					
Customer Involvement	end-users highly involved with project team, provide significant input	end-users play minor roles, moderate impact on system	minimal or no end-user involvement; little end-user input		
Customer Experience	end-users highly experienced in similar projects; have specific ideas of how needs can be met	end-users have experience with similar projects and have needs in mind	end-users have no previous experience with similar projects; unsure of how needs can be met		
Customer Acceptance	end-users accept concepts and details of system; process is in place for end-user approvals	end-users accept most concepts and details of system; process in place for end-user approvals	end-users do not accept any concepts or design details of system		

(Continues)

Risk Factors and Categories	L—Low Risk Evidence	M—Medium Risk Evidence	H—High Risk Evidence	Rating (H/M/L)	Comments
Customer Training Needs	end-user training needs considered; training in progress or plan in place	end-user training needs considered; no training yet or training plan is in development	requirements not identified or not addressed		
Customer Justification	end-user justification complete, accurate, sound	end-user justification provided, complete with some questions about applicability	no satisfactory justification for system		
Contract Fit	contract with customer has good terms, communication with team is good	contract has some open issues which could interrupt team work efforts	contract has burdensome document requirements or causes extra work to comply		
Benefits Defined	benefits well-defined, with identified measures and baselines	some questions remain about benefits, or baseline is changing and measures doubtful	benefits not defined, no baseline established, unattainable or unmeasurable		
Budget/Cost Factors					
Project Size	small, noncomplex, or easily decomposed	medium, moderate complexity, decomposable	large, highly complex, or not decomposable		
Hardware Constraints	little or no hardware-imposed constraints or single platform	some hardware-imposed constraints; several platforms	significant hardware-imposed constraints; multiple platforms		

(Continues)

TABLE F-8 (Continued)
Risk Categorization Table Template

Risk Factors and Categories	L—Low Risk Evidence	M—Medium Risk Evidence	H—High Risk Evidence	Rating (H/M/L)	Comments
Technology	mature, existent, in-house experience	existent, some in-house experience	new technology or a new use or under development; little in-house experience		
Reusable Components	components available and compatible with approach	components promised, delivery dates unsure	components projected, but not available when needed		
Supplied Components	components available and directly usable	components work under most circumstances	components known to fail in certain cases, likely to be late, or incompatible with parts of approach		
Budget Size	sufficient budget allocated	questionable budget allocated	doubtful budget is sufficient		
Budget Constraints	funds allocated without constraints	some questions about availability of funds	allocation in doubt or subject to change without notice		
Economic Justification	completely justified and cost effectiveness proven	justification questionable or effectiveness not completely established	not justified or cost effectiveness demonstrated		
Cost Controls	well established, in place	system in place, weak in areas	system lacking or nonexistent		

(Continues)

TABLE F-8 (Continued)

Risk Categorization Table Template

Risk Factors and Categories	L—Low Risk Evidence	M—Medium Risk Evidence	H—High Risk Evidence	Rating (H/M/L)	Comments
Schedule Factors					
Delivery Commitment	stable commitment dates	some uncertain commitments	unstable, fluctuating commitments		
Development Schedule	team projects that schedule is acceptable and can be met	team finds one phase of the plan to have a schedule that is too aggressive	team projects that two or more phases of schedule are unlikely to be met		
Project Content					
Requirements Stability	little or no change expected to approved set (baseline)	some change expected against approved set	rapidly changing or no agreed-upon baseline		
Requirements Complete and Clear	all completely specified and clearly written	some requirements incomplete or unclear	some requirements only in the head of the customer		
System Testability	system requirements easy to test, plans underway	parts of system hard to test, or minimal planning being done	most of system hard to test, or no test plans being made		
Design Difficulty	well-defined interfaces; design well understood	unclear how to design, or aspects of design yet to be decided	interfaces not well-defined or controlled; subject to change		

(Continues)

Risk Factors and Categories	L—Low Risk Evidence	M—Medium Risk Evidence	H—High Risk Evidence	Rating (H/M/L)	Comments
Implementation Difficulty	algorithms and design are reasonable for this team to implement	algorithms and/or design have elements somewhat difficult to implement	algorithms and/or design have components this team will find very difficult to implement		
System Dependencies	clearly defined dependencies of the software effort and other parts of system	some elements of the system are well understood and planned; others are not yet comprehended	no clear plan or schedule for how the whole system will come together		
Documents Stability	documents will be available on time and will contain few errors	some documents may be late and contain minor errors	little chance of getting documents on time, many corrections and changes expected		
Performance Factors					
Test Capability	modular design allows for easy coverage test planning and execution	modular design aids developing test harnesses for unit test	No modular design or ability to easily establish test coverage planning.		
Expected Test Effort	good estimate available, readily fits system acceptance process	rough estimate of test time, may be a bottleneck in the process	poor or no estimate of test times, definite chance of bottleneck		
Functionality	highly functional, meets all customer needs	good functionality, meets most customer needs	little functionality, many customer needs not met		

(Continues)

Risk Factors and Categories	L—Low Risk Evidence	M—Medium Risk Evidence	H—High Risk Evidence	Rating (H/M/L)	Comments
External Hardware or Software Interfaces	little or no integration or interfaces needed	some integration or interfaces needed	extensive interfaces required		
Project Management Factors					
Approach	product and process planning and monitoring in place	planning and monitoring need enhancement	weak or nonexistent planning and monitoring		
Communication	clearly communicates goals and status between the team and rest of organization	communicates some of the information some of the time	rarely communicates clearly to the team or to others who need to be informed of team status		
Project Manager Experience	project manager very experienced with similar projects	project manager has moderate experience or has experience with different types of projects	project manager has no experience with this type of project or is new to project management		
Project Manager Attitude	strongly committed to success	willing to do what it takes	cares very little about project		
Project Manager Authority/Support	complete support of team and of management	support of most of team, with some reservations	no visible support; manager in name only		

(Continues)

TABLE F-8 (Continued)
Risk Categorization Table Template

Risk Factors and Categories	L—Low Risk Evidence	M—Medium Risk Evidence	H—High Risk Evidence	Rating (H/M/L)	Comments
Development Process Factors					
Alternatives Analysis	analysis of alternatives complete, all considered, assumptions verifiable	analysis of alternatives complete, some assumptions questionable or alternatives not fully considered	analysis not completed, not all alternatives considered, or assumptions faulty		
Quality Assurance Approach	QA system established, followed, effective	procedures established, but not well followed or effective	no QA process or established procedures		
Commitment Process	changes to commitments in scope, content, schedule are reviewed and approved by all involved	changes to commitments are communicated to all involved	changes to commitments are made without review or involvement of the team		
Development Documentation	correct and available	some deficiencies, available	nonexistent		
Use of Defined Engineering Process	development process in place, established, effective, followed by team	process established, but not followed or is ineffective	no formal process used		
Early Identification of Defects	peer reviews are incorporated throughout	peer reviews are used sporadically	team expects to find all defects with testing		

(Continues)

TABLE F-8 (Continued)
Risk Categorization Table Template

Risk Factors and Categories	L—Low Risk Evidence	M—Medium Risk Evidence	H—High Risk Evidence	Rating (H/M/L)	Comments
Change Control for Work Products	formal change control process in place, followed, effective	change control process in place, not followed or is ineffective	no change control process used		
Defect Tracking	defect tracking defined, consistent, effective	defect tracking process defined, but inconsistently used	no process in place to track defects		
Development Environment Factors					
Physical Facilities	little or no modification needed	some modifications needed; some existent	major modifications needed, or facilities nonexistent		
Hardware Platform	stable, no changes expected, capacity is sufficient	some changes under evolution, but controlled	platform under development along with software		
Tools Availability	in place, documented, validated	available, validated, some development needed (or minimal documentation)	invalidated, proprietary or major development needed; no documentation		
Configuration Management	fully controlled	some controls in place	no controls in place		

(Continues)

TABLE F-8 (Continued)

Risk Categorization Table Template

Risk Factors and Categories	L—Low Risk Evidence	M—Medium Risk Evidence	H—High Risk Evidence	Rating (H/M/L)	Comments
Security	all areas following security guidelines; data backed up; disaster recovery system in place; procedures followed	some security measures in place; backups done; disaster recovery considered, but procedures lacking or not followed	no security measures in place; backup lacking; disaster recovery not considered		
Vendor Support	complete support at reasonable price and in needed time frame	adequate support at contracted price, reasonable response time	little or no support, high cost, and/or poor response time		
Staff Factors					
Staff Availability	in place, little turnover expected; few interrupts for fire fighting	available, some turnover expected; some fire fighting	high turnover, not available; team spends most of time fighting fires		
Mix of Staff Skills	good mix of disciplines	some disciplines inadequately represented	some disciplines not represented at all		
Product Knowledge	very experienced at developing this type of product	some experience in developing this type of product	no experience in developing this type of product		
Software Development Experience	extensive experience with this type of project	some experience with similar projects	little or no experience with similar projects		

(Continues)

TABLE F-8 (Continued)
Risk Categorization Table Template

Risk Factors and Categories	L—Low Risk Evidence	M—Medium Risk Evidence	H—High Risk Evidence	Rating (H/M/L)	Comments
Training of Team	training plan in place, training ongoing	training for some areas not available or training planned for future	no training plan or training not readily available		
Team Spirit and Attitude	strongly committed to success of project; cooperative	willing to do what it takes to get the job done	little or no commitment to the project; not a cohesive team		
Team Productivity	all milestones met, deliverables on time, productivity high	milestones met, some delays in deliverables, productivity acceptable	productivity low, milestones not met, delays in deliverables		
Maintenance Factors					
Complexity	structurally maintainable (low complexity measured or projected)	certain aspects difficult to maintain (medium complexity)	extremely difficult to maintain (high complexity)		
Change Implementation	team in place can be responsive to customer needs	team experiences delays, but acceptable to customer	team is unable to respond to customer needs		
Support Personnel	in place, experienced, sufficient in number	missing some areas of expertise	significant discipline or expertise missing		
Vendor Support	complete support at reasonable price and in needed time frame	adequate support at contracted price, reasonable response time	little or no support, high cost, and/or poor response time		

5. Project Risk Reporting Format

Establish a regular risk report format for weekly project status meetings. At a minimum, show the status of the top ten risks with the ranking of each from the previous week and the number of weeks on the list. Show the risk response report and the risk change report. Table F–9 shows this report with the changing in rankings and the resolution progress.

TABLE F–9
Weekly Risk Change Report

Risk Item	Rank This Week	Last Rank	Number of Weeks on List	Resolution Progress
Too few engineering experts	1	1	2	Contract under discussion
Design schedule tight	2	2	2	Enforcing Delphi estimates
Report function weak	3	5	3	On agenda with customer
Interface too different	4	4	3	On agenda with customer
New requirements	5	3	4	Review each new one for cost
"Goldplating" threat	6	6	4	Reviewing each phase
Unknown quality	7	8	3	No second supplier found yet
Wall unstable	8	new		Contract for braces in process
Timing problems	9	new		Plan to stimulate in March
New technology risky	10	10	4	Reviewed requirements

6. Define Ongoing Project Risk Management

The final step is ensuring that risk management is an ongoing process within your project management. Monitoring and control must be done to the list of risks on a regular basis. The project manager and team must be aware of the identified risks and the process for resolving them. New risks must be identified as soon as possible, prioritized, and added to the risk management plan. High-priority risks must be worked on with respect to the overall project plan.

Software Risk Management Plan

Lift Controller

Excelsior Elevator Embedded Software Development Team

April 3, 2001

Version	Release Date	Responsible Party	Major Changes
0.1	20 January 2001	Team	Initial Risk Factor Release for Comment
0.2	15 February 2001	Team	Refined Risk Factors
0.3	1 March 2001	Team	First Draft of All Risk Steps
0.9	15 March 2001	Team	Alpha Document Release
1.0	3 April 2001	Team	Version 1.0 Release

Table of Contents

1. Introduction

The lift controller project was chartered for the express purpose of risk mitigation. The embedded controller in the elevator systems sold by Excelsior must be guaranteed to never open the door with no elevator present, and never allow the door to open while elevator is in motion. This risk management plan focuses only on proving the requirements model correct through the use of a theorem prover, Alloy.

2. Risk Categorization Table

Using the basic template, Table F–10 shows the ranking of the basic risk factors as related to the lift controller correctness proof.

3. Risk Ranking

Table F–11 shows the risk rankings for all areas of the baseline risk template used within the embedded systems group. Another column has been added to the baseline table to uniquely identify each risk. The unique number is made up of the risk factor identifier from Table F–12, the original risk ranking (H or M), and a sequential number.

TABLE F-10

Lift Controller Risk Categorization Table

Risk Factors and Categories	L—Low Risk Evidence	M—Medium Risk Evidence	H—High Risk Evidence	Rating (H/M/L)	Comments
Mission and Goals Factors					
Project Fit	directly supports organization mission and/or goals	indirectly impacts one or more goals	does not support or relate to organization mission or goals	L	
Workflow	little or no change to workflow	will change some aspect or have small effect on workflow	significantly changes the workflow or method of organization	L	
Organization Management Factors					
Organization Stability	little or no change in management or structure expected	some management change or reorganization expected	management or organization structure is continually or rapidly changing	M	
Development Team Stability	team chosen, little or no change expected	team chosen but members may change	team not chosen, no decision as to members	L	
Policies and Standards	development policies and standards are defined and carefully followed	development policies / standards are in place, but are weak or not carefully followed	no policies or standards, or they are ill-defined and unused	L	
Management Support	strongly committed to success of project	some commitment, not total	little or no support	L	

(Continues)

TABLE F-10 (Continued)
Lift Controller Risk Categorization Table

Risk Factors and Categories	L—Low Risk Evidence	M—Medium Risk Evidence	H—High Risk Evidence	Rating (H/M/L)	Comments
Performance Objectives	verifiable performance objectives, reasonable requirements	some performance objectives, measures may be questionable	no established performance requirements or requirements are not measurable	L	
Executive Involvement	visible and strong support	occasional support, provides help on issues when asked	no visible support; no help on unresolved issues	L	
Customer Factors					
Customer Involvement	end-users highly involved with project team, provide significant input	end-users play minor roles, moderate impact on system	minimal or no end-user involvement; little end-user input	M	
Customer Experience	end-users highly experienced in similar projects; have specific ideas of how needs can be met	end-users have experience with similar projects and have needs in mind	end-users have no previous experience with similar projects; unsure of how needs can be met	L	
Customer Acceptance	end-users accept concepts and details of system; process is in place for end-user approvals	end-users accept most concepts and details of system; process in place for end-user approvals	end-users do not accept any concepts or design details of system	L	

(Continues)

TABLE F-10 (Continued)

Lift Controller Risk Categorization Table

Risk Factors and Categories	L—Low Risk Evidence	M—Medium Risk Evidence	H—High Risk Evidence	Rating (H/M/L)	Comments
Customer Training Needs	end-user training needs considered; training in progress or plan in place	end-user training needs considered; no training yet or training plan is in development	requirements not identified or not addressed	L	
Customer Justification	end-user justification complete, accurate, sound	end-user justification provided, complete with some questions about applicability	no satisfactory justification for system	L	
Contract Fit	contract with customer has good terms, communication with team is good	contract has some open issues which could interrupt team work efforts	contract has burdensome document requirements or causes extra work to comply	L	
Benefits Defined	benefits well-defined, with identified measures and baselines	some questions remain about benefits, or baseline is changing and measures doubtful	benefits not defined, no baseline established, unattainable or unmeasurable	L	
Budget/Cost Factors					
Project Size	small, noncomplex, or easily decomposed	medium, moderate complexity, decomposable	large, highly complex, or not decomposable	H	
Hardware Constraints	little or no hardware-imposed constraints or single platform	some hardware-imposed constraints; several platforms	significant hardware-imposed constraints; multiple platforms	L	

(Continues)

TABLE F-10 (Continued)
Lift Controller Risk Categorization Table

Risk Factors and Categories	L—Low Risk Evidence	M—Medium Risk Evidence	H—High Risk Evidence	Rating (H/M/L)	Comments
Technology	mature, existent, in-house experience	existent, some in-house experience	new technology or a new use or under development; little in-house experience	L	
Reusable Components	components available and compatible with approach	components promised, delivery dates unsure	components projected, but not available when needed	H	
Supplied Components	components available and directly usable	components work under most circumstances	components known to fail in certain cases, likely to be late, or incompatible with parts of approach	L	
Budget Size	sufficient budget allocated	questionable budget allocated	doubtful budget is sufficient	M	
Budget Constraints	funds allocated without constraints	some questions about availability of funds	allocation in doubt or subject to change without notice	L	
Economic Justification	completely justified and cost effectiveness proven	justification questionable or effectiveness not completely established	not justified or cost effectiveness demonstrated	L	
Cost Controls	well established, in place	system in place, weak in areas	system lacking or nonexistent	H	

(Continues)

TABLE F-10 (Continued)
Lift Controller Risk Categorization Table

Risk Factors and Categories	L—Low Risk Evidence	M—Medium Risk Evidence	H—High Risk Evidence	Rating (H/M/L)	Comments
Schedule Factors					
Delivery Commitment	stable commitment dates	some uncertain commitments	unstable, fluctuating commitments	L	
Development Schedule	team projects that schedule is acceptable and can be met	team finds one phase of the plan to have a schedule that is too aggressive	team projects that two or more phases of schedule are unlikely to be met	M	
Project Content					
Requirements Stability	little or no change expected to approved set (baseline)	some change expected against approved set	rapidly changing or no agreed-upon baseline	L	
Requirements Complete and Clear	all completely specified and clearly written	some requirements incomplete or unclear	some requirements only in the head of the customer	L	
System Testability	system requirements easy to test, plans underway	parts of system hard to test, or minimal planning being done	most of system hard to test, or no test plans being made	H	
Design Difficulty	well-defined interfaces; design well understood	unclear how to design, or aspects of design yet to be decided	interfaces not well-defined or controlled; subject to change	M	

(Continues)

Risk Factors and Categories	L—Low Risk Evidence	M—Medium Risk Evidence	H—High Risk Evidence	Rating (H/M/L)	Comments
Implementation Difficulty	algorithms and design are reasonable for this team to implement	algorithms and/or design have elements somewhat difficult for this team to implement	algorithms and/or design have components this team will find very difficult to implement	H	
System Dependencies	clearly defined dependencies of the software effort and other parts of system	some elements of the system are well understood and planned; others are not yet comprehended	no clear plan or schedule for how the whole system will come together	L	
Documents Stability	documents will be available on time and will contain few errors	some documents may be late and contain minor errors	little chance of getting documents on time, many corrections and changes expected	L	
Performance Factors					
Test Capability	modular design allows for easy coverage test planning and execution	modular design aids developing test harnesses for unit test	No modular design or ability to easily establish test coverage planning.	M	
Expected Test Effort	good estimate available, readily fits system acceptance process	rough estimate of test time, may be a bottleneck in the process	poor or no estimate of test times, definite chance of bottleneck	H	
Functionality	highly functional, meets all customer needs	good functionality, meets most customer needs	little functionality, many customer needs not met	L	

(Continues)

TABLE F-10 (Continued)
Lift Controller Risk Categorization Table

Risk Factors and Categories	L—Low Risk Evidence	M—Medium Risk Evidence	H—High Risk Evidence	Rating (H/M/L)	Comments
External Hardware or Software Interfaces	little or no integration or interfaces needed	some integration or interfaces needed	extensive interfaces required	L	
Project Management Factors					
Approach	product and process planning and monitoring in place	planning and monitoring need enhancement	weak or nonexistent planning and monitoring	L	
Communication	clearly communicates goals and status between the team and rest of organization	communicates some of the information some of the time	rarely communicates clearly to the team or to others who need to be informed of team status	L	
Project Manager Experience	project manager very experienced with similar projects	project manager has moderate experience or has experience with different types of projects	project manager has no experience with this type of project or is new to project management	M	
Project Manager Attitude	strongly committed to success	willing to do what it takes	cares very little about project	L	
Project Manager Authority/Support	complete support of team and of management	support of most of team, with some reservations	no visible support; manager in name only	L	

(Continues)

TABLE F-10 (Continued)
Lift Controller Risk Categorization Table

Risk Factors and Categories	L—Low Risk Evidence	M—Medium Risk Evidence	H—High Risk Evidence	Rating (H/M/L)	Comments
Development Process Factors					
Alternatives Analysis	analysis of alternatives complete, all considered, assumptions verifiable	analysis of alternatives complete, some assumptions questionable or alternatives not fully considered	analysis not completed, not all alternatives considered, or assumptions faulty	L	
Quality Assurance Approach	QA system established, followed, effective	procedures established, but not well followed or effective	no QA process or established procedures	L	
Commitment Process	changes to commitments in scope, content, schedule are reviewed and approved by all involved	changes to commitments are communicated to all involved	changes to commitments are made without review or involvement of the team	L	
Development Documentation	correct and available	some deficiencies, available	nonexistent	M	
Use of Defined Engineering Process	development process in place, established, effective, followed by team	process established, but not followed or is ineffective	no formal process used	L	
Early Identification of Defects	peer reviews are incorporated throughout	peer reviews are used sporadically	team expects to find all defects with testing	L	

(Continues)

Risk Factors and Categories	L—Low Risk Evidence	M—Medium Risk Evidence	H—High Risk Evidence	Rating (H/M/L)	Comments
Change Control for Work Products	formal change control process in place, followed, effective	change control process in place, not followed or is ineffective	no change control process used	L	
Defect Tracking	defect tracking defined, consistent, effective	defect tracking process defined, but inconsistently used	no process in place to track defects	L	
Development Environment Factors					
Physical Facilities	little or no modification needed	some modifications needed; some existent	major modifications needed, or facilities nonexistent	L	
Hardware Platform	stable, no changes expected, capacity is sufficient	some changes under evolution, but controlled	platform under development along with software	L	
Tools Availability	in place, documented, validated	available, validated, some development needed (or minimal documentation)	invalidated, proprietary or major development needed; no documentation	H	
Configuration Management	fully controlled	some controls in place	no controls in place	L	

(Continues)

TABLE F-10 (Continued)

Lift Controller Risk Categorization Table

Risk Factors and Categories	L—Low Risk Evidence	M—Medium Risk Evidence	H—High Risk Evidence	Rating (H/M/L)	Comments
Security	all areas following security guidelines; data backed up; disaster recovery system in place; procedures followed	some security measures in place; backups done; disaster recovery considered, but procedures lacking or not followed	no security measures in place; backup lacking; disaster recovery not considered	L	
Vendor Support	complete support at reasonable price and in needed time frame	adequate support at contracted price, reasonable response time	little or no support, high cost, and/or poor response time	H	
Staff Factors					
Staff Availability	in place, little turnover expected; few interrupts for fire fighting	available, some turnover expected; some fire fighting	high turnover, not available; team spends most of time fighting fires	M	
Mix of Staff Skills	good mix of disciplines	some disciplines inadequately represented	some disciplines not represented at all	L	
Product Knowledge	very experienced at developing this type of product	some experience in developing this type of product	no experience in developing this type of product	L	
Software Development Experience	extensive experience with this type of project	some experience with similar projects	little or no experience with similar projects	L	

(Continues)

TABLE F-10 (Continued)
Lift Controller Risk Categorization Table

Risk Factors and Categories	L—Low Risk Evidence	M—Medium Risk Evidence	H—High Risk Evidence	Rating (H/M/L)	Comments
Training of Team	training plan in place, training ongoing	training for some areas not available or training planned for future	no training plan or training not readily available	H	
Team Spirit and Attitude	strongly committed to success of project; cooperative	willing to do what it takes to get the job done	little or no commitment to the project; not a cohesive team	L	
Team Productivity	all milestones met, deliverables on time, productivity high	milestones met, some delays in deliverables, productivity acceptable	productivity low, milestones not met, delays in deliverables	M	
Maintenance Factors					
Complexity	structurally maintainable (low complexity measured or projected)	certain aspects difficult to maintain (medium complexity)	extremely difficult to maintain (high complexity)	M	
Change Implementation	team in place can be responsive to customer needs	team experiences delays, but acceptable to customer	team is unable to respond to customer needs	M	
Support Personnel	in place, experienced, sufficient in number	missing some areas of expertise	significant discipline or expertise missing	H	
Vendor Support	complete support at reasonable price and in needed time frame	adequate support at contracted price, reasonable response time	little or no support, high cost, and/or poor response time	H	

TABLE F-11

Lift Controller Risk Categorization Table

Risk Identifier	Risk Factors and Categories	L—Low Risk Evidence	M—Medium Risk Evidence	H—High Risk Evidence	Rating (H/M/L)	Comments
BC_H_01	Project Size	small, noncomplex, or easily decomposed	medium, moderate complexity, decomposable	large, highly complex, or not decomposable	H	
BC_H_02	Reusable Components	components available and compatible with approach	components promised, delivery dates unsure	components projected, but not available when needed	H	
BC_H_04	Cost Controls	well established, in place	system in place, weak in areas	system lacking or nonexistent	H	
PC_H_01	System Testability	system requirements easy to test, plans underway	parts of system hard to test, or minimal planning being done	most of system hard to test, or no test plans being made	H	
PC_H_03	Implementation Difficulty	algorithms and design are reasonable for this team to implement	algorithms and/or design have elements somewhat difficult for this team to implement	algorithms and/or design have components this team will find very difficult to implement	H	
PF_H_01	Expected Test Effort	good estimate available, readily fits system acceptance process	rough estimate of test time, may be a bottleneck in the process	poor or no estimate of test times, definite chance of bottleneck	H	

(Continues)

TABLE F-11 (Continued)
Lift Controller Risk Categorization Table

Risk Identifier	Risk Factors and Categories	L—Low Risk Evidence	M—Medium Risk Evidence	H—High Risk Evidence	Rating (H/M/L)	Comments
DE_H_01	Tools Availability	in place, documented, validated	available, validated, some development needed (or minimal documentation)	invalidated, proprietary or major development needed; no documentation	H	
DE_H_02	Vendor Support	complete support at reasonable price and in needed time frame	adequate support at contracted price, reasonable response time	little or no support, high cost, and/or poor response time	H	
ST_H_02	Training of Team	training plan in place, training ongoing	training for some areas not available or training planned for future	no training plan or training not readily available	H	
MT_H_03	Support Personnel	in place, experienced, sufficient in number	missing some areas of expertise	significant discipline or expertise missing	H	
MT_H_04	Vendor Support	complete support at reasonable price and in needed time frame	adequate support at contracted price, reasonable response time	little or no support, high cost, and/or poor response time	H	

(Continues)

Table F-11 (Continued)
Lift Controller Risk Categorization Table

Risk Identifier	Risk Factors and Categories	L—Low Risk Evidence	M—Medium Risk Evidence	H—High Risk Evidence	Rating (H/M/L)	Comments
OM_M_01	Organization Stability	little or no change in management or structure expected	some management change or reorganization expected	management or organization structure is continually or rapidly changing	M	
CU_M_01	Customer Involvement	end-users highly involved with project team, provide significant input	end-users play minor roles, moderate impact on system	minimal or no end-user involvement; little end-user input	M	
BC_M_03	Budget Size	sufficient budget allocated	questionable budget allocated	doubtful budget is sufficient	M	
SC_M_01	Development Schedule	team projects that schedule is acceptable and can be met	team finds one phase of the plan to have a schedule that is too aggressive	team projects that two or more phases of schedule are unlikely to be met	M	
PC_M_02	Design Difficulty	well-defined interfaces; design well understood	unclear how to design, or aspects of design yet to be decided	interfaces not well-defined or controlled; subject to change	M	
PF_M_01	Test Capability	modular design allows for easy coverage test planning and execution	modular design aids developing test harnesses for unit test	no modular design or ability to easily establish test coverage planning	M	

(Continues)

TABLE F-11 (Continued)
Lift Controller Risk Categorization Table

Risk Identifier	Risk Factors and Categories	L—Low Risk Evidence	M—Medium Risk Evidence	H—High Risk Evidence	Rating (H/M/L)	Comments
PM_M_01	Project Manager Experience	project manager very experienced with similar projects	project manager has moderate experience or has experience with different types of projects	project manager has no experience with this type of project or is new to project management	M	
DP_M_01	Development Documentation	correct and available	some deficiencies, available	nonexistent	M	
ST_M_01	Staff Availability	in place, little turnover expected; few interrupts for fire fighting	available, some turnover expected; some fire fighting	high turnover, not available; team spends most of time fighting fires	M	
ST_M_03	Team Productivity	all milestones met, deliverables on time, productivity high	milestones met, some delays in deliverables, productivity acceptable	productivity low, milestones not met, delays in deliverables	M	
MT_M_01	Complexity	structurally maintainable (low complexity measured or projected)	certain aspects difficult to maintain (medium complexity)	extremely difficult to maintain (high complexity)	M	
MT_M_02	Change Implementation	team in place can be responsive to customer needs	team experiences delays, but acceptable to customer	team is unable to respond to customer needs	M	

4. Key Risk Identification

Table F–12 shows the high and medium risks. All low-risk items have been removed.

5. Project Risk Reporting Format

Table F–13 shows the format for the weekly risk review. The top ten risks or *all* the high-risk items are reviewed weekly for mitigation plans and reduction efforts.

6. Define Ongoing Project Risk Management

The process of weekly review of the top ten risks will continue until the project is completed or all risks are mitigated.

TABLE F–12
Risk Factor Description Key

Factor ID	Risk Factor Description
BC	Budget/Cost Factors
CU	Customer Factors
DE	Development Environment Factors
DP	Development Process Factors
MG	Mission and Goals Factors
MT	Maintenance Factors
OM	Organization Management Factors
PC	Project Content
PF	Performance Factors
PM	Project Management Factors
SC	Schedule Factors
ST	Staff Factors

TABLE F-13
Weekly Risk Change Report

Risk Identifier	Risk Factors and Categories	Rank This Week	Last Rank	Weeks on List	Rating (H/M/L)	Comments on Mitigation Plan
BC_H_01	Project Size	1	1	1	H	Re-scoping on internal controller instruction count
BC_H_02	Reusable Components	2	2	1	H	Prior calculus models
BC_H_04	Cost Controls	3	3	1	H	None
PC_H_01	System Testability	4	4	1	H	Z Compiler search
PC_H_03	Implementation Difficulty	5	5	1	H	Truth Table Generator from UML
PF_H_01	Expected Test Effort	6	6	1	H	None
DE_H_01	Tools Availability	7	7	1	H	None
DE_H_02	Vendor Support	8	8	1	H	University-developed tool
ST_H_02	Training of Team	9	9	1	H	More OJT time
MT_H_03	Support Personnel	10	10	1	H	None
MT_H_04	Vendor Support	11	11	1	H	None

Software Test Plan _____

Review Chapter 23, "Validation and Verification," in this practitioner's guide before filling in the software test plan template.

Software Test Plan

<Name of Project>

\<author\>

\<date\>

Version	Release Date	Responsible Party	Major Changes
0.1			Initial Document Release for Comment

Table of Contents

Build the table of contents here. Insert it when you finish your document.

1. Introduction

2. Test Plan

2.1 Test Items

2.2 Features to Be Tested

2.3 Features Not to Be Tested

2.4 Approach

- For each major set of features, specify the major activities, techniques, and tools which will be used to test them.
- The specification should be in sufficient detail to permit estimation and scheduling of the associated tasks.
- Specify techniques which will be used to assess the comprehensiveness of testing and any additional completion criteria.
- Specify the techniques used to trace requirements.
- Identify any relevant constraints.

2.5 Item Pass/Fail Criteria

2.6 Suspension Criteria and Resumption Requirements

2.7 Test Deliverables   Deliverables shall include:

- Test design specification;
- Test case specification;
- Test procedure specification;
- Test item transmittal report;
- Test log;
- Test incident report;
- Test summary report;
- Test input data and output data.

Test tools may be included as deliverables.

2.8 Testing Tasks   Identify tasks, inter-task dependencies, and any special skills required.

2.9 Environmental Needs   Specify physical characteristics (including hardware, communications and system software, mode of usage, and any other software or supplies), level of security, and special test tools or needs.

2.10 Responsibilities

2.11 Staffing and Training Needs

2.12 Schedule

2.13 Risks and Contingencies

2.14 Approvals

3. Test Design Specification

3.1. Features to Be Tested

3.2 Approach Requirements

3.3 Test Identification

3.4 Feature Pass/Fail Criteria

4. Test Case Specification

4.1 Test Items

4.2 Input Specifications

4.3 Output Specifications

4.4 Environmental Needs

4.5 Special Procedural Requirements

4.6 Intercase Dependencies

5. Test Procedure Specification

5.1 Purpose

5.2 Special Requirements

5.3 Procedure Steps   Examples of procedure steps are: log, setup, start, proceed, measure, shut down, restart, stop, wrap up, and contingencies.

6. Test Log

6.1 Description

6.2 Log Entries

- Executions
- Procedure results
- Environmental information
- Anomalous events
- Incident report identifiers

7. Test Incident Report

7.1 Summary

7.2 Incident Description   Specify inputs, expected results, actual results, anomalies, date and time, procedure step, environment, attempts to repeat, testers, and observers.

7.3 Impact on testing

8. Test Summary Report

8.1 Summary

8.2 Variances

8.3 Comprehensiveness Assessment

8.4 Summary of Results   List resolved and unresolved incidents.

8.5 Evaluation (by Test Items)

8.6 Summary of Activities

8.7 Approvals

Software Test Plan

Lift Controller

Excelsior Elevator Embedded Software Development Team

March 7, 2001

Version	Release Date	Responsible Party	Major Changes
0.1	15 January 2001	Team	Initial Document Release for Comment
1.0	28 February 2001	Team	Version 1.0 Release
1.5	7 March 2001	Team	Change in Proveability Theorem

Table of Contents

1. Introduction

The lift controller project's purpose is to develop the requirements proveability using formal methods for the embedded portions of the latest Excelsior Elevator software system. To that extent, this test document focuses solely on the testing of theorem baselines. Baselines are defined as project configuration items as defined in the SCMP.

2. Test Plan

2.1 Test Items

2.2 Features to Be Tested   Only lift controller baselines and tools used in the project will be tested. Each baseline will consist of the following:

1. Truth table showing the requirement feature set to be proved
2. Relational calculus describing the correctness tautology
3. End-user scenario or use case with appropriate UML diagrams
4. Alloy source code
5. Alloy run logs and execution audits
6. Alloy configuration tables for the run
7. Alloy tautology-proven results
8. Signed certificate of completeness by baseline engineer

Tools to be tested include Alloy and any automatic modeling tools. Each tool will be bench-marked upon first use with a vendor-supplied regression test set to ensure that the tool is functioning correctly. Calibration of software tools is critical in order to eliminate any tool-induced errors.

2.3 Features Not to Be Tested   All project documentation and artifacts other than baselines and tools will be tested by way of reviews and walk-throughs.

2.4 Approach   The approach to be used in testing is the best-practices approach used in formal language specification and proveability with the Z language.

2.5 Item Pass/Fail Criteria   A baseline passes when a tautology is proven. If a tautology cannot be proven, the "failed" baseline is archived and no other use may be made of its lambda or predicate calculus representation. Within the SCM system, no branches may be made from its source.

2.6 Suspension Criteria and Resumption Requirements   Tests may not suspend and resume. Tests must run to completion or be canceled and restarted. Restarting of formal proof tools is not a deterministic process and consistent results cannot be guaranteed.

2.7 Test Deliverables   A baseline package is the deliverable from each test. The baseline is the smallest test object and all of these pieces must be included:

1. Truth table showing the requirement feature set to be proved
2. Relational calculus describing the correctness tautology
3. End-user scenario or use case with appropriate UML diagrams
4. Alloy source code
5. Alloy run logs and execution audits
6. Alloy configuration tables for the run
7. Alloy tautology-proven results
8. Signed certificate of completeness by baseline engineer

2.8 Testing Tasks   Prove the correctness of the baseline package.

2.9 Environmental Needs   There are no special needs outside of the development systems. In this project situation, the development and test systems are one and the same, by design.

2.10 Responsibilities   There are none other than those specified in the SPMP and Excelsior Elevator embedded system development policies and procedures for systems that can cause injury to humans.

2.11 Staffing and Training Needs   More on-the-job training is needed in Alloy for algorithm development and testing.

2.12 Schedule   Refer to the SPMP.

2.13 Risks and Contingencies   Refer to the project risk management plan.

2.14 Approvals   All final baseline packages must be approved by the embedded systems executive.

3. Test Design Specification

Not required. Each individual baseline package will have its inherent testing documented as part of the baseline development.

4. Test Case Specification

Not required. Each individual baseline package will have its inherent testing documented as part of the baseline development.

5. Test Procedure Specification

Not required. Each individual baseline package will have its inherent testing documented as part of the baseline development.

6. Test Log

6.1 Description   The change management system has logging of individual baseline tests as a subtask. That system will be used for all test logging.

6.2 Log Entries   Each of the baseline acceptance tests will have the following information captured and entered into the database log system:

1. Executions
2. Procedure results

3. Environmental information
4. Anomalous events
5. Incident report identifiers

7. Test Incident Report

Test incident reporting is part of the test logging process for this project. An on-demand incident report is available from the database.

8. Test Summary Report

An on-demand test summary report is available from the database.

Software Configuration Management Plan (SCMP) _____

Refer to Chapter 31, "Software Configuration Management," in this practitioner's guide before filling in the SCMP template.

Software Configuration Management Plan

<Name of Project>

<author>

<date>

Version	Release Date	Responsible Party	Major Changes
0.1			Initial Document Release for Comment

Table of Contents

Build the table of contents here. Insert it when you finish your document.

1. Introduction

This section shall provide an overview of the plan.

1.1 Purpose   This subsection shall delineate the specific purpose of the particular software configuration management plan.

1.2 Scope   This subsection shall identify the software items to be produced and used, the organizations, the activities, and the phases of the software life cycle to which the plan applies.

1.3 Definitions and Acronyms   This subsection shall define or provide a reference to the definitions of all terms and acronyms required to properly interpret the SCMP.

1.4 References   This subsection shall:

1. Provide a complete list of all documents referenced elsewhere in the SCMP.
2. Identify each document by title, report number (if applicable), date, and publishing organization.
3. Specify the sources from which the referenced documents can be obtained.

2. Management

This section shall describe the organization and associated responsibilities.

2.1 Organization   This subsection shall describe the organizational structure that influences the configuration management of the software during the development, operation, and maintenance phases. This shall:

1. Describe each major element of the organization together with the delegated responsibilities. Organizational dependence or independence of the elements responsible for SCM from those responsible for software development and use shall be clearly described or depicted.
2. Include an organizational chart or list for the project that illustrates the structure for program/project/system management.
3. Describe the organization responsible for SCM during the operation and maintenance phases.
4. Describe the interface between the developing organization and the using organization, if any, with particular emphasis on the transfer of SCM functions in the operation and maintenance phases.
5. Specifically cover the organizational relationships with the configuration control board in the development, operation, and maintenance phases.

2.2 SCM Responsibilities   This subsection shall describe:

1. The organizational responsibilities for each SCM task; for example, identification, control, status accounting, and reviews and audits.
2. The relationships with software quality assurance, software development, and other functional organizations required to ensure delivery of the approved final product configuration.
3. The responsibilities of the users and developer/maintenance activity in the review, audit, and approval process during each phase of the life cycle.

4. Any SCM responsibilities of the representatives from each organization participating in the product development.

5. The overall responsibility of the configuration control board.

6. Any unusual responsibilities such as special approval requirements necessary to meet SCM requirements.

2.3 SCMP Implementation

This subsection shall establish the major milestones for implementation of the SCMP. Example milestones include the establishment of:

- The configuration control board;
- Each configuration baseline;
- Schedules and procedures for SCM reviews and audits;
- Configuration management of related software development, test, and support tools.

2.4 Applicable Policies, Directives, and Procedures

This subsection shall:

1. Identify all applicable SCM policies, directives, and procedures that are to be implemented as part of this plan. The degree of implementation of each shall be stated.

2. Describe any SCM policies, directives, and procedures that are to be written and implemented for this project.

Examples of material which may be covered by policies, directives, and procedures are:

- Identification of levels of software in a hierarchical tree
- Program and module naming conventions
- Version level designations
- Software product identification methods
- Identification of specifications, test plans and procedures, programming manuals, and other documents
- Media identification and file management identification
- Document release process
- Turnover or release of software products to a library function
- Processing of problem reports, change requests, and change orders
- Structure and operation of configuration control boards
- Release and acceptance of software products
- Operation of software library systems to include methods of preparing, storing, and updating modules
- Auditing of SCM activities
- Problem reporting, change request, or change order documentation for requirements, describing the purpose and impact of a configuration change

- Level of testing required prior to entry of software into configuration management
- Level of quality assurance; for example, verification against development standards, required prior to entry of software into configuration management

3. SCM Activities

This section shall describe how the following requirements for SCM shall be satisfied:

1. Configuration identification
2. Configuration control
3. Configuration status accounting and reporting
4. Configuration audits and reviews

3.1 Configuration Identification   This subsection shall identify the software project baselines (that is, the initial approved configuration identifications) and correlate them to the specific life cycle phases. For each baseline, the following shall be described:

1. The items which form each baseline (for example, software requirements specifications, deliverable software, etc.).
2. The review and approval events, and the acceptance criteria associated with establishing each baseline.
3. The users' and developers' participation in establishing baselines.

Elements of a baseline definition might include the following:

- Product name and nomenclature
- Product identification number
- For each new version release, the version release number, a description of the new changes, the change release vehicle, the changes to any support software, and the changes to the associated documentation
- Installation instructions
- Known faults and failures
- Software media and media identification

In this subsection delineate the project titling, labeling, numbering, and cataloging procedures for all software code and documentation.

3.2 Change Control   This subsection shall identify the routing of change proposals during each of the software life cycle phases. This may be provided in chart form with narrative support that does the following:

1. Describes the methods of implementing approved change proposals (to include changes in source and object code and documentation).

2. Describes the procedures for software library control including those procedures that provide for: access control, read and write protection for applicable baselines, file protection, file identification, archive maintenance, change history, and disaster recovery.

3. Describes the methods for identification and control, if patches must be used to change object code.

Define the role of each member of the change control board; for example, change review authority:

1. Specify their authority and responsibility.

2. Identify the chairperson and the membership in the organizations, if the organizations have been formed.

3. State how the chairperson and the members (and alternates) are to be appointed, if the organizations have not yet been formed.

4. State the relationships of the developers and the users to the CCB(s).

3.3 Configuration Status Accounting   This subsection shall:

1. Delineate how information on the status of configuration items is to be collected, verified, stored, processed, and reported.

2. Identify the periodic reports to be provided, and their distribution.

3. State what dynamic inquiry capabilities, if any, are to be provided.

4. Describe the means to implement any special status accounting requirements specified by the user.

Some examples of information normally desired are:

- Status of specifications
- Status of proposed changes
- Reports of approved changes
- Status of product versions or revisions
- Reports of the implementation of installed updates or releases
- Status of user-furnished property; for example, user-furnished operating systems

3.4 Audits and Reviews   This subsection shall:

1. Define the SCM role in audits and reviews to be performed at specific points in the software life cycle as defined in Section 1.2 of the SCMP.

2. Identify the configuration items to be covered at each of these audits and reviews.

3. State the procedures to be used for the identification and resolution of problems occurring during these audits and reviews.

4. Tools, Techniques, and Methodologies

This section shall identify, state the purposes, and describe (within the developers' scope of proprietary rights) the use of the specific software tools, techniques, and methodologies to be employed to support SCM on the specific project. This shall include the tools, techniques, and methodologies used to:

1. Identify software media and media documentation.
2. Bring documentation and media under SCM control and formally release it to a user.
3. Document the status of changes made to software and associated documentation.

It shall further define the tools, methodologies, and techniques to be used to prepare reports for various levels of management, such as the project manager, CCB, SCM, and the user.

5. Supplier Control

This section shall state the provisions for assuring that vendor-provided and subcontractor-developed software meet established SCM requirements. As a part of this, this section shall:

1. Indicate the proposed methods for control of subcontractors and vendors to the extent that it impacts the execution of this SCMP.
2. Explain the methods to be used to determine the SCM capability of subcontractors and vendors and monitor their adherence to the requirements of this SCMP.

At a minimum, the supplier shall be required to prepare and implement a SCM plan in accordance with this standard.

6. Records Collection and Retention

This section shall:

1. Identify the SCM documentation to be retained.
2. State the methods and facilities to be used to assemble, safeguard, and maintain this documentation. As part of this, identify any off-site backup facilities to be used.
3. Designate the retention period.

Software Configuration Management Plan

Lift Controller

Excelsior Elevator Embedded Software Development Team

March 15, 2001

Version	Release Date	Responsible Party	Major Changes
0.1	1 February 2001	Team	Initial Document Release for Content Check
0.5	15 February 2001	Team	Changes Information on CVS and Use of Central Linux Server
1.0	15 March 2001	Team	Version 1.0 General Plan Release

Table of Contents

1. Introduction

This SCMP will define the configuration management to be used for all the deliverables of the lift controller project. Those specific deliverables are:

1. Enumerate the lift problem use cases in English.
2. Write formal specification.
3. Determine Boolean expressions for the problem.

4. Translate use cases into Boolean expressions.

5. Write truth table for the Boolean expressions.

6. Review formal specification.

7. Code model and assertions into Alloy from Boolean expressions.

8. Run each assertion and verify that there are no counter-examples for the model.

9. Refine model until no counter-examples are found.

10. Final project review preparation and presentation.

Along with the deliverables, all formal methods tools will be under configuration management.

1.1 Purpose   The lift controller project provides the formal proof of correctness of the requirements gathered to control and move elevators in a building with three floors according to the following logic:

1. Each elevator has a set of three buttons, one for each floor. These illuminate when pressed and cause the elevator to visit the corresponding floor. The illumination is canceled when the elevator visits the corresponding floor.

2. The first and the third floors have one elevator button, while the second has two: one to request an up elevator and one to request a down elevator. These buttons illuminate when pressed. The illumination is canceled when an elevator visits the floor and then moves in the desired direction.

3. When an elevator has no requests, it remains at its current floor with its doors closed.

1.2 Scope   These project artifacts shall be maintained within the configuration management system:

1. Project management plan

2. Software requirements specification

3. Risk management plan

4. Test plan

5. Configuration management plan

6. Alloy source code

7. Alloy proof cases

The Alloy tool executable code shall be maintained within the configuration management system.

The project shall use the CVS system running on the Zorba Linux box located within the client secure DMZ portion of the Excelsior computing network. All project work product will be maintained on this system.

1.3 Definitions and Acronyms   None are used that differ from the industry-accepted IEEE definitions.

1.4 References

1.4.1 Lift Controller Project Plans

Software Project Management Plan, Lift Controller, Excelsior Elevator Embedded Software Development Team, Version 1.0, March 8, 2001

Software Requirements Specification, Lift Controller, Excelsior Elevator Embedded Software Development Team, Version 1.0, March 22, 2001

Software Risk Management Plan, Lift Controller, Excelsior Elevator Embedded Software Development Team, Version 1.0, April 3, 2001

Software Test Plan, Lift Controller, Excelsior Elevator Embedded Software Development Team, Version 1.5, March 7, 2001

2. Management

2.1 Organization   All members of the embedded systems team are responsible for the use of SCM on this project. The embedded system group change control board (CCB) will be the decision body for all changes to the base requirements in the SRS.

2.2 SCM Responsibilities   All configuration items have been identified in the SRS. All team members are responsible for adequate SCM. The CCB will function as per their charter within embedded systems.

2.3 SCMP Implementation   The CVS tool is currently operating within the secure partitions of Zorba. A separate repository named lift_ctrl has been defined and populated with the preliminary versions of all artifacts and their respective templates. All team members with development authority within the embedded systems network have been validated on the Zorba partition.

2.4 Applicable Policies, Directives, and Procedures   None beyond the standard development policies and procedures for mission-critical and life-threatening systems development. This project will adhere to the Level 10, highest level of correctness proving, for all of the final embedded code developed.

3. SCM Activities

3.1 Configuration Identification   Each baseline will consist of the following:

1. Truth table showing the requirement feature set to be proved
2. Relational calculus describing the correctness tautology
3. End-user scenario or use case with appropriate UML diagrams
4. Alloy source code
5. Alloy run logs and execution audits
6. Alloy configuration tables for the run
7. Alloy tautology proven results
8. Signed certificate of completeness by baseline engineer

3.2 Change Control   No baselines, once run and certified, can be changed. A baseline found to be unproveable will be stored as an unlinkable failed theorem proof. A new baseline will be defined to correct any unproven dead-end theorem paths.

All project artifacts other than baselines will have a version control sheet attached, and all past generations will be constructable at any point in its life.

Tools used in this project will *not* be modified unless there is a catastrophic error within the tool. If any tools are changed, all baselines must be rerun and recertified.

3.4 Audits and Reviews   The CCB is responsible for the approval of all changes to any project artifacts except baselines which must be redone.

The project sponsoring executive is responsible for certifying the correctness proveability of the entire project at its conclusion.

4. Tools, Techniques, and Methodologies

There are no specific changes from the standard operating procedures for Level 10 embedded software development.

5. Supplier Control

No external suppliers are to be used on this project.

6. Records Collection and Retention

All artifacts of this project and the tools and systems needed to reproduce them will be kept for 12 months after the last elevator using these embedded controls is decommissioned from service.

References _____

Boehm, Barry (1989). "Tutorial: Software Risk Management." IEEE Computer Society Press.

IEEE Std 1058-1998, "IEEE Standard for Software Project Management Plans," IEEE Computer Society, 8 December 1998.

IEEE Std. 1012-1986.

IEEE Std. 829-1983.

IEEE Std. 1008-1987.

Karolak, Dale (1996). "Software Engineering Risk Management." IEEE Computer Society Press.

Pritchard, Carl (1997). "Risk Management." ESI International.

Web Pages for Further Information _____

www.baz.com/kjordan/swse625/intro.html. Raymond Miller (1997). "Quality and Risk Management."

www.eas.asu.edu/~riskmgmt/intro.html. James S. Collofello. "Software Risk Management."

www.sei.cmu.edu/publications/documents/97.reports/97hb002/97hb002abstract.html. Brian Gallagher, Christopher Alberts, and Richard Barbour. "Software Acquisition Risk Management Key Process Area (KPA)"—Guidebook Version 1.0.

Joint Application Design in Use

Chapter 16, "Eliciting Requirements," described Joint Application Design (JAD). It is a registered trademark of IBM Corporation. As a team approach to requirements elicitation, it focuses on improving the group process and getting the right people involved from the beginning of a project. Toby Crawford and Chuck Morris at IBM developed the initial concept of JAD in 1977. Through a marriage of the IBM methodology, Business Systems Planning, and their own innovative methods, they got IT professionals and end-users to agree on requirement and design specifications. Since 1977, JAD has emerged as the most widely used tool for requirements definition. It isn't just for requirements though—it is employed in the creation of other plans, designs, and policies throughout the software life cycle. Development organizations now realize that a methodology with a high degree of user interaction leads to higher quality software.

JAD sessions are similar to brainstorming sessions, but they aren't quite the same animal. Brainstorming sessions last about two hours; JAD sessions tend to last about three days. Brainstorming sessions are about rapid-fire production of ideas; JAD sessions can produce high-level, but specific, software models of function, data, and behavior.

This description of the use of JAD in the real world of projects was sent to the authors by a Software Project Management Certification class member on remote assignment for her company. The names of all companies in this appendix have been changed. FastPak Universal (FPU) is the focus of this Appendix as JAD is used for the assessment of an integration project. FPU has acquired a company, Dakat, with expertise in the freight forwarding business— shipping containers and air freight versus small envelope-type packages that are the core business for FPU. Definitely complementary business models, but not complementary systems!

The JAD sessions were conducted in late May initiating a 6–8 week assessment process. With teams spanning the globe, the need to have a face-to-face kick-off meeting was considered critical. The focus of the JAD session, or workshop, was to put in place the framework from which the larger, world-wide teams would begin their assessment. The goals of the workshop were as follows:

- Identify short-term, highest return-on-investment opportunities;
- Establish a benchmark for the current situation with regard to Dakat's internal systems;
- Provide a context for future discussions about system integration with FPU and Dakat as the integration strategy evolves;
- Provide a blueprint for system changes for the long term and the user's priority.

The team was also very clear that the goals were *not*:

- Technical assessment only.
- Requirements gathering starting from scratch.
- Agreement on implementation strategy.
- Dakat/FPU-only exercise.

To keep it simple, the team designed and built its own templates to help the workshop move quickly and efficiently. These templates were the tools that the team leaders used to move through the assessment process. The "road map" document used is shown in Table G–1. This guide details the process the team used and provides a reference for all other JAD documents.

TABLE G–1
Team Leader's Guide

Process Step	Task	Responsibility	Tools	Activity or Deliverable
1. Orient Team				
1.1	Team member introductions	Team leader	Team bios (document 1.1)	Note to team that bios are available in notebook
1.2	Team list update	Team leader	Team member list (documents 1.2 and 1.2.1)	Team members review and update contact information
1.3	Review team meeting agenda	Team leader	Team meeting agenda (document 1.3)	Team members review agenda
1.4	Review team roles and responsibilities	Team leader	Roles and responsibilities matrix (1.4)	Review roles and responsibilities document in notebook
1.5	Review workshop preread materials	Team leader	Preread materials (section 2.1)	Review materials
1.6	Distribute any workshop handouts or additional reference material	Team coordinator	Handout materials (section 6)	Distribute to team
1.7	Review team goals statement	Team leader	Goals statement (document 1.5)	Review team goals
1.8	Review intra-team communications plan	Team leader	Intra-team communications plan (document 1.6)	Review with team
1.9	Review inter-team communications plan	Team leader	Inter-team communications plan (document 1.7)	Review with team

(Continues)

Process Step	Task	Responsibility	Tools	Activity or Deliverable
1.10	Review generic team project plan	Team leader	Team project plan (document 1.8)	Review with team
1.11	Review team meeting plan	Team leader	Team meeting plan (document 1.9)	Review with team
1.12	Review team quorum criteria	Team leader	Team quorum criteria (document 1.10)	Review with team
1.13	Team leader guide	Team leader	Team leader guide (document 1.11)	Review with team
1.14	Workshop survey	Team leader	Workshop survey (document 1.12)	Review with team
2. Transfer Knowledge				
2.1	Present current state of known systems	Team leader and cross-team liaison	TL/CTL presentation (document 2.2)	Present overview to team
2.2	Introduction of known system feature categories based on known state	Team leader and cross-team liaison	GBS functionality matrix (document 2.3)	Review with team
3. Brainstorm System Features				
3.1	Introduce known system features	Team leader and cross-team liaison	System feature master list (document 3.1 and 3.1 key)	Review with team
3.2	Record classification notes or function assumptions	Team coordinators	System feature comments (document 3.2)	Review with team

TABLE G-1 (Continued)
Team Leader's Guide

Process Step	Task	Responsibility	Tools	Activity or Deliverable
3.3	Brainstorm in defined categories	Team leader and team	Flip chart sheets and yellow sticky notes	Complete list of system requirements for defined categories
3.4	Brainstorm in requested categories	Team leader and team	Flip chart sheets and yellow sticky notes	Complete list of system requirements for requested categories
3.5	List system features in master sheet	Team coordinator	System feature master list (document 3.1 and 3.1 key)	All system features captured on master list
3.6	Prepare individual ranking sheets	CIT	Individual worksheet (document 3.3 and 3.3 key)	Individual worksheets prepared for team members
3.7	Individually rank system features	Team leader and team	Individual worksheet (document 3.3 and 3.3 key)	Team members will rank system features
4. Assess Features				
4.1	Assess applications or systems	Team leader and team	System feature master list (document 3.2)	Teams will complete a gap analysis for all systems using the master list worksheet. Teams may break into subgroups as appropriate.
4.2	Record individual ranking	CIT		

(Continues)

TABLE G–1 (Continued)
Team Leader's Guide

Process Step	Task	Responsibility	Tools	Activity or Deliverable
5. Group Ranking of System Features				
5.1	Rank system features	Team leader and team	System feature master list (document 3.2)	Team will rank system features for both short- and long-term features
6. Recommendation Prework				
6.1	Complete recommendations questionnaire	Team leader and team	Recommendations questionnaire (document 4.1)	Team will complete questionnaire
6.2	Prepare recommendations questionnaire	Team leader and team	PowerPoint template (document 4.2)	Team will complete presentation
7. Present Team Recommendations				
7.1	Make team presentation	Team leader	PowerPoint presentation (document 5.1)	Presentation should take 15 minutes, with 10 minutes for questions

Table G–2 is the team-recommended prework. This began to focus the team on the presentation they would give to the rest of the workshop participants, whose outline is shown in Table G–3. The team also developed a standard PowerPoint presentation template to use.

TABLE G–2
Team Prework

1. Are there systems capabilities or rankings that could not be assessed during the workshop? If so, list them.

2. Are there key regional or product questions still open? If so, list them.

3. Are there assumptions or constraints? If so, list them. (These items should be captured on the flip chart sheet as the meeting progresses.)

4. Are there nonsystem issues? If so, list them. (These items should be captured on the flip chart sheet as the meeting progresses.)

5. Are there nonsystem risks? If so, list them. (These items should be captured on the flip chart sheet as the meeting progresses.)

6. List action items to be completed before next meeting or conference call, not over the life of the project.

Step 1

Level of System Integration	Yes	No
Fredonia and Appleton interface at data level		
Fredonia uses Appleton system or Appleton uses Fredonia system		
Fredonia and Appleton codevelop common system		
Need more analysis		

Step 2

Explain in one paragraph why the above recommendation was chosen.

Step 3

List next steps within the context of the recommendation:

ID	Responsible Party

Step 4

List the top 10 short-term and top 10 long-term system features.

Step 5

List the top 5 assumptions and constraints.

Step 6

List the top 5 issues.

Step 7

List the top 5 risks.

TABLE G–3
Team JAD Session Presentation Format

Slide Number	Slide Contents	Questionnaire
Slide 1	Team name	
Slide 2	Team recommendation: level of system integration and justification	Steps 1 and 2
Slide 3	Top 10 short- and long-term system features	Step 4
Slide 4	Top 5 assumptions and constraints	Step 5
Slide 5	Top 5 issues and risks	Steps 6 and 7
Slide 6	Next steps	Step 3
Slide 7	Extra slide to be used as team chooses	

What the Team Did Right

- There was a well-defined process to get the teams from start to finish. The team had over 75 participants, 9 business areas to review, and 5 days. There is no doubt that the team would have failed without a highly-structured game plan. It is interesting to note that the participants seemed quite happy to have a great deal of structure and a clearly defined road map. The team even received feedback from those who did not attend the workshop but "heard good things" regarding its organization and outcome. The teams understood what they had to accomplish and how much time they had to do it.

- The team had enough support resources. The role of team coordinator on each team was filled by a senior project manager. These people kept the teams and team leaders on track. The team also had administrative help to document the teams' output. This help was vital—it is difficult to manage a JAD session while capturing all of the detail.

- There were clearly defined goals for what the team was, and just as important, what the team was not, trying to accomplish. These goals were in the opening presentation and every participant's notebook. The team members knew they were successful when the systems and IT participants would remind the line-of-business participants that the JAD session was to talk about *what* not *how*!

- The team had executive buy-in. This high-level support was reiterated several times throughout the week during group meetings and was visibly demonstrated as several senior executives visited.

- The organizers paid attention to non-workshop items—they planned group dinners, constantly restocked the hospitality suite at the hotels, gave out silly prizes. It mattered.

What the Team Would Change Next Time

- Team leaders would arrive a day early for training. Although the team had a dress rehearsal of the process via conference call, and team leaders were invited to participate, the team leaders were not as prepared as they could have been. The team coordinators were able to jump in and assist; however, the team had two teams go off track. One team lost time because the team leader accidentally skipped two steps in the process, and it took the team a couple of hours to refocus. The other team never accomplished one of the steps, the gap analysis, because the team leader arrived with his own agenda. Had the leaders understood, and been comfortable with, the JAD environment and assessment process, these glitches might not have occurred.

- The team would implement a better system to collect the individual votes regarding the importance of each feature. Table G–4 shows the format that was used. Participants voted on paper, and the assessment team entered the votes in the master list spreadsheet at 2:00 a.m.

The team adjusted this during the second round of team meetings by asking participants to submit their votes electronically; however, there was still a lot of cutting and pasting. You would think a bunch of technology project managers would be able to figure this one out!

TABLE G–4
Individual Data Collection Form

Item Number	Category	System Feature	Short	Importance Ranking	Primary Driver	Long	Importance Ranking	Primary Driver

Individual Work Sheet Key

Primary Driver Entries:

Legal

Financial

Regulatory

Revenue

Cost

Industry standard

Country request

Other

Short entries: Range 3 to 18 months

Long entries: More than 18 months

- Team coordinators and managers would be given a plan of action for the week to 10 days after the session. Although the team had a high-level idea for the next steps, the three coordinators and their manager were completely exhausted at the end of the week. By Friday afternoon they were unable to form complete sentences and would laugh hysterically at all suggestions. The team lost a bit of momentum while regrouping in the week after the workshop. A detailed list of next steps would have been difficult to formulate prior to the workshop because the team was not completely certain of the results; however, the team should have had a high-level plan in place.

JAD Team Documents

The following documents were produced by the JAD team during their integration assessment sessions.

Intra-Team Communications Plan

Objective: The intra-team communications plan details how the team members will communicate with each other and how team members can access information regarding the team's activities. (See Table G–5.)

TABLE G–5
Intra-Team Communications Events Schedule

Communications Event	Frequency	Description	Communication Method	Role Responsible
Kick-off meeting	One time for each team	Team information such as: goals, timelines, milestones, etc.	Email to all team members, and GBS Web site	Team leader, team coordinator
Meeting notices	One per meeting	Information regarding the next team meeting, including date, time, call-in number, etc.	GBS Web site	Team leader, team coordinator
Meeting minutes	One per meeting	Attendees, conclusions, issues, action items, next meeting schedule	GBS Web site	Team leader, team coordinator

Inter-Team Communications Plan

Objective: The inter-team communications plan details how the team will validate findings and recommendations with management and how team activities will be communicated to non-teammembers. (See Table G–6.)

Team Roles and Responsibilities

Table G–7 represents the roles and responsibilities of all the JAD session participants. This is an excellent tool providing a reset point for all session attendees.

Team Meeting Plan

Objective: The team meeting plan details the calendar or schedule for team meetings (see Table G–8), contact information, meeting minute format, and information sharing.

Contact information for all teams will be available on the project Web site in the "Team Information" folder.

The format for meeting minutes will be as follows:

- List of those attending meeting
- Agenda items
- Status of action items previously assigned
- Recap of agenda items and discussion points
- Updated list of action items, including owner and due date
- Information regarding next meeting
- Contact for questions regarding minutes

The project assessment Web site will be the primary point for sharing of information. Any documents or material that would be beneficial to the team should be posted on the Web site.

The team leader and the cross-team liaison have primary responsibility for identifying the documents they feel are appropriate for their teams. In addition, the team leader and cross-team liaison are responsible for categorizing the documents as preread, recommended reading, additional background information, or meeting handouts.

Team members or other subject matter experts can also contribute materials by sending documentation to the team leader or cross-team liaison. The team leader and cross-team liaison will decide if the material is appropriate, then categorize and forward it to the team coordinator for publication. The team leader and cross-team liaison will make the final decision whether to make the document available to the team, and, if so, how the document should be

TABLE G-6
Inter-Team Communications Events Schedule

Communications Event	Frequency	Description	Communication Method	Role Responsible
Team announcements	One time for each team	Information regarding who is assigned to each team and what their role will be.	GBS Web site	Team leader, cross-team liaison
Communications schedule	One time for each team	Schedule that teams will use to post communications. All communications will be posted within two business days of the event, unless otherwise noted.	GBS Web site	Team leader, team coordinator
Kick-off meeting	One time for each team	Team information such as: goals, timelines, milestones, etc.	Email to all team members and GBS Web site	Team leader, team coordinator
Summary status	One per week for each team	Weekly updates reporting ordinal status (red, yellow, green), accomplishments for the week and future events (what's scheduled for next week and significant milestones). Appropriate for senior management to determine if projects are on track.	GBS Web site	Team leader, team coordinator
High-level status update	One per month for each team	Brief milestone review with management and executive teams.	Conference call	Team leader, cross-team liaison
Conclusions	One time for each team	Recommendations from each team.	Conference call and GBS Web site	Team leader, cross-team liaison

TABLE G–7

Team Roles and Responsibilities

Role	Responsibilities
Cross-team liaison (CTL)	Provide consistency between assessments Ensure coordination between teams
Team leader (TL)	Direct team Oversee the assessment process Validate team needs Determine the desired state from both long-term and short-term perspective Present final team recommendations
Team coordinator (TC)	Develop team project plan Organize team Determine team resource needs Update project plan weekly Maintain project notebook Maintain team assessment procedures Report team status Coordinate team meetings Publish team meeting minutes Produce recommendation
Subject matter expert (SME)	Refine team plan and procedures Perform assessment tasks Analyze systems Review findings
Reviewer (REV)	Attend milestone review sessions Receive team communications

categorized. The team coordinator should not receive any materials from anyone other than the team leader or cross-team liaison.

The team coordinator is responsible for posting all documents on the GBS Web site.

Scheduled times for meeting conference calls must accommodate multiple time zones.

Team Project Plan

Figure G–1 is a graphic showing the collapsed project Gantt chart. This is used as the top-level graphic showing the project plan.

TABLE G–8
Team Meeting Schedule

Type of Meeting	Frequency	Description	Meeting Notice	Role Responsible
Kick-off meeting	One time for each team	Initial meeting with broader team including all SMEs. Focus of meeting will be to review team goals, timelines, and milestones. In addition, the recommendations of the Dallas workshop team will be presented for validation.	Email to all team members and GBS Web site	Team leader, team coordinator
Team meetings	As scheduled	Team meetings will be held as necessary to meet team timelines and complete milestones as described in the team project plan.	GBS Web site	Team leader, team coordinator

Team Quorum

Objective: The team quorum describes the number of team members who must be present to conduct meetings and make decisions.

TABLE G–9
Quorum Standards

Type of Meeting	Required Quorum
Dallas workshop or any follow-up meetings for workshop items	At least 75% of the team members
Team meetings	At least 35–50% of the team members

ID	ⓘ	Task Name	Duration	Start	Finish
1		**GBS Tactical/Detailed and Strategic/Preliminary Asse**	99.93 days	Mon 3/12/01	Tue 7/31/01
2	■	Preliminary Assessment	5 days	Mon 3/12/01	Fri 3/16/01
3	■	**Detailed Business Assessment**	48 days	Wed 3/21/01	Fri 5/25/01
4		Detail Assessment Kick-Off Mtgs	7 days	Wed 3/21/01	Thu 3/29/01
5		Form Teams	11 days	Wed 3/21/01	Wed 4/4/01
6		Define Assessment Process	6 days	Mon 3/26/01	Mon 4/2/01
7		Finalize Teams, Comm Plan, and Process Defn	2 days	Tue 4/3/01	Wed 4/4/01
8		Review Teams and Process	2 days	Thu 4/5/01	Fri 4/6/01
9		Prepare Team Orientation Materials	5 days	Mon 4/9/01	Fri 4/13/01
10	■	Cross-Team Dallas Mtg	5 days	Mon 5/21/01	Fri 5/25/01
11		**Full Team Assessments**	23.93 days	Tue 6/5/01	Mon 7/9/01
12		**FM Full Team Assessment**	19.93 days	Tue 6/5/01	Mon 7/2/01
13		**Orient Team**	0.5 days	Tue 6/5/01	Tue 6/5/01
22		**Transfer Expertise**	0.5 days	Tue 6/5/01	Tue 6/5/01
25		**Develop Shared Vision**	1.63 days	Wed 6/6/01	Thu 6/7/01
30		**Develop Assessment Work Plan**	2 days	Thu 6/7/01	Mon 6/11/01
38		**Assess Applications**	5.8 days	Mon 6/11/01	Tue 6/19/01
47		**Develop High-Level Potential Solution**	6.25 days	Tue 6/19/01	Wed 6/27/01
52		**Make Recommendations**	3.25 days	Wed 6/27/01	Mon 7/2/01
57		**CM Full Team Assessment**	19.93 days	Wed 6/6/01	Tue 7/3/01
102		**TM Full Team Assessment**	19.93 days	Thu 6/7/01	Thu 7/5/01
147		**EDI Full Team Assessment**	19.93 days	Fri 6/8/01	Fri 7/6/01
192		**PO Full Team Assessment**	19.93 days	Tue 6/5/01	Mon 7/2/01
237		**FGV Full Team Assessment**	19.93 days	Wed 6/6/01	Tue 7/3/01
282		**WMS Full Team Assessment**	19.93 days	Thu 6/7/01	Thu 7/5/01
327		**CorpRef Full Team Assessment**	19.93 days	Fri 6/8/01	Fri 7/6/01
372		**SFA/CS Full Team Assessment**	19.93 days	Mon 6/11/01	Mon 7/9/01
417		**GBS Integrated Solution**	16 days	Mon 7/9/01	Tue 7/31/01
418		Recommendation Prep	15 days	Mon 7/9/01	Mon 7/30/01
419		Recommendation Formal Presentation	1 day	Mon 7/30/01	Tue 7/31/01

FIGURE G–1
Team Project Plan

Team rules are as follows:

- An associated region or business unit must have representation in team meetings.
- If a quorum cannot be reached after two successive attempts, it will be escalated to the program coordinator.

Charter for the Jakarta Workshop

Goals of the project assessment:

- Identify short-term, highest return-on-investment opportunities
- Establish a benchmark for the current situation with regard to Dakat's internal systems
- Provide a context for future discussions about system integration with FPU and Dakat as the integration strategy evolves
- Provide a blueprint for system changes for the long term and the users' priority

What the GBS Assessment is *not*:

- Technical assessment only
- Requirements gathering starting from scratch
- Agreement on implementation strategy
- Dakat/FPU-only exercise
- Just a workshop in Jakarta

Goals of the Jakarta JAD session:

1. Establish Teams
   - Workshop activities
   - Work with larger team
2. Develop high-level shared vision
   - Define the "ruler" for measuring the system's health
   - Understanding the *whys* behind the *whats*
3. Develop gap analysis
   - Determine the baseline of current state
4. Define action steps
   - Develop draft proposal for larger team
   - Remaining assessment activities
   - Preliminary recommendations
5. Gain better understanding of other team priorities

What the JAD session is *not*:

- The end of the assessment process
- The beginning of the assessment process
- A loosely organized, open format event

GLOBAL FEATURE AND FUNCTION ASSESSMENT—Jakarta

Session 1 _____ Session 2 _____

LOCATION/DATE _____ Jakarta, May 19–25, 2001 _____

TEAM LEADER (Specify)* _____

CROSS-TEAM LIAISON (Specify)* _____

SURVEY COMPLETED BY _____

(optional)

*If there was one person you worked with the most during the sessions.

SURVEY QUESTION	EXCELLENT	GOOD	FAIR	POOR
1 Rate the Pre-Meeting Communication and Registration				

Explanation _____
_____
_____

2 Rate the Meeting Facility				

Explanation _____
_____
_____

3 Rate the Hotel Meeting Facility				

Explanation _____
_____
_____

4 Rate the Hotel Accommodations				

(Hotel Name here) _____

Explanation _____
_____
_____

5 Rate the Knowledge Transfer Process/Presentation				

(Please provide an explanation)

Explanation _____
_____
_____
_____

6 Rate the Brainstorm Features/Functions Process				

(Please provide an explanation)

Explanation _____
_____
_____
_____

7 Rate the Individual Feature/Function Ranking Process				

(Please provide an explanation)

Explanation _____
_____
_____

8 Rate the Systems Gap Analysis Process				

FIGURE G–2
JAD Facilities Survey Form

Final JAD Documents

Team orientation	1
Transfer knowledge	2
Workshop worksheets—brainstorm system features, assess applications, and group ranking of system features	3
Recommendation prep work	4
Present team recommendations	5
Constraints, assumptions, and issues	6
Meeting handouts and additional information	7
Notes	8

FIGURE G–3
JAD Notebook Table of Contents

Item #	Category	System Feature	Feature/Function Importance						System Assessment			
			Short	Average	Rank	Long	Average	Rank	System 1	System 2	System 3	Other

Master List Key

Feature/Function Importance	Numeric Value	Description	System Assessment Ranking	Numeric Value
Mandatory	10	Mandatory legal or finance compliance requirement.		
Extremely critical/vital	8–9	Critical to business success. Significant revenue, cost savings, or customer satisfaction expected.	Excellent	9–10
Essential	6–7	Increased revenue, cost savings, or customer satisfaction expected.	Good	6–8
Desirable	3–5	Potential revenue, cost savings, or customer satisfaction expected.	Fair	3–5
Insignificant	1–2	Minimal business impact. Little revenue, cost savings, or customer satisfaction expected.	Poor	1–2
No positive impact	0	No change or impact to business if implemented.	Fails	0
Negative impact	−1	Negative effect, may hurt business if implemented.		

FIGURE G–4
System Feature Master List

(Continues)

Feature/Function Value Table

Feature/Function Importance	Numeric Value	Description
Mandatory	10	Mandatory legal or finance compliance requirement.
Extremely critical/vital	8–9	Critical to business success. Significant revenue, cost savings, or customer satisfaction expected.
Essential	6–7	Increased revenue, cost savings, or customer satisfaction expected.
Desirable	3–5	Potential revenue, cost savings, or customer satisfaction expected.
Insignificant	1–2	Minimal business impact. Little revenue, cost savings, or customer satisfaction expected.
No positive impact	0	No change or impact to business if implemented.
Negative impact	–1	Negative effect, may hurt business if implemented.

FIGURE G–4 (Continued)
System Feature Master List

Item #	Category	System Feature	System	Feature Criteria or Clarification

FIGURE G–5
System Feature Comments Table

Glossary

This glossary is a limited set of quality, software engineering, and project management terms. Only those terms used specifically in chapters within this guide are cited here. Please refer to the following referenced glossaries for a more in-depth treatment of the terminology within the body of knowledge.

Quality Engineering Glossaries

www.1stnclass.com/quality_glossary.htm. More than 250 common acronyms and terms related to quality management with their definitions, cross-linked for your convenience.

www.asq.org/info/glossary/. "American Society of Quality Glossary of Terms."

Software Engineering Glossaries

Freedman, Alan (2000). *9th Computer Glossary: The Complete Illustrated Dictionary* (with CD-ROM). New York, NY: American Management Association.

IEEE Standard 610.12-1990, *IEEE Standard Glossary of Software Engineering Terminology.* Identifies terms currently in use in the field of software engineering. Standard definitions for those terms are established.

Nader, Jonar C. (1998). *Prentice Hall's Illustrated Dictionary of Computing* (with CD-ROM). Upper Saddle River, NJ: Prentice Hall.

www.geocities.com/ikind_babel/babel/babel.html. "Babel: A Glossary of Computer-Oriented Abbreviations and Acronyms."

Project Management Glossaries

www.pmforum.org/library/glossary/index.htm. "Wideman Comparative Glossary of Project Management Terms v2.0."

www.pmi.org/publictn/download/2000welcome.htm. The Project Management Institute, Inc., "A Guide to the Project Management Body of Knowledge," 2000 edition.

Quality Software Project Management Practitioner's Glossary

Abstraction—(1) The level of technical detail of some representation of software. (2) A cohesive model of data or an algorithmic procedure.

Activity—An element of work performed during the course of a project. An activity normally has an expected duration, an expected cost, and expected resource requirements. Activities can be subdivided into tasks.

Adaptive maintenance—Activity associated with changing an application to make it conform to changes in its external environment.

Analysis—A set of activities that attempt to understand and model customer needs and constraints.

Analysis methods—A notation and heuristics for creating models of customer needs and constraints.

Architectural design—An activity that attempts to lay out the module "floor plan" for the software.

Baseline—A configuration item (where configuration may be one thing or a collection of things) that has been formally reviewed and agreed upon, that thereafter serves as the basis for further development, and that can be changed only through formal change control procedures (before this, changes can be made quickly and informally).

Behavioral modeling—Representing the mode of behavior (called states) of an application and the events that cause transitions from state to state.

Beta testing—Testing that is conducted by the user.

Black-box testing—Testing that does not focus on the internal details of the program but uses external requirements.

Business risks—The set of potential business problems or occurrences that may cause the project to fail.

CASE—Computer-aided software engineering.

Cause–effect graphing—A black-box testing method.

Change control—Combines human procedures and automated tools. A change control procedure may include these entities and activities: change request, evaluation, change report, change control authority, engineering change order, check out, changes, review, check in (access and synchronization control), baseline, testing, promoting changes for inclusion in the next release, rebuild of version, review of changes, inclusion of all changes, distribution of new version.

Change control board (CCB)—The person(s) who have responsibility for deciding whether a change is to be made.

Change report—Provides detail on the nature of work required to make a change.

Change request—Provides detail on the type of change that is requested.

Classes—A basic construct in object-oriented methods that categorizes elements of the problem.

Classic life cycle—A linear, sequential approach to process modeling.

Coding—The generation of source code.

Coefficient—A number or symbol multiplying a variable or an unknown quantity in an algebraic term, as 4 in the term $4x$, or x in the term $x(a+b)$; any of the factors of a product considered in relation to a specific factor, especially a constant factor of a term as distinguished from a variable.

Complexity—A quantitative measure of a program's complexity.

Component reuse—The ability to reuse a portion of a model, source code, test case, or similar item.

Configuration—The collection of programs, documents, and data that must be controlled when changes are to be made.

Configuration audit—Verifies that all required configuration items have been produced, that the current version agrees with the specified requirements, that technical documentation completely and accurately describes the configuration items, and that all change requests have been resolved. It may require answers to questions such as these: Do reviews of changes occur? Is the software process followed? Are naming conventions followed?

Configuration control—The evaluation, coordination, approval (disapproval), and implementation of approved changes in the configuration of an item.

Configuration item—An aggregation of hardware or software or any of its discrete portions that satisfies an end-use function and is designated for configuration management. Configuration items may vary widely in complexity, size, and type.

Configuration status accounting—The recording and reporting of the implementation of changes to the configuration. It requires answers to the classical what, who, and when questions.

Configuration status reporting (CSR)—An activity that helps software developers to understand what changes have been made and why.

Corrective maintenance—Finding and fixing defects that have been reported by users.

Correctness—Extent to which a program satisfies specifications and fulfills the user's mission objectives.

Curve fitting—The curve fitting problem is defined as: Given a general equation of a curve and a set of points that the curve passes through, determine the exact equation of the curve that passes through those points. For example, given the following:

A general equation: $y = Ax + B$

A set of points: (1,9), (2,12), (5,21)

The curve that fits this data is:

$y = 3x + 6$

It is generally not possible in real-world problems to have exact solutions because there are almost always errors in the points. Therefore, in curve fitting we are trying to optimize the error between the points and the fitted curve.

Considering the exact definition of an optimization problem as previously given, the curve fitting optimization problem is:

Curve fitting

Objective function—Minimize error between points and curve with calculated constants

Unknowns—The unknown constants in the general equation

Constraints—None (although sometimes the constants are limited to a specified range)

Many different methods are used to calculate the error between the points and the curve, but the most common (and the one used here) is the *least-squares* error. This is defined as the sum of the squares of the differences between a y-coordinate and the value of the curve at that x-coordinate. As an example, consider the line discussed previously:

A general equation: $y = Ax + B$

A set of points: (1,9), (2,12), (5,21)

Current values of unknowns: $A = 1$, $B = 10$

At each point, the difference in the y-coordinates is:

(1, 9) difference $= 9 - 11 = -3$

(2, 12) difference $= 12 - 14 = -2$

(5, 21) difference $= 21 - 15 = 6$

Square each of the differences and then sum the squares, giving a total error of 49 attempts to fit a set of data (x and y vectors of numbers) to a straight line, polynomial, or other function of x. For the moment, we will consider only the case of fitting to a line and ignore the issue of whether the model was, in fact, a good fit for the data.

In a standard linear least-squares fit, we have a set of (x,y) data points that we want to fit to the model $y = m\, x + b$ by adjusting the parameters m and b to make the y values calculated from the formula be as close as possible to the actual y values in the data set. (In a polynomial fit, the model is instead, say, $y = a\, x^3 + b\, x^2 + c\, x + d$. In a multilinear fit, we have data points of the form (x_1, x_2, x_3, y) and our model is $y = a\, x_1 + b\, x_2 + c\, x_3 + d$.

In the model formula, variables such as x and x_2 are called the *independent variables*, and y is the *dependent variable*. Variables such as m, a, and b are called the *parameters* of the model.

Customer—The person or group that has requested the software and will be paying the bill for its development.

Data design—An activity that translates the data model developed during analysis into implementable data structures.

Data dictionary—A database that contains definitions of all data items defined during analysis; see also, *requirements dictionary*.

Data flow diagram (DFD)—A modeling notation that represents a functional decomposition of a system.

Data modeling—An analysis method that models data objects and their relationships.

Data objects—An input or output that is user-visible.

Debugging—The activity associated with finding and correcting an error or defect; a lack of conformance to requirements found in the software after delivery to the customer.

Defect—A problem found in a later phase or process than when it was introduced.

Design—An activity that translates the requirements model into a more detailed model that is the guide to implementation of the software.

Design specification—A document that describes the design.

Design walkthrough—A formal technical review of the design.

Detail design—A design activity that focuses on the creation of an algorithm.

Documents—Deliverables produced as part of the software engineering process.

Efficiency—Amount of computing resources and code required to perform a function.

Effort—The work-time product (e.g., person-days) associated with a project.

Enhancement—An extension of functional or performance requirements.

Equivalence partitioning—A black-box testing method.

Errors—A lack of conformance found before software is delivered to the customer.

Estimation—A project planning activity that attempts to project effort and cost for a software project, or a problem found in the current phase or process.

Exponent—A number or symbol, as 3 in $(x + y)^3$, placed to the right of and above another number, symbol, or expression, denoting the power to which that number, symbol, or expression is to be raised. In this sense, also called power.

Fail-safe—The property of avoiding damage during a failure.

Fault-tolerant—The property of being able to recover from certain errors and keep operating.

Flexibility—Effort needed to modify an operational program.

Formal technical reviews—A structured meeting conducted by software engineering with the intent of uncovering errors in some deliverable or work product.

Function points—A measure of the utility delivered by an application.

Functional decomposition—A technique used during planning, analysis, and design; creates a functional hierarchy for the software.

Hawthorne effect—Those involved in metrics programs must be aware of the possibility of incorrect conclusions because people may perform differently just because they are being measured. Studies have shown that workers under observation appreciate the attention, form team bonds, and generally perform better. Bias may be introduced into the data simply because the measurement is taking place.

The Hawthorne Studies (or experiments) were conducted from 1927 to 1932 at the Western Electric Hawthorne Works in Chicago (now closed), where Harvard Business School professor Elton Mayo examined productivity and work conditions.

The studies grew out of preliminary experiments at the plant from 1924 to 1927 on the effect of light on productivity. Those experiments showed no clear connection between productivity and the amount of illumination, but researchers began to wonder what kind of changes would influence output.

Specifically, Mayo wanted to find out what effect fatigue and monotony had on job productivity and how to control them through such variables as rest breaks, work hours, temperature, and humidity. Mayo took six women from the assembly line, segregated them from the rest of the factory, and put them under the eye of a supervisor who was more a friendly observer than disciplinarian. Mayo made frequent changes in their working conditions, always discussing and explaining the changes in advance. He changed the hours in the working week, the hours in the workday, the number of rest breaks, and the time of the lunch hour.

Throughout the series of experiments, an observer sat with the observed team in the workshop noting all that went on, keeping the team informed about the experiment, asking for advice or information, and listening to them.

The experiment began by introducing various changes, each of which was continued for a test period of 4 to 12 weeks.

Output of the workers went up when improvements in working conditions were made, and output continued to go up when the improvements were taken away. Explanations of this phenomenon are that the individuals became a team, performing well together and giving themselves over to the experiment. The team members perceived that they were autonomous. Without pressure from management, they became responsible for product delivery and developed their own techniques for production.

Mayo discovered that the upward trend in production was independent of the changes made in working conditions. He realized that workplaces are social environments and that people are motivated by much more than economic self-interest. In his studies, the observer, who was tracking productivity, also became involved in the group's social atmosphere.

The workers who were "measured" felt a sense of self-esteem. Because their supervisor included them in plans, they felt as if they were truly a part of his team. This newfound cooperation and loyalty explained why productivity rose even when workplace improvements were removed.

The positive effects noted by the Hawthorne experiments showed that benign supervision and concern for workers, and their coalescence as a team, raised productivity—the changes in working conditions had little or nothing to do with it.

A lesson from the experiment, particularly relevant for software project managers embarking upon or engaged in a metrics program, is that participants in a test, trial, or study have a good experience because they receive attention, which is gratifying to them. Therefore, better results are forthcoming, regardless of any changes made.

Independent test group (ITG)—A group of people whose primary responsibility is software testing.

Integration—The specific approach to integration testing.

Integration testing—A testing step that constructs the software while testing it.

Integrity/security—Extent to which access to software or data by unauthorized people can be controlled.

Interface control—The evaluation, coordination, and approval (or disapproval) of all proposed changes to established functional and physical interfaces, as defined in specifications. It seeks to identify change, control change, ensure that change is being properly implemented, and report changes to those who have an interest.

Interoperability—The degree to which one application communicates or interfaces with another.

Joint Application Design (JAD)—A specific requirements elicitation technique.

Levels of abstraction—The degree of detail with which some representation of the software is presented.

Line-of-code metrics—Measures of quality or productivity that are normalized using lines of code produced.

LOC—Lines of code.

Maintainability—The degree to which a program is amenable to change.

Maintenance—The activities associated with changes to software after it has been delivered to end-users.

Measurement—Collecting quantitative data about the software or the software engineering process.

Metrics—A specific measurement.

Milestones—A point in time that is used to indicate progress during a project.

Modular design—A design approach that stresses modularity.

Modularity—An attribute of a design that leads to the creation of high-quality program components.

Multiple regression—Regression in which one variable is estimated by the use of more than one other variable.

Object-oriented—An approach to software development that makes use of a classification approach and packages data and processing together.

Object-oriented analysis (OOA)—A technique for defined classes of objects, their relationships, and their basic structure.

Object-oriented design (OOD)—A technique for translating the OOA model into an implementation model.

Objects—A named element of the problem domain containing data and processing.

Perfective maintenance—Enhancement.

Portability—The ability to transport software from one target environment to another.

Preliminary design—Creates a representation of the data and architecture.

Problem—Deviation from specifications or expected results.

Procedural design—Creates representations of algorithmic detail within a module.

Process error—Incorrect output of a process, resulting in an incorrect state or condition.

Process failure—Event in which a faulty resource used by the process produces an error in its output that is eventually observed.

Process fault—Fault that resides in the resources used in a process and is viewed as an input to a process; represents an incorrect state or condition of the system to which the process belongs.

Processing narrative—A natural language description of a model (program component).

Productivity—Work output per unit time.

Project control—The control of quality and change.

Project database—The place where configuration items are kept.

Project planning—The activity that creates the project plan.

Project risks—The set of potential project problems or occurrences that may cause the project to fail.

Project scope—A statement of basic requirements of the software to be built.

Project size—An indication of the overall effort to be expended or the number of people working on the project.

Project tracking—The activity that enables a manager to understand the status of a project.

Prototyping—The creation of a mock-up of an application.

Quality—The degree to which a product conforms to both explicit and implicit requirements.

Quality metrics—Measures of quality.

Re-engineering—A series of activities that transform legacy systems (with poor maintainability) into software that exhibits high quality.

Regression analysis—Suppose that a relationship or correlation between two or more things is suspected. That suspicion can then become a theory that one thing causes another. For example, if it were suspected that grams of sugar consumed are related to number of cavities, then a causal hypothesis would be that grams of sugar consumed *causes* cavities.

Statisticians set out to prove that a theory is not false rather than attempting to prove that it is true. A null hypothesis is constructed, which claims that the suspected relationship is not statistically significant. There is an attempt to show statistically that the probability is high that the relationship is significant. A false null hypothesis then lends credence to the idea that the relationship does indeed exist and can be used to explain the behavior of observed phenomena. If a relationship is established, statistical analysis can be used to measure the strength of association between the variables.

Consider the example where the null hypothesis is that there is no relationship between grams of sugar consumed and number of cavities experienced by a person. If people were interviewed and data was gathered for the variables mentioned, you could plot data points over a period of time. If grams of sugar consumed in one year were plotted on the x-axis of a graph and the number of cavities sustained for the year were plotted on the y-axis, the graph might look like a scatter plot. If a line were fitted through the points, a clear relationship might emerge in a linear graph where cavities increase as sugar consumption goes up.

The implication is that more sugar consumed contributes in a causal fashion to more cavities. The algorithm used in simple linear regression analysis attempts to best fit the line through the data points. The equation for the line can be expressed by the formula:

$C = K + S \times I$

where:

C = an observed number of cavities in an individual

K = a constant number

S = grams of sugar consumed by the individual

I = the increase in cavities per gram of sugar consumed

In this example, cavities are plotted on the y-axis, the constant is the y-intercept, grams of sugar consumed are plotted on the x-axis, and increase in cavities per gram, I, is the slope of the line. The slope may be thought of as the number of units of change in y relative to a unit increase in x, or the ratio of the change in y due to the increase in x. A linear relationship exists if the slope of the regression line is not zero. Knowledge of x will contribute to a meaningful estimate of y. In the statistical relationship, cavities, C, is the dependent variable, and sugar, S, is the independent variable. There is a direct linear relationship because the dependent variable increases when the independent variable increases. The test for the null hypothesis is that the slope of the regression line is equal to zero. That is, if the slope is not equal to zero, the null hypothesis is false and a relationship does exist.

Multiple regression involves the simultaneous analysis of more than one independent variable. In the real case at hand, involving software maintenance, the function is:

$$MC = K + \Sigma \, B_i \times CM_i$$

Regression testing—Tests that are conducted repeatedly to ensure that a change has not introduced side effects.

Reliability—Extent to which a program performs with required precision.

Requirements analysis—A modeling activity whose objective is to understand what the customer really wants.

Resources—Anything that is required to get the project done, including people, hardware, materials, and information.

Reusability—The ability to reuse an already-existing program component in another application.

Reusable components—Configuration items that are reusable.

Reverse engineering—Trying to develop design models or an understanding of design using program code as a starting point.

Revision—A new version intended to supersede the old. Revisions typically occur in linear order, but older ones are not thrown away—they are kept in case new bugs are introduced.

Risk—A potential problem or occurrence that put a project in jeopardy.

Risk analysis—Techniques for identifying and evaluating risks.

Robustness—The property of being tolerant of bad inputs.

Scheduling—The activity that lays out a timeline for work to be conducted on a project.

Scope—A bounded statement of what must be accomplished.

Selective testing—Testing only a selected set of program paths and data inputs.

Side effects—Errors that occur because of changes.

Software—Programs, documents, and data.

Software engineering—A discipline that encompasses the process associated with software development; the methods used to analyze, design, and test computer software; the management techniques associated with the control and monitoring of software projects; and the tools used to support process, methods, and techniques.

Software failures—Failures that originate with design defects/errors (system and software), coding defects/errors, clerical mistakes, debugging inadequacies, and testing mistakes.

Software metrics—Quantitative measures of the process or the product.

Software project management plan (SPMP)—A description of the management approach for a project.

Software quality assurance (SQA)—A series of activities that assist an organization in producing high-quality software.

Software Quality Engineer (SQE)—ASQ certification for having a quality approach to software engineering.

Software requirements specification (SRS)—A deliverable that describes all data, functional and behavioral requirements, all constraints, and all validation requirements for software.

Software testing—A set of activities conducted with the intent of finding errors in software.

Spiral model—An evolutionary software engineering paradigm.

State transition diagram (STD)—A notation for behavioral view modeling.

Statistical quality assurance—Techniques for process improvement that are based on measurements of the product and the process.

Status accounting—Notation of the status of the latest revisions and changes. It typically involves reporting document activity (number of documents approved or released, number of changes processed, number of changes approved and incorporated).

Stepwise refinement—A technique for accomplishing functional decomposition or procedural design (also called partitioning).

Structured programming—A design method that limited design constructs to only three basic forms and constrains program flow for better quality.

Task—A generic term for work that is not included in the work breakdown structure but that potentially could be a further decomposition of work by the individuals responsible for that work. Also, the lowest level of effort on a project.

Technical risks—The set of potential technical problems or occurrences that may cause the project to fail.

Test plan and procedure—A description of testing strategy and tactics.

Testability—Effort needed to test to ensure that something performs as intended.

Testing—A set of activities that attempt to find errors.

Tools—Application software used to perform software engineering tasks (e.g., design tools, testing tools); see also CASE tools.

Total quality management—A company commitment to develop a process that achieves high-quality product and customer satisfaction.

Unit testing—Part of the testing strategy that focuses on tests to individual program components.

Usability—Effort required to learn, operate, prepare input, and interpret output.

User—The person who actually uses the software or the product that has software embedded within it.

Validation—Tests to ensure that the software conforms to its requirements.

Version control—Procedures and tools to manage different versions of configuration objects. A version has a set of attributes that describe it, such as a number, a date, and indication of changes.

White-box testing—A test case design technique that makes use of knowledge of the internal program logic.

Work breakdown structure (WBS)—The set of work tasks required to build the software; defined as part of the process model.

Bibliography

This bibliography is a limited set of quality, software engineering, and project management references used throughout this practitioner's guide. Please refer to the following referenced bibliographies for a more comprehensive set within the specific body of knowledge.

Print Bibliography

Abdel-Hamid, Tarek, and Stuart E. Madnick (1991). *Software Project Dynamics: An Integrated Approach*. Upper Saddle River, NJ: Prentice Hall. Abran, Alain, and James W. Moore, eds. (2001). Trial Version 0.9 of the SWEBOK (2001). Los Alamitos, CA: IEEE Press.

Abreu, F.B. (1993). "Metrics for Object-Oriented Environment." *Proceedings of the Third International Conference on Software Quality*, Lake Tahoe, NV, pp. 67–75.

Ackerman, Phillip L., et al., eds. (1990). *Learning and Individual Differences: Process, Trait, and Content Determinants*. Washington, DC: American Psychological Association Books.

Adams, John R. (1997). *The Principles of Project Management*. Sylva, NC: PMI Publication Division.

Akao, Y., ed. (1990). *Quality Function Deployment*. Cambridge, MA: Productivity Press.

Albrecht, A.J., and S.H. Gaffney (1983). "Software Function, Source Lines of Code and Development Effort Prediction: A Software Science Validation." *IEEE Transactions on Software. Engineering*, 9(6):639–648.

Alderfer, Clayton P. (1972). *Existence, Relatedness, and Growth: Human Needs in Organizational Settings*. New York, NY: Free Press.

Allen, Paul (2000). *Realizing e-Business with Components*. Reading, MA: Addison-Wesley.

Allport, Gordon W. (1960). *Personality and Social Encounter: Selected Essays*. Boston, MA: Beacon Press.

Allport, Gordon W. (1961). *Pattern and Growth in Personality*. New York, NY: Holt, Rinehart and Winston.

Archibald, Russell D. (1992). *Managing High-Technology Programs and Projects*, 2nd ed. New York, NY: John Wiley & Sons.

Baber, Robert Laurence (1991). *Error-Free Software: Know-How and Know-Why of Program Correctness*. New York, NY: Wiley.

Bache, Richard, and Gualtiero Bazzana (1994). *Software Metrics for Product Assessment*. New York, NY: McGraw-Hill.

Baker, A.L., et al. (1990). "A Philosophy for Software Measurement." *The Journal of Systems and Software*, 12(3):277–281.

Barns, Michael G. (1993). "Inheriting Software Metrics." *Journal of Object-Oriented Programming*, November–December, pp. 27–34.

Baron, Renee, and Elizabeth Wagele (1994*). The Enneagram Made Easy: Discover the Nine Types of People*. San Francisco, CA: Harper Collins Press.

Basili, Victor R., and R.W. Selby (1987). "Comparing the effectiveness of software testing strategies." *IEEE Transactions on Software Engineering*, SE-13(12):1278–1296.

Basili, Victor (1980). *Tutorial on Models and Metrics for Software Management and Engineering*. New York, NY: Institute of Electrical and Electronics Engineers.

Basili, Victor, and Barry T. Perricone (1984). "Software Errors and Complexity: An Empirical Investigation." *Communications of the ACM*, 27(1):42–52.

Basili, Victor, and D. Hutchens (1983). "An Empirical Study of a Complexity Family." *IEEE Transactions on Software Engineering*, 9(6):664–672.

Basili, Victor, and D. Weiss (1984). "A Methodology for Collecting Valid Software Engineering Data." *IEEE Transactions on Software Engineering*, SE-10(6):728–738.

Basili, Victor R., et al. (1994). "Goal/Question/Metric Paradigm." *Encyclopaedia of Software Engineering*, Volume 1. New York, NY: John Wiley and Sons, pp. 528–532.

Basili, Victor R. (1990). "Viewing Maintenance as Reuse-Oriented Software Development." *IEEE Software*, January, pp. 19–25.

Basili, Victor R. (1984). "A methodology for collecting valid software engineering data." *IEEE Transactions on Software Engineering*, SE-10(6):728–738.

Bass, Len, et al. (1997). *Software Architecture in Practice*. Reading, MA: Addison-Wesley.

Bass, Len, Paul Clements, and Rick Kazman (1998). *Software Architecture in Practice: The SEI Series*. New York, NY: Addison-Wesley.

Batini, Carlo, et al. (1991). *Conceptual Database Design: An Entity-Relationship Approach*. Reading, MA: Addison-Wesley.

Becker, Shirley, and Mitchell Bostelman (1999). "Aligning Strategic and Project Measurement Systems." *IEEE Software*, 16(3):46–51.

Beizer, Boris (1984). *Software System Testing and Quality Assurance*. New York, NY: Van Nostrand Reinhold.

Beizer, Boris (1990). *Software Testing Techniques*, 2nd ed. New York, NY: Van Nostrand Reinhold.

Beizer, Boris (1995). *Black Box Testing: Techniques for Functional Testing of Software and Systems*. New York, NY: Wiley.

Berard, E.V. (1993). *Essays on Object-Oriented Software Engineering*, Volume 1. Reading, MA: Addison-Wesley.

Berg, Cindy, and Kim Colenso (2000). "Work Breakdown Structure Practice Standard Project—WBS vs. Activities." *PM Network*, April.

Bias, Randolph G., and Deborah J. Mayhew, eds. (1994). *Cost-Justifying Usability.* Boston, MA: Academic Press.

Binder, Robert (1993). "Scenario-Based Testing for Client/Server Systems." *The Software Testing Forum*, 1(2):12–17.

Binder, Robert V. (1999). *Testing Object-Oriented Systems: Models, Patterns and Tools.* Reading, MA: Addison-Wesley.

Black, Rex (1999). *Managing the Testing Process.* Redmond, WA: Microsoft Press.

Boar, Bernard (1984). *Application Prototyping: A Requirements Definition Strategy for the '80s,* 1st ed. New York, NY: John Wiley & Sons.

Boegh, Jorgen, et al. (1999). "A Method for Software Quality Planning, Control, and Evaluation." *IEEE Software*, 16(2):69–77.

Boehm, Barry (1976). "Software Engineering." *IEEE Transactions on Computers.* Los Alamitos, CA: IEEE Computer Society.

Boehm, Barry (1981). *Software Engineering Economics.* Englewood Cliffs, NJ: Prentice Hall.

Boehm, Barry (1988). "A Spiral Model of Software Development and Enhancement." *IEEE Computer*, 21(5):61–72.

Boehm, Barry W., and Rony Ross (1989). "Theory W Software Project Management Principles and Examples." *IEEE Transactions on Software Engineering*, 15(7):902–916.

Boehm, Barry W., et al. (2000). *Software Cost Estimation with Cocomo II.* Englewood Cliffs, NJ: Prentice Hall.

Boehm, Barry, and Alexander Egyed, et al. (1998). "Using Win Win Spiral Model: A Case Study." *IEEE Computer*, 31(7):33–44.

Boehm, Barry, et al. (1978). *Characteristics of Software Quality.* New York, NY: American Elsevier.

Boehm, Barry, et al. (1997). "Developing Multimedia Applications with the Win Win Spiral Model." *Proceedings, ESEC/FSE 97 and ACM Software Engineering Notes,* November. New York, NY: Association for Computing Machinery.

Boloix, Germinal, and Pierre Robillard (1988). "Inter-Connectivity Metric for Software Complexity." *Information Systems and Operation Research*, 26(1):17–39.

Booch, Grady (1994). *Object-Oriented Design with Applications.* Reading, MA: Addison-Wesley.

Booch, Grady, et al. (1998). *Unified Modeling Language User Guide.* Reading, MA: Addison-Wesley.

Booch, Grady, James Rumbaugh, and Ivar Jacobson (1999). *The UML Modeling Language User Guide.* Reading, MA: Addison-Wesley.

Bourque, Pierre, et al. (1999). "The Guide to the Software Engineering Body of Knowledge." *IEEE Software*, The IEEE Institute, November/December, pp. 35–44.

Bowan, Jonathan P., and Michael G. Hinchley (1995). "Ten Commandments of Formal Methods." *Computer*, 28(4):56–63.

Bowditch, James L., and Anthony F. Buono (2001). *A Primer on Organizational Behavior,* 5th ed. New York, NY: John Wiley & Sons.

Briand, Lionel C., Sandro Morasca, and Victor R. Basili (1996). "Property-Based Software Engineering Measurement." *IEEE Transactions on Software Engineering*, 22(1):68–86.

Brooks, Fred (1975). *The Mythical Man-Month: Essays on Software Engineering,* 1st ed. Reading, MA: Addison-Wesley.

Brooks, Fredrick P. (1987). "No Silver Bullet: Essence and Accidents of Software Engineering," *IEEE Computer,* 20(4):10–19.

Brooks, Fredrick P. (1995). *The Mythical Man-Month: Essays on Software Engineering,* anniversary ed. Reading, MA: Addison-Wesley.

Brown, Karen A., and Nancy Lea Hyer (2001). "Mind Mapping as a WBS Development Tool." PMI 2001 Seminar and Symposium, Nashville, TN.

Buck, F.O. (1981). "Indicators of Quality Inspections." *IBM Corporation Technical Report.* IBM TR21, 802, September.

Bush, Marilyn (1990). "Improving Software Quality: The Use of Formal Inspections at the Jet Propulsion Laboratory." *Proceedings, 12th International Conference on Software Engineering.* Nice, France, March 26–30, pp. 196–199.

Buzan, Tony (1991). *Use Both Sides of Your Brain,* 3rd ed. New York, NY: Penguin Putnam.

Buzan, Tony, and Barry Buzan (1996). *The Mind Map Book: How to Use Radiant Thinking to Maximize Your Brain's Untapped Potential.* New York, NY: Penguin Putnam.

Buzan, Tony, Tony Dottino, and Richard Israel (1999). *The Brainsmart Leader.* Burlington, VT: Gower Pub.

Calero, Henry H. (1979). *Winning the Negotiation.* New York, NY: Hawthorn Books.

Cantor, Murray R. (1998). *Object-Oriented Project Management with UML.* New York, NY: John Wiley & Sons.

Cantor, N., and J.F. Kihlstrom (1987). *Personality and Social Intelligence.* Englewood Cliffs, NJ: Prentice-Hall.

Card, David N., and Robert L. Glass (1990). *Measuring Software Design Quality.* Englewood Cliffs, NJ: Prentice Hall.

Carmel, E. (1995). "Cycle Time in Packaged Software Firms." *Journal of Product Innovation Management,* 12(2): 110–123.

Cassel, Paul, and Pamela Palmer (1999). *Sams Teach Yourself Access 2000 in 21 Days.* Indianapolis, IN: Sams.

Chapin, Ned (1974). "A New Format for Flowcharts." *Software—Practice and Experience,* 4(4):341–357.

Chapin, Ned (1979). "A Measure of Software Complexity." *Proceedings of the AFIPS National Computer Conference,* Spring 1979, pp. 995–1002.

Chapin, Ned (1985). "Software Maintenance: A Different View." *Proceedings of the 1985 National Computer Conference.* AFIPS Press, pp. 507–513.

Charette, Robert N. (1990). *Applications Strategies for Risk Analysis.* New York, NY: McGraw-Hill.

Chen, J.Y., and J.F. Lu (1993). "A New Metric for Object-Oriented Design." *Journal of Information and Software Technology,* 35(4):232–240.

Chen, Peter (1977). *The Entity-Relationship Approach to Logical Database Design.* Wellesley, MA: Q.E.D. Information Sciences.

Chevrier, Sylvia, as reported by Larraine Segil in "Global Work Teams: A Cultural Perspective." *PM Network,* March 1999.

Chidamber, Shyam R., David P. Darcy, and Chris F. Kemerer (1998). "Managerial Use of Metrics for Object-Oriented Software: An Exploratory Analysis." *IEEE Transactions on Software Engineering*, 24(8):629–639.

Christensen, K., G.P. Fitsos, and C.P. Smith (1981). "A Perspective on Software Science." *IBM Systems Journal*, 20(4):372–387.

Cleland, David I. (1994). *Project Management: Strategic Design and Implementation*, 2nd ed. New York, NY: McGraw-Hill.

Coad, Peter, and Edward Yourdon (1991). *Object Oriented Analysis.* New York, NY: Prentice Hall Yourdon Press Computing Series.

Coad, Peter, and Edward Yourdon (1991). *Object Oriented Design.* New York, NY: Prentice Hall Yourdon Press Computing Series.

Coad, Peter, et al. (1996). *Object Models: Strategies, Patterns and Applications*, 2nd ed. New York, NY: Prentice Hall Yourdon Press Computing Series.

Codd, E.F. (1970). "A Relational Model of Data for Large Shared Data Banks." *Communications of the ACM*, 13(6):377–387.

Codd, E.F. (1990) *The Relationship Model for Database Management*, Version 2. New York, NY: Addison-Wesley.

Cohen, Herb (1980). *You Can Negotiate Anything.* Secaucus, NJ: L. Stuart.

Connell, John, and Linda Shafer (1986). "Reducing Software Maintenance Costs." *Computer Programming Management.* Auerbach Publishers.

Connell, John, and Linda Shafer (1987). *The Professional User's Guide to Acquiring Software.* New York, NY: Van Nostrand Reinhold.

Connell, John, and Linda Shafer (1989). *Structured Rapid Prototyping: An Evolutionary Approach to Software Development*, 1st ed. Englewood Cliffs, NJ: Prentice Hall.

Connell, John, and Linda Shafer (1995). *Object-Oriented Rapid Prototyping.* New York, NY: Prentice Hall Yourdon Press Computing Series.

Connolly, Thomas, Carolyn Begg, and Anne Strachan (1998). *Database Systems—A Practical Approach to Design, Implementation, and Management.* Reading, MA: Addison-Wesley.

Conte, S.D., H.E. Dunsmore, and V.Y. Shen (1986). *Software Engineering Metrics and Models.* Menlo Park, CA: Benjamin/Cummings.

Cook, Jonathan E., Lawrence Votta, and Alexander L. Wolf (1998). "Cost-Effective Analysis of In-Place Software Processes." *IEEE Transactions on Software Engineering*, 24(8): 640–649.

Curtis, Bill (1979). "In Search of Software Complexity." *Proceedings of the Workshop on Quantitative Software Models for Reliability,* pp. 95–106.

Curtis, Bill (1980). "Measurement and Experimentation in Software Engineering." *Proceedings of the IEEE*, 68(9):1144–1157.

Curtis, Bill, Herb Krasner, and Neil Iscoe (1988). "A Field Study of the Software Design Process for Large Systems." *Communications of the ACM*, 31(11).

Dart, Susan A., et al. (1987). "Software Development Environments." *IEEE Computer*, 20(11):18–28.

Daskalantonakis, Michael K. (1992). "A Practical View of Software Measurement and Implementation Experiences Within Motorola." *IEEE Transactions on Software Engineering*, 18(11):998–1010.

Date, C.J. (1999). *An Introduction to Database Systems*, 7th ed. Reading, MA: Addison-Wesley.

DeMarco, Tom (1979). *Structured Analysis and Systems Specification*. New York, NY: Prentice Hall Yourdon Press Computing Series.

DeMarco, Tom (1982). *Controlling Software Projects*. Englewood Cliffs, NJ: Prentice Hall.

DeMarco, Tom (1995). *Why Does Software Cost So Much? and Other Puzzles of the Information Age*. New York, NY: Dorset House.

DeMarco, Tom, and Barry W. Boehm (1998). *Controlling Software Projects: Management, Measurement, and Estimates*. Englewood Cliffs, NJ: Prentice Hall PTR/Sun Microsystems Press.

DeMarco, Tom, and P.J. Plauger (1985). *Structured Analysis and System Specification*. New York, NY: Prentice Hall Yourdon Press Computing Series.

DeMarco, Tom, and Timothy Lister (1987). *Peopleware: Productive Projects and Teams*. New York, NY: Dorset House.

Deming, W. Edwards (2000). *Out of the Crisis*, 1st ed. Cambridge, MA: MIT Press.

Deming, W. Edwards (2000). *The New Economics: For Industry, Government, Education*, 2nd ed. Cambridge, MA: MIT Press.

Department of the Air Force, Software Technology Support Center (1996). *Guidelines for Successful Acquisition and Management of Software Intensive Systems*. Version 2.0, June.

DeSantis, Richard, John Blyskal, Assad Moini, and Mark Tappan (1997). SPC-97057 CMC, Version 01.00.04. Herndon, VA: Software Productivity Consortium.

Deutsch, Michael S., and Ronald R. Willis (1988). *Software Quality Engineering: A Total Technical and Management Approach*. 1st ed. Englewood Cliffs, NJ: Prentice Hall PTR/Sun Microsystems Press.

Devor, Richard E., et al. (1992). *Statistical Quality Design and Control*. New York, NY: Prentice Hall.

Dijkstra, Edsger Wybe (1976). *A Discipline of Programming*. Englewood Cliffs, NJ: Prentice Hall.

Dorfman, M., and R.H. Thayer, eds. (1997). *Software Engineering*. Los Alamitos, CA: IEEE Computer Society Press.

Doyle, Michael, and David Straus (1982). *How to Make Meetings Work: The New Interaction Method*. New York, NY: Penguin Putman.

Dumas, Joseph S., and Janice C. Redish (1999). *A Practical Guide to Usability Testing*, rev. ed. Portland, OR: Intellect Books.

Dutoit, Allen H., and Bernd Bruegge (1998). "Communication Metrics for Software Development." *IEEE Transactions on Software Engineering*, 24(8):615–628.

Dyer, Michael (1992). *The Cleanroom Approach to Quality Software Development*. New York, NY: Wiley.

Ebenau, Robert G., and Susan H. Strauss (1994). *Software Inspection Process*. New York, NY: McGraw-Hill.

Eriksson, Hans-Erik, and Magnus Penker (1998). *The UML Toolkit*. New York, NY: John Wiley & Sons.

Fagan, Michael E. (1976). "Design and Code Inspections to Reduce Errors in Program Development." *IBM Systems Journal*, 15(3):185–211.

Fagan, Michael E. (1986). "Advances in Software Inspections." *IEEE Transactions on Software Engineering*, 12(7): 744–751.

Fairley, Richard E. (1985). *Software Engineering Concepts*. New York, NY: McGraw-Hill.

Fairley, Richard E. (1992). "Recent Advances in Software Estimation Techniques." *IEEE 14th International Conference on Software Engineering*, Los Alamitos CA: IEEE Computer Society Press, pp. 382–391.

Fenton, Norman (1991). *Software Metrics: A Rigorous Approach*. New York, NY: Chapman & Hall CRC Press.

Fenton, Norman, and Martin Neil (1999). "A Critique of Software Defect Prediction Models." *IEEE Transactions on Software Engineering,* 25(5): 55–67.

Fenton, Norman E., and Martin Neil (1999). "Software Metrics: Successes, Failures and New Directions." *Journal of Systems and Software*, 47(2–3):149–157.

Fenton, Norman E., and Shari Lawrence Pfleeger (1997). *Software Metrics—A Rigorous and Practical Approach*, 2nd ed. Boston, MA: PWS Publications.

Fisher, Roger, and William Ury (1991). *Getting To Yes*, 2nd ed. New York: NY: Penguin Books.

Flavin, Matt (1981). *Fundamental Concepts of Information Modeling*. New York, NY: Prentice Hall Yourdon Press Computing Series.

Florac, William A. (1992). *Software Quality Measurement: A Framework for Counting Problems and Defects*, CMU/SEI-92-TR-22. Pittsburgh, PA: Software Engineering Institute, Carnegie Mellon University.

Florac, William A., and Anita D. Carleton (1999). *Measuring the Software Process*. Reading, MA: Addison-Wesley.

Florac, William A., et al. (1996). *Practical Software Measurement: Measuring for Process Management and Improvement*, CMU/SEI-97-HB-003. Pittsburgh, PA: Software Engineering Institute, Carnegie Mellon University.

Frame, J. Davidson (1987). *Managing Projects in Organizations*. New York, NY: Jossey-Bass.

Frame, J. Davidson (1994). *The New Project Management*. New York, NY: Jossey-Bass.

Franken, Robert E. (2002). *Human Motivation*, 5th ed. Pacific Grove, CA: Brooks/Cole.

Freeman, Daniel, and Gerald Weinberg (1990). *Handbook of Walkthroughs, Inspections, and Technical Reviews*, 3rd ed. New York, NY: Dorset House.

Friedman, Michael A., and Jeffrey M. Voas (1995). *Software Assessment: Reliability, Safety, Testability.* New York, NY: Wiley.

Gacek, Cristina, Ahmed Abd-Allah, Bradford Clark, and Barry W. Boehm (1995). "On the Definition of Software System Architecture." *Proceedings of the First International Workshop on Architectures for Software Systems*, Seattle, WA.

Garmus, David, and David Herron (2001). *Function Point Analysis: Measurement Practices for Successful Software Projects*. Boston, MA: Addison-Wesley.

Gause, Donald C., and Gerald M. Weinberg (1989). *Exploring Requirements: Quality Before Design*. New York, NY: Dorset House.

Gilb, Tom (1977). *Software Metrics*. Cambridge, MA: Winthrop Publishers.

Gilb, Tom, and Dorothy Graham (1993). *Software Inspection*. Reading, MA: Addison-Wesley.

Goldratt, Eliyahu M., and Jeff Cox (1993). *The Goal: A Process of Ongoing Improvement*, 2nd ed. Aldershot, Hampshire, England: Gower.

Goodman, Paul (1992). *Practical Implementation of Software Metrics*. New York, NY: McGraw-Hill.

Gorden, Raymond L. (1998). *Basic Interviewing Skills*. Prospect Heights, IL: Waveland Press.

Grable, Ross, et al. (1999). "Metrics for Small Projects: Experiences at the SED." *IEEE Software*, 16(2):21–29.

Grady, Robert B. (1987). "Measuring and Managing Software Maintenance." *IEEE Software*, 4(4):35–45.

Grady, Robert B. (1992). *Practical Software Metrics for Project Management and Process Improvement*. New York, NY: Prentice Hall.

Grady, Robert B. (1997). *Successful Software Process Improvement*. Englewood Cliffs, NJ: Prentice Hall.

Grady, Robert B., and Deborah L. Caswell (1987). *Software Metrics: Establishing a Company-Wide Program*, Englewood Cliffs, NJ: Prentice Hall.

Graham, Ian (1995). *Migrating to Object Technology*, 1st ed. Reading, MA: Addison-Wesley.

Grant, Richard (2000). Instructor, University of Texas Software Quality Institute Certificate Program, Sequence XI, Session 3.

Guinta, Lawrence R., and Nancy C. Praizler (1993). *The QFD Book*. New York, NY: AMACOM Books.

Haag, Stephen, M.K. Raja, and L.L. Schkade (1996). "Quality Function Deployment Usage in Software Development." *Communications of the ACM*, 39(1):41–49.

Haley, Tom, et al. (1995). "Raytheon Electronic Systems Experience in Software Process Improvement." *Software Engineering Institute Technical Report*, CMU/SEI-95-TR-017, November.

Hall, Anthony (1990). "Seven Myths of Formal Methods." *IEEE Software*, September, 11–20.

Hall, Tracy, and Norman Fenton (1997). "Implementing Effective Software Metrics Programs." *IEEE Software*, 14(2):55–67.

Halstead, Maurice H. (1977). *Elements of Software Science*. New York, NY: Elsevier.

Hammer, Theodore F., Leonore L. Huffman, and Linda H. Rosenberg (1998). "Doing Requirements Right the First Time." *CrossTalk, Journal of Defense Software Engineering*, December.

Harmon, Paul, and David A. Taylor (1993). *Objects in Action: Commercial Applications of Object-Oriented Technologies*. Reading, MA: Addison-Wesley.

Harrison, Warren, and Kenneth Magel (1981). "A Complexity Measure Based on Nesting Level." *ACM SIGPLAN Notices*, 16(3):63–74.

Hatley, Derek J., and Imtiaz A. Pirbhai (1988). *Strategies for Real-Time System Specification*. New York, NY: Dorset House.

Hauser, John R., and Don Clausing (1988). "The House of Quality." *The Harvard Business Review*, May–June, pp. 63–73.

Hergenhahn, B.R. (1990). *An Introduction To Theories of Personality*. Englewood Cliffs, NJ: Prentice Hall.

Hersey, Paul, and Kenneth H. Blanchard (1993). *Management of Organizational Behavior*, 6th ed. Englewood Cliffs, NJ: Prentice-Hall.

Hersey, Paul, Kenneth Blanchard, and Dewey Johnson (1996). *Management of Organizational Behavior: Utilizing Human Resources*, 7th ed. Upper Saddle River, NJ: Prentice Hall.

Herzberg, Frederick, Bernard Mausner, and Barbara Bloch Snyderman (1993). *The Motivation to Work*. New Brunswick, NJ: Transaction Publishers.

Hetzel, William C. (1988). *The Complete Guide to Software Testing*, 2nd ed. Wellesley, MA: QED Information Sciences.

Hetzel, William C. (1993). *Making Software Measurement Work: Building an Effective Measurement Program*. Boston, MA: QED Pub. Group.

Hirsh, Sandra, and Jean Kummerow (1989). *LIFETypes*. New York, NY: Warner Books, Inc.

Howard, Jr. Baetjer (1997). *Software As Capital: An Economic Perspective on Software Engineering*. Los Alamitos, CA: IEEE Computer Society.

Humphrey, Watts (1989). *Managing the Software Process*, 1st ed. Reading, MA: Addison-Wesley SEI Series in Software Engineering (reprinted with corrections, August 1990).

Humphrey, Watts (1995). *A Discipline for Software Engineering*. Reading, MA: Addison-Wesley, SEI Series in Software Engineering.

Humphrey, Watts S., and W. L. Sweet (1987*). A Method for Assessing the Software Engineering Capability of Contractors*, Technical Report #CMU/SEI-87-TR-23. Software Engineering Institute, Carnegie Mellon University, September.

Hunter, Michael R., and Richard D. Van Landingham (1994). "Listening to the Customer Using QFD." *Quality Progress*, 27(4): 55–59.

IEEE (1993). "IEEE 1044 Standard Classification for Software Anomalies." *IEEE Software Engineering Standards Collection*. New York, NY: Institute of Electrical and Electronics Engineers.

IEEE (1993). "IEEE 1058 Standard for Software Project Management Plans." *IEEE Software Engineering Standards Collection*. New York, NY: Institute of Electrical and Electronics Engineers.

IEEE (1995). "IEEE 1044 Standard Classification for Software Anomalies." *IEEE Software Engineering Standards Collection*. New York, NY: Institute of Electrical and Electronics Engineers.

IEEE 1008-1987 (1987). "IEEE Standard for Software Unit Testing." New York, NY: The Institute of Electrical and Electronics Engineers.

IEEE 1016.1-1993 (1993). "Guide to Software Design Descriptions." New York, NY: The Institute of Electrical and Electronics Engineers.

IEEE 1016-1998 (1998). "Recommended Practice for Software Design Descriptions." New York, NY: The Institute of Electrical and Electronics Engineers.

IEEE 1045-1992 (1992). "IEEE Standard for Software Productivity Metrics." New York, NY: The Institute of Electrical and Electronics Engineers.

IEEE 1061-1992 (1992). "IEEE Standard for a Software Quality Metrics Methodology." New York, NY: The Institute of Electrical and Electronics Engineers.

IEEE 1074-1997 (1998). "IEEE Standard for Developing Software Life Cycle Processes." New York, NY: The Institute of Electrical and Electronics Engineers.

IEEE 1233 (1998). "Guide for Developing System Requirements Specifications." *Software Engineering Standards Collection*. New York, NY: Institute of Electrical and Electronics Engineers.

IEEE 1320.1-1998 (1998). "Standard for Functional Modeling Language—Syntax and Semantics for IDEF0." New York, NY: The Institute of Electrical and Electronics Engineers.

IEEE 1320.2-1998 (1998). "Standard for Conceptual Modeling Language Syntax and Semantics for IDEF1X97 (IDEFobject)." New York, NY: The Institute of Electrical and Electronics Engineers.

IEEE 1471-2000 (2000). "Recommended Practice for Architectural Description of Software Incentive Systems." New York, NY: The Institute of Electrical and Electronics Engineers.

IEEE 610.12-1990 (1990). "IEEE Standard Glossary of Software Engineering Terminology." *Software Engineering Standards Collection*. New York, NY: The Institute of Electrical and Electronics Engineers.

IEEE 729-1983 (1983). "IEEE Standard Glossary of Software Engineering Terminology." New York, NY: The Institute of Electrical and Electronics Engineers.

IEEE 829-1983 (1983). "IEEE Standard for Software Test Documentation." New York, NY: The Institute of Electrical and Electronics Engineers.

IEEE 830-1998 (1998). "IEEE Recommended Practice for Software Requirements Specifications." *Software Engineering Standards Collection*. New York, NY: The Institute of Electrical and Electronics Engineers.

IEEE 982.1-1988 (1988). "IEEE Standard Dictionary of Measures to Produce Reliable Software." New York, NY: The Institute of Electrical and Electronics Engineers.

IEEE 982.2-1988 (1988). "IEEE Guide for the Use of IEEE Standard Dictionary of Measures to Produce Reliable Software." New York, NY: The Institute of Electrical and Electronics Engineers.

Ilich, John, and Barbara Schindler-Jones (1981). *Successful Negotiating Skills for Women*. Reading, MA: Addison-Wesley.

Ince, Darrel (1989). "Software Metrics." *Measurement for Software Control and Assurance*, New York, NY: Elsevier Applied Science.

International Function Point Users Group (1990). *Function Points as Asset Reporting to Management*.

International Function Point Users Group (1994). *Function Point Counting Practices Manual*, Release 4.0. IFPUG Standards.

International Function Point Users Group (1994). *Guidelines to Software Measurement*, Release 1.0. IFPUG Standards. Ishikawa, K. (1976). *Guide to Quality Control*. Tokyo, Japan: Asian Productivity Organization.

Ishikawa, K., and D.J. Lu, trans. (1988). *What is Total Quality Control? The Japanese Way*, 1st ed. Englewood Cliffs, NJ: Prentice Hall.

Jackson, Michael (1998). "Will There Ever Be Software Engineering?" *IEEE Software*, 15(1):36–39.

Jacobson, Ivar (1994). *Object-Oriented Software Engineering: A Use Case Driven Approach*. Addison-Wesley Object Technology Series.

Jacobson, Ivar, Grady Booch, and James Rumbaugh (1999). *The Unified Software Development Process*. Reading, MA: Addison-Wesley.

Jacobson, Ivar, et al. (1992). *Object-Oriented Software Engineering: A Use Case Driven Approach*. Reading, MA: Addison-Wesley.

Jazayeri, A. Ran, and F. van der Linden (2000). *Software Architecture for Product Families*. Reading, MA: Addison-Wesley.

Jennerich, Bill (1999). *Joint Application Design: Business Requirements Analysis for Successful Reengineering*. Berwyn, PA: Bluebird Enterprises.

Jensen, Howard A., and K. Vairavan (1985) "An Experimental Study of Software Metrics for Real-Time Software." *IEEE Transactions on Software Engineering*, SE-11(2):231–234.

Jones, Capers (1978). "Measuring Programming Quality and Productivity." *IBM Systems Journal*, 17(1).

Jones, Capers (1986). *Programming Productivity*. New York, NY: McGraw-Hill.

Jones, Capers (1997). *Applied Software Measurement: Assuring Productivity and Quality,* 2nd ed. New York, NY: McGraw-Hill.

Kafura, Dennis (1985). "A Survey of Software Metrics." *Proceedings 1985 Annual Conference of the ACM,* Denver, CO, October 14–16, ACM Press, pp. 502–506.

Kahler, Taibi, and Hedges Capers (1974). "The Miniscript." *Transactional Analysis Journal,* 4(1):27–42.

Kan, Stephen H. (1995). *Metrics and Models in Software Quality Engineering.* Reading, MA: Addison-Wesley.

Kaner, Cem, et al. (1993). *Testing Computer Software,* 2nd ed. New York, NY: Van Nostrand Reinhold.

Karolak, Dale (1996). *Software Engineering Risk Management.* Los Alamitos, CA: IEEE Computer Society Press.

Karras, Chester L. (1993). *Give and Take: The Complete Guide to Negotiating Strategies and Tactics.* New York, NY: HarperBusiness Publishers.

Katz, Daniel, and Robert L. Kahn (1978). *The Social Psychology of Organizations,* 2nd ed. New York, NY: Wiley.

Kearney, Joseph K., et al. (1986). "Software Complexity Measurement." *Communications of the ACM,* 29(11):1044–1050.

Keil, Mark, and Erran Carmel (1995). "Customer-Developer Links in Software Development." *Communications of ACM,* 38(5):33–44.

Keirsey, David (1998). *Please Understand Me II: Temperament, Character, Intelligence.* Del Mar, CA: Prometheus Nemesis Book Company.

Keirsey, David, and Marilyn Bates (1984). *Please Understand Me: Character and Temperament Types.* Del Mar, CA: Prometheus Nemesis Book Company.

Keirsey, David, and Marilyn Bates (1984). *Please Understand Me, An Essay on Temperament Styles,* Amherst, NY: Prometheus Books.

Kelvin, W.T. (1891–1894). *Popular Lectures and Addresses.*

Kemerer, Chris F. (1987). "An Empirical Validation of Software Cost Estimation Models." *Communications of the ACM,* 30(5):416–429. New York: NY: Association for Computing Machinery.

Kennedy, Gavin (1998). *The New Negotiating Edge: The Behavioral Approach for Results and Relationships.* Sonoma, CA: Nicholas Brealey Publishing.

Kerzner, Harold (1998). *Project Management: A Systems Approach to Planning, Scheduling, and Controlling,* 6th ed. New York, NY: John Wiley & Sons.

King, David (1992). *Project Management Made Simple: A Guide to Successful Management of Computer Systems Projects.* Englewood Cliffs, NJ: Yourdon Press.

Kirchof, Nicki S., and John R. Adams (1982). "Conflict Management for Project Managers." *Principles of Project Management.* Upper Darby, PA: Project Management Institute.

Kitchenham, Barbara, and B. Littlewood, eds. (1989). *Measurement for Software Control and Assurance.* New York, NY: Elsevier Applied Science.

Kitchenham, Barbara, and Shari Lawrence Pfleeger (1996). "Software Quality: The Elusive Target." *IEEE Software,* January, pp.12–21.

Kitchenham, Barbara, Shari Lawrence Pfleeger, and Norman Fenton (1995). "Towards a Framework for Software Measurement Validation." *IEEE Transactions on Software Engineering,* 21(12):929–944.

Knight, J.C., and E.A. Meyers (1993). "An Improved Inspection Technique." *Communications of the ACM*, 36(11):51–61.

Koltzblatt, Karen, and Hugh R. Beyer (1995). "Requirements Gathering: The Human Factor." *Communications of the ACM*, 38(5):30–32.

Krasner, Herb (1999). "Teamwork Considerations for Superior Software Development." *Constructing Superior Software*, 1st ed. Indianapolis, IN: Macmillan Technical Publishing. p. 180.

Krasner, Herb (2001). "Implementing Software Quality." *Software Project Management Certificate Program Sequence XI*, Session 32. Software Quality Institute, The University of Texas at Austin.

Kroeger, Otto, and Janet Theusen (1992). *Talk Type at Work*. New York, NY: Delacorte Press.

Kruchten, Philippe (1996). "A Rational Process." *CrossTalk*, 9(7):11–16.

Kruchten, Philippe (2000). *The Rational Unified Process: An Introduction*. Reading, MA: Addison-Wesley.

Kummerow, Jean M., et al. (1997). *Work Types*. New York, NY: Warner Books.

Lakshmanan, K.B., S. Jayaprakash, and P.K. Sinha (1991). "Properties of Control-Flow Complexity Measures." *IEEE Transactions on Software Engineering*, 17(12):1289–1295.

Landsbaum, Jerome B., and Robert L. Glass (1992). Measuring and Motivating Maintenance Programmers. Englewood Cliffs, NJ: Prentice-Hall.

Larman, Craig (1998). *Applying UML and Patterns: An Introduction to Object-Oriented Analysis and Design*. Reading, MA: Addison-Wesley.

Lavold, Gary D. (1998). "Developing Using the Work Breakdown Structure." *Project Management Handbook*, 2nd ed. New York, NY: Van Nostrand Reinhold.

Leonard, Nancy H., et al. (1995). "A Self Concept-Based Model of Work Motivation." *Proceedings of the Academy of Management Annual Meeting*, Vancouver, B.C., Canada.

Leveson, Nancy, and Clark S. Turner (1993). "An Investigation of the Therac-25 Accidents." *IEEE Computer*, 26(7):18–41.

Lewicki, Roy J., et al. (1996). *Think Before You Speak: The Complete Guide to Strategic Negotiation*. New York, NY: John Wiley & Sons.

Lewicki, Roy J., et al. (1999). *Negotiation*, 3rd ed. Boston, MA: Irwin/McGraw-Hill.

Lewin, Kurt (1975). *Field Theory in Social Science: Selected Theoretical Papers*. Westport, CT: Greenwood Press.

Lewin, Kurt (1997). *Resolving Social Conflicts; Field Theory in Social Science*. Washington, DC: American Psychological Association.

Lewis, James P. (1995). *Project Planning, Scheduling, and Control: A Hands-On Guide to Bringing Projects in On Time and On Budget*, rev ed. Chicago, IL: Irwin.

Lewis, James P. (1998). *Mastering Project Management: Applying Advanced Concepts of Systems Thinking, Control and Evaluation, Resource Allocation*. New York, NY: McGraw-Hill.

Lewis, James P. (1998). *Team-Based Project Management*. New York, NY: American Management Association.

Lewis, James P. (2000). *The Project Manager's Desk Reference: A Comprehensive Guide to Project Planning, Scheduling, Evaluation, and Systems*. New York, NY: McGraw-Hill.

Lind, Randy K., and K. Vairavan (1989). "An Experimental Investigation of Software Metrics and Their Relationship to Software Development Effort." *IEEE Transactions on Software Engineering,* 15(5):649–653.

Lyu, Michael R., ed. (1996). *Handbook of Software Reliability Engineering.* New York, NY: McGraw-Hill.

Maccoby, Michael (1988). *Why Work: Leading the New Generation.* New York, NY: Simon and Schuster.

Maier, David (1983). *The Theory of Relational Databases.* Rockville, MD: Computer Science Press.

Manley, John H. (1984). "CASE: Foundation for Software Factories." *COMPCON Proceedings,* IEEE, September, pp. 84–91.

Maples, M.F., and C. Sieber (1998). "Gestalt Theory." *Counseling and Psychotherapy: Theories and Interventions.* Boston, MA: Merrill-Macmillan.

Marciniak, John J., ed. (1994). Encyclopedia of Software Engineering. New York, NY: John Wiley and Sons. pp. 131–166.

Marick, Brian (1995). *The Craft of Software Testing.* Englewood Cliffs, NJ: Prentice Hall.

Marqulies, Nancy (1991). *Mapping Inner Space: Learning and Teaching Mind Mapping.* Tucson, AZ: Zephyr Press.

Martin, Charles C. (1976). *Project Management: How to Make it Work*: Amacom.

Martin, James (1981). *An End-User's Guide to Data Base.* Englewood Cliffs, NJ: Prentice Hall.

Martin, James (1982). *Computer Database Organization.* Englewood Cliffs, NJ: Prentice Hall.

Martin, James (1991). *Rapid Application Development,* 1st ed. New York, NY: Macmillan.

Martin, James, and Carma McClure (1983). *Software Maintenance: The Problem and Its Solution.* Englewood Cliffs, NJ: Prentice Hall.

Martin, Roger J., and Wilma M. Osborne (1992). "Guidance on Software Maintenance," NBS Special Publication 500-106. National Institute of Standards and Technology.

Maslow, Abraham H. (1971). *The Farther Reaches of Human Nature.* New York, NY: Viking Press.

Maslow, Abraham H. (1999). *Toward a Psychology of Being,* 3rd ed. New York, NY: John Wiley & Sons.

Maslow, Abraham Harold (1954). *Motivation and Personality,* 1st ed. New York, NY: Harper.

Maxwell, John C. (1999). *The 21 Indispensable Qualities of a Leader: Becoming the Person that People Will Want to Follow.* Nashville, TN: T. Nelson.

McCabe, T., and Charles W. Butler (1989). "Design Complexity Measurement and Testing." *Communications of the ACM,* 32(12):1415–1424.

McCabe, Thomas J. (1976). "A Complexity Measure." *IEEE Transactions on Software Engineering,* SE-2(4):308–320.

McCall, James A., et al. (1977). "Metrics for Software Quality Evaluation and Prediction." *Proceedings of Second Summer Software Engineering Workshop,* Greenbelt, MD, September 19.

McCall, John, et al. (1977). "Factors in Software Quality," NTIS AD-A049-014, 015, 055, November.

McConnell, Steve (1996). *Rapid Development: Taming Wild Software Schedules,* 1st ed. Redmond, WA: Microsoft Press.

McConnell, Steve C. (1993). *Code Complete: A Practical Handbook of Software Construction.* Redmond, WA: Microsoft Press.

McFarlan, Warren F. (1974). "Portfolio Approach to Information Systems." *Harvard Business Review,* January/February, pp. 142–150.

McFletcher Corporation (1993). *WorkStyle Patterns™ Inventory.* Scottsdale, AZ.

McGregor, Douglas (1960). *The Human Side of Enterprise.* New York, NY: McGraw-Hill. pp. 33–34.

McMenamin, Stephen M., and John Palmer (1984). *Essential Systems Analysis.* New York, NY: Prentice Hall Yourdon Press Computing Series.

Mellor, Stephen J., and Paul T. Ward (1989). *Structured Development for Real-Time Systems: Implementation Modeling Techniques.* New York, NY: Prentice Hall Yourdon Press Computing Series.

Mendonta, Manoel G., and Victor R. Basili (2000). "Validation of an Approach for Improving Existing Measurement Frameworks." *IEEE Transactions on Software Engineering,* 26(6):484–499.

Meredith, Jack R., and Samuel Mantel, Jr. (2000). *Project Management: A Managerial Approach,* 4th ed. New York, NY: Wiley.

Metzler, Ken (1996). *Creative Interviewing: The Writer's Guide to Gathering Information by Asking Questions.* New York, NY: Allyn & Bacon, Pearson Education.

Miller, Ann (1992). *Engineering Quality Software: Defect Detection and Prevention.* Reading, MA: Addison-Wesley, Motorola University Press Six Sigma Research Institute Publications.

Miller, George A. (1956). "The Magic Number Seven, Plus or Minus Two." *Psychological Review,* 63:81–97.

Mills, Harlan (1976). "Software Development." *IEEE Transactions on Software Engineering.* SE-2(4):265–273.

Mills, Harlan, et al. (1987). "Cleanroom Software Engineering." *IEEE Software,* 5(5):19–24.

Mintzberg, Henry (1983). *Structures in Fives: Designing Effective Organizations.* New York, NY: Prentice-Hall. p. 11.

Moder, Joseph J., et al. (1983). *Project Management with CPM, PERT, and Precedence Diagramming,* 3rd ed. New York, NY: Van Nostrand.

Moller, K.H., and D.J. Paulish (1993*). Software Metrics: A Practitioner's Guide to Improved Product Development,* 1st ed. New York, NY: Chapman & Hall.

Mosley, Daniel J. (1993). *The Handbook of MIS Application Software Testing: Methods, Techniques, and Tools for Assuring Quality through Testing.* Englewood Cliffs, NJ: Prentice Hall.

Murray, Mike (2000). University of Texas Software Quality Institute Certificate Program, Sequence XI, Session 22.

Musa, John D. (1993). "Operational Profiles in Software Reliability Engineering." *IEEE Software,* 10(2):14–32.

Musa, John D. (1999). *Software Reliability Engineering: More Reliable Software, Faster Development and Testing.* New York, NY: McGraw-Hill.

Musa, John D., et al. (1987). *Software Reliability: Measurement, Prediction, Application.* New York, NY: McGraw-Hill.

Myers, Glenford J. (1979). *The Art of Software Testing.* New York, NY: John Wiley & Sons.

Nassi, I., and Ben Schneiderman (1973). "Flowchart Techniques for Structured Programming." *SIGPLAN Notices of the ACM,* 8(8):12–26.

National Aeronautics and Space Administration (1993). *Software Formal Inspections Guidebook*, NASA-GB-A-302, Office of Safety and Mission Assurance, National Aeronautics and Space Administration.

Neumann, Peter G. (1986). "On Hierarchical Design of Computer systems for Critical Applications." *IEEE Transactions on Software Engineering*, SE-12(9):905–920.

Nielsen, Jakob (1993). *Usability Engineering*. Boston, MA: Academic Press.

Nielsen, Jakob (1996). "Usability Metrics: Tracking Interface Improvements." *IEEE Software*, 13(6):12–13.

Nielsen, Jakob, and Robert L. Mack, eds. (1994). *Usability Inspection Methods*. New York, NY: John Wiley & Sons.

Nierenberg, Gerard I. (1986) *The Art of Negotiating*, 2nd ed. New York, NY: Simon & Schuster.

Nierenberg, Gerard I. (1987). *Fundamentals of Negotiating*. New York, NY: Perennial Library.

Nierenberg, Gerard I. (1991). *The Complete Negotiator*. New York, NY: Berkley Books.

Norden, Peter V. (1958). "Curve Fitting for a Model of Applied Research and Development Scheduling." *IBM Journal of Research and Development*, 2(3).

O'Brien, James J. (1969). *Scheduling Handbook*. New York, NY: McGraw-Hill.

Offen, Raymond J., and Ross Jeffery (1997). "Establishing Software Measurement Programs." *IEEE Software*, 14(2):45–53.

Offutt, A. Jefferson (1992). "Investigations of the Software Testing Coupling Effect." *ACM Transactions on Software Engineering and Methodology*, 1(1).

Ogren, Ingmar (2000). "Requirements Management as a Matter of Communication." *CrossTalk, The Journal of Defense Software Engineering*, 13(4).

O'Neill, Don (1997). "Setting Up a Software Inspection Program." *CrossTalk, The Journal of Defense Software Engineering*, 10(2).

Osborn, Alex F. (1983). *Applied Imagination*. Buffalo, NY: Creative Education Foundation.

Ouichi, William G., and Alfred M. Jaeger (1978). "Type Z Organization: Stability in the Midst of Mobility." *Academy of Management Review*, 3(2):159–168.

Oviedo, Enrique I. (1980). "Control Flow, Data Flow and Programmers Complexity." *Proceedings of COMPSAC 80*, Chicago IL. pp. 146–152.

Page-Jones, Meilir (1988). *The Practical Guide to Structured Systems Design*, 2nd ed. Englewood Cliffs, NJ: Prentice Hall.

Pall, Gabriel A. (1987). Quality Process Management. Englewood Cliffs, NJ: Prentice-Hall.

Palmer, Helen (1991). *The Enneagram, Understanding Yourself and the Others in Your Life*. San Francisco, CA: Harper.

Park, Robert, E. (1992). "Software Size Measurement: A Framework for Counting Source Statements." *Software Engineering Institute Technical Report SEI-92-TR-020*. Pittsburg, PA: SEI, Carnegie Mellon University.

Parnas, David L. (1972). "On the Criteria to be Used on Decomposing Systems into Modules." *Communications of the ACM*, 12(12):1053–1058.

Patel, Sukesh, William Chu, and Rich Baxter (1992). "A Measure for Composite Module Cohesion." *Proceedings of the 14th International Conference on Software Engineering*, Melbourne, Australia, pp. 38–48. New York, NY: Association for Computing Machinery.

Paulk, Mark C. (1994). "A Comparison of ISO 9001 and the Capability Maturity Model for Software," Technical Report # CMU/SEI-94-TR-012. Software Engineering Institute, Carnegie Mellon University.

Paulk, Mark C., Charles V. Weber, Bill Curtis, and Mary Beth Chrissis (1994). *The Capability Maturity Model: Guidelines for Improving the Software Process*. Reading, MA: Addison-Wesley SEI Series in Software Engineering.

Perlis, Alan, Frederick Sayward, and Mary Shaw, eds. (1981). *Software Metrics: An Analysis and Evaluation*. Cambridge, MA: MIT Press.

Perry, William E. (1986). *How to Test Software Packages*. New York, NY: John Wiley & Sons.

Pfleeger, Shari Lawrence (2000). "Use Realistic, Effective Software Measurement." *Constructing Superior Software*. Indianapolis, IN: Macmillan Technical Publishing.

Pfleeger, Shari Lawrence, and J.C. Fitzgerald (1991). "Software Metrics Tool Kit." *Support for Selection, Collection and Analysis. Information and Software Technology*, 33(7):477–482.

Pfleeger, Shari Lawrence, Les Hatton, and Charles C. Howell (2002). *Solid Software*. Upper Saddle River, NJ: Prentice Hall.

Pfleeger, Shari Lawrence, Ross Jeffery, Bill Curtis, and Barbara Kitchenham (1997). "Status Report on Software Measurement." *IEEE Software*, 14(2):33–43.

Pheatt, Chuck (2000). Computer Science CS 444. Emporia State University, Emporia, KS.

Playle, Greg, and Charles Schroeder (1996). "Software Requirements Elicitation: Problems, Tools, and Techniques." *CrossTalk, The Journal of Defense Software Engineering*, 9(12).

Plsek, Paul E. (1997). *Creativity, Innovation, and Quality*. New York, NY: McGraw-Hill.

PMI Standards Committee, William R. Duncan, Director of Standards (1996). *A Guide to the Project Management Body of Knowledge*. Newtown Square, PA: Project Management Institute.

Porter, A.A., et al. (1997). "An Experiment to Assess the Cost-Benefits of Code Inspection in Large Scale Software Development." *IEEE Transactions of Software Engineering*, 23(6):329–346.

Pratt, Philip J., and Joe Adamski (2000). *Concepts of Database Management*, 3rd ed. Boston, MA: Course Technology.

Pressman, Roger S. (2001). *Software Engineering: A Practitioner's Approach*, 5th ed. Boston, MA: McGraw-Hill.

Pritchard, Carl (1997). *Risk Management*. Arlington, VA: ESI International.

Project Management Institute (1996). *A Guide to the Project Management Body of Knowledge*. Sylva, NC: PMI Publication Division.

Putnam, Lawrence H. (1978). "A General Empirical Solution to the Macro Software Sizing and Estimating Problem." *IEEE Transactions of Software Engineering*, SE-4 (4):345–361.

Putnam, Lawrence H., and Ware Myers (1992). *Measures for Excellence: Reliable Software on Time, within Budget*. Englewood Cliffs, NJ: Yourdon Press.

Radice, R.A., et al. (1985). "A Programming Process Study." *IBM Systems Journal*, 24(2):91–101.

Rae, A.K., et al., eds. (1995). *Software Evaluation for Certification: Principles, Practice and Legal Liability.* New York, NY: McGraw-Hill.

Retting, Marc (1992). "Five Rules of Data Normalization." Poster for *Database Programming & Design.* San Francisco, CA: Miller Freeman Publications.

Richter, Charles (1999). *Designing Flexible Object-Oriented Systems with UML.* Indianapolis, IN: Macmillan Technical Publishing.

Rifkin, Stan (2001). "What Makes Measuring Software So Hard?" *IEEE Software*, 18(3):41–45.

Rising, Linda, and Callis, Frank, W. (1992). "Problems with Determining Package Cohesion and Coupling." *Software Practice and Experience*, 22(7):553–571.

Rob, Peter, and Carlos Coronel (1999). *Database Systems: Design, Implementation, and Management*, 4th ed. Cambridge, MA: Course Technology.

Rothwell, J. Dan (2001). *In Mixed Company: Small Group Communication*, 4th ed. Fort Worth, TX: Harcourt College Publishers.

Royce, W.W. (1970). "Managing the Development of Large Software Systems: Concepts and Techniques." *Proceedings WESCON*, Los Alamitos, CA, August.

Royce, Walker Jr. (1998). *Software Project Management, a Unified Framework.* Reading, MA: Addison-Wesley.

Royer, Thomas C. (1993). *Software Testing Management: Life on the Critical Path.* Englewood Cliffs, NJ: Prentice Hall.

Rumbaugh, James (1994). "Getting Started: Using Use Cases to Capture Requirements." *Journal of Object Oriented Programming*, September.

Rumbaugh, James, et al. (1991). *Object-Oriented Modeling and Design.* Englewood Cliffs, NJ: Prentice Hall.

Sawyer, Pete, Ian Sommerville, and Stephen Viller (1999). "Capturing the Benefits of Requirements Engineering." *IEEE Software*, 16(2):78–85.

Schach, Stephen R. (1999). *Classical and Object-Oriented Software Engineering: With UML and Java*, 4th ed. New York, NY: McGraw-Hill

Schein, Edgar H. (1980). *Organizational Psychology*, 3rd ed. Englewood Cliffs, NJ: Prentice-Hall.

Schein, Edgar H. (1992). *Organizational Culture and Leadership*, 2nd ed. San Francisco, CA: Jossey-Bass.

Schneidewind, Norman F. (1991). "Setting Maintenance Quality Objectives and Prioritizing Maintenance Work by Using Quality Metrics." *Proceedings of the Conference on Software Maintenance* (CSM91), October.

Schneidewind, Norman F. (1997). "Software Metrics Model for Quality Control." *Proceedings of the 4th International Software Metrics Symposium* (Metrics '97), Albuquerque, NM.

Schneidewind, Norman F. (1999). "Measuring and Evaluating Maintenance Process Using Reliability, Risk, and Test Metrics." *IEEE Transactions on Software Engineering*, 25(6):769–781.

Schutz, William (1996). *The Interpersonal Underworld.* Palo Alto, CA: Science and Behavior Books.

Shafer, L., and John Connell (1982). "Deriving Metrics for Relating Complexity Measures to Software Maintenance Costs." *Proceedings of the 1982 Computer Measurement Group International Conference.* pp. 134–141.

Shepperd, Martin, and Darrel Ince (1993). *Derivation and Validation of Software Metrics*. New York, NY: Oxford University Press.

Shepperd, Martin, ed. (1993). *Software Engineering Metrics—Volume I: Measures and Validations*. New York, NY: McGraw Hill, International Series in Software Engineering.

Shewhart, Walter A., and W. Edwards Deming (1986). *Statistical Method from the Viewpoint of Quality Control*, 1st ed. New York, NY: Dover Pubs.

Shlaer, Sally, and Stephen Mellor (1988). *Object-Oriented Systems Analysis: Modeling the World in Data*. New York, NY: Prentice Hall Yourdon Press Computing Series.

Shneiderman, Ben (1997). *Designing the User Interface: Strategies for Effective Human-Computer Interaction*. Reading, MA: Addison-Wesley.

Shooman, Martin L. (1983). *Software Engineering Design, Reliability, and Management*. New York, NY: McGraw-Hill.

Sommerville, Ian (2000). *Software Engineering*, 6th ed. New York, NY: Addison Wesley.

Sommerville, Ian, and Gerald Kotonya (1997). *Requirements Engineering: Processes and Techniques*. New York, NY: John Wiley & Sons.

Stevens, W.P., Glenford J. Myers, and Larry L. Constantine (1974). "Structured Design." *IBM Systems Journal*, No. 2, pp. 115–139.

Strehlo, Kevin (1996). "Catching Up with the Joneses and 'Requirement' Creep." *InfoWorld*, July 29.

Stuckenbruck, Linn C., and David Marshall (1985) "Team Building for Project Managers." *The Principles of Project Management: Collected Handbooks from the Project Management Institute*. Sylva, NC: PMI Publication Division.

Stuckenbruck, Linn C., ed. (1981). *The Implementation of Project Management: The Professional's Handbook*. Drexel Hill, PA: Project Management Institute.

Stutzke, Richard D. (2001). *Software Estimation: Projects, Products, Processes*. Reading, MA: Addison-Wesley.

Symons, Charles R. (1988). "Function Point Analysis: Difficulties and Improvements." *IEEE Transactions on Software Engineering*, 14(1):2.

Taylor, David A. (1990). *Object-Oriented Technology: A Manager's Guide*. Reading, MA: Addison-Wesley.

Taylor, David A. (1992). *Object-Oriented Information Systems: Planning and Implementation*. New York, NY: John Wiley & Sons.

Tervonen, Iikka (1996). "Support for Quality-Based Design and Inspection." *IEEE Software*, 13(1):44–54.

Thayer, Richard H., ed. (1997). *Software Engineering Project Management*. Los Alamitos, CA: IEEE Computer Society Press.

Thayer, Richard H., Merlin Dorfman, and Sidney C. Bailin, eds. (1997). *Software Requirements Engineering*, 2nd ed. Los Alamitos, CA: IEEE Computer Society Press.

Tieger, Paul D., and Barbara Barron-Tieger (1995). *Do What You Are: Discover the Perfect Career for You Through the Secrets of Personality Type*, 2nd ed. Boston, MA: Little, Brown.

Tomayko, James E. (1986). *Support Materials for Software Configuration Management*. SEI-SM-4-1.0, Carnegie Mellon University, Software Engineering Institute.

Tuckman, Bruce W. (1965). "Developmental Sequence in Small Groups." *Psychological Bulletin*, 63:384–399.

Tufte, Edward (1983). *The Visual Display of Quantitative Information.* Cheshire, CT: Graphics Press.

Tufte, Edward (1990). *Envisioning Information.* Cheshire, CT: Graphics Press.

Tufte, Edward (1997). *Visual Explanations: Images and Qualities, Evidence and Narrative.* Cheshire, CT: Graphics Press.

Ullman, Jeffrey (1982). *Principles of Database Systems.* Rockville, MD: Computer Science Press.

Ury, William (1993). *Getting Past No.* New York, NY: Bantam Books.

U.S. Department of Defense (1986). *Engineering Changes, Deviations and Waivers,* MIL STD-480. Washington, DC: U.S. Government Printing Office.

U.S. Department of Defense (1986). *Configuration Management Practices for Systems, Equipment, Munitions, and Computer Programs,* MIL-STD-483A. Washington, DC: U.S. Government Printing Office.

U.S. Department of Defense (1989). *Military Standard for Configuration Management,* MIL-STD-973. Washington, DC: U.S. Government Printing Office.

van Solingen, Rini, and Egon Berghout (1999). *The Goal/Question/Metric Method: A Practical Guide for Quality Improvement of Software Development.* New York, NY: McGraw-Hill.

Verma, Vijay K. (1996). *Managing the Project Team: the Human Aspects of Project Management.* Upper Darby, PA: Project Management Institute.

Verma, Vijay K. (1997). *The Human Aspects of Project Management.* Upper Darby, PA: Project Management Institute.

Voas, Jeffrey M., and Gary McGraw (1998). *Software Fault Injection: Innoculating Programs Against Errors.* New York, NY: Wiley.

Von Mayrhauser, Anneliese (1990). *Software Engineering: Methods and Management.* Boston, MA: Academic Press.

Vroom, Victor (1994). *Work and Motivation.* New York, NY: Wiley, Jossey-Bass Management Series.

Walston, C.E., and C.P. Felix (1977). "A Method of Programming Measurement and Estimation." *IBM Systems Journal,* 16(1):54–73.

Walters, Stan B. (1995). *Principles of Kinesic Interview and Interrogation.* Boca Raton, FL: CRC Press.

Ward, Paul T., and Stephen J. Mellor (1986). *Structured Development for Real-Time Systems: Essential Modeling Techniques.* New York, NY: Prentice Hall Yourdon Press Computing Series.

Warner, Paul (1998). "How to Use the Work-Breakdown Structure." *Field Guide to Project Management.* New York, NY: John Wiley & Sons.

Wasserman, Anthony I. (1982). "Rapid Prototyping of Interactive Information Systems." *Software Engineering Notes,* 7(5):171–180.

Wasserman, Anthony I. (1996). "Toward a Discipline of Software Engineering." *IEEE Software,* 13(6).

Watson, Arthur H., and Thomas J. McCabe (1996). "Structured Testing: A Testing Methodology Using the Cyclomatic Complexity Metric." *National Institute of Standards and Technology Special Publication 500-235.* Gaithersburg, MD: NIST.

Webster's College Dictionary. (1992) New York, NY: Random House.

Webster's Dictionary of the English Language. (1997) New York, NY: Lexicon Publications.

Weinberg, Gerald M. (1971). *The Psychology of Computer Programming.* New York, NY: Van Nostrand Reinhold.

Weinberg, Gerald M. (1992). *Quality Software Management, Vol. 1, Systems Thinking.* New York, NY: Dorset House.

Weinberg, Gerald M. (1997). *Quality Software Management, Vol. 4, Anticipating Change.* New York, NY: Dorset House.

Weller, E.F. (1993). "Lessons Learned from Two Years of Inspection Data." *IEEE Software*, 10(5):38–45.

Wheeler, David A., Bill Brykczynski, and Reginald N. Meeson, Jr., eds. (1996). *Software Inspection, An Industry Best Practice.* New York, NY: IEEE Computer Society Press.

Wiegers, Karl E. (1999). "Writing Good Requirements." *Software Development*, May.

Wiegers, Karl E. (1999). *Software Requirements.* Redmond, WA: Microsoft Press.

Wiklund, Michael E., ed. (1994). *Usability in Practice: How Companies Develop User-Friendly Products.* Boston, MA: Academic Press.

Wing, Janet M. (1990). "A Specifier's Introduction to Formal Methods." *Computer*, 23(9):8–24.

Wiorkowski, Gabrielle, and David Kull (1992). *DB2: Design and Development Guide*, 3rd ed. Reading, MA: Addison-Wesley.

Wirfs-Brock, Rebecca, et al. (1990). *Designing Object-Oriented Software.* New York, NY: Prentice Hall.

Wirth, Nicholas (1971). "Program Development by Stepwise Refinement." *Communications of the ACM*, 14(4):221–227.

Wohlin, Claes, and Per Runeson (1994). "Certification of Software Components." *IEEE Transactions on Software Engineering*, SE-20(6):494–499.

Wood, Jane, and Denise Silver (1989). *Joint Application Design: How to Design Quality Systems in 40% Less Time.* New York, NY: John Wiley & Sons.

Woodcock, Mike, and David Francis (1981). *Organization Development Through Team Building: Planning a Cost Effective Strategy.* New York, NY: Wiley. p. 3.

Woolf, Bob (1990). *Friendly Persuasion: My Life as a Negotiator.* New York, NY: Putnam.

Wycoff, Joyce (1991). *Mindmapping: Your Personal Guide to Exploring Creativity and Problem-Solving.* New York, NY: Berkley Books.

Wyllys, R.E. (2001). "Overview of Normalization: Introduction." LIS 384K.11, *Database-Management Principles and Applications.* The University of Texas at Austin Graduate School of Library and Information Science.

Yamaura, Tsuneo (1998). "How to Design Practical Test Cases." *IEEE Software*, 15(6):30–36.

Yoder, Cornelia M., and Marilyn L. Schrag (1983). "Nassi-Schneiderman Charts: An Alternative to Flowcharts for Design." White Paper, IBM Corporation, System Products Division, Endicott, NY.

Yourdon, Edward (1979). *Classics in Software Engineering.* New York, NY: Yourdon Press.

Yourdon, Edward (1988). *Managing the System Life Cycle*, 2nd ed. Englewood Cliffs, NJ: Yourdon Press.

Yourdon, Edward (1989). *Modern Structured Analysis.* New York, NY: Prentice Hall Yourdon Press Computing Series.

Yourdon, Edward (1994). *Object-Oriented Systems Design: An Integrated Approach.* Englewood Cliffs, NJ: Yourdon Press.

Yourdon, Edward (1997). "Metrics for Death-March Projects." *Proceedings of Symposium: Eighth International Conference on Applications of Software Measurement*, Atlanta, GA, October.

Yourdon, Edward (1997). *Death March: the Complete Software Developer's Guide to Surviving Mission Impossible Projects.* Upper Saddle River, NJ: Prentice Hall PTR.

Yourdon, Edward, and Larry L. Constantine (1979). *Structured Design: Fundamentals of a Discipline of Computer Program and Systems Design.* Englewood Cliffs, NJ: Prentice Hall Yourdon Press Computing Series.

Yukl, Gary (2001). *Leadership in Organizations*, 5th ed. Upper Saddle River, NJ: Prentice Hall.

Web Pages for Further Information

Analysis and Design

fiat.gslis.utexas.edu/~l384k11w/rw38411.html. R.E. Wyllys (2001). "Overview of Normalization." *Database-Management Principles and Applications*, LIS 384K. The University of Texas at Austin, Graduate School of Library and Information Science.

ola.aacc.cc.md.us/csi122/norm/datanorm.html. Kari Siner (2001). Personal Computer Database Management System with Microsoft® Access 2000, CSI 122. Anne Arundel Community College, Arnold, MD.

stein.cshl.org/genome_informatics/sql1/lecture_notes.html. Robert Peitzsch (1999). SQL and Relational Database Section, Genomic Informatics Class, CSHL. Stein Laboratory, Cold Spring Harbor Laboratory, Cold Spring Harbor, NY, Genome Informatics.

www.baldwinw.edu/~gbouw/courses/csc280/puppy.html. Gerardus Bouw (2001). Department of Math and Computer Science, CSC 280. Baldwin-Wallace College, Berea, OH.

www.omg.org. Object Management Group (OMG) (2000). Unified Modeling Language (UML) Specification, Version 1.3, March.

www.open.org/~prslkg/sy_chap.htm. Paul R. Seesing and ARMA International (1993). "Basic Systems Analysis Tools for Computer Users."

www.oracle.com/. Oracle Corporation.

www.rational.com/index.jsp. Rational Software.

www.sei.cmu.edu/architecture/definitions.html. Software Engineering Institute (2001). "How Do You Define Software Architecture?"

www.software.org/pub/darpa/darpa.html. Richard DeSantis, "Evolutionary Rapid Development," Software Productivity Consortium.

www.support.lotus.com/simsold.nsf/. Lotus Customer Support Technote (1998). "The Five Rules of Database Normalization." Number 127782.

www.sybase.com/. Sybase.

www.zoo.co.uk/~z0001039/PracGuides/pg_use_cases.htm. Edward Kenworthy, "Use Cases."

www-4.ibm.com/software/data/db2/udb/. DB2 Universal Database.

Building a Work Breakdown Structure

stsc.hill.af.mil/crosstalk/1996/apr/project.asp. Lynn Satterthwaite (1996). "Project Management: Some Lessons Learned—April 1996." Software Technology Support Center.

varatek.com/howtowbs0.html. "Work Breakdown Structure Development: How To Create A Project Work Breakdown Structure (WBS)." Varatek Software, Inc.

www.4pm.com/articles/wbs.html. "Work Breakdown Structure: Important Project Design Issue or Clerical Task?"

www.acq.osd.mil/pm/newpolicy/wbs/wbs.html. "Work Breakdown Structures (WBS) for Defense Material Items," MIL-HDBK-881.

www.pmi.org/publictn/pmboktoc.htm. PMI's A Guide to the Project Management Body of Knowledge (PMBOK® Guide), Chapter 6.

www.pmi.org/standards/wbspractice.htm. Cindy Berg and Kim Colenso (2000). "Work Breakdown Structure Practice Standard Project—WBS vs. Activities." PM Network, April.

www.worldbank.org/worldlinks/english/training/world/webproj/define/develop/develop2.htm. "Building a Collaborative Web Project." World Links for Development Program (WorLD) Training Materials.

Capability Maturity Model and Continuous Improvement

www.sei.cmu.edu/. The Software Engineering Institute (SEI).

www.sei.cmu.edu/activities/str/indexes/glossary/. SEI Glossary.

www.qualitydigest.com/mar01/html/ci.html. Craig Cochran. "Two Hidden Gems of Continual Improvement—With a pair of basic actions, you can lead your organization to true long-term improvement."

www.qualitydigest.com/may99/html/ci.html. Lee C. Bravener. "The Road to Continuous Improvement."

www.qualitydigest.com/jul/contimp.html#anchor112080. J. Chris White. "Reengineering and Continuous Improvement, in a complex system, relations dominate and primarily determine the success of the system."

Configuration Management

cm-solutions.com/cms/tools/application_development/joint_application_design-jad.htm. Management Consulting & Information Technology Solutions, JAD.

sourceforge.net/ SourceForge. A free service to Open Source developers offering easy access to the best in CVS, mailing lists, bug tracking, message boards/forums, task management, site hosting, permanent file archival, full backups, and total web-based administration.

www.cmtoday.com/yp/configuration_management.html. The "Yellow Pages" for Configuration Management.

www.mks.com/products/scm/si/2134.htm. Robert Bamford and William J. Deibler II. "Configuration Management and ISO 9001." Software Systems Quality Consulting.

www.sei.cmu.edu/legacy/scm/. The intent of this area is to share the configuration management research done by the SEI between 1988 and 1994 and to provide pointers to other useful sources of information on Software Configuration Management.

www.sei.cmu.edu/legacy/scm/papers/CM_Plans/CMPlans.MasterToC.html. The purpose of this document is to give an understanding of the importance of the role of the configuration management (CM) plan, to give the results from a set of informal discussions that shows how CM plans are used, and to provide an evaluation of three CM standards.

www.sei.cmu.edu/legacy/scm/scmDocSummary.html. Summary of available CM-related documents.

Estimating Costs and Estimating Effort

courses.cs.vt.edu/~cs3604/lib/Therac_25/Therac_1.html. Nancy Leveson and Clark S. Turner. "An Investigation of the Therac-25 Accidents." IEEE Computer, 26(7):18–41.

ifpug.org. International Function Point User's Group (IFPUG).

ourworld.compuserve.com/homepages/softcomp/fpfaq.htm. Frequently Asked Questions (and Answers) Regarding Function Point Analysis, Copyright 1996–1997 by Software Composition Technologies, Inc.

sern.ucalgary.ca/courses/seng/621/W98/johnsonk/cost.htm#SLIM. University of Calgary.

www.cpsc.ucalgary.ca/~hongd/SENG/621/report2.html#2.6.5. Danfeng Hong. "Software Cost Estimation." Department of Computer Science, University of Canada, Alberta, Canada.

www.dacs.dtic.mil/databases/url/key.hts?keycode=4:7&islowerlevel=1. The Data & Analysis Center for Software (DACS) is a Department of Defense (DoD), Information Analysis Center (IAC). Cost Estimation: Function Points Analysis.

www.jsc.nasa.gov/bu2/PCEHHTML/pceh.htm. Parametric Cost Estimating Handbook.

www.pricesystems.com/prices.htm. PRICE-S estimating tool from PRICE Systems.

www.qpmg.com/fp-intro.htm. Roger Heller. "An Introduction to Function Points." Q/P Management Group, Inc.

www.qsm.com/products.html. SLIM estimating tool from Quantitative Software Management, Lawrence Putnam, President.

www.rcinc.com/. Resource Calculations, Inc. Sizing and cost modeling tools include ASSET-R, SSM, SOFTCOST-R.

www.sciam.com/1998/1298issue/1298jones.html#further. Capers Jones. "Sizing Up Software: Unlike oil, steel or paper, software is an intangible commodity."

www.sepo.nosc.mil/revic.html. REVIC estimating tool.

www.SoftstarSystems.com/. Softstar Systems offers Costar, an automated implementation of COCOMO.

www.stsc.hill.af.mil/crosstalk/. Software Estimation: Challenges and Research.

www.sunset.usc.edu/cocomo2.0/cocomo.html. COCOMO estimating tool.

www.wwk.com/coolsoft.html. COOLSoft™ Quantitative Tool for Software Development Cost Estimation.

Leadership

www.typeworks.com/leadersh.htm. A discussion that relates the MBTI model to leadership.

Managing Subcontractors, Handling Intellectual Property, and Other Legal Issues

palimpsest.stanford.edu/bytopic/intprop/crews.html. Kenneth D. Crews (1992). "Copyright Law, Libraries, and Universities: Overview, Recent Developments, and Future Issues." Working paper presented to the Association of Research Libraries.

www.411legalinfo.com/. For all your legal needs.

www.abanet.org/. American Bar Association.

www.adr.org/. The American Arbitration Association is available to resolve a wide range of disputes through mediation, arbitration, elections and other out-of-court settlement procedures.

www.ed.gov/databases/ERIC_Digests/ed381177.html. Janis H. Bruwelheide (1995). "Copyright Issues for the Electronic Age." ERIC Digest # ED381177. Syracuse, NY: ERIC Clearinghouse on Information and Technology.

www.findlaw.com/. FindLaw. Web portal focused on law and government provides access to a comprehensive and fast-growing online library of legal resources for use by legal professionals, consumers and small businesses.

www.ilrg.com/. Internet Legal Resource Guide™.

www.ldrc.com/cyber6.html. Samuel Fifer and Chad J. Doellinger. Annotated Bibliography of Materials Concerning First Amendment and Intellectual Property Internet Law Issues."

www.mycounsel.com/. MyCounsel.com offers guidance from leading lawyers from around the country.

www.nolo.com/index.html. Nolo Press Website: To help people handle their own everyday legal matters.

www.richmond.edu/jolt/v2i1/caden_lucas.html. Marc L. Caden and Stephanie E. Lucas (1996). "Comment, Accidents On the Information Superhighway: On-Line Liability And Regulation." 2 RICH. J.L. & TECH. 3.

www.usdoj.gov/crt/ada/cguide.htm. U.S. Department of Justice. "A Guide to Disability Rights Laws."

Forms and Templates

dijest.editthispage.com/stories/storyReader$91. Phil Wolff's collection of forms and templates.

web.mit.edu/entforum/www/Business_Plans/bplans.html. "MIT Enterprise Forum's Business Plan Resource Guide." The guide is a list of resources focused entirely or substantially on writing a business plan.

www.atlsysguild.com/GuildSite/Robs/Template.html. This requirements specification template is used as a basis for specifications.

www.bplans.com/dp/. Developing a business plan.

www.ecofinance.net/bptemplate01.html. New Ventures Investor Forum. "Writing your Business Plan."

www.newgrange.org/. New Grange Center for Project Management, tools and templates sharing. A non-profit professional organization whose focus is on a hands-on, practical approach to project management. Sponsors and active email news and discussion service.

www.planware.org/bizplan.htm. White Paper: "Writing a Business Plan."

www.sb.gov.bc.ca/smallbus/workshop/sample.html. URL to sample business plan.

www.sba.gov/starting/indexbusplans.html. "The Business Plan, Road Map to Success." A tutorial and self-paced activity.

General

bcentral.com/resource/articles/bizplans/101.asp. C.E. Yandle. "How to write a business plan." Microsoft bCentral Business Plans.

dictionary.cambridge.org/. © Cambridge University Press 2000.

dictionary.com/. Dictionary.com, online English dictionary.

lifelong.engr.utexas.edu/sqi/index.cfm. Software Quality Institute.

search.kachinatech.com/index.shtml. SAL (Scientific Applications on Linux) is a collection of information and links to software that will be of interest to scientists and engineers.

stealthis.athensgroup.com/presentations/. Athens Group, Inc. (2001). "The Business Case and Methodology for Performance Management."

stsc.hill.af.mil/. Software Technology Support Center (STSC) of United States Air Force (USAF). "Guidelines for Successful Acquisition and Management of Software-Intensive Systems." CrossTalk, The Journal of Defense Software Engineering.

web.mit.edu/icrmot/. Sloan School created the International Center for Research on the Management of Technology.

www.acm.org. Association for Computing Machinery.

www.acq-ref.navy.mil/turbo2/index_ie.html. Turbo Streamliner is a repository of acquisition definitions, principles, best practices, lessons learned, references, sample contractual language, and related Web sites.

www.asq.org/standcert/certification/csqe.html#csqebok. CSQE BOK Information.

www.best.com/~wilson/faq/. alt.folklore.computers (1998). List of Frequently Asked Questions.

www.bjmath.com/bjmath/least/curve.htm. Richard Reid. "Curve Fitting." (Reference "Schaums Outline Series: Theory and problems of Probability and Statistics" by Murray R. Spiegal, Ph.D.)

www.computer.org/. IEEE Computer Society.

www.esi.es/. European Software Institute.

www.geraldmweinberg.com. Gerald M. Weinberg's Home Page.

www.geraldmweinberg.com/shape.html. The SHAPE Forum (Software as a Human Activity Practiced Effectively).

www.m-w.com/cgi-bin/dictionary. New York, NY: Random House.

www.m-w.com/netdict.htm. Merriam-Webster's WWWebster Dictionary.

www.seas.smu.edu/disted/sys/r.html. Southern Methodist University School of Engineering Systems Engineering Resource Sites.

www.software.org. Software Productivity Consortium.

www.spc.ca/. Software Productivity Centre.

Interaction and Communication

typelogic.com/. MBTI Type Information.

www.cba.uri.edu/Scholl/Notes/Conflict.htm. Richard W. Scholl (2001). "Conflict Resolution." Class notes for students in Management, Organizational Behavior, Labor Relations, and Human Resources, School of Management, University of Rhode Island.

www.cba.uri.edu/Scholl/Notes/Equity.html. Richard W. Scholl (2001). "Primer on Equity." Class notes for students in Management, Organizational Behavior, Labor Relations, and Human Resources, School of Management, University of Rhode Island.

www.cba.uri.edu/Scholl/Notes/Motivation_Expectancy.html. Richard W. Scholl (2001). "Expectancy Theory." Class notes for students in Management, Organizational Behavior, Labor Relations, and Human Resources, School of Management, University of Rhode Island.

www.cba.uri.edu/Scholl/Papers/Self_Concept_Motivation.HTM. Nancy H. Leonard, et al. (1995). "A Self Concept-Based Model of Work Motivation." *Proceedings of the Academy of Management Annual Meeting,* Vancouver, B.C.

www.humanmetrics.com/cgi-win/JungType.htm. Abbreviated MBTI test.

www.keirsey.com/. Abbreviated Keirsey Temperament Sorter test.

www.ndu.edu/inss/books/strategic/pt1ch5.htm. "Chapter 5: Framing Perspectives." Strategic Leadership and Decision Making. Washington, DC: National Defense University.

www.personalitypage.com/info.html. Information About Personality Types.

www.personalitytype.com/. Barbara Barron-Tieger and Paul Tieger, authors of four books on Personality Type.

Lessons Learned

info.nrel.gov/esh/manual/esh-27.shtml. NREL Lessons Learned Program.

standishgroup.com/visitor/chaos.htm. Standish Group, Chaos Report.

www.4pm.com/articles/pmtalk8-2-00.pdf. "Post-Project Reviews: Lessons Never Learned, Project Manager's Control Tower." PMTalk Newsletter.

www.ima.umn.edu/~arnold/455.f96/disasters.html. Two disasters caused by computer arithmetic errors.

www.lanl.gov/orgs/ism/lessons.html. Los Alamos / DOE Lessons Learned. This is a bit more than project post-performance analysis, but interesting reading. Thanks to the Society for Effective Lessons Learned Sharing.

www.nytimes.com/2001/05/20/business/20EXAM.html. Diana B. Henriques and Jacques Steinberg (2001). "Right Answer, Wrong Score: Test Flaws Take Toll." New York Times Online, May 20.

www.salon.com/tech/feature/2000/12/06/bad_computers/index.html. Cheryll Aimée Barron (2001). "High tech's missionaries of sloppiness, Computer companies specialize in giving consumers lousy products—it's the American way of techno-capitalism." Salon.com.

www.sei.cmu.edu/legacy/scm/abstracts/abscm_past_pres_future_TR08_92.html. Automated support for configuration management (CM) is one aspect of software engineering environments that has progressed over the last 20 years.

www.testing.com/writings/classic/mistakes.html. Brian Marick, testing consultant.

Life Cycles

itc.fgg.uni-lj.si/ICARIS/LIST/msg00007.html. "The Application of Multi-agent Systems to Concurrent Engineering." *Concurrent Engineering: Research and Applications (CERA).* West Bloomfield, MI: CERA Institute.

www.brainyquote.com/quotes/quotes/. Quotations.

www.informatik.uni-bremen.de/uniform/gdpa/vmodel/vm1.htm. V-Model Development Standard for IT-Systems of the Federal Republic of Germany.

www.software.org/pub/darpa/erd/erdpv010004.html. Evolutionary Rapid Development.

www.stsc.hill.af.mil/crosstalk/1996/aug/isoiec.asp. Lewis Gray (1996). "ISO/IEC 12207 Software Lifecycle Processes." *CrossTalk*, August.

Metrics

hissa.ncsl.nist.gov/. Center for High Integrity Software Systems Assurance—NIST International Software Metrics Symposium.

irb.cs.uni-magdeburg.de/sw-eng/us/. Software Measurement Lab at the University of Magdeburg.

irb.cs.uni-magdeburg.de/sw-eng/us/index.shtml. Software Measurement Laboratory.

mijuno.larc.nasa.gov/dfc/societies/Ispa.html. The International Society of Parametric Analysts.

satc.gsfc.nasa.gov/support/STC_APR96/qualtiy/stc_qual.html. 8th Annual Software Technology Conference, Utah, April 1996.

sel.gsfc.nasa.gov/website/documents/contents.htm#1. Software Engineering Laboratory, Section 6: Software Measurement.

stsc.hill.af.mil/. U.S. Air Force's Software Technology Support Center (search "software metrics").

www.cmg.org. Computer Measurement Group Inc.

www.iese.fhg.de/ISERN/. International Software Engineering Research Network (ISERN).

www.ifpug.org. International Function Point Users' Group.

www.incose.org. International Council on Systems Engineering.

www.instmc.org.uk. The Institute of Measurement and Control.

www.m2tech.net/rsm/default.htm. Resource Standard Metrics.

www.nist.gov/. National Institute of Standards and Technology.

www.psmsc.com. Practical Software and Systems Measurement Support Center.

www.qucis.queensu.ca/Software-Engineering/Cmetrics.html. Programs for C Source Code Metrics.

www.sigmetrics.org/. Association for Computing Machinery SIG Metrics.

www.softwaremetrics.com/Articles/default.htm. Longstreet Consulting Inc.

www.spr.com/index.htm. Software Productivity Research provides software measurement, assessment, and estimation products and services. Capers Jones, chairman and founder.

www.ssq.org. Society for Software Quality.

Project Management: Documenting Project Plans, Scheduling, Monitoring Development, and Tracking Project Progress

www.allpm.com/. Provides details of resources available on project management.

www.ee.ed.ac.uk/~gerard/Management/art8.html. Gerard M. Blair. "Planning a Project."

www.fek.umu.se/irnop/projweb.html#top. WWW-Guide to Project Management Research Sites.

www.hq.nasa.gov/office/hqlibrary/ppm/ppmbib.htm. NASA PPM Library. Program/Project Management Resource Lists originally written for the NASA project management community.

www.infogoal.com/pmc/pmchome.htm. The Project Management Center.

www.michaelgreer.com/bibliog.htm. Greer's Bibliography of PM, ID, and ID/PM References.

www.michaelgreer.com/postmortem.htm. Consultant Michael Greer's PM Resources Web site.

www.pmforum.org/. WWW Project Management Forum. The Project Management Forum is a non-profit resource for information on international project management affairs dedicated to development, international cooperation, promotion and support of a professional and world wide project management discipline.

www.pmforum.org/library/glossary/PMG_P12.htm. PM Forum's glossary of project management terms.

www.pmi.org/. Project Management Institute (PMI®).

www.pmi.org/certification/. PMP Certification Requirements.

www.pmi.org/pmi2001/papers/quality.htm. Howland Blackiston (2001). "Quality in Project Management: Organizing for Continuous Improvement in Project Management." PMI, Nashville, TN, November.

www.pmi.org/publictn/pmboktoc.htm. PMI's A Guide to the Project Management Body of Knowledge (PMBOK® Guide).

www.pmibookstore.org/. Online PMI Bookstore contains over 1,000 of the finest project management books and products available, including a complete listing of PMI books.

www.project-manager.com/. The Project Manager Web site. PM resources and information.

www.spmn.com/. SPMN Mission: To seek out proven industry and government software best practices and convey them to managers of large-scale DoD software-intensive acquisition programs.

www2.umassd.edu/SWPI/sei/tr25f/tr25_12c.html. Software Project Tracking and Oversight.

Project Teams

www.afirstlook.com/docs/Schulz. Em Griffin (1991). *A First Look at Communication Theory,* McGraw-Hill.

www.enneagraminstitute.com/. The Enneagram Institute.

www.humanmetrics.com/JungType.htm. Human Metrics, Jung and MBTI topology.

www.humansource.com/trendspotting/19990201.htm. Interviewing.

www.keirsey.com. Closely related to MBTI is the Keirsey Temperament Sorter, derived from the work of David Keirsey in his book Please Understand Me.

www.purenlp.com/whatsnlp.htm. Richard Bandler (1996). "What Is NLP?" The First Institute of Neuro-Linguistic Programming™ and Design Human Engineering™.

www.selbymillsmith.com. Selby MillSmith, Chartered Occupational Psychologists, FIRO-B Instrument.

www.sol-ne.org/res/wp/toc. Edgar H. Schein (2000). "Kurt Lewin's Change Theory in the Field and in the Classroom: Notes Toward a Model of Managed Learning." Society for Organizational Learning.

www.tajnet.org/articles/kahler-miniscript-addendum.html. Taibi Kahler. Article discusses correlating drivers, ego states, psychological needs, life positions, rackets, script injunctions, scripts, roles, games, and myths.

Publications

computer.org/software/. IEEE Software Magazine.

kapis.www.wkap.nl/kapis/CGI-BIN/WORLD/journalhome.htm?1382-3256. Victor R. Basili. Empirical Software Engineering.

sel.gsfc.nasa.gov/website/documents/contents.html. National Aeronautics and Space Administration (NASA) (1998). "Annotated Bibliography of Software Engineering Laboratory (SEL) Literature." Goddard Space Flight Center (GSFC), Greenbelt, MD.

sqp.asq.org/. ASQ Software Quality Professional.

www.4pm.com/. Project Managers Watch Tower. PM resources and information.

www.acm.org/jacm/. Association for Computing Journal of the ACM.

www.acm.org/sigsoft/. Association for Computing Machinery SIG Software Engineering.

www.acm.org/tosem/. Association for Computing Transactions on Software Engineering and Methodology.

www.adtmag.com/. Application Development Trends.

www.soft.com/News/TTN-Online. Testing Techniques Newsletter.

wwwsel.iit.nrc.ca/SPN/. Software Process Newsletter.

Quality

acis.mit.edu/acis/sqap/sqap.r1.html. An SQAP prepared by MIT for NASA.

akao.larc.nasa.gov/dfc/qfd.html. E.B. Dean (1997). "Quality Function Deployment from the Perspective of Competitive Advantage."

hissa.ncsl.nist.gov/. Center for High Integrity Software Systems Assurance—NIST.

qaiusa.com. Quality Assurance Institute.

satc.gsfc.nasa.gov/homepage.html. Software Assurance Technology Center.

www.acq-ref.navy.mil/wcp/qfd.html. QFD.

www.asq.org. American Society for Quality (ASQ).

www.asq.org/info/library/faq/. Resource guides prepared by the Quality Information Center's librarians in response to frequent information requests on these topics. Each guide includes recommended articles, books, and web sites that provide relevant information on each topic.

www.asq-software.org. ASQ Software Division.

www.cs.uwf.edu/~wilde/gump/sqa.htm. This document describes the Software Quality Assurance (SQA) plan for the generic software maintenance process used in the Software Engineering graduate program at the University of West Florida (UWF).

www.dhutton.com/samples/sampqfd.html. QFD.

www.nauticom.net/www/qfdi/. The QFD Institute.

www.qaiusa.com/. Quality Assurance Institute.

www.qfdi.org/. Quality Function Deployment Institute.

www.qualitydigest.com/mar99/html/itech.html. Douglas L. Swanson, Ph.D.; Richard A. Esposito; and Jean Jester, Ph.D.. "Managing Quality for Information Technology."

www.sqatester.com. SQAtester.com.

www.sqazone.com/. Welcome to SQAZone.com. Everything you wanted to know about software testing and quality assurance is right here. This Web site is divided into various sections with classified information available, anytime you need.

www.sqe.com. Software Quality Engineering.

www.ssq.org/. Society for Software Quality.

www-sqi.cit.gu.edu.au/. Australian SW Quality Research Institute.

Reliability

members.aol.com/JohnDMusa/. J.D. Musa (1998) (updated regularly). "More Reliable Software Faster and Cheaper (Software Reliability Engineering)."

rac.iitri.org/. The mission of the Reliability Analysis Center (RAC).

www.asq-rd.org/. American Society of Quality, Reliability Division.

www.cs.cmu.edu/~koopman/des_s99/sw_reliability/. Jiantao Pan (1999). "Software Reliability," Carnegie Mellon University, 18-849b Dependable Embedded Systems, Spring.

www.ieee.org/organizations/society/rel.html. IEEE Reliability Society is concerned with the problems involved in attaining reliability, maintaining it through the life of the system or device, and measuring it.

www.ima.umn.edu/~arnold/455.f96/disasters.html. Two disasters caused by computer arithmetic errors.

www.nytimes.com/2001/05/20/business/20EXAM.html. Right Answer, Wrong Score: Test Flaws Take Toll.

www.nytimes.com/2001/05/21/business/21EXAM.html. When a Test Fails the Schools, Careers and Reputations Suffer.

www.sre.org/. Society of Reliability Engineers.

Requirements

brainstorming.org.uk/tutorials/usenewpeople.html. Brainstorming tutorials.

edweb.sdsu.edu/triton/guides/Brainstorming.html. Brainstorming.

members.ozemail.com.au/~caveman/Creative/Techniques/brainstorm.htm. Brainstorming

Quality Function Deployment from the Perspective of Competitive Advantage.

sunset.usc.edu/research/WINWIN/winwin_main.html. Barry Boehm, Alexander Egyed, et al. (1998). "Using WINWIN Spiral Model: A Case Study." IEEE Computer, 31(7):33–44.

www.acq-ref.navy.mil/wcp/qfd.html. QFD.

www.advisorteam.com/user/ktsintro.asp. Keirsey Temperament Sorter.

www.brainstorming.co.uk. Infinite Innovations Ltd, Brainstorming.

www.brainstorming.org.uk/tutorials/usenewpeople.html.

www.cpsc.ucalgary.ca/~danah/kaw96/FINAL.html. Daniela Elena Herla. "Users' Involvement in the Requirements Engineering Process." Knowledge Science Institute, University of Calgary.

www.dhutton.com/samples/sampqfd.html. QFD.

www.directedcreativity.com. Brainstorming.

www.imappl.org/crest/requirement.html. Department of Systems and Computer Science at Howard University.

www.inspiration.com/. Mind Mapping.

www.mcli.dist.maricopa.edu/authoring/studio/guidebook/brain.html. Brainstorming.

www.mindjet.com/. Mind Mapping.

www.ozemail.com.au/~caveman/Creative/Mindmap/. Features a selection of mind-mapping related sites.

www.processimpact.com/articles/qualreqs.html. Karl E. Wiegers, "Writing Quality Requirements." Process Impact (originally published in Software Development, May 1999).

www.qfdi.org/. Quality Function Deployment Institute.

www.sdmagazine.com/documents/s=758/sdm9905c/9905c.htm. Writing Good Requirements.

www.sei.cmu.edu/pub/documents/92.reports/pdf/tr12.92.pdf. Michael G. Christel and Kyo C. Kang (1992). "Issues in Requirements Elicitation," Technical Report CMU/SEI-92-TR-12 ESC-TR-92-012, September.

www.thebeenet.com/bluebird/jaddoc.htm. Bill Jennerich (1999). "Joint Application Design: Business Requirements Analysis for Successful Re-engineering." Berwyn, PA: Bluebird Enterprises.

www.zoo.co.uk/~z0001039/PracGuides/pg_use_cases.htm. Edward Kenworthy. "Use Cases."

Risks

www.cs-solutions.com/riskplus.htm. Risk+ Add-on for MS Project.

www.eas.asu.edu/~riskmgmt/intro.html. James S. Collofello. "Software Risk Management."

www.palisade.com/html/risk.html. @Risk Add-on for Excel or MS Project.

www.sei.cmu.edu/programs/sepm/risk/.

www.sei.cmu.edu/publications/documents/97.reports/97hb002/97hb002abstract.html. Brian Gallagher, Christopher Alberts, and Richard Barbour. "Software Acquisition Risk Management Key Process Area (KPA)—A Guidebook Version 1.0."

Software Engineering—Defining the Product and Understanding Development Activities

liinwww.ira.uka.de/bibliography/index.html. This is a collection of bibliographies of scientific literature in computer science from various sources, covering most aspects of computer science.

mingo.info-science.uiowa.edu/soft-eng/. World Wide Web virtual library of software engineering.

sunset.usc.edu/. The Center was founded in June of 1993 by Dr. Barry W. Boehm for the purpose of providing an environment for research and teaching in the areas of large-scale software design and development processes, generic and domain specific software architectures, software engineering tools and environments, cooperative system design, and the economics of software engineering.

www.best.com/~wilson/faq/. alt.folklore.computers (1998). List of Frequently Asked Questions.

www.computer.org/tab/swecc/. ACM, IEEE Software Engineering Coordinating Committee. The IEEE-CS/ACM joint task force on Software Engineering Ethics and Professional Practices (SEEPP) has developed a Code of Ethics for Software Engineers. It contains eight sets of guiding principles.

www.cs.queensu.ca/Software-Engineering/. World-Wide Web archives for USENET newsgroup comp.software-eng, including the Frequently-Asked Questions (FAQ) postings.

www.cs.umd.edu/projects/SoftEng/tame/. The Experimental Software Engineering Group (ESEG) of the University of Maryland views the study of software engineering as a laboratory science. Specific research projects are centered on formalizing various aspects of (a) the Quality Improvement Paradigm (QIP), (b) the Experience Factory (EF), and (c) the Goal/Question/Metric approach (GQM).

www.faqs.org/faqs/software-eng/. Software Engineering FAQ.

www.qucis.queensu.ca/Software-Engineering/reading.html. This is the hypertext version of the Software Engineering reading list posted regularly to comp.software-eng.

www.swebok.org/. Since 1993, the IEEE Computer Society and the ACM have been actively promoting software engineering as a profession, notably through their involvement in the IEEE Computer Society and ACM Software Engineering Coordinating Committee.

Standards

standards.ieee.org/index.html. IEEE Standards.

www.ansi.org/. American National Standards Institute.

www.iso.ch/9000e/execabstract.htm. ISO 9000 Information.

www.iso.ch/9000e/plain.htm. ISO 9000 and 14000 Explained.

www.iso.ch/infoe/intro.htm. ISO Organization Information.

www.iso.ch/iso/en/ISOOnline.openerpage. International Organization for Standardization (ISO).

www.nist.gov/. National Institute of Standards and Technology.

www.nssn.org. National Standards Systems Network.

Tools

argouml.tigris.org/. The goal of the ArgoUML project is to build an object-oriented design tool that is: a joy to use, actually helpful to designers when they are making design decisions, completely open source Java, leading edge (supports the latest UML specifications), modular and extensible, integrated with the web and other Tigris tools.

ca.com/products/superproject.htm. Computer Associates.

cvshome.org/. The Concurrent Versions System is an open-source network-transparent version control system.

iatek.com/WebPM/default.asp. ProjectLab.

silver.sdsmt.edu/~fmatejci/kcqc~1.htm. Statistical Process Control. Detailed examples of ancient tools, approaches for computing means, standard deviations, X-bar charts, R charts, and S charts are included.

sourceforge.net/foundry/tcl-foundry/. Foundry for Tcl (Tool Command Language), a cross-platform (Unix/Windows/Macintosh/and more...) scripting language.

www.aonix.com/content/index.html. Aonix.

www.construx.com/. Software engineering tools and software development resources provided by Construx and other organizations.

www.cs-solutions.com/riskplus.htm. Risk+ Add-on for MS Project.

www.eproject.com. eProject.

www.eroom.com. eRoom: Virtual Team Collaboration Tools.

www.gedanken.demon.co.uk/cxref/. Cxref is a program that will produce documentation (in LaTeX, HTML, RTF, or SGML) including cross-references from C program source code.

www.gnu.org/software/emacs/. GNU Emacs is an advanced, self-documenting, customizable, extensible real-time display editor for Emacs.

www.imagix.com/products/metrics.html. Imagix Power Software.

www.incose.org/tools/tooltax/riskmgt_tools.html. Risk Tool Summary.

www.inventx.com. InventX: Web-based Enterprise Project Management.

www.it.swin.edu.au/projects/jmetric/products/jmetric/. JMetric aims to bring current OO-metrics, and metrics tools research to the practitioner.

www.li.org/. Linux International is a non-profit association of groups, corporations, and others that work towards the promotion of growth of the Linux operating system and the Linux community.

www.lotusnotes.com. Lotus Notes Software.

www.lysator.liu.se/~alla/dia/dia.html. Dia is a gtk+ based diagram creation program released under the GPL license. Dia is designed to be much like the commercial Windows program 'Visio'. It can be used to draw many different kinds of diagrams. It currently has special objects to help draw entity relationship diagrams, UML diagrams, flowcharts, network diagrams, and simple circuits.

www.man.deakin.edu.au/rodneyc/XLStats.htm. XLStatistics is a set of Microsoft Excel (ver 5+) workbooks for statistical analysis of data designed to replace and enhance the tools provided with Excel's Data Analysis Toolbox add-in.

www.mccabe.com/main.htm. McCabe & Associates.

www.methods-tools.com/. Software Methods and Tools.

www.microsoft.com/ms.htm. Microsoft tools.

www.microsoft.com/Office/Project/PRK/2000/Six/70ct.htm. MS Project Central: Collaborative.

www.netcomputing.de/html/main.html. AnyJ is a cross platform Java IDE & Sourcecode Engineering Solution.

www.open.org/~prslkg/sy_chap.htm. Paul R. Seesing and ARMA International (1993). "Basic Systems Analysis Tools for Computer Users."

www.oracle.com/. Oracle Corporation.

www.palisade.com/html/risk.html. Majors include: @Risk Add-on for Excel or MS Project.

www.perl.com/pub. Perl is an interpreted language optimized for scanning arbitrary text files, extracting information from those text files, and printing reports based on that information.

www.ping.be/bertin/abs.shtml. Abs is a stand-alone state of the art spreadsheet designed to run on any UNIX platform.

www.qsm.com/. Quantitative Software Management (QSM).

www.qualitydigest.com/apr99/html/excel.html. William A. Levinson, P.E. Using Excel Control Charts with Varying Sample Sizes, Spreadsheets can actually exceed the capabilities of many commercially available SPC packages.

www.qualitydigest.com/june97/html/cover.html. J. Michael Crouch. "Essential Tools for Quality Managers, Or, What I Wish I Knew Before I Took This Job."

www.qualitydigest.com/pdfs/2001src-software.pdf. "2001 Software Quality and Calibration Guide." Separate sections for calibration software and services, document control, flowcharting and process simulation, and ISO 9000 software.

www.quicklist.org/. QuickList is a free (GPL) gtk+ program for any un*x system with gtk+ 1.2 or better that allows novice and experienced users to keep track of "things" without any help from a system administrator.

www.rational.com/index.jsp. Rational Software.

www.resourcedesigninc.com/RDImain.html. Ecomodeler—automated front-end project building software for World Construction Set from Viewscape3D Ltd.

www.scitools.com/. Scientific Toolworks, Inc.

www.soft.com/AppNotes/TestWorksIndex/index.html. TestWorks Quality Index.

www.softwareqatest.com/TOP. Rick Hower. The Software QA/Test Resource Center lists dozens of automated tools to help with dynamic testing of multiple application types. It is a thorough, and annotated list, containing a web site for each tool.

www.spmn.com/rsktrkr.html. Risk Radar—MS Access-based risk tracking.

www.spr.com/. Free web-based assessment service provides insight into a software organization.

www.sre.org/sresoft.htm. The Reliability Test Planner (RTP) software simplifies the construction of statistical reliability test plans for the exponential and binomial distributions.

www.stat.umn.edu/~luke/xls/xlsinfo/xlsinfo.html. Lisp-Stat is an extensible statistical computing environment for data analysis, statistical instruction and research, with an emphasis on providing a framework for exploring the use of dynamic graphical methods.

www.stgcase.com/. AxiomSys is an implementation of the Structured Analysis method, including the Hatley-Pirbhai Real-Time extensions. It also includes the Hatley-Pirbhai Architecture modeling capabilities.

www.sybase.com/. Sybase.

www.turbocase.com/. TurboCASE/Sys for Windows automates the system requirements and architecture methods developed by Derek Hatley and the late Imtiaz Pirbhai.

www.verilog.com/. Verilog HDL is a hardware description language used to design and document electronic systems.

www-4.ibm.com/software/data/db2/udb/. DB2 Universal Database.

zing.ncsl.nist.gov/WebTools/. Web Metrics.

Verification and Validation

rexblackconsulting.com.

satc.gsfc.nasa.gov/fi/fipage.html. NASA's Formal Inspections Process.

sel.gsfc.nasa.gov/website/index.htm. Software Engineering Laboratory.

stsc.hill.af.mil/CrossTalk/1998/dec/oneill.asp. Don O'Neill (1998). "National Software Quality Experiment, A Lesson In Measurement: 1992–1997." CrossTalk: Journal of Defense Software Engineering, December.

world.std.com/~jr/Papers/QW96.html. Johanna Rothman (1996). "Measurements to Reduce Risk in Product Ship Decisions." Proceedings of the Ninth International Quality Week, Software Research, San Francisco, CA.

www.chasmgroup.com/.

www.cse.dcu.ie/. Centre for Software Engineering, Ltd., Dublin City University Campus, Dublin, Ireland.

www.geraldmweinberg.com. Gerald M. Weinberg's Home Page.

www.ics.hawaii.edu/~johnson/FTR/. Formal Technical Review Archive.

www.ics.hawaii.edu/~siro/. Software Inspections and Review Organization.

www.io.com/~wazmo/qa/. Software Testing Hotlist, Brett Pettichord, ed.

www.iso.ch/iso/en/ISOOnline.openerpage. International Organization for Standardization (ISO).

www.jrothman.com.

www.kaner.com/. Dr. Kaner is the senior author of Testing Computer Software.

www.kaner.com/coverage.htm. Cem Kaner (1996). "Software Negligence and Testing Coverage." STAR 96 Proceedings, May.

www.mtsu.edu/~storm/. Software Testing Online Resources.

www.nist.gov/. National Institute of Standards and Technology (NIST).

www.nstl.com/. National Software Testing Labs.

www.ondaweb.com/sti/. The Software Testing Institute.

www.ondaweb.com/sti/newsltr.htm. Software Testing Newsletter.

www.ondaweb.com/sti/stivend.htm. A Professional Software Tester's Resource Guide.

www.qaiusa.com/. Quality Assurance Institute.

www.satisfice.com/articles/good_enough_quality.pdf. James Bach (1997). "Good Enough Quality: Beyond the Buzzword." Software Realities column, IEEE Computer, August.

www.satisfice.com/articles/software_reality.pdf. James Bach (1999). "What Software Reality is Really About." Software Realities column, IEEE Computer, December.

www.satisfice.com/articles/test_automation_snake_oil.pdf. James Bach (1996). "Test Automation Snake Oil." Windows Tech Journal, October.

www.softwareqatest.com/TOP. Software QA/Testing Resource Center.

www.softwareqatest.com/WEB_SECURITY. Testing of World Wide Web sites.

www.spmn.com. Software Program Managers Network

www.sqe.com/index.asp. Software Quality Engineering.

www.stlabs.com/~marick/root.htm.

www.stqemagazine.com/featured.asp?stamp=1129125440. James Bach (1999). "Risk-based Testing." Software Testing and Quality Engineering Magazine, 1(6).

www.stqemagazine.com/webinfo_detail.asp?id=102. Brian Marick (1999). "Web Watch: Automating Testing." Software Testing and Quality Engineering Magazine, 1(5).

www.stsc.hill.af.mil/CrossTalk/1998/dec/oneill.asp.

www.stsc.hill.af.mil/SWTesting/gilb.html. Tom Gilb documents.

www.testing.com/writings/automate.pdf. Brian Marick (1988). "When Should a Test be Automated?" Proceedings of International Quality Week, May.

www.testing.com/writings/classic/mistakes.html. Brian Marick (1997). "Classic Testing Mistakes." Proceedings of STAR 97, Software Quality Engineering, Jacksonville, FL.

www.testing.com/writings/coverage.pdf. Brian Marick (1999). "How to Misuse Code Coverage." International Conference and Exposition on Testing Computer Software, June.

www.testing.com/writings/effective.pdf. Brian Marick (1998). "Working Effectively With Developers." STAR West Conference, October.

www.testing.com/writings/experience.pdf. Brian Marick (1991). "Experience with the Cost of Different Coverage Goals for Testing." Pacific Northwest Software Quality Conference, October.

www.testing.com/writings/purpose-of-testing.htm. Brian Marick. "The Testing Team's Motto."

www.testingcraft.com/exploratory-pettichord.html. Bret Pettichord (1999) "An Exploratory Testing Workshop Report." July.

www.useit.com/.

www.zdnett.com/pcmag/pctech/content/17/17/tu1717.001.html. Neil Randall. "Making Software Easier Through Usability Testing: Software companies take a rigorous approach to determining how easy their products are to use." PC Magazine Online.

www2.ics.hawaii.edu/~johnson/FTR/. The WWW Formal Technical Review Archive.

www2.ics.hawaii.edu/~siro/. Software Inspections And Reviews Organization.

Index

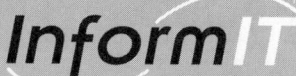
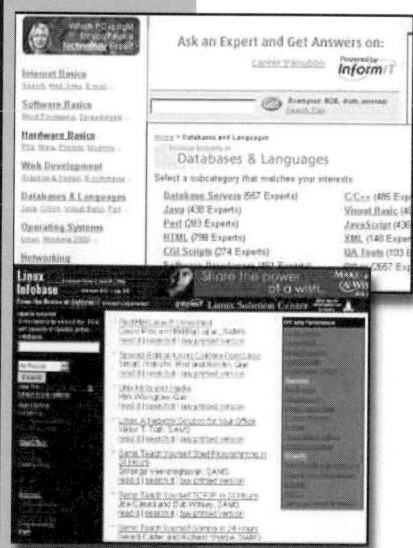

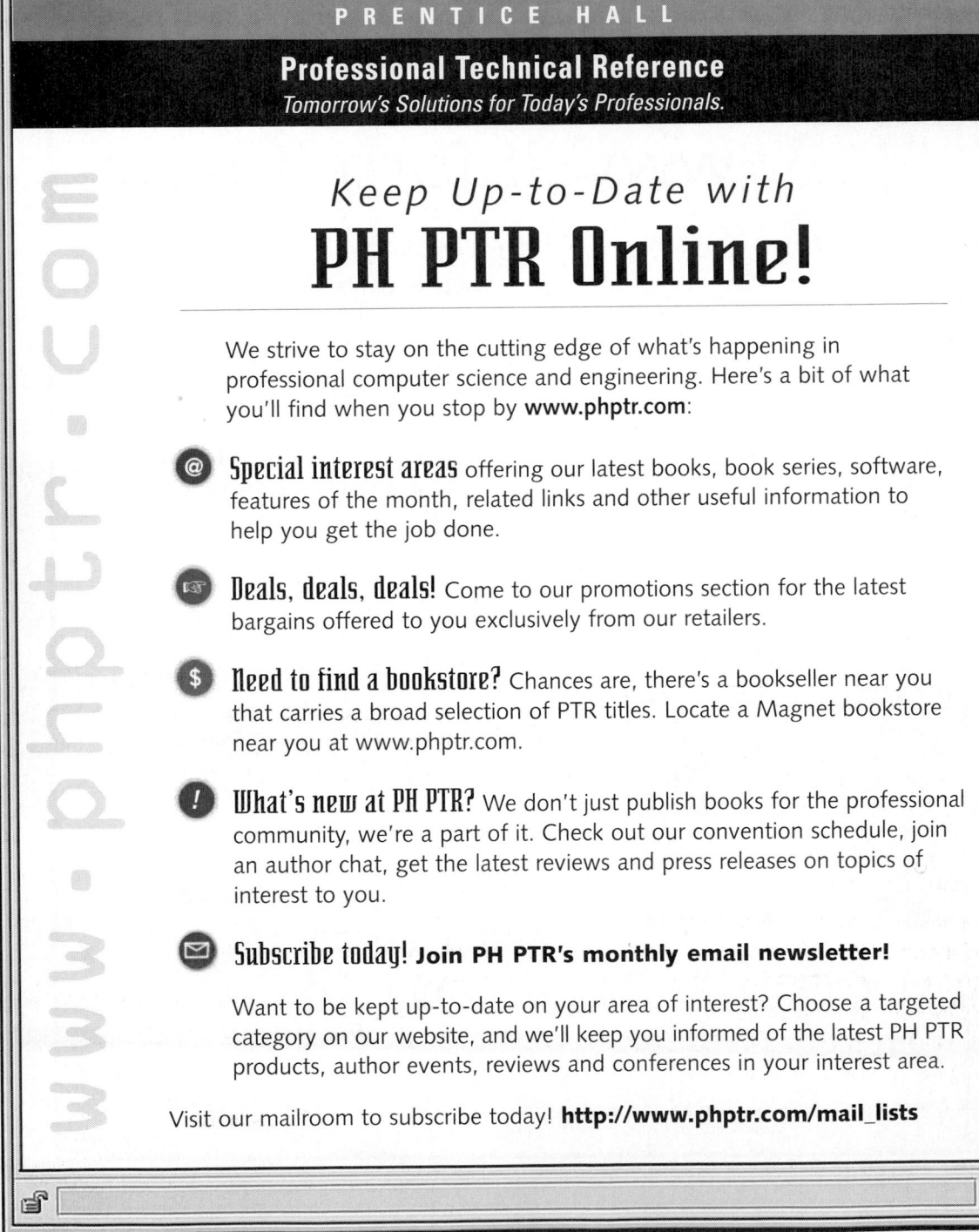